Jonathan Periam

The national cyclopedia

A dictionary of useful and practical information for the farm, home and school

Jonathan Periam

The national cyclopedia

A dictionary of useful and practical information for the farm, home and school

ISBN/EAN: 9783337224363

Printed in Europe, USA, Canada, Australia, Japan

Cover: Foto ©Paul-Georg Meister /pixelio.de

More available books at **www.hansebooks.com**

THE
NATIONAL CYCLOPEDIA:

A

DICTIONARY OF USEFUL AND PRACTICAL INFORMATION

FOR THE

FARM, HOME AND SCHOOL.

BY

HON. JONATHAN PERIAM,

FOR FORTY YEARS A PRACTICAL FARMER; LATE EDITOR PRAIRIE FARMER; ASSOCIATE EDITOR FARM, FIELD AND STOCKMAN; EX-MEMBER ILLINOIS DEPARTMENT OF AGRICULTURE; PROFESSOR OF HYGIENE, ETC., CHICAGO VETERINARY COLLEGE; HONORARY MEMBER ILLINOIS VETERINARY MEDICAL ASSOCIATION; LIFE MEMBER AMERICAN POMOLOGICAL SOCIETY, ETC., ETC.

ILLUSTRATED.

VOL. III.

CHICAGO:
R. S. Peale & Company.

quince, the latter an elegant flowering sort and a fair hedging plant. The cut shows the flower of the Japan quince natural size. They are deep crimson, and appear before or at the time of the first leaves. The quince delights in a cool, moist but well drained soil, and rather humid atmosphere, hence it is but little cultivated in the prairie regions of the West, or in other dry intercontinental climates. There are, however, special localities near the great lakes, congenial to it, and in these situations the crop is very profitable, since the scarcity of the fruit causes it to sell at high prices. The quince is largely used as a stock upon which to bud the pear to dwarf it for cultivation in gardens and other small places. But when this is done, they should be worked so low that they may be planted below the junction of the bud or graft, else they are short lived.

QUINCE CURCULIO. *Conotrachelus crataegi.* The insect resembles the plum curculio, and belongs to the same genus, but differs remarkably in its habits from either the apple or plum curculio. It makes a direct puncture as a nidus for the egg and the larva, feeds near the surface of the fruit, and does not approach the core. It passes the winter in the larva state, and does not change to a pupa until a few days before it issues as a beetle. As with the plum curculio jarring the insects upon a sheet is the remedy, say from the first of June until the middle of August in the North.

QUINCUNX. In the following order with one at each corner, and a fifth in the center of the square. (See Orcharding.)

QUININE. The active principle of Peruvian bark, a white crystalline alkaloid.

QUINSY. Inflammation of the tonsils. This is common inflammatory sore throat; it is not infectious. It begins with pain on one side of the throat and swelling of the tonsils, attended by febrile symptoms, which sometimes run high, especially as the tumefaction advances; there is great restlessness and anxiety, and often the utmost difficulty of swallowing even liquids and of breathing. The disease has proved fatal by producing suffocation, but it generally terminates in resolution or suppuration; in the latter case the abscess breaks, and a great deal of pus is discharged, and the patient is at once relieved of all urgent symptoms; but it occasionally happens that the other side of the throat becomes affected and goes through the same stages. Quinsy in hogs is prevalent and often fatal; when attacked, injections of four ounces of sulphate of magnesia and two drachms of oil of turpentine in half a pint of soap-suds, should be given to relieve the bowels. Cast and tie the hog firmly, and with a sharp knife scarify the skin over the swelling, to draw blood freely, and assist the bleeding with cloths rung out of hot water. Give also internally in gruel two ounce doses of turpentine, if the hog will eat, if not, swab the throat with a feather dipped in equal parts of turpentine and oil.

QUITCH GRASS. Couch grass. (See Grasses.)

QUITTOR. This is a fistula of the coronet, caused by calking, a bruise, suppurating corns, irritation between the sole and wall caused by any foreign substance. The horse may go lame for a long time; finally a tender swelling will make its appearance at the coronet, above the hoof, which, when it bursts discharges a whitish watery matter, difficult to heal. Often the fibrous network covering the bone and elastic tissue of the foot will be completely involved, canals leading thence to the main issue. If there is inflammation reduce this by poulticing. The probe will show somewhat the extent of the disease. Give the treatment into the hands of a veterinary surgeon, if one is to be had. The inflammation being partly reduced, inject three or four times in a day, of the following: Five grains of bichloride mercury, twenty drops of muriatic acid, one ounce of alcohol. The next day inject the mixture twice, and thereafter once a day until the fistula becomes superficial, when it may be kept covered with wet tow or lint. Severe cases may require the knife. If so, a competent surgeon should be called. Everything about the stall should be kept sweet and clean, and the animal's bowels kept in a natural state by grass, bran mashes or a gentle laxative.

QUOIN. The corner of a building. Oblong blocks of wood used to lock printers' form.

R

RABBET. A moulding.

RABBIT. The common gray rabbit, really a hare, *Lepus Americanus*, is one of the most noxious animals of the farm, and should be exterminated wherever found. This may easily be done, or at least they may be kept well under by means of a common box trap with a floor. The trap may be made of boards seven inches wide for the sides, with a door in the top for introducing the hand, the box to be placed on a bottom of tight boards. The box should be about eighteen inches each way, and set with a common figure four, and weighted, so the rabbit can not move off its foundation. The bait used may be a piece of sweet apple. (See Hare.) The varieties of domestic rabbits, *Lepus cuniculus*, are numerous, and of many colors; white, black, blue, gray, and parti-colored. The lop-eared varieties are among the most curious. A rabbit warren is built by excavating the soil and using six inches of pounded glass or tin waste to prevent burrowing out, and covered over with about six inches of earth, boarded up and the top covered with slats. A suitable box should be provided for breeding, and the males must be kept separate from the females except during the rutting season. Rabbits breed at the age of six or seven months. The doe goes with young thirty to thirty-one days, producing from four to seven or eight young at a litter. The rabbit, like the female hare, has a double matrix, and therefore can carry in the womb two separate litters. In the hare super-fœtation is common, but in the rabbit much less so.

RABBIT FOOT. One of the names of Welsh or stone clover. *Trifolium arvense.* It is a worthless plant and should be eradicated wherever found. It is a native of Europe, a one-seeded legume, flowering and bearing seed twice in a season. Being an annual plant, its eradication is not difficult to a farmer who gives clean cultivation. (See article Clover.)

RACEME. In botany, a form of inflorescence, in which the flowers are stalked along a common unbranched axis, as in the hyacinth.

RACEMIC ACID. An old name for a tartaric acid; the paratartaric acid.

RACHIS. A branch which proceeds in nearly a straight line from the base to the apex of the inflorescence of a plant. It is also applied to the petioles of the leaves of ferns.

RACK. A railed place formed above the manger in a stable for holding hay. It should be constructed with openings at the bottom for the seed or dust to pass through.

RACKING. Decanting; separating the clear portions from the dregs. The barrel into which the fluid is racked should be perfectly clean and fumigated with sulphur.

RADIANT. A luminous spot or body.

RADIATION. (See Meteorology.)

RADICAL. A base in chemistry. Compound radical is a compound base in organic bodies.

RADICLE. In botany, that portion of an embryo which eventually becomes the descending axis or root. It is the lowest of the two opposite cones of which an embryo plant consists.

RADISH. *Raphanus sativus.* A hardy annual plant, originally from China, perfecting its seed the first season. It is broken now into many varieties, generally round, ovoid, or fusiform, some varieties being exceedingly long and slender. The varieties generally in cultivation require to be sown in rich, warm land, early in spring so the growth may be early in the season, to have them tender and succulent. The seed may be sown in shallow drills, one foot apart, and rather thickly in the rows; thinning out as necessary, and gathering for use as soon as they get to be the size of the little finger. For a very early crop the seed may be sown in a gentle hot-bed the latter part of February, using a turnip rooted variety. So at the time of sowing in the open ground, sow turnip rooted, either early white or scarlet, and at the same time sow long scarlet and French breakfast radish. For autumn and winter use sow Black Spanish, and Rose-colored Chinese, from July 25 to August 10 in the West, and later South. To keep over winter pack the roots in barrels tops down, and pour air-dried sand about them. An ounce contains about 3,500 seeds retaining vitality five or six years. Seed one or two years old do not make such strong tops as fresh seed.

RADISH, WILD. The charlock, a weed.

RADIUS. The length of a straight line drawn from the center to the circumference of a circle.

RADIUS BONE. One of the bones of the forearm.

RAFTER. A timber of the roof.

RAFTERING LAND. Plowing only half the land, and turning the grass side of each furrow-slice upon an unplowed bed.

RAG. Woolen rags are very useful as a manure. They are chopped fine, and used at the rate of half a ton to the acre. They last four or five years, and advance vegetation, especially the hop. The rags, by decay, become converted into carbonate of ammonia, in the same way as hair and horns, with which manures they are identical.

RAGGED ROBIN. *Centaurea cyanus.* Blue bonnets of the Scotch, a pretty flower, an annual introduced from Europe, and naturalized, in many places as a weed. In England and the Continent, it is regarded as a troublesome weed in grain, and care should be taken that it does not spread from gardens.

RAGWEED. *Ambrosia trifida,* great ragweed, and, *A. artemisiæ,* bitter weed or ragweed. The first a coarse, ugly, native weed common in uncultivated places. The second well known as springing up in stubble fields, especially after wheat. The land being in grass, it gives no trouble, but on good wheat soil it springs again when the land is plowed for crops.

RAIL. Great Red-breasted Rail. *Rallus elegans.* A fresh-water bird living and breeding in the inland Southern States, and rarely appearing in the North, but is at home in the Gulf States. They scarcely wander far, but are in the habit of returning to the same nests year after year. The length of the bird is nineteen inches and the expanse of wings twenty-five inches. Their flesh is good, and the eggs excellent. *R. crepitans,* sometimes confounded with the former, inhabits salt marshes from New Jersey south, along the coast. The Sora Rail and the Virginia Rail are both found in the West. They are plainly colored, dark brown, very swift, and at the approach of cold weather emigrate south. The food of all the species is insects and aquatic seeds.

RAIN. It has been said that drought scares the farmer, but that too much water absolutely destroys his hopes. This has especially been found to be a truism in the West, and hence the impetus given to surface and tile draining within the last few years, especially the latter, since it not only quickly rids the soil of superfluous moisture, but in times of drought, through intercirculation and condensation of vapor in the pores of earth, causes the accumulation of moisture within the soil. In relation to the rainfall of the country it has been determined that throughout the Northern States the fall of rain during the summer varies from nine to fourteen inches. The region including all the great lakes from the mountains of northern New York and valley of Lake Champlain to the western extremity of Lake Superior, extending along the southern border of Lake Ontario and the east end of Lake Erie, then passing southeast to include almost all of Pennsylvania west of the Susquehanna, the high region of Virginia to the border of North Carolina, eastern Kentucky, northeastern Ohio, all of Michigan, a small portion of Indiana, and the borders of Lakes Michigan and Superior, in Wisconsin, appear to be favored with a smaller fall of rain during the summer than any other parts of the vine-growing districts of the United States east of the Mississippi. Over this region, which may also properly include the coast of New England, there occurs in summer the average of about ten inches of rain. There is a district over which nine inches only are deposited, but it is quite limited, and extends from Rochester west to the end of Lake Ontario, and not much further south than Buffalo. A similar contracted district of eight inches summer rainfall occurs in the mountains of Virginia. As regards the fitness of the latter for vine-growing we have no information. The region over which the fall of nine to ten inches of summer rain extends includes all the localities where the cultivation of the vine has, in the northern section of our country, been attended with the largest share of success. At Cincinnati and St. Louis the fall of rain for the summer months is about fourteen inches, and this deposit of moisture occurs over most of southeastern Virginia, the Carolinas, where it reaches fifteen inches; most of Kentucky, middle Tennessee; but equaling that of the Carolinas in the western part of the two last-named States, the southwestern corner of Ohio, the southern border of Indiana, all the south, southwestern and western parts of Illinois, including one-half of the State; southeastern Iowa, and all the eastern half of Missouri to the Ozark mountains. Between the northern border of the rain district of fourteen inches thus appropriately designated, and which can only be properly defined upon a map, and the district of ten inches fall before noted, there is interpolated a very irregularly shaped region, over which there is deposited in the average of summers about twelve inches of rain. This extends over almost all of New Hampshire, all of Vermont except the northwest corner and valley of Lake Champlain, all of New York except the northeast mountain region, the valley of the St. Lawrence and lake borders before noted, as having nine and ten inches fall, and the lower valley of the Hudson, where eleven inches are deposited. It also includes all of eastern Pennsylvania and southern New Jersey, the northern part resembling the valley of the Hudson, and passing southwestwardly between the two districts before named, extends in a narrow belt through Maryland and Virginia, crosses the mountains in western North Carolina, ranges along the west boundary of Virginia, extends over southern, middle, and western Ohio, nearly all northern and middle Indiana, all northeastern Illinois and Wisconsin, except the lake borders, and over most of Iowa and Missouri not before excepted. The table page 776 will be interesting not only to those living in the regions directly named, but generally, since it shows that the opinions usually current, in regard to the rainfall of the great plains have been erroneous. This table as given also affords unexpectedly favorable results, particularly in regard to the critical seasons of spring and summer. Of more than twenty stations near or on the plains, but two or three show marked deficiency of rain, even in summer; and in spring, April and May at the South, and May and June at the North, are always marked by a fair amount of rain. A report to the United States government a few years since says: There is, it is true, need of observation at a much greater number of places, and conducted for longer periods. A few years more of the present fullness of observation will warrant more decisive judgments as to the quantities anywhere at hand to be utilized in some way more than is done at present. If, at the localities of Fort Atkinson, Fort Kearney, and Fort Sully; on this side of the plains, a summer aggregate of ten inches or more is to be relied upon, and at Fort Lyon, Golden City, Laramie, and Cheyenne, five to seven inches can be relied upon for the same season, the assurance is certain that forest growth may be anywhere maintained after the first efforts and dangers of planting are past. Comparing these quantities with the records of rainfall in Europe, the facts appear in a still more striking light; the whole interior, and indeed much of the west of Europe, having a small quantity of rain. The following are condensed results by seasons, and generally derived from long periods of observation.

Locality.	Spring.	Summer.	Autumn.	Winter.	Year.
	Inch.	Inch.	Inch.	Inch.	Inch.
London, England	4.09	6.00	6.15	4.45	20.69
Marseilles, France	4.67	2.17	8.00	5.23	20.16
Berlin	5.66	7.21	5.45	5.24	23.56
St. Petersburg	2.89	6.73	5.11	2.93	17.65
Simferopol, Crimea	3.22	6.01	3.40	2.20	14.83
Lougan, South Russia	3.57	4.99	3.02	2.28	13.87

The whole central area of Europe exhibits like small quantities of rain, and the simple measurements of quantity on the plains of the United States by no means sustain the idea that such aridity exists as to require irrigation. Yet the small number of rainy or cloudy days, and the sudden outflow of the water in streams, as well as its rapid evaporation in the somewhat caustic atmosphere that sweeps over the plains, reduce the practical value of the rain falling to little more than half the quantity when deposited elsewhere. At Niagara and Rochester, N. Y., the quantity of rain in spring is less than seven inches, and that of summer eight and a half to nine inches only. At Council Grove, Fort Riley, and Fort Atkinson, positions reaching westward from the settled border of Kansas, the quantity is fully equal to or exceeds that at Rochester. Even at Golden City, Fort Lyon, and Denver, great altitudes, it is nearly equal in spring, though deficient in summer. The actual proportion of the rain falling on any district, thrown off in the ordinary surface-drainage, has been calculated with care in many cases as a basis for the construction of works for the supply of water to cities. The results are variously stated at from fifty to seventy-five per cent. of the annual fall, in average districts of the Atlantic States. Ellet calculated the discharge of a stream called Anthony's Creek a tributary of the Greenbrier river of Virginia, by daily measurements for one year, to be seventy per cent. of the quantity falling in that year, and sixty-five per cent. of the average fall for a period of years. In all these localities of the Eastern States a fair proportion of woodland, and also of loose soil and cultivated surface, would be included, thus affording conditions much more favorable to the retention of moisture, and its absorption into the soil, than those existing on the general surface of the plains. If the rainfall of Maryland, at forty-four inches, should average to throw off sixty per cent. as a basis of available drainage for water-supply to reservoirs, there would be twenty-six and a half inches of waste, or of ordinary flow into rivers, and seventeen and one half inches permanently diverted by absorption and evaporation. And of the quantity thus retained and re-supplied to the air some portion would inevitably be re-deposited in rain; and thus the primary rainfall, as it may be called, may at the season of showers receive considerable augmentation. And this increase

DEPTH OF WATER FALLING IN RAIN AND SNOW (IN INCHES AND HUNDREDTHS) AT VARIOUS STATIONS ON OR NEAR THE PLAINS.

Stations.	Latitude.	Longitude.	Altitude.	Years.*	January.	February.	March.	April.	May.	June.	July.	August.	September.	October.	November.	December.	Spring.	Summer.	Autumn.	Winter.	Year.
	° ′	° ′	Feet.																		
Fort Towson, Arizona	34 0	95 33	300	14	3.19	2.99	4.38	5.33	5.84	5.78	4.62	3.96	3.41	4.59	4.23	2.84	15.55	14.36	12.23	8.94	51.08
Fort Arbuckle, Indian Ter.	34 27	97 09	1,000	9¾	0.89	2.98	1.12	2.39	4.46	3.16	3.13	4.12	3.38	2.08	2.97	1.57	7.97	10.83	8.43	5.44	32.69
Fort Belknap, Texas	33 08	98 48	1,600	5 5-6	0.47	2.29	1.32	0.88	4.21	3.98	2.49	2.97	2.77	2.92	2.65	1.10	6.41	9.44	8.34	3.86	28.05
Fort Scott, Kansas	37 45	94 35	1,000	10¼	1.92	1.18	1.79	3.70	7.08	8.13	4.55	3.69	2.30	2.66	3.46	1.69	12.57	16.37	8.42	4.79	42.15
Council Grove, "	38 40	96 30	1,200	6	1.17	2.31	1.81	3.16	5.14	5.33	5.19	6.39	4.59	3.11	1.75	1.14	10.11	16.91	9.45	4.62	41.09
Manhattan, "	39 15	96 40	1,100	9	0.52	1.63	1.36	3.10	2.37	4.86	4.90	3.52	3.35	1.69	1.52	1.06	8.50	13.08	6.56	3.21	29.69
Fort Riley, "	39 03	96 85	1,300	14	0.77	1.01	0.75	1 74	3.01	3.93	3.00	3.22	3.09	1.21	1.15	0.74	6.83	10.15	5.45	2.52	23.62
Fort Atkinson	37 47	100 14	2,330	1	0.04	0.49	0.98	3.38	9.34	4.35	3.00	2.80	3.85	6.81	1.39	1.60	13.68	10.15	12.05	2.13	38.01
Bellevue, Nebraska	41 20	95 57	1,250	8	0.89	1.57	0.79	1.92	3.76	3.58	3.91	3.82	3.18	1.76	1.36	2.10	6.47	11.31	6.30	4.56	28.64
Omaha Mission, Nebraska	42 05	96 10	1,500	6½	1.03	0.84	1.42	2.56	4.42	3.00	4.42	3.57	3.06	1.68	1.67	1.13	8.40	10.99	6.41	3.00	28.80
Fort Kearney, "	40 38	98 57	2,360	14¼	0.59	0.43	1.25	2.26	4.30	3.69	4.74	2.70	2.29	1.57	0.97	0.46	7.81	11.13	4.83	1.48	25.25
Fort Randall, Dakota	43 01	98 12	1,456	8 5-6	0.49	0.42	0.99	1.10	2.67	2.30	1.78	2.56	2.43	1.09	0.47	0.30	4.76	6.64	3.90	1.21	16.51
Fort Laramie, Wyoming	42 12	104 31	4,519	12⅓	0.61	0.46	0.64	1.06	3.74	1.90	1.63	1.37	1.17	0.97	0.84	0.57	5.64	4.90	2.98	1.64	15.16
Denver, Colorado	39 40	105 10	5,000	2	0.81	0.97	1.26	2.80	1.45	0.29	0.51	0.20	2.85	0.54	1.82	0.75	5.51	1.00	5.21	2.53	14.25
Fort Lyon, "	38 08	102 50	4,000	1	0.32	0.12	0.16	2.09	4.84	1 40	2.53	0.37	0.04	0.00	0.07	0.15	7.09	4.30	0.11	0.59	12.09
Golden City, "	39 45	105 20	5,240	1	....	1.00	1.40	2.80	5.40	2.10	2.37	0.45	2.20	....	....	....	9.60	4.92	....	....	....
Fort Massachusetts	37 32	105 28	8,365	5	0.34	0.86	0.81	1.15	1.19	0.71	2.01	2.84	1.80	0.87	3.61	1.07	2.95	5.56	6.28	2.27	17.06
Great Salt Lake City, Utah	40 46	112 06	4,320	5⅚	1.68	2.25	2.47	1.39	1.34	1.49	2.54	1.01	1.37	2.20	2.35	3.76	5.20	5.04	5.92	7.69	23.85
Camp Douglas, Utah	40 39	111 42	4,800	3¼	2.77	1.53	2.87	1.11	1.58	0.80	0.84	0.60	0.99	1.79	1.71	4.18	5 76	2 04	4.49	8.48	20.57
Fort Defiance, Arizona	35 43	109 10	6,500	8½	0.98	0.70	0.84	0.67	0.52	0.74	2.44	2.73	1.86	0.70	1.16	0.87	2.03	5.91	3.72	2.55	14.21
Fort Ruby, Nevada	40 01	115 35	5,924	1¾	2.24	0.23	1.63	1.57	2.04	0.59	0.59	1.82	0 53	3.33	0.94	1.76	5.24	3.00	4.80	4.23	17.27
Deer Lodge City, Montana	46 15	112 30	6,000	2¾	1.45	1.81	1.64	1.40	2.28	1.97	0.58	0.58	0.86	0 48	1.38	0.49	5.32	3.13	2.72	3.75	14.92
Helena, "	46 45	111 50	4,150	1⅗	2.12	0.43	1.15	1.80	4.30	3.50	0.07	0.20	1.80	2.61	0.50	1.00	7.25	3 77	4.91	3.55	19.48
Fort Benton, "	47 52	110 40	2,674	1⅙	1.01	0.37	1.11	1.81	2.86	1.14	4.62	0.61	1.82	....	....	1.30	5.78	6.37	5.00	2.68	19.83
Fort Sully, Dakota	44 39	100 40	1,491	⅓	....	....	....	....	2.98	2.34	6 48	1.58	0.21	....	....	....	....	10.35	....	....	20.00
Cheyenne, Wyoming	41 12	104 42	6,000	1	0.02	0.27	6.38	1.61	1.99	1.84	3.90	2.05	1.08	....	....	....	3.98	7.79	....	....	16.00
Corinne, Utah	41 30	112 18	5,000	1	0.70	2.42	0.55	1.43	2.66	0.47	0.11	1.04	0.14	0.35	3.22	4.04	4.64	1.62	3.71	7.16	17.13

* The rainfall is the average for the years mentioned in the column, and not for particular years, since these would give an excess in particular years, and a light rainfall in other years.

once established, it becomes permanent so long as the surface continues favorable,' increasing the humidity of the local atmosphere and the cultivable capacity of the soil. Applying this analogy to the plains, a quantity of twenty inches now found falling on the dry surface, and of which seventy to ninety per cent. is immediately thrown off in the streams and rivers, may, by covering the surface with forests in part, and by breaking up the hardened turf in cultivation, diminish the waste from eighty to sixty, or even fifty per cent., retaining, say, six or eight inches of this quantity in some form, and at least preventing the immediate waste from which no secondary benefits can now be derived. The practical value of the primary water-deposit can not fail under such change of surface to be equivalent to an addition of ten per cent. to such original quantity; sufficient in many cases to secure important results, and to obviate deficiencies that are now decisively adverse to whole classes of crops. A further measure may be suggested here, in the construction of what may be called temporary reservoirs, in which the surplus of the profuse showers falling in spring and early summer may be retained to be distributed by channels of irrigation, or to secure general benefits by simple retention. The cost of such works need not be great, nor need they be more than such temporary obstruction of the smaller drainage-channels as is within the power of a few settlers at any locality to construct at any time. For these, as for all preliminary works of the kind, the agency and means of the railroad companies may be easily and effectively employed. Whatever may be found practicable in this respect, it is clear that eight to ten inches of rainfall in the three or four months of most rapid growth can be utilized to a much greater extent than to permit eighty per cent. of the quantity to run off at the moment it falls, affording no useful result, and only flooding the valleys of great rivers and their tributaries just at a time when no surplus is wanted in such valleys. It is a common mistake to suppose that the rainfall of England is greater than that of the United States. Recent observations in this country enable us to make the comparisons between the fall of rain in the two countries with considerable accuracy, not only as to the amount which descends annually, but, what is more important, as to the amount in each particular season of the year. The average rainfall of England is, in general, much less than that of the United States. In the eastern portion of England the annual fall of rain is estimated at twenty inches; in the middle portion, at twenty-two inches; in the southern and western, at thirty; in the extreme southwestern, at forty-five inches. In Wales it is estimated at fifty inches; in the eastern portion of Ireland, at twenty-five inches, and in the western at forty inches. The rainfall in the United States, as shown by Blodgett's rain chart, is in the basin of the great lakes, thirty inches; on Lake Erie and Lake Champlain, thirty-two inches; in the valley of the Hudson, on the headwaters of the Ohio, through the middle portions of Pennsylvania and Virginia, and western part of North Carolina, thirty-six inches; in the extreme eastern and the northern portions of Maine, northern portions of New Hampshire and Vermont, southeastern counties of Massachusetts, central New York, northeast portion of Pennsylvania, southeast portions of New Jersey and Delaware, also on a narrow belt running down from the western portion of Maryland, through Virginia and North Carolina to the northwestern portion of South Carolina, thence up through the western portion of Virginia, northeast portions of Ohio, northern Indiana and Illinois, to Prairie du Chien, forty inches; on the east coast of Maine, eastern Massachusetts, Rhode Island, and Connecticut, and middle portion of Maryland, thence on a narrow belt to South Carolina, thence up through eastern Tennessee, central Ohio, Indiana, and Illinois, to Iowa, forty-two inches, and the same down through western Missouri and Texas to the Gulf of Mexico; from Concord, N. H., through Worcester, Mass., western Connecticut and the city of New York, to the Susquehanna river, also at Richmond, Va., Raleigh, N. C., Augusta, Ga., Knoxville, Tenn., Indianapolis, Ind., Springfield, Ill., St. Louis, Mo., thence through western Arkansas, across Red river to the Gulf of Mobile, forty-five inches; from the belt just described, the rain fall increases inland and southward until at Mobile it is sixty-three inches; the same amount also falls in the extreme southern portion of Florida. The rainfall of New England, it is perceived, is about double that of the eastern and middle portions of England. Observations at London, by Dalton, for forty years gave an average fall of 20.69 inches, while observations for forty-three years at New Bedford, Mass., gave 41.03. The most striking difference as to the fall of rain in the two countries is found in the quantities which fall in single days. While we have vastly more rain in our country, we have far less rainy days. In the United States we have either decided rain, or bright, fair weather; while in England, though it seldoms rains hard, there is much of the time a fog, a mist or a drizzling rain. The records at all points of observation are unfortunately too brief to afford any proper means of determining whether the quantity of rain is greater now than it was ten years since; though great force attaches to the almost universal belief in such increase on the part of the more intelligent residents and observers in the interior. The range of non-periodic variation is very great in all parts of the temperate latitudes, and it is possible that our earliest practical experience on the plains was in a period characterized by a succession of dry seasons. In Utah it is quite clear that practically the warmer seasons have become far more profuse in rainfall than they were fifteen years ago; and at the eastern foot of the mountains, the settled localities, as Denver, and the districts both south and north of the original center of settlements, afford marked evidence of improvement. But there are no statistics of measurement which afford any positive evidence; the periods observed at the military posts being quite irregular, and not sufficiently extended to establish any law of increase. On no point of practical results are both writers and observers more thoroughly agreed than in affirming the value of forests, as agents of at least local amelioration of climate. An essential condition of the growth or improvement of a soil by chemical decomposition of its elements and by the deposit in or on it of vegetable mold, is the constant permeation of its strata by the water of rains and snows. These waters bear more or less ammonia always with them, which is the chief agent of rock decomposition, and in practical experience the forest-soils of the Central States are found deeply decomposed and fertilized. They are also free in absorbing water, holding it long, and yielding it slowly by subsequent evaporation and by drainage through the surface strata in permanent springs. The first result of too great and general clearings of the forests is to dry up the springs, and next to harden the surface-soil, forming a stiff mass which sheds the water of ordinary rains, and can only be permeated by water and by the roots of plants when thoroughly broken up and fertilized by artificial means. After long periods of exposure the surface becomes so hard and refractory as to bear little or no resemblance to the soft, moist, deep soil of the original woodland. The denudation of the hills and upland plains of any one of the Central States will show a marked decline in productive capacity, from that belonging to the original or first occupancy. At that time the wealth of the soil had not been wasted, nor had the general exposure of the surface deprived the crops of the shelter of adjacent woods, preventing the dry and caustic winds from exhausting the vitality of every plant exposed to them. The ordinary condition of the atmosphere, as it sweeps in general progress eastward, is that of an absorbent of moisture. When rain is not actually falling the air is taking up moisture, and if nothing is offered to it by ordinary evaporation from the surface the condition soon becomes arid, or deficient in the quantity necessary for favorable action on vegetable growths. Though a desert surface intensifies the aridity, yet an ordinary dry and denuded surface yielding no moisture by evaporation soon renders the surface atmosphere unduly dry and caustic. The summer winds may even approach a sirocco in quality, and those of winter are piercing and destructive. The water surface of any one of the great lakes is quite sufficient to neutralize either extreme for the countries lying on the line of atmospheric circulation across those lakes; and while the actual rainfall of Buffalo, Niagara, and Lockport is but small, the air is rarely or never biting in its aridity, as when it reaches the eastern and cultivated border of the plains after traversing hundreds of miles of surface destitute of water, forests, or other moisture-yielding conditions. The practical question is whether, with a general climate of constant rainfall, the smaller quantity of such rainfall can be diffused and distributed so as to sustain the constant vegetation of the Central and Eastern States. What may be accomplished by replacing that which we are accustomed to regard as the natural covering of the soil in the forests? And what further by cultivation, by special irrigation, and by shelter from the present unrestricted sweep of surface winds? In answer, it may at least be assumed that important ameliorations of the local and surface conditions are certainly within control. And the whole field of action is in a climate especially mild as compared with the north of Europe. The denuded uplands of Germany, the exposed mountain districts of Scotland, and other localities of the Eastern continent where cultivation struggles to reclaim every inch of surface that may be made to yield the smallest product for human support, present examples of deterioration. The entire area of the plains, and all the plateaux, mesas, and basins of the interior need nothing but water to make them productive in valuable staples. Everywhere within the United States it is warm enough, and the natural soil is rich enough. So great is this natural capacity that every observer and writer who has visited these districts believes that irrigation would be profitable in every case where it would be possible; the general presumption being that many of the valleys and river bottoms near the mountains will continue to be deficient in rain, and can only be cultivated by the aid of irrigation. The concentration of settlements in the basin districts of Utah and Idaho has fortunately tested this capacity for profitable cultivation by irrigation very thoroughly, and it is pronounced successful in all cases. The mountain streams are abundant and permanent, showing a profusion of summer as well as winter rains on their summits. The rain which would be sufficient, probably, if equally distributed over valleys as well as mountains, is condensed by attraction on the higher ranges, and therefore is not constant in the valleys. In short, it is not the general average supply that is so much at fault as the local distribution. But the districts on the eastern slope of the greater mountain-plateaux are probably the most difficult to deal with. The great ranges have exhausted most of the moisture of the aërial volumes from which the summer rains fall, and until their disturbing influence has been wholly exhausted the deficiency of rain continues. Probably a belt at Denver and near the eastern foot of the mountains has the quite insufficient quantity of fifteen inches of rain annually, and another, stretching two hundred to three hundred miles eastward, has but twenty to twenty-four inches. This is not of itself decidedly adverse, and cultivation might here succeed without irrigation, if adequate shelter and local amelioration could be introduced, at least for the cereal crops, and many others not requiring much moisture. Saussure the celebrated Swiss meteorologist states that, in ascending the sides of a mountain into the region of the clouds, he has seen globules of water as large as small peas floating in the air, which, from their levity, were evidently hollow spheres, similar to small soap bubbles. From this observation the idea became prevalent that the water of a cloud was in a vesicular condition, or, in other words, that cloud consists of minute hollow spheres of liquid water, filled with air, which is rendered more buoyant by the rarefaction due to the heat of the sun; and this opinion was strengthened by the fact that clouds do not give a decomposition of the rays of light sufficient to exhibit the phenomena of the rainbow. In what manner such a condition of water can be produced, and how it can be retained by any principle of science, has not, so far as we are informed, been explained. A soap bubble soon becomes too thin to retain its globular form, and is resolved into the condition of soap water. Ordinary water is still more unstable, and can not be retained for an instant in a hollow spherical form. We shall therefore be on the safe side if we adopt an hypothesis apparently more in accordance with known and established principles, and, if this does not furnish a logical account of all the phenomena, we must wait until further research, or light from collateral branches of science dispels the obscurity with which this point may be involved. The suspension of the clouds can be explained by taking into account the extreme minuteness of the particles of which they are composed. In the case of mists, which are sometimes formed at the surface of the earth, and afterwards become clouds in being elevated into the atmosphere by a wind blowing between them and the earth, the particles are of such extreme tenuity as to be invisible to the naked eye, and their presence is only rendered evident by looking through a stratum of considerable thickness. The simplest method of measuring the rain, which any one may practice for himself, is to catch the water in a cylindrical vessel, a straight-sided tin pail, and to measure the depth in inches and tenths of an inch after each shower. It is hardly necessary to remark that the vessel should be so placed that it may not be screened by trees, buildings, and other obstacles from the wind which bears along the falling drops. The object of the investigation is to ascertain the number of inches of water which fall from the clouds on a given space, in a given time—for example, a year or a season. In relation to signs foretelling rain, much has been said and written. The Signal Service of the United States now predicts storms with tolerable accuracy forty-eight hours in advance. It is probable that in the near future the science of meteorology will have been so far perfected that the peculiarity of seasons may be foretold with a considerable approximation to reality. Certain phenomena in the air and peculiarities of birds have long been known to indicate a change in the weather. Many years ago the learned Dr. Jenner embodied these in verse, in reply to an invitation from a friend with whom he had planned an excursion the following day. It embodies about all that is known to-day upon that branch of the subject, and we reproduce it as being reasonably correct:

The hollow winds begin to blow,
The clouds look black, the glass is low;
The soot falls down, the spaniels sleep,
And spiders from their cobwebs peep.
Last night the sun went pale to bed,
The moon in halos hid her head;
The boding shepherd heaves a sigh,
For, see, a rainbow spans the sky;
The walls are damp, the ditches smell,
Closed is the pink-eyed pimpernel.
Hark! how the chairs and tables crack,
Old Betty's joints are on the rack;
Loud quack the ducks, the peacocks cry;
The distant hills are looking nigh.
How restless are the snorting swine,
The busy flies disturb the kine;
Low o'er the grass the swallow wings;
The cricket, too, how sharp he sings;
Puss, on the hearth, with velvet paws,
Sits, wiping o'er her whisker'd jaws.
Through the clear stream the fishes rise,
And nimbly catch th' incautious flies;
The glow-worms, numerous and bright,
Illum'd the dewy dell last night.
At dusk the squalid toad was seen,
Hopping and crawling o'er the green;
The whirling wind the dust obeys,
And in the rapid eddy plays;
The frog has chang'd his yellow vest,
And in a russet coat is dressed.
Though June, the air is cold and still;
The black-bird's mellow voice is shrill.
My dog, so alter'd is his taste,
Quits mutton bones, on grass to feast;
And see, yon rooks, how odd their flight,
They imitate the gliding kite,
And seem precipitate to fall—
As if they felt the piercing ball.
'Twill surely rain, I see with sorrow,
Our jaunt must be put off to-morrow.

RAINBOW. A display of the prismatic colors in the air, produced by the action of particles of water on the sun's rays.

RAIN GAUGE. An instrument to measure the amount of rainfall. (See article Rain.)

RAISING PLATE. The timber to which the upper ends of the rafters are nailed.

RAISINS. Grapes allowed to dry on the vine. As soon as they are ripe, the leaves are pruned off, and none but sound fruit left. The stalk is also half cut through. When dry they are plucked, dipped in a solution of lye, and dried on frames.

RAKE. There are so many uses to which hand rakes may be put that, notwithstanding the almost universal use of horse rakes in gathering crops, the industry connected with the manufacture of wooden, iron and steel rakes is immense. Since the introduction of the lawn mower, the lawn rake with its sharp edged teeth has almost disappeared and has been superseded by one similar to the old time hay rake, but with teeth as close again. In gardening six and eight inch rakes, in connection with wheel hoes, have nearly in like manner displaced the common. In buying a garden rake many persons select goose-neck hoe and the Sutch or Scuffle hoe, cast iron implements on account of their cheapness. It is poor economy. It is far better to pay the difference and get the lighter and stronger steel implement. Two sizes are all that are required, one of eight inches and another of twelve inches in width. The latter to be used only in fining the soil. In buying a rake see that the handle is long, tough and flexible, since in working the soil fine, the backward movement is of more consequence than the forward movement. Thus with a tough flexible handle, the gardener may do double the work, and in a better manner than with a rigid one. So in buying a wooden rake, see that the handle, and especially the teeth, are of tough, second growth wood if possible. Then as fast as a tooth breaks out put in another, and when not in use, whatever the implement, see that it is put away clean, dry, and in a dry place.

RAM. The male of sheep, as distinguished from the ewe. Sometimes the word buck is used, and the word doe for the female. It is manifestly incorrect and should not be persisted in. (See article Sheep.)

RAMENTA. Thin, brown scales seen on ferns and young shoots.

RAMIE. This fiber plant has attracted much attention in the South within the last twenty years, and especially so within the last ten years, as also has the other coarser fiber plant of the East Indies, jute, which see. The chief difficulties in the way of the manufacture of these articles has been in economically separating the fiber. So important has this matter long been felt that the British government has offered immense rewards in cash to the inventor of a properly and economically working machine. Until this is accomplished the cultivation of ramie can not be successfully engaged in, in the United States, on account of the high price of manual labor. In India and China, with their wonderfully cheap labor, the cost of separating the fiber is $150 per ton. Its value when prepared is about $375 per ton in England. In 1875, a machine was exhibited which it was claimed would separate the fiber at a cost of $30 per ton. Yet but little seemed to come of it, from the fact that like machine-manufactured flax, the quality of the article for fine dress goods was worthless. Later, however, by the combination of chemical means and improved machines, it seems that inventive talent is in a fair way to accomplish the object sought. When so, the cultivation both of ramie and jute will be immensely profitable in the Gulf States, and in California where the climate is adapted to the growth of these plants. In relation to the ramie plant and its preparation, the following article, prepared for the United States government, by an expert, Emile Lefranc, will be interesting. The writer is enthusiastic and sanguine, nevertheless, there are facts of interest aside from this to those in the South who wish to engage in this new industry. We quote from the writer as follows: Introduced into Louisiana toward the fall of 1867, the ramie has had ample time to prove its vitality and toughness as a perennial growth. With little or no care it has thriven alone since then, and whenever attention has been given to it, its propagation has been considerable. In some rich and elevated soils the plant has stood and propagated without the least cultivation for the last six years. The stems die in winter, and multitudes of others shoot forth every spring. Where the bushes are regularly cut three or four times a year, the more vigorous and luxuriant is the growth. All these facts sufficiently prove the perennial and hardy vitality of the plant, as also its adaptability to our soil, and the congeniality of our climate. Therefore the agricultural problems and the questions of acclimation are also solved and settled. If the ramie industry did not unfold sooner the advantage of the plant, it was solely on account of the unprofitable or inefficient methods of extracting the fiber. When first introduced on this continent, the treatment of the ramie-plant was erroneously assimilated to that of the nettle family. The universal opinion was that it should be treated like jute, flax, hemp, and other textiles of the cannabis variety, which are disintegrated lengthwise from the stems by the simple process of water fermentation. The error was soon discovered. Ramie fiber admits of no rotting action on the stalks. Steeped and fermented in water or exposed to the air, it is decomposed and reduced to a short and weak fiber, saturated with tannic acid and spotted with tan-bark. Moreover the process is tedious and anti-economical. It has been found that the envelope of the ramie-fiber contains some sulphuric and carbonic elements, which dissolve the joints of the cellulose when the stem is subjected to the acetic degree of fermentation or rotting. Then, some chemists resorted to the process of neutralizing those dissolving elements by means of an acidulated bath for the plants. But those different systems were of no avail, because they required the additional intervention of machinery to break and hackle the filament, which was otherwise more or less injured in its quality by the unnatural treatment to which it was subjected. In face of the despotic exigencies of economy in labor, and the absolute necessity of a large production, none of those methods were practicable. What is the process of the Chinese, who for centuries have monopolized the trade? Their process consists in stripping the ramie-plant and scraping the bark containing the filament. The contrivance that cleans ramie, and furnishes a product similar to that of China, is founded on that true principle, as follows: Revolving cleaners, provided with a peculiar sort of knives, receive gradually, by means of a circular carrier, bunches of stems, which are doubled down and hooked in the middle. The carrier withdraws them from the rotary action of the cleaners, and delivers them in the form of clear ribbons, of a light yellow color, as fine as the imported China-grass. English manufacturers have monopolized the ramie or China-grass trade in Europe and America, and kept somewhat secret the process of finishing and weaving the fiber. Almost all the dress-goods, mixed with brilliant materials and imitating silk fabrics, are made in part of ramie. Leeds and Bradford are the principal manufacturing centers that use that staple as a substitute for silk in many sorts of goods. It is a common error to consider ramie as a substitute for cotton. The observation of the following rules will be absolutely necessary for the cultivation of ramie, and for drawing from the rich plant all it can yield: For nursery purposes or for cultivation, the land must be sufficiently elevated to receive the benefit of natural drainage, because the roots will not live long in a watery bottom. The soil must be deep, rich, light and moist as the sandy alluvia of Louisiana. Manure supplies the defects in some lands in these respects. The field must be thoroughly cleared of weeds, plowed twice to the depth of eight or ten inches if possible, harrowed as much as a thorough pulverizing requires, and carefully drained by discriminate lines of ditches. Water must not be allowed to stand in the rows of the plant. The land being thus prepared, planting becomes easy and promising. December, January, and February are the best months in which to plant. Roots, rattoons, and rooted layers are the only available seed. They are generally four or five inches long, carefully cut, not torn, from the mother-plant. The dusty seed produced by the ramie stalks in the fall can be sown, but it is so delicate and requires so much care during the period of germination and growth that it seldom succeeds in open land. The regular germinating power of that seed is also questionable. The Department of Agriculture vainly tried, a few years ago, to diffuse this seminal cultivation by distributing imported seed, which never germinated. In the presence of these difficulties, and of the sure propagation obtained from fractional roots, sowing has been abandoned and replanting adopted as follows: Furrows five or six inches deep and five feet apart are opened with the plow. The roots are laid lengthwise in the middle, close in succession if a thick stand of crop is desired, but placed at intervals if nursery propagation is the object in view. The first mode will absorb 3,000 roots per acre, but will save the labor of often filling the stand by propagation. The second mode will spare three-fourths of that amount of roots, but will impose the obligation of multiplying by layers. Being placed in the furrow closely, or at intervals, the roots are carefully covered with the hoe. Pulverized earth and manure spread over the roots insure an early and luxuriant growth in the spring. When the shoots have attained a foot in height they are hilled up like potatoes, corn, and all other plants that require good footing and protection from the fermenting effect of stagnant water. The intervals between the rows being deepened by the hilling have also a draining influence, which can be rendered still more effective by ditches dug across from distance to distance, say fifteen feet. Good crops are obtained by thickening the stands. The stems are then abundant, fine, straight, and rich in fiber. Close planting is then necessary, inasmuch as it prevents the objectionable branching of the stalks.. Crooked and branchy ramie is unfit for mechanical decortication; it causes waste and yields an inferior quality of fiber. The period at which the plant is ripe for cutting is indicated by a brownish tinge at the foot of the stems. At that early stage the plant, though greenish, yields a fine and abundant filament; it also produces three or four crops according to soil and climate. The first cutting may be unprofitable on account of the irregularity and sparseness of the growth; but if the stand is well razeed and manured over the stubbles the ensuing cuttings will be productive. For that purpose the field must be kept clear of grass until the growth be sufficiently dense to expel the parasites by its shade. That necessary density is obtained by means of the important laying process. This consists in bending down, right and left along the growing stand, the highest switches, and in covering them with earth up to the tender tip, which must not be smothered. One of the causes of the perennity and of the vigor of the plant is the nourishment it draws from the agencies of the atmosphere. Consequently the leaves of the layers should never be buried under ground. When properly performed, laying is very profitable; it creates an abundance of new roots, and fills up rapidly the voids of the stand. After two years the plants may be so thick as to spread out in the rows. Then the plow or the stubble-cutter has to chop in a line, on one side, the projecting rattoons. If well executed this operation leads to notable advantages: It extracts roots or fractional plants suitable for the extension of the cultivation elsewhere. It maintains, as a pruning, a vigorous life and develops a luxuriant growth in the stand. If always applied on the same side of the row, this sort of stubble-cutting has the remarkable advantage of removing gradually the growth toward the unoccupied land in the intervals, and of pushing it into a new position without disturbance. That slow rotation preserves the soil from rapid exhaustion, and the ramie from decay, through the accumulation of roots under ground. Of course this lateral plowing will not prevent the opposite row from receiving the benefit of hoeing after each crop. Experiments made in Louisiana have demonstrated the efficiency of that method; to which are due the preservation and propagation of the plant in that State, while it has been destroyed in other sections for want of similar care. It is through such judicious methods that the old land of China has preserved sufficient fertility to produce constantly the ramie for many centuries. After each cutting Chinese planters plow on one side and make cleanly the stand; then they cover it with a thick coat of manure. That maintains the moisture and fertility of the soil, and, at the same time, preserves the plant from excessive heat or extreme cold. That protective system permits in winter ramie cultivation in latitudes corresponding to those of Maryland and Virginia. It could even be undertaken farther north by another Chinese application. In some cold regions of the northwestern parts of the Celestial Empire, China-grass is cultivated like potatoes. Planters dig up the stand every fall, after the last cutting, and store the roots in cellars to replant them in the spring; yet they generally obtain two crops by such an unfavorable process. We have given this subject prominence for the reason that when cheap means for successfully reducing the fiber is invented and perfected, it may take as prominent a stand as one of the principal productions in the Gulf States, as hemp once did in Kentucky; such means have not yet been found, and the fiber must be separated in a great measure, as is still done in China and India, where labor costs but a few cents a day. Hence, there can be no competition here as against such labor until machinery comes to our aid. That this will at length be done, there is no doubt, and in this light those who are ready to avail themselves of cheap means of reduction, when it comes, will reap profits equal to that on cotton, following the invention of the cotton gin. The British government, years ago, offered a reward equal to $200,000 for machinery that would successfully reduce fibers like that' of ramie, for use in India, yet, we believe, it has never yet been awarded.

RAMOSE. Branched.

RAMPION. *Campanula ranunculus.* This is cultivated to a limited extent, for its roots. It is cultivated like radishes, and is fit for use in September and the fall. The soil should be rather moist The roots are eaten raw, in salads, sliced with the leaves, or they may be boiled and treated as asparagus.

RANIDÆ. The reptiles resembling the frog (*rana*).

RANUNCULUS. Plants resembling the butter-cup and crowsfoot. They are bad weeds in meadows, many of them being acrid and poisonous. Some of the improved varieties are cultivated in gardens for their blossoms.

RAPE. *Brassica rapa.* The cultivation of rape for its seed, from which an oil is expressed, formerly used for its superior illuminating power, and for its other uses in the arts, has, of late years, considerably declined even in Europe. The best varieties for oil are the biennial species, notably *B. campestris olifer.* None of the biennials are hardy in the North. Hence in the cultivation of this plant, chiefly in Wisconsin, an inferior annual variety, the German smoothed-leaved, with upright pods, *B. Præcox*, is sown. The seed may either be sown broadcast or in drills, three pounds drilled or six pounds broadcast. The most economical way, however, is to sow in drills. It is harvested by reaping, and dried and threshed similar to flax. It is comparatively little cultivated now, though at one time there were mills at Fond du Lac, Wis., capable of working 100,000 bushels of seed in a season. Land under fair culture will yield ten to eighteen bushels of rape per acre, though thirty-five bushels per acre have been obtained. The seeds yield about two gallons of oil per bushel. The crop leaves the soil in excellent condition, and the chaff, when mixed with roots, makes an excellent cattle food. The rape-seed cake is highly valued in Europe for feeding dairy cows. In case a crop of grain gives indications of failure, it can be turned under in season for raising a crop of rape in its place, which is subject to no disease or insect enemy. Its broad leaves shade the soil and stifle any weeds that may spring up after it gets fully established, and it prepares the soil admirably for winter wheat; it requires no labor during its growth, and may be cut with a cradle scythe or mower, and harvested at a most convenient time, in the first half of September, after the summer harvests are out of the way, and before the corn and potato harvest begins. One bushel yields about two gallons of oil, superior to the best lard or sperm as an illuminating oil, besides being a good lubricator, and enduring an intense degree of cold before solidifying. The only conditions unfavorable to the entire success of rape as a general farm crop are, that it will not succeed on foul land, where it would be choked out by weeds in its early growth, and that it must be harvested just as the pods are turning from green to yellow or much of the seed will be lost.

RAPHE. A suture. Parts which appear as though they had been united. In botany, the thread passing from the ovule to the placenta.

RAPHIDES. Crystals of oxalate of potash and other salts found in the juice of rhubarbs, docks, and other plants.

RAPTORES, ACCIPITRES. Birds of prey, as the hawk, owl, eagle, etc.

RAREFACTION. The act of diminishing the density of air or other bodies; it is done by the air-pump in the case of air.

RASORES. Scratchers; gallinaceous birds, such as the fowl, turkey, pheasant, etc.

RASPBERRY. *Rubus.* Our native raspberries are the Thimble Berry or Black Cap, (*Rubus occidentalis*), and the Red raspberry (*R. s rigosus*). The raspberry is common in some of its forms in nearly every part of Europe and the United States. The variety from which the principal European sorts have their origin, is *Rubus Idæus*, said originally to have been introduced into the gardens of the south of Europe from Mount Ida, hence its name. The five varieties most extensively cultivated throughout the United States are the Mammoth Cluster, the Orange, the Philadelphia, Purple Cane, and American Black. In the West, the Turner is now the favorite for hardiness and prolific bearing, added to fairly good quality. The cultivation of the raspberry is simple. Plant in rows five feet apart by three and one-half feet in the row, in rich, rather moist (not wet) soil. When the plants are three feet high pinch out the tip to make them more stocky. Give clean cultivation, eradicating all suckers, and do not allow those sorts which propagate from the tips to take root. Where the climate is very cold the more tender varieties will need protection, and the more slender sorts must be tied to stakes. It is, probably, its sturdy nature and hardy character that makes it a favorite, since in quality it is below the Mammoth Cluster, and far inferior to such delicate sorts as Knevet's Giant, Imperial Red, and Orange. On page 783 we have illustrated one of the old and, for market, still largely cultivated varieties, Doolittle's Black Cap. It is of small size, but quite hardy, enduring the winters well North, and firm enough to carry long distances. On page 784 is shown the Herstine, a berry of the largest size, obtuse in form, a red berry of excellent quality, but not sufficiently firm for carrying by railway. It is also tender, as, indeed, are all first-class berries. Where protected, however, and the proper conditions for growth and health are present, it is valuable as a fine-flavored, prolific, and large berry. Nevertheless, neither of these cuts are given as showing the best sorts of either black or red raspberries, but as types of each. Soil, climate and situation have so much to do with success and failure in small fruits that the farmer had better take the advice of some respectable nurseryman (not a mere tree pedlar), as to varieties that will probably do well in his locality.

RASPBERRY WINE. (See Gallizing.)

RAT. *Mus Rattus.* The rat now usually found, is an importation said to be originally from Norway. They are on account of their fecundity and voracity, the most destructive of verminous animals, calling for every possible means for their destruction. In large cities rat-catching is made a regular business, and it has been said that when business became dull, the sagacious rat catcher would turn loose those caught in one place upon another. The most successful means of destroying rats is by ferrets, kept for the purpose, (See Ferret). Yet this means will not soon come into general use, since ferrets require to be kept and fed, and it requires some skill to work them in hunting rats. Terrier dogs, with the aid of traps, baiting and poisoning the rats, will generally keep the farm buildings measurably clear. When poisoning, however, is followed care must be taken that farm animals, and especially children, do not get near it.

RATCHET. A small lever which plays into the teeth of a ratchet-wheel, and allows it to turn freely only in one direction.

RAT'S TAIL. A disease in horses, in which the hair of the tail is permanently lost.

RATTLESNAKE. Snakes of the genus *Crotalus.* Their bite is extremely venomous. The wound should be cut out and scarified, and the patient sustained by brandy and ammonia.

REAPERS. Reaping by machinery is mentioned so long ago as the time of Pliny, the elder, or more than 2,000 years ago. This graphic writer says: In the extensive fields of the lowlands of Gaul, vans of large size, with projecting teeth on the forward edge, are driven on two wheels through the standing corn (grain) by an ox yoked in a reversed position with the machine forward of the ox. In this manner the heads or ears are torn off and fall into the van. Coming from Pliny's time, and through the dark ages, to about a century ago, a machine was worked in England, driven forward by a horse hitched in the rear, which, as it passed forward, clipped the heads which fell into a box in the rear. When full this was hauled to the granary and deposited, and was the germ perhaps of the modern header. The great statesman of England, Gladstone, is credited with having taken out a patent in England for a reaper which cut the grain and delivered the straw in gavels, to be bound by hand. Curious, is it not, that it should have taken over two thousand years to bring so useful and necessary a machine to its present perfection, and yet not more singular than the parallel history of the perfection of the plow, that has been in use in some crude form since the days of the ancient Egyptians, if indeed they did not get their idea, probably, from the more remote civilization of the Chinese. To come down to the present time. To Mr. Obed Hussey and to Mr. McCormick, are due the merit of first elaborating ideas that have made reaping and mowing machines practi-

DOOLITTLE'S BLACK CAP RASPBERRY.

RASPBERRY — VARIETY HERSTINE

cable. Successive inventors have, with them, carried the improvements forward until, in 1878, machines cut, bound, and delivered the grain ready for shocking far cleaner and better than it could be done by hand. In California, headers are still much used, that dry climate allowing the grain to stand until so ripe that the heads may be safely ricked, or threshed, directly from the machine. In self-binding reapers, their perfection by human means may be said to have been about reached. The history of reaping, and the laurels added from time to time to American machines, have been thus tersely stated. The sickle, which was in almost universal use till within a very recent date, is undoubtedly one of the most ancient of all our farming implements. Reaping by the use of it was always slow and laborious, while from the fact that many of our grains would ripen at the same time, there was a liability to loss before they could be gathered, and practically there was a vastly greater loss from this cause than there is at the present time. It is not, therefore, too much to say that the successful introduction of the reaper into the grain-fields of this country has added many millions of dollars to the value of our annual harvests, by enabling us to secure the whole product, and by making it possible for the farmer to increase the area of his wheat-fields, with a certainty of being able to gather the crop. Nothing was more surprising to the mercantile community of Europe than the fact that we could continue to export such vast quantities of wheat and other breadstuffs through the midst of the late civil war, with a million or two of able-bodied men in arms. The secret of it was the general use of farm-machinery. The number of two-horse reapers in operation throughout the country, in the harvest of 1861, performed an amount of work equal to about a million of men. The result was that our capacity for farm production was not materially disturbed. The credit of the practical application of the principles involved in this class of machines undoubtedly belongs to our own ingenious mechanics; for though somewhat similar machines were invented in England and Scotland many years ago, they had never been proved to be efficient in the field, and had never gained the confidence of the farmers, even in their neighborhood; while the patent issued to Obed Hussey, of Cincinnati, in 1833, and another issued to McCormick, of Virginia, in 1834, not only succeeded in the trials to which they were subjected, but in the face of difficulties gained a wide and permanent reputation. Many patents had been issued in this country previously, the first having been as early as 1803, but they had not proved successful. Hussey's machine was introduced into New York and Illinois in 1834, into Missouri in 1835, into Pennsylvania in 1837, and in the next year the inventor established himself in Baltimore. McCormick's machine had been worked as early as 1831, but it was afterwards greatly improved, and became a source of an immense fortune to the inventor. He took out a second patent in 1845, fifteen other machines having been patented after the date of his first papers, including that of the Ketchum, in 1844, which gained a wide reputation. The first trial of reapers, partaking of a national character, was held under the auspices of the Ohio State Board of Agriculture in 1852, when twelve different machines and several different mowers were entered for competition. There was no striking superiority, according to the report of the judges, in any of the machines. A trial had been held at the show of the New York State Agricultural Society, at Buffalo, in 1848, but the large body of farmers who had witnessed it were not prepared to admit that the work of the machines was good enough to be tolerated in comparison with the hand-scythe. Some thought they might possibly work in straight, coarse grass, but in finer grasses they were sure to clog. The same society instituted a trial of reapers and mowers at Geneva in 1852, when nine machines competed as reapers and seven as mowers. Only two or three of the latter were capable of equaling the common scythe in the quality of work they did, and not one of them all, when brought to a stand in the grass, could start again without backing to get up speed. All the machines had a heavy side-draft, some of them to such an extent as to wear seriously on the team. None of them could turn about readily within a reasonable space, and all were liable to tear up the sward in the operation. The old Manning, patented in 1831, and the Ketchum machines were the only ones that were capable of doing work that was at all satisfactory. One or two of the reapers in this trial did fair work, and the judges decided that, in comparison with the hand-cradle, they showed a saving of eighty-eight and three-fourths cents per acre. Here was some gain certainly, a little positive advance, but still most of the reapers, as well as the mowers, did very inferior work. The draft in them all was very heavy, while some of the best of them had a side-draft that was destructive to the team. The inventive genius of the country was stimulated by these trials to an extraordinary degree of activity. Patents began to multiply rapidly. Local trials took place every year, in various parts of the country, to test the merits of the several machines. The great International Exposition at Paris, in 1855, was an occasion not to be overlooked by an enterprising inventor, and the American machines, imperfect as they were at that time, were brought to trial there in competition with the world. The scene of this trial was on a field of oats about forty miles from Paris, each machine having about an acre to cut. Three machines were entered for the first trial, one American, one English, and a third from Algiers, all at the same time raking as well as cutting. The American machine did its work in twenty-two minutes, the English in sixty-six, and the Algerian in seventy-two. At a subsequent trial on the same piece, three other machines were entered, of American, English, and French manufacture, when the American machine did its work in twenty-two minutes, while the two others failed. The successful competitor on this occasion, says a French journal, did its work in a most exquisite manner, not leaving a single stalk ungathered, and it discharged the grain in the most perfect shape, as if placed by hand, for the binders. It finished its piece most excellently. The contest was finally narrowed down to three machines, all American. Two machines were afterwards converted from reapers into mowers, one making the change in one minute, the other in twenty. Both performed their task to the astonishment and satisfaction of a large con-course of spectators, and the judges could hardly restrain their enthusiasm, but cried out, good, good! well done! while the excitable people who looked on hurrahed for the American reaper, crying out, that's the machine! that's the machine! The report of a French agricultural journal said: All the laurels, we are free to confess, have been gloriously won by Americans, and this achievement can not be looked upon with indifference, as it plainly foreshadows the ultimate destiny of the New World. Five years after the Geneva trial there was a general desire to have another on a scale of magnificence that should bring out all the prominent reapers and mowers of the country. The United States Agricultural Society accordingly instituted a national trial at Syracuse, N. Y., in 1857. More than forty mowers and reapers entered, and were brought to test on the field. It was soon apparent that striking improvements had been made since the meeting at Geneva. The draft had been very materially lessened in nearly all the machines, though the side-draft was still too great in some of them. Most of the machines could now cut fine and thick grass without clogging, and there was a manifest progress in them, but of the nineteen that competed as mowers, only three could start in fine grass without backing to get up speed. The well known Buckeye, patented only the year before, won its first great triumph here, and carried off the first prize. Every year now added to the list of new inventions and improvements. In 1839 the Wood mower was invented, and soon gained a high reputation. By the year 1864 there were no less than a hundred and eighty-seven establishments in the country devoted to the manufacture of reapers and mowers, many of them very extensive, and completely furnished with abundant power, machinery and tools of the most perfect description, while the work had become wisely and thoroughly systematized. The people directly sustained by these factories exceeded sixty thousand, while the value of their annual product exceeded $15,000,000, the number of machines amounting to one hundred thousand. Nine years after the Syracuse trial, another exhibition of mowers and reapers, national in its character, was held at Auburn, N. Y., under the auspices of the New York State Society, in July, 1866. The number of mowers that entered, single and combined, was forty-four; the number of reapers, thirty; or seventy-four in all. It was plain, at a glance, that a decided improvement had taken place in workmanship and mechanical finish. The mowers were more compact, simpler in construction, lighter, and yet equally strong; they ran with less friction; the draft was easier, and the machines generally were less noisy; they cut the grass better, and were capable of working over uneven surfaces. The committee say in their report: Those who had been present at former trials were astonished at the general perfection which had been attained by manufacturers of mowing machines. Every machine, with two exceptions, did good work, which would be acceptable to any farmer; and the appearance of the whole meadow, after it had been raked over, was vastly better than the average mowing of the best farmer in the State, notwithstanding the great difficulties that had to be encountered. At previous trials, very few machines could stop in the grass and start without backing for a fresh start. At the present trial every machine stopped in the grass and started again without backing, without any difficulty and without leaving any perceptible ridge to mark the place where it occurred, thus leaving a clean cut. We may here note the rapid progress of these most valuable labor-saving machines, for while, in the earlier trials, only one or two mowers met with any success whatever, no one doing what practical farmers could call good work, in this trial forty-two of the forty-four machines entered did their work well. In the early contests even a partial success was the rare exception; in the late, failure was the equally rare exception. In 1850 less than five thousand machines had been made and put to use, and few, if any of them, gave satisfaction. Now there is scarcely a farm of any size in the country but has its mowing machine. It is one of the grandest agricultural inventions of modern times, and yet we see that it is less than twenty years since doubts were freely entertained as to whether it would ever become practically useful, whether the numerous mechanical obstacles would be entirely overcome. Its triumph has been complete. We have now many mowers that have not only a national but a world-wide reputation. The successful introduction of these machines was an immeasurable step in advance upon the old methods of cutting grass. They come in at a season when the work of a farm is peculiarly laborious, when labor is held at higher than the usual high rate of wages, when the weather is often fickle, either oppressively hot and trying to the physical system, or catchy and lowering, and they relieve the severest strain upon the muscles at the time of harvest. Our reapers are at the same time self-rakers. We can reap and gather from fifteen to twenty acres a day in the most satisfactory manner. This brings us up to 1870, about which time inventive talent was earnestly directed to self-binding machines. The first successful attempt in this direction was the Marsh harvester, which cut the grain and carried it to tables from which two expert binders would tie the bands as fast as delivered, working from eight to twelve acres per day according to the heft and standing of the grain. It will not be necessary to follow inventive talent further in the perfection of reaping machines, suffice it to say, the ideas of the earlier inventors have been improved on and elaborated. Lightness of draft combined with great strength; the avoidance of undue friction and lost motion; the power of starting with a clean cut in heavy, and, indeed, green and tangled bottom; automatic raking, and more later automatic binding, and the delivery of the bound sheaves in piles ready for shocking—all these points have been successfully elaborated within the last decade. Besides this, machines do not now easily get out of order, so that from the perfectness of the working parts, twenty or more machines may be put to work in a harvest, working one after the other on consecutive cuts, as illustrated in Landed Estates and Farms, and with almost as much certainty of retaining their respective places in line as may a string of gang plows, as illustrated in the article Plowing. In fact they can be kept as well under control, almost, as stationary appliances.

REAR HORSE. *Mantidæ.* True orthopterous insects which have their legs peculiarly adapted for walking, and known under various expressive names, as Rear-horse, Camel-crickets, or Praying mantids; all, as well as the specters or walking-sticks, are beneficial to agriculture, since they destroy all such insects as they can catch and overcome. They are all insects belonging to the South rather than the North, being seldom found much above the latitude of St. Louis. *Mantis Carolina* is common in Southern Illinois and South. They are of a greenish or grayish-brown color, their heads horizontal, their eyes large and globular, antennæ thread-like, and the body long, linear, and oval, with the abdomen much wider than the thorax or front part of the body, and of a depressed form. The upper wings of the male are long, and have numerous veins. The under wings are thin and net-veined with long parallel veins. The wing-covers of the females are considerably shorter than those of the male, and do not reach the end of the abdomen. When disturbed, this singular insect elevates or rears the fore part of its body almost perpendicularly, fixes its large staring eyes full upon the disturber, and turns its head sideways in a peculiarly human, yet ludicrous manner, so as to follow every movement of its tormentor with at least one eye. If a small object, such as a blade of grass, be then presented, it will either strike out vigorously with its saber-like fore feet, or else retreat to what it considers a safe distance. These insects are especially remarkable in the formation of their fore feet, which are much longer than the others, and are formed particularly for catching and holding their prey, which consists of other insects. The thighs are robust, and armed with a double row of spines, the shanks are short, spiny, and curved so as to fit into the under side of the thighs, when closed, like a clasp-knife. When in pursuit of its prey the insect moves almost imperceptibly along, and steals toward its victim like a cat approaching a mouse, and, when sufficiently near, the fore leg is extended at its full length, the insect immediately caught and impaled by the spines between the thigh and shank, carried to the mouth, and deliberately eaten piecemeal while yet alive and struggling to escape. If gently treated and daily accustomed to the sight of its feeder, this insect may readily be tamed so as to take flies from the hand, and from the oddity of its actions and apparent intelligence makes a most interesting pet. The eggs are clustered together in an irregular brownish mass or case, about an inch long, and fastened to the branches or trunks of trees, on palings, or walls, and even on the under side of window-sills, in Washington, where the insects are very common. Wherever such cases are found, they should be protected and not destroyed, as is generally the case, (being mistaken for the eggs of leaf-destroying caterpillars), as the insects produced from them do no injury whatsoever to vegetation, but, on the contrary, are very beneficial as destroying injurious insects, from their earliest infancy, as when young they feed upon plant-lice and other minute insects. These young rear-horses are so carnivorous that almost as soon as they are hatched and their skins a little hardened by exposure to the atmosphere they will devour their younger and softer-bodied brethren, and we have seen frequently a young mantis of a day old mercilessly devour the young of its own kind when just emerged from the egg-case. When older, these insects disperse and feed at first on very small insects, such as plant-lice and similar small game, until they acquire size and strength sufficient to master small caterpillars and flies. When fully grown, the females, being much larger, stronger, and more rapacious than their mates, the males, will frequently sieze and kill them, and afterward make a good meal from their quivering bodies. Allied to these are the specter or walking-stick insects, *Phasmidæ.* These insects in this country do very little, if any, injury to the farmers, as they generally live on the shoots and foliage of wild shrubs or trees in the woods. The most common species is the common walking-stick insect, (*Diapheromera femorata*), so named from the close resemblance the insect bears to a dead twig or stick. The egg-sac is said to be flattened, elliptic, with a lid in front, which can be pushed open by the imago when about to hatch. These eggs are deposited in autumn. The young insects resemble the old ones in form and habits, differing only in size. The species never acquire wings, and merely crawl from limb to limb; they are of very sluggish habits, and the males are considerably smaller than the females. When stretched out motionless on a twig, with fore feet and antennæ extended, they can scarcely be distinguished from the twigs themselves, and city visitors, who see them for the first time, can scarcely be persuaded that they are not real twigs, gifted in some mysterious manner, with life and motion. These insects are said to be able to reproduce some of their limbs when accidentally broken off. They feed upon the buds, shoots, and foliage of various trees and shrubs, but are not sufficiently numerous to cause much injury.

RECEPTACLE. In botany it has four different significations: That part of a flower upon which the carpels are situated; or, in other words the extremity of the fruit stalk. The axis of the theca of *Trichomanes* and *Hymenophyllum,* among ferns. That part of the ovarium from which the ovula arise, and which is commonly called the placenta. That part of the axis of a plant which bears the flowers when it is depressed in its development; so that, instead of being elongated into a stem, it forms a flattened area, upon which the flowers are arranged, as in compositæ.

RECLAMATION OF LAND. The history of the reclamation of swamps and marsh lands, more especially by shutting out the water of floods, is as old as civilization itself. Its condensed history is given both as showing its antiquity and the importance always attached to such reclamation, from the great fertility of such soils. The periodical overflow of the Nile to uncertain limits necessitated the controlling of the waters within defined boundaries, and this control was most undoubtedly exercised by means of embankments. The Phœnicians—the people of Tyre and the ancient sea-ports of the East, the Greeks and the Romans, erected extensive works on their sea-coasts to protect their cities and ships from ocean storms and foreign enemies, and no doubt they enclosed low-lying lands in many instances for the purpose. The Romans, during their occupation of Britain, raised immense lines of embankments at several points along the coast, the remains of which are still in existence. In fact, all nations, as they advanced in civilization seem to have recognized in reclamation a means of extending the area of land to be distributed among the people without necessitating an emigration of surplus inhabitants. This has been the case in India and China, where the dense population manages to accommodate itself to the limits of those countries, and it is only within the last few years that we have seen any signs of a movement by these people to other countries. The original settlers of the Netherlands were the descendants of those wandering tribes whose emergence from their homes in the North heralded the downfall of the Roman empire, and laid the foundation of the nationalities which at present checker the map of Europe. The first steps toward erecting barriers against the tidal overflow in Holland are stated to have been taken in or about the second century of the Christian era. It is probable that the vanguards of the great army of invasion which in later times overran Europe from the north had begun to move forward and occupy in small bodies the country lying along the northern coast. As the population increased, and the groups of mud huts grew into large towns and cities, the necessity for placing under cultivation more extensive areas of land became imperative. The more valuable these settlements grew to the people, the more desirous were they to guard them against destruction by the sea, and the attention of the government and people was directed to the general and permanent embanking of the whole coast. How they have succeeded we all know. The country which was once a desolate marsh is now a garden. Visitors passing through it acknowledge that in no part of the world is scientific agriculture better understood or applied, although the fields and dwellings are in many places twenty feet below the level of the sea. It was not alone necessary to embank against the sea, but also against the waters of some of the great rivers whose sources are to be found in the very heart of Europe, and which would overflow all the low lands they traverse had not the precaution of confining them to their natural channels been taken by the Hollanders. Many works have been written which give detailed descriptions of the manner in which the diking of the Netherlands was carried on. The foundation of the work was laid by nature. The superstructure was the work of man. Along the coast exposed to the great ocean storms a bank of sand was washed up by the action of the waves, and a natural barrier was erected against the incursion of the tidal waves. A belt of wood which grew along the coast, and against which the sand was heaped, assisted the early toilers in their labors by affording both shelter and material. This wood has since disappeared to a great extent in the constant repairs rendered necessary by the action of the waves in stormy weather. Beyond strengthening and connecting these mounds or banks of sand, and securing the lands in the immediate neighborhood of the ocean from tidal overflow, little was done in the beginning on the main embankment along the coast, while the river banks were left wholly exposed. The great work once initiated, however, it has progressed steadily to the present day, and we find that after a struggle lasting many centuries, the energy and perseverance of man have wrested a kingdom from the sea. Writers on the subject of the early condition of Holland tell us that the country was covered with lakes, varying in size, which have been drained and converted into fruitful farms. The most important operation lately and successfully completed is the draining of the Harlem lake, which covered an area of about 45,000 acres. A description of this work was given in the report of the Department of Agriculture for 1866. Extensive tracts on the western coast of England, called the Fen country, have been embanked and drained, and added to the cultivable land in that section. As many as 680,000 acres of fen have been reclaimed, and the works rival those of Holland in extent. The Encyclopædia Britannica says: This fen country has for centuries been the scene of drainage operations on a stupendous scale. The whole surface of the great basin of the fens is lower than the sea, the level varying from four to sixteen feet below high-water mark in the German Ocean. The difficulty in draining this flat tract is increased from the circumstance that the ground is highest near the shore and falls inward toward the foot of the slope. These inland and lower grounds consist of a spongy peat, which has a natural tendency to retain water. The rivers and streams which flow from the higher inlands discharge upon these level grounds, and originally found their way into the broad and shallow estuary of the wash, obstructed in all directions by bars and sand-banks. These upland waters, being now caught at their point of entrance on the fens, are confined within strong artificial banks, and so guided straight seaward, and are thus restrained from flooding the low grounds, and by their concentration and momentum assist in scouring out the silt from the narrow channel to which they are confined. The tidal waters are at the same time fenced out by sea-banks, which are provided at certain intervals with sluice-doors by which the waters escape at ebb tide. When this does not provide such a drainage as to admit of cultivation, the water is lifted mechanically by wind or steam mills into the main aqueducts. In the district called Marsh, in Norfolk, extending between the Ouse and the New, in that called South Holland, in Lincolnshire, stretching between the New and Welland, northward of Spalding, and also northeast of Boston, there are considerable tracts of marine clay soil. In Marshland this is chiefly arable land, producing large crops of wheat and beans; but in Lincolnshire it forms exceedingly fine grazing land. This tract lies within the old Roman embankment, by which the district was first defended from the ocean. Outside this barrier are the proper marsh lands, which have been reclaimed in portions at successive periods, and are still intersected in all directions by ranges of banks. The extraordinary feature in this tract is that the surface outside the Roman bank is three or four feet higher than on the inside, and the level of each new inclosure is more elevated than the previous one. The land rises step by step as the coast is approached, so that the most recently reclaimed land is often twelve and sometimes eighteen feet higher than the lowest fen land in the interior, the drainage from which must, nevertheless, be conveyed through these more elevated marshes to the sea.¹ These extensive works are represented by many hundreds of miles of river embankments, and the sea-coast line embanked exceeds one hundred and thirty in length. This fen land, once, like that of Holland, a wild, marshy tract, impassable to man or beast, is now a fertile farm, rich in agricultural products, and inhabited by a healthy and wealthy population. Another instance of successful reclamation is to be found in England; the Bedford level, called after the Earl of Bedford, who in the year 1634 expended over £100,000 to reclaim these lands, and whose son completed the work at an additional cost of £300,000. These lands have since that time been kept perfectly free of water by means of windmills and other pumping engines. Extensive drainage operations have been carried on in many parts of Europe, particularly in France and Italy. The celebrated Pontine marshes, near Rome, are mentioned by early historians as a source of great danger to the public health, and several unsuccessful attempts were made to reclaim them. The popes at different periods renewed these efforts, and their success, though partial, proved that the drainage could be effected with sufficient capital. In Ireland, immense tracts of peat-bog have been drained and converted into arable land. The bog of Allen is an extensive area of peaty soil, extending into several counties, and covering many thousand acres. In the southern part of Ireland, along the rivers and shores of the main estuaries, large areas of alluvial deposits have been inclosed by embankments, and a rich soil made available for cultivation. The cotton lands in the valley of the Mississippi are exceedingly fertile when properly protected by levees from the periodical overflow of the river. The construction and maintenance of these levees are often the subject of discussion in Congress, and it would seem proper that the nation's representatives should interest themselves in what forms so important a protection to the agricultural interests of several of the States of the Union. In Canada the question of reclaiming the marsh lands is receiving considerable attention from both the government and the people. Extensive works are about to be commenced, with a view to these reclamations; and vast areas of fertile soil will be added to the lands of the New Dominion. In the United States the question of utilizing marshes has not attained the importance it deserves. In the neighborhood of New York, a considerable tract of land, known as the Newark Meadows, lying between the Newark and Paterson range of hills, on the west side, and the Palisade ridge of Bergen hill on the east side, has been embanked and otherwise drained and reclaimed within the past fifteen years. Mr. Jerome J. Collins, a civil engineer of New Jersey, who has had large experience in reclaiming the tide water lands between New York, Newark, and Hackensack, originally unproductive salt marshes, but now most valuable and high priced gardening soil, gives the general principles of reclamation as follows: In effecting the reclamation of a tract of marsh land, three distinct objects must be attained before the work can be considered complete. First, the exclusion of all waters, having their sources of supply or operating from the outside of the limits of the marsh land reclaimed. Second, the collection and expulsion, by means of drains, ditches, sluices, and pumps, of all waters lodged on the marsh or having their sources inside its limits. Third, the control of all waters that may afterward accumulate on the marsh from springs, rains or other causes, so that the danger of drowning the land may be avoided and the cultivation of the soil be uninterrupted. Each of these conditions must exist to insure the harmonious working of the other two; the absence of one is fatal to the usefulness of the others. In case of the first condition, when we undertake to exclude waters having their sources outside the limits of the marsh to be reclaimed, it is necessary to erect a dike; but the shape, size, and mode of construction will be governed by the locality, material, and the amount of resistance the dike must offer to the return of the excluded water. The collection and expulsion of waters accumulated on the marsh from rains, or the interception of that deriving its source from springs within the marsh limits, will depend considerably on area, location, and outfall, as well as on the power and capacity of pumps and other water-engines. The control of the water in the soil and its removal for agricultural purposes will depend on the excellence and completeness of the other works, but will also be affected by climate and the character and treatment of the crops raised. The location of the marsh with respect to high lands is of the utmost importance, as, when adjoining upland, it receives the rainfall of the hills in addition to its own, and unless precautions are taken to control this irregular addition to its own waters, the land shall not suffer from it, the third condition for a complete reclamation can not be said to be complied with. Embankments are necessary for the exclusion of water from an area where the source of that water is above the level of the surface to be kept dry. For instance, the embankment of a reservoir must of necessity be above the level of the river, spring, or other reservoir from which the first receives its supply, unless, indeed, the discharge from the latter be equal to that which it uniformly receives, and its embankments lose their retaining character, and become simple diverters of the stream. In like manner, any space enclosed by an embankment for the purpose of excluding water must have that embankment higher than the highest level of the encroaching water, if an inland stream, or the highest known range of the tide, if on a tidal river bank, or the sea-coast, unless, in the case of the inland stream, the water becomes simply guided in its course, and not confined. As our principal marshes requiring embankments are located along the shores of the large bays and inlets, or on the banks of tidal streams, remarks will be confined to such marshes and their requirements. In erecting a dike to resist the pressure of the tide, the shape, the size, and the mode of construction of the dike must vary with the location and the range of the tide. Location affects it because the bank may at one point be sheltered from the eroding action of the waves, while at another point it may be exposed to their full force. It is therefore evident that some dissimilarity must exist between the work to be done by the two sections of the bank, and a consequent difference becomes necessary in their shape, strength, and mode of construction. Many plans have been projected for the erection of dikes, sea-walls, and embankments, each possessing some peculiar merit, while failing to fulfill equally important requirements. No particular form of dike can be recommended for all cases, as the necessity of each case demands special treatment. The Dutch engineers favor long slopes for sea-banks, constructed of sand or other light material, but the length of the exterior slope can be safely diminished, where a durable material, like stone, can be procured, with the additional security of piles and other protection; it is also certain that where the material is not adhesive and durable, long slopes, especially facing the waves, are advantageous when not exposed to the face of the ocean waves, as on the coast of Holland. A base of about five to one, divided between the internal and external slopes, in addition to the width of the bank on top, would afford ample base for an embankment. Thus, if we require an embankment six feet high to resist the encroachment of the tide, we can not with absolute safety construct it with a base of less than thirty-five feet to resist effectually the wash of the waves. This width of base would admit of, in the first place, a width on the top of the embankment of five feet and external slope of three feet and a half to one, and an internal slope of one and a half to one. The bank with a thirty-five foot base is suited to exposed situations, where wind and wave act directly but moderately. Where the bank is subject to a heavy blow from the waves, the slope will be so graduated as to receive and gradually deaden the effort of the wave as it traverses its surface. The shape of the bank is of as much importance as its construction and dimensions, because, if by unsuitable proportions we subject the very best material and workmanship to extreme and unnecessary strains, it can not be expected that the work of resistance will be performed as effectually as if due consideration were given to the relations which should always exist between the shape, material, and amount of resistance the bank is expected to offer to the water. Durable material is not always to be had where wanted for embankments, but in the case of salt marshes, with very few exceptions the soil excavated forms a superior material for their construction. This is generally the case along the shores of large rivers and estuaries, where the silt from the river is continually being washed against the bank, and during high tides carried over and deposited on the surface of the marsh along the river-banks, forming a compact soil, which, when used, in the construction of a bank and dried, becomes hard, durable, and water-tight—the three most important requirements for an embankment. The fitness of these marsh soils for embankments has been tested, and where used not the least trouble has been experienced with them either by a settlement or breach, but the shape of the bank has been preserved unchanged after severe winters and heavy rain storms. When banks are erected to exclude water, they must be made perfectly impermeable to that element. The least leakage is but the forerunner of a burst, unless quickly attended to. These leaks are frequently caused by the imperfect construction of the bank itself, where the material is not packed close, or some of the joints between the sods of soil have not been thoroughly closed by the workmen. Another cause may be the shrinkage of the material when drying in the bank, joints that were close while the moisture swelled the material of the bank being opened by the shrinkage of the soil, and admitting tiny streams, which soon become serious leaks, and finally the cause of the destruction of the bank. Of the two causes, either may be guarded against by proper care in constructing the bank. There is still another cause of leakage and the failure of a bank—the penetration of the bank by muskrats and other boring animals, whose attacks must be steadily resisted by constant vigilance and the adoption of some plan of construction which will defeat their operations. Several attempts which have been made at reclamation in this country owe their failure to the muskrats. These animals are not to be despised as enemies to marsh reclamation. As workers they are unrivaled in perseverance, for they will return again and again to the attack on the same point of an embankment, until they succeed in boring it to their satisfaction, or are killed by a lucky shot. On the Newark meadows, New Jersey, they were defeated effectually by means of the iron plate inserted in the embankment, and covering the space between the range of high and low water. The rats penetrated the bank in many places, but were stopped by the plate, and they either gave up their excavation or cut their way over the plate at a level above that of high water, and the consequent injury to the bank was slight and easily repaired. A core composed of a less expensive material than iron would answer the same purposes, and a well-constructed dike core of wood, hemlock for instance, will probably be found fully equal to all requirements. There are conditions, however, under which the iron core might be preferable. To accomplish the second important condition, the collection and removal of all waters lying stagnant or otherwise, and having their source of supply within the limits of the marsh, a series of main and intermediate ditches or drains must be cut through the marsh, for the collection and conveyance of these waters to points on the line of the main embankments, from which it can be forced or drained out. In the case of tide marshes, where the range of the tide brings the low-water level sufficiently below that of the marsh surface to admit of the drainage of the soil to a proper depth, and a fair outfall for the water collected in the ditches, a number of well-placed and properly-constructed sluice-gates will assist considerably in draining the land, as the volume of water drained into the river or bay will be in proportion to the fall and capacity of the sluice to discharge it. Although many advantages are derived from the use of sluices on marsh lands, they are not to be compared in efficiency with a well-constructed pump, worked by steam-power. No matter how well constructed a sluice may be, or of what material, there is always a weakness about it and a liability to accident that must impress itself upon the observer. The connection made between the embankment and the wood-work or masonry of a sluice is, in nine cases out of ten, the site of numerous leaks, which are continuously enlarging and are the more dangerous on account of their apparently trifling character. The material of a sluice may be iron; it corrodes and gets easily clogged by slight obstructions, such as small branches of trees or tufts of grass. If made of wood, it is liable to rot away under water, and be unexpectedly destroyed by a violent storm or other cause. The stone-work setting of a sluice, on account of the alternate wetting and drying process that goes on, particularly during the winter frosts, will work out all the mortar or cement from the joints, and the whole sluice is liable to be undermined by the action of the current passing through the sluice twice in every twenty-four hours. If the sluice is self-acting, it is a source of danger, as it is liable to be obstructed by floating wood, grass, weeds, etc., and is certain to be frozen up in winter time, and in case it should be so prevented from working properly, the sluice being set to low water, the obstruction to the free flow of the water or to the closing of the gate against the rising tide will not be discovered until, in the latter case, the tide begins to flow in through the sluice, when the obstruction is placed out of reach. In this way considerable damage may be done to young crops by an overflow of salt or brackish water. If the sluice is worked by hand, it is equally dangerous, as neglect will result in a general overflow of the reclaimed land and a probable destruction of valuable property. The best provision that can be made against an overflow from a neglected or defective sluice-gate is the use of pumps exclusively for the drainage of tidal marshes. A considerable saving is also effected by using a pump, as fuel can be economically used and only when required, while the cost of pumping from one station will be much less than sluicing from a dozen points, when a larger staff of workmen is required. The general plan of the ditches and drains is regulated as much by the location of the outfall as by the actual wants of the land. The object being to remove the water as quickly as possible from the place where it accumulates, and by that means to save every inch of the fall, the ditches should be laid out with that object, and every part of the tract to be drained should be connected with the outfall as directly as possible. It is also desirable to keep a current flowing through the ditches to the outfall as uniformly constant as possible, so that no deposit can occur in the drain to obstruct the passage of the water. This uniformity of motion and direction can not be obtained by the use of sluices, or rather can be obtained by no other means than by pumping-power, which has no cause for stoppage by reason of the ebb and flow of a tide, the effect of prevailing winds, or any other obstacle to the free and constant flow of water through a sluice-way. By the use of pumps a uniform and unbroken line of embankment is presented to the outside water, having no weak places to cause a fear for its stability, no wood-work to rot away, iron-work to corrode, or masonry to be destroyed. Complete control is obtained over all accumulations of water that may occur after rain storms; a deeper drainage of the land is possible, as the level of low water outside does not affect the operation; and in the case of heavy rains due preparation can be made by the engineer to deal with the water, for when the barometer indicates a change of weather or the approach of a storm he can pump his ditches dry if necessary, and keep the water very low during the heaviest rains; on the other hand, the pump need not be worked more than one day in the week during dry weather. When certain conditions favor the adoption of the sluice in preference to the pump, it is wise to adopt that system; there are some cases where no choice can be exercised. Where springs are found on these marshes, either isolated or in groups, it is proper to connect them with a main drain through a lateral ditch; and when found in groups to surround them with a ditch by which their waters may be removed as fast as discharged, and not permitted to saturate the soil for any distance around. The removal of water from the soil for agricultural purposes is the last and most important condition to be fulfilled in the work of reclamation. The fitting of soil such as is found on our marsh lands for the reception of suitable crops calls for the exercise of considerable skill on the part of the agriculturist. He finds a virgin soil in the formation of which almost every fertilizing element is employed. His experience of upland farming may be very extensive; but here he has land that requires peculiar treatment, but no manure, no invigoration, to call forth its productiveness; in fact, nothing except the ditching tool and the plow, and the farmer's personal care and management, is required to achieve success equal to the highest expectations. An excess of moisture in a soil hurts vegetation by keeping the temperature of the subsoil low, and weakening the effect on the plants of the various chemical constituents that assist in the development and support of vegetable life. The remedy for this evil must necessarily be drainage. The absence of a proper moisture is equally damaging to vegetation, as many of these chemical constituents of soils are brought into active operation by the water in the soil and the vitality of the plant is thereby sustained. Water is the principal constituent of the sap of plants, and its absence in proper quantity must cause an exhaustion to the vegetable similar to that produced in the animal life by loss of blood. The want of natural moisture is usually supplied artificially by what is known as irrigation. We must seek a mean between the two conditions of excess and total absence of moisture, in order to arrive at that in which a soil is best fitted for the production of a healthy vegetation. Some soils, owing to their formation, will retain moisture more readily than others, and, therefore, require a different style of cultivation. Sandy soils are dry and represent the opposite extreme to the marsh in point of humidity. This is due to the composition of the soil. Sand, being purely granular, permits water to pass easily through it until it sinks to the level of some denser substratum. Marsh soil, especially alluvial or vegetable deposit, is absorbent; its particles are so minute as to form a closer and more compact combination not easily penetrated by any foreign matter moved by the force of gravity alone, insoluble, and possessing in a high degree the property of inducing capillary attraction. Nothing but deep incisions into the surface of this soil creates that positive disconnection of the mass which is necessary for the liberation of the water held in the soil by the sponge-like substance which enters so largely into its composition. The low situation of marshes and bogs is not a reason for the presence in excess of moisture in their soils. In many instances these bogs are found on high lands or the tops of high mountains. Tracts of peat bog in various parts of Ireland and England, where the surface is soft and shaking, are as high as eight feet above the level of the adjoining dry and arable land, and the water of these bogs rarely interferes with the dry land in the immediate vicinity, as it is held by the soil of the peat bog by capillary attraction stronger than gravity itself, which latter force asserts itself wherever the particles of soil are incapable of losing their identity by being blended in a general mass. The action of this capillary force on the water in the subsoil and the result in favor of vegetation has already been stated in this article and needs no further explanation. When an outfall is secured, and a regular system of main drains established, the freeing of the excess of moisture for the purposes of cultivation is accomplished by the smaller drains, which intersect the areas not immediately affected by the main drains. The size and capacity of these sub-drains will of course be suited to the area affected and the degree of humidity of the soil. In some parts of the same marsh tract the soil differs so considerably in its nature as to necessitate a variation in the plan of drainage. The proximity of high lands, woods, springs, or other causes of excessive moisture in the soil, must be taken into consideration and provision be made accordingly, but the general principles by which the detail drainage of the land is affected must be observed. A general inclination or fall of all minor drains to a main drain is as necessary as the fall of the main drain to the outlet, sluice-way, or pumping station. Where tile drains are laid, a fall of one foot in two hundred is sufficient to carry off the water, but as there are many cases in which drain pipes can not be employed, it is desirable that, while affecting as much ground as possible by a drain, every advantage should be taken of a good fall on the line of each drain, whether a main or an intermediate drain. Various plans for intermediate drains have been suggested and adopted from time to time. Among them may be mentioned one that is formed by a simple trench, cut with a shoulder to support a covering sod, laid grass down, and covered to the surface with the excavated soil. This drain does not last long, but is an economical form. Another kind of drain is made by leaning the flat tiles bridgewise against one another on top, the apex of the triangle so formed being covered with a thick sod, and the remaining part of the trench filled with broken stone and excavated soil. The tile-and-shoe drain has been used extensively in many parts of England. It is a horse-shoe tile, resting on a flat tile, thereby forming a kind of arched drain, from one to four inches in diameter. This style of drain is not now used so much as the simple circular drain pipes, with collared joints, where such a precaution is necessary to preserve the efficiency of the drain. These drain pipes are of burnt clay, about fourteen inches in length and from one to fourteen inches in diameter. In very humid soils it is necessary to provide a sufficient number of drains to carry off the water after heavy rains as fast as it soaks into the ground. Experiments will soon establish the proper positions and distances apart for these drains. As it is necessary to the productiveness of a soil that the warm rainwater should penetrate below the line of vegetation, the drains should be laid at such a depth as to be clear of the plow and spade, and the frost and the tap roots of larger plants. As soils are very rarely broken below eighteen inches from the surface, and roots are known to reach down as far as the soil is rich, while the frost penetrates to an average depth of three feet, it would be safe in districts affected by frost to lay drains four feet under the surface, and in warmer climates at a depth of one foot below the line of cultivation. With a suitable connection between the main and the drains, no soil, no matter how wet it may be, can fail to be reduced to a condition fit for cultivation. As localities differ widely in their physical features, and various circumstances compel special treatment in almost every case, it is not practicable to designate, beyond the general principles that should govern the construction and arrangement of reclamation works, any form of embankment, drain, sluice, or pump to be adhered to under all circumstances. Locality, prevailing winds, climate, range of tide, strength and velocity of local currents, the nature of the soil and vegetation, all combine to alter the character of the works, and a common standard would be impossible. It may be said of all these that locality is the one on which all the others depend for their importance. We find as we traverse the Atlantic coast of this continent a great many varieties of soil in the marshes. This is owing to the different kinds of vegetation produced on these marshes, or which composed their soil originally, and the rapidity of decomposition of this vegetable material in the soil. With locality, climate varies considerably, and climate regulates the character and growth of plants, their development, their time of maturity and of decay. A natural result of all this influence must be that in localities possessing warm climates the vegetation is more varied, more luxuriant, and consequently enters more largely into the composition of the soil than in places where the climate is less favorable for the development of vegetation. The rapid growth and quick succession of crops must tend to a large annual deposit of vegetable matter on the surface, which, before it becomes thoroughly decayed, is itself a soil, from which other plants spring, and the deposit becoming in this way more rapid than the decay which should convert it into vegetable mold, a soil is formed many degrees less dense in its structure than that of a place where the climate is colder and the growth of vegetation is slower and less luxuriant. It has been remarked that spongy, vegetable soils will retain water, when sandy and porous soils will not, and the work of drainage will be increased in proportion to the quantity of vegetable matter found in the soil. It also occurs that this rapidly formed soil is less fitted for the construction of water-tight embankments than that of a more gradual deposit, on account of its being more permeable to water, and it is often found necessary, therefore, to reject the soil we propose to reclaim, as a material for the embankment, and use that from another place. While locality and climate materially affect the manner of reclamation, prevailing winds also exercise an influence by their action on the tidal wave. In exposed situations, the winds exercise this influence to such a degree as to necessitate a complete change in the plan of reclamation, especially on the tidal marshes along the coast and the shores of our rivers. According to the course of the river, against the overflow of which embankments are erected, as well as the direction of the opening by which the waters reach the sea, the wind at certain seasons, causes a raising of the tide wave above its ordinary level, and of course necessitates higher and stronger embankments to resist it. Reference is not made to the semi-monthly occurrence of spring tides, but to the powerful effect of strong winds on the surface of water, forcing it in the direction in which it blows. When a strong wind and a spring tide occur at the same time, the tide will be raised over the level of spring tide in proportion to the strength of the wind; and when both meet a heavy freshet after a rain storm, the increased volume of the stream is not unlikely to overflow the banks, and inundate the surrounding country for many miles, doing much damage to property, and sometimes causing loss of life. In level countries the wind blows in a downward direction at an angle of something over 18° with the horizon. The pressure of the wind is in proportion to its velocity—the former increases as the square of the latter. The following table of velocities and pressures of the wind is taken from Burnell's Hydraulic Engineering:

Character of wind.	Velocity per second.		Effect per yard square.
	Ft.	In.	Pounds.
Light breeze, hardly perceptible	1	0	0.04989
Gentle breeze	3	0	0.19756
Light wind	6	0	0.79130
Rather a rong wind, best for sailing	18	0	6.06996
Strong wind	33	0	20.06690
Very strong wind	66	0	80.26760
Tempest or storm	70	0	101.62790
Great storm	90	8	146.34430
Hurricane	118	4	260.05870
Hurricane able to tear up trees, etc., etc.	150	8	405.51180

An instance of the effect of strong wind on water is mentioned by Franklin. A pond, nine miles wide, and of an average depth of three feet, was acted on by a strong wind, which forced the water from one side so that it was laid bare, and the depth of water on the other side was increased to six feet. Next to the influence of winds and waves on reclamation works, is the action of currents. Where the shore is concave, it would be imprudent to erect embankments close to the water-line, unless some protection in the shape of masonry or piling be placed against the wearing action of the current; while, on the other hand, when the shore is convex, the embankment may be placed even at the water's edge, as the fore-shore will continue to gain in the latter case as it loses in the former. In like manner, on sea-coast embankments, where the bank is likely to be washed by any of the numerous currents created by the movement of the tides, the greatest caution should be exercised in protecting the works from injury, and the exterior slopes should be strengthened in the best manner to resist the action of the water. To preserve the embankment against the damaging effects of frost, it is well to cover the face of the exterior and interior slopes with thick sods, by which a protection is afforded to the bank by the covering of grass, and the frost is not permitted to penetrate so deep into the soil composing it. In California it is estimated that there are 3,000,000 acres of swamp lands, which when drained will be the most valuable in the State.

Since 1870 this work has been prosecuted with energy, one company alone having a nominal capital of $12,000,000, and owning, in 1872, 120,000 acres of land in the delta of the Sacramento and San Joaquin rivers, and embracing we believe, both salt water and fresh water tide land. In the West there are large areas of what are known as low prairie, not marshes, but lands suffering from excess of water in the spring and interspersed through with ponds seldom dry. In Iroquois county, Ill., vast areas have been reclaimed by a careful system of drainage, rendering them among the most valuable lands in the State. In Iowa there are large tracts of the same nature requiring comparatively little expense to fit them for the plow, also many river bottoms of large extent, subject to overflow in floods occurring both in spring and summer. A good beginning has also been made in that State in the reclamation of these lands by surface drainage and by embankments. In the West there has been so much unoccupied land requiring no drainage, that until within a few years, but little attention has been paid to systematic drainage. It is now found that these lands are the richest in the several States, and that they may be reclaimed at a comparatively light cost. Hence, capital and energy have sought these channels of industry, and have acquired large tracts worth many millions of dollars in the aggregate, and adding a large yearly surplus of agricultural products for export, or for consumption at home, through being fed to fattening cattle and swine. There is another class of soils, the richest in the world, lying along the great rivers of the Mississippi valley, especially those vast areas near the Mississippi and Missouri rivers, subject to overflow in great freshets, because lying below the high water line, that if protected at all must be so by expensive systems of levees, requiring large outlays of capital. This system has been in operation in the South many years, and yet only imperfectly accomplished, since with streams carrying a large amount of sediment, the natural consequence of diking the banks, is to cause a deposit of sediment at the bottom of the stream, so that the bed of the river may come to be ultimately higher than the land itself. This is found to be the case in some of the streams of Europe, that have been diked for many centuries. The same effect seems to be going on in the lower Mississippi, the result being that the levee must be raised constantly higher and higher. Natural reasoning will show that there is a limit beyond which human art may not strive, and already, a number of schemes have been advocated to take the pressure from the banks. The recurrence of destructive inundations like those in the last decade, (1876 and 1881), in the upper Mississippi, and in 1881 along the Missouri as well, would seem to point to the fact that some means must be taken to ease the pressure of water, in very high floods, by straightening the channel, and causing a freer flow, with increased velocity, in connection with higher and more substantial embankments. The floods of 1881 would seem to teach this plainly. Another fact seems plain. The lands lying along the Mississippi are of sufficient value to bear a large outlay in perfecting the embankments. For whatever the cost, it must be done thoroughly. The damage by the flood of 1881 would undoubtedly cover the entire cost of the system of embankments or levees, or at least the recurrence of another such a one certainly would. It would seem to be a wise course that such disasters to property be prevented, if possible, in future.

RECTIFICATION. A second distillation.

RECTRICES. The tail feathers of a bird.

RECTUM. The lowest intestine, ending in the anus.

RECUMBENT. Leaning down.

RED BIRD. The cardinal grosbeak is a southern species, sometimes called the Virginia nightingale. They have been accused of mutilating orchard fruits, for the seeds, and also of catching bees. That they are destructive to a considerable extent there is little doubt. Yet the stomachs of those shot, have been found to contain principally the seeds of wild plants.

RED BUD or JUDAS TREE. *Cercis Canadensis.* Is one of our prettiest early spring flowering ornamental trees, growing from fifteen to thirty-five feet high. The flowers appear before the leaves, small, numerous, covering the branches, bright red in color, fading to a pale pink. The tree is common along the banks of streams, in the latitude of central Illinois and south. A European species, *C. siliquastrum* is similar, but not so handsome as the American species.

RED CLOVER. (See Clover.)

RED LEAD. A mixture of the protoxide and peroxide of lead, used as a paint.

RED SPIDER, PLANT MITE. *Acarus telarius.* A small red insect which spins a net, and lives on the juices of many plants and trees, attaching itself to the lower side of the leaf. It is especially injurious in hot-houses. They are destroyed by frequent syringing with cold water, by fumigations and washes of whale-oil soap and water.

RED-TAILED BUZZARD. (See Buzzard.)

RED TOP. A name sometimes given to herd's grass, and also to a dry perennial grass of the Middle States (*Tricuspis*) of little or no value.

RED WATER. (See Black water of Cattle.)

RED-WINGED BLACKBIRD. (See Blackbird.)

RED WORM. An old name for the wireworm.

REED. The genus *Arundo*, tall, aquatic, and boggy grasses. They may be destroyed by draining the soil, by liming and ashes.

REED BIRD. *Icterus agripennis.* This sprightly summer visitor is known by a variety of names in different parts of the country. In Louisiana as meadow bird, in the Carolinas, the rice-bunting. As the reed bird in Pennsylvania, and as the bob-o-link in New York and East. In the West, it is known both by the names of reed bird, bob-o-link and skunk blackbird. Its song is a sprightly chatter familiar to all, and once commenced by one will be answered by each other male bird within hearing. Its food is principally seeds, but it is also very destructive to the cereal grains when in the milk. In the South, it is the execration of the rice planter, and yet who can help loving the gay, familiar, and chattering skunk blackbird.

REED GRASS. Canary grass.

REFLECTION. The throwing back of the rays of heat or light by a polished surface or mirror.

REFLEXED. Bent back, turned back.

REFRACTION. The action exerted by water, glass, and all transparent bodies of changing the direction of rays of light, so as to make them appear bent.

REMIGES. The quill feathers of birds.

REMIPES. An order of coleopterous insects which are capable of swimming.

REMITTENT FEVERS. Fevers which are subject to periodical paroxysms, as the ague, bilious fever, etc.

RENAL. Relating to the kidneys.

RENIFORM. Kidney-shaped, of the shape of a kidney bean.

RELATIVE GROWTH OF TREES. It is not generally known how fast trees will grow and make timber in a fertile soil. It is not necessary in this article to go into an argument to prove the value of tree planting in treeless regions. It is an accepted fact. As showing the growth of timber in twenty years, we give a table as prepared, some years since, by the late H. H. McAfee, a well known cultivator. It is as follows:

Species.	Diameter of trunk—inches.	Height in feet.	Cord feet in fuel.
Cottonwood (*monilifera*)	24	50	5¼
Cottonwood (*quadrangulata*)	26	50	6
Lombardy Poplar	23	60	4¾
Elm (*Americana*)	17	44	3¾
Elm (*Fulva*)	18	39	3
Maple (*dasycarpum*)	18	39	3¾
Maple (*niger*)	11	37	1
Walnut (*cinerea*)	20	38	3¾
Walnut (*niger*)	14	37	2¾
Honey Locust	4	40	3
German Pine	14	33	2

Thus, actual test shows that cottonwood will make three-fourths of a cord; that even the slow growing black maple will make one-eighth of a cord, while the ash-leaved maple (*negundo*) will make five-eighths of a cord to the tree in twenty years' growth. The same trees if grown in groves thickly, would probably not make more than half the quantities named, which would in time come nearer to the figures as given above. The following will, we think, be a safe estimate for groves or broad belts, in twenty years, planted, say, four by four feet, and thinned out as their good deserves, to a maximum distance of sixteen by sixteen feet for the fast growing varieties, and eight by sixteen feet for the slower ones:

Species.	Cords.
Cottonwood	70
Ash-leaved Maple	60
White Walnut (Butternut)	50
White Maple	44
Elm	43
Honey Locust	35
White Pine	32
Black Walnut	30
Black Sugar Maple	20

A very simple and easy way to plant and cultivate, either for wind-breaks or groves, is to bring the ground into a good deep tilth by plowing and harrowing, and then plant the trees of two, three, or four years' growth, in straight lines, and at a distance of four feet apart. Cultivate with an ordinary two-horse cultivator so long as you can stride the rows, if the trees be small enough when set, or with double-shovel plow, if larger. Continue this until it is no longer easy to get between them with a horse. All the willows will grow readily from cuttings, so will the cottonwoods, and Lombardy poplar; but, do not plant Lombardy poplar, it is good neither for shade, timber nor fuel. Walnut, either white or black, does not transplant unless raised in the nursery, root pruned and moved at two years old. It is better that you raise them from roots yourself. The same is true of hickory and all the oaks. They seldom succeed transplanted; never under ordinary circumstances. All the other trees named in the list transplant kindly—especially when small. Other trees that will be found valuable for timber are, white, black, green, blue, and, on moist soils, red ash. Of evergreens, White Pine and Norway Spruce do well generally in the West. Of deciduous coniferous trees, European larch should not be omitted. When it attains a fair size—and I have seen it grow to a diameter of twelve inches in thirteen years—it is valuable for all purposes except burning. This it is said to be almost impossible to do. Basswood or Linden is also valuable. As a shade tree it is unexcelled. The cultivation of timber is not the terrible task it has been represented to be; certainly not when undertaken systematically, as one would a crop of corn. Too many of the failures are made in consequence of planting trees too large. Evergreens two years old may be bought by the thousand at very light cost. These should be placed in a nursery bed, at a distance of six by twelve inches, and protected by a scaffold, high enough to work under, and over which enough boughs should be placed to keep off the direct rays of the sun. At the end of two years they may safely be planted where they are to stand, and at a distance of four by four feet. Other trees should be planted at an age of from one to three years from seed, according to the habit of growth. Plant wind-breaks of a width as directed; not necessarily along roads, but where they will afford shelter to orchards, farm buildings, pastures and field crops. We repeat—what we have heretofore frequently said—there is no safer investment for money, nor a better heritage for children in a prairie country, than wind-breaks and plantations of valuable timber. If the plantation is strictly for timber uses, many waste places unfit for cultivation, such as the tops of knolls, steep hill sides, along ravines, etc. For soft wooded trees, as willow, cottonwood, etc., the edges of ponds are admirable; whitewood grows admirably on sandy ridges sufficiently out of water so they are never wet. Hickory, black walnut, butternut, maple, beech, and elms do well on any prairie soil that is dry, and the two latter on soils somewhat moist. Thus we think you may be able to decide not only whether it will pay you to plant, but also what to plant, for in this respect every man must be the judge of his own action.

REMOVING FRUIT AND OTHER TREES. Unless much care is taken, the greater part of the small or fibrous roots of fruit trees are destroyed in digging; or if not thus destroyed, they are allowed to get dry, and consequently become worthless for the purpose for which nature intended them—that of supplying sap to the tree. This is especially the case with the evergreen tribe. Once dry, they can not be soaked into life again. The small roots are sometimes, though incorrectly called spongioles. The true spongioles—or root-hairs, as they have sometimes been called—are of annual growth, and are said to die with the fall of the leaf. They are supposed to extract plant-food from the earth, to be conveyed by the roots proper to the stems, branches, and leaves of the plant. The leaves have been called the lungs of the plant. They, however, decompose the air-consuming the carbon and nitrogen, and liberating the oxygen. So, also, in the decomposition of water; they hold the hydrogen only. Animals are said to liberate heat, vegetables to imprison it, and therefore it is by antithesis, and not by harmony that the relation exists. Science is gradually throwing more and more light upon the economy of plant life, but the road seems as yet dark and wearisome to travel. But to return to the tree. If, when carefully dug, the roots being kept from the air and quite moist, they are honestly planted and thoroughly mulched, but little loss will ever ensue, even should the entire tops be left upon the tree. In fact, we have always had better success where we have left the top intact—cutting out only the irregular and superfluous branches—than we have ever had by the old method of excessive trimming. There is no doubt but that foliation stimulates activity in the root. The roots should be spread naturally, and fine soil packed carefully about them. If the ground is dry, a little water may be added and the earth leveled and mulched. If the tree is likely to be blown about, it should be staked. Trees so planted never fail to reward their owners.

RENNET. The membrane of the stomachs of the suckling young grass-feeding animals, including swine, furnish the secretion called rennet, as used for coagulating milk in the manufacture of curd and cheese. Rennet skins, as these membranes are called, are better at one year old, or when thoroughly cured, than when green, or fresh, and that of the suckling calf is superior to all others. Rennet, in its broad sense, may therefore be called an infusion of animal membrane. This infusion, as prepared, is slightly acid, yet it is not the acid that curdles the milk, since if the rennet be made slightly alkaline by the addition of potash, and milk rendered alkaline, even so the whey will show an alkaline reaction, it will be curdled by rennet. The presence of lactic acid, however, from the conversion of milk sugar, does facilitate coagulation. Rennets should not be saved from calves less than a week old, since before this time the stomach is not normal and those of the age of from three to four weeks furnish the best rennets. The stomach of no animal out of health should ever be used. The rennets should be taken out immediately after the animal is killed, turned inside out without washing, thoroughly cured with dairy salt, perfectly dried, and then kept in strong paper sacks until wanted for use. For use the rennets should be soaked in clean whey, saturated with salt for twenty-four hours before using, frequently squeezing them with the hand, that they may become thoroughly macerated. After being soaked, the liquor should be kept as cold as possible, and in tight

RHEUMATISM 796 RHUBARB

covered vessels until used. In regular dairies the rennet is prepared to a given strength and this strength ascertained, a definite quantity may then be relied on to produce the coagulation in a given time. Another point, in preparing rennets, is that the liquor may be smelt of and tasted without experiencing anything disagreeable. A very good old recipe, omitting the spices or not according to taste, is as follows: Rennet never should be taken from the calf till the excrement shows the animal to be in perfect health. It should be emptied of its contents, salted and dried, without scraping or rinsing, and kept dry for one year, when it will be fit for use. It should not be allowed to gather dampness, or its strength will evaporate. To prepare it for use, into ten gallons of water (blood warm) put ten rennets, churn or rub them often for twenty-four hours, then rub and press them to get the strength, stretch, salt and dry them as before. They will gain strength for a second use, and may be used when the weather will admit of soaking them to get the full strength. Make the liquor as salt as can be made, strain and settle it, separate it from sediment, (if any,) and it is fit for use. Six lemons, two ounces of cloves, two ounces of cinnamon, and two ounces of common sage are sometimes added to the liquor to preserve its flavor and quicken its action. If kept cool in a stone jar, it will keep sweet any length of time desired, and a uniform strength can be secured while it lasts. Stir it before dipping off to set milk, take enough of it to curdle milk firm in forty minutes. (See also article Cheese.)

REPENT. Running on the ground.
REPTILIA. Cold-blooded vertebrate animals, as snakes, tortoises, frogs, lizards, etc.
RESIN. An inflammable product of the vegetable kingdom, rich in carbon and hydrogen, soluble in alcohol, but insoluble in water. There are a great number of species, some of which are used in varnishes.
RESERVOIR. A tank or artificial excavation to hold water. (See Irrigation and Watering Stock.)
RESOLUTION. In farriery, the discussion or dispersion of inflammatory gatherings or abscesses, by applying leeches, poultices, and fomentations.
RESPIRATION. The act of breathing. It is accomplished by the movements of the diaphragm and muscles of the chest. Atmospheric air passing into the lungs is changed, oxygen being separated from it and absorbed into the blood, and four per cent. of carbonic acid thrown out. Water also passes off from the lungs. By these changes heat is produced. The effect of respiration is to alter the color of the blood from dark to bright red; it begins at the commencement of life, and any interruption of the function is rapidly fatal.
RETICULATE. Like a net.
RETICULUM. The honeycomb stomach of ruminants.
RETINA. The nervous layer at the back of the eye which receives the image of objects.
REVOLUTE. Rolled backward.
RHAPONTICIN AND RHEIM. Substances obtained from the roots of rhubarb.
RHEUMATISM. Horses, cattle and swine are subject to rheumatism, a disease often confounded with founder or stiff disease, as it is called by many persons. Rheumatism is an inflammation of the joints, tendons, ligaments, and muscles, accompanied with stiffness and lameness, and changing from one part to another. It would seem to be hereditary in some cases, but if not, is generally found in old animals, or those weak, and is generally brought on succeeding colds, or else accompanies catarrh, influenza, and other disorders of a like nature. It may be acute or chronic. Acute rheumatism is known as rheumatic fever. There is sudden lameness, with or without swelling, of a joint or joints. There is fever, with quickened pulse, sweats, thirst, scanty urine and constipated bowels. The treatment is to keep the body well clothed, the stable warm, using slings, if necessary, to support the animal. If the constipation is strong, move the bowels. Good nursing and care is the strongest point in this disease. In addition to this, give three or four times a day, mixed in a pint of water or gruel, one ounce each of salicylic acid and bicarbonate of soda.
RHIPIPTERANS. An order of insects, the *Strepsiptera*; having wings which fold like a fan.
RHIZANTHS, RHIZANTHÆ. A small order of plants resembling fungi, but having sexes.
RHIZOMA. A root stock like that of the flag.
RHODIUM. A rare metal, of great hardness, found in some of the platina ores.
RHODODENDRON. It is to be regretted that these noble flowering plants should be so little cultivated in the grounds of our wealthy citizens, who could give them the conditions of moisture and partial shade they so much desire. Those who saw the admirable and extensive collection from an English propagator, as shown at Philadelphia, at the Centennial, will not soon forget the magnificent display. Unfortunately, those varieties that are hardy East, even as far north as Long Island, require protection—removal to a light cellar preferable—in the winter. With this care they may be grown about any farm homestead, and well repay the labor devoted to them. Thus treated, even the so-called half hardy ones may be grown. There are nearly thirty species, and many varieties, some of the newer ones, and also the hybrids with azalia, a close relation, are magnificent when in bloom, as well as attractive in their foliage.
RHUBARB. Pie-Plant. *Rheum. Rheum Rhaponticum*, is the medicinal rhubarb, a native of the interior of Asia, introduced into England, and now broken up into many garden varieties, and within the last fifty years universally used in spring for tarts, pies and sauce. Its cultivation is exceedingly easy, requiring only plenty of water and plenty of manure, the more of the latter in the shape of strong compost the better. The eyes should be planted three feet apart each way, and covered about four inches deep. In the autumn cover the crowns with litter, removing it early in the spring. They will furnish plenty of stalks, and the plants will get larger and larger until five years old, when they should be separated and removed to new soil. Many persons get inferior stalks for want of attention. The only secret is to dig in plenty of manure every year, and to keep the soil about the plants deeply and frequently stirred. The stalks are separated from the attachment, by a quick, sharp, sidelong jerk. The stalks are sometimes partly blanched by put-

ting a headless barrel over each plant and allowing the stalks to grow up through it. Thus they are tender and succulent. If the old stools, not less than three years old, are lifted with earth about the roots in the fall, set thickly over the cellar bottom, they will produce tender blanched shoots sometimes by midwinter, and give a succession for some time. A better way is to force them in a gentle hot bed, or under the staging of a greenhouse.

RIBAND GRASS. Canary grass, and the striped leafed *Phalaris;* grown as an ornament in gardens.

RIB GRASS. A name for the plantain (*Plantago major.*)

RIBS. The curved bones attached to the vertebræ behind, those which meet at the chest and are articulated to the sternum are called true ribs; those whose extremities are only furnished with cartilage are the false ribs. In building, curved timbers for roofing.

RICE. *Oryza. Oriza sativa*, and its varieties have been cultivated from time immemorial in Oriental countries as human food. It ranks next to wheat, as a sustenance for the human family as a constant food, however, it is only used by the nations of hot climates, containing a dense population. Asia, Africa, and sub-tropical North and South America are its principal areas of cultivation, though it has been grown in the United States as far north as Virginia on the coast, and in the west as far north as Illinois. Alluvial bottoms that may be flooded at will, or tide lands above brackish water are the best lands for the cultivation of the varieties of aquatic rice. The leaves of rice are broad and leek like, the seed stems of the plant from four to six feet high, terminating in a panicle, not altogether unlike a panicle of oats. A species, adapted to dry land, *O. Mutica*, has occasionally been cultivated in the United States, even as far north as Virginia and Illinois, but its cultivation was unprofitable, the product being inferior; in some Oriental countries this species is extensively cultivated. Indian rice, *Zizania*, or water oats, of several species, *Z. aquatica, Miliacia,* and *fluitans*, common in all suitable waters in the West as far north as Minnesota, in ponds, shallow still streams, and ditches of gently and constant running water. It is not cultivated, but was an important article of sustenance to the Indians, who would tie the heads together in bundles just before ripening and when the seed was mature, beat it upon blankets laid in their canoes. The green plants are eaten greedily by all kinds of farm stock, who will wade into water up to their backs in order to get the last blade. It also makes the best of fodder when it may be obtained without too much labor. (See illustration, Wild Rice.) Since the late war the cultivation of rice has declined in the Southern States, and other crops have taken the place of this once important industry there, perhaps, from the well known unhealthy nature of the industry. Within the last year or two, however, attention has again been directed to this crop. Therefore the means used in irrigation on the coast, and also in the delta of the Mississippi, those two systems will be sufficient to designate the proper means, in connection with different water systems. On the Savannah river tide water, the plan is as follows: Main canals, having sluices on their mouths, are dug from the river to the interior, about twenty feet in width; and, as they very frequently extend across the whole breadth of the swamp, they are more than three miles in length. The rice plantations are subdivided into fields of about twenty acres each. The fields have embankments raised around them, with sluices communicating with the main canal, that they may be laid dry or under water separately, according as it may be required. Numbers of open ditches are also dug over the grounds for the purpose of allowing the water to be more easily put on or drawn off. In all cases the water is admitted to the fields as soon as the seed is sown, and when the young shoot appears above ground, the water is drawn off In the course of a week the crop usually receives another watering, which lasts from ten to thirty days, according to the progress the vegetation makes. This watering is chiefly useful in killing the land weeds that make their appearance as soon as the ground becomes dry. But, on the other hand, when the field is under water, aquatic weeds, in their turn, grow up rapidly, and to check their growth the field is once more laid dry, and the crop is then twice hand-hoed. By the 1st of July the rice is well advanced, and water is again admitted and allowed to remain on the fields until the crop is ripe. This usually takes place from the 1st to the 10th of September. The water is drawn off the day previous to the commencing of reaping. It will be seen that large capitals are necessary in the culture of rice on the tidal swamps. A great expenditure of labor is constantly required to maintain the banks in good order, and to clear out the drain and canals, as well as to keep the sluices and valves in repair. The fact, however, of the rice grounds being higher than any land devoted to any other crop, is quite sufficient to attest the profitableness of rice culture. On rice grounds of the delta of the Mississippi, the culture is carried on differently from that followed in the tidal swamps of Carolina. The Mississippi usually begins to swell in the delta about the end of February, and continues to rise till the 1st of June, from which time it again gradually subsides. It is thus in flood during the hot season. A ditch having a sluice on its mouth, is dug from the river toward the swamp. The land immediately behind the levee being the highest, is cropped with Indian corn and potatoes; but at a little distance from the river, where the land is lower and can be flooded, it is laid out in narrow rice fields, parallel to the river, inclining off from the river's edge. The narrow strips are banked all around, so that they can be laid under water after the rice is sown. The land is plowed in March, and shortly afterward it is sowed and harrowed. As soon as the young plants appear above ground, the water is admitted for the purpose of keeping the weeds in check. The crop grows rapidly, and the depth of the water is gradually increased, so as to keep the tops of the plants just above it. There is a constant current of water flowing from the river into the fields and over the swamp, so that there is no stagnation, and the fields are not laid dry till the crop is ready to cut. The only labor that is bestowed in the culture of the crop is to pull up by hand the weeds, which are mostly grasses; and this operation is effected, by men going to the fields knee-deep in water. The produce varies from thirty to sixty

WILD RICE—ZIZANIA AQUATICA.

bushels of rice in the husk. The quality, however, is not equal to that of Carolina rice. The lands adapted to rice, the preparation of the swamps, the cultivation, harvesting, and cleaning, from a paper on the subject written for the United States Government, is as follows: In this article we will confine our attention chiefly to what is known as golden or Carolina rice. There is a species of bearded white rice, known as Highland rice, but as it is unknown to commerce, of very limited culture and inferior quality, and not suited to the system of cultivation herein to be described, it will not command our attention. The best lands adapted to growing rice in swamps and rush lands lying immediately adjacent to tide-water rivers, between twenty-nine degrees and thirty-five degrees north latitude. For the purpose of economical and successful irrigation they must be perfectly level. They are always alluvial, and consist of blue clay, yellow mottled clay, or black bay lands. The former two contain a large per cent. of isinglass, highly important to their value. There is another class of lands adapted to rice culture, known as inland swamps. These are large basins or lakes, surrounded by highlands, having water leads running into them, by which they are inundated. These basins, being drained, are easily reclaimed, and a portion is usually set aside as a reservoir for holding a sufficiency of water for irrigating purposes. These lands, though not usually so prolific as the river swamps or tide-water lands, generally, under good management, produce a heavier grain, which is much sought after for seed. As a general rule they have heavier soils, are harder to cultivate and not so remunerative as the river swamps. Tide river plantations are usually located a little above the junction of salt and fresh water, and extend up the banks of the rivers so far as the rise and fall of the tides are sufficient for flooding and draining. This rise and fall should not be less than three or four feet, and six or eight feet is to be preferred, on account of the more perfect drainage these latter figures afford. Rice plantations are located above the junction of salt and fresh water, from the fact that rice, being an aquatic plant, requires a vast amount of fresh water during its growth; salt water being fatal to it at all stages. These swamps are usually reclaimed by means of embankments or levees, which are made high and strong enough to effectually bar out the river. Smaller embankments, called check banks, subdivide that portion of the plantation lying between the main river embankment and the highland, into squares or fields, generally from fifteen to twenty acres in area. These squares are all subdivided again into beds or lands, of twenty-five or thirty feet width, by a system of main ditches and quarter drains. Canals from twelve to thirty feet wide and four or five feet deep, are sometimes cut from the river embankment, through the center of the plantation, to the high land, for the purpose of introducing or draining off the water to or from those fields situated far back from the river. These canals also form a very conspicuous feature in the harvest scene, as they serve as a medium of navigation for the large flat-boats which convey the rice to the stack-yard in quantities of eight or ten acres at a load; and as rice usually yields from two to three tons of straw per acre, the value of this immense water carriage can be easily conceived. Flood-gates or trunks having doors at both ends are buried in the embankments on the river, as well as in the canal embankments and the check banks, those at the outlet of canals being so constructed as to permit the flat-boats to pass into the river. By means of these flood-gates or trunks the whole system of irrigation is carried on under the complete control of the planter, and the lands are flooded or drained at will. The canals and ditches being all carefully cleaned out, down to the hard bottom—the banks neatly trimmed and free of leaks—the flood-gates and trunks all water-tight, either to hold out or hold in water—the planter commences his operations, as early in the winter as possible, by plowing. These lands, being yearly enriched by alluvial deposits from the river, do not require deep plowing, four or five inches being generally sufficient to furnish a good seed bed, and on account of the numerous ditches subdividing the fields, a single mule plow is always preferable. When lands are plowed early in the winter and nicely shingled, it is of very great advantage to put in a shallow flow of water, and suddenly draw it off, in severe weather, for the benefit of freezing the furrow slices. But it is not a good practice to flood deep, as the weight of water packs the land, which becomes run together by the action of the waves, and renders good harrowing afterward an impossibility. Harrowing is usually begun only a few days previous to planting, in order that the seed-bed may be as fresh as possible, to encourage germination and, by its pliancy, permit the young roots to expand rapidly and take good hold on the soil, in order that the plant may resist the birds and a tendency to float. The operation of harrowing is perhaps one of the most important to the crop, and no consideration must induce the planter to slight it, as this is the golden opportunity afforded him for killing his potent and pernicious enemy—i. e., grass—his dread all the summer time. By breaking up every clod now, and exposing its roots and seeds to the action of the sun, half the battle is won. Immediately after the harrow comes the crusher, which implement is not abandoned until the field is reduced to garden order. About the 10th or 15th of March, up to the 10th or 15th of May, the process of drilling is carried on—seeding from two and a half to three bushels of clean seed per acre. At this juncture two antagonistic systems are encountered, one known as covered rice and the other as open trench rice. Both have their advocates. The first system, or covered rice, is where the grain is covered up in the soil two or three inches deep, as fast as it is drilled in, which thus protects it from birds, floating away, etc. The other, open trench, consists in leaving the rice entirely uncovered in the drill, and taking the risks alluded to, in order to save time and labor, the grain being soaked in thick clay water before seeding, to hold it to the ground. The seed being deposited, the flood-gates are immediately opened, and, if it be covered rice, and the ground pretty moist, the water is taken in as rapidly as the capacity of the gates may afford; and when it has attained a depth of twelve or eighteen inches, or deeper, if the check banks can bear it, the water from the river is then shut off, and the inside gate is closed, to hold in what water is on the field. The trash now rapidly rises and floats toward the banks, and it must be immediately hauled up with rakes, before it settles down on the rice. In the course of a few days the seed is carefully examined, and as soon as the germ or pip appears the water is drawn off the field to the bottom of the ditches, and kept out until the rice has two leaves. If the grain is planted open trench, as soon as the seeding is done, the water is leaked into the field gradually, until the land sobs and the rice sticks, then it is flooded slowly until the above-mentioned depth is attained; the water is then held until the rice has good roots, or begins to float, and is then drawn off carefully. Here all difference in the culture ceases. The rice having two leaves—or earlier, if the field is inclined to be grassy—the water is again let in to the same depth as before, completely submerging the plants, and is held to this gauge from seven to ten days, the planter being governed by the weather. If warm, seven; if cool, ten days. Then a leak is put in the gate and the water let off gradually, until a general verdure is seen floating all over the field. At this point the water is stopped and a mark set upon the gate as a gauge mark. To this gauge the water is rigidly held for sixty or sixty-five days from the day it first came on the field. This flow, when properly managed, effectually destroys all tendency to grass, and promotes a vigorous growth of rice. It sometimes happens that, during this flow, the crop takes a check and stops growing. In this event to take off the water is fatal, as it will produce foxed rice, it must be held firmly to the gauge, and in a few days the plant will throw out new roots and go on growing. If the maggot attack it in this flow the water is drawn off for a day or two and replaced. And where water is abundant and easily handled, the maggot can generally be avoided by beginning, about the thirtieth day, to change the water once a week. To do so skilfully, both gates must be simultaneously opened at the young flood. The stale water will thus rush out and fresh water come immediately back with the rising tide to float the rice leaves and prevent them sticking to the ground in their fall. If the maggot gets serious the field has to be dried immediately and thoroughly. The maggot is a tiny white worm, which is generated by stale water, and attacks the roots of the plant, causing serious injury to the crop. The presence of the maggot may always be suspected by the stiff and unthrifty appearance of the field. If the land is fertile at the end of the sixty-day flow, it will be found, on drawing off the water, that the rice has attained a vigorous growth of about three feet, and is well stocked with tillers, while also, if the field is level, and the harrowing and pulverizing was thoroughly attended to before planting, no grass will be seen, nothing but rice and the clean soil beneath. The field is kept dry now for about fifteen or twenty days, or until the land dries off nicely and the rice takes on its second growth. And if there be no grass it ought not to be disturbed with the hoe, as the hands, at this stage, often do more harm than good. This, however, does not apply to cattails and volunteers, which should, of course, be carefully pulled up by the roots, and sheafed and carried to the banks, to be disposed of by the hot sun. At the end of fifteen or twenty days, as above mentioned, the water is returned to the field as deep as the rice and banks can bear, never, however, topping the fork of the former. This water, where circumstances permit, is changed every week or two, by letting it off on one tide and taking it back on the next, and increasing the gauge with the growth of the rice. When the heads of the rice are well filled and the last few grains at the bottom are in the dough, it is fit to cut, and as little delay is permitted as possible, as the rice now over-ripens very rapidly, and shatters in proportion during the harvest. The water may be drawn off the field from three to five days before cutting the grain, and the land will be in better condition for harvesting. The rice is cut from twelve to eighteen inches from the ground, depending on its growth, usually from four to six feet high, and the gavels laid evenly and thinly upon the stubble, for the purpose of curing and permitting the air to circulate beneath it. Twenty-four hours in good weather is usually required to cure the straw, and the binding does not commence before this period, and never while the dew is on the straw. It is safer always to cut from sunrise to twelve o'clock, and bind the previous day's cutting from that hour to sunset. As soon as bound the rice is shocked up in wind-cocks, and at the end of a week taken to the barnyard and stacked up in ricks, thirty feet long, eight feet wide, and ten feet high. A stake, four feet long, is put into the rick at each end for daily examination and as long as the stake does not become too hot at its point to be held by the hand, when suddenly drawn out, the rick is not to be interfered with, otherwise it is to be pulled down, aired, and re-stacked. So soon as the temporary heat is over the grain is fit for the thresher. As soon as the rice is taken from the field attention is immediately given to sprouting volunteer and shattered rice, providing the crop has not been allowed to remain in the field for an indefinite period beyond the week alluded to above. This is best accomplished by instantly flooding the field quite shallow, so as to promote fermentation, and drying it again every twelve or fifteen days, for a day or two at a time. This process is continued until freezing weather sets in, and if the season has not been remarkably cool it will be found that most of this grain is destroyed. Threshing as performed by steam power is generally done with great neatness and despatch. The main building is commonly built on a brick foundation, about sixty feet long by forty feet wide, having two stories and an attic; the first story being fourteen and the second twelve feet high, with what is called by workmen a square roof. At the side of this building is the engine house and boiler room; and in front of the main building, a little distance off, is the feeding room, which is connected with the second story of the same by a covered way which protects the feeding cloth. In the second story is placed the thresher, which, for a first-class machine, consists of a cylinder forty-two inches in diameter and thirty-six inches wide, armed with 1,000 teeth. In the rear of the cylinder follow six revolving rakes with spring teeth, all of a diameter and width corresponding to the cylinder. Under the rakes is a hopper which conveys the grain down to two large fans in the first story; from these the grain is taken by elevators and carried to the third, or screening fan, on the second story, whence by elevators and spouts it is deposited into large bins ready for shipment. The feeding cloth consists of an endless canvas, bound with band leather and having slats riveted on it. It extends from the cylinder down to the feed room in the stack-yard. The rice is brought in sheaves from the ricks to the feed room, where several hands are stationed for the purpose of placing it on the feed cloth in close succession. The revolutions of the cloth thus keep a continuous stream of grain flowing into the cylinder, which in turn is relieved by the rakes seizing the straw, and after tossing out the grain they throw it out of a window in the rear into straw wagons below, kept ready to receive and carry it away. A good engine, with machinery of this description, will thresh and clean, ready for market, 1,000 bushels of rice per day. Now the grain is called rough rice; and is generally shipped to market from the plantation in cargoes of from 3,000 to 5,000 bushels at a time. On arriving there, if rough rice is in demand, it is immediately sold in that condition either to European buyers or city millers. The former export it to the European mills, and the latter pound it in their own, and again bring it into market as clean rice, in tierces averaging 600 pounds net. Good, well-cleaned rough rice, weighing forty-five pounds to the bushel, will take about twenty bushels to make a tierce of 600 pounds clean rice. As rice pounding mills are very costly affairs, they are seldom erected by the planters themselves. The building is a much larger one than that mentioned for threshing, and the capacity of the engine and boilers very much greater. The rough rice is first ground between very heavy stones, running at a high speed, which partially removes the rough integument, or hull chaff. This chaff is passed out of the building by spouts, and the grain by similar means conveyed into the mortars, where it is beat or pounded for a certain length of time by the alternate rising and falling of very heavy pestles, shod with iron. These are operated by a revolving cylinder of huge dimensions, armed with powerful levers, which, passing into a long opening in the pestle, about fifteen feet in length, raise it and let it fall suddenly into the great mortars below. From the mortars elevators take the rice to the fans, which separate the grain from the debris. From thence it goes through other fans that divide it into three qualities, known as whole rice, middling rice, and small rice. The grain is finally passed through a polishing screen, lined with gauze wire and sheep-skins, which, revolving vertically at the greatest possible velocity, embellishes it with that pearly whiteness in which it appears in commerce. From the screen it falls immediately below into a tierce, which is kept slowly rotating, and struck on two sides with heavy hammers, all the time it is being filled, for the purpose of obtaining its greatest capacity. The tierce, as soon as full, is removed and coopered ready for market. The cost of such a mill was $1,000 per pestle—fifty pestles being considered a good market mill. Good strong land, at a fair pitch of the tides, well managed and worked with labor that can be depended upon at all times, will average from forty to fifty bushels of clean rough rice per acre, valued at about one dollar per bushel. And ten acres to the hand, with good animal force, and only corn enough for provisions, is easily handled by a good planter, making an aggregate of from $400 to $500 per hand, gross. With the provisions alluded to above, the rice is one of the most agreeable and profitable to cultivate; but, on the other hand, if they are wanting, disappointment and failure are the natural results.

RICE BIRD. (See Reed Bird.)

RICE, PERUVIAN. QUINOA. *Chenopodium quinoa.* A plant of the Andes, similar to the goose foot, the leaves of which are used as spinach. The seeds are very nutritious, and are eaten boiled in soups. In Chili and Peru, the seeds are eaten in porridge or gruel, and made into cakes.

RICE WEEVIL. *Callandra oryza.* An insect very similar to the grain weevil, and which pro-

RICINUS.

duces much destruction in crops of rice and wheat at the South; it is destroyed by kiln-drying the grain.

RICINIC ACID. An oily acid, produced by distilling castor oil at a high temperature.

RICINUS. As a decorative plant, some of the varieties of the castor oil plant are highly ornamental. Their great stature, and magnificent leaves presenting a fine picture of tropical luxuriance. To produce the best effect, however, the seeds must be planted in pots in a hot-bed, about the first of March, and repotted as they need it, being transferred to a warm, sheltered place about the first of June. If dry weather intervenes, the plants should be watered to thoroughly soak the soil, about once in ten days. But one plant should be allowed to grow in a place, and this is better tied to a strong stake if the situation is at all windy. Thus it will throw up its great flower and seed spike the last part of September, and give full satisfaction for the care and trouble. Among the best sorts for garden cultivation are *R. sanguinarius*, though *R. communis* is sometimes used where the season is too short to ensure maturity. The cut will show the form of the leaves and flower spike. (For field cultivation, and for the seed, see Castor Oil Bean.

RICK. A long stack.

RIDDLE. A coarse sieve to separate grain or other substances from trash, etc.

RIDGE. The upper timber in a roof, against which the rafters pitch.

RIDGING. Laying up the soil in narrow ridges.

RIDGLING. A male animal imperfectly castrated.

RIGGIL. An imperfect sheep.

RIME. White, or hoar frost.

RIMOSE. Resembling the broken appearance of the bark of old trees.

RINDERPEST. Fortunately this terrible scourge of cattle beyond the Atlantic has never been introduced into America. Probably it is only a question of time, until our country will be desolated with this scourge of horned cattle, for if the equally dreaded, and as contagious Pleuro-Pneumonia could be twice introduced, why not, this. For this reason we give an abstract of the report to the United States government in 1879, of this disease as it is known in Europe, introducing the subject with something of its history. The rinderpest (cattle plague, *pestis bovilla*) appears to have been carried from central Asia to Europe as early as the fourth century, but the first exact description of this disease dates from the year 1711, two years after an extensive epizootic outbreak of the same in most European countries. It is estimated that in the course of the eighteenth century, not less than two hundred million head of cattle were carried off by the cattle plague. In the beginning of the present century, Prussia, Schleswig-Holstein, Saxony, and France, were visited by the plague, which was observed to have followed the movements of armies during the wars of the first Napoleon. In 1828, 1829, and 1830, during the Russo-Turkish and the Russo-Polish wars, the rinderpest was carried from Russia into Poland, Prussia, and Austria. In 1865 the plague appeared in Holland, and was carried thence to England. In both countries the disease carried off one hundred thousand head of cattle in the course of a few months. In 1867, Germany was again visited by the plague, which, however, was prevented by timely measures from spreading beyond the eastern provinces of Prussia. In 1870, soon after the outbreak of the Franco-German war, the rinderpest appeared in Germany in consequence of importations of cattle from Russia, and spread over Germany and France, following the movements of the armies. In the beginning of the year 1877, the disease was again carried into Germany by Russian cattle, and made rapid progress, because the imported animals, apparently healthy, but already infected, were allowed to reach the markets of Breslau, Berlin, and Hamburg, from which cities the infection was gradually communicated to other places. In Dresden the disease spread at once through the whole market. Towards the end of August, 1877, the rinderpest was reported by our consular officers as extinguished in the German Empire; but the danger of its reappearance in consequence of possible movements of cattle from the steppes of southern Russia to the borders of Germany, though much lessened by the stringent sanitary regulations adopted by the Russian Government, is not regarded as entirely obviated. Fleming, in his work on Veterinary Sanitary Science, says that, in recent years, several of the most competent veterinarians have endeavored to ascertain the home of the cattle plague, but without much success. Unterberger throws much doubt upon Russia and its steppes being the source of the malady, and he asserts that it is a purely contagious disease in Russia-in-Europe, and also, perhaps, in the whole Russian-Empire. It has been seen in southern Russia, the Asiatic Steppes, in different parts of India; in Mongolia, China (south and west), Cochin China, Burmah, Hindostan, Persia, Thibet, and Ceylon. It is as yet unknown in the United States, Australia, and New Zealand. So far as Europe is concerned the geographical limits of the disease may be given as follows: Beyond the Russian frontiers, and even in every part of that empire, the steppes excepted, the cattle plague is evidently a purely contagious malady. It is never developed primarily in Europe, either in indigenous cattle or in those originally from the steppes, and it has not yet been positively demonstrated that it may be primarily developed in the Russian Steppes; the most recent observations even tend to prove that in the European portions of these regions the affection is only present through the transmission of a contagium. Consequently, the plague is a malady which is perhaps primarily developed in the Russo-Asiatic Steppes—perhaps elsewhere—but is never seen in Europe except by the importation of its contagious principle. Nothing certain or definite as to the causes which develop the cattle plague are known. In Western Europe it relies solely for its introduction and diffusion to the presence of a contagium, carried either by animals suffering with the disease, those which have been in contact with them, or media of different kinds which are contaminated with the virus. Once introduced, it spreads from its point of introduction as from a center; each newly-infected animal becomes a focus whence the disease may radiate in every direction, and it usually attacks those animals which are nearest the foci. It spreads with more or less rapidity as the animals or vehicles charged with the contagium are moved about; even the air may, within a certain distance, be credited as an active agent in the diffusion of the deadly malady. The nature of the contagious matter (contagium), has also so far baffled all the efforts of investigators. Neither microscopic examinations nor chemical analysis of the tissues, blood, and mucous discharges of the infected animals, have led to the discovery of the principle of contagion. It is known, however, that from the very beginning of the disease a contagious matter is formed, which attaches itself to every part of the diseased animal. It is principally contained in the secretions of the mucous membranes, but, being volatile, attaches itself also to the urine, the dung, the blood, the skin, and the breath. It may be communicated to the atmosphere by exhalations from any part of the sick animal, or its carcase. Experience has shown that healthy cattle may be infected by coming near the sick animals, or near anything contaminated by their excrements or exhalations, without actual contact with them. The contagious matter has no effect in open air at a distance of twenty to thirty paces, because the air either dilutes or modifies it so as to deprive it of its power. But in cases where a current of air comes directly from an accumulation of infected matter, and also in inclosed spaces the contagion may be carried to greater distances. Therefore, the disease may be communicated in a large stable to a healthy animal quite a long distance from the diseased one, or may be carried from one stable to another as far as a hundred feet apart. This happens only when the exhalations are carried over directly from one stable to the other, by a current of air so rapid as not to allow time for the air to dilute or modify the contagious matter. Where one stable is separated from another by a partition which is not air-tight, the contagion is very easily transmitted. Besides these direct means of infection, the disease may be carried to healthy animals indirectly, in many ways. For instance, objects which have come in contact with infected matter, may be carried to a distant place and there spread the disease. Porous substances, such as woolen clothing, wool, hay, straw, etc., are particularly liable to absorb the contagious matter, which may diffuse itself after some time in a distant place. Thus butchers, drovers, and other persons who visit infected stables, may carry the disease from yard to yard, and from village to village. In railroad trucks, the woodwork absorbs a considerable amount of the contagious matter, and, if not thoroughly disinfected, may communicate the disease to animals subsequently placed therein. The dung of diseased animals may spread the contagion to distant places by being carried away on the wheels of vehicles or the shoes of persons. Dogs and cats may carry it in their fur and birds in their plumage. A small quantity of blood or dung on the sole of a shoe or on the tip of a walking-stick has sometimes been sufficient to carry the disease to a great distance. The modes of possible transmission are, in fact, so numerous and involved as to render it, in many instances, a matter of extreme difficulty to account for the cause of an outbreak of the plague. The vitality of the contagious matter is variable, according to circumstances. Air is its most potent and reliable destroyer. Hay and straw which have lain above the stables of sick animals have been often used as fodder with impunity after an airing of twenty-four hours. Wool, impregnated with the mucus from the nostrils of sick animals, was found to be innocuous when thoroughly aired for five or six days. Stables and pasture-grounds will be thoroughly disinfected in a few weeks by the action of the atmosphere. In the same way clothing and other porous substances become entirely disinfected by airing. The stronger the current of air the more prompt its disinfecting action. On the contrary, if infected porous substances are not exposed to currents of air, the contagious matter is preserved for a long time. Closely-packed hay and straw, the woodwork and floors of closed stables, manure-heaps, packed-up clothing, etc., may remain infected for several months. A case is recorded of the rinderpest breaking out anew in a stable which had stood empty for four months, but had not been disinfected after a previous outbreak. The flesh and hides of carcases which had been buried for over three months were found to be capable of infecting healthy animals. Very high temperature has the same effect in destroying the power of the contagious matter as currents of air, but summer heat is effective only in so far as it promotes the drying up of the contagious particles, and renders them more volatile and more easily diluted by the air. The contagious matter is not destroyed by cold, not even by frost; on the contrary, its power is preserved, as the drying up of the substances containing it is thereby hindered. Dung frozen through the winter spreads the contagion upon thawing in the spring. All ruminating animals are liable to the rinderpest, but goats and sheep are less commonly and less severely affected by it than neat cattle. The disease does not affect non-ruminating animals, nor is it in any way dangerous to man. The rinderpest breaks out generally on the fifth or sixth day from the time of infection, sometimes as early as the fourth, and frequently as late as the eighth or even ninth day. According to some observations, the period of incubation may extend to two or three weeks, but the instances of so protracted an incubation are to be considered as entirely exceptional. The spread of the disease in a herd of cattle is usually slow in the beginning. Often when the contagion is introduced only a single animal is infected. This one, after the few days required for the incubation, becomes sick and commences to evolve the contagious matter, which infects one or more of the animals in the same stable or herd. Then, again, an interval of time elapses before the disease is developed in the new victims. As soon as several animals are diseased, the contagion spreads more rapidly, and many are attacked at the same time. Want of proper caution on the part of stable-men and other attendants is often the cause of an exceedingly rapid progress of the contagion, which is carried in their clothing from one end of the stable to another. Dr. J. Burdon Sanderson, one of the commissioners appointed by the English Government to investigate this disease during its last invasion of Western Europe (1865), in speaking of the phenomena of cattle plague and the general character and progress of the malady during the life of the affected animal, says that it is an essential or general fever, and that it can be shown, more clearly than in any human disease of the same class, that the disturbance of the system which is understood by the term fever may exist independently of local changes occurring in particular organs; and in this respect a fact new to pathology has been discovered, i. e., that the increase of the temperature of the body, which is the one and only symptom which all fevers have in common, exists for several days before any other derangement of health can be observed. Although constitutional or general in its origin, the disease is attended with local alterations of structure, some of which are so constant and invariable that no definition of the malady can be complete which fails to recognize and include them. One or two days before any other change occurs in the condition of the infected animal there appears an increase of temperature, which is most readily detected by means of a thermometer introduced into the rectum. The temperature is found to have risen by 2° to 4° Fahr., from the normal temperature of 102°. At the same time symptoms of fever are observed, such as shivering, muscular twitchings, dryness of the skin, a staring coat of hair, an unequal distribution of temperature throughout the body, and changes of temperature, which are particularly noticeable at the base of the horns. A very important and characteristic symptom at an early stage of the disease is a peculiar alteration of the mucous membranes. This alteration is very soon noticeable in the vagina of cows, which becomes spotted or striped with red. The next day small yellowish-white or gray specks are clearly seen on the red spots and stripes. These specks are formed by the loosening of the cuticle, which can be rubbed off or detached by the finger, leaving in its place a dark-red depression. The same red spots and stripes and yellowish or gray specks appear in the mouth and nose of the sick animals of either sex. The next day after the appearance of the peculiar eruption upon the mucous membranes, there is a disinclination to eat and ruminate, and with cows a diminution and soon a total absence of milk. Two days after the manifestation of the above described symptoms, marked changes in the general appearance of the diseased animal are apparent. It lies down very frequently; when standing it draws the hind legs forward as if suffering from colic. The look is distressed, the head drooping, the ears hanging, the breathing oppressed; the pulse becomes rapid and weak, the discharges from the eyes, the nose, and the mouth become thick and purulent, the breath fetid. The iris, which at the commencement of the fever is generally inflamed and cherry red, resumes its natural color with the increase of secretions from the lachrymal duct. Cows far advanced in pregnancy generally calve in this stage of the disease. On the second or third day diarrhœa sets in. The feces, at first thin and watery, then thick and slimy, are filled with detached masses from the mucous surface very fetid and more or less tinged with blood. When the diarrhœa has lasted two or three days the disease advances with rapid strides. The animal is so weak as not to be able to rise, the evacuations of excrements are involuntary, the breathing is uneven and rapid, the beatings of the heart are no longer perceptible, the pulse becomes very feeble and the temperature rapidly falls. Death usually occurs on the fifth day from the first visible signs of the disease. Sometimes the course of the disease is so rapid as to reach its culmination within two days. On the average seventy, to seventy-five per cent. of the diseased animals die. Those that survive have not had the disease in its most malignant form. Once convalescent the animals recover very fast; but the diarrhœa continues for several days after the disappearance of all other symptoms. In summer, when the cattle are grazing, the disease is less severe than in winter, when they get dry fodder and are kept in close stables. The symptoms and progress of the disease are the same with goats and sheep as with neat cattle, but the percentage of fatal cases is somewhat less. Many of the symptoms of rinderpest occur in the lung disease (*pleuro-pneumonia*), the malignant catarrhal fever, and the mouth-and-foot disease. The lung disease is distinguished from the rinderpest by the absence of the characteristic eruptions upon the mucous membranes; the malignant catarrhal fever, by the dimness of the transparent cornea, which in the rinderpest remains clear; the mouth-and-foot disease by the ulceration of the foot, the less degree of fever; and its peculiarly rapid spreading from one animal to entire herds. Among the lesions observed after death there are several, though no more constant than several of the prominent symptoms, that materially assist in establishing a proper diagnosis. The age and general condition, the state in which the animals were kept before they were affected, their breed, the character and intensity of the disease, all appear to have some influence on the seat and seriousness of the lesions. These vary according to the period at which death takes place. Fleming says that if the animal is killed at the commencement of the malady, and the symptoms have been comparatively mild, there will nevertheless be found, on examination after death, such alterations in the mucous membranes as congestion and ecchymoses. The latter are more particularly observable on the free border of the mucous folds in the fourth compartment of the stomach (true stomach) and around the pylorus, although they also exist to a less degree in the small intestine, and often in the vagina. When, however, an animal has died from the disease, or been killed when it had attained a certain degree of intensity, the changes are more marked, the body becomes quickly inflated after death, and sometimes even before death occurs. The rectum is elevated and its lining membrane is tumefied and of a deep red color; the tail and hinder extremities are more or less paralyzed during life, and are therefore usually soiled by the feces. The skin exhibits the characteristic eruption, and in those places where there are neither glands nor hair, as on the teats, it is injected in irregular patches of variable dimensions, the epithelium is thickened, soft or friable, and the integument is often cracked. On removing the skin the vessels which are cut are generally filled with a dark colored fluid blood, and the flesh is red, blue, or violet-tinted. The peritoneum in some cases may be slightly injected or ecchymosed in patches. The whole of the intestines are generally greatly distended with gas, and in some cases the small intestine may be reddened. In the interior of the digestive canal are found the most marked evidences of the disease, though they are not always constant and equally intense in every portion of the mucous membrane. In the mouth, pharynx, true stomach, small intestine, and rectum, they are most frequently present. They are least conspicuous and often absent in the œsophagus, the three first compartments of the stomach, and in the cæcum and colon. They may be so trifling as to resemble the lesions of a slight catarrh, while in other instances they are unmistakable and pathognomonic. In the mouth and pharynx are observed the alterations in the lining membrane and the epithelial changes. It is chiefly where there has been much friction or local irritation that they are most exaggerated, and deep erosions, with loss of texture of the derm of the mucous membrane, may be noted. The œsophagus is rarely affected, though it is not always exempt. In the rumen the quantity of food may be found a little larger than usual. The epithelium on the mucous membrane lining it and the next compartment may be more easily detached than in a healthy state, and a microscopical examination of the cells prove them to have undergone a similar change to those of the mouth. The mucous membrane in these compartments is also frequently injected in a general manner, though more deeply in some places than in others. It is not rare to find on this membrane round, oval, or irregular-shaped eschars, disposed separately or in groups, varying in color from a dark brown to a greenish hue. The elimination of these eschars, takes place gradually from around their borders, and cicatrization occurs, even in cases which have a fatal termination. Submucous extravasation is probably the cause of these gangrenous patches. Around them the tissues are infiltrated, and more or less injected, while beneath the texture is injected or ecchymosed, and red or green in color. The third compartment sometimes contains food, which is hard, dry, and friable; at other times it is soft and pulpy. In the first case, the epithelium of the leaves is readily detached, and adheres to the cakes of aliment removed from between them. This epithelium also exhibits granulo-adipose degeneration. The leaves themselves are injected wholly or partially, and ecchymoses and eschars may be present in them; they are also easily torn. In the fourth compartment and small intestines the contents are at first normal; but they soon change, and there is found a small quantity of thick, yellow, brown, or even blood-colored fluid. The mucous membrane is covered by a viscid, grayish-yellow, or reddish mucus. The cæcum and colon at this period contain a frothy mass of a brownish, sometimes sanguinolent fluid. The rectum has a thick viscid mucus adhering to its inner surface. If the disease pursues its course, the débris detached from the intestine is mixed with exudations and extravasations to form a viscid, albuminoid, whitish-yellow, brown, or red fluid, in which are shreds and the detritus from the membrane. When an animal has been killed in the early stages of the disease, and the mucus has been carefully removed from the mucous membrane of the stomach, it is found that the surface of the latter is irregular, and that its tissue is infiltrated and injected to a degree corresponding with the seriousness of the attack and the stage the malady has reached. The abnormal color, varying from a brick-red to a reddish brown, is generally diffuse, but is most marked at the pyloric portion, attaining its maximum of intensity towards the free borders of the folds. Submucous extravasation are also frequently met with in this part, differing in size from a fine point to a large patch. In the small and large intestines there also exist, at this period, analogous alterations; but, while the redness of the abomasum is usually diffuse, in the small intestine it generally appears in the form of transverse striæ, which are crossed by lighter colored longitudinal streaks, this intercrossing forming a somewhat regular pattern. These extravasations are common in the small intestine, but the infiltrations and exudations are not so frequent in the abomasum. In the duodenum the alterations are usually more intense than in the remainder of the intestine, and it is not rare to find in it a very marked diffused redness and much sanguine effusion. The congestion is often greatest around the solitary glands and Peyer's patches, whose volume is more or less increased. Frequently the areolated aspect of these patches is most conspicuous at the termination of the first period. The same lesions are found, but in a less degree, in the large intestines. In these the most salient portions, such as the borders of the valvulæ, are the parts which are the most deeply colored and most extensively ecchymosed. The infiltration is greatest if diarrhœa has not been present. In cases where the disease has made considerable progress, the lesions are still more characteristic. The mucous membrane of the abomasum and intestine is deeper colored, often blue or black, and in the duodenum of animals which have succumbed, it may even be uniformly black, while the petecchiæ and ecchymoses are more numerous. In the abomasum, but oftenest in the intestine, toward the fifth day of the disease, there appears a pigmentation, varying from a bright gray to a slate color, or even darker, and which takes the place of the abnormal color due to the blood. This appearance is first noticed in the rectum, and in the intestines generally its tints seem to be related to the intensity of the blood coloration, of which these parts have been the seat. It is therefore in the duodenum, and especially near the pylorus, that it is deepest-tinted and most extensive. In the duodenum it is diffuse, but in the remainder of the small intestine it is limited, as a rule, to a double series of perpendicular zones more or less incomplete, and in the rectum is usually in the form of longitudinal lines. This coloring matter is deposited in the most superficial layer of the mucous membrane, and is constituted by minute irregular granules, which, according as they are disposed separately or in clusters, give rise to the different shades. Around the orifices of Brunner's glands, and in the texture of the villi, this deposit appears to be most localized. The epithelium of the fourth compartment of the stomach rapidly undergoes changes analogous to those observed in the mouth. Their intensity depends upon the part examined, as well as the gravity of the attack and its stage. In the first and last portions of the small intestine, in the cæcum, in the first section of the large colon, and in the rectum, they are generally more developed than elsewhere. In mild cases the epithelium, though not yet detached, is always less adherent to the derm than in health. In more serious cases this layer is found completely detached over a considerable surface, and especially in the small intestine. The excoriations thus produced vary both as to extent and number, and are generally covered by a gray, red, or dark colored viscid mucus. The matter is tenacious, and adheres firmly in flakes to the membrane. The extent of these flakes is generally from a quarter to two inches in length. The color is gray, yellow, red, brown, or black; their free surface is smooth, and more or less convex; their variable consistency is less at the border than the center; the membrane beneath them is injected and spotted with small extravasations, and their margin, in consequence of the retraction of the flake, is separated for a short space from the border of the erosion. The mortification which may invade the intestinal wall does not usually go beyond the mucous membrane. In rare and very severe cases it extends to the submucous connective tissue, or even to the muscular layer. The liquefaction of the mortified patches causes a loss of substance in the membrane, and these places are designated excoriations or erosions, according as the derm remains intact or not. Their number is as variable as are the patches. The viscid masses covering the surface of the intestine, as well as the flakes, are produced by the utricular glands of the gastric and intestinal mucous membrane, which are greatly altered and tumefied. Peyer's glands undergo alterations of a particular character. They lose their epithelial covering, and, in the majority of epizootics, undergo changes analogous to those of the solitary glands; though in other epizootics they are rarely affected, and when they are the lesions are not always equally marked. Sometimes they are merely covered with a mucus layer, like the other parts of the intestine, and are injected; at other times they are more salient than usual from tumefaction; and they then may contain contents like that of the solitary glands; again, they may be covered by a croupal exudation or false membrane, several lines in thickness, and gray, yellow, red, or blue in color, adhering by its central part to the mucous membrane. The presence of these patches is not a constant feature in the pathological anatomy of the disease; in certain epizootics it is almost always present, while in others it is exceptional. Among the conditions which appear to have an influence in its production only one is known, and that is the condition of the animal before infection; if it has been well nourished these deposits are most likely to be present. The prominent alterations in the glands of the mucous membrane appear to consist in an exaggerated proliferation of their cell elements, accompanied by a prompt granulo-adipose destruction of the newly formed cells. The liver is seldom much altered, but the gall-bladder is very often distended with bile, and its mucous membrane is in somewhat the same condition as that of the intestines. The mucous membrane of the air-passages is greatly altered. That lining the larynx, the trachea, and also the bronchia is injected and marked by extravasations which, particularly in the trachea, appear in the form of longitudinal striæ. The lungs are frequently emphysematous (interlobular) to a degree corresponding to the intensity of the malady. This condition is chiefly noticed about the borders of the lungs and in the mediastinum, and, passing along the large blood-vessels toward the lumbar region, it may reach the loins. The lungs are also occasionally œdematous. The pleura, like the peritoneum, is occasionally congested in places, and even ecchymosed. The heart is usually flabby, dark or clay colored, and friable, and at times there are subendocardial extravasation towards its base; the blood is darker colored than in health, and coagulates imperfectly, or not at all. The kidneys may be tumefied, congested, and more friable than usual. The bladder is rarely empty, but generally contains a quantity of urine, which may be pale, dark colored, or muddy, and have suspended in it shreds of epithelium. Its mucous membrane may also be congested and ecchymosed and covered with viscid mucus. The vulvo-vaginal mucous membrane presents a very marked redness, which generally extends to the cervix of the uterus. As in the mouth, there are little elevations of altered epithelium on this membrane, with erosions covered by viscid matter. The udder, frequently congested, sometimes contains a small quantity of thick milk. According to Reynal, the latest observations on the pathological anatomy of cattle plague are those of Damaschino, who has made a complete study of the histological alterations occurring in the disease. This investigator states that the ulceration of the mucous membrane is due to a unique process, which presents a great resemblance to that of pharyngeal diphtheria of man. At the commencement, the lesion consists in an exaggerated production of epithelial cells, which are infiltrated with an amorphous substance, become deformed, throw out multiple prolongations, and acquire an abnormal adhesion, which finally gives them a pseudo-membranous aspect. But beneath these false membranes the young epithelial cells do not submit to the same alterations. Instead of the prolongations adhering to each other, and becoming matted together, they are the seat of a purulent transformation, whence results less adhesiveness, and soon the casting off of the pseudo membrane. At this moment ulceration commences, and as these tissues are softened it happens that there is found implanted on this surface fragments of hairs, which are recognized by the microscope. The loss of substance is not always superficial. On the tongue, sometimes, the lesion ceases at a portion only of the thickness of the papillæ, but in other cases it extends throughout their texture. In the stomach it is often deeper, comprising a portion of the substance of the glandula, and even the entire thickness of the mucous membrane to such a degree that, without the presence of a thick layer of adipose tissue at these points, the stomach would frequently be found perforated. On the surface of these ulcerations the adipose tissue exhibits all the characters of inflammation proper (nuclear proliferation in the conjunctival parietes). In two cases there was found a lesion of the venal and hepatic parenchyma, consisting in a granular degeneration of the glandular elements. In the liver, the lesion, as is usual, showed a predilection for the periphery of the lobules in the vicinity of the vena portæ; there the cells were found in a very advanced stage of granular degeneration. The epithelium of the kidneys, more especially, showed the peculiar tumefied troubled appearance already indicated, though the granular condition was less marked. The muscular alterations consisted in the presence of numerous elongated bodies, very abundant in the right side of the heart, and incontestably situated in the substance of the muscular fiber. These bodies are blunt at one end, pointed at the other, and are composed of a regular mass of cylindrical cells lying together in such a manner that at the pointed extremity there is only a single cell, at the obtuse end two cells, and in the other part sometimes two, sometimes three cells, clustered on a given segment. It is surmised that these minute bodies are entozoa in their primary stage of development. There being no remedy known for this disease, human intervention in dealing with it has thus far been necessarily restricted to measures for its prevention and extinction. Most European governments have passed laws and prescribed regulations for the purpose of protecting their respective countries from the invasions of the plague, and for its speedy extirpation on the occurrence of an outbreak. Of all these enactments the regulations now in force in the German Empire are considered as the most complete embodiment of the results of experience and scientific investigation in regard to this subject.

RING-BONE. Splint and ring-bone in the pathology of the disease are the same, produced by the same causes, and preceded by the same stages of morbid action. From the relation of the parts, however, ring-bone at its forming stage shows earlier and greater lameness, while splint may perhaps go forward and escape attention except from a critical eye, unless the bony tumor be felt in pressing the hand over the part. Ring bone shows itself in lameness, with the first inflammation, and the earliest effusion calls the attention of the horseman. In all diseases resulting in exostosis, or the formation of bone matter, it is essential to take it in the inflammatory stage. Rest is essential; use a high-heeled shoe if the animal inclines to walk on the toe, and a shoe thin at the heel when the animal walks on the heel. Absolute rest from labor is necessary sometimes for months. If the inflammation is active, reduce it with a persistent application of cold water, or with warm embrocations. Then apply the following blister: twenty grains corrosive sublimate, twenty grains camphor, ten drops muriatic acid, one ounce oil of turpentine. The blister must be carefully watched and when sufficiently raised the mixture should be washed off to prevent chance of blemish. Firing should not be resorted to except by a veterinary surgeon. If so the iron should burn in spots, rather than over the whole surface. If the first blister does not suffice apply again when the old one is healed. It is better to keep the blister running as long as possible, by means of simple cerate or plantain leaves.

RINGENT. A name given to the personate corolla, as in the genus *Antirrhinum.*

RINGING FRUIT TREES. This operation has long been known as a means of inducing fruitfulness and increasing the size of the fruit on the particular branch operated on. At one time it was extensively practiced on the grapevine. The fruit sometimes under this system will attain great size, but lacks in flavor, the texture of the fruit is coarse and the skin thick, and as formerly practiced it resulted usually in the subsequent death of the branch. The operation consisted in cutting out a ring of bark, more or less wide up to a quarter of an inch, down to the wood but not into it, since this will certainly kill. This arrests the flow of sap, checks too active inflorescence, and favors the setting and subsequent growth of the fruit. Roots are sometimes so acted upon, to induce the formation of fibrous roots. The modern application of this system of increasing fruitfulness, under expert hands has been found to be very successful, and not injurious to the tree. The system is advocated by such practical men as Messrs. Turner, Spalding, and Weir, of Illinois. We have operated successfully on shy bearers, like yellow bell-flower, and without final injury to the tree. Trees of any bearing size are girdled just before the season of inflorescence, especially those varieties that blossom and yet are inclined to shed the fruit. In some cases a fine saw is driven carefully just through the bark, but not so as to injure the wood. Generally a ring of bark is carefully excised with a sharp knife, varying in width from an eighth to a quarter of an inch in width, and sometimes the wound is protected from the air by wrapping. In other cases strips of bark are left to connect the upper and lower portions of the bark. Sometimes a section is taken half round the tree on one side and a little above, another half round on the other side. Again a simple incision is made about the tree with a sharp knife, down to the wood, and again another, or not, as the case may be, a little above, allowing the upper cut to run to nothing when it meets the first incision next the wood. If the ringing is done in June, or when the tree is in its full elaboration of sap, the wood will invariably heal. In fact there are numerous instances of the bark being maliciously stripped from trees at this season even up to the branches and without subsequent injury. The practice, however, is dangerous, and will kill if the succeeding weather is hot and dry; even ringing is not to be commended except under the direction of one experienced in the performance, and sufficiently well versed in horticulture not to err.

RINGS, FAIRY. Rings of green grass, enclosing a less fertile spot; they are produced by the growth and decay of fungi, the green grass appearing where the fungi have just died.

RIPPLE GRASS. The smaller plantain.

RIPPLING FLAX. Separating the seeds by beating the plants against a board or other contrivance.

RIVOSE. A surface marked with irregular furrows.

ROAD HORSES. The possession of wealth in the Northern States, both East and West, almost invariably shows itself in the desire to possess horses for driving single or double, and that may combine handsome form, style and docility, with a high and continued rate of speed. The wants of business men require horses possessing all these characteristics, but in a lesser degree; still another class, the sons of well-to-do farmers, and those of other producing classes, require horses that will be either above or below the business man's horse, according to the state of their respective purses. This has created a demand for horses sufficiently well bred to unite speed, stoutness and style, and many intelligent farmers have of late years turned their efforts, and with profit, to the breeding of such horses; these are now called road horses, in contradistinction to the trotting horse, which, if he can go fast enough, is a fortune to his possessor, even without the added qualification of style and beauty of form. The roadster, like the trotting horse, is essentially an American invention. American horsemen have taken the initiative in the breeding of these horses; and in no other country in the world will be found either roadsters or trotters capable of doing what these American bred horses will do, either on the trotting course, the road, or on the pleasure drives of our parks. The passion for driving upon the road is undoubtedly one of the means through which our trotting horses were developed, and it seems more than probable that thus were developed some of the best traits that have descended to many of the best trotting horses. Thus a horse of the style of Edward Everett, (see cut), combined with bottom and speed, would be far preferable to a faster horse, but not so handsome. The faculty of fast and natural trotting has been called the trotting instinct. To our mind the trotting instinct is more due to generations of horses, trained to trotting, and which through heredity becomes a fixed characteristic, than anything else. This, with high breeding, careful training, and a cool temper, both in horse and horseman is what has produced the wonderful speed and endurance, both in the American trotting horse and in the American roadster. For light driving, the descendants of Hill's Black-hawk, and many others of the Morgans, may be regarded as almost the perfection of this class of horses. Where greater range of stoutness, and faster work is required, we must look to the descendants of Messenger, Bellfounder, Duroc, etc. Hambletonian, for instance, stands for all that is excellent as a trotter (See Trotting Horses), but his head, if perpetuated in a descendant, would be against him as a stylish road horse. In relation to breeding trotters from roadsters, or rather the development of the trotting stock of our country, Mr. Helm, a practical horse breeder, and author of American Roadsters and Trotting Horses says: It is important to note the fact that, while we recognize the blood of Messenger as the great trotting blood of our country, this trotting quality has come to us mainly, if not altogether, from the sons and daughters of Messenger that were either part bred or kept and bred from in localities where the horse was used as a roadster; and that, of his thoroughbred sons and daughters used for racing purposes, for which they were also distinguished, a much smaller percentage of trotting qualities has been disseminated. Carrying out the supposed teachings of experience in this same matter, it is also claimed that to produce great trotters with certainty and success, the parents must both be trained and developed in the way that our great trotters are trained, and that as a sequence of this doctrine such animals alone can be relied upon for the highest degree of success as breeding animals. Whether it is true that this high degree of development in sire and dam is beneficial or can be relied on with increased confidence, is a matter of uncertainty, and also one of some difficulty to determine with any degree of satisfaction. Whether the process of training and fitting which we call the grand preparation for the great struggles of the race-course, do tend to give the nervous and physical organism the same degree of fixed character and constitute such traits into the permanent elements of the animal nature and being as the regular and constant use as a roadster and fast trotter in daily road work, we can hardly decide. Theory and practice might not agree—the doctrine started with, may not correspond to the results of experience. There may be many reasons why a fair test can not be expected. It takes so many years to develop the trotters, and bring them to the highest degree of excellence, that before they are ready to be transferred from the department of performance to that of reproduction, their age unfits them for the greatest excellence in the latter. Thus far but a small number of great trotters have produced stallions that approach the front rank. Princess enjoyed a short career on the trotting turf after several years use as a roadster, in both of which departments she was distinguished, and then produced the stallion Happy Medium, who undoubtedly displays much of the trotting quality for which she was noted. Sally Miller, the dam of Long Island Black Hawk, was a trotter and road mare of distinction in her day, her claims to that rank being founded both in her performances at one and two-mile heats, and in her being either a granddaughter or a great-granddaughter of Messenger. Flora Temple has also left a son that has some claims to trotting excellence, but is yet not known to rank as a distinguished stallion. Lady Thorn has left a son yet too young to settle the question whether her high degree of perfection as a trotter was in her favor as the dam of a great stallion, and the same observation will apply to the son of Lucy, her distinguished companion and old-time competitor. It is certainly true that the renown of Lady Thorn as a trotter, and her brother Mambrino Patchen as the sire of trotters, in large part originated in the fact that their dam was a highly bred and fully developed road mare, in constant service and of great reputed excellence. Amazonia, the dam of Abdallah, was the most noted road mare of her day; bred from the most noted road stock, but without any of the so-called development in any way, except hard and constant use on the road, where she had no peer. In her blood constituents, and in her acquired and steadily maintained excellence, she was the worthy maternity of the greatest trotting family of our country, but not less distinguished, in each of the above respects, was the Charles Kent mare, the dam of Hambletonian. She was deeply in-bred in the best trotting blood—herself a daughter of one of the best natural trotters our country then had, and for many years was as much famed on the road as the distinguished dam of Abdallah. From such parentage it is no strange phenomenon, in breeding, that there came the founder or progenitor of a trotting race or family the greatest the world has yet seen. The dam of Alexander's Abdallah, the most successful of the sons of Hambletonian, for his short existence, was a developed road mare, but not entitled to be classed as anything beyond. So was the granddam of Volunteer, the dam of George Wilkes, the dam of Ericsson and granddam of Clark Chief, the dam of Trustee, who trotted the twenty-mile race, and the dam and granddam of Knickerbocker. The dam of Gov. Sprague, in addition to the qualities of a fast road-mare fully developed, had the additional element of being a daughter of Hambletonian. The dam of Mambrino Chief, by her good qualities as a roadster, first proved herself to be worthy to produce so great a stallion, and in later years, by the qualities of her descendants, also fully established her claim to the double distinction of possessing as good blood as was on the calendar. From her Abdallah would have produced the peer of Hambletonian, and, perhaps, a more generally successful stallion. The dams of Aberdeen, Cuyler, Middletown, Mambrino Star, Argonaut, and many other distinguished stallions, came from superior road-mares—the first on the above list, from a trotter of considerable distinction. It is rare indeed that a truly great road-mare of good breeding has failed. when bred to a good sire, to produce something worthy of her own excellence, and still more rare, that a really great stallion can be shown whose dam was an unused and idle mare, whose blood qualities had never been called into exercise and proved by actual use and the capacity for hard work. Many mares in the breeding farms of this country have no other claim to superiority than a pedigree showing the blood of distinguished families. That many such fail may be owing to the fact that they never wore a collar or performed a day's work in their lives. It might be that many of these long-pedigree mares would acquire the harmony of nerve organism and blood traits which they seem to lack, if they were put into actual service on the road for a long and uninterrupted period. Nothing else, perhaps, would call out the dormant qualities of nerve and muscle which they carry hidden and unseen. It seems to be a law of animal existence, not confined to the human race, that without labor there is no great excellence, and that it is the trials and contests of life that call out and develop the capabilities of a race. The reader will find elegant photo-illustrations of Lakeland Abdallah, and also of Edward Everett. These horses will serve as object lessons of first-class horses, either for the course or the road.

ROADS AND ROAD MAKING. The question of good roads is one of the most important of any outside the farm proper, for without roads upon which fair loads may be hauled, the produce of the farm can not be carried to market, nor can the general traffic of the country be carried on. In the settlement of a new country the ridges and dryer portions of the country are used for roadways, often causing deviations from the shortest lines, and very often these roadways remain after the settlement of the country, to the great inconvenience of the traveling public and the owners of farms, near villages these detours are gradually shortened, and straight roads are laid out, properly graded and, at length, ballasted with suitable material. In alluvial countries such as the prairie regions of the West, the greatest difficulty is experienced in making roads that shall be solid and constant in their nature during wet and dry weather. Fortunately, the soil is of such a nature, that during the dry months of the year, or from June to November, the earth when kept properly graded forms smooth and tolerably firm roadways. And in winter, also, when frozen, they are soon worn smooth. In older settled countries engineering talent is brought into constant requisition in the making of roads and various materials, gravel, cinders, broken stone, slag from furnaces, blocks of wood or stone, and planking are used. In England, in some places, burned clay has been successfully used in the ballasting of roads, it having the peculiarity once thoroughly burned that it does not again come into a plastic state but acts on plastic soils, in the nature of sand and gravel, forming under the pressure of travel a tolerably firm roadway. It would require a large volume to treat the important subject of roadways and road making exhaustively. It is more the study of the civil engineer than the private individual. Nevertheless, the subject is so important to farmers especially, that we append the chief points relating to earth road, and road making, as originally suggested by Mr. W. J. Edwards, who was eminently fitted to understand the whole subject, both as inventor of road-making machinery and a practical road-maker. Without good roads there can be no material development, beyond that mediocrity which mere civilization gives. Even the most degraded savages have well defined trails; and the knowledge of the conservation of manual force, which it would almost seem that they possess intuitively, leads them, from point to point, over the easiest grades consistent with a direct route. So, the early settler finding soon the necessity of roads, first blazes a bridle path through the timber, or else, follows the trail of the Indian across the plain. Speedily, however, the wagon or cart must be used for the transportation of crops and other goods, and these usually follow the ridges or higher lands, until, with the further settlement of the country, water courses are bridged, sloughs are ditched, and at last continuous tracks, and next roads, crude and imperfect, it is true, but yet distinctly defined, are made from point to point. Nature knows no roads; and savages, like some species of animals, wear tracks only. Therefore, it may be set down as an axiom, that one of the first indications of increasing civilization in man, is the steps he takes to improve the roadways over which he must travel; and therefore the completeness of the roads are as landmarks, which show the degree of enlightenment which a nation has reached. Not only this, the higher the civilization, the nearer approach to true utility in designing and forming the road beds of a country—if we except mere pleasure roads, as seen in private grounds and also in landscape gardening. However pleasing curved lines may be, or however delightful the views caught here and there, however charming the vistas that now and again appear in the driveways of the wealthy man's estate, yet, in the formation of public roads, all this must be sacrificed to the tyrant, utility. They may not be employed in purely ornamental driveways, even without some apparent cause, artificial though it be, for the curvature of the road. A change of level in the ground, a pond, a tree, a group of shrubbery, or some similar natural or artificial obstruction, must be present to afford an opportunity to demand a change of line. Thus, in landscape gardening, where the ground is irregular, the deviations from a straight line necessary to follow an easy grade and at the same time adhere as closely to the natural surface of the ground as possible, will generally develop graceful curves. And in no case should any but the easiest curves in long sweeps of roadway be attempted on a level surface; for they would be just as incongruous as would be a Gothic cottage, with its acute angles, standing in the middle of a marsh, or a fine mansion in a wilderness. Granted, then, the necessity for roads, both useful and ornamental, let us explain how roads develop a country. First, they render traffic practicable. Even the mere bridle path to the nearest mill does this, but in a country where no other roads are asked for, the inhabitants will too often be found carrying a stone in one end of the sack to counterbalance the peck of corn in the other, if, indeed, they do not pound their grist between two stones. Their village will be irregular; their implements of the crudest kind; education among them will be wholly wanting. The men will be barbarians: the women slaves;

while the land itself will be divided between wild beasts and savage tribes. But soon the inventive faculty of the settler devises a rude vehicle, for he finds that the log may be rolled far easier, than it can be drawn lengthwise. The inventor, from his superior intelligence, acquires wealth more rapidly than his fellows, and with wealth comes the desire for luxuries. His compeers are stimulated to like efforts. Fields are opened, improved implements are devised, villages are built, and so roads must be made to them, and, lo! the problem of civilization is at last solved. In the formation of roads for the carriage of loads, or those of utility, they should go as directly from point to point as the nature of the ground will permit. This portion of the work is the first duty of the engineer. He must survey the country, and the various obstacles; figure upon the relative economy of passing over, through, or around them, and so form his grades as to present the least possible obstacle to the passage of teams. In this direction, and in spanning chasms; passing around or through mountains; bridging great rivers, or tunneling under them, some of the greatest engineering feats in the history of the world have been performed. It is obvious, that, as a rule, the roads of a country should be built of the material found in the vicinity, and that will combine in the greatest degree, cheapness, indestructibility and smoothness of surface, with the requisite degree of firmness. And whatever kind of roads are made, they must present a slightly convex surface, be of easy grade, and also be thoroughly drained, else the labor of their construction is expended in vain. In localities where sharp gravel is obtainable, there is no doubt but that a covering of from ten to fifteen inches upon a perfectly graded and well drained road is one of the best and most economical; at the same time it is easier to keep in repair for country roads, for the reason that it costs merely the digging and hauling. Washed and rounded gravel should not be used, for it will never cement together to form an even surface. It may, indeed, in time become so incorporated with the soil as to increase the solidity of the roadway, but it can never become a really efficient medium over which loaded vehicles can pass at all seasons of the year. In California, which is well known for the miry nature of its soil, during the rainy season, even in the mountains, a covering of sharp gravel, twelve to eighteen inches thick, over carefully graded road beds, has proved entirely satisfactory, and it is quite well known that, for ordinary travel, there are no roads more agreeable to travel on, than carriage ways, carefully drained, graded, and then ballasted with sharp, strong gravel. Some years since plank roads were all the rage. It is scarcely necessary to notice them here, since they are expensive to build, annoying and costly to keep in repair, quickly wear out, are absolutely torturing to animals driven fast over them, rack vehicles severely, and are little less than horrifying to those travelers who are compelled to ride over them. These two classes of roads, if we except the poor make-shifts usually found, patched here and there, by throwing irregularly to the center of a roadway a ridge of earth scooped from the sides, with no definite idea of the first principles of road making, have been made to do duty as roads. The first is found only at long intervals; the second is, happily, now a thing of the past. The third, or earth roads, if properly made and kept in repair, would, at a comparatively light cost, add infinitely to the average value of the farm lands of the entire prairie region of the West. The proper construction of roads adapted to continuous and heavy traffic by loaded teams at all seasons of the year, must depend measurably upon local circumstances; for their perfection and durability will be in direct ratio to the materials used, other circumstances being equal. In large cities, and near great marts of trade and commerce, the first cost of such roads is only a secondary consideration. They must perforce be perfect at any reasonable expense. Fortunately timber is cheap, and had plank roads served no other purpose, they should be respected as being the initial movement toward the Nicholson pavement that is now held in such justly high repute in the great cities of the West. The next in point of endurance and easy travel is, undoubtedly the Telford pavement; next, the MacAdam roadways; next, gravel roads; and last, but not least, will be the roads of loam, clay, or other materials which form the natural soil of the prairie region. To briefly describe the more artificial roadways that can only be made under the direction of competent engineers and trained workmen, would seem desirable, but before proceeding to this, there are some questions that suggest themselves, which may well be considered here. The first requisite in any road, as has been before stated, is drainage. The second is the sub-road or foundation, but since this must always be of the soil natural to the country, it may safely be left until that class of roads is considered. Drainage must be absolutely perfect. For any road, if water soaked, however great the expense incurred in its construction, will not stand. This drainage may be made by open ditches or gutters at the side, if the water be carried away from the vicinity of the road bed at every available point. Whenever practicable the fall should be made both ways from a point as nearly central as may be, and each water way should be extended to a point of discharge lower than the plane; but if the distance between such points of discharge be so great as to lead to the fear of the washing of the road bed, the proper means must be taken to prevent this, no matter what the cost. Where gradients are so steep that the water will flow along the road in spite of the rounded surface, then catch or water bars, transverse gutters must be provided to carry the water into the proper channels at the sides of the roadway. The transverse grades of roads is a most important consideration. On perfectly hard roads, such as the Nicholson, Telford, MacAdam, or others with so hard and uniform a surface, that they will not under any circumstances wash, a very slight decline only from the center to the sides should be given, for much lateral slope is one of the most objectionable features in hard roads, and is permissible at all, simply to carry off moisture; therefore, in every case this should be reduced to a minimum on the last slope consistent with the perfect drawing of the water of rains into the gutters at the sides of the road. Consequently, it is scarcely practicable to give any rule that will meet even a moiety of the constantly changing conditions, or that will meet even approximately the cost of the various materials of which roads are made. Some ancient nations carried road making to a high state of perfection. They were made of as various materials as they are at the present time, including gravel, asphalt, and numerous concretes. On these it will be useless to expatiate, since the civilization that called those roadways into existence has passed away, and nothing remains save the traditions. There are, however, two systems of roadways of nations that lived and bound together ancient and modern times—the Chinese and the Roman—whose roads were of the most solid and enduring nature. Those have been the basis from which our system arose. The Chinese roads are perfect to-day, because that nation still exists to keep them in repair. The remains of some of the Roman roads still stand in a state of good preservation, although centuries have elapsed since the nation which made them as perfect as they were enduring, became a thing of the past. The system which the Chinese adopted in building their roads was to grade the roadway and then cover the whole with hewn blocks of stone, carefully jointed and cemented together so that the entire surface presented a perfectly smooth plane. They are immensely costly to build, and indestructible by time. The block pavements of modern days are of this type. They would not, however, be tolerated now, since teams have but little traction power on these roads, owing to the hard, smooth surface of the exterior, and horses are liable to slip, fall and injure themselves. The Roman roads were built by laying a concrete foundation of proper thickness and then cementing therein blocks of stone or other material. The knowledge of engineering was superior and the sums of money they expended prodigious. We are all conversant with the feats of Hannibal in his passage of the Alps. His engineers forced a passage over rocky promontories by heating the surface and then disintegrating it by means of acids (vinegar). Modern science, in road making, is as far superior to the ancient as is gunpowder, nitro-glycerine and dynamite to the old method of blasting by heat and the application of acids. The Nicholson pavement undoubtedly combines more excellencies than any other form of pavement for vehicles. It is easily laid, durable, and also easy of repair, is pleasant for travel, comparatively noiseless, and not especially injurious to the hoofs of horses. In constructing these pavements the first step is to grade the roadway; a layer of sand or fine gravel is laid smoothly and evenly over; inch to inch and a quarter boards are then placed over the sand so as to break joints; this is now thoroughly swabbed with boiling gas tar. Four inch timbers are then accurately sawed to a length of eight inches, and laid either directly or diagonally across the roadway, and securely nailed to the planking beneath, or to the narrow strips used to divide the lines of block, thus leaving a space of an inch between the upper half of the row of blocks. These interstices are filled with fine gravel of uniform size, gas tar at nearly a boiling point is then poured in, and the whole rammed compactly with suitable implements. A layer of gravel of a quarter to a half inch size is then thinly strewn over the pavement. The whole is swept so as completely to fill the interstices, and then we have a type of the best roadway ever devised by man. Many variations have been made from this plan, as laying the blocks directly on the bed of sand or gravel beneath, doing away with the narrow strips, etc., etc. They have some advantages, but the real improvements on the original plan more than counterbalance them. It would appear, however, that if the foundation could be made on the Telford plan, and this be covered with sufficient fine gravel to thoroughly cement the whole and the wooden pavement laid directly over all, it would leave little to be desired either in point of solidity, permanence or facility for repairs. The expense of such pavements, however, preclude their adoption except in cities and their vicinity where the travel is heavy and constant, for the interest on the cost and wear and tear of any road can only be fixed on a just percentage of the traffic thereon. In making MacAdam roads, in tenacious soils the surface on which to place the broken stone should be at least one foot above the bottom of the waterways. The margins and slopes must be of such a nature that they will not wash or abrade, and if an under-drain be placed at each side of the rock covering, so much the better. Indeed, the value of under-drains beneath any road, with lateral drains at suitable intervals, into the waterways at the sides of the road, are not appreciated as they should be by many otherwise good engineers. The stone with which the road is ballasted should be broken so that the most of it would pass through a two-inch ring, this being found by experiments made both in England and other countries to be the largest size allowable. Indeed, MacAdam himself declares that cubes of one and one-quarter inch are better than a larger size; but in speaking of cubes of a certain size it is neither understood that absolutely square pieces are meant, nor that the sections of rock shall be of uniform size. In fact, a considerable irregularity of size and shape is more conducive to a perfect cementing of the whole, so that when settled by rolling and travel it shall form a continuous, even surface, over which vehicles may be easily propelled. Years ago the laborious process of breaking the stone by hand formed an item of considerable expense in the formation of these roads. Later, machines were invented which perform this work most perfectly. In the application of the broken stone to the road-bed care should be taken that the earth's surface has not been worn into ruts, for if this be the case it will inevitably cause the road to settle unevenly, and such depressions can not be mended save by picking up, remetaling and again ramming. In this case the stone should be rather smaller than that used in the building of the road. The same rule will also apply to all the repairs of the road. Whenever depressions or ruts are worn, the surface must be picked to sufficient depth to permit the packing used to thoroughly cement with the metal below. To cover or metal a mile of road twenty feet wide to a depth of twelve inches, will require something more than 903 cords of stone or other material, so that, given the cost of the rock, and knowing the value of labor, it will be easy to figure the cost of the superstructure. So the rule will also apply to any portion of the labor required to form any road. The conditions are so varying, that even an approximation can not be reached; and these always mislead. The exact conditions must be studied by the commissioners as they always are by contractors. If this be done, there will seldom be much difference between the contracting parties. For ballasting or metaling roads, as it is called, limestone is most generally used, probably for the reason that it is the most evenly distributed, and when available, being of easy and even fracture, it is cheaply prepared for the road-bed. Nevertheless, it is not the best material. Granite, from its extreme hardness, is much superior; but this rock, being one of the primary formations, is comparatively rare at the surface of the earth. As it will not pay to convey the metaling long distances, the most available rock near by must, perforce, be used. The surface of the road having been properly ballasted, a dressing of clay, from one to two inches, should be laid over all, and the whole surface thoroughly and continuously rolled with a heavy roller, until the superstructure is alike even and compact, and the angularities of the metal have been thoroughly interlocked and rendered solid, before vehicles are allowed to pass over it. Many object to this surfacing, but without this or some other binding covering, the top will be a long time in coming into a smooth surface, and is far more likely to be worn into ruts, especially if it be a country road, where there is comparatively little turning out from the center to avoid teams going in a contrary direction. Another advantage of the clay surfacing, besides its binding action, is that it prohibits passing wheels from destroying the angularity of the broken rock, and thus preventing cohesion, by reducing them to the shape of water-worn pebbles; for it is well known that stones once worn round never after cohere and bind together to form a perfect surface. Another advantage of this clay surfacing is, that it at once renders the road comparatively water-proof; and, gradually working down, does not in the least add resistance to the draft of teams, as has been claimed, but, on the contrary, does render the draft much easier, at first, than if the rock surface were on top. A width of twenty feet of rock is ample for any travel, except in isolated cases, where a road is thronged with teams constantly passing and re-passing, as is the case in large cities or contiguous to them. On all roads there should be side tracks corresponding with and forming an unbroken grade with the macadamized portion of the roadway. This metaled surface may be diminished, both in width and thickness, down to a width of eight feet and a thickness of six inches, to meet cost to be expended on the requirements of travel. The great cost of hauling material of any kind to form the superstructure of a road, renders it imperative that the most careful calculation be made as to the amount of traffic thereon. If, for instance, the heavy travel be nearly all one way, as in country places, ten feet of ballasted portion will be ample; fourteen feet will easily allow for turning out, and for the passage of loaded teams; eighteen to twenty feet will allow teams to go in contrary directions continuously; and twenty-four to thirty-two feet will admit of the road being thronged in both directions, and yet leave sufficient room for turning out and the passing and repassing of light vehicles, swiftly driven. When the earth of the roadway consists of gravel of proper size, and clay in due proportion, or if there be an admixture of cementing material, as combinations of iron, etc., as is sometimes found, the work of making the road is comparatively easy. It has merely to be graded by the proper machines, (and these should be employed in every town, whether metaled or natural roads are to be used,) and then the material, by repeated rollings, cemented firmly together. Of course, in making any road, it is understood that the proper engineering must first be employed, the gradients established, sharp hills leveled or passed around, valleys filled, natural obstacles cut away and removed, so that, whatever grade be established as the maximum, the surface may be made to correspond. This is the work of the surveyor. This done, the proper slope of the road adjusted, the drainage provided for, the culverts established, and other minutia attended to, all the contractor then has to do is to carry out the plan according to the specifications. Unfortunately for the constructing of perfect roadways in alluvial countries, this variety of soils rarely exists; but if unfortunate in this respect, the disability is amply compensated for by the exceeding richness of the soil. A country composed of material suitable for superior roads, is never worth much for anything else—certainly not for agricultural purposes. But, as before stated, we propose to show here how the whole prairie portion of the West, may have roads good enough, during the seasons of principal travel, to allow the carrying of 4,000 pounds per team of two horses; and this can be done at an exceedingly light cost for labor. While its soil is one of the richest on the face of the earth, there are few countries where the material can be made into as good roadways as there. They have only to be properly drained, graded and compacted to form most admirable roadways, that will rarely become bad for travel, except, it may be, a short season in the early winter and spring. In the construction of gravel roads, as in all others, the sub-stratum must be, of course, the natural soil of the locality. The drainage must be as well attended to, and the engineering must be the same as for other roads. The lower portion of the road-bed may be of any material that will make a solid foundation for the upper strata, or the whole may be composed of gravel of different sizes, the larger being placed and kept at the bottom. For light traffic and easy travel, both for teams and individuals, there is no question of the superiority of well made and well kept gravel roads over all others. A combination of the Telford foundation with a gravel surface, when the cost may warrant it, will, undoubtedly form the perfection of a roadway for ordinary travel. At the bottom, on a properly graded sub-way, may be placed the rough foundation of the road-bed, consisting of irregular stone, or small boulders, from the size of a man's fist to a two-quart measure, or larger, according to the amount of travel expected. Over this the top work of smaller gravel should be laid, still keeping the larger gravel at the bottom and evening up with the smallest. Great care should be taken to secure the foundation properly. The large pieces of rock forming this should not be laid in at random, or in rows, and never on their flat side; but should be placed so as to break joints, as it were, and yet be left sufficiently even on top to receive the covering of gravel. This is done by breaking away those projections of rock which rise much above the general surface; or when square, they may be embedded in the soil beneath. There is one fact which should never be lost sight of; and that is, the foundation must ever remain pervious to water, so that whatever moisture finds its way through the surface, may immediately pass to the soil below, and thence easily percolate to drains which should always be provided, unless the nature of the soil and subsoil be such that the drainage is naturally thorough. It is essential that the foundation of any road be rolled when laid. It is absolutely imperative that the surface covering be so rolled, until the whole is entirely compacted into one cohesive mass. The very best roads are made thus, whether with a covering of gravel, or macadam, or any other cohering material; the larger in the bottom, and the finer on top, while no material the size of a hen's egg should ever be allowed within four inches of the top; and the harder the rock material the smaller the cubes or fragments of rock or gravel may be, for a complete cementing of the whole. Now, as the perfection of a road made of broken stone is, to have a foundation of coarse, angular fragments, followed by a covering of two-inch cubes, surfaced with cubes of one inch, or smaller, sure to the elements, make it valuable when it is readily obtainable. In Paris, France, and its vicinity, asphalt is extensively used, but the dust arising from it is obnoxious in the extreme. Concrete roads are made under several patents, and are composed of a great variety of materials, gas tar, and gravel, and cements of several kinds, with gravel; often with some form of lime as the base, or entirely of lime or plaster. As mere pleasure walks or lawn drives, to be covered with gravel, they may answer for a makeshift, where nothing better can be obtained. Concrete, of which lime is the base, made upon the road, and laid to the depth of six inches, and then covered with gravel, pressed into it before it sets, is excellent as a foundation, where stone can not be procured. There are remains of old Roman roads so made, that are sound to-day. We have so far carried the reader through some of the more expensive kinds of roads in use in various countries. We now proceed to give tables and other data from actual experiments made by celebrated engineers in Europe. These might be multiplied indefinitely, and quotations made from such authorities as Law Morin, MacNeill, Sir H. Parnell, Bevan, Edgeworth, Flachet, Gerstner, Kassak, Minard, Navier,

		Character of the vehicle.		
CHARACTER OF ROAD.	Carts.	Trucks, four horses.	Stage coaches.	Two-horse carriages.
Firm soil covered with gravel, four to six inches deep............	1-12	1-9	1-8	1-8.
Firm embankment covered with gravel 1¼ to 1½ inches deep.....	1-16	1-11	1-10	1-10
Earth embankment in very good condition......................	1-41	1-29	1-26	1-26
Bridge flooring of thick oak plank...............................	1-70	1-46	1-41	1-42

Broken Stone Road.		Walk.	Trot.	Walk.	Trot.
In very good condition, very dry, compact and even.............	1-75	1-54	1-48	1-41	1-49	1-42
A little moist or a little dusty......................................	1-53	1-38	1-34	1-27	1-34	1-27
Firm, but with ruts and mud.......................................	1-33	1-24	1- 1	1-18	1-22	1-19
Very bad, ruts 4 to 4½ inches deep, thick mud..................	1-19	1-14	1- 2	1-10	1-12	1-10
Good pavement { Dry...	1-90	1-65	1-57	1-38	1-59	1-30
Good pavement { Covered with mud.........................	1-69	1-50	1-44	1-33	1-45	1-34

according to the hardness of the material, so the most complete gravel roadway is made by placing the larger stones at the bottom, over which the smaller are laid; the whole to be finished with that of less and less size, until the surfacing shall be the smallest sharp gravel obtainable. It will not be necessary to speak of the various concrete and cement roads, except in the way of mere mention, since they are valueless for heavy and steady travel, unless we except the so-called cinder roads, or those composed of the scoria from blast furnaces. These do make excellent mediums for ordinary travel. The material, when obtainable, cements most perfectly, and is pleasant to travel over, if kept free from dust; but, from the soft and porous nature of the material, under heavy work, they soon wear out. For the foundation of road-beds this scoria is most valuable, and is extensively used in the vicinity of Chicago and other places where smelting furnaces, rolling mills, or other works for the melting of iron are in operation. Asphalt is used in many combinations in the formation of roads. Its cementing qualities and the indestructible nature of the materials, through expo-

Perdonnet, Poncelet and others. The four first named, however, must suffice. They establish important facts that should be known to all who have anything to do with the making or the management of roads. The experiments of Morin, made in 1838–41, appear to have been made with a painstaking degree of care and accuracy, thus leaving nothing more to be desired, and the table, as given, an extract from his results, will be found valuable as showing that fraction of the weight of the vehicle and load, which is required to move them on a level road. As an example, suppose a truck weighed, with its load, 9,000 pounds, how many pounds traction will be required to move the same? On firm soil, gravel four to six inches deep, that is a newly repaired road as we often find it, (one-ninth by table) 1,000 pounds; on best kind of embankment (one-twenty-ninth by table), 310.3 pounds; on broken stone roads in good condition (one-fifty-fourth by table), 166.6 pounds; on broken stone roads, deep ruts and mud (one-fourteenth by table), 643 pounds; on a good pavement (one-sixty-fifth by table), 138.5 pounds. Or since the tractive force of a medium horse, when working all day, is said to be about 125 pounds, we need in the first case, eight horses; in the second case, two and a half horses; in the third case, about one and a quarter horses; in the fourth case, about five horses; and in the fifth case, only one good horse to move the same entire load all day with ease. The following are the general results of the experiments made by M. Morin, at the expense of the French government, on traction: The traction is directly proportional to the load, and inversely proportional to the diameter of the wheel. Upon a paved or hard macadamized road the resistance is independent of the width of the tire, when it exceeds from three to four inches. At a walking pace the traction is the same, under the same circumstances, for carriages with springs or without them. Upon hard macadamized and upon paved roads, the traction increases with the velocity; the increments of traction being directly proportional to the increments of velocity, above the velocity of 3.28 feet per second, or about two and a quarter miles per hour. The equal increment of traction thus due to each equal increment of velocity is less, as the road is more smooth, and the carriage less rigid or better hung. Upon soft roads of earth, or sand, or turf, or roads fresh and thickly graveled, the traction is independent of the velocity. Upon a well made and compact pavement of hewn stones, the traction at a walking pace is not more than three-fourths of that upon the best macadamized road under similar circumstances; at a trotting pace it is equal to it. The destruction of the road is in all cases greater, as the diameter of the wheels are less, and it is greater in carriages without than with springs. Experiments made by Sir John MacNeill, with an instrument invented by him for the purpose of measuring the tractive force required on different descriptions of road, under various circumstances, will be of value. The general results which he obtained are given in the following table, the numbers in which exhibit the tractive force in pounds requisite to move a weight of a ton, under ordinary circumstances, at a very low velocity upon the several kinds of road mentioned:

Description of Road.	Force.
On a well made pavement.	33
On a road made with six inches of broken stone, of great hardness, laid either on a foundation of large stones, set in the form of a pavement, or upon a bottoming of concrete	46
On an old flint road, or a road made with a thick coating of broken stone laid on earth	65
On a road made with a thick coating of gravel, laid on earth	147

Mr. H. Law, C.E., in the work—Construction of Roads, edited by Rob't Mallet, C. E., etc.—gives the table, on next page, which is of importance, as showing the comparative disadvantages of hilly roads, with light and heavy travel. It is also valuable as showing the resistance upon various grades, and also the angle which these grades will present to the horizon. It shows, with sufficient exactness for most practical purposes, the force required to draw carriages over inclined roads, and the comparative advantage of such roads and those which are perfectly level. The first column expresses the rate of inclination,

and the second the equivalent angle; the two next columns contain the force requisite to draw a common stage wagon weighing, with its load, six tons, at a velocity of 4.4 feet per second (or three miles per hour), along a macadamized road in its usual state, both when the hill ascends and when it descends; the fifth and sixth columns contain the length of level road which would be equivalent to a mile in length of the inclined road, that is, the length which would require the same mechanical force to be expended in drawing the wagon over as would be necessary to draw it over a mile of the inclined road; the four next columns contain the same information as the four last described, only with reference to a stage coach weighing with its load, three tons, and to travel at the rate of 8.8 feet per second, or six miles per hour. The following table will show the force required to move a ton, the limiting angle of resistance, and the greatest inclination which should be given to the roads named. The values of the resistances on which the table is calculated, are those quoted previously:

Description of road.	Force in pounds required to move a ton.	Limiting angle of resistance.	Greatest inclination which should be given to the road.
Well laid pavement	33	°0 '50	1 in 68
Broken stone surface on a bottom of rough pavement or concrete	46	1 11	1 " 49
Broken stone surface laid on an old flint road	65	1 40	1 " 34
Gravel road	147	3 45	1 " 15

As indicating something of the cost of the construction of roads, as also their repairs, the following condensed account will be interesting and valuable for reference: According to all the returns from different States, the average construction of gravel roads is $2,241 per mile, and the average annual cost per mile for repairs is $103. It appears, from the reports, that only a very few of the roads are improved by a gravel bed, and neither the width of the beds so improved, nor the quantity of material applied, is given. We may reasonably infer, however, that neither is greater than is absolutely required, and yet we find the cost of construction, per mile, to range from $700 to $4,000, and to average $2,241. The annual outlay per mile varies from $4 to $200, the average being, as above stated, $103. By reference to the table, showing the cost of repairs to common roads per mile, throughout the country, we find it to vary from $1 to $59, and the general average is $18 11 per mile. The returns show that the average cost of construction of macadamized roads in the different States from $500 to $336. The average annual cost per mile for repairs of macadamized roads, as reported, is $40—varying from $10 to $100 per mile. The average cost of construction of plank roads per mile is reported to be $3,000, and the average annual cost of repairs per mile is $550. The table, page 816, compiled

		FOR A STAGE WAGON.				FOR A STAGE COACH.			
Rate of Inclination.	Angle with the horizon.	Force required to draw the wagon up the incline.	Force required to draw the wagon down the incline.	Equivalent length of level road for an ascending wagon.	Equivalent length of level road for a descending wagon.	Force required to draw the coach up the incline.	Force required to draw the coach down the incline.	Equivalent length of level road for an ascending coach.	Equivalent length of level road for a descending coach.
		lbs.	lbs.	Miles.	Miles.	lbs.	lbs.	Miles.	Miles.
1 in 600	0° 5′ 44″	286	241	1.085	.9150	372	350	1.030	.9890
1 " 575	0 5 59	287	240	1.088	.9116	373	340	1.032	.9676
1 " 550	0 6 15	288	239	1.093	.9074	374	349	1.033	.9662
1 " 525	0 6 33	289	238	1.097	.9029	374	349	1.035	.9648
1 " 500	0 6 53	291	237	1.102	.8979	375	348	1.037	.9629
1 " 475	0 7 14	292	235	1.107	.8926	376	347	1.039	.9605
1 " 450	0 7 38	294	234	1.113	.8869	377	347	1.041	.9588
1 " 425	0 8 5	295	232	1.120	.8801	377	346	1.043	.9563
1 " 400	0 8 36	297	230	1.128	.8722	378	345	1.046	.9535
1 " 375	0 9 10	300	228	1.136	.8642	380	344	1.049	.9506
1 " 350	0 9 49	302	225	1.146	.8543	381	342	1.053	.9489
1 " 325	0 10 35	305	222	1.157	.8433	382	341	1.056	.9431
1 " 300	0 11 28	309	219	1.170	.8301	384	339	1.061	.9381
1 " 290	0 11 51	310	217	1.176	.8245	385	338	1.064	.9358
1 " 280	0 12 17	312	216	1.182	.8179	386	338	1.066	.9335
1 " 270	0 12 44	314	214	1.189	.8111	386	337	1.068	.9314
1 " 260	0 13 13	315	212	1.196	.8039	387	336	1.071	.9286
1 " 250	0 13 45	317	210	1.204	.7963	388	335	1.074	.9259
1 " 240	0 14 19	320	208	1.212	.7876	390	334	1.077	.9226
1 " 230	0 14 57	322	205	1.222	.7785	391	3·32	1.080	.9192
1 " 220	0 15 37	325	203	1.232	.7684	392	331	1.084	.9156
1 " 210	0 16 22	328	200	1.243	.7573	394	330	1.088	.9115
1 " 200	0 17 11	331	197	1.255	.7451	395	328	1.092	.9071
1 " 190	0 18 6	334	193	1.269	.7319	397	326	1.097	.9024
1 " 180	0 19 6	338	189	1.283	.7171	399	324	1.103	.8968
1 " 170	0 20 13	343	185	1.300	.7004	411	321	1.109	.8906
1 " 160	0 21 29	348	180	1.319	.7814	404	320	1.116	.8839
1 " 150	0 22 55	353	174	1.341	.6587	406	317	1.123	.8761
1 " 140	0 24 33	360	168	1.364	.6359	410	314	1.132	.8673
1 " 130	0 26 27	367	160	1.392	.6079	413	310	1.142	.8573
1 " 120	0 28 39	376	152	1.425	.5752	418	306	1.154	.8451
1 " 110	0 31 15	386	142	1.451	.5491	423	300	1.169	.8308
1 " 100	0 34 23	398	129	1.510	.4903	429	294	1.185	.8142
1 " 95	0 36 11	405	122	1.537	.4634	432	291	1.195	.8045
1 " 90	0 38 12	413	114	1.565	.4336	436	287	1.206	.7937
1 " 85	0 40 27	422	106	1.600	.4004	441	282	1.219	.7801
1 " 80	0 42 58	432	96	1.637	.3629	446	278	1.232	.7677
1 " 75	0 45 51	443	85	1.680	.3204	451	272	1.247	.7522
1 " 70	0 49 7	456	72	1.728	.2719	457	266	1.265	.7345
1 " 65	0 52 54	470	57	1.784	.2161	465	258	1.285	.7143
1 " 60	0 57 18	488	40	1.851	.1505	474	250	1.309	.6908
1 " 55	1 2 30	508	19	1.926	.0736	484	239	1.337	.6630
1 " 50	1 8 6	533	....	2.019	....	496	227	1.371	.6283
1 " 45	1 16 24	562	....	2.133	....	511	212	1.412	.5871
1 " 40	1 25 57	600	....	2.274	....	530	194	1.464	.5324
1 " 35	1 38 14	648	....	2.456	....	554	170	1.530	.4690
1 " 34	1 41 8	659	....	2.499	....	559	164	1.546	.4535
1 " 33	1 44 12	671	....	2.544	....	565	158	1.562	.4370
1 " 32	1 47 27	684	....	2.598	....	572	152	1.580	.4193
1 " 31	1 50 55	697	....	2.644	....	578	145	1.599	.4007
1 " 30	1 54 37	712	....	2.699	....	586	138	1.618	.3805
1 " 29	1 58 34	727	....	2.758	....	593	130	1.640	.3592
1 " 28	2 2 5	744	....	2.820	....	602	122	1.663	.3363
1 " 27	2 7 2	762	....	2.888	....	610	113	1.688	.3129
1 " 26	2 11 42	781	....	2.960	....	620	103	1.714	.2854
1 " 25	2 17 26	801	....	3.038	....	630	93	1.743	.2566
1 " 24	2 23 10	823	....	3.120	....	641	82	1.774	.2267
1 " 23	2 29 22	847	....	3.213	....	653	69	1.806	.1919
1 " 22	2 36 10	874	....	3.313	....	666	56	1.844	.1554
1 " 21	2 43 35	903	....	3.423	....	681	42	1.884	.1150
1 " 20	2 51 21	933	....	3.538	....	698	26	1.926	.0730
1 " 19	3 0 48	970	....	3.677	....	714	8	1.977	.0221
1 " 18	3 10 47	1010	....	3.876	....	734	....	2.032	....
1 " 17	3 21 59	1058	....	3.991	....	756	....	2.092	....
1 " 16	3 34 35	1102	....	4.178	....	780	....	2.160	....
1 " 15	3 48 51	1157	....	4.368	....	807	....	2.234	....
1 " 14	4 5 14	1221	....	4.699	....	839	....	2.322	....
1 " 13	4 23 56	1294	....	4.906	....	875	....	2.423	....
1 " 12	4 45 49	1379	....	5.229	....	918	....	2 540	....
1 " 11	5 11 40	1480	....	5.611	....	968	....	2.679	....
1 " 10	5 42 58	1600	....	6.067	....	1028	....	2.846	....
1 " 9	6 20 25	1747	....	6.623	....	1101	....	3.048	....
1 " 8	7 7 30	1929	....	7.315	....	1192	....	3.300	....
1 " 7	8 7 48	2162	....	8.199	....	1308	....	3.621	....

from replies to circular issued by the Department of Agriculture, United States, shows the average annual cost per mile of repairs of common roads in the respective States:

State.	Cost per mile.
New York	$21 82
New Jersey	27 50
Massachusetts	59 16
Rhode Island	33 75
Michigan	23 60
Wisconsin	24 70
Pennsylvania	18 28
Maine	40 00
Connecticut	9 00
New Hampshire	16 00
Vermont	25 00
Maryland	11 00
Delaware	14 50
Virginia	6 00
North Carolina	6 50
South Carolina	1 00
Georgia	7 58
Florida	18 00
Alabama	4 84
Mississippi	8 00
Louisiana	2 00
Texas	7 95
Arkansas	6 43
Tennessee	17 00
West Virginia	8 40
Kentucky	13 57
Missouri	10 59
Illinois	10 31
Indiana	38 24
Ohio	23 60
Minnesota	20 00
Iowa	20 00
Kansas	8 00
Nebraska	5 00
Utah	43 00
Colorado	
California	23 00
Nevada	10 00
Oregon	25 00

It has often been asserted that the West could never have a good system of roads, for the reason that, except in widely scattered localities, good gravel could not be found, and that it was still more rare to obtain rock suitable for the formation of roads. This very scarcity of what has heretofore been deemed indispensable to road-making, has led to the perfection of implements for casting up from the sides of the road-bed a continuous ridge of earth, leaving the grade perfect, the slopes of the roadway light or heavy at will, the sides gradually descending to the ditches or gutters, so that the whole surface, and even the water ways, when not wet, may be made use of as a roadway. Indeed, the making of earth roads by machinery may be said to have been reduced almost to a science; since, given the miles of clear surface to be graded, the cost of making the road may be estimated to within a fraction of the cost. We think it will be admitted to be beyond contradiction that the prairies, composed as they are of a strong loam, that, when dry and under pressure, will compact, will make a smooth, even surface, upon which the wheels of loaded vehicles scarcely make an impression, and this fact ought to have suggested their admirable nature for this purpose long ago. Certain it is that during the droughts of summer, and when frozen and worn smooth in winter, they are among the best of any natural causeways in the world. Upon any of our well drained, carefully graded, and tolerably well traveled prairie roads, there is but a small portion of the year—say a short time in the spring, when the frost is just coming out, and another equally short time, when it is freezing and thawing in the fall—that a good team can not haul 3,000 pounds with ease. Therefore, given good drainage, an even grade as to the slopes of the sides, and a soil that will pack solid, the question of good roads is solved. It has also been objected to by those who have studied works on drainage, where certain gradients being determined on by the engineer, every slope of the various undulations must be cut away, and the materials used to fill the slight hollows, so that the road when completed shall present a continuous line of equal rise and fall, like a railroad. Indeed, railroad engineers are beginning to find out that it is cheaper to run over rather light grades than always to cut through them; and hence railroads have become practicable where once it was believed it would not pay to build them. It has furthermore been found, in practice, that the ordinary undulating surface of our prairies offer no obstacle to the continuous running of roads, and that the grades may follow the surface, unless, in exceptional cases, where a sharp, high ridge may intervene. These may require some cutting, but far less than has generally been supposed. As a rule the grading may be made continuous over hill and dale, and seldom will it be found necessary to deviate from a straight line in order to avoid serious obstructions. Therefore no engineering is required; nothing but good implements, a set of flags by which to drive, sufficient team and men to operate the machine, and the work may go on continuously at the rate of a mile to a mile and a half per week of road completed, perfect in its slopes and drainage, through valleys and over the gentle slopes that are found everywhere on our grand prairies. The superior drainage which this system of roads would give to prairie farms is itself one of the most eloquent pleas possible for its general adoption. But valuable as this one point really is, it is but an integer of its final value to the entire West, and really almost insignificant in comparison with the development that would follow. The wealth that a system of building first-class earth roads would create, is simply enormous. How to do this to the best advantage, is the question. One of the mistakes, but still a very pardonable one, where the work is done with old fashioned implements, is that the road-beds are commenced too narrow. When it becomes necessary to widen them, as it inevitably does, in order to accommodate increased travel, not only the original labor is lost, but where the ditch once was it can with difficulty be made solid, since here must be placed a thick layer of comparatively soft earth, and adjoining on each side the ridge of compact earth that formed the original road-bed. It is, therefore, advisable that the road-bed be made at least twenty-five feet wide, with the ditches not less than seven feet wide, and nine feet is preferable. This extreme width for road-beds and water-ways will leave twelve and one-half feet on each side for the planting of such shade trees as may be needed, and yet give ample space for the passage of pedestrians. The ditches should commence at nothing, running gradually back until the extreme depth, eighteen inches to two feet, is reached. This should be at a point only so far from the extreme width as to correspond with the height of the bank, so that the rise to the bank may be as one to one, or an angle of forty-five degrees. In making a road by means of a machine, it must be arranged so it will carry the earth directly to the center of the road and drop the material excavated continuously as the machine passes forward, to correspond with the width of the ditches; so continue until you have the ditches or water-ways of sufficient depth and regularity, and the whole is ready for spreading or finishing. This finishing is done by taking an eight by ten inch square timber, twenty-four feet long, and drawing it diagonally, the rear end in the water-way, up and back. This will spread and grade the earth evenly over the required space for the road-bed, leaving the surface crowning to the middle just as may be required. It is not necessary in every case that it be cast all over the roadway, so that if only a narrow track is required the bermes next the ditches may be left of any width desired, and still preserve the integrity of the transverse grades. Start a road and run it clear through a township, if possible. Why not? A machine with eight horses and two men should grade a first-class road six miles in thirty working days, and at an expense for labor of not more than fifteen cents per rod. Plenty of cases might be cited where an average of a mile in four days has been easily accomplished, and this with green teams. The impression wished to be conveyed is, that the time has come when perfected machines are doing this work in the very best manner, and at a cost of about twenty-five cents on the dollar for what it would cost with the plow and old fashioned scraper; that roads made with modern implements stand more and rougher usage than the old style of roads, and with far less expense for repairs; that the drainage supplied to the adjacent farms by a good system of roadways on every section line, necessarily will add materially to the productiveness of the soil, and the increased facilities for travel will diminish the cost of transportation fully one-half. In fact, it is the want of good drainage, and the difficulty in transporting produce to market, that is doing more to reduce the profits of farming than any other two causes combined. Therefore, what the low value of the land years ago would not allow to be done may now be accomplished at so light a cost per capita as to form no objection to the making of earth roads, at least, over the whole prairie region of the West. Let us now examine for a moment the advantages of carrying the grades of roads over the undulations of the surface. One of the difficulties over the old system of simply grading the hollows is, that on the declivities and acclivities where there are no lateral slopes to the roadway, the water seeks the ruts, if there be such, or if the roadway be smooth, then the middle of the roadway; since, being without grade, these must soon become the lowest portions of the road. Gullies are formed which wear larger and larger, until the road becomes impassable, and a new track has to be sought. So the process goes on and on, until the whole width of the roadway is ruined. The grade being carried continuously up and down the slopes, and over the summits of the undulations as well as in the valleys, the crowning surface of the road conveys the water naturally to the water-ways at the side. If the soil be of a sufficiently yielding nature to be abraded easily, protection against this may be readily applied. If the slopes are so steep as to require cutting down, to render the gradient more easy, when this is done the road grade to the ditches may then, be established as on an ordinary surface, remembering always, as a rule, that the steeper the grade the more rounding the roadway should be, and this for very obvious reasons. The following figure will show a cutting through a sharp ridge, and the grade of the road. Again, suppose it be easier to go round a hill than through it; then the figure of the road will be as given in the following cut; a ditch being needed only on the side next the hill. These, however, are only isolated cases, and will never be required in a gently undulating prairie region, except, perhaps, in the descent to and ascent from a river, ravine, etc. In the hilly portions these cuts will often be found necessary, and in rare cases in other sections. The illustrations are given so that with a little study of the tables previously given, and a simple level and plumb, the gradients can be at once established and the cuttings made by any

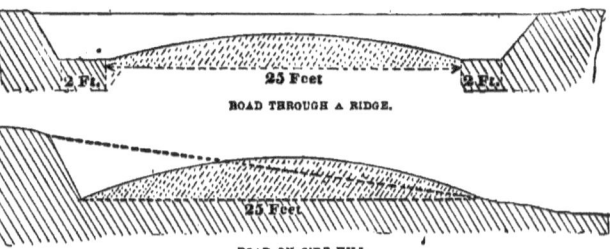

ROAD THROUGH A RIDGE.

ROAD ON SIDE HILL.

intelligent man. Again, if from the nature of the country the grades must be made so steep that the water will not run easily to the gutters on the sides, catchways may be provided as previously shown to arrest and convey the water to the ditches. These must be formed of some firm and unyielding materials. This course will be necessary in isolated cases, where the character of the country is exceedingly difficult. One of the most common errors in road making is, that the ditches are left deepest in the middle and rise alike towards the road and the bank. This is entirely wrong. They should slope gradually to a point next the bank, and corresponding to the height from the bottom of the ditch to the bank as heretofore stated. From thence they should rise sharply to the bank. The reason is plain: If the lowest point of the gutter be half way between the bank and the road-bed (the outside of it), and there is enough water carried to wash at all, there will be danger that the roadways may become abraded or eaten into by the flowing water; but if near the bank, then the

A PERFECT EARTH ROADWAY.

water will wear away from rather than toward the roadway, and all the danger of washing will be avoided. Thus the whole, when completed, should present an appearance as shown in full page cut. When it is necessary to carry the water of the ditches through slight rises of ground the additional work of excavating a channel will be comparatively slight. It may either be spaded and cast out, or a strong horse and plow going back and forth will loosen the earth so that it may be thrown out with a shovel. Thus a slight way once made, the water will speedily wear a channel that will never become choked. One of the most important essentials in road making is sluice ways or culverts, at proper intervals, so that the water may readily be conveyed from one side of the road to the other as the conformation of the surface may demand, to keep up the continuity of the drainage; for, if water be permitted to stand in the ditches at all, the roadway must remain moist and consequently soft. One of the greatest nuisances is the rough and uncouth wooden abomination miscalled a culvert. When these ditches receive the accumulated water of fields, as when the roadway crosses natural water courses, substantial culverts or bridges must be provided; but when the accumulation is simply the drainage of the road, with, perhaps, some addition from the adjacent land, a simple line of tile sunk to the level of the bottom of the ditch, and extending across and under the road, is all that is necessary. These, besides offering no obstruction to travel, are far cheaper than even the simplest culverts formed of wood. These should always be of vitrified tile and may be ordered in any city. They are made of any size, from six inches to two feet or even larger in calibre. If one is not enough, lay two or more alongside each other, and do away with the severe shocks that torture horses, drivers and passengers, whenever the wheels strike those plank water ways. Grade the road as wanted before building your sluices. Then excavate to the desired depth, level the bottom accurately, making it concave to fit the convexity of the tile. Lay them carefully, pack the earth firmly around them until they are so securely held that they can not move; lay a plank upon the soil, say from four to six inches over the tile, and then fill in the earth so that the grade may correspond with the rest of the road. There will then be no danger that the heaviest loaded teams will injure the tile, and there is no reason why they should not last as long as the road itself. We have thus far endeavored to show something of the various ways of making roads, the materials used, and the adaptability to the various needs, seeking to avoid technicalities and elaborate computations that serve only to confuse those not educated to the science of engineering. We have, however, given such data and tables as we deemed serviceable to road-making farmers, road-overseers and commissioners of highways. Our principal aim has been to give you an idea how easy it is to make good earth roads, and to call attention to the fact that improved machinery is now doing as much for the road makers as improved implements have done for the farmers. Arrange for the width of the road and ditches, by means of grade pegs and flags along the edges of the required ditches. Set flags along the center of the road to guide the operators somewhat in spreading the earth. Plow the entire width of the ditches throwing the furrows toward the roadway. Now scrape the furrows well to the center, spreading evenly. Plow again, narrower than before, being careful not to get too deep next the road; again scrape, and so proceed to plow until you have the earth necessary to form the roadway being careful to preserve the bottom of the ditch so that it shall slope very gradually to within about eighteen inches of the outside of the ditch, and rise sharply to the banks next the fences. Thus finished, the work should present the appearance as seen in cut. Illustration on page 818 shows a completed road, with figures indicating the several proportions. Thus, the width of ditches, nine feet; width of ungraded surface, four feet; width of grade, sixteen feet; height of grade, fifteen inches; width between fences being sixty-six feet. Suppose this road be in a slough with slopes rising each way, longitudinally with the road. The accumulation of water will fill the ditches and overflow the road; but a culvert, or a line of tile, according to circumstances, running transversely on, from ditch to ditch, and ending in an open or covered ditch, running down the line of the slough a sufficient distance to form an outlet for the water, establishes your drainage, and your road must, as a matter of course, remain dry. When graded, the surface should be repeatedly dragged with a heavy harrow to smooth all unevenness, and then rolled until it is quite even and hard. Then, when once worn by teams, it will ever after remain almost impervious to water, unless it is allowed to get out of repair. It will probably surprise many to be informed that some years ago it was seriously argued that owing to the spongy nature of the soil, tramways would have to be established over the West to enable the farmers to get their produce to market. We presume there would be few now to advocate this system, in those towns and other sections, where a connected system of earth road-ways has been established. One of the great difficulties in organizing a perfect and uniform system of roads, is the multiplicity of overseers in our towns. It is an onerous position at the best, and one bringing loss rather than profit to the incumbent. These are, or are supposed to be, farmers or business men, who have a direct interest in keeping the roads in repair. From the fact that the position is an onerous one, no man who has business of his own, likes to take it. If a responsible man does, it is simply on account of his public spirit, and they are but seldom men who possess a practical knowledge of road-making. But each does have an indefinite idea of how a road should be made, and immediately proceeds to carry out these ideas. If there are three or a dozen different overseers in a township, there will be as many different kinds of roads. Consequently there never can be, under this system, any uniformity in the road-ways, nor perfection in drainage. The next year comes a new set of overseers, and they proceed to practically demonstrate their ideas. So it goes on from year to year, and our roads, in too many instances, continue to be a horror to travelers; rutted and full of holes in dry weather, and miry and dreadful when wet. The men are not to blame. They are, as a rule, honest and honorable men. They are not road-makers, but farmers, mechanics or business men, who can not be expected to leave their occupations to work upon the public ground, especially when, after their best endeavors, they are compelled to endure the censure of imperfect work. Who, then, is to blame? Well, no one specially. It is the law which made the system. Suppose we change this system, and in lieu of a multitude of road-makers, place the whole matter of road-making in the hands of one competent commissioner in each town, who shall be paid liberally for the labor performed. He may give bonds, if necessary, for the faithful handling and judicious disbursement of the money. Let the commissioners of a county meet at some time in the winter to compare notes and experiences, devise ways and means, report upon improvements, estimate the necessary amount of money required to be raised for the current year, and agree as near as possible upon a uniform system to be pursued. How long would it be before improved drainage and improved roads had added ten times the cost of the work to the value of the lands of the State? Suppose a good road was built on every section line in a township of six miles square, at a cost of fifty cents per rod, or $160 per mile. It can be done for much less. There would be seventy-two miles of road in the town. This, at $160 per mile, would be $5,760. Add as much for bridges and sluice-ways, and we have $11,520. There are 23,040 acres in a township. Thus the roads and bridges have added the enormous sum of fifty cents per acre to the cost of the farms. The value of the drainage alone would pay the bill and leave the roads as clear gain. Will any farmer say that it will not increase the value of his farm by at least five dollars per acre? With this view of the case, would there be any difficulty in inducing every property holder to vote the money necessary to bring about this much to be wished for result? Undoubtedly not. But to do this the law must be changed, and the old system of doing the work by property owners, under the direction of a multiplicity of overseers, working without concerted plans, must be abolished. To do this, the people of the several States, for they are the real power, must be made to see that the benefits arising therefrom, will be at least commensurate with the cost.

ROBIN. (See Thrush.)
ROBINIA. (See Locust.)
ROCHELLE SALT. Tartrate of soda and potassa; used as a gentle purgative.
ROCK CRYSTAL. Transparent quartz.
ROCK SALT. The coarse native salt, found in immense masses in some parts of the globe. It consists of salt chiefly, but adulterated with chloride of calcium, gypsum, and marl.
ROD. The same as a pole, sixteen and one half feet. Four of these make Gunter's chain.
RODENTS, RODENTIA. Gnawing quadrupeds, with two long chisel teeth in the front of either jaw. Rats, rabbits, and squirrels are of this class.
ROLLER. An implement of simple construction, the main object of which is to render smooth the surface of arable lands. It is an implement in which greater diversity of form is found to exist than in most agricultural machines. Rollers are of all sizes, weights, and lengths; and the material of which they are made is occasionally iron, sometimes stone, but most commonly wood. Of these, the first is undoubtedly the best, and particularly for the jointed roller, by which the operation of turning at the ends of the ridges is materially facilitated, and the crowding of the earth which would otherwise take place on the head-lands, not only to their great detriment, but in the increase of labor to the team, is thereby prevented. The use of the roller is now confined to compressing the soil, and except on roads, walks, and causeways, is less used than formerly. It having been found in practice that this implement seldom crushes the clods of hard earth, but simply presses them level with the surface. Hence, other implements which grind as well as press, have in a great measure, taken their place. One of the best of these is a plank twelve or fourteen inches wide, to which the team is hitched, and upon which the driver rides. Another implement for leveling and grinding is made of three two-by-four hard wood scantling, fastened together by rods, and placed about ten inches apart, answers excellently. A roller formed by a series of discs placed together in two ranks, the rear rank cutting between the tracks of the forward ones, grinds hard clays admirably, but is heavy and tedious, and compacts the soil too firmly. Hence farmers are now depending more on fall plowing, in tenacious soils than formerly, using the roller simply to compress the earth about the seeds, and render the surface uniform.

ROOD. A square measure, equal to forty perches or square poles. The fourth part of an acre.

ROOK. *Corvus frugilegus.* The gregarious crow, almost domesticated in England in rookeries. They live, for the most part, on insects. The young are sometimes eaten.

ROOT. That part of the central axis of a plant which is formed by the descending fibers, and whose function is to attract liquid food from the soil in which it is found. It differs from the stem in not having leaves or buds upon its surface, and in its tendency to burrow under ground, retreating from light; nevertheless, some kinds of roots are exclusively formed in air and light, as in the ivy, and other such plants. Roots are of various figures, as fibrous; spindle, as in the radish; knotted, etc. The rhizome of the flag and the tuber of the potato are not roots, but subterranean stems. The cormus of palms and aroideæ is a mere expansion of tissue, which is neither a root nor stem.

ROOT CROPS. By root crops we understand the cultivation of those crops, the roots, bulbs, or tubers of which are used as food for man or farm stock. In England the turnip forms the most important root crop in cultivation, since it has been made the means of feeding stock and acting as a cleaning and fallow crop in the regular rotation. The climate of the United States is not adapted to the extensive culture of the turnip, and Indian corn takes its place as a feeding crop. As a field root crop, potatoes are the most important in the United States, next the onion, then beets, parsnips, carrots and salsify, all these being used for culinary purposes except beets and carrots. No root crop should have green manure applied to it the same year of cultivation. Potatoes and onions suffer least from the application of green manure. It is apt to make the first knobby, and the second thick necked. All the spindle-shaped roots as beets, carrots, etc., are pretty sure to have forked and ill-shaped roots from the application of green manure. A good plan is to precede the cultivation of root crops with Indian corn heavily manured, and give a good surface dressing of well rotted manure or compost the fall preceding the planting of the roots, to be well worked in the soil the succeeding spring. (See articles on varieties.)

ROOT PRUNING. The principal objects sought to be gained by root pruning is, first to so check the growth as to induce early fruitfulness; second, to induce the formation of fibrous roots, third, to prevent blight, and fourth, as a means of preparing a tree for subsequent removal with a mass of earth attached. Root pruning has the direct effect of at once cutting off a supply of sap. Therefore the work should be performed understandingly. The leaves not being furnished with their usual quantity of sap, the branches are checked in growth, and as a fruit bud is well known to be but a modification of a leaf bud, it naturally follows that the energies of the tree being checked, that fruit buds are apt to be formed for the next season's growth. It would therefore follow that root pruning to induce fruitfulness should be performed early in the season or before the full season of growth. To induce the formation of fibrous roots and to check early blossoming, the pruning may be done in the latter part of winter or as early in the spring as the ground is well settled. For the prevention of blight the late Dr. Hull, one of the most successful of Illinois' orchardists, has stated the following: If root pruning the pear is to be done to induce tardy bearing trees to become fruitful, then the pruning should be at such time, and with sufficient severity, to cause the trees to produce their leaves fully grown at least six weeks before frost in autumn. But when the pruning is be done to ward off the attacks of blight, then the roots must be so much shortened that the tree will show terminal buds on leading shoots, at the earliest period that trees are known to show the effects of blight in the sap wood. No rule based on time can be given, since each mile, north or south, would make some variation necessary. Or, to be more explicit, the degree of maturity would be reached earlier South than North. For instance take Seckel trees making moderate growth. These in latitude 39° would show terminal buds, at the ends of the latest growing shoots, about June 1; 3° south, the 15th to the 20th of May; while a similar condition of growth as far north as the 43° could not occur earlier than July 1. For these and similar reasons any rule made as a guide for root pruning must have reference to conditions rather than time. The conclusions given above are based on microscopic examinations, also on observations made on root pruning, extending through a period of more than twenty years. Dr. Hull believed that in no instance can pear tree blight materially injure a tree on which all the leaf growth is well developed by the time the first branch growth of slow growing Seckel trees is ended; provided a second growth is not made. Excellent examples in support of this view may be found in the Seckel growing on poor soils. Under such conditions the trees form terminal buds on the strongest of the current year's shoots at the time we have named. It is probable that these slow growing Seckel trees could not blight, in fact do not, until a second flow of sap occurs. Thus, Seckel, and other trees of similar habits of growth, could be kept in health by a moderate shortening of the roots; while trees which continue branch and leaf growth to a later period, must be more severely root pruned. Theoretically considered, especially for the South, pruning to secure early maturity of wood growth is wrong; since trees which naturally go to rest early, after they have been a short time inactive, generally cast their leaves and then make a partial second growth, which is injurious or fatal to them. Observation, however, has taught the important lesson that root-pruned trees make but one growth the same season. When severe top pruning is done, then the roots grow slowly until the balance in the top and roots is again restored. In like manner, trees which are deprived of a part of their roots push only a part of their germ branches, these are soon grown. After this branch growth has ceased the leaves continue a long while active and change leaf to fruit buds; a large number of buds are so changed. After which, all further growth of the season, if there be any, goes to restore the loss of the roots. Trees pruned as directed, do not again restore the balance between the top and roots before the end of the second season. Hence it was conceded that root-pruned pear trees, growing under any of the conditions described, could not blight until the third summer. For this reason, shortening the roots once in two years, in accordance with the rule it was claimed, would protect the trees from injury by blight. Among other advantages gained by root pruning, besides preventing blight, may be named the following: Root-pruned pear trees generally resist leaf blight. Tardy bearing trees, perfect fruit buds the first summer, after their roots have been cut, and produce full crops of fruit the next. The size of the fruit is much increased. The pears on root pruned trees are smooth-skinned and free from russet patches and bands, and on ripening, color finely; in this respect rivaling the California pears, which they also greatly excel in quality. Root-pruned pear trees, on pear roots, may be dwarfed to almost any extent desired. Trees of any age after they have been several times root pruned, may be safely transplanted. The operation is thoroughly performed as follows: Root pruning may be performed from November to April. The latter part of winter or spring is best, as the subsoil is then easily penetrated by a spade. For trees the circumference of which is twelve inches at one foot above the ground, mark a circle around the tree, the semi-diameter of which shall not exceed eighteen inches from the trunk. For trees larger than twelve inches, for each additional three inches of girth, enlarge the diameter of the circle three inches. Next, with a sharp spade open a trench outside of the circle to the depth of not less than three feet, cutting all lateral roots to that depth. For a tree measuring twelve inches, this will leave a round ball of earth of the diameter of forty inches to contain the lateral roots left after pruning. After having the work inspected, fill the trench with top soil and give thorough cultivation until August at the north part of Illinois, latitude 42°, and until October in latitude 38°. Once in two years repeat the operation enlarging the diameter of the circle three inches with each additional operation. The effect of this pruning is to force the trees to form their terminal buds on the leading shoots by the time the blight first appears, which in the latitude of St. Louis occurs about May 25 to the 1st of June. Root pruning, for the purpose of rendering a tree safe to remove, though the formation of new roots should be performed early in the spring, or better late in the previous fall, so as to allow a full season's growth previous to removal. In root pruning, however, as in ringing, the operator must understand the nature of the tree to be operated on, as well as to have a correct idea of the changes that are to occur. For general orchard work a subsoil plow, with the coulter ground sharp, is simply run deeply both ways in the orchard, cutting the earth in squares about the trees. In more restricted grounds, a sharp, long-bladed spade is thrust deeply in the earth in a circle about the tree. This often has fully as good an effect as the more scientific pruning, and is applicable to all trees and shrubs of rampant growth. In the fruit garden it will pay, when it may not do so in extensive orchard culture, and for one reason that finer varieties are usually grown there than in the commercial orchards.

ROOT STOCK. The rhizome of the flag, ginger, arrow-root, etc.

ROSACEÆ. A large and important natural order of plants, the species of which are, for the most part, inhabitants of the cooler parts of the world. They are in some cases trees, in others shrubs, and in a great number of instances herbaceous, perennial plants; scarcely any are annuals. No natural orders contain more species of general interest, in the beauty of their flowers, or their perfume; there is the rose itself, and various species of the genera *Rubus, Spiræa, Potentilla, Geum*, and *Pyrus*. The apple, pear, plum, cherry, peach, nectarine, apricot, raspberry, strawberry, and similar valuable fruits are the produce of others. As medicinal plants, some are of considerable importance. Prussic acid is obtained from the leaves and seeds of the bitter almond, peach, plum, and other species. This important assemblage of plants is distinguished by having several petals; separate carpels; distinct, perigynous, numerous stamens; alternate leaves, and an exogenous mode of growth.

ROOTS AND VEGETABLES, PITTING. Many farmers in the West, even of those who pay proper attention to the kitchen garden, do not have the cellar room they ought to have; and this, often, from the difficulty and expense in procuring stone for the walls. This, however, need not prevent any one from having a good supply of vegetables during the winter. They may be kept in pits, or, covered on the surface of the land, in the best possible condition, if the proper plan is adopted for keeping them intact; that is, to keep such as are injured by slight freezing, warm enough, and those which will not be so injured, cool enough. Potatoes, for instance, are ruined by the least frost, so when they receive their final covering for winter the pits should have no ventilation. On the other hand, beets, and especially swedes and common turnips, should be kept quite cold; if of the two latter varieties they may be partially frozen, and yet come out intact, if allowed to thaw naturally; indeed, we usually allow them to freeze slightly, and place on additional covering to keep them so frozen. Parsnips and salsify, also, are better so frozen, and so are onions; but beets and carrots, if frozen, are injured. In cold, long winters, pits of potatoes will often freeze, though covered with a great depth of soil. Our rule is to cover with plenty of hay or straw, then with six inches of earth, then another layer of straw, and again six to eight inches of earth. Thus covered we have never had pits frozen, even in the extremest winters; but in very long, cold spells, we usually add a covering of litter over all. The philosophy is this: The frost penetrating to the first covering of straw, is held by the dead air there, and seldom enters the second layer of earth to any great extent. Parsnips and salsify may be safely left in the ground where they grow, all winter; but enough should be put in the cellar, or pits, to last till spring. It is a mistaken notion that these roots are not good until frozen. They are undoubtedly better in the spring; but if left thus until then, the season is so short that but little good is had of them. Late celery is saved and blanched for winter use by digging shallow trenches about two feet wide, and placing the plants upright therein, as closely together as possible, and yet allow to have earth packed firmly about the plants, and nearly to the tops. When so packed the whole should be covered with rails, so that the litter over all, to keep out the frost, will not press heavily on the plants. It is some trouble to keep celery, but the satisfaction of having this delicious vegetable in winter well repays the cost. When wanted for use the end last packed may be broken into, as much as is desired taken out, and the whole again covered secure, remembering that fifteen degrees of frost kills this plant.

ROOT CROPS FOR FEEDING. Very few farmers estimate the relation in value of root crops, to the other crops of the farm. The cultivation of beets in France and Germany, has added one quarter to the number of cattle that may be fed; and also added twenty-five per cent. per acre to the production of wheat in those countries. Why? Nothing is exported but the sugar of the crop. The beet pulp after the sugar is taken, is one of the most valuable of foods for cattle; and the cattle fed return large quantities of rich manure to the soil. Crops of beets are among the best fallow crops known; for the land must be put in first rate condition and kept absolutely free from weeds. This done, there is no difficulty in raising great crops of anything which follows. Among a very important class of western men, the cultivation of root crops might be of great value. These are stock breeders and dairymen. Fortunately this class can afford to cultivate them systematically. Our extreme summer droughts render the cultivation of turnips impracticable. Not so other roots, and especially beets. We do not advocate the cultivation of roots by the general farmer, although if done to such a degree that each horse, sheep, head of swine or cattle kept, could have a certain quantity each day in connection with other food, it would be found profitable in enhanced health to the stock. If Short-Horn herds received a quota of roots every day in the winter, and if milch cows were fed roots during the same season, we should hear much less of infertile animals among the farmers, and of abortions, and that class of disabilities among this class of stock. For this reason we shall give the most feasible plan of cultivation, for experimenting with such crops by these classes. The cultivation and preparation of the soil, it will not be necessary to resume, except to say that the soil must be deeply worked, well manured, and free from the seeds of weeds. Among the implements of culture, a leveler and a roller are indispensable. A leveler is thus made: Take two 4x4 hard wood scantlings, eight feet long. Fasten them together with strong one and a half inch pins, so they shall be two and a half to three feet apart. To the forward piece fasten a chain so that it may form a V to draw by. Put a walking board on the pins, between the scantling, to stand on. Thus by taking proper positions, you may make the leveler draw more or less diagonally, catching the earth at the high places and moving it to the lower. Go over the land both ways if necessary, and you will be surprised at the result, if you have not heretofore known this. Accuracy in marking the land, that rows may be perfectly straight, and at equal distances from each other, is indispensable. A strong plank eight feet long, with runners and a tongue attached, will make five marks, two feet apart, and will run steady if you attach a stout rope of proper length from the near and the off hame rings of the harness, to the outside of the marker. If the marker be sawed into three sections, and again joined with strong strap hinges, it will fit inequalities in the ground. Let the markers be of sled runner shape, as they will press the earth rather than stir it, making the marks as shallow as possible, and so that they can be seen. Having passed once through, in returning keep one shoe accurately in the last track made; and then with a little care your plat will be ready for the drill. Any of the better class of garden drills will sow your seed accurately and perfectly. So soon as the seed appears above ground, work as closely to the rows as possible with a stirrup, wheel, hoe or other suitable implement, and as soon as the plants gain a little size, thin them with a narrow hand hoe; if beets or ruta-bagas, into squares of six inches apart. The latter, however, are better thinned entirely by hand, at the time of weeding. We have given the distance of two feet apart for the rows, since at this distance a common one-horse cultivator may be shut close enough to clean between the rows if care be used, and after the plants get some size there will be little difficulty in working the crop. In seeding, sow thick, not less than four pounds of carrots or parsnips, and six to eight of beets per acre, many sow twelve. It is far easier to thin than to lose a stand, for replanting never pays. Sow from the first to the tenth of May, north of the latitude of southern Iowa, or Central Illinois, Indiana and Ohio. In these latitudes the last of April will be proper. If South, still earlier. Ruta-bagas should be sown about the 25th of May, in the latitude first named, since it is difficult to get a stand if sown later, on account of the fly, drought, etc. If you lose the first crop, sow again. Beets should not be sown more than an inch deep; carrots and parsnips one-half inch, and rutabagas still more shallow. Roll the whole surface even, after planting, since this will make the cultivation easier. The theoretical value of any food is the dry matter it contains. Its real value consists in the power of the animal organism to assimilate the organic matter contained. The amount of the several proximate organic bodies in a ton of kernels of corn, dry, according to the analysis of Salisbury, are:

Organic Matter.	Pounds.
Sugar and extract	266.40
Starch	1186.00
Fiber	17.80
Matter by Potash	119.80
Albumen	85.80
Casein	1.60
Zein	33.80
Dextrine and gum	65.20
Oil	72.00
Water	169.90
	2018.10

The per cent. of dry matter in 100 parts of the kernels of white flint corn, according to the same authority, is 62.56, and 37.44 per cent. water. A proximate analysis of mangold, fresh, by Horseford and Krucker, in 100 parts, gave:

Albuminous matter	2.04
Sugar	12.26
Cellulose and other nitrogenous substances	2.56
Mineral substances	0.89
Water	82.25
	100.00

Thus we have in beets, of solid matter, 17.75 per cent. as against 62.56 in corn, or three and a half times as much. So, theoretically, 100 pounds of corn should go as far as 350 pounds of beets; but practically, 250 pounds of beets will feed as far as 100 pounds of corn, for this reason: the beets are more perfectly digested than the corn. Again, it will require under the most favorable circumstances, the labor of a man and team two and a half days to raise and crib a ton of corn, or an acre; this will represent at $3.00 per day, $7.50. Under equally favorable circumstances four tons of beets may be raised for the same money. But let us look at the matter in another light. We have shown that a ton of corn, which corresponds to a good crop, contains per acre, exclusive of water, 1848.20 pounds of solid matter. According to Johnson, twenty tons of mangold, an average yield per acre, under ordinary circumstances, contain 4,950 pounds of starch, sugar, etc.; 900 pounds of gluten, etc.; 900 pounds of fiber, and 450 pounds of saline matter, equals 7,200 pounds, or about four times the amount contained in the acre of corn. An acre of corn costs $7.50; the acre of beets, if raised by hand, will cost $30; and thus, again, we are even, allowing that both are equally assimilated, which every man knows we are not, unless the corn is ground. The point lies just here: To reach the best results, the grain and vegetable food should be fed together, since one contains largely of fatty matter, and the other of nitrogenous matter, and so one assists the other. For ourselves, we have reached the best results in feeding a half bushel of roots, and a peck of meal, to each fattening ox per day. This was near Chicago, where mills were plenty, and when the culture of roots could be economically carried on. Different results might be obtained where corn was cheaply raised, and roots difficult of culture. Still this does not alter the question of value in the animal economy.

ROSE. This queen of flowers is almost universally cultivated in some form. Every garden however small has its rose bush, too often, however, of old and discarded varieties that have but little merit compared with the varieties of later years. The well known June rose, annual bloomer, is perfectly hardy, and may now be had of splendid varieties, including standard, moss, climbing and pillar roses, or half climbing. Unfortunately, once they have cast their short lived bloom, they bloom no more until the next season. The hybrid perpetuals, however, after their summer bloom is passed, if cut back, will again bloom in the fall, and the color, variety, and substance of their flowers is all that could be desired. They, however, require protection during the winter, North. Without this they are liable to winter-kill. Roses require a deep, rich humus, but moderately compact soil. Pot roses like a soil rather lumpy, that is a soil not sifted. Two parts of rich, black loam, and one part of rotted cow manure, with the addition of a little sharp sand serves them admirably. The monthly or Chinese rose and its hybrids, generally known as monthly roses, are still more tender than the perpetuals. They may be perfectly well wintered in a pit, three or four feet deep, covered with glass, and protected from severe frost, if a little air is given them in winter. So also they may be wintered in a well lighted cellar. They are the roses principally grown in window gardens. The only objection to growing roses in rooms is the prevalence of insects, especially the green fly and red spider, destroying their usefulness and beauty. Semperflorens is among the best for a single variety; for two, add Indica Alba; three, add Eugene Beauharnais; four, add Indica (common daily); five, add La Superbe; and for six, add Jacksonii. These are all firm and free blooms. The tea roses are exquisite and fragrant. Odorata, Saffrano, Compte de Paris, and Adam are among the good reliable sorts. The Bourbon roses, sometimes called China-perpetuals are a fine class, vigorous in growth and hardier than the China rose. Queen of Bedders, Souvenier de la Malmaison, and Hermosa are fine. All the roses described may be wintered in a pit or cool cellar as described. They may be planted out in the ground about April first, in latitude forty two degrees, and taken up before hard and continuous freezing occurs.

ROSE BAY. The handsome *Rhododendron maximum.*

ROSE CAMPION. (See Cockle.)
ROSE MALLOW. (See Mallow.)
ROSEMARY. Handsome species of plants cultivated for their scented leaves and their essential oil. They are not hardy in the North. South these plants have been used occasionally as hedge plants. There are three principal varieties, the green, golden striped, and silver striped. The latter two are ornamental varieties.

ROSIN. The resin remaining after distilling the spirits from turpentine. Colophony.

ROSTELLUM. The name given to the retractile sucking tube of apterous insects.

ROT. This is a name given to a disease in sheep, when infected with the fluke, *distomum Lanceolatum*, and *Fasciola Hepatica* which inhabit the gall bladder and ducts, and passes to the substance of the liver. Once the disease becomes apparent, immediate remedies must be used. This is known by the comjunctiva, or membrane covering the eye-ball in front, and lining it, becoming pale and yellow; in a healthy sheep it is brilliantly red and is of a natural color. As the disease progresses the sheep become pot bellied, rough, ragged, and finally die. When developed there is no cure. As a preventive, or in the very early stages of the disease, give every fourth day for two weeks a wine-glass full of the following mixture, and several hours before food is given: Take one and one-half ounces saltpetre, one ounce powdered ginger, one-half ounce carbonate of iron, one pound salt, three quarts boiling water, mix, and when nearly cool, add nine ounces spirits of turpentine, bottle for use, and shake well before giving it. Badly drained pastures, musty hay or that badly cured, are supposed to be favorable to the flukes. Keep sheep in high, solid, well-drained pastures, feed plenty of salt, and if the fields are suspected keep the sheep off the pasture except when the grass is free from moisture. The foot and mouth disease in cattle is sometimes incorrectly called rot, and, also, hoof rot—the latter comes from unclean usage of cattle. (See Apthous fever.) Rot is a common term used to denote the decay of the growing fruit on the tree, from stings of insects followed by the attack of fungi, or from original epidemic fungi. There is no known remedy except a change of atmospheric conditions.

ROTATION OF CROPS. In all countries when agriculture has advanced to a condition where the same land is occupied from year to year, a rotation of crops comes to be looked on as indispensable, and for the simple reason that all such cultivated and carried from the land, sooner or later exhaust the soil of the elements of fertility required to perfect the species. Hence those crops which are carried off, root, branch and seed, exhaust the soil quicker than those, a portion of which are left on the field or are returned to it. Consequently the poorer the soil the more care must be taken to diversify the crops, and from the well known fact that different plants exhaust different constituents of the soil. Among the ancients rotation was less attended to than manuring, and rest and fallow. In more modern times the value of rotation became more generally known, and in Great Britain and on the continent of Europe, most elaborate systems of rotation in connection with the feeding of cattle, and special manures have been adopted. In the United States, and especially in the West, from the generally fertile character of the soil, careful rotation has been less attended to, yet even on the richest soils of the West, it is quickly found that special crops, as wheat, may not be cultivated year after year, on the same soil, without quick deterioration. In the East and South the system of rotation is in special cases quite elaborate, yet as a rule, our farmers generally depend more on the simple rotation from grain to grass, in connection with manure than any other. In the West, where the fattening of stock is one of the most important industries of the farmers, this simple system has been found fully adequate, and from the fact that nothing is carried away from the farm except the stock fed, and farms being stocked with all the animals they will feed, grass becomes fully half the area of farms, consequently the rotation becomes simplified to a three fold rotation, Indian corn, meadow and pasture, the amount of grain carried away from

RYE.—Rank and yield of the States, with average annual product for the past nine years.

Rank.	States.	Total value of Crop	Value per Acre.	No. of Acres.	Amount of Crop. Bush.	Yield per Acre. Bush.
1	Pennsylvania	$ 2,599,677	$ 11.08	235,180	3,261,652	13.8
2	New York	1,994,974	10.73	191,399	2,576,662	13.6
3	Illinois	1,470,089	9.37	155,656	2,613,750	16.7
4	Wisconsin	1,084,740	9.34	120,328	1,906,650	15.6
5	Kansas	1,062,281	8.08	131,341	2,637,600	20.0
6	Kentucky	808,384	8.63	94,766	1,105,785	11.9
7	Ohio	401,196	9.23	41,875	608,245	13.5
8	New Jersey	386,575	10.52	36,844	483,686	13.1
9	Connecticut	371,147	14.73	25,880	378,930	14.7
10	Missouri	356,848	9.13	40,036	605,362	15.1
11	Virginia	325,195	6.80	48,508	484,550	10.1
12	Indiana	294,106	9.57	31,067	441,635	14.3
13	Nebraska	289,812	5.95	51,092	905,393	17.3
14	North Carolina	279,598	6.78	41,235	343,401	8.3
15	Massachusetts	269,925	14.25	20,391	308,592	15.4
16	Tennessee	242,708	8.32	29,653	295,343	9.0
17	Maryland	220,653	9.19	24,084	302,055	12.5
18	Iowa	216,300	7.88	27,823	475,603	17.0
19	West Virginia	213,743	9.49	23,080	287,007	12.5
20	Georgia	200,255	11.57	18,319	130,000	7.4
21	Michigan	170,345	9.97	17,165	248,125	14.4
22	California	97,724	15.89	6,181	100,871	16.5
23	Minnesota	65,887	9.91	7,617	144,475	18.9
24	Vermont	64,992	15.98	4,118	70,215	17.1
25	South Carolina	60,419	9.15	6,670	43,012	6.4
26	Texas	50,800	16.91	2,980	48,343	16.1
27	Arkansas	49,800	13.33	3,637	47,705	12.2
28	New Hampshire	45,144	17.22	2,628	42,512	16.8
29	Maine	37,048	17.24	2,195	35,175	16.1
30	Alabama	31,065	14.50	2,133	21,250	10.0
31	Mississippi	24,138	15.91	1,520	15,155	10.0
32	Rhode Island	19,156	14.02	1,114	20,475	11.2
33	Delaware	9,314	9.47	1,012	12,450	12.5
34	Oregon	8,647	17.61	481	9,817	21.5

the farm being small in comparison to that fed. In England and on the continent of Europe, turnips, cabbages, beets, carrots, potatoes, vetches, and in fact all the roots and many of the vegetables, here cultivated only in market gardens, enters into the rotation. As showing something of this, we append a system of rotation for seven years, as prepared at the request of the French government, soon after the Revolution, and also for the purpose of showing the elaborate system in vogue nearly a century ago, and as having relation to the clean culture necessary to grow them. Other points as to their ameliorating nature, and as showing their diversified character in view of preventing undue loss in any of the elements of the soil, will be found as interesting as they are important. As showing that grass is the basis of fertility in all countries in the rotation, we give the experience of various sections of the United States, East, West and South; premising with the fact that in Flanders, celebrated for its great yield of crops, and where every thing, liquid and solid, in the shape of manure is returned to the soil, the soiling of green crops and the turning under of others, enabling them in fact to get a rotation even in one season of certain crops, so that it is not uncommon for plowing, sowing and reaping to be carried forward at one and the same period of time, there, as elsewhere, grass or its equivalent, green crops being the basis of fertility. It is said that by the same or similar alternations of crops that many farms in Norfolk county and other sandy regions of England, once very poor and unproductive, have been converted into the most fruitful, wealthy, and populous districts of that kingdom. This same system has wrought similar changes of agricultural improvements in Scotland and Germany, and it will, if properly and perseveringly pursued, produce equally beneficial results in our own country. There is nothing in farming that requires a nicer judgment, or on which the farmer's profits more depend, than upon the order in which the various farm crops cultivated are made to succeed each other upon our fields. The green manuring and alternating husbandry, so successful in Flanders, has been adopted to a considerable extent in nearly all the other countries of Europe, and is constantly growing in favor there. Turnips in those countries have been used quite generally as a soil-renovating crop with great advantage, their large, spreading leaves drawing more nourishment from the atmosphere than their roots do from the soil. Sheep are turned into the fields and eat off the tops or leaves of the turnips, and as many of the roots as they wish, leaving their manure upon the ground evenly distributed, and the field in good condition for a succeeding crop of grain. One of the difficulties in the way of a perfect rotation is, that owing to peculiar seasons, it is impossible to closely follow any established rule, yet, the intelligence of the cultivator will enable him to provide for such contingences and follow the system which he may have found beneficial, without serious breaks. For instance, we have known extensive meadows to be destroyed by the larva of the May beetle, *Lachnosterna quer*-

First Year. Acres.	Second Year. Acres.	Third Year. Acres.	Fourth Year. Acres.	Fifth Year. Acres.	Sixth Year. Acres.	Seventh Year. Acres.
30 Wheat	{ 5 Turnips. 5 Cabbages 2½ F'ld beet 2½ Carrots. 10 Potatoes. 3 Vetches. 2 Beans }	10 Oats 5 Barley	15 Wheat	{ 5 Turnips.. 5 Cabbages. 2½ F'ld beet 2½ Carrots }	15 Wheat	{ 10 Potatoes. 3 Vetches.. 2 Beans }	30 Wheat.
15 Clover	15 Wheat	{ 10 Potatoes. 3 Vetches.. 2 Beans }	30 Wheat	10 Oats 5 Barley	15 Clover
5 Turnips. 5 Cabbages. 2½ Field beet. 2½ Carrots.	10 Oats 5 Barley	15 Clover	{ 10 Potatoes. 3 Vetches.. 2 Beans }	15 Wheat	{ 5 Turnips.. 5 Cabbages. 2½ F'ld beet 2½ Carrots.. }	10 Oats 5 Barley.
10 Potatoes.. 3 Vetches.. 2 Beans	15 Clover	15 Wheat	{ 5 Turnips.. 5 Cabbages 2½ F'ld beet 2½ Carrots.. }	10 Oats 5 Barley	15 Clover	{ 10 Potatoes. 3 Vetches.. 2 Beans }

Lucerne, which lasts indefinitely, may be substituted on any ten acres, in the rotation, during the whole course. Very proper for trial in California, in the Southern States, and other localities where lucerne is grown; afterwards to be plowed down and succeeded by wheat.

cina, usually known as the white grub. This destruction is sometimes so complete, that the turf eaten from one to two inches below the surface, may be rolled up like a carpet; and, since the grub requires three years to attain its growth from the egg, it may easily be seen how this and other causes may seriously interfere with rotation. Nevertheless, this need not prevent an intelligent farmer from keeping a rotation comparatively intact, even under the most adverse conditions, either from insect enemies, drought, or flooding. And more especially when, as may be the case in the West, the rotation is confined to two years of meadow, one year of pasture, one year corn, and one year wheat, and mixed crops, to be varied, according to the stock kept, if for dairying, requiring more pasture, and if for stock feeding, more corn. Let us take a farm of 160 acres. A good Western farmer has recommended the following. Allowing twenty acres of this amount for timber-land, and ten more for farm-buildings, yards, calf and hog pastures, and lanes, there would remain 120 acres to be specially devoted to crop culture and rotation. These 120 acres divide into six lots, containing twenty acres each; three to be kept constantly in clover, or clover and timothy; one in pasture in connection with the timber-lot; the other two grass-lots to be cut for hay. Of these the oldest seeded may be used for fall pasture, and the other mowed for a second crop of hay or grass-seed. The lot used for summer pasture having been in grass for three years, should be broken up in the spring following for a crop of corn, potatoes, and other hoed crops; this for restoring exhausted, overworked soils. Of course, virgin soils require no close rotation of crops; but the raising of grain should invariably be conducted with a view to the future introduction and cultivation of the grasses and to a regular system of rotation of crops. The rotation of Mr. W. S. Thorp, of Vermont, may be taken as indicative of a good rotation for the New England States. He believes that an eight-year rotation might be used with profit generally. This, allowing the farm twenty acres of woodland, would leave eight ten-acre fields. As labor is scarce and high, all wish to manage with as little help as possible. On that account grass may be grown with as much profit as anything, so apply grass to the rotation if convenient. This course, in going around the eight ten-acre fields in eight years, would allow one to have one ten-acre field in corn or roots; second year in wheat, barley, oats, or some other grain-crop seeded to grass; the next two years mowed for hay, and the next four years in pasture. This is about equally divided for the keeping of stock summer and winter, supposing the owner to feed all the crops on his farm. By using a rotation and feeding all our produce on the farm, we can keep two-thirds more stock than the majority of farmers do at the present time, and farms would be all under cultivation. We should have ten acres in hoed crops, ten acres in grain, and at a very low estimate we should get 300 bushels of potatoes, or 1,000 bushels of rutabagas or mangolds per acre, and four or five hundred bushels of grain annually. In regard to a rotation in the South, grass must still be the basis of reclamation, or of a system to keep the fertility intact. Of late years, the attention of southern planters has been especially directed to this subject, and investigation and trial have shown that the South is not at all deficient in valuable grasses, even outside of clover, alfalfa and cow-peas, which are sometimes erroneously ranked as grass. A writer of repute on Southern agriculture, and one who writes from experience as a cotton planter in one of the Gulf States, in illustrating his views says: A great defect of southern planters is that they do not keep, in the way of fertility, what they get. That is to say, when they make a piece of ground, they afterward continue to work it in exhausting crops until all the richness is gone. They can not get possession of a goose without ripping up the poor bird. The true policy is not merely to keep the ground rich, but to make it richer. To illustrate: If a piece of rich land is put in cotton, it may be followed with corn, small grain, with clover being sowed among the corn in August. If the clover is allowed to occupy the ground for two years, and to go to seed, even under a longer rotation than the above, it will not be necessary to sow it again. As soon as the ground is at rest, it will be covered with young clover. Three years ago, on this farm, a piece of ground was put in turnips, manured in the drill with farm-yard manure. The turnips were eaten on the ground by sheep. The next year it was put in corn, the next in cotton worked very clean, and this year in oats. After the oats were cut a fine stand of red clover appeared. This seed was never sown, but must have been in the manure applied three years since to the turnips. This is not a solitary case. Many similar instances have occurred. It is such plants as clover and peas that not only hold but increase the fertility of the soil. As one suited to the agricultural condition of the South, we will suppose a farm of 500 acres of open land under fence. Let 250 acres be devoted to arable purposes, and the rest to grazing. The rotation might be as follows: 1. Cotton and corn in the same field in suitable proportions. 2. Oats sown in August on the cotton and corn land. 3. Rye, or rye and wheat, sown in September, the land having been twice plowed in order to kill the germinant oats. 4 and 5. Clover, if the land is in sufficient heart to produce it; if not, the fourth year rest ungrazed, and the fifth year sheep and cattle penned upon it every night during the year, using a portable fence. An ordinary farm of 500 acres will support 500 sheep, besides the crops in the above rotation. The oats and rye will feed them during the winter nearly or entirely, without injury to the grain. Five hands would be sufficient to work such a farm and take care of the live stock. During the first year, our authority thinks, the following results might be expected from an ordinary farm, without manure:

25 acres in cotton, 12 bales, at 15 cents....................	$900
25 acres in corn, 250 bushels, at $1......................	250
50 acres in oats, 500 bushels, at 80 cents............	400
25 acres in rye, 200 bushels, at $1....................	200
25 acres in wheat. 150 bushels, at $1.50.............	225
Increase and mutton sales of 500 sheep.............	500
Wool, 3 pounds per head, at 33 cents per pound....	495
Manure, at $1 per head...........................	500
	$3,470

Separately each of these products is small, still the aggregate result is more than $600 per hand. Yet this is nearly three times the average products per hand in the cotton States. That average in Georgia, was estimated to be $209; in South Carolina, $202; in Virginia, $211; in North Carolina, $214. These are the lowest averages. The farm products given in the case above supposed are the result of the first year of the rotation. The next year the cotton and corn would be more than double by penning 500 sheep at night on fifty acres. It is the writer's experience that ten sheep regularly penned will manure well one acre in a year. Five hundred would, therefore, manure well fifty acres. The appearance of the ground would not indicate this high manuring; but it should be remembered that the liquid manure, which is equal in value to the solid, is not visible. If, in addition, a stock of cattle were kept and penned on the same fifty acres, then fertility would be increased in proportion. It should never be forgotten that accumulating, saving, and applying manure, is as serious a business of the farm as making corn or cotton. At the end of the fifth year of this rotation the change in the farm would be equal almost to a transformation, the crops being doubled or trebled, without (which is a most important point,) any material increase of labor or other expense. This improvement of the soil, accompanied at first by moderate profits, and with a great diminution of vexations and unreliable labor, should be the great end of the Southern planter. It involves a double profit from increased production and increased salable value of the soil. (See Supplement, page 1114.)

ROUND-UP. This is a term used by herdsmen, for the gathering together, at regular seasons, the vast herds of cattle in Texas and on the great plains of the West, for the purpose of identification of stock and the branding of young animals. In the article Landed Estates and Farms, on page 550, is given a graphic illustration of a round-up.

ROWAN-TREE. The mountain ash, (*Pyrus aucuparia*).

ROWEL. A seton; also the sharp wheel of a spur.

ROWEN. A name for after-math hay.

RUBBING-POST. An appendage sometimes found in feeding yards, but a poor apology for the curry comb, or card.

RUBBLE-STONE. Fragments of brickbats, loose stones, etc.

RUBEFACIENTS. Substances which produce redness on the skin without blistering.

RUBIGO. Rust in plants. (See *Uredo*.)

RUDDLE. An ochreous clay, reddle.

RUE. *Ruta graveolens*. A fœtid shrub; the leaves are reputed as of use as an antispasmodic. It grows readily in a clay soil without manure, and is propagated by slips.

RUMEN. The paunch, or first stomach, of ruminating quadrupeds.

RUMINANTS. Animals having four stomachs, having parted hoofs and which chew the cud. The ox, sheep, deer, and camel are well known ruminants. Rumination is the act of chewing the cud. In feeding, the animals simply gather the food, and swallow it without greater mastication than simply to moisten it, and work it into masses fit for swallowing. It enters the first stomach, is moistened still further in the second stomach, is worked and moulded into balls, raised again to the mouth by regurgitation, leisurely chewed, and swallowed, this time, entering the third stomach, and in the fourth stomach, it is digested. Ruminant animals require leisure for the act, and rumination being interrupted the animal may be known to be out of health.

RUNCINATE. In botany, hooked back, or curved in a direction from the apex to the base, as the lobes of the leaf of the dandelion.

RUNNER. The stolon, or running stem, as in the strawberry.

RUNT. A variety of common pigeon; small black cattle of Wales and Scotland; decrepid pigs.

RUPTURE. A hernia or sinking of the bowels through, so as to form a large, soft tumor. (See Hernia.)

RURAL ECONOMY. The management of all things pertaining to the farm.

RUSHES. The family of sedges, called by botanists *Juncus* and *Scirpus*, growing in rich wet lands; they are destroyed by draining, tillage, and liming. Rushes make excellent mats, coarse basket-work, and bottoms of chairs.

RUSSIAN CATTLE. In Russia there are no distinctive breeds of cattle that have been considered of sufficient good form and substance to warrant importation into the United States. They are principally long-horned, large-boned, rough cattle, better in hide and tallow than meat. The vast plains of the Ukraine, and other inter-Russian southern provinces, furnish grazing grounds for great herds of cattle. The principal races there are enumerated as follows: The Ukraine; Wallach, or Podolian; Little Russian; Donian; and the Black Sea breeds. All these denominations are local; but the original character, which nearly resembles that of the Hungarian race of cattle, has been preserved. They are distinguished for their strength, adaptation for field labor, and facility of taking on flesh and fat. The latter singularity consists in the fat not growing so much on the outside, but penetrating the flesh itself, rendering it juicy and more delicate, especially when the beeves have been fed in the rich prairies of the Caucasian line. It is for this reason that butchers in large towns give preference to this beef over that of the other cattle. The cows, however, yield but little milk. This breed is to be found from Podolia to the Ural, but the finest type is found at Karlowka, in the government of Poltawa. It is also met with in some places in the province of Ekathérinoslaw, near the river Samara, and further northward in the provinces of Little Russia, but of not so fine appearance, from the want of good keeping. The Kalmik breed is intermediate between the Ukraine and Russian races. It is of small size and fine flesh, and is able to endure any change of climate. All the year round, such cattle can live on the steppes, and during winter subsist on grass, which they obtain from under the snow, except when, after rain has fallen and the snow is frozen, they can not break through the ice, and are deprived of food. In many districts of country on the Don, the inhabitants prefer this race to the Ukraine, though they are less valuable for the purposes of the dairy and for labor. The Russian race, properly so called, has no peculiar characteristics, as its original type is not easily to be distinguished. In general, the cattle of this race are ill-shaped, diminutive in size, and not well reared. They are found in the middle, northern and western provinces, where they are kept for their milk. In the province of Wologda, and in the vicinity of St. Petersburg, this race is improving from better management. To the above races may be added the Lithuanian breed, which is small, but strongly built, giving an abundance of milk. Among the foreign races introduced into Russia is the Cholmogory breed, of Dutch origin, distinguished by its fine form and good milking qualities. It is found pure only in the districts from which it takes its name, in the Government of Archangel. The heavy bodies of the oxen render them unfit for labor. In general, the cows require good keeping and great care, so that the expenses of their support are rather excessive, which must be redeemed out of the proceeds of their milk. The Foigtland race, introduced into some districts of the Baltic provinces, is remarkable for its medium size and fine appearance. The cows content themselves with a rather common food, and give plenty of milk. The oxen are well adapted for work. The Frisland race begins to be multiplied among the Mennonite settlers of Molotchan. The cows produce a fair yield of milk. The Tyrolese, Scotch and English breeds have been introduced and acclimatized in the provinces of the Baltic. The Swiss breed is extensively diffused, as is also the Tyrolese, in the kingdom of Poland. A cross between the Cholmogory and the indigenous breeds is also found in some districts of the government of Archangel, as well as those of Wologda, Kalouga, Twer, Kostroma, Jaroslaw, and in the districts near the capitals.

RUST. 1. The oxydation of any substance through the action of the oxygen of the air on its surface, in connection with moisture, or during that portion of the day when the atmosphere is moist. Articles do not rust readily when in motion, and bright surfaces withstand the action of rust more easily than others. To prevent rust, a coating of oil, or better, lampblack and oil, should be used on the iron surfaces of planes and other implements when not in use 2. Rust as applied to vegetation, is the effect of fungus in connection with heat and moisture.' The rust in wheat is usually produced by a fungus known as *puccinia graminis;* blight, smut, or brand, by *Uredo segetum,* the dry rot of timber is caused by the fungus *Merulius lachrymans.* etc. The natural remedies against rust are dry air, and circulation of air.

RUSTIC-WORK. In building, a term applied to work jagged out into an irregular surface. Work, also, which is left rough.

RUT. To cut a line on the soil with a spade. The copulation of deer in the rutting season; the track of a cart-wheel.

RUTA-BAGA. *Brassica campestris vars.* Known also as Swede, Russian, and French turnip. A biennial plant forming its large, fleshy bulb the first season, and maturing its seed the second. It is extensively raised throughout Northern Europe, and in Great Britain as part of the rotation, and as food for cattle, sheep, and for culinary use. In the United States it is not much raised, only for culinary use, except in some portions of the Eastern States. It is much better-adapted to the climate of the United States than the common turnip, though except in the extreme North the bulbs are apt to be long necked and tough. This, however, does not naturally injure them for feeding. For stock, the seed should be sown in rich soil, about the middle of June, at the rate of about two pounds per acre, in drills two feet apart, and thinned to six inches in the row. They must be watched when young for the ravages of the turnip fly, and dusted with dry ashes, soot, or sulphur and flour when the dew is on. The cultivation simply consists in keeping the ground mellow as to its surface, weeding, and thinning the rows. Just before the ground freezes they must be pulled, their tops placed together in double rows, and cut with a sharp spade, then the bulbs stored for winter, in a cold cellar, or in slightly covered pits, but so they will not freeze severely.

RYE. *Secale cereale.* Rye forms a rather unimportant product of American husbandry. It is but little used for bread; Indian corn has usurped its place for distilling, as it has for one other of its important uses in some of the Eastern States, notably Pennsylvania, as food for horses. In the northern parts of Europe, especially Russia and Germany, it is the principal bread grain of the inhabitants. In the United States its cultivation is principally to furnish green forage, except in the extreme North, and upon some sandy soils not so well adapted to the cultivation of other grain. The proportion of rye raised in the United States is as one to fifteen of wheat, and as one to seventy-five of Indian corn, in bushels, per year. It is usually sown broadcast, in October, at the rate of one and one-half bushels per acre, or if drilled, at the rate of one bushel per acre. For late fall and early spring feed, it is often sown among corn at the last cultivation, or if not then, in August, between the rows. The average price of rye per bushel ranges from seventy-five cents to one dollar, the yearly export varies between 200,000 and 500,000 bushels yearly. In 1873-74, however, there was exported 1,568,362 bushels, at an average value of one dollar per bushel, and 59,820 barrels of rye-flour, valued at $6.50 per barrel. As a forage crop, it is superior, and is adapted to a great variety of soils not really wet. The best grain for flour, however, is raised on rather dry, sandy soils. (See Supplement.)

RYE BROMUS. (See Chess.)

S

SACCHARIC ACID. An uncrystallizable acid, produced by the action of nitric acid on sugar. Its salts are called saccharates.

SACCHAROMETER. An implement for taking the specific gravity of syrups and worts for brewing, etc. Baume's hydrometer is chiefly used.

SACCHAROULMIN AND ULMIC ACID. A brown, brilliant substance obtained by digesting sugar for a long time in dilute nitric or sulphuric acid.

SACCHOLACTIC ACID. Mucic acid is obtained by treating sugar of milk with nitric acid.

SAC OF THE EMBRYO. In botany, the small enclosed body in which the embryo is placed during its growth.

SACRUM. The lower portion of the spine.
SAFFLOWER. (See Saffron.)
SAFFRON. A bulbous, perennial plant, *Crocus sativus,* growing wild in Sicily. The stigmas, or pistils of the plants are collected and kiln dried, and pressed into cakes for use in medicine. It is now not much esteemed. Safflower, or bastard saffron, is an annual plant, *carthamus tinctoria,* the deep red fecula of the flowers forming the colors known as Spanish red and China lake. The meadow saffron belongs to the genus *colchicum.*

ST. JOHN'S WORT. *Hypericum.* The common St. John's wort, *H. perforatum,* is too well known to need description; an acrid and pernicious weed, difficult to extirpate. There are many species, none of them of any value. *H.*

corymbosum, a southern species, has some merit as an ornamental plant, blooming early in the spring at the South, flowers yellow, berries red. In 1881, 3,000 plants were distributed by the Department of Agriculture, Washington. Fortunately it did not prove hardy at the North, and hence that section escaped acclimating another weed.

SAFFRON, MEADOW. Colchicum.

SAGAPENUM. A fœtid gum resin from a species of ferula.

SAGE. *Salvia*. A class of plants containing many species of value, whether we regard it medicinally, as a condiment, or for the splendor of its flowering varieties. As a gargle it is most useful. In China it was once regarded with favor, being used as we use tea, holding a large trade between Chinese and Dutch merchants. The old monks would seem to have thought it a specific for all human ills. Now-a-days it is but little used, except as a gargle, and for flavoring cheese, sausage, etc. The broad-leaved, green sage, Balsamic sage, is esteemed for medical uses, and the narrow-leaved, green sage, Sage of Virtue, is the mildest in flavor. The variety most generally found in gardens is the red-leaved, and the green-leaved sage, *Salvia officinalis*. The cultivation is simple. The seeds should be sown in a gentle hot bed, early in spring, and transplanted, when large enough, in rows twenty inches apart by twelve inches in the row. Keep clean from weeds and cut when in bloom for use. The plants must be covered in winter, since they will not survive freezing and thawing. Thus the bed will continue to produce several years, but it is better to renew the plantation every three years. Another plan is to sow in drills, in May, and thin to the requisite distance, but the plants will be much weaker, and are not apt to furnish a cutting the first season. A subvariety of the common, green, leaved sage, and also of the red-leaved variety, have handsome variegated leaves, and must be propagated by cuttings under a moist heat, as indeed may the other varieties. None of the species, however, are entirely hardy in the West. The flowering varieties are splendid objects, and flourish admirably in the open ground in the West, from June until frost, being covered with a profusion of flowers in August and September. *Salvia splendens*, and *Alba* are the varieties most cultivated, the first-named is red, the second white. *S. gesneriflora* is a soft-wooded labiate, and a most elegant decorative ornament for the greenhouse and conservatory, growing from two to three feet high and compact, the leaves a bright, rich green, and well clothed with abundant deep scarlet flowers, during the whole winter and spring.

SAGITTATE. Shaped like an arrow head, as the leaves of some water plants.

SAGO. A starchy farina from the pith of several palm-trees, as the *Sagus farinifera*, *Rhumphii*, etc. It is a good, wholesome food, and much esteemed for puddings and gruel. In England, a gruel of sago is often given to horses after a hard run. The Florida arrow-root is a kind of sago obtained from the pith of the *Zamia integrifolia* and *pumila*, indigenous plants.

SAL AMMONIAC. A salt of ammonia much used in the arts. Very soluble in water, and has been used as a steep; one pound, added to one gallon and a half of water, is sufficient for one bushel of seed. A small amount of it exists in putrescent fluids.

SALEP. The farinaceous product of the roots of the *Orchis mascula*.

SALICIN. A neutral crystalline body existing in willow bark.

SALICYL. A hypothetical compound radical, existing in salicylous acid, etc., bodies derived from salicin.

SALIFEROUS. Containing salt; a name given to the new red sandstone formation.

SALIFIABLE BASE. A substance which combines with acids to form salts.

SALIVA. Spittle. It is prepared by the parotid and other glands, and mixed with the food during mastication. According to Liebig, it is a means of introducing oxygen into the stomach to accomplish the first step in digestion.

SALIVATION. An excessive discharge of saliva, slobbering; change of food, with salt, are preventives in cattle.

SALMON. The salmon, as a fish for artificial breeding, has of late years attracted much attention, and they have been successfully transferred to many of our deep and larger waters. The author of American Fish Culture gives full information in relation to the habits of this celebrated fish from which we extract the following: Salmon commence to make in toward the rivers from which they migrated at rather a later period than shad. Of course those of a more southern latitude are earlier comers. On the Bay of Fundy, for instance, at St. John, N. B., some are taken in May, in June they are abundant. If they are introduced in the Hudson and Connecticut they might, doubtless, be taken in Long Island Sound and in the lower bay in April. They continue to come in schools and ascend the rivers all summer, the earlier comers being the earlier spawners, while the late spawners frequently remain in the river all winter, and go to sea in the spring. The latter, as has been ascertained in Scotland, may not spawn the ensuing fall, a period of two years expiring before they reproduce. From the information gained in the British Provinces, I am of opinion that there is only one, and that an annual, migration of the same fish to and from sea on this side of the Atlantic. This is necessarily the case, as most of the rivers are rigidly closed with ice for some months, and many of them for half of the year. On the coast of Great Britain, where the rivers are always open, their migrations occur nearly every month; still there is a throng time when the greater number enter fresh waters. Smolts and grilse have frequently been marked and have gone to sea and returned in six or eight weeks. In Ireland there are fresh run fish in January and early fly-fishing in February. In the rivers of the British Provinces north of us there is also what may be termed a throng time. This is generally when the first schools come in. In some rivers they are found at the lower rapids within a week (earlier or later) of the middle of June, and in others, even of the same latitude or district of country somewhat later. There are different runs up to the middle of September; the schools being influenced by easterly storms to enter the bay, and by a rise in the river to ascend. Unlike the shad, which are deterred or driven back by a freshet, salmon seem to delight in a heavy rise, after which, there is always good fishing as the water clears. When a school of salmon, coming from sea, reaches a bay or the mouth of a river entering the sea, some weeks are occupied in working up toward the head of tide, the fish in the meanwhile undergoing a change of system which fits them for their habitation while in the fresh water. During this time they feed on smelts, sparlings, and other small fish as well as crustacea. After entering fresh water no food is to be found in their stomachs; notwithstanding, they will rise occasionally at a natural or artificial fly, and

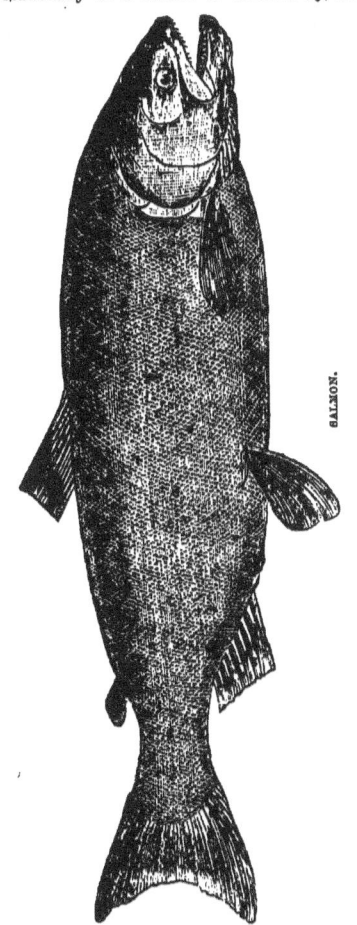

SALMON.

will sometimes take a worm bait. In their journey upwards they generally linger on the way, at the foot of many a rapid or just above, until they reach their native spawning-grounds, or go beyond. They lose the silvery brightness which they bring from sea, and continue to grow darker and fall off as the summer advances. A fish that was a twenty-pounder, when fresh run, in three weeks will be one of seventeen pounds, and so on to the time of spawning, when they have lost half of their weight and are scarcely fit for food. If their native water is some inconsiderable brook, which is frequently the case, they will wait for a rise, or wriggle over shallows scarcely the depth of their bodies. When the young salmon frees itself from the shell it is about three-fourths of an inch long, and has the same umbilical sac which we observe in the fry of brook trout. This it carries for about six weeks, during this time it refuses all food. As soon, however, as this sac is absorbed, its predaceous instinct is observed, rising eagerly at the smallest insect or atom, and seizing animalculæ beneath the surface. In pisciculture the food of the fry is much the same as those of the trout. Although the incubation of salmon ova is similar to that of the trout in breeding them artificially, the manipulation of the fish is different on account of the large size and vigor of the salmon, requiring two and sometimes three persons to perform the operation. If the fish is held pendent by the head, the ova, if mature, will distend the lower portion of the abdomen; and some of it flow without pressure; and this, from all we can learn, is the position in which the salmon is generally held when it is being operated on. The young of the salmon, as long as it retains what are known as the finger-marks on its sides, is called a parr. When these marks are no longer visible, and it assumes a silvery coat, it is a smolt, and is sufficiently advanced for its first migration to sea. On its return, which may be after six or eight weeks, or not until the following summer, it is a grilse, its average weight being about four pounds. After its second visit to its marine feeding-grounds, it is a salmon, weighing from eight to fifteen pounds. Immediately after spawning it is called a kelt, or a black fish; the latter appellation is given to a fish that has spawned and remains in the river for any length of time, which generally occurs in the winter months.

SALLENDERS. (See Mallenders.)

SALSIFY. Vegetable oyster, (*Tragopogon porrifolium.*) This is one of the most valuable of esculent roots for the kitchen garden, as hardy as parsnip, and like that plant may be left in the ground all winter. It should be sown as early in the spring as possible, and requires the whole season's growth. The soil must be deep, mellow, and fertile, as for all the spindle-shaped roots. Sow in drills two feet apart, and thin to about five inches in the row for large roots. It is a perennial, seeding the second year, and has rather handsome flowers. The root is the part used, after the first year's growth, in the winter and early spring, but the tender shoots of the second year's growth, when six inches or less high, are sometimes used as a substitute for asparagus. The roots cooked have the reputation of being good for persons inclined to diseases of a wasting nature as consumption. It is cooked as follows: After the roots have been scraped, and laid in water for several minutes to abstract a part of the bitter flavor, it is to be boiled tender, and either cut in thin slices, or grated and pressed into little cakes, of the size of oysters. Dip the slices, or cakes, into a batter made of wheat flour, milk and eggs; roll them in crumbled bread or crackers; and then drop them into hot lard. When of a light brown color, they are sufficiently cooked, and ready to

SAND 831 SANFOIN

be carried to the table. Or they may be sliced, cooked tender in milk, and served on toast.

SALT. *Chloride of sodium.* Chemically, salt is a compound of one atom of chlorine and one of sodium, and occurs naturally in every part of the globe as a rock, interstratified with marls, sandstones, gypsum, etc.; also as an element of springs and salt lakes; Salt Lake, in Utah, being the most remarkable of this latter, its water being a saturated solution of salt. The proportion of the constituents of salt are chlorine, 60.4 per cent. and sodium 39.6 per cent. Its impurities, as found in rock salt, are gypsum, oxide of iron and clay, chlorides of calcium, potassium and magnesium, and sulphates of soda and magnesia. The ocean contains notable quantities of salt, and is one principal source of the supply of salt by evaporation. A peculiarity of salt is its power of transmitting heat, clear rock salt transmitting ninety-two parts out of one hundred, while plate glass transmits but twenty-four parts. Salt is the only mineral substance universally regarded as an article of food by man, and the higher orders of the animal kingdom. As a preservative also it is indispensable, and as a manure it is of growing importance, especially in inter-continental climates. In the United States, the principal sources of supply are from the salt springs of New York State, and those of Michigan, though more or less salt is manufactured in various States. In 1797, the first salt was made at Onondaga, New York. At least that was the first date of the lease; 25,474 bushels were manufactured in that year. In 1849, the amount was 5,083,369 bushels; in 1855, it was 6,082,885 bushels. Since then the quantity has fluctuated above and below these figures. Since 1860 the salines of Michigan have supplied the West with a large and increasing quantity of salt. The three principal salines of Michigan are the Salina, the Michigan salt group and the coal measures—of these the Michigan salt group supplies the largest number of productive wells. These salines lie at an average of about 800 feet, the brine being often at or near the saturation point, and practically inexhaustible.

SALT MARSHES. Marshes washed by sea water; the herbage is coarse, but often very nutritious, and preferred by cattle.

SALT OF LEMONS. Binoxalate of potash, used in removing iron mold from linen.

SALTPETRE. (See Nitrogen.)

SALTS. Chemical compounds, which are usually (oxysalts) formed of a base and acid, and possess neither acidity nor alkaline action. Haloid salts are those which are binary, containing a metal in combination with an electro-negative element.

SALTWORT. The genus *Salicornia*, which grows on salt marshes; the ashes yield barilla.

SALVE. An ointment.

SALVER-SHAPED. Hypocrateriform. A monopetalous corolla, with a long tube and spreading limb at the top.

SAL VOLATILE. Sesquicarbonate of ammonia, or smelling salts.

SAMARA. An indehiscent, few-celled seed, with an expansion of tissue resembling wings, as the pods of the ash and ailanthus.

SAND. Finely divided silicious matter usually constitutes common river and sea-sand; particles of other substances are often blended with it, and sometimes it becomes calcareous from the prevalence of carbonate of lime. Sand is sometimes employed as a divisor by the cultivator of poor, hungry clays, especially if the sand be calcareous. (See Soils).

SANDAL WOOD. *Pterocarpus santalinus.* Red saunders, a dye wood, but giving fugitive reds.

SAND BATH. A quantity of sand heated by a flue, and used in the laboratory.

SAND-CRACK. Sand-crack is a fissure in the hoof, which begins at the coronet, the thin edge first breaking away. It is a disease of nutrition, the horn of the foot being secreted in diminished quantity and impaired quality. The break, small at first, is extended until it may divide the entire hoof. It usually occurs in the quarter, and perhaps most frequently at the inner quarter. It has been asserted that the whole difficulty is produced by bad shoeing. Low condition, impure state of the blood, and lack of care are predisposing causes. In this conjuncture slight injury to the coronet may be followed by such deficient secretion of horn at that place, that the weakened part may give way and sand-crack take place. If possible, the animal should be given entire freedom from work, and should be turned into a small paddock, or have a loose box, in which he may move somewhat. He should have nutritious food, and sufficient green food or bran mash to keep his bowels free. During the early stages of the disease, and while efforts are being made to restore the soundness of the foot, the horse is better without shoes, as the natural movements of the parts tend to restore their vitality. The bar-shoes, recommended by some writers, are useful only in those cases of long standing which are essentially incurable, and where the horses are to be put to slow work. The part should be interfered with as little as possible; there should be no cutting, paring, or burning; and care should be taken to keep dirt, gravel, etc., from the open sore. The healthy condition of the open and granulating surface should be maintained by frequent washing with soap and water, and the application of the solution of chloride of zinc, three grains to the ounce of water. If the animal is in use, before being taken out the crack should be filled with lint saturated with the solution, which should be confined in place by a strip or cloth completely covered with tar. This should be removed as soon as the horse returns, and the wound be cleansed, if it is at all foul, and carefully dressed again. If treatment is commenced early, a fair degree of expectation of recovery may be entertained; but, in many cases, through neglect or lack of proper treatment, a permanent deficiency of the hoof remains. In such cases, by the use of a bar shoe, properly adjusted, the animal may be made of some use.

SANDSTONE. A rock made of sand cemented together, or merely compressed together.

SANDWORT. Plants of the genus *Arenaria;* they are succulent and harmless.

SANFOIN. *Hedysarum onobrychis.* A perennial forage plant, native of Europe, up to latitude 51°, a legume which has the property of binding light, dry, sandy and chalky soils, by its roots. English and continental writers agree as to its nutritious qualities for stock, and also as to its value as a crop to shade the soil and for plowing under. It has been tried from time to time in the United States, both North and South, but has not met with favor in any locality. In the North it winter kills, as it does in the West. In the Middle States it can not compete with clover, and in the South it is reported to be feeble in growth.

SANICLE, SANICULA. A genus of umbelliferous weeds.

SANIES. A thin, fœtid discharge from sores.

SAP. The circulation of the sap of plants has been the cause of many elaborate theories, each of which in turn has been exploded. Indeed, but little is really known of the precise causes acting in this abstruse problem. Prof. Burrill, of the Illinois Industrial University, who has given much patient attention to the subject of vegetable physiology, (see Vegetable Physiology,) in a lecture before the Illinois Horticultural Society, in relation to sap, stated as follows: The movements and office of sap in the plant have always been interesting topics in vegetable physiology. The physicist, observing the rise of fluids through small tubes by what is called capillary attraction and being also acquainted with the force exerted by liquids of different densities through membranes, (called osmosis,) readily satisfies himself that these are sufficient to account for the rise of the sap in the woody structure of plants. With his laboratory experiments to start upon, he soon learns to modify them sufficiently to meet and explain the ordinary indications of motion of fluids in the tree. Now, it is certainly true that these fluids do not move without some kind of mechanical force to cause them to do so. Being lower in organization than the animal, we might naturally suppose that the forces of the inorganic world would have more direct application in the plant than, for instance, in man, yet we believe the blood is propelled through our bodies by a sufficient mechanical (or chemical?) force. Though the vital powers, whatever they are, preside over and cause the contraction of muscles, the act in itself is a mechanical one, controlled by the laws, as to limit of power, etc., that apply to dead substances. Without material substance to work through, the will or life force, if that term is more suitable for us, can not cause blood or anything else to move through our organs. Then, it is inconceivable that vitality, separate and apart from the laws of matter, can cause the sap to move regularly or irregularly through the plant tissues. There must be somewhere and somehow a power behind the throne. There must be a reason, and a sufficient one, for water, whose course is usually down hill, to change its direction and flow vigorously upward in spite of the down-hill tendencies of gravitation. Do, however, the physical laws before cited and the others generally advanced meet the case? Does sap move because of capillary attraction, or of *osmosis*, or of both combined, or from evaporation from the leaves? There are evidences to the contrary. It is found that the fluid passes through the cells and not through tubes, so that the notion of capillary attraction is not consistent with the fact. It is likewise found that two plants, standing side by side, begin to send up from the roots water at very different times and under very different conditions. According to President Clark's experiments at the Massachusetts Agricultural College, each species of tree from which sap flowed upon puncture had its own time of beginning and maximum. Thus the sugar maple begins to flow in October, reaches its maximum about April 1, and ceases about May 1. The black birch begins about the last of March, reaches its maximum the last of April, and ceases about the middle of May. The grape has similar dates in May 1, May 20 and June 1. These experiments accord with our own common observation as to the difference of leafing in different species, but, it will be noticed, are not parallel with them. The maple is not very forward in showing its leaves in the spring, though ahead of all other trees in the flow of sap from a wound. There are other things of similar import which might be adduced here, but with this alone, how is it possible for us to hold to the idea that *osmosis*, the term applied to the passage of fluids through membranes, causes the gorging of the trees in spring time? Neither is it evaporation from the leaves, for at this season of the year there are no leaves. We indeed have reached a partial explanation, but it may as well be confessed that we do not know all about it. The physical laws to which the phenomenon is generally attributed may be in the main the immediate cause, but, if so, they are controlled and directed by a something else. There is, furthermore, no positive clew to the cause of another motion of the fluids in plants, so far as my information goes; I mean the rotation that takes place in an individual cell. The plant, indeed, has a maze of motions going on in its tissues, of which we should be totally ignorant were it not for the microscope. It is more than possible that even this instrument has not revealed all to us yet, and that future investigators will wonder at our ignorance and blindness. But the practical thing here is to so manage our plants that the movement of sap can take place freely. If we had all the facts, doubtless this could be better done, for it is groping in the dark to find how before we find why. This is evident: if fluids are to pass through cell walls, the thinner the walls are the easier the passage. Then, from what we know of the plant growth, the newer these cells are the better this flow. The movement takes place more freely in a young shoot than in an old trunk, and this is the philosophy of the rapid growth seen in sprouts from the side of a tree, and is also a good part of the so-called pruning for vigor. A branch once started to growing rapidly has an advantage over the less fortunate ones, even though afterward having an equal supply of food. A plant from a good seed, capable of throwing out a vigorous shoot, will distance its fellow from a smaller seed far beyond the difference in the food supplied. So, too, when a plant wilts from lack of moisture, the cell structure may be so impaired as to prevent ever after full, healthy action. A tree checked in its growth by transplanting has much more to do than to restore its mangled roots. The whole structure has to be surrounded with new tissues before the normal action is restored. It is not, then, a simple question in transplanting as to what percentage live, but how well they live and perform the first year the full functions of growth. Why, it may now be asked, all this motion of the fluids upward, downward, sidewise, endwise, and around, repeatedly, the confines of a cell? In the higher animals, there are vessels for a regular and continuous flow, and until recently it was supposed the plant juices made a similar circuit from the root to the leaves, through the wood fibers, thence downward through the bark and adjoining tissues. But analogy often leads us wrong. While there may still be something in this specification of tissues in plants, there is certainly nothing comparable to the organs of animals. The latter have a double railroad track, so to speak, upon which freight trains pass and repass without colliding; but the plant gets along, for the most part, with one, switching and backing and jostling, now making time one way, now the other. The change of water and dissolved inorganic substances into sap is another of the mysteries connected with the physiology of plants; but it is believed, upon good grounds, to be effected only in presence of the chlorophyl or green portion of the plants; hence, the material entering the root must in the main reach the leaves, and of course the immense evaporation from the leaves must be supplied by the root. Here, then, is cause enough for motion and reason enough for poor growth, when by any means the fluids are not given the fullest freedom. It is true that the materials which enter the root are forthwith changed to some extent, being no longer simply water and earthy salts; but whether the root itself has any power of changing these newly attained elements is an open question. Since the root has sometimes different properties from the rest of the plant, it is argued that it does modify the food elements; but if so, it is a very different thing from that which takes place in the leaves. The green tissues, in the sunshine, rend asunder the particles bound by chemical ties, working against their ordinary affinities, and make them over anew. The chemist, in a well equipped laboratory, accomplishes wonderful things, but fails utterly in competition with a leaf. This is the function of plants, the one property that gives them value to us, and the one alone that makes them indispensable to our use, and the one end as well toward which all the motion and commotion in the structure is directed. Maturing and ripening are only other terms for the completion of this work, and are very different things from simple cessation of growth. A large leaf surface and recent and healthy cell structure are, therefore, the requirements of plant culture.

SAPAN WOOD. A dye wood resembling Brazil wood.

SAPHENA. The large vein of the thigh.

SAPROPHAGANS. A tribe of coleopterans, many of which feed on decaying matters.

SAP SAGO CHEESE. Zapzeiger. A Swiss cheese, flavored with Mellilot.

SAP-SUCKER. The word sap-sucker is incorrectly applied to various birds of the woodpecker family, indeed, to any birds thought to be addicted to sucking the sap of trees and plants. The only true sap-suckers are insects of the so-called louse family, aphis, bark louse, mealy bug, red spider, etc. The woodpecker tribe, with one exception, are all innocent of any damage to trees, except so far as may result from the necessary endeavor to extract borers and other insect depredators. This exception is the Yellow-bellied woodpecker (*Picus varius*), known by the bright red spot on the head, and in the male also on the throat. The nuthatches have been ignorantly called sap-suckers by a majority of farmers. They are among the most beneficial of birds, as insect eaters. The name sap-sucker should be discarded by all. Bark-eater would be a more appropriate name, since it is on the cambium, or inner bark, that the Yellow-bellied Woodpecker principally lives, yet to their credit it must be said that in the stomachs of birds shot, together with vegetable matter, have been found the grubs of boring beetles, the beetles themselves, and ants.

SAP WOOD. The alburnum, or new wood.

SARCOCELE. A tumefaction of the testes.

SARCOCARP. The fleshy substance of fruits.

SARCOCOLLA. A kind of gum.

SARMENTUM. A runner, as the strawberry.

SARSAPARILLA. The roots of several species of Smilax growing in tropical America; the decoction is used as an alterative.

SASH. In building, a piece of framing for holding the glass in a window. It is of two sorts, viz., that called the French sash, which is hung like a door to the sash frame; and that in which it moves vertically, from being balanced by a weight on each side, to which it is attached by lines running over pulleys at the top of the sash-frame. When, in a window, both the upper and lower sashes are movable, the sashes are said to be double hung, and single hung when only one of them moves.

SASSAFRAS. *Sassafras officinale.* The sassafras is widely distributed over the United States, but attains its best development south of 40° and in rich bottoms. It is hardy up to the northern line of Illinois. In Southern Illinois it has attained a size of two feet in diameter, and in the extreme south has been found much larger. The wood fine grained and durable, is said to be vermin proof. The bark of the root is less used now than formerly for its supposed blood purifying qualities. It is propagated by seed or suckers. If by the seed, it is better sown in boxes placed on the north side of a fence and kept moist, since if planted in the open soil it does not always vegetate the first year.

SATURATION. A chemical expression, signifying either that no more of a given substance, or salt, can be dissolved; or that, in a compound, the combination of its parts is complete or saturated.

SAUERKRAUT. Cabbage sliced thin and packed closely in barrels, with salt, and sometimes spices, is called sauerkraut (sour krout). It was formerly one of the specifics against scurvy in long sea voyages, but modern improvement has given better agents, and it is now but little used. It is still, however, regarded with favor as an article of diet in many parts of the country, and is prepared as follows. In October, or before severe frosts, the cabbage is to be cut from the stumps, the outside and loose leaves cut off and the heads quartered and thrown into a tub of clear water, from which they should be taken, one piece or more at a time, and placed in a small box, open at top and bottom, and running in the grooves of the krout machine, which is about four feet long, one foot wide, and six inches deep. The box runs over three or four knives, sometimes made of old scythes, fixed

SAWING TIMBER IN THE WOODS.

diagonally across the bottom of the machine. The edges of the knives are slightly raised above the level of the bottom, and when the box is moved backward and forward in the grooves, and pressure made with a small piece of board on the cabbage, the latter is cut into thin, small slices, which drop into the tub beneath the cutter. As the cabbage is cut, it is transferred to a clean barrel (a pork barrel is preferable) and pounded with a heavy wooden mallet. The more closely it is packed the better; and, with care, from 250 to 300 pounds of cabbage may be put into a barrel of forty gallons. One pint of fine salt to the barrel is sprinkled with the cabbage as it is packed down. No addition of water is required. Fill the barrel to a point two inches from the top, cover the krout with large cabbage leaves, and place over the whole a wooden cover small enough to be inserted within the barrel, where it must be kept firmly, by a heavy stone, until the process of fermentation is past. Place the barrel within five or six feet of the kitchen fire, and in a few days fermentation will commence, which may be hastened by the addition of a little blood-warm water; a frothy scum will rise and run off, when the krout is all right and ready for use, and the barrel may he set in the cellar, porch, or shed. Freezing does it no injury, and it will keep in the cellar until March or April without depreciating, and longer in a cooler place. A barrel of krout can he made in two hours by two men. There are various modes of cooking it, while some prefer it raw, eating it as a salad. It is frequently boiled, three hours or more, with salt pork cut into small pieces. Perhaps the nicest style is to fry it in pork fat or with the gravy from roast pork. For frying, it should be boiled two hours to make it tender. It is a wholesome, hearty food, and is particularly appreciated by men requiring a substantial diet, while it is also relished by many of more fastidious taste.

SAVING AND APPLYING MANURE. The value of manure lies in its soluble parts, except in so far as its mechanical action may change the condition of the soil. So, the value of any given soil, aside from its mechanical texture, is contained in its soluble parts given up through vegetable decompostion, or the chemical action and re-action constantly going on through the growing season. Arthur Young, the celebrated English agricultural writer and experimenter, years ago took five equal portions of a field. One portion of this he manured with dry cut straw; a second with straw soaked five hours in strong urine; a third soaked in like manner for fifteen hours; a fourth treated for three days; to the fifth plat he added nothing. The whole field was plowed alike, sown with grain, and treated alike. The grain product of the first plat was thirty-nine; of the second, fifty; that of the third sixty-three; of the fourth 126; and of the fifth, that left without manure, only nine of grain. The weight of grain and straw in the several portions in the order as before named, was 100, 120, 300, and 48. The straw undoubtedly had some mechanical effect, but could have rotted only so partially as to have produced little effect upon the crop except from its soluble portion. Thus the wonderful effects of manure from this experiment, was due chiefly from the liquid manure with which the straw was saturated; in the extreme case giving in weight of grain as nine to one hundred and twenty six, or thirteen times; that of straw and grain was as forty-eight to three hundred, or six-and-one-half times. The lesson here taught shows: If manure is worth anything it is worth saving in the best manner possible. In other words, it should not be allowed to lie about the yards and run to waste, as is too often the case, especially in the West. In the West especially upon our ordinary prairie clays and loams, the sooner manure is hauled upon the land the better. It should be applied to corn, potatoes and other gross feeding crops, in its green state, and, principally from the reason, that thus we get the full benefit, both of its mechanical effects upon the soil through decay, while at the same time it is giving up its soluble properties to the crops tilled. When green, also, it contains a minimum amount of water, and consequently is lighter to haul than when soaked to its full capacity with water. Still again, it has given but little if any of its fertilizing properties to the air, through heating, which always ensues to a greater or less degree when vegetable substances are saturated with moisture. In locations unlike the West, where the necessity of manure is paramount; where sheds and buildings for saving it are used, and where the manipulations attending its mixing and fitting are intricate and expensive, much art is bestowed in scientific handling and its preparation. What would be good practice and economical there, would be the reverse here. Nevertheless, manure is far too valuable anywhere to be wasted; and hence good and careful cultivators everywhere are careful to keep and apply all that is made. This should always be remembered. About the only cost of manure in the West is the hauling and spreading on the field. However rich the soil it will well repay the cost of adding manure to the meadow, the corn field and other crops which are greedy for manure. However rich the soil, unless reinforced, it is surely becoming poorer and poorer each year it is cropped. So, the farmer who constantly takes from it and adds nothing, in the end, finds himself with an impoverished farm, that costs more to bring back to a state of fertility, than it would have cost to keep it so originally.

SAURIANS. The subdivision of the animal kingdom, including the crocodiles, lizards, etc.; they have four legs, and are covered with a scaly epidermis.

SAVANNAHS. Extensive alluvial flats; the prairies.

SAVIN. *Juniperus sabina.* The leaves are a powerful drug. In the United States, the red cedar is called savin.

SAVORY. The summer savory (*Satureja hortensis*) is an annual, and propagated by seed; the winter (*S. montana*) is perennial, and managed in the same way as sage, which it greatly resembles. They are labiate plants.

SAW. The use of the saw has, without doubt, exerted a greater influence in the art of building, than that of any other implement or tool ever used therein. It has enabled all inside and outside finish to be elaborated to the greatest degree, and of late years, steam and water-propelled gang saws, scroll saws, and other perfected forms have not only cheapened the price of lumber the world over, but rendered it available for a great variety of purposes, not previously attainable. Now, so simple has machinery for sawing purposes become, that mills for sawing timber may be set up directly in the forest, and the lumber made us fast as the trees are felled. This is often done, especially in sawing hard wood. The illustration gives a fair representation of the manner of work, including chopping the trees, sawing off the logs, loading, and ripping by means of the steam circular saw. The history of the saw is especially interesting, and hence we give some information relating to this implement, from Appleton's New Cyclopædia. It says: The Egyptians used saws of bronze, and applied them to cutting out planks from logs. The saw was single-handed, and the log was placed on end and secured to posts set in the ground. The inventor of the saw was deified by the Greeks, and called by some Talus and by others Perdix. The saws of the Grecian carpenters were like the straight frame saws of modern times, the blade set across the middle of the frame, with the teeth perpendicular to its plane. The block of wood to be sawn was clamped down upon a bench, and the workmen stood on opposite sides of this, one at each end of the saw. Saws are of various forms and sizes, according to their intended use. The older forms are straight strips of steel, either set in a frame, or simply provided with handles at each end, so as to be moved forward and back by two persons; or the plate is made stiff enough for a single handle to answer, when it is worked by one person holding it in one hand. In modern times saw blades are often circular, the teeth cutting as the saw revolves constantly in the same direction. The teeth are variously shaped for different saws. The most simple are made by angular notches, the angle at the apex of the notch being of 60°. This is most convenient for sharpening, as the common triangular or three-square file is just adapted to its figure. When the teeth are made with equal sides, they are said to have an upright pitch; and when they make a zigzag of alternating long and short lines, they are said to be flat or to have considerable pitch. The former are adapted for cross-cut saws, worked by two men, one at each end. Such teeth lack the chisel-like effect of those of a low pitch, and rather scrape away the wood than tear into it like the latter, which cut only when the saw is moved in the direction toward which the teeth point. Hand saws in the United States and England have the teeth pointed from the handle; in Asiatic countries and in Greece they have always been made with teeth pointed the other way. A straight cut upon a line can probably be made better by the thrusting cut, and in this the sawdust is thrown out more freely; but the force is certainly applied to better advantage as regards the saw in pulling it in the line of its greatest strength than in pushing; and for very slender saws, in which it is an object to dispense with all unnecessary width and thickness, as in the keyhole and other similar sorts, it would appear decidedly better to adopt the East Indian practice. Some large saws are notched at a sharper angle than 60°, and for these special files made for the angle are used, and are known as mill-saw files. Teeth made at a low pitch in large saws would become clogged with sawdust unless the spaces between them were enlarged, and the various forms in which this is done give distinctive names to the teeth. In large mill saws and circular saws the space between the teeth, which may be two or three inches, is hollowed out in a curve, and the outline is much like a fish hook in form, the shank of the hook bending back to make the back of one tooth, and the point curving round to form the under side or face of the next. All saws used for cutting wood require some provision against their liability to become jammed and the teeth clogged in the narrow passage they make for themselves. This is sometimes effected by making the blade thinner toward the back, but the most effectual mode is in the set given to the teeth. The earliest notice of saws being run by power is contained in a manuscript of the 13th century in Paris, in which is a representation of the saw mill with a self action turned by a water wheel. Beckmann finds evidence of saw mills worked by water power in Augsburg, Germany, as far back as 1322. In the island of Madeira one is said to have been in operation in 1420, and the first one in Norway was built in 1530. In Holland they were in use more than one hundred years sooner than in England; and the Dutch furnished the English with lumber. The operation of one at Lyons in 1555 is described by the bishop of Ely, then British ambassador at Rome. The first recorded attempt to establish a saw mill in Great Britain was made near London in 1663 by a Dutchman; but the enterprise was abandoned on account of the opposition of the hand sawyers. In 1700 the advantages offered by this improvement was set before the public by one Houghton; but no one ventured to introduce it till 1767 or 1768, when by the desire of the society of arts a saw mill was built at Limehouse by James Stansfield. It was soon destroyed by the mob. In the American colonies the importance of this expeditious means of obtaining sawed lumber was generally felt; and efforts were early made to obtain the necessary machinery, such as was used in Holland. In 1634 a saw mill was put in operation at the falls of the Piscataqua, between Berwick and the Cocheco branch of that river, and this is supposed to have been the first mill of the kind in New England. In New York as many as three mills were constructed by the Dutch West India company about 1633, to run by water power or by wind. One of them was on Nut or Governor's island, which was leased in 1689 for 500 merchantable boards yearly, half oak and half pine. Another was on Saw Mill creek, a small stream which flowed into the East river from the pond know as the Collect. On the Delaware, saw mills were erected by the Dutch and Swedes before the arrival of Penn.

SAWDUST. When rotted in the compost heap, or with lime and earth, it forms a good manure for improving the texture of soils. When partially rotted it forms an excellent mulch, and is often used as a divisor for manure in making hot beds.

SAW FLIES. An extensive family of hymenopterous insects, of the genera *Cimbex*, *Tenthredo*, *Selandria*, etc. The perfect insects, resembling bees and wasps, are seen in summer hovering over the plants they feed on. The female lays her eggs in a slit made in the young stem, or in leaves; the larvæ feed on leaves and buds, and are extremely voracious. In eight weeks, they descend to the ground and form a web either among the dead leaves, in the bark, or under ground. They are very destructive; whale-oil, soap water, tobacco water, and lime are used to destroy them.

SAXIFRAGE. Flowering plants of the genus *Saxifraga*.

SAXON BLUE. A solution of indigo in sulphuric acid, used as a dye.

SCAB IN SHEEP. It is more than probable that the disease is occasioned by neglect. That in ill-kept sheep it quickly assumes a virulent form there is no doubt, since on fat sheep, or those in the full flush of growth, it is evident, as in other farm animals, the parasites can not get control of the body of the sheep. Scab is known by the generally ragged appearance of the sheep, and by bare patches of the skin; by their rubbing the irritated parts, and, if closely examined, by reddish, pimply spots, upon which a small blister or vesicle forms. The infested sheep also are rest less, and rub themselves against trees and posts to relieve the intolerable itching. Later sore places will be found, the appetite fails, and if relief is not given the animal dies. The mange affecting the horse, ox, dog, and cat, depends upon the presence of insects. There are different insects, known as *acari*, infesting different animals, having distinctive characteristics in each, and generally confined to that species of animals; yet the mange from a dog is said to have been communicated to man, and a horse has been infested with mange by means of the skin of a mangy cat. The sheep acarus does not bore galleries in the skin, but remains on the surface, clinging to the wool, and finding shelter among the masses of scab produced by the drying of exudations from the wounds inflicted by these parasites. Experiment has shown that increase of temperature hastens the hatching of their ova; fourteen days, according to Prof. Brown, of England, sufficed to hatch a lot in a bottle carried in the trowsers' pocket, while two months' time was required with some kept under glass in a room. The young have six legs; the fully grown, after several changes of skin, have eight. The microscope reveals numerous sucking-caps or disks in the legs, enabling the parasite to cling to the wool and skin of the sheep; and renders fully apparent the action of these structures, showing, as the feet advance, how the disks are expanded to grasp the substance over which the acarus is moving, apparently retaining their hold in obedience to the volition of the animal. Thus its structure adapts it for crawling over and adhering to the skin, instead of burrowing beneath it. Burrowing acari, like the itch insect in man, are always armed with cutting teeth, set in strong jaws, and their legs are very short. The body of the female of the sheep acarus is larger than that of the male, rounder in form, the fourth pair of legs are developed nearly as well as the third, and are supplied with terminal sucking disks. The accompanying illustrations represent a female acarus magnified one hundred diameters, and a young six-legged acarus, also magnified one hundred diameters. Mature mites are visible to the naked eye as pellucid points of the size of a pin's head. Various experiments have been made to ascertain the rapidity of the growth and reproduction of these parasites. The young acari have been detected in fourteen days from the direct transference of the acarus to the skin of the sheep. In a month the disease had spread over a space of five inches; in ten to twelve weeks pretty nearly over the whole body. A greater or less amount of time may be required under different circumstances of temperature, and other modifying influences.

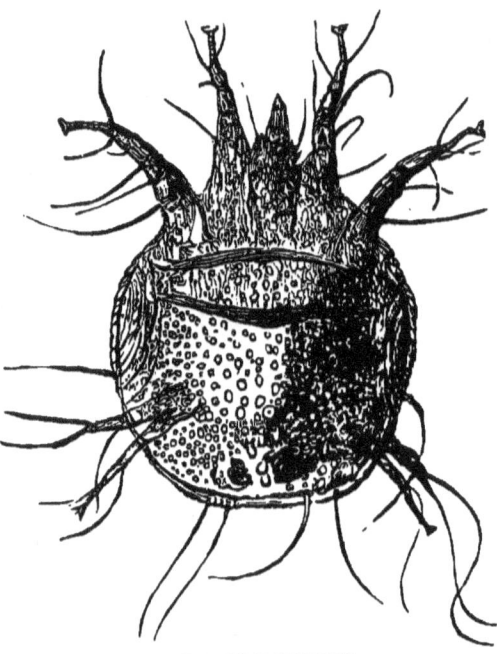

FEMALE ACARUS OF SHEEP SCAB.

The first sign of the existence of scab is rubbing against any projecting body within reach; as it extends, sheep bite themselves, kick with their hind feet at their sides and shoulders. If one is caught and the hand placed on the mouth, while infected parts are scratched, gratification is evinced by nibbling at the hand, and when the infection is severe or general this nibbling movement is regarded as an infallible sign. Examination will disclose spots on the skin, white and hard, the center marked with yellow points of exudation, which adheres to the wool, matting the fibers together. The wool may be firm on these spots, and no scabs are seen at this stage.

Then the yellow moisture, evaporating, gives place to a yellow scab, which adheres firmly to the skin and wool. Raw places appear at points which the animal can reach with his teeth and hind feet. The disease is complicated in summer by the presence of the larvæ of the blow-fly, the maggots burrowing under the scab. The animal becomes nervous, excited to wildness, and can not obtain properly either food or rest, thus losing flesh and becoming reduced to a skeleton, from constant irritation and lack of nutrition, only the strongest animals recovering if left without treatment. Destruction of the parasite and its eggs is the only object of remedial treatment. Arsenic and mercury are often employed very effectually, but they are poisonous, and therefore injurious and dangerous to the sheep. These and other solutions are used both as washes and dips. Sudden changes of weather and locality, or a deficiency of food after such treatment, often induce serious or fatal results which can not be guarded against. Whole flocks have thus been lost. Mercurial ointment, with olive oil and a little turpentine,

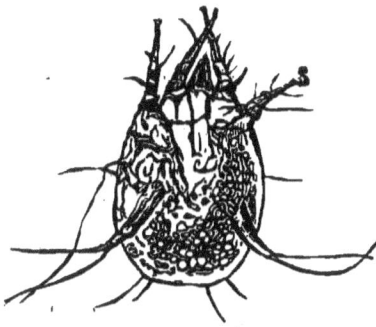

YOUNG ACARUS.

is popular in England, nevertheless, and is regarded as improving the yield of wool. Experiment proves that the acarus will live in arsenic and sulphur for some hours; potash is more fatal, and tobacco is more deadly still, killing in a few minutes. But carbolic acid is probably the most potent remedy used. When combined with one hundred times its bulk of water, it has killed acari in two minutes; when used with fifty times its bulk of water, a degree of potency harmless as a dip, it kills in forty to ninety seconds. Prof. Brown thus describes the manufacture of the carbolic acid dip, which, it is claimed, has never failed when properly used: First, it is necessary that carbolic acid should be obtained of uniform strength, and experience has proved that the crystalline product is less efficacious in the destruction of parasites than the liquid residue, which is sold under the name of terebane, or cresylic acid, which can always be obtained of the manufacturers. The liquid is, when fresh, of a very light straw color, becoming dark brown on exposure to the atmosphere. The pure carbolic acid was employed in many experiments, at first with only partial success, but even had it proved to be superior to the liquid terebane, the price would have been a serious objection; terebane, however, is very much cheaper, and in every experiment was found to be more active as a remedial agent than the pure carbolic acid, while its fluid condition at all temperatures renders it more easy of manipulation. To effect perfect combination between the terebane and the water used for dilution care is essential, as imperfect mixtures are capable of doing injury, and may cause the death of some of the sheep, particularly of those which are first introduced into the bath. The reason of this is obvious. An incomplete mixture allows the separation of the terebane, which floats on the surface of the fluid in the form of a brownish, oily, or rather tarry scum; the first few animals which are dipped become covered with the undiluted acid, which acts at once and energetically as a caustic, causing prostration and death, unless immediately on observing the symptoms of distress means are taken to wash off the agent with warm water and soap; this treatment is not, however, at all times successful. An accident of the kind never ought to occur and, in fact, never can occur if the dip is properly prepared and used. It is not probable that the average farmer will attempt to make the compound; the following directions, therefore, may be taken as meant for the instruction of the practical chemist or the veterinary surgeon who has charge of the diseased flock. A quantity of terebane, proportioned to the number of sheep to be dipped, is to be placed in a convenient vessel of iron or earthenware, and, if possible, the vessel should be suspended in a larger one containing water, and so arranged that heat can be applied. In all chemical laboratories a water-bath will be available; but for the purpose of making small quantities of the dip, an iron bucket suspended in an ordinary copper filled with water, which may be kept hot, but not up to the boiling point, will answer perfectly well. As soon as the terebane is placed in the temporary water-bath, a certain proportion of soap, one bar weighing over two pounds to each gallon of terebane, is to be added. The mixture should be stirred with a wooden rod until the soap is entirely dissolved, care being taken that the fluid does not boil. When the solution is complete the compound should be removed from the fire, and as soon as it ceases to give off vapor, oil of turpentine is to be added in the proportion of one pint to each gallon of terebane. The mixture, when cold, may be poured into carboys or casks ready for use. While the above remedies may be entirely efficacious, and are to be recommended as the best, it may not be amiss to give a few which have been popular heretofore: An infusion of arsenic, half a pound of the mineral to twelve gallons of water. The sheep should be washed in soap-suds and then dipped in the infusion. This treatment is preferred by Mr. Spooner. Mercurial ointment, incorporated thoroughly with four times its weight of lard, rubbed upon the head and upon the skin (the wool being carefully parted) in parallel lines from head to tail, four inches apart. The mixture applied should not exceed two ounces, and a half an ounce may be enough for a lamb. A light second application is sometimes necessary. It is preferred by Youatt. One pound of sulphur gradually mixed with half a pound of oil of tar, the mixture rubbed down with two pounds of lard, may be applied in the same way. Mr. Randall would prefer this, because not poisonous, if sure to be effectual. Another mixture contains a half pound of corrosive sublimate, three-fourths pound of white hellebore, six gallons whale oil, two pounds rosin, and two of tallow. This is powerful, and should be sparingly applied. Tobacco decoctions are much used in this country and quite effectually, if thoroughly applied after the wool is taken off.

SCABIOUS. Plants of the genus *Scabiosa*, at one time celebrated for curing the itch.

SCABROUS. Rough, from minute inequalities.

SCAFFOLDING. The temporary frame-work put up in buildings.

SCALDED CREAM. Clotted cream; cream raised from milk by heating.

SCALE INSECT. (See Lice.)

SCALPEL. A small knife, convenient for dissection or surgical operations.

SCAMMONY. The gum resin of the *Convolvulus scammonea*. It closely resembles jalap.

SCANDENT, SCANDENS. Climbing branches. Or having climbing branches, as Cobœa scandens, which climb by adhesive tendrils of the branches.

SCANSORIALS, SCANSORES. Climbing birds, as the woodpeckers; they have two toes before and two behind on each foot.

SCAPE. A flower stem or peduncle rising from the ground, as in the hyacinth, flag, etc.

SCAPHOID. Shaped like a boat.

SCAPULA. The shoulder-blade.

SCAPULARS. The shoulder feathers which cover the sides of the back in birds.

SCAPUS. The stem of a feather. In architecture, a shaft.

SCARABÆIDANS. A family of lamellicorn beetles.

SCARCEMENT. A rebate, or set back in a wall, or bank of earth.

SCARFING. The union of two timbers, to answer as one.

SCARFSKIN. The epidermis, a delicate covering of the true skin.

SCELIDES. The posterior or lower extremities.

SCHEELES GREEN. Mineral green, arsenite of copper.

SCHIST. A coarse slate.

SCIATIC. Relating to the hip joint, as the sciatic nerve.

SCIENTIFIC AGRICULTURE. There is no such thing as a science of agriculture, and never will be in an exact sense, since the conditions present to-day are changed to-morrow, and the conditions, are ever varying, not only with the seasons, but from year to year, and from generation to generation. Hence, science in agriculture, must ever be more or less experimental, like medicine. Scientific agriculture, however, as is science in agriculture, are both important, and necessary studies, since the practical application of the facts elicited by scientific inquiry from generation to generation, have made up the sum of all agricultural knowledge. Until within the last few years, comparatively, agricultural science has been largely theoretical. It is so yet, to a considerable degree, and must in every instance be so since theory must always precede practical investigation. Yet inductive experiment, the only true plan, is being carried out more carefully year by year, by such organizations as agricultural colleges, boards of agriculture, agricultural congresses, and other bodies of a like nature. The province of every practical farmer, should be to foster such organizations, by every means in his power, and especially by assisting them in carrying forward simple experiments as may be designated, with a view of adding new facts carefully stated, which aggregated together and confirmed until a law is established, is really all there is in science in any of its departments. (See also article Agriculture.)

SCION. A bud, or buds on a branch. A stick of buds ready for grafting is called a scion. (See Grafting.)

SCIRRHUS. An indurated gland; it becomes a cancer when suppuration occurs.

SCIURINES. The squirrel family.

SCLEROTICA. The white membrane of the eye.

SCOLOPENDRE. The genus of centipedes.

SCOPIPEDS. A tribe of melliferous insects, some of which have the posterior feet furnished with a scopa, or little tuft of hair.

SCORE. Twenty pieces, or twenty pounds.

SCOTCH CATTLE. The Scotch breeds have been summarized by Youatt as follows: Scotland contains several distinct and valuable breeds of cattle, evidently belonging to our present division, The Middle Horns. The West Highlanders, whether we regard those that are found in the Hebrides, or the county of Argyle, seem to retain most of the aboriginal character. They have remained unchanged, or improved only by selection, for many generations; indeed from the earliest accounts that we possess of Scottish cattle. The North Highlanders are a smaller, coarser, and in every way inferior race, and owe the greater part of what is valuable about them to crosses from the Western breed. The Northeastern Cattle were derived from, and bear a strong resemblance to, the West Highlander, but are of considerably larger size. The Ayrshire breed is second to none for milking. The Galloways, which scarcely a century ago were middle-horned, and with difficulty distinguished from the West Highlanders, are now a polled breed—increased in size, with more striking resemblance to their kindred, the Devons—with all their aptitude to fatten, and with a great hardiness of constitution.

SCRUB CATTLE. This is a term applied to mixed cattle, that through the hardship incident to having to care pretty much for themselves, as in some thickly timbered regions of the country, have degenerated into dwarfed, scrawny stock, of no particular use, either for beef, labor or milk. (See Native Cattle.)

SCOURING. In colts and calves this is usually produced from some disability of the dam, or in the case of calves, from improper food. This must be remedied according to the nature of the case. Diarrhœa in horses is produced by a variety of causes, as indigestible or irritating food, disorder of the liver, or from constitutional tendency or weakness. It must be met according to the nature of the case. It is often an effort of nature to get rid of injurious matter in the system. If so, as soon as discovered, give a moderate dose of linseed oil, say from a half to one pint, but if the discharge has proceeded naturally for some time, such remedy would not be indicated. As a general remedy, two drachms of spirits of camphor, one drachm tincture chloride of iron, and one ounce of ether would be indicated. If the discharges are sour and fetid, take one ounce each of powdered chalk and bi-sulphite of soda, to be mixed in the food two or three times a day. If the diarrhœa is the result of over purging by medicine, give two ounces each of laudanum and powdered chalk, mixed in gruel of flour, every three hours until an effect is produced. For horses or cattle where a more astringent effect is required to counteract an irritable relaxed condition of the bowels, give the following in gruel or linseed tea: One drachm each of powdered kino, powdered opium, powdered gentian, and bi-carbonate of soda. Or it may be made up into a ball and given. For scouring in calves, give in milk or linseed tea, four drachms of calcined magnesia, twenty grains powdered opium, and two drachms of powdered rhubarb. Useful remedies are also strong teas of willow bark, with the addition of a little ginger or calamus root. For lambs troubled with diarrhœa, take one drachm of powdered opium, one-half ounce of powdered ginger, and two ounces of prepared chalk; mix these in a pint of calamus or mint tea, and give a tablespoonful twice a day until relieved. If this fails, to the foregoing add one ounce of powdered catechu, and give as before directed.

SCRATCHES. (See Grease.)

SCROFULA. A disease of the glands about the neck, followed by debility and skin diseases.

SCRUPLE. Twenty grains; the third of a drachm.

SCUFFLER. A light scarifier, or horse hoe.

SCUTATE. Protected by large scales.

SCUTELLIFORM. Of the figure of a shield; leaves having the foot-stalk terminating in the center of the lamina.

SCURVY GRASS. *Cochlearia offici·alis*. A plant belonging to the same genus as the horseradish.

SCUTCHING. Breaking flax or hemp. (See Flax.)

SEAM. In geology, a thin layer of a given rock between large masses. Also a measure of eight bushels, or a horse load of wood.

SEBACEOUS GLANDS. The minute glands of the skin, which excrete a fatty matter.

SEBACIC ACID. An acid produced during the destructive distillation of fats.

SECHIUM. A vegetable resembling a small squash in size, but different in flavor and structure, said to be from the *Sechium edulis*, a South American plant.

SECONDARY ROCKS. The formations lying above the coal and between it and the tertiary series. They are fossiliferous and stratified.

SECRETION. The separation from the blood or sap of certain products, by a glandular or other apparatus; the perspiration, urine, bile, saliva, etc., are secretions. They perform important offices in the economy, and can not be arrested without the occurrence of disease.

SECUNDINE. The second envelope of the ovule in plants. The word secundines also means the membranes which cover the animal fœtus.

SECURIFERS, SECURIFERI. The name of a tribe of *Terebrantia*, or boring hymenopterous insects, comprising those in which the females have a saw-shaped or hatchet-shaped terebra or appendage to the posterior part of the abdomen for the purpose of preparing a place to receive the eggs, and of depositing them therein.

SECURIPALPS, SECURIPALPI. The name of a family of coleopterous insects, comprehending those in which the maxillary palps terminate in a joint which is elongated and hatchet-shaped.

SEDATIVES. Medicines which produce sleep and diminish pain, as henbane, camphor, morphia, etc.

SEED. The seed is the perfected fruit of the plant, capable of again reproducing itself through germinations and growth. They may be divided into six principal classes: 1. Those of the cereal grains, beans, peas, etc., contained within dry coverings, and which are prepared directly for use. 2. Those contained in fleshy envelopes, as fruits, pumpkins, squashes, etc., the envelopes being the edible part. 3. The seeds of plants, the tubers, bulbs. leaves or foot stalks of which are eaten. 4. The seeds of plants used for flavoring. 5. The seeds of medicinal plants. 6. The seeds of plants cultivated for their foliage or flowers. In a more restricted sense the fruits of plants are not considered the seeds, the fruit being generally termed the edible portion. In the present article it will only be necessary to notice the seed in its relation to the improvement of the species, other questions having been discussed in the articles acclimation, foods, germination, etc., which see. The vitality of seeds is determined by the length of time required to disorganize them as kept under ordinary circumstances, with care as to dryness, and partial exemption from the effects of the oxygen of the air; seeds remain vital for twice or three times the number of years as ordinarily given in the table. Kept entirely from contact with air and moisture, there is practically ño limit to the length of time they may be kept intact. As to the amount of cold which the seeds of plants will withstand without impairing their vitality, if dry, there is practically no limit. Prof. Wartman, of Geneva, Switzerland, more than twenty years ago, placed nine varieties of seed, some of them tropical, in hermetically sealed tubes, and submitted them to freezing as severe as science can produce. Some remained fifteen days in a mixture of salt and snow, others were plunged into a bath of liquid sulphuric acid, rendered as cold as possible by artificial means. They were then taken out and sown in pots in the open air and all germinated. Those which had been submitted to the severest cold germinated as kindly and made as good and healthy plants as those not submitted to this extreme test. Nevertheless, seeds as usually kept, like plants, have a limit beyond which they will not stand cold, or a degree of cold at which their cells are ruptured, provided always, however, they contain a sufficient amount of moisture for this purpose. In relation to the germination of seeds and tests of their quality, M. Charles Appelius, of Erfurt, in a memoir furnished the Imperial Society of Horticulture, France, says: The value of a sample of seeds is often determined solely by their specific weight and density. This method is no doubt good, but not infallible; besides, the weight of the same kind of seed may vary from year to year, according to the manner in which it is grown. It may even vary upon the same plant; it does so particularly in an ear of maize, the grains situated in the center of the ear of that plant having a greater specific gravity than those above or below. Now, the latest experiments of Dr. Hellriegel go to prove, first, that in accordance with the general opinion of cultivators the best formed seeds have the greatest specific gravity; and, in the second place, that the heaviest seeds produce the strongest plants. Every one knows that in order to ascertain the specific gravity of seeds quickly and easily it is the custom to throw them into water, and to collect as the best those which, from their greater weight, fall to the bottom, whilst those which float are rejected as bad. However, too much confidence must not be placed in this method of proving seed by water. It may frequently mislead, particularly in the case of seeds in which the specific gravity differs little from that of the fluid. For example, those of cucurbitaceous plants, which are produced during cold seasons, float upon the water, and nevertheless germinate very well. It is known, too, says M. Appelius, that the seeds of these plants bear more female flowers than younger plants; that is to say, the plants are more prolific than those raised from seeds gathered in a cold season and planted shortly after they have ripened. Good seeds of the melon and gourd lose weight as they grow old; at first they will sink in water, and by the sixth year half of them will float, without having become bad. We conclude, therefore, in this case, as in many others, that trial by water is not a sure test. In general the heaviest seeds are those which contain the most starch, such as those of cereals and leguminous plants, etc. The specific gravity of oily seed is often nearly the same as that of water, although in some cases they are heavier; as, for example, those of cabbages. The lightest seeds are those of umbelliferous plants, such as carrots, parsnips, chervil, aniseseed, etc., and of composites, such as lettuces, scorzoneras, etc. In the first of these families the lightness of the seeds arise from the presence of an oil in the case which encloses the seed, and of air in the last. With a few exceptions all shining seeds are heavier than water. Many cultivators, before buying seeds, test them by making them germinate upon damp blotting paper, at a temperature of 59° to 75°. This process is convenient and tolerably sure for the kinds which are quickly raised, such as clover, peas and cereals, but does not answer for those which require a long time to germinate. For these the best practical plan is to grow a sample in a pot. But even this will not always give a strictly correct indication of the germinating power of seeds, since the result depends, all other circumstances being equal, upon the care taken in sowing, the temperature of the air, the depth at which seed is sown and the time of the year, etc. Thus the pips of apples and pears almost always germinate badly and in very small quantities when trials are made of them in pots soon after they are ripe, whilst they answer perfectly if they are sown at the end of October or in March in beds in the open air. For this reason it often happens that a sample is pronounced bad when in reality it is excellent. This is the case with the generality of woody plants, the seed of which come up the first year, conifers excepted. The soil which is used to cover the trial seedlings also considerably affect the result. If, for example, the ryegrass seed (Lolium perenne) is sown in soil which retains moisture with average tenacity, and is buried one inch below the surface, seven-eighths of it grow in twelve days; if two inches, seven eighths also grow, but in eighteen days; if three inches, six-eighths in twenty days; if four inches, four-eighths germinate in twenty-one days; at five inches, three-eighths in twenty-two days; and at six inches, the proportion of the seeds which germinate is reduced to one-eighth in twenty-three days. On the other hand, when ryegrass is sown and simply harrowed in, it germinates, almost without exception, in five days. M. Appelius' memoir contains, in the form of a table, the length of time necessary to germinate the seeds of many plants at a temperature of 54° to 55° in the sun, and 54° to 64° in the open air. This table shows plainly, says the German author, that those seeds which are lighter than water require a longer time to germinate than those which are heavier. A tolerably large number of seeds come up slowly, and even with difficulty; they are generally those which have a thick, tough skin. In this case it is a good plan to soak the sample in hot water, from 167° to 185°, allowing it to cool naturally to 60° for four and twenty hours, and not to sow it until after it has been prepared in this manner. Their germination may be assisted by notching, a more delicate operation than the first, because care must be taken not to injure the embryo. Unless one or the other of these methods is adopted, it will generally be one or two years before such seeds come up. The seeds of palm trees usually grow very well placed on damp sawdust, the germinating end downwards, and kept in a damp, warm atmosphere. The spores of ferns and the seeds of orchids, which are very minute, come up rapidly, if they are scattered on pieces of peat placed in a pan with water. For hardy plants M. Appelius recommends, as by far the best plan, to sow them in lines. In his opinion, the reason of the frequent failure of seeds in gardens is that they are sown in earth too dry and buried too deep. Besides, if care is not taken to press the earth lightly together before sowing the seed, heavy rains falling directly after will force some of the seed deeper in, and so occasion greater inequality in germination. For perfectly hardy annuals, the best plan is to sow them late in the autumn, or, at least, very early in the spring; if the seeds are not in the ground before April you run the risk of seeing them flower very late and very badly. Seedlings which are obliged to be raised in hotbeds or under frames, cause much disappointment, and consequently complaint of the quality of the samples. M. Appelius does not hesitate to say, in that case, the want of success arises more often from bad management than from the badness of the seeds. In his opinion it is a mistake to sow many kinds of flowers in high bottom-heat, such as stocks, asters, phlox, heartsease, petunias, etc., which do far better in a very gentle hot-bed, and produce stronger plants, less likely to die off. On the other hand, it must not be forgotten that the dung with which a hot-bed is made, after it has given off its first heat, absorbs the moisture from the earth with which it is covered; that the surface of this earth under the frame generally slopes toward the south, and the greater part of the shower from the watering runs down this incline, the end of which is that the earth in which the seeds are embedded is often too dry, or, at least, it is so with that next to the back of the hot-bed. In this case, says M. Appelius, if you sow those seeds which germinate slowly and require constant damp, such as phlox and heartsease, at the bottom or in the front of the bed, and those which grow more readily at the top or back, the result will be good; but it will be quite the contrary if the reverse is done. Finally, the success of seedlings raised under frames depends principally upon the regulation of moisture. Another precaution, and one of the utmost importance in this case, is not to sow thick; a plant raised among a lot of crowded seedlings is very apt to die before it has made its fourth leaf. This seldom happens if, on the contrary, seeds are sown thin, and a little powdered charcoal mixed with the earth. Wheat, and the other cereal grains, if not injured by insects, or damp, retain their vitality perfectly three or four years, but seeds of the previous year's growth are best. Grass seeds should not be depended on for more than one year. The oily seeds unless kept quite dry and from contact with air soon deteriorate. The seeds of all the cucumber family, including melons, squashes, etc., are better after four years old. As to the time that seeds may ordinarily be kept intact, the following table of the seeds of vegetables and herbs will show:

Seeds.	Years.
Artichoke	5 to 6
Asparagus	2 to 3
Beans, all kinds	2 to 3
Beet	3 to 4
Broccoli	5 to 6
Carrot	2 to 3
Cress	3 to 4
Corn kept on the cob	2 to 3
Cucumber	8 to 10
Egg plant	1 to 2
Endive	5 to 6
Leek	2 to 3
Cauliflower	5 to 6
Celery	2 to 3
Chervil	2 to 3
Corn salad	2 to 3
Onion	2 to 3
Parsley	2 to 3
Parsnip	2 to 3
Pea	5 to 6
Pumpkin	8 to 10
Rhubarb	3 to 4
Squash	8 to 10
Lettuce	3 to 4
Melon	8 to 10
Mustard	3 to 4
Okra	3 to 4
Spinach	3 to 4
Tomato	2 to 3
Turnip	5 to 6
Pepper	2 to 3
Radish	4 to 5
Salsify	2 to 3

HERBS.

Seeds.	Years.
Anise	3 to 4
Balm	2 to 3
Basil	2 to 3
Caraway	2
Coriander	1
Dill	2 to 3
Fennel	2 to 3
Hyssop	3 to 4
Lavender	2 to 3
Sweet marjoram	2 to 3
Summer savory	1 to 2
Sage	2 to 3
Thyme	2 to 3
Wormwood	2 to 3

In sowing seeds, a good rule for those not practically acquainted with the proper depth at which to sow seeds is to cover them four times their diameter. Very minute seeds should be simply pressed into the ground and kept moist until they sprout. Wheat, for instance, germinates best at a depth of three-quarters to one inch in depth. Below the depth of two inches it must partially exhaust itself in reaching the surface, and in throwing out its superficial roots. At the depth of six inches, it reaches the surface nearly or quite exhausted, if it indeed do not perish in the attempt. In light soils, however, seeds may be sown one-quarter deeper than in heavy, compact soils. The following tables of the time of sowing, the average seed or pounds sown per acre, the time of harvest and the best soil, gathered from a variety of sources will be found valuable. The table of averages of seeding and product in the different States, with the time of planting and harvesting, and prices of the various articles, is compiled from a number of returns in the different States; and in some instances, perhaps, eight or ten—in others, not more than four to six; and in one or two instances, perhaps, not more than two. The extremes are given, and the replies ranged from these; but in many instances there was almost an entire similarity in the judgments formed in the case of the prominent crops. In respect to some of the crops, also, regard must be paid to the different varieties cultivated. In the potato crop, both the common and sweet potato are embraced in the replies from certain States; and this fact deserves recollection when the disparity of seeding is mentioned. For a few of the States, as no returns were received there are no records made. The other tables, relating to estimates of the proportions of cultivated land to uncultivated, of corn stalk and straw fodder to the grain, the rotation of crops, and the cost of raising different crops, with amount of consumption, and the prices of various agricultural products and wages of labor, can of course be viewed only as the results of the conclusion of a few in each section of the country. Yet many of those who have furnished this information are among the prominent successful agriculturists, in their respective districts; or practical farmers, who show that, though the subject is new to them, they duly appreciate its importance, and have gladly lent their aid to promote the object. The replies, generally, relate to a county or district, though in a few instances, perhaps, they have been confined to a single town. The number of the returns were not sufficient to allow a condensation in a tabular statement, in respect to some of these subjects; and they have, therefore, simply been drawn out and entered in the order of the States. It is not claimed that the quantities of seed stated, or, the land adapted to the cultivation of the crops are a sure guide except in a general sense. Yet approximately they are correct. Allowance must be made for climate. For instance, a crop doing well in a cool and rather stiff soil in the South might require a warm and rather light soil in the North, and *rice versa*. So in the quantity of seed different soils and localities require different quantities of seed. Though defective in many respects, yet at the same time they are of value, in a general sense, especially in relation to costs, quantities sown and time of harvesting.

WHEAT.

States.	Time of sowing or planting.	Average bushels or pounds of seed per acre.	Time of harvest.	Best soil.
Maine	May 15 to June	1½ bush	August 20 to 30	Sward corn stubble; high ridges; dry pasture.
New Hampshire	April to May 10	1½ to 2 bush	August 1 to 20	Clay loam; new upland; diluvial; black loam.
Massachusetts	April 10 to 25	1¼ to 2 bush	June 25 to Aug. 10	
Vermont	May 1 to September	2 to 2½ bush	Last Aug. to Sept. 1	Loam clay; clay loam
New York	May 10 to September 1	1¼ to 2 bush	July 2 to Aug. 10	Sandy loam; clay loam; loam mixed with gravel.
New Jersey	Sept. 1 to October 15	1½ to 2 bush	June 28 to July 7	Friable loam; loam; clay loam; sandy loam, rather stiff
Pennsylvania	Sept. 1 to October 15	1¼ to 2 bush	June 15 to July 15	Light sandy; clay soil; sandy loam; limestone; do. clay, mixed with gravel; clay; do.; clay and gravel.
Delaware		1 1-6 to 2 bush		
Maryland	October	1½ bush	June	Rich loam; clay.
Virginia	Sept. 15 to Nov. 30	1 to 2 bush	June 15 to July 15	Clay; do do.; clay and lime.
South Carolina	October and Nov.	50 lbs	June 1	Clay.
Georgia	September 15 to Nov.	¾ to 1 bush	June 1	Red mulatto.
Alabama	September to Dec.	½ to 2 bush	June to July	Loam; oak and hickney.
Tennessee	October 12	1 to 1½ bush	June 15	Dark loam; all kinds.
Kentucky	September and Oct.	75 lbs	July	Clay.
Ohio	Sept. 1 to Oct. 25	1 to 1½ bush	June 28 to July 20	Oak and maple land; clay; do.; very warm; limestone: clay loam; yellow clay; clay; sandy.
Indiana	September to October	1 to 2 bush	June 15 to July 20	Sand and loam; clay loam; clay; improved clay; loam do.; clay; sandy loam.
Illinois	August to Sept. 30	1 to 1½ bush	May to July 1	Sandy loam; clay; oat or clover stubble; clover; rich loam.
Michigan	Sept. 3 to Oct. 1	1¼ to 1½ bush	June to July 30	Marl Clay; clay and sand; oak; clay loam.
Iowa	August 20 to Sept. 15	90 lbs. to 1¾ bu.	July 5 to 20	
Texas	October 1 to Dec. 15	¾ bush	May 1 to June 10	Lime soil.

BARLEY.

Maine	Last of May	2 bushels		
New Hampshire	April; May	2½ to 4 bush	August	Black loam.
Massachusetts	May	2½ to 3 bush	July 30	High, warm land.
Vermont	July 1	2 bushels	August 1	Dry.
New York	April 10 to May 10	2 to 3 bush	July 1 to August	Loam; warm loam; loam and muck; sandy loam; black sandy loam.
Pennsylvania	March 15	1½ to 2 bush	June and July	Heavy clay; sandy loam.
South Carolina	September	2 bushels	May	Clay.
Tennessee	March 1	1 bushel	July 1	
Ohio	April 1 to May 1	1½ to 2 bush	July 1 to 25	Clay, mixed with sand; clay loam; loose do.
Indiana	April to September	1¼ to 2½ bush	June 25 to August	Clay; do. loam; dry, sandy loam.
Michigan	April 15 to May 1	½ to 2 bush	July 7 to August 1	Sandy loam; rich loam.
Iowa	March to April 1	1¼ bushel	July 1	

OATS.

Maine	April to May	2½ to 3 bush	August 10 to 30	Dry; gravelly.
New Hampshire	April and May	3 to 4 bush	August 1	Clay; sandy; free.
Massachusetts	April 10 to May 10	2½ to 3 bush	July 15 to August 20	High, warm land.
Vermont	April to May 15	3 bushels	August	Light; sandy.
New York	March 15 to May 25	1½ to 3 bush	July 10 to August 15	Loam and muck; loam; deep, black muck; rich, sandy loam.
New Jersey	April 1 to 15	2 to 2½ bush	July 20 to August 1	Sandy loam; clay.
Pennsylvania	March 15 to April 15	1 to 3 bush	July 10 to August 1	Sandy loam; light; sandy; sandy loam; limestone; do.
Delaware				Rich; moist.
Maryland	April	2 bushels	July	Dry loam; clay and lime; sandy loam; do.; do.
Virginia	February to April 1	1½ to 2½ bush	July 10 to August 10	
South Carolina	Dec. to February	1 bushel	June 1 to last June	Moist; sandy.
Georgia	January to March 1	1 to 1½ bush	June to July 1	Slate loam.
Alabama	November to April	¾ to 1 bush	May and June	Sandy loam.
Mississippi	October to February	1 bushel	July	Light do.; clay.
Tennessee	Feb. 15 to March	1½ bushels	July 10	Black loam, thin.
Kentucky	March and April	48 pounds	July	
Ohio	March and April	2 bushels	June to August 1	Loose loam; do. do.; clay loam; sandy loam; oak and hickory loam.
Indiana	March to May 1	1¼ to 2 bush	July 1 to August	Sandy loam; loam; clay; do.; do.; sandy.
Illinois	March 20 to April 4	1½ to 2 bush	June to August 1	Sandy loam; light loam; sandy do.
Michigan	April 10 to 30	2 to 3 bus	July 7 to August 1	Clay or sand; rich loam; sandy.
Iowa	April	2 to 4 bush	July 15 to August	
Texas	February	1 bushel	May	

RYE.

States.	Time of sowing or planting.	Average bushels or pounds of seed per acre.	Time of harvest.	Best soil.
Maine	Fall and Spring	1½ bush		New, burnt land.
New Hampshire	September and April	1 to 2 bush	July and August	Sandy; silicious; newly cleared land.
Massachusetts	August to September	1 to 1½ bush		High, warm, light land.
Vermont	September	1¼ to 1½ bush	Last July to August	Light.
New York	September 1 to Nov	1 to 2 bush	July 10 to 25	Sandy and slate; sand; sandy loam, or gravel; gravelly loam.
New Jersey	September 1	1 bushel	July 1	Light, sandy loam.
Pennsylvania	September 1 to 15	1 to 1½ bush	Last June to July	Gravel; serpentine; stubble.
Maryland	October	1 bushel	June	Light.
South Carolina	October	⅝ bushel	June	Gray land.
Georgia	September	⅝ bushel	July	Mulatto.
Alabama	October	½ bushel	May	Light.
Mississippi	September	½ bushel	May and June	Rich loam.
Tennessee	September 1	1 bushel	June 15 to July	Black, thin loam.
Ohio	September and Oct	1 to 1½ bush	June to July	Clay; clay, light; sandy and warm oak and hickory clay.
Indiana	September to Oct	1 to 1¼ bush	June 20 to July	Dry; just cleared.
Illinois	October and Nov	2 to 2½ bush	June 20 to July	Clay; or sandy loam.
Michigan	October 10	1½ bush	July 15th	Clay or loam.
Iowa	September	2 bushels	July	

BUCKWHEAT.

Maine	Middle of June	½ bush		
New Hampshire	June	½ bushel	August; September	Silicious.
Vermont	July 1	¼ to ½ bush	September	
New York	June 10 to July 20	½ to 1 bush	September 15 to Nov	Rich, sandy loam; sand and loam; deep black muck; light sandy.
New Jersey	July 13 to last of June	½ to 1 bush	September 15	Sandy.
Pennsylvania	June 1 to last July	½ to 1 bush	Sept. 1 to Oct. 15	Slate; sandy loam; gravel or slate.
Tennessee	May 20	1 bushel	October 15	Mountain.
Kentucky				
Ohio	Middle June to July 1	½ to 1 bush	Sept. 20 to Oct. 1	Loose loam; sandy; black, thin and compact loam.
Indiana	July 1 to August 1	½ to 1 bush	September to Oct. 1	Clay; black loam.
Illinois	June to July 1	18 to 25 ℔s	September	Sandy loam; wheat stubble; black muck.
Michigan	June 15 to July 5	½ to 2 bush	Aug. 10 to Oct. 10	Light loam; light sandy do.
Iowa	June 20	½ to 1½ bush	September 20	

INDIAN CORN.

Maine	May 20 to June 6		September	Dry, warm, deep, clay loam; gravelly.
New Hampshire	May 20	½ bushel	September and Oct	Warm, rich, silicious; any except clay.
Massachusetts	Last April to May 20		Last of Sept. to Oct	
Vermont	May 10 to 20	6 to 8 quarts	September and Oct	Sandy loam; dry loam; black slate.
New York	May 1 to June 10	4 to 12 quarts	September to Nov	Gravelly loam; sand and loam; clay loam; black, gravelly; warm loam; gravelly; sandy loam; gravelly loam; do. with sand.
New Jersey	May 2 to 10	4 to 6 qu rts	Sept. 20 to Oct. 15	Sandy loam; do.
Pennsylvania	April 15 to May 15	½ to ¼ bush	Sept. 15 to Nov	Sandy loam; sand and slate; limestone; sandy; do.; do.; loam; light; sandy; shale.
Delaware				
Virginia	March 25 to May 15	½ to ¼ bush	September and Nov	Low bottom and sandy loam; sandy loam; do.
South Carolina	March a'd April	1-10 bushel	October	Clay sub-soil grounds and bottom lands.
Georgia	March 15 to May 1	½ bushel	October	Red Hickory land; red, black loam.
Alabama	February to May 1	1-10 to 1 peck	September and Oct	Alluvial; light.
Mississippi	February to May		October	Rich bottom.
Tennessee	March to April	1-10 bushel	September and Nov	Black loam; best.
Kentucky	April and May		October and Nov	
Ohio	April and May	1-9 to ½ bush	October and Nov	Alluvium; do.; bottom land; do.; black ground; loam; sandy; black loam; loose land.
Indiana	April 1 to May 1	5½ qts. to 1¼ bu	Oct. 1 to Nov. 30	Rich, black loam; black loam; sandy bott m.
Illinois	March to May 25	6 to 10 ℔s	October to Dec	San y loams; do.; alluvial bottoms; buttoms.
Michigan	May 1 to 20	4 to 5 quarts	Sept. 20 to Oct. 15	Warm, sandy; intervale loam.
Iowa	April and May	4 qts to ½ bush	September t Nov	
Texas	February and March	1-10 bushel	Early in Aug.to Sept	

POTATOES.

States.	Time of sowing or planting.	Average bushels or pounds of seed per acre.	Time of harvest.	Best Soil.
Maine	April to June	10 bush	September	Dry.
New Hampshire	May to June 1	10 to 15 bush	September and Oct.	Gravelly; old pasture land, without manure.
Massachusetts	April and May	10 to 20 bush	September and Oct.	Dry.
Connecticut	April and May	10 bush	September and Oct.	
Vermont	April 6 to June 30	10 to 20 bush	September	Loamy, if manured; sandy, with plaster; marl.
New York	April 15 to June	8 to 15 bush	Last May to Nov. 1	Black, gravelly; sandy loam; loam; dry, sandy loam and muck.
New Jersey	Last week in March to June 10	2½ to 10 bush	July 1 to Oct. 30	Sand; loose sandy loam; loam.
Pennsylvania	April and May	2½ to 10 bush	August to October	Sandy loam; do.; light loam; light; common; sandy; do.
Maryland	May	10 bush	September	
Virginia	February to June 20	2 to 10 bush	July to November	Sand and loam; do.; calcareous loam.
South Carolina	February to April	3 to 5 bush	September to Dec.	Fresh light; grey moist.
Georgia	February to May	3 to 5 bush	Sweet, Oct. 15; common, October	Sandy; grey.
Alabama	Sweet, April		October	Light.
Mississippi	Sweet, April; common, January	Sweet, 10 to 15; common, 4 bu.	November	Sandy loam.
Tennessee	April and May	3 to 4 bush	October 15	Clay; sandy; rich.
Kentucky	April and June			
Ohio	April to June 1	8 to 20 bush	Sept. 15 to Oct. 30	Bottom; loam; sandy; stiff; rich; alluvial.
Indiana	May 1 to June 20	3 to 20 bush	July 1 to last Sept	Rich, dry, sandy loam; sandy; black loam; light, sandy; black loam.
Illinois	March and June	Common, 8 to 12; sweet, ¼ to ½ bushel	July and October	Wet clay; new and alluvial; sandy.
Michigan	May 1 to June	5 bushels	October 10	Intervale; muck or loam.
Iowa	April and May		Sept. to Nov. 1	
Texas	February 1 to 20			

HAY.

Maine			July 15 to Aug. 15	
New Hampshire		¼ bushel	July and August	Diluvial and moist; clay; moist.
Massachusetts	April and May	10 lbs. clover; 1 peck timothy	July and August	Cultivated meadows.
Vermont			July and August	Wet.
New York		½ bushel	June 25 to Aug. 20	Deep, black muck; clay loam; moist alluvial.
New Jersey	March 1	¼ bushel	June and July	Meadow; sandy loam.
Pennsylvania		½ bushel	June and August	Limestone; light loam; sandy loam; clay for timothy; loam for clover.
Maryland			July	
Virginia	In the fall	6 lbs. clover; 4 lbs. timothy	June to August 15	Sandy loam for timothy; clay for clover; sand and loam; limestone.
Tennessee	August 10	1 bushel	June and July	Low swamp for herds grass; rich clay for clover.
Kentucky				
Ohio	September or March	1-10 to ¼ bush.	Last June to Aug. 1	Loose land; bottom; black swamp; clay loam; clay; do.; limestone.
Indiana	September to Feb. 1	4 to 10 quarts	June to August 1	Sandy; stiff table land; clay; damp clay; clay; do
Illinois	February	10 quarts	June and August	Wet clay; sandy.
Michigan			July 1 to October 10	Clay; do.
Iowa		6 lbs.	June 1 to July 1	

HEMP OR FLAX.

Vermont	May	½ bushel	July	
New York	April	¼ to 1 bush	July and August	Clay sand; alluvial.
Tennessee	April 4	2 bushels	May 20	
Ohio	April to May 1	1 to 2 bush	Last July to August	Sandy
Indiana	April 1	¼ to 1 bush	July 1	Loam; clay.
Michigan	April 15 to May 20		September 1	

TOBACCO.

Maryland	May to August		September	Sandy loam.
Virginia	May to June			
Tennessee	February 20		August 1 to Sept. 20	Rich.
Ohio	April	1 bushel	August	Hickory and white oak.
Indiana	June		September	Loam.
Illinois	February		September	Manured lots.

COTTON.

States.	Time of sowing or planting.	Average bushels or pounds of seed per acre.	Time of harvest.	Best soil.
Virginia	May 1	2 bushels	October 1 to Dec. 15.	
South Carolina	April	75 pounds	Sept 1 to end Dec.	Dry and light.
Georgia	April 1	2½ bushels	Fall	Sandy; do.
Alabama	March and April	1 to 4 bush	Fall and winter	Grey.
Mississippi	March 15 to April 15	3 bushels	August till March	Black loam.
Tennessee	April 20 to May 1	2 bushels	October	Clay, light.
Texas	March and April	Not material, if plenty	August 1	

RICE.

South Carolina		100 pounds	September	
Alabama	March	½ bushel	September	Branch lands.
Tennessee	April 20	2 bushels	August	Swamp.

One of the mistakes in sending seeds long distances, except it be in the case of regular seedsmen, who understand their business, is, they are packed nearly air tight, and often in a damp state. The same is often true of seeds kept for sowing or planting. The consequence is they mold and even rot. The proper rule to be kept in view in the saving of all seeds for great lengths of time is, first, perfect dryness, at a temperature of not less than 100°, nor more than 130°, then packed in paper bags, enclosed in canvas sacks, and kept as near the freezing point as possible, and at the same time in a dry atmosphere. Hermetically sealing, and other methods of excluding the air, are not only useless but positively injurious. The following table of weights per bushel, time of sowing in the North, and quantity per acre, will be found valuable, and correct. The letter *a* signifies the months when they may be sown:

Weight per bushel.	Seed.	March.	April.	May.	June.	July.	August.	September.	October.	Quantity per acre.
60	Red clover	a	a	..	..	..	..	..	..	8 to 10 pounds.
45	Timothy	a	a	..	..	..	a	a	..	⅓ to ½ bushel.
14	Red top	..	a	a	..		a	a	..	½ to 1 "
14	Ky. blue grass	..	a	a		a	a	..	..	1½ to 2½ "
50	Hung. grass	..		a	a	..	.	.		⅓ to ½ "
50	Millet	..		a	a		..	..	..	¼ to ¾ "
45	Sorghum seed	..		a	a	..	..	..		2 quarts.
56	Flax seed	..	a	a	a	..	..		..	1 to 3 bushels.
56	Corn	.	a	a	a	..	..	..	..	4 to 6 quarts.
56	Rye	a	a	..	..	..		a	a	1 to 2 bushels.
60	Wheat	a	a	.	.	..	a	a	..	1 to 2 "
48	Barley	a	a	a	..	..	a	a	..	1½ to 2 "
32	Oats	a	a	a		..	..	..	..	2 to 3 "
52	Buckwheat	.	..	..	a	a	..	..	..	½ to ¾ "
60	Potatoes	a	a	a	a	a	..	..	.	10 to 15 "
55	S. Potatoes	..	.	a	a	..		..	..	Transplant.
..	Beets	..	a	a	a	..	..	..	.	4 to 10 pounds.
..	Carrots		a	a	a	..	..	.	.	2 to 3 "
55	Turnips	a	a	a	..	..	a	a	..	½ to 1 "
	Parsnips	a	a	a	a		..	.	..	2 to 3 "
..	Onions	a	a	..		..	.	..	..	4 to 6 "
60	White beans	..	..	a	a		..	..	..	½ to 1 bushel.
60	Pease	a	a	..	..	.	..	..	..	1½ to 2½ "

The larger quantity of flax should only be sown when the lint exclusively is wanted, and then only on exceedingly rich and mellow land. Sweet potatoes, if in hills three feet each way, will require per acre 4,840 plants. If in ridges four feet apart by sixteen inches in the row, it will take 8,166 plants. Beets, carrots, and parsnips should not be planted in June, except for the purpose of getting small and tender roots for family use. The greater number of pounds per acre is used only in field culture where many plants are necessarily lost. The quantity of peas is, for sowing broadcast, when drilled, from one to one and a half bushels only will be required. Potatoes should not be planted in June and July, except early maturing sorts. These will usually produce excellent crops after the nights become cool in the fall. It is better to plant any potatoes in March and April, than in May—except in very high latitudes. As a rule, the earlier we seasonably plant our crops in the West, the better the crops will be, except turnips, buckwheat, etc., which require cool weather to mature in. The later these are sown, having time to mature, the better the crop. The following table explains itself, and will, as well as the others given, be found valuable for reference:

	Seeds, per oz.	Length of Drill, per oz.	Vitality. Years.
Asparagus	1,000 to 1,200	50 feet.	4 to 6
Beet	1,200 to 1,500	100 "	6 to 8
Carrot	20,000 to 24,000	200 "	1 to 3
Cabbage / Cauliflower	8,000 to 12,000	Transplant.	4 to 6
Celery	50,000 to 60,000	Transplant.	3 to 5
Egg plant	5,000 to 6,000	Transplant.	5 to 6
Endive	20,000 to 24,000	Transplant.	8 to 10
Lettuce	25,000 to 30,000	400 feet.	5 to 6
Okra	500 to 600	50 "	5 to 6
Onion	7,000 to 8,000	200 "	1 to 2
Parsnip	5,000 to 6,000	200 "	1 to 2
Radish	3,000 to 4,000	100 "	4 to 5
Salsify	2,500 to 3,000	100 "	4 to 5
Spinach	2,000 to 3,000	100 "	4 to 5
Tomato	About 20,000	Transplant.	4 to 5
Turnip	8,000 to 12,000	200 feet.	6 to 7

Dwarf beans will run from 1,200 to 4,000 seeds per quart, according to the variety; Lima, Scarlet runners and other large pole varieties are much larger. The seed required per acre is from thirty-six to fifty quarts. Pease will run from 1,200 to 2,000 seeds per acre, the large marrows giving the lesser and the dwarf varieties the greater number. The seed required per acre is from thirty-six to fifty quarts of garden seed, the quantities per acre given above are more than are required to mature, but enough must be planted to insure a crop. Of potatoes, eight bushels will plant an acre in hills three feet apart each way—two pieces in each hill—if cut small, but fifteen bushels will be used in drills three feet apart, by about fifteen inches in the drill, if cut to two to three eyes. The seeds of vegetables should be attended to as they ripen, and be carefully taken care of. Thus peas, when ripe, should be pulled, and after becoming dry in the sun, ought to be immediately threshed and spread in some airy place to season. The same rule will apply to beans. Top onions may be cut and hung up, or laid in rows to cure. Shallots, black seed, and potato onions should be pulled when the tops are generally dry, but not yet withered, and placed in windrows to mature. Garlic should be tied in bunches, and hung up to dry in the shade. Lettuce, parsnip, oyster-plant, etc., should be cut and dried in the shade. If possible do not wait until the seeds are all ripe. If you do, many of the best seeds will be lost. Corn should be plucked as soon as the husk begins to dry and hung up in the air to ripen. Tomatoes and other pulpy fruits should be allowed to become entirely ripe and then broken, and macerated in water to separate the seeds. Cucumber seeds should be washed in this way. Do not allow undue fermentation, however, as it blackens the seeds. In cleaning wheat, oats, barley, and other small grain, save only the best for seed. The time to save the seed is when you are marketing your grain. Pot herbs should be cut while green, carefully and thoroughly dried in the shade, and then laid away in paper bags for future use. It will pay every farmer to grow vegetables, and also to save some of the more important seeds thereof.

SEEDING. One of the most important operations of the farm, is the equal distribution of the seed over the land, whether in drills or broadcast, so there shall be no bare spots, and that each plant may have equal room, measurably at least. In the old way of seeding by hand this was a difficult matter, even by the most practiced sowers, either from an inequality of the several casts, and especially from the contingencies of wind, and other causes beyond the control of the operator. In this direction, agricultural ingenuity has fully kept pace with invention in other directions, relating to the farm. We have now machines adapted to sowing the finest grass seeds in accurate proportions per acre, or the most bulky grains and seeds, either in drills or broadcast, and at any given depth, and in the case of drills, from the most minute garden seeds, one drill at a time to the young field seeder, which will finish twelve acres a day, leaving the seed covered at any

COMBINED SEEDER AND CULTIVATOR.

required depth, and the drills exactly equi-distant one from another. Above we give a cut of a combined seeder and cultivator. In the planting of seeds in hills or check-rows, there would seem to be little desired, the better class of check-row attachments doing away with all marking of spaces previous to planting.

SEED LIP. A sowing basket.
SEED LOBES. The fleshy substance of the seed, the *cotyledons;* there are two in dicotyledonous or exogenous plants, but one in endogens, such as grasses, cerealia, palms, etc.
SEDGES. Plants of the genus *Carex,* perennial; coarse, false grasses, growing generally in marshes and wet places.
SEGMENT. A slice, a portion cut from a solid by a line or plane
SELECTION OF SEED. (See Seed.)
SELENITE. Crystallized sulphate of lime.

SELENIUM. An elementary body closely resembling sulphur. Selenic acid is isomorphous with sulphuric acid; it is very rare.

SEMEIOTIC. Relating to the signs or symptoms of diseases.

SENECA SNAKEROOT. *Polygala senega.* A perennial-rooted, common plant, especially in the South, the roots of which are used as an expectorant.

SENNA. *Cassia senna.* A small leguminous shrub of Africa and Arabia, the leaves of which are much employed in decoction as a purge.

SENSIBLE FROG. The part of a horse's hoof immediately above the bony covering; the fleshy sole.

SENSITIVE PLANT. Plants or shrubs of the genus *Mimosa*, whose leaves fold when touched, or shaded from the sun.

SEPALS. The leaflets of the calyx.

SEPTARIA. Large nodules or masses of a marly clay found in some geological formations; when burned they form Roman cement which has the property of hardening under water.

SEPTIC. Substances or causes which hasten putrefaction.

SEPTUM, SEPTA. A partition, especially in a seed vessel.

SEQUOIA. A genus of plants to which the giant trees of California, *S. gigantia*, and the redwood, *S. Sempervirens*, belong. They are difficult to transplant, and not hardy in the North, and neither of them will probably be valuable for cultivation in the United States outside their native habitat.

SERICEUS. Silky, covered with short, soft hairs.

SERICIC or MYRISTIC ACID. An oily acid obtained from the butter of nutmegs.

SEROSITY, SEROUS FLUID. (See Serum.)

SERRICORNS. A coleopterous family, many of which have serrated antennæ.

SERUM. The fluid portion of the blood; it consists of a solution of albumen in soda, with salts, and contains seven per cent. solid matter.

SESAMOID. Small bones not larger than a pea, found at the joints of the toes and fingers.

SESQUI. One and a half. *Sesquioxide.* An oxide containing three equivalents of oxygen, and two of metal.

SESSILE. Without stalk, sitting on the stem.

SETA. A term used by botanists in various senses. It is the stalk that supports the theca, capsule, or sporangium of mosses; the awn or beard of grasses, when it proceeds from the extreme point of a palea or glume; sometimes the glandular prickles of roses, and also the abortive stamens or rudimentary perianth of cyperaceous plants.

SETACEOUS. Bristle-like. *Setose*, bristly.

SETONS. These are generally made of tapes, though sometimes fine wire or strong thread is used. Their object is to produce a running sore and constant irritation, to cure some disease, strained sinews, or in healing fistulas. They are inserted by means of a seton needle, and are to be smeared daily with some irritating ointment, and also moved forward at the same time. The ends, of course, must be knotted together to prevent their dropping out. A good ointment is made by taking one part each of oil of turpentine, and powdered cantharides, and digesting them together in a closed vessel, and then adding eight parts of Canada balsam; or the seton tape may be smeared with either oil of turpentine, or citrine ointment, according as a mild or sharp irritant is desired, or they may be mixed in the proportion of one part of turpentine to three of citrine ointment.

SEXES. In plants, the stamens and pistils; the former being called the male, and the latter the female organs, from a fanciful analogy.

SHADDOCK. An inferior but very large orange; the fruit of the *Citrus decumaria.*

SHAFT. The trunk of a column, the entrance or downward excavation of a mine; a handle.

SHAKES IN TREES. Fissures, clefts, rents, or black and rough places in trees or timber.

SHALE. A loose, rotten, or crumbling slate.

SHALLOT. *Allium ascalonicum.* A species of onion, the bulbs of which are of small size, of mild flavor, something resembling the leek, which are cultivated by planting the small sets in precisely the same manner as onion sets. They are but little cultivated.

SHANK BONE. The femur.

SHARE OF A PLOW. The point.

SHARP-SHINNED HAWK. (See Buzzard.)

SHEARLING. A sheep once shorn.

SHEEP. The antiquity of sheep, as kept for their flesh and wool, is coeval with the first dawn of civilization of mankind. The original wild type is lost in obscurity, and naturalists have conjectured in vain as to when the original race was indigenous, and from what race or races domestic sheep have sprung; some asserting the mufflon (*Ovis musmon*) of Barbary, Crete, Corsica, Sardinia, and the islands of the Grecian Archipelago to be its origin; others, the argali (*Ovis ammon*) of Siberia; while others again, consider it likely that more than one wild species have commingled to form the numerous domestic breeds. Whatever may have been the type of our common sheep, there can be no doubt that they are naturally mountainous animals. For, if left to themselves, it is always observed that they prefer hill-sides and rocky mountains to valleys and low plains; and, in the former situations, they thrive better, although they acquire less flesh than on more luxuriant soils. The domesticated sheep is pre-eminently a wool-bearing animal; yet many races seem to be destitute of this covering, particularly in tropical climates, and to be clothed with wool, so closely resembling hair as not to be distinguishable from it unless by means of a powerful lens. The mufflons and argali, that is, the wild species, are covered with a harsh kind of hair, having beneath it, at its roots, a short, spiral wool, which, in winter, becomes longer and more full. Mr. Bell, an English writer, considered the harsh hair as essentially wool in its structure, presenting the imbrications which the microscope shows to be the characteristic of wool, and on which its felting property depends; and he regards the short under-coat as composed of hair, and not of wool. Mr. Youatt makes the contrary statement, and, notwithstanding the appearances noticed by Mr. Bell, one might be inclined to the opinion of the former; for, as is well known, in the Cashmere and Angora goats, the long outer covering is hair; the under-coat exquisitely fine down, or wool. In other down or wool-bearing animals, as the beaver and otter, a similar arrangement prevails; and we know, moreover, that, in some neglected breeds of the domesticated sheep, the wool becomes mixed with long, coarse hairs, by which it is more or less obscured. Both in its natural and domesticated state, the sheep is a gregarious animal, collecting in flocks of greater or fewer numbers, according to the nature of the district it frequents, and the abundance of pasture. The more the sheep is neglected, and the less its range of pasture is circumscribed, the more will it acquire habits of independence, and the more will its instincts be drawn forth and put into exercise. In wild and mountainous districts, it has been remarked that sheep unite in self-defense, and form themselves into a phalanx in opposition to a strange dog, or a prowling fox, the rams heading the array, and presenting a formidable front to the foe, while the ewes and lambs crowd together in the rear. Should the intruder venture within a certain distance, they rush upon him and commence a violent assault. On the mountains, they display considerable boldness and agility in leaping from crag to crag, and frequently climbing about the whole surface of the almost perpendicular sides of the precipitous rocks, by treading upon the narrow ledges and projections, which scarcely afford them room to stand. In these apparently dangerous situations, sometimes at a height of several hundred feet, and with the billows of the ocean roaring beneath them, they show that they are not such cowardly and stupid beings as they have been described. They exhibit great intrepidity, and a full confidence in their skill, vieing with the goat in sureness of step and strength of spring, when they are ascending to the summit by repeated bounds. With regard to the courage of sheep may be instanced the boldness with which the ewe not unfrequently defends her offspring from danger, and the desperate combats often occurring between the rams, actuated by a feeling of mutual jealousy; for, as soon as they come together, they rush headlong at each other with immense force, the concussion of their heads being audible at a very considerable distance. The skin of sheep is composed of three textures. Externally is the cuticle or scarf-skin, which is thin, tough, devoid of feeling, and pierced by innumerable minute holes, through which pass the fibers of the wool and the insensible perspiration. It seems to be of a scaly texture. This is plain to be seen when the sheep have the scab. Below this is the *rete mucosum*, a soft structure, its fibers having scarcely more consistence than mucilage, and being with great difficulty separated from the skin beneath. This seems to be placed as a defense to the terminations of the blood-vessels and nerves of the skin, and these are in a manner enveloped and covered by it. Beneath is the cutis or true skin, composed of innumerable minute fibers crossing each other in every direction, highly elastic, in order to fit closely to the parts beneath, and to yield to the various motions of the body. Judging from the mixture of wool and hair in the coat of most animals, it is thought by some that the primitive sheep had a hairy covering. It is said that there are, at the present day, varieties of sheep that are clothed outwardly with hair of different degrees of fineness, and underneath the external coat is a softer, shorter, and closer one that answers to the description of fur, but which really possesses all the characteristics of wool. It is, therefore, highly improbable that the

sheep, which has now become, by cultivation, the wool-bearing animal, should, in any country, have ever been entirely destitute of wool. Sheep of almost every variety have at times been in the gardens of the Zoological Society of London, but there has not been one on which a portion of crisped wool, although exceedingly small, has not been found at the bottom of the hair. The filament of the wool has scarcely pushed itself through the pores of the skin, when it has to penetrate through another and singular substance, which, from its adhesiveness and color, is called the yolk. It is found in greatest quantity about the breast and shoulders, the very parts that produce the best and most abundant wool, and in proportion as it extends to any considerable degree over other parts, the wool is then improved. It differs in quantity in different breeds; it is very abundant in the Merino. The yolk being a true soap, soluble in water, accounts for the comparative ease with which the sheep, that have the natural proportion of it, are washed in a running stream. The fiber of the wool having penetrated the skin and escaped from the yolk, is of a circular form, generally larger toward the extremity and also toward to root, and in some instances very considerably so. When the animal is in good condition, and the fleece healthy, the appearance of the fiber is brilliant, but when the state of the constitution is bad the fiber has a dull appearance, and either a wan, pale light, or sometimes scarcely any, is reflected. The age of the sheep is generally determined by their teeth. When they are about one year and a half old, they shed their two center teeth of the incisors, and two wide ones grow out and take their place. The next year the next two are shed, and when the sheep is three years old the four central teeth are fully grown. At four years they have six teeth, and at five years the teeth are perfectly developed. This is one year before the horse or ox can be said to be fully mouthed. This rule for the age of sheep will hardly ever fail in ewes, but sometimes will in the case of rams. If not too old, their age may be determined by the growth of their horns each year. The difference caused in the shedding of their teeth may be by the manner in which the sheep are cared for. If well fed and kept in a thriving condition, they will shed them faster, and *vice versa*. Some sheep with the full mouth will hold their teeth much longer than others. The natural age of sheep is about ten years, to which time they will thrive and breed well if in good health. Sheep husbandry was early undertaken in the United States, but has been subjected to great vicissitudes. Sheep were imported into the colony of Virginia as early as 1609, and they increased by 1648 to three thousand. The Dutch West India Company introduced them about the year 1625, but they proved to be too much of a temptation for dogs and wolves, for it is recorded that in 1643 there were but sixteen in that whole colony. They were kept upon the islands in Boston Harbor as early as 1633, and two years after there were ninety-two in the vicinity of Portsmouth, N. H. It became the universal practice in the good old days of homespun for the farmer to keep a number sufficient to clothe his family. The old native sheep was a coarse, long-legged, and unprofitable animal, and there was no improvement made in the breeding till toward the close of the last century, when, in 1793, the first merinoes, or fine-wooled sheep, were imported by William Foster, of Boston. They were wholly unappreciated, were given to a gentleman to keep, and he, knowing nothing of their value, simply ate them, and a few years after was buying the same class of sheep at $1,000 per head. The embargo of 1808 induced many to turn their attention to fine-wooled sheep, and soon very large numbers of merino sheep were imported and distributed throughout the United States, and our modern sheep-husbandry, now grown up to its proportional importance, may be said to date from these importations. The finest wooled sheep are now most extensively produced in the United States and in Australia. Next comes France, and then Spain. Mutton sheep have been carried to great perfection in England, and of late years, this industry has been a constantly increasing one through the importation of the best representatives of the middle and long-wooled breeds. Of the English breeds, the report to the Government of the United States, following the Vienna Exhibition, states the characteristics of prominent English breeds as follows: The British breeds are most naturally divided according to altitudes and fertility of their habitat. The large breeds, white, hornless, and bearing long wool with small felting property, occupy the rich alluvial districts, the lands reclaimed from the sea, and the highly cultivated and very productive farm-areas. These are the Leicester, Lincoln, Romney-Marsh, Cotswold, the few remaining of the Devonshire Notts, the Roscommon, and similar Irish sheep. Next should be classed the sheep of the chalk-downs, the commons, and forests, suited to a dry and temperate climate. There are the Downs of several families, perhaps now to be taken as breeds, the Dorsets and their congeners, the pink-nosed Somersets. They produce a short, felting-wool, suited to inferior grades of goods. The Ryeland, formerly found in the western counties, and esteemed for producing the finest cloth-wool of England, is now almost extinct. The third general division comprises the mountain breeds, first the Cheviots of the hills of the North of England and borders of Scotland; the Black-face of the central chain of mountains and moors northward from Derbyshire to the mountains of Scotland; and two varieties of Welsh mountain-sheep, and the Kerry and other mountain-breeds of Ireland. There are many local remnants of the ancient stock allied to the above, but there are none worthy of special mention. The weight of fleece of British sheep averages about five pounds. The Lincolns may be placed at eight pounds, the Cotswolds nearly the same, the Leicesters at seven, the Downs at four, the Cheviots at three, the Black-faces at two and one-half, and the Welsh at two. The Leicesters are most numerous, exceeding one-third of all; the Downs one-sixth, the Black-faces nearly as many, Cheviots one-eighth, leaving about one-fifth for other breeds. The heavy breeds of eighty years ago, modified mainly by the Leicester, now furnish lighter fleeces. For instance, the Lincoln, as reported by Hon. Robert R. Livingston, then yielded eleven pounds; the Teeswater and Cotswold, nine pounds. These are, of course, average weights, as rams as well as pampered ewes and wethers, greatly exceed the average. The weight of carcase exceeds by twenty per cent. the weight of imported mutton, and averages sixty pounds; by some estimates, sixty-five pounds. A brief reference to this improvement, with the characteristic points and present status of the principal breeds, will indicate more fully the progress of the century in sheep-husbandry. Leicesters.—The Leicestershire sheep, in the beginning of the Bakewell era of improvement, were known by their names, the old Leicesters, the new Leicesters, or Dishleys, (the latter from Bakewell's place of residence,) and the forest-sheep. The Dishley experiment commenced in 1755, and was continued so successfully that the rams of this famous flock ultimately commanded $15,000 as hire for the season, giving an impetus to the improvement which was perpetuated by the permanence and desirability of the results achieved, until the breed assumed a position which has been maintained to the present time. The original Leicester upon which Bakewell commenced his experiment was an animal of large frame, with heavy bone and coarse-grained meat, a flat-sided carcase, and legs large and rough. It was a slow feeder and necessarily late in reaching maturity, weighing at two or three years old 100 to 120 pounds. Seeing the necessity of obtaining, in addition to the fleece, the largest possible increase of flesh in proportion to the food consumed, in the shortest period of time, he bred by selection most persistently and skillfully for these objects. With these aims always in view, he chose with rare judgment, yet with a broad latitude as to breed or family, such animals as would approximate his ideal of compactness and symmetry, refinement of bone, a reduction of the proportion of unprofitable parts, and higher capacity for rapid conversion of food to flesh. After securing this result by animals of characteristics so widely differing from those of the original stock, he found necessary a rigid adhesion to the practice of in and in breeding to keep the advantage gained, until a fixedness of type had been secured which should impress itself surely and indelibly upon any race which might be selected for improvement. In accomplishing results of such practical value, with all possible care to retain the sound constitution and great hardiness of the old stock, there was perhaps inevitably induced a comparative delicacy, a reduction in size, a decrease in prolificness and excellence as nurses. These defects have indeed demanded the wisest judgment in the infusion of fresh strains of blood, by which the stamina of the race has been fortified, and its popularity maintained until the present day, to such a degree that the Leicester blood is far more widely diffused than that of any other breed, even modifying essentially all the long-wool races, and to some extent the mountain breeds, and some families of the short-wool Downs. The true type of this breed, as understood by Youatt, is thus described: The head should be hornless, long, small, tapering toward the muzzle, and projecting horizontally forward. The eyes prominent, but with a quiet expression. The ears thin, rather long, and directed backward. The neck full and broad at its base, where it proceeds from the chest, so that there is, with the slightest possible elevation, one continued horizontal line from the rump to the

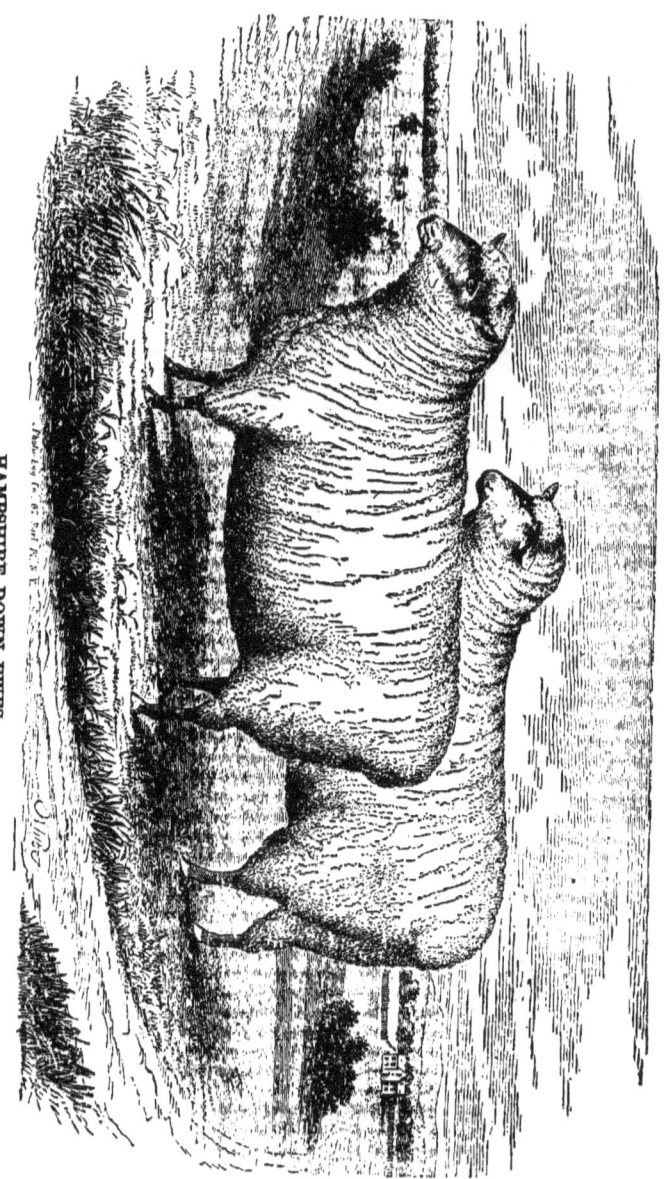

HAMPSHIRE DOWN EWES.

(851)

poll. The breast broad and round, and no uneven or angular formation where the shoulders join either neck or the back; particularly no rising of the withers or hollow behind the situation of these bones. The arm fleshy through its whole extent, and even down to the knee. The bones of the leg small, standing wide apart; no looseness of skin about them, and comparatively bare of wool. The chest and barrel at once deep and round, the ribs forming a considerable arch from the spine, so as in some cases, and especially when the animal is in good condition, to make the apparent width of the chest even greater than the depth. The barrel ribbed well home; no irregularity of line on the back or belly, but on the sides; the carcase very gradually diminishing in width toward the rump. The quarters long and full, and, as with the fore legs, the muscles extending down to the hock; the thighs also wide and full. The legs of a moderate length; the pelt also moderately thin, but soft and elastic, and covered with a good quantity of white wool. The Leicester requires less food in proportion to weight than any other race. They are mostly sold early in the summer or early autumn after their first year, many wethers at twelve to fifteen months weighing twenty to twenty-five pounds per quarter; and at two years they attain the weight of thirty to thirty seven pounds. The fleeces are valuable as fine combing-wool, and, if well grown, weigh from seven to eight pounds each. The earliest record of this breed in the United States is a mention by Custis of the Bakewell ewes on the estate of Washington, from which, through a cross by a Persian ram, was derived the somewhat famous Arlington long-wooled sheep. The influence of this and other long-wool flocks of Virginia gave a popularity to the English races which has continued to the present day, though the preference at present appears to be given to the Merinoes, especially since the war and its accompanying destitution and lack of thrift. Kentucky also gives a preference to the Leicester, as a fit companion to the short-horn bullock upon the blue-grass pastures. They are to be found in small numbers in the Middle and Ohio Valley States, generally in a semi-degenerate state, not bred up to the modern standard of the perfect Leicester in his English home. The mutton of Leicesters is too fat to suit American taste, yet that of grades is quite palatable, though coarse-grained, with too much outside fat. Even in England must of animals two years old is less valuable than that of lambs or shearings; and the price is always materially lower than mutton of Southdowns and the mountain races. Border Leicesters.— More than a century ago some of the sheep-folds of the border were reinforced by Leicestershire sheep of established repute. Early in the present century representatives of the Dishley stud began a contribution to the improvement, which has been continued until they have won a distinct position in the show-yard and in popular esteem. The characteristics of this breed, as given by Mr. John Wilson, are extraordinary aptitude to fatten and early maturity. He says: The most marked feature in their structure is the smallness of their heads and of their bones generally, as contrasted with their weight of carcase. They are clean in the jaws, with a full eye, thin ears, and placid countenance. Their backs are straight, broad, and flat; the ribs arched, the belly carried very light, so that they present nearly as straight a line below as above; the chest is wide, the skin very mellow, and covered with a beautiful fleece of long, soft wool, which weighs, on the average, from six to seven pounds. On good soils, and under careful treatment, these sheep are currently brought to weigh from eighteen to twenty pounds a quarter at fourteen months old, at which age they are now generally slaughtered. At this age their flesh is tender and juicy, but when carried on until they are older and heavier, fat accumulates so unduly in proportion to the lean meat as to detract from its palatableness and market value. Cotswolds. —This is one of the largest English breeds, though the improved race is smaller than the originals, on account of the influence of the Leicester element in its amelioration. As a breed it is of great antiquity. It has gained in fleece and form, and comes to maturity earlier; is more prolific than the Leicester, and has greater strength of constitution; is often fattened at fourteen months, yielding fifteen to twenty pounds per quarter, and twenty to thirty if kept till two years old. The fleece is six to eight inches in length, and sometimes much longer; is strong, somewhat coarse, of good color, and yields a heavy fleece. The mutton is superior to that of the Leicester, with a smaller proportion of fat, and the sheep are also superior to that popular breed in weight of wool, size, hardiness, and vitality. They are possessed of good figure, have a large head, well set on, a broad chest, a well-rounded barrel, and a straight back. They are often used for crossing upon other breeds, and for obtaining earlier market-lambs, both in this country and in Europe. They are more widely disseminated in this country than any other long-wool, and preserve well the popularity which they have attained here. Some imported sheep of this breed have borne fleeces in this country of eighteen pounds. Lincolns.—The old Lincolns, of the fertile meadows of Lower Lincolnshire, were remarkable beyond any contemporary breed for coarse and heavy forms and length of wool, the fleeces weighing ten to twelve pounds. They were hornless, with large limbs, hollow flanks, and flat sides. They shared with the Romney-Marsh sheep the alluvial and fen districts, consumed largely their rank pasturage and fattened slowly. When the fame of Bakewell at Dishley was rising to its zenith, recourse was had to his improved Leicesters for improvement in the flesh-taking property, and this course of crossing was pursued to the close of the eighteenth century, and indeed to the present time, as found necessary, for the purpose of securing a better form and earlier maturity without losing wholly their peculiarities of size and length of fiber. For at least a quarter of a century a sharp contest was waged between the supporters of the old and the new, the former fearing the loss of hardiness and local adaptation, as well as its unrivaled peculiarities of fleece, while the latter were quite willing to risk any or all of these results in the belief that more mutton and wool and money could be realized upon each acre of area than with the modified Lincolns. And the latter ultimately prevailed, and verified the correctness of their theory. The effect of this change upon the wool has been to make it shorter and finer, and to diminish somewhat its softness of fiber. It is a question whether the peculiar quality of the wool could have been retained in larger degree without essential injury to its mutton producing quality. This district of country still continues to produce the largest sheep of Great Britain, with fleeces superior in weight and value to any other. They are not equal in earliness of maturity to the Leicesters, but they are profitable, and suitable to the rich lands they occupy, wethers frequently attaining the enormous weight of fifty to sixty pounds per quarter. Romney-Marsh.—There is another breed of English sheep inhabiting the rich alluvial soil of Kent, known as the Romney-Marsh sheep, which pertinaciously retains its distinctive features, though modified and improved by recent breeding. It is a large sheep, not very symmetrical in form, having narrow forequarters and flat sides, and coarse bone and muscle. It has a white face, a long and thick head, and a tuft of wool on the forehead. The wool is of more value than the mutton, perhaps, (but not being profitable without it,) being long, fine and lustrous, and in demand at good prices for export to Flanders and to France, for the manufacture of cloth of gold and similar fabrics. Other breeds have been introduced upon the marshes, but can not maintain themselves in competition with the Romneys. The country is flat, open to the east, and very bleak, yet these sheep live through the winter in the open fields, and have little protection or supplied food. The ewes are comparatively prolific, about thirty per cent. of doubles being expected in reproduction. The lambs come late, after the severity of the winter is over. With a good course of turnip feeding after the first wintering they can be brought to seventeen pounds, sometimes to eighteen pounds, per quarter, yet they are more frequently kept over a second winter. They are not very early in maturing, and grass is the main reliance for growth if not for fattening. There are cattle on the farms, but sheep greatly predominate and furnish the principal profits. The pasture lands of the marsh differ greatly in productiveness. There are feeding lands, keeping two or three ewes in winter and twice as many in summer; and the fattening lands keep four or five sheep per acre. The original Sussex or Southdowns have probably the purest blood, free from admixture during the long period which covers the rise and development of the British wool-manufacture and the increase of meat production, of any race of British sheep. Their improvement has been long-continued and is still continuing, apparently without the necessity of recurrence to any foreign blood for amelioration of a single objectionable point. While they have been greatly improved, progress has invariably been in the direction indicated in the distant past, and not by radical and violent changes. It has been carried on, there is little reason to doubt, solely by selection, there being little, if any positive evidence that the Leicester or other blood has aided in the amelioration. In the production of Hampshire and Shropshire and other breeds bearing the Down name, it is well known that other blood has been effectively used; but it should be remembered that these families, or rather breeds, are not really improved Downs, but have come from selected individuals of other hardy, primitive breeds, molded into a modification of the Southdown type by large and repeated infusion of that blood, with occasional dashes of Leicester to give greater size and aptitude for fattening. The changes effected in the true South (or Sussex) Downs have been mainly these: Speckled faces have been changed to a uniform tint of brown or fawn color, sometimes almost a gray; the forehead and cheeks have been partially covered with wool; a greater symmetry of form has been obtained; a larger size and greater fattening aptitude. The flock of Lord Walsingham exhibits some deviation from the Sussex type, having somewhat greater length and a decided development of the forequarter, giving greater weight at the expense of somewhat reduced value to the butcher. They are splendid animals, and have been largely sought by continental purchasers, though disapproved by many breeders of pure Southdowns. By reason of its purity the Southdown, perhaps, has stamped its peculiarities on its cross-bred offspring more certainly and strongly than any other of the English breeds; and for this reason, together with its hardiness and the unsurpassed quality of its mutton, it is deemed of greater practical value in its crosses than in its pure-bred flocks. But for the fact that quantity and quickness in lamb production are of more pecuniary value than superior quality, it would far surpass the Leicester in its prevalent use for cross-bred early lambs. It is now considerably more than one hundred years since Mr. Ellman, of Glynde, Sussex, sought a more symmetrical and profitable form, and a superior flesh and fat producing habit, without injury to constitution or fecundity; and he pursued his object slowly, cautiously, with a judgment, patience, zeal, and intelligent liberality that insured success. The light forequarters, narrow chests, and long necks and limbs were totally changed. This is the description given by Mr. Ellman, himself, to his improved sheep: The head small and hornless; the face speckled or gray, and neither too long nor too short; the lips thin, and the space between the nose and the eyes narrow; the under jaw, or chop, fine and thin; the ears tolerably wide and well covered with wool, and the forehead also, and the whole space between the ears well protected by it as a defense against the fly; the eye full and bright, but not prominent; the neck of medium length, thin toward the head, but enlarging toward the shoulders, where it should be broad and high, and straight in its whole course above and below. The breast should be wide, deep, and projecting forward between the fore legs, indicating a good constitution, and a disposition to thrive. Corresponding with this, the shoulders should be on a level with the back, and not too wide above; they should bow outward from the top to the breast, indicating a springing rib beneath and leaving room for it, the ribs coming out horizontally from the spine, and extending far backward, and the last rib projecting more than the others; the back flat from the shoulders to the setting on of the tail; the loin broad and flat; the rump long and broad, and the tail set on high, and nearly on a level with the spine; the hips wide, and the space between them and the last rib on either side as narrow as possible, and the ribs, generally speaking, presenting a circular form like a barrel; the belly as straight as the back; the legs neither too long nor too short; the forelegs straight from the breast to the foot, not bending inward at the knee, and standing far apart both before and behind; the hocks having a direction rather outward, and the twist, or the meeting of the thighs behind, being particularly full; the bones fine, yet having no appearance of weakness, and of a speckled or dark color. The belly well defended with wool, and the wool coming down before and behind to the knee and to the hock; the wool short, close, curled, and fine, and free from spiry projecting fibers. The Dorsets.—A very ancient race of sheep is found in the county of Dorset, which formerly included a large tract of country. It has some resemblance to the Merino in form, but none in other respects. In 1749 they were described by Ellis as having white fleeces, white and short legs, broad loins, and fine curled wool. They still have white legs and faces, and show some increase in length of limb and in weight of fleece, which averages about four pounds of fine wool without sufficient softness for goods of first quality. Its great distinguishing peculiarities, which prevent its extinction as a breed, are its early breeding and fecundity, rendering it popular for early lambs, dropped in October, and fit for table at Christmas. There is a paying demand for them raised as house-lambs for the London market. Either Leicester or Southdown rams, preferably the latter, are generally employed, making the lambs a Dorset cross. Some have attributed their peculiarities to an origin in a warm climate; others to the comparative mildness of climate, a calcareous soil, and to the abundance of thyme and aromatic plants in the herbage. These sheep are hardy, food well, subsist on scanty pasturage, and wethers at three years old furnish mutton weighing eighteen pounds per quarter. While their range has been reduced by the predominance of the modern Leicesters and Southdowns, they maintain a better footing in the county of Somerset than in Dorset itself, exhibiting here slight difference in type, especially showing a pink-colored nose like the Merino, and often called the pink-nosed Somerset. They have also somewhat greater length of wool, larger lambs, and mutton heavier per quarter. Other varieties of the Dorset group, inhabiting the older commons of the south and west of England, are nearly extinct, though traces of them may still be found. One variety, inhabiting the isle of Portland, still exists in a state of purity. They are small, gentle, of good form, with a tinge of dun on the face and legs. Their wool is of medium fineness, weighing two pounds per fleece. The wethers often produce mutton weighing ten pounds per quarter. Welsh mountain-sheep.—The Welsh is another mountain-breed, indigenous, and still unmodified in the higher elevations, while they are the basis of the more cultivated flocks inhabiting the more productive valleys. They are small, weighing as store-sheep about seven pounds per quarter. The head is small and well set up, the poll clean, except sometimes a tuft upon the forehead; the females generally hornless; the faces unusually white, with occasional instances of gray, speckled, or rusty brown. They are narrow-chested, low-shouldered, high-rumped, long-tailed, active in movement, having little regard for fences or hedges, hardy and thrifty on scanty herbage. The wool is fine, though not very even in quality; fleeces weighing about two pounds. They are not prolific, as one lamb is enough for a mother to care for in mountain pastures, but are good nurses, and are sought for on that account for breeding fat lambs from Leicester or Down crosses. In the winter, just before the lambing-season, the ewes are brought down from the mountain-wilds and supplied with small quantities of hay or oats; if the latter, sheaf-oats are used, as the little Welsh sheep would not know what to do with clear grain. Lambs kept in the flock are shorn in July or August; and after weaning, the mothers are milked for a month or two, and butter is made, or the milk is used to improve skim-cheese. They are too wild for ordinary farm economy of the lowlands, a new lot brought home disappearing in all directions if allowed the opportunity to scatter, and sometimes found on the roofs of neighboring cottages. Cheviots or other breeds do not thrive in their mountain-home, rendering it probable that they will not be superseded, though they may be modified. Cheviots.—As the Black-faces monopolize the higher mountain-lands, the Cheviots occupy the lower elevations, the hills of the border counties between England and Scotland. They have been systematically improved by the use of carefully selected rams of Lincolnshire, before the day of the improved Lincoln race. It has been claimed that the Leicester blood produced the improvement, but the hardiness of the breed and the testimony of the breeders tend to invalidate the opinion. They were formerly light in bone and wool, of scraggy frame, but with a constitution wonderfully hardy. Draining of lands, provision of shelter, and a greater abundance, both of summer and winter food, have aided the efforts of the breeder, and the result has been one of the most useful and profitable of known breeds of sheep. No animal has contributed so much to the prosperity of the Scottish border and hill farms as the Cheviot sheep. Their mutton ranks very high in Smithfield market, and some people give it a preference over the game-flavored mutton of the Black-face. These sheep obtain their name from a range of hills running through the border counties of England and Scotland. The original improver of greatest repute is William Robson, of Bilford, who commenced his operations a century ago, and his flock became the nucleus of the ram-supply of all that region for many years. They are considered very useful for crossing with border Leicesters. Roscommons.—Connaught has been for a long period the principal sheep-breeding section of Ireland, and the source of supplies furnished to the great Ballinasloe fair for the graziers of all other parts of the green isle. Culley described the original stock of Connaught as the most awkward and ungainly sheep to be found in the kingdom, with nothing to recommend them but their size. These sheep are supported by very long, thick, crooked, gray legs; their heads long and ugly, with large, flagging ears, gray faces, and sunken eyes; necks long, and set on below the shoulders; breasts narrow and short, hollow before and behind the shoulders; flat-sided, with high, narrow, herring-backs, hind quarters drooping, and tail set low; in short they are almost in every respect contrary to what be apprehended a well-formed sheep should be; and it is to be lamented that more attention has not been paid to the breeding of useful stock in an island so fruitful in pasturage as Ireland. The spirit of improvement reached this district; the smuggling of English animals, the importation of which was strictly prohibited, begat a desire for superior style and more satisfactory returns. At length the restriction was removed, and their improvement was very vigorously conducted, the first means employed being a Leicester cross, by which the form was improved and the wool lost much of its coarseness. When it assumed the distinctive and fixed peculiarities of a new breed, it took the name of the Roscommon sheep. The breeders manifested much judgment in perfecting its points and skill in selecting the individuals by which it was accomplished. For the past generation the progress made has been remarkable, compelling the Royal Agricultural Society and the Royal Dublin Society, which for a long time admitted them in a mixed class to their shows, to recognize them as a distinct breed of long-wools. The following statement of their present status is given by the editor of the *Irish Farmer's Gazette:* The old Connaught breed of sheep were never fattened until they were three or four years old, when they made great weights, but the mutton was coarse. In consequence of the improvement which has been made in the breed, shearling-wedders, are now sold fat to the butcher, making from twenty-five pounds to over thirty pounds per quarter; but, as a general rule, the Roscommon graziers hold them over until they are thirty months old, at which age they are generally sold in Ballinasloe fair, at prices varying from three to four guineas each, to Leinster graziers, by whom the sheep are kept until they are about three years old, when, they make from thirty-six pounds and upward per quarter. Draft ewes, fed after being cast for breeding, weigh from thirty-four pounds to forty pounds per quarter, and the quality of the mutton is unexceptionable. It must be understood that the Roscommon sheep are, in general, reared entirely upon grass, with the help of some hay during winter. Turnip-feeding does not, as in Great Britain, form a material point in sheep-farming as conducted in Roscommon, there being only one acre of turnips grown in that country to each 109 acres of area. These sheep, from first to last, are for the most part reared and fattened without seeing a turnip. In all cases where turnip-feeding is pursued, the Roscommon sheep prove that early maturity, along with heavy weights, has become one of their characteristics; so that if turnip-growing were extended in the west of Ireland, it is only reasonable to believe that Connaught would produce much larger supplies of sheep. A breed of sheep has long been known with enlarged and very fat tails, and were at one time regarded with considerable favor. They are now extremely rare, being unprofitable in both flesh and wool. The American Merino is acknowledged to be the best fine-wooled sheep in America, if indeed it now has a superior in the world. It has been disseminated into every State and Territory of the United States and Canada, and has been largely exported to every

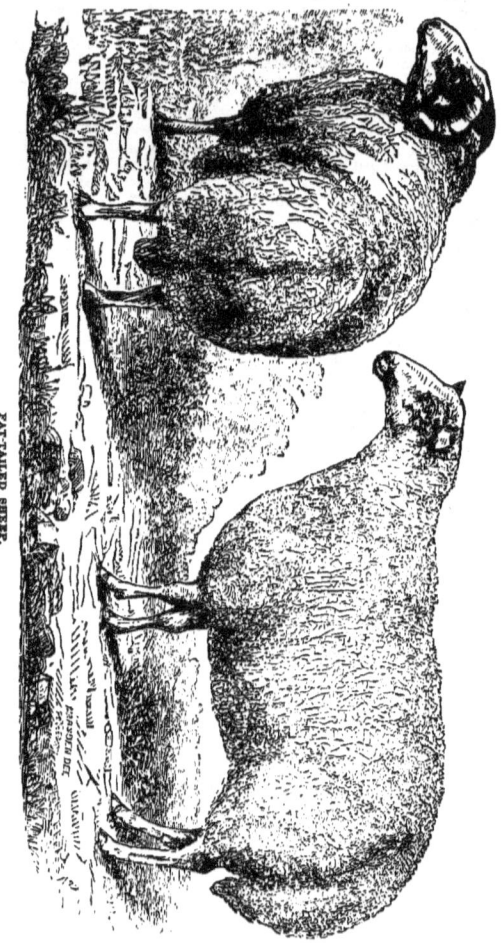

FAT-TAILED SHEEP.

country in the world, where the raising of fine wool is made a leading industry. The introduction of fine wooled sheep into the United States, and the establishment of the American Merino was principally brought about by the introduction of Spanish blood. The history of their introduction is as follows: Wm Foster, of Boston, Mass., imported three Merino sheep from Spain into that city in 1793. They were given to a friend, who killed them for mutton! In 1801 M. Dupont de Nemours, and a French banker named Delessert, sent four ram lambs to the United States. All perished on the passage but one, which was used for several years in New York, and subsequently founded some excellent grade flocks for his owner, E. I. Dupont, near Wilmington Del. The same year, Seth Adams, of Zanesville, O., imported into Boston a pair of Spanish sheep which had been brought from Spain into France. In 1802, Mr. Livingston, American Minister in France, sent home two pairs of French Merinos, purchased from the Government flock at Chalons. In 1809 and 1810, Mr. Jarvis, American Consul at Lisbon, bought and shipped to the United States about 3,850 sheep. Of these, 300 were Aqueirres, 200 Escuriels, and 200 Montarcos, the rest Paulars and Negrettis. French Merinos, and also Saxon Merinos, were also introduced. These crosses, however, worked damage wherever introduced. The incomparable American Merinos that have shown themselves so well adapted to a great range of climate and conditions, have been the result of careful crossing of selected animals with reference to weight and fineness of wool, perpetuated for the last fifty years by careful selection. Thus, as at present constituted, they would suffer by crossing upon any other breed, and they will hold their own with the best flocks of any country, all things considered. In relation to the general management of sheep, the following extracts from a carefully written article by Mr. T. M. Younglove to the Department of Agriculture will be found to carefully cover all the essential points. He says: I know of no more definite way of arriving at the profits of wool-growing than to refer to the common custom of letting sheep. Occasionally a flock of ewes are let to double in three years. This is an annual interest of thirty-three and one-third per cent. The more common practice is to let them for two pounds of wool per head annually, returning the original number. Assuming the ewe to be worth three dollars per head, and the wool an average of forty cents per pound, it gives eighty cents for the use of one sheep, or twenty-six and two-thirds per cent. This is certainly a very good interest for the owner of the sheep. Now let us see what the taker has for his care and trouble. With reasonable care he can count upon raising three lambs from every four ewes, or seventy-five per cent. increase; which, if they be worth $1.50 per head, would be over $1.12 cents per head for the increase of each ewe. This, added to the wool left after paying the two pounds to the owner, (assuming that they would shear four pounds,) is eighty cents—making one dollar and ninety-two and one-half cents for his portion. The cost of keeping a single sheep for the entire year is variously estimated at from one dollar to one dollar and fifty cents per head. Taking the highest figure, it still leaves over forty cents clear profit, after paying the owner over twenty-six per cent. annual interest. But this is only upon a flock of breeding ewes, which may be set down as about two-fifths of each flock. The other three-fifths will pay a little more than pay for their keeping. Allowing them to shear four pounds, at forty cents, gives one dollar and sixty cents. But this portion of the flock will shear more in proportion to their weight of carcase,

and require much less care and attention than the breeding ewes. Upon this branch of wool-growing very much depends. Upon the form of the carcase depend not only the powers of endurance, but the capability to produce the greatest possible amount of wool to the least weight of carcase. It is quite as impossible to put a strong and healthy constitution as it is to put a heavy fleece upon a sheep with long, slender legs and neck, and a thin, lathy, loose body. In order to secure the many desirable good qualities which go to make up a first-class flock of sheep, great care is taken in the selection of a buck with reference to the particular flock of ewes with which he is to be put. As one buck is sufficient to serve from one to two hundred ewes, very much depends upon him, as he is to impart, in a great measure, his qualities to the entire flock. Some bucks, although possessing all the desired qualities of form and fleece, yet fail to infuse into their stock their many good qualities, and are, therefore, rejected as not good stock bucks. But when one is found that seems to impart all the valuable qualities of the sire to the entire stock, he is very properly termed a decided stock-getter, and is prized accordingly. One hundred dollars is not deemed an excessive price for a good stock buck. In some cases fancy prices even beyond this have been paid. It is not uncommon for a buck in prime of life, weighing from one hundred and twenty-five to one hundred and fifty pounds, to shear twenty pounds annually of unwashed wool. Bucks that are valued highly are not risked the exposure of a cold bath for the purpose of washing the wool upon the sheep. Constitutional defects of body or fleece in a flock of ewes can easily be corrected by using a buck that shows strength where the other is weak. A common custom is to turn the buck loose with the flock of ewes which he is desired to serve, and to give them no further attention. This will do very well where only a few ewes are to be served by one buck; but when it is desired to have one buck serve a large number, it may be done much more effectually by keeping the buck up, and ewes only taken to him when in heat, such being selected from the flock, by the aid of a buck, with an apron called a teaser. Some allow the buck to run with the flock during the daytime, and keep him up through the night. From observation of the different modes, I think the better way is to allow the buck to run with the ewes from the time the flock is brought to the yard at night until they are turned away in the morning, and so keep the buck in the stable during the day. This gives the buck an opportunity to go through the flock before they lie down at night and again in the morning, and not only the buck, but the whole flock of ewes are allowed to feed at their leisure through the day. There are few males in the whole of the animal race more cruel or abusive to the female than the buck, for he will follow and butt or hook until both are worried down. From this practice an observing breeder will readily see that extraordinary exertion of the ewe brings her readily to the wants of the buck. In case it is desired to have the ewe ready for the buck when put together, it can easily be effected by driving the flock of ewes briskly for a half or a whole mile before being brought to the yard. They will then be found in a particularly pleas-

NUMBER ENGAGED
In all Gainful Occupations, and the Relative Percentage in each.

TOTAL LABORING POPULATION, 17,392,099.

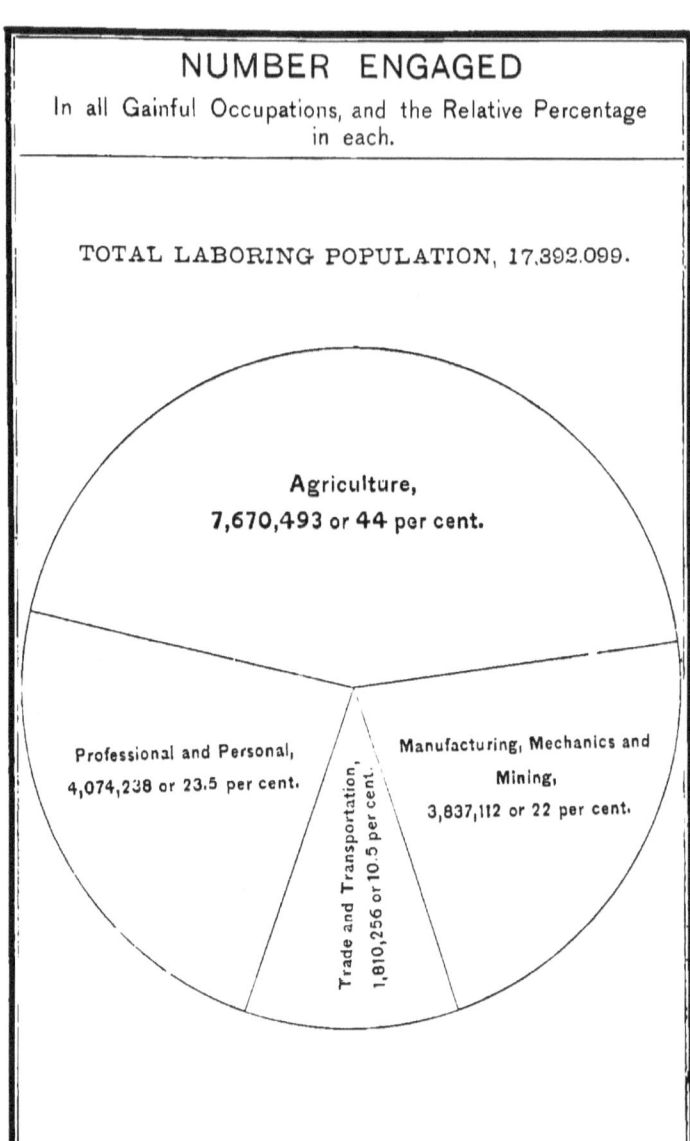

Agriculture, 7,670,493 or 44 per cent.

Professional and Personal, 4,074,238 or 23.5 per cent.

Manufacturing, Mechanics and Mining, 3,837,112 or 22 per cent.

Trade and Transportation, 1,810,256 or 10.5 per cent.

ant mood. If the buck is stabled, and the ewes brought to him in this manner, he is served much labor, and will consequently serve more ewes in a given time, without fatigue or exhaustion of the system, than if allowed to run with the flock. A buck treated in this manner will serve one hundred ewes without materially impairing his condition or the offspring, and will be as strong and healthy at the close of lambing as at the beginning. Lambs should be dropped at the particular season when the ewe first obtains a scanty supply of grass, and consequently must be varied in different localities. If allowed to drop earlier, the ewe gives but a poor supply of milk, many of the young ones, and those in low condition, none at all. In this case many of the ewes that have no milk will refuse to own the lamb, and many of the lambs get a stunt, of which they recover, if at all, but slowly, and the flock will be of all sizes. If allowed to drop later in the season, when the ewe has obtained sufficient grass to enable her to give a flow of milk, and the whole system becomes invigorated by it, the offspring too often attains an over growth, so that even the services of the most skillful midwife are not sufficient, and frequently both mother and lamb die from this cause. Another serious difficulty of late lambing is, that unless the lamb draws both teats soon after its birth, the ewe suffers from an over abundance of milk, and frequently inflammation follows. The lamb should be castrated at from one to three days old. The lamb should be held by an assistant, who should set the lamb upon his back just back of the hips, taking the fore and hind legs of each in each hand, putting the fore legs outside of the hind, and hold them firmly just above the knee joints. The operator takes hold of the pouch and pulls it gently, so as to get as much as possible of it, and then with a sharp knife at a single stroke takes off the pouch pretty close to the testicle. Then take a firm hold of each testicle separately between the fore finger and thumb of the right hand, and pull it out with all the cord that adheres to it. This completes the operation. The reason for cutting off all the pouch that can be easily pulled beyond the testicle is, that it leaves a much evener surface for shearing than if only a little is taken off. This operation should be performed in the morning, and the lambs then turned out to move about, which will, in a great measure, prevent any disposition of swelling or stiffening of the parts, which is frequently the case if they are allowed to lie still for a time afterward. Docking should be done as soon as they are well of the castration, generally about three days afterward. This operation should be performed with a single stroke of a sharp knife, and in the evening, allowing the flock to lie down and keep quiet and still, so that they may lose the least possible amount of blood. By morning the wound will be sufficiently dried that no fear of bleeding need be entertained, unless by accident. In no case should they be driven or put to any extra exertion immediately after being docked, for if so, many will bleed to death. If these hints, which are simple and easily put in practice, are carefully heeded, not one lamb in a hundred need be lost by both operations. At from ten to fifteen days old he should be entirely well of both, and will go on thriving. At about three months old the lamb should be taken from the ewe. The flock should be brought to the yard in the forepart of the day and turned away just at evening, while they are hungry. Much anxiety of both is avoided by this simple practice, for both flocks will go quietly to feeding, and finally lie down satisfied, which they would not otherwise do. The lambs should be picked from amongst the ewes and allowed the liberty of a larger yard, while the ewes are kept more closely confined during the latter part of the day, the two flocks separated by a sheep rack, or open fence. The lambs' yard should be furnished with a feeding trough, supplied with a mixture of salt and bran. This is very palatable, and they will learn to eat from a trough the same day their supply of milk is taken from them. This yard and trough should be convenient for the flock of lambs to run to, and should, as often as twice a week, be supplied with something palatable, which learns them to eat from a trough, and goes far towards taming and attaching them to the shepherd. If the yard is not contiguous to the pasture, the trough may and should be moved to the pasture where the lambs are to make their future home. As the season advances and the nights become frosty, or during heavy storms, the flock of lambs should be herded, and the yards supplied with racks and troughs sufficient for them to feed without crowding too much. Occasionally a little hay, or oats in the sheaf, should be put in the racks. This teaches them to use the yard and and rack ere it is needed; and when the first severe storm of winter covers the ground, as only a cold winter storm can do, they will take hold with a keen relish. If they are left in the field until the winter sets in and makes it necessary to fodder, they are brought to the yard strangers alike to the arrangements and the food they are to use. Many will become discouraged and stand with drooping head and ears, and will only eat when reduced to a reeling skeleton. They thus begin the winter under serious disadvantages and frequently never regain it, but drag along a miserable winter, toppling over every obstacle, to be lifted to their legs, and finally die, as the first warm days of spring take from them the miserable remnant of appetite which idly lingered about them. This negligence in the early education of the sheep is like neglecting the education until the tender and pliant years of childhood are past. When the fully-matured man acquires a business that must be done, he sets about learning to do it. There is however, this difference; the man can get a competent person to do it for him, but the unlearned sheep can get none to eat for him that will supply the wants of nature. When the lambs are fairly in their winter quarters, their education may be considered complete, as their treatment in the after part of the winter may be in every respect like older sheep only a little more care and attention; and like older ones grain is not lost upon them, although too high feeding is not recommended. During the winter, care should be taken not to allow too many to run in one flock, for the stronger continually overrun the weaker, picking out the most delicate portions of the food, and leaving that less palatable and of inferior quality to those which should have the best. The usual mode is to allow from one hundred to one hundred and fifty in a flock. While some keep them in close yards and water and feed them, others allow them to roam over the fields during the day and bring them to the yard at night. Such as are allowed a free range usually pick quite a portion of their winter living, but it is of an inferior quality, and a flock allowed to roam will not usually keep in as good condition as when they are carefully yarded, housed, and properly fed. If sheep are divided into small flocks of about twenty-five, and are selected with reference to size and strength, and kept in close confinement through the winter, giving them only room enough to move about, they will require less food than if allowed more liberty, and allowed to run in larger flocks; but whether the increased amount of labor will offset against the difference in the supply of food can only be determined by the circumstances and conveniences of the grower. Before the sheep are changed from hay to grass in the spring they should be carefully looked over, and all horns and hoofs that threaten to be troublesome carefully removed. The hoofs can be taken off with pruning shears, but a fine saw is needed for horns. The sheep is then laid upon his back in a kind of saw-buck, with a board nailed to each side, forming an easy place for the sheep to lie, and convenient for the operator. It should be high enough for the sheep to run under without oversetting it. A basket is then placed at the end to receive the tag locks as they are taken off. A portion of the wool should then be taken from the stern of each sheep in such a manner as to allow the manure to drop free without finding any stray locks or loose raw edges of wool to obstruct it in its passage. The wethers should have a small portion of wool removed from the belly, to allow the urine a free passage. This is quite as important as any part of the tagging, and yet is neglected by many. When the entire flock have received this attention, they are ready to be changed from the yard to the pasture. A ewe should not be required to move about much for a few hours after lambing. If her teats are closed against the efforts of the lamb, squeeze them out with the wetted fingers. If they have been cut off in shearing and are grown up, reopen them with a delicate blade, inserting it no further than is necessary. The sucking of the lamb will generally keep them open; but if they become inflamed, the ewe must be held for the lamb to suck, and some cooling lotion applied to the part. If the udder is hard and hot, it should be fomented by frequently and continuously applying to it a cloth dipped in hot water. Repeated washings with cold water produce the same effect, but more slowly, and with a greater tendency to dry up the milk. If the lamb is dead, and there are indurated tumors in the udder, apply iodine ointment. A ewe which disowns her lamb, or one which is required to adopt another should be confined alone with it in a dark place, and out of hearing of other sheep, and she should be held several times a day for it to suck. Frightening a ewe when with her lamb, by showing her a strange dog, or a child wearing a bright colored mantle, sometimes arouses her dormant maternal instincts. If a ewe's dead lamb is skinned, and the skin tied on a living lamb, she will generally readily adopt it. If she hesitates, rubbing some odor on her nose and also on the lamb will facilitate the process. Docking and castration should be performed when the lamb is not more than two or three weeks old, and before warm weather comes on; and it is an excellent plan to smear the wounds with a compound of tar, butter, and turpentine. The tail should be cut off so that no part of the bone is left uncovered. Castration is an operation sufficiently familiar to most farmers. It is generally held by those who have tried it that early shearing is preferable for sheep, if they can be subsequently housed in case of severe storms or unusually cold nights. As early washing is improper in cold climates, it is urged that sheep should be shorn unwashed. This is a question on which the wool-grower should be allowed to exercise his own judgment; nor should any buyer attempt to compel washing, or to take advantage of its omission by insisting on a particular and fixed rate of shrinkage on unwashed wools. The shrinkage on every lot should be proportioned to its actual condition, as deduction is made on wheat, other products, or foreign wools which contain impurities. The mode of washing sheep does not require to be here described. Merino sheep generally require to have their feet trimmed at least once a year. Some do this at washing, when the feet are clean and soaked soft; others immediately after shearing.

SHEEP DIPPING. Dipping is a term used for immersing sheep, after shearing, to free them from vermin, and used also as a means of curing them from the scab or mange insect. When but few sheep are kept, the cure is accomplished generally by anointing them with any of the preparations in common use for this purpose. For those who prefer ointments, the following will be found good: One pound mercurial ointment, one-half pint oil of turpentine, one pound resin, and six pounds of lard. Dissolve the resin in the turpentine; dissolve the lard by gentle heat, mix the mercurial ointment thoroughly with it, and when cold rub both preparations well together. In applying this, the wool must be parted well down to the skin from between the ears to the tail. From this similar partings should be made along the shoulders and thighs to the legs and also parallel ones along the sides. These furrows must have the ointment lightly rubbed into the skin as made. On the great Western plains, and in Australia, vast herds of sheep are kept, often with but little in the way of buildings to show the wealth of the proprietor. On page 858 is an illustration of such an establishment, the sod-house, yards and sheep dipping apparatus comprising the sole outlay. In the article Scab will be found popular recipes for sheep dipping.

SHELL LIME. Lime procured from burning shells. If it is well made, it is excellent for agricultural purposes, as it contains nearly two per cent. of bone earth, and is free from caustic magnesia.

SHELL MARL. This is very rich in the remains of shells; when especially so it may often be profitably burned for lime.

SHELTERING STOCK. We provide ourselves with comfortable clothing in winter to ward off the effects of cold. We eat fat meats for the same reason. The more northern and colder the climate, the more of fatty substances are consumed. The Esquimaux drink train oil. These substances contain much carbon, and carbon produces heat. Farm stock in the winter crave oily grains, as corn, for the reason that they assist in keeping up the animal heat. Is it not poor economy, in view of these facts, to let your cattle, colts and sheep winter at the lee side of some bleak hill, or in the fence corners, when a little time and money expended at odd times would provide them with comfortable stables, or at least, with warm sheds? The money paid for this will pay for itself each season, to say nothing of the satisfaction of knowing that you have done all in your power to make your farm stock as comfortable as possible. The farmer knows full well that a plant once stinted while young can never after recover to fully develop itself. It is the same with live stock, only in a greater degree. If allowed to stop growing and get thoroughly poor while young, they never, however well fed thereafter, fully recover. Our most successful and most money-making feeders continue to feed liberally from younglings to maturity. It will make a pig as heavy at ten months old as he would become, under ordinary feeding, in eighteen, and the full fed steer will be as heavy at three years, as the lighter fed one will be at five. It takes a certain amount of waste to supply the animal economy, and the waste is in proportion to the length of life. It costs just twice as much to prolong this waste two years as it does one, and more goes to waste in cold weather than in warm, hence the economy of providing warm shelter and plenty of food. Animals so provided will be sleek and healthy, while the others will be gaunt and shivering, and their coats staring. Stablemen understand the economy of keeping fine horses warmly clothed in winter. It is only another name for preventing waste. Too many ordinary farmers fail to see it. Try sheltering your stock one winter and see how you and they like it. We know of no experiments having been undertaken in the West with a view of determining this question accurately; that is, under different given ranges of the thermometer. We do know, however, that animals kept in stables when the temperature is at fifty degrees, have their coats soft and sleek, and that as the temperature falls below forty degrees, their coats begin to get rough and staring. A rough coat, however, is not always indicative of ill health; for an animal may be kept in good health out of doors in the winter, if it be provided with shelter where it may be protected from the direct force of the wind, and against storms of rain and sleet. Nevertheless it is always at the expense of an extra quantity of food, and this in just proportion to the temperature, force of the wind, or the effect of rain on the animal; for the escape of animal heat is in just proportion to the effects of the conditions mentioned above, and this wasted heat must be kept up by an extra supply of carbonaceous food. Hence the well-known maxim, stock can not be wintered in the West on hay and straw, when exposed to the inclemencies of the weather. On the other hand, John Johnston, the well-known farmer of New York State, long since asserted—and this is well known to practical men—that he could keep his cows in milk during the winter, on good sweet hay, by attending to the warmth of the stable. A certain portion of the food eaten by animals is consumed in keeping up the vital warmth; another portion in supplying the natural waste of tissue, etc., the rest goes to make flesh and fat. So, food is consumed in due proportion to the waste of heat, from low temperature or exposure. Experiments made some years ago in the comparatively mild, or rather equable, climate of England, is thus stated: One hundred sheep were fed in a shed twenty pounds each of Swedish turnips per day; another hundred in the open air or field were fed twenty-five pounds each per day; and yet the former on one-fifth less food had gained at the end of a few weeks three pounds each of flesh more than the others. Five sheep were fed in the open air between the twenty-first of November and the first of December, consuming ninety pounds of food per day, the temperature being at forty-four degrees At the end of this time they weighed two pounds less than when first exposed. Five sheep were then placed under a shed in a temperature of forty-nine degrees. At first they consumed eighty-two pounds of food per day; then seventy pounds; and at the end of the same time as the others, they had gained twenty-three pounds. Again, five sheep were placed in a shed as before, and not allowed to take exercise. They ate at first sixty-four pounds a day, then fifty-eight pounds, and increased in weight thirty pounds. Thus it will be seen that the first lot on the largest amount of food lost flesh, and that additional warmth not only decreased the amount of food eaten, but they increased largely in flesh. Our experience is that animals will for fattening thrive best in warm and moderately dark stables. And however cheap or abundant the forage, it pays to provide warm shelter, whether for stock or fattening animals. This fact is more noticeable with milch cows than with other stock. We have known them to shrink fully one-half in their mess from being inadvertently exposed to a cold storm of rain; and they did not regain their full flow of milk again for several days after being again placed in the stable.

SHERDS. Fragments of garden pots, used to under-drain the soil of boxes, pots, etc.

SHETLAND PONIES. The Shetlands, the smallest of the pony breeds, are round, closely ribbed up, with heads bony and well shaped, but wide at the brow, and often with the basin-shaped face of the true Arab. The ears are small, erect, well shaped and placed, eyes large, bright and intelligent; the neck short, strong, and with long, coarse, thick manes; the shoulders thick, but sloping; the withers low; back slightly hollowed, loin strong and wide, tail exceedingly long and thick like the mane; the quarters are strong, with particularly good legs and hoofs. Their endurance is wonderful, and for such animals their speed is considerable, they being capable of performing journeys of forty miles a day upon the rocky, hilly pathways of their native country. When petted and treated kindly they become much attached to their masters, are gentle, sagacious, easily trained, but like the mule, will resent abuse sometimes with their heels. In color they are generally dark sorrel, brown and black. Yet many are now found parti-colored, with considerable white. When reared in a semi-wild state they are often reduced to extreme straits, for want of food, even subsisting on kelp and sea weed along the sea shore, but quickly respond to better care and treatment. The Shetlands of the smallest size combined with the most perfect form are said to be found in the extreme northern islands of Unst and Yell. Many of them are not more than seven or eight hands in height, the average being not more than nine or ten hands, or thirty-six to forty inches. In fact it is held that no true Shetland ever reached the height of eleven hands.

SHIELDS. In botany, little colored cups or lines with a hard disk, surrounded by a rim, and containing the sporules, or seeds of lichens.

SHOCKS. Assemblages of sheaves, from six to twelve or more. Shocks of corn are composed of from eight to twelve hills square, or from sixty-four to one hundred and forty-four hills.

SHOEING HORSES. The proper shoeing of horses, when employed on city pavements or hard roads, is one demanding the most earnest attention of every horse owner. Nevertheless, not one in a hundred ever take the pains to inform themselves as to the correct manner of doing this, but trust to horse-shoers, many of them as ignorant of the varying necessities of the case, according to the shape and quality of the hoof, as is the owner. On soft roads, and on all work in soft ground, the hoofs are undoubtedly better without shoes, and hence many good farmers properly allow the horses worked on the farm to be shod in summer, except those that are to be driven on stony or other hard roads. Some years since, Mr. George Fleming, Veterinary Surgeon Royal Engineers, England, prepared a paper on Horse Shoes and Horse-shoeing, that has been accepted as one of the best monographs on the subject extant. We therefore give it nearly entire as well worthy of study: It would take us rather beyond the limits of our subject if we attempted to point out the very important part the horse plays in the world and in the progress of civilization, and to what an extent mankind has to rely on him for most essential services, rendered in peace or in war. Neither need we dwell on the share this creature has taken in the development of civilization, and in the great events which have marked the history of our species. Suffice it, therefore, to state, that on no other animal has devolved, or could be imposed, the same onerous duties, and to no other creature is man indebted for so many services and benefits. These could never have been rendered but for the fact, discovered at a very early period in the history of man, that the horse was gifted with a special conformation, which adapted him for the most varied uses under the most diverse circumstances, and that the chief point in this conformation was the presence of a solid foot cased in tough, elastic horn. The varied uses to which the horse has been subjected since he was taken from a wild condition, and the willing and cheerful manner with which he has undergone fatigue and performed duties which are, one would think, quite foreign to his nature, have certainly all been owing to his combined and unequal qualities of strength, courage, speed, fidelity, and obedience, as well as docility; and though his great value has mainly depended upon a just disposition of these, yet it cannot be doubted that to the presence of a wonderfully contrived foot the horse largely owes his exalted position above all those creatures which have submitted themselves to domestication and toil for the benefit of the human species. The history of mankind abundantly testifies that every possible use and application of this animal, whether in war, commerce, or pleasure, seems to have been anticipated by the most ancient peoples; and old-world nations which, ages ago, most largely employed the horse, were the great centers of antique civilization. Indeed, it may safely be asserted that but for the horse the human race could not have reached its present state of progress or refinement, or have been able to contend against the numerous obstacles to advancement and material happiness which surrounded it; and it has been well said that, next to the want of iron, the want of horses would have been one of the greatest physical barriers to the perfecting of the arts of civilized life. And but for the horse being endowed with a continually growing hoof, which covers the most beautiful and delicate structures, and which, being solid, and a slow conductor of heat and cold, eminently fits him for traveling in snow and ice during the winter of northern regions, and in the burning sands of tropical climates, he would scarcely have proved himself worth the trouble of domesticating. For, notwithstanding his other grand qualities, no invention or device of man could have compensated for the absence of his solid, hoof-cased foot. Therefore it has happened that, from the earliest ages, the attention of horsemen has been largely centered on the feet of the horse; and no matter how perfect the other points of his conformation may have been, if these organs were defective all was bad, as none of his good qualities could then be made effective. And from these ages to the present time, when the uses to which the horse can be put have become so multiplied, and so much more necessary for our business or pleasure, this truth has been daily receiving further confirmation, until the aphorism, no foot, no horse, has become a painful reality in modern days; though it is but a re-echo of what was, no doubt, enunciated centuries beyond two thousand years ago. For the manifestation of his strength and the due development of his other good qualities the horse must rely upon the soundness of his feet, as in them are concentrated the efforts created elsewhere, and on them depend, to a great extent, the solidity and just equilibrium of the whole animal fabric. So that it is wisely considered that the foot of the horse is one of the most, if not the most, important part of the body, and that all the splendid qualities possessed by the noble creature may be diminished in value, or hopelessly lost, if through disease or accident, natural or acquired defects, or other causes, this organ fails to perform its allotted task. Seeing, then, the great interest and importance which attach to this animal, in its being of all creatures most concerned with man in promoting a progressive and long-continued civilization, and to the means and appliances which have from time to time been brought to bear in increasing the utility of this devoted servant, it cannot but be a matter of public interest to inquire into an art which, however insignificant it may generally appear, yet increases a hundred-fold the usefulness of the horse. I refer to the art of shoeing, through which, in arming that portion of the hoof which comes in contact with the ground and sustains the whole weight and propelling power of the animal, injury is not only averted, but the power of the horse is greatly developed. An art which has indirectly exercised much influence on the destiny of mankind, and lent its aid to the restless wave of human action, surely deserves some notice; and if it be looked upon as a modest and obscure art, it nevertheless merits the attention of the humane no less than that of the utilitarian, in consequence of its being so closely related to the comfort and the preservation of this animal, whose value is every day becoming more appreciated and exaggerated. It may be said that with the horse in a state of nature the hoof requires no protection. The solidity and toughness of the material of which it is composed; the absence of artificial roads; nothing but the weight of the body to be supported; and the horn never being subjected to any other influences than those it is naturally adapted to resist, maintain it in health and uninjured. But, in connection with climate, domestication alters more or less the conditions on which the horse depends for the horn's integrity as an efficient protection to the living and extremely sensitive parts it encloses. In several regions of the world, which have a dry climate and a soft soil, and where the hoofs are firm in texture, shoeing is seldom, if ever required. When the journeys are long, however, and the labor severe, some kind of artificial protection is needed, or the animal's feet become denuded of horn, and lameness results. Among the Mongols this accident is repaired by the horseman exchanging his pony for one whose hoofs are not worn; or, if he has a number, he rides another until the cripple has had time to grow a new supply for wear. In some regions, as with the North American Indians and the Tartars, raw hide is used on such occasions, and even the horns of other creatures; and in Japan, when a traveler is about to start on a long journey, a bundle of rice-straw slippers for his steed, is tied to his saddle, and these he attaches to the animal's feet from time to time, as they become worn. Strange to say, the Japanese knew nothing of attaching an iron shoe to the hoof by means of nails until some troop farriers were sent from North China to that country in 1860, to attend to the horses purchased for the expedition to Pekin. These farriers introduced the art into Japan. But even in the most favored countries the usefulness of the horse can be but limited without some means of protecting the hoof from undue wear. And doubtless this fact was soon recognized by the people who, at a very early period, trained and employed this animal, and who, no doubt, were compelled to resort to various devices to protect it from inefficiency from this cause. For, with the increasing spread of civilization, the demands upon the services of the horse became more urgent and heavy, and the diversities of climate to which he was carried, as well as of races which resulted, would lead one to suppose that greater wear and modification in the nature and consistency of the hoof would render some kind of defense absolutely necessary. This necessity led to the bold and efficient method now in vogue, of attaching a metal rim to the lower border of the hoof by means of nails driven through the horn, a device which the nineteenth century can not improve, and one which, to the individual who proposed or first practiced it, must have been a feat of no ordinary magnitude; while to us it has proved to be an invention scarcely inferior to that of the steam engine in importance. But, like so many other inventions, this one is lost in the obscurity of ages; and archæologists and antiquarians have for nearly two centuries puzzled themselves in vain in trying to arrive at the period when the art of horseshoeing was introduced; while ancient writers afford little or no assistance in enabling us to judge whether the art was practiced even in their day. Up to a recent period horse-shoeing was traced no further back with certainty than the ninth century, though the legends, traditions, and superstitions relating to it proved that it was very old. But the great advances made in archæology now make it manifest that shoeing was known to the Romans and the ancient Gauls; and though it is persistently stated in every-day books of reference, such as Haydn's Dictionary of Dates, that the farrier's art was introduced into Britain by William the Conqueror, it is certain that during the Roman occupation of this country horses were shod in a similar manner to what they are now-a-days. Horse-shoes have been discovered repeatedly in the camps and graves of ancient Gaul, and even in battle fields of these people. They have been found in numerous instances with Roman relics, such as arms, brooches, lamps, coins, etc., in France, Switzerland, and Belgium; and in this country many have been discovered in excavations in London, in the streets of some of our towns at considerable depths, in Roman camps, roads, villas, and various other situations; and as a further proof that horse-shoeing was known in this country before the arrival of the Normans, we find that in the ancient laws of Wales the court farrier was an important personage, and had certain valuable privileges conferred upon him while he shod the king's horses. Indeed my researches have carried me as far back as about 300 years before our era, when a coin of Tarentum was struck, which was evidently designed to represent something in connection with the farrier's art; perhaps it was intended to commemorate the birth of the art itself. I may also mention that there can be no doubt that a temporary protection for the hoofs was sometimes resorted to, as we find it mentioned by different Roman writers under various names. This protection was in all likelihood something of the same kind as that now used by the Japanese; but it would also appear to have been made of iron, and to be something of a sandal. Often with the ordinary Roman horse-shoe, sometimes alone, there have been found articles of different shapes, though alike in some particulars, which have been designated, hipposandals, by those who believe them to have been these temporary protections. It is questionable whether many of these could have been used for such a purpose, however; while it is not at all improbable that others may have been attached to the hoofs of the horse for some other purpose than that of a sandal. A word with regard to the Roman horse-shoe. In the description of my work on horse-shoeing I had occasion to examine and to read the description of very many of the shoes which undoubtedly belonged to the Roman period, and I was surprised to find they all bore the greatest resemblance to each other; so much so, indeed, that if they had been laid together any one who did not know that they had been collected in France, Switzerland, Belgium, and England, would be likely to assert that they were made by the same artisan; and there is also a wonderful uniformity of size amongst them, which would go to prove that the horses then applied in these countries were small. The shoe is of the simplest kind, being merely a narrow strip of iron bent like the shoe now in use, the ends of the branches being rolled over to form calks, and there are nearly always three holes on each side to receive the nails. The holes and nails form the distinctive features of the shoe, however, and have led me to consider such shoes as peculiar to the Romano-Gallic or Romano-British period. At each nail-hole is a wide oval indentation, in the middle of which the round hole for the nail is made. This indentation was intended to and did receive the base of a large flat-headed nail which it supported, and prevented from being twisted out of the shoe. With the two calks, each foot in this way stood on eight distinct points, which insured a good foothold. But in making the oval cavity for the nail head the narrow rim of metal was bulged out at each hole, and thus the border of the shoe presented an undulating appearance, which is exceedingly of these shoes. Toward the middle ages the art of shoeing acquired much importance in Western Europe. Armor of a heavy description began to be worn; horses of a large size, to carry the increased weight, were bred, and they had to be protected with heavier shoes. So important did the art become that the farrier or his superintendent was often a high officer of the royal household; and kings, princes, and nobles did not disdain to be taught and to practice that art upon which so much depended in those days. Noblemen received their titles and names from their connection with the craft, as Marshal, Ferrers, Laferriers, and Ferrier; and gifts were bestowed and tenures held in connection with horse-shoes and horse-shoeing, more especially in England during the reign of William the Conqueror. Northampton and a large tract of country was held by Simon St. Liz on condition that he provided shoes for William's horses; and it is probably in connection with this peculiar tenure that the Northamptonshire militia wear a horse-shoe on their pouches. And for superintending the shoeing of the same monarch's steeds, Henry de Ferrarus, or Ferrers, had bestowed upon him the honor of Tutbury, in Staffordshire. In other parts of the country tenures were held on similar terms; and even in your own city of London, in 1235, during the reign of Henry III., Walter le Bruin, or Brun, a farrier, or marechal, as the shoer was then designated, had a piece of land granted him in the Strand, in the parish of St. Clement's Danes, whereon to erect a forge, on condition that he should render at the exchequer, annually, for the same a quit rent of six horse-shoes, with the nails (sixty-two) thereto belonging. This curious payment was made twice during the reign of Edward I., and is continued up to the present time, the shoes and nails being paid on the 30th September, at the swearing in of the newly-elected sheriff of London and Middlesex, to the representatives of the sovereign for the said piece of ground, though it has long been city property. Noblemen and others had horse-shoes on their coats of arms and seals, and even towns sported the hoof-iron, as is seen in the old corporation seal of Gloucester, in use during the reign of Edward III. But we need not pursue the history of the art any further, except to remark that the grooved or fullered shoe came into use in this country about four or five centuries ago; though shoes of this kind, of a much earlier date (fifth century), have been found in graves in Burgundy, the groove having evidently been made by the same tool that cut the furrows in the formidable scramasaxs, or swords worn by the warriors, for the farrier was often also the armorer. The shoes were ponderous and clumsy, and the hoofs appear at a later period to have become subjected to serious mutilations by the farrier's boutoir, or buttress, as the hoof-cutting implement was named. In this country, towards the end of the last and commencement of this century, an attempt was made to place the art on a scientific basis, but, unfortunately, wild theories with regard to the functions of the horse's feet were promulgated; the hoof alone was studied, and no regard was had to the important structures it contained, and to which it was a mere shell; fantastic notions as to the expansion of the hoof at the heels, the descent of the sole, and other strange ideas, were carried into practice; and shoeing on what was, and is still, termed improved principles—though the improvement was an infraction of nature's laws—proved a veritable curse to horses. The hoof was reduced to the thinnest film where it should have been left strong, and was pared away until it yielded on the sole to the pressure of the thumb, or until the blood came oozing through; a knife was devised to search into the inflexions at the heels, which were so many natural bulwarks, and the elastic cushion at the back part of the hoof was recklessly sliced away, until at last the foot was so robbed of its natural covering that it required great skill and an artificial protection between it and the shoe to enable the animal to travel for a few years. The shoe was beveled off on the upper surface, so as not to press on the tender sole, and this threw all the strain of the weight and exertion upon the margin of the foot. In short, no treatment devised to ruin horses prematurely in their feet could have been more appropriate and successful, so far as the lower surface of the hoof was concerned. With regard to the outer part, this was rasped and chiseled away to make fine work, until there was scarcely sufficient material left to drive the nails through; consequently these had to be increased in number. The evils horse-shoeing thus introduced have continued, and are as prevalent now as they were fifty years ago. The number of horses rendered useless by improved farriery is very great, and only too frequently inefficiency is brought about at an early period of the horse's career. The farriers only too frequently work by rule of thumb, and on no fixed principle. Their knowledge is mainly traditional, passed from father to son, or from an elder to an apprentice, without cultivation, or without being enhanced by educated observation. This is due to the neglect into which the art has fallen for many centuries; and yet this neglect is somewhat unpardonable. Not very many years ago the farrier was the only authority on the diseases of animals, and to his tender mercies was entrusted their restoration to health and soundness when they were sick or lame. Science has relieved him of this responsibility, and transferred it to the medically-trained veterinary surgeon, who, from the general and professional education, should be better fitted for such a duty. But this deprivation has still further lowered the status of the farrier, and, it is to be feared, his art; for he has not the same incentive to maintain his ancient position, and to be a shoer of horses is to rank very inferior indeed; while the veterinary surgeon, from the many subjects he has to study while at college, and the far too brief period he spends there, has no time to acquire even elementary notions of the horse's foot and the best means of keeping it sound. He therefore imagines this matter is of but little moment; and I fear some members of the veterinary profession think it rather degrading to pay any attention to what they consider such an humble mechanical handicraft. This is deeply to be regretted, when we know how many horses are prematurely ruined through mismanagement of their feet; how many suffer the most horrible torture, for perhaps years, through bad shoeing; and how many are rendered more or less inefficient and worn out in their limbs from badly adjusted, ill-constructed, or far too heavy shoes. There is no remedy for this unfortunate state of affairs but teaching the farriers their art in some school or college presided over by competent teachers, and licensing them when they are able to carry the principles they have been taught into practice. A certificate of competency would be a guarantee that the possessor had devoted some attention to the theory of his art, and was so far acquainted with the anatomy and physiology of the organ with which he had to deal, that if he could not treat it as a surgeon when it was diseased, he would yet be in a position to prevent much disease in it. It does seem strange that, in a country like our own—the home of the best and most valuable horses in the world—and among a horse-loving people such as we are, some such an establishment has not been instituted. If the Society of Arts wished to confer a great service upon horse-owners and upon the noble beast itself, and through them upon the entire public, it could not do better than propound a scheme for supplying educated farriers to all parts of the country. The Society would have abundant support, and nothing would tend more to improve the minds and elevate the position of the farriers themselves. Though the end of the horse's limb is named the foot, yet it has no analogy to the human foot, except that both rest on the ground and are essential instruments in progression. The fore foot of the horse is, in fact, the extremity of the middle finger of man's hand, and the hind foot is the analogue of the middle toe of his foot; while the nail on each represents the horse's hoof. In this way the horse's knee is the human wrist, and the hock the human ankle and heel. It is sometimes useful to bear this distinction in mind. A sort of conical semi-lunar bone fills the anterior two-thirds of the hoof, and to it the hoof is moulded, as well as firmly attached. This is the foot-bone—admirably adapted for its purpose in being light, yet strong, and affording ample protection to the large blood vessels which supply the organ in such profusion. Above this bone is the small pastern-bone, and behind it, between the wings of the crescent, is another narrow bone—the navicular or shuttle bone, as the old farriers used to name it. Over this bone the powerful flexor tendon of the foot passes, to be inserted into the lower surface of the foot bone; and this tendon again rests upon, and is supported at this its weakest part by a large mass of elastic substance, which plays a very necessary part in the function of the foot. From each wing of the foot-bone spring two wide, cartilaginous plates connected with the elastic cushion; and these, rising above the heels of the hoof, have a large share in promoting springiness, and obviating injury to the organ. The whole of the foot within the hoof is covered by an exquisitely sensitive membrane, which secretes the horn. The hoof consists of three parts—wall, sole and frog. The wall is attached to the foot-bone by means of a very large number—over six hundred—of very sensitive and vascular leaves, which run from above to below, and are received between similar, but horny, leaves on the inner surface of the wall. This union is of the most intimate and beautiful character, and I regret that time will not allow me to show you how wonderfully adapted it is for the end in view. The wall itself, as indeed is the whole of the hoof, is composed of very minute cells, not unlike those which compose the skin; but differently arranged to form fibers, which pass from the top to the bottom. These fibers can be distinguished by the naked eye on a very close inspection, and to form them the cells are laid lengthways, or vertically, while the fibers themselves are united by interfibrous cells, which lie horizontally, so that we have cells laid in two directions; and this not only affords a better resistance to wear, but prevents splitting. The wall grows from the coronet, or upper part of the foot, and this growth is incessant. The outer, or surface fibers, are very dense and smooth, but the deeper they are situated the more soft and spongy they become—a fact of much importance in shoeing. At its upper part the wall is covered by a soft, elastic horn, which protects it while it is being formed. The sole is formed of fibers passing in the same direction, and constructed in the same manner as in the wall, but it differs from the latter in one important point. When it has attained a certain thickness, the superficial horn becomes detached in flakes, which, even in a semi-detached state, serve a useful purpose in retaining moisture for the growing horn beneath, and acting as a springy defense against injury from loose stones. The wall, on the contrary, grows to an indefinite length, or rather depth, when indeed it is not worn away by contact with the ground—another important fact to be remembered. The frog is also fibrous, but the horn of which it is composed is different in quality, being soft, dense, and elastic, like india rubber. It is an essential constituent of the elastic apparatus of the foot, and in situation and function it is analogous to the pad on the foot of the dog, cat, and other animals, and the cushion beneath man's heel. The elastic apparatus of the foot also consists of a cushion of springy material around the top of the organ, and which fits into a recess at the upper margin of the wall, so that we not only have elastic cartilages and cushions at the back part of the foot, but an excellent contrivance all round the top to break the primary shock of contact with the ground. The fore foot, when well formed, is nearly circular in shape, but the hind one is oval, otherwise there is not much difference between them. The angle or slope of the wall varies, but it is generally between fifty and fifty-two degrees. This is as much of the anatomy of the foot as we now have time to notice; but I may tell you that perhaps no organ of the animal body will better repay a careful study, if only to trace the evidences of design so wonderfully displayed in every part and combination of parts. With regard to function, it may be sufficient to mention that the wall sustains the largest portion of the weight, and is the part chiefly exposed, as it is that which is mainly designed to encounter wear. The sole also shares in weight bearing, but a wider surface participates on soft than on hard ground, owing to its concave shape. The frog has also to sustain weight to a great extent, but its most important duty is undoubtedly to support the flexor tendon of the foot through the intermediate cushion, to prevent slipping, and also to assist the animal in suddenly checking its pace when moving rapidly. The lower border of the hoof does not expand to any appreciable extent when the animal is in motion. For years this has been taught, but it is a fallacy, and many circumstances prove it to be so. The expansion takes place at its upper border, and towards the heels, where the chief elastic apparatus is situated. The function of the fore foot is chiefly to support weight, that of the hind foot is to propel the body. Now as to shoeing: It is obvious that the horse's foot was designed to meet every natural demand, so far as the animal's weight and movements are concerned; but when a heavy load is imposed on his back, or attached behind, and when he is compelled to travel, particularly over hard roads, in all kinds of weather, nature's arrangements are overtaxed, and the wear of the hoof is greater than the repair. Consequently, art must step in to assist nature. The part of the hoof which suffers most from undue wear is that which was intended to encounter it, the wall; and when this is too much worn the sole becomes broken around its margin, and the sensitive parts within wounded and contused. Therefore all that the hoof requires, in order to enable the horse to remain serviceable, is merely some kind of protection for the lower border of the wall; but this protection should not be heavy, else the muscles, which were designed to move a marvelously light foot, will be unduly strained, as will also tendons and ligaments, for the muscles —the moving power of the limb—are all situated at the upper part of the leg, and act upon short levers, the mechanical means being designed rather for speed than strength. This protection must be durable; it should not damage or interfere with the functions of the foot, but allow every part to perform its office unimpaired; it ought to be easily applied, and secure when attached to the foot; it should not render the animal less sure-footed, if possible, than before it was applied; and, finally, it ought to be simple and cheap. Grave charges have been brought against this method of preserving the hoof from the effects of wear, by men whose absurd theories, when carried into practice, inflicted most serious injury to the foot; but we may dismiss these and all other charges by the declaration that it is not the use, but the abuse, of the method which is to be inveighed against. The abuses are due to the farrier trying to improve, not to assist nature, and to make improvement costly. The most serious abuse is the very unreasonable and barbarous mutilation of the hoof. This is often carried to an excess scarcely credible. The sole is robbed of its natural protection until it yields to the pressure of the thumb, or even until the blood is passing through it. The frog is cut away to a shred to make it look neat: the bars are carefully removed; and then a shoe is put on much too small for the hoof. This leaves a portion of the wall projecting beyond the outer margin of the metal; and to make the foot fit the shoe, the horn is removed by means of a rasp from the front of the wall, which is consequently considerably weakened at the very part of all others where it should be strong, to support the nails which retain the shoe. Not only this, but the dense resisting outer fibers being removed, the soft, spongy inner horn is exposed, and this being acted upon by external influences, cracks and splits, until there is scarcely any sound material to retain the nails, which have, consequently, to be driven higher and nearer to the sensitive parts; and this, in time, leads to disease and deformity. A hoof so maltreated has an unmistakably ugly and ragged appearance. In addition to this mutilation of the hoof in the vicinity of the shoe, the farrier, in order to complete a fine job, as he imagines it, rasps the outer surface of the wall as high as the hair, and in this way not only destroys the horn so rasped, but impairs the growth of that from the coronet, which becomes weak and brittle; so that at length the workman has to employ his utmost skill to fasten on the shoe without laming the horse, and has also to employ a greater number of nails, which immensely exaggerates the evil. These mutilations and their consequence are quite common, and one can scarcely pass a horse in the streets of London without noticing them, and the majority of the shoes which are applied to the hoofs are no more reasonable in their construction. Great clumsy, unsightly masses of iron, the weight of which is perfectly outrageous, are attached to the feet of horses which have to travel sometimes at a rapid pace, carrying or drawing heavy loads. This weight is not only injurious to the feet, through the strain it imposes on them, but is extremely fatiguing to the muscles; so that a large portion of the animal's power is expended in carrying about unwieldy clogs of iron. And the useless weight is not the only objection to very many of the shoes in daily use. In order that the denuded sole may not suffer injury from the pressure of the shoe, this is beveled away on its upper surface, until there is only a narrow rim left on which the foot rests; so that in reality the whole of the weight bearing is thrown upon the wall; and in consequence of the thickness of the shoe, neither sole or frog ever come in contact with the ground, and sustain their fair share of the weight and strain. In this way the horse is compelled to travel as no other animal does, or was ever designed to—on the outer margin of its feet. The space between the shoe and the sole is admirably adapted for the lodgement of stones, dirt, etc., and in heavy, stiff ground wonderfully increases suction. So much for the upper surface of the shoe; the lower, or ground surface, is not much less defective. It is usually a large, wide, smooth surface of metal, well contrived to promote sliding and slipping, furnished with a groove near its border, in which the nail-holes are punched, but which groove is a mere waste of labor and time, for the farrier to make, as it is useless. Sometimes, with a view to prevent slipping, two projections, or calks, are raised at the end of the branches of the shoe; and these, though they may to a trifling extent answer their purpose, nevertheless throw the foot and limb into a most unnatural and uncomfortable position, the pain and inconvenience of which we may realize by walking in very high-heeled boots. These are only some, not all, of the evils of shoeing as commonly practiced, and it must be confessed that they are very serious, and sooner or later lead to painful traveling for the horse, as well as impaired efficiency; and yet this art, which the farrier makes so difficult and costly, both directly and indirectly, should be neither. To shoe a horse properly, if we take observation and a study of nature's plans into consideration, is certainly not a very difficult operation, and neither need it be a very expensive one. Our object should be to protect the hoof from wear—nothing more; and in doing so we ought to maintain the integrity and soundness of the hoof, while we do not overburden or disturb the natural direction of the foot and limb; and, as a secondary object, we should endeavor to increase the animal's foothold on the ground, if possible. The first object is attained by leaving the sole, frog and bars in their natural condition; as I have already explained that when they have acquired a certain thickness the outer surface falls off in flakes of dead horn, so that they never become too thick. It is different with the wall, which would grow to an indefinite length, because it is not thrown off in flakes, and the shoe prevents it from being worn. This, therefore, every time the horse is shod, has to be reduced in length at its lower border to a degree corresponding to the growth which has taken place since the previous shoeing; and the manner in which this is done, as well as the extent, constitutes, in my opinion, the chief test of the farrier's skill. If the wall is too much reduced, generally, injury will follow; if too much at the toe or front, the heels will be naturally high, and this will alter the animal's gait, particularly in the fore feet, and make its paces uncomfortable to the rider; if too much at the back part of the heels, it throws the unnatural strain on the fetlocks and some other joints; and if one side is lowered more than another, it leads to twisting of the limbs and strain on the lateral ligaments of the joints. All these can be avoided by the skillful artisan; and yet, strange to say, the normal position or direction of the limb and foot is seldom taken into consideration, and we see numbers of horses of all descriptions with these more or less crooked in consequence. The unmutilated hoof only requires as much iron as will protect the lower border of its walls, say for a month or six weeks, and insure security of foothold—nothing more—and all beyond this is loss or injury; while, if possible, the sole and frog should be allowed to play their part. A shoe and method of shoeing which admirably answer these ends is that introduced some years ago by M. Charlier, a Parisian veterinary surgeon. A narrow rim of iron is imbedded in a recess formed by removing the wall only, to a certain depth of its lower border; the iron, in fact, takes the place of the removed wall, and is retained securely by a small number of very small nails. The first, I believe, to try this method of shoeing in this country, I have continued its use, but in a modified form, up to the present time, and can affirm that it is, for many horses, the best method of shoeing known. In principle it is founded on a sound physiological basis, and in practice I can testify to its great utility. My modification consists in having only a short rim of metal passing round about two-thirds of the wall, and imbedded on a level with the sole, leaving that and the frog to reach the ground, and the heels free of iron—in all respects, in fact, as though the foot were in an unshod state. The rim weighs about one-third of the common shoe, and is retained firmly in position by only four of the very smallest nails, and yet it wears longer than the heavy shoe, which requires eight, ten, and sometimes twelve nails. This is easily accounted for by the fact that horn and iron wear together in this instance, and that the limbs are not fatigued, but move lightly and easily. Traveling is also safer on slippery roads, as there is only a very small portion of metal exposed, and the frog prevents slipping. The saving in manufacture, nails, and iron is also very great. If this shoe can not be employed, then we ought to resort to one in conformation the opposite of that now adopted, in so far that it should be much lighter, be concave on the ground surface and flat towards the foot, and instead of having a groove, have merely the nail-holes punched for the reception of the nail-head. This would assure a safer footing, diminish the strain on the wall by allowing the sole to share in sustaining the weight, as it was intended it should do, and obviate the effects of suction in heavy ground, as well as picking up stones, etc. A shoe I have devised meets these ends, and is merely an imitation of the lower border of the wall, sole and bars. I have tested its utility among troop horses and in the hunting-field for a number of years, and it has proved a good shoe for road work. The bevel on the ground surface suddenly ceasing within an inch or so of the end of the branch leaves a catch, which imitates the angles of the bars, and acts like them in assisting the horse to check his motion suddenly. The nails should be as few and as small as possible, and be driven only a short distance into the wall, which, if reduced to its proper dimensions before the shoe is put on, will not, and ought not to, receive any further rasping, especially on the face, as the shoe should be fitted full to the circumference. A word as to fitting. To secure a perfect coaptation between the shoe and hoof is not an easy matter, and requires much time and tact; and when it has been obtained the shoe is far from being as secured as is desirable, particularly if the hoof is exposed to wet. The fitting is greatly simplified, and an accurate adjustment, as well as a solid surface for the shoe, secured, if the latter be used in a hot state to prove the evenness of the surface on which it is to rest, as well as to fuse or char the immediate ends of the fibers, which are thereby hardened, and resist pressure and the effects of moisture to a wonderful degree. Persons ignorant of the subject imagine this injures the foot, but in all my experience I have never observed any harm to follow. Horn is a very slow conductor of heat, and provided the shoe is sufficiently hot to leave its imprint when momentarily applied, and the hoof is not mutilated to a shred of horn, no injury can or will follow. With regard to security of foothold, and adding to the horse's power in draft, particularly with those horses which travel at a slow pace with heavy loads in our cities, there can be no doubt that calks are necessary, but their utility is greatly diminished, and they do harm to the limbs and joints if a toe-piece is not added. In nearly every town and city in this country, with the exception of London, the claw-shoe, as it has been termed, is in use; and without it the horse would be much more liable to falls, and would draw much less loads with quite as much fatigue. This shoe is not worn in London, and we see horses not drawing half the loads those in these places do, and yet are scarcely able to keep their feet. Surely this is short-sighted policy. With a toe-piece, the hind foot of the horse has a powerful aid in seizing the ground securely, and its propelling muscles can then be brought into full play in moving the load to which it is attached, instead of expending half its force in maintaining equilibrium. Various contrivances have been from time to time proposed to give the horse a better foothold, but none have proved so successful and so cheap as the calks and toe-piece. In connection with this subject of slipping, which is chiefly observed in the streets of our towns and cities, it must be confessed that the manner in which these are paved only too frequently does us little credit as a humane or economical people. Certainly economy has much to do with their construction; but it is short-sighted economy, and chiefly in favor of the rate-payer, not of the community in general, or yet of horses. Indeed, looking at the variety of pavements and their difficulties in the matter of traffic, one must feel that the horses which have to travel on them must be greatly perplexed, and if they have any reflective power they will doubtless consider their masters as very stupid and embarrassing road-makers. Some of the streets in London are infamously cruel to horses. Those paved with granite may be cheap to lay, but they are most objectionable in every respect, and the most expensive of all to horse and carriage owners. They are at all seasons very dangerous and fatiguing for horses in the matter of slipping; they inflict great injury to the limbs and feet from concussion; traction upon them is heavy: they are extremely noisy, and the jar and vibration they occasion to carriages wear these out more rapidly than any other kind of road. When wet and muddy, they are as dangerous to human passengers as to horses. In fact, though granite blocks make a very durable pavement, yet, on the whole, looking at such a pavement from an equestrian point of view, it is the most expensive and dangerous of any in use. As to macadamized roads, there is certainly a better foothold upon them, but their traction is heavy; in wet weather this is increased, and the mud is most objectionable; while in dry weather the dust is a great drawback, and watering is a nuisance and expensive. Noise is also considerable, and repair must be frequent. The asphalt pavement is in many respects objectionable; traction is, no doubt, easy, but when the surface of the pavement is damp there is no foothold for horses, and the danger from serious falls is great. It is not at all a noiseless pavement; sprinkling sand over it to render it more safe increases the noise and the traction, and makes its surface disagreeably dirty. Besides, asphalt does not at all answer on hilly streets. The best pavement, perhaps, ever introduced for horse traffic is that of wood, such as is laid down at Ludgate hill. From the fact that the cubes of wood are so laid that the fiber is vertical, that the interspaces are filled with pitch and gravel, and that they are laid upon diagonal planks, we have not only a very safe and comfortable pavement, so far as the horse's footing is concerned, but the nature of the material and the manner in which it is disposed render it a most humane roadway, with regard to obviating jar and concussion to the feet and legs. Traction upon it is easy. There is comparatively little noise, dirt or dust; and, altogether, for the human and equine population of our towns and cities, perhaps no more economical, safe, and agreeable pavement could be devised. [This fully coincides with the opinion in the article Roads, by an authority thereon.—Editor.] The farrier must do his best to preserve and protect the horse's feet by shoeing, but we have a right to expect that the engineer will not fail to second his efforts by constructing roads which, while insuring safety to horses traveling upon them, will not counteract the advantages of good farriery. The more frequent use of brakes for carriages, and particularly omnibuses, is pulling up suddenly, and also in going down hills, would prove of great benefit to horses, in connection with shoeing and slipping. This matter of roads and brakes for carriages is one of great moment, but particularly the former. It is painful to witness unfortunate horses unable to keep their feet on the horrible pavements with which the majority of streets are laid, and brutal drivers plying their unmerciful whips on the poor creatures' skin for no fault whatever, but merely because a stupid and mistaken economy will persist in constructing a particular kind of road, upon which it is impossible the animals can travel with anything like safety, and at the same time exercise their powers in draft. This consideration brings me to winter, or frost shoeing. In a climate so uncertain and fickle as Great Britian it is difficult to make more than a guess as to the kind of winter we may have in any year, and therefore no provision is made against the occurrence of frost. Indeed, in some winters we may have no frost at all, and the ordinary shoeing suffices for the whole season; but at other times the temperature may suddenly fall, and frost and snow appear; and then all is confusion, partial suspension of traffic, dangerous traveling, serious accidents, and such other incidents as hard winters provide in abundance. The ordinary method of roughing the shoes, as it is termed, consists in taking them off the hoofs, turning up a sharpened calk, and perhaps adding a sharp toe-piece, and putting them on again. This is a slow and expensive process, and of course requires the aid of the farrier either in the stables or at the forge; it is very injurious to the hoofs, takes a good deal of time, and, in consequence of the projections being only soft iron, must be repeated at short intervals. Besides, in the hurry which always exists at this time, the shoes are often badly put on, and get loose or are lost, or the nails are driven into the quick. To obviate all these disadvantages and inconveniences, various contrivances have been proposed. A very temporary one consists in inserting some large, sharp headed nails in the place of others withdrawn. These also injure the hoof. Another is the insertion of sharp studs screwed in at the heels of the shoe. These are convenient, but somewhat expensive, and are liable to break at the neck, leaving the screw portion immovably fixed in the shoe. Other more or less expensive and inefficient appliances have been proposed, but have not succeeded in meeting the requirements of those whose horses must do regular work during frost. This winter-shoeing has attracted my attention for many years. During a campaign it is sometimes of the utmost importance that horses should be able to travel on ice—indeed, the fate of an army or the success of some great movement may depend upon it. I may point to the French retreat from Moscow, in November, 1812, as described by Thiers, when the terrible disasters that occurred were largely due to the absence of some contrivance for enabling the horses to travel on the slippery roads. We may also read with profit the Danish retreat from Schleswig to Sonderburg on the night of February 5, 1865. I have tried every method proposed, but have found none which was economical, efficient and speedily applicable when required, and without the necessity of taking off the shoes. Three years ago I ventured to experiment with a method which has certainly proved to be the nearest to perfection in these respects. During last winter it was very extensively used, and reports were most favorable. This method consists merely in punching a square hole at the end of each branch, and, if thought desirable, at the toe of the shoe, and inserting into it a square, slightly tapering, plug of steel, with a sharp point projecting beyond the lower surface of the shoe. The plug may be of any reasonable length, from one to three inches, but it must fit the hole somewhat accurately and tightly, and must not go quite through the shoe to the hoof. It should be well tempered at the point, to give it durability; and then nothing more is necessary than to insert it into the hole, give it a slight tap on the point, to fix it until the horse puts its weight on it and drives it home, when it is firmly retained, every step keeping it tighter in. This stud rarely falls out if properly made, and when required to be removed, as to be re-sharpened, replaced by another, or left out altogether, a few taps on each side will generally start it, owing to the taper on that portion which fits into the shoe. A set of studs will last four or five days, and the simple square hole takes but little time to punch. At the commencement of winter—say November—all shoes put upon my troop horses are provided with these holes, and the farriers have their studs ready. Should the frost suddenly set in, all the horses can be made proof against slipping on sheet ice, even in a few minutes, and, with a good supply of studs, may travel for weeks without going near a forge, or requiring the farrier. When the frost disappears the studs can be taken out again, and they may be removed every night in the stable, and inserted in the morning before going to duty. I must now conclude what I have to say concerning horse-shoeing in general, and the principle on which it should be based. I have made

SHORT-HORN CATTLE 868 SHORT-HORN CATTLE

no mention of the different kinds of shoes sometimes required for particular hoofs, nor what we may term pathological horse-shoeing, for the cure of disease or defects, natural or acquired, of the feet and limbs. This, though a most interesting and important section, nevertheless comes more within the domain of the scientific veterinary surgeon, and is of too extensive and perhaps technical a character to be here introduced.

SHORE. A piece of timber which props up a wall.

SHORT-HORN CATTLE. The history of this wonderful breed of cattle, once as eminent for their combination of milk and flesh producing qualities as they have in later years been made to excel as strictly beef producers, is very much mixed up, writers, both English and American, having endeavored to cast discredit upon certain strains of blood, either to subserve their own particular views, or to bring into repute the stocks of particular breeders. The following, from the work of Mr. Lewis T. Allen, editor American Short-Horn Herd Book, is undoubtedly as nearly correct as it can now be had. He says: For some centuries anterior to the conquest of England by the First William, (of Normandy,) the northeastern counties of England, Northumberland, Durham and York, (then called Northumbria,) had been possessed, with occasional interruptions, by the Danes, and other Scandinavians of northwestern Europe. They were a warlike people, not only conquering, by their bold raids, the countries along the continental coast to the south of them, even into Holland, but pirates and sea kings as well, carrying their devastations across the water into Northumbria, and some adjoining parts of Britain. While they held the frontier coast of England they established trade in many articles of merchandise and agricultural products, and shipped them to and from both sides of the ocean channel. Among these were cattle in considerable numbers. Southern Denmark, Jutland, Holstein, and Utrecht, long held by the Danes, possessed a breed of cattle—short-horns essentially—having their general appearance, and peculiar colors, but coarse in their form and flesh, yet yielding largely of milk. It is supposed by a majority of the earlier English writers on agriculture and cattle, who paid particular attention to these subjects, that it was from these foreign cattle, imported at that early day from the neighboring continent, that the present race of short-horns are descended, and that for some centuries they inhabited that part of England only. The earliest accounts we have seen, first found them there. Holderness, a district of Yorkshire, was said to number these cattle in considerable herds. They possessed a great aptitude to fatten, in addition to their milking qualities, yet their flesh was coarse, accompanied by a large amount of offal. That they possessed valuable characteristics in their high and broad carcases, and contained within themselves the elements of refinement, when brought within the conditions of shelter, good fare, and painstaking, we may well conjecture. The people of those days were rude and uncultivated, and the cattle must have been rude also. Oftentimes pinched with poverty and scant fare, subject to the storms and blasts of an inclement winter climate, unsheltered, probably, in all seasons, except as the woods or hollows of the land could protect them, the worst points in their anatomy took precedence in their looks, and they were but a sorry spectacle to the eye of an accurate judge, or breeder. Following down to near the middle of the last century, we find that some of the authors named speak of these cattle, on the banks of the river Tees, a stream dividing the counties of York and Durham,) existing in a high degree of improvement, and superior to almost any others which they had seen. As we have before remarked, it is not surprising that they were found in these counties only, as every district in England had its own local breeds to which their people were partial, and cattle were not interchanged as now, except for the purposes of feeding, and going to London, or other large seacoast markets, for consumption. No doubt, in the agricultural progress of the country, these cattle had received considerable attention, and were much improved in their forms, flesh, and general appearance by their breeders, until they arrived at a considerable degree of perfection. Here, then, we find them existing in several excellent herds, and bred with much care. Some pedigrees can be traced, more or less distinctly, back to the year 1740, or even earlier. The late Mr. Bates, in one of his accounts of these cattle, says, in 1784 the estates of the Earl of Northumberland had fine short-horns upon them, for two hundred years previous to that time. Let us see: Bailey, in his survey of Durham, written in the year 1808, says that, seventy years since (1738,) the colors of the cattle of Mr. Milbank and Mr. Croft, were red and white, and white, with a little red about the neck, or roan, as related to him by old men who knew them at the time. Cully also states the same fact. Milbank and Croft were both noted cattle breeders of that day, and into their herds many modern cattle trace their pedigrees. The Duke of Northumberland had good short-horns on his estate at Stanwick, in that county. The Aislabees, of Studley Park, and Sir William St. Quintin, of Scampston, also kept excellent short-horns; and the Stephensons, Maynards, Wetherells, and many others, too numerous to mention, were breeders. As the merits of these cattle became more known, they rapidly increased among the local breeders and farmers of those counties, but they did not obtain anything like a general reputation over the country, until Charles and Robert Colling came on to the stage and commenced breeding them. They were young farmers, brothers, and their father had been a short-horn breeder before them. They established themselves as farmers and cattle-breeders about the year 1780, each having separate herds, but working more or less together, and interchanging the use of their bulls. Charles, the younger, was the more enterprising, but not a better breeder than his brother. With great sagacity and good judgment, they picked up some of the best cows and bulls from the herds of the older breeders around them, and for many years bred them with success and profit. They early possessed themselves of a bull, afterwards called Hubback, claimed, by some, to be the great progenitor of the improved short-horns. He proved a most excellent stock-getter while in the hands of the Collings, as well as before they obtained him, and after he left them. The possession of Hubback proved fortunate for the Collings, as some of their best cattle traced into his blood, which was more or less participated in by the breeders around them. The blood of this bull —Hubback—became so famous, indeed, that any good and well bred beast which could trace its pedigree to him, was counted of rare value. This breed of cattle early attracted attention in America. Soon after the Revolutionary war, cattle supposed to be pure Short-horns were imported into Virginia, cattle as remarkable for their milking qualities as for the flesh they carried since it reported that individual animals gave as high us thirty-two quarts of milk a day. As early as 1797 the produce of these cattle were taken to Kentucky by a Mr. Patton, that soon became widely disseminated over the West as the Patton breed. The editor of this work nearly forty years ago saw descendants of this stock in Illinois, having all the characteristices of the short-horns and they were known as the Patton breed. Among those having them may be mentioned the late Rev. Mr. Morrison, near Momence, Ill. These cattle were still famous for their large size and milking qualities. Indeed those imported up to fifty years ago were remarkable for their milking qualities, and particular herds and strains of this stock still exist excellent in this quality as well as in their flesh making aptitude. As to the further history of the short-horns in America, Mr. Francis M. Rotch, of New York, a gentleman perfectly well qualified, in a report to the United States Government in 1861, says: The majestic size, proud carriage, and beautifully variegated colors of the Short-horn render him easily recognized by the merest tyro; but few who thus admire and recognize them are aware how many qualifications go to make up this splendid whole, or how carefully each point has been weighed and discussed, and its relative value decided; how the useful parts are divided from the ornamental and fashionable, and how systematically the whole has been carried out. The high caste short-horn should have a small head, a broad, flat forehead, with no projection of the frontal bones; the face should be well cut out below the eyes, tapering to a fine muzzle with open nostrils; the nose must be flesh or chocolate colored; any discoloration hinting towards black or blue is very objectionable, though occasionally seen in some of the highest bred families; the eye must be bright, prominent, and yet placid; a small, piggish or hollow eye, or one showing viciousness or nervousness, are alike to be avoided, the latter indicating a bad feeder almost invariably; the horn should be well set on, curving forward, not too heavy, and of a waxy, yellow color at the base; the body should be square, massive, and symmetrical, set on short legs which should be straight and well under the animal; the fore legs should be small in the bone below the knee, whilst the forearm must be broad and tapering downwards, fitting level into the girth; the hind legs must be nearly straight; if the hocks are too much bent, turn inward, or not well under the body, it not only gives an awkward gait in walking, but is generally a sign of weakness; the neck is moderately long, clean in the throat, and running neatly into the shoulders, which should not be too prominent at the points, nor too wide at the top, else the crops will be certain to seem defective; they should mould nicely into the forequarters, and be well covered with flesh on the outside; the neck vein should be well filled up with flesh, and form on smoothly to the shoulder points; the chest must be broad and deep, and full back of the elbows, which secures a good girth and consequent room for the most important vital organs; the brisket should be full and broad rather than narrow and projecting; it is of inferior quality as beef, yet, as a point of beauty and as indicating a propensity to fatten, must not be overlooked. We now come to the upper portion of the frame, carrying the best beef, and here we must have width and thickness and length; the crops must fill up level with the shoulders and back; the ribs must spring level and full from the back, and fill well up to the hips, (the short-horn is apt to be loosely ribbed up). The loin must be broad and well carried forward into the crops, and covered with thick flesh moulding nicely on to the hips, which though wide must not be too prominent, but slope away gradually to the rump or side bones at the tail; a quarter badly filled up between hips and rumps or scooped-out, as it is termed, is very objectionable; the back must be level from neck to tail, with no drops back of the shoulders, nor any rise where the tail is set on; the rumps must be well laid up but not too high, else when the animal is fat we shall have those large masses of fat aggregated about them so common among the breed some years since, but now deservedly stigmatized as had; the twist should be well filled out in the seam, wide and deep, the outside thigh full, the flank deep, and forming with the fore-flank and belly (the latter well supported by its plates) a parallel line with the animal's back. The whole frame must be evenly covered with flesh, of a mellow elastic nature, readily yielding to the fingers, yet following them as the pressure is withdrawn; the skin must be of a moderate thickness, neither papery (too thin) nor thick enough to be stiff and hard; it must be covered with a coat of thick, soft, mossy hair. As regards color the latitude is very great, from deep blood-red through all the intermediate shades and mixtures to pure white, but any other colors, as brown, black, or dun, are never met with in thoroughbreds. Fashion has vindicated the rich red and purple roan as the most desirable colors, and after them red. White is sometimes objected to, under the impression that it is apt to spread through a herd and overpower the other colors; but this fear is more common in this country than in England, where white bulls are often used. Red and white, in blotches, with defined edges not running into roan, is disliked, and the term patchy is applied to it. This discrimination, however, as regards color, is entirely arbitrary, animals of equal excellence and breeding being found of all these colors. We may gather from the foregoing pages that the essential peculiarities of the improved short-horns are, early maturity, a great disposition to fatten, a remarkable evenness on laying on their flesh, a gentle, quiet temper, and, in some tribes and families, a large secretion of milk. It has been claimed by some of their more zealous advocates in this country that they make good oxen, but we hardly think, however docile and powerful they may be, that they can compete in activity and speed with some of the other breeds. Taking into consideration these characteristics, we see how admirably adapted they

SHORT-HORN BULL.

SHORT-HORN COW.

(870)

are for the larger portion of our country. Wherever there is fair pasturage, good water, and shelter from the extremes of heat and cold, there the short-horn thrives. Over the broad prairies and blue grass pasture of the west, in the rich valleys of our great rivers, he roams and flourishes as though in his native vale, and readily adapts himself to the change of situation and climate. But it is to the crosses of the short-horn that we must look for the most general adaptation and dissemination of the breed. The high value of the thoroughbreds for breeding purposes must for many years prevent their universal adoption, and it is only by crossing them upon our so-called natives that we can reap immediate benefit from them. Fortunately for us, no breed more promptly and strongly stamps its impress upon other blood than this one. All the writers on cattle unite in this opinion, and some even advocate crossing the short-horn or other pure races, with a view to their improvement. We shall usually find, however, the most remarkable and satisfactory results when a short-horn is put upon a mongrel or a lately established breed, as then the deep breeding of the sire will obliterate the numerous thin strains of the dam's blood, and the produce will resemble the superior race. The cross between the native cow and the short-horn bull almost always produces good milkers, and, as a whole they afford more milk of a better quality than other beef breeds, and, when dry, they feed quickly and make excellent beef. In this connection we extract from the Fifth Annual Report of the Massachusetts Board of Agriculture a portion of a statement made to them of the dairy performance of some grades of short-horns belonging to Mr. Robinson, of Barre. The cows were half and three-quarters bred. Seven of them yielded, during the first seven days in June, 2,207¾ pounds of milk, averaging forty-five pounds per diem to each cow. From this milk 232 pounds of cheese was made, averaging one pound of cheese to nine and a half pounds of milk. The same cows gave during the three following days 955 pounds of milk, from which forty-one pounds nine ounces of butter was made, averaging one pound of butter to twenty-three pounds of milk. It will be seen that the milk that makes one pound of butter will make two and a half pounds of cheese. These cows had no extra feed during the trial, having been turned to pasture on the 15th of May. This instance is selected not as a very extraordinary performance, but as a well-authenticated and carefully-conducted experiment. We may, without fear of contradiction, pronounce the females of the cross of the short-horn and native as essentially and almost uniformly deep milkers. The original strong predisposition to milk that marked the race, which is shared by none of the other pure races, is admirably fitted to combine with the occasional and accidental quality in the native and in the progeny to assure pre-eminence on this point. The steers are thrifty, and lay on flesh rapidly and evenly, and are ready to turn off at two and a half or three years old. They are hardy as their native parent, and bear transportation and driving admirably, shrinking less than the thoroughbreds. The greater proportion of the cattle now brought from Ohio, Indiana Illinois, Iowa, and further west, to supply markets of the seaboard cities, and for exportation, are crosses of this character, and none pay the feeder better, and again the butcher is rarely disappointed in the fifth quarter. Among the eastern importations were those of 1815, 1822, 1823, 1828, 1835, 1839, 1849-50 into the State of New York. Into Massachusetts, in 1818, 1820, 1823. Into Kentucky, in 1817, and again in 1837-38 and '39. In 1834, large importations were made into Ohio, and again in 1885-86. These were widely distributed, and that they were good animals may be inferred from the fact that they were sold at prices varying from $500 to $2,500 each. The first direct importation of short-horns from England to Illinois was in 1858. These were superior animals and sold at satisfactory prices. Since that time the work of importing and breeding has been carried on all over the North, the Middle States, the West, the Northwest and the northern line of States South, until the time came when animals superior to those English bred were sent back to England, at prices all the way up to $30,000 for single animals. In the breeding of short-horns Canada has not been behind the United States. Since 1885, importations have been common, from England. The breeding has been prosecuted most successfully, and of late years there has been many interchanges of blood between the Dominion and the United States, back and forth, and with satisfaction to all parties concerned, and to-day there are no higher bred or better short-horns in the world than are to be found in the United States and Canada. The points of short-horns, and which will apply in judging all beef animals, with slight variations, are worthy of a somewhat minute description. The points are of two classes, those observed with the eye and those felt with the touch. By the eye we observe the general contour of the animal, size, length, breadth, thickness, fineness of body, head and limb, the loin, back, thigh, the spring of the rib and the manner in which the animal is ribbed close to the hip bones. The touch, that is the feeling under the touch, shows length and quality of the hair, thickness and elasticity of the skin. Thus, the eye and expression of countenance is indicative of disposition and temper; an elastic, mellow, and yet firm hide of medium thickness, shows thick, well marbled flesh. A floating, soft skin of blubbery fat, indicates a bad feeder and often an animal of dark colored flesh. The butcher, in buying an animal for beef has now-a-days but a single object in view. The animal that will turn out the greatest amount of lean meat, in the prime parts with the least offal, and only a moderate amount of fat, for fat is now one of the cheapest portions of the animal. Years ago in the days of tallow candles, the reverse was the case. The back, loin and ribs are the choice bits, next the rump and thighs, then the shoulders, while the neck and head are comparatively worthless. The sagacious breeder while keeping this constantly in view, seeks to add early maturity to good flesh. He who comes nearest to this has the best animal whatever the breed, or the pedigree of the particular breed, for, the butcher's block is the final and the crucial test. Derived from a large breed, the improved short-horn is heavy, less in height than the originals of the Tees, rounder and deeper in the trunk, the limbs shorter, chest and back broader, appearing less in bulk, while really greater in weight. The skin is light-colored, hair reddish brown or white or mixed, the muzzle flesh-colored, the horns shorter and lighter-colored than the former breed, the skin soft to the touch, the form square, the shoulder upright, and the hind-quarter large. The color can not be characterized by a single term, varying greatly from a pure white to a rich red, a mixture being quite common as roan or strawberry. The skin should he velvety and not too thin, while the hair should be plentiful and of a mossy softness. The head of the female is finer and more tapering than that of the male, the neck thinner and lighter, and her shoulder inclining to narrow towards the chine. The short-horn looks smaller than he is. He excels all other stock in facility of fattening, making good and heavy beef in thirty months, and even in two years. Henry Strafford, an excellent judge, thus sums up his points: The head of the male animal is short, but at the same time fine; very broad across the eyes, but gradually tapering to the nose, the nostril of which is full and prominent; the nose itself of a rich flesh color, neither too light nor dark; eyes bright and placid, with ears somewhat large and thin. The head, crowned with a curved and somewhat flat horn, is well set on to a lengthy, broad, muscular neck; the chest wide, deep, and projecting; shoulders fine, oblique, and well formed into the chine; fore legs short, with the upper arm large and powerful; barrel round, deep, and well ribbed up towards the loins and hips, which should be wide and level; back straight from the withers to the setting on of the tail, but still short, that is, from hip to chine, the opinion of many good judges being that a short-horn should have a short back with long frame. Well treated and kept, both alike in the same pasture, with equal winter forage and shelter, at eighteen months old the native may acquire a weight of 600 to 800 pounds, while the short-horn will weigh 1,000 to 1,200 pounds. At two and one-half years the native may have attained a weight of 1,000 pounds, and the short-horn of 1,200 to 1,400 pounds. The latter will be in a profitable bred-condition, while the former will be immature and not fit for market. By adding another year to their keeping, the native arrives at perhaps 1,200 pounds and the short-horn at 1,500 to 2,000 pounds, the former being still unripened, while the latter is at full maturity, and will sell at one or two cents per pound higher than the native. The common steer, at less than four and one-half years, is not fully ripe as a market-animal, and then, with the capital and interest invested in him, together with the risk of disease or death, and the additional forage for the extended time, he brings less money than a short-horn a year younger. These facts, together with the fact that the short-horn has but a small amount of bone and offal according to its weight, and gives a much larger percentage of choice meat than the native, slaughtered at whatever age, prove that the short-horn is more profitable for the breeder, the grazier, the feeder, and, what is quite as important, the consumer.

SHOULDER LAMENESS. Dr. Dadd says: Lameness is more apt to arise in the shoulder than in the corresponding part of the hind extremities; the latter having a bony union to the body, which prevents, or rather limits, undue extension of the muscles. The lameness may exist in the muscular tissues, or at the point of articulation between the shoulder blade and the *os humeri*. The principal symptom is, that the horse, instead of advancing the leg straight forward, moves it in a circular manner; and the action of the shoulder is quite different from that of the other side; it will be observed also, that the animal throws the weight of the body as much on the sound side as possible. The treatment of shoulder lameness will depend altogether on the nature of the case; if it be one of muscular origin, caused by heavy drawing, violent tugging, or galloping on hard roads, rest, fomentations, and a light dose of medicine are indicated. Should the animal still be lame after the inflammatory symptoms have subsided, use the following liniment: one pint linseed oil, one ounce chloric ether, one-half ounce oil of cedar; mix, and apply to the shoulder night and morning. If the disease is confined to the joint, counter-irritants are indicated: some recommend blisters, or use the acetate of cantharides, to be applied occasionally over the parts effected. A stimulating liniment may, however, answer the purpose, composed of equal parts olive oil, spirits camphor and tincture of ginger.

SHREW MICE. *Sorex.* The family of shrews are properly insectivorous, and from the fact of their being nocturnal are seldom seen, even where they are most numerous. They should be protected. The young are blind and naked at birth. Their general characteristics are as follows: The body slender, legs short, the feet and nails resembling those of a mouse; neck short and powerful, and the head stout, terminating in a long, pointed nose, extending much beyond the teeth, the slender, but strong, cartilaginous point of which is movable. The eyes are exceedingly small, and usually hidden by the fur. The lower incisor teeth project horizontally forward from the jaw, at the base, and are curved upward near the tip; the points of the teeth usually of a dark color. The body is densely clothed with soft, glossy fur. On each side are glands, which secrete a fluid of peculiar odor; these glands being more fully developed in the males. The short-tailed shrew, *Sorex blarina*, Cooper's shrew, *S. Cooperi*, and Arnold's shrew, *S. eximius*, are varieties.

SHRIKE. Butcher bird. *Callyria borealis.* The shrikes closely resemble the jays, and get their name, butcher bird, from their habit of impaling their prey on thorns or sharp branches of bushes. It is, however, more than a match for the jay in rapacity. Its food is large insects, small birds, and such small animals as it may be able to overcome. It inhabits most of the Middle and Southern States, coming North in summer to breed. The nest is lodged in the fork of a small tree, often an apple tree. The female lays six eggs, the general appearance being a dirty lead-colored white, dashed with spots of brown at the larger end.

SHRUB. A small, low, dwarfish tree, which, instead of one single stem, puts forth from the same root several sets of stems. A collection of these, tastefully arranged, is a shrubbery.

SHUCK. The husk, or collection of involucra about the corn ear. Shucks are much esteemed for fodder, being very superior to straw and corn fodder. When cut into shreds, they make a good material for mattresses.

SHY. Starting aside, in horses; the result of fear, produced by strange objects.

SIALAGOGUES. Drugs which produce salivation, or an increased flow of saliva.

SILEX, SILICIC ACID. Pure sand, rock crystal. An acid, consisting of one equivalent of silicium, (32.22), a body resembling in appearance charcoal, and three equivalents of oxygen, 46.22. In the cold it is inactive, but at a white heat it forms an exceedingly active acid, combining with bases, and displacing most other acids, except the phosphoric and boracic. The silicates are nearly all insoluble in pure water; glass and common earthen-ware are specimens of silicates, but they gradually decay in the presence of acids, and of carbonic acid and water. But the compounds of silicic acid, with two or three times its weight of carbonate of potash or soda, are soluble silicates, and have been recommended as manures for the cerealia, which always contain a large amount of silicic acid in their stems, leaves, and husks. Most of the minerals and rocks of the earth are silicates, this acid forming from one-quarter to one-third of its entire solid mass. Soluble and other silicates are formed by fusing together sand and the desired chemical body, usually in the state of carbonate, in a black-lead crucible, at a full red heat. Potash, soda, lime, and magnesia in the soil which supply plants with saline matters, are often in the form of silicates; these are slowly decomposed under the influence of the carbonic acid of the air, or from decaying vegetable matter, which converts them into soluble carbonates, whereby they gain access to the plant.

SILICATES. Salts containing silicic acid, usually flinty and insoluble; slate, feldspar, and granite are specimens.

SILIQUA, SILIQUE. A one or two-celled, many-seeded, linear fruit, dehiscent by two valves separating from a septum; the seeds are attached to two placentæ adhering to the septum, and opposite to the lobes of the stigma. The seed pods of the mustard is an example.

SILIQUOSE PLANTS. Improperly applied to leguminous plants, but properly to the cruciferous family.

SILKWORM. The Silkworm has attracted so much attention in all civilized countries where it may be propagated and raised for the silk which is obtained from the cocoons spun by the larvæ, and especially in the United States, where much money has from time to time been spent in establishing this industry, that more than a passing notice is deemed necessary. There is no reason why the rearing of silkworms may not be practiced in any portion of the United States south of 40°, the only question being the cost of labor in attending them. We believe the only two States where the industry is profitably carried on at present is in California and Kansas. The importance of the silk industry and the increasing demand for these products, as wealth increases, will undoubtedly prevent any glutting of the market, since the price of silk fabrics has steadily increased for the last forty years until now the possession of real silk fabrics, unmixed with other material, for dresses is beyond the reach of any but the more wealthy. So important was this industry considered that Dr. Riley was employed by the government of the United States to write a manual on the habits and rearing of the worm and the puperation of the cocoons, and the food-plants of the worms, to which the reader is referred for information not contained in this article. From Dr. Riley's manual, we extract as follows: The Silkworm proper, or that which supplies the ordinary silk of commerce, is the larva of a small moth known to scientific men as *Sericaria mori*. It is often popularly characterized as the Mulberry Silkworm. Its place among insects is with the *Lepidoptera*, or Scaly-winged insects, family *Bombycidæ*, or Spinners. There are several closely allied species, which spin silks of different qualities, none of which, however, unite strength and fineness in the same admirable proportions as does that of the mulberry species. The latter has, moreover, acquired many useful peculiarities during the long centuries of cultivation it has undergone. It has in fact become a true domesticated animal. The quality which man has endeavored to select in breeding this insect is, of course, that of silk producing, and hence we find that, when we compare it with its wild relations, the cocoon is vastly disproportionate to the size of the worm which makes it or the moth that issues from it. Other peculiarities have incidentally appeared, and the great number of varieties or races of the Silkworm almost equals those of the domestic dog. The white color of the species; its seeming want of all desire to escape as long as it is kept supplied with leaves, and the loss of the power of flight on the part of the moth, are all undoubtedly the result of domestication. From these facts, and particularly from that of the great variation within specific limits to which the insect is subject, it will be evident to all that the following remarks upon the nature of the Silkworm must necessarily be very general in their character. The silkworm exists in four states—egg, larva, chrysalis, and adult or imago. The egg of the Silkworm moth is called by silk-raisers the seed. It is nearly round, slightly flattened, and in size resembles a turnip seed. Its color when first deposited is yellow, and this color it retains if unimpregnated. If impregnated, however, it soon acquires a gray, slate, lilac, violet, or even dark green hue, according to variety or breed. It also becomes indented. When diseased it assumes a still darker and dull tint. With some varieties it is fastened to the substance upon which it is deposited, by a gummy secretion of the moth produced in the act of ovipositing. Other varieties, however, among which may be mentioned the Adrianople whites and the yellows from Nouka, in the Caucasus, have not this natural gum. As the hatching point approaches, the egg becomes lighter in color, which is due to the fact that its fluid contents become concentrated, as it were, into the central, forming worm, leaving an intervening space between it and the shell, which is semi-transparent. Just before hatching, the worm within becoming more active, a slight clicking sound is frequently heard, which sound is, however, common to the eggs of many other insects. After the worm has made its exit by gnawing a hole through one side of the shell, this last becomes quite white. Each female produces on an average from three to four hundred eggs, and one ounce of eggs contains about 40,000 individuals. It has been noticed that the color of the albuminous fluid of the egg corresponds to that of the cocoon, so that when the fluid is white the cocoon produced is also white, and when yellow the cocoon again corresponds. The worm goes through from three to four molts or sicknesses, the latter being the normal number. The periods between these different molts are called ages, there being five of these ages including the first from the hatching and the last from the fourth molt to the spinning period. The time between each of these molts is usually divided as follows: The first period occupies from five to six days, the second but four or five, the third about five, the fourth from five to six, and the fifth from eight to ten. These periods are not exact, but simply proportionate. The time from the hatching to the spinning of the cocoons may, and does, vary all the way from thirty to forty days, depending upon the race of the worm, the quality of the food, mode of feeding, temperature, etc.; but the same relative proportion of time between molts usually holds true. The color of the newly-hatched worm is black or dark gray, and it is covered with long stiff hairs, which, upon close

FULL-GROWN LARVA OF SILKWORM.

examination, will be found to spring from pale-colored tubercles. Different shades of dark gray will, however, be found among worms hatching from the same batch of eggs. The hairs and tubercles are not noticeable after the first molt and the worm gradually gets lighter and lighter until, in the last age, it is of a cream-white color. When full grown it presents the appearance of Fig. 1. It never becomes entirely smooth, however, as there are short hairs along the sides, and very minute ones, not noticeable with the unaided eye, all over the body. The preparation for each molt requires from two to three days of fasting and rest, during which time the worm attaches itself firmly by the abdominal prolegs. In front of the first joint a dark triangular spot is at this time noticeable, indicating the growth of the new head; and when the term of sickness is over, the worm casts its old integument, rests a short time to recover strength, and then, freshened, supple, and hungry, goes to work feeding voraciously to compensate for lost time. This so-called sickness which preceded the molt was, in its turn, preceded by a most voracious appetite, which served to stretch the skin. In the operation of molting, the new head is first disengaged from the old skin, which is then gradually worked back from segment to segment until entirely cast off. If the worm is feeble, or has met with any misfortune, the shriveled skin may remain on the end of the body, being held by the anal horn; in which case the individual usually perishes in the course of time. It has been usually estimated that the worm in its growth consumes its own weight of leaves every day it feeds; but this is only an approximation. Yet it is certain that during the last few days before commencing to spin, it consumes more than during the whole of its previous worm-existence. It is a curious fact, first noted by Quatrefages, that the color of the abdominal prolegs at this time corresponds with the color of the silk. Having attained full growth, the worm is ready to spin up. It shrinks somewhat in size, voids most of the excrement remaining in the alimentary canal; acquires a clear, translucent, often pinkish or amber-colored hue; becomes restless, ceases to feed, and throws out silken threads. The silk is elaborated in a fluid condition in two long, slender, convoluted vessels, one upon each side of the alimentary canal. As these vessels approach the head they become less convoluted and more slender, and finally unite within the spinneret, from which the silk issues in a glutinous state, and apparently in a single thread. The glutinous liquid which combines the two, and which hardens immediately on exposure to the air, may, however, be dissolved in warm water. The worm usually consumes from three to five days in the construction of the cocoon, and then passes in three days more, by a final molt, into the chrysalis state. The cocoon consists of an outer lining of loose silk known as floss, which is used for carding, and is spun by the worm in first getting its bearings. The amount of this loose silk varies in different breeds. The inner cocoon is tough, strong, and compact, composed of a firm, continuous thread, which is, however, not wound in concentric circles, as might fairly be supposed, but irregularly, in short figure-of-eight loops, first in one place and then in another, so that in reeling, several yards of silk may be taken off without the cocoon turning round. In form the cocoon is usually oval, and in color yellowish, but in both these features it varies greatly, being either pure silvery-white, cream or carneous green, and even roseate, and very often constricted in the middle. It has always been considered possible to distinguish the sex of the contained insect from the general shape of the cocoon, those containing males being slender, depressed in the middle, and pointed at both ends, while the female cocoons are of a larger size and rounder form, and resemble in shape a hen's egg with equal ends. The chrysalis is a brown, oval body, considerably less in size than the full-grown worm. In the external integument may

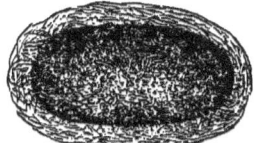

SILKWORM COCOON.

be traced folds corresponding with the abdominal rings, the wings folded over the breast, the antennæ, and the eyes of the enclosed insect—the future moth. At the posterior end of the chrysalis, pushed closely up to the wall of the cocoon, is the last larval skin, compressed into a dry wad of wrinkled integument. The chrysalis state continues for from two to three weeks, when the skin bursts and the moth emerges. With no jaws, and confined within the narrow space of the cocoon, the moth finds some difficulty in escaping. For this purpose it is provided, in two glands near the obsolete mouth, with a strongly alkaline liquid secretion with which it moistens the end of the cocoon, and dissolves the hard gummy lining. Then, by a forward and backward motion, the prisoner, with crimped and damp wings, gradually forces its way out, and when once out the wings soon expand and dry. The silken threads are simply pushed aside, but enough of them get broken in the process to render the cocoons, from which the moths escape, comparatively useless for reeling. The moth is of a cream color, with more or less distinct brownish markings across

MOTH OF SILKWORM.

the wings. The males have broader antennæ, or feelers, than the females, and may, by this feature, at once be distinguished. Neither sex flies, but the male is more active than the female. They couple soon after issuing, and in a short time the female begins depositing her eggs, whether they have been impregnated or not. Domestication has had the effect of producing numerous varieties of the Silkworm, every different climate into which it has been carried having produced either some changes in the quality of the silk, or the shape or color of the cocoons; or else altered the habits of the worm. Some varieties produce but one brood in a year, no matter how the eggs are manipulated; such are known as Annuals. Others, known as Bivoltins, hatch twice in the course of a year; the first time, as with the Annuals, in April or May, and the second, eight or ten days after the eggs are laid by the first brood. The eggs of the second brood only are kept for the next year's crop, as those of the first brood always either hatch or die soon after being laid. The Trevoltins produce three annual generations. There are also Quadrivoltins, and in Bengal, a variety known as Daccy which is said to produce eight generations in the course of a year. Some varieties molt but three times instead of four, especially in warm countries and with Trevoltins. Experiments, taking into consideration the size of the cocoon, quality of silk, time occupied, hardiness, quantity of leaves required, etc., have proved the Annuals to be more profitable than any of the polyvoltins, although Bivoltins are often reared; and Mr. Alfred Brewster, of San Gabriel, Cal., says that he found a green Japanese variety of these last more hardy than the Chinese Annuals. Varieties are also known, by the color of the cocoons they produce, as Greens, or Whites, or Yellows, and also by the country in which they flourish. The white silk is most valuable in commerce, but the races producing yellow, cream-colored, or flesh-colored cocoons are generally considered to be the most vigorous. No classification of varieties can be attempted, as individuals of the same breed exported to a dozen different localities would, in all probability, soon present a dozen varieties. The three most marked and noted European varieties are the Milanese (Italian), breed, producing fine, small, yellow cocoons; the Ardèche (French), producing large yellow cocoons, and the Brousse (Turkish), producing large white cocoons of the best quality in Europe. Owing to the fearful prevalence of *pébrine* among the French and Italian races for fifteen or twenty years back, the Japanese Annuals have come into favor. The eggs are bought at Yokohama in September, and shipped during the winter. There are two principal varieties in use, the one producing white and the other greenish cocoons, and known respectively as the White Japanese and the Green Japanese Annuals. These cocoons are by no means large, but the pods are solid and firm, and yield an abundance of silk. They are about of a size, and both varieties are almost always constricted in the middle. Another valuable race is the White Chinese Annual which much resembles the White Japanese but is not as generally constricted. We have already seen the importance of getting healthy eggs, free from hereditary disease, and of good and valuable races. There is little danger of premature hatching until December, but from that time on, the eggs should be kept in a cool, dry room in tin boxes to prevent the ravages of rats and mice. They are most safely stored in a dry cellar, where the temperature rarely sinks below the freezing point, and they should be occasionally looked at to make sure that they are not affected by mold. If at any time, mold be perceived upon them it should be at once rubbed or brushed off, and the atmosphere made drier. If the tin boxes be perforated on two sides and the perforations covered with fine wire gauze, the chances of injury will be reduced to a minimum. The eggs may also, whether on cards or loose, be tied up in small bags and hung to the ceiling of the cold room. The string of the bag should be passed through a bottle neck or a piece of tin to prevent injury from rats and mice. The temperature should never be allowed to rise above 40° Fahr., but may be allowed to sink below freezing point without injury. Indeed, eggs sent from one country to another are usually packed in ice. They should be kept at a low temperature until the mulberry leaves are well started in the spring, and great care must be taken as the weather grows warmer to prevent hatching before their food is ready for them, since both the Mulberry and Osage Orange are rather late in leafing out. One great object should be, in fact, to have them all kept back, as the tendency in our climate is to premature hatching. Another object should be to have them hatch uniformly, and this is best attained by keeping together those laid at one and the same time, and by wintering them as already recommended, in cellars that are cool enough to prevent any embryonic development. They should then, as soon as the leaves of the food plant have commenced to put forth, be placed in trays and brought into a well-aired room where the temperature averages about 75° Fahr. If they have been wintered adhering to the cloth on which they were laid, all that is necessary is to spread the same cloth over the bottom of a tray. If, on the contrary, they have been wintered in the loose condition, they must be uniformly sifted or spread over sheets of cloth or paper. The temperature should be kept uniform, and a small stove in the hatching-room will prove very valuable in providing this uniformity. The heat of the room may be increased about two degrees each day, and if the eggs have been well kept back during the winter, they will begin to hatch under such treatment on the fifth or sixth day. By no means must the eggs be exposed to the sun's rays, which would kill them in a very short time. As the time of hatching approaches, the eggs grow lighter in color, and then the atmosphere must be kept moist artificially by sprinkling the floor, or otherwise, in order to enable the worms to eat through the egg-shell more easily. They also appear fresher and more vigorous with due amount of moisture. The room in which the

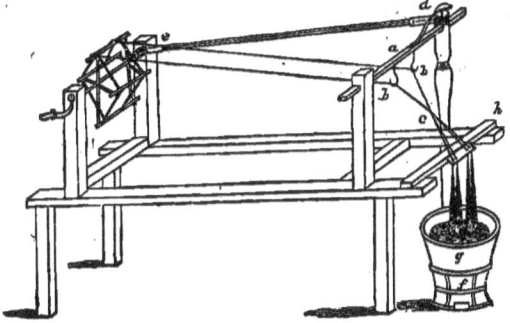

PIEDMONTESE SILK REEL.

rearing is to be done should be so arranged that it can be thoroughly and easily ventilated, and warmed if desirable. A northeast exposure is the best, and buildings erected for the express purpose should, of course, combine these requisites. If but few worms are to be reared, all the operations can be performed in trays upon tables, but in large establishments the room is arranged with deep and numerous shelves from four to eight feet deep and two feet and six inches apart. All wood, however, should be well seasoned, as green wood seems to be injurious to the health of the worms. When the eggs are about to hatch, mosquito-netting or perforated paper should be laid over them lightly. Upon this can be evenly spread freshly-plucked leaves or buds. The worms rise through the meshes of the net or the holes in the paper and cluster upon the leaves, when the whole net can easily be moved. In this preparation for moving, paper has the advantage over the netting; it is stiffer and does not lump the worms together in the middle. They may now be spread upon the shelves or trays, taken to give them plenty of space, as they grow rapidly. Each day's hatching should be kept separate in order that the worms may be of a uniform size, and go through their different moltings or sicknesses with regularity and uniformity; and all eggs not hatched after the fourth day from the appearance of the first should be thrown away, as they will be found to contain inferior, weakly, or sickly worms. It is calculated that one ounce of eggs of a good race will produce 100 pounds of fresh cocoons; while for every additional ounce the percentage is reduced if the worms are all raised together, until for twenty ounces the average does not exceed twenty-five pounds of cocoons per ounce. Such is the general experience throughout France, according to Guérin Méneville, and it shows the importance of keeping them in small broods, or of rearing on a moderate scale. The young worms may be removed from place to place by means of a small camel's-hair brush, but should be handled as little as possible. The best mode of feeding and caring for them is by continuing the use of the feeding-net first mentioned. As the worms increase in size the net must have larger meshes, and if it should be used every time fresh food is furnished, it will save a large amount of time and care. It entirely obviates the necessity of handling the worms, and enables the person having charge of them to keep them thoroughly clean; for, while they pass up through the net to take their fresh food, their excrement drops through it and is always taken up with the old litter beneath. It also acts as a detective of disease; for such worms as are injured, feeble, or sickly, usually fail to mount through the meshes and should be carried off and destroyed with the refuse in the old net below. Placing on of the new net and carrying away of the old is such a great convenience and time-saver that, in France, for many years, paper, stamped by machinery with holes of different sizes, suited to the different stages of the worms, has been used. The paper has the advantage of cheapness and stiffness, but a discussion as to the best material is unnecessary here, the aim being to enforce the principle of the progressive rise of the worms. Details will suggest themselves to the operator. Where the nets are not used, there is an advantage in feeding the worms upon leaf-covered twigs and branches, because these last allow a free passage of air, and the leaves keep fresh a longer time

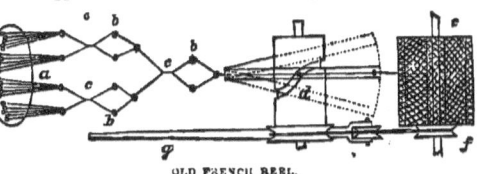

OLD FRENCH REEL.

than when plucked. In thus feeding with branches consists the whole secret of the California system, so much praised and advocated by M. L. Prevost. The proper, stamped paper not being easily obtained in this country, mosquito-netting will be found a very fair substitute while the worms are young, and when they are larger I have found thin slats of some non-resinous and well-seasoned wood, tacked in parallel lines to a frame just large enough to set in the trays, very serviceable and convenient—small square blocks of similar wood being used at the corners of the tray to support the frame while the worms are passing up through it. Coarse twine-netting stretched over a similar frame will answer the same purpose, but wire-netting is less useful, as the worms dislike the smooth metal. Where branches, and not leaves, are fed, the Osage Orange has the advantage of Mulberry, as its spines prevent too close settling or packing, and thus insure ventilation. It is recommended by many to feed the worms while in their first age, and, consequently, weak and tender, leaves that have been cut up or hashed, in order to give them more edges to eat upon and make less work for them. This, however, is hardly necessary with Annuals, although it is quite generally practiced in France. With the second brood of Bivoltins it might be advisable, inasmuch as the leaves at the season of the year when they appear, have attained their full growth and are a little tough for the newly-hatched individuals. In the spring, however, the leaves are small and tender, and nature has provided the young worms with sufficiently strong jaws to cut them. Many rules have been laid down as to regularity of feeding, and much stress has been put upon it by some writers, most advising four meals a day at regular intervals, while a given number of meals between molts has also been urged; but such definite rules are of but little avail, as so much depends upon circumstances and conditions. The food should, in fact, be renewed whenever the leaves have been devoured, or whenever they have become in the least dry, which, of course, takes place much quicker when young and tender than when mature. This also is an objection to the use of the hashed leaves, as, of course, they would dry very quickly. The worms eat most freely early in the morning and late at night, and it would be well to renew the leaves abundantly between 5 and 6 a. m. and between 10 and 11 p. m. One or two additional meals should be given during the day, according as the worms may seem to need them Great care should be taken to pick the leaves for the early morning meal the evening before, as when picked and fed with the dew upon them they are more apt to induce disease. Indeed, the rule should be laid down, never feed wet or damp leaves to your worms. In case they are picked during a rain, they should be thoroughly dried before being fed; and on the approach of a storm, it is always well to lay in a stock, which should be kept from heating by occasional stirring. Care should also be taken to spread the leaves evenly, so that all may feed alike. During this first and most delicate age the worm requires much care and watching. As the fifth or sixth day approaches, signs of the first molt begin to be noticed. The worm begins to lose appetite and grow more shiny, and soon the dark spot already described appears above the head. Feeding should now cease, and the shelves or trays should be made as clean as possible. Some will undoubtedly undergo the shedding of the skin much more easily and quickly than others, but no feed should be given to these forward individuals until nearly all have completed the molt. This serves to keep the batch together, and the first ones will wait one or even two days without injury from want of food. It is, however, unnecessary to wait for all, as there will always be some few which remain sick after the great majority have cast their skins. These should either be set aside and kept separate, or destroyed, as they are usually the most feeble and most inclined to disease; otherwise, the batch will grow more and more irregular in their moltings and the diseased worms will assuredly contaminate the healthy ones. It is really doubtful whether the silk raised from these weak individuals will pay for the trouble of rearing them separately, and it will be better perhaps to destroy them. The importance of keeping each batch together, and of causing the worms to molt simultaneously, can not be too much insisted upon as a means of saving time. As soon as the great majority have molted they should be copiously fed, and, as they grow very rapidly after each molt, and as they must always be allowed plenty of room, it will probably become necessary to divide the batch, and this is readily done at any meal by removing the net when about half of the worms have risen and replacing it by an additional one. The space allotted to each batch should, of course, be increased proportionately with the growth of the worms. The same precautions should be observed in the three succeeding molts as in this first one. As regards the temperature of the rearing-room, great care should be taken to avoid all sudden changes from warm to cold, or vice versa. A mean temperature of 75° or 80° F. will usually bring the worms to the spinning-point in the course of thirty-five days after hatching, but the rapidity of development depends upon a variety of other causes, such as quality of leaf, race of worm, etc. If it can be prevented, the temperature should not be permitted to rise very much above 80°, and it is for this reason that a room with a northern or northeastern exposure was recommended as preferable to any other. The air should be kept pure all of the time, and arrangements should be made to secure a good circulation. Great care should be taken to guard against the incursions of ants and other predaceous insects, which would make sad havoc among the worms were they allowed an entrance, and all through the existence of the insect, from the egg to the moth, rats and mice are on the watch for a chance to get at them, and are to be feared almost as much as any other enemy the Silkworm has. The second and third casting of the skin takes place with but little more difficulty than the first, but the fourth is more laborious, and the worms not only take more time in undergoing it, but more often perish in the act. At this molt it is perhaps better to give the more forward individuals a light feed as soon as they have completed the change, inasmuch as it is the last molt and but little is to be gained by the retardation, whereas it is important to feed them all that they will eat, since much of the nutriment given during the last age goes for the elaboration of the silk. At each successive molt the color of the worm has been gradually whitening, until it is now of a decided cream color. Some breeds, however, remain dark, and occasionally there is an individual with zebra-like markings. During these last few days the worms require the greatest care and attention. All excrement and litter must be often removed, and the sickly and diseased ones watched for and removed from the rest. The quantity of leaves which they devour in this fifth age is something enormous, and the feeding will keep the attendant busily employed. Summed up, the requisites to successful Silkworm raising are: 1. Uniformity of age in the individuals of the same tray, so as to insure their molting simultaneously. 2. No intermission in the supply of fresh food, except during the molting periods. 3. Plenty of room, so that the worms may not too closely crowd each other. 4. Fresh air and as uniform temperature as possible. 5. Cleanliness. The last three are particularly necessary during the fourth and fifth ages. While small, the frass, dung, and detritus dry rapidly, and may, though they should not, be left for several days in a tray with impunity, but he who allows his trays to go uncleaned for more than a day during the ages mentioned will suffer in the disease and mortality of his worms just as they are reaching the spinning-point. With eight or ten days of busy feeding, after the last molt, the worms, as we have learned before, will begin to lose appetite, shrink in size, become restless, and throw out silk, and the arches for the spinning of the cocoons must now be prepared. These can be made of twigs of different trees, two or three feet long, set up upon the shelves over the worms, and made to interlock in the form of an arch above them. Interlace these twigs with broom-corn, hemlock, or other well-dried brush. The feet of each arch should be only about a foot apart. The temperature of the room should now be kept about 80°, as the silk does not flow so freely in a cool atmosphere. The worms will immediately mount into the branches and commence to spin their cocoons. They will not all, however, mount at the same time, and those which are more tardy should be fed often, but in small quantities at a time, in order to economize the leaves, as almost every moment some few will quit and mount. There will always be a few which altogether fail to mount, and prefer to spin in their trays. It is best, therefore, after the bulk have mounted, to remove the trays and lay brush carefully over them. The fact that the worms already mounted make a final discharge of soft and semi-fluid excrement before beginning to spin makes this separation necessary, as otherwise the cocoons of the lower ones would be badly soiled. As the worms begin to spin they should be carefully watched, to guard against two or three of them making what is called a double or treble cocoon, which would be unfit for reeling purposes. Whenever one worm is about to spin up too near another, it should be carefully removed to another part of the arch. In two or three days the spinning will have been completed, and in six or seven the chrysalis will be formed. Eight days from the time the spinning commenced, it will be time to gather the cocoons. The arches should be carefully taken apart, and the spotted or stained cocoons first removed and laid aside. Care should be taken not to stain the clean ones with the black fluids of such worms as may have died and become putrid, for there are always a few of these in every cocoonery. The outer cocoons of loose or floss silk are then torn from the inner cocoons or pods, and the latter separated according to color, weight, and firmness of texture; those which best resist pressure indicating that the worm has best accomplished its work. Too much care can not be taken to remove the soft or imperfect cocoons, as, if mixed with the firm ones, they would be surely crushed and soil the others with their contents. The very best of the firm cocoons are now to be chosen as seed for the next year, unless the raiser prefers buying his eggs to the trouble of caring for the moths and keeping the eggs through the winter. Eggs bought from large establishments are, however apt to be untrustworthy, and it is, well for all silk-raisers to provide their own seed. These cocoons should be chosen for their firmness, and the fineness and color of the silk, rather than for their size. Mr. Crozier says: If white, take them of the purest white, neither soft nor satin-like; if yellow, give preference to the straw-colored, which are the most sought after; and, last, if they are the green of Japan, the greener they are, of a dark, sharp color, very glossy, the better is the quality of the thread. Discard the pale shades in the last breed. If there are any double or treble cocoons in the batch, of the right color, quality, and consistency, they should be used before the others, as they are just as good for breeding purposes, though unfit for reeling. In estimating the quantity that will be required, the following figures will be of use: The general estimate is always made of 40,000 eggs to the ounce, and also that each female lays from 300 to 400 eggs. Taking the higher estimate, it will require only 100 females to lay an ounce of eggs; taking the lower, it will require 133. It will, therefore, not be safe to take fewer than 200 cocoons, half males and half females, if an ounce of seed is desired, and from that to 225 would be safer. While it may not always be possible to determine the sex of the cocoons by their shape, we may approximately separate them by weighing. The whole quantity set aside for breeding purposes is first weighed in order to get the average, and then each one is weighed separately, and all above the average may be pretty accurately considered females and all below it males. These breeding cocoons should now be either pasted upon card-board on their sides, or strung upon a string. great care being taken to run the needle through the silk only and not deep enough to injure the chrysalis, the object being in both cases to secure the cocoon so that the moth can the more readily make its escape. They can be laid aside in a rat-proof place to await the appearance of the moths, and in the mean time the other cocoons should be taken care of. In most silk-producing countries the parties who raise the cocoons sell them to the reeling establishments before suffocation is necessary, as these establishments have better facilities for this work than are to be found in private families. If, however, the reeling is done by the raiser, or some time must elapse before the cocoons can be sent to a reeling establishment, some means must be used to kill the contained chrysalis before the cocoon is injured for reeling purposes by the egress of the moth. This can be done by stifling them with steam or choking them by dry heat. Steaming is the surest, quickest, and best method, if the facilities are at hand. It can be done at any steam mill. The cocoons are laid upon shelves in a tightly-sealed box and the steam is turned in. Twenty minutes will suffice to do the required work, and the cocoons are then dried in the sun. The dry heat method occupies a much longer time The cocoons are placed in shallow baskets and slipped on iron drawers into an oven which is kept heated to a temperature of about 200° Fahr. This should not be increased for fear of burning the silk. This operation lasts from two to twenty-four hours. A certain humming noise continues so long as there is any life, and its cessation is an indication that the chrysalids are all dead. Where the choking is well done there is little loss, only about one per cent, of the cocoons bursting at the ends. After choking in this manner, the cocoons should be strewn upon long, wooden shelves in the shade, with plenty of air, and, for the first few days, frequently stirred. After remaining on these shelves for about two months, with occasional stirrings, the chrysalids become quite dry and the cocoons will preserve indefinitely. They are, however, still subject to the attacks of rats and mice, and the little beetles known as museum pests, belonging to the genera *Dermestes* and *Anthrenus*, are attracted by the dead chrysalids within and will penetrate the cocoon, injuring it for reeling purposes. In the warm, Southern States the dry heat choking can be accomplished by simple exposure to the sun. This was done by M. L. Prevost, in Southern California, and is practiced habitually by Mr. Crozier in Silkville, Kansas, who says: Here the cocoons need only to be fully exposed to the rays of the sun, from nine o'clock in the morning till four o'clock in the afternoon. Two or three days of such exposure are sufficient. But, as some time strong wind can annihilate the effect of the sun's warmth, it is good to have for that purpose long boxes, four feet wide, sides six inches high, to be covered with glass frames. This will increase the heat, and, by absorbing the air of the box, stifle your chrysalis most surely. Ed. Müller, another California grower, (Nevada county), always makes use of this method of stifling by the sun's rays, but says that the glass cover of the box should be left cracked open to allow the evaporation of the moisture, which otherwise would collect in large drops upon the glass, and, falling back upon the cocoons, would keep them moist for a longer time. Do not, however, allow the ants to creep in at the crack, as they too will penetrate the cocoon to feed upon the chrysalis. In the colder climates it has been suggested that the chrysalis could be well choked, with no injury to the cocoons, by placing them in a vacuum box and exhausting the air. Chloroform has been used to a certain extent, and experiments are now being made in France with sulph-hydric acid gas, a vapor which is evolved from the mixture of dilute sulphuric acid and sulphide of iron; also with bisulphide of carbon. In from to twelve to twenty days from the time when the worm commenced to spin, the moths will begin to issue from the cocoons laid aside for breeding purposes. They issue abundantly during the early morning hours, from four to eight o'clock, and as they appear, they should be taken by the wings and the sexes kept apart for a short time. The males may be readily distinguished from the females by their broader antennæ and smaller bodies, as also by the incessant fluttering of their wings. The females remain comparatively quiet, their abdomens being heavy and distended with eggs. A few hours after issuing, the sexes, in equal numbers, may be placed together, great care being taken to destroy any that are at all deformed, in order to keep the breed as fine as possible. They should be placed upon paper or card-board, and the room should be kept as dark as possible in order that the males shall not uncouple themselves. For the complete impregnation of the eggs, the sexes should be kept together six hours, neither more nor less, and occasionally visited in order to replace those males which may have become separated. Should there, on this day, more males than females issue, the superfluous males may be put in a closed box and kept till the next day, when the state of things may be reversed. Should there, on the other hand, be a superfluity of females, a sufficient number of the strongest and most vigorous males should be uncoupled at four hours and placed with the unpaired females for six hours more. As the pairs are uncoupled at the end of six hours, care should be taken to injure neither sex. The female should be held by the wings with one hand and the abdomen of the male gently pressed with the other. The males may then be laid aside in a box, as there may be use for them before all the moths have appeared. After all the females are impregnated, however, they may be thrown away. These last, as soon as separated, should be placed for a few minutes upon sheets of blotting-paper, where they will free themselves of a quantity of greenish-yellow fluid. From the blotting-paper they should be transferred to trays lined with cloth upon which the eggs are to be laid. This cloth should be of the smoothest sort of woolen stuff rather than of linen or paper, if it is desired to remove the eggs at a future time, as they will stick so fast to the latter that it will be difficult to remove without bruising them. Upon these trays they may be placed in rows, and will immediately commence depositing. It is advisable to tip up the trays at one end so that they incline a little, as the moths are then more apt to lay their eggs uniformly. They should also be kept in the dark, in accordance with the nocturnal habit of the moth. The temperature of the room should be kept at about 75°, and plenty of air given during oviposition. All of the thoroughly impregnated eggs will be laid in about twenty-four hours, and the moth should be removed after that length of time. She may continue depositing a short time longer, but the eggs should be kept by themselves and not mixed with the others. It will be well, also, if the best and purest breed be desired, to keep the eggs of those moths which were coupled with males that had been used before, separated from the eggs laid by those which were coupled with virgin males. The eggs are best preserved on the cloth where originally deposited, as they are protected by a natural coating of varnish, and, being fastened, the worms, when hatching, eat their way out better. For commercial purposes, however, they are usually detached during the winter by immersing the cloth containing them in cool, soft water for a few moments; the moisture being then drained off by means of blotting-paper, and the eggs gently removed with a paper-knife. They are then washed in soft water, thoroughly dried, and put away for keeping. All eggs which swim on the surface are considered bad and discarded. The Japanese producers sell their eggs on cards or cartoons made of coarse silk. The cards are placed in wooden frames, the rims of which are varnished, so that the moths—disliking the varnish—are made to confine their eggs upon the cards, which are consequently covered in a very regular and uniform manner. The egg retains the characteristic color of the unimpregnated ones—light yellow—for twelve or fifteen days, when it gradually acquires the gray, lavender, or greenish tint of impregnation. The moths live but a few days after having perpetuated their kind.

SILVER. A well-known metal; it is soluble in nitric acid, the salt, nitrate of silver, being used as a caustic in farriery, and in the laboratory as a test for chlorine, with which it produces a white, curdy compound, chloride of silver, that is soluble in ammonia, and blackens by exposure to light.

SILVER GRAIN, IN WOODS. The bright markings; the medullary rays.

SILVER WEED. *Potentilla anserina.* A perennial running weed with yellow flowers, and five-parted, silvery leaves, generally growing on poor soils.

SINAPISM. A mustard poultice or other preparation.

SINCIPUT. The forehead.

SINUS. A cavity; the veins of the brain are so called.

SINUOUS. Full of cavities, tortuous.

SIT-FAST. In farriery, an ulcerated sore in which a part of the skin has turned horny; if a healthy tone can not be gotten up by rubbing with mercurial ointment, it must have a mild blister applied, which will cause it to suppurate. It generally proceeds from a warble or little tumor resulting from the presure of the saddle.

SIZE. A thin glue made from skins.

SKELETON. The bony frame on which the muscles and soft parts are placed.

SKID. A drag chain; ways for loading logs.

SKIN. The external coat of animals. It consists of a scarfskin, or epidermis, a *rete mucosum*, which is thin and colored, and the *cutis vera*, which forms the substance, and from which hairs, etc., proceed.

SKIRTING. In building, the narrow, horizontal board running along the walls of a room at the floor.

SKUNK. *Mephitis mephitica.* This well-known animal inhabits the entire United States, east of the Rocky mountains and north of Texas, preferring the banks of streams and open woods, or some secluded situation near dwellings. Where there is no suitable place for burrows, it will take up its habitation in a wood pile, under out buildings, or even under dwellings. Its mephitic odor, secreted from glands situated below the root of the tail, is its means of defense. From the two orifices the secretion may be ejected several feet. Its principal food is insects and small verminous animals, also eggs when it can get at them. The injury it does in destroying eggs is trifling, and were it not for its terrible odor it would become one of great benefit from its persistency as an insect destroyer. West of the plains, in California, Oregon, and Texas, the common species East is replaced by two other species, *Mephitis occidentalis* and *M. Bicolor.* The skunk may be rendered very tame, and by the removal of the secreting glands it will no longer have the power of giving out its terrible odor, which, however, is never done except when angry or frightened. Its skin and fur are valuable, if not tainted with its odor, and large numbers are collected by the fur companies.

SKUNK CABBAGE. *Symplocarpus fœtidus.* Marsh cabbage. A large-leaved plant of the family *Aroidæ,* growing in wet places at the North; it has an unpleasant odor, and is reputed antispasmodic.

SLATE. Any rock which has a close texture and is readily split into slabs. The term is more particularly applied to the fine aluminous slates used in roofing and for writing upon.

SLEEPER. Timbers on which are laid the ground joists of a building or railway.

SLEET. A cold rain mixed with snow.

SLIPS. Twigs or small branches taken from a tree or bush for the purpose of propagation.

SLOE. In Europe, this name is given to a small wild plum, the *Prunus spinosa,* which is used as a dwarf stock for grafting plums. In the United States it is given to the *Prunus pygmæa,* and also the *Viburnum prunifolium.*

SLOUGH. A name given to decayed matters separating from a wound: proud flesh; a muddy hole.

SLUG. A name applied to various larva, those of saw-flies, for instance, known by their slimy appearance, and which are particularly injurious to the pear, rose, and it is said in Europe an allied species attacks the cereal grains. The remedy is dusting with white hellebore, (*veratrum,*) or fresh slaked lime, the latter for large trees, and the former for small shrubs and plants. Snails and ground slugs are said to be attracted to small pots, sunk nearly even with the ground, and partly filled with a mixture of starch and iodine. They are said to be attracted by the emanations of iodine for considerable distances.

SLUICE. A water-way of stone, brick, plank, or other material for conveying water; in irrigation, connected with a head-gate. (See Irrigation.)

SMOOTH BROME GRASS. (See Chess.)

SMUT. The best preventives known are to keep the lands occasionally limed or salted, never using too much rank stable manure without some saline matters; and, secondly, steeping the seeds before sowing in solution of sulphate of copper, (blue vitriol). One ounce and a quarter of the salt is used to a bushel of wheat; it is dissolved in just enough water to wet the grain, which is steeped for three quarters of an hour, and dried by being spread out. A strong brine and milk of lime are also used with good success; but the copper solution is superior.

SMUT IN GRAIN. Smut is a fungus, or parasite, developing or replacing, where it develops, the organs in which it is developed. The seeds (spores) are exceedingly minute, and can not be recognized singly, except under a considerable magnifying power. It attacks the leaves and stems of plants, of all the grains, but is especially destructive to the seed itself; and seemingly develops preferably in oats, barley, and Indian corn, but is not so much dreaded in Indian corn, by the farmer, since sinutty ears of corn may be easily thrown out. In barley it is separated by washing before malting, so that only in our bread grains are means usually taken to prevent its ravages. There is no conclusive evidence to show that the various compounds used for soaking wheat actually kill the smut. On the other hand, evidence would seem to show that any wash strong enough to kill smut (*uredo*) will also destroy the vitality of grain. The probability is, rather, that, as smut germinates quickly, the soaking and subsequent liming gives the proper impetus to germinate them, and the lime forming a proper *nidus,* material growth ensues; and, subsequently, having no proper substance to sustain itself, it perishes before the smut is enabled to seize the growing plant. Klippart mentions placing smut balls in a solution of nitrate of potash, dilute nitric acid, sulphate of iron, of copper, and of zinc, and even in dilute sulphuric acid. The smut so treated invariably manifested undoubted signs of vitality when surrounded by proper conditions. Therefore, it is not safe to simply moisten wheat with lime or other washes. The simplest and surest plan, to prevent smut in wheat, is to make a solution by using one pound of blue vitriol (sulphate of copper) to every two gallons of water. Make a sufficient quantity so it may stand above the wheat. Stir the whole to allow the light material to rise. Skim, and at the end of an hour spread the wheat on a dry floor, and sprinkle with quick lime, previously so slaked with chamber lye as to leave the lime in powder. So continue until you have all the wheat treated. In this state it may be heaped and remain several days before sowing, if the heap be occasionally turned. If the wheat remains damp, it must be still further dried before sowing, if it is to be drilled, so it will pass easily from the drill. Many farmers use brine. In this case the solution should not be stronger than a pound of salt to the gallon of water. Proceed as before directed, and dry with lime. Some persons claim good success by sprinkling the wheat with a solution of five pounds of blue vitriol to six gallons of water, using this quantity for twenty bushels of wheat, turning the same until every grain is moistened, and sowing without further trouble. The way we have indicated is the surest, and in the end the cheapest, since the liquor can be used over and over again until exhausted.

SNAKEROOT. *Aristolochia serpentaria.* A perennial-rooted plant, growing wild in woodlands, the root of which is used as a bitter and tonic.

SNEAD or SNATHE. The handle of the scythe.

SNOW BIRD. *Junco hyemalis.* Several small sparrows which remain in the North late in the autumn and return early in the spring or late winter, and which breed, in the extreme northern limits of the United States and in Canada, are called Snow birds. Some seasons, the Snow birds remain all winter in the West, and before snow storms, or in extremely cold weather, gather in considerable flocks about houses and farm buildings.

SOAP. A chemical compound of fat or oil, animal or vegetable, with potash or soda. Various plants were used in ancient times for their cleansing qualities, among others, the juice of a plant called *Struthium* by the Romans. Pliny ascribes the invention of soap to the Gauls and credits the ancient Germans with making both hard and soft soap. Among plants known to the moderns for their saponaceous and detergent and cleansing qualities, are the berries of the soap tree, *Sapindus saponaria;* the bark of the *Quillaia saponaria,* both natives of South America. The juice of *Saponaria officinalis,* Bouncing Bet, has long been used in England, for cleansing dresses. In California, the bulbous root of *Phellangium pomaridianum* has been extensively used in the place of soap for washing clothes, since the settlement of the country. Of the two alkalies employed for making soap,
56

soda is used for hard soap and potash for soft soap. The more solid fats, as tallow and suet, make firmer soaps than the soft fats which contain more oleic acid. In connection with potash, the soap fats make a still softer and watery soap. To harden these a small quantity of fused crystals of sulphate of soda are used. So if the soap is too hard rape or linseed oil, or rosin combined with the tallow will soften the product. Lard and soda make a very hard, white, and excellent toilet soap. Castile soap is made with olive oil and soda, and the peculiar marbled appearance is given it, the dark by stirring into it a solution of sulphate of iron, which, on and near the outside of the bars, by being oxygenated by the air, gradually assumes a reddish appearance; the streaks and patches are produced by the black oxide separating from the water after being stirred in the soap when in a semi-fluid state. Other colors and marblings are given this and other fancy soaps, by rubbing up vermilion or ultramarine olive oil in soap. A small portion is taken up with a spatula or thin knife and worked into the mass of melted soap and stirred about until the proper effect is produced. So turmeric is also employed for coloring, or any innocent coloring matter may be employed. Transparent soap is made from the hardest fats and soda. The soap is then dissolved in alcohol, filtered and evaporated to the proper consistency. Soap balls are made by dissolving soap in a very little water, and then working into balls with starch. The cleansing and detersive qualities of soap may be increased by the addition of ammonia, camphor, spirits of turpentine, perfumes being added to disguise the smell of the chemicals. Soap varies in its quality according to its power of taking up water in the making. Castile soap should not contain more than fourteen to fifteen per cent. of water. The soaps made of cocoanut oil often contain nearly seventy-five per cent. of water. Ordinary soft soap contains nearly forty-eight per cent. of water, while the ordinary hard washing soaps contain from thirty-five to twenty-three per cent. of water, according to quality. The proportions of fat and alkali in making soft soap, is, for 450 pounds, 200 pounds of clean fat or oil, and 72 pounds of potash in lyes of specific gravity 1.110. Lye that will just bear out an egg is called weak lye, and if it bears out an egg buoyantly or of the size of a shilling piece, it is called strong lye. When of the proper consistency of soft soap, or when it forms a half solid, jelly-like substance, when cold, it may be converted into hard soap, by adding two pounds of salt, in the form of strong brine, to each pound of fat or oil used. Add the solution of salt gradually into the boiling mass, stir, and the sodium of the salt will take the place of the potassium in the soap, and uniting with the chlorine, goes into the lye, which readily separates from the soda soap. Following are good recipes for making hard and soft soap: After the raw soda or barilla is ground or pounded, it is placed in a vat in alternate layers with unslacked lime, the bottom layer being lime. Water is allowed to infiltrate through those layers, and the lye is secured as it trickles through a hole in the bottom of the vat. The lime absorbs the carbonic acid of the soda, making the lye caustic or fit for the soap-kettle; and the quantity of lime applied must be in proportion to the quantity of carbonic acid in the soda. To every twenty pounds of tallow add one gallon of weak lye, and boil until the lye is spent. The mass must then cool for one hour, the spent lye drawn off, and another gallon of strong lye added; the mixture again boiled until the second dose of lye is spent; and the same process must be repeated for several days, until the mixture, if properly managed, is converted into white tallow soap, which should be allowed to cool gradually and settle, when it is poured into molds, and when solid it is cut into the bars which are found in our markets. Twenty pounds of tallow ought to make thirty pounds of first-quality hard soap, allowing three pounds of soda-ash for every twenty pounds of tallow. The balance of the weight is made up by the large quantity of water which enters into combination with the grease and alkali in the course of saponification. When yellow or resin soap is required, the hard soap has to be made in the usual manner, and at the last charge of lye, or when the soapy mass ceases to absorb any more lye, one-third the weight of pounded resin is introduced, the mixture constantly stirred, and the boil kept up vigorously until the resin has become incorporated with the soap. The whole must stand until it settles, and soap then dipped out. Resin soap, when well made, should be a fine, bright color. The principal difference between hard and soft soaps is, that three parts of fat afford, in general, fully five parts of hard soda-soaps; but three parts of fat or oil will afford six or seven parts of potash-soap of a moderate consistence. From its cheapness, strength, and superior solubility, potash-soap is preferred for many purposes, particularly for the scouring of woolens. The lyes prepared for making soft soaps should be made very strong, and of two densities, as the process of making potash or soft soap differs materially from that of making soda or hard soap. A portion of the oil or fat being placed in the boiling-pan and heated to near the boiling-point of water, a certain portion of the weaker lye is introduced and the fire kept up so as to bring the mixture to the boiling point; then some more oil and lye are introduced alternately, until the pan is filled. The boiling is continued gently, strong lye being added until the saponification is complete. The fire should then be removed, and some good soap, previously made, added while cooling down, to prevent any change by evaporation. One pound of oil requires about one-third of a pound of American potash, and will make one and three-quarters to two pounds of well-boiled soap, containing about forty per cent. of water. Sixty pounds of lard will make 100 pounds of first class soft soap by using one and a half cans of concentrated lye, made from salt, which is a soda lye.

SOAPER'S WASTE. The refuse of the soap-works has been much used as a manure. The nature of the manure depends on the use of ashes or soda ash in the manufacture; in the first case, it is a very valuable amendment; in the latter, considerably less so. The first contains a large quantity of ash, the chloride of potassium; the second contains but little soda salts, and when barilla is employed, the ash is merely calcareous matter; of the latter ashes, in the fresh state, from sixty to 200 bushels have been used on grass lands with effect. If ashes and common salt have been used, ten to twenty bushels of refuse will be enough.

SOBOLE. An underground creeping stem.
SOD. A turf of grass.
SODA, PROTOXIDE OF SODIUM. An alkali very analogous and isomorphous with potash. It is constantly found, in the ashes of plants performing the same function as potash; but in the vine and some other plants it is not equally serviceable. In the mineral kingdom it is abundant as a silicate, in the form of chloride of sodium, or salt, the nitrate, which is an important manure, is also abundant in certain places. Kelp, barilla, and soda ash all owe their value to the carbonate of soda, which is used in making hard soaps. The carbonate of soda resembles pearlash very closely in its properties, but is less active.

SOIL. Soil is distinguished from earth in that it contains a greater quantity of organic vegetable matter than the sands, gravels and clays, which constitute so large a portion of the upper surface of the earth's crust. The earths originally were composed of the detritus or decomposition of the various rocks. Until this wearing away and decomposition became partial at least no vegetation could subsist. This is primarily brought about by the action of the oxygen of the air, by the action of rain, running water, floods, but more generally by the grinding power of glacial action which at some time seems to have been present on nearly every portion of the earth's surface. Upon the relations of Geology to Agriculture—Hon. James Shaw, in an address to the Northern Illinois Horticultural Society, truly said: Soils are derived from the decomposition of the rocks. The silent processes of nature, to-day, as in past geologic ages, are grinding rocks into soils, and re-cementing and hardening soils into stratified rocks. There was a time when the earth was, indeed, rock-ribbed; but atmospheric and chemical agencies and aqueous forces kept in constant action, processes of slow decay, and the soils were gradually formed as precipitates and sediments in ancient geologic seas. We all know the old proverbs about the constant dropping that wears away the stone, and the file of time that wears and makes no noise; but few realize how important a part these peaceful agencies have taken in the creation of the present order of things. The frost and the rain, and other like agencies and energies of nature, are all powerful to bring about the mightiest results. If undisturbed by mechanical forces, the superficial clays, loams, sands, subsoils and soils covering the underlying rocks would be nothing but the residuum left after the removal by the percolation of the water of the more soluble portions of the rocky ledges, which had decayed. The soil would be *in situ*. It would bear a close resemblance to the rocks from which derived. The geologist, by an examination of the rocks, could tell the nature of the soil with which they were covered, and, by an examination of the soils, could describe what rocks they concealed. Primarily, all soils are derived from fire rocks; secondarily, many of them are derived from water rocks. The first resemble, in composition, the primary rocks; the second, having first been granites, then, by the decay of the granites and the transportation of water, becoming stratified rocks, whose decay and chemical combinations and separations, separated and assorted by the elements, oftentimes do not resemble the first at all. The general proposition is, however, true, that rocks differ from each other, and soils also resemble the rocks from which they are derived. In small patches, and to a limited extent, this is true of the soils of the West. The alluvial bottoms of our rivers are generally sedimentary soils, sometimes hungry sandy soils, but often black, fat, sedimentary deposits. The latter produces great crops of Indian corn, when dry enough to cultivate; but, when low and wet, it grows heavy crops of the coarse prairie and slough grasses. But the most marked illustration of the proposition under discussion, may be noticed in localities underlaid by the Cincinnati shales. Here the soil and subsoil, if undisturbed, is a close grained, finely comminuted, buff or straw-colored clay. It is so compact and tenacious that it becomes water-soaked, and has not the power to rapidly absorb surplus moisture. The best soil is the formation known as Loess, by western geologists. It caps, and in most cases, makes up a large proportion of the bluff ranges along the Mississippi river, and some of the internal streams in that part of Illinois; it sometimes extends back for some miles from the bluffs into the interior; but, in the latter case, it is seldom pure, but is mixed with other sands and clays. It is white, buff-colored silt, of extreme fineness of texture, where purely developed; but it often consists of marshy, sandy deposits, and various mixtures and clayey combinations—for vines and deep-rooted trees no better deposits exist in the State. It owes its origin to the silt washed up by broad sea-like lakes and wide lake-like rivers. It affords little resistance to the penetrating rootlets of trees, is well-drained, and is unsurpassed, either for wheat, fruits, grapes or vegetables. The foregoing remarks are based on the argument that soils are derived from the decay of the underlying rocks. An examination of the soils of the prairie region of the West, however, will soon convince any one that this statement, as a matter of fact, is true to only a limited extent; it will do for fragmentary patches and driftless regions. Over wide stretches of country the decay of the rocks has not formed the soils covering them. Transportation of soils, a universal mingling of materials derived from widely different sources, is a fact susceptible of easy demonstration. That tremendous force which tore the bowlders from their parent outcrops in the distant Lake Superior regions, and drifted them along on their southward journey, which grooved and planed the surface of the solid rocks, which strewed, for hundreds of miles, beds of clay and sand and gravel, whether floes and bergs of ice, borne by winds and currents loaded with stones and detrital matter, or strong water currents mingling and wearing the moving beds of abraded materials, or the procession of the slow, silent, all-powerful glaciers, grinding the solid stones into soils, as wheat is ground to flour between the upper and nether mill-stones, whether one, or all these causes combined, it mingled, mixed, transported and formed the soils to such an extent as to well nigh destroy their separate and characteristictic origin, and greatly increase the difficulty of their proper classification. In attempting to classify soils and earths thus made and mingled there is no end to the distinctions and divisions. Soils are light or heavy, warm or cold, dry or wet, compact or porous, fine or coarse, hungry, leachy, loamy, sour, sweet, clayey, sandy, limy, marly, and various combinations of these too numerous to mention. Silica, or the earth of flints; alumina, lime, magnesia, potash, and various salts and metalloid compounds unite in various combinations to make up these soils. The humus, which gives richness and blackness of color, is chiefly derived from successive growths and decays of grasses and other vegetations. The question as to what soils will produce and mature good and constant crops depends not only upon the nature of the soils themselves, but also upon climatic influences, and upon the nature and properties of subsoils. If the subsoil is gravelly, marly, porous, leachy, sandy, or of such a texture as not to retain water too easily, almost any soil will produce trees and fruits. But, if a hardpan, or other tough, impervious clay, happens to be the subsoil, so as to retain the surplus moisture, the best soil in the world unless a very deep one, will not respond to a liberal cultivation, with a generous supply of good, vigorous, healthy, and sure crops. The best soils for wheat are dry, firm, but easily disintegrable, and rather compact soils, such as contain a good proportion of lime and clay. The best Indian corn is raised upon the deep humus, prairie soils and river bottoms of the West, but a good wheat soil is also a good corn soil if the summer is long enough to ripen the crop. In this connection the classification of soils, their composition and their organic and inorganic matter will give a good idea of what constitutes soils for cereal crops. A loess soil, as heretofore stated, is admirable for the grains, grasses, and for fruit. The classification of Boussingault is excellent and is as follows:

Soils according to composition.	Usually designated.	Clay.	Sand.	Lime or Chalk.	Humus.
Clay with humus...	Rich wheat land...	74	10	4	11.5
" " "	" "	81	6	4	8.5
" " "	" "	79	10	4	6.5
Marly soil..........	" "	40	22	36	4
Light soil, with humus.	Meadow land......	14	47	10	27
Sandy soil........	Rich barley land...	20	67	3	10
Argillaceous land..	Good wheat land...	58	36	2	4
Marly soil........	Wheat land........	56	30	12	2
Argillaceous land..	" "	60	38	....	2
Stiffer "	" "	48	50	....	2
Clay.............	" "	68	30	....	....
Stiff argillaceous land.	Barley land, 1st cl's	38	60	....	2
Stiff argillaceous land.	Barley land, 2d cl's	33	65	....	2
Sandy clay........	" "	28	70	....	2
" "	Oat land..........	23.5	75	....	1.5
Clayey sand.......	" "	18.5	80	....	1.5
" "	Rye land....	14	85	....	1
Sandy soil........	" "	9	90	....	1
" "	" "	4	95	....	0.75
" "	" "	2	97.5	....	0.5

Specific gravity is also one of the tests of a good soil, since it will show if the soil be finely comminuted the presence of a good proportion of clay. The percentage of clay and sand in various soils from pure clay (pipe clay), to humus soils and peaty soils is as follows: Pure clay, pipe clay, sixty per cent. silica, forty per cent. alumina, oxide of iron chemically combined. Strongest clay soil, brick clay, pure clay with five to ten per cent. of sand which can be separated. Clay loam fifteen to thirty per cent. fine sand and pure clay. Loamy clay thirty to sixty per cent. sand and pure clay. Sandy loam sixty to ninety per cent. sand and pure clay. Sandy soil containing no more than ten per cent. of pure clay. Marly soils, in which the proportion of lime is more than five, but does not exceed twenty per cent. of the whole weight of the dry soil. Calcareous soils, in which the lime exceeding twenty per cent. becomes the distinguishing constituent. Vegetable soils from garden mold, which contains from five to ten per cent., to the peaty soil in which the organic matter may amount to sixty or seventy per cent. These soils again may be clayey, loamy, or sandy, according to the predominant character of the earthy admixtures. A fertile soil, therefore, consists of three earths, clay, sand, and lime mechanically combined, organic matter from the decay of plants, etc., which may be resolved into carbon, oxygen, hydrogen and nitrogen, and the inorganic elements, in combination, chemically, with metals, hydrogen, oxygen, chlorine, and sulphur. These are in small quantities. Thus chlorine produces the chlorides, iodine, the iodides, sulphur, the sulphurets, and sulphuric acid; phosphorus, the phosphoric acid; potassium, the potash; sodium, the soda and common salt; calcium, the lime; aluminum, the clay; silicon, the sand; and iron and manganese, oxides and sulphurets. The mechanical texture of the soil has a strong influence upon its practical fertility, very heavy clay, and very light sands, being both, for opposite reasons, apt to produce badly. The soil in which the particles are the finest, so that the air can enter, and the roots spread without difficulty, is, other things being equal, the best. In clay soils this division of the particles must be produced by the plow and other mechanical means; while in loose sands it is too great, and must be amended by an admixture of clay and other substances. The cause of the great and lasting fertility of prairie soils, is, first, its extreme comminution—fineness—and its large proportion of clay, sand, and organic and inorganic elements. The color of the soil is not always an indication of its fertility. As a rule, however, dark soils are the most fertile. The absorbing power of soils is another indication of fertility, since a porous, or other soil that will easily absorb water and hold its vapor, is generally a fertile soil. The following table from Schubler, shows the relative absorbing power of the soils named:

Kinds of earth.	1,000 grains of earth on a surface of fifty square inches absorbed in			
	12 hours.	24 hours.	48 hours.	72 hours.
	Grains	Grains.	Grains.	Grains.
Silicious sand...	0 water	0 water.	0 water	0 water.
Sandy clay......	21 "	26 "	28 "	26 "
Loamy clay.....	25 "	30 "	34 "	32 "
Brick clay......	30 "	36 "	40 "	41 "
Gray pure clay..	37 "	42 "	48 "	49 "
Garden mold....	35 "	45 "	50 "	52 "
Arable soil......	16 "	24 "	23 "	21 "
Humus	80 "	97 "	110 "	120 "

Thus while sandy lands may suffer from long continuance of dry weather, a neighboring field abounding in humus may absorb sufficient moisture from the air to serve all the requirements of vegetation. The power of saturation by water, and the retention of moisture, vary in the same manner, and nearly in the same degrees. An-

other important property of soils is their power to absorb oxygen from the air. According to Schubler:

Grains.	Kinds of earth.	Cubic inches.	
1,000	Silicious sand, in a wet state, absorbed oxygen............	0.24	From fifteen cubic inches of atmospheric air, containing twenty-one per cent. of oxygen.
1,000	Sandy clay.....................	1.39	
1,000	Loamy clay....................	1.65	
1,000	Brick clay.....................	2.04	
1,000	Gray pure clay.................	2.29	
1,000	Garden mold...................	2.60	
1,000	Arable soil....................	2.43	
1,000	Humus........................	3.04	

Soils lose, in drying, the property of absorbing oxygen from the air, but regain it in the same proportion as before, on being moistened. The action of organic manures, and the production of carbonic acid, depend on the existence of oxygen in the soil. Capillary attraction or power, means the power by which a liquid ascends in the interior of a capillary tube, or tube of small bore, above the surface of the liquid which surrounds it. The phenomenon occurs in solid bodies which are capable of being wetted. Thus, when water is poured into the basin of a flower-pot, the soil gradually sucks it in, and becomes moist even to the surface. The same takes place in the soil in the open fields. The water from beneath—that contained in the subsoil—is gradually sucked up to the surface. Where water is present in excess, this capillary action keeps the soil always moist and cold. Evaporation takes place from the surface of the land, and as each atom of moisture is taken up into the atmosphere, its place is supplied by another atom, communicated by the contact of the particles of soil, the more superficial acting on the deeper particles like so many pumps, to elevate the water, and supply the loss. Thus a naturally porous soil may be kept injuriously wet by an impervious subsoil several feet below. Drainage counteracts this. The capillary action of the soil, however, is an important action of the soil, since thus the vapor of water is constantly passed upwards from below, to supply that lost by evaporation at the surface during droughts. A moderately compact, and yet porous soil, has strong capillary power; and hence, again, another reason for its fertility, since a soil, when abundantly dry, is always unproductive; and for one principal reason, that it is only in a soluble form, that is in combination with water, that the elements of plant food can become available. Thus, given a virgin and fertile soil, capable of producing those crops natural to a climate, it would seem to be of the utmost importance that the farmer keep it up to the original standard. This is accomplished by fallowing, manuring, or by a proper succession of crops, or better, by a combination of the three. (See articles Fallow, Manure, and Rotation.) There is another agent fully as important, and that is disintegration. This enables natural agents to act promptly in restoring lost fertility, both summer and winter. These are heat, electricity, moisture, carbonic and other acids formed in the soil, and the complex chemical changes constantly going on in a soil in which heat, moisture, and porosity are present in normal conditions. This being the case and the elements of fertility present in due proportion we have a fertile soil.

SOILING. Soiling, as applied to farm animals, is the cutting and feeding, green, such forage crops as may be economically raised in contradistinction to pasturing. The principal soiling crops in the North are clover, rye, Indian corn and roots, as beets, carrots, etc. In California, these, with the addition of lucerne, and in the South the first named, with the addition, perhaps, of cow peas. The system has never been profitable except where only a little stock could be kept, and in situations where pasturage was not practicable.

SOILING CROPS. (See Soiling.)

SOLANACEÆ. A natural order of herbaceous or shrubby exogens, inhabiting all parts of the world, excepting the arctic regions. This order contains nightshade, henbane, mandrake, tobacco, stramonium, the potato, and the tomato, the leaves of all which are narcotic and exciting, but in different degrees, from *Atropa belladonna*, which causes vertigo, convulsions, and vomiting; tobacco, which will frequently produce the first and last of these symptoms; henbane and stramonium, down to some of the solanum tribes, the leaves of which are so inert as to be used as kitchen herbs. Even in the potato plant, the narcotic acrid principle is found in the stem and leaves, and even in the rind of the tuber. But the principal part of the latter consists of starch, and the small quantity of deleterious matter being volatile and near the surface, is readily driven off by the heat used in cooking.

SOLIDUNGULATES. Animals with an undivided hoof, as the horse.

SOLUTION. The diffusion in water, or other menstrua, of the particles of a solid or other body. The amount dissolved is definite at the same temperature, and is usually increased by heat. A fluid already holding in solution a given substance will not dissolve so much of a third as if pure, and sometimes none at all.

SOOT. Soot is a complicated and variable mixture of substances produced during the combustion of coal or wood. Its composition, and consequently its effects as a manure, vary with the quality of the fuel, with the way in which it is burned, and with the height of the chimney in which it is collected.

SORE EYES. (See Eyes, Inflammation of.)

SORE THROAT. Colds often are accompanied with inflammation and swelling of the air passages, and in the acute form are sometimes dangerous. The breathing is difficult and hoarse, the nose is protruded, the eyes bloodshot, the ears are cold, and cold sweats break out over the body. Relief should be obtained by fomenting the throat with cloths wrung out of hot mustard water, and the animal should be made to inhale the steam from a bucket of boiling water. When the fomentation is through, paint the throat with thin mustard and water. The difficulty in swallowing will probably prevent giving medicine, but the following mixture may be made and smeared on the tongue three or four times a day: One ounce of powdered guaicum, four ounces of powdered chlorate of potash, and one-half pint of molases.

SORGHUM. The importance which the cultivation of Sorghum has assumed as a crop in the West, within the last ten years, and more particularly within the last six years, through improved processes in its manufacture, by which a fair amount of crystallizable sugar may be produced, ranging from seventy to ninety per cent. of the mush sugar in concentrated syrup, has caused many to again undertake this industry, who from twenty to twenty-five years ago gave up the manufacture as unprofitable, as carried on with the crude apparatus then at hand. When the same capital and appliances are given to the production of sugar from sorghum in the North, and especially in the West, as are applied to sugar cane in the South, and to the manufacture of beet sugar in Europe, there is no reason why it should not enable the West to add immensely to her productive capacity, and in fact give the world as cheap sugar as she now does cheap grain. That the time is near at hand when the intelligent use of large capital will be so employed, and remuneratively, there is no doubt, and first from the fact that the climate and soil of the West are admirably adapted to the crop, and second, mechanical talent is now actively engaged in producing economical apparatus for condensing, as chemical talent is in cheaply neutralizing the acid qualities, and separating impurities from the juice. It is not necessary here to go into a long historical account of sorghum, and its varieties. It is now nearly forty years since sorghum was introduced from France to the United States, and disseminated as a crop that might be profitably worked into syrup. We believe the first seed was brought to New York in 1853, and sent out. In 1856 the writer received a small package from a friend, planted it in Cook county, Illinois, and made a kind of syrup by crushing it between crude rollers, and boiling down in a five pail kettle. The next year and the succeeding years it began to be disseminated all over the then settled portions of the West. In 1857 Mr. Leonard Wray brought to New York several varieties of Imphee, which he had procured from Natal, South Africa. This, it was confidently said, would produce sugar. It did not with the crude apparatus and the imperfect knowledge of the chemical requirements then known. Nevertheless, the sugar was there, and has since been brought out of it. The failures and losses have not been nearly so great as those attending the introduction and manufacture of beet sugar in Europe. Yet Europe now furnishes one-third the crystallizable sugar produced on the earth, and the beet crop has revolutionized the agriculture of the countries producing it; and added fully twenty-five per cent. to the product in other crops. How? By the clean cultivation of the beets required, by feeding the refuse to cattle, and by the manure made. Let us see how this industry has figured in the past. From the report of the Commissioner of Agriculture for 1876, we find that the aggregate of syrup reported from the census of 1860 was 6,749,123 gallons. The first State in production was Iowa. It reported 1,211,512 gallons, followed by 881,049 in Indiana, 806,589 in Illinois, 796,111 in Missouri, 779,076 in Ohio, and 706,663 in Tennessee. For the census of 1870 the aggregate was 16,050,089 gallons. Indiana reported 2,026,212; Ohio, 2,023,427; Illinois, 1,960,473; followed in the order of decrease by Kentucky, Missouri, Tennessee, Iowa, and West Virginia. Iowa, the first in production in 1859, but the seventh in 1869, returned 1,218,636 gallons, an advance only of 7,124. But the State census of 1867 gives for 1865 an area of 21,452 acres, producing 1,436,605 gallons; and for 1867, 25,796 acres, producing 2,094,557 gallons. The State census for 1875 gives, for 1874, 15,768 acres, yielding 1,386,908 gallons. The definite statistics for the State of Ohio, annually published since 1861, afford a fair illustration of the gradual advance in production up to about 1866 and the subsequent gradual decline throughout the section between the Ohio and the Missouri, and including Missouri. The production in Ohio for the years named was as follows:

Years.	Acres.	Sugar.	Syrup.
		Pounds	Gallons
1862	30,872	27,488	2,6 6,151
1863	31,255	27,339	2,34,578
1864	29,302		2,8,9,798
1865	37,042	41,660	4,083,754
1866	43,101	102,313	4,629,570
1867	17,814	20,094	1,255,807
1868	25,257	28,668	2,001,055
1869	5,63 7	27,048	1,683,042
1870	23,150	2,988	2,187,673
1871	23,052	23,305	1,817,043
1872	12 83.2	34,599	968,131
1873	9,426	38,846	692,314
1874	12,108	36,410	941,510
1875	13,114	21,768	928,100

In the Ohio valley there has been a tendency to decrease the area of sorghum since 1869, while there has been a marked increase in the South and west of the Missouri. For fourteen years, ending with 1875, the average product of syrup in Ohio has been 2,054,605 gallons, a little more than the crop of 1869; the average area is 25,868 acres, and the yield 79.4 gallons of syrup and 1.39 pounds of sugar per acre. As an illustration of the increase in new Western States, the product, in 1875, in Kansas is reported as 2,542,512 gallons; in 1869, by the census returns, 449,409 gallons. The crop of 1875 was produced on 23,026 acres; average per acre, 110 gallons. Georgia reported the same year 15,905 acres, yielding seventy-three gallons per acre, or 1,161,065 gallons, averaging sixty-six cents per gallon, and estimated to cost twenty-eight cents per gallon. A larger quantity of syrup is extracted as experience is acquired and processes improved. As an estimate for twenty-one years since the introduction of sorghum, 11,000,000 gallons of syrup per annum might approximate the product. At an average value of sixty-five cents, (it is less now,) the value of the annual product would be $7,150,000. The sugar of the sorghum is a small item, yet in fourteen years, in Ohio alone, it amounts to 506,000 pounds. Including sugar and forage, the annual value must be not less than $8,000,000, and the aggregate value $168,000,000 since its introduction by the Department of Agriculture. Within the last few years much has been written upon corn as a sugar plant. That its juice is rich in saccharine, and that it could be made into syrup has long been known. That it contains notable quantities of crystal sugar has lately been demonstrated. That it can do more than add something to the length of the sugar making season—being earlier in ripening—is hardly probable. That sugar making from corn, where the ears, when in milk, may be utilized for canning and drying, may be made profitable there is no doubt, and fortunately, at the time the corn is in the early milk, and from this time while the corn is in perfection for eating green, sugar corn is in the best state for producing crystallizable sugar. At such time Stowell's Evergreen gave a specific gravity of 10.60; showed 11.34 of crystallizable

EARLY AMBER SORGHUM.

sugar, and 1.56 of uncrystallizable sugar. Eight rowed yellow corn gave respectively 10.60, 11.42 and 1.65. These results were, we suppose, obtained by means of the polariscope, an instrument for testing saccharine juices. In the practical working, even where the best appliances are used, including a vacuum pan, some loss ensues, with any saccharine juices, including the beet and sugar cane. If five per cent. of crystal sugar can be obtained it will pay. Six per cent. will leave a handsome profit and seven per cent. give large returns for the capital invested. From what has been accomplished in Ohio, Illinois, Missouri, Kansas, Iowa, and especially Minnesota, and without the best appliances, this product would seem to be fairly attained; with more perfect apparatus better results would seem to lie in the future. All sugar plants seem to suffer from an excess of nitrogen in the soil. This was especially found to be the case in the manufacture of beet sugar in Illinois. A soil rich in the elements of fertility was selected, one capable of producing from seventy to one hundred bushels of corn per acre in good seasons. Its strong nitrogenous qualities destroyed, by reducing the out come of sugar. Nitrogenous manures, therefore, should be avoided. The best soils are those deep, rich, well drained, calcareous soils—the wheat producing, rolling prairies, and the loess soils of our rivers and bottoms, are excellent. The range of production for sorghum is anywhere where the Dent corn of the West will ripen, Minnesota being the northern limit. Where manure is necessary, those abounding in the phosphates should be used—superphosphate of lime, bone dust, etc. Lime and gypsum would also be indicated. The varities of cane used generally in the West have been Chinese, Liberian, and white and red Imphee. The Liberian and white Imphee have been favorites in the West from their power of standing heavy winds without much prostration, but they are late in maturing. The Chinese is most productive. The Amber cane of late years has proved most successful. It is early, productive in sugar, and seems well adapted to the soil of the West. Whatever the variety, early planting on well drained soil, say immediately preceding corn planting, careful attention while young with deep cultivation early in the season and shallow cultivation later is essentially necessary to the best success, since as the plants gain strength they acquire a mass of superficial roots, necessary to the production of sugar. The Chemist of the Department of Agriculture, in 1877, analyzed a sample of Early Amber sugar cane from Minnesota, given as follows: Cane sugar (saccharose) 88.8934; grape sugar (glucose) 5.6100; water, (by drying at 110 Centigrade thermometer), 5.8250. Thus showing nearly eighty-nine parts of sugar, and over five and one-half parts of glucose in 100. In Minnesota the yield of sugar is from five to six pounds from one gallon weighing thirteen and one-quarter pounds, and the yield varies from 125 to 150 gallons of syrup per acre. The following table prepared by Mr. L. L. Stewart, of Pennsylvania, for the Department of Agriculture, will show the composition of several varieties of sorghum juice. It will not be necessary in this article to go over the ground of preparation, grinding, defecating, evaporating and finishing the juice for crystallization. It would fill a large volume, and year by year improvements are being made that must be taken advantage of. Mr. Stewart, who has given much thought and attention, as a chemist, to saccharine juices, especially corn, says, in regard to crystallization, that, sorghum syrup should be reduced to a density that, after a lapse of from twenty-four to forty-eight hours, when kept in a warm room, it will become an almost solid mass of sugar. It requires then a special mode of treatment, the crystals being fine and held together by only a small quantity of molasses. When in this condition, the mass is to be thrown into a large tub or mixing-vessel, and a small quantity, (about one-tenth of its volume) of a fair, thin syrup, prepared from sorghum juice of a density of say about 30° Baumé, when cold, is to be poured upon it and thoroughly incorporated in it, by means of a wooden stirrer. This will bring it to a semi-fluid state, if the room in which the operation has been performed has been kept heated. The syrup dilutes the uncrystallized sugar sufficiently to render it mobile, and does not dissolve the cane sugar. The mass may then be drained in a centrifugal, the inner drum of which is very clearly but minutely perforated and running at the highest rate of speed. A number of linen and coarse muslin sacks are provided, of any convenient size, but their length should be about two and one-half times their width, say twenty by fifty inches; each sack is to be about one-third filled with this sugary mixture, folded once on itself in the middle, and flattened by placing it upon a table upon a sheet-iron plate with rounded corners, a little larger on every side than the partially flattened half of the sack and its contents; the loose half being folded under. The open end of the sack may be folded twice if necessary. The plate and sack are then to be placed within a frame on the bed of a powerful screw-press, and

VARIETIES.	STAGE OF GROWTH.	Specific gravity.	Crystallizable sugar.	Uncrystallizable sugar
			Per cent.	Per cent.
Chinese (regular)	Flower just expanding	10.42	6.72	2.18
" "	In flower a few days { Butt joints	10.60	11.30	1.60
	{ Top joints	10.53	9.75	1.25
" "	Seed ripening	10.58	11.52	1.18
" "	Seed quite ripe { Upper and middle joints	10.63	12.72	0.78
	{ Lower joints	10.55	10.57	0.93
" "	Mixed juice, ripe and unripe	10.60	11.94	1.56
Red Imphee	Seed in early milk	10.53	9.93	0.08
" "	Ripe	10.60	11.92	0.98
Black Imphee	Coming in flower	10.53	9.98	0.92
White Imphee	Not yet in flower	10.59	10.90	1.90
" "	Flower just expanded	10.57	10.30	2.20
" "	Seed nearly ripe	10.60	10.65	2.24
Chinese Imphee {	Cut and stored (lower joints)	10.82	14.97	3.53
	Whisks (upper and middle joints)	10.82	16.13	2.31

a series of such sacks and interleaved plates laid neatly one upon another, being turned in opposite directions, and subjected to pressure gradually applied, at first, to avoid rupture of the sacks, and afterwards with sufficient power to remove all the syrup and leave the sugar nearly dry. This fine dried sugar is then to be transferred without further drying to a heating vessel, and about one-tenth of its weight of pure water mixed with it. Here it is to be heated very gradually, with frequent stirring, to diffuse the heat through the mass, and when it has partially remelted and it is in

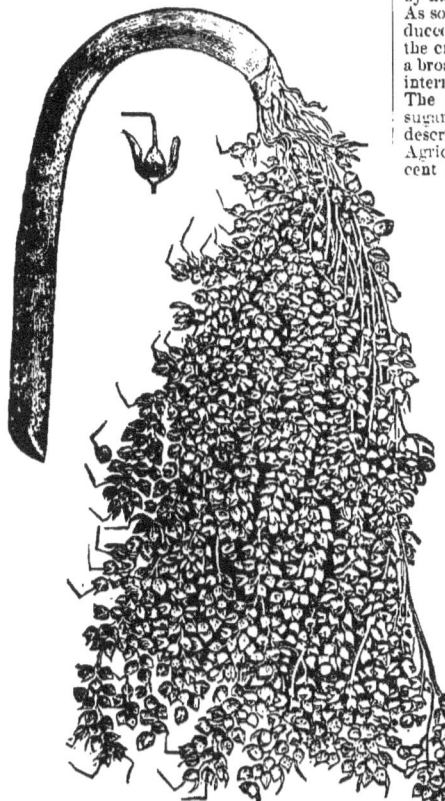

WHITE LIBERIAN CANE.

the liquefied state, it is to be poured finally into the crystallizing boxes, in a room heated about 90° F., where it will form a solid mass of crystals as soon as it becomes cool. The result is a very coarse-grained, beautiful sugar of a high grade. If properly prepared, it will be almost white, and the immediate yield is almost double that which may be secured in any other way without reboiling. The sugar prepared from sorghum in this way has the additional advantage of not being contaminated with the secondary products usually formed by reboiling; the final crystallization is attended by no risk, is easily and cheaply done, and in quality, with due care should rank nearly or quite equal to vacuum sugar. The very small quantity of syrup left in contact with the crystals will drain off from the crystallizers, and, being almost free from glucose, will crystallize gradually if exposed in broad trays at the temperature of the room. If the production of sugar of a softer or more open grain is desired, it can readily be accomplished by a mode of treatment almost identical with the stirring off process adopted by maple sugar producers but with better results. As soon as the half-liquefied sugary mass, produced as already mentioned, has been poured in the crystallizing-boxes, it should be stirred with a broad oar-shaped wooden instrument, without interruption, until it is cool and the sugar dry. The process of experimental manufacture of sugar from both corn and sorghum in 1878, is thus described by the chemist of the Department of Agriculture, and also the results including per cent of syrup. He says: The following tabulated results of my experiments are valuable in this especially, that they were conducted quantitatively throughout. The cornstalks were from a common field-corn, said to have been a cross between a yellow and white. The ears had been plucked from the stalks and sold in our own markets as green corn some three weeks before the stalks had been cut and brought to me for the making of sugar. The sorghum was a variety known as the Minnesota Early Amber. Both corn and sorghum were in a condition of vigorous growth when cut, the leaves being green. The seed of the sorghum was sufficiently mature to warrant its preservation, and indeed the last lot received shelled slightly upon handling. The sorghum had not been planted or cultivated so as to produce even a fair average in size, as will be seen by the results appended. The mill made use of in expressing the juice was an old sorghum mill of common construction, which, through previous use and misuse, had been rendered quite unfit to give satisfactory results. After most of our experiments below given were concluded, it was repaired, so that afterward its working was very much better, as will be seen by the subsequent results given further on. The apparatus used in the experiments, besides a few barrels and pails for holding the juice, consisted of a copper tank of the following dimensions: four feet three inches long, two feet three inches deep, two feet three inches wide; a galvanized iron pan nine feet long by eight inches deep, and three feet six inches wide. This iron pan was entirely surrounded by a wooden frame of two-inch plank, so as to support the sides, and pan was placed in brick-work with chimney, and so arranged as to permit a fire to be kept below it in direct contact with the bottom. In the case of the copper tank the flame played about the sides also, so as to heat the contents more rapidly. The galvanized-iron pan was such as could readily be constructed by any ordinary tinsmith or mechanic. The copper tank was used for defecation with lime; the galvanized-iron pan for evaporation. The process in brief is as follows: After topping or stripping the corn or sorghum, it was passed through the mill, and when sufficient juice had been obtained it was heated in the copper tank to a temperature of 82° Centigrade—182° Fahrenheit. After the juice had reached this temperature there was

HEAD OF CHINESE SORGHUM.

added to it, with stirring, cream of lime until a piece of litmus paper dipped in the juice showed a purple or bluish-purple color. The heat was now raised to the boiling point and so soon as the juice was in good ebullition the fire was drawn, and a thick scum removed from the surface of the juice. After a few minutes the sediment from the juice subsided, and by means of a syphon the clear liquid was decanted off, leaving a muddy sediment which was equal to about one-teuth to one-twentieth of the bulk of the juice. This muddy sediment was drawn off by means of a stopcock, and filtered through a plaited-bag filter, and the clear filtrate therefrom was added to the liquid previously syphoned off. The clarified juice, which, during the above operation, is not allowed to cool below a temperature of 66° Centigrade, or 150° Fahr., was now emptied into the evaporating-pan, and there was added to it, with stirring, a solution of sulphurous acid in water, until the lime present was neutralized, as was shown by the reddening of litmus paper when it was dipped in the juice. The evaporation was now hastened as much as possible, and the juice concentrated to a syrup at a boiling point of 108° Centigrade equal to 226° Fahrenheit, or thereabout. It was the intention to concentrate the syrup still more (to a boiling point of 112° Centigrade, equal to 235° Fahrenheit) but it was found impracticable to do so in the evaporator, as the danger of scorching it was great, over a naked flame which could not well be controlled. When the syrup reached the density above indicated, it was drawn off into wooden tubs, the fire having previously been drawn from beneath the evaporator. Owing to the fact that each successive lot of stalks was a new experiment, I was unable to wait for the process of filtration of the sediment from the defecator to be completed, and therefore in every case lost a portion of the juice, which of course could have been saved in a continuous process such as would be practically carried out. This will explain what is meant by the juice utilized, as compared with that obtained. It was intended to have still further concentrated the syrups in a smaller pan of galvanized iron, so arranged that by a slide the heat could be instantaneously removed to prevent the scorching of the syrup; but before this pan was completed it was found that the several tubs of syrup were crystallizing, and they were therefore allowed to stand; and the sugar was obtained by pressing out the molasses by means of an ordinary screw press, the mass of molasses and sugar from the tubs being enclosed in an ordinary grain-bag. The sugar thus obtained was very greatly improved in appearance by the addition of five or ten per cent. of water, and stirring it into a mush, and again subjecting the mass to pressure, by which operation the adhering molasses was almost entirely removed, and the sugar obtained was, in the case of sorghum, nearly white, while in the case of corn it was of a rich golden yellow. I may add that in no case, either with corn or sorghum, did I fail to obtain satisfactory results in the way of crystallization, although of course the molasses still contains a very large percentage of crystallizable sugar, which will, at least in great part, be obtained by further concentration. I omit mention of seven experiments with comparatively small quantities of corn-stalks and sorghum, only saying that the results obtained were such as to fully warrant the more extended experiments here recorded; and it is unfortunate that the value of these experiments is vitiated somewhat by the imperfect apparatus employed, as also by the inferior material, which, however, was all that was obtainable in this vicinity. It is greatly to be desired that another season may find the department amply equipped with all

HONDURAS CANE.

necessary means to carry these important questions to complete solution. The point which these experiments have fully settled is, that there exists no difficulty in making from either corn or sorghum a first-rate quality of sugar, which will compare favorably with the best product from sugar cane grown in the most favorable localities. The experiments here given clearly indicate the probability that sugar may be thus made at a profit, and it is desirable that nothing be spared in continuing an investigation giving such fair promise of success. In 1879, and previous, the Commissioner of Agriculture, Gen. Le Duc, caused many experiments to be made in reducing the juice of the cane, and in ascertaining the best varieties for planting. We have reproduced four of those considered best, including the old Chinese and the deservedly popular Amber. The report of the chemist of the department is given in connection as explanatory so far as relates to these varieties with some of the conclusions arrived at. The chemist says: During the past season there have been made several series of investigations for the purpose of determining the development of sugar in varieties of sorghum, maize, and of pearl millet. These investigations appear to demonstrate that

stalks, all the results of which only confirmed the general principle above stated, viz., the practical equality and great value of every variety of this plant. The illustrations, as we have given them, show varieties of sorghum grown during the past season on the grounds of the Department of Agriculture at Washington, and used in the experiments of the chemical division as detailed in the report. The drawings were made by a gentleman employed in the department. The designations given them are somewhat different from those current in some parts of the country, but are conformed to what are believed to be the most authoritative standards. The cut, page 886, represents the Early Amber Sorghum, a favorite with planters in Minnesota and the Northwest. What is now called the Minnesota Early Amber cane is claimed as an improvement upon the Early Amber varieties grown formerly in different parts of Minnesota, by Hon. Seth .M. Kenny and Mr. C. F. Miller of that State. Acting on the theory that cane in a high latitude will degenerate if grown continuously from its own seed, these gentlemen selected the finest specimens of seed from their own crops and sent them to a southern latitude to be grown. The seed products of this southern growth was

Number.	Kind of Stalk.	Pounds of raw stalks.	Per cent. of juice in raw stalks.	Pounds of juice used.	Specific gravity of juice.	Pounds of syrup made.	Per cent of syrup in juice.
1	Corn-stalks, stripped and topped.............................	2,353	25.29	520	1053	74	11.03
2	Corn-stalks, stripped and topped.............................	2,60	28.91	591	1061	101	19.93
3	Corn-stalks, (butt ends), stripped and topped................	3,368	29.04	971	1053	143	14.62
4	Corn-stalks, (top ends), stripped and topped.................	2,517	19.94	483	1050	65	13.48
5	Sorghum, stripped and topped................................	2, 52	37.97	1,090	1057	146	13. 9
6	Sorghum, stripped and topped................................	1,v 0	3.1.04	808	105.7	135	16.71
7	Sorghum, topped, but unstripped.............................	3, 31	36.75	958	......	148.5	15.50
8	Sorghum (butt ends), unstripped.............................	1.3 4	47.29	445	1.59	73	16.41
9	Sorghum (top ends), unstripped..............................	3,52	43.16	398	1057	58.5	14.70
10	Sorghum (butt ends), unstripped.............................	1,24	41.99	346	1062	57	16.47
11	Sorghum (top ends), unstripped..............................	1,128	34 60	291	105.1	41.5	14.94
12	Sorghum, small stalks, stripped..............................	963	56.20	538	1086	101	18.95
13	Sorghum, large stalks, stripped...............................	515	58.55	299	1091	60	20.09
14	Sorghum, small stalks, stripped..............................	1,623	55.87	781	1086	156	19.97
15	Sorghum, large stalks, stripped...............................	1,549	58.11	711	1084	158	22.12

there exists little difference between the various kinds of sorghum as sugar-producing plants; and, what is quite a surprising result, each of them is, at a certain period of its development, nearly if not quite as rich in sugar as the very best of sugar-cane. It is a matter, also, of extreme practical importance that this maximum content of sugar is maintained for a long period, and affords sufficient time to work up a large crop. Another result of these investigations has been to satisfactorily explain the cause of repeated failure in the production of sugar during the past quarter of a century, and to give the assurance that in the future such failure need not attend this industry. For the purpose of making clear the above points, the results obtained in the laboratory and in out-of-door experiments are appended. The varieties of sorghum grown and subjected to continuous investigation during the season were Early Amber, White Liberian, Chinese, and Honduras and Pearl Millet. Besides the above there were made very many examinations of other specimens of sorghums and corn-

returned to Minnesota. By this alternation of seed, and by other intelligent processes of culture they have succeeded in establishing a new and permanent variety, which they claim to be more productive in weight of cane and to contain a higher per cent. of saccharine matter than any other grown in that State. This claim needs to be substantiated by more careful and extended observations before it can be said to be fully established. Messrs. Kenny and Miller describe the Early Amber cane as presenting the characteristics of both sorgho and imphee. By sorgho they mean the Chinese sorgho, page 889, and by imphee, the White Liberian, page 888, and its kindred African varieties. The Early Amber receives its name from its early ripening and from the bright amber color which characterizes its syrup when properly made. The Early Amber cane on the department grounds did not grow quite so tall as the White Liberian. Its seed-heads were of moderate fullness and dark in color. Page 889 shows the Chinese Sorghum grown on the department grounds. Its height is about that of the

Early Amber. Its seed-heads are fuller and more compact and somewhat resembles a head of sumach; hence the synonym Sumach Cane. It is also known as Chinese Cane. Page 888 shows the White Liberian Sorghum grown on the department grounds. This variety is rather taller than the Early Amber. The stalk curves at the top leaving the head pendent; hence the synonym Gooseneck. The seed-heads are shorter, more compact, and of lighter color than the Early Amber. Page 890 shows Honduras, grown on the department grounds. It grows about one-half taller than either of the above varieties Its seed-top is reddish brown and spreading; hence the synonym Sprangle Top. It is also called Mastodon and Honey Cane. The Early Amber, Chinese, Liberian, and Honduras Sorghums and the Pearl Millet examined, mentioned as having been grown upon the department grounds, were all planted the same day, May 15, 1879. The relative weights of the different kinds of sorghum experimented upon are as follows:

Name.	Pounds.
Early Amber, average of 40 stalks	1.73
White Liberian, average of 38 stalks	1.80
Chinese, average of 25 stalks	2.00
Honduras, average of 16 stalks	3.64

Since these were all grown side by side and upon land presumably of equal fertility, it will afford the data for calculating the relative amount of each variety, as required, to be grown per acre. An average of all the examinations made of these four sorghums, during these periods when they were suitable for cutting, gives the following results: Early Amber, from August 13 to October 29, inclusive, fifteen analyses, extending over seventy-eight days, 14.6 per cent. sucrose; Liberian, from August 13 to October 29, inclusive, thirteen analyses, extending over seventy-eight days, 13.8 per cent. sucrose; Chinese, from September 13 to October 29, inclusive, seven analyses, extending over forty-six days, 13.8 per cent. sucrose; Honduras, from October 14 to October 29, inclusive, three analyses, extending over sixteen days, 14.6 per cent. sucrose. Besides the investigations above mentioned, there have been made thirty-five experiments in making sugar from cornstalks, sorghums, pearl millet, etc., in all of which there have been used over twenty-three tons of stalks. The result of these experiments has been to fully confirm all the experiments, not only of the previous year, but also to help towards the solution of certain questions of the highest practical importance. In every case it has been found that the quality of the syrup obtained has been precisely such as the previous analysis in the laboratory of the juice used made probable. An average of the nine best syrups obtained showed a percentage of cane-sugar present equal to 92.7 of the amount originally present in the juice, while an average of the nine poorest (i. e., containing the lowest percentage of cane-sugar) showed a percentage of cane-sugar present equal to 90.1 of the amount present in the juice.

SORREL. Field sorrel. Sheep sorrel, *Rumex acetocella*, well known from the acid nature of its weeds. It is supposed, erroneously, to be indicative of a want of lime in the soil, and liming has been recommended as a means of driving out this and other acid plants. It is natural to sandy soils, and those under which water slowly finds its way. It is not common in the West. Draining, cultivation, and manuring are the remedies.

SOUP. A nourishing and healthful food to be taken as the first course at dinner. Lean meat only should be used for soup. The conditions to be observed in boiling meat, both as respects its quality as food, and also when it is intended for soup, are as follows: If the mass of flesh intended to be eaten be introduced into the boiler when the water is in a state of brisk ebullition, if the boiling be kept up for a few minutes, and the pot then put in a warm place, so that the temperature of the water be kept at one hundred and fifty-eight to one hundred and sixty-five degrees, we then have united the conditions for giving to the flesh the qualities which best fit it for being eaten. When it is introduced into the boiling water the albumen of the flesh is immediately coagulated on the surface, and to a certain extent inwards, thus forming a skin or shell which no longer permits the juice of the meat to flow out nor the water to penetrate the mass. The flesh continues juicy and well flavored, the greater part of the savory constituents being retained in the meat. On the other hand, if the mass of flesh is set on the fire with cold water, and this slowly heated to boiling, the flesh undergoes a loss of soluble and savory matter, while the soup becomes richer in these. The albumen is gradually dissolved from the surface to the center; the fiber loses, more or less, its quality of tenderness, and becomes hard and tough. The thinner the piece of meat the greater its loss of savory constituents. This explains the well known observation that the mode of boiling which yields the best soup gives the toughest, driest, most vapid meat, and that in order to obtain well-flavored and eatable meat we must relinquish the idea of making good soup from it. If finely chopped meat be slowly heated to boiling with an equal weight of water, kept boiling for a few minutes, and then strained and pressed, we obtain the very strongest and best-flavored soup that can be made from flesh. When the boiling is longer continued some little organic matter is dissolved, but the flavor and other properties of the soup are thereby in no degree increased or improved. By boiling, mutton may be regarded as losing about one-fifth of its weight, and beef about one-fourth. By roasting, mutton and beef lose each about one-third of their weight; mutton is, however, the most nutritious meat.

SOUR DOCK. (See Dock.)

SOUTH AMERICAN CATTLE. The Rev. G. D. Carrow, some years since, when superintendent of the missions of the Methodist Episcopal Church in South America, contributed a graphic account of South American Cattle, and cattle farming in the Pampas, which we reproduce as showing the origin of South American Cattle, their management, and much other interesting matter of general interest. The Reverend author writes as follows: There are two classes of men, discoverers by land and sea, and pioneers in new fields of tillage and commerce, who though almost invariably distinguished for great and good qualities, seldom realize an adequate return for their services to their country and to mankind. The truth of this statement is confirmed by many facts belonging to the history of the discovery and colonization of this continent. Were we not so strongly assured of the contrary, we might suppose that the discovery and exploration of the three greatest rivers of this continent and of the globe, were events certainly calculated to insure solid comfort to their authors during the brief period of their mortal life, as well as immortal fame on the pages of history. What are the facts which so sternly forbid this natural supposition? Fernando de Soto was the first white man who explored the banks of the Mississippi, and saw that father of waters roll beneath the boughs of the primeval forest to the sea. But only a few days after his passage of the mighty stream he had ceased to live; his body, to conceal his death from his enemies, was wrapped in his mantle, and, at the hour of midnight, was silently sunk in the middle of the current. The wanderer, says Mr. Bancroft, had crossed a large portion of the continent in search of gold, and found nothing so remarkable as the place of his burial. Francisco de Orellana, striking a stream that wound itself along through the rugged passes of the Peruvian Andes, built a mere raft of green wood, launched it, and drifted with the current. Onward it bore him through plain and forest, mountain gorge and fertile valley, ever growing deeper and wider, till, at the end of seven months, and at a distance of four thousand five hundred miles, his frail and rudely constructed vessel felt the heaving, and his experienced eye surveyed the great expanse, of the Atlantic Ocean. He called the river Amazon. Marvellous was the adventure, and immortal the fame. But, ten years later, the discoverer perished in an expedition designed to locate and further explore the river, whose course he had followed from its birth in the mountains to its death in the sea. In 1515, Juan Dias de Solis, crossing the equator, and steering boldly to the south, in the teeth of the terrific gales which sweep northward from the latitude of Cape Horn, entered what he soon perceived to be the mouth of a great river, and finding, or hoping to find, silver among its sands, called it El Rio de la Plata. But venturing ashore a few days after the discovery, he was put to death by the native savages. The explorers were in search of the precious metals, but died at the height of their career in poverty and disappointment. Posterity, however, was to reap incalculable advantage. Harvests of grain and cotton are now gathered in the valley of the Mississippi more valuable than the produce of the mines of Potosi. Harvests of fruit, corn and cotton are to be gathered in the valley of the Amazon worth more than all the gold which streaks the mountains whence that river flows. And from the far-reaching plains of La Plata's basin, supplies of meat and clothing might be drawn in quantities sufficient to meet the necessities of more than half the world. The pampas form the larger portion of that great river's basin. Of their wool-producing capabilities, and of the extent to which they are already laid under contribution, the writer has given some account in the report of 1864, Department of Agriculture. In the present communication his purpose is to give to agriculturists of the valleys of the North some information on the subject of horned cattle breeding on the great plains of the South American continent. There were no horned cattle either in the northern or southern division of this continent prior to the discovery. The first ever seen in the new world were imported by Columbus in 1493. Respecting their importation into the northern section of the southern continent, Lieutenant Gibbon, in his Exploration of the Valley of the Amazon, says: This pampa looks like a great pasture field, enclosed by the Mamoré ditch on the south, and the Securé on the north. Under the shade of the trees stand the cattle of the field. They have gradually clambered over the Cordilleras from the flats of Guayaquil, through the table lands of Oruro, and from the salt district of Charcas. The creoles drove them down by the side of the Mamoré river, and let them out into the grassy prairie lands of Chiquitos and Mojos. When the cattle came among the Indians they knew not what to make of them. There were no such animals in their wild lands. The fierce tiger, and the poisonous serpent which they had worshipped, were outdone. The cow interfered with the belief they previously had, that the largest animals were God's favorites, particularly those which had the greatest means for active aggression or self-defence. The cow helped to change such a religion. By degrees they learned that she neither bit, clawed, nor stung; that she carried a bag full of milk; that her teeth were given her to cut the pampa grass, and not to devour the flesh of a human being; that she was docile and friendly to man, and not his enemy. The Jesuits (missionaries) taught the Indians how to milk the cow and how to use her milk. They soon learned how to tend cattle, to lasso them, to yoke them by the horns, so that they may drag along a bundle of drift wood from the edge of the river to the middle of the plain. In this way they kept cattle near them, while herds roamed through the pampas, became wild, and are now so scattered through the lands that it is difficult to count them. The pampas described in the lieutenant's report form the central and southeastern departments of the present republic of Bolivia, and he is doubtless correct when he states that the first horned cattle introduced into that part of the continent came from the Pacific coast. In 1551 horned cattle were first brought into Paraguay from the coast of Brazil. These Sir Woodbine Parish regard as the progenitors of the numberless herds that for three centuries have roamed the southern plains. For the original importation Paraguay was, doubtless, indebted to the Jesuits, as was that country, and, in fact, the whole interior of the southern continent, for almost all the elements of their early civilization. Sir Woodbine is mistaken, however, in asserting that the whole pampas stock originated from the breed imported into their mission grounds by the Jesuits of Paraguay. Prior to the date to which that importation is assigned, settlements of Europeans had been effected in southeastern Peru, and the colonists, as Mr. Gibbon suggests, had brought cattle with them from the west coast. The present stock, therefore, may be regarded as the combined results of the two original importations, one from the Atlantic, and the other from the Pacific shore. As to the particular character of the original stock, it, no doubt, consisted of the common black cattle of Spain and Portugal. There is a very common mistake in regard to what some writers designate as the wild cattle of the south. The writers themselves are mistaken, and have led their readers to the same erroneous conclusion. The opinion is, that from an early period after the conquest, herds of straying and unclaimed cattle were allowed to run wild, and that these were, in the course of many years multiplied into countless millions, roaming wild and fierce through the forests and over the plains. It is true that portions of herds, which had never received proper care, or that by some special and violent cause had been separated and scattered, have become wild in their habits and fierce in their dispositions. But being regarded as common property, both Indians and white settlers have hunted them till the breed can no longer be said to exist, and the only wild cattle now are the few, comparatively, that have wandered away from the farms during the absence of the herdsmen in times of revolutionary commotion. The general characteristics of the present native stock are about the same as those of unimproved stock in this country. The principal points of difference are in the legs and horns; the legs being longer, and the horns longer and wider at the tips than those of our native breed. Their average weight is about the same as that of our ordinary farm cattle. In a large herd almost all shades of color may be distinguished, the prevailing hues being light and dark red, and black, and dark brown. Steers frequently attain a fine size, are very symmetrical in their proportions, and when broken to the yoke and put to service are gentle in their dispositions, and rapid and graceful in their motions. In regard to the qualities of the cows for the production of milk, but little can be said with certainty. On the cattle farms milk is but seldom used, and so little attention is paid to the cows that are kept by milkmen for the purpose of supplying the towns and cities, that the quantity of milk they yield can not be taken as a fair sample of their natural capabilities. The milk itself is very rich and has an excellent flavor. The town and city traffic in that article is somewhat noteworthy. Certain police regulations are made to prevent adulteration; but they are not very effectual. Every morning quite a troop of milkmen's horses may be seen in line before the door of the police officer, and after due examination, the charge of adulterating being brought home, the contents of the cans are condemned and confiscated. But the adulteration of milk, like the adulteration of whisky, is found to pay so well that the rogues can afford to suffer the penalty of the law quite as often as a policeman can be found sharp enough to detect and sufficiently conscientious to arraign them. It must, indeed, be rather an extreme case of milk and water to be thought grave enough to be presented for the action of municipal authority. Hence it is worthy of note, as another peculiarity belonging to this traffic, that many of the milkmen will confess to the faces of their customers the sin of adulteration. The vachero who supplied the family of the writer, frankly acknowledged that he regularly brought three kinds of milk to market. I have, said he, a double share of cream for my customers who pay me an extra price, no cream for those who pay the regular price, and milk and water for such as may not pay anything. For reasons that will be stated in connection with another point remaining to be noticed, no attempt has been made to improve the native stock by the cattle breeders of the pampas. This, to many, may seem strange; for, considering the facilities afforded for such an experiment by the climate and pasturage of the country, it might prove successful there beyond precedent in those countries where, by crossing and careful treatment, stock has been brought to its highest degree of perfection. If the writer mistake not, there is a handsome fortune in store for any intelligent, enterprising cattle farmer who would go to that country and invest a moderate capital in the improvement of native stock, both for domestic supply and foreign exportation. An estancia, or cattle farm, varies in extent from one thousand to fifty thousand square leagues, the square league containing five thousand seven hundred and sixty English acres. In the districts adjacent to the cities and towns, and in those which lie upon the margin of the Plate and Parana rivers, sheep are rapidly taking the place of horned cattle. The largest estancias for cattle, in fact, are now to be found only in the interior, and in such sections as are far from the great water-courses. The cattle farms abound in what the natives distinguish as strong grasses. These coarse grasses gradually disappear whenever the land is appropriated to sheep. In their place there comes a rich supply of smooth-stalked meadow grass, *Poa pratensis*, and meadow foxtail, *Alopecurus*. Horned cattle, like sheep, prefer these, but thrive very well on the trefoil, wild barley, and other varieties of coarse grass which abound throughout the plains. The coarse grasses are more hardy, and stand the dry season better than finer ones, but contain less nutriment; and while stock fed upon them are preserved in a healthy and plump condition, they neither fatten so quickly nor so abundantly as when favored with their choice pasture. Pasture is most abundant in winter, the rainy season of that climate, and of best quality during the months of summer and autumn. On a single estancia is frequently pastured a stock consisting of a hundred thousand head. The general herd is divided into smaller ones containing, each, from three to twelve thousand. A herd of three thousand can be properly cared for by one man. The entire herd is collected every evening at a spot near the farm house. This gathering place is called, in Spanish, *rodeo*. And one marked peculiarity to be observed when the stock has been assembled for the night is, that each animal is careful to select precisely the same spot on which it laid the night before, and every night, probably, since it took its place among its full grown companions. The immense herd will all lie or stand together thus, each in its own place, without enclosure of any kind, and will not separate for the day's grazing until eight or nine o'clock in the morning. Cows calve once a year; heifers as early as at two years old. With regard to the longevity of horned cattle, no exact information can now be obtained. Farmers have not recorded nor perhaps even made any observations on that subject. In the opinion of Mr. Van Blarcom, an experienced and intelligent observer, the average age of animals may be set down at fifteen or twenty years. Neither the proprietors nor the men they employ will eat the flesh of an old cow or steer, and as stock is not bred to any extent either for milking or labor, there is no inducement to preserve animals till they have grown old, especially as the heifers and younger cows are preferred for the purpose of breeding. For these reasons but very few animals are allowed to grow old; and such as receive this privilege are permitted to die of neglect, or are killed for the hide and tallow, the carcase being thrown to the dogs and buzzards. To secure comfort and success in cattle breeding, water is a prime consideration. The most desirable land, therefore, for this purpose, is that which is situated in those slightly undulating districts of the great plains where large ponds of water collect during the rainy season. These, however, evaporate in most cases during the heat of summer, and water must be obtained from wells. In cases where care had not been taken to provide a sufficient number of these, great destruction of stock has sometimes been the consequence. In the province of Entre Rios, in 1846, there was a general drought, unusually prolonged and disastrous. The grass was literally reduced to dust. Cattle, suffering from thirst, wandered off from their accustomed pasture grounds in search of food and water. Some farmers lost five thousand, some ten, and some as many as fifty thousand animals. It is stated, indeed, and is doubtless true that at one estancia, an English gentleman, lost one hundred and fifty thousand head. In seasons of protracted drought cattle will stray in quest of water hundreds of miles. If they find water, and remain long enough in its neighborhood to calve, they will never return. But if the drought ceases before they calve, they will return to the grounds of their owners. Protracted droughts are not of frequent occurrence; and yet they are sufficiently so, one would think, to induce the farmers to adopt all suitable precautions. The immigrant farmers do provide wells sufficient to meet ordinary exigency. But the native proprietors in this, as in all things else, are disposed to take the world easy, and are perfectly willing that the morrow should provide for itself, or even prefer that it should be a day of disaster rather than to-day should be devoted to care and toil. Besides this, native labor is exceedingly scarce. The great pampas are very sparsely populated; and the necessaries of life are so cheaply and easily obtained that the few who are dependent upon their own exertions for a livelihood will do but little work. In one particular, both foreign and native proprietors are alike to blame. Dependent as they frequently are upon their wells, they have not adopted any modern improvements for pumping water. The horse-bucket system still prevails. An author very familiar with the modes and customs of the pampa cattle farmers thus describes the process: Over the well is a framework from which is suspended a pulley through which a rope is passed, one end being secured to the bucket and the other fastened to a horse. The bucket is made of hide, very long, and of a peculiar form; the adjustment of the rope is so secured that when the horse reaches the extreme length of the rope one mouth of the bucket leans into a cistern or trough, into which it empties itself. By this primitive and tedious process it takes one man and two horses eight hours to water two thousand head of cattle. So if there should be only fifty thousand head on a particular farm, and there is frequently double that number, it would require a day's work for twenty-five men and fifty horses to give the entire herd a single drink of water. There is one custom peculiar to horned cattle which the natives call standing rodes. The explanation is this: if one farmer lose a herd, or any portion of one, and sets out in search of the missing animals, every farmer he visits in the course of his search is required by an ancient law, enacted expressly for that purpose, to drive up his herd for the inspection of his unfortunate neighbor, that he may see whether he can identify any of his lost animals. This is what is meant by standing rodes. In a country where there are no fences, and causes are constantly occurring that tend to scatter the herds, it will be perceived that the law in question is very proper and necessary. As there are neither ditches nor fences of any kind to separate adjoining farms, each animal must be stamped with the mark of its owner, so that in case of occasional straying, or a general stampede, or other causes producing an intermixture of herds and great consequent confusion, each proprietor may distinguish and claim his own. Patterns of the various marks or brands adopted by the estancieros of a political department are preserved in the office of the *comandante*, with the names of the parties that use them; and to counterfeit or alter a mark is a penal offence of the same grade as forgery, or counterfeiting money. The season of marking is one of great sport for the young men and boys and even the girls of a family. It corresponds, in its way, to the cornhuskings and quiltings that were so highly appreciated and keenly enjoyed by our grandfathers and grandmothers. The process is very simple. The cattle are driven into a large pen; a man or half grown boy mounts a horse; the Spanish saddle is fastened very strongly with stout and broad leather straps; in the central strap, about half way between the horse's back and belly, there is an iron ring; to this the lasso (a strong, plaited raw-hide rope) is attached; the other end is formed into a noose which the rider throws over the horns of the animal, and the horse dragging it from the herd its legs are then securely fettered, and being thrown upon its side the red-hot brand is produced and the owner's mark is stamped indelibly upon its smoking flesh. The catching of a single animal for domestic use frequently presents an exciting scene. The particular one desired is singled out, and perceiving itself, as by instinct it frequently does, to be the object of some dangerous design, it breaks from the herd and bounds off into the plain. The horsemen duly equipped with a lasso clasps the spur to his steed and bears down upon the flying fugitive. Having gained a point within convenient distance, he swings the lasso several times around his head to give it momentum, and then throws the noose around the horns of his victim. This is done while horse and steer are at the top of their speed. The moment the noose lodges on the head of the steer the horse stops and wheels to receive the shock which is often so violent that the animal is thrown headlong and bellowing to the ground. The precision with which many horsemen throw the lasso can hardly be conceived by one not familiar with the customs of that country. The Indian's arrow or tomahawk scarcely speeds more directly to its mark. The performance is to be explained as are all the feats of human dexterity. Early training and long practice supply the horsemanship, the steady hand, and the unerring aim. The lasso is the native child's first toy; and one of his earliest amusements is found in throwing its noose over the heads of the dogs, cats, and tame sheep that follow him about his play grounds. Another method of catching cattle is with the bolas. This instrument is prepared in the following manner: Three round stones or iron balls, each the size of an egg, are covered with raw hide; one is fastened to each end of a forked strip of hide, about ten feet long; the third ball is secured to a strip, attached to the main one, about five feet long. The horseman takes this in his hand, and, as in the former case, pursues the animals. When he comes within easy reach of his object, he takes hold of the end of the rope, and swinging the other, that has the balls attached, several times around his head, throws the whole contrivance at the animal's legs In an instant it is entangled, and the more it endeavors to escape the more securely it is fettered till it falls. The bolas may be thrown fifty or sixty yards with certainty; and if the pursuit be rapid, the fleetness of the horse adding force to the throw, an animal may be struck with tolerable precision at a distance of eighty or ninety yards. An ordinary herdsman, or other laborer, receives per month from twelve to twenty silver dollars. The entire estancia, with all its arrrangements, is placed under the superintendence of an experienced and well tried major-domo, whose salary differs, according to the wealth of the proprietor and the responsibilities of the situation, from three to five hundred Spanish dollars per annum. In killing cattle for home consumption the butchers first hamstring them and then cut their throats. In dressing them they are not suspended, but flayed on the ground. Some years ago the Buenos Ayrean city fathers prepared a slaughter-house of the same style and conveniences as are common in other countries, but the butchers refused to occupy it, and steadfastly adhered to the old custom of hamstringing and throat-cutting in an open pen. The carcase is divided in a mode somewhat peculiar. The tenderloin is taken out and sold by itself. Beef is never weighed in market, nor even measured, except by the butcher's eye, who acquires great exactness in subdividing the quarters of an animal so as to make the pieces suit the daily, bi-weekly, or tri-weekly demands of his customers. The beef market of the pampas was in former years probably the cheapest in the civilized world. So recently as twenty years ago an ordinary cow or heifer could be bought for one silver dollar, and a large fat steer for two dollars and a half. Now, the prices of the same animals range from eight to twenty dollars. In 1858 a piece of sirloin, weighing ten pounds, could be purchased in the market of Buenos Ayres or Montevideo for fifty cents, and in the towns of the interior for half that sum. The natives are very partial to roast beef, which they term *asado;* but their mode of preparing it is peculiar to themselves. They take the best roasting pieces and cut away the flesh till the rib is reduced to nearly the thinness of an ordinary sparerib of pork, according to our method of butchering. This is done to suit their mode of roasting, which is never in accordance with that which obtains in Paris, London, or New York. Instead of the oven, they still use the more primitive spit. This is a piece of iron about four feet long. It is run through the meat, and, if the meat be prepared in the open air, is stuck into the ground at such an angle as brings the meat into contact with the tip of the flame; or, if the meat be prepared in the kitchen, the spit is inclined against the chimney in about the same position. The fire is kindled with weeds or small dry faggots cut from the paradise or peach tree. As this consumes very quickly, fresh fuel is constantly supplied. When the fat of the flesh ignites and blazes, the cook seizes the spit, blows out the flame, and then returns it to its place. This is repeated till the meat is nearly done, when the spit is laid across two large bricks, and the process of cooking is completed by toasting a few minutes over the fresh coals. Meat cooked in this way is somewhat smoked and a good deal blackened, but it has a juiciness and a peculiar flavor which could not fail to commend it to the palate of a finished epicure. Some travelers complain of the toughness of the native roast, but the writer's experience is altogether in conflict with their statements, and his impression is that they must have fallen into the hands of a very unskillful cook, or upon the carcase of an animal that had been toughened by poverty and leanness or unusual length of days. The qualities of the beef are very superior. English residents, generally, do not esteem it; but this is owing to that intense national egotism from which few, even of traveled Englishmen, ever entirely recover. They will roundly assert that neither first-rate beef nor mutton can be found beyond the limits of the British isles. But many Americans, who have traveled extensively on both continents, consider the best pampas beef fully equal, if not a little superior, to the best beef ever brought to an English market. It has not the same amount of fat, nor is the fat so thoroughly distributed through the lean portions of the carcase, but it is sufficiently fat to meet the demand of any delicate and well-educated palate. The tissues are so fine as to render the flesh peculiarly tender, and, when cooked, it has a flavor akin to that which distinguishes the flesh of the wild duck from that of the flock which is hatched in the poultry house, and reared in the barnyard. It is also very easily digested. A feeble, dyspeptic stomach may take as much as the appetite of a hungry man will ever crave and not be oppressed by the indulgence. Pampas beef, as well as pampas air, might safely be prescribed for all invalids who are suffering from dyspepsia, and assailed by its veteran ranks of horrors attendant on dyspepsia or ennui. An establishment for salting and curing jerked beef is called a saladero, literally, salting tub. The mode of slaughtering the cattle and preparing the beef is very simple. As in the case of marking, the herd is driven into a large pen. A man or boy, with a lasso attached to his saddle girth, throws the noose around the horns of the animal. The lasso traverses a pulley, suspended from a cross-beam resting on two strong upright posts. The horse draws the head of the animal directly up to the beam where a man or boy sits with a long knife. The moment the head touches the beam the knife severs the spinal cord just back of the horns, and the animal drops on a movable platform which runs on a tramway, and is immediately drawn out of the pen by hand and placed under an open shed, where two men, without hanging the carcase, quickly flay it right and left; two others take out the intestines, cut off the head, divide the trunk into four quarters,

COMPONENT PARTS OF NATIONAL WEALTH.

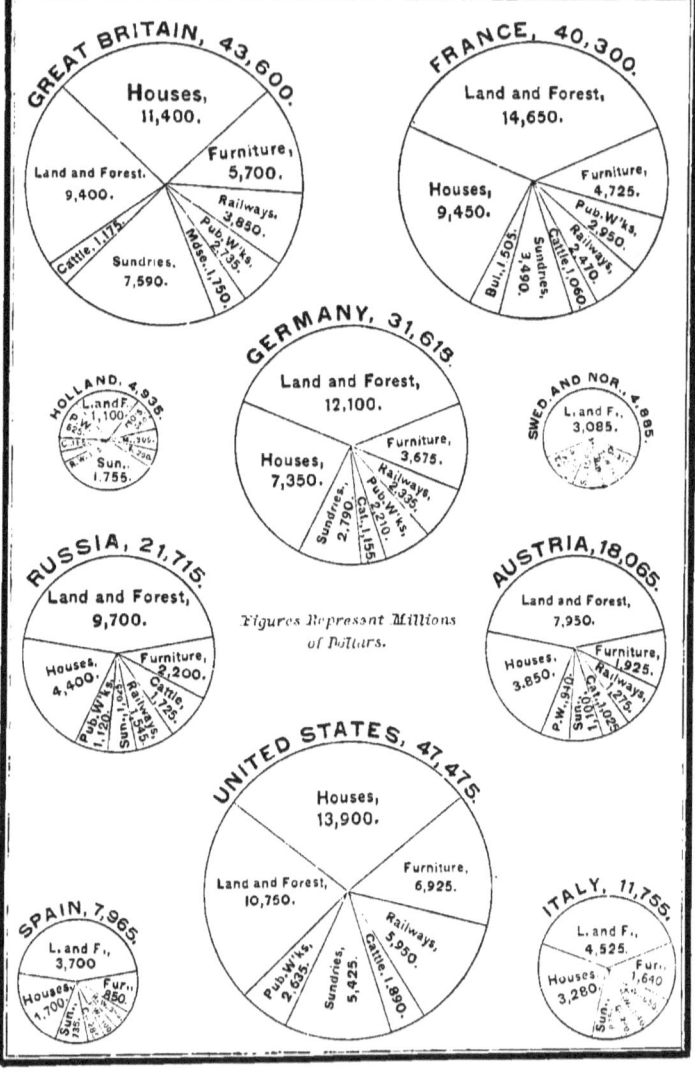

hang them on hooks, cut them in slices, throw them into a handbarrow, and, while one wheels off the flesh to be salted, another conveys the hide, bones, horns, and tallow to their appropriate places. In the salting shed is a large tank filled with strong pickle. The slices are deposited in this for a short time, in order to wash them from all blood. They are then hooked out and packed under the shed in alternate layers of meat and salt. The slices take sufficient salt in about a week. They are then removed to another part of the shed, turned, and piled again. This moving and piling is repeated several times. The meat is then hung on poles in the sun for a few days, when it is again piled for the last time, and looks in this, its last stage of preparation, in the separate pieces, very much like codfish or sole leather; and, in the aggregate pile, very much like a stack of cornhusks that has stood the storms of a New England winter. And now, perhaps, the reader is ready to inquire whether, in its finished condition, it is a savory article of food. In reply, he may be reminded, in general terms, that taste is almost altogether a matter of education. At first, but very few persons relish tomatoes; and yet there is scarcely any one who does not learn to esteem them as one of the most delicious of all vegetables. Codfish, to an uncivilized palate, is at first about as agreeable as would be fine splints of pine board steeped in fermented and half putrid brine. Yet some civilized people esteem codfish a dish worthy to be set before a king. Tobacco stands among the very first articles on the long and varied list of human luxuries. But who does not remember the retching that followed the first chew, or the first cigar? On the same principle we should not be surprised to learn that jerked beef is highly esteemed where it has been longest and most generally used. The people that manufacture it, however, will not eat it at all. It is mostly exported to Cuba and Brazil, and is appropriated to the use of the negroes who cultivate the sugar and coffee plantations. Cattle are in the best condition in March, which is the first month of autumn in that hemisphere. The principal killing season is from November to March. But most of the saladeros are continued in moderate operation all the year around. These establishments for the manufacture of jerked beef were first founded in 1815, and were among the first fruits of the immigration that flowed into the country immediately upon the achievement of its independence. During the first few years of their existence, it was rarely the case that as many as a hundred animals were slaughtered at one establishment in a single day. Now, there are, probably, nearly a hundred such establishments, at each of which are slaughtered from two to four hundred head per day. The cost of a saladero capable of slaughtering four hundred head per day would be scarcely less than thirty thousand dollars. Take four men, skilled in such labors, and in fifteen minutes by the watch they will convert a living animal, standing in the pen, into jerked beef, salted in the common pile. The writer has measured the process, watch in hand, and is satisfied that four such workmen will average an animal to every fifteen minutes during the working hours of the day. Dried hides are from cattle that are killed for domestic consumption. The drying of them is rather a tedious operation, and one that requires a good deal of care. Those

57

intended for German and English markets are stretched lengthwise only, by which the hide acquires a much greater thickness than it would if stretched both ways. As many as twenty-four or twenty-six stakes are used for fastening the extremities of the hide to the ground. The dry hides designed for Spain, and other markets requiring thin leather, are staked so as to stretch them both laterally and longitudinally as much as possible. Hides shipped to Liverpool and Antwerp are generally twenty per cent. heavier than those intended for other ports; and those which are sent to the Spanish markets are said to be ten per cent. better in quality. Salt hides are first steeped in brine, then washed, and after the washing are packed away in alternate layers of hide and salt. Thus prepared they will keep well for at least one year after being taken from the salt. As to the quality of the pampas hides, it may safely be affirmed that better are not known to the commerce of the world. They may owe some of their superior qualities to the climate, some to the pasture, but the principal reason for their superiority is, that the breed of cattle have never been improved. The finer the animal, the thinner and less valuable the general qualities of the hide. This is mainly the reason why the most enterprising estancieros of the south have made no attempt to improve the native breed of cattle. What would be gained in flesh and tallow they think would be lost in hide and labor, and, probably, they are not wrong in this opinion. Every part of an animal is made available—horns, hoofs, hair, bones, and tallow, as well as the flesh and hide. The tallow is one of the most important items belonging to the general traffic. As soon as the flesh is sliced from the carcase, the bones and fat are deposited in vats, in alternate layers, for the purpose of being steamed. The bones are so arranged as to leave apertures through which the steam may quickly penetrate. The door of the vat is then closed, and the steam turned on. In twelve hours or more, according to the size of the vat, the liquid is drawn off by means of a brass tap. The condensed steam, in the form of a greasy liquid, is discharged first, and afterwards the liquid tallow, which is received in tubs, and thence conveyed to a large cast-iron boiler, in which it is purified. From the purifying boiler the tallow is conveyed through a shoot into a large iron tank, where it is allowed to cool down. After this it is drawn off into casks, and is then ready for shipment. Steaming for the purpose of extracting tallow was commenced about thirty-five years ago, and the process has undergone great improvement. The general arrangements necessary for steaming are quite expensive. A saladero, costing thirty thousand dollars, would require a steaming apparatus that would cost, at least, one-half that sum. Cattle are always paid for in cash. The risk of delivery is with the purchaser, as stock is invariably bought as it stands on the farm. There is a class of professional drovers in the country. Unlike the same class in this country, however, they are not proprietors, but are simply hired by the purchasers to convey their droves to market. One capitaz (chief drover) with four or five assistants will convey to market a herd of five or six hundred head. The price per head for this service will be twenty-five to seventy-five cents, according to the distance. When taken from their accustomed pasture grounds, cattle are sometimes restive and disposed to scatter. When any special causes of disturbance occur many are lost—in a few instances whole droves have broken away from their drivers and dispersed in the plains beyond chance of recovery. While en route for market, the custom is to halt for the night on some spot where the feeding is good. The drovers sleep and ride round the herds by turns. On stormy nights it is particularly difficult to keep the herd together, and whenever a general stampede occurs it is usually at such times. Cattle in good condition will stand driving twenty-five miles per day without injury. If pushed beyond this, the effect is very perceptible in what is called tired beef. Cattle once delivered, either at the city markets or the saladeros, receive no further attention; and, when the supply is large, animals are allowed to remain in the pens for a week without a blade of grass or a drop of water. If they do not starve long enough to produce per cent. on the sum total of the exportation. It will readily be perceived from these facts that the barraca business is one of the most important branches of the general trade of the country. It is pretty equally shared by natives and foreigners. Some very sharp men are engaged therein. They can tell all about a hide when it is yet warm and whole on the back of the steer; or what the quality of a fleece is, and how many pounds it contains before the shears have touched it. While passing through the plaza, observing without being observed, the writer has often been reminded of the accuracy of the woodman's eye and judgment, by which he correctly estimates how many square feet of ship timber or how many cords of wood there are in a standing tree. The extent and importance of this will appear from an annual statement. During one year the produce of five hundred and sixty-two thousand head of cattle was shipped at the port of Montevideo alone.

SOUTH DOWN RAM.

shrinkage of flesh, the proprietors do not care for the sufferings of the poor beasts. Excepting live stock, the produce of the country is offered for sale in a public plaza or market-place. Sometimes the farmers themselves act as their own salesmen, but the general usage is to employ a broker. The broker is styled a barraquero, and his warehouse a barraca. When a mercantile house wishes to obtain hides, wool, or other produce of the country, a barraquero is employed to attend the sales in the plaza and make the purchase. The articles are then conveyed to his barraca. If it be wool, it is packed (or baled, rather) with a hydraulic press. Hides are simply stored in piles; and at the proper time the barraquero attends to the shipment of the cargo. The merchant has only to provide the money and keep the accounts, and the broker, for the entire cost and trouble of his agency, charges only one That city is the capital and chief port of the republic of Uruguay. And something of the great wealth of that state, in horned cattle, may be inferred from such an annual shipment, especially when it is considered that the revolutionary has become its chronic and prevailing condition. The total number of hides exported from the river Plate and the Rio Grande for one year was one million five hundred and eighty thousand; another year, one million six hundred and fifty thousand. The amounts included in this statement are nearly all the product of the great pampas lands lying on the eastern and western shores of the river Plate and its tributaries.

SOUTH DOWN SHEEP. That the South Down sheep make the most superior mutton of any known breed, there is no doubt, yet superior as is their mutton, except in the vicinity of large

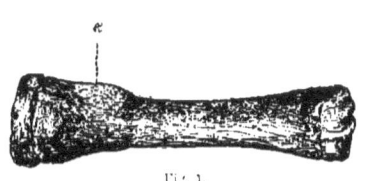
Fig. 1.

Fig. 2.

Fig. 3.

Fig. 4.
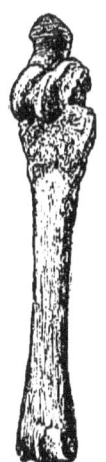
Fig. 5.

Fig. 6.

Fig. 7.

Fig. 7.

ILLUSTRATIONS OF SPAVIN

depth of six inches. For fallowing, it was really an excellent implement, but, unfortunately, it would not cover trash however slight, and the draft was excessive.

SPADIX. A form of inflorescence, in which the flowers are arranged around a fleshy rachis, enclosed within a kind of bract called a spathe, as in palms and araceous plants. The Indian turnip is an instance.

SPANISH CATTLE. (See Texas Cattle.)

SUSSEX CATTLE. Youatt says of the Sussex cattle, undoubtedly a subfamily of the Devons, that the Sussex ox holds an intermediate place between the Devon and Hereford, with much of the activity of the first and the strength of the second, and the propensity to fatten, and the beautiful fine-grained flesh of both. Experience has shown that it possesses as many of the good qualities of both as can be combined in one frame. The Sussex ox is of a deep chestnut-red—some, however, prefer a blood-bay; deviation from this color indicates some stain in the breed. The hide of the true Sussex is soft and mellow; a coarse, harsh, thick hide denotes here, as in every other district, an ill-bred or an unthrifty beast. The coat is short and sleek. There is seldom found on the Sussex ox that profusion of soft and wavy, and, occasionally, long hair, which, although it may have the appearance of roughness, is consistent with a mellow and yielding hide, and one of the truest indications of more than usual propensity to fatten. The Sussex cow, like the Hereford one, is very inferior to the ox; she seems to be almost another kind of animal. The breeder has endeavored, but with comparatively little success, to give to the heifer the same points that the ox possesses. The Sussex cow ought to have a deep red color, the hair fine and the skin mellow, thin and soft; a small head, a fine horn, thin, clean and transparent, which should run out horizontally, and afterwards turn up at the tips; the neck very thin and clean made; a small leg; a straight top and bottom, with round and springing ribs; thick chine; loin, hips, and rump wide; shoulder flat—but the projection of the point of the shoulder is not liked, as the cattle subject to this defect are usually coarse; the legs should be rather short; carcase large; the tail should be level with the rump. The Sussex cow does not answer for the dairy. Although her milk is of very good quality, it is so inferior in quantity to that of the Holderness or the Suffolk, that she is little regarded for the making of butter or cheese. There is one great fault about the Sussex cows seemingly inconsistent with their propensity to fatten, and which can not be remedied. Their countenance indicates an unquiet temper; and they are often restless and dissatisfied, prowling about the hedge-rows, and endeavoring to break pasture, and especially if they are taken from the farm on which they were bred. They are principally kept as breeders, all the use being made of them at the same time as dairy cows of which circumstances will admit. And it can not be denied that they are generally in fair condition, even while they are milking; and that no beasts, except their kindred, the Devons and the Herefords, will thrive so speedily after they are dried. The secretion of milk being stopped, the Sussex cow will fatten even quicker than the ox. It must, however, be acknowledged that the Sussex cows are not perfect even as breeders. Some of the ancient Britons sought refuge from the attacks of their invaders, amid the fastnesses of the Weald of East Sussex. Thither they drove, or there they found some of the native cattle of the country; and they anxiously preserved them free from all admixture. The resemblance between the Sussex and the Devon oxen is very great. They unquestionably betray the same origin. The Sussex ox has a small and well formed head, compared with many other breeds, and even with the Hereford, but evidently coarser than that of the Devon; the horns pushing forward a little and then turning upward, thin, tapering and long—not so as to confound this breed with the long horns. The eye is full, large and mild in the ox; but with some degree of unquietness in the cow. The throat clean, and the neck, compared with either the long horns or the short ones, long and thin, yet evidently coarser than that of the Devon.

SPANISH FEVER. (See Texas Fever.)

SPAN WORM. More properly geometers, *geometræ*, from their peculiar manner of moving, by arching the back, while they bring up the hinder part of the body. Attaching themselves, the body is stretched to the utmost length, and so progression proceeds by a series of movements by which they seem to measure the ground. They have only ten legs; six jointed and tapering under the fore part of the body, and four fleshy prop legs behind, the three intermediate pair of prop legs being wanting. They are all destructive insects, feeding on leaves, often defoliating trees and plants. The dreaded canker worm is a true geometer.

SPASMODIC COLIC. (See Blown.)

SPAVIN. Spavin, ringbone, and in fact any enlargement of the bone, by deposit of bony matter, may be referred to similar causes, and should be treated alike, first to allay the inflammation, and then to excite absorption. Firing, (burning the parts,) and all like heroic treatment, should be condemned; and disused, as a barbarous relic of the inhuman past. Bog spavin, and wind galls are produced by the same cause, congestion, inflammation, and resulting enlarged *Bursæ mucosæ*, and are relieved by cooling lotions in their first stages, and followed by bandaging of the parts. Blood spavin is a local venous congestion, and is to be met in the early stages, by cold water, and cooling lotions, later by strong infusions of bayberry bark, or brandy and salt applied through a considerable period of time. Wind galls, are difficult of cure, and do not constitute unsoundness. Of the nature of spavin the late Dr. Dadd says: it is a compound of two diseases, known as *exostosis* and *anchylosis;* the former signifies hypertrophy of bone, (*hyperostosis,*)—morbid enlargement; anchylosis signifies stiff joint—absorption of inter-articular cartilage and substitution of bone. Anchylosis, however, does not take place in what is properly understood as the hock joint, composed of the *tibia* and *astragalus*—although a very common occurrence in the human subject; but it generally occurs beneath the true joint, within its collateral or inferior articulations, known as the tarsal bones. Spavin, therefore, may commence in exostosis and end in anchylosis, and *vice versa*. The seat of spavin, then, is on the inside of the hock, in the region of the tarsal bones, and beneath the true joint, from which point it may both spread and acquire magnitude. Hypertrophy, or enlargement of the bone beneath the tarsal articulations, occurring on the upper part of the cannon, does not constitute spavin. Spavin has two origins, hereditary and exciting. Facts have proved conclusively that spavin, as well as predisposition, morbid tendency to the same, is transmitted from parents to offspring. It is probable, however, that predisposition is more frequently transmitted than actual disease; for the latter does not make its appearance so early as it otherwise would were it transmissible. Spavin is not peculiar to colthood, but to adult life, and even then can often be traced partly to an exciting cause, strain, injury, over-work, etc. Predisposition may not always have an hereditary origin; still it will not differ in its mode of action from the former; for all predisposing causes produce in the economy certain changes which may be said to prepare it for disease; and therefore, predisposition, whatever its source, may be considered as the incubative stage of disease. Exciting causes are those from which this disease seems to have direct origin, such, for example, as strain, injury, overwork, etc.; yet these fail to produce spavin in a great majority of cases; in confirmation of which we have only to look into the history of our truck horses, particularly those used for several years in the shafts. The herculean strength necessary to back a load which requires the united strength of two or three to draw would, one would think, be likely to produce spavin; yet a great proportion of such are exempt from this disease; therefore we may infer that exciting causes are in some cases inoperative, unless conjoined with predisposition. Unfortunately for the poor brute, lameness is not generally of that character which incapacitates him for work; and thus he is urged to the performance of his duties, the disease progressing, and his sufferings increasing, until at last the owner sees that the lameness is not to be driven off. The generality of non-professional men are unwilling to believe in the existence of spavin, unless they can both see and feel it, and are therefore more prone to refer primary spavin lameness to some other joint, until, after a few months of intermittent lameness, they are, by ocular demonstration, convinced. Spavin commencing in inter-articular cartilage is not demonstrable in this manner; there is no circumscribed tumor, nor irregularity; our diagnosis must, therefore, be made up from the signs revealed—from the heat and tenderness about the part, of a subacute character—from the absence of tumor—from the manner of catching up the limb—and from the intermittent nature of the lameness, which is progressive, yet fluctuating. The history of the case, also, must be considered. If a sort of irregular lameness has existed for some months, referable to no other joint than the hock, and the difficulty has of late gradually increased, so that the joint appears stiff, all doubts are set aside, for anchylosis is hastening toward completion; after which we may expect to observe a tumor on the inside of the hock. A tumor once formed in the region already referred to needs no wise man to point it out; it can be both seen and felt; and this, accompanied with hock lameness and ligamentary tumefaction, is the diagnostic symptom of spavin in its exostotic stage. In illustration of the subject of bony formation we shall find that original inflammation of the bony tissue is comparatively rare, while that of the periostial investment of the bone is quite frequent. A variety of causes may account for this. Perhaps the most common is the evil of overwork. Hard driving on a hard road, as on a plank road, on the frozen ground, or on the ice, or the strain of draft, as too heavy a load, may excite periostial inflammation, and from this as a commencement we may have splint, spavin, ringbone, nodes, etc. Splint (Fig. 1 a) is a bony tumor at some point about the cannon and splint bones. The knee-joint is formed at its inferior part, between the lower row of carpel bones and the cannon and splint bones, the two latter forming a considerable portion of the joint. As the leg is flexed these bones slide upon the cannon bones, contributing to the elasticity of the step. When the motion is violent and long continued, especially with striking upon a hard surface, irritation first and inflammation afterward may be produced in the periostial membrane covering these bones. Bony matter is thrown out in the immediate vicinity of their adjacent surfaces, and the result is a sealing together of the bones and the formation of a bony tumor. Unfortunately the condition is frequently overlooked until the change is complete and the disease beyond a remedy, for when the bony union is thoroughly consolidated it can not be remedied. For a time, while the deposit is fresh callus, and the circulation active, measures to abate the inflammation and to excite the absorption of the deposit may restore the integrity of the part. In the pathology of the disease, (Fig. 1 and 2) splint and ringbone, as before stated, are the same. They have the same causes, and are preceded by the same stages of morbid action; but, from the relation of parts, ringbone, at its forming stage, gives rise to earlier and greater lameness. Attention is earlier called to the disease, and treatment is usually sooner applied. Splint may go on to its final stage of bony consolidation without giving rise to much lameness and without attracting attention to the diseased part, which may escape observation unless the hand is passed over the small tumor; but in ringbone usually the lameness appears with the inflammation, and the earliest effusion over the region calls attention to the seat of the disease. Spavin, (Fig. 4, 5 and 6,) when it consists in the deposit of bony matter about the hock joint, and the consequent cementing together of the tarsal bones, or the destruction of the tarso-metatarsal joint, is a similar disease, having essentially the same causes. This form of disease may exist in every degree, from a slight exostosis near the joint to such an amount as will entirely destroy the joint, and so invade the soft tissues that the slightest movement is productive of great suffering. Fig. 7 and 8 shows, in spavin, the lower tarsal bones, cementation by the deposit of bony matter. In the treatment of spavin, ringbone, splint or any disease of the joints or limbs involving inflammation, rest is absolutely necessary. If the disease has progressed, and bony matter has formed, there is absolutely no cure. Pain, however, will not be severe after the bony process is completed. Hence the wonderful cures, by various nostrums, applied at such stage, and which would have resulted naturally in a so-called cure. The treatment is, in the first stage of the inflammation, cold water applications thoroughly applied, as for any other inflammation. Then to cause absorption. A good resolvent is four ounces mercurial ointment, one-half ounce of powdered cantharides, and two drachms of oil of rosemary. Triturate these thoroughly together, and use daily. Thoroughly rubbing the part with oleate of mercury, from day to day, will soon dissipate whatever has not already become bone. If before these are applied, when bony formation has commenced, it would be well to insert a narrow bladed bistoury under the skin and scarify the seat of the spavin freely.

SPAYING. Spaying is extracting the ovaries of female animals, for the purpose of fattening. If operated on about the season of periodic heat, and when in full flow of milk, spaying prolongs indefinitely the period of giving milk and increases the flow. Thus cows have been known to continue in milk for years, and, of course, without subsequent period of heat. Experiments with twenty-seven cows varying in age from six to fifteen years, showed an increase in milk of thirty-three per cent. Spaying does not so much depend upon the instruments used, as upon the skill of the operator. It should never be undertaken until the operator first makes himself acquainted with the anatomy of the parts, or until he has had instructions from an experienced operator. Then the operation may be safely performed with a common knife, a crooked needle, and some waxed silk thread. Yet the regular instruments are better. The cow should be cast, securely fastened, and her head held firmly down by an assistant; an incision is then to be made through the muscles, skin and peritoneum large enough to admit the hand, which seizing the ovaries, in turn, they are brought up as far as possible, severed, and the wound closed with four or five interrupted sutures; that is the edges of the wound to be brought together, and pierced, through the lips, with a threaded needle, and tied, each stitch separately, and and the ends of the threads left three or four inches long, and the wound properly dressed. If the animal subsequently is irritable and refuses her food, prepare the following drink: two ounces of valerian and two quarts of water; when cool, strain, and add one quart infusion of marsh mallow, and give a pint every two hours. If the wound shows signs of pus, and does not heal kindly, wash with two ounces of pyroligneous acid, in two quarts of water. It is also well to prepare the animal by giving a scalded bran mash every night for a few days before the operation. M. Morin, a French surgeon, operated as follows: The eyes of the cow are covered, one strong man holds her by the nose and another by the horns. Her hocks are tied together and held by another assistant, who also holds the tail and pulls when the cow attempts to move. Then, says M. Morin, the cow being conveniently disposed of, and the instruments and appliances, such as curved scissors, upon a table, a convex-edged bistoury, a straight one, and one buttoned at the point, suture needle filled with double thread of desired length, pledgets of lint of appropriate size and length, a mass of tow (in pledgets) being collected in a shallow basket, held by an assistant, we place ourselves opposite to the left flank, our back turned a little toward the head of the animal; we cut off the hair which covers the hide in the middle of the flanks, at an equal distance between the back and hip, for the space of thirteen or fourteen centimetres (a centimetre is forty hundredths of an inch), in circumference; this done, we take the convex bistoury, and place it open between our teeth, the edge out, the point to the left; then, with both hands, we seize the hide in the middle of the flank, and form of it a wrinkle of the requisite elevation, and running lengthwise of the body. An assistant seizes with his right hand the right side of this wrinkle. We then take the bistoury, and cut the wrinkle at one stroke through the middle; the wrinkle having been suffered to go down, a separation of the hide is presented of sufficient length to enable us to introduce the hand; thereupon we separate the edges of the hide with the thumb and fore finger of the left hand, and, in like manner, we cut through the abdominal muscles, the iliac, (rather obliquely,) and the lumbar, (cross,) for a distance of a centimetre from the lower extremity of the incision first made in the hide; this done, armed with the straight bistoury, we make a puncture of the peritoneum, at the upper extremity of the wound; we then introduce the buttoned bistoury, and we move it obliquely from above to the lower part up to the termination of the incision made in the abdominal muscles. The flank being opened, we introduce the right hand into the abdomen, and direct it along the right side of the cavity of the pelvis, behind the paunch and underneath the rectum where we find the horns of the uterus; after we have ascertained the position of these viscera, we search for the ovaries, which are at the extremity of the *cornua*, or horns, (fallopian tubes,) and when we have found them, we seize them between the thumb and fore finger, detach them completely from the ligaments that keep them in their place, pull lightly, separating the cord, and the vessels (uterine or fallopian tubes) at their place of union with the ovarium, by means of the nails of the thumb and fore finger, which presents itself at the point of touch; in fact, we break the cord, and bring away the ovarium. Again introduce the hand in the abdominal cavity, and proceed in the same manner to extract the other ovarium. This operation terminated by the assistance of a needle, place a suture of three or four double threads, waxed, at an equal distance, and at two centimetres, or a little less, from the lips of the wound; passing it through the divided tissues, we move from the left hand with the piece of thread; having reached that point, we fasten with a double knot; we place the seam in the intervals of the thread from the right, and as we approach the lips of the wound, we fasten by a simple knot, being careful not to close too tightly the lower part of the seam, so that the suppuration, which may be established in the wound, may be able to escape. The operation effected, cover up the wound with a pledget of lint, kept in its place by three or four threads passed through the stitches, and all is completed. It happens, sometimes, that in cutting the muscles, we cut one or two of the arteries, which bleed so much that there is necessity for a ligature before opening the peritoneal sac, because, if this precaution be omitted, blood will escape into the abdomen, and may occasion the most serious consequences. The best time for spaying cows, with a view of making them permanent milkers, is between the ages of five and seven, especially if they have had two or three calves. If intended to be fattened for beef, the operation should not be performed until the animal has passed its fourth year.

SPEAR GRASS. (See grasses).
SPEARMINT. Common green mint, *Mentha viridis*; also the weed *Mentha tenuis*.
SPECIES. In natural history, an individual or individuals, whether plant or animal separated from others of a genus. Thus, the genus *Bos* embraces the buffalo, the bison and others, the sub-genus, or species *Bos taurus*, being the ox, or the various varieties of our horned cattle. In plants the same rule follows. The genus *triticum*, for instance, contains a number of species among which are wheat, (*T. vulgare*). Thus, individual plants or animals, so much like each other that they may be conceived to have a common origin are species. Below this again are varieties, or sub-species as the varieties of cattle, or of the rose.
SPECTRUM. An image, usually applied to the image of the sun seen through a prism, and which consists of seven colors.
SPECULUM. A reflector or mirror of metal.
SPEEDWELL. The genus *Veronica*, perennial plants, often with beautiful spikes of blue flowers.
SPELT. Spelter wheat. An inferior variety of wheat having the chaff strongly attached to the grain, and requiring milling to separate it. It is cultivated in some parts of Europe not adapted to the growth of the better varieties. In Germany it is called *dinkel*, and is of two varieties both bearded and smooth, one having a smooth, the other a rough berry or kernel. It is one of the oldest varieties and was known to the ancient Egyptians.
SPERMAPHILE. The prairie squirrel.
SPERMATIC ANIMALCULES. Minute, thread-like animalcules found in the secretion of the testes.
SPERMATIC CORD. The collection of blood-vessels passing from the abdomen to the testes.
SPERMIDIUM. The same as akenium, a small seed vessel resembling a seed.
SPHACELUS. Mortification, gangrene.
SPHAGNUM. A genus of mosses growing in bogs, and forming a great deal of the peat.
SPHENOID BONE. A bone in the base of the skull.
SPHINCTER. The name of muscles which close the natural openings of the body.
SPICE WOOD. *Laurus benzoin*. An indigenous shrub, four to ten feet high, the wood of which yields an aromatic smell. It grows in damp places.
SPIDER. The whole family of spiders *Arachnida*; except mites and scorpions, are on the whole beneficial to agriculture on account of the insects they destroy. There are some venomous kinds in the South that must be guarded against, as the tarantula. The spiders are between the crustaceans and the insects proper. The body is divided into two parts, the thorax and the abdomen; the head is continuous with the chest and there is no abdomen. The sexes are separated, and the young are produced directly from the egg, without undergoing an intermediate larval state. Spiders are divided into terrestrial and aquatic, species of each being spinning, and sedentary, lying in wait near their nets for their prey, and also predaceous, or hunting spiders. Some of the species have sought to be made available, in thin silk, but so far not success fully. Spiders are eaten by some tribes of savages, including our Digger Indians, and some southern species are large enough to overcome small birds.
SPIKE. 1. Incorrectly applied to lavender. 2. A large nail. 3. An ear of Indian corn, wheat, etc. 4. A shoot. 5. In botany, a species of inflorescence in which sessile flowers are alternate on a common simple peduncle, as lavender, whence the common name of lavender.
SPIKE-LAVENDER. (See Lavender.)
SPIKENARD. A name applied to various plants producing fragrant, essential oils, as *Aralia racemosa*, in the United States, and in England to *Andropogon nardus*; to *Valeriana spica*; to several species of *Baccharis, conyza*, etc.
SPINACH. *Spinacia oleracea*. Plants, the succulent leaves and stems of which are used for boiling as greens. The seed should be sown pretty thickly or about four to the inch, in drills fourteen inches apart, early in the spring, and the plants cut at the roots as soon as the leaves are nearly or quite fully grown. The best varieties are the large prickly seeded spinach and the round leaved or summer spinach. South of forty degrees the seed of the first named variety are sown in autumn and the plants covered during winter.
SPINDLE-SHAPED, FUSIFORM. Roots which taper at both ends, as the radish.
SPINDLE-TREE. *Euonymus Europæus*. A small tree or shrub, the wood of which is extremely hard, and used for spindles. It is improperly called strawberry-tree by some nursery men.
SPINE. The vertebrated column of quadrupeds. It is composed of forty or more pieces, or *vertebræ*, articulated by cartilage; through these runs the spinal marrow or pith, which sends off at every bone a pair of spinal nerves, which distribute the sensation of touch and the power of movement to the skin and muscles, over which they are distributed.
SPINES. In botany, imperfect branches.
SPIRACLES. The breathing openings or pores of insects.
SPIRAL VESSELS. In plants, elongated cellules, which contain a delicate internal thread, spirally wound, and capable of being drawn out.
SPIRIT. Any distilled alcoholic product.
SPIT OF EARTH. A spadeful, as dug from the soil.
SPLANCHNOLOGY. An account of the viscera of animals.
SPLAYED. In building, an angle cut off obliquely.
SPLEEN. A spongy viscus, of an oval form, the use of which is not well known; placed in the human subject in the left hypochondrium, between the eleventh and twelfth false ribs.
SPLINT. (See Ringbone.)
SPONGIOLE. The small spongy extremity of the rootlets.
SPORADIC. Springing up singly, or in small numbers. Diseases are sporadic which are not epidemic or endemic.
SPORANGIUM. The case or receptacle containing the spores.
SPORIDIA. The covering of the spores, the spore-like bodies of algæ.

SPORULES, or SPORES. The minute, simple, reproductive grains of cryptogamic plants.

SPRAINS AND STRAINS. These arise from violent exertion severely taxing the muscles or sinews, or even from long continued slight exertion of some particular muscle or sinew. The consequent disuse of the part, as in shoulder lameness, causes a falling away of the muscles, causing what is known as sweeny. This may, indeed, continue so long that the muscles from permanent disease become atrophied. If this continue, after acute lameness has ceased, mild blisters, and a long rest at pasture are the means of cure. Those who claim to cure sweeny in any other way, and especially by the application of secret specifics, are charlatans, and should be avoided. In the treatment of sprains or strains the first thing is to reduce the inflammation. This is best done by the application of cold water faithfully applied or by hot fomentations, perfect rest being of course understood, until the animal is again sound. The next step is firm and steady pressure of the parts by bandaging, with cooling lotions, until the inflammation is entirely passed. Next counter-irritations and gentle, regular exercise to avoid stiffness and wasting of the muscles (sweeny). A good, cooling lotion is one ounce of acetate of lead, one pint of vinegar, and one pint of rain water. For stiffness, pain and swelling, after the inflammation has passed, one-half ounce of iodine, two ounces each of glycerine and mercurial ointment and six ounces of olive oil will be found excellent. It will also be found good for chronic rheumatism, enlarged glands, goitre, and the slow form of strangles.

STRAIN OF THE BACK. Strain of the back or lumbar region arises from causes very evident to those who pay attention to the anatomical structure of the horse. The symptoms of this strain are: pressure over the lumbar region elicits symptoms of pain; the part feels hot and the horse shows great pain. The proper treatment is rest, application of cold water, light diet, and cream of tartar water as a drink. The day of plasters, in human as well as veterinary practice, has gone by; they are now only used by those who have never taken the trouble to understand the exhalatory function of the skin—which plasters obstruct; the wet sheet next the skin, and a blanket over it, will be more likely to do good than a plaster. Should the horse show more than ordinary symptoms of pain, a fomentation of hops should be resorted to; if, after a day or so, the pain is still manifest, the trouble is something more than mere strain, and the owner had better consult a veterinarian.

SPRAY. The young branches or twigs of trees.

SPRINGS. The usual acceptation of the word spring, is a bubbling fountain of water at the surface of the ground; yet, in digging, if a vein of water is met that rises in the well, it is quite as truly a spring as that other one that seeks the surface through a natural fissure in the soil or rock. So, also, those jets of water, rarely found, that, from the pressure on the reservoir below, spout into the air, are as truly springs as those which bubble gently at the surface, or which simply ooze slowly to the surface and pass slowly away. Among the more noted springs of the globe are those, hot and cold, which, containing mineral matter of real or supposed utility, are sought by invalids for the cure of diseases, or else as places of fashionable resort during the hot season of the year. Spouting springs are termed geysers. As illustrating this class, we give a cut of the great geyser of the National, or Yellowstone Park, in the Rocky mountains, one of

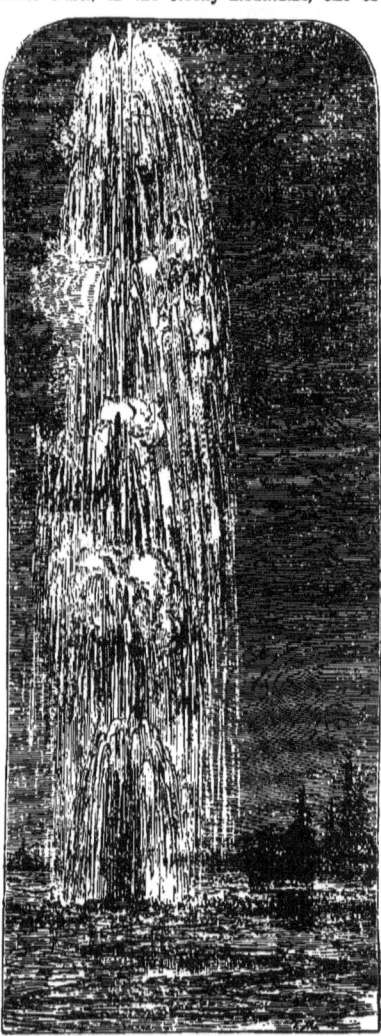

GREAT GEYSER OF THE YELLOWSTONE.

the most remarkable on earth. In the endeavor to get a permanent supply of water at or above the surface, large outlays are often made, either in the erection of wind or steam power for pumping, or else, when feasible, in boring to a depth sufficient to find water, the natural pressure upon which is sufficient to force it to or above the surface. These are termed artesian wells, and are of incalculable value in many regions, which without them would be uninhabitable.

SPRING BEETLE. (See Elater.)

SPRUCE. Fir. *Abies*. The spruces proper are plentifully distributed in the Northern States, and also found in northern Europe and Asia. In ornamental planting they are useful, combining a regular conical form with a more or less drooping habit. The Norway spruce, *Abies excelsa*, and the Hemlock spruce, *A. Canadensis*, are the two most valuable for planting. The first succeeds in a great variety of soil and climate, and is the favorite for general planting and windbreaks. The Hemlock is one of the most beautiful of evergreens. Unfortunately it does not succeed generally in the West when transplanted.

SPUD. An implement used in cutting up weeds, as dandelion, burdock, etc., in sward or turf. A chisel-formed tool, about two inches wide on the cutting edge inserted into a handle of four or six feet in length.

SPUR. The short, fruit-bearing branches of apples and pears. The hind toe of gallinaceous birds. A well known implement used by horsemen. In botany, an elongated appendage of the corolla.

SPURGE. The genus *Euphorbia*, the juice of which is usually acrid. Many species are ornamental.

SPURGE LAUREL. *Daphne laureola*.

SPUR OF RYE. Ergot. (See Rye.)

SPURRED RYE. Ergotted rye. (See Ergot.)

SPURRY. *Spergula arvensis*. An annual plant in considerable repute in Germany and France as a forage plant, being well adapted to soils, especially sandy land, too poor and thin to bear clover. It has been called the clover of poor sands, and it is said will, if sown in March, May, and July, and the three crops plowed in, fit a barren soil for clover. In France, Belgium, Germany and the North of Europe it is used not only as a fertilizer, but as a forage crop, both green and dry. Spurry is a native of America as well as Europe, being indigenous to the Middle States. In the United States it has not met with favor and is treated as a weed.

SQUAMA. A scale; rudimentary scale, like leaves or other parts of a plant. *Squamous* is scaly, or scale-like.

SQUARROUS. Ragged in appearance.

SQUASH. Squashes as generally cultivated in gardens are divided into three classes. The Summer or bush squashes, the Autumn Squashes, and the Winter or late keeping varieties. Of the bush varieties, the Summer Bush, Warted Crookneck, and the Early White Bush Scalloped Squash, are the varieties most cultivated. Of these the latter is the earlier and the former the best. Of the autumn varieties the Autumnal Marrow, sometimes called Boston Marrow, and the Turban are superior. The former being the best variety for steaming, and the latter one of the best of all the squash tribe for baking. The Autumnal Marrow will keep until about January, and the Turban until February. There are late winter varieties which keep until spring with proper care, on shelves in a perfectly ventilated cellar, dry, and not sinking below about 50° Fahr. A room that will not freeze is still better. Of these our preference for quality is, first, Hubbard, and second, Marblehead. This latter variety is variable in quality, like the so-called Sweet Potato Squash. If but one variety is cultivated for autumn and winter use, cultivate the Improved Turban by all means. The squash requires the whole season in which to mature. If started in six inch pots in a gentle hot bed and transplanted when in the rough leaf, the ravages of the striped bug may often be entirely avoided. They will scarcely feel the check of the removal if watered when transplanted. We have transplanted large fields of them, from troughs made by nailing sections of six inch siding upon sections of fencing each three feet long. Thus the back of one trough makes the front of another, and the plants may be carried any distance in them without danger. In transplanting break apart into six inch squares, as they were planted. A warm, rich, dry soil must be given to the whole family of squashes, and in addition they must be liberally manured in the hill, with rich compost manure. The hills for summer squashes are made four feet apart, and those of the autumn and winter varieties twelve feet apart.

SQUILL. *Scilla*. An extensive genus of interesting bulbous plants. A light soil is most suitable for them; and they are readily increased by offsets from the bulbs. The leaves are radical, linear. The flowers in clusters, blue, purplish, or white.

STABLE. The proper site for stables is as necessary as care in construction and ventilation. They need not necessarily be hidden entirely from view from the house, even in suburban places of the more pretentious order. Neither on the farm, need they be necessarily posted in the same yard with the house; or, if so, they should be at such distance as to be somewhat hidden by planting, and a separate entrance to them from the road is especially essential where they are intimately connected with the storage of grain and forage. Every quarter-section farm should have the horse stable a separate building from the barn. The cattle stable may occupy the basement of the barn when a side hill basement is practicable. In the article Farm Buildings, we have treated of the subject of stables in general. In this article it will not be necessary to do more than indicate what is necessary in the economy of space to be considered, leaving the details of construction to the architect, and the good sense of the builder and the owner. The cost of a stable will of course be indicated by the taste and wealth of the master. Nevertheless no stable can be economically complete if it be not comfortably warm, and well ventilated, and this can be measurably well secured in a comparatively cheap structure, if not quite as well as in the most costly one. To illustrate as to the value of warmth and ventilation in the case of cattle, (and with horses the rule will apply with greater force), the following from a German experiment will give a good idea of our meaning: Cows were placed in a stable that could be artificially heated, and fed on hay. The temperature of the stable was changed at intervals of ten days, the changes ranging from 41° Fahr. (nine degrees above freezing point) to 65.75°. During the ten days at the lower temperature the hair became rough and without gloss; the skin was drawn close and occasional shiverings were observable, and there was a loss of twenty-two pounds in the total weight of the two cows. At 54.5° to 59° the hair became smooth and the hide attained its former luster, softness, and looseness. The effects of unfavorable temperatures were also visible in diminished appetite and in variations of the milk product. The heat of the animal system is thrown off principally from the body, and not as many suppose from the breath expired from the lungs. The heat thrown off from the body does not necessarily injure the animal unless the ventilation of the stable is so bad that the vapor given off from the lungs can not be passed away. The ventilation therefore, must have reference to the animals kept, horses requiring more air than cattle. It must also become a question whether fuel or increased grain feed may be cheapest, in cold countries. This being settled, the question of the height of the stable walls must be considered. Less than eight feet for horses is not admissible; ten feet is better, since in a low stable the vitiation of the atmosphere is more than counterbalanced by the increase of heat from the animal's body. A cool, still air is better than a warm, close, moist atmosphere. It should be dry enough to readily pass off the insensible perspiration, and warm enough to dry a horse easily when sweated, and under the hands of the person who is rubbing the animal. There should also be abundant light by means of windows. These, if tolerably high, may be a part of the system of the ventilation employed. The floor of the stable of whatever material it be made should not soak up the urine. A floor composed of small broken limestone, say of one inch diameter, filled with cement, and covered with the fine material left in breaking, forms an excellent floor. A hard dry earth floor is altogether better than plank or cobble stone, since on the farm there is an abundance of straw for bedding by which the animals may be kept dry. This understood, the following will give a most excellent arrangement for farm or draft horses. The stable should not be less than eighteen feet wide, the stalls of such length as will allow six feet standing for each horse, and five feet in width. The walls should be eight feet high. The horses stand in a single row, and the harness is hung on pegs in the wall behind them. This width admits of thorough ventilation to the stable without subjecting the horses to drafts. Each standing should be parted off by an upright post reaching from the ground to the ceiling rafter, placed three feet from the wall at the horse's head. The partitions should be closely boarded up three feet above the manger and hay-crib to prevent the horses quarrelling about the food and biting each other. To each of the posts a bale, eight feet long and twenty inches wide, should be hung by a strong chain to divide the standings and suspended by another strong chain at the hinder end from the ceiling rafter. Each chain should have a hook and eye within reach that may be readily unfastened. This arrangement will leave the whole space opposite the head of each horse available for feeding purposes. The manger for grain and chaff (cut feed) may be two and a half feet long. It should be two feet wide at the top, one foot two inches at the bottom. The hay and straw, need a larger receptacle, which should be three feet six inches long, two feet wide at its upper part and half that width below. It should be so constructed that while it is even with the manger above, it should reach to the ground, two feet above which should be fixed to the wall a bottom, sloping to one foot above the ground in front, where some upright opening should be cut to allow the escape of seeds and dirt. At the top of this hay and straw crib, an iron rack with bars six inches apart, should be so hung as to open up and fall back against the wall to let the fodder be put in, and then be put down upon it for the horse to eat through. It should be so much smaller than the opening that it can fall down with the fodder as it is consumed, by which means not a particle is wasted. The manger may be constructed of yellow pine one and a half inches thick for the front, back, and ends; the bottom of iron, or if of wood, two inches thick. The top of the front and ends should be covered with half round iron, two and a half inches wide, screwed on to project over the front, a quarter of an inch outside and three-quarters of an inch inside the manger. This prevents the food being tossed out and the manger being gnawed. A short post must be put up as near the centre of the standing as possible to support the manger, into which a large screw ring must be put to let the chain or rope of the headstall pass freely up and down without constant friction. The manger may be three and a half feet from ground to top; the hay-crib of course the same height. The paving of the standings to three and a half feet from the head, should be flat, then with a fall from both sides to the centre, where an angle iron drain of four inches wide from end to end, with a removable flat iron cover fitted to the inside of it, should be placed straight down the standing, with a fall into another larger cross main drain ten feet six inches from the head, so placed as to carry away the urine from all the smaller drains into a tank outside the stable. This main drain so placed, takes the urine from the mares, and has a loose cover also fitted to it, easily removed for sweeping out when necessary. In the article Barns, the subject of stable economy is quite fully treated, and if the reader will refer thereto, excellent illustrations will be found showing both horse and cow stables, simple and of modern construction.

STAG. In natural history the stag is the male of the red deer or hind. It is also sometimes applied incorrectly, to a colt or filly. As we understand the term, it is only used to denote a male animal castrated after he has attained near or full maturity. Frequently applied to animals of the ox kind, which are castrated at such an age as to preclude their gaining the full size of an ox. In commercial parlance used to designate an outside irregular dealer in stocks, not a member of the exchange.

STAG BEETLES. These are closely allied to the lamellicorn beetles, and they may be easily recognized by the cut we give of *Lucanus dama*. The late Dr. Le Baron says: Notwithstanding their conspicuous size, but little is known of the habits of the perfect insects. The few observations on record go to show that their ordinary food consists of honey dew, or the exudations of the leaves and bark of trees, which last they are said to pierce with their pincer-like mandibles, but the force with which these organs are brought together does not seem to be sufficient for this purpose. They have been known to feed readily, in confinement, upon moistened sugar. The larvæ are found in rotten wood, and some of them have been known to bore into the solid roots of trees. But in the United States they have never been known to be seriously injurious.

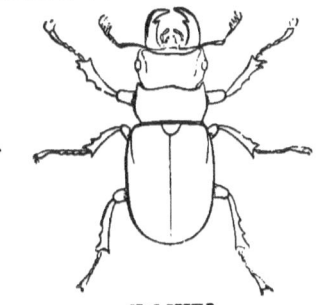

STAG BEETLE.

STAGGERS. (See Indigestion.)
STALL FEEDING. The stall feeding of animals intended for human consumption is the natural outgrowth of the massing of populations in cities, and the accumulation of wealth. In England the stall feeding of sheep is regularly practiced. In this country the feeding of sheep, fat, is yearly increasing near all the great centers of population. Cattle and swine will undoubtedly long continue to be the chief source of meat supply, or at least until the population shall approximate in density that of England, a contingency yet in the somewhat far future, since there are yet vast areas of land in the United States to be settled and brought under cultivation. Until within the last ten years, the stall feeding of cattle—that is, their confinement in restricted areas, where the light was restricted, and exercise could not be taken—was almost unknown. Even to-day the great bulk of our fat cattle in the West are fed in open lots more or less protected by timber. The best feeders, however, are careful to give shelter from snow and rain. It is simply a question of cheapness of food as against shelter. There are still large areas in the West where feeding in confined stables will not soon give place to feeding in open lots from the cheapness of grain. Under this system, however, animals can not be made what is called ripe. They attain a certain degree of fat, and are undoubtedly the best beef that can be made, lacking only that degree of succulence combined with tenderness, attainable when they are fed in stables. In the article Stable we have noticed the importance of ventilation, warmth and cleanliness. In the stall feeding barn less ventilation is necessary; warmth up to 60°, and not below 45° is essential to success. Ease of cleaning the stable and means to keep the animals from being soiled, are of fully as much importance. Standing places so arranged that the urine may flow easily into gutters, is also essential. The stanchions or other means of securing cattle, will easily suggest themselves, as will also the most economical feeding places, according as whole grain, ground feed, roots, steamed food, or a combination of a part or the whole is intended. In removing cattle to the stables for feeding, it should be done before there is any shrinkage from the drying up of the herbage. So long as the grass is good the cattle should have it, if they can be comfortable at night and be protected from cold storms. The best feeders prepare their cattle during the previous summer for stall feeding, by allowing them grain or meal whenever the pasture is not flush, and especially do they give additional feed during the autumn before they are finally removed to the barns. This not only keeps the steers growing, but it tends also to harden the flesh, so they do not shrink so much when first put up. It also gradually enures them to the change from succulent to dry food, not the least of the several points to be considered. The subject is beginning to be of sufficient importance in the West, so that a careful study of the subject will well repay every intelligent farmer. Cost of buildings, price of labor, facilities for watering in the stable, the grinding and hauling of grain, and many other minor considerations must be carefully considered. With corn at twenty-five to thirty cents per bushel, and help scarce and high, the experience of our best experimental farmers would seem to be in favor of feeding in well sheltered lots, therefore, except in the case of animals intended for special markets or for exhibition, as prize animals, stall feeding has not been much practiced in the West. In other sections of the country the case is different. It will be but a comparatively short time, in the older settled regions of the West, when stall feeding will also have become profitable there.

STAMENS. The male apparatus of a flower. They are situated immediately within the petals, and consist each of a filament, the anther, and the pollen; of which the two latter are essential, and the former not. They are a modified form of the petal, and are placed next it on the inside, towards the center of the flower. Independently of their physiological importance, they are much used as good marks of discrimination in systematical botany.

STAMINATE. Having stamens only.
STARCH IN PLANTS. The principal constituent in plants is carbon in some of its many forms. Starch is present in notable quantities in all that class most useful as food for man and farm animals. The source of alcohol in plants is primarily starch. Thus any plant which either in its seeds or fiber contains notable quantities of starch, may be economically used in the production of alcohol, by first changing the starch to the peculiar substance, called fructose or glucose according to the source from which it was obtained. So also the starch producing grains and vegetables, as corn, potatoes, etc., are the source of the starch of commerce. In chemical composition starch and cellulose are identical. So also is dextrine, and may be artificially manufactured from starch. The chemical composition of starch is as follows:

Carbon... 44.44
Hydrogen... 6.17
Oxygen... 49.39

                                                  100.00

Gum is another substance closely allied to starch. So is sugar, and all the substances herein named are mutually convertible in nature and to a considerable extent in the laboratory of the chemist,

STARCH IN PLANTS 909 STEAM PLOWING

of the manufacturer. Thus we find in germination that the starch of the seed is converted into dextrine and glucose, and passing into the young plant is changed into cellulose and starch. In the sugar beet, under certain diseased conditions, the sugar is changed to starch, but being originally true sugar, this can not be again converted from starch to sugar, but may be converted into glucose or starch sugar. In the work How Crops Grow the average amounts of albuminoids and carbo-hydrates in various vegetable substances is given. The carbo-hydrates are composed of carbon, oxygen and hydrogen, and are subdivided into woody fiber, starch, sugar, gum, oil, and jellies; they are all near enough alike, so far as the animal economy in feeding is concerned, to be included here. The carbo-hydrates and albuminoids are the most important, the first furnishing heat and fat, and the second important in connection with the formation of muscle, have been compiled as given below:

Substances.	Albuminoids.	Carbohydrates.
Wheat	13.0	67.6
Indian Corn	10.0	68.0
Oats	12.0	60.9
Rice	7.5	76.5
Rye	11.0	69.2
Millet	14.5	62.1
Peas	22.4	52.3
Beans	26.5	45.5
Wheat Straw	2.0	30.2
Rye Straw	1.5	37.0
Barley Straw	2.0	39.8
Oat Straw	2.5	38.2
Pea Vines	6.5	35.2
Bean Vines	10.2	33.5
Corn Stalks	3.0	39.0
Pea Hulls	8.1	36.6
Potato (Irish)	2.0	21.0
Beets (common)	1.1	9.1
Rutabagas	1.6	9.3
Turnips (white)	.9	5.9
Wheat Bran	14.0	50.0
Wheat Flour	11.8	74.1
Wheat Chaff	4.5	33.2
Linseed Cake	28.3	41.3
Hay.		
Lucerne, in blossom	14.4	22.5
Red Clover, in blossom	13.4	29.9
Vetches, in blossom	14.2	35.3
Orchard Grass, in blossom	11.6	40.7
Tall Meadow Oat Grass, in blossom	11.1	35.3
Blue Grass, in blossom	8.9	39.1
Timothy, in blossom	9.7	48.8
Average of all the Grasses, in blossom	9.5	41.7
Green Fodder.		
Grass, before blossom	3.0	12.9
Grass, after blossom	2.5	15.0
Red Clover, before blossom	3.3	7.7
Red Clover, in full blossom	3.7	8.6
White Clover, in full blossom	3.5	8.0
Lucerne, very young	4.5	7.8
Lucerne, in blossom	4.5	7.0
Oats, in early blossom	2.3	8.8
Rye	3.3	14.9
Corn Forage	1.0	9.8
Peas, in blossom	3.2	8.3

The principal grains contain the following amounts of starch:

Barley contains starch			57.5
Corn	"	"	59.0
Oats	"	"	46.6
Rye	"	"	59.7
Wheat	"	"	59.5

Thus we see why Indian corn is found to be practically one of the best as it is the cheapest of our cereal grains for fattening purposes.

STAR-WORTS. Composite plants of the genus *Aster*.

STATICE. (See Grasses, ornamental.)

STATION AGRICULTURE. (See Agricultural Education.)

STAVES. Staves for spirit puncheons are of white oak, for sugar hogsheads of red oak, but ash and white oak are also used. They are cut of several lengths to make into hogsheads, puncheons, and tierces. The largest size is seventy-two inches long, seven inches wide and three inches thick; for puncheons, tierces, brewer's casks, pipes, etc., staves are thirty-three, forty-two, forty-five, fifty-four inches long, and from three-quarters, one and one-quarter, one and one-half, two and one-half, to three inches thick. The most usual dimensions are seventy-two, forty-two, and thirty-three inches, with three, one and one-half, and one inch thickness; these measures are exclusive of sapwood. They are now exclusively made by machinery, any width and length, and dressed ready for use.

STEAM PLOWING. The cultivation of the earth, both as respects the cultivation before, and subsequent to plowing has for many years occupied the attention of the best agricultural inventive talent both in England and the United States. The solution of the problem has been fairly accomplished in England, so that plowing, as well as some of the processes of subsequent cultivation, has become an economical fixture, where the nature of the land, and peculiar conditions required to be brought about, might be fairly met by the agency of steam. In the United States, although our abundant prairies are admirably adapted to steam cultivation, no machine has yet been brought out that could successfully compete with horse power, partly from the fact that it requires skill not possessed by the ordinary farm hand to run the engine and operate the machinery, but principally because our soil is so easily plowed, not requiring to be worked to the depth at which the steam machines are most economically worked. Nevertheless, it is certain that before many years certain crops may be economically prepared for by means of the steam plow. Therefore something of the history of steam plows, and steam plowing will be pertinent. The history of attempts to introduce the use of steam in cultivating the soil, is really of considerable antiquity. The sixth patent granted in England, and the first in which the power of steam was sought to be used in cultivating the soil, was January seventeenth, 1618, over 250 years ago, and was originally described in these follows: Newe, apte, or compendious formes or kinde of engines or instruments and other pfitable invencions, wayes and meanes for the goode of our commonwealth, as well as to ploughe grounde without horse or oxen, and to enrich and make better and more fertill as well barren peate, salte and sea sande, as inland and upland grounde within our kingdomes of England and Ireland, and our domynyon of Wales, as also to rayse waters from anye lowe place to highe places for well watering of cittyes, townes, noblemen's and gentlemen's houses, and other places nowe much wanting water, with lesse charges than ever hath bene heretofore; and to make boates for the carryage of burthens and passengers runn vpon the water as swifte in calmes, and more saff in stormes, than boate full sayled in greate wynes. The history of steam plowing has been written by Prof. Brainard, Examiner in the United States Patent Office, up to the year 1865. From it we extract the salient points: The hauling plow, so called because the engine that operates the plow is placed upon one side of the field, and moves along a headland; the plows, generally a gang with two sets, turn furrows in the same direction in moving back and forth over the field. Upon the opposite side of the field is placed a movable capstan or windlass, which is moved forward upon a headland, and the plows are drawn back and forth by means of wire ropes or chains, as shown on page 747. At each set of furrows the engine is moved forward upon the headland upon one side of the field, and the capstan upon the other, the width of a set of furrows, when the plows are drawn again across the field. This method of cultivating or working the land by steam power, was first patented in the United States by E. C. Bellinger, of South Carolina, November 19, 1833, but from some cause the invention never went into general use. About the year 1854 John Fowler, of England, improved upon this general plan of Bellinger's, and was so far successful that a number of machines were put in operation. In 1856 and 1857 Fowler took out patents in the United States for his improvements, but up to this date but two of them have been brought into use in this country. As a special encouragement, Congress was induced to pass a bill allowing the introduction of steam plows free of duty. Another method of steam culture has been attempted, in which the engines are designed to travel over the field, drawing the plows behind them, usually in gangs, and many patents have been granted for alleged improvements in this mode of culture. Among the earlier of these adventurers may be named Henry Corning, 1850; David Russell, 1855; Judd Stevens, 1858; J. D. Howell, 1859; B. Crawford, 1857, and many others. Their efforts at improvement have been directed chiefly to the construction of an engine that was capable of traversing the field, and drawing a gang of plows; but hitherto insurmountable difficulties have been experienced. It has not been found impracticable to construct an engine capable of running over a common road, but in a cultivated field, where the soil is soft and yielding, it has been found that nearly the entire power of the engine has been expended in its own propulsion, and hence its inability to overcome the resistance of the plows. The cause of the failure of traction engines to perform their work in plowing can be explained upon the following hypothesis: We will suppose that an engine of ten-horse power, fully equipped for the field, will weigh eight tons. If it has four driving wheels one-foot tread each, there will be forty-eight inches of effective contact with the earth. Now, a single furrow, twelve inches wide and ten inches deep, will present a resisting surface of 120 square inches; consequently the resistance, even with a single plow, would be greater than the applied traction power of the engine. But a team of ten pairs of oxen would be able to turn a furrow of prairie turf of the width and depth named, say at the rate of an acre a day for a single plow. Ten pairs of oxen would be equal to a ten-horse power engine, and their united weight, when fitted for service, would equal that of the engine—say eight tons. The foot of an ox has an effective contact with the earth of about eight inches, and we may safely estimate that one-half the number of feet while under draft will be constantly in contact with the earth; hence we have 40 × 8 = 320 inches; that is, the eight tons' weight of the team is distributed over a surface of 320 inches of contact of balance against 120 inches of resistance in the furrow. An acre of land contains 43,560 square feet. A team turning a single furrow twelve inches wide and ten inches deep will, upon an average, travel one mile in an hour. A furrow one mile long and twelve inches wide contains 5,280 square feet of surface, and hence it follows that the distance traveled by a team in plowing one acre with a width of furrow of twelve inches, will be a little over eight miles, which is about a fair day's work. A steam engine of a stationary power equal to that of ten pair of oxen must, to be equally effective for draft, have a corresponding amount of contact with the earth; that is the weight of the engine must be distributed over 320 superficial inches of surface in order to be equal to a team of the same weight with the same amount of earth contact. But an increase of surface contact would give a corresponding increase of power within certain limits—say to double the amount; that is, if an engine could be so constructed as to have 640 inches of traction surface for eight tons' weight, it would be capable of doing twice the amount of draft labor that it would with half that amount of surface. A team needs care and feed when it is of the least service. The short duration of animal life, and the risk of premature death, add not a little to the cost of animal power. Mr. J. Boydell, of England, in 1846, constructed an engine that laid its own track as it traveled over the ground. This he accomplished by hinging together a number of stout, flat, wooden rails, so that they would form a polygon outside, and in the same plane with the driving wheels. These hinged rails were so attached to the wheels that they revolved with them, each rail in turn being laid down in front and taken up behind its proper driving wheel, thus forming a track, composed of an endless belt of short rails hinged end to end. By means of this ingenious expedient Mr. Boydell was able to get traction, but, unfortunately, at the sacrifice of a great amount of power. In 1854 Mr. Boydell made considerable improvement in his machine, but for some cause it has never been introduced into general use, but, like many others of its kind, has been laid aside. About the year 1858, Mr. Thomas H. Burridge, of St. Louis, Mo., a man of remarkable genius, invented and built a traction steam engine, intended chiefly for field culture. It consisted of a large cylinder, about ten feet in diameter and ten feet in length, and made of heavy boiler iron. A shaft was supported in the centre by means of rods or spokes at each end, and at equal distances from each end was secured an interior cog gear. In 1851, Messrs. Calloway and Purkis, of England, with a view to improvement in steam culture, constructed a neat locomotive, with two main traction wheels of eighteen inches' tread, with a truck forward for a steering apparatus. One patent has been taken out in the United States, by E. G. Otis, for improvements in this steam plow, but it has never been put in successful operation. The plan invented by Bellinger, commonly called cable traction, and subsequently improved upon by Fowler, consisting chiefly in his balancing gang plow frame, has undoubtedly been received with more favor, and has gone more extensively into use than any other in England. Among the steam plows invented in this country, that of John W. Fawkes, of Lancaster, Pa., has attracted the greatest attention. Fawkes's locomotive was of the high-pressure kind, and carried two steam cylinders of nine inches diameter each, with fifteen inches stroke, consequently the maximum force was about eleven horse-power. The weight of the locomotive was seven tons, about five of which rested upon the journals of a traction cylinder six feet in diameter and six feet in length. The amount of effective earth contact was, therefore, seventy-two inches. Eight yoke of oxen, weighing in the aggregate eight tons (much below the standard weight), are capable of plowing eight furrows of the width and depth named, at the rate of eighty-eight feet per minute, or one mile per hour, and in doing this they have a traction contact with the earth of 256 inches. Now, without allowing any deduction for the consumption of power by the increase of speed from one to four miles per hour, it would require 1,024 inches of contact, or thirty-two pairs of oxen, to drive eight plows at the rate of four miles an hour. The resistance offered by one plow, in sward ground like that upon which Fawkes's plow was tried, is about 400 pounds. It requires one horse power to raise 33,000 pounds one foot per minute; therefore, to raise 400 pounds (the draft of a single plow) one foot in one minute will require one eighty-second (1-82) of a horse power. Now, 3,200 pounds is eight times 400 pounds (the draft of Fawkes's eight plows), hence it will take eight eighty-seconds (8-82) to move 3,200 pounds one foot per minute. Fawkes's plows were said to move at the rate of four miles per hour, which is 352 times one foot per minute; therefore it will require three hundred and fifty-two (352), times eight eighty-seconds (8-82) or a horse power to drive his eight plows four miles per hour, which is thirty-four and a half horse power, about twenty-three more than the maximum of Fawkes's engine, and this without subtracting anything for propelling his engine of seven tons weight. It therefore follows that Fawkes's engine, in order to come up to the standard of an ox team of equal tons weight, should have had an increase of traction contact of 184 inches over the seventy-two of the driving wheel, thus equaling 256 inches (which is that of the team under draft), about a hundred less than the estimated power of Fawkes's engine required to develop its full working capacity of eleven horses. Hence it follows that Fawkes's locomotive should have had a traction surface of 352 inches, instead of seventy-two, and to this deficiency may be attributed his want of success. Among the various appliances to overcome the difficulties from want of traction may be mentioned the revolving screw, operating not unlike the screw propeller in steamships. But experience has shown that the friction of the blade upon the soil consumed too much of the power of the engine to make its use successful as a means of propulsion. A patent was granted to J. R. Gray, in 1857, for a machine of this character. In 1863, A. W. Hall, of St. Louis, Mo., was granted a patent for a steam plow, so nearly allied to cable traction as to render it worthy of notice, in which the points of novelty were directed to means for overcoming the hitherto almost insurmountable difficulties experienced from want of traction. The locomotive, consisted of a framework, supported upon four wheels, of suitable strength to bear the weight of the boiler and other parts of the machine. As he did not depend upon the weight of his locomotive for traction, it was built as light as was consistent with the required power. There are two sets of rollers placed horizontally in pairs, transversely to the frame of the machine, and rotated in opposite directions at a uniform speed, by means of two sets of cog gears, which are driven by two reciprocating engines, located upon opposite sides of the boiler. The rollers are grooved in the center to receive a rope which passes between them, and is held from slipping by the strong bite of the rollers. The rope is anchored at each side of the field to be plowed, the anchors being moved forward from time to time on head lands as the plowing progresses. In 1868, P. H. Standish, of California, invented a novel steam cultivator or triturator. The peculiar features of this apparatus consisted in the manner of cutting or breaking the ground; it is not done by shares turning furrows, nor by spades lifting and dumping the earth; but by four knives, or spits, set at right angles vertically in a head-block of cross-bars, revolving horizontally in a perpendicular shaft, tearing and stirring the earth in a transverse direction to the movement of the machine, something in the manner of a rotating harrow. Two or three, or more, of these implements are worked, and follow the engine according to its power, and as may be desired. In 1869 there were patents issued for five steam plows. The same year the plow of Mr. Minniss of Pennsylvania was tried in Iowa, which revolved upon an endless chain track. It plowed five furrows at a time, but failed, as all others had before and since, in doing the work economically in comparison with horses. As we remarked in the beginning of this article, steam plowing probably will not supersede the use of horses, except the time come, requiring extraordinary deep plowing. Then if inventions can overcome some of the chief difficulties of traction, steam plowing practically considered may become a fixed fact on our prairie soils. Within the last ten years other patents have been issued either on steam plows or improvements in steam plowing. Yet the feeling that success was to be met with was dying out. It is needless to say that none of them showed development that would supersede horse power, and they were short lived. That the large amounts of money spent in this direction have been entirely sunk, except to the parties directly interested, it would be wrong to say. Perhaps some future inventor profiting by the failure of his successors, may hit upon an idea that may make steam plowing a practical success, on the broad prairies, and, in the hands of the half section farmer. In conclusion we would call attention to the articles, Plows, Plowing, Cultivating, etc., and also to the illustration of the operation of steam plowing, on page 747, as practiced in Great Britian.

STEARIN. The solid part of fats. Stearate of glycerine.

STEARIC ACID. The acid obtained by saponizing stearin, and decomposing the soap by a dilute acid. It is a brilliant white, soft body, insoluble in water.

STEATITE. Soapstone.

STEATOMA. A fatty tumor.

STEER. (See Ox.)

STELLATE. Star-shaped, resembling a star.

STEM. In botany, the upward prolongation of the axis of a plant. It is distinguished from all other parts by bearing buds.

STENELYTRANS. A family of coleopterous insects, many of which have the elytra narrow at the posterior part.

STEREOMETER. An instrument for taking specific gravities.

STERNUM. The breast bone, to which the ribs are attached.

STETHOSCOPE. An instrument used to assist the ear in determining the character of the sounds of respirations and other functions occurring within the body, to form an opinion of the disease.

STHENIC DISEASES. Those of increased action or inflammation.

STIGMA. The upper extremity of the style, or female organs of plants: it has almost uniformly a humid surface. It is the part upon which the pollen falls, and where it is stimulated into the production of the pollen tubes, which are indispensable to the act of impregnation.

STILE. In building, an upright piece in framing. A set of steps, to allow the passage of men, but not of animals.

STIMULANTS. Substances which produce increased circulation or heat, as alcohol.

STIPULE. A small leaf or scale situated at the base of the leaf-stalk (*petiole*) of some plants.

STIRRING OF THE SOIL. In the articles Cultivation, Plows, Plowing, and Harrowing, this subject has been fully treated, in so far as relates to the preparation of the soil, and also partially so in relation to implements for keeping it clean. The present article, therefore, will only treat upon stirring the soil, for the eradication of weeds springing up in a crop, and also as a means of keeping the land in the best con-

HORSE HOE.

dition for the nourishment of the roots. The three implements in general use are the harrow, the single and double shovel plow, the five tooth cultivator, and what is now known as the two-horse or straddle row cultivator. Harrowing is used for preparing a tilth, and for covering the seed, and also for stirring the surface of the land before rowed crops are up, or soon after, as in the case of corn, potatoes, etc. The five toothed cultivator and horse hoe are used by passing up and back, between rows so narrow that the straddle cultivator can not work, but generally in garden crops where the two-horse implements are not used. The double shovel plow is used when a deeper tilth is required, and when considerable earth is to be cast to the crop, and the single shovel plow, with wings,

DOUBLE SHOVEL PLOW.

when still more hilling is necessary. For corn and field crops generally, the principal implement now used is the two-horse cultivator, in which may be used either riding or walking. The cut on the next page shows one of these modern implements adapted either for walking or riding.

STOCK. Live stock, or animals of the farm.

STOLON, STOLE. A running stem which throws off young plants at certain points, as the strawberry. Stoloniferous is a derivative.

STOMACH. The cavity or pouch in which food is digested. In most animals there is one stomach only, but in ruminants there are four. In the stomach, properly so-called, a fluid termed the gastric juice is secreted, which serves to digest the food.

STONE CLOVER. (See Rabbitfoot.)

STOVER. Coarse fodder.

STRAINING PIECE. A timber intended to keep two posts or other pieces at a certain distance.

STRAINS, SPRAINS. Injuries produced by over-stretching the ligaments or muscles; they are often very severe, and require cupping and leeching. Occasionally fomentations are sufficient, with rest, and bandaging the part tightly. (See article Sprains.)

STRAMONIUM.—*Datura stramonium.* This plant is known under a number of popular names, as the Jamestown weed, Stink weed, and thorn apple, and in the South, and even south of $40°$, is as troublesome as it is a noxious weed. There are two varieties, one with green and the other with purple stems, tender annuals, but the seeds surviving and growing freely in favorable situations as far north as, even well up into, Wisconsin in the West and to the New England

States in the East. Both the leaves and seeds are violent poisons, and hence should be destroyed wherever found. As a medical remedy it is valuable, and the chipped root has been smoked as a palliative in asthma. It has been planted to some extent, for poisoning the moths of the tobacco worm, poisoned honey being dropped into the open blossoms, which are attractive to the moth. This, however, is not safe where there are children, and would also be fatal to bees. There are other ways of killing the moth, as by lighted fires in the evening, and if the poisoned flowers of Stramonium are used, they should all be cut and burned at sunrise. There are a number of ornamental varieties, which are started in the greenhouse or hot bed for summer decoration, but they are hardly to be commended unless sparingly used.

STRANGLES. This is a disease prevalent in young horses, under the common name of distemper. It used to be thought that horses must at some age have the distemper. The same thing used to be held in regard to measles in the human family. Both are, however, fallacious. The disease is highly contagious, and hence when an animal in a stable is affected, all are liable to attacks. The liability depending on the more or less virulence of the attack. M. Reynal, professor at the Alfort School, submits a number of observations corroborative of the contagious character of Strangles. He states that young horses having strangles, put into stables with horses of adult age, doing regular work, have communicated the disease to those of the latter who have stood in adjoining stalls, though some few have only exhibited the disease in a catarrhal form. Even the foal has been known to suck the disease from its dam. Experiments have been to, to inoculate for strangles. M. Damalix smeared with a sponge, impregnated with matter taken from the abscess of strangles, twice daily, both sides of the pituitary membrane and the internal surfaces of the linings of the eyelids, in a sound horse, about to be cast for spavin. This was continued for seven days. On the eighth, he remarked, the horse had lost his appetite, had commenced running from both nostrils, coughed softly and loosely, had swelling under the jaw, which ended in resolution; all the symptoms terminating eight days from their commencement. It has been remarked that strangles is more surely communicated at an early than a late stage, and in a certain form more readily than in others. Strangles will assume the herpetic character, will simulate farcy and glanders, will settle in the mesenteric glands, or may follow castration. In regard to contagion may be mentioned, as most readily communicable, that form of strangles, which assumes the character of eruptions on the lips, nose, and pituitary membrane. Strangles usually commences like a common cold. There is a cough, sore throat, the animal is dull, loses appetite, and swallows with difficulty. Then there is quickened pulse, rapid breathing, and running at the nose. A hot, tender swelling will appear within the lower jaw bone, sometimes on one side and sometimes on both, in which latter case the whole cavity is filled. If the attack is virulent, the swelling is sudden and great, filling up the mouth, and the animal shows those signs of strangulation from which the disease takes its name. There is great distress, the breathing (difficult) is accompanied with a loud blowing noise, and unless the animal soon gets relief, it dies of suffocation. If the attack is light, but little will be required, except to keep the animal warm, and to apply warm fomentations and poultices, to the swollen glands, allowing an ounce of saltpetre to the pail of water, night and

RIDING AND WALKING CULTIVATOR.

morning. Give soft, easily eaten, and digestible food. When the tumor comes to a head and bursts, keep it poulticed to induce suppuration. If it seems indolent, put on a fly blister to bring it to a head, when it may be opened with the knife. Again, if the swelling is languid and does not come to a head, it may be painted with the iodine, or it may be rubbed with iodine. In the treatment of strangles, the condition must be kept up with good food and stimulants, if necessary. Avoid medicines which deplete the system. If suffocation is imminent, the windpipe may be opened and a silver, or even a tin tube may be inserted as a last resource, to enable the animal to breathe. (See Tracheotomy.)

STRANGURY, or SUPPRESSION OF URINE, INCONTINENCE OF URINE, BLOODY URINE. Strangury may arise from an injury done to the kidneys, or to the bladder, by strains, or by the absorption of irritating matters. Allow the horse absolute rest; give mashes, gruel, and other soft food; give tepid water to drink. Bloody urine should be treated in the same way. Some horses have such a natural or acquired weakness of kidneys, as to stale blood with their urine on every occasion of over-exertion. The means frequently used for relief are such as aggravate the complaint, and, indeed, are often the occasion of it, which are diuretics. Strong diuretics injure horses more than strong physic, and benefit them less than any other of the popular means made use of. In retentions of urine, but particularly in the case of bloody urine, they are absolutely improper.

STRATH. A small valley.

STRATUM. A bed of rock, or other deposit.

STRAW. The value of straw in the economy of the farm, will depend upon a variety of circumstances, as nearness to a market, where it may be sold for bedding, packing, the stuffing of articles of use, filling mattresses and the various uses to be found for it in and near large cities. The burning of straw as practiced in all new settlements should never be allowed, at least, not after stock can be procured. Then it may be liberally thrown about the yards to be trampled down and thus converted into manure. As a rule, one ton of straw will make three tons of manure. It is true, the want of manure is not seriously felt in countries where the soil is virgin, yet, the time will come when it will be felt, and the farmer who saves and applies his manure, finds himself still with a soil rich in all the elements of plant growth, when his more indolent neighbor is lamenting that his farm is run out. As a feeding material, wheat straw dried at 212 degrees, contains in 100 parts 2.05 muscle forming substances, and 35.06 of heat producing substances. The first representing nitrogenous matter; the second, carbon in a state for assimilation; the balance, is woody fiber 56.87, and mineral substances 6.02. Yet straw alone will never support the life of an animal during the winter season, yet, if properly saved, and fed in connection with grain and hay, it is a most valuable adjunct thereto. In seasons of a scarcity of hay or where hay is wanted for sale, and corn is cheap, horses, cattle and mules, may be brought through the winter in admirable condition on straw fed in connection with corn. As illustrating this we quote a statement of a farmer in New York, in feeding wheat straw to cows in connection with wheat bran and corn meal. Commencing the middle of December, his cows being then in fine condition, and drying off, he fed six quarts of wheat bran daily, with all the straw the animals would eat, giving two meals per day and continuing this treatment six weeks. Afterwards he changed the bran feed to corn meal and bran, one measure of the former to two of the latter giving four quarts of the mixture daily. This grain feed was gradually increased toward calving, and a small allowance of hay was given in the morning after the straw and before the grain feed. Under this treatment the animals maintained a good appetite and were kept in thriving condition. The experiment is quoted as an illustration of the advantages which would result from a judicious use of good bright wheat straw in times of high prices of hay. Though the experiment was confined to cows not in milk, he considers it as pointing to the more limited availability of straw in winter feeding of cows in milk and beef cattle. With these classes of stock more grain should be given. And with any description of stock there should be proper discrim-

Number.	NAMES.	Size.	Sex.	Color.	Form.	Flesh.	Season.	Origin.	Nova scotia	New Brunswick.	Maine.	New Hampshire.
1	Agriculturist	l.	P.	d. c.	r. c.	f.	M.	Am.				
2	America	l.		d. c.	r. c.	f.	E.	Am.				
3	Burr's New Pine	m.	P.	b. r.	r. c.	s.	E.	Am.				
4	Boston Pine	l.	H.	d. c.	r. c.	f.	M.	Am.	*			
5	Black Defiance	l.	H.	d. r.	r. o. c.	f.	M.	Am.				
6	Charles Downing	l.	H.	d. s.	c.	f.	M.	Am.				
7	Col. Cheney	l.	P.	b. s.	r. ov	f.	M.	Am.	*			*
8	Downer's Prolific	m.	H.	b. s.	r. c.	s.	E.	Am.				
9	Early Washington	m.						V. E.	Am.				
10	Fillmore	m	P.	d. s.	o. c.	f.	M.	Am.				
11	Forest Rose	l.	H.	b. s.	c.	f.	M.	Am.				
12	French's Seedling	m.	H.	b. s.	r. c.	s.	M.	Am.				
13	Green Prolific	l.	P.	l. c.	r. o. c.	a.	M. L.	Am				
14	Hovey's Seedling	l.	P.	b. s.	r.	f.	M.	Am.	*		*	
15	Jenny Lind	m.	H.	d. c.	c.	f.	E.	Am.				
16	Jucunda	l	H.	b. s.	o. c.	f.	L.	Am.			*	
17	Kentucky	l.	H.	b. s.	r. c.	f.	L.	Am.				
18	Large Early Scarlet	s.	H.	l. s.	r. c.	s.	E.	Am.				
19	Leunig s White	m.	H.	w. t	r. o. c.	s.	M.	Am.				
20	Longworth s Prolific	l.	H.	l. c.	r.	f.	L. M	Am.				
21	Mary Stewart											
22	Monarch of the West	v l.		b. r.	r. o. c.	f.	M.	Am.				
23	Nicanor	m.	H.	b. s.	r. o. c.	f.	E. L.	Am.				
24	President Wilder	l.	H.	b. s.	r. o. c.	f.	M.	Am.				
25	Russell s Prolific	l.	P.	r.	c.	s.	M.	Am.			*	
26	Seth Boyden	l.	H.	r.	o. c.	f.	M.	Am.				
27	Sterling	l.	P.	b. s.	c.	f.	M.	Am.				
28	Triomphe de Gand	l.	H.	l. c.	o. c.	f.	M.	F.	*		*	
29	Victoria	l.	H.	l. c.	r. c.	f.	M.	F.				
30	Wilson s Albany	l.	H.	d. c.	r. c.	f.	E. L.	Am.	*		*	*

ination in management—feeding the straw chiefly in early winter, and from time to time making some variations in the food given. We have wintered work horses and mules almost entirely on straw and grain without any apparent diminution of their working powers, nevertheless, except in times of scarcity, should not advise more than half a ration of straw a day. To return to straw as manure, very few farmers are liberal in the use of straw for bedding. It is poor economy, with straw as plenty as it is, to allow any of the farm animals less than will completely soak up all the urine. Even when bedding is scarce, it takes no more straw to furnish a liberal bed than half enough, since none of the straw need be thrown away except that which becomes soiled, and even in this case it may be dried and used again.

STRAWBERRY. It seems strange that a fruit so well adapted to a variety of soils, so easily cultivated, if in long rows where horse implements may be used, which children would gladly gather if the head of the family would only plant and cultivate, should scarcely ever be found in abundance upon the tables of our farmers. Yet such is the fact, while our cities are now fully supplied with the finest fruit, and at a cost to the consumer often as low as eight cents a quart for good, and five cents for ordinary, and this at a profit, including setting, picking, boxing, transportation, and commissions. The reason probably is that when planted, in a majority of cases, like the rest of the garden, strawberries are allowed to take care of themselves. One other reason is that many varieties are planted, it not being generally known that the strawberry is peculiar as to varieties adapted to the soil, the Wilson, perhaps, only excepted. The cost of picking well cultivated strawberries will not exceed from one to one and one-half cents per quart where girls are hired. Industrious girls, when the berries are properly grown, have averaged eighty quarts a day, and in some instances 130 quarts per day. With such berries the cost of picking need not be more than three-quarters to one cent per quart. Hence it is that good cultivators make money, while poor cultivators condemn the cultivation of strawberries as a trifling business. The yield of strawberries under good cultivation, and in good soil is enormous. There are plenty of instances on record of crops of 150 up to 200 bushels, and even to over 200 bushels per acre. Mr. O. B. Galusha, secretary of the Illinois Horticultural Society, has given special and successful attention to the cultivation of this crop for market. In his elaborate report to the Society in 1879-80, he says: The plants set in spring should be about eighteen or twenty inches apart in the rows, which should be three feet apart. Thorough cultivation should be commenced early and be continued well through autumn, running a narrow shovel-plow deep in the center of the space, and pulverizing and leveling with cultivator, leaving the row of plants from one foot to eighteen inches wide. At first hoeings the plants should be layered along the row within this limit, and all others treated as weeds. In late autumn, and after the ground has frozen so as to bear a team, the mulch may be put on, which may consist of horse-stable litter—using only that made where prairie hay is fed. Where this is not obtainable, planing chips, cut corn stalks, slough grass, whole corn stalks, or oat straw can be used. He uses corn fodder cut short with a horse-power cutter. Shaken from large baskets over the plants, it settles into the spaces between the leaves and gives sufficient protection without smothering the plants, and does not require removal in spring, but remains as a summer mulch to keep the vines fresh and the fruit clean, and as it gradually decays gives stimulus to growth and fruitage. In addition, sow along the rows a mixture of ashes, plaster, and hen-manure, adding a little salt—using six to eight bushels of this mixture per acre. This is applied early in spring, and sometimes a slight sprinkling, thoroughly pulverized and mixed, is again applied just at blossoming time. After the crop is harvested—as soon as condition of soil will admit—plow the spaces with a one-horse moldboard plow, turning two furrows together, and harrow the entire ground level. The runners will then occupy the spaces, and early in autumn they may be again plowed, or, if it is desired to renew the plantation, the old strips may be plowed under and leave the young plants only for next year's fruiting. Where uncut mulch is used it is opened from over the rows in spring and left in the spaces until after the crop is gathered. Treated in this way a half dozen or more successive crops may be taken from the ground. The strawberry-worm should be carefully hand-picked, and killed by crushing, from the vines several times during the season of cultivation. This practice, which costs but little, will if carefully and persistently carried out, keep these pests well in check. The strawberry-leaf folder is almost everywhere present among the vines, and sometimes so numerous as to almost entirely defoliate them. His attacks, unlike those of the strawberry-worm, are not made until after the crop is gathered; and hence he can be more surely destroyed. It has been recommended by some writers, and practiced to a small extent in the West, to cover the vines during a dry time and just before the earliest leaf-folders change from the larval to the pupal state by spreading straw over the plants, and burn straw, plants and insects together. This seems harsh treatment. It would not seem safe to practice this destructive cultivation during a drought, but only when the condition of the soil is such as to insure a quick succeeding growth. He finds with nearly all varieties the best fruit is obtained from rows not more than eighteen inches wide; and where the best berries will command extra prices. He would confine them to one foot in width, so as to give more light and a better circulation of air for the fruit and foliage. With such rank, dense growers as Crescent, Windsor Chief, Miner, Crystal City, Centennial Favorite, Sharpless, Duncan, Glendale, Cumberland Triumph and Star of the West, full exposure in narrow rows is essential to secure large fine fruit; while Wilson, Kentucky, Downing, Pioneer, Duchess, Col. Cheney, Durand's Beauty, Cinderella, Continental, Seth Boyden, Forest Rose may be grown with profit if planted three and a half to four feet apart and allowed to occupy strips two to two and a half feet. There is no species of fruit grown in our country of which there is such a diversity of opinions in respect to the real or comparative value of varieties as the strawberry; and it is safe to say that nine-tenths of this difference is due to the fact that this fruit is more capricious or rather more particular and discriminating as to soils and modes of culture than any other. This holds good in respect to nearly all vareties in cultivation. Varieties of first berries ripened in central Illinois as follows; but the first general picking of each was five or six days later: May 26, Charles Downing; May 27, Crescent, Black Defiance; May 28, Cumberland Triumph; May 21, Prouty, Duchess; June 1, Capt. Jack, Champion, Duncan, Cinderella, Col. Cheney, Monarch of the West; June 4, Centennial Favorite, Wilson; June 5, Continental, Forest Rose, Springdale, Windsor Chief; June 7, Great American, Miner's Great Prolific; June 8, Kentucky. Cowing's Seedling, Sterling, Pioneer, Star of the West, and Seth Boyden ripened their first fruit about medium season. The following varieties, in the order named, will generally be found valuable in the West. For strong clayey, Loess and rich prairie soils, for near market and home use: Crescent, Miner, Charles Downing, Duchess, Windsor Chief, Cumberland Triumph, Sharpless, Champion, Captain Jack, Duncan, Continental, Seth Boyden, Great American, Prouty. For sandy-loam soils, near market and home use: Crescent, Charles Downing, Windsor Chief, Duchess, Black Defiance (home use), Centennial Favorite, Miner, Kentucky, Sharpless, Cinderella, Champion, Crystal City, Capt. Jack, Col. Cheney, Seth Boyden, Cowing's Seedling. For distant market: Sharpless, Capt. Jack, Chas. Downing, Wilson, Continental, Prouty. For high cultivation in hills or single rows for home use and for fancy berries: Sharpless, Great American, Crescent, Seth Boyden, Miner, Monarch of the West, Essex Beauty, Centennial Favorite. There are other varieties which produce large, fine fruit, and have high local reputation; among which are Pioneer, Star of the West, Springdale, Sterling, Forest Rose, etc. The tables, pages 914 and 915, show varieties in general cultivation in the several States of the Union as reported at a late meeting of the American Pomological Society. The columns explain: Size—l., large; s., small; m., medium, Sex—H., hermaphrodite; P., pistillate. Color—d. c., deep crimson; d. s., deep scarlet; b. a., bright scarlet; w. t., whitish tinted with red; l. c., light crimson. Form—r. c., roundish conical; o. c., obtuse conical or coxcomb form; c. conical; r., roundish; r. o. c., roundish obtuse conical. Flesh—s., soft; f., firm. Season—E., early; M., medium; L., late; E. L., early to late. Origin—Am., American; F., foreign. *, signifies doing well; **, great superiority and value; †, new and recently introduced for trial. The strawberry of late years, especially where cultivated extensively for market, has been subject to very numerous insect enemies, among the most destructive of these is the Strawberry Crown Borer, *Analcis fragaria*, see cut, a, larva; b, beetle, side view; c, beetle, back view, the hair lines showing the natural size of the insect. As the name indicates, it bores into and kills the plant by destroying the crown. The best remedy is to dig out infested plants and burn them. Another injurious insect, and much more widely distributed than the crown borer is, what is familiarly called the Strawberry worm, *Emphy-*

tes maculatus. The cut shows, at 1, ventral or lower side of pupa; 2, side view, hair lines showing natural size; 3, perfect fly enlarged; 4, larva, natural size; 5, perfect fly, natural size; 6, larva on leaf, at rest; 7, cocoon; 8, antenna enlarged,

STRAWBERRY CROWN BORER.

showing joints; 9 egg, enlarged. The flies gather over the vines in the spring, the female deposits the eggs in the stems of the plant, and when hatched, the young feed on the leaves, making innumerable small holes, the maggots

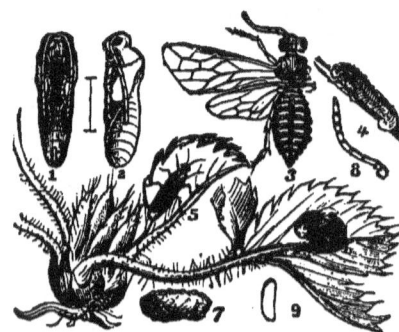

STRAWBERRY WORM.

often changing their skin four times; and when fully grown, measuring three-quarters of an inch in length.

STRAWBERRY WINE. (See Gallizing.)

STRENGTH. In mechanics, is used in the same sense as force or power. Thus, strength of animals is the muscular force or energy which animals are capable of exerting; strength of materials is the resistance which bodies oppose to a force acting upon them. It is obviously a matter of much importance to be able to estimate with tolerable accuracy the efforts which an animal of the average strength employed in labor is capable of exerting, and accordingly, very numerous observations have been made on the subject; but this species of force is subject to variation from so great a number of circumstances, both physical and mechanical, that the results given by different authors present very little agreement with each other, though they are of great value as affording data for determining the modes in which animal labor is most advantageously employed. Of all animals employed as first movers, the horse is, beyond question, the most useful, and that whose labor is susceptible of the most numerous and varied applications. For the purpose of determining his muscular power, the dynamometer may be conveniently used; but, as the action of the animal is very quickly reduced by continued exertion, it is more usual to estimate it according to the amount of daily labor performed. Desaguliers and Smeaton estimate the strength of a horse as equivalent to that of five men; the French authors have commonly stated it as equal to seven men; and Schulze makes it equal to fourteen men in drawing horizontally. According to Desaguliers, a horse's power is equal to forty-four pounds, raised one foot high in one minute. Smeaton makes this number 22,916; Hachett 28; and Watt 33. The last estimate is commonly understood by the term horse-power as applied to steam engines. The quantity of action which a horse can exert diminishes as the duration of the labor is prolonged. Tredgold gives the following table, showing the average maximum velocity with which a horse unloaded can travel according to the number of hours per day:

Time of March in Hours.	Greatest Velocity per Hour in Miles.	Time of March in Hours.	Greatest Velocity per Hour in Miles.
1	14.7	6	6.0
2	10.4	7	5.5
3	8.5	8	5.2
4	7.3	9	4.9
5	6.6	10	4.6

STRENGTH OF MATERIALS. There are four different ways in which the strength of a solid body may be exerted: first, in resisting a longitudinal tension, or force tending to tear it asunder; secondly, in resisting a force tending to break the body by a transverse strain; thirdly, in resisting compression, or a force tending to crush the body; and, fourthly, in resisting a force tending to wrench it asunder by torsion. Mr. Hodgkinson gives the following results of his experiments on the resistance of a crushing force of short pillars of some of the most common descriptions of wood, the force being applied in the direction of the fibers.

Description of Wood.	Strength per square inch in pounds.
Alder	6,831 to 6,960
Ash	8,683 " 9,363
Bay	7,518 " 7,518
Beech	7,733 " 9,363
English birch	3,297 " 6,402
Cedar	5,674 " 5,863
Red deal	5,748 " 6,686
White deal	6,781 " 7,293
Elder	7,451 " 9,973
Elm	10,331
Fir (spruce)	6,499 " 6,819
Mahogany	8,198 " 8,198
Oak (Quebec)	4,231 " 5,982
Oak (English)	6,484 " 10,058
Pine (pitch)	6,790 " 6,790
Pine (Red)	5,395 " 7,518
Poplar	3,107 " 5,124
Plum (dry)	8,241 " 10,493
Teak	12,101
Walnut	6,063 " 7,227
Willow	2,898 " 6,128

STRINGHALT. This is a name given to a sudden jerking up of one of the hind legs, or of both, in the act of walking or trotting. In mild cases the paroxysm passes off after the animal has got fairly under way. Sometimes it shows itself only when the animal is turned to one or the other side, or when unduly excited. It is a nervous disease and the cause of its origin is obscure. It increases with age and if pronounced is an unsoundness. There is no known cure; but its paroxysms may be in a measure alleviated by any means used to prevent undue excitement.

STRIPED MAPLE. (See Maple.)

STRONGYLUS. A genus of parasitical intestinal worms.

STRONTIA. An alkaline earth, very similar to lime.

STRUMA. A swelling.

STRYCHNIA. An extremely poisonous vegetable alkaloid, obtained from the nux vomica and other strychnous plants. It produces violent convulsions and death.

STUBBLE. The roots and stems of grain plants left in the soil after harvest.

STUD. A post or upright in a building; an establishment for horses.

STYLE. The stem which supports the stigma; it is the upper portion of the carpels.

STYLOBATE. An uninterrupted base common to many columns.

STYPTICS. Substances which when applied to small wounds, restrain the flow of blood, as alum. The word scarcely differs from astringents.

SUBCLAVIAN. Any part under the clavicle or collar bone.

SUB-EARTH VENTILATION. (See Ventilation.)

SUBERIN. The substance of cork. By digesting it with nitric acid, it is converted into suberic acid.

SUBLIMATION. A process by which solids are by the aid of heat converted into vapor, which is again condensed, and often in the crystalline form. This operation is frequently resorted to for the purpose of purifying various chemical products, and separating them from substances which are less volatile.

SUBLINGUAL. The parts lying under the tongue.

SUBSOIL. The earth immediately below that which is tilled. The value of land depends almost as much on the subsoil as the tilth; if it be wet and full of stagnant water, it must be underdrained; if it be hard and rocky, the surface soil dries readily to a dust; if it be deep and too light, water and fluid manures may drain away.

SUBSOILING. Loosening the subsoil by a plow without any mold-board to turn it. A heavy plow is first run along the field some six or eight inches deep, and a subsoil plow follows in the bottom of the furrow, deepening it to fourteen or sixteen inches in all. This differs from trench plowing, in which the subsoil is cast up and mixed with the surface, by which the soil is either benefited or injured, according to the nature of the subsoil. The principal effect of subsoil plowing is, that the earth is deepened to a considerable depth, and root culture is much improved; in loose, gravelly or sandy soils subsoil plowing is often very injurious. By the tillage of years, the treading of cattle, and the pressure of the sole of the plow and rolling, the surface soil becomes compact, and holds water and manure sufficiently for the crops; but by subsoiling these advantages are thrown away, and a thirsty, loose soil again established.

SUBSOIL PLOW. An implement used to follow in the furrow after a turning plow, to loosen the subsoil without inverting it, thus leaving it directly in the bottom of the furrow. Trench plowing is sometimes erroneously called subsoiling. (See articles Plowing and Trench Plowing.)

SUBSTANTIVE COLORS. Coloring matters which stain the texture or yarn permanently, without the necessity for a mordant; the latter being called adjective colors.

SUBSTITUTION. In chemistry, the doctrine advanced by Dumas, that, in many organic and complex compounds, one element can take the place of another without changing the relations of the others.

SUBSTRATUM. The stratum of a different geological kind immediately below the surface.

SUBULATE. Awl-shaped, round, and tapering to the end.

SUBULICORNS. A family of neuroptera, with awl-shaped antennæ.

SUBULIPALPS. A section of caraboid beetles, some of which have the exterior palpi awl-shaped.

SUCCORY. (See Chiccory.)

SUCCULENT. Fleshy, full of water.

SUCKERS. The shoots from the roots of trees or plants near the stem.

SUDORIFICS. Medicines which produce increased perspiration.

SUET. Fat which contains a large proportion of stearin, from the loins or kidney of the sheep and the ox.

SUFFOLK CATTLE. Of this once famous breed of cattle, Youatt says: The Suffolk Dun used to be celebrated in almost every part of the kingdom, on account of the extraordinary quantity of milk that she yielded. The dun color is now, however, rarely seen in Suffolk, and rejected as an almost certain indication of inferiority. The breed is polled. The Suffolk, like the Norfolk beast, undoubtedly sprang from the Galloway; but it is shorter in the leg, broader and rounder than the Norfolk, with a greater propensity to fatten, and reaching to greater weights. The prevailing and best colors are red, red and white, brindled, and a yellowish cream color. The bull is valued if he is of a pure unmingled red color. Exaggerated accounts have been given of the milking of the Suffolk cow, and she is not inferior to any other breed in the quantity of milk that she yields. In the height of the season some of these cows will give as much as eight gallons of milk in the day; and six gallons is not an unusual quantity. The produce of butter, however, is not in proportion to the quantity of milk. The bulls are rarely suffered to live after they are three years old, however excellent they may be, for the farmers believe that if they are kept longer they do not get a stock equally good, and particularly that their calves are not so large after that period. Nothing can be more erroneous or mischievous. A bull is never in finer condition than from four to seven years old. Having obtained, by accident or by exertion, a good breed of milkers, the Suffolk people have preserved them almost by mere chance, and without any of the care and attention which their value demanded. The Suffolk cow, poor and angular as she may look, fattens with a rapidity greater than could be expected from her gaunt appearance. Whence she obtained the faculty of yielding so much milk, is a question that no one has yet solved. Her progenitor, the Galloway, has it not. The Holderness could scarcely be concerned; for more than a hundred years ago, the Suffolk dun was as celebrated as a milker as the breed of this county is at present, and the Holderness had not then been introduced into the county of Suffolk. The fattening property derived from the northern breed is yet but little impaired. The cow is easily fattened to 500 to 600 pounds, and the quality of her meat is excellent.

SUFFRUTEX. An under shrub, a small bush, a portion of whose annual stems die away. *Suffruticose* is like an under shrub.

SUGAR. By the term sugar is usually meant cane sugar. Before the war this industry reached (in 1861) a total in Louisiana of 528,321,500 pounds. In 1862 and 1863 it dwindled to nothing. In 1864, 7,668,200 pounds were manufactured, which in 1870 reached 166,613,150 pounds, then again running down until in 1876 the production was 190,672,570 pounds; in 1877, 167,-161,941 pounds; in 1878, 250,094,160 pounds, the total consumption being about 1,731,573,558 pounds. Since this time these figures have not varied materially, so it will be seen that the consumption of sugar is seven times greater than the home production. Even supposing that the yearly sugar production will again reach the figures before the war, we shall with our increasing population have to import three, four or five times as much as we produce, unless the difference can be made up by the production of sugar from sorghum, maize or beets, or all combined, since the production of maple sugar can not possibly be extended, and this from the increasing scarcity of maple trees. If the better cultivation of cane and improved processes for manufacture could be backed up by capital, then indeed there is no doubt but the sugar producing district of the South, narrow as is the strip along the Gulf, might easily be made to produce sugar enough to supply the wants of the nation. The northern limit of cane sugar production in the United States, may be given as belonging to Florida and the gulf region of Georgia, Alabama, Mississippi, Louisiana and Texas. It is true that cane sugar has been made in Arkansas, and even in Missouri, yet the manufacture can never be profitably carried on outside the Gulf States. Even Louisiana gives only 1,200 to 1,800 pounds of sugar per acre, while in the West Indies, 3,000 and even 5,000 pounds per acre is produced, and in the Mauritius, and in the East Indies the product sometimes runs up to 7,000 per acre. Australia is earnestly pushing her young sugar industry and if we may credit reports from there, her lands are but little if any less productive than the more favored regions of the West Indies. The sugar production of the world has not kept pace with the increasing wants of the population; yet there are twenty-four principal sugar countries in the world, six of these are European ones in which are produced beet sugar to over one-half the amount of the entire cane sugar production of the whole world. The real difficulty in the way of the production of cane sugar in the United States does not really lie so much in the want of land available for sugar, so much as in the fact, that laborers will not work in a climate so unhealthy as a cane sugar climate must necessarily be, so long as they can find more congenial labor. Where slave labor is employed, the case is different. If they die others can be bought, and, revolting as is this system of labor, it is the only one yet found except that of peonage, serfdom, caste, and that other one of enforced labor from superabundant population, where sugar making has really given steadily large profits to the planters. The following table will show the countries of the world producing cane sugar and also those producing beet sugar. It will be seen that the great cane sugar producing countries are those where the labor is either owned or enforced by means entirely beyond the control of the laborers. The tables give the yield for the year 1875, which for all practical purposes may be taken as an average one of the productions of the world. The first table shows crop of cane

Country.	Tons.
Cuba	700,000
Porto Rico	80,000
British, Dutch, and Danish West Indies	250,000
Java	200,000
Brazil	170,000
Manila	130,000
China	120,000
Mauritius	100,000
Martinique and Guadeloupe	100,000
Louisiana	75,000
Peru	50,000
Egypt	40,000
Central America and Mexico	40,000
Reunion	30,000
British India and Penang	30,000
Honolulu	10,000
Natal	10,000
Australia	51,000
Total tons	2,186,000

sugar in round numbers and the second that of beet root sugar. We may therefore assume that the South will not again be a great producer of cane sugar without a change in the present labor system. It is true, she has land enough, so has

Country.	Tons.
German Empire	346,646
France	462,259
Russia and Poland	245,000
Austria and Hungary	153,922
Belgium	79,796
Holland and other countries	30,000
Total tons	1,317,623

every other country where sugar is produced, and in the most of which the annual yield per acre is double that of the South. Yet even there, with the yearly increasing price of sugar, there is not the expansion one might expect. The risk to health is too great except in those cases where the labor is enforced. The steadily growing feeling in all enlightened communities against this system of labor, would alone prevent great expansion in sugar production if other disabilities did not exist. There seems but one way in which the South can extend the area of cane cultivation and largely increase her production of cane sugar. This is by allotting land to tenants, and with the aid of owners of small tracts of land, raise the cane to be carried to central factories to be worked up, at an agreed price, or on shares, as has of late been done to a considerable extent with sorghum cane in the North, and which system has proved valuable in the French West Indies. Where capital can be secured in legitimate investment it is not slow to seek remunerative channels, and plenty of it might be forthcoming to put the sugar lands of the South on a paying basis if first there could be an assurance that the cane sufficient would be grown from year to year; and second, that capital might be secure from destructive influences. How well this system works in the French West India islands, the following synopsis of a communication to the Department of State, of the United States, will show. It is as follows: A system of central factories has been adopted in the French West India islands of Martinique and Guadeloupe, for the manufacture of sugar. The system is a substitute for the long practiced method of making the sugar by individuals upon the plantations where the cane is produced. The design is to separate agriculture from manufacture, and by a concentration of capital, somewhat upon the co-operative system, to accomplish what the isolated planter was unable to do. The experiment, made upon a large scale during a series of years, it is maintained, has fully demonstrated the soundness of the principle. The central factories, or *usines*, as they are called, are owned by joint-stock companies, by which the sugar cane is taken from the plantation and transported to the mill upon railroads, or tramways, constructed by those companies, a certain per cent. of the value of the cane being allowed the planter, the price being regulated by the market at Point-à-Pitre at the time the cane is delivered. The system seems to have proved a success, affording to the manufacturing interest a handsome profit, and, by leaving the planter free to devote himself to his peculiar vocation, largely increasing the cultivation of the cane. The government of the island of Jamaica recently appointed a commission to visit the French islands and inquire into the working of this central sugar factory system. The Department of Agriculture has received, through the Department of State, the report of these commissioners. Their examinations were made during the last summer, and the results, as stated by them, are not without interest and value to the sugar-producers of the United States. The largest central factory in the French islands is that which is commonly called the Usine d'Arbousier, at Point-à-Pitre (Saint Louis), the chief commercial station of the island. The factory is in the suburbs of this seaport, and is constructed upon the grandest scale, having all the improvements in machinery and manufacture of sugar devised by modern science. The cost of it was upward of a million of dollars, and its capacity of manufacture is equal to 10,000 tons of sugar during the first six months of the year, which is the manufacturing season. The process of manufacture, as described by the commissioners, is as follows: The canes are brought by the planter to a siding of the main tramway on his estate. The wagon generally carries two tons of canes, and one mule on a good level ordinary tramway can draw easily two wagons. The wagon, when brought to the mill itself, conveys the canes to the rollers. The bagasse being elevated by power to a platform over the boilers, the juice, on leaving the mill-bed, falls through three strainers into a tank, which has a double bottom, heated by steam. It is treated here with a little bisulphite of lime, and is then run into a montejus. This montejus, by steam, sends the juice up to the clarifiers, where it is heated in the ordinary way and tempered with lime properly. From this it is passed to the charcoal filters, through which it gravitates, and then passes by a gutter into a receiver. From this it is passed to a montejus and is thrown up by steam into a cistern over what is known as the triple-effet. From this cistern it gravitates into the triple-effet, passing from the first to the second, and from the second to the third boiler, as the attendant wishes. When it leaves the boiler it is immediately passed over new reburned charcoal. It gravitates through this and falls into another receiver, from which the vacuum-pan takes it up and boils it to sugar. The first-quality sugar is generally crystallized in the pan, and then is dropped into sugar-boxes, which stand seven feet from the ground; under these boxes a little charging-vessel runs on a railway that is hung from the bottom of the said boxes, and this vessel conveys the sugar over the centrifugals, where it is cured, the molasses from this being boiled up, when found in good condition, with the syrup of the following day. When this molasses is thick and clammy it is boiled into a jelly by itself and dropped into sugar boxes, where it is allowed to granulate for a number of days. This makes the second-quality sugar, and the molasses from this, along with the skimmings and subsidings of clarifiers, goes to make rum. The juice that leaves the clarifiers does not pass over fresh charcoal, but follows the syrup from the triple-effet, thus assisting to wash out the sweets which may have been left by the syrup. The weight of canes delivered at the factory last year was 75,000 tons, although it was a season of drought. The factory can receive 100,000 tons a year. Last year 5,325 tons of sugars were obtained from 68,725 tons of cane, or about seven and three-quarters per cent. In April last the factory company declared a first dividend of twenty-four per cent. In other words, a net profit of $181,585 was made upon the manufacture of 68,745 tons of sugar and 182,798 gallons of rum. The processes of manufacture in all the factories, both in Guadeloupe and Martinique, are identical, the only difference being the adoption in the new factories of the appliances of modern science, and improved mechanical and other arrangements. The clarification of the juice, its reduction to a syrup at a low temperature, the perfect crystallization and color of the sugar, and a maximum return, are obtained by repeated filtration through animal charcoal, the triple-effet and vacuum-pan processes, and, last of all, centrifugal machines. In Martinique the mean weight of canes was found to be equal to twenty-eight tons per acre, producing, say two and a quarter tons of sugar, and the sugar sells at $200 a ton. The central factories, or usines, are represented as in the highest popular favor. Capital, both local and in France, is freely subscribed to establish new usines upon a large and extensive scale. Eight of the factories, at considerable cost, have been erected within the last few years, and others are now in process of erection. They seem everywhere, by increasing

WEALTH OF THE UNITED STATES,

TOTAL AND PER CAPITA.

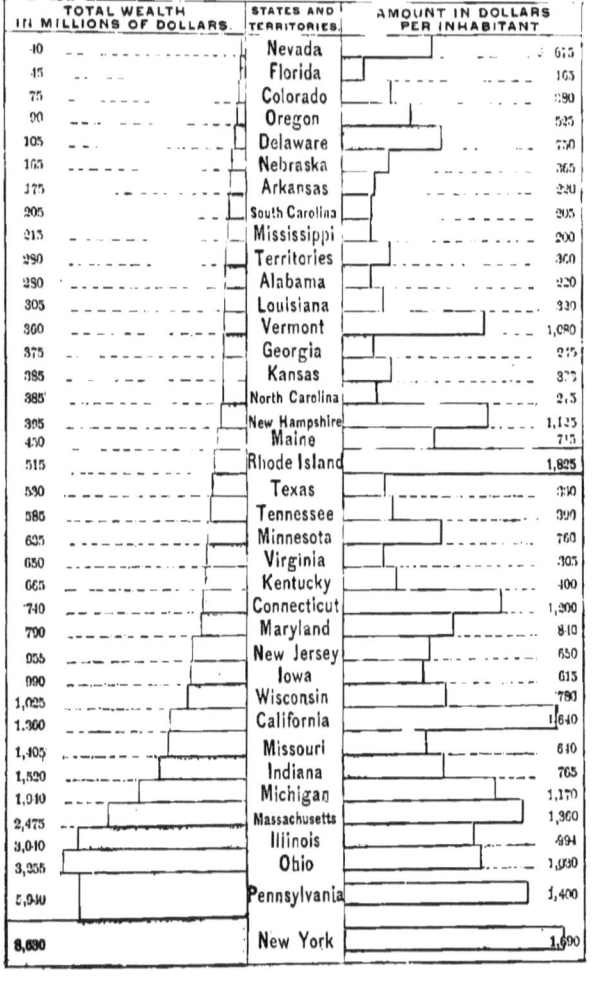

TOTAL WEALTH IN MILLIONS OF DOLLARS.	STATES AND TERRITORIES.	AMOUNT IN DOLLARS PER INHABITANT
40	Nevada	675
45	Florida	165
75	Colorado	290
90	Oregon	525
105	Delaware	750
165	Nebraska	365
175	Arkansas	230
205	South Carolina	205
215	Mississippi	200
250	Territories	300
280	Alabama	220
305	Louisiana	330
360	Vermont	1,080
375	Georgia	215
385	Kansas	375
385	North Carolina	215
395	New Hampshire	1,125
450	Maine	715
515	Rhode Island	1,825
530	Texas	390
585	Tennessee	390
625	Minnesota	760
650	Virginia	305
665	Kentucky	400
740	Connecticut	1,200
790	Maryland	840
955	New Jersey	850
990	Iowa	615
1,025	Wisconsin	780
1,360	California	1,640
1,405	Missouri	640
1,520	Indiana	765
1,940	Michigan	1,170
2,475	Massachusetts	1,360
3,040	Illinois	994
3,355	Ohio	1,030
5,040	Pennsylvania	1,400
8,630	New York	1,690

the facilities of manufacture, to have stimulated the planters to increased production of the cane. In speaking of the difference between the tillage of those who sell their canes to the usines and those who manufacture at home, it is remarked that in the one case the canes are no sooner out of the fields than the gangs and stock are at work, preparing the land for the next crop, and all the fields are tidy and clean. In the other case, fields are left to take care of themselves until the crop season is over. Estates which, before the establishment of the usines, were in debt, are now said to be in a flourishing condition, and others which had almost fallen out of cultivation are now making excellent crops. In most of the factories hydraulic or other presses are employed for extracting the remnants of juice from the skimmings. (See Sorghum Sugar, page 1117.)

SULCATE. Marked with furrows, or parallel deep lines.

SULPHATES. Salts of sulphuric acid. The principal in agriculture are the sulphate of lime, (see Gypsum) the sulphate of soda, (Glauber's salt); and the sulphate of potash, serviceable as a steep, or as a manure in gardens for the cruciferous plants. The chief value of the sulphates as manures arises from the necessity for sulphur in plants, especially the cruciferous and leguminous families.

SULPHITES. Salts of sulphurous acid.

SULPHOCYANATE OF POTASSIUM. A solution of this body is used to protect iron, with which it forms a brownish-red color.

SULPHOSINAPISIN. A pungent body obtained from mustard, containing both sulphur and nitrogen.

SULPHUR. Brimstone. A solid, fusible, insoluble, yellow elementary body, it is a non-conductor of electricity, and powerfully electro-positive in its compounds. It is very inflammable, uniting with oxygen, and forming the white, suffocating vapors of sulphurous acid. With three equivalents of oxygen it forms sulphuric acid, or oil of vitriol, a dense, oily acid, of great causticity, and well known in the arts. Sulphur unites directly with metals at a heat below redness, forming sulphurets. The gaseous compound of one equivalent of sulphur with one of hydrogen, or sulphuretted hydrogen, is remarkable for its great fœtor; it is given off by decaying organic matters containing sulphur, and, with the sulphuret of ammonium, constitutes the principal cause of the stench of putrefying animal matters. Sulphur is abundant in the mineral kingdom about volcanoes. It is present in all vegetables, existing in albumen, caseine, and analogous bodies. It has been used to destroy insects. When burned, the pungent, sulphurous acid destroys life, but is also injurious to vegetation. It has the property of bleaching many colors, and especially that of straw. A solution, formed by boiling equal parts of quicklime and sulphur in twenty or thirty times their weight of water, is extremely fœtid and poisonous to insects; it is called the hydrosulphuret of lime and cheaper bought than made at home.

SULPHURETS. Compounds of sulphur with metals.

SULPHURETTED. Containing sulphur chemically united. A solution of sulphuretted hydrogen gas in water is much used as a test for metals in solution.

SULPHURIC ACID, OIL OF VITRIOL. It should be colorless, but is often brown; is caustic, destroying the skin instantly. When water is added, the mixture becomes quite hot. It combines with all oxides, forming sulphates. It is used to dissolve bones, but is inferior to muriatic acid. One hundred pounds of the best acid dissolve, after much time and with repeated stirrings, about 200 pounds of fine bone dust, converting it in part into sulphate of lime (gypsum), and into superphosphate of lime, which is soluble.

SULPHURIC ÆTHER. Common ether.

SULPHUROUS ACID. It is composed of sulphur 16.1, oxygen 16. It is a gas readily condensed, soluble in water, and very sour, with the odor of sulphur. In contact with oxygen and moisture it readily becomes changed into sulphuric acid.

SUMACH. *Rhus.* This family of plants has of late years attracted attention from the amount of superior tannin contained in the dried leaves and young stalks of the current year's growth. In Sicily, which has long furnished the greatest amount of sumach, used for tanning morocco and other fine leather, the leaves are said to be discarded, and only the twigs and bark are used, after grinding fine in a mill adapted to the purpose. Why the leaves should be refused it is difficult to understand, since analysis shows them to be valuable in tanning material. The family Rhus contains some

CUT LEAVED SUMACH.

poisonous species. These, however, are but two, the Poison Elder, or Dogwood Sumach (*R. venenata*) and the Poison Oak or Ivy (*R. toxicodendron*). The other northern species, and those valuable for their tannin, are Staghorn

Sumach (*Rhus typhina*), Smooth Sumach (*R. glabra*) and Dwarf Sumach (*R. copallina*). There is another variety, a low, straggling bush, known by its aromatic leaves, the Fragrant Sumach (*R. aromatica*). The two first named of the sumachs furnishing tannin are those most common and most easily gathered for market. Sumach not only contains tannin, but coloring matter, the latter used in calico printing as a substitute for nut galls. The average amount of tannin in European sumach from six analyses, as stated by Gauhe, is thirteen per cent. Though fine samples of Palerma will yield twenty-two to twenty-four per cent. of tannin, several samples of sumach, gathered in from different localities in Virginia, gave according to the analysis of the chemist of the Department of Agriculture respectively, in 100 parts, 20.80, 18.25, 23.50, and 28.20, or an average of 22.68 per cent. A sample of Missouri Sumach gave tannin 28.20, so that it will be seen that the idea prevalent that European Sumach is richer than ours is not only erroneous but that our varieties are even richer in tannin. Wagner has given the average for European Sumach respectively at 16.50 per cent. for first quality, and 13.00 per cent. for second quality. Where sumach is plenty, it is prepared for market by cutting the twigs of the current year's growth, together with the leaves, drying them, without being wetted by rain, running them through a cutting machine and pressing them in sacks for market. The price paid varies from twenty to fifty dollars per ton. The valuable southern species, not heretofore mentioned, are *Rhus pumila*, a dwarf species of the pine barrens from North Carolina to Georgia, *R. metopum*, found in Florida, growing fifteen to twenty feet high, *R. cotinoides*, found in Alabama, and supposed to be allied to the Venetian or exotic species, *R. cotinus*. *R. glabra* is the variety used as a mordant for red colors, the bark of which contains the essential elements. This and *R. typhina* are the varieties most used for tanning. The cut, page 921, shows an ornamental variety of *Rh. glabra*, or cut leaved sumach, sometimes grown for ornament. Until within the last fifteen years, almost the entire amount of sumach used for tanning in the United States was imported. Since that time the value of American sumach has been better understood. The difficulty has been that it has been gathered wild in the woods, no attempts at cultivation having been made. Until within five years, almost the entire amount of sumach used in this country was imported from Europe, and still the larger proportion in use is of foreign growth and manufacture. It has been supposed that the American species were deficient in tannic acid, this opinion being the result of the want of care and skill in gathering the leaves, and their preparation at the manufactories. More care having been used in gathering and preparing sumach, it was long since demonstrated, and acknowledged by consumers in our own country, and dealers in Europe, that American sumach, from the best mills, excels in quality and equals in preparation any in the world. An importing house, having branches in New York, Philadelphia, and Savannah, impressed with the importance of further developing the native Sumach interest in this country, and being convinced of the value of our native species, by actual investigation, determined to moot the question of home production and in a circular to the trade, as long ago as 1869, said:

We would call the attention of the trade to a very fine Virginia sumach now being received, equal in every respect to the finest Sicily. We recommend its use from the following comparison in the analysis:

FINEST SICILIAN.

Lead Seal, Pojero, and Ne plus ultra.

Tannin 23.65
Sand 1.00
Vegetable fiber 75.35

                                                    100.00

FINEST AMERICAN.
Virginia.

Tannin 30.00
Sand .... .50
Vegetable fiber 69.50

                                                    100.00

This would seem to set at rest the idea that the American article is inferior. In fact, all the analyses we have found show it to be superior to the best imported. The gathering and shipment east of western sumach, and thence out of the country, in connection with that gathered east, is not inconsiderable; Iowa and Missouri being the principal States from which shipments have been made. The first shipment was made from Missouri, in 1872, consisting of 12,000 pounds, going to New York, and thence to St. Johns, New Brunswick. It would seem to be an interest that ought to bear the test of experiment in cultivation. One curious feature in connection with sumach is that manufacturers, usually so alert, have not taken hold of the matter with the view of cheapening the principal agent in tanning morocco, now one of the important industries of the North, and especially of the West.

SUMMER FALLOW. A fallow made during the warm months to kill weeds. A green fallow.

SUNFLOWER. *Helianthus annua*. This well known plant of many gardens, generally grown for its immense head of flowers would seem to have capabilities not generally estimated by the mass of cultivators. The seeds are excellent for fowls, and valuable for their oil, the dried leaves are reported to be useful in pulmonary diseases when smoked from a common pipe. The leaves and stalks contain a large per cent. of potash, and the uses of these plants when grown in masses should be better known than they are for their value in warding off the effects of miasma, being only second in this respect to the Australian gum tree; unfortunately these trees are not hardy north of Louisiana, except in some parts of California. In some sections of Europe where the sunflower is extensively cultivated for its oil product, especially in Russia, the yield is fifty bushels per acre, average. The oil is palatable—as it is well known the seeds are clear and flavorless, and is extensively used in adulterating olive oil. The seeds of native species, are used by many barbarous and semi-barbarous tribes, and also by the American savages, as food, either eaten raw or boiled.

SUPERPHOSPHATE. (See Phosphate.)

SUPPOSITORY. A solid medicine introduced into the rectum to produce purgation.

SUPPURATION. The common healthy termination of inflammations of the cellular tissues, in which pus is formed. It should be thoroughly evacuated as soon as formed.

SUPRACRETACEOUS. The formations above the chalk, now called tertiary.

SURVEYING. In agriculture, the determination of the contents of any piece of ground or estate; it is usually done in a rough way by a compass with sights, or a plane table and chain of 100 links, or twenty-two yards. The external boundaries of the field are measured by the chain along straight lines determined by setting up the compass, level, and a staff. The distance between these is ascertained in chains and links; every turn or angle of large size is determined by its bearing with the compass and staff, and a measurement of the length of the straight line, made as often as there are sides or angles. In this way a plan is obtained, giving the angles, bearings, and lengths of the sides bounding the field. This is plotted and a calculation made of the contents by the ordinary rules of mensuration. For this purpose the contents are divided into triangles, the side of any of which can be measured on the ground, to assist or correct the reckoning. The chain contains 100 links of 7.92 inches. A square chain forms the tenth of an acre; the calculation is therefore made in links, which are a decimal portion of the acre; and the resulting area being reduced by three figures, gives the number of acres in a field. But in better examinations the theodolite is used, and the distances determined by trigonometrical observations, and not by measurements with a chain.

SUTURES. Wounds or incisions after having been cleansed and prepared have their edges brought together and fastened, by means of stitches through the lips of the wound. These are called sutures, and are of two kinds, the interrupted and the twisted suture. In the case of the interrupted suture the needle is passed through the two edges of the wound, the ends tied and cut close to the wound. In the twisted suture, pins are run through the lips of the wound, and thread or horse hair, dipped in the blood, or fine wire is then woven back and forth to hold all firmly. As a rule they should be removed in four or five days or as soon as the parts are united. To promote this they should be bandaged to prevent tearing. All wounds should be closed with sutures, since the operation is so simple that any intelligent person may easily understand the operation. Our preference is for the interrupted suture for extensive lacerations, pins generally being used only for more shallow and short wounds.

SWAMP. A low place or morass in which trees grow.

SWAMP MAPLE. (See Maple.)

SWAN. As an ornamental bird, in the ponds and lakes of parks and large private grounds, the Swan has been universally admired. Their snow white color, and easy grace in the water, making them great favorites wherever introduced. Like the goose, they are long lived, sometimes, it is said, attaining the age of a hundred years. They breed readily in confinement, laying seven or eight white eggs, which being incubated, produce young birds, ash colored at first and for some months, until they have attained their first molt. When incubating they are sometimes dangerous to approach, since they fight desperately, and a blow from their wings has been known to fracture the leg of a man. There are now introduced a number of ornamental varietes, among others, the black-necked swan from Chili. The head and neck jet black, and the body, wings and tail pure white, the bill having a red knob or protuberance. The black swan is from Australia.

SWARD GRASSES. A name given to the genus *Poa*, which forms the best natural meadows.

SWATH. Grass cut in mowing.

SWEATING HAY. The slight fermentation which occurs when fresh grass, clover, etc., are placed in heaps. It is attended with considerable heat if the quantity is great, and should, therefore be looked after. Fruits and grain also undergo a sweating process, if heaped soon after collection. It is the best method to prepare the different kinds of hay.

SWEENY. (See Sprains and Strains.)

SWEET BRIAR. *Rosa rubiginosa.* A plant hardy everywhere in the United States, and well known for its fragrant foliage. In many places it is so well naturalized as to have run wild, and to become troublesome from its half climbing habit and its sharp spines.

SWEET FLAG. *Acorus calamus.* The root is pleasantly aromatic.

SWEET-SCENTED SHRUB. *Calycanthus Floridus.* A pleasant, fragrant shrub with dark flowers.

SWIFT. (See Swallow.)

SWINE. *Sus scrofa.* The origin of the domestication of swine, like that of the horse, cattle and sheep, is lost in obscurity. In a wild state, however, it has been known from the remotest times in Europe, Asia and Africa. The great fecundity of the species, its well known character of being fully able to protect itself against animals of prey; its strong gregarious habits and determined courage, and the added fact that it can live in any country where it may find nuts, plants, or roots during the winter, would easily account for its being found universally almost in the countries named. In America, Australia and the islands of the southern Pacific, however, swine were unknown until introduced after the discovery of these countries by white men. Once introduced, however, they quickly increased and spread, so that that there are few timbered regions of America where swine have not run wild, attaining all the characteristic ferocity of other wild races. That the swine of Europe, Asia and Africa have a common origin is evidenced from the fact that all the species breed together, the progeny propagating the species, with unimpaired vitality. In fact the greatest improvements introduced into our native breeds, is the result of crossing with the domestic hog of China, of Italy, and probably, those of Turkey. Thus the three great continents of the East have contributed to the improvement of our modern domesticated swine. In England the wild species has long been extinct, and it is only in some parts of Germany, Denmark and the mountainous and sparsely settled districts of southern Europe, in Asia Minor, and Africa, where they are now met. The teeth of the hog number forty-four, and may be represented by incisors, six upper and six lower; canines or tusks, two upper and two lower; molars, including what were formerly called wolf teeth fourteen upper and fourteen lower. Fustenburg, a well known German authority, has given the means of determining the age of swine by their teeth, as follows: Born with eight teeth, four corner incisors and four tusks, on the eighth or tenth day the second or third temporary molars appear. The four nippers, two on the upper and two on the under jaw, appear at four weeks old. At the fifth or sixth week the first temporary molars appear in the upper and lower jaw. At the age of three months, the intermediary incisors appear. At the sixth the so-called wolf teeth are seen, and also the third permanent molars. At the ninth month the permanent corner incisors, the permanent tusks, and the second permanent molars will be seen. At twelve months the permanent nippers will have appeared, and by the thirteenth month, the three temporary molars will have been shed, and the permanent ones will be seen; at fifteen months these will be fully up. At the age of eighteen months the permanent intermediary incisors and the permanent rear molar will show, and at the twenty-first month these will be fully developed, thus completely finishing the permanent dentition. The three great swine producing and Essex. In relation to the various reputable breeds created here or introduced, the second session of the National Swine Breeders, through an appropriate committee fixed upon the following as characteristic of the breeds. The history of the breed of swine known as the Poland-China breed is as follows: In the early history of swine breeding in the Miami Valley, in Ohio, it is clear from the best written authorities available, and from oral testimony, that there were two breeds which, to a great extent, had been profitably crossed with the common bristled breed of the country. These were the Russian and Byfield breeds. The Bedford breed is also named in connection with the other two; to what extent it was used can not now be readily determined. In 1816, we have positive proof from an unquestioned source that the Shakers of Union Village, situate in Warren county, O., and being four miles from Monroe, in Butler county, purchased at Philadelphia one boar and

CHESTER COUNTY SOW — BREEDER.

States are Illinois, Ohio and Iowa. In 1878, Illinois produced 3,355,500, Ohio, 2,341,411, and Iowa, 2,224,800 head, or nearly one-quarter of the production of the United States, which was 30,362,500 head of swine. Of this vast number there were packed at Chicago over 5,000,000, or one-sixth of the whole number contained in the United States. In 1879-80, from November 1, to March 1, 6,946,151 hogs were packed at the principal receiving centers of the United States. Each section of the United States and Canada has its favorite breeds of swine, though representatives of all the reputable breeds may be found in every State. Thus, in the East, the Suffolks, Berkshires, and Chester county breed seem to meet with the most favor. In the great pork producing region of the West, the great bulk of the swine raised are Berkshires, and Poland China, and their grades among large breeds and among the small breeds the Suffolk three sows, of what was, at the time, believed to be pure China. They were represented to be either imported, or the immediate descendants of imported stock. They were called Big China hogs. These animals were the first China hogs ever brought into southwestern Ohio. Subsequently other China hogs were introduced and extensively used. The Shakers and other judicious breeders in Warren and Butler counties continued to use the breeds at command, and produced, by repeated crosses, a hog of exceedingly fine qualities for that period, which was generally known as the Warren county hog. These hogs, continually increasing in good qualities, were bred in both counties, and the very best specimens were carefully and interchangeably used, so as to make the best crosses. Such was the progress that had been made in forming the ground work of a good specimen of a hog. This condition of the breed continued until about the year 1835 or 1836, when Mr. Munson Beach, of Warren county, first introduced the Berkshires, which were obtained from C. M. Bement, of the State of New York. Other lots of Berkshires continued to flow into the Miami Valley, until, about 1841. The Berkshire blood was liberally infused into the stock existing not only in southwestern Ohio, but in Kentucky also. Crossing with the Berkshires was almost exclusively done until about 1838 or 1839, when Mr. William Neff, of Cincinnati, imported some choice specimens of the Irish Grazier. This breed soon grew into high favor, and, as a consequence, was liberally used in making crosses with the best specimens of the crosses previously made. This intermingling of blood—this crossing of breeds—continued for some time. In a few years, however, the use of the pure blooded Berkshire was entirely discontinued, and there were no further importations made of the Irish Grazier. The breeders of swine in the Miami Valley settled down to the conviction that the basis of a good breed of hogs had been established, and that in the future judicious and discriminating breeders could use and, if necessary, modify the material furnished, so as to meet the highest demands of the public. For more than thirty years no new blood has been introduced into this breed, and no effort made to obtain a new supply of the blood of either breeed previously used. While this is true, the breeders have not been indifferent to the further improvement of the breed. Stimulated by their success, they have perseveringly aimed to improve what they had been so successful in forming. The best points or qualities have been preserved, and when practicable, have been made even more excellent. All defective points or undesirable qualities have been corrected or improved by the care, skill, and judgment of experienced breeders. The best specimens have good length, short legs, broad, straight backs, deep sides, flanking well down on the leg, very broad, full, square hams and shoulders, drooping ears, short heads, wide between the eyes, of spotted or dark color; are hardy, vigorous, and prolific, and when fat are models, combining the excellences of both large and small breeds. The Chester Whites, as a breed, originated in Chester county, Pa. The first impulse to the improvement of swine in this county was given by the introduction of a pair of fine pigs, brought from Bedfordshire, England, by Capt. James Jeffries, and placed upon his farm near the county seat, in 1818. Some of the enterprizing farmers of the neighborhood were encouraged to commence the improvement of their swine; and by crossing these pigs upon the native white hog of the county, their progeny with the best specimens attainable, and by a course of careful and judicious crossing and selection for many years, the present valuable breed of well formed, good sized, easily fattened hogs, known as Chester Whites, was produced and made an established breed. Some twenty-five years ago an attempt was made to introduce into that county the Suffolk and also the Berkshire breeds of swine, and a few of the Chester Whites were crossed with them; but after a few years' trial both were rejected, not being considered any improvement upon the Chesters. The following may be given as characteristics of these hogs: Head, short and broad between the eyes; ears, thin, projecting forward, and lopping at the point; neck, short and thick; jowl, large; body, lengthy and deep; back, broad; hams, full and deep; legs, short and well set under the body for bearing the weight; coat, thin, white, and straight; (if a little wavy it is no objection). Small tail and no bristles. The family of pigs known as Victorias originated in Saratoga county, N. Y. They were made by crossing the Byfield hogs with the native, in which there was a strain of the Graziers, Subsequent crosses were made with the Yorkshire and Suffolk, the result being a purely white hog of medium size. These pigs, if pure bred, should all have a direct descent from a sow called Queen Victoria, which may be said to be the mother of the family. She was pronounced by good judges to be almost perfect, and was the winner of a number of first prizes. Breeders in the Eastern States have long felt the need of a medium sized white hog, with all the good points of the English breeds without their objectionable features, a breed which would mature early, and be covered with a good coat of hair to protect it from the cold in winter and the heat in summer. The color is pure white, with a good coat of fine, soft hair. The head thin, fine, and closely set on the shoulders. The face slightly dishing. The snout short. The ears erect, small, and very light or thin. The shoulders bulging and deep; legs short and fine. The back broad, straight, and level, and the body long. The hams round and swelling, and high at the base of the tail, with plaits or folds between the thighs. The tail fine and free from wrinkles or rolls. The skin is thin, soft, and elastic. The flesh fine-grained and firm, with small bone and thick side pork. The pigs easily keep in condition and can be made ready for slaughter at any age. Cheshire hogs, it is said, originated in Jefferson county, N. Y., and it is claimed by some of the breeders that they started from a pair of hogs bought of Mr. Wolford, of Albany, N.Y., which were called Cheshires. However that may be, there is no such distinctive breed of hogs known as Cheshires in England, and there is no record of any hogs of this name having been imported into this country. Yorkshires have been imported into Jefferson county from time to time, and the so-called Cheshires have been improved by crossing with them and hogs bought in Canada. This family of hogs are pure white, with a very thin skin, of pink color, with little hair. They are not uniform in this respect, as pigs in the same litter differ widely in the amount of hair. The snout is often long, but very slender and fine. The jowls are plump, and the ear erect, fine, and thin. The shoulders are wide and the hams full. The flesh of these hogs is fine-grained, and they are commended on account of the extra amount of mess-pork in proportion to the amount of offal. The tails of the pigs frequently drop off when young. The positive origin of the Jersey-Red and Duroc swine is unknown. They have been bred in portions of the State of New Jersey for upwards of fifty years, and with many farmers are considered to be a valuable variety. They are of large size and capable of making a heavy growth, 500 and 600 pounds' weight being common. They are extensively bred in the middle and southern portions of New Jersey. In neighborhoods they were bred quite uniform, being of a dark red color; while in other sections they are more sandy and often patched with white. They are probably descended from the old importations of Berkshires, as there is no record of the Tamworth, the red hogs of England, ever having been brought into this country; nor is this likely, as the Tamworth were not considered a valuable breed, and were confined to a limited breeding. The Reds resemble the old Berkshires in many respects, but are now much coarser than the improved swine of this breed. A good specimen of a Jersey-Red should be red in color, with a snout of moderate length, large lop-ears, small head in proportion to the size and length of the body. They should be long in the body, standing high and rangy on their legs; bones coarse, hairy tail and brush, and hair coarse, inclining to bristles on the back. They are valuable on account of their size and strong constitutions, and capacity for growth. They are not subject to mange. There is another family of sandy hogs called Durocs, bred in Saratoga county, N. Y., which are finer in the bone and carcase than the Reds. They have been bred with their crosses in that region of country for about twenty years; are extremely hardy and ultimately attain a large size. Berkshires have been bred in Berkshire, England, from a very early period. The family which was the basis of this breed was of a sandy or buff color, about equally spotted with black, of large size, a slow feeder, maturing at two and a half to three years. It was esteemed for a comparatively greater proportion of lean to fat, and the superior weight of its hams and shoulders, and for the superior fitness of the whole carcase for

SUFFOLK BOAR.

SUFFOLK SOW.

smoking. Some time during the past century, as tradition affirms, the Siamese boar, then recently imported into England, was fixed upon for the purpose of improving the existing Berkshire. The Siamese is described as varying from a clear jet-black to a dark-slate or rich plum. It was of medium size, quick to mature, fine in all its points, short legs and head, thin jowls, a dished face, slender ears, compact body, well ribbed, extra heavy hams and shoulders, slender tail, thin skin, and firm flesh. The following standard of characteristics is given of the

Berkshires: Color black, with white on feet, face, tip of tail, and an occasional splash of white on the arm. While a small spot of white on some other part of the body does not argue an impurity of blood, yet it is to be discouraged, to the end that uniformity of color may be attained by breeders. White upon one ear, or a bronze or copper spot on some part of the body, argues no impurity, but rather a re-appearing of original colors. Markings of white other than those named above are suspicious, and a pig so marked should be rejected. Face short, fine, and well dished, broad between the eyes. Ears generally almost erect, but sometimes inclining forward with advancing age; small, thin, soft, and showing veins. Jowl full. Neck short and thick. Shoulder short from neck to middling deep from back down. Back broad and straight, or a very little arched. Ribs long and well sprung, giving rotundity of body; short ribs of good length giving breadth and levelness of loin. Hips good length from point of hips to rump. Hams thick, round, and deep, holding their thickness well back and down to the hocks. Tail fine and small, set on high up. Legs short and fine, but straight and very strong, with hoofs erect, legs set wide apart. Size medium. Length medium; extremes are to be avoided. Bone fine and compact. Offal very light. Hair fine and soft; no bristles. Skin pliable. The following standard of characteristics of Suffolks is given: Head small, very short; cheeks prominent and full; face dished; snout small and very short; jowl fine. Ears small, thin, upright, soft, and silky. Neck very short and thick, the head appearing almost as if set on front of shoulders; there is no arching of crest. The chest wide and deep; the elbows standing out; the brisket wide, but not deep Shoulders and crop: shoulders thick, rather upright, rounding outwards from top to elbow; crops wide and full. Sides and flanks: ribs well arched out from back, good length between shoulder and ham; flank well filled out and coming well down at ham. Back broad, level, and straight from crest to tail, not falling off or down at tail. Hams wide and full, well rounded out; twist very wide and full all the way down. Legs small and wide apart, in sows just keeping the belly from the ground; bone fine, feet small, hoofs rather spreading. Tail small, long, and tapering. Skin, hair, and color: skin thin, of a pinkish shade, free from color; hair, fine and silky, not too thick; color of hair pale yellowish white, perfectly free from any spots or other color. Size small to medium. The Essex is a black hog, originating in the south of England, small or medium in size, with small soft ears; carcase long, broad, and deep, hams heavy and well let down, bone fine, hair thin. They are remarkable for easy fattening, and are great lard producers. They are fair nurses and prolific breeders. The Neapolitan is distinguished as the basis of improvement of several of the best breeds of English swine, and produces that striking uniformity of characteristics among different individuals which marks a long-established breed as well as good breeding. Martin credits the great improvement of English swine, during many years, chiefly to the agency of the Neapolitan and Chinese breeds. Like the thoroughbred horse, the Neapolitan has a delicate look, a peculiar grace and stylishness, a look of intelligence, with a vivacity and sprightliness unusual in swine, and which in this breed do not seem to be incompatible with surprising aptitude to lay on flesh, or to grow rapidly on a small amount of food. In the vicinity of New York many gentlemen, who in their travels have eaten the pork of Naples and vicinity, have imported Neapolitans and bred them for their own use, on account of fine grain and delicious flavor of the pork. The breed is of great antiquity, and imparts its peculiarities with great uniformity. This is one of the purest and most valuable of known breeds—easily kept, but difficult to keep down in good breeding condition; one of the gentlest and most easily managed, and least fastidious in its food; the sows are good mothers, furnishing abundance of milk, and reasonably prolific; they furnish juicy hams and shoulders, well marbled and not coated with masses of fat, abundance of leaf-lard, and the most delicate of side-pork for family use, while the offal is a minimum quantity. Their characteristics are: Head small; forehead bony and flat; face slightly dishing; snout rather long and very slender; ears small, thin, standing outward and forward nearly horizontally, and quite lively; jowls very full, but not large; neck short, broad and heavy above, with a small dewlap; trunk long, cylindrical, and well ribbed back. Back flat, and arching even in low flesh. Belly horizontal on the lower line. Hindquarters higher than the fore, but not very much so. Legs very firm, the bones and joints being smaller than those of any other breed. Hams and shoulders well developed and meaty. Tail fine, curled, flat at the extremity, and fringed with hair on each side. General color, slaty or bluish plum-color, with a cast of coppery red. Skin soft and fine, nearly free from hair, which when found upon the sides of the head and behind the forelegs is black and soft and rather long. Flesh firm and elastic to the touch.

SWING PLOW. The plow without a wheel under the beam.

SWINGLE-TREE, WHIPPLE-TREE. The bar of wood or iron to which the traces of each horse are fastened, and which are hitched on to the vehicle, plow, or other implement to be drawn.

SWISS CATTLE. Aside from an occasional importation by curious amateurs, the Swiss cattle have never gained a foothold in our country, and yet they bear a high reputation in many parts of Europe. In France, especially, they are much esteemed, and at the agricultural school of Grignon their performances at the pail are said to compare well with those of the common short-horns, which were considered the best milkers in the establishment. An accurate observer says they are robust, hardy animals, usually of a dun color, or dun and white, with medium heads, hanging dewlaps, rather coarse shoulders, and broad hips and quarters, with well-developed udders. Removed from their native mountains, they manifested little impatience at the change, and though kept in stables and soiled, they seemed to thrive, and carried a good coat of flesh; when dry, they are said to fatten readily. In Switzerland they are wintered in the valleys, on the coarsest food, and as soon as the snow melts from the southern slopes of the mountains are driven to their pastures, which, as the season advances, are gradually changed for the higher ranges. For four months in the year they are kept on the most elevated feeding grounds, and there, attended by a single man, uniting in his person the offices of cowherd and dairy-man, they feed on the close, sweet herbage, often at the very edge of the snow fields, till their short summer is over, and they are driven by the autumn storms to the more sheltered pastures again. Cheese is the chief product, and its manufacture is conducted in the lonely chalet, perched on the mountain side, in the most primitive manner. A few pails and tubs and an iron kettle are the only utensils required. The best cows yield from ten to twenty quarts of milk daily, and each cow produces, by the end of the season of four months, on an average, 225 pounds of cheese. The best cheeses are made upon pastures 3,000 feet above the sea level! How far the introduction of these cattle into our country might be of advantage is a question; but there are districts which, though not absolutely alpine in their character, are sufficiently rugged and bleak to require for their profitable occupation a breed of this kind, especially as with better keeping and a milder climate they, proportionably improve in both milk and form.

SWITCHING HEDGES. Cutting off the year's shoots. This is done with a sharp hooked blade called a switching-hook, or with large hedge shears.

SYCAMORE. *Platanus occidentalis.* Western sycamore. Button wood. Plane tree. This is one of the most majestic of western forest trees, delighting in rich alluvial soils. It is not much valued for timber, though it is sometimes used for posts, etc. The Greater maple, *Acer Pseudo platanus*, sometimes called sycamore, is an introduced tree, but less handsome than our sugar maple or the Norway maple.

SYCON, SYCONUS. A fruit consisting of a fleshy disk or hollow receptacle, as in the fig.

SYENITE. A granite with black spots of hornblende, which takes its name from Syene in upper Egypt.

SYMBOL. In chemistry, the abbreviation used to distinguish an element or chemical body. It usually consists of the initial letter, sometimes of the first and second.

SYMPATHY. A veterinary and medical term used to express the existence of certain symptoms in a disease which are remote from the parts injured.

SYMPATHETIC NERVE. A grand connection of nerves from one end of the body to the other, furnished with nervous centres or ganglia, by which some physiologists suppose a uniformity in the operations of the different viscera is maintained. It is also called the trisplanchnic nerve.

SYMPIESOMETER. A kind of barometer.

SYN. A common prefix in descriptive words, meaning united.

SYNAPTASE. The white matter of almonds freed from oil, albumen, and other matters.

SYNCARPOUS FRUITS. Such as contain several carpels united, as the apple, pear, etc.

SYNCHONDROSIS. The junction of bones by a cartilage.

SYNCOPE. Fainting, whenever the circulation and respiration become feeble for a time.

SYNGENESIA. The composite family of plants, in which, according to Linnæus, the anthers are united into a tube, the filaments being usually separate and distinct.

SYNOCHA. Continued inflammatory fevers.

SYNOVIA. The albuminous or serous fluid secreted in the joints, to diminish the friction of the extremities of the bones; it is poured out from little pouches, called synovial bags.

SYNTHESIS. In chemistry, the production of a compound body by a union of its elements or parts.

SYRIAN GOAT, (See Goat.)

SYRINGE. A small cylinder with an airtight piston or sucker, which is moved by a handle The lower end of the cylinder terminates in a small tube, through which a fluid is forced into the body of the cylinder by the atmospheric pressure when the handle is drawn up, and then expelled in a small jet, by pushing the handle in the opposite direction. The syringe acts on the principle of the sucking pump. The syringe is also used as a pneumatic machine for condensing or exhausting the air in a close vessel, but for this purpose it must be furnished with two valves. In the condensing syringe the valves open downward and close upward; in the exhausting syringe they are closed downward and opened upward. The garden syringe, useful for watering plants, and removing caterpillars, red spiders, and other insects, is a large syringe of a quart size or larger, which discharges fluid from a rose or perforated end instead of a point.

SYRPHUS FLY. Beneficial insects, which deposit eggs upon plants infested with lice, which hatching into larva, subsist thereon. The grub is blind and discovers its prey by means of its feelers. The parent fly is two-winged, about seven-tenths of an inch across them. It has a curious habit of hovering, stationary, over or near flowers during the day, darting away if disturbed, but soon returning and resuming its former attitude. They should be sedulously preserved, since they tend to keep down the spread of plant lice, both the woolly ones and others, which sometimes swarm by millions.

SYRUP. A thick solution of sugar, as the boiled down juice of vegetables and plants containing saccharine, as the beet, watermelon sorghum, Indian corn, sugar cane, etc., which see. The juice evaporated to a thick consistency becomes a syrup, also called molasses. This latter term is not, however, correct, except as applied to the drippings or uncrystallizable syrup of sorghum sugar, beet sugar, sugar cane, and other true sugar producing plants.

SYSTOLE. The contraction of the heart, the diastole being its dilatation. These two alternate movements produce the beating.

T

TACAMAHACA. The *Populus balsamica* of Canada, which yields a resinous, balsamic exudation in the spring.

TAG. Tags are the masses of dirt that accumulate on the wool of the tail; the process of removing them is called tagging, and sometimes, when they cause the tail to be fastened to the body, that state is called tagbelt or pinning.

TAGLIA. A combination of pulleys, a tackle.

TAGLIACOTIAN. Any operation in which the skin is nearly cut from one part and made to cover another.

TAIL DRAIN. The main drain, which receives the water of the lesser drains.

TALC. A mineral closely resembling mica, but not elastic.

TALLOW. The melted or rendered fat of the ox or sheep. The fat of horses, amounts to eight or ten per cent. Its composition is similar to that of oils, but the stearine is in excess.

TALLOW-TREE. *Croton sebiferum*. A large lauraceous tree of China, the seeds of which, when pressed, yield a fatty body very similar to tallow. Some specimens of this tree are found growing in the shrubberies of the Southern States.

TALUS. A heap of rubbish accumulated at the foot of a cliff or steep rock.

TAMARAC. (See Larch.)

TAMARIND. *Tamarindus Indica*. A large tree of the leguminous family, native of the tropical East and West Indies. The prepared pods are preserved in sugar.

TAMARIX. The genus *Tamarix;* small, ornamental shrubs.

TAMPING. In blasting, filling the hole with sand and pieces of rock after a cartridge has been introduced.

TANAGER. *Pyranga rubra.* This is a well known summer visitor in the Atlantic States north, but more sparingly seen as yet West of the Alleghanies, an active insect destroyer, delighting in copses near swamps.

TANK. In gardening a cistern or reservoir used for collecting and preserving water during a scarcity or drought. They are sometimes built in the ground, and lined with cement. Where wells can not be sunk, and water is scarce, in some seasons, tanks are necessary appendages to a house. A current of air is said to promote the purity of water in tanks, which is easily effected by the earthenware or other pipe which conveys the water from the roof being of six or eight

TAPE WORM   929   **TEA**

inches in diameter, and an opening left for the surplus water to run away; and where the prevailing winds do not blow soot and leaves on the house, the water remains good, even for drinking, without clearing out the rubbish more than once a year; but, in some cases, filtering by ascension may be found useful, and effected by the water being delivered by the pipe at the bottom of a cask or other vessel, from which it can not escape till it has risen through the holes in a board covered with pebbles, sand, or powdered charcoal.

TANNIN. The astringent principle of galls, sumach, catechu, and numerous barks. It is very soluble in water, and possesses the property of uniting with albuminous matters, and forming tanno-gelatine, or leather. When separated from the other substances in bark, it is found to be a white, astringent powder, with acid reaction, and known as tannic acid; by the action of moisture and air it absorbs oxygen, and becomes converted into the insoluble gallic acid. It is tribasic, and its salts are called tannates. The value of any specimen of bark for tanning and certain dyes is ascertained by the amount of tannic acid they contain. The amount, in 480 parts, in the barks mentioned is:

Varieties.	Pounds.
Oak bark contains	29
Spanish chestnut	21
Leicester willow (large)	33
Elm	13
Common willow (large)	11
Ash	16
Beech	10
Horse-chestnut	9
Sycamore	11
Lombardy poplar	15
Birch	8
Hazel	14
Blackthorn	16
Coppice oak	32
Inner rind of oak bark	72
Oak cut in autumn	21
Larch cut in autumn	8
Sicilian sumach	78
Nut galls	127
Catechu	261

TANSY. *Tanacetum vulgare.* A well known garden plant, cultivated for its bitter aromatic properties. Escaping from cultivation, it has become a common, but not an essentially troublesome weed.

TANYSTOMES. A family of dipterous insects, most of which have a projecting proboscis.

TAPETUM. A coat of the eye under the black pigment, and peculiar to quadrupeds.

TAPE WORM. This is the mature form of an entozoa, the cysts in measly swine being an immature stage of the worm. The parasites in their mature state may inhabit the intestines of any of the vertebrate animals. In their transition or immature state they occur as cysts in the tissues of such animals as feed upon those which bear them. They have been produced in many carnivorous animals to which the encysted forms had been artificially fed. The eggs of the mature worm being set free, are carried into water, manure, etc., and may be taken into the system on grass, by animals, or on salads by man. The eggs taken into the stomach produce the encysted state, as measles in swine, or as the trichina. Dogs are the most prolific source of spreading the eggs of the tape worm, so also are all animals which feed upon flesh that may contain the encysted worm. (See Measles in Swine.)

TAPIOCA. A starchy farina from the root of the *Jatropa manihot.* There are two varieties; one with a bitter, poisonous root; the other with a sweet root.

TAP ROOT. The main root which descends vertically from trees.

TAR. A dark-brown, viscid liquor, obtained by charring the wood of the pitch pine tree. It consists of resin, empyreumatic matters, and acetic acid. When inspissated by boiling, it is converted into pitch. The manufacture is simple; a conical hole, usually in the side of a bank, being made, roots and billets of pine are let into the cavity, and the whole is covered with turf, which is beat firmly down above the wood. The wood being kindled, a slow combustion takes place. A cast-iron pan at the bottom of the cavity receives the fluid, and has a spout which projects through the bank and carries the tar into barrels. As quickly as the barrels are filled they are closed with bungs, when the material is ready for exportation. This manner of preparing tar has been derived from the earliest ages. Tar is a very compound substance; it contains modified resin, and oil of turpentine, acetic acid, charcoal, water, etc. Tar is used in medicine as well as in the arts. It is an excellent topical stimulant, when made into an ointment with lard, in dry skin diseases. These two substances, tar and pitch, are of extensive use in the arts.

TARES. Corn Spurry. Devil's Flax. *Spergula arvensis.* This plant is cultivated in Europe as fodder, cattle and sheep being fond of and thriving on it. It is there credited with enriching the milk of cows fed on it, and of making superior mutton. Here it is a weed and should be so treated. The vetch (*vicia sativa*) is also called tare, and is prized in Europe. We have so much better plants that it is here regarded as a weed.

TARO. A cultivated *Arum* of the Columbia river.

TARRAGON. *Artemesia dracunculus.* A bitter pot-herb, of the same genus as the tansy.

TARSUS. The bones articulated to the tibia, and forming the upper part of the foot.

TARTAR. The sediment of wine casks.

TARTAR, CREAM OF. Supertartrate of potash, obtained by purifying tartar.

TARTAR EMETIC. Tartrate of potash and antimony, a powerful emetic, sedative, and expectorant.

TARTARIC ACID. The acid of grapes or of tartar.

TAXICORNS. A family of coleopterans, in many of which the antennæ enlarge towards the upper ends.

TAXIS. The replacement of parts by the hand.

TEA. *Thea viridis.* A plant belonging to the *camelliaceæ*, and known wherever civilization extends as the source of the green and black tea of commerce. It is indigenous to many portions of China and is reported to have been introduced to Japan by a Buddist priest in the sixth century. Its native country is unknown, the only country where it has certainly been found wild is Assam. Tea has been grown in the Southern States, in a small way for many years, the leaves

59

being gathered for the family beverage, and said to be superior to that imported. Within the last few years its cultivation has been attempted under the patronage of the government, large quantities of plants having been propagated and sent out (20,000 in 1876) with a view of making it a national industry. This, however, will hardly be accomplished until machinery can be invented to compete with cheap East Indian and Chinese labor. Tea was first imported to Europe by the Hollanders in the seventeenth century. In 1661 it was introduced into England, and came to America as soon as the wealth of the settlers enabled them to buy it. The Chinese tea-plant —*Thea viridis*, Linn.; *Camellia therifera*, Griff. (Chinese, *Chak;* Assamese, *Phalap*) is described by botanists as a polyandrous plant, of the natural order *Ternstroemiaceae*. The flowers, which open early in the spring (appearing upon the plant about a month), are smaller in size and much less elegant than those which render some species of the *Camelia* so attractive. They are slightly odorous, and of a pure white color; they proceed from the axils of the branches, and stand on short foot-stalks, or at the most two or three together, but usually solitary. There are five or six imbricate sepals or leaves supporting the blossom, which fall off after the flower has expanded, and leave from six to nine petals surrounding a great number of yellow stamens that are joined together in such a manner at their bases as to form a sort of floral coronal. The

numerous branches bearing a very dense foliage, and in its general appearance not unlike the myrtle, though not so symmetrical as that plant. The wood is light-colored, close-grained, of great comparative density, and when freshly cut or peeled gives off a strong smell resembling that of the black currant bush. The leaves are alternate, on short, thick, channeled foot-stalks; coriaceous or leathery, smooth and shining; of a dark green color, and a longish elliptic form, with a blunt or notched point, and serrated except at the base.

MATE. PARAGUAY TEA.

The black and green teas of commerce are produced from this plant. The opinion was at one time quite prevalent that there existed several species of *Thea*, but it is now known that the different sorts in market are indebted to artificial manipulations for much of their apparent variety and distinctive qualities. Many of the names attached to teas are merely descriptive of the locality or country where they are produced, the condition of the leaves when gathered, and the mode of preparing them for market. Thus there is Java tea, Japan tea and Assam tea; bohea tea, from coarse leaves; gunpowder tea, made from the small, close-curled young leaves; and green tea, colored to suit its name. In the preparation of black tea, the freshly gathered leaves, being partially dried by brief exposure in the open air, are thrown into round, flat iron pans, and exposed to a gentle fire heat for five minutes, which renders them soft and pliant, and causes them to give off a large quantity of moisture. They are then emptied into sieves, and while hot they are repeatedly squeezed and rolled in the hands to give them their twist or curl. They are next placed in the open air, in the shade, for a few days, and finally they are completely dried in iron pans over a slow fire. Green tea, when genuine, is prepared in a

CHINESE TEA PLANT.

seeds are enclosed in a smooth, hard capsule, of a flattish triangular shape, which is interiorly divided into two, three, and even five cells, each containing a firm, white, and somewhat oily nut, from the size of a pea to that of a hazel-nut, of a nauseous and bitter taste. They ripen in some localities as early as October; in others not until January. The stem is generally bushy, with

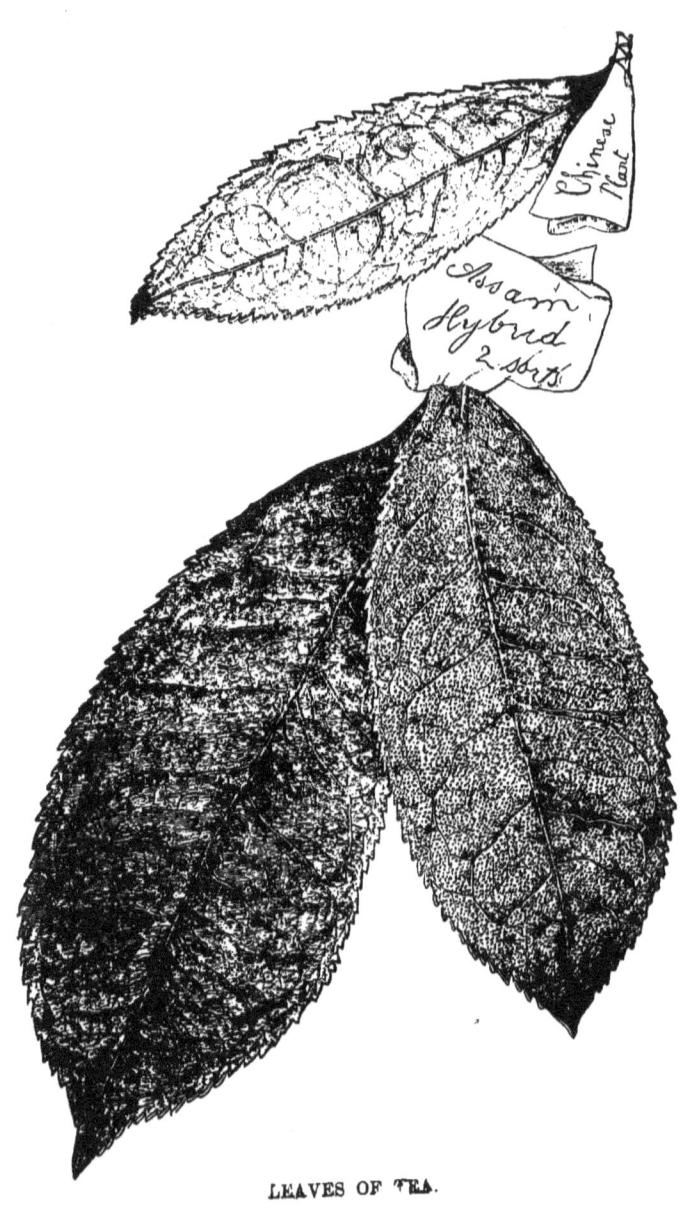

LEAVES OF TEA.

YOUNG TEA PLANT AND ROOT.

similar manner, except that it is dried with more care, and by a slower process, but the greater part of the green tea consumed in Europe and America is colored by the Chinese to suit the demands of foreign trade. There are about a dozen varieties of tea in commerce, but, besides the preceding distinction of color, they consist merely of different sizes obtained by sifting. The active principles in tea are theine and a volatile oil, to the latter of which its flavor and odor are due, and which possesses narcotic and intoxicating properties. It also contains fifteen per cent. of gluten or nutritious matter, and more than twenty-five per cent. of tannin. On page 932 will be found a cut of the young plant and root. Every civilized nation, and some barbarous tribes, have plants the infusion of which is drank. Among the more noted of these we find the following: Paraguay tea, or *Yerba de mate, Ilex Paraguayensis, (Aquifoliaceæ.)*—The leaves of this South American tree are used in furnishing the beverage, yerba mate. They yield the same active bitter principle called theine which is found in the leaf of the Chinese tea plant, and form a commercial product that occupies the same important position in the domestic economy of South America as the famed China plant does in this country, and is consumed to the extent of several thousand tons annually. The leaves are prepared by drying and roasting, not in the fashion of making Chinese teas, but by cutting large branches from the trees, which are placed on hurdles over wood fires, and kept there until the leaves are sufficiently roasted, when they are removed and placed on a hard floor, and the dried leaves knocked off by beating the branches with sticks. The leaves are then gathered up, reduced to powder in wooden mills, and packed for market. This tea is often packed in sacks made of raw hides, which are sewed together in a square form. The powdered leaves are pressed into the sacks with great force, and when full they are sewed up and exposed to the sun, where the hide dries and tightens over the contents, forming a package nearly as hard and heavy as stone. There are several grades or sorts of mate tea in the South American markets, valued according to the age of the leaf and the modes of preparation. It is prepared for use by placing a small quantity of the powder in a cup, and pouring boiling water over it; the decoction is quaffed or sucked through a *bombilla*, or tube having a bulb perforated with minute holes. It has an agreeable, slightly aromatic odor, rather bitter to the taste, but very refreshing and restorative to the body after undergoing great fatigue. It is highly relished by travelers, and it is almost impossible for those who become accustomed to its use to discontinue it. It acts in some degree as an aperient and diuretic, and, if taken in over-doses, it occasions diseases similar to those produced by strong liquors. It is supposed that there are several species of Ilex, the leaves of which are gathered for tea; *Ilex theezans, Ilex gongonha,* and *Ilex amara* are known to be used in Brazil and other places The Yerba, produced by, and known to the Brazilians as Herva de Palmeira, is specially renowned for its excellent qualities. The plant yielding Faham or Angrecum tea is *Angræcum fragrans,* an epiphytal orchid of the Island of Bourbon, where it is used under the name of Faham. It has been introduced and used as a beverage in France and other European countries. In taste it differs greatly from that of the Chinese tea, having an aroma of great delicacy, and producing quite an agreeable perfume similar to that of the tonka bean. It has tonic and digestive qualities; and it is recorded that in the aromatic principle of the plant there is a diffusible stimulant capable of deadening nervous sensibility; in the bitter principle an excellent stimulant to revive the strength of the nutritive organs; and in the mucilage a demulcent to relax the tissues. Jesuits' tea, is the leaf of *Psoralea glandulosa, (Leguminosæ,)* a native of Chili, a small shrubby plant. The infusion of the leaves is slightly aromatic, and is valued more for its medicinal qualities than for its agreeable flavor. It is used as a vermifuge, and is pronounced to be a good remedy for asthma. The leaves are used in Chili for making poultices for wounds, and an infusion of the roots is emetic and purgative. The leaves are also dried and smoked like tobacco. Arabian tea is prepared from the leaves of *Catha edulis, (Celastraceæ,)* a small tree or shrub, seldom growing over eight feet in height, native of Arabia. Under the name of cafta, small branches of this plant, with leaves still attached, form a considerable article of commerce among the Arabs, who cultivate the plant to a great extent in the interior of their country. A decoction of the leaves produces effects similar to those following the use of strong green Chinese tea, only that they are more pleasant and agreeable. The leaves are also chewed when in the green state, and are said to have a tendency to produce great hilarity of spirits, and also to act strongly as a preventive of sleep. The use of cafta in Arabia is supposed to be of great antiquity, and to have preceded the use of coffee. Bencoolen tea is a beverage prepared from the leaves of *Glaphyria nitida, (Myrtaceæ,)* a native of the Malayan Islands, where it inhabits high elevations and attains a great age. The leaves are eagerly sought for use in the preparation of a kind of tea. Brazilian tea is prepared from the leaves of *Stachytarpha Jamaicensis, (Verbenaceæ.)* It is not known that any peculiarly favorable result attaches to the use of this as a tea, but it is known that Chinese tea is frequently adulterated by mixing with the leaves of this vervain. The green leaves are used as an application to ulcers. Bush tea is an infusion of the leaves of *Cyclopia genistoides, (Leguminosæ,)* a small bush, native of South Africa. Its use seems to partake of a medicinal character, and is recommended in cases of consumption and chronic catarrh; it has an agreeable tea-like smell, with a sweet astringent taste. Theezan tea is prepared from the leaves of *Sageretia theezans,(Rhamnaceæ,)* a Chinese plant of shrubby growth, having smooth shining-green leaves, somewhat resembling those of the true tree, and is employed as a substitute for it by the poorer classes in Southern China. Labrador tea.—A preparation of the leaves *Ledum palustre, (Ericaceæ,)* a small spreading shrub, native of Labrador. Mexican tea.— A name applied to the infusion of the young shoots and leaves of *Ambrina ambrosioides, (Chenopodiaceæ).* It is entirely medicinal, having antispasmodic, vermifuge, and carminative properties. *A. anthelmintica* is much used as a vermifuge. Mountain tea is the leaf of *Gaultheria procumbens, (Ericaceæ,)* a small creeping plant familiarly known as winter green in the United

States and Canada. All parts of the plant possess a pleasant peculiar aromatic odor and flavor, due to a volatile oil, which, when separated by distillation, is known as wintergreen oil. The leaves are used either as a flavor to genuine tea, or an infusion alone, which partakes of an astringent character, and is useful medicinally.

TEASEL. *Dipsacus fullonum.* The teasel ot commerce, in the finishing of woolen fabrics, from blanketing to the finest broadcloth, is used for the purpose of raising the knap, for which their hooked spines abundantly fit them. Until about the year 1848 they were imported for use in the United States almost entirely from foreign countries. They began to be cultivated in a small way only, since 1835, in the State of New York. About 1850 their cultivation was extended in New York, and, in 1865, the cultivation, principally in New York and the southern New England States, generally supplied the demand of this country. It is, however, a crop subject to many contingencies, not the least of which is freezing out, being a biennial like our wild teasel. The wild teasel, *Dipsacus sylvestris*, however, has spines straight, instead of recurved; and like the cultivated teasel, should be destroyed whenever found in waste places.

TECTRICES. The small feathers which cover the quill feathers.

TEDDER. The hay tedder is an implement supported on two wheels, with a seat for the driver. The working parts consist of an eccentric crank-shaped shaft, mounted with a series of levers armed with spring teeth, which, revolve on the cut grass, whether in swaths, windrows, or as left by the mowing machine. Thus the grass is tossed into the air, falling again in the lightest possible condition, by which the sun and air is admitted, curing it perfectly in a short time. In good hay weather the horse rake may follow in about two hours, and the hay is ready for the barn or stack the same day. The tedder has not come into general use in the West. The fine harvest weather usually experienced, allowing the hay to be, as a rule, easily cured. There is no doubt, however, that its use would pay on every farm where much hay is cut.

TEETH. (See Horse.)

TEETH, FOUL. (See Lampas.)

TEGMENTA. The scales of winter buds.

TEGUMENT. In anatomy, the general covering of the body. In entomology the term is applied to the coverings of the wings of the order *Orthoptera*, or straight winged insects.

TEMPERATURE. The question of temperature has been somewhat treated of in the articles Earth, Germination, Meteorology and Soil. It is an important subject, for upon temperature, as one of the prime factors, rests the question of the proper ripening of crops. Thus soils, exposed to the rays of the sun, have varying powers of absorbing warmth and holding heat, as a rule, those which absorb fastest, soonest give it up. To ripen the cereal crops an average temperature of 56° Fahr. is required. Yet this rule is not a constant one, for in the Red river country, west of lake Superior, in latitude 50°, the mean annual temperature is 32°, and yet in consequence of a clear tropical heat of sixty days, wheat and other valuable cereals are ripened. So we can not take the establishment of a general rule as correct, for the decrease of temperature as we proceed north, as indicating the climate that may be expected. In central Europe, the change in mean annual temperature is said to be a lowering of the temperature of one degree for every seventy miles of northing. In the United States, in the valley of the Mississippi, it is reported as one degree for every forty miles. Yet in the valley of the Mississippi, in consequence of the great and continued heat of summer, certain crops are ripened perfectly, that can not be ripened in a corresponding latitude in central Europe; but, again, certain crops, as grapes, are ripened as to particular varieties, in Europe, that can not be in a corresponding latitude in the United States. In the planting of crops where special earliness is desired, sandy soils are recognized for their value. Drying easily in the spring, they consume heat, as can not be expected in dark, peaty or stiff clay soils. So the protection of hedges, wind breaks, fences and glass structures are resorted to, to increase and conserve the heat of the sun. Thus the temperature is raised during the day to 70 and 80 degrees in the months of March and April and conserved during the night, through the prevention of radiation, by means of the covering, and by the aid of bottom heat. Thus all the more tender plants such as cucumbers, tomatoes, peppers, egg plant, etc., are forced. The heat to which the soil is often raised by the sun's rays alone is but little understood by the people generally. The range favorable to vegetation is from 34° Fahrenheit to 140°, in like manner, too, the very germination or first vital action of the seed must have between 34° and 40°, so that there be no danger of decomposition, and sufficient warmth to maintain circulation. The common pea, requires at least 40°, and when it is forced for early use the temperature is from 45° to 50°; that of the air to keep it growing healthily is at 60°, and after it has flowered from 52° to 70° is necessary to mature its pods. An ordinary greenhouse, which contains a miscellaneous collection of hardy plants and shrubs flowering in the winter months, may be regulated to advantage, if its temperature be not lower than 45°, but by the sun's rays in the day-time it may rise to 65°, or even higher, to fall again to 45°, or a little below. The cooler temperature of the night-time is favorable to all plants, inviting them to repose, by diminishing their excitability. Prof. James F. W. Johnston, in one of his lectures on the general relations of science to practical agriculture, delivered before the New York State agricultural society, states that, in this country, the temperature of the earth, five feet below the surface may be warmed by the sun to 100° and a half an inch below the surface sometimes rises as high as 140° Fahr. Such statements seem scarcely credible; yet, according to Dr. Coulter, plants grow on the banks of the Rio Colorado which occasionally endure this intense heat. Sir John Herschel found the soil in his bulb garden at Cape Good Hope, on the 5th of December, 1837, between 1 and 2 o'clock p. m., raised to 159° of heat, and at 3 o'clock p. m., it was 110°, and even in shaded places 119°. The temperature of the atmosphere in the shade in the same garden at the same period was 98° and 92° Fahr. At 5 o'clock p. m. the soil of the garden, having been long shaded, was found to have, at four inches in depth, a temperature of 102°. On the 3d of December, a thermometer was buried a quarter of an inch deep, in contact with a seedling fir of the year's planting, quite healthy, and having its seed leaves, marked as follows: at twenty-five minutes past 11 o'clock a. m., 148.2 ; at forty-eight minutes past 12 p. m., 149.5 ; at thirty-four minutes past 1 p. m., 149.8 ; at fifty-four minutes past 1 p. m., 150.8 ; and at forty-six minutes past 2 o'clock p. m., 148 Fahr. Similar statements were made by Prof. William Henry Harvey, in his lectures on botany before the Lowell Institute, at Boston Massachusetts, in 1849, when he also stated that desiccation of the soil in consequence was so great that severe labor was requisite to lift the bulbs of the amaryllis, gladiolus, and kindred genera from the earth, and that each year's successive decay of leaves formed an envelope around the bulbs which served as protection, and preserved their vegetative powers. From accidental circumstances it has been proved that a similar drying process will not injure the gladiolus in cultivation, but rather seems to serve as a stimulus to activity on application of moisture. Gardeners have long resorted to similar expedients to induce certain succulent plants to flower, by delaying their seasons of repose and rest by heat and dryness. Such well observed facts confirmed the previous statements of Bruce, that the temperature in the sun at Gondar has been as high as 113 ; at Benares, 110°, 113°, 118°, according to Harvey; and at Sierra Leone, 138 , according to Winterbottom. In the relation of heat to germination there is a lowest and a highest point, and also a temperature of most rapid germination. This latter is about ten degrees greater, than half the sum of the lowest and the highest temperature of germination and the temperature of healthy germination about ten degrees above the lowest temperature of germination. The range of temperature for agricultural plants in the north, to ensure active and healthy germination, may be stated to be at about 55 for the more hardy to 90° for the most tender. Goppert found no seeds of plants, usually sown, to germinate below 39°, and Sachs gives the lowest temperature at from 41° to 55°, and the highest range at from 102° to 116° So also he found the point of most rapid germination to be between 79° and 93° of temperature. There are, of course, some plants that germinate at a very low temperature and others that require a much higher one. Some arctic plants germinate when the temperature stands at or exceeds thirty-two degrees, and the cocoanut is said to germinate certainly only when the heat of the soil is 120 degrees. What we have been indicating, relates to plants cultivated in temperate and sub-tropical climates. The following table will elucidate our meaning, as showing temperatures of germination:

	Lowest Tempera-ture.	Highest Tempera-ture.	Temp. most rapid Germination.
Wheat and barley	41° F.	104° F.	84° F.
Pea	44.5.	102.	84.
Indian corn	48.	115.	91.
Scarlet bean	49.	111.	79.
Squash	54.	115.	93.

With wheat may really be placed all the cereal grains, peas, and all hardy vegetables, as radish,

parsnip, turnip, lettuce, etc. With Indian corn all that class which actual freezing will destroy, including all the dwarf beans. With the squash may be included all the more tender plants, including lima and other running beans, tomatoes, egg plants, etc. Among the cereal grains oats, perhaps, should be excepted. Oats should rather be placed with the pea, and with this, or rather between this class, and Indian corn, all the half hardy plants, as flax, Hungarian grass, celery, beets, onions, etc. Potatoes are susceptible to frost. They require about the same temperature for germination as Indian corn, but they may be planted very early in the season, since until the ground gets warm, germination goes on so slow that they do not appear above ground until all danger of frost is generally over, and if the soil be not sodden with water they will not decay. So, also, the seeds of any grain if sown early, and not exposed to become water-soaked in the soil, they will germinate when the proper temperature is reached, and growing, will be more hardy than when they sprout more quickly after being sown. Thus Haberlandt found that with a temperature of forty-one degrees, rye formed rootlets in four days, the other cereals and clover in from five to seven days, and at fifty one degrees the time was shortened one half. At this latter temperature kidney beans required eight, Indian corn eleven, and tobacco thirty-one days to commence active germination. At sixty-five degrees the cereal grains, clover, flax, and peas, begin to sprout in one or two days; beans, corn, and sugar beets in three days, and tobacco in six days. (See articles Heat, Light, Electricity, Germination, etc.

TEMPERATURE OF ANIMALS. The animal heat (of the body) in health is ninety-eight degrees, and deviation from this heat, even to that of a few degrees, shows good ground for supposing that there is disability present. If the temperature sinks we have a chill, and if it rises we have fever. Thus, an alternate sinking and rising of the temperature gives chills and fever.

TEMPORAL BONES. The temple bones.
TENACITY. Cohesion. The power of resisting a pulling force.
TENACULUM. A simple small hook, used to seize bleeding vessels in operations.
TENDRIL. A clasping stem, as that of the vine, passion flower, etc.
TENESMUS. A straining and ineffectual effort to relieve the bowels; it is a symptom of irritations and inflammations of the bowels.
TENON. The end of a rail introduced into a mortice.
TENSOR MUSCLES. Those which tighten.
TENT. A plug of lint or sponge introduced into wounds to dilate them, or to stop hemorrhages.
TENTACLES. Prehensile, thread-like organs in the lower animals. Usually arranged around their mouths.
TENUIROSTERS. Insessorial birds, with a slender bill.
TEREBRANTIA. A section of hymenopterous insects, the females of which are furnished with a terebra, or borer, with which they bore into the bark of trees, or the bodies of animals, to deposit her eggs. The ichneumons, wheat insect, etc., are of this class.
TERETE. A term applied to round stems, antennæ, etc.

TERGUM. In insects, the upper part of the abdomen or back.

TERMITES. A genus of insects inhabiting tropical Africa and America, allied to the ants.

TERRACE. A raised bank, for a promenade and ornamental objects.

TERTIARY FORMATION. Strata situated above the chalk and green sand, disposed in basins, and for the most part sedimentary, but containing some hard rocks. It is divided into three portions, the eocene, miocene, and pliocene.

TESSELATED. Marked into squares, or trapezoids; a pavement laid with square stones of different colors.

TEST. In chemistry, anything by which we distinguish the chemical nature of substances from each other; thus, infusion of galls is a test of the presence of iron, which it renders evident by the production of a black color in water and other liquids containing that metal; in the same way, sulphuretted hydrogen is a test of the presence of lead, and nitrate of baryta, of sulphuric acid. In metallurgy and assaying, the porous crucible which absorbs the liquid vitrifiable oxide of lead and other metals combined with it is sometimes called the test.

TESTA. The shell or integument of a seed.

TESTACEANS. Animals provided with a shell; pertaining to shells.

TESTES. The glands which produce the reproductive secretion of male animals.

TESTUDINATA. A tribe of animals like the tortoise, furnished with a carapace or horny covering. Testudinate, roofed or arched.

TETANUS. Locked jaw.

TETHERING. Fastening cattle or horses by a rope, or chain, to a post or tree, to give them a limited pasturage.

TETRADYNAMIA. Having four long and two short stamens, as the cruciferous plants.

TETRAGONA. The New Zealand spinach.

TETRAGYNIA. Having four pistils.

TETRANDRIA. With four stamens.

TETTER. This is a skin disease in the horse called eczema, a moist tetter, showing red and inflamed, and often torn by the animal. Blisters arise which discharge. Tetter somewhat resembles mange, and is often mistaken for that more serious disease. It differs however, in that it is not produced by an insect, and is not contagious. The remedy is, to open the bowels with a moderate dose of aloes, and if the bowels continue irregular thereafter with fœtid dung, give night and morning a ball composed of one half ounce of powdered gentian and one ounce of bisulphate of soda. As an application for the tetter, good also for other skin disorders, an ointment composed of equal parts of soft soap, tar and alcohol is good. Paint the tetter with this, and also the surrounding parts, twice a day.

TETTIGONIANS. The *Cicadians*, or locusts.

TEXAN CATTLE. Texan cattle are now-a-days too well known in the principal beef markets of the United States and along the lines of our trunk railways to need particular description. Originally derived from the Spanish cattle brought over by early adventurers, they covered all the great grazing plains of Mexico, Texas, and California, becoming to all intents and purposes, feral or wild cattle. So that, from the time of their introduction, about the year 1500, notwithstanding the immense numbers annually killed, and until within a few years, principally for their hides and tallow, they had increased in the State of Texas alone, in 1870, to the number of over 4,000,000 head, and at that time consti-

GROUP OF TEXAN CATTLE.

COST OF GOVERNMENT

AS SHOWN BY

The Taxation of various Nations.

NATIONS.	Per Inhabitant.	Total Amount in Thousands.
Denmark	13.25	20,150
Portugal	9.75	41,100
Sw. and Nor.	7.50	52,400
Holland	13.00	52,500
Belgium	12.50	68,250
Spain	12.25	203,500
Austria	10.00	368,500
Italy	13.00	371,500
Russia	5.00	424,500
Germany	11.50	517,050
Great Britain	17.75	618,865
France	19.25	720,225
United States	13.25	799,000

The full colors represent Local Taxes.
The light colors represent National Taxes.

tuting about one-seventh of the cattle of the United States and Territories. Impatient of restraint, never becoming really domesticated, they are reared in great herds and within the last fifteen years have been driven north in vast numbers, furnishing cheap, and, when properly fattened, it must be confessed, good beef. A fair estimate of the average of these cattle, as they are sold in our markets, may be put at 1,000 pounds live weight, of which the flesh and bone, as sold to the consumer, may be 400 pounds, the balance being hide, offal, and a very little tallow. Corn-fed for some months, they will come to the average of 1,200 pounds, live weight, with possibly 600 to 700 pounds of marketable meat and bone, as weighed from the butcher's block. They are principally corn-fed in the States of Kansas, Iowa, and Illinois, the plan generally practiced being to feed them in herds in the open fields. Some attempts have been made to stallfeed them, but it has not proved satisfactory. In 1868-69 the editor fed 450 in central Illinois in stables specially prepared therefor, having water conducted in pipes to them, with tramways for carrying grain and hay. They were dragged into the stables with lariats, tied to the stanchions, and remained there until fat, at the end of five months. The stables were kept partially darkened, no strangers were allowed admittance, and every means used to ensure their quiet. They came out ripe, and sold in New York at the very highest price of prime beef; out of the 450 put in, only about thirty being classed lower than fat. The experiment, however, was not repeated, since the larger price required to be paid for good grade short-horns yielded a better profit for the feed consumed. The typical Texan steer is being less and less met with year by year and now the acclimatization of pure bred bulls in Texas is being more and more shown in the improved form and fattening qualities of these semi-wild Texan stock. The most improved plan of acclimating bulls taken from the North and West is to select healthy calves in the autumn after all danger of Texas fever is past. Ship them to the point where they are to be kept, being careful not to crowd too many in one car. Arrived at their destination they are fed meal, bran, and crushed oats, with plenty of corn leaves or good hay, and with access to pure running water to drink. If possible, a run should be allowed on a field of green barley or oats, sown for the purpose. They must also be kept in dry lots and carefully housed from northern and other storms. Prompt attention must be paid to any symptoms of fever. If this is shown, charcoal and ginger may be administered in the proportion of a tablespoonful of charcoal and a teaspoonful of ginger. If they are gotten safely along through January they will generally be safe until the spring rains. During this time and until July they must not be exposed to storms or sun, and must be carefully watched for ticks and other vermin. These must be immediately destroyed by an application of crude petroleum and lard in the proportion of one part of the former to two parts of the latter. Thus, if they are carried safely, until two years old, with proper care, they may thereafter be kept for breeding purposes.

TEXAS FEVER. This is a malignant disease that has been characterized by a number of names, as Spanish fever, Texas fever, Splenic fever, and also by the general name of Texas plague. It is a disease originating in the lowlands of Texas and Mexico, a contagious fever, in some respects said to resemble, in its effects on the system, the rinderpest of Asiatic Russia. It is, however, less destructive and less contagious, since cattle affected in one pasture will not communicate it to those in another pasture, if divided by an impassable barrier. The contagion is communicated by cattle passing over the feeding grounds of Texans, or by traveling over roads infected. It is destroyed by the first frost that occurs, and it is fairly well demonstrated that northern animals affected, do not communicate the disease to others. The organs principally affected are the fourth stomach, the spleen, and the bowels, and the period of incubation varies from four to six weeks. There is slight fever, dulness, drooping of the head, glassy and watery eyes, arched back, loss of appetite, cough, trembling, increased heat of the system, the urine becomes high colored, and then very dark, the mouth and rectum become a dark red or copper color, the dung is hard, and sometimes coated with blood. The animal continues to get worse and worse, and at length dies in a stupor or convulsions. As a rule treatment has not been found effectual. If taken early, and the animals removed to a clean pasture, it is recommended to give them the following dose two or three times a day: One-half ounce chlorate of potash, one ounce tincture of chloride of iron, in a quart of water, and if there is much weakness, to stimulate the system freely with whisky. As soon as the animal begins to mend, light and nourishing food should be allowed, and the following tonic twice a day: one-half ounce of sulphate of iron and one ounce of tincture of ginger, in a quart of water. Prof. Gamgee, who made an elaborate report of this disease to the United States goverment, upon the great outbreak of the disease in the West, in 1868, advises shelter, friction of the limbs, the bowels to be moved by injections and ounce doses of laudanum during the first few days, to be followed by stimulants of one half ounce of sulphuric ether, four ounces of solution of acetate of ammonia, to be given in a quart of linseed tea or water, three times a day. The disease, where spread by Texas cattle, is so deadly that but little can be done, once it makes its appearance, except to prevent its spread. The following, from the proceedings of the National Convention, convened at Springfield, Ill., following the last great outbreak in the West, will serve as a guide, as the proper repressive measures. The action there taken seems to have resulted in the preventing of a repetition of the disease. The report of the action of the convention is taken from the transactions of the Ohio agricultural report of 1868. As early as 1849 a disease was noticed among cattle on the western borders of Missouri, which was attributed to a contagion spread from droves of Texan cattle which about that time began to be brought into the State. For several years the importation of these cattle into Missouri and Kansas steadily increased, while the disease referred to prevailed only in some seasons. In 1858 this cattle trade was greatly extended and the cattle disease increased in proportion. So serious was the evil, and so manifestly did it depend on a contagion spread from imported cattle, that, in 1861, the Legislature of Kansas attempted to stay its ravages by restrictive enactments. The importation of cattle was totally interrupted during the late war, but promptly resumed after its close, and with this resumption there was a return of the disease among the native cattle of Kansas and Missouri. This was followed by protective legislation in Missouri, and additional restrictions upon the trade in Kansas. During the season of 1868 Texas cattle were still more largely imported, immense stock yards had been opened at Abilene, on the Union Pacific Railroad, in Kansas, from which upwards of two thousand car loads of cattle were carried to the grazing States, or to the eastern market. Another route was opened by New Orleans, and up the Mississippi river by steamboat, and still another by land to the mouth of the Red river, and thence up the Mississippi. By these routes not less than 100,000 head of Texas cattle were brought into the State of Illinois, in 1868. With this influx of cattle from Texas the Texas fever appeared with great violence in the States of Illinois, Indiana and Ohio in the months of June and July, and was soon heard of in other states both east and west. The loss to stockholders became ruinous in the extreme, and excitement widely prevailed. In the town of Tolono, on the Illinois Central Railroad, 778 head of native cattle died; in the single county of Champaign, Illinois, there was a loss of 7,000 head, and in the fifth ward of the city of Chicago, the death of cows by this disease amounted to nearly 700. In some herds the loss exceeded ninety per cent., while others were wholly swept off by the pestilence. One of the most marked symptoms of Texas fever is a greatly accelerated pulse, from forty beats in a minute, which may be taken as the average for healthy oxen and cows; in this disease it sometimes rises as high as 120 beats in a minute. Another symptom usually present is a decided increase of the temperature of the animal after the fever is fully developed, but this is generally preceded during the formative stage by a chill. The excretions from the intestines and bladder are diminished in quantity and usually high colored or bloody; the secretion of milk is nearly suspended. A yellow mucous is discharged from the mouth and nostrils; the animal has a dejected look, hollow flanks, un arched back, an unsteady gait, and a rough coat. Many of these symptoms are also common to other cattle diseases. It may be presumed, therefore, that the most expert veterinarian would hesitate to pronounce a case one of Texas fever without taking into account all the attending circumstances. This presents no evidence of disease of the lungs or air passages, but little that is unnatural can be found in the first three stomachs; the fourth stomach usually shows congestion, and the intestines are still more engorged and blood stained. The liver is not often materially affected, but the gall bladder is almost always filled with dark colored and thickened bile. The spleen is always enlarged; in health it weighs in mature animals from one pound to a pound and a half; while in cattle that die of Texas fever it sometimes weighs as much as eight pounds. The kidneys are congested and their secretion in the bladder is bloody or blood stained. The contagious character of the disease is supposed to be established by the following evidence: There is no such disease known in any part of the country through which Texas cattle have not passed, and whenever the disease has appeared among native cattle it is only among such as have pastured upon lands previously grazed or traveled over by Texas cattle, or that have used water running from a field in which Texas cattle were kept or watered. The disease does not appear to be communicated through the atmosphere alone, but only when cattle come in contact with, and can take up with their food or drink the excretions of Texas cattle. When Texas cattle have been brought from their homes during the winter months there is no evidence that the fever has followed in their trail, but when they arrive in the northern States as late as June or July, the native cattle of these States that are exposed, die almost universally. Doubt of the contagious nature of this disease or of the contagion originating with Texas cattle has existed in some minds, because it is an admitted fact that some of the cattle which have been supposed to communicate the disease, have no manifestations of it themselves. Can cattle communicate a disease without having it? is urged as though it were a question impossible to answer in the affirmative. To this it may be replied that the history of some of the diseases affecting the human subject afford cases precisely analogous. Prisoners confined in ill-ventilated dungeons before the days of prison reform, have often given typhus fever to a whole court at the time of trial, while the prisoners themselves had been steeped so gradually in the poisonous atmosphere that their system had become accommodated to it, and hence they have escaped altogether, although the poisonous exhalations from their bodies have spread death all around. A person protected by vaccination from small-pox may have that modified and trifling form of disease known as varioloid, but such a person may communicate fatal small-pox to another person not protected by vaccination. It may therefore be presumed that Texas cattle have come so gradually under the influence of the cause of the mischief or have in some way become comparatively insusceptible to its action so that they escape the deadly form of the malady, and yet can transmit its seeds to more susceptible animals. Others have hesitated to admit the contagiousness of the disease, because the attack does not appear in some cases until a long time after the exposure. This, however, presents no difficulty to persons familiar with the history of other contagious diseases. Many of them require a period sometimes definite, sometimes indefinite, after the exposure, for the incubation of the disease. This period varies greatly, and in Texas fever it may extend to forty days, and even more. The above recital of symptoms, post mortem appearances, and evidence of the contagious character of the Texas fever, the disease must still be regarded as unsatisfactory, without additional light on the true cause and source of the mischief. Happily for us the microscope has done in this case what it has done in so many others, it has brought to view and made us acquainted with very potential agencies which are altogether invisible to the unassisted eye. Dr. M. Morris, of New York, one of the board of health of that city, read to the convention an exceedingly interesting paper, giving the results of examinations with the microscope of both solids and fluids of hundreds of animals that had died or had been killed while laboring under Texas fever. These investigations disclose the fact that the fluids of animals affected with this disease, the urine, the blood, and more especially the bile, are infested and practically destroyed by the spores of a minute cryptogam or fungous plant. These spores which take the place of seeds in more highly organized plants are multiplied by a simple process which admits of unlimited continuation and of almost inconceivable rapidity. They have the form and organization of simple cells, each cell or spore under favorable circumstances would produce the little plant known to microscopists as *Tilletia caries*, the plant in turn would produce other spores but under different conditions, as for example, when immersed in animal fluids the spore does not produce a plant, but multiplies itself after the manner of simple cells. Each spore contracts at the center, then divides, and either end has at once the power and activity of its parent, and the process of multiplication by what is called fission, goes on indefinitely, or so long as the fluid in which it is immersed has fresh organic matter to sustain the life of new cells or spores. In relation to this cryptogam, it was said to be found abundantly in the blood and bile of every animal that died of the fever or that was killed while suffering from its effects. Cattle of the Northern States, while unaffected by Texas fever, have no such cryptogamous parasites in their fluids, but the same parasite was to be found invariably in Texas cattle, although regarded as healthy. It was also stated that this, or at least, allied fungous growths had been observed growing parasitically upon the grasses native to Texas, so that it might readily pass into the bodies of animals with their food. While the vigor of the animals is maintained at a natural standard the growth of the parasite is restrained, but when the animal is subjected to hard driving and scarcity of food and water, all of which diminish his vitality, then the parasite has less and less to overcome, until all the nutritious and recumentitious fluids are destroyed or vitiated. That the animal, while allowed to remain in circumstances where his vital force is unimpaired, should be able to resist the injurious influence of the parasite, but should succumb to its attack when debilitated by hard usage is in correspondence with innumerable facts in the history of other diseases. To some in the Springfield convention it seemed incredible that a minute, and to the unassisted eye invisible organism could, by any possibility, destroy the life of an animal as strong and as large as the ox; the same doubt will probably be suggested to the mind of many who will read reports of the proceedings. It should be borne in mind, however, .ha what are called the lower forms of life, such as cryptogamia and protozoa, rank lower than other organisms only in regard to some of the manifestations of vitality, their reproductive force is vastly greater than that of more perfect beings. The structure of the cryptogam being very simple, it is almost limited in its functions to the one end of reproduction, and this is carried on with singular energy. Its attack, therefore, is not from without but from within. The nutritious fluids of the animal are assailed, and all appropriated to the uses of the little parasite until the animal that harbors its myriads must ultimately die of starvation, if death, in more violent form, does not sooner occur. Comparatively recent discoveries claim to have established that all epiphytic and epizootic diseases, as well as all contagious epidemics, and many of the endemic diseases to which humanity is liable, are of cryptogamic or protozoic origin. The oidium that has almost destroyed the grape crop of Europe, the potato rot, cholera, small pox, measles and intermittent fever are notable examples said to depend on such causes. Whether these claims be all admitted or not, they open a most interesting field of inquiry for patient and truth loving investigators. It may, perhaps be some relief to timid persons to learn that no facts were presented to the convention by the health officers of New York or Chicago, showing that Texas fever or any other sickness was given to persons who unwittingly used the flesh or milk of animals affected with this disease. Whatever entozoon should conceal himself in our food, so long as that food is properly cooked there is no probability that it can do mischief to the human subject. Carbolic or phenic acid, the product of the distillation of coal tar, is one of the most powerful antiseptics known. It is especially inimical to the lower forms of vegetable and animal life; a solution so dilute as to contain not more than half of one per cent. the acid being sufficient to destroy such organisms almost instantly. It can not be administered to any animal in large quantity, but it has been supposed that it might be administered and taken into the circulation in quantity sufficient to destroy the parasites without materially injuring the health of the animal. The result of the experiment appears to have been in some instances what was desired, and persons have become quite sanguine of the success of this treatment. It is perhaps safer to say that the result is sufficiently favorable to warrant further trial; but the facts thus far observed do not justify us in regarding the carbolic acid or anything else as a specific. This disease affords a marked example of the soundness of the old proverb, that an ounce of prevention is worth a pound of cure. The Texas fever can be effectually kept from any locality only by keeping out the cattle by which it is introduced. There is no disinfectant known that can be absolutely relied on to prevent the communication of the disease. The convention, with entire unanimity, recommended to the legislatures of all States liable to be visited by Texas cattle, to pass stringent laws prohibiting their importation or transportation during the summer months. The recommendation of the convention relative to this subject is in the following terms:

Whereas, A malignant disease among cattle, known as Texas fever, has been widely disseminated by the transit of southwestern cattle through the Western and Northwestern States during the warm season of the year, occasioning great loss to our farmers, and possibly endangering the health of our citizens; therefore,

Resolved, That this convention earnestly recommend the enactment, by these States, of stringent laws to prevent the transit through their limits of Texas or Cherokee cattle, from the first day of March to the first day of November, inclusive.

Resolved, That the interests of the community require the enactment of laws making any person responsible for all damages that may result from the diffusion of any disease from animals in his ownership or possession.

In addition, to these resolutions, the following draft of a bill was adopted and recommended to such States in the East or on principal routes of transportation as might require its provisions. The first article provides for the appointment of three commissioners, or such other number as may be necessary, by competent authority, to hold their office for five years, and report annually to the legislature. Such commissioner shall have power to watch over the general welfare of animals within the State for which they are appointed, and particularly to prevent the spread of dangerous diseases among them, and to protect the people of the State from the dangers arising from the consumption of diseased meat. They may from time to time appoint such assistant commissioners to aid them in the discharge of their duties, as the public good may require. They should have power to administer oaths, and to prescribe from time to time such rules and regulations as may be necessary to accomplish the object of their appointment. They shall give public notice of the outbreak of any dangerous disease, and such practical directions for its avoidance as they may deem necessary. They may either place such diseased cattle in quarantine or cause them to be killed, as may seem necessary for the public protection; but in the latter case they shall cause an appraisal of such cattle to be made, and the county or State shall pay such proportion of the appraised value as may be provided by law. The second article provides that the commissioners, or any assistant commissioner, located on the frontier of any State, shall have power, at such times as may be prescribed by the commissioners, to inspect all the animals brought into such State, whether by railroad cars, vessels or common roads, and shall have power to detain such railroad cars, vessels and drovers of animals on common roads, long enough to make a proper investigation of them, for the purpose of ascertaining their sanitary condition. No animal shall be permitted to enter the State which shall be deemed by such assistant commissioner to be capable of diffusing dangerous diseases, or of injuring the health of the inhabitants. No train shall be allowed to proceed unless the animals contained therein have been supplied with food, water and rest within twenty-four hours next preceding the time of such inspection. All animals shall have rest and have access to food and water for twenty-four hours after having traveled a similar period. The railroad companies shall provide the suitable yards for feeding, watering and resting animals traveling on the trains, and for quarantine purposes, which shall be kept cleanly and in wholesome condition, to the satisfaction of the commissioners. Each train, on leaving its point of departure, shall have certificates, signed by an assistant commissioner, which shall certify that all the animals therein contained were in a healthy condition at the time of its departure, and also the exact time of leaving; and such certificates and endorsements thereon of the time of resting and time of departure of the train at subsequent resting and feeding places, shall be exhibited to the proper authorities whenever required. Proper penalties should be inserted to prevent the bribery of officers charged with the execution of these provisions; and also for those who interfere with or resist the officers charged with the execution of these duties.

TEXTILE CROPS. The principal textile crops produced in the United States are cotton, flax and hemp. Flax indeed can hardly be ranked as a textile crop, since the fiber is only considered a secondary product anywhere. Generally it is regarded simply as a waste product. Jute and ramie are still in the experimental stage of progression. Among the plants the cultivation of which has been undertaken in the South and abandoned, sisal hemp *Agave sisalana*, and the pulque plant, *Agave pulque*, may be mentioned. The first is used exclusively for its strong fiber, and the latter furnished the Mexican liquor pulque and its fiber the paper of the ancient Aztecs. So also the attempt to introduce the cultivation of the Indian mallow *Abutilon avicenna* in Illinois is worthy of mention. It was hoped that this plant, which has become a noxious weed might be allowed since the method of preparation of the fiber was very much similar to that of flax. Yet the cultivation did not prove remunerative. Among the textile and cordage fibers not generally known, and mostly the production of tropical and subtropical countries may be noticed. *Agave Mexicana*, or aloe; the *Heliconea Caribea*, or Brasilier; *Musa textilis*, or abaca; hemps of Saigon, a species of *Urtica*, or nettle, from Cochin China; also string made from the fiber; *Coir*, or cocoanut fiber, of which a coarse rope is made; fiber, of the *Ananas*, or pineapple, apparently very good; *Battenbong* and *Suntang*, hemp-like fiber from Cochin China—very fine and apparently strong; fiber made from the stalks of the *Hibiscus esculentus*, or the common okra of our gardens; also, fiber made from the *Brom·lia karatas* (?) and banana. A curious kind of fibrous cloth is also made by beating the inner bark of the *Brousonetia papyrifera*, or paper mulberry in Tahiti, as likewise from the *Dawron* bark and *Ficus prolixa* from New Caledonia. As showing the annual production of textile fibers in the United States, including wool and silk, the following table for three decennial periods will be interesting as evidencing the status of these products:

Year.	Cotton.	Hemp.	Flax.	Wool.	Silk cocoons
	Bales.	Tons.	Pounds.	Pounds.	Pounds
18·0	2,469,093	34,871	7,709.876	52,5 6,959	10,843
1·60	5,387,052	74,493	4,740,145	60,364,113	11,044
1870	3,011,996	12,746	27,133,034	100,102,387	3,837

In 1878 there was produced, cotton, 5,200,000 bales of 450 pounds each. Flax, fiber, hemp and silk have grown less, though the acreage and yield of flax for seed holds its own. It will be seen from the table we have given, that outside of cotton the fiber crops of the United States do not aggregate a large sum. It seems quite safe to say that for many yet to come that the two staple fibers, of the United States will be cotton in the South and wool in the North. If machinery can be devised for cheaply converting other fiber crops into merchantable fibers of high quality, then, flax in the North, hemp in the Middle States, and ramie and jute in the South will take important rank, and other tropical and subtropical plants will also be brought into active importance.

THALAMUS. In anatomy, the part of the brain from which the optic nerves have part of their origin. In botany, the part on which the ovary is seated. The succulent red center of a strawberry, the core in the fruit of a raspberry, are the thalami of these plants. Some botanists call it receptacle of the fruit.

THALLUS. The leaf-like expansion of lichens, sea-weeds, etc. Hence these plants are sometimes called *Thallogens*, or *Thallophytes*.

THATCH. Straw, or any other dry vegetable substance, laid on the top of a building, rick, etc., to keep out the wet. There are many different materials that may be made use of as thatch, but the straw of wheat and rye, when well laid, forms the neatest and most secure covering for general purposes. The reed is a highly valuable article for the purpose of thatch, where a lasting roof is required; but is much too expensive at first, although it is cheapest in the end. Reed is also thought to be too stubborn for common purposes. In relation to the economy of thatching it is unfortunately true, that farmers often lose money for want of some waterproof covering to stacks and ricks. Very few stackers are able so carefully to lay a stack that it will not take more or less rain, especially when accompanied by driving winds. Yet if the crown of the stack is carefully topped, and thatch of some material carried well down to the shoulders of the stack, but little difficulty will be experienced. Cornstalks, leaves and all, laid with the butts up, commencing at the lower end of the slope, and so lapped that only about one-third of the stalks are uncovered, make a good thatch. Where lumber is cheap we have seen wide boards used, lapped as in siding, with good effect. The mode of thatching in a rough way will readily suggest itself to the intelligent farmer.

THECA. A case, usually the urn of mosses, in which their spores are situated.

THECOSTOMES. The class of insects which have their suckers surrounded by a sheath or case.

THEINE. The active principle in tea, *Thea viridis*, giving it its invigorating or stimulant quality. It is the same in coffee, *Coffea Arabica*. In coffee it is called caffein, the leaves containing more than the berries. The fruit of *Paullinia sorbilis*, a plant found in the valley of the Amazon, belonging to the family *Sapindaceæ*, contains a remarkable quantity of *Theine*, the alkaloid, being known as *Guaranine*. The kola nut, *Cola acuminata*, and Paraguay tea, also contain notable quantities of *Theine*. Good black tea contains of *Theine* 2.13 per cent.; various samples of coffee beans, 0.8 to 1 per cent.; dried coffee leaves, 1.26; *Guarana*, 5.07; kola, 2.13. Paraguay tea contains 1.25 per cent. of *Theine*. Thus it will be seen that one of the substances named is more than twice as rich as tea and another equal to it. (See article Tea.)

THEODOLITE. A surveying instrument for measuring both vertical and horizontal angles, necessary in accurate surveys.

THEORY. The expression of a general law based all on numerously ascertained facts. An hypothesis is merely a guess, without any basis on fact.

THERAPEUTICS. The science which treats of the action of medicines.

THERMOMETER. An instrument for measuring variations of heat or temperature. Fahrenheit's thermometer is the one generally used, the freezing point of which is 32° and the boiling point 212° at the sea level. In the arts and sciences, and especially in chemistry, Reaumer's and the Centigrade are often used. The following table will show the correspondence between the thermometers of Reaumer, Centigrade and Fahrenheit:

Reaum.	Cent.	Fahr.	Reaum.	Cent.	Fahr.
80	100.	212.	29	36.25	97.25
79	98.75	209.75	28	35.	95.
78	97.5	207.5	27	33.75	92.75
77	96.25	205.25	26	32.5	90.5
76	95.	203.	25	31.25	88.25
75	93.75	200.75	24	30.	86.
74	92.5	198.5	23	28.75	83.75
73	91.25	196.25	22	27.5	81.5
72	90.	194.	21	26.25	79.25
71	88.75	191.75	20	25.	77.
70	87.5	189.5	19	23.75	74.75
69	86.25	187.25	18	22.5	72.5
68	85.	185.	17	21.25	70.25
67	83.75	182.75	16	20.	68.
66	82.5	180.5	15	18.75	65.75
65	81.25	178.25	14	17.5	63.5
64	80.	176.	13	16.25	61.25
63	78.75	173.75	12	15.	59.
62	77.5	171.5	11	13.75	56.75
61	76.25	169.25	10	12.5	54.5
60	75.	167.	9	11.25	52.25
59	73.75	164.75	8	10.	50.
58	72.5	162.5	7	8.75	47.75
57	71.25	160.25	6	7.5	45.5
56	70.	158.	5	6.25	43.25
55	68.75	155.75	4	5.	41.
54	67.5	153.5	3	3.75	38.75
53	66.25	151.25	2	2.5	36.5
52	65.	149.	1	1.25	34.25
51	63.75	146.85	0	0.	32.
50	62.5	144.5	1	1.25	29.75
49	61.25	142.25	2	2.5	27.5
48	60	140.	3	3.75	25.25
47	58.75	137.75	4	5.	23.
46	57.5	135.5	5	6.25	20.75
45	56.25	133.25	6	7.5	18.5
44	55.	131.	7	8.75	16.25
43	53.75	128.75	8	10.	14.
42	52.5	126.5	9	11.25	11.75
41	51.25	124.25	10	12.5	9.5
40	50.	142.	11	13.75	7.25
39	48.75	119.75	12	15.	5.
38	47.5	117.5	13	16.25	2.75
37	46.25	115.25	14	17.5	0.5
36	45.	113.	15	18.75	1.75
35	43.75	110.75	16	20.	4.
34	42.5	108.5	17	21.25	6.25
33	41.25	106.25	18	22.5	8.5
32	40.	104.	19	23.75	10.75
31	38.75	101.75	20	25.	13.
30	37.5	99.			

THERMOSCOPE. A general term, including any instrument for measuring heat.

THIBITIAN GOAT. (See Goat.)

THICK LEG. (See Shot of Grease.)

THINNING OUT. Removing some plants, branches of a tree, or fruit to give the rest a better opportunity of growing large. It is an important operation in the orchard, as a tree over-burdened with fruit will not produce such fine specimens as one that has fewer to perfect.

THISTLE. *Circium*. There are numerous species, ten principal ones being enumerated in the North. They are all more annoying than noxious, except the dreaded Canada thistle. All are marked by the stalks, leaves and flower-heads being more or less prickly, by the heads being many-flowered, of a reddish purple or cream color, by the leaves on the stalks being sessile, alternate, often pinnatifid, and prickly, and by the seed being armed with *pappus*, or hairs, uniting in a ring, by which they are carried by the wind. Of the principal species, the common thistle. *C. lanciolatum* is naturalized from

Europe, *C. muticum* is the swamp thistle, *C. pumilum* is the pasture thistle, *C. horridulum* is the yellow thistle, and *C. arvense* is the Canada thistle.

THORAX. The chest. The cavity of the chest is termed the thoracic cavity, and contains the heart and lungs. In entomology, the second segment of the frame.

THORACIC. Relating to the chest. The thoracic duct is a vessel which receives the contents of the lacteals and absorbents, and conveys it to the blood by the subclavian vein.

THORN. A name given to the hawthorn, and also generally applied to all spined, and even imperfectly spined plants, used for hedging.

THORN APPLE. Jamestown weed, Jimson weed, stink weed, *Datura stramonium*. A dangerous, unsightly and noxious weed, naturalized all over the United States, a member of the nightshade family, and known by its bad odor, large, funnel-shaped flower with plaited border, and by the spined, dark green seed pods. Children eating the seeds are poisoned, often fatally. The plant is valuable in medicine, but should be exterminated when found. It is a native of Asia and tropical America, but being an annual, readily propagates itself by seed. Some greenhouse species are very handsome.

THOROUGHBRED. The word Thoroughbred does not mean, as many suppose, an animal of pure blood, that is unmixed. If so, any wild animal would be a thoroughbred. The word thoroughbred is used to designate animals bred from the best blood, but originally derived from a mixture of races, as the short-horn cattle, and racing horses. In the articles Blood Horse, American and English, and in the article Horse, and in the article Short-horns, will be found matters of general interest relative to thoroughbred horses and cattle. In this article it will only be necessary to notice the essentials in thoroughbreds as applied to the horse. Mr. J. H. Walsh, (Stonehenge) a well known and competent English authority, in relation to the object for encouraging the breed of horses writes graphically and logically upon the thoroughbred. It will be of interest. The great object of encouraging the breed of racehorses, our authority states, is lost sight of, if suitable crosses for hunting, cavalry, and hack-mares can not be obtained from their ranks. In these three kinds, soundness of the feet and legs is all important, together with a capacity to bear a continuation of severe work. These qualities are highly developed in the Arab, and until lately were met with in his descendants on the English turf. Even now a horse with a stain in his pedigree will not bear the amount of training which a thoroughbred will sustain, his health and spirits soon giving way if forced to go through the work which the race horse requires to make him fit. But the legs and feet of the latter are the drawbacks to his use, and the trainer of the present day will generally be sadly taxed to make them last through a dry summer. Our modern roads are also much harder since the introduction of macadamization, and thus, in proportion to our greater demands, is the absence of the material to meet them. A hack that is not pretty well bred is now neglected, except for high weights, because his paces are not soft and pleasant, and he does not satisfy the eye. But how many of the fashionable sort will bear constant use on the road without becoming lame? And how many sound horses are there to be met with out of a hundred, taken at random from the ranks of any kind, tolerably well bred? Every horse proprietor will tell you, scarcely five per cent.; and some will even go so far as to say, that a sound horse is utterly unknown. Even though the thoroughbred horse is well fitted to compete with others in all cases where speed is the chief point of trial—as in flat-racing, steeple-chasing, hunting, etc.,—and yet he is not so well qualified for some kinds of harness work, or for road work of any kind, as the horse expressly bred for these purposes. There is no doubt that thoroughbred horses might be selected and bred solely for speed, without much reference to these other qualities, it is useless to expect much improvement; but, on the contrary, they may be expected to become yearly more and more soft and yielding. For many purposes the Eastern horse is wholly unfit—as, for instance, for heavy and dead pulls; here his high courage, light weight, and hasty temper are adverse to the performance of the task, for he is far excelled by the old English, or modern improved cart-horse. No thoroughbred horse would try again and again at a dead pull like many of our best breeds of cart-horses; and therefore he is little calculated for work which requires this slow struggling kind of exertion. The pull of the Eastern horse, or his descendant, is a snatch; and though it may to a certain extent be modified by use, yet it can never be brought up to the standard of the English cart-horse, even if the weight of carcase and size and strength of limb of the former could be sufficiently increased. Such then are the general qualities of the thoroughbred horse and the purposes to which he can be beneficially applied. It remains now to consider the formation and specific characteristics best adapted to the turf, which is his chief arena; and also to the hunting-field, which now absorbs a very large number of his breed. Finally, it will be necessary to consider him as a means of improving other breeds, such as the cavalry-charger, hack and harness horse, and for the stable. In the first place purity of blood must be considered as a *sine quâ non*, for without it a horse can not be considered thoroughbred, and therefore we have only to ascertain the exact meaning of the term blood. It is not to be supposed that there is any real difference between the blood of the thoroughbred horse and that of the half-bred animal; no one could discriminate between the two by any known means; the term blood is here synonymous with breed; and by purity of blood is meant purity in the breeding of the individual animal under consideration; that is to say, that the horse which is entirely bred from one source is pure from any mixture with any other, and may be a pure Suffolk Punch, or a pure Clydesdale, or a pure thoroughbred horse. But all these terms are comparative, since there is no such animal as a perfectly purely bred horse of any breed, whether cart-horse, hack, or racehorse; all have been produced from an admixture with other kinds, and though now

THOROUGHBRED STALLION VOLTIGEUR.

THRESHING BY STEAM.

kept as pure as possible, yet they were originally compounded from varying elements; and thus the racehorse of 1700, was obtained from a mixture of Turks, Arabs, and Barbs. Even the best and purest thoroughbreds are stained with some slight cross with the old English or Spanish horse, as has been heretofore shown; therefore it is only by comparison that the word pure is applicable to them or any others. But since the thoroughbred horse, as he is called, has long been bred for the race course, and selections have been made with that view alone, it is reasonable to suppose that this breed is the best for that purpose, and that a stain of any other is a deviation from the clearest stream into one more muddy, and therefore impure; the consequence is, that the animal bred from the impure source fails in some of the essential characteristics of the pure breed, and is in so far useless for this particular object. Now, in practice this is found to be the case, for in every instance it has resulted that the horse bred with the slightest deviation from the sources indicated by the stud-book, is unable to compete in lasting power with those which are entirely of pure blood. Hence it is established as a rule, that for racing purposes every horse must be a thoroughbred; that is, descended from a sire and dam whose names are met with in the stud-book. On page 943 we give a life-like illustration of the well-known racer, Voltigeur, which will show the admirable make-up of this wonderful subfamily of horses.

THOROUGH PIN. Thorough pin is a dropsical effusion, or enlargement of the sheath of the tendon which passes along the upper and posterior side of the hock joint, a synovial effusion in the bursa of the flexor muscle, and is similar to bog spavin and wind galls; both may exist, or be found separately without occasioning lameness. The best means of relief is by pressure, and cold applications alternately. The best means, unless a veterinarian is employed, is as given, the horse to wear a high shoe to relieve pressure, and a spring truss with rest. The difficulty with all this class is that the swelling is apt to return when the pressure is removed.

THRESHING. The old-time plan of threshing with the flail, is now only resorted to in those cases where it is necessary to save the straw of full length, and practically unbroken. This being the object, hand threshing by the flail has not been practically superseded by the use of machines. So again the most ancient practice of threshing by tramping with animals, is not now practiced except to a limited extent, and then generally only in the case of oats, when the straw is required for feeding cattle, it being well known that stock will eat straw better from under the feet of horses than if thrashed in any other way. The steam threshing machine of to-day is probably the perfection of swift, clean, and cheap threshing, many of the larger class of steam driven machines working up to 1,000 bushels, and even more in good wheat, per day; the practical limit of horse machines being less than half this amount, the grain being winnowed in the most perfect manner, and the straw at the same operation being delivered, by means of an automatic carrier, directly on the straw stack. Various devices have been patented for threshing by means of power machines, among them beaters and rotating flails. The spiked cylinder

is, however, in most general use, being faster than any other known device. The chief improvements of late years in threshing have been in perfecting the winnowing apparatus, especially in regulating the blast from the fan, which is sometimes so strong as to blow the grain off the riddle. These devices have in view an automatic arrangement of the entrance passage for air, whereby, when the machinery moves rapidly, the size of the passage is decreased and the quantity of air admitted thus diminished, the operation being analogous to that of a governor of a steam engine, although the appliances nowhere resemble it. The theory of operation observed in several of these is this: The blast from the fan is directed against a flap, which communicates, by means of a lever, with a valve on the air opening. When the blast is moderate the valve, which is weighted, remains open; but when the blast becomes violent, owing to the rapid motion of the fan, the flap is moved, and the lever connection closes the valve wholly or in part. As the machinery moves more slowly the force on the flap is withdrawn, and the valve opens automatically by reason of the weight. Most farmers in the West are practically acquainted with steam threshing. Not so all in older settled countries where small farms are the rule. To illustrate threshing by steam, we give on page 944 a cut of steam engine, thresher, and gearing, with elevator for carrying the straw to the stack. Every bushel of grain, of whatever kind, sent forward from the farm in anything but the most merchantable condition, costs the farmer a loss precisely in accordance with the freight on, and the handling of the trash contained; the cost of recleaning, and the added depreciation in value from reduction in the weight of the standard bushel; added to this the lower price obtained, from the general inferior appearance of the grain from all these causes combined. Added together, the whole amounts to three or four times the cost of careful recleaning at home. Threshers, who, in fair to good grain, always work by the bushel, of course wish to make as much measure as possible, by rushing the grain through, often imperfectly threshed, and of course full of dust, dirt, straw, and light grain. The first four causes constitute a dead loss to the farmer, whether he recleans or not. The light grain, if sold with the good, always causes depreciation in quality more than enough to counterbalance its weight. Thus the farmer really has no one to blame if he allows it to be so. A little intelligent supervision will obviate all but the latter evil of light grain. This may be made right by recleaning; for, if the grain be conscientiously threshed and cleaned, still a dead loss must ensue to the farmer if he allows the grain to go from him without recleaning, since all the light grain and trash, inseparable from the best machine work, counts as nothing to the miller who makes the flour. Retained at home, this is all available as feed in some shape, and will pay the cost of recleaning with a heavy percentage added. It will indeed pay alone in the freightage of the trash, since this never realizes the transportation charges; these charges are no inconsiderable item, when thousands of miles are estimated. Thus he retains the light grain at home, and saves freights, for light grain counts for nothing in the markets of the world. So he saves in the enhanced value of clean grain—the most important of all. Last, but by no means least, he has the satisfaction of knowing that he is reaping enhanced profits honestly earned, by sending his products to market in the best possible condition. Then again, the straw in many sections of the Northwest is coming to be of value, both as winter bedding for stock and as partial winter feeding. As taken from the carrier of the machine, it should be carefully stacked, tramping the middle of the stack as much as possible, keeping the center well up meanwhile, with the longer straw as much as possible at the outside, and carrying the ricks as high as feasible, without expending too much labor. These, if built pretty broad, and in L shape, or, as three sides of a hollow square, will afford excellent shelter for stock in winter, and at the same time make excellent winter feed for cattle, horses and mules, with the addition of a little corn or other grain. There is one other thing in this connection, not generally well understood by farmers; grain once in the stack, and well protected, should not be threshed sooner than six weeks after. It takes about this time to get through the sweat that always ensues after stacking, however dry the grain may be. The same may be said of hay. It should never be fed to stock while it is undergoing this sweat. If grain is to be threshed at once, it should be done directly from the shock. If the grain, after being in a heap over night, or longer, shows any disposition to heat, it should be thoroughly aired by being thrown from one side of the barn floor to the other, or by being run through the fanning mill; this process to be continued from time to time, until it is thoroughly dry. A little attention to the details we have mentioned, will save many dollars yearly to individual farmers. (See page 1120.)

THRIPS. These are minute orange-colored insects found in growing wheat heads, and said to subsist by sucking the juices of the unripe grains, causing them to shrivel. A usual remedy is to thoroughly dust the field with air-slaked, but dry lime. A species of leaf hopper, *Erythroneura*, is popularly but erroneously called the grape vine thrip, it sometimes severely injures the foliage of the vine by sucking the juices, causing them to assume a withered and spotted appearance, and sometimes to shed their leaves. The Entomologist of the Department of Agriculture, Washington, in one of the late reports says: The *Thripidæ* were placed by Westwood in a separate order called *Thysanoptera*, or fringed-winged insects, from their wings being ciliated or fringed. Packard places them in the *Hemiptera*. These insects possess two setiform, horny mandibles, which, by their juncture at the tip, form a two-valved syphon. They are of very small size, with bodies long, linear, and depressed; the four narrow wings are fringed with hair, and, when at rest, are laid horizontally along the back. By some naturalists they are said to injure wheat, etc. Dr. Packard says they are very injurious to grain and flowers, eating holes in the leaves or corollas, and sucking the sap from the flowers of wheat, in the bottom of which they hide. With a lens we have seen the sap oozing out of small punctures made by these insects on grape-leaves. Harris says, they live on leaves and flowers, in buds, or in the crevices of the bark of plants. Their punctures poison plants and often produce deformities in the leaves and blossoms.

Curtis in his work on farm-insects states that the European species, *Thrips (Limothripps) cerealis*, once destroyed one-third of the wheat-crop in Piedmont, and that the shriveled grains of wheat are caused by the thrips extracting the milky secretion. Westwood says that, the thrips infest wheat to a mischievous extent, causing the grain to shrink. These are only a few extracts from reliable authorities, to show that by some it is considered an injurious insect, and yet on the other hand Mr. Walsh once said he did not believe the true thrips to be a vegetable feeder, but that on the contrary they are cannibal insects preying upon injurious larvæ; and again he says, these insects have hitherto been considered to be vegetable-feeders, but are generally, if not universally, insectivorous, and feed upon the eggs of the wheat-midge (*Diplosis tritici*) and on gall-making larvæ. A small yellow thrips is mentioned in Mr. Riley's second report as destroying the eggs of the curculio or plum-weevil. From the above statements it appears that in certain cases the true thrips (not the insect generally known by the name of the grape-thrips, and which is a leaf-hopper), is in some degree beneficial by destroying other insects: but it appears to be very questionable if advantage from the few insects destroyed by them is at all commensurate with the injuries they inflict on our grain-crops, grape vines, fruit trees, and vegetation in general. The remedies suggested for the destruction of these insects, in gardens and greenhouses, are the same as those suggested for plant-lice (*Aphides*), such as dusting with slaked lime, syringing with whale oil, soap and water; or strong soap suds, tobacco water, or a decoction of aloes or quassia and water and soapsuds, taking care not to wet the fruit, when on grape-leaves. It must, however, here be again remarked that the insect, generally known as the grape-vine thrips, is a homopterous insect or leaf-hopper, which, when disturbed, leaps with great activity from the leaves, and is not of the same long, linear form as the true thrips, which generally remains stationary upon the leaf, or, at most, crawls slowly over it, and never flies in such swarms as the *Erythroneura*, or grape-vine leaf-hopper, whenever the vines are disturbed.

THROAT. Faux, the commencement of the tube of a personate or labiate flower.

THROWING FOR OPERATIONS. When any painful operation is to be performed on an animal, it must be securely fastened. This is done by hobbling and casting the animal, and then securely tying. For operations not requiring a long time, a pen may be made, three feet wide six feet long, with strong posts where the limbs will stand. To these the limbs may be securely bound, and the animal may be supported, if necessary, with slings. Secure the head, and he can neither bite nor kick. The manner of throwing is described in the Horse Owners' Cyclopædia as follows: Hobbles consist of four broad padded leather straps, provided with strong buckles, and long enough to encircle the pasterns. To each of these an iron ring is stitched, and to one of them a strong, soft rope, six yards in length, is securely attached. Provided with four, or, if possible, five assistants, the operator buckles the hobble with the rope attached to the near foreleg, and the remaining three to the other legs. Then passing the rope through their rings, and through the first also, it is held by three assistants, the nearest of whom stands about a yard from the horse, so as to pull upwards as well as away from him; a fourth assistant holds him by the head to keep him quiet, and to be ready to fall on it as soon as he is down, and the fifth stands at his quarters, ready to push him over on his off side. This place is sometimes occupied by the operator himself when short of hands. Casting should never be attempted on any hard surface, a thick bed of straw being necessary to prevent injury from the heavy fall which takes place. The hind legs should be brought as far forward as possible before beginning to pull the rope, and when the men do this they should do it with a will, but without jerking, so as to take the horse off his guard, when he will resist much less stoutly than if he is allowed more time. As soon as the legs are drawn up together, the man at the quarters is quite safe from injury, and he may lean forcibly against that part, and force the horse over to the off side, upon which he falls: the assistant at the head keeping that part down, no further struggling takes place, and he is secured by passing the end of the rope under the hobble rings between the fore and hind legs, and securing it with a hitch. Something more, however, is necessary to be done before any of the usual operations can be performed, as all of the legs are at liberty to a certain extent and the scrotum can not be reached in safety. The following further precautions must therefore be taken, varying according to the part to be operated on. For castration the horse should be cast on his near side, with a web halter in the usual place of a collar. The rope of the halter is then passed through the ring of the hobble on the off hind leg, and using it as a pulley the foot is drawn forcibly forward beyond the arm and firmly secured to the webbing around the neck, and bringing it back again it may be passed around the thigh above the hock (which should be guarded from friction by a soft cloth or leather), and again secured to the webbing. By these precautions the scrotum is completely exposed, and the hind legs can not be stirred beyond the slight spasmodic twitch which extends to the whole body. To perform any operation on the fore leg it must be taken out of its hobble, and drawn forward upon the straw by a webbing attached to its pastern, where it must be held by an assistant, the horse having little or no power over it in this position. The hind leg is secured in the same way as for castration, unless the fetlock is to be fired, when webbing must be applied to the thigh above the hock only. With most horses, however, firing can be performed without casting, by buckling up the fore leg, or by having it held by a competent assistant. When the horse is to be released, the hobbles are quietly unbuckled in succession, beginning with the undermost hind leg. Several improved hobbles have been invented, but they are suited rather for the veterinary surgeon than for the ordinary horsemaster, who will only require them for castration and minor operations. The side line is sometimes used for securing one hind leg thus: the long rope and single hobble only are required, the latter being buckled to the hind pastern, which is to be secured. The rope is then passed over the withers and brought back around the bosom and the shoulder of the same side as the leg to which it is secured, and then passed inside the first part of the rope. By pulling at the end of this cord the hind leg is drawn up to the shoulder, and secured there with a hitch, but the plan is not nearly so safe as casting.

THRUSH. This is a diseased condition of the frog, commencing at the cleft, and extending over the whole frog, attended by a fœtid discharge. It is brought about by foul stables, and neglect of the feet. Clean and excise the diseased growths, and a leather shoe should be worn, to support the layer of tar with which the diseased frog may be covered.

THYME. Two species of thyme are cultivated, the common garden thyme, *Thymus vulgaris*, and the Lemon or Evergreen Thyme, *T. citriodorus*; are perennial plants of low growth, called hardy, but not wintering well in the west without winter protection. It is one of the few sweet herbs, in common cultivation, the others being Sage, Summer Savory, (*Saturjea viminea*), and Sweet Marjoram, (*Origanum majorana*). The cultivation for all the species named is alike, gardeners generally raising them as a secondary crop by transplanting, strong seedlings, or by division of the roots. (See article Sage for cultivation.

THYROID GLAND. A gland situated in front of the throat.

THYRSUS. An inflorescence similar to that of the common lilac.

TIBIA. The largest of the two bones of the fore leg. In entomology, the fourth joint of the leg.

TICKS. Among vegetable productions what is known as Beggar ticks are the ripe seeds of *Bidens chrysanthemoides*, and also the seeds of Spanish Needle, *B. bipinnatus*, is sometimes so called. Sheep ticks, *Hippobosca* (*Mel-phagus*) *ovina*, is a small louse fly, without wings, often exceedingly troublesome, especially to lambs, the insect leaving the mother sheep for the lambs, while sucking. All sheep should be examined occasionally for ticks. When not numerous they may be removed by picking. They may be destroyed by dipping the sheep (with the exception of the face and head) in a mixture of arsenic, soft soap, potash, and water, or other arsenical preparations; but they, being highly poisonous, are very unsafe remedies, and can not be recommended for general use. Decoctions of tobacco, applications of brimstone, lard, paraffine oil, etc., about the neck, are common remedies. Snuff or sulphur in powder, rubbed thoroughly into the wool, is sometimes used with good results, and a bath made by steeping tobacco in water, about two pounds to ten gallons of water, in which the lambs are immersed, (except the face,) is said to be effective, but in some cases has proved injurious to the health of the lambs. In the case of lambs, therefore, it would be proper to reduce the strength. It should, however, be observed that the weakness produced by the tobacco most usually passes off in a short time. Of Cattle ticks, one of those most usually found is the common *Ixodes*, and which at one time was popularly believed to be the cause of the Spanish fever in cattle. They are not common in the north except when distributed by Texan cattle, which often are covered with them, when driven from the south. The remedy is by picking. The late lamented Dr. Walsh, in referring to these insects, gave the probable facts in the case as follows: There is a prevailing opinion amongst certain classes, that the ticks which are found on the cattle which die of Texas fever are actually the cause of the disease. In view of this fact, specimens of these ticks have been sent us for examination, from different localities in Illinois, and they are identical with those we have ourselves examined upon diseased cattle in St. Louis, and are but the common cattle tick. It is exceedingly improbable that they have anything to do with the disease, although it is barely possible that they may communicate the infection from the Texas cattle to our native herds.

TIE. In building, a timber or metal used to bind together two parts which are liable to separate.

TILE. (See Drainage.)

TILLAGE. (See Cultivation and Plowing.)

TILLER. Branching off stems from the root.

TILTH. Firmness and preparation of the soil.

TIMBER. In the article Forestry and in the description of the more important species of useful trees, we have noticed those species generally cultivated for profit or ornament. Upon the importance of the timber resources of the country and the yearly increasing scarcity, and the need of planting for continued supply, we append a statement from an address, in 1871, by the editor, before the Illinois State Horticultural Society, and which is of as great force now as then in view of the continually diminishing supply, and also from the facts gathered in relation to forestry: It was remarked by Humboldt that, in felling trees which cover the crowns and slopes of mountains, man in all climates seems to be bringing on future generations too calamities at once—a want of fuel and a scarcity of water. The destruction of timber and the dense mass of natural grasses with which the prairies were originally covered, has added another most serious one—meteorological disturbances which are constantly modifying the climate, and if persisted in without compensation, must ultimately result in depopulating the country by rendering it unfit for human habitation. It was asserted twenty years ago [now thirty—Editor] that, before the United States reached a population of 50,000,000 that, through the waste of valuable timber, the folly and short-sightedness of the age would meet with a degree of censure and reproach not pleasant to contemplate. This point was reached before the census marked 40,000,000; and it is due principally to the causes just mentioned; which may be illustrated by the following deductions based upon facts: Heated air saturated with water in the form of vapor, gives up a portion of it if cooled, or absorbs more if its heat is increased. This power is doubled with each increase of temperature of twenty-seven degrees of Fahrenheit; therefore, if a warm current meets a colder one, both saturated, a portion is condensed and forms clouds and rain. If in falling this rain passes into a dry current of air, it may be absorbed partially or wholly before reaching the earth; or, falling through a saturated atmosphere, from high elevations or cold strata, its intensity may be increased by aggregation. All open countries are subject to violent atmospheric alternations; but if clothed with vegetation, especially timber, the changes are less violent, and the temperature is equalized. The solar rays have more power to heat plowed soils, than those unplowed; and just in proportion to their powers of absorption, will be their power to give up this heat again. In the cool recesses of the forest, evaporation goes on more slowly than in the open plain, for the reason that the rays of the sun seldom reach the earth, and hence their power of holding moisture and giving it out slowly by percolation to feed the springs that always abound in such regions. This cooler atmosphere, condensing moisture from the currents of heated and saturated air flowing in from the more open country, often causes the gentle rains incident to such localities. Evaporation causes latent heat, precipitation sets it free again or renders it sensible; and, thus nature by increasing the capacity of air to both hold and give up heat and moisture prevents those deluges that would otherwise occur, stores up heat and moisture to be given out regularly and slowly, unless influenced by violent meteorological convulsions. These are of infrequent occurrence in timbered districts, but are frequent, and often devastating, in open countries. While timbered regions have equal and gentle rainfalls, the open country beyond is visited with rain at unequal intervals, and torn by terrible winds accompanied by violent electrical phenomena. Forests modify all this, and although they may have no marked effect upon the amount of annual rainfall, they do cause it to be more equally and gently distributed, than is the case in countries where there is but little timber. Wide regions entirely destitute of timber have little or no rain, and become deserts often, not from their want of fertilizing inorganic and organic elements, but for want of that great fertilizer, water. I am well aware that Professor Henry is reported as saying that the records of the Smithsonian Institute do not indicate an annual diminution of rainfall, during the last twenty years. Annual granted, but its irregularity and also its infrequency is becoming more and more noticeable each year, and is apparent to the most ordinary observer; and it is this irregularity that is constantly harassing the farmer and horticulturist, more and more with each successive year. The meteorological changes incident to the destruction of forests seem to be well known to the ancients, and hence the many mythological tales that have come down to us through the old Hindoo, Chinese, and other writings. Alluding thereto, the poet Bryant says:

The groves were God's first Temples.

Abraham and his children planted groves in which to worship. Upon the re-occupation of the soil by the Hebrews, they cut them down because pagans worshipped there. The denudation constantly going on, the once fertile Canaan, land of groves and meadows, flowing with milk and honey, became an arid waste. The vast deserts of the earth, from the fossil woods occasionally found therein, were probably once fertile regions. The valley of the Nile, once famous for its forests, at length became useful for cultivation only by means of irrigation; later, through the planting of some millions of forests trees by the Pachas of Egypt, this country has again been visited by rain. The modern civilized man will leave deserts in his path much sooner than did the ancients, because his wants are more multifarious, and because he has the means of much quicker and more sure destruction of the forests. What he leaves, is more surely destroyed by desolating fires driven by tornadoes occasioned by meteorological changes which certainly follow this destruction. These changes are already beginning to show themselves in California in one direction, just as surely in Utah in another direction; in California by increasing drought through denudation, and in Utah, as in Egypt, by an increasing rainfall through replanting. The vast treeless plains of the far West were once clothed with timber, at least portions of them, else why the dry beds of rivers which have again become living streams by settlement and the protection of timber; an illustration of which may be found at Denver, Colorado. Look at modern Persia, prostrate with gaunt famine and without possibility of help, since the regions adjacent are desert and uninhabited, except by marauding barbarians; these tracts must be traversed by primitive pack-mule or camel trains, consuming their loads ere they could reach these famishing and dying wretches. What has lately befallen Persia, may be the fate of regions now abounding in agricultural and horticultural wealth, in succeeding generations, if the progress of destruction in our forests, and the denudation of our natural grasses is allowed to go on without replacement. Let us look for a moment at the destruction going on in a single section of our country, the lumber region of Michigan and Wisconsin, bounding upon lakes Michigan and Superior; for in the limit of this paper I can but touch upon facts. To write up the subject fairly would require a large volume. The records are many of them already written, and the curious in such matters have but to read to find them. According to the report of the Commissioner of Agriculture for 1870, there are 10,000,000 acres of land in Wisconsin and the upper peninsula of Michigan, north of the forty-fourth degree of north latitude, which, previous to the settlement of that portion of these states, were covered with heavy growths, valuable for timber and fuel. Since that time at least one-half of this growth has been cut off, and the timber brought into market and sold; and 1,000,000 acres of hard wood timber has been felled and burned upon the land by the settlers, while clearing up their farms. About 4,000,000 acres remain undisturbed. From the mills in that territory, there have been annually shipped 750,000,000 feet of lumber. To the ports of Lake Michigan, in 1869, there was brought the enormous quantity of 1,250,000,000 feet of lumber, and with that shipped east through the Straits of Mackinaw, the grand total of lumber annually sent from the forests of northern Wisconsin, and the upper peninsula of Michigan, is 1,750,000,000 feet. Does any one apprehend the immensity of these figures? We may arrive at it by synthesis. Suppose a machine, capable of making and counting one hundred strokes per minute, were to run night and day without stopping, it would count 52,596,000 in one year; consequently to count this number it must work uninterruptedly for nearly thirty four years or, more exactly, thirty-three years, three months, twenty days, twenty-one minutes, and nearly five seconds. The average yield of pine timber in this region is usually estimated by practical lumbermen, at 300,000 feet per forty acres. Some place it higher. Reckoning 330,000 feet, it will be seen to require a little more than 200,000 acres for the annual timber supply. Add to this quantity 100,000 acres for railroad ties, telegraph posts, hewn timber, and shingles, determined by actual amount received in the Chicago market, and 30,000 acres for the amount cut and burned in clearing the land, and we have 330,000 acres denuded annually. At this rate of consumption, all the valuable timber remaining on these tracts, (at the time this estimate was made, 1869,) would be consumed in twelve years. The destruction of these forests by a great conflagration has been estimated to be equal to a ten year's supply of timber, all of which will be a total loss, except in so far as the lumbermen may be able to immediately work up the charred remains. This ten years' supply would amount to 10,750,000,000 feet, worth, at twenty dollars per thousand, $215,000,000. Add to this the destruction of personal property, and the sum will approximate $250,000,000; and thus we have destroyed, in one short month, including the losses in Chicago, over $500,000,000 as one of the items of loss, aggravated by climatic changes incident to the artificial denudation of our forests and our natural grasses. The remedial means that are being used to increase our timber are principally in the prairie regions. It is estimated that there have been annually sent out from the districts just ranged by fire, 100,000,000 trees; also 50,000,000 of nursery-grown forest trees are annually shipped—one firm alone, in Illinois, furnishing 10,000,000 to 15,000,000 a year, the balance being made up by the other nurserymen throughout the West. Besides this there is some stock annually imported from Europe, but in the aggregate this is not appreciable, and owing to the losses sustained thereon, these importations are growing less each year. Therefore, we have in round numbers, 150,000,000 of trees planted each year, which at 1,000 trees per acre, would give 150,000 acres per year, not half enough planted in all the prairie States, to replenish the waste in two small districts. In a money point of view, it will therefore be seen that there is no more profitable occupation that can be followed, for the next fifty years at least, than the raising of timber for sale. If we ever arrive at a practical solution of this question, it must be because it will enrich the pocket. Looked at from an æsthetic standpoint, it meets our most pleasant approbation. As a sanitary measure, it is of great value. That it ameliorates and modifies climates, there is no longer a question; and the money value of timber plantations to the planter is also so well assured by experiments, both in this country and in Europe, that there need be no longer hesitation on this score. The only questions remaining are how to work so as to secure the greatest area of plantations, where to plant, and how to plant. The first can only be accomplished by concert of action among the agricultural classes. The second question, where to plant, may be answered—upon knolls, on the steepest hill sides, above rocky bluffs, along the margins of regular and irregular streams, the dry beds of former streams, sloughs, and other low places, occupying each site with timber appropriate to its situation. Plant in rows if practicable—and there are comparatively but few places in the West where it is not so—upon thoroughly prepared land, so thickly as to soon shade the soil, and give good cultivation from three to six years, according to the variety of timber planted. One more question occurs here, and that is as to how much to plant. It is estimated in Europe that at least one-fifth of the area of a country should be covered with trees, to insure the best results in general tillage. This would give forty acres for each farm of two hundred acres. A large area for many farmers to look at, but let them remember there is money in it, and with modern appliances for cultivation after the planting is once done, it simply means so many acres less of corn. If this area were planted it would not be twenty years before each farm would have its system of springs and rivulets, and from having one of the worst watered, we should have one of the fairest climates, the best watered, and most beautiful country that the sun ever shone upon. Nature has bestowed here a region lacking only trees to make it a paradise. It is filling up with the human energy, and intelligence, and skilled labor of the nations of the earth. Absolute freedom, both civil and religious, is the prerogative of all, under the law. We have only to heed the lessons that nature and events are constantly teaching us, to become not only one of the most prosperous and happy, but also the greatest and most far-sighted people upon the face of the earth. The prosperity of nations rests upon their agricultural resources, and one of the pillars of that agriculture is wealth of timber. And no nation can continue permanently great without it. It devolves upon this generation to lay the foundation of the prosperity of succeeding ones. Nature clothed the earth with timber and grasses, and in the fact that it takes generations to produce the monarchs of the forest, is the lesson that man may not with impunity destroy these without replacement; They have been destroyed heretofore, the destruction is still going on, but at what a terrible price! and how fearful the lesson to the destroyers in every era! Let those who are curious read its history in every land. If we expect assistance from the general government I fear we are bound to be disappointed. Unlike some European ones, which we are sometimes pleased to term despotic, ours being subject to periodical change, the politicians have no time to look at the future; present perquisites absorb the thoughts of too many; it is only a far-seeing few who take heed to the hereafter. The State governments of Illinois, Missouri, Kansas, and Iowa, have done something; they should do more by assisting individuals and corporations, (by every means in their power) upon whom must devolve the task of clothing these vast plains with forest growths. Parents desire to leave their children prosperous and happy, and what better heritage can a father leave his child, next to a good name, than a well kept farm, sheltered by pleasant groves, within whose cool recesses are born living springs that issuing forth gratefully slake the thirst of flocks and herds, and trickling to the valley form the rivulet, which, swollen along its way by other brooks from other homestead groves, turns in its laughing course hundreds of mills busy with their wealth of productive industry. This is no improbable picture, but is simply a view of the certain results of conformity to Nature's laws of cause and effect; and we know from history as

well, that such tree-planting as I have here recomended will surely produce the blessings enumerated. The opposite of this picture we are already beginning to see in the drying up of streams once used for turning mills, in the accumulative force of, and constantly increasing destruction from tornadoes, in the extreme heat and drought of our already tropical summers, followed by the cold winds of arctic winters, alternated with torrents of rain or fearful storms of snow. The children of those barbarous nations which followed the civilization that destroyed the ancient forests, retained the traditions relating thereto. As succeeding civilization advanced, these traditions were woven into fables, incorporated into their religions, and gods and goddesses made the avengers of the sacrilege. Shall the destruction of the great forests of the western continent again depopulate nations? We think not. The printing press has given wings to science, and science has already shown the means of recuperation but not until that recuperation may also afford the means of wealth. We have spoken of the attention which some of the European governments are paying to the protection of timber. With them the industries are of paramount importance. England the greatest manufacturing nation on the face of the earth, is beginning to be alarmed at the exhaustion of her coal-fields, which is expected to take place any time between the years 2800 and 3000, as her facilities for deep mining may be more or less increased. The total denudation of our great forests may be fixed at a much nearer date by estimating the constantly increasing demand upon our timber, far exceeding both the natural and artificial growths, and yet we are not giving the heed to the subject that its importance demands. I do not hesitate to say that if this denudation is allowed to go on without adequate replanting, this generation will see the almost total destruction of our more valuable hard and soft-wood trees. Believing our forest wealth practically inexhaustible we have gone on perfecting wonderful machinery, marvelous in its perfection for the working of wood. For this industry is one of the paramount ones, and actually pays more than one half of our internal revenue. But if as we go on perfecting our machinery we do not also increase our supply of the raw material, this very perfection will eventually bring disaster upon the whole industry. In Prussia, France and Bavaria it is estimated that there are about 10,000,000 acres of state forests. One-half of these belong to Prussia. In this country, as well as in other European ones, there are schools of forestry. At the head of the schools, as in other schools of technology, are placed men eminent for their practical attainments in these several branches of human knowledge, and as an item, in one direction, resulting from the schools of forestry we may note, as an important fact, that the annual revenue derived by France from her state forests before the war, was over three dollars per acre, or $8,700,000 per year from 2,700,000 acres. The subject of tree planting may now be considered as one of paramount importance. As affecting us physically, in the present and future it is so, and it is fast becoming so in a money point of view. We have shown from statistics what the average acre of timber will produce in lumber under the destructive means employed in all new countries for its manufacture. If multiplied by the present prices, and the other economics connected with forestry are estimated, even aside from any and all social considerations except money value, it may readily be perceived that the planting of the waste tracts that may always be found upon every farm will pay better in the future than any other crop that can be grown. The Hon. J. M. Edmonds, another writer, in relation to this subject of forest waste says: Maine, Michigan, Wisconsin, Minnesota, and Florida are the only States east of the Mississippi which now export any appreciable quantity of timber more than they import, and the reserve in these States is being rapidly cut away. The mountain and plateau region, occupying the interior of the continent, has only a moderate supply. No supplies can be drawn from this region for the older States, or even for the great plains; without exhausting a reserve which is already below the immediate prospective demand. In the Pacific States and Territories there is still an adequate supply, but not beyond the early prospective wants of their own people. The States bordering the Mississippi on the west have no surplus, and most of them are at this moment importing to meet the demands of even their sparse population. Arizona, New Mexico, Colorado, Wyoming, Montana, Idaho, and Dakota have but a meager supply, not sufficient for a population as dense as now occupies Ohio, Indiana, or Illinois. Only the newly acquired Territory of Alaska remains to be considered. Very little is known of its timber resources, but, in much the largest portion, it is known that its rigorous climate precludes the growth of valuable forests, but it is not too much to presume that the timber in that Territory will be sufficient to meet the demands of the trade now opening with the great populations of China and Japan. Considering, then, the present and the prospective forest products in this country in the light of their necessity for domestic purposes, and for the protection of men, animals, fruits, and grain, and of their value in inducing moisture, protecting the soil, and tempering the climate, it is, indeed, important that every section of the country should retain, if it has them, and if does not have them, should immediately engage in their production, at least to the extent of supplying local use and protection. In upper Egypt, the rains, which eighty years ago were abundant, have ceased since the Arabs cut down the trees along the valley of the Nile towards Libia and Arabia. A contrary effect has been produced in lower Egypt, from the extensive planting of trees by the Pacha. In Alexandria and Cairo, where rain was formerly a rarity, it has, since that period, become more frequent. Prof. R. C. Kedzie, of the Michigan State Agricultural College, in an address—The Influence of Forest Trees on Agriculture—delivered not long since before an agricultural society in that State, gave a very earnest warning against the wasteful destruction of forests, citing, at the same time, the well known facts of current history. It is noticeable as a hopeful fact, that prominent agricultural societies, in various sections of the country, have recently been emphatically directing public attention to this matter. In 1864 the British government founded an improved general system of forest administration for the whole Indian empire, having in view the preservation and development of state forests. All superior government forests are reserved, and made inalienable, their boundaries marked, and forest rules and penalties defined. Surveys have been made, and are still in progress, towards establishing data as to the nature and extent of the timber resources. Several thousand mahogany trees have been raised in the Terai. Large tracts have been planted to wood for the purpose of supplying the railways, which consume immense quantities for fuel. Puget Sound, Washington Territory, is well known as a principal source of the lumber export of the North Pacific coast. Besides amounts consumed within our own territories, many cargoes of lumber are annually shipped from thence to ports in China, the Sandwich Islands, Australia, and South America. The following statement in regard to the resources of Puget Sound is on the authority of Mr. Joseph Cushman, receiver of public moneys at Olympia, situate at the head of the sound: The time is not far distant when nearly all the ship building on the Pacific coast will be done on the shores of Puget Sound. From the Cascade range to the Pacific, comprising about one-half of Washington Territory, the surface is densely covered with the finest forest growth in the world. Some of the trees, straight as an arrow, are four hundred feet in height, and fourteen feet in diameter near the ground. Varieties of the fir predominate, interspersed with spruce, hemlock, tamarack, white cedar, maple, ash, white oak, and, on some of the mountain slopes, white pine. The yellow fir (*Abies Douglasii*) is a tree peculiar to the North Pacific coast from the forty-second parallel to Alaska, and is found only east of the Cascade range, north of the boundary of forty-nine degrees. This is the timber principally used at the saw mills on the Sound, and is both strong and durable; in fact it is the strongest timber on the coast, both in perpendicular pressure and horizontal strain.

TIMBER TREES, RANGE OF. The statistical atlas of Gen. Walker contains a careful analysis of our forest wealth, prepared by Prof. Brewer, of Yale College. It will be found valuable, in connection with the articles Forestry and Timber. Considered botanically, the flora of the United States is very rich in woody plants. The actual number of species is not known, but 800 is perhaps not too high an estimate. There is no dividing line in nature between trees and shrubs; the arbitrary rule adopted by most botanists is to call trees only such species as grow to thirty or more feet high; less than that are shrubs. Sometimes, however, the habit of the plant will place among the trees a plant which, from size alone, would be called a shrub. An examination of various authorities shows that upwards of 300 indigenous species of trees are known to botanists growing within the limits of the United States, which attain the height of thirty feet. About 250 of these are, somewhere in the United States, tolerably abundant, or, at least, not rare. If for our purpose we exclude all the smaller trees that never attain a height of fifty feet, also those tropical species, however large, which occur with us only in extreme Southern Florida, also a few Mexican trees found only along our extreme southern border, also such rare species as may occur only in Alaska, also all those very rare species nowhere common, and consider only the larger trees which are somewhere in our territory tolerably abundant, we have still about 120 species, of which about twenty species attain a height of 100 feet, twelve a height of 200 feet, while perhaps five or six may attain a height of 300 feet and over. Of the 120 species indicated, about fifty belong to the *Coniferæ*. How many of these species are of special importance in commerce, or in the home industries (of other use than for fuel), it is impossible to say, but it is a very large proportion of the whole number. Many of the smaller species, however, and of the larger shrubs, give special character to large areas of woodlands, and can not be ignored in any discussion of American trees, whether considered botanically or economically. A glance at the map shows large regions either treeless or very sparsely wooded. It is possible to cross the continent, from the Pacific to the Gulf of Mexico, without passing through a forest five miles in extent, or large enough to be indicated on the map. Then, again, the woodlands of the East are separated from those of the West by a broad, treeless plain from six to fifteen degrees wide. The forests and woodlands on the two sides of this gap are entirely unlike in their aspect and in their botanic characters. On the eastern side, broad-leaved, hard wood species predominate, both in abundance of individuals and in number of species, the forests of large areas consisting entirely of such kinds. On the west, the forests are entirely of *Coniferæ;* other species occur, some of great value, but they nowhere (or at most in only rare cases in the extreme west) form a conspicuous or even noticeable element in the forests of both sides; the nearest approach to it is the aspen, (*Populus tremuloides*), which is a common tree in the North from the Atlantic to the Pacific. Two species of cottonwood are also abundant in some localities, and form an important element in the fringe of wood bordering streams, but are never otherwise a conspicuous element in the forests of the West. These three species of poplar are the only broad-leaved trees that figure as trees on both sides of the central treeless plains; but others stray across as mere shrubs on one side Among the *Coniferæ*, one cedar is found on both sides as an abundant wood in places, but it is a low, crabbed growth west. a large shrub oftener than a tree. Neither beech, nor elm, nor hickory, nor mulberry, nor basswood, nor tulip-tree, nor magnolia, nor sassafras forms an element in the forests of the Rocky mountains and westward. For convenience in discussing the kinds of wood, we may divide our domain into ten geographical divisions, viz.: 1. New England; 2. The Middle States; 3. The Southeastern region; 4. The Northwestern region; 5. the Southwestern; 6. The Plains; 7. The Rocky Mountain region; 8. Arizona, New Mexico, and the Great Basin; 9. The Pacific region, and 10. Alaska. Only native species are considered in the following discussion of the kinds of wood. So much confusion exists in the popular and commercial names of many of our trees that the botanical name is given where necessary for precision. One example is sufficient to illustrate this confusion of names. The most widely spread and valuable of western timbers, *Abies Douglasii*, which grows from British Columbia to New Mexico, is known in its different localities under the various names of Douglas fir, red fir, black fir, Douglas spruce, red spruce, black spruce, hemlock, Oregon pine, western pitch, Bear River pine, swamp pine, and perhaps others; moreover, nearly all of these names are also applied to other species. Similar confusion exists in the popular names of not a few species. New England was originally entirely wooded, and has about eighty or eighty-five species of trees, of which about sixty may reach fifty feet in height. Maine is a great source of pine-spruce lumber, but, as a whole, hard wood species predominate, particularly south of the forty-fourth parallel. Many of these hard woods are noted for their durability and texture, and form the raw material for a great variety of manufactures, particularly of carriages and various tools and implements where tough wood is an essential part. The extent and variety of manufactures in wood is relatively greater in this region than elsewhere, and ship building is an important industry. The large timber used in house and ship building is unquestionably rapidly diminishing, but the area of woodlands is not decreasing in the same ratio. In many places the large trees suitable for sawing, are cut without clearing the land of the smaller growth, leaving it still woodland; and as such it is shown on the map, in article Forestry, page 369. As a whole, the area of woodlands in this region is but slowly, if indeed at all, diminishing, and in large districts it increases from year to year. This is particularly the case in portions of the western part, where hilly regions, formerly largely in tillage and pasturage, are now growing up with trees, mostly of hard wood kinds. Some of the timber thus grown is considered peculiarly valuable in manufactures, where strength and durability are needed. This extension of woodland areas is by natural process. Few, if any, forests have been planted, except on the sandy regions along the southern part and on the islands, where pines have been planted to some extent. The extensive planting of trees for shade and ornament, however, increases largely the actual amount of wood in this region. To appreciate how much it is only necessary to see many of the New England villages and cities from some height in the summer, where the abundance of trees gives the appearance of a forest to the scene. Some of the cities have more actual wood growing in their streets and parks than is sufficient to be termed a heavy forest of timber in the sparsely wooded regions of the West. In New England, the elm, and perhaps the sugar maple, attain their finest development and greatest abundance. The Middle States have about 100 to 105 species of trees, sixty-five to sixty-seven of which sometimes reach fifty feet in height. The region was originally entirely wooded. Over much of it the forests were very heavy, and there are still immense quantities of timber available. The forests of this region are usually made up of quite a number of species; in some places the broad leaved species predominating, in others the *Coniferæ;* but both kinds commonly grow together, the *Coniferæ* usually less abundant in the southern and western portions. The deciduous oaks, chestnut, beech, two species of ash, and perhaps the white pine, attain in this district their greatest size. The original forests are noted for their grandeur, and, with some of the secondary forests, for the diversity of their timber products. On the ridges of the Appalachians, which cross Pennsylvania and New York, while the hard woods may not attain their greatest size, some of them, particularly white oak, white ash, and some of the hickories are believed to attain their greatest perfection as regards strength and durability, or at least they are only equaled by the timber of the same species extended on the line of these ridges beyond this district in both directions. This is a matter of great importance in ship and boat building, and in the manufacture of railroad cars and of agricultural implements, all of which industries are here prominent. In portions of New York and Pennsylvania there are still large forests of excellent timber yet almost untouched by the axe; but, as a whole, the woodlands and forests are rapidly diminishing, both in area and in aggregate value, and there is as yet no corresponding compensation. Probably the price of timber must advance considerably before adequate means will be taken to produce a future supply by growth. How much this may be aided by wise legislation is still a problem. The southeastern region, extending from Virginia to Florida, is the richest in species, is of peculiar interest to the botanist, and of first class importance in commerce. (We can not say that any one wooded region is more important than others, inasmuch as wood is a prime necessity in every civilized community.) This region, originally entirely wooded, has upward of 130 species of trees, (a much larger number, indeed, if we include the larger shrubs and the tropical species of extreme Southern Florida,) seventy-five of which attain a height of fifty or more feet, and perhaps a dozen species attain a height of 100 feet. A belt of pine timber extends nearly the whole length of this district, of varying width, occupying a part of the region between the mountains and the sea. This is the great source of hard pine timber, (known in commerce as hard pine, yellow pine, heavy pine, pitch-pine, southern pine, and Georgia pine.) State statistics show that the annual export from Georgia alone now amounts to from 200,000,00 to 300,000,000 of feet per annum. The trade is yearly growing, and the adjacent States are contributing largely to the supply. But this is not the only commercial lumber of this district. The live-oak of Florida has a reputation throughout the world as ship-timber. The hard woods of the mountain-ridges have been less utilized than the growth of the regions already spoken of; but this is not owing to any inferiority of the wood itself. It is believed that the white oak attains its greatest development of strength in certain parts of Virginia and West Virginia, hardly equaling in size, however, its greatest development in the States immediately north. While pine is abundant along the belt mentioned, and is at present of greater commercial importance, the broad leaved species are the most abundant element in the forests. Here we find the magnolias and many flowering trees and shrubs in their greatest development and beauty. The area of woodlands, as a whole, has not probably much diminished of late years; but the trees suitable for hewing and sawing are decreasing under the heavy drafts made by commerce. In very many cases the land is despoiled of only its best timber trees; the others are left, so that it is yet woodland, and in due time a new crop of timber will result. The data for the preparation of the report of this region are more imperfect than for either of the regions before enumerated.

The northwestern region extends from Ohio to Iowa and Minnesota, inclusive. In its original state it had every variety of forest feature represented, from the heavy forests of broad leaved species of the Ohio bottoms and the dense *Coniferæ* forests of Michigan, through every gradation of lighter forests, openings and belts, along the streams, to the grassy prairie and the treeless plains which everywhere terminate this district on the west. It is represented by about 105 to 110 species, about sixty-eight or seventy of which may reach a height of fifty feet. In southern Ohio and Indiana, the forests are of broad leaved species; oaks and various hard woods grow to magnificent size and of good texture, while black walnut, bass wood, white wood (or tulip tree), attain here their greatest development. The pine region may be said to begin in northwestern Ohio and extend across Michigan and Wisconsin to northern Minnesota. The northern parts of the three States last mentioned now furnish a larger quantity of sawed lumber than any other part of the country. The census of 1870 gave the total production of sawed lumber in the United States at 12,750,000,000 feet, and of this Michigan furnished over 2,250,000, and Wisconsin over 1,000,000, the two States producing upward of one-fourth of the whole yield of the country. The Chicago Lumberman's Exchange gives as the receipts of lumber at that city over 1,000,000,000 feet for each of the three years following that census. This is sawed lumber, exclusive of laths, shingles, and all forms of hewed timber. A prominent journal devoted to the lumber trade, gives the production of logs, for a single river during the winter of 1873-'74 as 433,000,000 feet, and deplored the dull trade, as shown by such a short crop. To illustrate the capacity for sawing lumber, it may be stated that a single mill in Michigan, on June 3, 1874, as a test of capacity, sawed 179,718 feet of lumber in three working hours, the actual running time being two hours and forty minutes. (This was given on the authority of a local journal.) Many mills boast a capacity of 50,000 to 150,000 feet per day. But these examples of production tell a story of destruction also; and great as is the supply of pine in this region, it is so rapidly diminishing under the demands of the growing cities of the West, that serious apprehensions are awakened of a scarcity within a comparatively few years. The data for northeastern Minnesota are very meagre. Between the pine forests and the treeless plains, the prevailing trees are of broad leaved species, sometimes forming forests of considerable density and size. Sometimes the limits of prairie and woodlands are well defined; at others there is a regular gradation, through glades and openings, from the actual forest to the prairie. It must be remembered that the uncolored portions of the map are by no means always treeless. A region with less than forty acres woodland per square mile, if sparsely settled, may have sufficient timber and wood for the ordinary wants of such a population. Again, there are other regions without actual trees, but with low shrubs, sufficient for fuel and many other uses. The prairies of this region are the typical prairies of the country. Respecting their origin and the conditions which have rendered them treeless there have been many theories, which it is not necessary here to discuss. Periods of excessive drought, fires, the physical texture of the soil, are the leading theories, some advocating one, and some another. Where the prairies are uncultivated or have at most but a sparse population, the patches of wood (where they occur) are doubtless diminishing in number and area through man's agency. Where, however, a prairie region is largely occupied by settlers and a considerable part is under cultivation, the amount of wood is doubtless rapidly increasing. This is brought about in part by checking the fires which would otherwise kill the trees while young, in part by fostering in various ways any spontaneous growth of wood that may occur, and in part by actual planting In some places the aspect of the country has been entirely changed in this character by the settlement of the country; and in the more fertile regions there seems no good reason why a future supply of wood and timber may not be produced on lands originally treeless, whenever the price is sufficiently enhanced to make a successful growth profitable. The southwestern region extends from Kentucky and Missouri to Alabama and thence westward to the western edge of the timber in Texas. Originally the eastern and southeastern portions were heavily wooded, prairies, however, occurring far eastward in the district, increasing in number and area westward, until the dry and treeless plains are reached which skirt the whole western border. It has about 112 to 118 species, sixty to sixty-five of which attain a height of fifty feet. The belt of pine of the southeastern States extends into this region near the gulf of Alabama, thence running west and leaving the coast, extending into the Indian Territory and Texas. This belt is not continuous, however, west of Mobile bay, and there are other detached areas of considerable extent with valuable pinelands. In this district are swamps having an immense growth of cypress. Although so much of *Conifera* may be found, broad leaved species constitute by far the most abundant element of the forests, embracing both hard and soft woods, and some species, which are shrubs or small trees elsewhere, attain in this district large dimensions. Sassafras, which is but an insignificant tree in New England, in Missouri becomes a tree sometimes three or more feet in diameter, equaling camphor-wood for the manufacture of chests for household use. Black walnut is also abundant in places and grows to great size, and various species of timber trees are abundant over large parts of this district. This region has not furnished so much wood or timber to commerce as either of the districts before considered. This is not due to any deficiency in quantity or quality of its woods but entirely to other causes. In this district, as in the northwestern, the woods diminish westward, and finally fade out in the oak openings and crosstimbers of Texas and the fringes of wood that follow the streams far beyond the other trees into the plains west. Over most of this district, particularly the better wooded portions, the area of woodlands is not seriously diminishing, but, as elsewhere in places most available for commerce, the better timber trees are disappearing. In the western borders, where the supply is at best sparse, it grows yearly less by the destruction or use of the scanty supply, and no efforts are made to replace it. West of the districts described, the treeless belt already spoken of, separates entirely the wooded portions of the two sides of the continent, a belt extending from Mexico to the Arctic ocean. It is fully 350 miles wide in its narrowest part, between latitude 36° and 37°, widening to our northern boundary where it is eight hundred miles wide, or wider if we include a few outlying patches of timber on some of the northern ridges and mountains. Different parts of this belt, the plains in common language, vary greatly in their aspect. Sometimes they are absolutely treeless, as far as the vision extends; in others a fringe of timber from a few rods to several miles wide skirts streams, while the spaces between are treeless; and again others, particularly northward, some of the intervening hills are dotted with scattered cedars, usually shrubby and crabbed, but in places attaining the size and dignity of trees. The Black Hills have heavy forests of pine and spruce, and appear like a forest-island three hundred miles long rising out of this sea of plain far from the forests of either side. A few other similar though smaller detached forests occur in this treeless waste. The causes which have left this great area so bare are, without doubt, mostly climatic. Although in places the character of the soil is unfavorable, the great cause is doubtless the scanty or capricious rainfall of the region. What can be done toward clothing this with trees by artificial means is an entirely unsolved problem. The Rocky Mountain region lies near the chain so-called and north of latitude 36°. From the Columbia river northward to Alaska, forests clothe the whole mountain belt, except where too high or on limited parks and prairies. On our northern boundary the treeless plains suddenly cease at the eastern base of the chain, (about longitude 113° 40' west,) and heavy forests are almost continuous thence westward to the Pacific south of the Columbia river (about latitude 38° north) the forests of this chain are everywhere separated from those near the Pacific by dry and treeless plains and valleys of greater or less width. The forests of the northern part of the chain are continuous from Alaska southward to about latitude 42° 40' north, where a nearly treeless belt about a hundred miles wide cuts entirely through them from the bare plains east to the more barren basin in the interior. South of this belt, forests begin again and extend southward from southern Wyoming across Colorado and into northern New Mexico, more than four hundred miles, with a width of two hundred to two hundred and fifty miles. This forest is of varying degrees of density and interspersed in it, are many treeless, or nearly treeless valleys called parks. This forest is surrounded on every side by treeless areas, the limits usually sharply defined except along the southern and southwestern edge, where they shade off more gradually in density. The northwestern part of this forest is continuous with the forests of the north slope of the Uintahs, and these again with the forests of the Wasatch of Utah. Southwesterly in New Mexico and Arizona, are detached forests of similar character, clothing in each case mountain chains. These forests are everywhere of *Conifera*. The whole tree vegetation consists of twenty-eight or thirty species, about one-third of which are broad leaved kinds and two-thirds conifers, the latter constituting the forests. Of the former, box-elder (*Negundo aceroides*) occurs most abundantly along the eastern base of the mountains; two kinds of cottonwood, along the streams of the plains or in the parks; alders along streams but higher in the mountains; the aspen as a small tree (locally known as *Asp*) in the mountains and on the margin of the parks. No oaks occur as trees, but a scrubby form, (*Quercus alba*, var. *Gunnisonii*,) rarely more than ten to twenty feet high sometimes occurs on the foothills of the south. These and a few other species known to the botanist but not abundant as wood, and usually here as stragglers from some other region, make up the ten or eleven broad leaved species. The great Colorado forest spoken of consists essentially of five species of conifers, viz., *Pinus ponderosa*, (called here yellow pine,) *P. contorta*, (called tamarack, and red pine,) *Abies Engelmanni*, (really a spruce, but called white pine, as it is a soft white wood,) *A. Mengiesii*, (called here balsam,) and *A. Douglasii*, (called by a variety of names). These five species are by far the most abundant, large areas often being covered almost exclusively by but one or two of them. Other species not here named, are frequently met with; not rare, as the botanist would say, but of vastly less economic interest than the species enumerated. On the outlying spurs and ridges which extend into the woodless region on every side, scrubby cedars are found, and in the drier valleys the nut pine or pinon (*P. edulis*) is abundant, particularly southward—a low, scrubby tree, usually less than twenty and rarely more than thirty-five feet high. These, with a few others, make up the eighteen or twenty species of *Coniferæ*. The timber of this region is diminishing much faster than a legitimate use demands. Where one tree is cut for use, ten perhaps are killed by fires, which destroy great forests nearly every year, kindled by the carelessness of the whites, or perhaps as often by the Indians, who sometimes fire the forests to drive out game, sometimes to annoy an enemy, and sometimes no one knows why. Whatever may be the cause, blackened trunks disfigure many hundreds of square miles. For that portion of the Rocky mountain region lying between the forty-third and forty-ninth parallels accurate information is, as a whole, rather meager. For Idaho and the Yellowstone region, they are more complete and reliable, but for the region north and east of the Wind River mountains they are scant and unsatisfactory. The species of the northern Rocky mountain region are perhaps the same as those south, but varying in relative abundance. The two magnificent firs *Abies grandis*, (called white spruce, but in Oregon yellow fir,) and *A. amabalis*, become more abundant. In the northern part, particularly in the Kooskooskie region, heavy pine forests are reported. West of the Rocky mountains is another treeless or sparsely wooded region, which extends from the Columbia river to Mexico. Its northern portion narrows northward, but forms an important part of the valley of the Columbia and its tributaries; it embraces the whole of the great basin except insignificant edges of the rim; it throws out an eastern branch entirely through the Rocky mountains, and southward it is continuous with the treeless or sparsely wooded region which extends across the continent along our southern frontier. In this area occur the driest and the most inhospitable deserts of our country. It is of too varied character to admit here of details. Some portions are grassy prairies, some are plains of lava, others are deserts of drifting sand, others are half naked rock cut by canons, others are alkali plains and short valleys, others are great areas covered with sage brush and grease-wood, others pass into chapparal, in fact, there is every gradation, from naked barrenness to great forests. Some of the mountain chains found in this area are as bare of trees as are the valleys themselves; others have large shrubs of scrubby pines or cedars, while others are clothed with forests. The extreme northern part consists largely of lava plains. South of this the Blue mountains of Eastern Oregon have heavy forests of pine, fir, and spruce of the same species found in the northern Rocky mountains. Still south of this are the sage plains and deserts. In Nevada the valleys are treeless, (with very rare exceptions,) the ridges sometimes bare, sometimes dotted with shrubs and scrubby pines, the actual amount of wood being small, yet of inestimable value to a country so rich in minerals and so poor in wood. Over parts there is a crabbed, shrubby growth, becoming in places, chapparal, but oftener of scattered shrubs, attaining in favorable places the size of small trees. One of these, called mountain mahogany, (*Cercocarpus ledifolius*,) is often over thirty feet high, with a base two feet in diameter, the wood very hard, close-grained, dark-colored, and taking a beautiful finish when wrought. The shrubby vegetation of the region, including as it does the sage bushes, grease-woods, creosote bush, etc., is of great interest to the botanist, but can hardly claim further notice here. South of latitude 35° are a few species of small trees of much greater value. Of these, first in importance is the mesquite, (*Prosopis* (*Algarobia*) *glandulosa s.*) thriving in hot, dry places in the valleys and on the mesas, but is rare on the steeper slopes. The tree has a spreading habit, rarely more than thirty feet high and twelve inches in diameter. The very hard and durable wood is used for a great variety of purposes. Posts in use for fifty years are still sound, and its value for railroad ties must ultimately be great. The fruit, of eight to twelve beans, in a long, sweet, pulpy pod, like that of the carob (or St. John's bread) of the Old World, is a valuable food for animals, and even for man, while in Western Texas a considerable trade has sprung up in mesquite-gum, which is similar to gum-arabic. This species extends from California to Texas, and in the future will doubtless be extensively planted and cultivated. The tornillo or screw-pod mesquite (*Prosopis pubescens*) is smaller and of more restricted range, but of similar use. Another small tree, called arbol de hierro, or iron wood (*Olneya tesota*) is of much local value, and may become a commercial wood. Other broad leaved trees occur; cottonwoods and sycamores are common along the streams. In parts of this region are several *Cacti* on one *Yucca*, attaining a tree-size, more picturesque in the landscape than useful to man. The higher mountains of Arizona are well timbered with conifers. The prevailing species are red spruce (*Abies Douglasii*) and yellow pine, (*P. brachyptera*). The most notable of these forests (the limits of which have lately been demonstrated by the explorations of Lieut. Wheeler) extends nearly 400 miles. Other isolated forests, occupying mountains, are indicated on the map. On many of the lower ridges, the pinon (*Pinus edulis*) abounds, furnishing food to the Indians and fuel to the whites. It is a crabbed shrub, rather than a tree, usually less than twenty or twenty-five feet high. Other trees occur of more limited range or abundance, the actual number known to botanists in the whole of this vast region amounting to about thirty-five species. The Sierra Nevada and Cascade mountains lie nearly parallel with the coast of the Pacific, with their eastern base 100 to 200 miles distant from it. This chain is nearly continuous from the northern frontier southward to latitude 35°, a distance of about 1,000 miles, everywhere a broad and high chain, its summits far above the line of tree vegetation, often in the perpetual snow, culminating in the loftiest peaks in the United States. Its broad western slope is everywhere heavily timbered. Along the coast for the same distance are the Coast Ranges, a system of mountain chains more or less connected together, but broken by gaps and separated by valleys, and usually rather steep on the ocean side. They form a belt twenty-five to fifty miles wide, and are mostly between 2,000 and 4,000 feet high, but with numerous points rising to twice that height. The Coast Ranges are generally wooded. Between these two mountain systems a series of valleys extend their whole length, from Puget Sound to Southern California, cut across by a few ridges, so that it is not a single continuous depression, but rather a succession of valleys. North of the Columbia this valley is heavily wooded. The forests are open, but the trees are large, and little prairies are interspersed. Passing southward, the valley of the Willamette is largely prairie, but there is an abundance of wood for all uses. Between the Upper Willamette and the Upper Sacramento, several ridges cross from the Coast Ranges to the Cascades, and forests and prairies alternate. The former are heavily timbered. The great central valley of California is by far the largest of the series, and is treeless, or but sparsely wooded, for an area 420 miles long by thirty to sixty miles wide. The northern half of this has more wood than the southern, where large areas are absolutely treeless, except a very narrow fringe along the few streams. This region of mountain and valley, as a whole, and in all its relations, economic, scenic, and botanic, has, perhaps, the most interesting tree vegetation known. The whole number of species known to botanists amounts to eighty-eight or ninety, but a vastly smaller number are found in any one botanical or commercial district. Many of the more noted species are very restricted in their range, and not more than three or four important timber trees extend the whole length of the region. It is therefore necessary to treat its parts more in detail than in the case of the other districts. In this district are, perhaps, the grandest forests on the globe. In Washington Territory, they are made up of but few species, of which *Abies Douglasii*, (called here red fir,) is the most important. Commonly 150,or more feet high, and four or more feet in diameter, but sometimes fifteen feet (in extreme cases even over twenty feet) in diameter and over 300 feet high, straight growth, the wood firm, elastic, holding spikes with great tenacity, it produces the most noted timber of the Territory. Oregon cedar, (*Thuja gigantea*,) yellow or punkin pine, (*P. ponderosa*,) yellow fir, (*Abies grandis*,) black spruce, (*A. Menziesii*,) are the next most abundant species, all attaining a great size. The popular names are much confused, the generic terms of cedar, pine, spruce, and fir are all very loosely and capriciously applied. The finest of the forests are about Puget Sound, and on the western flanks of the Cascades. On the Coast Ranges, the forests are denser, and with tangled undergrowth, but the trees not of such large average size. Regarding the wonderful quantity of wood produced, one authority, (for many years Surveyor-general of the Territory) states that the whole region west of the summit of the Cascades to the Pacific, and north of the Columbia, will yield an average of 32,000 feet per acre of merchantable lumber. He states that about one-thirty-second part of this area is prairie. The following extracts from the annual reports of the Commissioner of the General Land-Office of the United States relate to this Territory: The land will produce from 25,000 to 300,000 feet per acre, and there are vast tracts that would cover the entire surface with cord-wood ten feet in height; there are localities that would afford double. Again, the reports speak of the forests of pine, fir, and cedar which grow thickly, from one to fifteen feet in diameter and 200 to 300 feet high; and again, of the forests of red and yellow pine of gigantic growth, often, attaining a height of 300 feet and from nine to twelve feet in diameter. Similar testimony could be greatly extended. In the extreme northeastern part, and east of the Cascades, are forests of pine; these forests are in character more like those of the Rocky mountains, with which they are continuous. Passing south of the Columbia river, the same species occur; but the forests are not so heavy, although individual trees may be as large. Prairies become more numerous and larger, and oaks and other broad leaved trees become more common in the valleys. In places, larch (*Larix occidentalis*) is abundant, and the yew (*Taxus brevifolia*) attains in Oregon and Northern California a height of fifty or seventy-five feet, a greater size than is attained by any yew elsewhere in America. As a whole, Oregon is very heavily timbered. Passing southward to California, the tree vegetation changes still more, and becomes the richest in species of any region west of the great plains, embracing a total of over eighty species. Some fifty species of *Coniferæ* have been enumerated by botanists, embracing several species, and even genera, found elsewhere. All the conifers of Washington and Oregon are found here, but not in the same relative abundance or size. The yellow pine (*P. ponderosa*) attains its greatest development, and is often over 200 or 250 feet high, and four to eight (sometimes twelve) feet in diameter. The sugarpine (*P. Lambertiana*) is perhaps the most valuable pine of the State; is abundant, of excellent quality, and great size. There are four firs (*Abies* of the section *Picea*,) three large spruces, and about twelve species of pine, more or less abundant. (More than twice that number of supposed species have been described by botanists.) The big trees (*S. quoia gigantea*) occur on the western slope of the Sierra Nevada, and are too well known to need notice here beyond the remark that the case with which they are propagated, and their valuable timber and rapid growth, will doubtless give them great value for cultivation in the future. Of more present value is the red-wood, (*Sequoia sempervirens*,) which only grows very near the sea, between latitude 36° and 43°, and on portions of this coast forms forests rivaling, if indeed not exceeding, any found elsewhere on the earth. The trees are often ten, and sometimes exceed more than twenty feet in diameter, very straight, 200 to 300 feet high; and the wood, which is light, is straight-grained, very durable, and adapted to many uses. It is extensively cut, and the lumber shipped to South America, the Pacific islands, China, and even to New Zealand. It is rapidly diminishing in quantity, and the only slight compensation is that when cut a new growth sprouts from the stump, which is not true of any other timber tree belonging to the *Coniferæ*. California cedar (*Libocedrus decurrens*) occurs in the mountains of large size. Several species of cypress, (*Cupressus*,) the California nutmeg, (*Torreya*,) and cedars of smaller size abound. Among the broad leaved trees there are many of great beauty, but there is a great lack of hard woods. The laurel, (*Tetranthera Californica*,) has been sparingly used in ship building; an ash, one maple, (neither abundant,) and some of the oaks do service where smaller hard woods are needed, but the supply is deficient. But among these trees are some of marvelous beauty, particularly among the oaks. Two cottonwoods, two sycamores, the Madrona, (*Arbutus Menziesii*,) and other trees are not rare. The data for Alaska are insufficient to construct a map of distribution and density of timber with reasonable accuracy; so the attempt is not made. Some portions of that extensive territory are heavily wooded, other portions are treeless, and there is every gradation, but the relative areas of each, and their boundaries, are unknown. Official reports speak of the forests as being really magnificent, covering the lower hills and uplands with dense masses of pine, spruce, fir, hemlock, cedar, and other valuable timber, principally evergreens. Again, that the forests extend almost to the water's edge along the southern shores, but north and east of the Alaskan peninsula they exist only in the interior, except at the heads of bays and sounds, while the inland forests are abundant, extending to within a short distance of the Arctic Ocean. In establishing the United States military post of Fort Tongas, in clearing the timber for this post, a magnificent growth of yellow cedar trees, eight feet in diameter and 150 feet in height was found. Nearly the whole of the Yukon district is well supplied with timber; and much more appears to the same effect. Of the species on the Yukon, Mr. Dall states that the white spruce, (*Abies alba*,) is the largest and most valuable tree found in the Yukon district. The next in importance is the birch (*Betula glandulosa*). Various other species are mentioned.

TIMOTHY GRASS. *Phleum pratense* Meadow cat's-tail grass. In rainy weather it too readily imbibes moisture. It gives very sweet and early herbage for sheep in spring, and mixed with other grasses, is found very useful in laying down land to pasture for a few years. The soil which suits timothy grass best is a good, moist, and rather stiff loam. On gravel it soon dies off. It is scarcely to be recommended without a mixture of other grasses, although very heavy crops of it have been grown; and from its strong stem when full grown, it should always be fed off when young, or cut for soiling horses and cattle before the stem has acquired its full growth. In rich land which is tired of clover it may form a very good substitute, to cut up green and depasture afterward. The seed is usually sown on wheat in the spring, or it may be sown with oats. Two pecks are commonly used, but it is better to use three pecks, or even a bushel when other grasses are not used. Clover and timothy do well together; eight pounds of clover and eight quarts of timothy seed may be used. (See Grasses.)

TISSUE. A membrane, or expansion of a cellular structure in animals or plants.

TITMOUSE. *Parus*. The small black cap titmouse or chickadee and the tufted titmouse are the two common species. Their principal food is the eggs of insects, found in the crevices of the bark of trees, and small insects. They are beneficial birds and should be scrupulously preserved. The tufted titmouse has a series of pretty notes.

TOAD. *Bufo*. The common toad of the North, West and South is perfectly harmless so far as containing venom inimical to the human family is concerned. The warty excrescences contain an acrid fluid, which exudes when crushed. It is unfounded, the vulgar idea that this fluid will produce warts upon the hands. The food of the toad is insects, even including the hated potato beetle; they are naturally retiring and inoffensive, seeking damp, dark places where insects abound. They will become quite tame if not injured and soon clear a garden of insects if protected. Gardeners are beginning to learn this fact and act accordingly.

TOADFLAX. Weeds of the genus *Antirrhinum* and *Linaria:* they are usually perennial, and should be extirpated.

TOBACCO. *Nicotiana*. There are many species of tobacco, fourteen being enumerated by Loudon. The two principal under cultivation with their varieties are *N. Rustica*, grown in the colder portions of Europe, and *N. Tabacum*, cultivated in the United States, of this latter, the Cuba, and the Connecticut seed leaf are the varieties principally cultivated in the United States for cigars. These varieties are not so rich in oil are lighter, and more bulky than varieties used for manufacturing into plug and other chewing, and pipe smoking tobaccos. Of the manufacturing tobaccos, there are innumerable varieties. The principal States for the production are Virginia, Kentucky, Tennessee, Missouri and Ohio. Of the sections named, Kentucky produces by far the largest quantity. The cotton States produce but little tobacco, but, at the centennial exposition twenty-one States were represented, which besides the hung leaf exhibited ninety specimens of pressed leaf, the best sample being from Virginia and valued at four dollars per pound. In cigar tobaccos, Connecticut produces the best, and Wisconsin the next best tobacco, if we may except Florida which produces comparatively but a small quantity, but of a high grade for wrappers and fillers to cigars. It is now thought that there are soils in Arizona that when opened to culture will produce very superior tobacco, as there is in California. Indeed, no crop is so much influenced by soil and climate as tobacco. When greater care in the selection of soils, manures, cultivation and especially in curing come to be more carefully attended to, there is no reason why tobacco from particular valley districts in the South, in the granitic formation, should not produce tobacco fully equal to the famous Yara of Cuba. Inattention to these plants and ignorance on the part of many cultivators, who have undertaken the cultivation of tobacco, has caused a glut of common tobacco which of late years have operated strongly against the profits of the crop. This will be evident by United States statistics which show the fact that, in 1869 the crop of the United States amounted to but about 324,000,000 pounds against, in round numbers, 412,000,000 in 1870; 410,000,000 in 1871; 505,000,000 in 1872; 502,000,000 in 1873; 358,000,000 in 1874; 520,000,000 in 1875; also 482,600,000 in 1876; and 581,500,000 in 1877; the conclusion is that, year by year, with slight variation, the planters have gone on increasing the crop until they have glutted the markets of the world. In relation to the product per acre 2,500 pounds have been produced, yet for the decade ending with 1878, 700 pounds was the average. The average price being five to six cents per pound. This average will cause continued loss to the planter. A good cultivator should get 1,500 pounds. At 700 pounds the acre brings but $38.50, a losing business; at 1,500 pounds, the acre brings $82.50. This leaves little margin for profit; but, if the 1,500 pounds be of superior quality the price will be raised to eight, ten, and even thirty cents per pound, and the profits are amply secured. The planter will thus see the necessity of never undertaking this crop until by experiment he is assured first that his soil, climate and situation—including protection from sweeping winds—is right, and also that he thoroughly understands the cultivation, curing and packing in the best possible manner and also that he has the necessary capital for carrying the whole forward. The following synopsis of the necessities in tobacco raising in the tobacco belt, say between 36° and 40°, we take from a statement by one of the most intelligent tobacco planters of the South. These general rules will apply wherever tobacco may be grown: Select good land for the crop; plow and subsoil it in Autumn to get the multiplied benefits of winter's freezes. This can not be too strongly urged. Have early and vigorous plants and plenty of them. It were better to have 100,000 too many than 10,000 too few. To make sure of them give personal attention to the selection and preparation of the plant bed and to the care of the young plants in the means necessary to hasten their growth, and to protect them from the dreadful fly. Collect manure in season and out of season, and from every available source—from the fence-corners, the ditch-bank, the urinal, the ash pile. Distribute it with a liberal hand; nothing short of princely liberality will answer. Plow it under (both the home-made and the commercial) in February, that it may become thoroughly incorporated in the soil and be ready to answer to the first and every call of the growing plant. Often (we believe generally) the greatest part of manure applied to tobacco—and this is true of the bought fertilizer as well as that made on the farm—is lost to that crop from being applied too late. Don't wait to apply your dearly-purchased guano in the hill or the drill from fear that, if applied sooner, it will vanish into thin air before the plant needs it. This is an exploded fallacy. Experience, our best teacher, has demonstrated beyond cavil that stable and commercial manure are most efficacious when used in conjunction. In no other way can they be so intimately intermixed as by plowing them under—the one broadcasted on the other—at an early period of the preparation of the tobacco lot. This second plowing should not be so deep as the first; an average of three to four inches is about the right depth. Early in May (in the main tobacco belt to which this article chiefly refers, that is to say, between the thirty-fifth and fortieth parallels of north latitude), re-plow the land to about the depth of the February plowing, and drag and cross-drag, and, if need be, drag it again, until the soil is brought to the finest possible tilth. Thus you augment many-fold the probabilities of a stand on the first planting, and lessen materially the subsequent labor of cultivation. Plant on lists (narrow beds made by throwing four furrows together with the mold-board plow) rather than in hills, if for no other reason than that having now, if never before, to pay wages in some shape to labor, whenever and wherever possible horse-power should be substituted for man-power—the plow for the hoe. Plant as early as possible after a continuance of pleasant spring weather is assured. Seek to have a forward crop, as the benefits claimed for a late one from the fall dews do not compensate for the many advantages resulting from early maturity. Make it an inflexible rule to plant no tobacco after the 10th of July—we mean, of course, in the tobacco belt we have named. Where one good crop is made from later planting, ninety-nine prove utter failures. Far better rub out and start afresh the next year. Take pains in transplanting, that little or no re-planting may be necessary. The cut-worm being a prime cause of most of the trouble in securing a stand, hunt it assiduously and particularly in the early morning when it can most readily be found. Keep the grass and weeds down, and the soil loose and mellow by frequent stirring, avoiding as much as possible cutting and tearing the roots of the plant in all stages of its growth; and more especially after topping. When at all practicable—and, with the great improvement in cultivators, sweeps, and other farm implements, it is oftener practicable than generally supposed—substitute for hand-work in cultivation that of the horse. The difference in cost will tell in the balance sheet at the close of the operation. Attend closely to worming for on it hinges in no little degree the quality and quantity of tobacco you will have for sale. A worm eaten crop brings no money. So important is this operation that it may properly claim more than a passing notice. Not only is it the most tedious, the most unremitting, and the most expensive operation connected with the production of tobacco, but the necessity for it determines more than all other causes the limit of the crop which in general it has been found possible for a single hand to manage. Therefore bring to your aid every possible adjunct in diminishing the number of worms. Use poison for killing the moth in the manner so frequently described in treatises on tobacco, to wit, by injecting a solution of cobalt or other deadly drug into the flower of the

Jamestown or jimson weed (*Datura stramonium*), if necessary planting seeds of the weed for the purpose. Employ at night the flames of lamps, of torches, or of huge bonfires, in which the moth may find a quick and certain death. In worming, spare those worms found covered with a white film or net-like substance, this being the cocoon producing the ichneumon fly, an enemy to the worm likely to prove a valuable ally to the planter in his war of extermination. Turn your flock of turkeys into the tobacco field, that they, too, may prey upon the pest, and themselves grow fat in so doing. If these remedies should fail, sprinkle diluted spirits of turpentine over the plant through the rose of a watering pot, a herculean task truly in a large crop, but mere child's play to the hand-picking process, for the one sprinkling suffices to keep off the worms for all time, whereas the hand-picking is a continual round of expensive labor from the appearance of the first worm until the last plant has been carried to the barn. We have no idea that such sprinkling will at all affect the odor or flavor of the tobacco when cured. If, as stated by a writer in a California paper, the well known yellow-jacket be useful in destroying tobacco worms, by all means win it as an ally. As proving its usefulness, the writer asserts that one of his neighbors, Mr. Culp, during fifteen years growing tobacco, has never expended a dollar for labor to destroy the worm, trusting all to this little workman, who, he says, carefully searches the plants for the worms, and never allows one to escape its vigilance. We can not speak from our own experience as to many of these suggested means for overcoming the horn-worm, but we have no hesitation in saying to the farmer, try any, try all of them rather than have your crop eaten to shreds, and the labor of more than half the year brought to naught in a few days, it may be, by a single glut of worms. Prime high and top low. While open to objection in particular cases, even with the character of tobacco chiefly under consideration, and altogether inadmissible, it may be, in the management of other varieties of tobacco, this is a safe rule, we think, to follow in general practice. We favor priming by all means; for when no priming is practiced the lower leaves (made worthless by constant whipping on the ground) serve only as a harbor for worms, which are the more difficult to find because of the increased burden of stooping. Moreover, if the bottom leaves be saved on the cut stalk, as most likely they will be, there is always the temptation to put them on the market. Yet another advantage to be gained by the removal of these bottom leaves, which is what the planter terms priming, is the increased circulation of air and distribution of light thereby afforded, both essential factors, the merest tyro knows, to the full development of plant life. Topping (the pinching off with the finger-nail the bud at the top of the plant) is an operation requiring considerable skill and judgment. Let it be performed only by hands having these prerequisites. That as many plants as possible may ripen at the same time (a desideratum not to be undervalued in aiming, as all should, at a uniform crop) wait until a large number of plants begin to button before commencing to top. Going about through the crop, topping a plant here and there because it may chance to have buttoned before its fellows, is a damaging process not to be tolerated. No inflexible rule can be given for the number of leaves that should be left on a plant. All depends upon the variety of tobacco, the strength of the soil, the promise of the particular plant, the probable seasons and time left for ripening, etc. One of the most successful growers of heavy dark tobacco we have ever known once stated to us his conviction, after years of observation and practice, that one year with another, taking the seasons as they come, eight leaves would give a better result than any other number. Our own experience has tended to confirm this judgment. See to it that the suckers are promptly removed. It is work quickly done, and with worming may constitute a single operation. We come now to consider the last operation in the field, cutting the crop. In this, as in topping, a man of judgment, experience, and fidelity is needed. An inexperienced hand, one without judgment, and particularly one who is indifferent to the interests of his employer, will slash away, right and left, not knowing or caring whether the tobacco he cuts be ripe or green, doing more damage in a few hours than his whole year's wages would compensate for, even could they be garnisheed. Therefore, be on hand to see for yourself, and do not delegate the duty to any less interested party, that a crop managed well, it may be, so far, from the initial plant-bed, shall not be spoiled in the closing work by an incompetent or unfaithful cutter. Be there, too, to see, in this supreme hour, that injury from sunburn is warded off by the timely removal, to the shade, of the plants that have been cut, or by a proper covering, where they lie, against the scorching rays of the sun. The neglect of this precaution has played havoc with many a crop when brought under the auctioneer's hammer. We should have no space to describe the different methods of curing tobacco, as for instance, sun-curing, air-curing, flue-curing, open-fire-curing, etc., even though the whole subject had not been gone over again and again in previous reports of this department. We can only say of this operation, as of all others connected with the production of tobacco, that much depends on its proper doing and that, as much as possible, it should have the personal superintendence of the owner. But the crop may have been brought along successfully even to the completion of this operation and lack one thing yet, if it be not now properly manipulated. Therefore, go yourself, trust no other into your barns, see with your own eyes, and not through the medium of others; handle with your own hands, and know of a surety that the tobacco hanging on the tier-poles is in proper order for striking and bulking, and act accordingly. When, later on, it is being stripped, sorted, and tied into bundles, or hands, as they are often called, be there again, *propriâ personâ*, to see that it is properly classed, both as to color and to length, the lugs going with lugs, the short with short, the long with long, etc. Instruct those sorting that when in doubt as to where a particular leaf should be put to put it at least one grade lower than they had thought of doing. Thus any error will be on the safe side. Prize in hogsheads to weigh what is usually called for in the market in which you sell, and, above all, let the tobacco in each hogshead be as near alike as possible, uniform throughout, so that the sample, from whatever point it may be taken, can be relied on as representing the whole hogshead, and that there be left no shadow of suspicion that nesting has been attempted, or any dishonest practice even so much as attempted. Again, manuring is important. If guano, poultry droppings, or other special manures are used, they must be followed by a liberal application of stable manure and the plowing under of green crops. For manufacturing tobacco, chewing, snuff, etc., twelve loads of sheep manure, twenty loads of horse, thirty loads of cattle, or thirty loads of hog manure would be indicated, the first mentioned being preferable. For cigar or other smoking tobacco: sheep manure, eight loads; horse manure, fifteen loads; cattle manure, twenty loads. If the soil is sandy the cow manure being indicated, guano may be applied also, 200 pounds, or poultry droppings 400 pounds per acre. Land in good heart, say capable of producing fifty or sixty bushels of corn per acre, being understood to start with. The tobacco house must be of ample size to properly cure the tobacco without crowding. The building having

TOBACCO HOUSE.

fifteen feet posts, a space twenty-four by thirty feet is not too much for each acre of heavy tobacco. Barns and outbuildings may be utilized to some extent, but tobacco can not be properly cured in them, since the crop sometimes requires firing—that is, drying by fire heat. Tobacco in the South is usually packed in hogsheads; in the North in cases. For cultivating and curing cigar tobacco, as practiced in the North, the following synopsis will give an intelligent idea: Ground can not be too rich. Barn yard manure is, beyond dispute, the most preferable, if not the only reliable fertilizer. Gypsum, wood ashes, etc., are good auxiliaries. Sandy loam, preferable to a stiffer soil, and thorough cultivation are the great requisites. Without this, a paying crop can not be expected. Fall plowing, or early spring desirable. When ground is thus prepared, say about May twentieth, it should be ridged in rows, three and a half feet apart, or four feet, if the ground is very rich. After ridging cut out indentations to receive the plant, say three and a half inches deep on the row, and from twenty-two to thirty inches apart, as experience may dictate, a medium between the two being, perhaps, as good as any, depending, of course, on soil, season, etc. The plants should be set below the general level of the row, as by future hoeing the higher portions will be cut down to a level. All other cultivation should be the same as that for corn or other hoed crops, thorough and frequent. No weeds dare be allowed at any time. In an average season the plant will mature sufficiently by the early part of August to dispense with further cultivation of ground, as the plant shading it will check the growth of weeds. Whenever the plant develops from fourteen to sixteen leaves, break off the top, don't cut it off. This arrests the further production of leaves, but will promote the growth of suckers, which will have to be removed, after attaining a length of three to four inches, as often as they appear. It may be well to refer here to two formidable enemies of the plant, viz: the black cut-worm and the green tobacco worm. The former will attack the root of the plant as soon as it is put into the ground. The depredations of this worm sometimes necessitate frequent re-planting. They must be hunted and destroyed until they disappear, which they will do as the season advances. The last named generally appears about July first, and feeds on the leaf until the crop is secured in the sheds. In fact, they frequently, if not picked off clean, cling to the leaves after the stalk is hung up. About these there is but one advice to give, pick them off and destroy them, going over the field for this purpose daily, as the ravages of the green worm do more to injure the quality, perhaps, than any one thing. Usually, from three to four weeks from the time of topping, the plant will mature and be ready to cut. Uniform size of leaves, and a stiffness of the leaf, making it liable to break by bending and handling, are the surest signs of maturity. Cut after the dew is off, but not during the middle of the day, when the sun is bright, as you must guard against burning while it is undergoing the wilting process, preparatory to spearing and handling in the removal to the shed. When sufficiently wilted, the plan most in practice is spearing or stringing upon laths four feet long, five or six plants to each lath, and then removing same into shed and hang up for curing. Distance between lath, general arrangement of shed and management thereof, as to ventilation, admission of light, etc., must be attended to. Air and light having a great influence on the curing and fixing of color, must be used to the best advantage in catering to the tastes of the trade, which, by the way, are subject to frequent changes; sometimes light tobacco is in demand and again dark only will meet a ready sale. Strange, but true, frequently when we have it dark the buyers want it light, and vice versa. In removing plants to the shed after cutting various devices are used. Sleds, wagons in various styles, any way in which you succeed without breaking or bruising the leaf, is a good, and the quickest way, with these ends accomplished, is the best. By the middle of December, and after, whenever the plant is sufficiently pliable by moisture to strip or handle it without

HAND OF TOBACCO.

WHEAT.—Rank and yield of the States, with average annual product for the past nine years.

Rank.	States.	Total value of Crop.	Value per Acre.	No. of Acres.	Amount of Crop. Bush.	Yield per Acre. Bush.
1	California	$32,760,147	$14.91	2,199,796	28,534,250	12.9
2	Illinois	30,084,369	13.15	2,336,591	30,488,354	13.2
3	Ohio	28,313,381	16.15	1,746,386	24,715,591	12.9
4	Indiana	26,983,689	14.32	1,874,287	25,283,745	13.3
5	Iowa	22,927,414	8.45	2,794,352	29,828,230	10.9
6	Pennsylvania	22,686,436	17.99	1,268,184	17,541,175	13.
7	Michigan	22,417,201	17.36	1,291,858	19,510,415	14.9
8	Minnesota	21,178,528	11.93	1,851,196	26,228,608	14.5
9	Wisconsin	19,966,528	12.18	1,632,733	21,588,100	13.2
10	Missouri	15,232,943	11.64	1,324,232	16,030,675	11.9
11	Kansas	14,541,661	10.76	1,377,997	19,055,135	13.8
12	New York	12,318,591	19.29	639,664	9,443,050	14.6
13	Tennessee	11,405,014	8.81	1,333,146	10,551,450	8.0
14	Virginia	8,843,927	10.34	860,131	7,229,570	8.3
15	Kentucky	7,985,582	11.50	691,240	7,442,900	10.9
16	Maryland	7,508,906	15.79	478,756	5,711,355	11.9
17	Nebraska	5,901,158	9.19	741,455	9,221,625	12.7
18	Oregon	4,725,464	16.03	295,251	5,288,955	18.5
19	Georgia	4,317,748	11.35	386,234	3,095,115	7.8
20	North Carolina	4,011,842	9.46	428,107	3,144,912	7.3
21	Texas	3,814,688	18.14	260,533	3,751,150	14.3
22	West Virginia	3,766,697	12.39	310,773	3,294,075	10.7
23	New Jersey	2,801,287	19.63	145,259	2,021,575	13.9
24	Alabama	1,562,058	10.61	153,042	1,195,670	7.9
25	Arkansas	1,412,324	11.21	150,070	1,356,250	9.3
26	South Carolina	1,349,288	12.01	112,481	865,721	7.0
27	Delaware	1,082,868	17.08	63,770	803,450	12.5
28	Vermont	663,186	21.40	27,460	453,875	16.5
29	Nevada	525,050	20.52	18,259	357,800	20.0
30	Maine	517,388	22.55	23,279	326,900	14.0
31	Mississippi	459,061	13.33	40,817	358,000	8.7
32	New Hampshire	301,877	25.00	12,207	185,390	15.3
33	Connecticut	52,861	25.57	2,244	36,849	16.4
34	Massachusetts	30,394	28.10	1,458	25,482	18.4

injury, you can strip it; assorting leaves is one of the prominent features in the stripping process. All solid leaves should be kept separate as wrappers, and these sorted into hands of ten or twelve leaves, each hand tied at the butt by a single leaf. All leaves in the same hand should be of uniform length. The hands should then be assorted with reference to length into two or three sizes. All defective leaves should be treated alike and put up separately, the respective qualities being bulked up separately ready for market. The packing or casing is generally done by parties buying it from the grower.

TOBACCO. (See Supplement for quantities, value and distribution.)

TOMATO. *Lycopersicum esculentum.* Like the lycopersicum family generally, the tomato is a native of America, the southern half of the continent being its home. It was introduced into England in 1596, and from there found its way to India. Until within, comparatively, a few years, it was considered poisonous, or at least unfit for food. Now it is cultivated in every garden, and has become an indispensable adjunct to the table, whether in its fresh state or canned. It is easily susceptible to frost, but of the easiest cultivation. The plan most successful on ordinary loam or clay, being to throw up rather high ridges five feet apart. Set the plants three and a half feet on these ridges, keep clean, and allow the vines to droop along the sharp sides of the ridges. Thus the sun and air is admitted, rot is prevented, the trouble and cost of trellising is avoided, and as large crops, (sometimes 500 bushels per acre) may be raised as in any other way. The seed should be sown in a hot bed as early as the first of March, and the plants pricked out six inches apart, as soon as large enough, transplanting to the open ground as soon as the days and nights become permanently warm. When the first frosts kill the vines in the fall, if the tomatoes are gathered and spread under glass, they will continue to ripen for a month. Select some of the large, smooth, red varieties for table use and canning, and the yellow plum variety for preserving.

TOMATO WINE. (See Gallizing.)
TOMENTOSE. Covered with down hair.
TON. A weight formerly of twenty cwt., or 2,240 pounds; now 2,000 pounds.
TONGUE. The soft, fleshy organ of taste. It is covered by nerves and blood-vessels.
TONICS. Those medicines which improve the general health and appetite. They are commonly called bitters.
TONKA BEAN. The fruit of the *Dipterix odorata*, used to flavor snuff.
TONSILS. Small glands situated in the throat.
TOOL HOUSE. An indispensable building, (either separate or attached to some other) dry and well ventilated, where tools, implements, machinery, etc., may be stored, when not in use. Such tools as are required for use every day, or at short intervals, should occupy such a position as to be easily accessible. The work shop may naturally occupy a portion of this building, and be provided with a carpenter's bench, saw horses, saddler's seat, and the tools, such as axes, planes, chisels, bits, augurs, needles, awls, thread, etc., for repairing.

TOP DRESSING. Top dressing is that form of manuring where the fertilizing material is applied to the surface of the earth, instead of being plowed under, as for instance, in the case of meadows, pastures, young wheat, and other cereal grains, young grass, orchards, etc. It may be intended to act simply as a fertilizer, or to effect the two-fold purpose of a mulch to protect a crop during the winter, and at the same time produce fertilization. In the latter case green manure may be applied in the autumn, and the long straw be raked together, and carted away in the spring, unless the crop is of such a nature that it will readily grow through. If a meadow or pasture, it should be raked off. If grain, it may be applied more thinly, and the grain will grow through. As a rule, however, a top dressing should consist of well rotted manure or compost. Of mineral substances, ashes, lime, gypsum, and salt are used; of commercial fertilizers, superphosphate, guano, poudrette, and other manures of like nature, should be lightly harrowed in, to save waste. Liquid manure is always used as a top dressing. It is one of the most valuable in the whole category of manures, and prompt in its action. Of these, the diluted urine of animals, leakage from compost heaps, and sewage waste are most generally used. In relation to the philosophy of top dressing, Prof. Johnson says: Fresh stable manure contains some seventy per cent. of water, twenty-five per cent. of vegetable and animal matters, and five per cent. of salts and mineral substance. If we put it on a cloth strainer, and slowly wash it with the rain of a watering pot, we shall dissolve out a portion of the organic matter, (some two per cent.,) and a portion of the salts, (some four or five per cent.) and we shall, besides, drive through the cloth some of the fine particles of the manure that do not actually dissolve; but the coarse parts will remain on the strainer. The same happens on the ground. The most active fertilizing elements are carried into the soil in solution, the undissolved matters which exist in a state of fine division are mechanically carried into the soil to an extent depending upon its porosity, while the coarse matters—the straw of the litter—remain on the surface. Now, what happens to dissolved matters, consisting of humic acid, which gives the brown color to dung liquor, and of carbonates, phosphates and sulphates, of ammonia, potash, lime, magnesia and soda? Are they liable to run to waste? No more, it would appear, than if the manure was buried in the soil. Not so much, in fact, as in the latter case, because they have more soil to pass through before they can escape into the springs. If the soil is fine in texture, has enough fine earth, or rather that retentive power over the soluble matters of manure which reside in the fine earth, and which enables good soil to filter out and hold in its pores these soluble matters, so that you can put dung heap liquor into a leach tub half full of such earth, and pure drinkable water will run out below, then you need fear no waste. But if the soil is coarse in texture, and water runs through it very rapidly, and dung heap liquor is not much clarified and sweetened by passing it, then the manure may suffer decided loss. Yet again, in case of the coarse, open soil, if it be full of grass roots or grain roots, which are ready to absorb the dissolved matters as soon and as fast as the spring rains descend, you may lose, indeed, some manure; but you may also do well to lose a part of it, in order to put another greater part where the growing crops will be certain to pay back for all the expenditure and give a margin of profit besides. On light, unretentive land, bare of vegetation, do not apply manure to the surface during the winter. A principal benefit of stable manure to such soil consists in mixing with the bulky, insoluble matters of the dung and litter which are of the most porous and moisture holding character, and which operate to counteract the leachy and droughty qualities of the soil. On such land hold the manure in reserve, carefully protected by cover if practicable, and bury it in the soil where the pushing roots of the new sown crops will find it, and where it will be food to the plant not only, but drink also, in virtue of its hygroscopic nature, all the summer through. The presence of abundance of stable manure in such a soil enables it to hold a much greater proportion of the rain that falls upon it; less rain runs off into the streams; there is less leaching, therefore, of plant food; at the same time there is increase of plant drink. This point can only be appreciated when we know that the evaporation of water through the foliage of crops amounts to 5,000,000 pounds per acre every season, and must go on whether there is rain to supply it or not. After having, by any proper system of management, so altered the texture of leachy soil that it will hold almost all the water that falls upon it; after having incorporated with it vegetable matter in considerable quantities, and mixed with coal ashes—leached ashes, perhaps—so that the soil has a great many fine pores, and so that the rain penetrates it slowly, and but little runs away altogether, then we have practically a different condition of things, and need not fear loss by drainage. The more the soil approaches that state which is implied by the term loamy, the more we can risk our manure upon the surface when the crop is not there. One effect of surface manuring upon soils which are in grass or occupied with crops or upon soils not thus occupied, if they are retentive of the element of fertility, has been mentioned by Dr. Hatch, that is, a decided effect on the texture of the soil. The German farmers have a special word for it; they call it fermentation, and have written books upon it. There is a kind of texture which is proper to land in good condition, something like that which you find in a well-cultivated garden. It is a thing which it is rather difficult to describe; but, when you once understand what it is, you can easily identify it. It is a sort of mellowness of the soil. If you take up a board which has been laying in a walk, you will see a difference between the soil underneath that board and the soil close at hand. There is a friability, a fineness, or something about that soil which is apparently very agreeable to the roots of plants. Dr. Hatch remarked that sod upon which manure had been laying through the winter broke up more easily and was a different sort of thing from sod where this had not happened. This quality depends chiefly upon the protection which the cover, be it board, stone or, manure, affords against the dashing of the rain, which compacts and puddles the surface, and against the drying effects of sun and wind, which tend to form a crust. The shelter keeps the earth uniformly moist, and as friable at the surface as it is below, or as its nature admits. It also favors the burrowing of earth-worms, grubs and other insects at the surface, which otherwise must go deeper to enjoy the moisture they require. This shelter, then, of surface-strewn litter is a cheap tillage, or takes the place of tillage to some extent; and on soils of certain texture is very favorable, or at least is thought to be by many intelligent, practical men. Speaking of the value of night-soil as a fertilizer, Mr. Clift said: I have been in the habit for five and twenty years of utilizing night-soil—taking the contents of the privy as prepared, and spreading them in the garden, upon my mowing-fields, and using them in the cultivation of almost all kinds of crops, especially garden crops, and I have eaten, and my family have eaten very freely of the various kinds of vegetables and fruits which have grown on this soil, which is pretty thoroughly saturated with night-soil. I have never discovered that it has done me or them any harm. The celery that is grown with this kind of fertilizer I know to be of very fine flavor, and I prefer to use it rather than any other in the cultivation of celery in trenches, where the application has been not only of the solid contents of the privy, but the liquid manure, of course very greatly diluted, applied to the growing crop. It makes very good celery, it makes good potatoes, it makes good sweet corn, good cabbages, good turnips, and good everything that I want to grow in the garden; and if it has ever done my family any harm, I have never found it out. Dr. Riggs spoke as follows of the earth-closet system and the value of night-soil when prepared in this way: The earth-closet system is true in theory, and it is true in every way; but, unhappily, it has never been applied until lately, and now not perfectly. The vaults of our privies should be so arranged that they should be regular manure factories, and so that a man can go into them in the winter time and manipulate the manure by mixing dry earth with it. This earth —no matter if it is nothing but light, loamy soil, what we call yellow dirt is just as good—should be dry. When it is dry, it mixes with the night-soil and deodorizes it completely, so much so, that you could carry it in a snuff box and present it to your neighbor, and he could not tell of what it was composed. Now, other manures should be deodorized in the same way, but night-soil especially should have that treatment. The cellar for composting of that material should be so arranged that it can be easily removed; we should have it under control. Coal ashes have considerable alkali, but it is in the form of carbonate of lime. The composition of coal ashes is carbonate of lime, alumina, and oxide of iron —valuable as far as it goes, and very valuable on light, sandy soil. Like the application of other carbonates, it makes light land heavier and more adhesive, and it has the contrary effect on clays; but it should not be composed with any manure any more than should lime. A point in which I think they are lacking in the stables we have visited, although the management is excellent, is this; the manure lacks packing. It is the carbonate of lime that causes that evaporation or the development of gases, and if it was thoroughly packed by those pigs, (that is their true field of action) they would find their manure much richer and much stronger when they undertook to get it out than they will under the present arrangement. That has been my experience. I have tried lime in compost heaps where there was nothing but vegetable matter, and it is very valuable, but in night-soil it is perfectly destructive to the fertilizing qualities; that is, in the main. I think it causes loss, so that it is not as good, or certainly no better, than road scrapings, or the soil that we get by the side of our fences. I think that we ought to have a proper reservoir made, not merely large enough for the excrement, both liquid and solid, to be kept during the year, but to give room for its manipulation, by throwing on this dry earth to deodorize it. Copperas, sulphate of iron, is very good, better than anything else, to deodorize a vault. You may take the strongest manure, and put in a few quarts of pulverized copperas, either in the form of a solution or a fine powder, and it will deodorize it so completely without any earth at all that you will hardly know what you are shoveling. It is better than plaster in a cellar like the one of which I am speaking. It costs more, but you can buy it by the quantity at about a cent and three-quarters or two cents a pound. You will find that copperas water or copperas sprinkled over it, will deodorize it so completely that your men will not object to working in it. Mr. Weld, of New York, gave his method of securing and preserving the contents of the privy as follows: I think a vault is a nuisance. There is a box which slides under the privy, which I originally had on runners, but I found it more convenient to knock the runners off, slip the box on a stone-boat and carry it off. The box is four and one-half or five feet long, two feet wide, and fourteen inches deep. There is a constant supply of dry earth kept in the privy, and when any member of my family uses the closet a dipper of earth is thrown in. It is not a very disagreeable thing to do, nor is there any thing disagreeable about keeping the box clean. The stone-boat is brought down, the box is raised with a crow-bar, for it is rather heavy to lift, the stone-boat shoved under, and the box is carried off, and the contents put on the top of the ground, or worked right into the garden. The manure does not deteriorate if left on the surface. The box is emptied a good many times a year, although I have but a small family. And the more dirt goes in it the better it is. It works easily. I frequently go in, and to the disgust of the man whose business it is to keep the earth box full, throw on half the contents of the box so as to be sure to have dirt enough. It is always crumbling, so that there is no trouble about applying it. The foregoing will apply to the saving of all offensive manures in their natural state. All such manures are also most valuable for top dressing, but are better if slightly covered under.

TORMENTIL. *Potentilla officinalis.* An exotic with an astringent root.

TORREFACTION. Roasting mineral bodies, usually under a red heat.

TORTRICES. A tribe of nocturnal lepidoptera, the larvæ of most of which conceal themselves by rolling up leaves and living in the interior.

TORUS. The end of the flower branch on which the carpels are situated.

TOURMALINE. A gem, valued from its property of polarizing light.

TOURNIQUET. A bandage which may be tightened to any extent by means of a screw, so as to exert pressure upon a cushion, and compress the arterial trunks to which it is applied. It is chiefly used to prevent hemorrhage in the operations of amputation.

TRACHEA. The windpipe.

TRACHEÆ. The spiral vessels of leaves and insects.

TRACHELIDANS. A family of coleoptera, in many of which the head is supported on a kind of neck.

TRACHEOTOMY. The operation of tracheotomy is described by the late Dr. Dadd as follows: The operation consists in making an opening into the windpipe to admit air to the lungs, when the natural passage is obstructed by foreign bodies, or when its calibre is lessened by tumefaction occasioned by disease. In severe cases of laryngitis, strangles, and their kindred diseases, when the patient seems almost suffocated, tracheotomy should be immediately performed. In performing the operation, we select a spot about six inches below the throat, in front of the neck, and over the region of the windpipe; an incision is to be made with a common penknife, (in lieu of a better instrument,) to the extent of two or three inches, in a downward direction, so as to lay bare the trachea; having exposed space sufficient, a circular piece between two rings, corresponding to the size of the tube, is to be cut out, and a short tube inserted, which can be confined in position by means of tape passed around the neck. When the obstruction is removed, or the fauces restored to their natural state, remove the tube, bring the edges of the integuments together, and sew them up.

TRACHYTE. An ancient lava.

TRAGACANTH. A gum, which swells, but is not soluble in cold water.

TRAM ROAD. A road set with stone flags, wood, or iron ways, at such distances that the wheels of wagons, etc., may continually roll on them.

TRANSITION ROCKS. The extensive series of stratified and ancient rocks lying between the granitic series and the coal. It consists of slates, gneiss, and crystalline limestones.

TRANSPLANTING. Transplanting is the art of so removing plants that they shall receive the slightest possible check in the removal. The objects in transplanting is, first, to increase the season of growth of exotic plants by previous forcing in hot beds and greenhouses, that we may get easier and longer continued flowering and fruitage; second, the economical and better care certain classes of plants may receive, by growing them while young in confined spaces, as cabbage, cauliflower, celery and other plants, which indeed mature perfectly in the North; third, in the case of trees that may be more easily grown in masses or narrow rows while young; fourth, to increase the root fibers by successive transplantings, thus inducing a more stocky growth of plants, and earlier fruitage. This latter may be also accomplished by root pruning. The whole art of transplanting during the season of growth is simply to keep sufficient moisture at the roots to compensate the exhalation from the roots until new feeding roots can be thrown out. Some plants have been known to transpire twice their own weight in a day. Hence plants not naturally supplied with fibrous roots, tap rooted plants, and those having soft and succulent leaves are, as a rule, difficult of transplantation. As a rule, plants will in favorable weather throw out new roots in twenty-four hours after being moved. Thus, to facilitate this action, they are usually moved during cloudy weather or just before night, after the sun has lost its power. It may, therefore, be taken as an axiom that to secure success in transplanting of plants with their foliage that it will depend upon the preservation of as many fibrous roots as possible and the prevention of excessive evaporation. In the case of trees and shrubs which drop their leaves periodically, there is little difficulty experienced during their season of rest. The same may be said of evergreens. Keep the roots moist and success is pretty certain. As a rule, transplanting is not as difficult as is generally imagined. The great and yearly losses sustained in the transplantation of the various plants usually purchased of the gardener, florist and nurseryman, make it very important that a few plain directions be given relating thereto. When sent out by respectable propagators and growers, plants are usually in good condition. It is to the interest of the grower that they shall be so. One of the most fatal mistakes, made by novices in the art is, that transplanting must be done when the earth is wet. If you can so time your work, that you transplant just before a shower, you will have hit the mark exactly, but if not, wait until the land is again in good working order. Never set out plants in the mud. Just at night or in cloudy weather, is the best time. If the plants are small keep the roots in water, until they are planted. If larger protect from the sun and air. We have known evergreens especially killed by contact with the sun and wind for five minutes. For ourselves we never wait for rain for transplanting, but have water near, hauled in barrels if necessary, for extensive planting. One hand plants, or rather fastens the plant, by drawing earth enough around it, for the purpose, another pours sufficient water about it to thoroughly wet it about the roots. When it has disappeared the planting may be finished by drawing over and around it dry or moist earth. Be sure and press the earth firmly about the roots when planted, but leave the surface light and mellow. Some of the more delicate plants, or those not easily transplanted, may need shading for a day or two, if you are very particular for perfect success, but under ordinary circumstances, it will not be needed. The same rules here indicated will apply to all larger plants, shrubs and trees. Keep the roots as much as possible from the sun and air. Give water at the roots when transplanted, draw over all dry, or only moist earth, mulch thoroughly, and nature will do the rest. In this connection, cast away the old fogyish notion that the top must be cut away to correspond to the rest. It is a relic of superstitious ignorance. The roots of a tree are its feeding mouths. The leaves are its lungs and stomach. Mutilate either unduly, and it is fatal to the prospect for health, and just in proportion to the top, in just such proportion will be formation of root surface. Never buy trees and plants at any price that have been unduly mutilated at the root, and the roots being fairly supplied, never cut away more of the top than just sufficient to bring the tree into as symmetrical shape as possible, for again we say, just in proportion to the leaf surface, so will be the power of the plant or tree, in forming new roots, or rather spongioles for feeding. We are thus particular because there is really no reason for the great annual loss which is sustained in the transplantation of trees and plants.

TRAPA NATANS. The water chestnut.

TRAP ROCKS. Ancient rocks of fusion occurring in mountains and large seams. They consist of various mixtures of hornblende and feldspar, and when containing much iron are very destructible, but usually resist the action of weather for an immense time.

TRAUMATIC. Relating to or arising from a wound.

TRAVELER'S JOY. *Clematis vitalba.* A climbing shrub with white flowers.

TREFOIL. *Trifolium.* A name applied to clover and also to lucerne, melilot clover, and formerly to all plants of the pulse family having three leaves like the common clover. The word is now scarcely used, the proper name of the individual species being applied. See articles Clover, Lucerne, Vetch, Melilotus, etc. The tick trefoil, desmodium, has many varieties, all noxious weeds, bearing bean-like pods, covered with hooked hairs, which fasten persistently to animals and the clothing of men.

TREES IN CITIES AND VILLAGES. We constantly hear complaints from citizens that the trees they have spent so much money in having planted and cared for, give but little satisfaction. A large majority die in the course of a few years, or at least become dingy and unhealthy from the effects of the smoke of the bituminous coal used so universally in the West. Evergreens are especially sensitive to disability from this cause. Among deciduous trees, the elm soonest shows blackening and stoppage of the pores, although all lose vigor to a greater or less degree from this cause, and notably all those having rough or hairy leaves, and this, undoubtedly, from the fact that these rough surfaces are not so easily washed by rains and showering as are the smooth and glossy leaved varieties. It is unfortunate, for in no place is the sanitary need of oxygen-giving plants more necessary than in our densely populated cities. Among the trees that longest resist the effects of city air, the cottonwoods bear the palm. The most serious objection to this tree is, the habit of discharging cotton, as the downy covering of the seeds is called. This, however, may be obviated, by selecting cuttings from the male tree, which does not throw off this substance. It has the added advantage of being healthy in a great variety of soils. The Plane (button wood) is also a most eligible tree for street planting in soils congenial to it. Its habit of throwing off its old bark annually, thus leaving its trunk smooth, gives this tree a peculiarly clean and fresh appearance, possessed by none outside this family. It also exposes a large leaf surface to the atmosphere, and exhales oxygen correspondingly. Ash leaved maple, *Acer negundo*, so far as our observation goes, also does well as a street tree. In fact all the maples do so measurably. The fact that the Ash leaved maple never grows to a great size we do not consider a special disability. It grows quickly, and that is what is wanted. If it were generally understood, great size is not what is wanted in street trees. These may be well for parks, and also waste places, but our streets and yards should be planted with smaller, quick-growing varieties, that will stand the smoke and dust of our crowded thoroughfares. In villages and country places, the inhabitants may have a wider selection. Here elms and hard maples, beech, sycamore and linden, the oaks, walnuts and hickory, may have full scope to grow and spread, giving shade and adding grandeur to the scenery. It is one of the pleasantest features of farm life that the prairie home may be shaded with varieties that in time will become giants, and yet which will, while growing, shade the lawn about the homestead, and furnish a grateful resting place from the noonday heat, or a pleasant place where the family may gather after the labors of the day to enjoy the summer twilight while engaged in pleasant chat, or listening to the evening song of the birds which are drawn thither. No less pleasant is the merry music of these feathered messengers at early dawn, when their joyous warblings fill the fragrant morning air with melody.

TREES OF THE UNITED STATES. In the articles Forestry, Timber, Timber Trees, range of, etc., will be found much valuable information which has not been commonly known to the general reader, and indeed which has not come under the reading of many who take a special interest in forestry and tree planting. At the centennial exhibition, at Philadelphia in 1876, special pains was taken by the United States Government, to collect specimens of the trees of the country; showing sections of the wood, together with such information as could be had as to their distribution, characteristics and peculiarities as could be obtained. Data relating to these was subsequently collated and digested and made public in a report of the Department of Agriculture, and we here reproduce the substance, for reference, in the interest of that large class whom it specially interests. The arrangement is by Dr. George Vasey, the accomplished botanist of the Department of Agriculture, Washington. As collector for the Southern States, Mr. A. H. Curtiss, of Liberty, Va., a well-known botanist, was engaged. A large number of the trees of the Middle States were obtained in the vicinity of Washington. Of these, thirty species were procured from a part of the General Washington estate at Mount Vernon, now owned by Dr. E. P. Howland. The trees peculiar to the New England States were procured by Mr. C. G. Pringle, of Charlotte, Vt. As collector for the Western States, Mr. John Wolf, of Canton, Ill., was employed. In making the collection in Colorado, he was assisted by Mr. C. W. Derry, of Granite, Lake county, Col Again, the semi-tropical trees of Southern Florida were obtained by Dr. A. W. Chapman, of Apalachicola, during a two months' cruise by schooner on the west coast, among the various keys and inlets, and far into the interior by the Caloosahatchee river. A portion of the trees of Texas were obtained by Dr. S. B. Buckley, of Austin, whose labors in developing the botany of that section are well known; and a portion were collected by Dr. F. G. Lindheimer, a veteran botanist, whose collections of Texas plants, made many years ago, enrich the principal herbaria of the country. In Utah, Mr. L. F. Ward, botanist of the survey of the Colorado river by Messrs. Powell and Thompson, made the collection of the trees of that region. The trees of the high sierras of California and Nevada were procured by Mr. J. G. Lemmon, of Sierra county, Cal. The magnificent coniferous trees of that region are represented by large wedge-shaped sections of trees from four to seven feet in diameter, the preparation of which cost a great amount of toil and expense. The immense trees had to be felled, and the desired sections removed by sawing and splitting with wedges until the portions were reduced to proper size. The trees of the Pacific slope, in California, were collected by Mr. G. R. Vasey, with valuable aid and assistance from Dr. Kellogg, of San Francisco, Dr. J. G. Cooper, and others. Dr. Edward Palmer made the collection for the southern portion of California, Arizona, and Southern Utah. Mr A. J. Dufur, centennial Commissioner for Oregon, collected the peculiar trees of that State. After the woods were received at Washington, they were taken to a mill and reduced to the uniform length of two feet; then each section was divided by sawing longitudinally into two pieces, which were planed on the sawed surface, one arranged to show the outer or bark surface and the other to show the grain of the wood, its color, density, etc. The corresponding botanical specimens for each species are displayed in frames arranged in the immediate vicinity of the trees to which they belong. By this means, an intelligent view of the appearance and properties of every species of the trees of the country may be obtained Great difficulty, says the compiler, was experienced in deciding upon the limitations of height and size which should characterize a tree. It is well known that certain plants which are only shrubs in some places become large trees in other places; sometimes the difference depending on climate and sometimes on other circumstances. Thus, *Magnolia glauca*, or White Bay, grows and matures its flowers and fruit in some portions of Massachusetts, where it attains only the size of a large shrub. It, however, steadily increases in size in situations farther south, until in Georgia and Florida it attains the size of a large tree. In some places, the same plant appears as a shrub or a tree, under different circumstances, in closely contiguous localities. Dr. Chapman, who made the collection of trees of South Florida, says: I was much disappointed in the size of most of the forest growth in that region. A peculiarity of these tropical trees is, that for miles they occur to you as mere shrubs, when at some other locality you find them lofty trees. As a general rule, there has not been admitted into the collection any tree which does not, under favorable circumstances, attain a height of twenty feet and a diameter of four inches. Yet, in a few cases, to more fully illustrate a family, a tree has been admitted which would fall below that standard. The list given below enumerates about 400 species, the greater portion of which are represented by specimens in the collection. Some portions of the country have been so incompletely explored that our knowledge of their vegetation is imperfect; yet it is probable that this catalogue presents, with great accuracy, our present knowledge of the trees of the United States. In two or three instances only, foreign species have been admitted, because of their extensive naturalization, in some sections. The two largest genera of trees are the oaks and the pines, of which we have about thirty species of each. Of coniferous trees, including the pines, firs, cedars, larches, cypress, sequoias, etc., we have about sixty species. The rose family, including the plums, cherries, thorns, etc., is represented by over thirty species. Of the order *Leguminosæ*, or trees of the pod-bearing family, we have over twenty, embracing the locusts, acacias, redbuds, mesquits, etc. Of ericaceous trees we have eight species, including the Californian manzanita and madrone trees, the sorrel tree of the Southern States, and others. Of maples we have eight; of magnolias, seven; of ash, eleven; of elms, six; of walnuts and hickorys, thirteen; of poplars, eight; and of birch, six species. The usual difficulty has been encountered in deciding as to the standing of certain forms which some botanists regard as species and others as only varieties. In most well marked cases, these are entered in the catalogue under distinct numbers, either as species or as varieties, as the evidences in the case seemed most convincing. The range, or botanical region of each species, is indicated in a general manner, thus: Those trees which occur more or less extensively over the whole or the larger portion of the country east or the base of the Rocky mountains or east of the Mississippi river are marked eastern United States. This region is sub-divided, by a line running eastward from the mouth of the Ohio river to the Atlantic, into two portions, one of which is called Northeastern United States, and the other Southeastern United States. Other localities are indicated as Southern States, New England States, Western States, Alleghany mountains, etc. The western portion of the United States and Territories is marked in detached regions, as follows: Rocky Mountains of Colorado, or Rocky Mountains of Colorado and Utah; Sierra Nevada Mountains of California, Oregon, and Washington Territory; California; Southern California; Arizona. The portion of the country adjoining the Mexican border is indicated by the locality Western Texas and Westward. Certain portions of our country have not yet been sufficiently explored to determine accurately all the species of trees thereto belonging. This is the case with respect to the southern portion of Florida. Some species which at one time were thought to be indigenous to that region have not been confirmed by any late investigations, and will probably have to be erased from the list. The same difficulty occurs with respect to some of the trees of the Rocky mountains and the western coast, particularly the conifers and the willows. In a short time allotted to making this collection, it did not seem possible to obtain wood specimens of every species given in the catalogue. The number wanting, however, is but a small percentage of the whole. Among the good results growing out of this work, we may mention, first, that much information has been gained respecting species hitherto imperfectly known: and, secondly, that four or five new species, or species before unknown to our flora, have been obtained. These are mainly in South Florida, and include two exogens, viz, an anona or custard apple, and a chrysophyllum or star apple; and one endogen, a palm of the genus *Thrinax*. The arrangement is as follows:

MAGNOLIACEÆ.

Magnolia grandiflora. Evergreen Magnolia. Southern States. A large and beautiful tree, with thick, glossy evergreen leaves and large white flowers, which are exceedingly fragrant.

M. glauca. Sweet Bay White Bay. Massachusetts southward. Northward, this is only a small tree or shrub, but in the South it attains a large size, and the leaves become evergreen.

M. Umbrela. Umbrella Tree. Southern States, Alleghany mountains.

M. acuminata. Cucumber Tree. New York, South and West. This species has a greater range to the north and west, where it sometimes attains a large size.

M. cordata. Yellow Cucumber Tree. Southern States.

M. Fraseri. Long-leaved Cucumber Tree. Southern States.

M. macrophylla. Large-leaved Umbrella Tree. Southern States.

Liriodendron tulipifera. Tulip Tree. Yellow Poplar. Eastern United States. One of the largest and most beautiful of North American trees. In the Western States, it attains an immense size. It is found principally in the rich bottom lands of the large rivers, where its wood is extensively employed for building purposes and for the manufacture of furniture. As an ornamental tree, it is hardly surpassed by any other; its form being regular, its foliage peculiar and pleasing, and its abundant flowers, though not highly colored, are yet very beautiful.

ANONACEÆ.

Anona. Custard Apple. Southern Florida. Discovered by Dr. Chapman, in South Florida. It grows fifteen to twenty feet high. The fruit is small and eatable when full ripe. The species is undetermined.

Asimina triloba. Papaw. From Pennsylvania South and West. A small tree, very common in the Southern States, less frequent at the North. It produces an oblong pulpy fruit about four inches long, which, when ripe, has a rich luscious taste.

CAPPARIDACEÆ.

Capparis Jamaicensis. Caper Tree. South Florida. A shrub or small tree of South Florida, also growing in the West Indies. The true capers of commerce are the fruit of the Old World species.

CANELLACEÆ.

Canella alba. White Wood; Wild Cinnamon. South Florida. A small tree in South Florida. In the West Indies, it is abundant, and called Wild Cinnamon and White Wood. The bark is aromatic and tonic, and is much employed in medicine.

TAMARISCINEÆ.

Fouquiera splendens. Western Texas and Arizona. Grows in Western Texas, and thence westward to Southern California. In our borders, it is usually only a shrub; but in Mexico it grows twenty to thirty feet high and on account of its spiny branches is used for hedges and fences.

GUTTIFERÆ.

Clusia flava. South Florida. A West Indian tree, said to have been found in Florida, but not recently observed.

TERNSTROMIACEÆ.

Gordonia lasianthus. Loblolly Bay. Southern States. A tree thirty to fifty feet high, growing in swamps near the seacoast from North Carolina to Florida and Louisiana. The leaves are evergreen; the flowers showy white, and sweet-scented. The bark is much employed in tanning, as a substitute for oak-bark.

G. pubescens. Mountain Bay. Southern States. A small tree over thirty feet high, found in Georgia and Florida, and quite rare. It has been introduced into cultivation, and is hardy as far north as Philadelphia. When in bloom, it is beautiful, and it flowers continuously for two or three months.

TILIACEÆ.

The Tilias in Europe are called Lime trees, or Linn. Our species are commonly called Basswood. They are large trees, and have a wide range, being found probably in every State east of the Rocky mountains. It is, however, not abundant, except in some localities. The wood is white and soft, and is employed to some extent in the manufacture of furniture, etc.

T. Americana. Basswood; Linden. Eastern United States.

T. heterophylla. White Basswood. Eastern United States

T. pubescens. White Basswood. Eastern United States.

ZYGOPHYLLACEÆ.

Guaiacum sanctum, Lignum Vitæ, South Florida. A small tree, quite rare in South Florida, but common in the West Indies. It is very similar to, and has the same properties as the *G. officinale* of the West Indies, which

ZANTHOXYLACEÆ.

Zanthoxylum Americanum. Prickly Ash; Toothache Tree. Northeastern United States. A shrub or small tree. The bark is very hot and aromatic, and is somewhat used medicinally.

Z. Carolinianum. Southern Prickly Ash. Southern States. A small tree found from South Carolina to Florida and westward. The bark is aromatic and tonic. The young stems are spiny, and the old ones more or less covered with tubercles, which have developed from the spines.

Z. Floridanum. Satin Wood. South Florida.

Z. Pterota. False Lion Wood; Yellow Wood. The Gulf States. A small shrubby tree occurring from Florida to Texas. The wood is yellow and close-grained.

Ptelea trifoliata. Hop-tree. Eastern United States. This is seldom more than a tall shrub. The fruit, a wafer-like seed, grows in clusters, is a bitter tonic, and has been used as a substitute for hops.

P. angustifolia. Narrower-leaved than the preceding. Rocky Mountains; Texas to California.

SIMARUBIACEÆ.

Simaruba glauca. Quassia; Bitter-wood. South Florida. Found in South Florida by Dr. Blodgett. It occurs in the West Indies with another species, the *Simaruba amara*, the bark of which is medicinal, and possesses the same properties as quassia.

BURSERACEÆ.

Bursera gummifera. West India Birch; Gummo Limbo. South Florida. The largest of the South Florida trees, abounding in gum.

Amyris Floridana. Torch Wood. South Florida. Mostly a shrub, but becoming a small evergreen and elegant tree.

OLACINEÆ.

Ximenia Americana. Hog Plum. South Florida. Mostly shrubby but sometimes twenty feet high. It bears a drupe the size of a plum, which is yellow and pleasant-tasted.

MELIACEÆ.

Melia Azederach. Pride of India; Bread Tree. Naturalized in Southern States. A native of Persia, but quite freely naturalized in some parts of the South. It is there one of the commonest ornamental trees. The wood is of a reddish color, solid, durable, and taking a beautiful finish.

ILICINEÆ.

Ilex opaca. Evergreen Holly. Southern States. In favorable localities this tree attains a pretty large size, frequently forty feet high, and twelve to fifteen inches diameter. The wood is very heavy, compact, and fine-grained. It is employed in some parts of cabinet work. It very closely resembles the European Holly.

I. Dahoon. Dahoon Holly. Southern States.
I. decidua. Deciduous Holly. Southern States.
I. monticola. Holly. Southern States.

CELASTRINEÆ.

Schaefferia frutescens. Crab-wood; False Box. South Florida. A small tree of South Florida; the wood is close and fine grained, and is said to be exported from the West Indies as a kind of box wood.

Euonymus occidentalis. California Spindle Tree. California.

E. atropurpureus. Waahoo. Southern and Western States.

RHAMNACEÆ.

Frangula Caroliniana. Alder Buckthorn. Virginia and southward.

F. Purshiana. Oregon Buckthorn. Western coast.

F. Californica. California Coffee-tree. Western coast. This much resembles the *F. Caroliniana*. In California, the berries of this species have been employed to some extent as a substitute for coffee. Some persons recommend it; others have been made sick by its use.

Ceanothus thyrsiflorus. California Lilac. Western coast. One of the most showy shrubs or small trees of California.

C. divaricatus. California.

Zizyphus setifolia. Texas Jujube-tree. Texas and westward.

Scutia ferrea. South Florida.

SAPINDACEÆ.

Æsculus glabra. Ohio Buckeye. Tennessee and Western States. This tree attains, in favorable situations, twenty to thirty feet height, and is much in use as an ornamental tree. It is not found wild east of the Alleghany mountains; its favorable locality being the banks of the Western rivers, in Ohio, Illinois and Kentucky. The wood is light, soft and useless. The nuts are said to be poisonous to cattle eating them.

Æ. flava. Sweet Buckeye. Southern States. This tree prevails more to the southward than the Ohio Buckeye. It is abundant in the mountainous districts of North and South Carolina and Georgia. In favorable situations, it frequently attains a height of fifty to sixty feet, and the trunk a diameter of two to three feet. The flowers are of a light agreeable yellow and quite ornamental. The wood is soft and perishable.

Æ. paria. Red Buckeye. Southern States. This species has nearly the same range as the preceding, but is usually only a shrub of eight or ten feet height; sometimes, however, becoming a small tree.

Æ. Californica. California Buckeye. California. This is the only buckeye of the Pacific coast. It forms a low, spreading, bushy tree from fifteen to twenty ft. ct high.

Ungnadia speciosa. Spanish Buckeye. Texas and Westward. This is a large shrub or small tree, a native of Texas and New Mexico. The chestnut-like fruits have an agreeable, sweet taste, but are strongly emetic. The foliage resembles that of the hickory, (*Carya*).

Sapindus marginatus. Soap Berry. Southern States. This tree varies from twenty to forty feet in height. It occurs along the coast in Georgia and Florida, also in Arkansas and Texas. The berries are smaller than those of the next species, but, like that, the black hard nuts of the berries are sometimes strung for beads and crosses.

Saponaria. White Wood. South Florida. This species was found by Dr. Chapman in south Florida. In the West Indies, the berries and the roots are used as a substitute for soap. The berries are used to intoxicate fish.

Hypelate paniculata. Madeira Wood. South Florida. A small tree found in South Florida. The wood is very like mahogany, and is highly valued.

Acer saccharinum. Sugar Maple; Hard Maple. Eastern United States. The well known Sugar Maple, from the sap of which in the Northern States and in Canada large quantities of sugar and syrup are made annually. It is one of the noblest of American trees, both for the value of its wood and the beauty of its form and foliage. It is much employed as an ornamental tree.

A. saccharinum, var. *nigrum.* Black Sugar Maple. Eastern United States. This variety differs little from the common form except in a darker wood.

A. dasycarpum. Silver-leaf Maple. Eastern United States. One of the most beautiful of maples; much used as a shade-tree on account of its rapid growth and beautiful foliage.

A. rubrum. Red Maple. Eastern United States. More compact in form and less rapid in growth than the preceding, but, like it, a favorite for street planting and ornament.

A. Pennsylvanicum. Striped-bark Maple. Northeastern United States. A small tree, the young bark with longitudinal stripes of green and black. Rare and little known outside of the Northeastern States.

A. macrophyllum. Oregon Maple. California and Oregon. This occurs in the mountainous districts of California and Oregon. In Oregon, it attains a large size, and the wood abounds in that peculiarity of grain which is called Bird's-eye and Curled Maple. For cabinet purposes it is thought to be equal to mahogany.

A. circinatum. Vine Maple. Oregon and Washington Territory. This species has a low and frequently reclining or prostrate trunk, which sends forth branches, at first upright, then bending down to the ground, and forming almost impenetrable thickets.

A. grandidentatum. Great-toothed Maple. California and Oregon. A small tree or shrub of the Rocky mountains.

Negundo aceroides. Box Elder. Eastern United States. This is a fine ornamental tree, of rapid growth, not commonly growing more than twenty to thirty feet high. It is rare east of the Alleghanies, but found along all the rivers of the West, reaching into Kansas, Missouri and Nebraska, and even northward to Minnesota and the British possessions. The sap contains a large amount of sugar. The wood is fine and close-grained, and has been used in cabinet work.

N. Californica. California Box Elder. California. This species is confined to the Pacific coast. It does not seem to differ greatly from the preceding species.

Staphylea trifoliata. Bladder Tree. Eastern United States. A large shrub or small tree ten to fifteen feet high, with trifoliate leaves, peculiar three-lobed bladdery pods.

ANACARDIACEÆ.

Rhus typhina. Stagborn Sumach. Eastern United States. The Sumachs are large shrubs or small trees mostly with pinnate leaves. The leaves and young twigs, are employed in tanning and are thought to be equal in strength to those of the Sicilian Sumach.

R. glabra. Smooth Sumach. Eastern United States.
R. microphylla. Small leaved Sumach. Texas and Southwest.
R. copallina. Dwarf Sumach. Eastern United States.
R. Metopium. Coral Sumach. South Florida. This grows in South Florida, where it atta ns a height of twenty to thirty feet. It is very poisonous. In the West Indies, it is called Mountain Maochineel and Burnwood.
R. venenata. Poison Sumach. Eastern United States.
R. integrifolia. One-leaved Sumach. South Carolina. This species and the succeeding do not have pinnate leaves. They are found in Southern California. The red berries of this ep cies are used by the Indians to make a cooling acid drink.
R. Laurina. Laurel Sumach. South California. A low spreading tree, much branched and ve y leafy, and exhaling to a considerable distance an aromatic odor. The flowers are somewhat showy, and the plant would be fine in cultivation.
Pistacia Mexicana. Mexican Pistacia-tree. Texas.
Schinus molle. Pepper Tree. Southwestern United States. Cultivated as an ornamental tree in California and in Mexico. It is probably introduced. The berries have the taste of black pepper.

VITACEÆ.

Vitis æstivalis. Summer Grape. Eastern United States.
V. cordifolia. Winter or Frost Grape. Eastern United States.

LEGUMINOSÆ.

Robinia Pseudacacia. Common Locust. Pennsylvania and southward. Hardly found north of the fortieth degree of latitude except in cultivation. It is chiefly found in the Alleghanies and the mountainous parts of Kentucky and Tennessee. It is a beautiful tree, attaining a height of fifty feet and upward. The wood is hard, compact, and very durable, much used in ship building.
R. viscosa. Clammy Locust. Virginia and southward. A smaller tree than the preceding. and much more rare. being confined to the mountains of Georgia and North Carolina.
R. Neo-Mexicana. New Mexican Locust. New Mexico and Arizona. A small tree, rarely exceeding twenty feet. Very thorny. Grows in stony ravines at the foot of mountains in New Mexico and Arizona.
Olneya tesota. Palo de Hierro. New Mexico and Arizona.
Piscidia Erythrina. Jamaica Dogwood. South Florida. A tolerably large tree of South Florida; also grows in the West Indies. Its blossoms resemble those of the Locust. The wood is heavy, coarse-grained und durable.
Cladrastris tinctoria. Yellow wood, Tennessee and Kentucky. This is one of the handsomest flowering-tr es of the Locust kind. It grows chiefly in the mountainous regions of Kentucky and Tennessee. The wood is yellow, and has been used in domestic dyeing. The tree rarely exceeds forty feet in height and one foot in diameter. It is well worthy of cultivation.
Sophora affinis. Texas and Southwest.
S. speciosa. Texas and Southwest. Our two Sophoras are small trees of Texas and New Mexico, seldom over six inches in diameter. They produce an abundance of showy flowers very early in the season. The *Sophora speciosa* has evergreen leaves, and beautiful red beans, which are said to be p isonous.
Gymnocladus Canadensis. Kentucky Coffee-tree. Eastern United States. A tall, large and handsome tree, rare in Western New York, Pennsylvania, and the States north of the Ohio river; more common in Kentucky and southwestward. The wood is very compact and closegrained, and valuable for cabinet work. The large beans of the pods have been used for coffee.
Gleditschia triacanthos. Honey Locust. Eastern United States. This is a large and handsome tree; the trunk and branches generally beset with long and formidable spines, on which account it has been employed as a hedge-plant. The long pods contain a sweetish pulp, and have been used in fermenting a kind of beer, but are of no practical value. The wood is heavy, and affords excellent fuel, but is not considered durable as a timber. The tree is rare in the Atlantic States, but rather common west of the Alleghanies, in Tennessee, Kentucky, and the tributaries of the Ohio and Mississippi.
G. monosperma. Water Locust. Illinois and southward. This is a smaller tree than the preceding, growing in swamps in the Southern States and in the vicinity of the Ohio river. The pods are short, roundish, and only one-seeded. The tree is thorny, like the Honey Locust.
Cercidium florid m. Green-bark. Western Texas and Arizona. This is the Palo Verdi of the Mexicans and the Green-barked Acacia of American t avelers. The bark is smooth and green on the young trees. It is a small, wide-spreading tree, with many branches, rarely seen a foot through, and twenty to thirty feet high.

Parkinsonia aculeata. Jerusalem Thorn. Western Texas and Arizona. Mostly a shrub; quite ornamental, and frequent in cultivation in the region bordering on Mexico.
P. microphylla. Western Texas and Arizona.
Cercis Canadensis. Redbud or Judas Tree. Eastern United States. The Redbuds are small trees; very ornamental. This species is frequent east of the Mississippi. The next is found principally on the Pacific Coast.
C. occidentalis. Western Redbud. Western United States.
Prosopis glandulosa. Mesquite. Texas to California. A scrubby, small tree, seldom more than twenty-five to thirty feet high; sometimes constituting extensive forests. It produces an abundance of bean-like pods, which contain a sweet pulp. Both beans and pulp are eaten by Indians and often by whites, but they are used chiefly as food for horses, which eat them with avidity. The wood is very hard and durable, dark brown, and resembles mahogany. Fences made of this timber are very durable. The wounded bark in spring exudes a gum of the same quality as gum arabic.
Strombocarpus pubescens. Screw-bean. Texas and westward. This tree is very similar to the preceding, but of smaller size. The pods are two to three inches long, and twisted like a screw. They are eaten by the Colorado Indians, powdered to a coarse meal, and made into a kind of bread. They are also good food for the horses.
Leucæna retusa. Texas and westward.
Acacia Farnesiana. Texas and westward.
Pithecolobium Unguis-Cati Cat's-claw. South Florida. In South Florida, mostly a shrub, rarely a small tree. The bark has medicinal properties.

ROSACEÆ.

Prunus Americana. Wild Yellow or Red Plum. Eastern United States. This is the common wild plum of the country east of the Rocky mountains, from Mississippi to Minnesota, in the valley of the Mississippi, and particularly southwestward, the two next named species also occur.
P. rivularis. Wild Plum. Mississippi Valley and westward.
P. Chicasa. Chickasaw Plum. Southeastern United States.
P. umbellata. Small Wild Plum. South Carolina and southward. A small purple or black plum, sour and bitter, growing from South Carolina to Florida.
P. Pennsylvanica. Wild Red Cherry. Eastern States. A small tree, or often a shrub, with sour, unpleasant fruit.
P. serotina. Wild Black Cherry. Eastern United States. A fine, large tree, of wide range, frequent in the Northern and Western States, and along the Alleghany Mountains in the Southern States. The wood is compact, fine-grained, and highly esteemed for cabinet work. The fruit is small, rather sweet and pleasant when fully ripe.
P. Virginiana. Choke-cherry. Eastern United States.
P. Caroliniana. Mock Orange. North Carolina and southward. A small tree with evergreen leaves, growing from North Carolina to Florida and in the Gulf States. It closely resembles the Cherry Laurel of Europe. It is a beautiful tree for cultivation, but probably would not bear a northern climate.
P. demissa. Rocky Mountain Choke-cherry. Rocky Mountains and California.
P. Andersonii. Desert Plum. California and Nevada.
P. ilicifolia. Holly-leaved Cherry. California.
P. mollis. Oregon. This is the principal wild cherry of Oregon and the northwestern coast. It grows to the height of twenty to thirty feet. The fruit is astringent and unpleasant.
Nuttallia cerasiformis. California.
Adenostom sparsiflora. Chinisell. California.
Cercocarpus ledifolius. Mountain Mahogany. Rocky Mountains. A low, spreading tree, not usually over ten to fifteen feet high, but sometimes forty feet high, and two and a half feet thick. The leaves are evergreen; the wood is a dark red, like mahogany, extremely compact and heavy. It is frequent on the mountains of Utah, Nevada, and California.
C. parvifolius. Small Mountain M hogany. California. A much smaller tree or shrub than the preceding; the wood quite similar.
Pyrus coronaria. American Crab Apple. Eastern United States. The common wild crab apple of the United States, growing in grades and frequently forming extensive thickets. The fruit is variable, but seldom palatable or serviceable. It is used, however, in new portions of the country for preserves or for making cider.
P. angustifolia. Narrow-leaved Crab. Pennsylvania southward and westward. Perhaps only a variety of the preceding, with narrower leaves and rather smaller fruit.
P. Ameri ana. American Mountain Ash. Northeastern United States. A small tree growing in swamps and mountain woods, sparingly in the Alleghany Mountains,

most common in New England and northward. It is frequently seen in cultivation, and much resembles the European Mountain Ash. The clusters of bright-red berries are very ornamental, and remain on the tree until winter.

P. rivularis. Oregon Cr b Apple. Oregon and Rocky Mountains. This is a small tree, ranging from California northward into Alaska. The fruit is . f the size of a cherry, of an agreeable flavor, and used, particularly in Alaska, by the natives of the country for food.

C. tomentosa. Black or Pear Thorn. Eastern United States.

Cratægus spathulata. Wild Thorn. Virginia and southward. Of wild thorns, we have numerous species, most of which are small and shrubby. About twelve species and varieties of the country east of the Rocky mountains may be counted as small trees, and two of the Rocky mountains and western coast.

C. apiifolia. Wild Thorn. Virginia and southward.
C. cordata. Washington Thorn. Virginia and southward.
C. arborescens. Wild Thorn. Southern States.
C. coccinea. Scarlet-fruited Thorn. Eastern United States.
C. tomentosa. Black or Pear Thorn. Eastern United States.
C. tomentosa, var. *punctata.* Black Thorn. Eastern United States.
C. tomentosa, var. *mollis* Gr. Wild Thorn. Eastern United States.
C. Crus-galli. Cockspur Thorn. Eastern United States.
C. æstivalis. Wild Hawthorn. Southern States.
C. flava. Summer Haw. Virginia and southward.
C. glandulosa. Wild Hawthorn. Virginia and southward.
C. rivularis. Western Hawthorn. Rocky Mountains.
C. sanguinea. Oregon Thorn. Oregon.
Photinia arbutifolia. Laurel Hawthorn. California. A beautiful evergreen shrub or small tree of the Pacific coast. It sometimes attains the height of twenty or twenty-five feet and a thickness of trunk of twelve or fifteen inches.

Amelanchier Canadensis. Service or June Berry. Eastern United States. Usually, a small tree, but sometimes becoming thirty to forty feet high, with a diameter of ten or twelve inches. It is found mostly by the banks of mountain streams. There are several varieties, some of them used as ornamental shrubs.

A. alnifolius. Service Berry. Rocky Mountains. This is usually a shrub; in Oregon and Washington Territory, it is said to be a small tree, yielding abundance of berries, which are largely employed as food by the Indians.

HAMAMELACEÆ.

Liquidambar styraciflua. Sweet Gum or Bilsterd. Eastern United States. A large and beautiful tree, with singular star-like leaves, somewhat resembling the maple. It grows in the Atlantic States in rich, low woods; also in the Mississippi valley, but not far north of the Ohio. The wood is compact and fine-grained, but not durable. It is a fine ornamental tree, and deserving of cultivation.

RHIZOPHORACEÆ.

Rhizophora Mangle. Red Mangrove. South Florida. Commonly a low, spreading tree in South Florida, also in Louisiana and on the coast of Texas. On the Thousand Islands, it attains a height of forty to sixty feet. All the low keys become high and are covered by this tree. It sends down roots from its germinating fruits, which take root upon reaching the earth, and thus forms an impenetrable thicket like the Banyan tree of India.

COMBRETACEÆ.

Conocarpus erectus. White Button Wood. Florida. A small tree of the West Indies and South Florida. It furnishes almost the only fuel used in South Florida, and extends north as far as Ancelote Keys. (Dr. Chapman.)

Laguncularia racemosa. Black Button Wood. South Florida. Found by Dr. Chapman in South Florida; a small tree everywhere; is a mere shrub, except among the Thousand Islands and north of Cape Sable, where it forms a large tree.

MYRTACEÆ.

Eugenia buxifolia. Iron Wood. South Florida. The Eugenias are in Florida small trees, reaching twenty to twenty-five feet in height. They belong to the Myrtle family, and the flowers of some species are very fragrant. The wood is close-grained, hard, and applicable to cabinet work.
E. monticola. Iron Wood. South Florida.
E. procera. Iron Wood. South Florida.
E. dichotoma. Stopper Wood. South Florida.
Psidium pyriforme. Guava. South Florida. The Guava is a well known fruit in the West Indies, where it is highly esteemed, and eaten either raw or formed into preserves. Dr. Chapman f und the tree extensively naturalized at Tampa Bay, Fla.

CACTACEÆ.

Cereus giganteus. Tree Cactus. Western Texas and Arizona. The specimens for this order are from southern Arizona, where they are striking and characteristic features of the country. The *Cereus giganteus* grows fifty to sixty feet in a straight column, and finally divides into several naked-looking branches. The wood of this and other large Cacti presents a singular net-work of fibers in distinct layers.

C. Thurberi. Thurber's Cactus. Western Texas and Arizona. *Opuntia arborescens.* Tree opuntia. Western Texas and Arizona.

ARALIACEÆ.

Aralia spinosa. Angelica Tree or Hercules' Club. Eastern United States.

CORNACEÆ.

Cornus florida. Flowering Dogwood. Eastern United States. This is usually a small tree, but sometimes acquires a height of forty or fifty feet, and a diameter of trunk of one and one-half feet. It flowers in spring before the full development of the leaves, and then presents a beautiful appearance. It deserves to be more generally cultivated.

C. Nuttallii. White Dogwood. California and Oregon. This species, which is confined to the Pacific coast, has rather larger flowers than the preceding, and is perhaps more showy. The wood of both is hard and valuable. Grows sometimes fifty or sixty feet high.

C. Pubescens. Western Dogwood. California and Oregon. This rarely becomes a small tree, twenty-five to thirty feet high, on the Pacific coast. We have five or six other species of dogwood which do not attain tree size.

Garrya Fremontii. Tassel-tree. Oregon and California. The Garryas are mostly shrubs, though under favorable circumstances the *Garrya elliptica* gains a height of twenty to thirty feet.
G. elliptica. Satin Tassel-tree. California.

Nyssa multiflora. Black or Sour Gum; pepperidge. Eastern United States. A middle-sized tree, growing from Massachusetts to Illinois and Southward. The fibers of the wood are so interwoven that it is almost impossible to split it; hence it is used for wheel hubs, rollers, and cylinders. (Bryant.) It is quite ornamental in cultivation.

N. aquatica. Water Tupelo. Southern States. This species grows in low, wet ground, chiefly in the Southern States, but is found also in New Jersey and Pennsylvania. The wood is very tough, and has been used in the manufacture of wooden bowls, etc.

N. uniflora. Large Tupelo. Virginia and southward. This is the largest tree of the genus. It is confined to the Southern States, growing in swamps. It bears a dark-blue plum-like fruit nearly an inch long. The wood is soft and extremely light. The roots are also extremely light and soft, and have been used as a substitute for cork. The wood is only used to make bowls and trays.

N. capitata. Ogeechee Lime. Southern United States. This species is found in swamps in Georgia and Florida and westward near the coast. It bears an oblong red plum-like fruit, which is agreeably acid, and can be employed as a substitute for the lemon. The tree is small and the wood without value.

CAPRIFOLIACEÆ.

Sambucus glauca. California Elder. California and Rocky Mountains. This species of elder in California forms a low tree, sometimes thirty feet high, with a stem two feet in diameter. Indians and birds eat the berries.

Viburnum prunifolium. Black Haw. Eastern United States. The haws are small trees or large shrubs, with smooth, glossy leaves and handsome flowers. They are worthy of cultivation

V. Lentago. Sweet Viburnum or Sheepberry. Eastern United States.
V. obovatum. Wild Haw. Virginia and southward.

RUBIACEÆ.

Cephalanthus occidentalis, var. *Californica.* Button-bush. California. This is seldom more than a shrub; but in California it sometimes grows twenty-five to thirty feet high, with a trunk twenty to twenty inches in diameter.
Guettarda Blodgettii. South Florida.
Randia lusif. lia. Seven-year Apple. South Florida.
Pinckneya pulens. Georgia Bark. South Carolina to Florida. A small tree in the lower districts of Georgia and in Flo ida, rarely exceeding the height of twenty-five feet and a diameter of six inches. The bark is extremely bitter, and has been employed in the treatment of intermittent fevers. It is closely related botanically to the

Cinchona, from which quinine is made, and which furnishes the Peruvian bark of commerce.

ERICACEÆ.

Vaccinium arboreum. Farkleberry. Virginia and southward. A shrub or small tree sometimes twenty feet high, growing from Virginia and Southern Illinois southward
Oxydendrum arboreum. Sourwood or Sorrel-tree. Pennsylvania and southward. This tree grows chiefly in the mountainous districts of the Alleghanies from Pennsylvania southward. In fertile valleys, at the foot of the mountains, in North Carolina and Tennessee, it attains a height of fifty feet. The common name sour-tree is derived from the acidity of its leaves. The flowers are white, and in spikes five or six inches long. They are very ornamental, and begin to be produced when the tree is five or six feet high.
Kalmia latifolia. Calico-bush or Mountain Laurel. Pennsylvania and southward. A beautiful evergreen shrub, sometimes attaining the size of a small tree. It is very ornamental and deserving of cultivation.
Rhododendron maximum. Rose Bay or Great Laurel. Pennsylvania and southward. Like the preceding, an evergreen shrub of great beauty. It has been much improved by cultivation. Some of the hybrids are most elegant, and a great variety are now sold by nurserymen. It has been hybridized with azalia, and the result of this cross, once supposed to be impossible, has given us many splendid varieties.
R. Catifornicum. California Rhododendron. Pacific coast.
Arbutus Menziesii. Madrone-tree. California and Oregon.
A. Texana. This species or variety grows in Texas. It is mostly a large shrub; sometimes, however, becoming twenty-five feet high and eight or ten inches in diameter. The leaves are smaller and the flowers less panicled than in the California species. The timber is said to be almost imperishable.
Arctostaphylos glauca. Manzanita. Oregon and California. There are several species of this genus on the western coast, mostly shrubs or small trees, which have been much confused. The specimen under this number is from Southern California, and has a large drupe-like fruit, with a consolidated nut. These berries are pleasant to the taste, and much employed as food by the Indians of that region.
A. tomentosa. Manzanita. California and Rocky Mountains.
A. pungens. Manzanita. California and Rocky Mountains.

STYRACACEÆ.

Halesia diptera. Snowdrop-tree. Georgia and Florida. The Snow drop-trees are found in the Southern States from the Ohio river southward, near the Alleghanies, and on the river-banks in Georgia and Florida. They are usually smallish trees, but sometimes grow forty or fifty feet high, and one and a half to two feet in diameter. They are very desirable for ornamental trees, producing a profusion of white bell-shaped flowers, even when quite small.
H. tetraptera. Silverbell-tree. Virginia and southward.
Symplocos tinctoria. Horse Sugar or Sweet-leaf Virginia and southward. A small tree with oblong evergreen leaves, and clustered racemes of small white flowers. It grows in low, damp woods and pine barrens in North Carolina, Georgia, and Florida, and attains a height of twelve to twenty feet, with a diameter of eight to ten inches. It is one of the most beautiful trees of the southern forest. (Nuttall.)

CYRILLACEÆ.

Cyrilla racemiflora. Iron-wood. North Carolina and southward.
Cliftonia liqustrina. Buckwheat-tree. Georgia and southward. An elegant small tree, growing from ten to twenty feet high, of about the same range as the preceding. It is evergreen, and exceedingly ornamental when in flower. After flowering, the tree presents a curious appearance, from the abundance of triangular winged capsules, resembling buckwheat, from which the tree receives its popular name.

EBENACEÆ.

Dyospyros Virginiana. Persimmon. Eastern United States. A well known tree, most common in the Southern states, but growing as far north as New York. It grows from thirty to sixty feet high, with a very hard fine-grained wood, which has been used for various purposes. It bears a plum-like fruit an inch or more in length, which when fully ripe is edible and palatable.
D. Texana. Persimmon. Western Texas. This is called Sapote-pieto by the Mexicans and Black Persimmon by the Americans. It is a shrub or middle-sized tree, often with a black, ebony-like core. The fruits are black, and of the size of a cherry and larger, melting, and very sweet. (Dr. Lindheimer.)

SAPOTACEÆ.

Sideroxylon pallidum. Mastic. South Florida. A middle-sized tree of South Florida called Mastic, probably from the production of a gum resembling mastic.
Dipholis salicifolia. South Florida.
Chrysophyllum microphyllum. Jacq. Golden-leaf. South Florida. A small tree of the West Indies, found lately by Dr. Chapman in South Florida. The leaves have a beautiful, golden, satin-like surface on the under side.
Mimusops Sieberi. Naseberry. South Florida. This is one of trees called Naseberry in the West Indies. It is common in South Florida where it becomes a large tree. Dr. Chapman invariably found the large trunks to be hollow. The fruit is delicious and highly flavored.
Bumelia lycioides. Iron-wood Kentucky and southward. The Bumelias are shrubs or small trees, of no special value.
B. parvifolia. Iron-wood. South Florida.
B. lanuginosa. Iron-wood. Southern States.
B. tenax. Iron-wood. Southern States.
B. reclinata. Iron-wood. Texas and westward.

THEOPHRASTACEÆ.

Jacquinia armillaris. Currant-trees. South Florida. A small tree of South Florida and the West Indies. The wood is curiously grained.

MYRSINACEÆ.

Myrsine Floridana. South Florida. Mostly a shrub, rarely a small tree.
Ardisia Pickeringii South Florida. Mostly a shrub, but on the keys a small tree. It is an evergreen tree, with laurel-like leaves, and panicles of showy-white, purple-tinged flowers.

BIGNONIACEÆ.

Catalpa bignonioides. Cutalpa. Southern States. A tree well known in cultivation, and hardy as far north as latitude 40°. It is native in the Southern and Southwestern States. In Southern Illinois and Indiana the variety *speciosa* is hardy, also, well up into Wisconsin, and attains a height of fifty or sixty feet, and a diameter of one and a half to two feet. The leaves are large, and the flowers showy, and when in bloom the tree is extremely ornamental. The wood is light, but of a fine texture, and capable of receiving a fine polish. It is very durable, and is growing in favor year by year.
Chilopsis linearis. Texas and Arizona. Usually a shrub, but sometimes attaining a height of twenty-five feet. It has long willow-like leaves, and is very ornamental when in flower.
Tecoma radicans. Trumpet-vine. Southern States. This beautiful woody vine sometimes acquires a woody trunk of a foot in diameter or more.

VERBENACEÆ.

Citharexylum villosum. Fiddle-wood. South Florida. Rarely a small tree, of no economic value.
Avicennia tomentosa. Black Mangrove. South Florida. This and the next species are called Black Mangrove, observed by Dr. Chapman at Cedar Keys and the Thousand Islands. They are low evergreen trees, forming impenetrable thickets on the muddy shores of the sea.
A. oblongifolia. Black Mangrove. South Florida.

ORDER BORRAGINACEÆ.

Cordia bullata. South Florida.
Ehretia Buerreria. South Florida.
E. elliptica. Texas Mostly shrubby, but sometimes a tree two feet in diameter; fruit an orange-yellow berry, of the size of a pea; much liked by children and birds. The evergreen rough leaves are used to rub and destroy eruptions of the skin. (Dr. Lindheimer.)

OLEACEÆ.

Olea Americana. Devil-wood; American Olive. Southern States. This is a small evergreen tree, with thick, leathery leaves, and small, white, fragrant flowers. It is related to the olive-tree of the eastern world, but its fruit has no value. It is impossible to split, and hence the vulgar name of Devil-wood.
Chionanthus Virginica. Fringe-tree. Middle and Southern States.
Fraxinus Americana. White Ash. Eastern United States. A large and valuable tree ranging over the eastern portion of the United States. The wood is tough and elastic, and much employed in various manufactures. It is a handsome and ornamental tree.

F. pubescens. Red Ash. Eastern United States. A smaller tree than the preceding, perhaps more common. The wood is said to be equally as valuable as that of the White Ash.

F. viridis. Green Ash. Western States. A middle-sized tree, of vigorous and rapid growth, and the wood has the same qualities as the preceding.

F. sambucifolia Black Ash. Northern and Western States. A large tree, usually growing in moist soil, and hence often called Swamp Ash. The wood is more elastic than that of any other species. It splits easily into thin, narrow strips, which are used for making baskets and hoops for barrels.

F. quadrangulata. Blue Ash. Western States. This species is not found in the Atlantic States. It is found from Ohio to Wisconsin and southward to Kentucky and Tennessee. It is a large tree, growing from sixty to seventy feet high, with a diameter of two feet or more. The wood is quite as valuable as that of the White Ash, and is said to be much more durable when exposed to the weather; hence its value for fence-rails, posts, etc.

F. platycarpa. Carolina Water Ash. Southern States. This species grows in swamps or marshy banks of rivers. It is usually twenty-five or thirty feet high, but sometimes becomes a large tree. The wood is remarkably light and soft, and probably has no economic value.

F. Curtissi. Southern States. Mr. Curtiss found at Eufaula, Ala., a large Ash with remarkably small fruit. This species is provisionally called F. Curtissi. It requires further investigation.

F. Oregona. Oregon Ash. California and Oregon. The common ash of the Pacific coast. It grows sixty to seventy feet high. Is of equal value with the White Ash of the Eastern States.

F. dipetala. California Flowering Ash. California and Oregon.

F. pistaciæfolia. Texas and westward.

F. anomala. Single-leaf Ash. Utah and Arizona. This ash is seldom more than a shrub ten to fifteen feet high, growing in ravines among the foot-hills of southern Utah and Arizona. The leaves are simple, not pinnate, as in the other species.

F. coriacea. Thick-leaved Ash. Utah and Arizona. A smallish tree, with thick, leathery leaves, growing in southern Utah and Arizona.

Forestiera acuminata. Southwestern States. A large shrub or small tree, of no economic value.

F. ligustrina. Southern States.

NYCTAGENIACEÆ.

Pisonia obtusata. South Florida. A small tree of Florida and the West Indies.

POLYGONACEÆ.

Coccoloba uvifera. Seaside Grape. South Florida. This and the following species are low and spreading trees along the coast in Florida and the West Indies. It is remarkable for the grape-like clusters of pear-shaped purple berries, which have an agreeable subacid taste, and which are much employed. The wood is heavy, hard, and valuable for cabinet work.

C. Florida a. Seaside Grape. South Florida.

LAURACEÆ.

Persea Car liniensis. Red Bay. Southern States. This species occurs from Southern Virginia to Florida and the Gulf States. It is found in the vicinity of swamps and swampy river borders. In favorable situations it grows to fifty or sixty feet high and fifteen to twenty inches in diameter. The leaves are large, shining, evergreen. The wood is of a beautiful rose-color, of a fine, compact grain, and finishes almost equal to mahogany.

P. Catesiyana. Catesby's Bay. South Florida.

Sassafras o fficinale. Sassafras. Eastern United States. This tree is found over a large portion of the United States. It is usually a small tree, but sometimes attains a large size. The wood is not very strong, but is fine-grained and durable. It is valuable for cabinet work. The bark of the root has a spicy, aromatic taste, and has some reputation as a medicine.

Creodaph e Californi a. California Myrtle. California and Oregon. The California Laurel is a fine ornamental evergreen tree, growing in open places from fifty to sixty feet high. In thick woods, it has been found shooting up to one hundred or one hundred and twenty feet. The leaves have a very pungent odor, which produces headache in some persons. The wood is very beautiful, and is used for fine cabinet work.

ELEAGNACEÆ.

Shepherdia argentea. Buffalo-berry. Rocky Mountains. A large shrub or small tree, growing in thickets on the banks of streams in the Rocky mountain valleys. The scarlet berries have an agreeable taste, and are employed as food by the natives.

EUPHORBIACEÆ.

Hippomane Mancinella. Manchineel. South Florida.

Stillingia sebifera. Tallow-tree. Naturalized in the Southern States. The Tallow-tree is a native of China, but has become extensively naturalized in the East and West Indies, and also in several of the Southern States along the seacoast. In its native country, its seeds and pods are bruised and then boiled, which causes a kind of tallow to rise to the surface. This tallow is much employed in making candles.

Excæcaria lucida. Poison-wood. South Florida.

Drypetes crocea. A small tree of South Florida and the West Indies. The leaves are evergreen, and have much the flavor of tea.

D. Glauca. South Florida.

URTICACEÆ.

Morus rubra. Red Mulberry. Eastern United States. The Red Mulberry is found throughout the greater part of the United States east of the Mississippi, and also some of the States west of that river. (Bryant.) It is commonly a smallish tree, sometimes, however, attaining a large size. The berries are quite palatable, and are eaten eagerly by birds, and also have a place in the markets as a second-rate fruit. The wood is strong, compact, and extremely durable.

M. parvifolia. Small-leaved Mulberry. Texas and westward.

Maclura aurantiaca. Osage Orange. Arkansas and Southwest. This tree, which is a native in Arkansas and Texas, has been quite generally introduced over the country, chiefly from its extensive employment as a hedge-plant. The early French settlers called it Bois d'arc or Bow-wood, from its use by the Indians for bows. The fruit is of the size and color of a large orange, but is not edible. The wood is very hard, elastic, fine-grained, and durable.

Ficus aurea. G m-tree; Wild Fig. South Florida. There are many species of wild fig in the West Indies, but this species of South Florida has not been identified with any of them. It is a large tree, full of milky juice, which forms a kind of India rubber, whence it is also called Gum-tree. The fruit is very small and insignificant.

F. pedunculata. Wild Fig. South Florida. This tree is also a native of the West Indies, and, like the Banyan of the West Indies, it sends down aerial roots, which become fixed in the soil. The fruit is larger than the preceding, being the size of a large cherry.

F. brevifolia. Wild Fig. South Florida.

Ulmus Americana. White Elm. Eastern United States. One of our most common and valuable trees, very popular as a shade tree on account of its graceful form. It is one of the largest of the deciduous trees of the United States, attaining sometimes the height of 100 feet. The wood is employed for various purposes, but it is not considered durable when exposed to the weather.

U. fulva. Slippery Elm. Eastern United States. This is usually a smaller tree than the White Elm. It is not as much esteemed as an ornamental tree. The wood, however, is said to be of better quality and more durable. The inner bark is very mucilaginous, and is extensively used for medical and surgical purposes.

U. racemosa. Corky White Elm. Northern States. This tree is limited to the northern portions of the United States, being found sparingly in New England, New York, and westward to northern Illinois and Wisconsin. It closely resembles the White Elm, but may be distinguished by the corky wings of the smaller branches which extend on both sides in grotesque and rough. Dr. N. H. Wright, of Penn Yan, N. Y., says it grows as rapidly as the White Elm, and he thinks will become as large. He has seen some young trees over two feet in diameter. The wood is tougher and finer-grained than the White Elm.

U. alata. Winged Elm. Southern and Western States. This species does not grow in the Northern States except on the line of the Ohio river. It is a smallish tree, and has smaller leaves than the other kind. The branches have a broad and thin corky wing on the opposite sides. The wood is finer-grained and more compact than the White Elm.

U. Floridana. Florida Elm. Florida.

U. crassifolia. Thick-leaved Elm. Texas and Southwest.

Planera aquatica. Planer-tree. Southern States. This tree is found in the Southern States and in Kentucky and Tennessee. It is a tree of medium size, with foliage somewhat like that of the European Elm. It is not a common tree, and the wood is not known to be applied to any useful purpose.

Celtis occidentalis. Sugar or Hackberry. Eastern United States. This tree is rare in the New England

States, but rather common in the Southern and Western ones. There are several varieties, one of which is usually a low and straggling bush. In the Western States, it often becomes a lofty tree. It somewhat resembles the elm in foliage and the ash in bark. It produces a dryish kind of berry about the size of a pea. The wood is white, but is not considered durable.

C. Mississippiensis. Mississippi Hackberry. Mississippi valley.

C. reticulata. Net-leaved Hackberry. Texas and Southwest. This is a western species, occurring in Texas and the Rocky mountain region. It is a small tree, often a mere shrub.

C. pallida. Pale-leaved Hackberry. Texas.

PLATANACEÆ.

Platanus occidentalis. Sycamore. Planetree. Eastern United States. It is probably one of the largest deciduous trees in the United States. It occurs throughout the Eastern, Southern and Western States, and extends beyond the Mississippi river. In the rich bottom-lands of the western rivers, it sometimes attains the enormous circumference of forty to forty-five feet. It much resembles the European Plane tree, and is thought to possess a richer foliage, and to afford a deeper shade. As a timber tree it is of little value, as the wood is liable to warp, and decays early.

P. racemosa. California Sycamore. California. This is the sycamore of the Pacific coast, extending from Central California to Mexico. Although a large tree, it does not attain the size of the eastern species. The wood is said to be more valuable, receiving a good polish and being more durable

P. Wrightiana. Wright's Sycamore. Arizona.

JUGLANDACEÆ.

Juglans nigra. Black Walnut. Eastern United States. This tree occurs in the Atlantic States, but attains its greatest perfection and abundance in the valleys of the Ohio and Mississippi. It has been so much in request for the timber that it is much less common than formerly The wood is used for the inside finish of houses, for cabinet work, for gun stocks, and many other purposes. It produces a nut much like the English walnut, but of stronger oily flavor. They are greatly relished by many persons.

J. cinerea. Butternut; White Walnut. Eastern United States. This is more limited in range than the preceding. In Pennsylvania, New York, and New England, it probably attains its greatest perfection. It is a smaller tree than the Black Walnut. It is also found in the Western States. The wood is of a light-brown color, fine-grained, and easily worked. Although less valuable than the Black Walnut, the wood is well adapted to many uses. The nuts are not as highly esteemed as those of the Black Walnut.

J. Californica. California Walnut. California. The California Walnut attains, in favorable situations, a height of fifty to seventy-five feet, and a diameter of two or three feet. It does not seem to be abundant, and we know nothing respecting the value of its wood. It has recent y been distinguished as a different species from the walnut of Arizona and New Mexico.

J. rupestris. Small Black Walnut. Texas and Arizona.

Carya olivæformis. Pecan nut. Mississippi valley. This tree grows in the valley of the Mississippi and its tributaries, on the Arkansas, the Illinois, the Wabash, and the Ohio, for some 200 miles above its mouth. The wood is coarse-grained, heavy, and compact. It is a beautiful tree, with a straight and well-shaped trunk. The but is well known in the markets, and is sought by some to be superior in flavor to any other nut known.

C. alba. Shell bark Hickory. Eastern United States. This species becomes a lofty tree, eighty feet high, with a diameter sometimes of two feet. It is one of the most valuable of the hickories for timber and for fuel. It furnishes most of the hickory nuts of commerce. They are pleasant flavored and highly esteemed. On large trees, the bark hangs off in long, narrow plates, whence the common name of the tree. The wood is heavy, elastic, and strong, and for handles of axes and agricultural implements, is unequaled. There is little difference in the quality and value of many of the different species of hickory.

C. sulcata. Western Shell-bark. Western States.

C. tomentosa. Mocker nut. Eastern United States.

C. amara. Bitter nut. Eastern United States. This is a large tree, growing from sixty to seventy feet high. The timber is said to be inferior to the preceding species, and the nuts are thin-shelled, bitter, and not hollow.

C. porcina. Pig nut Hickory. Eastern United States. A large tree, with small, pear-shaped fruit, the nuts blisterish and unpalatable. The wood is tough and valuable.

C. microcarpa. Small-fruited Hickory. Eastern United States.

C. myristicæformis. Nutmeg Hickory. Southern States. This species grows in swamps in the Southern States. The fruit resembles a nutmeg, whence the name of Nutmeg Hickory. It is somewhat like that of the Bitter nut tree, but much thicker.

C. aquatica. Swamp Hickory. Southern States. A species growing in swamps in the Southern States, with astringent, bitter fruit, and brittle, worthless timber.

CUPULIFERÆ.

Quercus macrocarpa. Bur Oak; Overcup Oak. Western States. This species is rare in the Eastern States, but common in Michigan. Illinois, Wisconsin, and Minnesota. It is a large tree, and when growing on low ground assumes a rounded and handsome form. It has very large acorns, which are usually deeply immersed in the cup; the border of the cup fringed with loose scales. The wood is open and brittle as it occurs in the prairie country, but valuable for fuel.

Q. alba. White Oak. Eastern United States. This is one of the noblest, largest, and most useful oaks of this country. The wood is strong, compact and durable, and is only second to that of the Live Oak. It is extensively employed in ship building, in manufacturing, and for many purposes.

Q. lyrata. Southern Overcup Oak. Southern States. Much resembles the Bur Oak, but is chiefly confined to the Southern States.

Q. stellata. Post Oak. Eastern United States. This species grows mostly upon poor clay lands. It is a middle-sized tree; the wood is yellowish, strong, fine-grained, and more durable than the White Oak.

Q. bicolor. Swamp White Oak. Eastern United States.

Q. Michauxii. Michaux's Oak. Southeastern United States.

Q. prinus. Chestnut Oak. Eastern United States. A species including several varieties. It is usually a large and lofty tree. Its timber is inferior to that of the White Oak in strength, but is still very valuable for many uses.

Q. prinus, var. *monticola.* Rock Chestnut Oak. New England and Middle States.

Q. prinus, var. *acuminata,* Yellow Chestnut Oak. Northern and Western States.

Q. Douglasii. Douglas's Oak. Rocky mountains, California. This and the next two succeeding species are the California White Oaks, extending into Oregon and Columbia. They are probably of equal value with the eastern species.

Q. Garryana. Garry's Oak. California and Oregon.

Q. lobata. California White Oak. California.

Q. undulata. The Rocky Mountain Oak. Rocky mountains. This is the common oak of the Rocky mountains, usually small and scrubby, but sometimes forming a moderate-sized tree. It is very variable in the foliage.

Q. densiflora. California Tan-bark Oak. California. An anomalous species found in California, between an oak and a chestnut. In open ground, it is a beautiful spreading, pyramidal tree, with a trunk sometimes five to six feet in diameter. Among the forest-trees, it rises to 100 feet or more in height.

Q. agrifolia. California Field Oak. California. This is commonly known in California as Evergreen Oak. It grows usually in open ground, with a wide, spreading, apple-tree-like top. It is usually a small tree, sometimes a mere shrub, and occasionally becoming forty or fifty feet high.

Q. chrysolepis. Canon Live Oak. California. An evergreen oak, growing in rocky canons and on mountain sides. It is sometimes shrubby; sometimes, like the last, becoming forty to fifty feet high. It furnishes the hardest oak-wood of the Pacific coast, and is used in making ox-bows, ax handles, etc.

Q. oblongifolia. Oblong-leaved Oak. Arizona, California.

Q. Emoryi. Emory's Oak. Arizona.

Q. hypoleuca. New Mexican Oak. Arizona.

Q. Durandii. Durand's Oak. Texas. This species approaches the Post Oak in general characters. The leaves are variable, being sometimes lobed, and sometimes entire.

Q. phillos. Willow Oak. Southern States. This species is confined to the States bordering the Atlantic and the Gulf; not, however, extending into the New England States. It is remarkable for its narrow, willow-shaped leaves. The wood is strong, but coarse-grained, and not durable.

Q. virens. Live Oak. Southern States. This is the famous Live Oak. It grows from southern Virginia to Florida and westward in the vicinity of the seacoast. The wood is more esteemed for ship building than any other. It is evergreen, and is a large tree with spreading branches.

Q. cinerea. Upland Willow Oak. Southern States. A small tree, growing in sandy pine-barrens from North Carolina to Florida. It is evergreen, with leaves like the Willow Oak, but thicker, and downy on the under surface.

Q. imbricaria. Shingle Oak. Eastern United States. A medium-sized tree, reaching to fifty or sixty feet high, and with a diameter of one and one-half to two feet. It grows principally, in open situations, from New Jersey to Illinois and southward. Its foliage is handsome, resembling that of the Laurel. The wood is coarse-grained and not durable.

Q. aquatica. Water Oak. Southern States. A middle sized tree, of the Southern States, growing on the borders of swamps; The leaves are perennial, of variable form, but always broadest at the upper portion and tapering to a point at the base.

Q. laurifolia. Water Oak. Southern States.

Q. nigra. Black Jack. Eastern United States. A small, scrubby tree, growing usually in poor clay soil. It is found in New Jersey, Maryland, and southward, as also in some of the Western States. The wood furnishes a good fuel, but is too coarse-grained and perishable for any use in the arts.

Q. falcata. Spanish Oak. Eastern United States. A large tree, attaining eighty feet or more in height, and sometimes four feet in diameter. It has about the same range as the Black Jack, not being found in New England nor in the northern part of the Western States. The wood is not valuable except for fuel.

Q. Catesbæi. Turkey Oak. Southern States. A small tree, with foliage much like the preceding. It is found in Florida. Georgia, North and South Carolina. The wood is good fuel, but of no value as timber.

Q. rubra. Red Oak. Eastern United States. This is one of the largest oaks of our country, and is diffused over all the eastern portion of the United States, but more especially to the northward. It is a beautiful tree, with reddish, coarse-grained wood, which is little used in the arts except for barrel staves.

Q. coccinea. Scarlet Oak. Eastern United States. The Scarlet and Quercitron Oaks do not differ much in their characters, and, indeed, are considered but as varieties of one species. They form large and handsome trees, and the bark furnishes a yellow dye which is used in the arts

Q. tinctoria. Quercitron. Eastern United States.

Q. palustris. Pin Oak. Eastern United States. A somewhat smaller tree than the preceding. The leaves are small, smooth, of a pleasant green color, very similar to those of the Scarlet Oak. The wood is stronger and more durable than that species. It is chiefly limited to the Northern States.

Q. Sonomensis. California Oak. Californi. This species is nearly related to the *Q. rubra* of the Eastern States. It grows in mountainous districts, and forms a pretty large tree.

Q. Wislizenii. California Live Oak. California. A smallish tree of California. with bright green persistent leaves, sometimes called Live Oak.

Q. dumosa. Dwarf Oak. California. This is a common dwarf oak in Southern California.

Q. reticulata. Dwarf Oak. Southern Arizona.

Castanea vesca, var. *Americana.* Gr. American Chestnut. Eastern United States. One of the noblest trees of the American forests. It occurs from Massachusetts to Michigan, and in the mountain districts of Pennsylvania. Virginia and Tennessee, but not in the prairie regions of the Western States. The wood is strong, elastic and durable, and is largely employed in the manufacture of furniture and for the inside finish of railroad cars and steamboats. The nuts are very sweet and palatable, and always command a good price in the markets.

C. pumila. Chincapin. Southern States. This may be called a dwarf chestnut, growing from New Jersey and Pennsylvania to Florida. Northward it is only a large shrub, but in South Carolina and Florida it becomes a tree of thirty to forty feet high, and twelve to fifteen inches diameter. The wood equals that of the chestnut, but the nuts, although generally eaten by children, are not comparable to those of the former.

Castanopsis chrysophylla. California Chestnut. California. A tree of Oregon and California, becoming sixty to one hundred feet high and two to three feet diameter. The bur is scarcely one-third as large as in the common chestnut, with shorter prickles. The shell of the nut is almost as large as the filbert.

C. chrysophylla, var. *pumila.* California Chincapin. California. This is mostly a shrub growing on open mountain -ides, and is sometimes called California Chincapin.

Fagus ferruginea. Beech. Eastern United States. The beech is one of our loftiest trees, sometimes reaching the height of 100 feet. It grows from Canada to the Gulf of Mexico. It is wanting in the prairie districts of the West. The wood is hard, fine-grained, and compact. It is largely used for shoe-lasts and handles of tools. It is also employed in the frame-work of buildings. The wood is in great repute as fuel. The nuts have a delicious flavor, but are too small to make them of much economic importance.

Carpinus Americana. Blue Beech. Eastern United States. A small tree fifteen to twenty feet high. The wood is white, compact, and fine-grained.

Ostrya Virginica. Hop Hornbeam; Iron-wood, Eastern United States. The Iron-wood is a small tree, but sometimes grows to a height of forty feet. The wood is heavy and fine-grained, and is used for mallets, wedges, levers, etc. Its growth is very slow.

Corylus rostrata, var. *Californica.* California.

MYRICACEÆ.

Myrica cerifera. L. Bayberry; Wax myrtle. Eastern United States. A shrub or small tree growing near the seacoast. The berries are coated with a waxy secretion, which is sometimes utilized in the domestic manufacture of candles and also in medicinal unguents.

M. inodora. Florida Bayberry. Florida.

M. Californica. California Bayberry or Myrtle. California. This species sometimes attains a height of forty feet, with a trunk two feet in diameter. It grows on the Pacific coast, from Puget Sound to Mexico.

BETULACEÆ.

Betula alba, var. *populifolia.* American White Birch. Northern and Northeastern United States. A small and slender graceful tree, fifteen to twenty-five high, growing from Maine to Pennsylvania, and sparsely on the great lakes.

B. papyracea. Canoe birch, Paper Birch. Northern and northeastern United states. A large and handsome tree, growing to the height of seventy feet, and with a diameter of three feet. It is limited to the northern portions of the country, ranging from Maine to Wisconsin on the northern border, and extending far northward into Canada. It has a brilliant white bark, from which Indians and traders construct canoes. The thin, external sheet of the bark forms the basis of a great variety of Indian fancy work.

B. lutea. Yellow Birch. Northern and northeastern United States. This is a beautiful large tree, growing in moist woods on our northern border. The wood is strong, fine-grained, and makes handsome furniture.

B. nigra. Cherry Birch; Black Birch. Northern and northeastern United States. This, like the preceding, is a large tree, chiefly of our northern borders, but extending also along the Alleghany region southward. The bark and twigs are highly aromatic. The wood is of a rosy hue, fine-grained, and valuable for cabinet work and for timber.

B. nigra, L. River Birch; Red Birch. Eastern United States. This becomes a large tree in favorable situations. It is found along the banks of rivers from Eastern Massachusetts southward to Florida, and westward to Kentucky, Illinois, and Iowa. The wood is similar to that of the preceding.

B. occidentalis. Western Birch. Rocky Mountains. This species is a small tree, rarely over twenty-five feet high and six inches in diameter. It is found in the Rocky mountains, along streams; in Colorado, Utah, etc.

Alnus incana. Speckled Alder. Northeastern United States. A shrub, or small tree. growing along streams in New England, New York, and northward. Of no particular value.

A. rhombifolia. California Alder. California.

A. Oregona. Oregon Alder. California and Oregon. On the Pacific coast, in California and Oregon. Often becoming a large tree, sixty to eighty feet high, with a trunk two feet in diameter.

SALICACEÆ.

Salix nigra. Black Willow. Eastern United States. This is almost the only willow of the eastern portion of the continent which attains a tree size. It grows from twenty to thirty feet high with a thick black bark. On the Pacific coast are several species which become tree willows.

Salix nigra, var. *Purshiana.* Willow. Texas.

S. Longifolia, var. California Long-Leaved Willow. California

S. Wrightiana. Wright's Willow. Texas.

S. lasiolepis. Willow. California.

S. lucida. var. California Shining Willow. California.

Populus tremuloides American Aspen. Eastern United States and Rocky Mountains. A small tree of the northern border and Canada, also found on the mountain sides through the Rocky mountains.

P. grandidentata. Great Toothed Aspen. Eastern United States. This is a larger tree than the preceding, common in the Northern States, and extending southward along the Alleghany mountains. It much resembles the European Silver Poplar.

P. monilifera. Cottonwood. Eastern United States and Rocky Mountains. This and the next species of cottonwoods have a wide range throughout most parts of the United States. Some botanists consider them to be but forms of one species. They are large, rapidly growing trees, particularly abundant in the prairie regions and Western river banks, extending even to the Pacific Ocean. The wood is light and soft, much employed for some of the Western States for building purposes, and for inside work of houses, under the name of Whitewood and Cottonwood.

P. angustata. Cottonwood. Southern States.

P. heterophylla. Swamp Cottonwood. Eastern United States. This species prevails in the Southern States, but extends northward as far as Delaware and Southern Illinois. It is a large tree, growing chiefly in swampy woods, and little valued.

P. balsamifera. Balsam Poplar. Northern and Western United States. This species grows mostly in higher latitudes, being found in New England and Northern New York, also in the Rocky mountains. It is a large tree; a variety of it is in cultivation.

P. angustifolia, James. Willow leaved Cottonwood. Rocky Mountains. This is now considered to be a variety of the preceding. It is found principally along streams in the Rocky mountains, where it is called Cottonwood, sometimes Willow-leaved Cottonwood.

P. trichocarpa. Cottonwood. California.

CONIFERÆ.

Pinus Banksiana. Banks' Pine; Scrub Pine. Wisconsin to New England. This species is found from the northern parts of the United States nearly to the Arctic ocean, and from Labrador to the Saskatchawan. In Wisconsin it becomes a middle-sized tree, and is used for timber when the trees are found of sufficient size.

P. contorta. Twisted Pine. Rocky Mountains. This tree is found in the Rocky mountains from Colorado to Oregon. It differs widely in regard to size in different localities. Near the Pacific coast it is often low and scrubby, bearing cones at five feet high. In Colorado it is found at an altitude of 7,000 feet, and attains a height of fifty feet.

P. contorta, var. *Bolanderi.* Bolander's Pine. California. This variety in the Sierra Nevada mountains at an altitude of 5,000 to 9,000 feet attains a height of 150 to 200 feet. It is variously called Tamarack, Twisted Pine or Black Pine.

P. inops. Jersey Pine; Scrub Pine. Eastern United States. A straggling tree fifteen to forty feet high, with spreading or drooping branches. It abounds in New Jersey, Maryland, and Virginia, also on the rocky hills bordering the Ohio in Kentucky, Southern Illinois and Indiana. The wood is of little value.

P. mitis. Yellow Pine. Eastern United States, chiefly south. This is a handsome tree, growing from New England to Wisconsin, and sparingly in Missouri, Kentucky, Tennessee, and southward to Florida. The timber is very valuable, commanding a higher price even than the white pine.

P. clausa. Florida. A small tree found by Dr. Chapman at Apalachicola, related to *Pinus inops.*

P. glabra. Spruce Pine. South Carolina and southward. A tree forty to sixty feet high, with smoothish bark and soft white wood, branching from near the ground. Resembles *P. mitis;* grows from South Carolina to Florida.

P. resinosa. Red Pine. Massachusetts to Wisconsin. A tree fifty to eighty feet high, with reddish bark, growing from Pennsylvania northward through Canada and Nova Scotia, also in Wisconsin and Michigan. The wood is compact, strong and durable, and for some uses is preferable to the white pine. It is also an excellent ornamental tree.

P. Elliottii. Elliott's Pine. South Carolina and southward.

P. pungens. Table Mountain Pine. This species grows on the Alleghany mountains from Pennsylvania southward; abundant in some parts of Virginia and North Carolina. A tree of forty or fifty feet height, and of very vigorous and rapid growth.

P. muricata. Bishop's Pine. California. A small tree thirty to forty feet high; grows near the coast north and south of San Francisco, and in other localities in that State.

P. edulis. Pinon Nut Pine. Rocky Mountains. A low tree with a spreading habit, growing in Colorado and Utah, and in New Mexico, Arizona, and Southern California. It is universally known by the Mexican name of Piñon. It has an edible nut, which is much used as food by the Indians, and the wood is rich in resin, making it excellent fuel.

P. monophylla. Nut Pine. Sierra Nevada mountains. This species is almost limited to the eastern slope of the Sierra Nevada mountains, at altitudes of 2,000 to 6,000 feet. It is a small tree of twenty to forty feet height. The seeds are eagerly collected for food by the Washoe and other Indians. The wood is excellent fuel.

P. Parryana. Nut Pine. Near the Mexican border southwest.

P. ponderosa. Yellow Pine. Rocky Mountains. A very variable pine; several of its extreme forms have been considered different species. It occurs in Colorado, Utah, and the Black Hills of Dakota. It is remarkable for its heavy wood, which makes excellent lumber. It is generally called Yellow Pine.

P. ponderosa, var. *Benthamiana,* Hart. Sappy Pine. California. This variety grows in the Sierra Nevada mountains, in damp valleys, and near streams. It is generally slender and tall, with low limbs, black bark, and sappy, tough wood. Used for building timber, flooring, etc. It has several names, as Swamp Pine, Sappy Pine, Black Pine, and Bull Pine.

P. ponderosa. Var. *Jeffreyi.* Jeffrey's Pine. California. This variety also grows on the Sierra Nevada mountains, and on the Coast Range of California. It often attains a height of 170 to 250 feet and a diameter of six to ten feet. It differs much in the qualily of the wood, but is used for all the purposes of other kinds. It is remarkable for the comparatively large size of its cones. It is called Yellow Pine, Pitch Pine, and Truckee Pine.

P. Australis. Long-leaved Pine. South Carolina and southward. A lofty tree, growing in the pine-barrens of the Southern States, attaining a height of seventy-five to one hundred feet. Next to the White Pine, this is perhaps the most valuable of the genus. The timber plays an important part in ship-building, is extensively used as a flooring, and in house-building. The chief value of this species is for the turpentine, tar, pitch, and resin which it supplies, and of which immense quantities are exported in addition to the home supply.

P. Coulteri. Coulter's Pine. California. A large tree of California, from eighty to one hundred feet in height, with large, spreading branches, and a trunk three or four feet in diameter. The cones are heavier than those of any other of the family, being frequently one foot long and six inches diameter, and weighing from four to six pounds. The large, nut-like seeds contained in the cones are nutritious, and used as an article of food by the Indians.

P. Sabiniana. Hard-nut Pine; Sabine's Pine. California. Grows on the foot-hills of the Coast Range and on the western foot-hills of the Sierra Nevada mountains of California. It is not very abundant, and is limited by the altitude of 4,000 feet. It grows from forty to one hundred feet high. The cones are large and heavy, and full of oily, nutritious nuts, which are used by the Indians. The timber is fit only for fuel. It is called Digger Pine, Foot-hill Pine, Gray-leaved Pine, etc.

P. Torreyana. Torrey's Pine. California. A species of Southern California, resembling the preceding, but smaller. The nuts are thick-shelled, but nutritious, and used as food by the Indians.

P. insignis. Monterey Pine. California. Grows along the coast south of San Francisco. Some old trees near Monterey are seventy or eighty feet high. It is quite an ornamental species, and is in frequent cultivation in California.

P. radiata. California.

P. tuberculata. Prickly-coned Pine. California. A small tree seldom attaining a greater height than thirty to forty feet, with a trunk of eight or ten inches diameter. It grows on the Coast Hills south of San Francisco, and in other places in the State.

P. rigida. Pitch Pine. Eastern United States. A medium-sized tree from thirty to seventy feet high, with dark, rugged-looking bark, and hard, resinous wood. The wood is knotty, and of little value for lumber, but gives an intense heat in burning on account of the quantity of resin which it contains.

P. serotina. Pond Pine. Southern States. This is closely related to the preceding, and is by some considered only a variety of it. It grows on the borders of ponds and swamps from Florida to North Carolina.

P. Tæda. Loblolly; Old-field Pine. Southern States. A species confined to the Atlantic States, growing mostly in damp, or in light, barren soil, frequently taking possession of old and neglected fields. It is variable in height, sometimes rising to seventy or one hundred feet high. The timber is said to be valuable, though less so than that of *P. australis.*

P. aristata. Prickly-coned Pine. Rocky Mountains. This species was first found in Colorado, near Pike's Peak, but it is now considered to be synonymous with the next.

P. flexifouriana. Balfour's Pine. Rocky Mountains. The specimen is from southern Utah, and grows on high, barren, sandstone mountains; it grows about fifty to sixty feet high. The tree is distinguished by its long branches, which are heavy, causing the ends to hang down. The tree is compact in appearance and of very dark-green color. It is thought by some that the tree of

Oregon, which has been described under this name, is a different species.

P. flexilis. Bull Pine. Rocky Mountains. This is the prevailing pine of the East Humboldt mountains, Nevada, and frequent in the Wasatch. It also grows in Colorado and on the San Francisco mountains of Arizona. In the Wasatch mountains it is found at high altitudes on limestone ledges, and has a branched and knotty habit, rendering it unfit for lumber. It is called by the inhabitants Bull Pine. It is a middle-sized tree, usually thirty to fifty feet high, but recorded by Fendler as sixty to eighty feet high near Santa Fe.

P. aloicaulis. White-barked Pine. Rocky Mountains. This species, although closely related to the preceding, is believed to be different. It grows only at extreme altitudes. It grows on the Cascade mountains of Oregon, on alpine peaks in the Sierra Nevada mountains, and on high mountains in Idaho and Montana. The name is suggested by the color of the bark of the tree, which Dr. Engelmann says is as white as milk.

P. Lambertiana. Sugar Pine. Sierra Nevada Mountains. Found sparsely growing on the Sierras of California, through their extent, at altitudes of from 4,000 to 10,000 feet. It is often 150 to 220 feet high, with a diameter of eight to fourteen feet. It is highly prized and eagerly sought by lumbermen for all articles of building lumber, and is fast being exhausted. It is called Sugar Pine from the sweet resin which exudes from partially-burned trees. It is also called Mammoth Pine and Shake Pine. It has enormous cones.

P. monticola. Soft Pine; Little Sugar Pine. California. Grows sparsely on the high Sierras, at altitudes of 7,000 to 11,000 feet. It sometimes attains a height of 150 to 200 feet, with a diameter of five to seven feet. It resembles the Sugar Pine, but with whitish, much furrowed bark, and smaller cones. The timber is similar to that of White Pine, but is seldom used, because the trees are so inaccessible.

P. strobus. White Pine; Weymouth Pine. Eastern United States. An old, well-known, and useful tree, extending from Canada to Virginia, but plentiful in New England, New York, and Pennsylvania. It is a large tree, becoming 100 to 150 feet high. It is the source of much of the lumber brought from the Northern States. It is not only very valuable on account of its wood, but is one of the finest ornamental conifers.

P. Chihuahua. Southern Arizona and Northern Mexico.

Abies alba. White Spruce. New England and Alleghany Mountains. A small tree, native of the northern portion of the United States and Canada, extending northward to the extreme confines of vegetation. It grows from twenty to thirty feet high, according to soil and latitude. It is frequent in cultivation, and is considered a handsome tree.

A. nigra. Black Spruce. New England and Alleghany Mountains. This tree has much the same range as the preceding, occasionally being found farther south on the Alleghanies. In favorable situations, it forms quite a large tree, about seventy-five feet high, tall and straight. The wood is light, elastic, and strong, and valuable for many purposes.

A. Canadensis. Hemlock. New England to Wisconsin. A well known tree of the Northern States, extending northward to Hudson's Bay, and southward along the mountains to North Carolina. It is one of the most graceful of spruces, with a light and spreading spray, frequently branching almost to the ground. The wood is coarse-grained, but is used in great quantities for rough work. The bark is very extensively employed in tanning.

A. Mertensiana. Western Hemlock. California and Oregon. This tree closely resembles the *A. Canadensis.* It grows from 100 to 150 feet high, and forms a roundish, conical head. The timber is said to be soft and white and difficult to split.

A. Williamsonii. Williamson's Spruce. California and Oregon. Grows on the Sierras of California and on the Cascade mountains of Oregon, on high peaks of 8,000 to 12,000 feet altitude. A very graceful tree, attaining a height of 150 feet. The wood is of excellent quality, but is too rare and inaccessible to be much known.

A. Douglasii. Douglas's Spruce. Rocky Mountains This species grows through the Rocky mountain region from Colorado to Nootka sound. On the Pacific coast it sometimes attains the immense size of 200 to 300 feet in height, and a diameter of trunk of eight to fifteen feet. Its timber composes the great lumber wealth of Oregon and Washington Territory. The wood is soft and easily worked, much prized for masts, spars, and plank for ship building, and is equally valuable for other building purposes. A tree cut by Mr. A. J. Dufur, was six feet four inches in diameter thirty feet from the base, and 321 feet long.

A. Douglasii, var. *macrocarpa.* Large-coned Spruce. Southern California. This was collected many years ago on the mountains east of San Diego, Cal.; in 1874 sent to the Department of Agriculture by Mr. F. M. Ring, of San Bernardino. Cal.; and again collected later by Dr. Palmer at San Felipe Cañon, east of San Diego. It has cones four or five times the size of *Douglasii,* and will probably be confirmed as a new species.

A. Menziesii. Menzies's Spruce. Rocky Mountains. This species has a wide range in the Rocky Mountains from Colorado and Utah to Oregon and Sitka. It grows mostly at high altitudes, 7,000 to 9,000 feet. In Utah, Mr. Ward says, it is easily distinguished from the other firs by the dense masses of its long, pendant, dark-brown cones at the top of the tree, which frequently obscure the foliage. The wood is fine-grained and white, and would be valuable for timber but for the numerous slight curves in the trunk which render it impossible to obtain saw-logs of any great length. In some places it is incorrectly called Balsam, in others it is distinguished as spruce. Mr. Dufur, of Oregon, gives a somewhat different account of the tree as growing there. He says: It grows along the tide-lands and about the mouth of the Columbia river, and is seldom found at an elevation of more than 500 feet. The young trees make a beautiful evergreen of pyramidal form. The large trees grow from 150 to 200 feet high, and from two to six foot in diameter. The wood is soft, white, and free, much prized for lumber.

A. Engelmanni. Engelmann's Spruce. Rocky mountains. This species is found on the higher parts of the Rocky mountains, from New Mexico to the headwaters of the Columbia and Missouri rivers. In Colorado, it occupies a belt between 8,000 and 12,000 feet, reaching its fullest development between 9,000 and 10,000 feet. On the highest summits, it becomes a prostrate shrub. Mr. Ward, writing of the tree in Utah, says : Between 9,000 and 10,000 feet altitude it becomes a large and noble tree, and is of the greatest value for lumber, taking the place in that region of the White Pine of the Eastern States, and is alone known by that name among lumbermen. The wood is white, very light, and easily worked, and at the same time durable. Botanically, it is difficult to distinguish it from some forms of *A. Menziesii.*

A. balsamea. Balsam. New England to Wisconsin. This species grows in cold, damp woods and swamps, from New England to Pennsylvania, Wisconsin and northward. It is also a native of Canada and Nova Scotia. It generally grows about twenty to forty feet high. It is a very popular ornamental tree. A very aromatic liquid resin is obtained from this tree by incisions made in the bark, and is called Canada Balsam.

A. sub alpina. Sub-alpine Balsam. Rocky Mountains. This is one of the tallest and handsomest firs of the Rocky mountains, often attaining a height of eighty or ninety feet; perfectly straight, and without limbs for a great distance. The wood is white, soft, and of little value for lumber. It is known among the lumbermen of the Wasatch mountains as White Balsam, or Pumpkin-tree. Its nearest affinity is to *A. balsamea* of the Eastern States. It reaches to great altitudes, being sometimes found near the timber-line. It has been collected, and generally referred to *A. grandis,* the incorrectness of which has been but lately pointed out by Dr. Engelmann, who has proposed for it the name given above.

A. grandis. White Silver Fir. California and Oregon. This name is here applied to the tree of the Pacific coast. In Oregon, Mr. Dufur says, it grows on the low, moist land, along the small streams emptying into the Columbia river. Is seldom found at an elevation of more than 50 feet, and never on sandy or gravelly ridges. It attains a size of from two to four feet in diameter, and 200 feet in height. It has a light-colored, thin, smooth bark. It is a rapid grower, and the timber decays correspondingly fast when exposed to the wet. The wood is white, free and soft, but too light and brittle for general building purposes. It is used for clapboards, boxes, and cooperage.

A. concolor. White Silver Fir. Rocky Mountains. In the Wasatch mountains in Utah this tree is very valuable for lumber, and is called Black Balsam It is there a large tree, sometimes three or four feet in diameter and forty to fifty feet high. The wood is tough and coarse-grained, adapting it for building purposes and all substantial uses. It ranges from 8,000 to 9,000 feet in altitude. (Ward.) In southern Utah it is sometimes called Black Gum.

A. amabilis. Red Silver Fir. California and Oregon. Mr. Lemmon states, On the Sierra Nevada mountains, it forms dense, scattered groves, at altitudes of 7,000 to 10,000 feet. The largest trees are 250 feet high and six to ten feet in diameter. A truly beautiful and magnificent tree, sometimes called the Queen of the Forest. Mr. Dufur says it is found extensively along the western slope of the Cascade mountains, on sandy, gravelly, rocky, and dry elevations. Its usual size is from 150 to 200 feet in height, and from one to four feet in diameter. The wood is rather coarse, not elastic, strong, and hard. It is used extensively for coarse building purposes, and also for masts and spars for ship building. The wood has a peculiar odor, and spikes, nails, and bolts hold firm and never corrode in the timber.

A. Fraseri. Frazer's Balsam. Alleghany Mountains. This species inhabits the highest parts of the Alleghanies in North Carolina. It is said to be a small tree, ranging from twenty to fifty feet in height. The cones resemble those of *A. nobilis* in miniature.

A. Nobilis. The Noble Fir. Oregon. This is one of the magnificent conifers of our country. It is a majestic tree, forming vast forests on the mountains of Northern California and Oregon. The Indians give it the name of Big Tree. The timber is said to be of excellent quality. It is nearly related to *A. Fraseri*, but has cones five times as large.

A. bracteata. Bracted-coned Spruce. Oregon. This species grows on the higher mountains of Oregon. It was also found by Dr. Coulter in Southern California. It is little known. The cones are very curious and remarkable, being handsomely fringed by long leaf-like bracts, entirely different from those of any other species.

Larix Americana. American Larch. New England to Wisconsin. This species is seldom found so far south as Virginia; its favorite localities being the New England States, northern New York, westward to Wisconsin, and northward to Canada. In Canada, it is called Hackmatack; in some portions of New England and New Jersey, Tamarack. The quality of the wood is represented as being superior to any kind of pine or spruce.

L. Lyallii. Lyall's Larch. Oregon.

L. occidentalis. Western Larch. Oregon. Mr. Dufur says this species is found abundantly in the Blue mountains in Eastern Oregon, also well up to the Cascade and Coast Ranges, but seldom at an elevation of less than 3,000 feet. It is often found 250 feet high, and attains a diameter of five feet, frequently being found 200 feet to the first limb. The timber is very strong and durable, free to split, and used for all kinds of fencing and coarse building.

Torreya taxifolia. Yew-leaved Torreya. Florida. A small tree from twenty to forty feet high, found on the east bank of the Apalachicola river in Florida. It is called by the inhabitants Stinking Yew, from the unpleasant odor of the bruised leaves. The genus was named in honor of Dr. John Torrey, the late eminent botanist of New York. It is considered to be a very ornamental evergreen in cultivation.

T. Californica. California Nutmeg tree. California. This species grows near the coast in California. It sometimes attains the height of sixty feet, with a trunk four feet in diameter, but is usually a round-headed, small, compact tree, twenty to forty feet high. The timber is said to be heavy and fine-grained. It is, like the preceding, called the Stinking Yew, from the unpleasant odor of the bruised leaves. The seeds have a rugose and mottled appearance, resembling a nutmeg, whence the name.

Taxus brevifolia. Short-leaved Yew. California and Oregon. A tree of California and Oregon varying much in height in different localities. Dr. Newberry saw it forming an upright tree fifty to seventy-five feet in height and two to three feet in diameter. Mr. Dufur says it is found on the lowlands of Willamette Valley, is of slow growth, and seldom attains a height of twelve to twenty feet and a diameter of a foot. It is very scarce in all parts of Oregon. The small, red berries remain on the tree till late in fall, and are used for food by the Indians. The wood is very hard and durable, is capable of receiving a fine polish, and is much prized for its fine grain, durability, and beauty.

T. Floriana. Florida Yew. Florida. This species, so far as known, is confined to a very limited field on the Apalachicola river in Florida. It is a small tree, from fifteen to twenty feet high.

Thuja occidentalis. American Arbor Vitæ. New England to Wisconsin. This tree is well known in cultivation, but is a native state is rarely found south of New York. In Canada and along the lakes, it is known as the White Cedar, which is the name given in New Jersey to the *Cupressus thyoides.* The Arbor Vitæ grows twenty-five to fifty feet high, forming a handsome, conical tree. The wood is light and soft, but durable, and is considerably used for building purposes. It is frequently employed as a hedge-plant and as an ornamental tree.

T. gigantea. Giant Arbor Vitæ. Oregon and Northwest coast. This tree is found in the greatest perfection on the western slope of the Cascade and Coast Ranges in Oregon and Washington Territory, at an altitude of from 500 to 1,000 feet. It attains not unfrequently the enormous size of from ten to fifteen feet diameter and 200 feet in height. The timber is very soft, smooth, and durable. It makes the finest sash, doors, moldings, etc., and all kinds of building lumber. The young trees are beautiful ornamental evergreens, and make a handsome hedge.

T. plicata. Nee's Arbor Vitæ. Pacific coast.

Cupressus thyoides. White Cedar. Middle and Southern States. This tree is found in swamps chiefly in the Atlantic States from Massachusetts to Florida. It has also been found near the Great Lakes. The tree rarely exceeds seventy or eighty feet in height, with a straight, tapering trunk. The wood is light, fine-grained, exceedingly durable, and easily worked. In New Jersey, it is largely made into shingles.

C. macrocarpa. Monterey Cypress. California. This is found in the vicinity of Monterey, Cal., where it grows fifty to sixty feet high, with a diameter sometimes of three to four feet. It is one of the finest cypresses known.

C. Nutkaensis. Nootka Cypress. Oregon and the Northwest coast. This grows at Vancouver's Island and near Nootka Sound. It is a tall tree of eighty to 100 feet high. The timber is white, soft, and valuable.

C. Lawsoniana. Lawson's Cypress. Mountains of Northern California.

C. MacNabiana. McNab's Cypress. Mountains of California and Oregon.

Taxodium distichum. Bald Cypress. Southern States. This tree is found in all the Southern States, extending into Delaware and into Southern Illinois. In rich, alluvial bottoms, it frequently grows to the height of 120 feet. The roots often form large conical excrescences, called cypress knees, which rise above the surface of the soil to the height of two to four feet. The wood is fine-grained, soft, elastic, strong, and exceedingly durable. Large quantities are made into shingles, and marketed at the North. Its foliage is delicate and beautiful, but it is dropped during the winter.

Sequoia sempervirens. Redwood. California. This is the mammoth tree of the coast of California, second only to the next species. It rises to the height of 200 to 300 feet, and sometimes with a circumference of sixty feet. The wood is dark red, rather light and brittle, but exceedingly durable, and makes valuable timber.

S. gigantea. Giant Redwood. California. This is the mammoth or big tree of California, growing in several groves on the western slopes of the Sierra Nevada mountains, at an altitude of 5,000 to 9,000 feet. The largest trees are over 300 feet high, and over thirty feet in diameter.

Libocedrus decurrens. Bastard Cedar. California. This is sometimes called Red Cedar, or Post Cedar. It grows in the Sierras of California, at elevations of from 5,000 to 7,000 feet. It is a handsome tree, of low, conical form, tapering fast; four to six feet diameter at base; but only about 100 feet high. The wood is light and strong, and makes excellent cabinet work, boxes, etc.

Juniperus Virginiana. Red Cedar. Eastern United States. This is the Red Cedar of the eastern portion of the United States. It grows to the height of thirty or forty feet, generally with a compact, conical form. The timber is exceedingly valuable, being light, fine-grained, compact, and durable. The heart wood is of a handsome dark-red color. It is used for a great variety of ornamental work, and for fence posts is almost imperishable.

J. Virginiana, var. *Bermudiana.* Pencil Cedar; Florida Cedar. Coast of Florida. This variety, or species, as it is regarded by some, grows on the western coast of Florida. The wood is softer and freer from knots than the common form, and the pencil manufacturers obtain their cedar wood from this source.

J. Virginiana, var. *Montana.* Rocky Mountain Red Cedar. Rocky Mountains. A form or variety of Red Cedar found in Colorado and Utah. In the Wasatch mountains, eastern Utah, this tree grows along the canons containing water throughout the year, and not in dry places. Its form is there quite different from the Red Cedar in the East, being taller and with a looser and less symmetrical top. The people there say that the wood is not durable, and do not use it for fence posts, etc., as is done with the eastern variety.

J. occidentalis. Western Cedar. Rocky mountains. California, and Oregon. This is undoubtedly the cedar named by Dr. Hooker *J. occidentalis.* It grows on the east side of the Cascade mountains in Oregon and also in California. It is of slow growth, seldom attaining more than a foot in diameter and thirty feet in height. The wood is nearly all white, and harder than the Red Cedar.

J. occidentalis, var. *Texana.* Rock Cedar. Texas and westward. This forms extensive woods on rocky soil in western Texas. The trunk is sometimes over two feet in diameter, yearly rings eccentric. It branches low and forms almost impenetrable thickets. It is common fuel and fencing timber in western Texas. (Lindheimer.)

J. Californica. Sweet fruited Juniper. Southern California. A cedar growing from San Felipe Canon, in the Cuyamaca mountains, southern California, into Arizona and Mexico. It is a dwarf tree, and is very prolific of berries, which are as large as large peas, of a somewhat resinous but sweet taste. The Indians consume large quantities of them for food. The seeds are large, smooth, and free, one or two in each berry.

J. Californica, var. *Utahense.* Western Red Cedar. Utah and California. This is the prevailing cedar of the Wasatch mountains, and ranging into Nevada and southern California. In eastern and central Utah, this tree covers the slopes and foot hills at from 5,000 to 7,000 feet altitude. It is low and spreading at the base, with a dense pyramidal top, light-green foliage, and large, rather woody, berries, not so nutritious as those of the preceding kind. The wood is extremely durable, and used for fence posts. In southern Utah, the berries are eaten by the Indians. The bark was formerly used by them in manufacturing many articles of clothing.

PALMACEÆ.

Sabal Palmetto, Cabbage Palmetto. Coast of North Carolina and southward. The well known Palmetto tree of the Southern States, from North Carolina to Florida. It grows in sandy soil along the coast, with a stem from twenty to forty feet high. The leaves are five to eight feet long. In the Southern States, the wood of this tree, though extremely porous, is preferred to any other for wharves, and when constantly under water is almost imperishable, but when exposed to be alternately wet and dry, in the flowing and ebbing of the tide, it decays as rapidly as other wood.

Brahea edulis. Guadalupe Palm. Guadalupe Island. Guadalupe island is off the coast of Lower California, 200 miles from San Diego. It is about twenty-six miles long by ten wide. It is owned by a chartered American company for the raising of Angora goats. On the island there is a palm forest, of this species, of several thousand acres in extent. They grow from twelve to twenty feet high, and have a diameter of trunk of eight to fifteen inches. The fruit is about the size of a plum, hanging in clusters, like grapes, two feet long, weighing from thirty to forty pounds, growing from one to four bunches to a tree. The fruit is eagerly eaten by goats.

Pritchardia filamentosa. California Palm. Southern California. This palm has been in cultivation to some extent for several years, both in Europe and in this country, under the name of *Brahea filamentosa*. It has recently been decided to belong to a different genus, (*Pritchardia*). It grows on rocky canons near San Felipe, some seventy-five miles northeast of San Diego, Cal. It grows to the height of fifty feet. The fruit is small, (as large as peas,) black, and pulpy. Though containing little nourishment, they are used as food by the Indians.

Thrinax parviflora. Silver Palmetto. South Florida. This palm was found last fall by Dr. Chapman in south Florida. The stem is rarely six inches in diameter, yet they attain a height of thirty to forty feet. It occurs first at Cape Romans and is found sparingly on the mainland southward. It is more common on the keys, but I never heard of it before. (Chapman.) The wood is quite dense; the berries white.

LILIACEÆ.

Yucca brevifolia. Desert Yucca. Arizona and southern Utah. This singular tree grows in the deserts of Arizona and southern Utah. It is from ten to twenty feet high, with a trunk sometimes ten or twelve inches in diameter. It is fibrous in all parts, so that the whole plant may be converted to paper.

Y. Treculiana. Spanish Bayonet. Western Texas and westward. Sometimes with a stem over one foot diameter and fifty feet high, branching only near the summit, every branch bears a thyrsus of flowers three to four feet high, each consisting of several hundred white fleshy flowers, shining like porcelain. The fruit is edible, resembling the papaw. The leaves are two to four feet long, deeply channeled, and pointed by a sharp thorn. (Dr. Lindheimer.)

TRELLIS. Slats, wire, or other material, connecting two or more parts upon which any creeping or climbing plant is trained. When two trellises are connected together from the top it is called an arbor. Also any frame large or small, upon which a plant may be trained.

TREMBLES. This disease is known by a number of local names, one of the most common being milk-sick or milk-sickness. It has been ascribed to a variety of causes, mineral and vegetable. It is essentially a disease incidental to new settlements, seldom found north of forty degrees, and then only near timber, or in regions interspersed with groves. When pastures are fenced it disappears. Horses, cattle, and sheep are affected with it, and from using the milk of cows it is communicated to the human family, producing distressing and alarming symptoms, and even death. It has now almost entirely disappeared in the West, where it was once prevalent, especially in central Ohio, Indiana, and Illinois. Prof. N. S. Townshend, of the Ohio Agricultural and Mechanical College, who had actual contact with the disease, in his medical practice, from his investigations says: a severe attack of milk-sickness is characterized at the outset by persistent nausea and vomiting, a sense of chilliness is commonly experienced, and great pain and tenderness are felt over the region of the stomach. After a time fever comes on, the tongue, which was at first coated and perhaps yellow, becomes dry and red, and sometimes cracks and bleeds. The vomiting continues; the matter ejected is at first bilious, but becomes dark, like coffee-grounds. There is obstinate constipation of the bowels. The examination of cases where death occurred before relief could be obtained, showed the disease to be acute inflammation of the stomach, such as might have been produced by an irritant poison. The inner surface of the stomach was crimson red, with patches of darker color, or of a dull, leaden hue. Similar evidences of inflammation, though in a less degree, were found in other portions of the intestinal canal. That milk-sickness, as it occurs in the human subject, is caused by using the milk from cows that are diseased or poisoned, or by eating the flesh of animals slaughtered while similarly affected, seems to be established by facts for which it would be difficult to find any other interpretation. Of a family of six persons, five who had used the milk of the same cow had milk-sickness—the sixth person used no milk or butter, and escaped entirely. At the time of the illness of this family, a yoke of oxen belonging to them were sick with trembles, and both died. The cow that furnished the milk used by the family, and which had pastured in the same stubble-field with the oxen, was at the time severely sick, but finally recovered, perhaps because the poison was eliminated from her system with the lacteal secretion. Neither the family nor the cattle used other water than that of Lake Erie. A thorough examination of the bodies of the oxen showed that both had died of inflammation of their stomachs and bowels. This inflammation had been manifested, during life by loss of appetite, and especially by chills or rigors, such as usually precede inflammation. The cold or trembling stage in cattle is always long-continued, and constitutes the prominent feature of the affection, and hence the name—Trembles. This case, and others essentially similar, leave little room to doubt that milk-sickness is a direct consequence of using milk or other animal products that have in some way become poisonous. To the question, What is it that produces such poisoning or disease of cattle? various answers have been given. Some have supposed the cattle to be affected by malarial fever; others have attributed the disease to bad water, or poor pasturage; and still others to some poisonous plant eaten by the cattle with their food. The latter opinion, that Trembles is caused by a vegetable poison, is that more generally received. But what is the plant that does the mischief? To this query many answers have been made. One says it is *Rhus radicans*, or Poison Ivy; another says it is *Rhus toxicodendron*, or Poison Oak, etc., etc. Probably the most satisfactory answer to the question is given in the Ohio Agricultural Report for 1858, in a communication from Mr. Vermilya, of Ruggles, Ashland county, O. In the same report, it appears that Mr. John Rowe, of Fayette county, had reached a similar conclusion many years previously. The results obtained by these gentlemen, and other observers to whom they refer, fix upon the *Eupatorium ageratoides* (sometimes called White-Snake Root), as the cause of Trembles in cattle, and, therefore, indirectly, of milk-sickness in the human subject. In the report referred to, a description and engraving of the plant are given. The *Eupatoriums*, of which Boneset, or *Eupatorium perfoliatum*, is a well known example, are some of them very energetic in their action upon the animal economy, as any one who has taken boneset tea has doubtless experienced. The species *E. ageratoides*, among the most active, is, without doubt, sufficiently so to produce decidedly poisonous effects if taken in considerable quantity. Regarding milk-sickness as simply an inflammation of the stomach, set up by an irritant poison, the appropriate treatment is plain enough, but, unfortunately, not always successful, for in too many cases the poison has done its deadly work before the nature of the difficulty is understood or relief obtained. Usually the stomach has been relieved of its contents long before the arrival of the physician, whose endeavor then is to allay the nausea and vomiting, and arrest the inflammation. For such purpose pounded ice should be given as long and as freely as it proves agreeable. To relieve the burning pain in the stomach, a strong mustard-poultice over the seat of pain will be serviceable. As soon as the stomach will tolerate any medicine, laxatives, such as Seidlitz powders, should be administrated; or, if the constipation is obstinate, injections, containing one or more drops of croton oil, may be required. A more thorough knowledge of botany by farmers seems to be desirable. The character of plants, noxious and beneficial, their effect upon animal life, the uses to which they may be put, and the injuries they are capable of inflicting, should be more profoundly and more generally studied. The *E ageratoides* rarely grows in cleared and enclosed pastures, but only in woods and protected places; and even there is not abundant or widely distributed, and cattle do not readily feed upon it, and are only induced to do so in seasons of drought when good herbage is deficient. Were the plant well known, a few hours would be sufficient to eradicate it entirely from any farm.

TRENCH. A deep ditch. Trenching, is the preparation of soils by digging two or more spades, or plowing two or more furrows deep, and exposing the soil.

TRENCH PLOWING. Deep plowing; subsoiling.

TREPAN or TREPHINE. Instruments for removing a part of the skull in disease or accidents.

TRICHINA SPIRALIS. This parasite, found principally in the flesh of swine, is among animals used as human food, but probably also in that of all vermin, insect and garbage eating animals, is worthy of special mention, from the fact that, of late years, trichinosis has been known in quite a number of instances as destroying human life. The chief source from which it is taken into the system of swine, is, being allowed to feed on vermin, as rats, mice, insects, and on the garbage of slaughter houses. In the corn zone of the West it is comparatively rare, really almost unknown, from the fact that swine are fed on Indian corn and grass exclusively. If a law were passed against the feeding of slaughter house garbage, it would probably be unknown altogether. It is true that the parasite is found in warm blooded animals generally, but yet, except in flesh or insect eating animals, to so light an extent as to make it altogether probable that their presence is due to taking them into the system accidentally. Rats and mice, supposed to be the great means of spreading this parasite —a supposition naturally founded, since they are well known to be generally infested; and cats, feeding upon them, are often infested to an enormous extent, as will be seen from the extracts further on. From an extended article in a report of the Department of Agriculture we find that, according to Dr. Cobbold, Mr. H. Peacock, so long ago as 1828 observed certain minute gritty particles in the substance of muscles in dissecting-room subjects, and made a preparation of muscle displaying them. Mr. Hilton next observed these specks, and first described the bodies as probably depending upon the formation of very small *Cysticerci*. Mr. Wormald also observed the characteristic specks in human muscle, and furnished Prof. Owen with the specimens on which he drew up his article. Paget first actually determined the existence of the entozoön while a medical student, and read a paper before a society one week before Prof. Owen presented his article; it is to Owen that we owe the first scientific description and the name of the *Trichina spiralis*. The immature parasites, as seen in muscles under the microscope, are worms about one-twenty-fifth of an inch in length, spirally coiled up within globular, oval, or lemon shaped transparent cysts, which, according to the length of time they have been formed, are more or less covered with calcareous matter. According to Leuckart, however, the cysts are to be considered rather as abnormalities, developed some little time after the larvæ have reached their destination, as hundreds of specimens have been seen to coexist entirely free from cysts. Fig. 1, 2 and 3 show the parasite in various forms highly magnified. The number found in any one subject varies, but Leuckart estimated that one ounce of cat flesh which he observed must have harbored more than 300,000 parasites. Even if we assume that the forty-five pounds of muscle which an ordinarily healthy man possesses were infested with only 50,000 *Trichinæ* to the ounce, they would still contain more than 30,000,000. The sexually mature male *Trichina*, according to Cobbold, is about one-eighteenth of an inch long, while the adult female is one-eighth; the body is rounded, slender, and the head very narrow and sharply pointed. The mode of reproduction is viviparous. The muscular parasite, when introduced into the alimentary canal of man or animal, is set free in the process of digestion, and in two day's time reaches the adult condition. Leuckart states that in six days more the female brings forth a numerous brood of minute hair-like larvæ; these soon begin their wanderings by piercing the intestinal walls, after which they proceed through the system till they reach the muscles, into which they penetrate; here they develop so that in two weeks more, that is, in about three weeks from the time the infested food was taken, they present the appearance of the ordinary muscular *Trichina spiralis*. The sexually mature worms probably produce more than one brood of young; they have been found alive in the intestines eight weeks after the ingestion of the flesh in which they are contained. The larvæ remain in the muscles they have reached, and shortly become encysted as heretofore mentioned. Smoking the meat does not kill the parasites it contains; brine, if very strong and long applied, probably does; thorough cooking certainly does. Time also has its effect on them, though they are endowed with wonderful vitality. In some healthy subjects who died from accident, the larvæ and their enclosing cysts have been found to have undergone calcareous degeneration; but it is probably months, and even years, before the death of the parasite

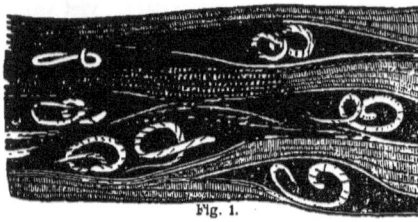

Fig. 1.
TRICHINA SPIRALIS.

occurs; in illustration of which, Virchow states that in one case he found them alive eight, and in another thirteen and a half years after infection. Prof. Zenker first discovered the consequences to which the presence of this parasite in great numbers gives rise. In January, 1860, a servant girl died in the Dresden hospital, after an illness of about a month. The case, in the first stage, presented the following symptoms: Lassitude, depression, sleeplessness, loss of appetite and fever, so that it was thought to be a case of typhoid fever; but there supervened excessive pain in the muscles, especially of the limbs, contractions of the knee and elbow, swelling of the legs, and finally pneumonia, which ended the patient's sufferings. On post mortem examination the muscles were found crowded with enormous numbers of the *Trichina spiralis*, and to be in a state of very marked (fatty) degeneration. The girl had been a servant in a family where two pigs and an ox had been killed for the Christmas festivities. Zenker, knowing that both animals were liable to the presence of this parasite, examined their flesh with the microscope, and demonstrated the presence of numerous *Trichinæ* in the pork. He also learned that all the patient's fellow servants had become more or less ill about the same time, and that the butcher who slaughtered the animals had ever since that event been seriously ill, suffering rheumatic pains in his limbs, and seeming to be paralyzed over his whole body. It is a habit among German butchers to taste the raw flesh of the animals they slaughter, and from this circumstance Zenker was led to believe that he also was a victim to this parasite. Numerous experiments with trichinous flesh (this girl's among others) made on animals have proved that Zenker's discovery is correct. Virchow, Leuckart, Davaine, Turner, Thudicum, Cobbold, Dalton, and others, have verified the fact. Nor has other and more serious corroborative evidence been wanting. Wunderlich has reported four cases among the butchers of an establishment, who were taken ill after eating some raw pork. At Planen, in Germany, thirty persons were attacked, of whom one died. At Calbe seven out of thirty-eight cases were fatal. In October, 1863, the town of Heltstadt was the scene of an outbreak of trichinosis, following a hotel dinner where one hundred and three of the citizens had partaken of smoked sausage. In these cases the disease was distinctly traced to a pig which had been purchased for the purpose of making the sausage to be eaten at this festival, and which had been considered by the owner not to be in good condition. On the day after the dinner several of the partakers were attacked with diarrhœa, prostration, and fever, and the cases increased so rapidly that in one month twenty of the party were dead, and eighty more were suffering from the fearful malady. Examination of a portion of the sausage revealed the parasites, and portions of muscle from some of the living sufferers and from the dead victims demonstrated the cause of the outbreak. When the epidemic ceased the twenty-eight cases had died, every appliance of the medical art had been tried, and the disease had been observed with such extreme care that its various features can hereafter be recognized without difficulty. The violence of an attack seems to depend considerably on the number of parasites introduced into the patient's intestinal canal; something also depends, probably, on the length of time the parent parasites live, or the number of broods they produce. The previous constitution and strength of the sufferer also modify this as they do other disorders. Cases which have occurred in the United States have closely resembled those

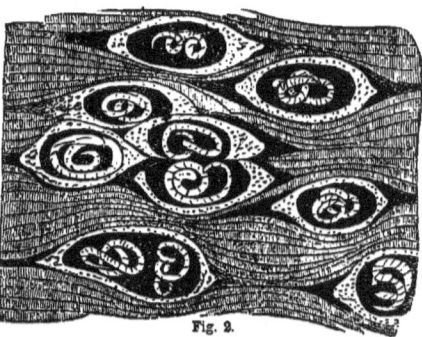

Fig. 2.
TRICHINA SPIRALIS.

recorded in Germany, of which that of the servant girl above mentioned may be taken as a type. The disease makes its appearance a few days after the introduction of infested food, with abdominal pain and tenderness, nausea or vomiting, a feeling of lassitude, loss of appetite and high fever. This condition of things is due to the development of the larvæ in the intestinal canal, and to the irritation produced by their penetration of its walls and contiguous membranes. Later in the disease, and as the traveling parasites reach their destination in the muscles, occur vague but severe pains, with marked stiffness. The muscles swell, become tense and hard, and are exceedingly painful on movement. As the case proceeds, from the third to the fifth week, there is frequently great difficulty in breathing, probably dependent on the invasion of the respiratory muscles by the parasite. Paralysis from the degeneration of the affected muscular tissues is found in some severe cases, and sometimes continues in a more or less degree for some time after the other symptoms have disappeared. Death is generally preceded by extensive inflammation of the lungs, and sometimes by delirium. Convalescence, in cases terminating favorably, is slow. The duration of an attack may be stated to be from four to eight weeks; that of recovery as much longer. In this country, so far, the disease has been almost exclusively developed in our citizens of German birth. American cookery is much more thorough, at least in the case of meats, than is that of Europe, especially in the West, where most of the epidemics of trichinosis have occurred among our adopted citizens, and it is perhaps fortunate that an amount of cooking which makes beef almost totally indigestible, is necessary to render pork fit for human consumption, even when unaffected by parasitic disease. The treatment of trichinosis in the human subject has so far been unsatisfactory in its results. In order to clear away any mature parasites which may be in the intestinal canal, the use of cathartics, such as castor oil, is recommended. Mozler and Niemeyer unite in advising that benzine, in doses of one or two fluid drachms, in gelatine capsules, should be given for its supposed efficacy against the intestinal Trichinæ. The pain may be modified by long continued hot baths. Quinine, in small doses, for the fever, stimulants for the prostration, and iron, in some form, for the anæmia during convalescence, are obvious resources. But far more good is to be accomplished by prevention than by treatment. Pork, in every form, should be thoroughly cooked before being eaten. If all meats presented for sale in markets could be examined microscopically before being sold, it would be the most

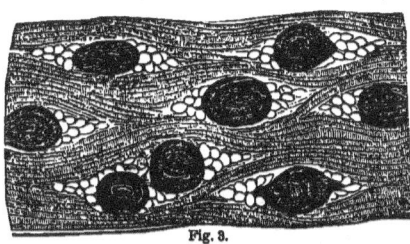

Fig. 3.
TRICHINA SPIRALIS.

efficacious means of preventing future epidemics. In many parts of Germany, but more particularly in Prussia, legal means of prevention have been attempted with considerable success. Either the butcher is compelled to own and use a microscope for the examination of the meat of the animals slaughtered by him, or to submit such meat to the inspection of a government official provided with proper instruments of investigation. Microscopes for the especial purpose of detecting Trichinæ are now manufactured and for sale throughout Germany, accompanied by such directions and descriptions as will enable any one of ordinary intelligence to detect the parasite in any of its forms. Of course severe penalties enforce the examination of meat exposed for sale, and several butchers have been punished for neglect or violation of the laws in this respect. Late investigations have not shown anything essentially different from the foregoing. Investigations made by the editor some years ago, on pork fed on grass and corn, exclusively, failed to show the presence of trichinæ. The flesh of a hog fed on slaughter-house refuse, showed many trichinæ, as also did the flesh of a hog kept in a close pen and fed on city garbage, principally hotel waste. The conclusion was that in both cases the trichinæ came largely from rats and other verminous animals consumed. So the late investigations made in Europe, have failed to show that American corn-fed pork is noxious. In fact, the parasites, in a majority of instances, have been traced directly to home-fed pork.

TRIMERANS. A section of coleoptera, many of which the tarsus contains three joints.

TRIMMER. In building, a piece of timber framed at right angles to the joists opposite chimneys or the well holes of stairs, which receive the ends of the joists intercepted by the opening.

TRIMMING JOIST. In building, a joist into which a trimmer is framed.

TROCAR. These are puncturing instruments, either cylindrical or flat, composed of a canula and stilet, so the stilet may be withdrawn, leaving the tube remaining, and used where a puncture becomes necessary to relieve hoven, or any obstinate accumulation of gas in an animal, and also in dropsy to remove the water.

TROPHI. A name given to the different instruments or organs contained in the mouth or closing it, and employed in mastication or deglutition. They include the labrum, labium, mandibulæ, maxillæ, lingua and pharynx.

TROPŒOLUM. (See Cress.)

TROTTING HORSES. The use of trotting horses dates back many years. As long ago as 1823 a distinct notice of a trotting course appeared in the *American Farmer* newspaper of that day, and it is recorded that the first time a horse ever trotted in public in the United States for a stake, was in 1818, the prize money being $1,000. But it was not until 1830 that the fast course was established and public purses offered in this country. In 1823 the rules for the New York Association for the improvement of the breed of horses; were made, founded upon an Act passed by the Legislature of New York, in 1821. The principal clause is as follows: Be it enacted by the people of the State of New York, represented in Senate and Assembly, that from and after the passing of this Act, the training, pacing, trotting and running of horses, upon regulated courses and upon private property in the county of Queens, is hereby declared to be exempted and freed, for and during the period of five years, from the passing of this Act, from the provisions and penalties of the Act, entitled An Act to prevent horse-racing and for other purposes. While there have been many fast trotting horses whose blood could not be distinctly traced to thoroughbred strains of stock, and while it is true that any active horse may be trained to trot fairly well, the wonderful performances, of late years, of horses bred closely to strains of thorough blood that have developed fast trotting qualities themselves, or which has appeared in their descendants, would seem to show that the thoroughbred horse is as wonderful in his adaptation to trotting as he is to running and leaping. Our transatlantic horse fanciers therefore need not feel badly, or rather they may look with pitying contempt upon that class of ill-bred snob-Americans, of which there are many abroad, traveling for the good of their country, who think it smart to assert that there are no trotting horses outside of America. Running horses would soon pound themselves out if obliged to run at speed on English roads. When American roads come to be generally of stone pavement, McAdam, or Telford, it is quite possible that our magnificent roadsters may become a thing of the past, and our trotting horses be confined to feats of the turf exclusively. Another fallacy which some otherwise good horsemen in the United States have fallen into, for the purpose of aggrandizing the performances of our trotting stock, is the assertion, and this time taken from English snobs, that the horse has but two natural gaits, the walk and the gallop. We suppose there are plenty of persons who have seen colts of every breed and degree start off at a square trot, when at play, or who trot naturally and quietly alongside their dams, when driven over the road, who could testify in favor of a trotting gait. The fact is, the gallop is never used by the horse except when pushed to escape some fancied or real danger, or upon some emergency, when speed is required greater than the natural trot. Education has indeed much to do with the gait of a horse, consequently some trotting strains of blood gallop most reluctantly; and on the other hand, horses long bred for running, use the trot reluctantly, often breaking from the walk directly into the running gait. It might as well be said of the elk, that he can not run. They are natural trotters, and this gait is solely used, except when hard pressed, then they will leap like the deer. The original sources of fast trotting blood is undoubtedly the thoroughbred, and for the simple reason that their great powers of speed and bottom, caused by a rare combination of bone, muscle, and lung power, had only to be modified as to gait. This conceded, it will also be conceded that to Messenger is due more than to any other horse, the transmission of the fast trotting gait to the horse of America. Next in the list probably comes Bellfounder. Messenger had as his first sire Mambrino, second sire Engineer, and third sire Sampson. His first dam, according to the English Stud Book, was by Turf; second sister to Figurant, by Regulus; third by Bolton Starling, running back in his sixth dam to the New Castle Turk, in the seventh to Byerly Turk, in the eighth to Taffolet Barb, and in the ninth to Place's white Turk, and out of a natural Barb mare, and according to the stud book, Messenger ran back beyond Sampson to Blaze, Flying Childers, and the Darley Arabian. Among the more remarkable families descended from Messenger, the author of Roadsters and Trotting Horses enumerates the following: Trustee gained reputation by the performance of a son trotting twenty miles within an hour but the dam of the trotter was a daughter of Winthrop Messenger. The Morse horse, sire of Norman, sire of Black-wood and Swigert, was descended on the dam's side from two different son's of Messenger. Rhode Island, sire of Gov. Sprague, derived all the known trotting blood he possessed from his descent from Romp, a daughter of Messenger. The family Royal Georges and Panics descended from Ogden's Messenger, and perhaps have a cross from Hambletonian, son of Messenger. Mambrino Chief and his family descended from Mambrino and Messenger Duroc, whose dam was a daughter of Messenger. The American Star family come from two and perhaps three daughters of Messenger. The great Hambletonian was a son of Abdallah, and an in-bred Messenger. The Bashaw and Clay families come from a branch of the descendants of imported Grand Bashaw, that extended backward to a daughter of Messenger. The trotting family of Cadmus descend from American Eclipse, whose dam was Miller's Damsel, the celebrated daughter of Messenger. The Morrils, Knoxes and Ethan Allen, the best of the trotters of Morgan descent, have crosses of Messenger blood. Coming to Bellfounder, about which horse there has been many conflicting statements: He was imported into Boston, in 1822. He was horse of fine trotting power, for that day, both at short and long distances, he having been recorded as having trotted, in England, two miles in six minutes, and also nine miles, some twenty-two seconds inside of thirty minutes. His dam, Velocity, is recorded to have trotted, in 1806, sixteen miles in a hour, and, in 1808, twenty-eight miles in an hour and forty-seven minutes. A direct descendant of Bellfounder, brought to Chicago about 1853, proved a getter of fine trotters. The Editor, at that time a breeder of blooded horses and cattle, had this Bellfounder horse stinted to two of his best mares, the colts both proving fast and easy going, smooth trotters, as elegant in form as they were fast. Duroc also is conceded to have exercised a good effect in forming some of our trotting families. He was a large horse, of great bone and muscle, courageous and resolute. At one time the wide-gait behind was eagerly sought for. This was a characteristic of the Duroc blood. The horse possessed some infirmities of blood, which showed themselves in a disposition to curbs, ringbones and sprains. The Duroc-Messenger especially, is noted as nicking kindly with the blood of almost any of the trotting families. The following description of some of the most famous, of the various high cast trotting families must suffice to close this article. They are taken from Roadsters and Trotting Horses, by Mr. Helm, previously quoted: By right of acknowledged pre-eminence, Hambletonian claims our consideration as the first on the list of great stallions. He was foaled on the 5th of May, 1849, at Sugar Loaf, Orange county, N. Y., and is now (March 1, 1876) nearing the day when he shall have attained the full age of twenty-seven years. With proper care and treatment he may survive several years longer, but his fame, and the renown of his family, will live in the breeding annals of this country for many generations yet to come. Having been employed in service to an extent greater, perhaps, than any stallion ever produced, his back has become much swayed, and this has worked a change in his form, constituting a wide departure from the magnificent original. For some months past he has also suffered from the effects of epizootic catarrh, which has operated much to depress the otherwise vigorous health of this most remarkable animal. But in the face of all the assaults of age, and these infirmities, incident to long service, and the inclemency of the season, he stands to-day a splendid exhibition of equine perfection. His coat is, ordinarily, of the brightest bay, his legs black, the black extending above the knees and hocks, with white socks behind (in size precisely alike), and a small white star in his forehead. His feet are neither small nor large, and as near the right model as I have seen anywhere. His pasterns not long or short, and from the sole of his foot upward he is as near perfection as I have ever known. His ankles and knees are large, and his cannon-bones flat, clean and hard to the touch, fine in texture and smooth on the surface. His hock is the firmest and the cleanest I ever grasped, and the large tendon, extending above, is very large and firm. I have not seen a horse, of any age, whose limbs and joints showed a finer texture or quality—more total absence of that gummy coarseness of cellular tissue which marks some even of the noted stallions of the day—his joints showing that perfect absorption of their synovial fluids, without which such an advanced age can not be obtained without great infirmity of limbs, and the development of marks and blemishes indicative of the imperfections so common in horses everywhere. There has been no firing nor blistering, and no resort to anything to stimulate absorption of synovial fluids, his own superior quality of bone, tendon, sinew, muscle, fiber and nerve, having been sufficient to exclude all approach of disease or tendency toward infirmity. He constitutes the best illustration I have ever seen of the highly-bred and finely-textured horse, as contrasted with the coarse-grained, soft, low-bred, beefy-limbed and gummy-jointed plug. His own perfection will be seen to better advantage, and more clearly illustrated, when we come to consider the qualities, high and low, of other stallions, even though some of them be the sons of this royal sire. Hambletonian has a knee thirteen and a half inches in circumference, a hock seventeen and a half inches; is fifteen inches around the smallest part of the limb and back tendon above the hock. From the center of the hip-joint to the point of the hock he is forty-one inches; from point of stifle to point of hock the length of his thigh is twenty-four inches; from the point of hock to center of ankle-joint he is sixteen inches; from center of foreankle to center of knee, eleven and a half inches; from center of knee to top of forearm joint, twenty and a half inches. His neck, from the notch in the vertebra on his withers to the extreme poll, is thirty-two inches, and on the underside his windpipe is only sixteen inches, giving him the appearance of a horse with a fine crest, but a very short neck. His shoulders extend forward at the point, very far and very strong and prominent, giving him a square, massive appearance, and one of great power. From hip to hip he is twenty-four inches, and in his back of medium length, round barrel, and massive, powerful hind-quarters, are found the completion of the powerful outline of this horse. Speaking of the Bellfounder blood Mr. Helm says: It is quite probable that the true character and genius of Bellfounder did not shine out in Hambletonian. In the Charles Kent mare and Abdallah blood, elements met which had some positive ingredients of dissimilarity. Although there is good reason, founded on many facts that come to my mind, for believing that Bellfounder and Messenger had a kindred origin, they had run in channels so far apart as to acquire certain diversities of quality, and their union in Hambletonian did not at the same time furnish the conditions to call out in full force the excressive and distinctive qualities of each. Both were there, but they could not both shine out with original brilliancy. Subsequently, in Goldsmith Maid, the Abdallah blood rose to its zenith, and shines to-day with a light that tells us how much has lain latent or hidden in the union of two bloods, whose brilliancy is often concealed by the very combination that is at the same time essential to the greatest fame and excellence of each. Thus it has been with this Bellfounder blood. Hambletonian was not a great success with mares strong in Bellfounder blood; but several of his sons have shown great success with mares remotely descended from Bellfounder. The dams of Bodine, St. Julien, Gazelle, Prospero, Reform, and others that have been previously named, run back to Bellfounder, and in their success testimony is found to prove the outlasting merit of this blood. It is one of the noteworthy facts in breeding that in regard to several of the important sources from whence we have derived our trotting blood the original fountain did not seem to give us as rich and beautiful currents as those that have sprung from later or more diluted branches. The native germ of excellence lay in the parent stock, but the most excellent manifestations of the blood are seen after it has been filtered through other forms and in part toned down or modified by other elements. It was so with the blood of Messenger. In itself, while it had two tendencies the trotting inclinations had to be freed in a measure from their native combination with the Arab elements that were blended with them. His success as a trotting sire is seen best in his more remote descendants, since the alliance of his blood with the other trotting elements have eliminated its real trotting excellence and presented the same ready for acceptable use in any combination. Likewise such was the case with Pilot the pacer. His blood was foreign and had to be naturalized by a commingling with that of the thoroughbred, after which it became an acceptable cross for any and all bloods which had original consanguinity with or toward the warm blooded families. Our experience with the blood of Bellfounder shows clearly that in its original form as presented fresh from the Norfolk trotter it possessed one element, a real drug that did not fuse readily in any combination. He was not, in his own immediate efforts in the introduction of his blood on this continent, an absolute success. Tested by his first fruits, and the essential transmitting qualities his own descendants seemed to possess, he was a failure. True, the Charles Kent mare was a trotter, and her power to transmit these qualities of the Bellfounder blood were enough to save him. The same may be said of the daughter that produced Harry Clay. Something may also be said of like import of one or two others, but these were all out of twenty years' service and a current popularity that surpassed any contemporary stallion. Abdallah was unpopular—almost discarded—

yet he left his powerful impress everywhere. Nevertheless of Bellfounder it may be said his success lies in the fact that he planted the germ, and in the later crosses of that blood its real force and value is coming out. Doubtless some of the sons of Hambletonian will in breeding display the richer qualities of the Bellfounder blood in greater force than it was displayed by him. The only trotters he left from mares of that blood that attained any distinction are Gazelle, and James Howell Jr., and their dams were by Harry Clay. His sons have been more successful in the same union thus far than he was. He has left several entire sons who were strong in the blood of Bellfounder, but not one of them has yet produced a 2:30 trotter; Rysdyk's Bellfounder, Manhattan, Idol, Electioneer—not one son of Hambletonian and a mare of Bellfounder blood has yet produced a 2:30 trotter; and only two of his own produce from such mares have trotted in 2:30, excepting, of course, daughters of his own sons. On the other hand, Volunteer has produced Bodine 2:19¼, St. Julien 2:22¼, Goldsmith's Abdallah 2:30, his grandam being a mare of Bellfounder blood, and he has produced Hickory, 2:30. Messenger Duroc has produced Elaine, 2:28, three years old; Hogarth, 2:26, four years old, and Prospero, 2:20. Jay Gould has produced King Philip, 2:21; all from mares of that blood. Belmont, by Alexander's Abdallah, was from a mare of Bellfounder blood, and he has produced three trotters with records respectively 2:23¼, 2:24¼, and 2:39. And one of the most promising two year olds by Almont was from a mare of similar composition. The value and true richness of the blood is now coming out in the more remote descendants, and that which has sustained so much odium is now returning to the flood tide of popularity. To-day it is the ascending current in popular estimation. By its union with other bloods, and especially with what would seem to be its kindred blood in the Messenger family, it has eliminated from itself the gross and cold elements which came from some inferior English road stock, and has also by the alliance thrown into the back ground the Arab tendencies of the Messenger strains, and the fusion thus presented now displays its trotting quality and its prepotent breeding capacities in far greater degree than they were seen in the first or original combinations. The dam of Florida having so much of this blended Messenger and Bellfounder character has presented in Florida an exact medium or intermediate between Hambletonian and Volunteer. He is much like each. Volunteer has been acknowledged by all to show more in his outward form and appearance of the Bellfounder type than any of the other sons of Hambletonian, which is, perhaps, owing to the fact that in the composition of his dam those conditions appeared that were required for calling into active force the essential Bellfounder elements; but in the dam of Florida, a daughter of this same Volunteer, were found still more nearly the essential conditions requisite to call into action the nerve force, temperament, physical and mental characteristics of the Bellfounder horse, as we have nowhere else seen them since the days of the original and greatly admired Norfolk trotter. I have seen in Kentucky a two year old—the Cromwell filly—by Almont, the grandam of which was by Bellfounder Jr., a son of the Ohio Bellfounder, that displayed in living colors the genuine Bellfounder type, as shown in a gait that will some day call to mind memories of the old Norfolk trotter, and at the same time will shine out with an original brilliancy in a new constellation that has appeared in the galaxy since his star went beneath the horizon. To an eye that has learned to revel in the excellence of this most lovely of trotting gaits, it is no rare sight to witness an exact and faithful exhibition of it at the rate of 2:40, in a two year old filly. Marvelous indeed must have been the high qualities of that sire that could, in his daughter, Goldsmith Maid, exhibit the purity and elastic richness of the finer Abdallah gait, and in his granddaughter, through the interposition of a remote cross, produce the genuine Bellfounder gait in all its nervous richness, and exhibiting a poise of body, and a steady, quick, and almost flying stroke, scarcely seen since the days of the great original. So of the Duroc-Messenger blood, writing of Administrator, Mr. Helm states as follows: His dam was by Mambrino Chief, whose dam may be set down as a granddaughter of Duroc. His third dam was by Duroc Messenger, a grandson of Duroc. This gives this horse two crosses of Duroc blood, which is visible in only one particular in his entire composition. He has a thigh twenty-four and one-half inches in length, but has scarcely a trace of the Duroc element in his gait. Instead of swinging his hocks wide out, and trotting with a sprawling, wide, open gait, as it is called, he trots as close and true as Lady Thorn with her twenty-three-inch thigh. His length from hip to hock, for so large a horse is not great—thirty-nine and one-half inches—but he lifts his foot up squarely, and spreads out his stifle, and sets each foot forward as truly in line as any son of Hambletonian in the land. This is entirely owing to the muscular conformation of his quarters, and their great proportions. His flank room is ample, and his muscle so works as to throw his stifle out wide, and yet his hocks are not widened enough to give him the appearance of a sprawler. His gait for a large horse is greatly admired and approved by all horsemen. This is contrary to the average Duroc characteristics, which generally are found in a flank of insufficient depth, and muscles so apportioned as to either beat the belly with the stifles, or go with wide, open gait. A gait of fair and reasonable width is desirable for clean, non-interfering action, but beyond that it is objectionable. In trotting he throws his feet well out in front, and bends his knees admirably without lifting them too high, and his hind feet extend well backward, but not so noticeably as in the Clay and Patchen families generally; while the steady and powerful stroke with which they are brought up under his body and sent forward, gives him the momentum of a very powerful trotter; yet for all that, his way of going betokens the greatest ease. The muscles of the body and of the limbs and quarters work in such perfect harmony as to secure this easy and steady appearance in his trotting action. While it is true that his double lines of Duroc blood are not the controlling elements in his composition, the real force and value of that blood is present in him in as rich a combination as can anywhere be found in this country. He is, in fact, a beau-ideal of a Duroc-Messenger. The three elements of his composition—Messenger, Duroc, and Bellfounder—are so finely inwrought and so completely blended as to form a perfect and homogeneous union, and work together in entire harmony and in the exuberance of the most absolute healthfulness. Not an infirm trait or tendency is manifest in him. He is a great strong horse, positive in his Messenger characteristics. He has that ready fusible and ever affiliating caste which distinguishes the union of the Messenger and Duroc bloods. He has also the rich qualities of the Bellfounder blood in a form and degree where they are more readily reached and applied—more yielding and fusible perhaps than they existed in Hambletonian himself. The composite of the first two bloods formed the truest and most suitable soil in which to reproduce the best fruits from the more uncertain and unyielding Bellfounder. While a Duroc-Messenger mare may not have been the equal of a Bellfounder in genuine trotting quality, such a mare would have furnished a field far more yielding and fruitful to the impress of any other blood. It was notably a union that readily impressed all other bloods and as readily swallowed them all up in any composition into which they all entered. We have never had an element in the American trotting horse that was so universally successful in uniting with any and all other bloods—in imparting richness to them, and in receiving all their good qualities—as this same union of Duroc and Messenger. The Bellfounder blood was a very coy element. It had no readiness for other strains, and it was not until it was filtered through distant and remote crossings that its dross was so far eliminated as to give us its pure gold, but when that state was reached, no gold Ophir, of the Sierra Nevada ever shone with such a radiance and enduring lustre. The strong Duroc-Messenger caste of the dam of Administrator was the field of more than alluvial fertility to the pent-up excellences of Hambletonian. The excellence of the union of the blood of Duroc and Messenger, for trotting purposes, was seen at an early day in the Eastern States. Duroc was taken to Long Island at a time when the daughters of Messenger were very abundant. The success of American Eclipse as a race-horse justified the opinion that they would excel in that branch of the turf. The large numbers of such mares that were sent to Duroc, and the early promise of the union for road purposes, served to make the cross a popular one. Steven's Messenger Duroc, and Stockholm's American Star, were both used for racing purposes at an early age, and both gave evidence of special adaptation to the trotting gait and of great excellence for road purposes. The former stood in the central portions of the State of New York, and gave us the dam of Mambrino Chief—a matter of which there can be hardly any reasonable doubt in the mind of the student of horse breeding who carefully and fairly considers the matter of locality, chronology and blood qualities in the respective families. The latter, known as the first American Star, from a daughter of the little Diomed horse, Henry, son of Sir Archy, gave us Seely's American Star. The grandam being by Messenger, the essential Duroc characteristics are in this family slightly modified, both by the Henry cross and the increased Messenger, but the Duroc-Messenger caste and type in the family prevails in such strong degree as to give the whole or predominant character to the family, even to the descendants of Hambletonian, that have come from Star mares—they are essentially Duroc-Messenger in their type qualities, both in matter of gait and blood traits. The high trotting quality of the Duroc-Messenger blood is displayed in eminent degree in the various branches of the families thus descended. They are bold and free drivers, going with a ready, open, and sweeping stride. They display their readiness for the trotting gait at a very early age, never lacking for courage and resolution, and showing much less nervous intractability than many other families. They bear early training, and can be forced to the utmost displays of speed with an ease and freedom from excitement shown by few families. They display a total absence of that hot-headedness which characterizes some otherwise valuable strains. While they require but little of the lash, they will bear it, and let out the last links they possess. These qualities render the Duroc-Messenger a class that bear training early, hence the earliness of their fame as trotters. They excel in the class of two and three-year-old performers. Their courage and pluck in the severe contests of a race never fail, and the name of quitter can not with any degree of propriety be applied to them. They are also distinguished for the success of this blood when crossed with other stock that are totally deficient in trotting action. The produce of stallions from this cross on thoroughbred and other highly bred mares is often marked with a high degree of excellence. Of Dexter, a Star-Hambletonian, it is only necessary here to give mention. His fame is one of pride to every lover of the American horse. Goldsmith Maid, of Abdallah blood, was in every respect a phenomenon. Her biography is given as follows: This Queen of the Trotting Turf, was foaled in 1857. She was bred by John B. Decker, of Sussex county, N. J. Her dam was one of those yellow-bay mares so common in the produce of old Abdallah. She was undersized, fretful, and of a nervous temperament, and up to the age of six years had performed no work of any kind, except to run occasional races about and on the farm, for the amusement of the boys. In 1863 she was sold by Mr. Decker for $260; the purchaser selling her again, on the same day, to Mr. Tompkins, for $360; and she was soon afterward bought by Mr. Alden Goldsmith, for $600. The eye of the practical horseman discovered that she was worth the handling. He discovered her ability, and soon brought the world to a knowledge of her value; under his careful and patient management, and the skillful drivers employed by him she soon displayed such speed and extraordinary qualities of game and endurance, that he was able to sell her, at about the age of eleven years, for the sum of $20,000. She was subsequently sold for the sum of $37,000. She has been matched against all the great trotters of her period; and, while she has occasionally lost a race, she has ultimately vanquished all competitors, and steadily lowered the record for trotting performances, and, at the age of eighteen, marked the marvelous, and thus far unapproachable, record of a mile in 2:14. Twice during the year 1876 she trotted in a race in 2:15, and although in her first race against the renowned Smuggler she was beaten, she by no means surrendered her queenly sceptre, for again, at Buffalo, she asserted her supremacy in the three fastest successive heats on record. Proudly does she command the sympathy and applause of all beholders when she hurls at her powerful competitor the defiant challenge, You may become King, but I am yet Queen. Goldsmith Maid is a bay mare fifteen and a quarter hands high, no white. She appears, at first glance, to be rather delicately made, but this conception is drawn from the form rather than the quality of her make-up. Her head and neck are very clean and blood-like; her shoulder sloping and well placed; middle piece tolerably deep at the girth, but so light in the waist as to give her a tucked-up appearance, and one would say a lack of constitution, but for the abundant evidence to the contrary; loin and coupling good; quarters of the greyhound order, broad and sinewy; her limbs are clean, fine-boned and wiry; feet rather small, but of good quality. She is high mettled, and takes an abundance of work without flinching. In her highest trotting form, drawn to an edge, she is almost deer-like in appearance, and when scoring for a start and alive to the emergencies of the race, with her great flashing eye and dilated nostrils, she is a perfect picture of animation and living beauty. Her gait is long, bold and sweeping, and she is, in the hands of a driver acquainted with her peculiarities, a perfect piece of machinery. She seldom makes an out-and-out break, but frequently makes a skip, and has been accused of losing nothing in either case. Aside from the distinction of having trotted the fastest mile on record, she also enjoys the honor of making the fastest three consecutive heats ever won in a race, which renders any comments upon her staying qualities unnecessary. She continued on the turf until past twenty years old, and after completing that age she closed her public career with the year 1877 by trotting during that year forty-one heats in 2:30 or better, and making a time record of 2-14¼. Her record stands at the close of her career at 2-14, with 332 heats in 2:30 or better. Her record and her career are the marvel of the age Of Voltaire Mr. Helm says, he is a stallion worthy of a place and a sketch among the first of his race and the age in which he lives, and adds: I find a sketch of Voltaire in a public print, which, with slight change, I here reproduce as part of my notice of this now justly celebrated stallion: Voltaire is a ten-year old dark bay stallion, by Tattler; dam Young Portia, by Mambrino Chief; second dam by Roebuck; third dam by Whip. He is a very dark bay, with no white; stands fifteen and a half hands high, a horse of great substance for his inches, weighing nearly one thousand one hundred pounds, in good road condition. He is upheaded, goes in great style, and is a hard one to whip in any class. Starting in June, without a record, he met and defeated some of the best horses on the turf, winning six successive victories, without a defeat, and winding up his trotting season at the National Breeders' Meeting, by winning the 2:20 stallion purse, beating such good ones as Blackwood, Jr., and Nil Desperaudum, and lowering his record to 2:21¼. His breeding represents three trotting crosses, and the balance thorough-bred blood, which helps to account for his wonderful staying qualities. He has beauty of form and color, very rapid action, fine disposition, and is as game a horse as ever looked through a bridle.

As a five-year-old he was started in one race which was won by the then famous Clementine, Voltaire's time being 2:34¼. As a six-year-old he did not appear in public, but in his seven-year-old form he trotted two races in one week, and was beaten by such horses as St. Julien and Orient, either of whom could trot close to 2:20. He did not start in 1876, being badly handled, and made his first appearance in 1877 at Mystic Park, Boston, June 5, in the 2:50 class, which he won after a had-fought contest of five heats, beating Powers, the hitherto invincible son of Volunteer, and gaining a record of 2:24. At Beacon Park, Boston, June 12, he again defeated Powers in a race of five heats, and trotted in 2:24. At Granite State Park, New Hampshire, June 19, Voltaire and Powers renewed the struggle, and Powers again met defeat, after a five-heat race, Voltaire winning the last three heats. August 28, at Charter Oak Park, he met and defeated such horses as Honest Harry, Tom Keeler, Richard, and Alley, another fast son of Volunteer. This race created great excitement, and was won by the pluck and indomitable courage of the Hartford stallion, in spite of a strong combination to beat him, and an effort to break down his sulky. This, as usual for him, was a five-heat contest, but it was in reserve for him to win an easy victory (the first of the season) the following week, at Mystic Park, which he did in three straight heats, over the same field of horses as at Hartford, and trotting the third heat in 2:24¼, the fastest of the race. His race at the National Breeders' Association Meeting, at Hartford, was won in great style, trotting the last three heats without a break, lowering his record to 2:21¼, and placing himself in the foremost rank of trotting stallions. He had in 1877 the fatest record in the State, beating Jefferson's record one and three-quarters seconds, and the second fastest record in New England, the famous Smuggler standing first. His career marks him as one of the most successful trotting stallions that have ever appeared on our trotting turf. Of Almont, Mr. Helm says: We now reach for consideration one of the most remarkable trotting sires this country has yet produced—a princely son of a royal sire, and worthy of a place in a household of kings and queens. Almont was bred at Woodburn Farm, the home of Alexander's Abdallah, either by Mr. Alexander or Mr. D Swigert—at that time the superintendent—and was foaled in 1864,and sold by Mr. Swigert, when four years old, to Col. Richard West, of Scott county, Ky. His dam was by Mambrino Chief; second dam by Pilot Jr.; and third dam, a very highly bred mare owned by Wm. H. Pope, of Louisville, Ky. For the latter mare no pedigree was given, but she was one of those very highly bred animals whose blood being unknown was often claimed for thoroughbred—and while, perhaps, not entitled to that rank, was nevertheless one of the best possible selections on which to start a structure composed of the best of trotting bloods and to culminate in a trotting sire of rare distinction and enduring fame. The next link in the chain is that of Pilot Jr., and he by the Canadian pacer Pilot, from a mare having much the same claims to high blood as the one above referred to. This Pilot Jr., cross, which will receive further attention during the progress of these chapters, was one that had the happy and very fertile, faculty of fusing and harmonizing well and readily with any trotting or even racing blood, and giving the product a ready tendency to the trotting gait, and at the same time interposing no real impediments in the way of crossbred or conflicting anatomy. It lacked fixedness and obstinacy, and served as a sort of amalgam to render opposite and unyielding fields pliant and fruitful, in union with more positive and controlling elements. It was an element that seemed to have affinities for every other, and all tending in a direction to promote ready trotting action, no matter what the combination. It possessed qualities that are difficult to comprehend. While the trotting quality came from an inferior and coarsely bred animal, it had, nevertheless, the faculty of engrafting a trotting action, to a very great degree, on the produce of other bloods far higher in quality. It even succeeded with thoroughbred crosses when the Hambletonian blood failed. Thus, for instance, the grandam of Crittenden, raised two daughters, one by Alexander's Abdallah, that has never been a success, and another by Pilot Jr., that breeds a colt of trotting action approaching the highest type—the latter is the dam of Crittenden. This is the only aspect or manifestation of the Pilot blood that is clearly visible in Almont, as we shall see further along. The next link in his pedigree brings us to his own dam by Mambrino Chief. Here we have a cross of royal trotting blood in the foreground, and one that was, like the Pilot blood, also noted for its readiness to amalgamate advantageously with any and all other elements, whether of the trotter or the thoroughbred. It was a blood that reached back in straight and short lines to old Messenger, by that process of reuniting, after a certain interval, two or more currents of the same blood, which, in breeding, is often found to secure an intensified manifestation of the leading or controlling qualities of the particular blood. This is nowhere better illustrated than in the case of the various families of trotters bred or descended from the Messenger family. Although it is true that now and then an able and intelligent critic of rare accomplishments, such as the fluent and versatile editor of the *Sportsman*, is found ready to detract from the great merits of the blood of Messenger as a trotting constituent, the concurrent testimony of so many others, and such vast numbers of great performances on the trotting turf, do attest the fact that the great trotting blood of the world is that which has come down to us from the great horse, imported Messenger. Almont is a deep or solid bay horse, standing fifteen hands two and one-quarter inches on his withers, and one inch higher on the rump, and weighs, in ordinary condition, 1,175 pounds. His points are black, and the color extends to and includes the knees and hocks; he has the Mambrino Chief badge of a grey right hind leg from the foot to the hock, although not yet very plain, but increasing with age. His mane is medium and his tail rather light. In his measurement and in his proportions he is almost exactly like Thorndale—his head is in length, twenty-six; his neck the same, thirty-five; his hindquarter is thirty-eight and one-half from hip to hock, and twenty-four and one-half in length of thigh—slightly longer; and in his fore leg his relative proportion is just enough different to make their gaits and that of all the Almonts clearly different—eleven and twenty-one; and let it be borne in mind that in this particular the variation of one-half inch makes a vast difference in the gait of a horse. It will be noticed that Almont is almost precisely the same in his fore leg measurement as Volunteer, and the old-time objection that I heard against the Almonts before I ever saw one of them, was that they pointed or dug too much with their forefeet. It is true that, like the Volunteers, they trot best with a light weight; but, as was shown in the case of that family, this clamor about not bending the knees is false in theory and needless in practice. Both families bend their knees enough to get to the end of the race in fast time. But the difference in the matter of elevation of the forefeet, between Thorndale and the Almonts, is very perceptible; while Almont might, without detriment, raise them a little more, Thorndale shows his well up and out in front in vigorous style. In the neck Almont appears slightly heavier than the Hambletonian model—his shoulder is heavy and very powerful, and extends well forward; his middlepiece is excellent, and, with his back and loin short and powerful, gives him the appearance of great compactness and power; but, like all of the best Hambletonians, the excellence of the animal appears to the greatest advantage in the hindquarter. His quarters are exceedingly muscular; and he carries it both on the outside and on the inside—and in this connection there is a family peculiarity pertaining to the Hambletonians worthy of notice. Many of our powerful trotters, especially those coming from Messenger, Hambletonian or Mambrino Chief blood, on Diomed or Archy crosses, show a great and very powerful muscular development of the outer quarters, and low down on the thigh or gaskin. Many of them widen out at a range with the stifle; but the Hambletonian family are marked from all others in the excessive development of the inside of the quarters and the back part of the great muscle of the quarters—I describe Hambletonian in that part as simply immense. The following record of performers in harness, unless saddle is mentioned, will show the capabilities of the trotting stock of America, both at short and long distances:

ONE MILE, IN HARNESS.

Maud S.	2:10¼
Goldsmith Maid	2:14
Rarus	2:14¼
Lula	2:15
Smuggler	2:15¼
Lucille Golddust	2:16¼
American Girl	2:16½
Occident	2:16¾
Gloster	2:17
Dexter	2:17¼

ONE MILE, TO SADDLE.

Great Eastern	2:15¼

TWO MILES, IN HARNESS.

Flora Temple—Eclipse Course, L. I., Aug. 16, 1859; 4:50½.
Dexter—Fashion Course, L. I., June 14, 1867; 4:51.
Geo. M. Patchen—Union Course, L. I., June 12, 1860; 4:53½.
Reindeer—Louisville, June 21, 1860; 4:58.
Gen. Butler—Fashion Course, L. I., July 23, 1867; 4:59.
Dreadnaught—Fleetwood Park, N. Y., June 29, 1870; 1:59½.
Tennessee—June 11, 1872; 5:00.
John Morgan—Louisville, Oct. 25, 1860; 5:00½.
Stonewall Jackson—Fashion Course, L. I., Oct. 4, 1864; 5:01.
Princess—Eclipse Course, L. I., June 28, 1859; 5:02.

TWO MILES, TO SADDLE.

Geo. M. Patchen—Fashion Course, L. I., July 1, 1863; 4:56.
Lady Suffolk—Centreville, L. I., Sept. 24, 1840; 4:59.
Shark—Union Course, L. I., June 27, 1866; 5:00¼.
Tacony—Union Course, L. I., Sept. 27, 1852; 5:02.
Silas Rich—Chicago, Sept. 9, 1867; 5:04.
Edwin Forrest—Philadelphia, May 6, 1840; 5:05.

TWO MILES, TO WAGON.

Gen. Butler—Fashion Course, L. I., June 18, 1863; 4:56¼.
Dexter Long Island, Oct. 27, 1865; 4:56¾.
Flora Temple—Centreville, L. I., Oct 17, 1855; 4:57.
Geo. M. Patchen—Fashion Course, L. I., June 18, 1863; 5:04.

THREE MILES, IN HARNESS.

Huntress—Prospect Park, L. I, Sept. 23, 1872; 7:21¼.

TEN MILES, IN HARNESS.

John Stewart—Riverside, Boston, June 30, 1868; 28:02½.
Prince—Union Course, L. I, Nov. 11, 1853 28:08½.
Captain Magowan—Cincinnati, O., Nov. 3, 1860; 28:11¼.
Gipsy Queen—Louisville, Ky., Oct. 27, 1861; 28:39.
Julia Aldrich—San Francisco, June 15, 1858; 29:04½.
Mattie Howard—San Francisco, Dec. 25, 1873; 29:13¾.
Duchess—1856; 29:17
Gen. Taylor—San Francisco, Feb 6, 1857; 29:41½.
Fanny Jenks—Oct. 2, 1844; 29:59.

TEN MILES, TO WAGON.

Princess—San Francisco, March 2, 1850; 29:10¾.

TWENTY MILES, IN HARNESS.

Captain Magowan—Riverside, Boston, Oct. 18, 1865; 58:25.
John Stewart—Fashion Course, L. I., 1868; 58:30.
Trustee—Union Course, Oct. 20, 1855; 59:35½.
Lady Fulton, Centreville, L. I., July 12, 1855; 59:55.

TWENTY MILES, TO WAGON.

John Stewart—Fashion Course, L. I., Sept. 22, 1868; 59:23.

FIFTY MILES, IN HARNESS.

Black Joke—Providence R. I., July, 1835; 3h, 57m.
Ariel—1846; 3h, 55m, 40½s.

FIFTY MILES, TO WAGON.

Spangle—Oct. 15, 1855; 3h, 59m, 4s.

ONE HUNDRED MILES, IN HARNESS.

Conqueror—Centreville, L. I., Nov. 12, 1853; 8h. 55m, 53s.
Fanny Jenks—Albany, N. Y., May 5, 1845; 9h, 38m, 34s.
Fanny Murray—Albany, N. Y., May 15, 1846; 9h, 41m, 26s.
Kate—Centreville, L. I., June 7, 1850; 9h, 49m, ¾s.
Tom Thumb Sunbury Com., Eng., Feb. 2, 1829; 10h, 7m.

ONE MILE, IN DOUBLE HARNESS.

Joe Clark and Mollie Morris—Mystic Park, Sept. 3, 1874; 2:26½.
Jessie Wales and Darkness—2:27¼.
George Wilkes and Honest Allen—Boston, July 4, 1871; 2:28.
Kirkwood and Idol—Prospect Park, May 31, 1870; 2:29
Jessie Wales and Honest Allen—Boston, Sept. 30, 1869; 2:29¾.
Black Harry and Belle Strickland—Narragansett, Oct. 5, 1869; 2:30.
Honest Allen and Kirkwood—Prospect Park, July 21, 1870; 2:30.
India Rubber Ben and Mate—Milwaukee, Sept. 30, 1869; 2:31¼.
Jessie Wales and Ben Franklin—Boston, Sept. 20, 1867; 2:32.
India Rubber Ben and Lady Walton—Boston, June 16, 1869; 2:32.
Kirkwood and License—Boston, June 9, 1870; 2:32¼.
Nabocklish and Medoc—Buffalo, July 31, 1868; 2:32¾.
Honest Allen and Myron Perry Boston, June 16, 1869; 2:33.
Dot and Ironsides—Philadelphia, Nov. 1, 1870; 2:35½.
Lantern and Whalebone—1856; 2:42.

ONE MILE, WITH RUNNING MATE.

Ethan Allen and Mate—Fashion Course, L. I., June 21, 1867; 2:15.
Honest Allen and Mate—Prospect Park, Sept. 15, 1870; 2:17¾.
Brown George and Mate—Milwaukee, Sept. 16, 1867; 2:20.

TWO MILES, WITH RUNNING MATE.

Lady Palmer and Flatbush Maid—Fashion Course, L. I., May 13, 1862; 5:01¼.
Lady Suffolk and Rifle—Philadelphia, May 31, 1842; 5:19.

TROUT. (See Fish Breeding.)

TRUCK FARMING. A name applied to that class of gardeners who make a speciality of raising those vegetables commonly consumed in families, and in contradistinction to the term gardener, as applied to those who cultivate all plants grown in gardens including flowers; just as the term florist is applied to those who grow or deal exclusively in flowers and flowering plants.

TRUFFLE. A subterranean fungus, of a roundish, oblong form, and a blackish brown color, much employed in cookery. It is found by dogs and swine, trained for the purpose, in soil beneath trees, especially beeches and oaks; it is, however, very local. It is propagated by spores included in sinuous chambers in the interior; but has never yet been cultivated with success, notwithstanding many attempts that have been made. The common kind is *Tuber cebarium.*

TRUNCATED. With the smaller parts cut off or removed.

TRUNCHEONS. Stout stems or trees, with the branches lopped off for rapid growth.

TRUNK. The shaft of a column; the body without extremities; the large stem of a tree. In entomology, the segment which lies between the head and the abdomen.

TRUSS. A bundle of hay or straw. A frame of timbers for supporting a beam or piece. Any bandage intended to support a part of the body, as in hernias.

TUBE. A pipe.

TUBER. The name applied to thickened, underground stems, as the potato, artichoke, dahlia, etc., having true buds, covered with scales. In the case of sweet flag, Solomon's seal, iris, the creeping grasses, etc., they are called root stalks. When the base of the leaves is thickened, as in the hyacinth, onion, lilly, turnip, etc., they are called bulbs. They are important in agriculture as furnishing food for both man and beast.

TUBERCLE. A roundish tumor of small size, and of the consistence of cheese, found in diseased structures.

TUCKAHOE. Indian loaf. An underground fungus, often two feet deep, but sometimes partly exposed, and from the size of a nut to a man's head, roundish and of a brown color. The *Lycoperdon solidus.* When fresh, it is of an acrid taste, but becomes eatable when dry.

TUFA. A volcanic rock, consisting of cemented scoriæ.

TUFO. A light, calcareous stone.

TULIP. A class of bulbous, hardy perennials, once among the most famous of garden flowers, and celebrated for the extraordinary prices once paid for particular varieties, and for the mania exhibited in the efforts to procure them. They are among the most brilliant of spring flowers, and of late years more and more attention is being attracted to them. They should form a part of every collection, since they are of the easiest cultivation, and are now very cheap.

TULIPTREE. *Liriodendron tulipifera.* White wood. It attains a great size on fertile bottoms, measuring even 150 feet in the Middle States, with a trunk of sixty to eighty feet without branches. The flowers are very attractive to bees and other insects. The wood is white or yellowish, and very soft; it is much used by cabinet makers and in building, under the name of poplar.

TUMBREL. A rough cart.

TUMOR. An unnatural enlargement. This term was formerly used to express any swelling or enlargement, as that of an abscess, or from a bruise; but it is now more strictly applied to enlargements of a more permanent nature, in which a change of structure takes place, or a new substance is produced, as fatty, fibrous, or bony tumors, in which the swellings are respectively formed of fatty, fibrous, or osseous matters. These being organic diseases, are not to be treated by poulticing or lancing, and seldom give way to any treatment but an entire removal by the knife.

TUN. A measure of 252 gallons, or four hogsheads. In weighing, 2,000 pounds.

TUNIC, TUNICA. A membrane or coat covering an organ.

TUPELO. The name given by Michaux to several species of *Nyssa*, or black gum.

TURBINATE. Whirled, and of a conical figure.

TURF. A term often applied to the green surface or sward of grass lands. Also the name given to peat, used as fuel. It varies much in its nature in different places, being sometimes hard and of a dark or black color, while in others it is soft and spongy.

TURKEY. *Meleagris.* Of this magnificent domestic fowl there are but two species. *M. gallapavo*, the common wild species, and from which our domestic varieties are descended, and *M. ocellatus*, a wild species, a native of Honduras, and indeed extended over various parts of Central America. In Mexico, is found *M. Mexicanus*, much resembling the common wild turkey. Since the discovery of America the wild turkey, as represented by the domestic varieties, have been carried to almost every civilized nation of the earth. Of the wild turkey, Mr. D. G. Elliot says that, the turkey was first introduced by the Spaniards from Mexico into Spain, and thence carried to England. In the reign of Francis the First, they were imported into France, and the first one eaten in that country was served up at the banquet given at the wedding of Charles the Ninth, in 1570. Bred with much care they rapidly increased, and soon were taken into Asia and Africa. It would be difficult to ascertain why its popular name was given to this bird, and it is to be somewhat regretted that such an appellation should ever have fallen to its lot, since it is apt to give rise to the supposition that it originated in Asia instead of America, the eastern in place of the western hemisphere. Not so much to be regretted, however, at the present time as formerly, for, since ornithology has taken its rightful place among the sciences, and its hidden things are investigated and explained by the researches of so many able minds, the results of whose labors dignify and elevate their subject, the origin of so noble a bird is not likely ever again to be lost sight of. At one time the turkey was pretty generally distributed throughout the United States, but like the Indian, it has gradually disappeared before the onward march of civilization, until now one must look for it amid the unsettled portions of our Western States, and the vast regions through which the Mississippi, Missouri, and their tributaries flow. It is still quite plentiful in the Southern States, many parts of which are yet covered with the virgin forest, while in the middle and Northern States it has almost if not entirely disappeared. The turkey may be considered as both migratory and gregarious; the first of these circumstances arising mainly from the exhaustion of their favorite food in any particular section of the country, or upon the opposite fact, of there being a great abundance of it in some other place. When this last is the cause of their migration they seem to be insensibly led towards the land of plenty by finding the supply increase as they advance, and not from any particular instinct of their own. Their food consists of maize, berries, fruits, grasses, acorns, and in that part of the country where it abounds, the pecan nut is preferred by them to everything else. When migrating, if they reach a river over which they desire to cross, they generally remain near the bank for a day or two previous to making the effort; seemingly either to consult upon the means of accomplishing their intention, or to recuperate their strength before undertaking the difficult feat. While they are thus waiting the males employ their time chiefly in gobbling continually, or in strutting pompously about with lowered wings and expanded tails, the females sometimes even imitating them in these movements. When they consider that the time has arrived for proceeding on their journey, the entire flock mount to the tops of the highest trees, and, at a given signal of their leader, launch themselves into the air and fly to the opposite shore. The old birds easily cross, but should the stream be wide, the young and feeble frequently miss the desired point and fall into the stream, when they proceed to swim ashore, which they accomplish with considerable dexterity, by closing their wings, using their expanded tails for support, and striking out rapidly with their long and powerful legs. Sometimes if the shore should be very steep, some are unable to ascend, and falling back from their unsuccessful attempts, perish in the water. Toward the latter part of February, the pairing season commences, and, then the females separate and endeavor to hide from the males, while the latter, with almost unintermitted gobbling, seek for them in all directions. Whenever the males meet while thus occupied, fierce battles ensue, ending, generally, in the death of the weaker party, unless he is fortunate enough to escape by flight. Of these fights Audubon says: I have often been much diverted while watching two males in fierce conflict, by seeing them move alternately backward and forward, as either had obtained a better hold, their wings drooping, their tails partly raised, their body feathers ruffled, and their heads covered with blood. If, as they thus struggle and gasp for breath, one of them should lose his hold, his chance is over; for the other, still holding fast, hits him violently with spurs and wings, and in a few minutes brings him to the ground. The moment he is dead, the conquerer treads him under foot, but what is strange, not with hatred, but with all the motions which he employs in caressing the female. The males do not always confine their attentions to one female; sometimes several of these may be seen accompanying one gobbler, until they commence to lay, when they hide themselves for the greater part of the day in order to save their eggs, which he would destroy whenever he obtained the opportunity. The nest, a very simple structure, is generally placed in some thicket to conceal it from the prying eyes of its various would-be despoilers, and the hen approaches it with great caution, rarely entering it twice from the same direction. The number of eggs deposited varies considerably, some nests having ten, others as many as twenty. They are of a dull cream color, profusely sprinkled with red spots. The young, when first hatched, are covered with a delicate hairy down, and are very tender; so susceptible to the influence of the weather that, should the season be rainy, great difficulty is experienced by the hen in raising them, for they rarely survive a thorough wetting. To guard against such a catastrophe the first night is generally passed by the young brood in the nest, and the mother then leads them to elevated dry places, reposing them at night under her outspread wings until they are two weeks old, when they roost upon the broad branch of a tree, still covered, however, by their watchful parent's wings. The turkey has many enemies beside man, and among those most feared by it are, perhaps, the lynx and great horned owl. The former sucks their eggs, and seizes both the young and old birds, his stealthy, noiseless progress enabling him to approach even so wary a bird unnoticed. The owl is equally dreaded, his soft plumage permitting him to fly about their roosting place without a sound, like some midnight sprite. The manner in which his attacks are evaded is both ingenious and successful, and is accomplished in the following way: As soon as the warning cluck of some watchful turkey has placed the whole number on their guard, they immediately stand upright upon the limb and observe every movement of their foe, who, soon selecting one of them for his prey, swoops upon it with the velocity of an arrow, and it would seem that the fate of that one was inevitable; but as rapid as was the owl's movement, still quicker is that of his intended victim; for, lowering his head and inverting his outspread tail upon his back, he meets his enemy with this inclined plane, over which he glides harmlessly, and the turkey drops to the ground and insures safety by running away. Many are the means employed to obtain possession of these birds, some of which are too often eminently successful; and also equally reprehensible, and although there may be instances, where turkeys are very numerous, that they may, to a limited extent, injure the growing crops, yet they are never so destructive as to render their almost complete extermination necessary. Many are trapped, sometimes whole flocks are captured at once in pens constructed for that purpose; and, in some parts of the country, man's ingenuity is exhausted in, seemingly, how to arrive, in the shortest possible time, at their extinction. The turkey is an extremely shy bird, taking alarm at the slightest sound; hence it can be readily understood how they would naturally shun man's presence, and prefer the depths of our great forests, or the solitude of the vast plains, and that, as a matter of course, they should become scarcer as the population near them increased, even though artificial means should be wanting to lessen their number. Audubon states that when he removed to Kentucky, rather more than a quarter of a century ago, turkeys were so abundant that the price of one in the market was not equal to that of a common barn fowl now; and that he has seen them offered for the sum of three pence each, the birds weighing from ten to twelve pounds. The average weight of this splendid bird is about fifteen to eighteen pounds (for the mature males), and the female from nine to ten. Some gobblers have been known to weigh much more than this estimate, and instances are not wanting where individuals have been obtained weighing thirty and forty pounds each; but this is rare. When full grown the male will measure four feet in length and nearly five feet in the stretch of its wings. The naked skin of the head and neck is blue, with the wattles red, as are also the legs. The feathers of the neck and body generally are a coppery bronze, changing in some lights to a greenish or purplish shade, and margined with an opaque line of velvet black. The back and rump are also black, with little reflection, while the sides, together with the upper and under tail coverts, are dark chestnut, barred with black near the end, and having metallic reflections of a rich purplish hue, while the extreme tips are opaque purplish chestnut. The tail feathers are dark chestnut barred with black, and tipped with a light chestnut. Near the end is a band of black, broadest on the outer feathers, and narrowing as it approaches the central ones. Between the bars on the feathers is a confused sprinkling of black. Neither upon the tail nor its coverts is there any white, and this is one of the ways by which the wild bird can always be distinguished from the domesticated. From the center of the breast hangs a long coarse hairy tuft, sometimes not found in the other sex. The female differs principally in being smaller in size, less brilliant in coloring, absence of the spur, and the small fleshy process at the base of the bill. But three species of this genus are acknowledged generally, the common wild turkey, already described, the Mexican Wild Turkey (*Meleagris Mexicanus*,) an inhabitant of New Mexico, resembling the preceding bird so closely that it would probably be considered identical by the casual or unscientific observer, and with habits also similar. The third species, called Ocellated Turkey (*Meleagris ocellatus*,) is a native of Honduras and other parts of Central America, is one of the most beautiful birds known to ornithologists, its feathers fairly blazing with metallic reflections of gold, green, blue, and bronze, while four series of ocellated spots, are found upon the tail and its upper coverts. But little is known of its habits, and comparatively few specimens have been obtained for scientific or other purposes. Careful breeding greatly improves the size of the turkey, especially in its native country. The heaviest turkey that has been known in England previous to 1853 weighed at death, thirty-two pounds. But that weight has been nearly doubled in this country. This result has been brought about by judicious crosses, and by reserving the best formed and heaviest birds of each year's raising for future breeding purposes. Experience also teaches conclusively that turkeys from two to five years of age are much better for breeding than young birds. The person who aims to breed good turkeys should select from two to six of the best females that he can procure, from two to three years of age; then procure a male turkey, not less than two years of age, and not related to either of his hens. Breed from the same birds for three or four years. During this time save a few of the finest young hens for future breeding, then when the old ones are discarded, procure another male turkey not related to the young hens. Afterwards it will only be necessary to procure a male bird once in three or four years, but never mate him with any of his own young. As to color, the breeder must select according to his own taste. Size of the young depends as much upon the hens as the cock. By following this simple rule, with high feeding and good care when young, the breeder will most assuredly have the satisfaction of increasing the hardiness and strength of the young chicks and the size of his mature Christmas roasters. The hen turkey possesses fair laying qualities, sits very steadily, and hatches in from twenty-eight to thirty days. As soon as the young poults are hatched, confine the turkey mother or hen in a large coop in a very dry, sunny place; never allow the young to run till after the dew is off, nor during rainy weather. One year old turkeys are found to be the best mothers, and gobblers should not be kept more than three years. The first day the chicks require no food. The second day they may have equal parts of egg and milk beaten together and baked into a custard, also what cracked wheat they will eat. This may be alternated with boiled oatmeal and milk. Green food must also be given them, such as chopped dandelion, lettuce, etc. They should be fed at least four times a day. The greatest care is required during the first two weeks of their growth, after which they may be allowed to ramble at will with the hen, being careful to feed them morning and evening. During the grasshopper season they will pretty well take care of themselves. The usual plan in the West is to allow the hen turkey to select her nest, hatch her brood, and pretty much care for them. In dry, warm, summer climates like the West, where there is plenty of range, we have found this the best, being careful to feed twice a day. In the autumn they may be fattened on whole corn or, better, be put in a tolerably dark place and fed with what cornmeal and oatmeal mush they will eat, being careful to supply them with clean, pure water. In raising turkeys they should be proportioned about ten or twelve hens to one cock. To save the trouble of watching them while seeking nests, prepare a yard of one-eight of an acre for every fifteen birds, wherein nothing else is allowed to go. The best arrangement for a nest is small houses, about three feet by three, gable-shaped, and three feet high in the center. Nests should be scattered about the yard, and, if convenient, partially hidden by brush. Turkeys, North, lay in April, and if two or three incline to one nest, set another box at right angles and adjoining the one they covet. Take away the eggs every night, and place them in parcels of sixteen or eighteen. Set several turkeys at the same time, as half a dozen flocks can be as easily cared for as one, and those hatched and taken off about the same time usually run together without fighting. As soon as they leave the nest they should have a yard twelve feet square for every two turkeys, by setting up boards, a foot wide, endwise. The mother must be washed with tobacco-juice, and the young chickens dusted with snuff, to kill the lice, or sulphur and snuff, mixed in equal parts, sprinkled over the nest soon after the turkey begins to sit, and, as opportunity affords, dust the turkey herself. The young ones must be fed sparingly, at intervals of an hour, with coarse-ground Indian meal mixed with scalded sour milk curds, and fine-chopped hard-boiled eggs; in six or eight weeks they will be able to master grains of corn. They require watching for two or three weeks after being turned into the fields, lest they wander into heavy, wet grass and perish; and should be driven up every night and shut into a stable or barn. They will soon get accustomed to coming home, and in due time will aspire to a roost.

TURMERIC. The root of the *Curcuma longa*. This root yields a fine yellow powder, which is occasionally used as a dye-stuff and in medicine; it also forms one of the ingredients of curry powder. Paper stained with turmeric is often used in the chemical laboratory, as a test of the presence of free alkalies and their carbonates, by which its yellow color is converted into brown.

TURNER'S CERATE. Melt half a pound of yellow wax with two pounds of lard, and when cool work into the mixture half a pound of prepared calamine. It is used for excoriations, or galled places, burns, and is a mild astringent.

TURNIP. In England the turnip has been called the basis of successful agriculture. In the United States it is but little cultivated except as a culinary vegetable. There are three principal reasons why the turnip can not be made profitable in the United States, either of which would be fatal to its cultivation: 1. It requires a moist cool season for its development, found only in some extreme northern sections of the West, and the Atlantic coast. 2. The cost of cultivation as contrasted with corn. 3. The impossibility of feeding on the land as in England, in consequence of the extreme winter weather. Hence Indian corn is almost exclusively used, as a feeding crop, as it is also one of the most important of our cleaning crops as preparatory to wheat. In garden cultivation the seed is sown early in the spring on sandy soil, in drills eighteen inches apart and thinned to three inches in the row, kept clean, with level cultivation, and the bulbs pulled when two inches or larger across. For late use they are either drilled or sown broad cast, from July twentieth to August first, succeeding other crops. They are difficult to keep over the winter, owing to the fact that they sprout at a very low temperature. Hence they must be kept dry, and cooled down to as near the freezing point as possible. To save seed select the finest bulbs, set them in rows two feet apart by one foot in the row, just so the crowns show, and gather when the first pods show signs of opening—dry and thresh. The best garden varieties are Early Flat Dutch, Purple Top and White Top Strap Leaf.

TURNIP CABBAGE. Kohl rabi, which see.

TURPENTINE. A transparent, oleo-resinous substance, which exudes naturally, but is chiefly obtained by incision, from various species of pine. There are several kinds of turpentine, namely, Common, Bordeaux, Canadian, Strasburg, Venice, and American White. The Chian turpentine is the product of the *Pistachia terebinthus;* but all of them possess the same general and chemical properties.

TUSSOCK MOTH. The white marked tussock moth (*Orygia leucostigma*) is often most destructive in orchards Dr. Riley, in his First Missouri Report, describes them as follows: During the winter little bunches of dead leaves are found to be quite numerous on our apple trees. They are generally fastened to the twigs, and upon examination are found to contain gray cocoons. The greater portion of these cocoons have an egg mass glued to them, which is composed of numerous perfectly round, cream-colored eggs, of about 0.03 diameter, and partly covered with glistening white froth-like matter; while the other proportion of these cocoons have no such egg mass. About the middle of the month of May these eggs begin to hatch in different parts of the orchard for over a month. The young caterpillar which hatches from these eggs at first measures 0.10 in length, and is of a dull, whitish gray color, with the underside paler or of a dirty white, and with the tufts on the back of a dark brown. In two days after hatching, orange spots commence to appear along the back. On the seventh day after having remained stationary for about two days, fastened to some part of the tree with silk, it casts its skin for the first time, after which operation the hairs are more numerous, the dark portions more intensely black, the orange parts of a brighter orange, and the two tufts near the head longer. As it approaches the time of the second molt, the underside becomes more glaucous, a yellow line begins to appear at the sides, and in some cases the orange marks become yellow, with the exception of a small, perfectly round spot on the ninth and tenth segments, which always remain orange; the neck or first segment, where it joins the head also becomes orange or yellow. Six days from the time of the first molt the second molt takes place, the worm having become lighter colored by regular stages, each day. Six days after the second molt the third molt takes place with but little change in the appearance of the caterpillar, further than that the different colors become still more bright and distinct and the different tufts still larger. Up to this time all the individuals of a brood have been alike, and of a size, so that it was impossible to distinguish the sexes. Six days from the third molt, however, the males measure not quite three quarters of an inch, and begin to spin their cocoons; while the females undergo a fourth molt about this time, and in about six days more they also spin up, having acquired twice the size of the male when he spun up. The annexed figure represents the full grown female caterpillar, it differing from the full grown male only in its larger size. At this stage of its existence the caterpillar is a most beautiful object, with its vermilion-red head and collar, its cream-colored brushes and its long black plumes. When young these caterpillars make free use of a fine web which they spin, and by which they let themselves down when disturbed, and it is quite amusing to watch them ascend again whenever they have become sufficiently assured that there is no danger. It may puzzle some persons to divine how such a hairy and tufted caterpillar can possibly cast off its skin and yet retain these pretty appendages. After having remained stationary without food for about two days, the old skin becomes dry and somewhat loose. If at this time this old skin be carefully removed, it will be found that an entirely new set of these

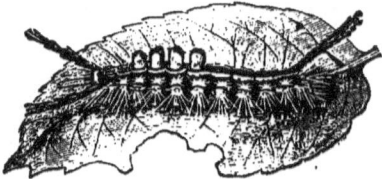

TUSSOCK MOTH CATERPILLAR.

appendages has been forming underneath it; the two long plumes curled over the head, down by the feet and up again to near the scaly collar; the four white brushes folded close together inwardly crossing each other; the anal plume folded below the anus, and all the other hairs laid in thread-like bunches close to the body in a posterior direction. In due time the old skin splits on the back, near the head, and the caterpillar gradually works it off posteriorly. The moment they are exposed the appendages which had been compressed, as described, to the body, commence to straighten out, and in a few minutes the new dress is displayed in all its beauty and freshness. The long plumes at the head do not straighten out of their own accord, however, for the caterpillar by a curious curling of the body, while resting on a few of its abdominal prolegs, cunningly brushes them with its tail end, first on one side, then on the other. It furthermore presses them, for the same end, one after the other, against any surface on which it is at the time walking, and having once thoroughly straightened out its toilet it rests a few minutes from its efforts and then commences to feed with surprising vigor, apparently determined to make up for its two days' fast. The male cocoon is white or yellowish, and sufficiently thin to show the insect within it. It is formed of two layers, the outer one having the tufts and plumes which adorned the maker, scattered through it. The female cocoon is twice as large and more solid and dense. Soon after completing his cocoon the male changes to a chrysalis. The female, in due time, changes to a very different chrysalis. In about two weeks after spinning up, the moths begin to issue. In this state the sexes are still more dissimilar. The male produces a winged moth, while the female is furnished with but the merest rudiments of wings, and is destined to simply crawl to the outside of her cocoon, where, after the male has met her, she deposits her eggs, gluing and protecting them with the white frothy matter, which, has every appearance of spittle. In relation to remedies, Dr. Riley says: Dr. Fitch has described two parasites, which attack this caterpillar, and that he is acquainted with seven others, making in all nine distinct parasites, which prey upon this species. In collecting the cocoons in the winter in order to destroy them, none but those which have the egg-masses on them should be taken, as all the others, either contain the empty male chrysalis or else some friendly parasite. From the fact that the female never travels beyond her cocoon, it becomes obvious that, since the insect can only travel in the caterpillar state, it would require over a century for it to spread even a hundred miles. Hence we may rightly conclude that it has been introduced to different parts of the country in the egg-state on young imported trees. How essential it is then to examine every tree in planting out a young orchard, and how easy it is with the proper precautions to forever keep an orchard free from its destructive work. As already stated, the young worms let themselves down upon slightly jarring the tree, and though after the third molt they lose this habit to a great extent, yet they may always be brought down by a good thorough shake, and where they have once invaded an orchard, this will be found the most feasible mode of killing them; though prevention by destroying the egg-masses in the winter when they are easily discerned, is infinitely the best and surest remedy against its attacks. In dealing with all insects destructive to vegetation it is necessary to take them early, since then two ends are served: the product upon which they feed is saved and the insects are prevented from doing further damage. Hence the persistence with which the best cultivators hunt and destroy the perfect insect or egg of any species. This is the easiest and best plan in any case, for from the great number of eggs laid by individual species, the destruction of the female moths, butterflies or beetles, as the case may be, would soon decimate the species.

TUSSOCKS OF GRASS. Clumps or hillocks of growing grass.

TWIG GIRDLER.

Fourth Illinois Entomological Report, says, of twig girdlers, the genus *Oncideres* contains three North American and many South American species. That known as the twig girdler, (*Oncideres cingulatus*) is the one known in the West, a cut of which is given: *b* shows the hole made by the insect; *c*, the manner of girdling below; *e*, egg natural size. The name is given from the habit of the female in girdling twigs below where she has deposited her eggs. It usually breeds in the hickory, but it has been known to girdle the twigs of the apple, the pear and the persimmon. The best remedy is to seek out and destroy the eggs, or better the female insect, wherever found.

TWITCH GRASS. Couch Grass.

TYMPANUM. The membrane of the ear which receives the vibrations of sound.

TYPES. In chemistry, a certain number of elements combined together, every one of which may be replaced by another and, indeed, every one in its turn, the arrangement of the elements in every case remaining the same with regard to each other, the type being no precise compound, but the manner of grouping. These new compounds (as when chlorine replaces hydrogen) have often the same properties as the original.

TYPHUS. Continued fevers, attended with great debility. They arise from impure air, bad food, etc., and are therefore often epidemic. Typhoid fevers, are those in which there is a tendency to great debility.

U

UDDER. The glandular organ of a cow, mare, ewe, or other animal which is destined for the secretion of milk. There are two or four teats, each of which consists of granular lobated glands, comprehending blood vessels, nerves, etc.

UDDER, INFLAMMATION OF. (See Garget.)

ULCER. An open sore discharging matter.

ULTIMATE ANALYSIS. The determination of the elements of an organic body.

UMBEL. In botany, a form of inflorescence in which all the pedicels proceed from a single point. If there is no subdivision, the umbel is called simple; but if the pedicels produce other umbels, as in parsley, the umbel is compound.

UMBELLIFEROUS PLANTS. *Umbelliferæ.* A race of great frequency in all cool or temperate climates, and even occur in hot ones, though much more rarely. They are known in general by their flowers being disposed in an umbel. They have an herbaceous stem; leaves usually much divided, often inflated when they join the stem; and they have universally a dry fruit, which divides into two seed-like pieces. Some of them are poisonous, as hemlock, fool's parsley and water dropwort; others are esculents, as celery, carrots and parsnips; many yield aromatic fruits, as caraway, coriander and anise; a few secrete a fœtid gum resin, of which assafœtida, ammoniacum and galbanum are examples. The species are extremely numerous, and difficult to recognize with accuracy; but those which grow in damp or wet places are to be suspected, whereas those that are aromatic and found in dry soils are often innocuous.

UMBILICAL CORD. In animals, the cord of blood vessels which passes between the placenta and fœtus; the navel string. In botany, the thread which attaches the seed to the carpel or placenta.

UMBILICUS. The navel.

UNCIFORM BONE. One of the bones of the wrist.

UNCONFORMABLE STRATA. The strata which do not incline or dip in the same direction as those below or above them.

UNDERDRAINING. A term applied to any covered drains, in which the flow of water may be more or less continuous. Stone, brush, slabs, boards, and other material facilitating the flow of water may be used, but tile is the best, as it is the cheapest material in the end where they may be procured. (See article Draining).

UNDERWOOD. Coppice, small trees, or shoots from old stools. Any thick undergrowth in forests.

AVERAGE YEARLY WAGES

OF THE

ARTISAN CLASSES.

TRADES.	NO. EMPLOYED.	AVERAGE YEARLY WAGES.	TOTAL YEARLY WAGES.
Hosiery and Knit Goods	28,885	$232	$6,701,475
Cotton Goods	183,472	245	45,014,410
Men's Clothing	160,758	286	45,940,350
Woolen Goods	86,501	300	25,836,292
Mixed Textiles	43,373	309	13,316,753
Tobacco, Cigars and Cigarettes	53,297	347	18,464,562
Paper	21,422	340	6,525,355
Book Bind'g and Blank Book Making	10,612	371	3,927,349
Glass	24,177	370	9,144,100
Boots and Shoes	133,810	381	50,995,141
Hats and Caps	17,210	385	6,635,522
Leather Tanning	23,812	387	9,204,243
Agricultural Implem'ts	39,580	388	15,359,610
Cars, Railroad and Street	14,232	388	5,507,753
Carriages and Wagons	45,094	400	18,088,613
Hardware	16,801	407	6,846,013
Furniture	48,717	418	20,388,794
Bread and Bakery Products	22,488	419	9,411,325
Cutlery and Edge Tools	10,510	422	4,447,349
Leather Currying	11,053	438	4,845,413
Foundries and Machine Shops	145,851	451	65,082,133
Carpentry	54,138	454	24,562,077
Malt Liquors	26,220	465	12,198,053
Marble and Stone	21,471	477	10,238,885
Jewelry	12,697	507	6,441,068
Printing and Pub.	58,178	509	30,531,697
Musical Instruments	6,575	692	4,603,193

UNGUIS. The claw or small extremity of a petal, where it is inserted into the stem.

UNGULATES. Those quadrupeds furnished with a hoof.

UNILOCULAR. Seed vessels which contain but one cavity.

UPAS. A Javanese tree (*Antiaris toxicaria*) from which the Upas poison is secreted.

UPONG. *Ilex vomitoria* and *cassena*. The black drink, medicine, or tea plant of North Carolina, used by the Indians.

UPRIGHT CHESS. (See Chess.)

UREA. A peculiar crystallizable substance held in solution in the urine. Urea is readily soluble in water, tasteless, inodorous, and when mixed with the other contents of the urine, very prone to putrefaction, the principal result of which is carbonate of ammonia.

UREDO. (See Fungus.)

URETERS. The tubes which convey urine from the kidneys to the bladder.

URETHRA. The passage from the bladder outward, for the discharge of urine.

URIC ACID, LITHIC ACID. An acid occurring in large quantity, combined with ammonia, in the urine of birds and reptiles, and to a small extent only in the urine of carnivorous quadrupeds. In the pure state it is a very insoluble white powder; it dissolves in nitric acid, and when evaporated to dryness and mixed with a little ammonia, gives a rich red color.

URINARY ORGANS, DISEASES OF. The diseases of the urinary organs are, in the horse, stone in the bladder, retention of urine or strangury, and profuse staling or diabetes. For stone in the bladder, a rare occurrence, a surgeon should be employed. The symptoms of the first are, stretching out, in an ineffectual attempt to urinate, with exhibition of pain. Sometimes the water will flow readily, and at other times scantily, or not at all. The ox tribe are also sometimes affected thus. In the latter case, it is better at once to fatten and kill. Strangury is occasioned from various causes, as paralysis of the bladder, meningitis, staggers, colic, and other acute diseases, and also from the effects of irritating drugs. If the difficulty is occasioned by palsy, the water may be drawn off by means of a catheter, but should be treated by a veterinary surgeon, the best means being by hypodermic injections under the skin. If it is due to general weakness of the bladder, two drachms of powdered camphor and one-half ounce of saltpetre may be made into a ball and given. If this do not give relief, try twenty grains of powdered cantharides and one drachm of powdered digitalis made into a ball with soap. For profuse staling, give the following, three times a day, in water: twenty grains of iodine, one drachm iodide of potassium, and four drachms carbonate of soda. For black water, a disease of the general system, but not common, to relieve the bowels, from four to six drachms of powdered aloes and one to two ounces of cream of tartar should be given in something less than a quart of water. If it do not act, repeat the dose, in any case assisting the operation by an injection of a quart of tepid soap suds to which is added three ounces spirits of turpentine. As the severe symptoms are relieved, assist the horse to rise, and use a tonic, say two drachms sulphate of iron and one drachm powdered nux vomica, given as a ball, with linseed meal and syrup.

Rest, light nourishing food and good ventilation are necessary in treating this disease.

URINE. A saline fluid secreted from the blood of animals by the kidneys, collected in the urinary bladder, and emitted by the canal of the urethra. Urine differs in different animals, and varies in its characters, according to the kind of food employed. The usual salts contained in it are, sulphates, phosphates, and chlorides, all of which are fertilizing substances. The urine of oxen and horses undergoes decomposition less rapidly than that of carnivorous animals. It contains hippurates, but no lithic acid, that substance which forms red gravel in man. Practically it is of the most valuable of all manures, as the following analysis will show: Human urine contains,

Water	93.30
Urea	3.01
Uric acid	0.10
Lactic acid, lactate of potash, and ammonia	1.71
Mucus	0.03
Sulphate of potash	0.37
Sulphate of soda	0.32
Phosphate of soda	0.29
Phosphate of ammonia	0.16
Chloride of sodium	0.45
Chloride of ammonia	0.15
Phosphate of lime and magnesia	0.11
	100.00

The following table from Sprengel shows the composition of cow's urine, in the first column, when fresh; in the second, when putrefied alone; and in the third column, when putrefied with water. The amount being parts in 100,000.

Components.	When fresh.	Putrefied alone.	Putrefied with water.
Urea	4,000	1,000	600
Albumen	10		
Mucus	190	40	30
Benzoic acid	90	250	120
Lactic acid	516	500	120
Carbonic acid	5256	16	1553
Ammonia	205	487	1624
Potash	664	664	664
Soda	554	554	554
Silica	36	5	8
Alumina	2		
Oxide of iron	4	1	
Oxide of manganese	1		
Lime	65	2	8
Magnesia	36	22	30
Chlorine	272	272	272
Sulphuric acid	405	388	332
Phosphoric acid	70	26	46
Acetic acid (vinegar)			20
Sulphuretted hydrogen		1	30
Insoluble earthy phosphates and carbonates		180	150
Water	92,624	95,442	93,481
	100,000	100,000	100,000

The next table will show the organic, inorganic, and total of solid matter in urine of several animals and man, and amount voided in twenty-four hours.

Urine of	Water in 1,000 parts	Solid matter in 1,000 parts.			Voided in 24 hours.
		Organic.	Inorganic	Total.	
Man	930 to 97	22 to 52	8 to 18	30 to 70	3 lbs.
Horse	888 to 940	27 to 79	33 to 45	60 to 124	8
Cow	880 to 930	50 to 70	20 to 47	70 to 120	40
Sheep	934 to 960	28 to 50	12 to 20	40 to 70	
Pig	926 to 983	9 to 56	9 to 18	18 to 74	

The urine of the horse is the most highly concentrated, that of the cow the most dilute, being double that of man, weight for weight, and twelve times that of the horse, depending, of course, upon the nature of the food used. It will naturally be seen, therefore, that urine should be applied in a very dilute state, since fresh urine is too concentrated to be applied directly to plants, and it is to the urea, which exists in much greater quantity than in other substances, that its fertilizing qualities are principally due. (See also articles Liquid Manure, Manure, and Top Dressing.)

URN. The small receptacle of mosses in which the sporules are placed. A vessel.

UROCERATA. The name of a tribe of the Terebrantia, or boring hymenopterous insects, in which the tenebra, or borer, of the females is sometimes very long and prominent, and composed of three filamentary processes, sometimes capillary, and coiled in a spiral form in the inter or of the abdomen.

USTILAGO. A name given to certain fungi which produce the appearance of burning on the leaves of plants; fire blight. This term was formerly applied to burned ear, a disease of grain.

UTERUS. The womb.

UTRICLE, UTRICULUS. A one-celled, one or four seeded, superior membranous fruit, often bursting by a transverse suture. A little bladder

UVA URSI. *Arbutus uva ursi.* Bear's berry. A small shrub, the leaves of which are used in medicine.

UVULA. The pendulous portion of the soft palate which hangs over the cavity of the pharynx.

V

VACUUM. A void space. The cavity of any vessel from which air has been extracted by the air-pump is called a vacuum.

VAGINA. A sheath; the passage from the uterus outward.

VAGINA, INFLAMMATION OF. This a rare disease; and usually due to injury to the parts by violence of the male, but occasioned by other violence, difficult labor, or by the presence of cancer or ulcers. There is tenderness, swelling of the parts and the extrusion of watery or purulent matter. In cases of simple inflammation if the discharge is foul, solution of sulphate of zinc, as recommended for inflammation of the yard, may be used, careful but repeated injections being made, so as not to further irritate the parts. In milder cases, slippery elm or linseed tea, with a drachm of sugar of lead to the pint may be used. If ulcerous, or cancerous, proceed as advised in inflammation of the sheath, always seeking the services of a veternarian if possible.

VALERIAN. *Valeriana officinalis.* A perennial herb, the root of which is a nervous stimulant.

VALLESNERIA. A genus of water weeds.

VALVE. In mechanics and zoology, a flap or small door opening only in one direction, and serving to close a tube or passage. There are many kinds of valves, as the door valve, the sliding valve. In botany, the pieces into which dry fruits or anthers burst naturally, are called valves.

VANILLA. The succulent fruit of the *Epidendron vanilla,* an orchideous climbing shrub of Mexico and tropical America. The seeds have aroma, and are used in flavoring.

VAPOR. The late Prof. Henry, Secretary of the Smithsonian Institution, Washington, has contributed much valuable literature on meteorology to what has been known before. The subject of vapor is an important one in agriculture, and hence we extract, from an article by the distinguished scholar, what relates to vapor: The great motive power which gives rise to the various currents of the aerial covering of our globe is the unequal distribution of the heat of the sun; the elevated temperature of the equatorial regions heating the air causes it to ascend and flow over toward the pole, while the cold of the frigid zone produces a condensation of the air, which gives rise to downward currents in that region, and a spreading out there in all directions toward the equator. The simplicity of this movement is first interfered with by the motion of the earth upon its axis, which gives to all the currents flowing towards the equator a curvature to the west, and to all those flowing from the equator a curvature to the east. Another perturbing influence, which has been mentioned, is the unequal heating of the several parts of the different zones of the earth, consisting as they do of alternations of land and water. But the great perturbing cause is the varying quantity of moisture which exists in the atmosphere, and which, by its increase and diminution, gives rise to the varying conditions of the weather, and produces the fitful and almost infinite variety of meteorological changes which occur at different times and in different places. We shall principally devote this article to an exposition of the phenomena of the vapor of the atmosphere, including that of the various aqueous meteors, such as rain, hail, hurricanes, tornadoes, etc. The meteorology of the United States, as well as its geology, is exhibited on a large scale, and affords one of the best fields on the surface of the globe for studying the general movements of the atmosphere. The subject has attracted much attention on this side of the Atlantic, and a number of laborers have devoted themselves to it with ardor and success; but we regret that the discussions, which unavoidably arise among different investigators, have not always been carried on with calmness and moderation with which the pursuit of truth should always be conducted. Indeed, meteorology has ever been an apple of contention, as if the violent commotions of the atmosphere induced a sympathetic effect in the minds of those who have attempted to study them. We have no hypothesis of our own to advocate; and while we attempt to reduce the multiplicity of facts which have been collected in regard to this subject to general principles, we shall aim at nothing but truth, and endeavor to select from the various hypotheses which have been proposed, such as, in our judgment, are well founded on the established laws of force and motion, and which give the most faithful and explicit expression of the phenomena. We shall be ready at any time to modify or change our views as soon as facts are discovered with which they are incompatible, and indeed we shall hold most of them as provisional truths, which may serve to guide our inquiries, and which are to be established, modified, or rejected by the results of subsequent induction. The statement may be repeated, which has been previously made, that while the general principles of meteorology are well understood, the facts relating to it, on account of the variations and multiplicity of condition, are the most complex of those of any branch of physical science. It has been properly said that astronomy is the most perfect of all branches of knowledge, because its elements are the most simple; and we may say, for a like reason, that meteorology is the least advanced, because its phenomena depend upon the concurrence of so many and such a variety of causes. The air at all times contains water in an elastic, invisible state, called vapor. To prove this, it is sufficient to pour into a bright metallic or glass tumbler a quantity of cold water, the outside of which will become covered with dew. If the vessel were pervious to the liquid, we might suppose the water which appears on the outside to come from within, but this can not be the case with a metallic or glass vessel, and the only source to which we can refer the dew is the atmosphere. The stratum of air immediately around the vessel is cooled by contact with its sides, and a portion of its vapor reduced to water. The air thus cooled becomes heavier, sinks down along the side of the tumbler, and gives place to a new portion of which the vapor is also condensed; and in this way the process is continued as long as the temperature of the water is below that of the surrounding air. If the water which trickles down the side of the vessel is chemically examined, it will be found in some cases almost entirely pure, and in others contaminated by animal and other effluvia which are diffused in the atmosphere. If the experiment be made on different days and at different seasons, we shall find a greater or less reduction of the temperature of the liquid within the tumbler is required in order to produce a deposition of the vapor. The greater the number of degrees of this reduction of temperature, the greater will be the evaporation from a given surface of water, and the more intense will be the different effects which depend on the relative dryness of the air. If the experiment be made in summer, and we find but a small reduction of temperature is necessary to produce the deposition of moisture on the outside of the tumbler; and if we attend to the state of our feelings at the same time, we shall experience that peculiar sensation which is referred to what is called the closeness or sultriness of the atmosphere, and caused, by the large amount of vapor with which it is charged. To understand even approximately the effects due to the vapor in the atmosphere, water in an aeriform condition as it exists by itself or separated from the atmosphere; and for this purpose we may employ the ingenious method devised by Dr. Dalton, of Manchester, England, to whose researches in meteorology and other branches of physical science we are more indebted than to those of almost any other individual of the present century. He employed in these researches, a glass tube of about forty inches in length, closed at one end, and filled with dry and warm mercury. The tube thus filled was inverted with its lower end in a basin of the same metal, and thus formed an arrangement similar to that of an ordinary barometer, in which the pressure of the air, as is well known, forces up the mercury and keeps it suspended at an elevation of thirty inches, when the experiment is made at the level of the sea. The space above the mercury is a Torricellian vacuum; that is, a space void of all gross matter, save a very attenuated vapor of mercury, which can also be removed by a reduction of temperature below the fiftieth degree of Fahrenheit's scale, but the correction on this account is so small that it may be neglected. Into this vacuum Dr. Dalton introduced a very small quantity of water, by forcing it from a small syringe into the mercury at the base of the column, whence it rose to the surface and was attended with an immediate depression of the mercurial column, which, when the temperature of the room was at 60°, amounted to nearly half an inch. By this experiment, it was proved that water, at the ordinary temperature, when the pressure of the air is removed, immediately flashes into steam or vapor, and that the atoms of this vapor repel each other, thus producing an elastic force which depresses the column of mercury. In this experiment; the quantity of water introduced was but a few grains, yet it did not all flash into vapor, but a portion of it remained in the form of a thin stratum of liquid on the surface of the mercury. Its weight, however, was insufficient to produce the observed descent of the column, and its effect in this respect could readily be calculated, since its weight was known. The descent of the mercury was therefore due to the repulsion of the atoms of vapor, and the former afforded an accurate measure of the comparative amount of this force. The tube, as we have stated, was forty inches long; and since the column of mercury at first occupied but thirty inches of its length, the extent of the vacuum before the introduction of the water was ten inches, and afterward ten and a half inches. That the depression of the mercury is an exact measure of the elastic force or repulsion of the atoms of the aqueous vapor, will be evident when we consider that if we remove the vapor the column will rise to thirty inches, and will then be exactly in equilibrio with the pressure of the external atmosphere; or, in other words, the two are in exact balance; but if, after the introduction of the vapor, the column is reduced half an inch in height, it is plain that the force which produces this effect must be just equal to the weight of this amount of mercury. Dr. Dalton next diminished the length of this vacuum by plunging the lower end of the tube deeper into the basin of mercury, and thereby causing the upper end of the column to be projected farther into the tube; but this produced no difference in the height of the column, the top of which was still depressed to half an inch below the normal height of thirty inches. From this experiment we infer that the repulsion of the atoms of vapor can not, like that of the atoms of air, be increased by external pressure, for when we attempt to coerce them into a smaller space by external pressure, a portion of them is converted into water, and the atoms which remain in the aeriform condition exert the same amount of presure as before. Dr.

Dalton next increased the temperature by surrounding the tube containing the mercurial column with a larger tube filled in succession with water of different temperatures; this produced for each temperature a difference in the depression of the height of the column; and when the water was at the temperature of 100°, the depression, instead of being half an inch, was almost precisely three times as much. The cut represents the apparatus employed by Dr. Dalton, in which a, is the barometer tube filled with mercury to the height of f, and its lower end plunged into the basin of mercury c. The graduated scale for measuring the height of the column is denoted by b. The larger tube around the barometer tube to contain the water of different temperatures is denoted by d. A thermometer, e, is inserted at its upper end by which to ascertain the temperature of the enclosed water and, consequently, that of the vapor within the barometer. With this simple contrivance, Dr. Dalton made a series of experiments to determine the repulsion of the atoms of steam; or, in other words, the elastic force of aqueous vapor, corresponding to the different degrees of Fahrenheit's scale from zero up to the boiling point. To facilitate the operations and to allow for any changes that might take place in the pressure of the atmosphere during the continuance of the experiment, another tube was placed beside the first, in the same basin, and the descent of the mercurial column of the first tube estimated from the top of that in the second, which, to render the measure more gradate, may be effected by means of a small telescope, sliding on an accurated rod, and movable in a horizontal plane. By placing water of a given temperature within the outer tube and then gradually cooling it after each observation, and finally filling the same tube with freezing mixtures, a table similar to the following was constructed. Dalton's experiments, however, have been repeated with additional precautions by other scientists and particularly by M. Regnault, from whose work the table on page 997 has been compiled, giving the elastic force of aqueous vapor, in English inches of mercury, temperature of Fahrenheit's scale's. The first column of the table gives the temperature of the water and vapor in the Torricellian vacuum for every ten degrees; the second, the depression of the mercury or the elastic force of the vapor, corresponding to the several degrees of temperature of the first column. The remaining columns give the depression of the mercury for the intermediate degrees, this arrangement being adopted to save space. For example, if we wish to know the elastic pressure

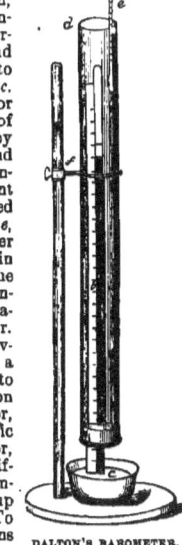

DALTON'S BAROMETER.

of vapor at the temperature of 70°, by looking opposite to 70°, in the second column, we find 0.733 or nearly seven-tenths and a third inches of mercury. Again, if we wish the amount of repulsive force of the atoms of vapor at the temperature of 86°, we cast our eye along the line of 80°, until it comes under the 6°, which is at the top of the table, and find 1.242 or very nearly an inch and a quarter as the height of a column of mercury which vapor of water will sustain without being condensed into a liquid, at the temperature of 86°. By looking along the table it will be seen that there are equal increments of elastic pressure. Thus, while the elastic force of vapor at 20° is sufficient to depress the mercurial column a little more than one-tenth of an inch, at 40° it supports nearly two and a half times as much, at 60° five times, at 80° ten times, and at 100° nineteen times. The reason of this is not difficult to understand, since it is evident that the elastic pressure of the vapor must be increased by the action of two causes: First, by increasing the temperature, the vapor tends to expand just as air would do under the same circumstances; and second, by the same increase of temperature, a new portion of water is converted into vapor, which, being forced into the same space, increases the density, and consequently, the elasticity of the vapor which existed there before. Dr. Dalton also showed that there is a remarkable difference between vapor which exists over water, and vapor separated from the liquid from which it is produced. In the first case, as we have seen, every increase of temperature causes the formation of a new quantity of vapor, which serves to increase the density and consequently the repulsive energy of the vapor previously existing. Hence, as we have shown before, the expansive power of vapor or steam increases in a geometrical ratio, while the temperature increases in an arithmetical ratio, that is, an addition of a few degrees of heat produces more than a proportional degree of elastic force. The case, however, is very different with vapor separated from the water from which it is produced; it then obeys the same law as atmospheric air, and increases in elasticity with equal additions of temperature. The atmosphere increases its elastic force by one four hundredth and ninetieth part for every degree of Fahrenheit above the freezing point; the vapor of water follows the same law. The table as given is limited to 100°, and is sufficient for resolving problems relative to the hygrometrical condition of the atmosphere. It is, however, important for the use of the steam engineer that it should be extended to a much higher degree, and accordingly experiments have been made for this purpose by a number of persons, and particularly by M. Regnault at the expense of the French government. From that table we may see that, at the temperature of 212°, the elastic force of vapor balances thirty inches of mercury and is then just equal to the pressure of the atmosphere. This fact gives the explanation of the phenomenon of boiling, since the vapor formed at the temperature of 212° has just sufficient repulsive power to expand beneath the pressure of the atmosphere, and to pass up in volumes through the water, giving it the peculiar agitation known as boiling. It is further evident from the same table that vapor is given off from ice, even at zero or 32° below freezing point; if, therefore, a lump of this substance in a cold day be placed under the receiver of an air pump, even when the apparatus is cooled down to zero, a portion of it will immediately spring into vapor, sufficient to fill the whole capacity of the cylinder, when the air is withdrawn; and if this vapor in its turn be removed by working the pump, another portion of the ice will pass into the state of vapor, and if the pressure of this be removed, another quantity of ice will be evaporated; and if the pumping be continued sufficiently long all the ice will be dissipated in vapor without passing through the intermediate condition of water. Instead of continuing to work the pump, in order to evaporate the ice, we may produce the same effect by placing within the receiver a broad dish containing sulphuric acid, which will absorb the vapor as fast as it is formed. We may, however, convince ourselves immediately of the evaporation of ice by exposing a given weight of it during a cold day in the shade while the temperature is below freezing. It will be found sensibly, though slowly, to diminish in quantity. The same effect, however, is exhibited in the process of drying clothes in cold weather, which though they may be stiffened by the frozen water with which they have been wetted, soon become dry and pliable by the evaporation of the ice. The apparatus of Dr. Dalton enables us to make the following experiment, which has an important bearing on some of the phenomena of meteorology: If, while the column of mercury is at the temperature, for example, of 60°, and a small quantity of water is resting on its upper end, the space above being filled with vapor due to this temperature, we place under the lower end of the tube beneath the surface of the mercury a small crystal of common salt it will rise through the mercury by its specific levity, and be dissolved in part or whole by the surface of water at the top. Now, as soon as this solution begins to take place, we shall see the column of mercury ascend; a portion of the vapor will be absorbed, and the tension of the remainder be diminished. In this case, the attraction of the salt for the particles of water neutralizes a part of their repulsive force and thus diminishes the weight of mercury the vapor can support. For the same reason, salt water boils at a temperature several degrees higher than 212°, though the vapor produced in this case has only the elastic force of that due to pure water. From the foregoing we conclude that the quantity of vapor from the surface of the ocean is less and has less tension and density, than that from the surface of fresh water lakes, at the same temperature. The table which was furnished by Dr. Dalton, and has since been corrected by more refined experiments, is of great value in various branches of science. The very simplicity of the method employed is an evidence of scientific genius of the highest character, and is well calculated to excite our admiration, as well as to call forth our gratitude, on account of the important truths it reveals. Dr. Dalton, although thoroughly imbued with a love of science for its own sake, and a profound thinker, was eminently a practical man, in the proper sense of the term. He had not only the sagacity to frame significant questions to be propounded to Nature, but also the ingenuity to devise simple means by which the answers to these questions would be given in terms the most precise and accurate. Again, there is another circumstance in regard to vapor which is of essential importance in understanding the part which it plays in producing the diversified changes of the weather, namely, the great amount of heat which it contains at different temperatures. It is well known that the quantity of heat that a body contains is not

Degrees Fahrenheit.	0° Fahr.	1° Fahr.	2° Fahr.	3° Fahr.	4° Fahr.	5° Fahr.	6° Fahr.	7° Fahr.	8° Fahr.	9° Fahr.
	In.	In.	In.	In.	In.	In.	In.	In.	In.	In.
0	0.043	0.045	0.048	0.050	0.052	0.055	0.057	0.060	0.062	0.065
10	0.068	0.072	0.075	0.078	0.082	0.086	0.090	0.094	0.098	0.103
20	0.108	0.113	0.118	0.123	0.129	0.135	0.141	0.147	0.153	0.160
30	0.167	0.174	0.181	0.188	0.196	0.204	0.212	0.220	0.229	0.238
40	0.248	0.257	0.267	0.277	0.288	0.299	0.311	0.323	0.335	0.348
50	0.361	0.374	0.388	0.403	0.418	0.433	0.449	0.466	0.483	0.500
60	0.518	0.537	0.556	0.576	0.596	0.617	0.639	0.662	0.685	0.708
70	0.733	0.756	0.784	0.811	0.839	0.868	0.897	0.927	0.958	0.990
80	1.023	1.057	1.092	1.126	1.165	1.203	1.242	1.282	1.323	1.366
90	1.410	1.455	1.501	1.548	1.597	1.647	1.698	1.751	1.805	1.861
100	1.918	1.977	2.027	2.099	2.162	2.227	2.293	2.361	2.430	2.501

actually measured by the thermometer or the temperature which it exhibits; for example, if a cubic foot of air at 60° be expanded without receiving or losing heat, its temperature will be much diminished, because the same amount of heat which was before contained in a given space is now distributed through a larger space. If an ounce of steam from boiling water, which indicates a temperature of 212°, be condensed in water at 60°, it will give out to the latter enough heat to elevate six times the quantity of water to the boiling temperature; that is, six times as much water through 152°, or the same amount of water 912°; or, in other words, after having given out more than 900° of heat in the act of being converted from a vapor to a liquid, it still retains a temperature of 212°. The heat which is thus set free, and has not been recognized by the thermometer, is called latent heat. In thus condensing a given quantity of vapor, from water at different temperatures, in a given quantity of cold water, and noting the elevation of temperature of the latter, it has been shown by Dr. Dalton and others that an ounce of vapor at all temperatures contains very nearly the same amount of heat, adding the latent and sensible heat together. This constancy of the amount of heat arises from the fact, that as we increase the thermometric heat a new portion of vapor is forced into the same space, its density increases, and the amount of latent heat is diminished; hence if the attenuated vapor from ice were received in a syringe, and suddenly condensed until its density became equal to that of boiling water, its temperature would be 212. On account of the great amount of latent heat of vapor, heat must be absorbed from all surrounding bodies during the process of evaporation; and in all cases of the reverse process, that is, of the conversion of vapor into water, an equal amount of heat must be given out. This absorption of heat by vapor at the place of its formation, and the evolution of an equal amount at the place where it is condensed into water, is one of the most efficient means of varying the temperature of different portions of the earth from that which they would naturally acquire under the regular periodical variation due to the changes of declination of the sun. In the evaporation of a cubic foot of water it is known from experiment that an amount of heat is absorbed equal to that evolved from the combustion of twenty pounds of dry pine wood, and consequently every cubic foot of rain water which falls from the clouds leaves in the air above an equal amount of extraneous heat, which tends to abnormally raise the temperature due to the elevation, and to produce powerful upward currents above, and horizontal motions of the air below. We may also recall in this place the fact that water, in passing from the state of ice to that of a liquid, absorbs 140° of heat, which is again evolved in the act of freezing, and that this also is an efficient means by which colder portions of the earth are mollified in temperature. We are also indebted to Dr. Dalton for another important series of experiments, which relate to the mingling of air and vapor. In the experiments before given the vapor was weighed and its temperature and tension determined in a separate state and unmingled with the air. To ascertain the effect which would be produced on the tension of vapor when suffered to be exerted in a space already occupied with air of different densities, Dr. Dalton employed the same method of experimenting previously described. A barometer tube was filled and inverted in a basin of mercury, a quantity of air was then admitted, which, rising into the Torricellian vacuum, pressed by its elasticity on the surface of the mercury and caused it to descend a given number of divisions of the scale, which were accurately noted; a small quantity of water was next admitted, which, rising to the top of the mercurial column, was, after a few moments, in part converted into vapor, while the mercury was observed to be depressed. When the experiment was repeated with different quantities of air above the mercurial column and at different temperatures, produced by varying the heat of the water in the external tube, or, which would amount to the same thing, by varying the temperature of the room, the remarkable fact was discovered that the depression of the mercurial column, due to the introduction of the water, was precisely the same at the same temperature as when the experiment was made with a vacuum; for example, at the temperature of 60°, whatever might be the elasticity of the air within the tube, the introduction of the water always gave an additional depression of half an inch. From this result the important fact is deduced, that the tension or elastic force of vapor in air is the same as that of vapor in a vacuum; from which we might also infer that the quantity of vapor which can exist in a given space already occupied with air is the same as that which can exist in a vacuum at the same temperature. Now, this fact may be directly proved. How? A determinate result may be obtained by the following method, which also gives us an independent means of determining directly the amount of vapor which exists in the atmosphere at a given time, and which may be employed for verifying the results obtained by other means: Let a tight cask, furnished with a stop cock near its lower part, be entirely filled with water, and let the small end of a tube, which has been drawn out in a spirit lamp, be cemented into the venthole above, so that no air can enter the cask except through the tube. Let this tube be filled with coarsely powdered dry chloride of calcium—a substance which has a great affinity for moisture—and the upper end put in connection with an open vessel containing air entirely saturated with moisture, which can readily be effected by agitating a quantity of the liquid in the vessel from which the air is drawn; let the stop-cock be now opened, and exactly a cubic foot of water be drawn into a measured vessel, it is evident that precisely a foot of air will enter the top of the cask through the tube and between the interstices of the pieces of chloride of calcium, moisture will be absorbed and its weight can be accurately ascertained from the increase of weight of the tube and its contents, which had previously been weighed for that purpose. By this simple experiment, as well as by the one we have previously given, we are enabled to conclusively prove that the weight of vapor contained in the air, in a given space, is the same as that which would exist at the same temporature in a vacuum. To render, however, the result of this experiment absolutely perfect, a slight correction must be made on account of the expansion of the air and the vapor due to the increased repulsive energy of the compound over that of the air itself. This will be evident from a due consideration of what follows. If into an extensible vessel, such as an India-rubber bag filled with air, a little water be injected, the bag will be suddenly expanded by the additional repulsive force of the atoms of vapor. Previous to the introduction of the water the bag will be pressed equally on the outside and on the inside; on the former by the weight of the external atmosphere, and on the latter by the repulsive or elastic force of the atoms of the enclosed air; when the water is introduced and a portion of it springs into vapor, the elastic force of the aqueous atoms must be added to that of the atoms of the air, and the interior will then be pressed outward with a force equal to the sum of the two repulsions. For example, if the experiment be made at sixty degrees and the air at its normal weight, the outward pressure within the bag previous to the introduction of the water will be equal to thirty inches of mercury, but after the water is injected it will be thirty inches and a half; hence expansion will take place and the bag will be distended until, by the separation of the interior atoms, the repulsion is so much weakened that the pressure without and within will again be equalized. The amount of the increase in bulk will be given by the following proportion: as the pressure of thirty inches of mercury is to the pressure of thirty and one-half inches, so is the original bulk of the India-rubber bag to its bulk after the introduction of the vapor. From experiments and observations it is evident that in free air the vapor exists as an independent atmosphere, being the same in weight and in tension as it would be in a vacuum of the same extent and the same temperature. That the same amount of vapor can exist in a space filled with air as in a vacuum, at first sight appears paradoxical, but when we consider that a cubic inch of water expanded into steam at 212° occupies nearly 1,700 times the bulk which it does in the form of water, also that air may be compressed into a space many hundred times less than that of its ordinary bulk, it is evident that the extent of the void spaces is incomparably greater than the atoms themselves, and, consequently, it is not difficult to conceive that the atoms of the vapor have abundance of space in which to exist between the atoms of air and the atoms of air between those of vapor. Dr. Dalton announces this important truth by stating that air and vapor and almost all gases are vacuums to each other. This enunciation is a true expression of the state of diffusion which gases and vapors attain after the lapse of a given time, but it does not truly express the phenomena of the act of diffusion. In a perfect vacuum a given space is filled with vapor almost instantaneously, or with a rapidity which has not yet been estimated, but this is not the same in a space already filled with air. In this case, though the vapor ultimately diffuses itself through the air as it would do in a vacuum, yet time is required to produce this effect; the result is as if there were a mechanical or some other obstruction to the free passage of vapor through the different strata of air, and, indeed, it would appear from the following experiments that a definite force similar to that produced by a slight attraction or repulsion, is offered in the resistance of a given thickness of this medium: In the laboratory of the Smithsonian Institution, a glass tube of about three feet in length, closed at its lower end, suspended vertically, and containing about an inch of water, has remained for several years undisturbed in this condition, without the least perceptible diminution in the amount of the liquid. In another experiment, a pane of glass was removed from an external window of a room, and the place of the glass supplied by a board, through the middle of which a hole of about an inch in diameter was made, and in this opening a tube was placed horizontally, one end being in the room and the other in the outer air. To each end of this tube a glass bulb was attached, airtight, the one within the room containing about an ounce of water, while the tube and the bulb on the outside were occupied with air. The temperature of the air within the room was, on an average, about seventy degrees, while that of the air without was, on an average, nearly thirty-two degrees, and although the experiment was continued for several months during the winter, not one drop of water was distilled over into the outer bulb. When, however, the latter was surrounded by a freezing mixture, a small quantity of vapor did pass over and was condensed into water and also when the vapor as contained in the outer bulb was absorbed by introducing a quantity of strong sulphuric acid into this bulb, the water in the other bulb gradually diminished in weight. From these experiments it would appear that there is more than a mechanical obstruction to the transfusion of vapor through air, and that if the difference of tension of vapor in two vessels only amounts to a certain quantity, no transfusion from one will take place to the other, or, in other words, for each inch or foot of thickness of a stratum of air, a certain amount of unbalanced repulsive energy is required for transfusion. The rapid mingling of vapor with air is due, in a considerable degree, to the currents produced by the mixture itself, and by variations of temperature. It is not upon the actual amount of vapor which the air contains at a given time or place that its humidity depends; but upon its greater or less degree of saturation. That air is said to be dry in which evaporation takes place rapidly from a surface of water or moistened substance. In an atmosphere entirely saturated with vapor, that is, in one which is filled with as much vapor as the space which it occupies can contain, the vapor already in the air by its elastic force presses on the surface of the moist body and neutralizes the repulsive action of the water; if, however, the temperature be raised, the elastic force will be increased and a new portion will be forced into the same space; the further, therefore, the condition of any portion of air is from saturation the more rapid will be the evaporation from the moist bodies which it surrounds. For example, a portion of air at a temperature of 100° would contain vapor of an elastic force, were it entirely saturated, equal to a pressure of two and a half inches of mercury. If the same air, however, only contained vapor of the elastic force of 60°, or, in other words, if the dewpoint was at 60°, the elastic force would be half an inch, and consequently there would be a force unbalanced by the pressure of vapor equal to the pressure of a column of two inches of mercury. The dryness, therefore, of the air is estimated by the difference of the elastic force of the vapor due to the temperature of the air, and of the elastic force due to the tension of the dewpoint. In meteorological works generally, when a portion of the atmosphere contains vapor equal in tension to that of the temperature of the air, it is said to be, as we have before observed, fully saturated, and its humidity is marked 100; but if the elastic force of the air as determined by the dewpoint is only one-fourth of that necessary to produce complete saturation, the relative humidity is marked 25. To find, then, the relative humidity at any time, we seek from the tables the tension of vapor due to the temperature of the air, and again due to that temperature to which it must next be cooled down in order to produce precipitation, or full saturation, which temperature, as we have seen, is that of the dewpoint. We then say, as the tension of the first temperature is to 100, so is the tension of the other temperature to the per centage of saturation. In this way comparative tables of relative humidity for different places are calculated from actual observation.

VARIETIES IN VEGETATION. This is an important subject and one in which every cultivator of the soil is interested. In addition to what has been heretofore given in this work we append a synopsis of facts and conclusions derived from various authentic sources, which will be of value. The origin of varieties is a subject of deep interest, and, perhaps, less understood than almost any other. A species, unlike a true hybrid, will always reproduce itself from its seed, and for an indefinite period. The plants which are raised from its seeds will not, however, be exactly like the parent species, but will differ in some particulars, as form, size, color, quality of fruit, but not in its original type, or material in its organic structure. These particular differences which have been enumerated constitute varieties, forms that are not monstrous, enduring only for a time and then disappearing, but the natural outgrowth of seed, not produced by a direct fiat of the Creator, as the species are supposed to have been, but by an inherent energy, acting by determinate laws, modified by the conditions in which they are placed, as soil, climate, and other extraneous influences which are too latent for us to comprehend. Varieties may also be obtained by cultivation and selection. It is sometimes said that God created the species of man and the varieties. There is no doubt that man, by means of cultivation, is a most powerful agent in the production of varieties. As the mind of man, when under powerful excitement, will make great intellectual efforts, such as it never made before, so a plant under the stimulus of high cultivation, will make an extraordinary development, often in a direction not expected, and produce a new variety which it never would have originated if it had been left alone in a wild state. The process pursued in this mode of producing varieties is to select the best fruit of any species or variety, and sow the seeds in a soil properly prepared for their most vigorous growth; then, again, selecting the best fruit from the new plants and planting the seeds, thus continuing the operation till the desired variety is obtained. Such varieties are sometimes called seedlings, because they are raised from the seeds, without any artificial process of hybridizing or cross-breeding. This process of producing new varieties has been carried on very extensively, and with wonderful results, and it would be very difficult to assign the limits to which the improvement may be carried. Prof. Von Mons, a distinguished pomologist, of Belgium, cultivated the pear very extensively in this way, and with good success. He began by sowing the seed of a healthy seedling pear which approximated nearest to the original species of any which he could find, without taking a wild one, supposing that by this course he could get some varieties different from any which had been seen before. In the fifth generation he obtained some excellent fruit, although he carried the process even to the seventh generation. He did not preserve every one of the multitude of plants which he raised from the seeds, till it matured fruit, but those which were feeble, or did not have the characters that he deemed essential for the production of good fruit, were destroyed; and so accurate had his observation become by long experience that, as he informs us, he could tell by the form of the leaf, the color of the branches, or the spreading of the top, whether the fruit would be good or not. He observed that, while the plant of the first generation was about seven years in coming into bearing, the time was diminished for each succeeding one, so that in the seventh it took only about four years. It would probably not be best for the common experimenter to begin by sowing the seeds of an uncultivated variety, as Prof. Von Mons did, but to select the best, thus appropriating to himself what had been gained by cultivation, although he might not, perhaps, obtain anything so entirely distinct from existing varieties as was done in the case of Prof. Von Mons. We have every reason to suppose that the Persian or European vine (*vitis vinifera*) has been brought to its present state of perfection from a wild grape; for it has been cultivated in Egypt from the remotest antiquity, and Egyptians declare that Osiris first taught them its use. It had been cultivated in Asia 800 years before those pious leaders and shrewd statesmen, Joshua and Caleb, visited the valley of Eshcol and brought away one cluster, so heavy that it was borne between two upon a staff. It grows to an enormous size when under cultivation. Schulz says he supped under a grape-vine in Palestine the stem of which was a foot and a half in diameter, the height thirty feet, and its branches formed a canopy thirty feet in diameter. The clusters, he adds, are so large that they weigh ten or twelve pounds, and the berries may be compared with our large plums. A gentleman from California, of undoubted veracity, informs me that he has seen a foreign vine in that State, planted a century or more ago by the Jesuit missionaries, which has a diameter even greater than this. There are few plants more inclined to vary or sport than the grape. All the European varieties, which vary so much in color and sweetness, have been produced from the same species, and sometimes white varieties and black have grown on the same stalk. The following are some of the varieties derived from the *Vitis labrusca:* The Adirondac Anna, Cassady, Catawba, Concord, Christine, Creveling, Diana, Dracut Amber, Hartford Prolific, Iona, Isabella, Israella, Ives' Seedling, Lydia, Muxatawny, Rebecca, Union Village, etc. From the *Vitis cordifolia*, originated the Clinton, Franklin, and Taylor's Bullet. From the *Vitis astivalis* we have the Alvey, Devereaux, Herbemont, Norton's Virginia and others. (See article Grape.) Many of our useful as well as ornamental plants vary much by change of habitat and by culture. The cabbage, in its wild state, had scarcely any head. The beet, carrot, parsnip, and turnips had roots no larger than the common thistle, (*Cirsium arvense*). The tubers of the potato were but little larger than the groundnut, (*Aralia trifolia,*) and the tomato bore fruit very much like the potato-ball, but now, by cultivation and selection, it has acquired a size of more than six inches in diameter. The strawberry has become many times larger than in its natural state. Prof. Buckman, of England, in a few years converted, by cultivation and careful selection, the wild parsnip into new and good varieties. M. Vilmorin produced the same change in the wild carrot in a few generations. Winter wheat and spring wheat may be converted into each other. M. Monnier sowed winter wheat in spring, and out of 100 plants four alone produced ripe seeds; these were sown and resown, and in three years plants were reared which ripened all their seed. Conversely, nearly all the plants raised from spring wheat which was sown in autumn, perished the first year, but a few were saved, and produced seeds and in three years this spring variety was converted into a winter variety. Running or twining beans may be reduced to bush beans by selecting the fruit that grows nearest the ground from year to year, and, on the contrary, their stems may be made to grow much longer by selecting pods from the top or end, and constantly planting. Cucumbers may be dwarfed in size, and almost stopped in running, by selecting seeds from those which grow near the root, and planting constantly. A farmer might very easily originate a new variety of wheat, by selecting some head which differed very much in size of kernel or length of spike, and sowing the seeds by themselves, from year to year, on well-prepared land, and weeding out, those heads which are not like the original type, and rejecting the small seeds. The same is true of maize, peas, beans, and, indeed, of all plants that are inclined to sport or vary. Single flowers which have a tendency to sport may be converted into double flowers by long cultivation in rich soil, and sometimes by keeping the seeds for several years, till they become weakened in their power of germination, and then planting them. Every tendency in the plant to vary must be carefully watched. When a valuable plant of any kind has been obtained, it is very desirable to preserve it, and cause it, if possible, to produce true seeds every year, and thus prevent it from reverting to its original or common form. This process is called by gardeners setting, and consists in planting the seeds, for several years, by themselves, and entirely unconnected with any other plants similar to it, and guarding at the same time against bees and other insects which may convey pollen to it. In this way, and by weeding out constantly, the plant becomes set, and will, with proper care, reproduce itself regularly from year to year. It must be remembered, however, that no variety will reproduce itself in every particular of shade of color, or taste, or other properties; and, therefore, when we wish to perpetuate a variety exactly, it must be done in the same manner as in the case of hybrids, by scions, cuttings, suckers, layers, etc. Varieties may also be produced by cross-breeding. We have already shown in what cross-breeding consists, how the operation is performed, and to what class of plants it is applied. It now only remains to explain its effects on the objects employed. All varieties, as has before been remarked, are perfectly fertile between one another, and it may be laid down as a general principle of universal application, except in cases where the relation is very close, that cross-breeding produces strength in the offspring, a result precisely the reverse of true hybridization, which always occasions weakness in some form. It has been said that the exception of close interbreeding, or cross-breeding, is obviously a wise provision of nature to prevent varieties from becoming too fixed in their habits, and differing too much from the original species; and, in the human race, to keep the members of families within the proper and natural limits of the marriage relation. The offspring produced by cross-breeding, as by hybridizing, is of a character nearly intermediate between the parents, the characters of the male usually being the most prominent; but the variety which possesses the greatest strength, and is nearest the type of the original species, finally predominates. It, therefore, has an important influence in obliterating individual differences, and giving uniformity of character to varieties of the same species. By repeatedly cross-breeding the different varieties of the same species, we could ultimately arrive very nearly at the original standard or type of the species. Varieties of plants may be improved by cross-breeding;

and even the same variety, when it is grown in different sections of the country for a few generations, and then the seeds are brought together and planted, will be invigorated and improved in size and quality. Cross-breeding has one advantage, and a very important one, over cultivation in the production of varieties, in the fact that they may be produced at once, with a very great degree of certainty, by uniting two known qualities in one individual. In this way we may combine directly, and at our pleasure, the desirable qualities of two known varieties, and produce a cross-breed sometimes far superior to either when taken alone. But, notwithstanding this, we must look to cultivation principally for originating the primary qualities, and to crossbreeding for blending them in beautiful and harmonious proportions. Although as yet by far the greater number of the best varieties of our fruits, and other plants, as the apple, pear, melon, and turnip, were probably obtained by cultivation, yet very many of the choicest were the result of the artificial cross-breeding of these primary varieties. Besides the advantages already named, cross-breeding improves the size and quality of the fruit of plants, their hardiness and prolificacy, and the beauty of their flowers. It has been found to be one of the most effectual means of acclimation, so that plants which could not endure the cold of the more northern climates are made perfectly hardy by this process. By it we may give to the hardy pears of the North the delicate sweetness of those of the South; to the insipid and watery grape the richness of the Black Hamburg; and to the white rose the delicate blush which the crimson imparts. The benefits derived from this art are summed up in the following extract from the London *Horticultural Magazine*: To it we owe some, indeed many, of our most beautiful garden flowers, as well as the most valuable of our fruits and vegetables. Among flowers, the most important qualities which can be impressed on the different races are greater hardiness of constitution, precocity or tardiness of flowering, the communication of odor where it is not possessed, increase in size, alterations in the forms of individual flowers, or greater prolificacy and improved arrangement, as regards their collective production. Modifications and the blending of colors, which are sometimes aimed at, seem to be the most paltry changes of any that are attempted. Among fruit and vegetables, the changes to be effected should be confined more to productiveness and quality than to appearance. Thus, the increase of size, together with improvement or modification of the sensible qualities, are the main objects to be sought, followed by such qualities of general application as hardiness, precocity, tardiness, productiveness, or increased inflorescence. It may be well to remark that it can not generally be known with certainty, when a new variety first begins to bear, whether the fruit will be of good quality or not. It usually takes several years for it to develop itself perfectly. If there should be any doubt at any time whether a plant is a hybrid or a cross-breed, it may generally be known by observing the following particulars: If it is intermediate between its parents and does not produce seeds, or produces such as will reproduce it only for a few generations, it is probably a true hybrid; but, on the contrary, if it is intermediate, and its seeds are perfect, and produce vigorous offspring continually, it is a classific hybrid or a cross-breed. The process of cross-breeding plants, although recent in its origin as artifically practiced, is of a very ancient date as carried on in the wide domain of the vegetable kingdom. Nature is continually carrying it on in the field, the orchard, and the garden. The pollen is passing from the flower of one variety to that of another of the same species; thus fertilizing countless numbers, the seeds of which will develop new forms and fruits unknown before. Hence a vast number of the new varieties of flowers and plants which are commonly supposed to be the result of some great and powerful effort of nature, may have been produced by this process of nature's cross-breeding. In the foregoing observations we have seen in what hybridizing and cross-breeding consist, the manner in which they are performed, the classes of plants to which they may be applied, and the beneficial results that have accrued to man from the introduction of a multitude of new plants into the vegetable kingdom, and yet it is sometimes more desirable to the practical agriculturist to know how to anticipate and avoid these intermixtures than to produce them. It becomes necessary, therefore, when we are about to cultivate different plants in the vicinity of one another to ascertain how nearly they are allied, or to what class or classes they belong. If they belong to species of different genera we may expect no trouble from any intermixture which they may occasion. The pea (*Pisum sativum*) and the bean (*Phaseolus vulgaris*,) the peach (*Amygdalus Persica*) and the apple (*Pyrus malus*,) the common potato (*Solanum tuberosum*) and the sweet potato (*Convolvulus batatas*,) the beet (*Beta vulgaris*) and the turnip, (*Brassica campestris*,) the parsnip (*Pastinaca sativa*) and the carrot (*Daucus ca ota*,) will never intermix with each other under any circustances, however much they may seem, in some respects, to be similar; for they are, as may be seen, species of different and remote genera, and nature has declared that they shall never unite. They may be cultivated in the closest proximity, but they can not intermix; and the seeds which each produces will be its own, peculiar and distinct from every other. Therefore, the first inquiry to be made in respect to any plants under consideration is, whether they belong to different genera. If they do, they will very rarely intermix, even with the present botanical classification. We may easily know to what genus or species any plant belongs, by turning to its name in any standard botany now in use. On this principle we are able to give a satisfactory answer to the inquiry whether one plant will turn into another; as chess (*Bromus secalinus*) into wheat, (*Triticum vulgare*) oats *Avena sativa*) into barley (*Hordeum vulgare*,) or the reverse. In the case of the first two plants, it will be observed that they are of different species, and also belong to different genera. It has been laid down as a law of nature that species are distinct, and were created so, and therefore can never change into one another. But these species belong to different genera, and we have seen that, when species are thus remotely allied, they will very rarely even hybridize. The two plants under consideration answer to both of these conditions, and of course one can not change into the other. But further, the experiment has frequently been tried to turn chess into wheat by high cultivation, but has always resulted in failure; the only change which has been effected being an improved variety of chess, without any change in its nature. In cases in which wheat is supposed to have changed into chess, there must have been some deception which escaped the observation of the cultivator. The seeds might have been carried in the manure, which was, perhaps, purchased at some neighboring stable in which chess mixed with the hay had been consumed by the horses or other animals. They may have been lying in the ground for many years, and from a greater depth of plowing than usual have been brought up to the light and heat of the sun, and thus made to germinate, since we know that the longevity of seeds is very great. Some new fertilizer may have been applied which has penetrated deeply enough to stimulate the dormant seeds into growth, and thus cause the chess to appear, on the same principle that applying ashes to fields, where no clover has grown for several years, will cause it to spring up in large quantities. The clover seeds had been lying dormant for years, in the earth and the ashes stimulated them into growth. In cases in which wheat was sown and chess grew in its place, the fact may be explained by supposing that the wheat perished from too much wet, or too great cold, or some other cause; and the chess, being more hardy, survived, and took its place. There must have been some fallacy of this kind; for no one who is familiar with the laws of reproduction can suppose that one of these would change into the other. In species of plants belonging to the same genus, there is frequently great difficulty to be encountered in preventing them from hybridizing. Although it is a general rule, previously laid down, that species of the same genus will not hybridize unless nearly allied, and that the cases in which they do are but exceptions to the general principle, yet, despite this repugnancy to hybridization, there are some which are classified as distinct species that intermix with almost equal facility as varieties of the same species, and it requires the most persistent watchfulness on the part of the agriculturist to prevent their union. As an instance of this kind we may mention the pumpkin (*Cucurbita pepo*,) and the squash (*Cucurbita melopepo*,) which are usually regarded as distinct but closely allied species. The question now arises—how can we know what species will hybridize, and what will not? It can be known only from experiments of our own or others; and it will never be safe to cultivate species of the same genus in the vicinity of one another without a previous knowledge of their relationship or alliance. The question is sometimes asked whether these two plants will change into each other. The answer may be safely given that they will not; but they will intermix, and form a classific hybrid which will resemble both plants, but will still be different from either. Since it is a law of hybridization that the hybrid partakes of the nature of both parents, and as a general rule the characteristics of the male parent predominate over the female, it is evident that when the squash is fertilized by the pumpkin the fruit grown from the seed of the fertilized plant will resemble the pumpkin more than the squash; and, on the contrary, when the pumpkin is fertilized by the squash the offspring will resemble the squash more than the pumpkin, though neither will be changed into the other. If, however, the pumpkin is the stronger plant in its specific character, the offspring may possibly in either case resemble the pumpkin more than the squash. None of the species of the squash and the pumpkin should be cultivated near one another. The muskmelon (*Cucumis melo*) and the watermelon (*Cucumis citrullus*) are liable to hybridize. It is said by some that the muskmelon and the cucumber (*Cucumis sativus*) will hybridize, but M. Sageret, an experienced hybridist, declares that he was unable to effect any union between them. All the species of the *Cucumis*, or melons, cucumbers, and colocynths, should not be cultivated together. The inquiry has frequently been made whether the Bush Bean (*Phaseolus nanus*) will change into the Pole Bean, (*Phaseolus vulgaris*). It will not. But, if it is fertilized by the Pole Bean, a classific hybrid will be produced resembling both, and doubtless will be a climbing bean, but not the same as the male parent, or Pole Bean. The Bush Bean is regarded by many as a variety of the Pole Bean, and therefore the two readily hybridize when cultivated near each other. Care should always be taken to separate them at considerable distance; and so with all the cultivated species of the *Phaseolus*, or beans. M. Sageret says the common cabbage (*Brassica oleracea*) will fertilize all the turnip-bearing species of the *Brassica*, as *Brassica campestris*, *Brassica rapa*, and *Brassica napus*; but none of them will fertilize the cabbage. Thus it may be seen that the cabbage will intermix with the turnip, but the turnip will not intermix with the cabbage. All the turnip-bearing species will, however, hybridize with one another. Therefore, when seeds are to be grown from the cabbage, turnip, colza, or rape, they should not be cultivated together. The intermixture of plants takes place only by means of their flowers, and consequently no cross-breeds can be produced from cultivating the tubers of different varieties together. The different varieties of the common potato will never intermix by their tubers, and they may be planted in the same hill without the least possibility of intermixture. They will, however, intermix through their flowers, like other plants, but no effect will be produced on the tubers by this intermixture; it is only in the seeds grown in the potato ball. The size of the tubers may be considerably increased by removing the flower-buds or the flowers from the stalks; and varieties that have never fruited may frequently be made to blossom by taking away a part of the tubers, that the nourishment may be thrown into the stalks and flowers. A greater profusion of flowers may also be obtained the next year from ornamental shrubs, than otherwise would have been, by breaking off the blossoms of the present year before they go to seed. The inquiry whether varieties of plants will degenerate or run out, as it is sometimes termed, is one that has created much interest at different times, and is really of great practical importance to the agriculturist. There is no doubt that they will degenerate, and the degeneracy may result from various causes. There is a natural tendency, which has been verified by long observation, in all plants to revert to their original species. They seem to be out of their natural sphere when brought into a high state of cultivation, and very much in the condition of the savage who has been taken from his forest home and educated in some seminary of learning. He is constantly uneasy, and when the first opportunity is presented escapes to his native haunts, and joins his old companions in their revels and vices. Therefore, great care should be taken that the largest fruit and the best ears of wheat and corn may be selected in order that the choicest seeds may be procured and sown; otherwise the plants will degenerate in time, and most if not all the excellent qualities which they possessed will be lost. Prof. Lindley says: In all cases where any importance is attached to the result, the plumpest and heaviest seeds should be selected if the greatest vigor is required in the seedling. They may degenerate for want of proper culture. As culture has much to do in developing new varieties, so the neglect of it will do much to destroy them, and there is no doubt that our best fruits, if removed from our orchards and gardens to their habitats in the forests, and reproduced from their seeds for a series of years, would be no better than the original species in a wild state. The delicious Newtown Pippin or the Pearmain would be no more agreeable in flavor than the little European crab-apple (*Pyrus malus*,) from which they probably originated. Prof. A. Gray, in his Botanical Text-book, says: The races of corn, wheat, etc., which now preserve their character unchanged, have become fixed by centuries of domestication. Even these at times manifest an unequivocal disposition to return to their aboriginal stock. Were cultivation to cease, they would all speedily disappear; the greater part, perhaps, would perish outright; the remainder would revert, in a few generations of spontaneous growth, to the form of the primitive stock. The improving hand of culture must be continually upon them, or they will lose all their good qualities and become worthless. The natural cross-breeding of different varieties with those of inferior qualities is a very frequent cause of deterioration. This is often observed in gramineous, leguminous, and curcubitaceous plants, which are raised annually from their seeds. All the varieties of maize are very liable to deterioration in this way. Those of the *Sorghum saccharatum* intermix so freely that cultivators have found it almost impossible to obtain pure seeds. From the same cause it is extremely difficult to preserve any of the varieties of the melon pure for any considerable time. No one can have any security of obtaining pure seeds unless they are planted many rods from all others, and the perfect flowers from which seeds are to be raised are covered with small tents of gauze of sufficient size to enclose each and protect it from insects. The judicious cross-breeding, however, of individuals of the same variety, when taken from a distance, will, as has before been observed, have a tendency to improve it. The mingling, even, of the sap of different trees, as in grafting, is sometimes not without its deleterious effects on the fruit of the engrafted scion; and the influence becomes more and more apparent the further we get from the purity of the parent stock. It seems allowable, observes Prof. J. Lindley, to infer that the goodness of cultivated fruits is deteriorated by their being uniformly worked upon stocks whose fruit is worthless. The common apple, when grafted upon trees bearing very austere fruit, is injured by the crude and bitter sap of the tree on which it has been grafted. On the contrary, it is improved by being grafted upon a stock superior to its own. A scion, also, taken from a young tree which has never fruited, will be hastened in its growth when grafted on a mature tree, and bear sooner than it would if it had been left to itself. They may degenerate from effect of climate. A vine, for instance, which produces very delicious grapes in Ohio or Missouri may become very inferior in New Hampshire or Maine. Certain fruits can not be perfected except in certain localities where the climate is particularly adapted to their growth and congenial to their nature. There are only a few countries where the grape will grow in perfection. There is no doubt that the climate has in many instances more influence than the soil in causing degeneration of plants. We look to the sunny skies and bland atmosphere of Italy, France, Palestine, or California, for the highest development of the grape and the pear, but for the apple perhaps there is no better region in the world than the middle section of the United States. Plants, then, should be selected that are adapted to the locality in which they are to be cultivated, or otherwise degeneracy must be expected, labor will be thrown away, and no satisfactory results can be obtained. The opinion is generally entertained by agriculturists that varieties which are raised from tubers and from scions or buds become weakened or degenerated by age. This was emphatically denied by Prof. J. Lindley, and as firmly maintained by Mr. T. A. Knight and others. Whatever the truth may be, the fact is obvious that varieties do degenerate by long-continued cultivation; but the change may generally be ascribed to other causes than to age. In the case of the potato the various elements of the soil that are peculiarly adapted to its growth may have been abstracted by frequent planting on the same ground, so that the plant is actually starved from year to year, and thus weakened in constitution and dwarfed in size. It is often induced, also, from selecting for seed small tubers that are imperfectly matured, and have not secreted starch in sufficient quantity to give adequate nourishment to the new plant before its roots have been sufficiently developed to enable them to draw the necessary nourishment for its support from the soil. Or, when the practice of dividing the tubers has been adopted, they may have been cut into pieces so small that they do not contain enough of the necessary elements to produce a healthy and vigorous plant. In order, then, that there should be no deterioration, tubers should be selected of good size, some of the largest, if they are sound and well formed, and cut into two or three pieces, if that plan is preferred to planting whole, according to their size. In this way the size vigor, and mealy qualities would be kept up, and a good and healthy crop be secured each year. Varieties of wheat, too, often degenerate for the same reason. A person who originates a new variety selects the ear, as we have before shown, which contains the best seeds; and he sows them from year to year, and keeps sowing and selecting them and no others, and soon he gets a variety which is much improved. But as soon as it goes into the hands of the cultivator, all the seeds, the perfect and the imperfect, are sown promiscuously and constantly, and the consequence is degeneration in a few years. Mr. Charles Darwin, in Variations of Animals and Plants, etc., volume 1, p. 379, says that, Colonel Le Couteur, in his persevering and successful attempts to raise new varieties by selection, began by choosing the largest ears, but soon found that the grains in the same ear differed so that he was compelled to select them separately, and each grain generally transmitted its own character. From this statement it is evident that the largest grains should be selected for sowing each year. This might be done at a trifling expense by sifting the grain through a sieve so prepared that the small kernels might pass through, and the large ones be retained in the sieve. Should this plan be pursued yearly there would doubtless be less complaint of the degeneration of this crop. The soil, no doubt, has very much to do with keeping up the size and vigor of the plant both in the case of the potato and the wheat. The necessary elements, such as lime, etc., which conduce to their growth, should be supplied with watchful care, and the labor would be rewarded by most ample and satisfactory results. Too much stress, in every department of agriculture, can not be laid on the importance of providing the proper elements for the food of plants, whatever kind may be cultivated. One person, perhaps, finds his orchard going to premature decay, while his neighbor's is thrifty and produces abundant crops. He supposes that the location of his own is more exposed to the cold winds of winter, or that by some singular fatality injurious insects infest his trees more, but the thought never occurs to him that they are starving for the food which their nature demands, when at the same time his neighbors are well fed. It may be true that neither orchard is enriched by manure from the stable, but one is located in a valley so as to receive a good manuring yearly by the hand of nature, while the other is on an elevation from which all the elements of growth wash away.

VEERING. A ridge made in plowing where two lands meet.

VEGETATION. The complex problems in vegetable life, and in the act of vegetation, have caused it to be made the careful study of some of the most profound thinkers of the present day. In the articles, Germination and Physiology, some branches of these questions are noticed. A plant from the time it begins its growth either from the seed or bud, simply multiplies cell growth until the limit of its vegetative powers are naturally reached, or until growth is stopped by some extraneous cause. The plantlet having reached the surface of the ground, moisture and heat must be supplemented with light, under which the stem and leaves become green and immediately begin to elaborate nutriment from the watery sap drained by the roots from the earth. The roots continue to extend, thus increasing their powers of absorption, the leaves above ground continue to multiply, thus increasing the power of elaboration, and as a rule in just proportion to the root, so will be the proportion of leaf surface of a plant. The seedling has all the organs of the perfect plant, except the blossom buds, and these, as have been shown in another part of this work, are simply modified leaf buds. Thus it simply has to grow and produce in duplicate, what it already possesses. Thus the stem is carried higher and higher, and in plants having more than a simple stem, side branches are produced, as in the oak, each branch, may each bud representing the ultimate perfect plant, each increasing, and with continued powers of increase, until the mature stage is reached and growth ceases. In the case of annuals, this occurs at the end of the season with the ripening of the seed. With biennials, it occurs at the end of the second year. With triennials the third year, and with perennials, this growth continues indefinitely, particular species of trees wanting 5,000 or even more years to complete their growth. Some plants die down to the ground at the end of the season, the nutriment for the succeeding year's growth being started from year to year, as in the case of herbaceous biennials and perennials, or as in the case of deciduous trees, that store elaborated sap next the bark, and in the buds, but drop their leaves at the end of the season. In the case of evergreens, the leaves remain persistent, for one or more years, sometimes for five or six years, the new growth being supplied from the annual buds, as in the cone bearing trees, or else buds open successively as in the case of some tropical forms of vegetation. Vegetation may therefore be divided into annuals, biennials, and perennials, since as a rule the so-called triennials are simply biennials, that under abnormal conditions survive to the third year. Annuals, then, store up their life-germs in the seed; biennials in the roots, the first season, expending this the second season in flowering and fruiting. By stopping the flowering, biennials may be made to continue to the third season, and some annuals may be changed into biennials, as in the case of winter wheat, strictly an annual plant. So biennial plants may bear fruit the first year. The organs of vegetation are three, the root, the stem, and the leaf. The form and appearance which these take are diverse, and yet however wonderful, still each may be traced to one of the three organs. This study is called morphology. The root is the simplest form, consisting of the primary root, and its branches, there are, however, subterranean, and aerial roots. Indian corn gives us an example among annual plants; the Pea-nut throws out aerial roots, which striking into the earth the nuts are formed thereon; the Banyan tree is an example among perennial trees, of aerial roots starting from the branches high in air, growing downward until they reach and pierce the soil, and forming additional props or trunks to the parent tree. So aerial roots are formed on a small scale by various climbing plants, as the Trumpet creeper, Poison ivy, the Virginia creeper, the English ivy, etc. So orchids or air plants, have nothing but aerial roots, and sustain themselves as parasites on other plants. The Mistletoe, Dodder, and various fungus plants, are well known parasitic plants. The stem as to form or kind is distinguished as belonging to herbs, shrubs and trees. It is herbaceous, if it die down in the autumn. It is denominated shrubby if it is woody, lives over the winter, and belongs to those trees denominated shrubs, or it is arborescent when belonging to tall trees of a single stem. It is upright when it grows erect; ascending when it rises in a slanting direction; declining when bent or turned to one side; decumbent when it lays along the ground but with the end turned more or less upward; procumbent when the whole stem trails along the ground; prostrate when it naturally lies flat on the ground; creeping, if postrate and taking root along its lower side where it rests on the ground; climbing when it rises by means of tendrils, as in the grape, or by twisting its leaf-stalk around the support, as in the Maurandia, or by its rootlets, as in the ivy; it is twining when the stem supports it by winding spirally about a support, as in the hop or bean. The Squash is a climbing plant, yet if it have no support it becomes a creeping plant, anchoring itself to the ground by roots thrown out at the joints. The Strawberry is a true running plant. It forms no tendrils, but does throw out runners, forming an independent plant at the end of the runner. The leaf of a plant forms the organ corresponding to respiration and digestion. These forms are almost endless in variety, and yet in a given species, afford a means for distinguishing the species. A complete leaf has a blade, the extended portion above the footstalk; a footstalk, the portion connecting it with the stem; and a pair of stipules, or a pair of little blades at the base of the footstalk next the stem. The quince has this perfect leaf, many leaves have no stipules, many have no footstalk but sit directly on the stem. Some indeed have no blade, but this is rare.

VEGETABLE CHEMISTRY. The chemical examination of all products of the vegetable world, as well as the functions of plants. (See Chemistry, Agricultural.)

VEGETABLE OYSTER. (See Salsify.)

VEGETABLE PHYSIOLOGY. An examination of the growth and functions of plants. (See Generation, Germination, etc.)

VEIL. Calyptra. A membrane connecting the pileus with the stem of some mushrooms.

VEINS. The vessels which convey blood that has circulated through the body back to the heart.

VELVET LEAF. (See Mallow.)

VENA CAVA. The great veins which discharge the venous blood into the right auricle of the heart.

VENTER. In entomology, the lower part of the abdomen.

VENTILATION. The subject of Ventilation is a most important one in connection with agriculture, since it bears not only directly upon the health of the family, the farm animals kept, upon the perfect saving of vegetables and seeds, and also upon the proper curing of cheese, and, in fact, upon all that pertains to a healthy condition inside any covering. Many complicated systems of ventilation have been and are constantly being invented, few of which long survive. In farm houses ventilation is not so abstruse a question as in city mansions. The chimney flues and the air spaces in the walls, together with the windows, will furnish ample means of ventilation. How to do this in the most economical manner, will depend upon the size of the house, and the number of inside rooms. When there are many, pure air may be forced in by a system of pipes leading to a main pipe, at the roof, turned to a right angle near the end, and terminating in an abrupt bowl or cone shaped opening, so provided that it may always turn to face the wind. Another series of pipes connecting with a main one leading out of the roof will convey away the impure air from the rooms. In ordinary farm houses pure air may be provided for by means of ventilators in the windows. The flues of the house, or the pipes leading to them, conveying away the impure air. Barns and stables should be provided with ventilating pipes or trunks not less than four feet square, and provided at the top with a good ventilating apparatus. These pipes will also serve as chutes through which hay and fodder may be passed to the feeding floors below. The stable floors should have a sufficient number of ventilating sashes, or, sashes hung by weights so that a proper amount of fresh air can be supplied at all times, and in such amount as may be necessary. Thus not only will ventilation be supplied, but also that necessary element, plenty of light. The ventilation of cellars, both those of buildings and of barns, and not less important of dairy buildings, where a cool current is necessary in summer, and pure air in winter, may probably be best conserved by the plan known as sub-earth ventilation, advocated and perfected by Mr. Wilkinson, of Illinois. This consists, substantially, in laying pipes or tile six inches or more in diameter from four to six feet under the surface of the ground, and of as great a length as may be desired, but not less than 400 feet, and where opening out at the surface of the ground, being provided with blowers, which will turn with the wind, and so the open side is kept always facing the wind. Thus the air in passing into the open mouth of the subterranean pipes, in its passage is cooled to the same temperature of the earth at the depth at which the pipe is laid, and passing out at the other end into the room to be ventilated, enters and cools the apartment to about fifty-five degrees, or in late summer to about sixty degrees Farenheit. This temperature being uniform, allows the curing of cheese in the most perfect manner, and at the same time the air of the room is kept perfectly sweet and cool. (See Supplement, page 1122.)

VENTRICLE. A cavity of the heart, brain, etc.

VENTRICOSE. Any part which appears blown out.

VERATRIA. An active alkaloid principle, from the *Veratrum album*, or white hellebore.

VERBENA. *Vervain.* Some years ago, and until this plant began to be severely attacked with rust, on the cutting bench, it was perhaps the most popular of plants both for the window and for bedding purposes. Its pretty trusses of flowers, in almost endless variety of color, and its profuse blooming, whether in the open ground in summer, or in the window in winter, made it universally sought after. It is adapted both to pot or vase, and will continue to bloom almost the whole winter if kept rather cool at night, and with plenty of sun during the day. Out of doors it will stand any temperature above actual freezing, and if protected during frosty nights will continue to bloom late in the fall. In the room 65° during the day, and not below 45° at night will keep the plants healthy, if care be taken to keep the leaves free of dust and insects. Water only when dry, and then liberally, never allowing water to stand in the saucers, and in mild weather give air in plenty, either by opening the window or setting them on the porch in a still atmosphere. It is usual now to depend upon seedlings. Sow the seed in a hot bed the first of March, prick out into three inch pots when large enough and transfer to the open ground as soon as danger of frost is over, setting the plants one foot apart. They should commence to bloom about the first of June and continue in bloom all the season. There are a number of species indigenous to the United States, North, among them, *Verbain angustifolia; V. Hastata*, or blue vervain; *V. urticifolia*, white vervain; *V. stricta*, hoary vervain; *V. officinalis*, common vervain; *V. bractiosa* and *V. anbletia*. The first, second and third named are found East and West. Officinalis was introduced from Europe. The rest are western species; the last named being a well known prairie flower, and is sometimes cultivated.

VERJUICE. The juice of green grapes or apples, from which a vinegar is made.

VERMIN. Destructive animals or insects.

VERNATION. The manner in which the leaflets of a bud are folded.

VERRUCOSE. Wart-like in appearance.

VERTEBRÆ. The bones of the spine, which is also called the vertebral column.

VERTEBRATES, VERTEBRATA. All animals having a spinal column.

VERTICAL. Upright, pointing to the vertex, or uppermost point overhead.

VERTICELLUS. A whorl. *Verticellate* is a derivative; disposed in a whorl.

VERTIGO. Badly fitting tight collars, especially if the horse be fat and full of blood, overwork in a hot sun, hereditary tendency to brain disorders, and various local disorders, will occasion the horse to stagger and sometimes fall in the harness. If produced by some other cause than a tight collar, the horse should not be used on the road since the difficulty increases with age, and constitutes a permanent unsoundness.

VESICANTS. Substances which produce blistering.

VESICLE. A small bladder.

VESPIDÆ. The family of wasps.

VESTIBULE. A porch or ante-room.

VETCH. *Vicia.* The cultivated Vetch, *V. Sativa*, or tare of Europe, has been tried from time to time in the United States, but its cultivation abandoned, and is now regarded as a useless weed. (See Tare.) The Kidney Vetch, or Sand Clover, *Anthyllis vulneraria*, has also been recommended as a forage plant, but in the United States has proved entirely worthless. The Milk Vetch, *astragalus*, as Indian pea, pop pea, ground plum, and rattle box weed, is abundant in the West and far-west. The peas are used boiled as food by the Indians. It should be destroyed wherever found, since the pods are obnoxious from adhering to the wool of sheep and injuring its quality.

VETCHLING. The genus *Lathyrus*, leguminous plants, frequently of great beauty, as the sweet pea.

VETERINARY SCIENCE. The care of sick animals on the farm requires more than ordinary prudence in its management. The dumb animal can not tell of its aches and pains, can not describe peculiar symptoms, except by brute signs, quite unintelligible to those who have not given particular study and attention to the phenomena presented in various cases. Pain in some instances is plainly enough intimated as to its near locality, by the animal turning its head to the part, or by striking at it with its feet. Yet the operator in veterinary art, must have studied much to be able always to tell the cause of that pain. Happily the days of bleeding and strong physic, the universal rule among a class of horse doctors, is now well past, and the modern veterinary surgeon depends more upon good care and nursing, with such remedies as may be needed to meet particular symptoms as they occur. Under their appropriate names, in the body of this work, are given such remedies and specifics as are proper for the diseases treated of, (those most usually appearing in farm animals) and in all difficult and critical cases the reader is advised to appeal to a veterinary surgeon if such can be had, and if not, then apply to the family physician, for no humane country physician will now-a-days refuse to minister to a dumb brute, for fear of being called a horse doctor. That day is happily passed except among a class who might almost be called unworthy the name of M. D. It really requires more science sometimes to understand the symptoms of a dumb brute than a human subject, and hence the physician who prescribes really shows himself not only humane, but of broad culture as well. As showing how the practice of the healing art on the human subject has been assisted by comparative investigations on the bodies of animals, and also as showing something of the benefits accruing from the study of comparative anatomy and physiology, we may quote from as old and well known an authority as Galen, who said: If medical men have been guilty of gross errors, it is because they have neglected to dissect brutes. Says Mr. Vines, speaking of some who have distinguished themselves as surgeons: They have transplanted to the medical profession the honor of discoveries that were made by trenching on the territory of the veterinary science. In experiments in transfusing the blood of one animal into that of another it was discovered that what were termed the globules of the blood were uniform in all animals of the same species, and yet presented different forms in animals of different tribes. In man, the particles of blood presented flat disks, resembling pieces of money, having a slight depression. In birds, reptiles and fishes the disks were oval, instead of being round, and instead of being depressed in the center, they were elevated on each side. From this experiment it was argued that the fitness of the blood of one animal to the uses of another of a different species depended on the formation of its globules. Experiments have frequently been made to test the truth of this theory, and it has been found to be correct. An eminent physiologist has remarked that, in order to arrive at an explanation of what is obscure in man, we must look to the lowest and simplest forms of creation. For though in man is combined, in a wonderful and unequaled manner, all the functions which separately exhibit themselves in various other animals, he is not the most favorable subject for observing their action; hence we are obliged to refer to a number of other tribes for the assistance we gain in the study of their comparative structures. There is not a single species of animal that does not present us with a set of facts which we should never learn but by observing them in such species, and many of the facts ascertained by the observation of the simplest and most common animals. Speaking of veterinary art, its general history, and the science as it existed twenty years ago, the late Dr. Dadd wrote: The veterinary science, like that practiced on man, was first called into existence by necessity; the many

diseases to which domestic animals were subject, and to which they, too frequently, fell victims for want of proper professional knowledge, and the great loss which agriculturists experienced in consequence, led them to seek for a remedy. In the year 1761, the first veterinary school was established at Lyons, under the patronage of government, whose fostering care the infant school for a time received. At the commencement of this embryotic enterprise, the populace looked on with indifference; but many of the liberal and scientific men of that day saw in the enterprise a boundless field for research, a broad road to usefulness and distinction, and many eagerly embarked in it with unflinching perseverance, overcoming every obstacle, with a view of making known those laws regulating the vital forces of domestic animals. The fruits of their labors are bequeathed as a legacy to the profession, and the names of the first cultivators of veterinary science are inscribed on the tablets of their country's history as public benefactors. Four years after the endowment of this, the first school in France, a similar one was established at Alfort. A regular system of veterinary medicine was there taught, under which students acquired an acquaintance with the various forms of disease, and the *modus operandi* of therapeutic agents on domestic animals. The novel enterprise was regarded by other nations of Europe with a watchful eye, and they were not slow in coming to the rescue; schools rapidly sprang up in Holland, Berlin, Copenhagen, Stuttgard, and in various other places, which proved equally successful and beneficial as the French schools. We now pass over a period of twenty-seven years, during which time the science had gradually enlisted in its ranks men of influence, talents, and research. And now an individual of French descent, named St. Bel, lands on the shores of England, having letters of introduction from the first men in France to Sir Joseph Banks and other influential individuals, to whom he made known his mission; which was, that of establishing the veterinary science, then unknown, and of course unappreciated, in the British dominions. He was encouraged, with very flattering assurances of success, to commence operations, and shortly after his arrival in London he published proposals for establishing a veterinary school; there seemed, however, to be a sort of indifference manifested among the masses, and consequently very little, beyond making known his object, was effected during the first year. In the following, he published proposals to read lectures on the science, and thus give the English nation an opportunity to judge of the value of the new project; but, alas! he was doomed to disappointment; his second proposal met with no better success than at first. The apparent failure of his primary labors has been attributed, by an eminent writer, to various causes, and it may be well for us to notice them, for the very same causes have been in active operation, diverting American skill and intelligence from embarking in a cause so worthy the attention and support of a free and enlightened nation. It was in consequence of the character of those who presumed, without the necessary qualifications, to practice the art, that the English husbandmen refused to put their shoulders to the wheel, and receive the offered boon. That country had been visited by diseases of a pestilential type, which had made sad havoc among the stock, and had swept them from the green hills and verdant valleys, as by the blast of a tornado. Their horses, too, did not escape the arm of the destroyer; they were constantly suffering and dying from insidious forms of disease, the history and characters of which were almost unknown. This state of things, together with the unfortunate occurrence that there were no legitimate practitioners, had opened a wide field for adventurers and quacks, whose barbarous systems, of medication, probably, was the cause of many deaths. These practitioners, in lieu of better, were taken as standards, and the people had, to a great extent, formed an estimate of the value of this art in exact ratio to the talents of the village farrier, and in proportion to the success that attended his labors. This is precisely the state of affairs in America. St. Bel gives us another reason for his failure, but it amounts to nearly the same thing. He says: The opulence of England offered a wide field for imposters of foreign origin, by whom the nation was daily imposed on, and repeated experience of such impositions naturally excited distrust towards foreigners in general; and because honesty of views was not written on his face, patience and perseverance became his only resources. At this stage of affairs St. Bel was fortunate enough to make the acquaintance of a gentleman who had a decided taste for the art, and who eagerly responded to the views of the professor, and bade him not despair of ultimate success; assuring him that by setting the matter in its right light before the people he would soon obtain all he desired. This assurance inspired St. Bel with new hopes, and he immediately issued a pamphlet of some twenty-eight pages, entitled, Plan for Establishing an Institution to Cultivate and Teach the Veterinary Art. This pamphlet was well received, and several agricultural societies paid the writer handsome compliments, and conferred on him honorary distinction. During the year 1790, several meetings took place between the members of agricultural societies and others favorable to the cause; at length measures were adopted for promoting the object. A resolution to this purport was now passed, which read as follows: That the parties had observed the good effects produced on the public mind by the exertions of the friends to the art, for its improvement, and approved of St. Bel's plan for establishing a public institution for that purpose. The result was, that an institution was soon endowed, which was named The Veterinary College of London, to which St. Bel was appointed professor. But, unfortunately, that distinguished individual had scarcely occupied the chair one year, when a sudden and brief illness terminated his mortal career, and he was consigned to the tomb ere the laurels had scarcely encircled his brow. Being thus cut off at such an early period, yet in the midst of his usefulness, the prospects of the infant institution became greatly affected—only for a short season, however. The college was considered to be in a flourishing condition; the Duke of Northumberland had already contributed a sum equal in our money to twenty-five hundred dollars, and the enterprise numbered among its staunch supporters such men as the Earl of Grosvenor, Mr. Penn, Earl Morton, Drs. John Hunter and Crawford. and subsequently that great surgeon and medical hero, Sir Astley Cooper. Medical men hailed the new enterprise as one not only calculated to ameliorate the condition of suffering domestic animals, but, what was of still greater importance to them and mankind, they perceived in it a fruitful field for the cultivation of comparative anatomy and physiology. With this object in view, Dr. J. Hunter assisted the friends of the new school both by his professional influence and from his private purse. Although the college had been in existence but a brief period, its pupils had gained sufficient knowledge of theory and practice to distinguish themselves; thus fully realizing the anticipations of its founders. Among the first students who sought to qualify themselves as efficient veterinary practitioners, we find recorded the names of Laurence, Blain and Clark. Each of these philanthropists has since left to the world a record of their labors, which, even in this enlightened age, serve as useful guides to the young aspirant for veterinary fame. The professorship made vacant by the death of the father of this science, St. Bel, was conferred on Mr. Coleman, who had previously devoted himself to physiological research; he, too, soon distinguished himself, and the college again assumed its former flourishing condition. A medical committee was now appointed, consisting of some of the most eminent practioners that the country could boast of, by whom the pupils were examined, and when found to have acquired sufficient knowledge of the art, certificates were granted accordingly. We are informed that this medical examining committee were lecturers of human medicine, and with a liberality that reflected great credit on them, permitting the veterinary pupils to attend their lectures on human anatomy free of charge. Thus did a band of really great and good men unite their efforts and interests, for the study of the science of life in all its diversities and forms. By this wise association of the sister sciences, its advocates aimed a death blow at ignorance, quackery, and superstition of the times, and they were successful to some extent; for a new order of practitioners took the field; they soon demolished the old landmarks set up by the ignorant farriers, and created in their stead beacons of light; thus spreading the illuminating rays of science broadcast, and the public, as well as domestic animals, were benefited thereby. The advantages under which the veterinary art can now be studied in England, France, and Germany are not inferior to those of the most favored university; and such astonishing discoveries, through the aid of chemistry and the microscope, are in such rapid succession surprising the medical world, and so splendid are the achievements in the departments of veterinary surgery, that the noble sons of Æsculapius (our brethren of the human school) are watching the labors of their kindred spirits with no ordinary interest. In the United States comparatively few graduates have entered the sphere of veterinary science. Some of our agricultural colleges have chairs of veterinary science, and yet to the American mind seeking an honorable profession the duties pertaining to veterinary practice do not seem to take kindly to it. Hence it is left principally to the graduates of European schools, who have emigrated hither. In our great cities every large stable has its paid veterinarian. In the country, especially in the more sparsely settled districts, it would be impossible for a veterinary surgeon to gain a living. Hence the greater need that every owner of animals should know something of the treatment of them, and hence again the reason why in this work we consider it important to give plain, simple, concise rules for the treatment of such diseases as generally come under the eye of the agriculturist, and which will be found treated of under their appropriate titles. Some of the family scales made at the present day are so nicely adjusted that they will answer for weighing drugs where the nicest accuracy is not needed. For this reason we give a table of apothecaries weights of quantities by utensils. Apothecaries weight is as follows: Sixty grains make one drachm; eight drachm one ounce, and sixteen ounces one pound. Where strict accuracy is not essential; sixty drops is equal to a teaspoonfull, and a teaspoonfull is a drachm; four teaspoonfulls make a tablespoonfull or half an ounce; two tablespoonfulls make an ounce; one wineglassfull, two ounces; one teacupfull four ounces; one tumblerfull, one half-pint, and two make a pint. So also the half pint and pint tin cup may be used as measures. Nevertheless, where much stock is kept it is better that the farmer provide himself not only with the proper scales, but also with a graduated fluid measure. So also it would be better that a few instruments should be kept, as for instance, a blunt pointed bistoury for operating under the skin or in cavities. A thumb lancet, as being better than the old fashioned fleam and safer than the spring lancet, gauging the depth with the thumb. A pair of forceps, for dressing wounds, catching and holding arteries for tying, etc. An aneurismal needle, blunt pointed for introducing small seton tapes, and if necessary for exploring wounds; a silver probe, however, blunt at one end and sharp at the other is better. A frog knife, such as is used by horse shoers, for cleaning and paring the hoofs, etc. A pair of curved scissors for trimming the edges of wounds, and cutting away hair close to the skin. A straight broad scalpel, which is useful in opening abscesses, as well as for castrating animals. These with a seton needle, a few surgical needles, and some white silk, linen thread, or fine catgut for tying wounds will provide amply for any case as ordinarily coming up on the farm, or when it may not be imperatively necessary to call a veterinary surgeon. A small collection of medicines to be kept will be found useful. White or opaque bottles should be used, since the action of light changes some substances. Keep everything well corked, and all corrosive substances in strong glass bottles with ground glass stoppers. So instruct the druggist of whom you buy. From five to ten doses of each will be sufficient. The annexed list of medicines as given by Dr. Law in his Veterinary Adviser will be found valuable for reference being arranged for all farm animals. Those marked by a star (*) will be found useful to have always at hand. The list is as follows:

Acetic Acid, antidote to alkalies, cooling astringent: Horse 1 drachm; ox 2 drachms; ass 1 drachm; sheep 1 scruple; dog 2 to 3 drops.

Tincture of Aconite, sedative, diaphoretic: Horse 20 to 80 drops; ox 30 to 40 drops; ass 15 to 20 drops; sheep 3 to 5 drops; dog 1 to 3 drops.

Alcohol, stimulant, diuretic, narcotic: Horse 1 to 3 ounces; ox 3 to 6 ounces; ass 1 ounce; sheep ½ ounce; dog 2 drachms. Cooling astringent.

Brandy, Whisky, and Gin, stimulant, diuretic, narcotic: Horse 3 to 6 ounces; ox 6 to 12 ounces; ass 2 to 5 ounces; sheep 10 ounces; dog ½ ounce. Locally cooling astringent.

Strong Ale, stimulant, diuretic, narcotic: Horse 1 to 2 pints; ox 2 to 4 pints; ass 1 pint; sheep ½ pint; dog 2 ounces. Locally cooling astringent.

Barbadoes Aloes, purgative: Horse 4 drachms; ass 3 to 4 drachms; dog ½ drachm.

Cape Aloes, purgative: Horse 5 drachms; ass 4 to 5 drachms.

Alum, astringent: Horse 2 to 3 drachms; ox 3 to 4 drachms; ass 2 drachms; sheep ½ to 1 drachm; dog ½ to 1 scruple.

Ammonia, Liquid, diffusible stimulant, antispasmodic, antacid, diuretic: Horse ½ ounce; ox ½ to 1 ounce; ass 2 to 4 drachms; sheep ½ to 1 drachm; dog 10 drops. Locally blister

Aromatic Ammonia, diffusible stimulant, antispasmodic, antacid, diuretic: Horse 1 to 2 ounces; ox 2 to 4 ounces; ass 1 to 2 ounces; sheep ½ to 1 ounce; dog 1 drachm. Locally blister.

*Carbonate of Ammonia, diffusible stimulant, antispasmodic, antacid, diuretic: Horse 2 to 4 drachms, ox 4 to 6 drachms; ass 2 drachms; sheep ½ to 1 drachm; dog 10 to 15 grains. Locally blister.

Muriate of Ammonia, stimulant, discutient, alterative, diuretic: Horse 2 to 4 drachms; ox 4 to 6 drachms; ass 2 drachms; sheep ½ to 1 drachm; dog 20 grains. Locally cooling discutient.

Acetate of Ammonia, Solution, diaphoretic, diuretic, stimulant: Horse 2 to 3 ounces; ox 3 to 4 ounces; ass 2 ounces; sheep ½ to 1 ounce; dog 2 drachms.

Anise-seed, stomachic, carminative: Horse 1 ounce; ox 1 to 2 ounces; ass 1 ounce; sheep 2 to 4 drachms; dog 1 to 3 scruples.

Antimony, Tartarized (Tartar Emetic), emetic: Swine 5 grains; dog 2 to 4 grains. Sedative, diaphoretic: Horse 2 drachms; ox 2 to 4 drachms; ass 2 drachms; sheep 1 to 2 scruples: swine ½ to 1 grain; dog ¼ to ½ grain. Locally blister.

Areca Nut, vermifuge, tæniafuge: Horse 1 ounce; ox 1 ounce; ass 1 ounce; sheep 3 drachms; dog ½ to 1 drachm.

*Arnica, Tincture, stimulant, diuretic: Horse 1 drachm; ox 1 drachm; ass ½ drachm; sheep 1 scruple; dog 10 drops. Locally cooling, soothing.

Arsenic, alterative, nerve tonic: Horse 5 grains; ox 5 to 8 grains; ass 3 to 5 grains; sheep 1 grain; swine ½ grain; dog 1-12 grain. Locally caustic, parasiticide.

*Assafœtida, diffusible stimulant, carminative, vermifuge and appetizer: Horse 2 drachms; ox 4 drachms; ass 1 to 2 drachms; sheep ½ to 1 drachm; swine ½ drachm; dog 10 to 20 grains.

Azedarach, vermifuge: Horse ½ to 1 ounce; ox 1 ounce; ass 3 to 4 drachms; sheep 1 to 2 drachms; swine 1 drachm; dog 20 grains.

Belladonna, anodyne, antispasmodic, narcotic: Horse 2 ounces; ox 2 ounces; ass 1 to 2 ounces; sheep ¼ ounce; dog 5 grains

Belladonna, Extract, anodyne, etc.: Horse 2 drachms; ox 2 to 3 drachms; ass 1 to 2 drachms; sheep ½ drachm; dog 1 to 3 grains.

Atropia (alkaloid of Belladonna), anodyne, etc.: Horse 1 to 2 grains; ox 1 to 2 grains; ass 1 grain; sheep ½ grain; dog 1-16 grain.

Balsam of Peru, stimulant, antispasmodic, expectorant: Horse 1 ounce; ox 1 to 1½ ounces; ass ½ to 1 ounce; sheep 2 drachms; dog ½ drachm.

Benzoin, stimulant, antispasmodic, expectorant: Horse 1 ounce; ox 1 to 1½ ounces; ass ½ to 1 ounce; sheep 2 drachms; dog ½ drachm.

Borax, nerve sedative, uterine stimulant: Horse 2 to 6 drachms: ox ½ to 1 ounce; ass 2 to 4 drachms; sheep ½ to 1 drachm; swine ½ drachm; dog 5 to 10 grains. Locally astringent, parasiticide.

Bismuth, Subnitrate, soothes irritation of the stomach and bowels: Horse 2 drachms; ox 2 to 4 drachms; ass 1 to 2 drachms; sheep 20 grains; swine 10 to 20 grains; dog 5 to 10 grains. Locally soothing, healing.

Blackberry Root, astringent: Horse 2 to 4 drachms; ox ½ ounce; ass 2 drachms: sheep 2 scruples; dog ½ scruple.

Bluestone (Copper Sulphate.)

Boneset, stimulant, tonic, diaphoretic: Horse ½ to 1 ounce; ox 1 ounce; ass ½ ounce; sheep 2 to 3 drachms; swine 2 drachms; dog ½ to 1 drachm.

Bromide of Potassium, nerve sedative: Horse 2 to 4 drachms; ox 4 drachms; ass 2 to 3 drachms; sheep ½ drachm; dog 5 to 10 grains

Buchu, stimulant, diuretic: Horse 4 drachms; ox ½ to 1 ounce; ass 3 drachms; sheep 1 drachm; dog 10 to 20 grains.

Buckthorn Syrup, purgative: dog ½ to 1 ounce.

Calomel, purgative: Horse 1 drachm; ox 1 to 2 drachms; ass 1 drachm; swine 1 scruple; dog 3 to 4 grains. Alterative: Horse 1 scruple ox 1 to 3 scruples; ass 1 scruple; swine 3 to 4 grains; dog ½ to 1 grain.

Camphor, calmative, antispasmodic: Horse 1 to 2 drachms; ox 2 to 4 drachms; ass 1 drachm; sheep 1 scruple. dog 3 to 10 grains.

Cantharides, stimulant, diuretic: Horse 5 grains; ox 5 to 10 grains; ass 3 to 5 grains; sheep 1 to 2 grains; dog 1-6 to ½ grain. Locally blister.

Capsicum, Cayenne Pepper, stimulant, aromatic: Horse 2 to 3 drachms; ox 2 to 4 drachms; ass 1 to 2 drachms; sheep 1 scruple; swine ½ to 1 scruple; dog 2 to 5 grains. Locally irritant.

Caraway Seed, stomachic: Horse 1 ounce; ox 1 to 2 ounces; ass 1 ounce; sheep 2 to 3 drachms; swine 2 drachms; dog 1 scruple.

Cardamoms, stomachic: Horse 1 ounce; ox 1 to 2 ounces; ass 1 ounce; sheep 2 to 3 drachms; swine 2 drachms; dog 1 scruple.

Cascarilla, stimulant, bitter tonic: Horse ½ to 1 ounce; ox 1 ounce; ass 4 to 6 drachms; sheep 1 drachm; dog 10 grains.

Carbolic Acid, sedative, anodyne, astringent, antiseptic, disinfectant: Horse ½ to 1 drachm; ox 1 drachm; ass ½ drachm; sheep 10 drops; dog 5 drops.

Castor-oil, purgative: Horse 1 pint; ox 1 to 1½ pints; ass 1 pint; sheep 3 to 4 ounces; dog ½ to 1 ounce.

Catechu, astringent: Horse 2 to 5 drachms; ox 3 to 8 drachms; ass 2 to 3 drachms; sheep 1 to 2 drachms: dog 10 to 30 grains.

Chamomile, stimulant, tonic: Horse 1 ounce; ox 1 to 2 ounces; ass 1 ounce; sheep 2 drachms; dog ¼ drachm.

Cherry Bark, wild, expectorant: Horse ½ ounce; sheep 2 to 3 scruples; swine 2 scruples; dog 1 scruple.

Chloral-Hydrate, sedative, antispasmodic: Horse ½ ounce; ass ¼ to ½ ounce; sheep 1 drachm; dog 20 grains. Soporific: Horse 1 ounce; sheep 2 to 3 drachms; dog ½ drachm.

Chloroform, sedative, antispasmodic, stimulant: Horse 1 to 2 drachms; ass 1 drachm; sheep 1 scruple; dog 5 to 10 drops. Anæsthetic.

Cinchona, Peruvian Bark, bitter tonic, antiseptic, antiperiodic: Horse 1 to 3 ounces; ass 1 ounce; sheep 2 to 4 drachms; dog 1 drachm.

Cinnamon, stomachic: Horse 4 to 6 drachms; ox ½ to 1 ounce; ass 4 to 6 drachms; sheep 1 to 2 drachms; dog 10 to 20 grains.

Cod-liver Oil, tonic: Horse 4 to 6 ounces; ox 6 to 8 ounces; ass 4 to 6 ounces; sheep 1 to 2 ounces; dog ½ ounce.

Colchicum, diuretic, sedative: Horse ½ to 1 drachm; ox 1 to 2 drachms; ass ½ drachm; sheep ½ scruple; dog 2 to 8 grains.

Colocynth, bitter purgative: Dog 2 to 5 grains.

Columbo, bitter tonic: Horse 4 to 6 drachms; ox ½ to 1 ounce; ass 2 to 3 drachms; sheep ½ to 1 drachm; dog 10 grains.

Conium, Extract, sedative: Horse 1 drachm; ox 1 to 2 drachms; ass ½ to 1 drachm; sheep 10 to 15 grains; swine 10 grains; dog 2 to 5 grains.

Copaiva, stimulant, diuretic, expectorant: Horse 2 to 4 drachms; ox 3 to 4 drachms; ass 2 to 3 drachms; sheep ½ to 1 drachm; dog 10 drops.

Copper, Ammoniated, tonic, antispasmodic, astringent: Horse 1 to 2 drachms; ox 1 to 2 drachms; ass 1 drachm; sheep 10 to 20 grains; dog 1 to 5 grains.

Copper, Iodide, tonic, discutient: Horse 1 to 2 drachms.

Copper, Sulphate, tonic, astringent: Horse ½ to 1 drachm; ox 1 to 2 drachms; ass ½ drachm; sheep 10 grains; dog 2 to 4 grains.

Croton Seeds, purgative: Horse 10 to 12; ox 15 to 20; ass 8 to 10; sheep 2 to 3; dog 1 to 2.

Croton Oil, purgative: Horse 15 to 20 drops; ox 20 to 30 drops; ass 12 to 18 drops; sheep 5 to 8 drops; dog 3 to 4 drops.

Cream of Tartar, diuretic: Horse 1 ounce; sheep 4 to 6 drachms; dog 1 drachm. Laxative: Horse 5 ounces; ox 5 to 8 ounces; ass 5 ounces; sheep 1 to 2 ounces; dog ½ ounce.

Dandelion Extract, Taraxacum, diuretic, laxative, bitter: Horse 1 to 1½ ounces; ox 2 ounces; ass 1 ounce; sheep 3 drachms; dog 1 drachm.

Digitalis, sedative, diuretic: Horse 15 to 20 grains; ox ½ to 1 drachm; ass 15 grains; sheep 5 to 15 grains; swine 2 to 10 grains; dog 1 to 3 grains.

Dover's Powder, sedative, diaphoretic: Horse 3 drachms; ox 3 to 4 drachms; ass 2 drachms; sheep 2 scruples; swine 1 scruple; dog 2 to 4 grains.

Ergot, checks bleeding, parturient: Horse ½ to 1 ounce; ox 1 ounce; ass ½ ounce; sheep 1 to 2 drachms; dog ½ drachm.

Ether, diffusible stimulant: Horse 1 to 2 ounces; ox 2 to 3 ounces; ass 1 ounce; sheep ½ ounce; swine 2 to 4 drachms; dog 1 drachm.

Fennel Seed, stomachic: Horse 1 ounce; ox 1 to 2 ounces; ass 1 ounce; sheep 2 to 4 drachms; dog ½ drachm.

Filix Mas., Extract, Male Shield-Fern, vermifuge, tænicide: Horse 1 ounce; sheep ½ drachm; dog 10 to 20 drops.

Galls, Oak, astringent: Horse 4 to 6 drachms; ox 1 to 2 ounces; ass 4 drachms; sheep ½ to 1 scruple; swine 1 to 2 scruples; dog 1 to 3 grains.

Gallic and Tannic Acid, tannin, astringent: Horse 1 to 3 scruples; ass 1 to 2 scruples; sheep 5 grains; dog 1 to 3 grains.

Gentian, bitter tonic: Horse 4 drachms; ox ½ to 1 ounce; ass 4 drachms; sheep 1 to 2 drachms; dog 10 to 20 grains.

Ginger, stimulant, stomachic: Horse 1 ounce; ox 2 ounces; ass ½ to 1 ounce; sheep ½ ounce; swine 2 drachms; dog 2 scruples

Glauber Salts (Soda Sulphate).

Henbane, Hyoscyamus, Extract, sedative, antispasmodic: Horse 2 drachms; ox 2 to 4 drachms; ass 1 to 2 drachms; sheep ½ to 1 drachm; swine ½ drachm; dog 5 grains.

Hemp, Indian, Extract, antispasmodic, soporific, narcotic: Horse ½ to 1 drachm; ass ½ drachm; sheep 10 to 15 grains; swine 5 to 10 grains; dog 1 to 2 grains.

Hydrocyanic Acid (Prussic).

Iodine, alterative, discutient: Horse 10 to 20 grains; ox 20 to 30 grains; ass 10 grains; sheep 5 to 10 grains; swine 5 grains; dog 1 to 2 grains.

Iodide of Potassium, alterative, diuretic: Horse ½ to 1 drachm; ox 1 to 2 drachms; ass ½ drachm; sheep 3 scruples; swine 1 to 2 scruples; dog 1 scruple.

Ipecacuanha, emetic, sedative: Swine 1 to 2 drachms; dog 15 to 20 grains. Diaphoretic, expectorant; Swine ½ drachm; dog 3 to 5 grains.

Jalap, purgative: Swine 1 to 2 drachms; dog ½ to 1 drachm.

Iron, Peroxide, tonic: Horse 2 to 4 drachms; ox 4 drachms: ass 2 drachms; sheep 1 drachm; dog 5 to 10 grains. Antidote to arsenic.

Iron, Sulphate, tonic: Horse 2 to 4 drachms; ass 2 drachms; sheep 1 drachm; swine ½ drachm; dog 2 to 5 grains.

Iron, Carbonate, tonic: Horse 2 to 4 drachms; ass 2 drachms; sheep 1 drachm; swine ½ drachm; dog 2 to 5 grains.

Iron, Iodide, tonic, discutient: Horse ½ to 2 drachms; ox 1 to 2 drachms; ass ½ to 1 drachm; sheep 15 to 30 grains; swine 10 to 20 grains; dog 1 to 8 grains

Iron, Tincture of Muriate, astringent, checks bleeding: Horse ½ to 1 oz; ox 1 to 2 ounces; ass ½ ounce; sheep ½ to 1 drachm; swine 10 to 30 drops; dog 5 to 10 drops.

Kino, astringent: Horse ½ ounce; ox ½ to 1 ounce; ass 2 to 4 drachms; sheep 1 to 2 drachms; swine ½ to 1 drachm; dog 10 grains.

Kousso, vermifuge: Sheep 2 to 3 ounces; dog 1 ounce.

Laudanum (Opium).

Lead Acetate (Sugar of Lead), astringent, sedative: Horse 1 to 2 scruples; ox 2 to 3 scruples; ass 1 scruple; sheep 10 to 15 grains; dog 2 to 5 grains.

Lime-water, antacid, astringent: Horse 4 to 5 ounces; ox 4 to 8 ounces; ass 4 ounces; sheep 1 ounce; dog 1 drachm.

Lime, Carbonate, Chalk, antacid, astringent: Horse 1 to 2 ounces; ox 2 to 4 ounces; ass 1 ounce; sheep 2 to 4 drachms; dog 8 to 12 grains.

Lime, Chloride, Chlorinated, checks tympany, disinfectant: Horse 2 to 4 drachms; ass 2 drachms; sheep 1 to 2 drachms.

Linseed Oil, laxative: Horse 1 to 2 pints; ox 1 to 2 quarts; ass 1 pint; sheep ½ pint.

Lobelia, sedative, antispasmodic, expectorant: Horse 1 to 2 drachms; ox 1 to 3 drachms: ass 1 drachm; sheep 15 grains; swine 5 to 15 grains; dog 1 to 5 grains.

Magnesia, antacid, laxative, antidote to arsenic: Horse 1 to 2 ounces; ox 2 to 4 ounces; sheep 1 ounce.

Magnesia, Sulphate, Epsom Salts, laxative: ox 1 to 2 pounds sheep 4 to 6 ounces.

Mallow, demulcent: Freely.

Mentha Piperita (Peppermint).

Mercury with Chalk, Hydrargyrum Cum Creta, antacid, laxative: Calf 10 to 15 grains; dog 5 to 10 grains.

Mercurial Pill, Blue Pill, laxative: Dog 5 grains.

Mercury, Subchloride (Calomel).

Muriatic Acid, Hydrochloric Acid, tonic, astringent, caustic, disinfectant: Horse 1 drachm; ox 2 drachms; ass 1 drachm; sheep 20 drops; dog 2 to 5 drops.

Myrrh, stimulant, tonic: Horse 2 to 4 drachms; ox 4 to 6 drachms; ass 2 drachms; sheep 1 to 2 drachms; dog 15 to 20 grains.

Nitre (Potassa Nitrate).

Nitric Acid, tonic, astringent, caustic: Horse 1 drachm; or 2 drachms; ass 1 drachm; sheep 20 drops; dog 2 to 5 drops.

Nux Vomica nerve stimulant, tonic: Horse 10 to 30 grains; ox 20 to 40 grains; ass 10 to 20 grains; sheep 5 to 15 grains; dog ½ to 3 grains.

Oak Bark, astringent: Horse 1 ounce; ox 2 to 4 ounces; ass 1 ounce; sheep 4 drachms; swine 2 to 8 drachms; dog 1 to 2 drachms.

Olive Oil, laxative: Horse 1 to 2 pints; ox 2 to 3 pints; ass 1 pint; sheep 3 to 6 ounces; dog 1 to 3 ounces.

Opium, narcotic, sedative, anodyne, antispasmodic: Horse ½ to 2 drachms; ox 2 to 4 drachms; ass ½ to 1 drachm; sheep 10 to 20 grains; dog ½ to 3 grains.

Opium, Tincture, Laudanum, narcotic, sedative, anodyne, antispasmodic: Horse 1 to 2 ounces; ox 2 ounces; ass ½ to 1 ounce; sheep 2 to 3 drachms; dog 15 to 30 drops.

Morphia, Muriate, narcotic, sedative, anodyne, antispasmodic: Horse 3 to 5 grains; ox 5 to 10 grains; ass 3 grains; sheep ¼ to 1 grain; dog ¼ to ½ grain.

Peppermint Oil, stomachic, antispasmodic: Horse 20 drops; ox 20 to 30 drops; ass 20 drops; sheep 5 to 10 drops; swine 5 drops; dog 3 to 5 drops.

Peruvian Bark (Cinchona).

Pepper, Black, White, stomachic, stimulant: Horse 2 drachms; ox 3 drachms; ass 2 drachms; sheep 1 to 2 scruples; dog 5 to 10 grains.

Pimento, stomachic, stimulant: Horse 2 drachms; ox 3 drachms; ass 2 drachms; sheep 1 to 2 scruples; dog 5 to 10 grains.

Podophyllin, purgative, sedative: Horse 1 to 2 drachms; ox 2 drachms; ass 1 drachm; sheep 10 to 20 grains; swine 6 to 8 grains; dog 1 to 2 grains.

Pomegranate Root Bark, vermifuge: Horse 1 ounce; ox 1 to 2 ounces; ass 1 ounce; sheep 2 to 3 drachms; swine 1 to 2 drachms; dog 20 to 30 grains.

Potassa Acetate, antacid, diuretic, diaphoretic: horse 6 to 8 drachms; ox 1 ounce; ass 4 to 6 drachms; sheep 1 to 2 drachms; dog 10 to 20 grains.

Potassa Nitrate, diuretic, febrifuge: Horse 6 to 8 drachms; ox 1 ounce; ass 4 to 6 drachms; sheep 1 to 2 drachms; dog 10 to 20 grains.

Potassa Bicarbonate, antacid, diuretic: Horse 6 to 8 drachms; ox 1 ounce; ass 4 to 6 drachms; sheep 1 to 2 drachms; dog 10 to 20 grains.

Potassa Chlorate, stimulant, diuretic, refrigerant, antiseptic: Horse 1 to 4 drachms; ass 1 to 2 drachms; sheep 20 to 40 grains; dog 5 to 15 grains.

Potassium Iodine (Iodine).

Potassium Bromide, nerve sedative: Horse ½ ounce; ass 2 to 4 drachms; sheep 2 drachms; swine 1 drachm; dog 20 grains.

Potassium Cyanide, sedative, antispasmodic: Horse 1 to 2 grains; ox 2 grains; ass 1 to 2 grains; sheep ½ grain; dog $\frac{1}{8}$ to $\frac{1}{4}$ grain.

Prussic Acid, sedative, antispasmodic: Horse 20 to 30 drops; ox 30 to 40 drops; ass 15 to 20 drops; sheep 5 to 8 drops; swine 5 drops; dog 1 to 3 drops.

Pumpkin Seeds, vermifuge, tæniafuge: dog ½ ounce.

Quinia, Sulphate, bitter tonic: Horse 20 grains; ox 20 to 30 grains; ass 15 to 20 grains; sheep 6 to 10 grains; swine 5 to 10 grains; dogs 2 to 6 grains.

Rhubarb, laxative, tonic: Horse 1 ounce; ox 2 ounces; ass 1 ounce; sheep 1 drachm; dog 20 grains.

Resin, diuretic: Horse 4 to 6 drachms; ox ¼ to 1 ounce; ass 4 to 6 drachms; sheep 2 to 4 drachms; swine 2 drachms; dog 20 to 30 grains.

Soap, diuretic antacid, laxative: Horse 1 to 2 ounces; ass 1 ounce; sheep 2 to 6 drachms; swine 2 to 4 drachms; dog 20 to 60 grains.

Soda, Bicarbonate, antacid, diuretic: Horse 4 to 6 drachms; ox 4 to 8 drachms; ass 4 drachms; sheep 1 to 2 drachms; dog 5 to 30 grains.

Soda, Sulphite, Bisulphite, Hyposulphite, antiseptic, disinfectant, alterative, relieves tympany: Horse 1 ounce; ox 2 to 3 ounces; ass 1 ounce; sheep 2 to 6 drachms; swine 2 to 4 drachms; dog 20 to 60 grains.

Soda Sulphate (Glauber Salts), purgative: Horse 1 to 1½ pounds; ox 1 to 2 pounds; ass ½ to 1 pound; sheep 6 ounces.

Sodium, Chloride (common salt), tonic, vermifuge, purgative: Horse 1 to 2 ounces; ox 2 to 4 ounces; ass 1 ounce; sheep 2 to 4 drachms; swine 1 to 3 drachms; dog 10 to 30 grains.

Santonin, Wormseed, Semen Contra, vermifuge: Horse ½ to 1 ounce; ass 4 drachms; sheep 2 to 4 drachms; swine 1 to 3 drachms; dogs 10 to 60 grains.

Squill, diuretic, expectorant: Horse ½ drachm; ox ½ to 1 drachm; ass 20 to 30 grains; sheep 10 to 15 grains; dog 1 to 5 grains.

Silver, Nitrate (Lunar Caustic), nerve tonic: Horse 5 grains; ox 5 to 8 grains; ass 2 to 4 grains; sheep 1 to 2 grains; dog ⅛ to ½ grain.

Spanish Flies (Cantharides).

Spigelia, vermifuge: Horse ½ to 1 ounce; ox 1 to 2 ounces, ass ½ to 1 ounce; sheep 2 to 4 drachms; swine 2 to 3 drachms; dog 1 drachm.

Strychnia, nerve tonic: Horse 1 to 2 grains; ox 1 to 3 grains; ass 1 grain; sheep ⅓ to 1 grain; swine ½ grain; dog 1-40 to 1-10 grain.

Sulphur, expectorant, diaphoretic: Horse 3 to 4 ounces; ox 5 to 6 ounces; ass 3 ounces; sheep 2 ounces; swine 1½ to 2 ounces; dog 2 to 8 drachms. Laxative, alterative: Horse 1 ounce; ox 1 to 2 ounces; ass 1 ounce; sheep 6 drachms; swine 4 to 6 drachms; dog ½ to 1 drachm. Parasiticide.

Sweet Spirits of Nitre, Spirit of Nitrous Ether, stimulant, antispasmodic, diuretic, diaphoretic: Horse 1 to 2 ounces; ox 3 to 4 ounces; ass 1 ounce; sheep 3 to 6 drachms; dog ½ to 2 drachms.

Stramonium, narcotic, sedative: Horse 20 to 30 grains; ox ½ to 1 drachm; ass 15 to 30 grains; sheep 5 to 10 grains; swine 4 to 6 grains; dog 2 grains.

Sulphuric Acid, tonic, refrigerant, caustic: Horse 1 drachm; ox 2 to 4 drachms; ass 1 drachm; sheep ½ drachm; swine 20 drops; dog 5 to 10 drops.

Tobacco, sedative, antispasmodic, vermifuge: Horse 4 drachms; ox 4 to 6 drachms; ass 4 drachms; sheep 1 drachm; swine ½ drachm; dog 5 to 6 grains.

Tar, expectorant, antiseptic: Horse ½ to 1 ounce; ox ½ to 2 ounces; sheep ½ ounce.

Turpentine Oil, stimulant, antispasmodic, diuretic: Horse 1 to 2 ounces; ox 1 to 1½ ounces; ass ½ ounce; sheep 4 to 6 drachms; swine, 1 drachm; dog ¼ drachm. Vermifuge: Horse 2 ounces; ox 2 to 3 ounces; ass 1 to 2 ounces; sheep 4 drachms; swine 2 to 3 drachms.

Valerian, diffusible stimulant, antispasmodic, vermifuge: Horse 2 ounces; ox 2 to 4 ounces; ass 2 ounces; sheep ½ ounce; swine 2 to 3 drachms; dog 1 to 2 drachms.

Valerianate of Iron, nerve tonic: Dog 4 to 5 grains.

Veratrum, sedative: Horse one scruple: ox ¼ to 1 drachm; ass ½ to 1 scruple; sheep 5 to 10 grains; swine 5 to 8 grains; dog 2 grains.

Wild Cherry Bark, expectorant: Horse 1 ounce; ox 1½ ounce; ass 1 ounce; sheep 3 drachms; dog 30 grains.

Zinc, Carbonate, astringent, tonic: Horse 2 drachms; ox 2 to 4 drachms; ass 2 drachms; sheep ½ to 1 drachm; swine ½ drachm, dog 10 to 15 grains.

Zinc, Sulphate astringent, tonic: Horse 1 to 2 drachms; ox 2 to 3 drachms; ass 1 drachm; sheep 15 to 30 grains; swine 10 to 20 grains; dog 2 to 3 grains. Emetic: Swine 15 grains to 1 drachm; dog 8 to 15 grains.

In explanation of the various terms and designations, used in connection with abnormal states of the system, the following explicit glossary is given, which will make everything clear to all readers:

Abnormal—Irregular.
Absorbents—Medicines used for absorbing; also the vessels of the body which suck up.
Acute—Sharp, severe.
Adipose—Fatty.
Adynamic—Debilitated.
Alae—Wings.
Alteratives—Medicines which change a disease for the better.
Anasarca—Dropsy of cellular membrane.
Anasarcous—Dropsical.
Anaemia—Bloodlessness.
Antiseptics—Medicines opposed to putrefaction.
Antispasmodic—Remedies opposed to spasms or convulsions.
Antiphlogistic—Opposed to inflammation.
Aperients—Medicines which open the bowels gently.
Aqueous—Watery.
Ascites—Dropsy of the belly.
Ataxic—Disordered.
Auscultation—Examination by sounding and listening.
Autopsy—Post-mortem examination.
Bifurcation—Division into two branches.
Bolus—A large pill.
Buccal Membrane—The lining of the mouth.
Canthus—Corner of the eye.
Capsule—Shell or case.
Carbonaceous—Containing carbon.
Carminatives—Medicines which relieve pain by expelling wind from the bowels.
Cartilaginous—Composed of cartilage.
Cathartic—Loosening.
Cellular—Cell-like.
Cerebellum—The brain.
Cerebrum—The brain.
Chancrous—Cancerous.
Clinical—Relating to individual practice.
Coma—Stupor.
Comatose—Stupefied.
Conjunctival Membrane—The membrane which lines the eyelids and covers the eyeball.
Cornea—Transparent coat of the eye.
Cranial—Pertaining to the skull.
Cranium—Skull.
Cracial—Shaped like a cross.
Decarbonize—To purify the air.
Diagnosis—The art of telling the nature of diseases.
Diaphoretics—Medicines which promote perspiration.
Diathesis—Predisposition to certain diseases.
Dietetics—Regulation of diet.
Diuretics—Medicines which increase the flow of urine.
Duct—Canal.

Dynomic—Relating to the vi al forces.
Emollients—Substances used to reduce inflammations.
Emphysema—Distention by gas or wind of certain portions of the body.
Emunctories—Organs which carry off waste matters.
Encephalon—The brain.
Enema—Injection.
Enzootic—Endemic diseases among animals.
Epizootic—Epidemic among animals.
Equilibrium—Balance.
Equi e—Relating to the horse.
Etiology—The doctrine of the causes of diseases.
Exc e:ne litiou—Useless.
E cr tor)—Relating to vessels which throw off useless matter.
Extravasation—Escape of a fluid of the body from its vessel into surrounding parts.
Exudation—Oozing through a membrane.
Fauces—The throat.
Fleam—An instrument used in bleeding.
Graminicorous—Feeding on grass.
Hema osine—The red coloring matter of the blood.
Hemorrhage—Bleeding.
Hippiatric—Relating to diseases of the horse.
Histology—General anatomy.
Hydrocephalus—Water in the head.
Hygiene—Preservation of health.
Ic.o.ou—Humory.
Idiopathic—Primary affections.
Idiosy rasy—Peculiarity of constitution.
Indurated—Hardened.
Inguinal—Belonging to the groin.
Intercostal—Between the ribs.
Inunction—The act of rubbing in.
Lachrymal Glands—Those which secrete tears.
Lancina ing—Shooting.
Laxatives—Loosening medicines.
Lesion—Disorder.
Ligament—The substance which joins bones together.
Mamm e—Breasts.
Maseeters—Muscles of the jaws.
Morbid—Diseased.
Morbific—Producing disease.
Navicular—One of the bones of the foot.
Neu o, athology—The nervous system in disease.
Nodulous—Like a knot.
Nosology—Classification of diseases.
Œdematous—Swollen.
Opa jue—Not transparent.
Os calcis—Bone of the heel.
Osseous—Bony.
Ooid In the form of an egg.
Polatine—Relating to the palate.
Panzootic—An epidemic affecting animals generally.
Pa asite—An animal which lives on another.
Parotid—Largest salivary gland.
Pathology—The study of the body in disease.
Pedicle—Narrow part of a tumor.
Petechial—Resembling flea-bites.
Phthisis—Wasting away.
Pituitary Membrane—Lining of the nostrils.
Pseudo-Membranous—Relating to false membranes.
Pus—Matter.
Pylorus—Entrance into intestines.
Rale—A watery sound heard in sounding the chest in some diseases.
Sanative—Health-giving.
Schneiderian Membrane—The lining of the nostrils.
Sebaceous—Of the nature of suet.
Sedatives—Medicines which produce sleep.
Serous—Watery.
Serum—Watery part of the blood.
Solvent That which dissolves.
Sporadic—Scattered.
Submaxillary—Beneath the jaw.
Sudamina—Small eruptions.
Supra-renal—Above the kidney.
Thoracic—Relating to the chest.
Thyroid—Shaped like a folding door.
Tonics—Medicines which give tone and strength to the body.
Tubercular—Relating to tumors in the structure of an organ.
Tumefaction—Swelling.
Turbinated Bones—Bones of the nose shaped like a top.
Turgescence—Great amount of humors in any part.
Vascular—Full of blood-vessels.
Ventricle—Cavity.
Virus—Poison.
Vis a Fronte—Force from the front.
Vis a Tergo—Force of propulsion.
Viscous—Sticky.
Voice-box—Larynx.

VEXILLUM. The standard: the upper petal of a papilionaceous or pea-like flower.

VIBRISSA. The pointed bristles which grow from the upper lip of animals, or from the jaws of birds, and are used as feelers.

VILLOSE. Woolly, covered with soft, flexible hairs, closely set.

VILLOUS. Having the appearance of a pile of velvet.

VINE. A class of climbing plants, which support themselves by their tendrils, aerial roots, or leaves to any object which they can grasp; also applied to twining plants, and those which run along the ground, taking root at intervals. (See Vegetation.) In pomology the term vine is applied especially to the grape.

VINEGAR. The juice of any fruit, especially that of the grape and the apple, which, having gone through the vinous fermentation, enters into the acetic fermentation, acquiring a more or less sharp acid taste. All reference to vinegar as a preservative must be understood as being made to a pure cider or wine vinegar. Chemical vinegars, such as are most commonly found in market, having various chemical properties, may either entirely fail to effect a preservation, or wholly consume the substance. For a good vinegar, to three gallons of pure apple cider add one gallon of soft water well sweetened with molasses, and expose to the sun or warm air till the acetic fermentation is nearly complete, then remove to a cool dry apartment. The cask should always be left uncorked. Vinegar can be made from the juices of almost any fruit containing either starch or sugar. In expressing the juice for any fruit wine the pulp retains a large percentage of starch well adapted to making vinegar. A German method of doing this with unripe fruit is as follows: They are to be grated, exactly as potatoes are prepared in the manufacture of starch, and the pulp passed through a moderately fine sieve, or through a coarse and open-meshed cloth. There is, thus, nothing left behind but the pomace proper, or cellulose, all the starchy matter having been passed through the sieve with the juice. This is next to be diluted with water in proportion to the quantity of starchy matter thus obtained; and the whole is then placed in the clean copper kettle, one or two per cent. of concentrated sulphuric acid being added, and heated long enough to transform the starch into grape sugar. The sulphuric acid is to be neutralized by means of carbonate of lime; the gypsum or the sulphate of lime thus produced allowed to settle, and the liquid to become clear, and then poured off. This liquid is to be left for fermentation to take place, either with or without the use of yeast. A liquid having eight or ten per cent. of sugar can easily be made to have four or five per cent. of alcohol after fermentation, which, by its subsequent acidification, will yield vinegar containing five to six per cent. of acetic acid, the usual strength. In the making of commercial vinegar, the basis of the manufacture depends upon alcohol, obtained from starch and sulphuric acid forming starch sugar, from weak alcoholic washes adulterated with sulphuric acid, or from alcohol obtained from the refuse wash of distilleries, or made direct from grain. Thus many years ago, a patent was taken for making vinegar from distillery wash as follows: The substance claimed is the swill grains or the exhausted liquor of distilleries. In all operations conducted in the large way, and especially where there are chemical processes depending on affinity, and that again on slight changes, such as strength of the materials, temperature, and other modifying causes, the chemical changes of one stage of the process are rarely completed before another is commenced; and thus more or less material is necessarily lost in all great manufacturing establishments. Thus in distilleries which to be profitable must be conducted on a large scale, the fermentation of the grain, in order to save the largest amount of alcoholic liquid, is disturbed before the process of fermentation is completed, and consequently a portion of sugar, of starch, and of dextrine, are left in the waste liquor or swill after distilling off the alcohol, which, if allowed to ferment again by a moderate temperature, will soon run into the acetic fermentation and vinegar will be produced. Hitherto the swill has been used only for feeding cows and swine; the inventor however, availing himself of the new German, or quick process of making vinegar, has been enabled by devices for separating the solid matters which would otherwise clog the apparatus and impede the process, to convert the swill into a vinegar to be used in the manufacture of white lead, sugar of lead, Paris green, and in other salts called acetates.

VINEYARD. The cultivation of vineyards has always occupied the attention of man from the earliest ages, and the grape has become one of the most celebrated fruits in history both from its product in wine, and from the value of its fruit in a sanitary point of view and as a dessert fruit. In the article Grape, we have given space to the cultivation of the grape with special reference to the value of the fruit as a market crop. In the article Wine, the manufacture of the juice is treated of. The home vineyard may be managed in the most simple manner. The commercial vineyard must be managed with scientific accuracy, to prevent loss in cultivation, pruning, gathering and marketing. In the home vineyard there can not be much choice of location. It must be near the house, for expeditious use, or the thought of a vineyard must be abandoned. In a commercial vineyard a site must be selected that will present the best conditions of soil, exposure, and facilities for marketing. At the home vineyard, the training and pruning may be pretty much to suit the whim of the cultivator. The trellis for particular reasons, being generally adopted, notwithstanding it has been time and again demonstrated that the simple system of training to poles is not only cheapest but also the best, though it must be confessed that if sufficient care be exercised, great crops may be grown either in the commercial or home vineyard upon trellises. The cut given will show the manner of training. In this article it will not again be necessary to go into the systems of cultivation. There are works extant that would fill a large library upon grape culture, and manuals devoted to each separate branch of the business, and also to the cultivation of special varieties. We shall, therefore, content ourselves, here, with a view, taken from United States statistics, showing the status of grape culture in the several States of the Union, embracing varieties popular as table fruit; wine grapes; varieties principally grown; those giving the heaviest must on the sugar scale; varieties most subject to rot; effect of shelter to prevent mildew; effect of soil in reference to rot in berry; soils chemically considered most favorable to health and perfection of fruit; effect of drainage, etc. To prevent confusion and as a means of separating the titles, they are presented in the form of questions and answers; varieties named being in order according to their estimated value:

What varieties are most popular as table fruit? Arkansas: Catawba, Delaware. Connecticut: Concord, Delaware. Delaware: Concord. Georgia: Herbemont, Scuppernong. Illinois: Concord, Delaware, Concord, Hartford Prolific, Isabella, Diana. Indiana: Concord, Catawba, Delaware, Hartford Prolific, Isabella, Diana. Iowa: Concord, Delaware, Hartford Prolific, Clinton, Creveling. Kentucky: Concord. Ives. Delaware. Kansas: Delaware. Missouri: Concord, Catawba, Delaware, Hartford Prolific, Isabella, Diana, Iona. Minnesota: Delaware. Michigan: Concord, Delaware. Massachusetts: Concord, Delaware. New Jersey: Concord, Isabella, Delaware. North Ca olina: Scuppernong, Catawba. New York: Delaware, Iona, Catawba, Isabella, Concord, Salem, Diana, Adirondac, Hartford Prolific, Rebecca, Maxatawny, Ohio: Concord, Catawba, Delaware, Isabella, Iona, Roger's

TRELLISED GRAPES.

No. 15. Pennsylvania: Concord, Isabella, Catawba, Iona, Hartford Prolific, Diana, Israella. South Carolina: Scuppernong, Catawba, Isabella, Lenoir. Tennessee: Catawba, Isabella, Concord.

What varieties are in highest repute as wine grapes? Connecticut: Delaware, Concord. Georgia: Scuppernong. Illinois: Concord, Norton's Virginia, Catawb , Clinton, Delaware, Ives, Iona, Hartford Prolific Herbemont. Indiana: Catawba, Delaware, Ives, Concord. Norton's Virginia, Isabella, Iona, Clin'on. Iowa: Concord, Delaware, Clinton, Catawba. Norton's Virginia, Roger's No. 4. Kentucky: Catawba, (in old v neyards) Ives, Delaware. Kansas: Delaware. Missouri: Nor on's Virginia, Concord Catawaa, Delaware, Herbemont, Clinton, Ives. Minnesota: Concord, Michigan: Delawa e, Concord. Massachusetts: Concord, Delawa e. New Jersey: Delaware, Cl n on. North Carolina: Scuppernong. New York: Delaware, Iona, Catawba, Isabella, Concord, Clinton. Oporto. Ohio: C tawba, Delaware, Con ord, Clinton. Norton's Virgini . Clinton. Pennsylvan . : Catawba, Delaware, Isabella, Conc or , Cl n on, Ives. South Carolina: Scuppernong, Clinton. Wisconsin: Isabella, Catawba.

VINEYARD

What varieties are principally grown? Arkansas: Catawba, Concord. Connecticut: Hartford Prolific, Concord. Delaware: Concord. Georgia: Scuppernong. Illinois: Concord, Catawba, Clinton, Hartford Prolific, Delaware, Norton's Virginia, Isabella, Herbemont, Iona, Diana, Ives. Indiana: Concord, Catawba, Isabella, Delaware, Ives, Norton's Virginia, Clinton, Diana, Hartford Prolific, Iona. Iowa: Concord, Clinton, Norton's Virginia, Catawba, Roger's No. 4, Delaware. Kentucky: (old vineyards,) Catawba; (new vineyards,) Ives, Concord, Delaware, Diana, Norton's Virginia. Kansas: Concord. Missouri: Concord. Norton's Virginia. Catawba, Delaware, Clinton, Herbemont, Isabella. Iona. Minnesota: Concord, Northern Muscadine. Michigan: Concord. Massachusetts: Concord. New Jersey: Concord, Isabella. North Carolina: Scuppernong; New York: Isabella, Delaware, Concord. Catawba, Diana Iona, Clinton, Salem, Hartford Prolific. Ohio: Catawba, Concord. Isabella, Delaware, Ives Norton's Virginia, Clinton, Hartford Prolific, Diana. Pennsylvania: Concord, Isabella, Catawba, Iona, Diana, Hartford Prolific, Clinton, Creveling. South Carolina: Scuppernong. Catawba. Tennessee: Catawba. Wisconsin: Concord, Delaware.

What varieties give the heaviest must on the sugar scale? Connecticut: Delaware. Georgia: Pauline, Herbemont. Catawba, Scuppernong. Illinois: Delaware, Norton's Virginia, Catawba, Rulander, Concord, Herbemont, Clinton. Indiana: Catawba, Delaware, Ives, Concord. Iowa: Delaware, Norton's Virginia, Catawba, Concord, Clinton. Kentucky: Norton's Virginia. Kansas: Delaware. Missouri: Norton's Virginia, Delaware, Concord, Catawba. Minnesota: Delaware, Iona. Michigan: Delaware. Massachusetts: Delaware, Clinton, Concord. North Carolina: Scuppernong. New York: Delaware, Iona, Diana, Clinton. Ohio: Delaware, Catawba, Norton's Virginia, Concord. Pennsylvania: Delaware, Iona, Isabella, Catawba. South Carolina: Catawba, Pauline.

What varieties are most subject to leaf diseases, and to what extent are they injured? Arkansas: Isabella, badly; Concord, slightly. Connecticut: All varieties more or less except Ives. Georgia: Pauline, Herbemont, and all the varieties of the *Vitis Labrusca*. Illinois: Catawba, Delaware, Clinton, Isabella, Rebecca, Diana, Iona, Ives, Hartford Prolific, Maxatawny, Israella, Creveling. Indiana: Catawba, Delaware, Isabella, Cuyahoga, Iona, Israella, Concord, Diana. Iowa: Clinton, Catawba, Diana, Isabella, Rogers's Hybrids, Allen's Hybrid, Iona. Kentucky: Roger's Hybrids, Delaware, Clinton, Tokalon, and all varieties if pruned in summer. Kansas: Delaware, Catawba, about three-tenths. Michigan: Isabella, Delaware, Israella. Massachusetts: Delaware, Creveling, Israella, Hamburg; Creveling, four-tenths to five-tenths. New Jersey: Delaware, Creveling, Rebecca, Iona, Diana, Allen's Hybrid, Maxatawny. New York: Delaware, five-tenths; Adirondac, four-tenths; Walter, three-tenths; Allen's Hybrid, three-tenths; Israella, two-tenths; Concord, one-tenth; Diana, one-tenth; Rebecca, one-tenth; Iona, one-tenth; Israella, one-tenth. Ohio: Catawba, Delaware, Iona, Isabella, four-tenths to five-tenths; Rogers's Nos. 3, 4, 15, three-tenths to five-tenths; Allen's Hybrid, four-tenths; Israella, three-tenths; Clinton, Iona, Diana, one-tenth to three-tenths. Always most injurious to plants that are overloaded with fruit; prevents ripening of wood, and weakens the vitality of the plant. Pennsylvania: All varieties are subject to leaf blight, sometimes to the extent of seven-tenths of the foliage, except Concord Hartford Prolific, and Northern Muscadine. South Carolina: Catawba, Isabella. Tennessee: Isabella, very badly. Wisconsin: Little or no disease.

What varieties are most subject to rot, and to what extent? Arkansas: Clinton. Connecticut: Diana. Georgia: Catawba, Isabella, six-tenths. Illinois: Catawba, seven-tenths to entire; Isabella, five-tenths to eight-tenths; Clinton, four-tenths to six-tenths; Creveling, five-tenths to seven-tenths; Diana, five-tenths; Taylor's Bullet, three-tenths; Tokalon, three-tenths; Iona, four-tenths; Rebecca, three-tenths; Concord cracks. Indiana: Catawba, three-tenths to eight-tenths; Isabella, three-tenths to eight-tenths; Diana, three-tenths to five-tenths; Concord, two-tenths. Iowa: Catawba, five-tenths to eight-tenths; Diana, four-tenths; Isabella and Clinton, three-tenths; Concord, one-tenth. Kentucky: Roger's Hybrids, Iona, Catawba. Kansas: Catawba rots badly in wet seasons. Missouri: Catawba, Isabella, Iona, Tokalon. Michigan: Catawba, Isabella. Massachusetts: Diana; very little in other varieties. New Jersey: Isabella in wet locations only. North Carolina: Catawba. New York: Catawba, three-tenths to four-tenths; Concord, one-tenth to two-tenths; Diana and Delaware on low, alluvial lands are subject to rot to a great extent. Ohio: Catawba, three-tenths to eight-tenths; Isabella, three-tenths to six tenths; Israella, three-tenths; Diana and Iona, three-tenths; Concord, one-tenth to three-tenths. Pennsylvania: Catawba and Isabella, very badly, frequently to the extent of eight-tenths. South Carolina: Catawba, Warren. Tennessee: Isabella and Catawba very badly after bearing two or three crops of fruit. Wisconsin: Allen's Hybrid, three-tenths.

What effect has shelter or protection, of any kind, in preventing leaf diseases? Arkansas: Sheltered trellis effectually prevents leaf diseases. Connecticut: Very little effect. Georgia: Always fair when grown in trees. Illinois: Favorable wherever tried; even slightly-covered trellis insures against mildew; protection will insure fair crops in the most unfavorable seasons. Indiana: Beneficial where tried. Iowa: Good where it has been tried. Kentucky: A beneficial effect to all tender-leaved varieties. Missouri: Where tried has exerted a favorable influence. Massachusetts: Beneficial by increasing the temperature. New York: Favorable where it does not prevent a free circulation of air. Ohio: Vines trained against buildings and on covered trellises are free from leaf diseases, instances are known of successful culture of uncertain varieties under shelter, successive crops for thirteen years having been raised. South Carolina: Most excellent effect; prevents leaf diseases. Tennessee: Vines protected by projecting eaves or copings always do well.

What effect has soil in reference to rot in the berry? Illinois: Low, wet soils almost invariably produce rot in the berry; rich lands also seem to induce rot in the berry. Indiana: Wet and rich soils are the prevailing causes of rot in the berry. Iowa: Undrained clay soils cause rot. Kentucky: Stiff, retentive subsoils, keeping water near the surface, produce rot. Kansas: Very rich soils cause rot in the grape. Missouri: Rot in the berries is very rare, and is seen on rich or heavy clay soils only. Massachusetts: Not liable to rot on dry soils. New Jersey: In wet seasons and on wet soils we have rot in the berries. North Carolina: The rot is frequently disastrous on rich or retentive soils. New York: Only on low grounds and wet subsoils. Ohio: Heavy wet soils are extremely pernicious, and thought to be the primary cause of rot; drained soils, even clays, are almost entirely exempt. Pennsylvania: The rot is most destructive on undrained, heavy clays, but is also induced by over-manuring and enriching the soil. South Carolina: Seldom escape rot in the berries, on heavy, damp soils.

What soils, chemically considered, are most favorable to health and vigor of plant, and perfection of fruit? Arkansas: A reddish clay soil, intermingled with sand, is the most congenial, so far as experience confirms; on pure clays the crop has failed. Connecticut: A good depth of limy, loamy soil is best. Georgia: Soils containing alkaline phosphates, and considerable humus, are most productive, and maintain healthy plants. Illinois: Silicious and calcareous soils are well suited; also gravelly clay soils, if somewhat rolling on the surface; clay subsoils are very good, if not too wet; especially so if they contain some iron and lime. Indiana: Grapes do well on clays if properly drained and limed; also very fairly on gravelly and sandy soils when properly worked. Iowa: The vines seem to do equally well either on silicious, calcareous, or gravelly soils, where the last is not too poor or light. Shales are very good. Clayey soils produce the richest fruit, but sandy soils the greatest amount of vine. Kentucky: Soils containing much oxide of iron seem to favor the rot. Kansas: A sandy clay soil is best for grapes. Missouri: The most favorable soils are those of a silicious and calcareous nature, containing magnesian limestone, with potash and phosphates; clay soils are very good, but they must be drained. Michigan: The earliest and sweetest fruit is produced on clay soils, but sandy soils give the largest and best yielding fruit. Massachusetts: Where the growing season is short, a dry sandy soil is preferable. North Carolina: A light sandy loam gives best results. New York: Calcareous and aluminous soils abounding in phosphates; shaly soils are always good. Ohio: Calcareous and aluminous soils, well drained; also rotten shales. Pennsylvania: Calcareous soils in combination with iron; shaly and silicious soils are very well adapted. South Carolina: The varieties of *Vitis estivalis* prefer silicious soils; the varieties of *Vitis vulpina*, those of an aluminous character; and the varieties of *Vitus rotundifolia* do equally well in either; as a general rule, light soils are best if supplied with lime and potash. Wisconsin: A loose limestone soil is perhaps the most favorable; sandy clay soils are also good, but very stiff clays are not so profitable.

What effects have been observed from mechanical conditions of soils, such as draining, subsoiling and other cultural operations? Arkansas: Subsoiling and trenching have worked wonders for good. Connecticut: Draining is indispensable in order to get the grape to grow in originally wet soils. Illinois: Draining, trenching, and good culture are necessary; the soil should be well pulverized and manipulated before planting. Indiana: Draining seems indispensable in most soils; subsoiling and good culture generally are always attended with marked results. Iowa: Deep plowing, in conjunction with draining and subsoiling, prevents rot to a very great extent. Kentucky: Draining and subsoiling pay well. Kansas: We find the best results on drained soils, and shallow after culture.

Missouri. The yield of fruit is largely increased by draining, trenching and subsoiling. Massachusetts: Draining is useful. North Carolina: Two products are greatly improved by proper stirring and culture of the soil. New York: Draining and subsoiling are of essential benefit, making the growth more certain, and preventing injury from drought. Ohio: Very dry soils are vastly improved by trenching; draining is indispensable in stiff clays, and subsoiling favorable; good clean culture will always be attended by best crops. Pennsylvania: Under-draining is always attended with good results in tenacious soils. South Carolina: Draining is absolutely necessary in clay soils; subsoiling is useful in alumi,ous lands, but of no use in silicious soils. Tennessee: Draining and deep culture, especially on poor soils, are of great benefit. Wisconsin: Deep culture is necessary in dry summers.

What effect has elevation upon the health of the vine? Give results of observations, and opinions as to the proper height above valleys. Arkansas: Other things being appropriate, we prefer low situations, because they are sheltered from heavy storms. Connecticut: No difference if the ground is dry in the valleys. Illinois: Elevated rolling lands are decidedly the best, but elevation is not so important when near large bodies of water; near small streams, or in valleys distant from water, an elevation of from one hundred and fifty to two hundred and fifty feet is much preferable; very liable to freeze in low grounds. Indiana: An elevated position is always the best; grapes are healthier, with much less disposition to rot, even to wet seasons. Iowa: An elevation of fifty to two hundred feet above streams has proved best. Kentucky: There is no question but that elevated sites are to be preferred, where the air can circulate freely, and be protected from slight frosts. Kansas: Elevations of fifty to one hundred feet above valleys, with grounds sloping to the south, are the best. Missouri: Elevations of from three hundred to four hundred feet above the water-level have proved the very best, for health and value of products. Minnesota: The best vines are those cultivated on elevations one hundred to two hundred feet above the river. Massachusetts: Side hills (of no great elevation) with southern slopes are most favorable; northern slopes and low frosty hollows must be avoided here. North Carolina: The Scuppernoug grape does best in low lands, but other varieties succeed only on elevations; on the mountain sides, where we are exempt from occasional late and early frosts, failure has never been known; in low valleys they are destroyed by blight and rot. New York: Our best vineyards are on considerable elevations, from fifty to four hundred feet above the valley. On these high lands we are not subject to early frosts in autumn, and the vine is healthier generally than in low grounds. Ohio: Elevations are considered good, but opinions differ as to height; some prefer being within range of fogs; fifty to three hundred feet above creeks and small streams exempts from early fall frosts, and vineyards are generally more healthy; where there are large bodies of water, elevation seems of but little consequence. Pennsylvania: Elevations of from two hundred to four hundred feet are safer in early and late frosts, and both the fruit and the vines are superior to the production of low grounds. South Carolina: The best grape region is that above the frost-belt on the mountain slopes; this is clearly indicated by the fact that a diseased grape leaf or berry has never been seen on these elevated lands. Tennessee: We find decidedly the best grapes on elevated positions. Wisconsin: Elevations are subject to destructive wind-storms.

Has any variety of the foreign grape proved remunerative in vineyard culture? The returns uniformly express a negative answer to this question.

What is the effect of summer pruning, and what method of winter pruning is best? Arkansas: Judicious summer pruning assists in developing the fruit; any system of renewal is good for winter pruning. Connecticut: Vines that are allowed to run all summer without pruning invariably yield large crops. Delaware: When summer pruning is judiciously performed, it has a tendency to increase the quantity and quality of the fruit; and also tends to promote maturity of growth. Georgia: We find summer pruning injurious. Illinois: All known methods of pruning are more or less practiced. Summer pruning is considered hurtful, according to its severity. Cases are cited of severe summer pruning causing the loss of half of the crop. Indiana: Summer pruning should be limited; it is injurious if severe. All methods of renewal and spur methods of winter pruning are practiced. Iowa: Summer pruning is injurious, if it involves the removal of much of the foliage. A moderate pinching of the points of fruiting shoots checks growth and improves the fruit. The renewal and other systems of winter pruning are practiced. Kentucky: On the whole, summer pruning is considered injurious, and should be abandoned. Kansas: Summer pruning should be strictly confined to pinching out the points of shoots, and not removing them entirely. Missouri: Summer pruning is practiced to a moderate extent. The winter pruning takes place in November.

All modes are practiced. Michigan: Summer pruning is deemed hurtful when carried to any considerable extent. The winter pruning is on the renewal system. Massachusetts: Very little summer pruning. Winter pruning on the spur system. North Carolina: Summer pruning severely injures, and sometimes kills the vine in this locality. New York: Summer pruning is injurious, except so far as to check the growth of rampant shoots, or remove superfluous wood. All systems of winter pruning are practiced, but the renewal mode is preferred. Ohio: Summer pruning is injurious as an unqualified system, but is favorable to the extent of removing superfluous buds, and checking over luxuriant growth. Many systems of winter pruning are practiced, but the renewal system is preferred. The system of horizontal arms with spurs has resulted in comparative failure. Pennsylvania: Moderate summer pinching is favorable to increase in the size of fruit, but is likely to increase the present at the expense of subsequent crops. Winter pruning is varied, both the renewal and the spur system in various modifications being practiced. South Carolina: Summer pruning is not practiced. The renewal system has been adopted in winter pruning. Tennessee: No summer pruning done. Wisconsin: Summer pruning is found to be beneficial when done with judgment. Winter pruning is done in November.

What insects are most injurious to the vine, and what is the extent of the injury; and what remedies have proved efficient? Arkansas: The leaf roller is somewhat troublesome on all varieties, except the Scuppernong and Clinton. Connecticut: The thrips is sometimes very injurious. Delaware: A small curculio, is very destructive. Georgia: No trouble from insects. Illinois: The leaf folder, thrips, borer, and curculio are occasionally found in vineyards. Shaking and hand-picking are the only known remedies for the last named. Indiana: Insects are not troublesome, although rose bugs occasionally devastate the young fruit bunches. Iowa: The leaf roller and thrips are the principal insect enemies. The first named can be destroyed by dusting with hellebore powder. Kansas: The thrips is sometimes seen, but not to any great extent. Missouri: The rose bug, thrips, and some other insects are to be seen, but not to any great extent. Minnesota: No injury from insects. Massachusetts: Rose bugs are troublesome. New Jersey: Rose bugs sometimes destroy the crops. North Carolina: The Scuppernong grape is exempt from all insect enemies; other varieties are sometimes injured. New York: The grape beetle, thrips, rose bug, and caterpillar appear. Whale-oil soap and dusting with lime are good preventives. Ohio: A worm that eats its way from one berry to another does considerable injury. The thrips is most destructive upon thin and smooth-leaved varieties. They have been prevented by washing the vines with a mixture of soft-soap and sulphur in the fall after the decay of the foliage; also by fumigating with tobacco smoke on their first appearance. Lime and sulphur sprinkled on the leaves are also effective. The rose bug, steel-blue beetle, and curculio are occasionally troublesome. Pennsylvania: Various insects make their appearance, but none of them are very injurious, except the thrips in some dry seasons. South Carolina: The thrips is occasionally troublesome. Tennessee: No insects of any moment. Wisconsin: The thrips to a small extent.

According to the above reports, the most popular varieties for table use are, first, Concord; second, Delaware; and third, Catawba. Those in highest repute for wine, are first, Delaware; second, Concord; third, Catawba, and Scuppernong in the Southern States. The varieties principally grown are the Concord and Catawba, but the newer varieties are rapidly being disseminated, and their representative merits will be tested in a few years. On the must scale the Delaware shows the greatest uniform amount of sugar, next the Iona; the Catawba and Norton's Virginia are also favorably mentioned in this respect. In regard to mildew and other leaf diseases, no variety appears to be entirely exempt; Concord, Ives, Hartford Prolific, and Northern Muscadine appear to suffer the least, and it is probably owing to this exemption from severe leaf injury that these varieties are so prominent. Rot in the berry is almost as universal as leaf blights, nearly all the varieties being liable under certain conditions. If any exceptions are made they refer to the family of summer grapes, the cultivated varieties of which are the Elsinburgh, Norton's Virginia, Lenoir, Cunningham, Herbemont, etc.; these appear to be noted for their freedom from rot. Old vines are also more generally liable to rot than those in young plantations. Shelter from dews and other atmospheric changes is considered advantageous in modifying leaf diseases. It has long been observed that plants growing under the partial protection of the overhanging eaves of a building, also those allowed to ramify unmolested on the branches of trees, are generally exempt from injury. Covered trellises seem to exert a similar influence. The effects of soil with reference to rot in the berry seems to be very decided. Soils that retain water, as undrained clays, are very likely to rot the fruit of grapes, more especially when the plants are over four or five years old. Very rich bottom lands are also conducive to this disease. Wet seasons are more fatal than dry on any soil, the primary cause appearing to be an excess of water in the soil. The chemical constitution of the soil does not seem to exert any very marked influence on the growth of the vine; clayey soils produce the richest fruit as also the earliest ripe; the latter, however,

vineyard culture, a fact which should be considered by those who are still experimenting with foreign wine grapes east of the Rocky mountains. The table given below will be found valuable as showing, at a glance, the status of viniculture in the several States of the Union.
VIOLET. *Viola.* The pansy or heartsease, *V. tricolor*, is, or should be cultivated in every garden, since if protected in winter, it will give abundant bloom from May to August, and again in the fall. If placed in a cool moist, shady situation it will bloom all summer. Some European varieties of violets are sweet scented, ours are not, but they make up in beauty what they lose in perfume. We have eighteen species. The dog-tooth violet, should not be included. It is an *erythronium*, and belongs to the lilly family. If the seeds of pansy are started early in a hot bed and transplanted, they will bloom early in the season, giving an abundance of flowers.
VIREO. The fly catchers, are among our most useful and innocent birds. The principal species are red-eyed vireo, *V. olivaceous;* the warbling vireo, *V. gilvus;* the white-eyed vireo,

STATES.	Number of counties reported.	Total acreage planted.	Total acreage bearing.	Grapes produced (tons).	Grapes sold (pounds).	Wine manufactured (gallons).	Average cost per acre.	Average product per acre (pounds).	Average age product of wine per acre (gallons).	Average product per acre years, (gals).
Arkansas....										
Connecticut...	1	43	35	20	10,000	15,000	$300 00	6,000		250
Delaware										
Georgia										
Illinois	87	2,711	1,515	1415½	615,500	234,412	285 20	5,072	200	318½
Indiana........	11	149½	104	81	10,000	6,922	274 00	6,666⅜	250	300
Iowa..........	7	178	111	26	19,000	2,740	320 00	6,200		180
Kentucky.....										
Kansas										
Missouri......	19	1,528½	993	944½	217,000	183,116	341 50	6,900	483½	540
Minnesota ...	1	5	1	2	1,000	80				
Michigan	2	45	13	12	8,000	1,575	197 00			
Massachusetts.	2	94	38	15	10,00	2,000	400 00	7,000		
New Jersey...	1	50	40							
North C. rolina	2	200				5,000	40 00		700	450
New York	9	7,473	4,367	7,338	2,322,000	234,250	247 14	4,571		416⅝
Ohio	23	10,000	7,387	4,330½	4,818,000	384,012	274 00	3,475	320	199½
Pennsylvania..	5	1,101	612	1,030	1,402,500	34,100	140 00	3,000		200
South Carolina.	2	500	475	50		1,000	100 00	2 000	150	275
Tennessee						500				

depending upon the moisture of the season; success evidently depends rather upon its physical quality. The conviction is gradually gaining ground that all grape soils should be artificially drained, unless they actually rest on an extremely porous strata; deep culture, or rather deep preparation of the ground, is also strongly recommended in connection with draining, the two operations being of much benefit only when simultaneously performed; draining being of little value unless the soil is deeply cultivated, and deep culture of but little value unless the land is drained. The effect of elevation upon the health of the vine is considered as favorable; the reports are nearly unanimous on this point. Not only are high lands more favorably disposed to drainage facilities, but the greater immunity from late spring and early fall frosts is of vast importance. Localities contiguous to large bodies of water are pre-eminently favored in this respect, but small streams in sheltered valleys have an injurious rather than a beneficial influence. The returns are entirely unanimous in regard to the failure of the foreign grape in

V. noreboracensis; the solitary vireo, *V. solitarius* and the yellow-throated vireo, *V. flavifrons.* The species are all trim, delicate in plumage, indefatigable in the pursuit of insects, and should be protected so they may feel entirely at home about the house, barns, garden and orchard.
VIRGIN'S-BOWER. *Clematis.* The common Virgin's-bower, *C. Virginiana*, from its habit of climbing to the tops of young trees and covering them with gossamer-like blossoms. The whole species are perennial herbs or vines, a little woody and climbing by the twisting of the leaf stalk. The following species are native North except *C. cylindrica*, which occurs at Norfolk, Va. and South. Northern species are, *C. ochroleuca, C. viorna* and *C. Pitcheri.*
VITELLUS. An occasional covering of the embryo in seeds. The white of an egg.
VITREOUS HUMOR. The fluid or humor which fills the posterior chamber of the eye.
VITRIOL. An old name for the sulphates.
VITRIOL, OIL OF. Sulphuric acid.
VIVES. This is a chronic enlargement of the glands of the lower jaw, and extending to the

FARM WAGES,
By the Month and by the Day, in Harvest.

WITHOUT BOARD.			WITH BOARD.	
Wages during Harvest.	Monthly Wages by the Year.	STATES.	Monthly Wages by the Year.	Wages during Harvest.
$1.08	$12.10	South Carolina	$ 8.10	$ .78
1.20	12.86	North Carolina	8.80	.85
1.10	12.86	Georgia	8.70	.80
1.05	13.15	Alabama	9.00	.80
1.30	13.75	Tennessee	9.49	1.00
1.27	13.96	Virginia	9.17	.99
1.23	15.10	Mississippi	10.09	.95
1.52	16.31	Maryland	9.80	1.15
1.12	16.64	Florida	10.20	80
1.10	18.20	Louisiana	12.09	.85
1.60	18.20	Delaware	12.50	1.25
1.54	18.20	Kentucky	11.75	1.18
1.31	18.50	Arkansas	12.25	1.03
1.30	19.16	West Virginia	12.16	1.00
1.39	20.20	Texas	14.03	1.08
1.50	22.30	Missouri	13.95	1.23
1.73	22.58	Pennsylvania	14.21	1.30
1.80	23.14	Indiana	15.65	1.58
1.75	23.37	Vermont	16.00	1.35
1.89	23.63	New York	15.36	1.47
1.70	23.85	Kansas	15.87	1.33
1.91	23.91	Illinois	17.11	1.54
2.09	24.25	New Jersey	14.20	1.74
1.95	24.45	Nebraska	16.20	1.55
1.79	24.55	Ohio	16.30	1.41
1.52	24.75	Maine	16.75	1.22
1.71	25.25	New Hampshire	16.79	1.35
2.13	25.76	Michigan	17.27	1.76
2.25	26.21	Iowa	17.95	1.91
2.50	26.21	Wisconsin	17.60	2.10
2.61	26.36	Minnesota	17.75	2.16
1.60	27.75	Rhode Island	17.00	1.30
1.65	27.90	Connecticut	17.37	1.33
1.75	30.66	Massachusetts	18.25	1.35
1.92	33.50	Oregon	21.75	1.50
2.21	36.50	Colorado	27.08	1.80
2.20	38.25	California	23.45	1.80

mouth. These becoming tender, at length discharge. This may generally be met by painting the affected parts with tincture of iodine. If not, prepare for application to the skin, over the swelling, an ointment composed of one drachm of biniodide of mercury, well triturated with an ounce of lard. This may be repeated daily until a free secretion from the skin is accomplished.

VIVIPAROUS. Producing living young, and not eggs.

VOLATILE ALKALI. Crude ammonia. (See Nitrogen.)

VOLUTE. In architecture, a scroll.

VOLVA. The wrapper or veil of certain fungi, as the agaricus.

VULTURE. The *vulturidæ* are represented in the United States by three or four species, only two of which are of importance in agriculture—the Crow, (see Crow) and the turkey buzzard, *cathartes aura*. This species is found everywhere South, more rarely north of the Ohio river, and living on dead carcases and putrid flesh as scavengers, are beneficial and tolerated. From being carefully protected in the South, they become quite tame. As compared with the crow, they are not nearly so beneficial, since the crow subsists in the North almost entirely on insects and small animals, only depredating on corn when other food fails. South the vulture is a beneficial bird. North it is not known.

W

WACKE. A hard basaltic rock.

WALKS. Walks, drives and roadways, in the vicinity of the farm or rural dwelling, should be so carefully made that they are good at all times, and should approach as directly to the object sought as possible, and without unnecessary curves, especially short ones. Within the house place, curved lines are admissible and beautiful, and here much elaboration may be spent, and once decided on they must be carefully formed and carefully kept, for nothing looks so slovenly as weedy, untidy, half-formed walks or drives through the grounds or garden. Thus unnecessary walks and roads should always be avoided. In relation to walks and roads on the farm, but specially about the homestead: It is true that the beauty of curved lines sometimes prompts to a deviation from the more available direct course; and, where it can be done without too great sacrifice of utility, it is not objectionable. But no walk should be turned from its obvious direct course without an apparently sufficient reason. A change of level in the ground, a tree or a group of plants, or other similar obstruction, will induce, and seemingly demand, a change of line. There are many locations where the straight line should be preferred as a matter of taste in design. As a connecting link between the strictly horizontal and the perpendicular lines of a building, and the irregular surfaces surrounding it, a perfectly straight walk is in the best taste and adds greatly to the effect of the architecture, while a frequently curving walk detracts from it. So also, a walk along the side of a straight boundary fence should not curve if both lines are visible at the same time. Most persons are aware of the great beauty of straight walks and avenues of trees; and for public parks of lesser order, enclosed by formal outlines, they can always be introduced with great effect, as well as convenience, where curving walks would be the reverse. In this case beauty depends upon harmony rather than contrast, and more than either upon utility. When roads or walks are carried over irregular surfaces, the natural turns and windings necessary to follow an easy or uniform grade, and keep as near the original surface of the ground as possible, will usually develop pleasing curves. A little studied attention in this matter of the course of a road will not only increase the beauty of curves by adding to them the grace of utility, but also deep and expensive cuttings, as well as heavy embankments, will be avoided, and easy grades and economical construction be more certainly secured. When it is necessary to branch a secondary road from the main line, it should leave the latter at as nearly a right angle as convenient, and at the same time be somewhat narrower, so that its appearance may convey the proper idea of its being subordinate, and so avoid confusion and mistake; otherwise the roads leading to the stable, ice house, or garden, may be mistaken for the road to the mansion. Under no circumstances should walks be made conspicuous in views of natural scenery. If it is essentially necessary that a walk should cross a lawn where it would interrupt a continuity of view, and destroy breadth of effect, it should be sunk beneath the line of vision by placing it in a slight excavation, which may be further assisted by throwing up a small mound on the side nearest the point of view. These expedients, as also that of planting thick groups of low-growing shrubs, will be effective and satisfactory if properly executed. In laying out curving roads it is not advisable to closely follow geometrical rules, or to set the curves out to any regular radius. This plan may occasionally prove perfectly satisfactory on a strictly level surface, but it will have quite an opposite effect where the ground is greatly undulating. The curves, to be pleasing, must be attractive—not too sudden or abrupt—and properly blended at their points of junctions. Very much of personal comfort and pleasure in rural residences depends upon good roads. A smooth, firm, dry road is one of the greatest conveniences and enjoyments; while a rough, soft, muddy road is one of the greatest drawbacks and annoyances of country life. Bad roads form the greatest obstacles to progress and permanent improvements in all the neighborhoods that are blasted with their presence; they have a demoralizing effect upon the inhabitants, and are a sure sign either of poverty or mismanagement, or both. Water is the worst enemy to good roads. It is, therefore, a leading principle in road making so to construct them that they may be kept dry. In absence of a timely recognition of this principle, many costly roads have proved to be failures; but where it has had prominent recognition and its value has been properly appreciated, good roads have been made at a trifling expense. After locating the road and marking out its course, the sides should be brought to the proper grade and finished by a layer of sod as a guide to further operations. In crossing a sloping surface it is not necessary to have both sides perfectly level, but the nearer this can be secured, with due regard to getting rid of surface water, the better it will admit of a neat finish and the more easily will it be kept in repair. The road bed is then formed by excavating and removing the soil to a depth of six inches at the sides, curving slightly higher in the center, and made perfectly smooth by rolling, producing a uniform surface upon which the material of the road is to be placed. The best stone for road metal is tough granite. Hard brittle stone is more readily reduced by pressure, but in a well kept road this difference is not important. It is, however, all important that the stones should be broken small. The largest should easily pass through a two-inch ring, and if one-half of them are small enough to pass through a ring of only one inch in diameter, the road will ultimately become all the more compact. The road bed should be filled with this broken stone to a level with the sides, increasing in depth toward the center at the rate of one inch to the yard. Thus, a road sixteen feet in width would have a depth of about nine inches in the center. The utmost care should be applied to regulating the surface, and the smaller stones should be used on top, in order to secure an even, compact, carefully moulded grade, which should be compressed by repeatedly passing a heavy roller over it, wedging every stone, and making a surface almost as smooth and solid as a pavement. A thin layer, not more than one inch in thickness, of fine clayey gravel should then be evenly distributed over the stones, and the roller again applied until the surface becomes homogeneous, firm, and close. The surface of the road will thus be higher than the sodded edgings; water will therefore pass readily from it, and one of the main points of keeping a good road will be secured. This will form a first class road for ordinary carriage drives, or for all purposes required in public parks or private grounds; and, if kept in good surface by frequent rolling, so as to prevent the forming of ruts while it is settling; and, if a facing of gravel is applied when necessary, it will permanently fulfil all requirements of a good road. The quality of gravel deserves notice. Wash gravel, consisting only of sand and rounded pebbles, should never be used. No amount of pressure will render it firm, and it is the most disagreeable material to walk upon. The best gravel is that to be found in banks composed of pebbles mixed with reddish clay; and the stones must be small. No detail in road making is of so much importance as this. If a wagon wheel or the foot of a horse press on one extremity of a stone the other end of it will probably be slightly raised, allowing small particles of sand to fall into the crevice, when the stone is loosened, and will roll on the surface; hence the necessity of using only very finely divided stones on top, so that they will be smaller than the pressing point, and not become disarranged from leverage or compound action. Where stone can not conveniently be obtained, the road bed may be filled with refuse matters of many kinds, such as coal ashes, clinkers from furnaces, and shells. Oyster shells are plentiful in many places near the sea-board, and form an admirable road; but the permanency, as well as efficiency of these materials in a road bed, will depend altogether upon the care of surfacing with proper gravel. Where it is impracticable to procure, or deemed inexpedient to use, any of the foregoing materials, an earth road may be rendered very serviceable by proper attention to the leading principle—that is, to keep it dry. In this case, instead of excavating a road bed, slight excavations should be made at the sides and the material spread over the center; and that surface water may pass to the sides more rapidly and thoroughly, a greater convexity may be given to the curve. In some sections of the country good roads are kept up in this manner, but they are carefully repaired whenever necessary, and all ruts and tracks are filled up as soon as they are formed. The same general principles apply to the formation of walks and foot paths. The depth of material, however, need not exceed a few inches. It is certain that much unnecessary expense is frequently laid out upon mere foot walks. A porous, gravelly, or sandy soil is in itself a good walk if properly shaped. Such walks admit of greater convexity than carriage roads, which is equivalent to a saving of material. Walks should be well filled up. There is no more disagreeable object, or one that conveys so meager an expression, as deep, raw edgings to a walk, looking as if they had been trimmed with a plow. Walks in this condition may be serviceable as water courses, but they are not comfortable foot paths. (See also Roads, and Landscape Gardening.)

WALL EYE. Opacity of the cornea; glaucoma.

WALL-PLATE. A timber lying on a wall on which girders, joists, etc., rest.

WALNUT. *Juglans.* The Walnut is represented by two species, the butternut, *J. cinerea*, and the black walnut, *J. nigra*. The walnut family, *Juglandaceæ* indeed includes *carya*, or the hickories, yet the name walnut is not generally applied except to the two species mentioned. (See Black Walnut and Hickory.)

WARBLER. The warblers, are as a class beneficial to the farmer, living almost wholly on the seeds of weeds and small insects. Our so-called snow birds, or winter sparrows, belong to this class, as also does our summer yellow bird. Some of the warblers remain north during mild winters, and hence are often seen in flocks with snow birds about houses and barnyards, driven thence in search of food in extreme weather. This class generally nest far north, returning late in the autumn. The principal species are the Blue Yellow-backed warbler (*Parula Americana*), the Maryland Yellow throat (*Geothlypis trichas*), Yellow-breasted Chat (*Icteria virides*), Nashville Warbler (*Helminthophaga ruficapilla*), Black-throated Green warbler (*Dendroica virens*), Yellow-rump warbler, or myrtle birds (*D. coronata*), Pine-creeping warbler (*D. pinus*), Chestnut-sided warbler (*D. pennsylvanica*), Yellow warbler or Yellow bird (*D. æstiva*), Black-pall warbler (*D. striata*), and the Prairie warbler (*D. discolor*)

WARBLES. Under this name, and also Grubs and Sitfast, are designated the presence of hard lumps, proceeding originally from swelling of the glands at the roots of the hair, occurring generally at the neck, withers and back and at the roots of the mane and tail, generally appearing in the spring. They are inflamed follicles, which break and suppurate, and often end in small ulcers difficult to heal, where they are irritated by the harness or otherwise. They sometimes assume a malignant character which may end in mortification, or an inflamed ring around a whitish central path. It is then termed sitfast and is difficult to heal. In the more simple forms of the disease, when the pimples are ulcerating, they should be poulticed to promote suppuration, but with this in any case to alter the secretions the animal's bowels should be prevented from becoming costive, and an ounce of sulphur should be given in the feed once a day. If the sores seem to need a greater stimulation than poulticing will give, the following resolvent may be used as an ointment: One part of biniodide of mercury and seven parts of neatsfoot oil. Rub all well together and apply every day with gentle friction until the skin is excited or somewhat inflamed. If the difficulty ends in sitfast, cut out the hard part or dead skin in the center, and cover the whole with crude petroleum, or better dress with an ointment of one drachm of carbolic acid and three ounces of lard.

WARREN. A place in which rabbits or other game are preserved, or in which they are naturally found.

WASH. The fermented liquor from which spirit is distilled.

WASHER. In building, a plate of iron set between a wall and timber, and the nut of a screw.

WASP. *Hymenoptera.* Insects having four membraneous wings, biting jaws and a sting in the extremity of the abdomen, bees, hornets, ants, gall flies, ichneumon flies and saw flies belong to the order, Hymenoptera. The class are mostly beneficial, the principal exceptions being the saw flies, (*Tenthredinida*,) the boring or wood wasps, (*Urocerida*,) and the gall flies (*Cynipidæ*.) When wasps build their nests, in trees near dwellings, or in the ground where their disturbance may be annoying, they may be destroyed in the first instance by syringing kerosene into their quarters at night and firing it. When found in the ground, pour kerosene over and into the nest and fire it immediately.

WATER. (See Meteorology, Moisture, Rain and Vapor.)

WATER CHESTNUT. *Scirpus tuberosus.* A rush cultivated in China and Italy for its root, which resembles a chestnut. It grows in ponds and ditches.

WATER CRESS. (See Cress.)

WATER PEPPER. (See Smartweed.)

WATERMELON. *Cucurbita citrullus.* Whatever has been said as to the cultivation of squash, muskmelon, etc., will apply to the watermelon. The varieties, generally cultivated, are the Carolina, Ice Cream, Imperial, and Mountain Sweet. The orange melon is small, early, of good flavor, the meat cleaving away from the rind. The Phinney, is one of the best early sorts and Haskell's, improved one of the best of the large late sorts. (See Melon).

WATER PEPPER. (See Smartweed).

WATER OF CRYSTALLIZATION. Water contained in crystals.

WATER PLANTAIN. The genus *Alisma,* consisting of useless water weeds.

WAVELLITE. A mineral of a radiated or stellated character, consisting of a hydrated phosphate of alumina.

WAX. Various plants are wax producing, among the most noted are the wax palm of Brazil, (*Copernicia cerifera*); the wax palm of New Granada, (*Ceroxylon andicola*); of Japan wax, produced from the fruit of (*Rhus succedanea*, and also *R. ve nicifera*); Peetha wax, from the fruit of the white gourd of India, (*Benincasa cerifera*;) Fig wax, a secretion of the (*Ficus cerifera*, a native of the island of Sumatra. Wax of the *Cordilleras*, a green resinous waxy matter secreted by the stipules which envelop the unexpanded buds of (*Escagia nitida*) (*Cinchonaceæ*) used as a varnish for various useful and ornamental objects. The candleberry or myrtle wax is yielded by the genus Myrica, widely prevalent in both hemispheres, principally in the temperate regions thereof; in the Azores, China, the Cape of Good Hope, Europe, Japan, Northern India, and North and South America. The North American species are, *Myrica cerifera*, and *M. Carolinensis*, the latter being the most valuable, yielding one pound of wax to four pounds of berries, and when burned diffusing a delightful odor, even some time after extinction.

WAYFARING TREE. The guelder rose. *Viburnum opulus.*

WEALDEN FORMATION. A portion of the upper secondary, consisting of heavy clays and green sand. It is remarkable for the great number of large saurians it contains.

WEASEL. *Putoria.* Usually regarded as verminous, and worthy of death wherever found, from the fact that they will destroy poultry. From the fact that they will destroy or drive away rats, wherever they are protected, the probabilities are that it should be classed among beneficial vermin, since it is easy to protect poultry against their ravages. The lesser weasel (*P. pusillus*) is the common species East and West. It is said to become white in the northern fur regions, but in more temperate regions it retains its brown color in winter. The small, brown weasel (*P. cicognani*) *fuscus*) is another common species and more destructive to poultry than the preceding. The white weasel or American ermine (*P. noveboracensis*) is common east of the Mississippi, in the North, and is fierce, cruel, and sanguinary, boldly attacking animals four or five times its size. Unlike the true ermine, its fur is worthless, and it should be destroyed whenever found.

WEATHER-BOARDING. Boarding nailed either upright or horizontally, and lapping on the outside of the framing.

WEATHER GLASS. A barometer.

WEB WORMS. Web worms are that class of caterpillars which feed on the leaves of trees,

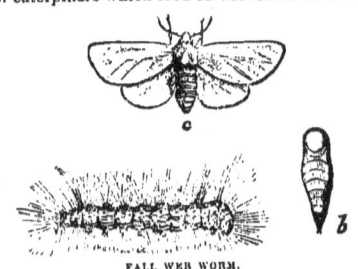

FALL WEB WORM.

and protect themselves by means of webs, within which they feed or else congregate at night. The webs are not only unsightly, as seen on the fruit trees, but they are among the most destructive of leaf-eating insects. They should be destroyed wherever found, and also should be carefully looked for that they may be destroyed while yet young, and before they have done much damage. The cut shows one of the most destructive of these caterpillars, the Fall Web Worm, (*Hyphantria textor*) *a*, larva or caterpillar, *b*, pupa, *c*, perfect insect or moth. The only remedy is by hand picking or thrusting a broom or brush into the webs, and winding them in it with their webs.

WEDGE. One of the simple mechanical powers, the efficiency of which is proportional to the length of the side. Knives are wedges.

WEED. (See Shot of Grease.)

WEEDS. Any plant growing where it is not wanted may truly be classed as a weed. The name, however, is only properly applied to those plants not valuable in agriculture. So long as the slovenly farmer, who grows weeds, can get nearly or quite as much for his illy cleaned grain, the work of extermination would seem hopeless. How serious this evil is the following facts will show, for if we consider the immense number of weed seeds that are mingled among our seeds, we would be at no loss to account for the growth of these pests in our fields. Prof. Buckman discovered, in a pint of cloverseed, 12,600; in broad clover, 39,440; and two pints of Dutch clover yielded, severally, 25,560 and 70,460 weed-seeds. Supposing these samples to be sown, here were seeds enough to stock the land with weeds for many years. If we take into account the great fecundity of some weeds, we will not feel the least astonished at the increase of the plants when the seeds are sown, and the plants allowed to arrive at maturity. Prof. Buckman has counted 8,000 seeds in a single plant of black mustard, and in a specimen of charlock 4,000 seeds. The common stinking chamomile produces 46,000, and the burdock 26,000 seeds; and the seeds of a single plant of the common dock produced 1,700 little docks. It is found that a single plant of the common groundsel will produce 6,500 seeds in one summer. The graceful corn cockle sheds 2,600 productive seeds; and the red poppy, which diversifies our corn fields and looks so gay upon our hedges, produces 50,000 minute but vital seeds. The corn sow-thistle launches out into the wind its 20,000 flossy parachutes to take root far away. The common dock lets fall 13,000 solid grains, each destined to shoot down a tap root into the soil. Dandelion produces nearly 3,000 seeds, each furnished with an inimitable apparatus for distant flight. The cow-parsnip, if neglected, will produce 5,000 plants; the meadow scabious, 4,000; the maywced, 45,000; the daisy, 13,500. Says the *North British Agriculturist*: Alexander II of Scotland denounced that man to be a traitor who poisons the king's lands with weeds, and introduces a host of enemies. Whoever was found to have three heads of common star-wort among his corn, was fined a sheep for each stalk. In Denmark the farmers are bound by law to destroy the corn-marigold, and in France a farmer may sue his neighbor who neglects to eradicate the thistles upon his land at the proper season. A law is in operation in Australia to the same effect, and it is proposed to introduce a similar enactment into the Canadian code. Nor have suggestions for such enactments been wanting in England. A clause enforcing the extirpation of weeds in hedges, or along the sides of roads, passed through the House of Commons, but it was for some reason negatived by the Lords. To come to the practical extermination of weeds in the United States, we have found that legislation is of but little avail, it is too difficult to enforce laws relating to the killing of weeds. Each person must exterminate weeds for himself. Fortunately those who do so most carefully are not only the best farmers, but also find their profit in so doing. As to what weeds are, they have been defined, as before stated, as being any plant whatever, out of place. That is wheat or Indian corn if growing anywhere, if not grown for profit, would be, or should be, considered a weed. Yet the more proper appellation of weeds are those plants noxious or not profitable to the cultivator. The late Dr. Darlington has given the most comprehensive and graphic monogram, originally written for the United States government, that we have seen, arranged according to the natural method or according to the plan adopted by Hooker, Torrey, Gray, etc., giving the authentic scientific names of the genera and species so all may be able to understand them, and also the common names so far as they can be traced. Our author has so classified them that the reader will find no difficulty in the reading. The list is given in the author's style and language as follows: In this article the plants are divided into *Phænogamous*, or flowering plants, and *Cryptogamous*, or flowerless plants; also into exogenous plants, or outside growers, as the oak; and endogenous plants, or inside growers, as Indian corn. (p.) denotes a perennial plant; (b.) a biennial; (a.) an annual, and (s.) a woody shrub or small tree.

DIPETALOUS EXOGENS—THE PETAL MOSTLY DISTINCT.

Ranunculus bulbosus. Buttercup, bulbous crowfoot, (p). This foreigner is extensively naturalized in grass plots, meadows, and low ground pastures along our streams, where it is regarded as a nuisance by the farmers. The fleshy bulb is highly acrid, and the plant when once introduced is difficult to subdue. The most effective remedy yet found is to get the plant closely depastured in early spring by stock, especially sheep. Another perennial species, viz: *Racris*, or tall crowfoot, is naturalized in New England, and is as obnoxious as its congener.

Delphinium consolida. Field Larkspur, (a.) This introduced plant has strayed from the gardens in many places, and is an unwelcome intruder in grain fields and other cultivated grounds. This and a kindred species (*D. ajacis*) have become so common in gardens that some attention is requisite to prevent them from trespassing on the farms. Plants which have matured their seeds in the garden should never be carried to the barnyard nor permitted to mingle with farm manures, otherwise the fields will be speedily infested with worthless and pernicious weeds. A slight plowing after the removal of the crops from the fields will favor the germination of the seeds, which will be destroyed by the regular plowing of the field.

Papaver eubium. Field Poppy, (a.) This foreigner has found its way into some districts, and, if unattended to, may become a troublesome weed, as it and the Corn Poppy (*P. rhoeas*) are in Europe. A similar remark is applicable to the Prickly Mexican Poppy (*Argemone Mexicana*) another kindred weed which has been introduced. This pl at should be extirpated by hand-weeding before the ripening of the seed. In Italy the prickly poppy became so obnoxious as to be called infernal fig.

Camelina sativa. Wild Flax, gold of pleasure, (a.) A naturalized foreigner, and, where neglected, becoming a great nuisance—formerly supposed by the simple and credulous to be a sort of transmuted or degenerate flax. It has been subdued by annual plowing, so managed as to allow the seeds to vegetate, and thus destroy the young plants before the seeds on them are matured.

Capsella bursa-pastoris. Shepherd's purse, (a.) A worthless little intruder from Europe, but the valuable grasses will generally choke out such small weeds.

Raphanus raphanistrum. Wild Radish, jointed charlock, (a.) A naturalized weed, becoming a nuisance in the Northern States. It has already invaded New England and Pennsylvania, and is tending westward. The seeds are contained in a jointed pod, and are thus protected from the severity of frost and concealed from birds until liberated by the process of decay of the pod.

Hypericum perforatum. St. John's Wort, (p.) A foreign weed, formerly supposed to cause cutaneous ulcers in white cows and on horses with white feet and noses; but, the disease disappearing, that notion seems to have become obsolete.

Agrostemma githago. Cockle, rose campion, (b.) A well known foreign weed infesting wheat fields. The black-coated seeds, when abundant and ground with wheat are injurious to the appearance of the flour. The root of this plant should be cut below the surface with a chisel fastened to a long handle and wielded by children. If this is neglected in the early part of the season, the fields should be scarified immediately after the removal of the crops to favor the germination of the seed, and ultimate destruction by fall ploughing and the frost. The seed obtained from the screening of cereals should not be thrown out upon the manure heap, but fed to fowls, and the refuse left by them should be burned the next day.

Abutilon avicennæ. Indian Mallow, velvet leaf, (a.) This foreigner, hitherto regarded as a worthless and troublesome intruder in Indian corn fields, potato patches, and other cultivated lots, has been recently announced (together with *Hibiscus moschatos* a malvaceous perennial, native of our maratime marshes,) as yielding a fibrous bark suitable for textile purposes, similar to the Jute of commerce, obtained from Asiatic species of corchorus, and employed in the manufacture of gunny bags. The economical value of this material, which is termed American Jute, must be ascertained by experience.

Rhus venenata Poison Sumach, poison elder.(a.) A noxious shrub frequent in moist, low grounds, by which many persons are liable to be badly poisoned. A similar cutaneous affection is often produced by the climbing variety of another species--the *Rhus toxicod ndron,* Poison Vine or Oak.

Trifolium arvense. Stone Clover, Welsh clover, rabbitfoot, (a.) This foreign plant is only entitled to notice on account of its worthlessness and prevalence in poor, old fields. Its presence is a pretty sure indication of a thin soil and neglected agriculture, and the obvious remedy is to improve both.

Potentilla Canadensis. Cinquefoil, fivefinger, (p.) The varieties of this are rather harmless, though worthless native weeds, and are merely indications of a neglected soil. There is also a coarse, erect, homely, annual species, *P. norvegica,* which is becoming a frequent weed in the Middle States, and seems to have migrated from the North.

Rubus villosus. Blackberry Bramble, common brier, (p.) Every one knows the common brier; the fruit in its season is a general favorite, and some remarkably fine varieties have been produced under careful culture. The tendency of the plant, however, to spread and take possession of neglected fields, causes it to be regarded as something of a nuisance where it prevails. Another and kindred species, the *R. cuncifolius,* or Sand Blackberry, has found its way into Pennsylvania, apparently from New Jersey, and bids fair to establish itself in the land of Penn. Fence angles and waste places in which the briers have obtained a foothold should be cleaned of a 1 weeds twice yearly, in spring and autumn. This will not only exterminate the briers, but admit air and light to the field borders, otherwise shaded.

Rubus Canadensis. Dewberry, running brier, (p.) Our American dewberry is a fine fruit, and generally preferred to all the blackberries proper, but it is not the dewberry of England, which is the *Rubus cæsius* of Linnæus. There is scarcely a farmer's boy in Pennsylvania who is not well acquainted with our plant, from having encountered its prickly, trailing stems with his naked ankles while heedlessly traversing the old fields where it abounds On well managed farms, however, this and all other species of brier, (not excepting our native raspberries) are becoming rare.

Rosa Carolina. This is often an obnoxious plant in wet meadows and low grounds, forming unsightly thickets with other weeds if neglected. Another native species, *R. lucida,* the Dwarf Wild Rose, is quite frequent in neglected grounds. The foreign Sweet Brier, *Rosa Rubiginosa,* is naturalized in many localities and deemed a trespasser.

Sicyos angulatos. One-seeded Star Cucumber. This climbing vine, with leaves resembling those of the cucumber, is a native weed, and a vile nuisance when admitted into gardens and cultivated lots.

Daucus carota Wild Carrot, (b.) When this wild variety of the common garden carrot becomes thoroughly naturalized, as it is now on many farms in the middle States, it is a troublesome weed, and requires persevering vigilance to get rid of it. It should be diligently eradicated before it ripens its seeds. In case of snow, with a smooth surface crust, the mature umbels break off and are driven by the wind to a great distance, and thus annoy an extensive district. Another umbelliferous nuisance is created by permitting the valuable garden parsnip *Pastinaca sativa,* to disseminate itself and multiply rapidly in adjoining fields, and along fence rows, giving to the farms a very slovenly appearance.

Archemara rigida. Cowbane, wild parsnip, (p.) This native weed occurs frequently in swampy meadows, and is reputed to be an active poison when eaten by horned cattle, which, however, probably seldom happens, unless the pasture is very deficient.

Ægopodium podagraria. Goat Weed, (p.) A foreign weed, troublesome and difficult to eradicate.

Cicuta maculata Water Hemlock, spotted cowhane, musquash root, (p.) The root of this is poisonous, and proves fatal to children who collect and eat it by mistake for the root of sweet cicely, *oemorrhiza longistylis.* It is found indigenous along rivulets and margins of swamps, and should be carefully eradicated.

Conium maculatum. Common or Poison Hemlock, (b.) A poisonous and dangerous weed, introduced from Europe, and occasionally met with about old settlements. It is supposed to be the identical herb with which the ancient Greeks put their philosophers and statesmen to death when they got tired of them.

GAMOPETALOUS EXOGENS—PETALS MORE OR LESS UNITED.

Sambucus Canadensis. Common Elderbush, (s.) This indigenous shrub is very tenacious of life, and inclined to spread extensively along fence-rows and hedges, giving the premises a very slovenly appearance.

Dipsacus sylvestris. Mill Teasel, wild teasel, (b.) This coarse European weed is completely naturalized in some localities, and is not only worthless, but threatens to become a nuisance if not attended to.

Vernonia noveboracensis. Wild Iron Weed, (p.) A coarse native plant, quite common in moist, low grounds, and along fence-rows The root of this must be cut like the Canada thistle before the flowering season in spring, or the danger will be imminent of its over-running the whole area in a short period by means of its floating seeds

Eupatorium purpureum. Trumpet Weed, joe-pye weed, (p.) Several varieties of this tall, stout weed are indigenous on our moist low grounds.

Aster ericoides. Heath-like Aster, (p.) Numerous species of this large American genus meet the eye of the farmer, in the latter part of summer, in his woodlands, low grounds, borders of thickets, etc., some of which are quite ornamental, but the little bushy one here mentioned is about the only one which invades our pastures to any material extent. In neglected old fields, it often becomes as abundant as it is always a worthless weed.

Erigeron canadense. Horse Weed, butter weed, (a.) This American weed has diffused itself all over our country, and it is said, has reached and pervaded all Europe. The cultivation of hoed crops will clear the fields of this pest. Other varieties of the same genus infest meadows, which, if the evil becomes too burdensome, must be plowed up.

Erigeron strigosum, Flea-bane Daisy, (a.) This very common native weed is apt to be abundant in the first crop of upland meadow after the usual routine grain crop. After that, especially in good lands, it becomes more rare, being probably choked out, like many other weeds, by the valuable grasses.

Solidago nemoralis. Golden Rod, (p.) Several species of golden rod occur along fence rows, borders of woods and thickets, and intrude upon neglected pasture fields.

Ambrosia trifida. Great Rag Weed, (a.) A coarse, ugly native weed, common in waste places.

Ambrosia artemisifolia. Bitter Weed, rag weed, (a.) This indigenous, bushy weed, occurs in most cultivated grounds, and is most abundant among the stubble, after a crop of wheat. But if the land be good, the plant seems to be smothered or choked out the next season by the usual succeeding crop of clover and the grasses. It is always ready, however, to make its appearance whenever the grassy turf is broken up by the plow.

Xanthium strumarium. Clot-weed, cockle-bur, (a.) This vile weed, of obscure origin, has the appearance of a naturalized stranger in our country, and seems, fortunately, not much inclined to spread. The burs are a great annoyance in the fleeces of sheep.

Xanthium spinosum. Thorny Clot-bur, (a.) This execrable foreign weed is fast becoming naturalized in many portions of our country, particularly in the southern States. It may be frequently seen also along the sidewalks and waste places in the suburbs of our northern seaports. It is stated that the authorities of a southern city a few years since enacted an ordinance against the

WEEDS

offensive weed, in which enactment it was denounced by the misnomer of Canada thistle. This plant may be destroyed with the hoe in the latter part of summer—in September.

Bidens frondosa. Bur Marigold, (a.) Worthless native weeds in gardens, corn fields, etc., and particularly disagreeable by reason of the barbed awns of the fruit, which adhere in great numbers to clothing.

Bidens bipinnatus. Spanish Needle, (a.) This, like the preceding, if not carefully watched and extirpated, is a great pest in cultivated lots. Another species, *B. Chrysanthemoides,* known as Beggar-ticks, is rather showy, with its head of yellow-rayed florets, and is frequently found along swamps and rivulets in autumn. They are all regarded as nuisances on account of their adhesive fruit.

Maruta cotula. May-weed, fœtid chamomile, (a.) A disagreeable little foreign weed, which is extensively naturalized, and in bad odor among us.

Achillea millefolium. Yarrow, milfoil, nose-bleed, (p.) English agricultural writers speak of it as a plant of some value in their pastures; but it is generally regarded in this country as a mere weed. Certainly it is far inferior to our usual pasture plants, and our cattle are rarely, if ever, observed to eat it.

Leucanthemum vulgare. Ox-eye, daisy, white weed, (p.) This intruder from Europe has obtained almost exclusive possession of many fields in eastern Pennsylvania, and the prospect of getting rid of it appears to be nearly hopeless. Its propagation and diffusion are so rapid and irresistible that one negligent sloven may become the source of a grievous annoyance to a whole neighborhood. The cultivation of hoed crops for a few years will rid a field of this obstruction to useful vegetation. The Corn Marigold, *Chrysanthemum segetum,* a kindred plant, which is said to be such a pest to the agriculture of the Old World, happily does not appear to have found its way as yet to the United States.

Erechthites hieracifolia. Fire Weed, (a.) This coarse native weed is remarkable for its prevalence in newly-cleared grounds, especially in and around the spots where brush-wood has been burnt; hence its common name of fire-weed.

Senecio vulgaris. Common Groundsel, ragwort, (a.) A homely worthless little herb, which Prof. De Candolle remarks migrates almost everywhere with European men. It is naturalized about the seaports of the Northern States, and has lately appeared in eastern Pennsylvania.

Centaurea cyanus. Ragged Robin, blue bonnets of our Scotch, (a.) This European plant is often seen in our gardens, and in some places is gradually straggling into cultivated fields. As it is considered a troublesome weed among the grain crops of the Old World, it should be watched here, so as to prevent the blue bonnets from coming over the border.

Cirsium lanceolatum. Common Thistle, (b.) This foreigner, which delights in a rich soil, is abundantly naturalized in Pennsylvania and in the northern States generally. It is a very objectionable weed on our farms, requiring constant vigilance and attention to exclude or keep it in subjection. If permitted to mature its fruit, the expanded pappus may be seen by thousands floating in the air, and disseminating the obnoxious intruder far and wide. The common thistle, having no creeping roots, is not so obstinate in resisting extirpation as some other varieties. It is easier destroyed if the roots are cut with sufficient care before its flowering season.

Cirsium horridulum. Yellow Thistle, (b.) This rugged, repulsive species looks like a stranger here, being hitherto chiefly restricted to the sandy seacoast of New Jersey. It is certainly desirable that it should continue to be a stranger to every agricultural district.

Cirsium arvense. Canada Thistle, (p.) This is perhaps the most pernicious and detestable weed that has ever invaded the farms of our country. Though miscalled Canada thistle, it is believed to be indigenous to Europe, and has probably acquired that name by reaching us via Canada. The rhizoma or subterranean stem (which is perennial and very tenacious of life) lies rather below the usual depth of furrows, and hence is not disturbed by common plowing. The rhizoma ramifies and extends itself horizontally in all directions, sending up branches to the surface, where radical leaves are developed the first year, and aerial stems the second year. The plant, that is, the aerial portion, appears to die at the end of the second summer like a biennial, but it only dies down to the rhizoma or subterranean stem. The numerous branches sent up from perennial rhizoma soon furnish prickly radical leaves, which cover the ground so as to prevent cattle from feeding where those leaves are. Nothing short of destroying the perennial portion of the plant will rid the ground of this pest; and this has been accomplished by a few years of continued culture, (or annual cropping of other plants which require frequent plowing or dressing with the hoe,) so as to prevent the development of radical leaves, and thus deprive the rhizoma of

1022

WEEDS

all connection or communication with the atmosphere. We have a few other thistles which are all worthless weeds; but not being so obnoxious as the preceding, it is not deemed necessary to notice them further here.

Lappa major. Burdock, (b.) Everybody knows this coarse, homely foreign weed; one of the earliest and surest evidences of slovenly negligence about a farm yard.

Cichorium intybus. Wild Succory, chiccory, (p.) This foreigner is becoming extensively naturalized. Some European agriculturists recommend it as a valuable forage plant, and cattle seem fond of it; though it is believed to impart a bad taste to the milk of cows which feed upon it. In Europe the roasted root is used as a substitute for coffee. In this country the plant is generally regarded as an objectionable weed.

Taraxacum dens-leonis. Dandelion, (p.) An introduced plant, and now so extensively naturalized in our grass-plots, fields, and meadows that although not very obnoxious as a weed, it will be found a difficult task to extirpate it. The leaves and flower buds are frequently used, wilted, as a salad, and boiled as greens, and the root has been much employed recently in domestic economy, and is esteemed a pleasant and salutary substitute for the coffee berry.

Lobelia inflata. Eye-bright, Indian tobacco, (b.) A native weed possessing acrid properties, and sometimes employed as an emetic, and as an expectorant in asthma.

Andromeda mariana. Stagger-bush, (s.) This native shrub is very abundant in the sandy districts of New Jersey, where it is reputed to be injurious to sheep when the leaves are eaten by them, producing a disease called the staggers. The evidence on this point is not quite conclusive, but if established would cause the bush to be deservedly ranked among the pernicious plants.

Plantago major. Common plantain, way-bread, (p.) This foreign plant is remarkable for accompanying civilized man, growing along his foot-paths and flourishing around his settlements. It is alleged that our aborigines call it the white man's foot, from that circumstance. Another foreign species, the *P. lanceolata,* known as English plantain, rib-wort, ripple-grass, and buckhorn plantain, is becoming particularly abundant in our upland meadows or clover grounds. The farmer should keep its seeds from mingling with those of the red clover, and thus injuring the sale of clover seed in the market

Peroma radicans. Trumpet-flower, (p.) This showy native climber is often cultivated and admired in the northeastern States, but in the West, along the Ohio river and its tributaries, it is regarded as an intolerable nuisance.

Verbascum thapsus. Common Mullein, (b.) An introduced, homely weed in our pastures and cultivated grounds. There is no surer evidence of a slovenly and negligent farmer than fields overrun with mulleins. As the plant produces a vast number of seeds it can only be kept in due subjection by eradication before the fruit is mature. There is another species called moth mullein, *V. blattaria,* more slender, and equally worthless, becoming frequent in our pastures.

Linaria vulgaris. Toad-flax, Ranstead weed. (p.) A rather showy, but fœtid weed, said to have been introduced into Pennsylvania by a Mr. Ranstead, from Wales, as a garden flower. It inclines to form large, dense patches in our pastures by means of its creeping roots, which take almost exclusive possession of the soil.

Nepeta cataria. Cat-mint, cat-nip, (p.) This is common about old settlements. Another perennial species, *N. Glechoma,* (Benth..) called ground-joy, and gill, is also common in moist, shaded places about farm houses.

Lamium amplexicaule. Dead nettles, hen-bit, (a.) A worthless little weed, abundant in and about gardens in the Middle States, requiring some attention to keep it in due subjection.

Leonurus cardiaca. Motherwort, (p.) A homely, obnoxious weed, found in waste places about houses and farm-yards.

Teucrium Canadense. Wood-sage, germander, (p.) This native plant, which is frequently seen in low, shaded grounds along streams, where it is harmless, has recently got into the fields of some of the best farms of eastern Pennsylvania, where it is now regarded as an obstinately persistent nuisance.

Echium vulgare. Blue-weed, vipers bugloss, blue devils, (s.) A showy, but vile weed, extensively naturalized in some portions of our country, especially in Maryland and in the Shenandoah Valley, Va. Wherever it makes its appearance the farmer should act promptly on the Ovidian maxim, *Principiis obsta,* etc.: Meet and resist the beginning of evil.

Echinospermum lappula. Stick-seed, beggar's lice, (a.) The slovenly farmer is apt to get practically and vexatiously acquainted with this obnoxious native weed in consequence of its racemes of bur-like fruit entangling the manes of his horses and the fleeces of his sheep.

Convolvulus arvensis. Bind-weed, (p.) This foreign plant has been introduced into some portions of our country, and will give the farmers much trouble if they do not carefully guard against it.

Cuscuta epilinum. Dodder, flax-vine, (a.) This remarkable parasitic plant, somewhat resembling copper-wire in appearance, was introduced with our flax crop, and was formerly a great pest in that crop, by winding round and entangling branches of stalks so as to spoil them; but the vine has become rare, and has nearly died out since the culture of flax has declined among us.

Solanum nigrum. Night-shade, (a.) Frequent in shaded, waste places about dwellings. It is reputed to be deleterious in its properties, and ought, therefore, to be excluded from the vicinity of all farm-houses, where its berries may tempt children to pluck and eat.

Solanum Carolinense. Horse Nettle, (p.) An exceedingly pernicious weed, and the roots are so penetrating and so tenacious of life that it is difficult to get rid of. It was probably introduced from the South by Humphrey Marshall into his botanic garden at Marshallton; Pa, whence it has gradually extended itself round the neighborhood, and forcibly illustrates the necessity of caution in admitting mere botanical curiosities into good agricultural districts.

Datura stramonium. Thorn Apple, Jamestown (or Jimson) weed, (a.) Two varieties of this coarse, fœtid, narcotic plant (which is probably of Asiatic origin) are common among us as an obnoxious weed, and they should be carefully excluded from the vicinity of all farm-houses.

Enslenia albida. Whitish Enslenia, (p.) This twining plant, allied to the Asclepias or Milk-weed family, and happily as yet unknown to the farmers of the Eastern States, is reported by Prof. Short, a distinguished botanist of Kentucky, to be an intolerable nuisance on the farms along the river banks in Ohio, Illinois, etc.

APETALOUS EXOGENS—COROLLA USUALLY WANTING.

Phytolacca decandra. Poke-weed, pigeonberry, (p.) This stout native is everywhere frequent in rich soil. The *turions*, or tender radical shoots, in the spring of the year afford a popular substitute for those of asparagus; nevertheless, the plant is regarded and treated as a weed by all neat farmers.

Chenopodium album. Lamb's Quarter, goose-foot, (a.) This coarse and rather homely weed has become common and quite troublesome in gardens.

Amaranthus hybridus. Pig-weed, (a.) A repulsive looking weed, an annoyance in gardens and cultivated lots in the latter part of summer. If permitted to mature its seed it soon becomes very abundant.

Amaranthus albus. White Amaranth, (a.) Another coarse weed in the farm-yards of the Middle States. Although supposed by some to be a native of Pennsylvania, it has a foreign habit and appearance, and probably came from tropical America.

Amarantus spinosus. Thorny Amaranth, (a.) This odious, bushy weed, supposed to be a native of tropical America is common in unfrequented streets and outskirts of our seaport towns, and is a vile nuisance wherever it appears. It can not be too sedulously guarded against. Hoeing on its first appearance is often effectual for its destruction.

Polygonum Pennsylvanicum. Knot-weed, (a.) A common worthless weed on road sides and in waste places about neglected farm-houses.

Polygonum puricaria. Lady's Thumb, spotted knot-weed, (a.) Resembles the preceding, and rather smaller, but equally worthless wherever introduced.

Polygonum hydropiper. Water Pepper, smart-weed,(a.) A naturalized weed as worthless as most of the species are, though this is even more obnoxious than the preceding, being a highly acrid plant, and sometimes causing obstinate ulcerative inflammation when incautiously applied to the skin.

Polygonum sagittatum. Arrow-leaved Tear-thumb, (p.) Mowers and haymakers are apt to be familiar with this annoying native weed in the second crop of swampy meadows. Another kindred species; viz: *Parifolium*, or Halbert-leaved Tear-thumb, is an accompanying and equally obnoxious weed. Ditching and draining are the remedies for the evil. Several other *Polygonums* occur, equally worthless, but rather less offensive.

Rumex crispus. Sour Dock, curled dock, (p.) An unsightly and objectionable foreign weed, too extensively known.

Rumex obtusifolius. Bitter Dock, broad-leaved dock, (p.) This foreign species is now more objectionable than the preceding, but it is not quite so prevalent. There is also a little foreign species, well known for its acidity, the *R. acetosella*, Field or Sheep Sorrel, (p.,) often so abundant as to be a nuisance on the farm. Improving the land, especially by adequate dressing of lime, is believed to be the best mode of expelling this and many other obnoxious weeds.

Euphorbia hypericifolia. Eye-bright, spurge, (a.) This is a common weed in dry pasture fields, especially in thinnish sandy soils, and has been suspected (how justly has not been determined) as the cause of the disagreeable salivation or slobbering with which horses are sometimes affected in the latter part of summer. There is another flatty, prostrate, bunching little species, *E. maculata*, often abundant in Indian cornfields and other cultivated grounds.

Urtica dioica. Nettle, stinging nettle, (p.) An exotic rather frequent in waste places about farm houses, well known to those who have come in contact with them.

ENDOGENOUS PLANTS—INSIDE GROWERS.

Symplocarpus fœtidus. Swamp Cabbage, skunk weed, (p.) A worthless native weed in wet and swampy meadows, readily known by its skunklike odor when wounded.

Saggittaria variabilis. Arrow-head, (p.) A common native plant of no value, found in sluggish ditches and swampy meadows. The roots, or base of stem, often produce large oval tubers in autumn, which tempt hogs to root for them, and thus disfigure the grounds on which they occur.

Anacharis Canadensis. Water-reed. (p.) This slender aquatic is supposed to be indigenous in our sluggish streams, where it often abounds, and may possibly become troublesome in our canals. It has been introduced into England, where its presence impedes the navigation of the canals to a serious extent.

Smilax rotundifolia. Green Brier, rough bindweed, (p.) This is common in thickets, and a variety of it, *S. Caduca*, (L.,) often abounds in poor, neglected old fields.

Ornithogalum umbellatum. Ten O'clock, (b.) This exotic from the gardens in many places multiplies its bulbs so rapidly as to alarm the farmer, if neglected. The bulbs are exceedingly tenacious of life, and when once in possession of the soil, it is an almost task hopeless to get rid of them.

Allium vineale. Field Garlic, crow garlic, (p.) Tradition says this species was introduced by the first Welsh immigrants to Pennsylvania for the purpose of affording an early pasture, particularly for sheep. It was formerly so abundant in some districts as to be quite an annoyance, by imparting a disgusting flavor to milk and butter, and injuring the manufacture of wheat flour. By good farming and a judicious rotation of crops the evil has been much abated.

Juncus effusis. Common or Soft Rush, (p.) There are numerous species of this worthless native weed, but this is the best known, and perhaps the most objectionable, as it has a constant tendency to form unsightly bunches, or *tussocks*, in moist low grounds. Mr. Elliott an eminent botanist, says that in South Carolina this Rush occupies and almost covers rice fields as soon as they are thrown out of cultivation.

Cyperus phymatodes. Grass of Florida, (p.) This species is not nately somewhat rare, as yet, in the northern and middle States, but it is a great pest to the agriculture of the South.

Cyperus hydra. Coco grass, nut grass of South Carolina, (p.) This is regarded by the southern planters as the most intolerable pest of their agriculture. Mr. Elliott says: It shoots from the base of its stem a threadlike fiber, which descends perpendicularly eight to eighteen inches, and then produces a small tuber. From this horizontal fibers extend in every direction, producing new tubers at intervals of six or eight inches; and these immediately shoot up stems to the surface of the earth, and throw out lateral fibers to form a new progeny. This process is interminable, and it is curious to see what a chain of network of plants and tubers can, with some care, he dug up in a loose soil. The only process yet discovered by which this grass can be extirpated is to plow or hoe the spots in which it grows every day throughout the whole season. In their perpetual efforts to throw their leaves to the light the roots become exhausted and perish; or, if a few appear the next spring, they can easily be dug up.

Carex tentaculata. Many-beaked Sedge, (p.) A very common species, in swampy low ground, of the large and unprofitable genus of sedges.

Carex stricta. Tussock Sedge, (p.) This is one of the most common, and most difficult to manage, of all our sedges. Its roots are apt to form large dense tufts or tussocks, in swamps. The careful farmers sometimes get rid of those tussocks by digging them out, and, when dry, collecting them in large heaps, burning them, and using the ashes as a manure. Of this remarkable and very numerous genus, (Carex,) Dr. F. Boott, an accomplished botanist of London, has now in hand one of the noblest and most elaborately illustrated monographs ever issued from the press.

Panicum sa guinale. Crab grass, finger grass, (a.) In the middle States this troublesome grass abounds in gardens in the latter part of summer, and is frequent also in Indian corn fields, but they may be kept in tolerable sub-

jection by the early and faithful use of the instrument known as the cultivator. The crab-grass is regarded as a serious pest in the plantations along the lower Mississippi.
Panicum capillare. Hair-like Panicum, Old Witch grass, (a.) This worthless species flourishes best in a light sandy soil, but is usually more or less abundant in corn-fields. In autumn the dry culms break off and the light-spreading panicles are rolled over the fields by the winds, until they accumulate in great quantities along fence and hedge rows.
Panicum crus-galli. Cock-foot Panicum, barnyard grass, (a.) This coarse homely grass is said to be an inhabitant of all quarters of the globe. It is usually found in the latter part of summer, rather abundant along drains of barnyards and other waste places.
Setaria glauca. Bristly Fox-tail grass, (a.) All our weed-like species of this genus are believed to be naturalised strangers here. This one usually makes its appearance in abundance among the stubble, after a wheat crop, and is frequent in pastures, orchards, etc., when not kept down by a more valuable growth. The *S. viridis,* called green fox-tail or bottle grass, is about equally worthless, but not quite so prevalent.
Setaria virticellata, (a.) The adhesive bristles of this species, frequenting gardens and neglected lots, are calculated to make it something of a nuisance if permitted to become abundant.
Cenchrus tribuloides. Bur grass, hedge-hog grass, (a.) This pestilential nuisance is quite abundant in the sandy districts of New Jersey and along the great northern lakes.
Cynodon dactylon. Dog's-tooth grass, Bermuda grass, (p.) Of this grass, which has found its way from Europe into Virginia and other southern States, Mr. Elliott remarks; The cultivation of it on the poor and extensive sand-hills of our middle country, (viz., in South Carolina,) would probably convert them into sheep-walks of great value; but it grows in every soil, and no grass is close, rich land, is more formidable to the cultivator. It must, therefore, be introduced with caution.
Bromus secalinus. Cheat, chess, broom grass, (a.) This is a well known intruder among our crops of wheat and rye, and often appears in the same fields for a year or two after the crops, but is soon choked out by the perennial grasses. This plant is an annual, and easy to overcome by care in sowing clean wheat, by keeping fence corners and field borders clear, and in establishing a proper rotation in cropping. The vulgar error that this grass is merely transmuted wheat, came to us with the earliest immigrants, and, notwithstanding the boasted march of mind, it yet prevails among a certain class of farmers to a considerable extent.
Triticum repens. Couch grass, Quitch grass, (p.) This species of *triticum,* which is quite distinct in habit from cultivated wheat, has found its way into some districts of our country, and is a pernicious intruder, when fully introduced, by reason of the exceeding tenacity of life in its rhizomas, or creeping subterranean stems.
Andropogon nutans. Wood grass, Indian grass, (p.) This and two or three other species of native Indian grasses are common in our sterile grounds, and are no better than mere weeds.

CRYPTOGAMOUS, OR FLOWERLESS PLANTS.

Pteris aquilina. Brake, bracken of the Scotch, (p.) This large fern is often abundant in moist woodlands and borders of thickets, and in our wild forests it affords a favorite shelter, or hiding-place, for deer and other game, but it is little better than a weed on the farm. Having thus disposed of the most prominent weeds in our agriculture, it remains merely to mention, very briefly, three or four of the injurious cryptogams, among the lower order of the fungi, viz:
Merulius lachrymans. Dry rot. This fungus, with some others which infest timber in places where a damp air is confined, as in houses and ships, is very injurious. It is said to be remedied by a wash of diluted sulphuric acid.
Ascophora mucedo. Mold, bread mold. This minute fungus usually abounds on moist decaying substances, and is well known to housewives as growing plentifully on bread and pastry which have begun to spoil; yet it is probable that many of them have never suspected it of being as genuine a plant as any weed that grows on the farm.
Uredo segetum. Blight, smut, brand. This is usually found within the glumes on fruit of wheat, barley, and other grasses, speedily filling the whole with a profuse black dust.
Puccinia graminis. Mildew, rust. This often operates injuriously on wheat crops in warm, close, foggy weather, near harvest time; especially where the crop is a little backward and mingled with grass or herbage.

WEEVIL. A name applied to various insects including many of the curculios, also to the pea weevil, and also to those attacking the bean. The Grain weevil, which attacks grain and the Rice weevil are similar. During the centennial exhibition the samples from some portions of Europe, especially from Spain, were literally honey combed with the European weevil and this pest was widely disseminated thereby. Various weevils and their habits, and remedies from their attacks have been collected from various sources as follows: The Northern granary and the Southern rice weevil differ but little in form to the ordinary observer, the latter being merely smaller, and having light brown spots on the wing cases. Curtis states a curious fact, that the granary weevil in England is destitute of the organs of flight, whilst the rice weevil has a pair of serviceable wings. Both of them are very injurious to grain and corn, and the rice weevil is very destructive to the Southern rice. The egg of the Northern granary weevil is deposited on the grain; the larvæ burrow inside and feed upon its inner substance; the perfect weevil makes its escape from a small hole bored through the outer skin. Curtis says, it is calculated that 6,045 individuals may be reared from one pair of European weevils in one summer. Dr. Harris says, that these insects are effectually destroyed by kiln-drying the wheat; the grain that is kept cool, well ventilated, and frequently moved, is said to be free from their attack; also by winnowing and shifting rice in the spring, the beetles can be separated, and should be immediately gathered and destroyed. Curtis states that placing the grain in close cellars is the worst of all proceedings, as the weevils delight in darkness and being undisturbed. He recommends frequently stirring or turning over the heaps of wheat; he also says that the scent or spirits of turpentine, or the fumes of sulphur, did not appear to incommode the insects. In an experiment tried, the odor of a few drops of chloroform killed both larva and weevil in some closely corked bottles of samples of wheat in the agricultural department; the same bottles being opened a year afterwards, retained the scent. Benzine would, perhaps, have the same effect, and be much cheaper, but, most probably, would also impart a nauseous taste and smell to the grain. Wheat kept in bottles, thus treated with chloroform for a week, germinated when planted. Curtis says that the larvæ as well as the weevils are destroyed at 190° Fahr. but it also scorches the grain; and that a room heated to 130° by hot water pipes has been constructed in Madeira, which answers every purpose and wheat subjected to this high temperature vegetated in the ground. He also says that fleeces of wool laid on the grain heaps attract and kill the insects. A larger weevil called the hunter-weevil, has been much complained of in certain localities, as eating the leaves of corn. A very similar insect is found near the Pedee river, in South Carolina, the larva of which feeds in the stalk of corn, thereby entirely destroying the plant. This is merely mentioned to warn farmers, in case they should find individual plants among their corn withering, and in a yellow, sickly state, that perhaps the larva of a hunter-weevil, or one very nearly allied to it, may be the cause of all the damage. The only remedy at present recommended is hand-picking and burning the infested plants. Another curculio (*Epicærus fallax*) is very injurious in the neighborhood of Washington, in the

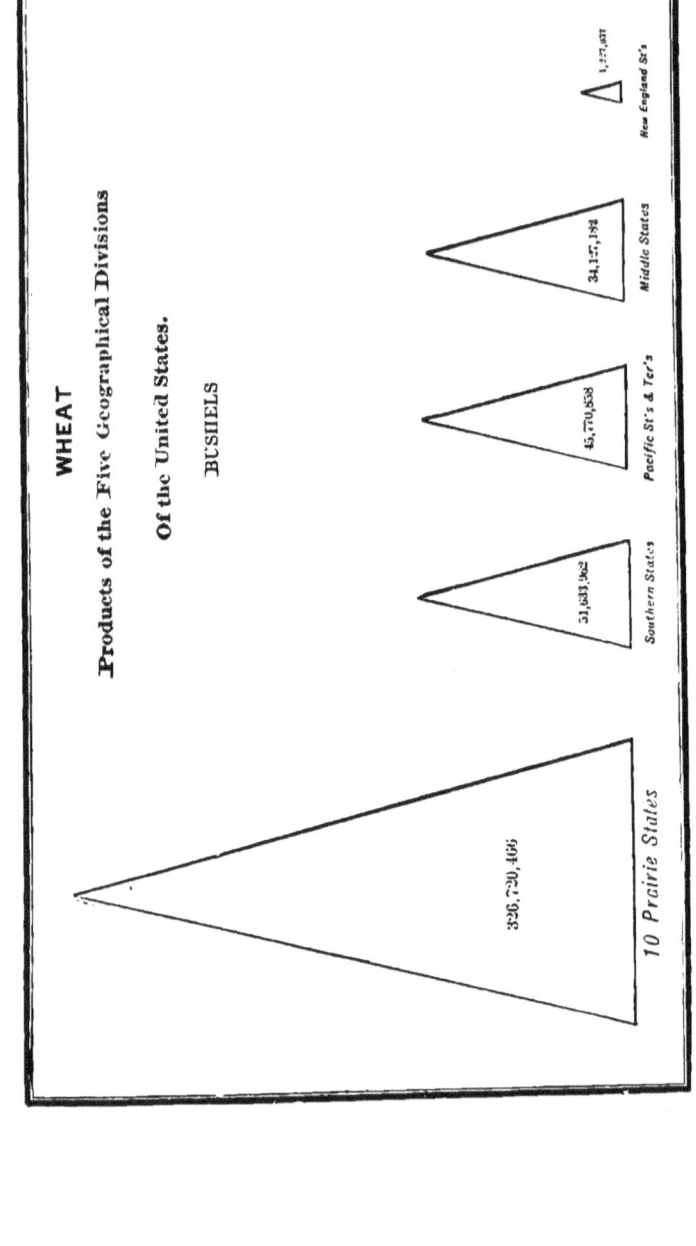

weevil or perfect state, to the leaves of young cabbages, clover, and various other plants. It appears, however, says our authority, to he local, no complaints were received except from Iowa, where it injures the foliage of the cherry and apple trees, and gooseberry bushes also. No remedies, however, have been recommended, as its habits have not been much investigated. The larvæ of the white-pine weevil injure pine trees by boring into the leading shoot, thus destroying the growth and symmetry of the tree. Harris recommends the injured leading shoot to be cut off in August, or as soon as it is perceived to be dead, and to burn it, together with its inhabitants. The larvæ of the pitch-eating weevil, and others, devour the substance under the bark of pine trees, and perhaps the method used for decoying the pine eating beetles in Europe may be practiced here with advantage. This consists in sticking some newly cut branches of pine trees in the ground in an open space during the season when the insects are about to lay their eggs; in a few hours these branches will be covered with the beetles, which may be shaken in a cloth and burned. The weevils inhabiting nuts, acorns, chincapins, and chestnuts, are distinguished by their very long projecting and slender bills or trunks. The egg is deposited in the young fruit, and the grubs are found in the interior. They afterwards enter the earth and change to pupæ and perfect weevils. No remedy has yet been found. The pea weevil destroys the interior substance or future seed-leaves of the pea, seeds of locust and other leguminous plants. The egg is deposited singly in punctures made by the female, on the pod. The larvæ, when hatched, penetrate through the pod and bury themselves in the pea opposite the puncture where they eat the interior of the pea. The pupa is formed in the pea itself, and in spring the perfect insect comes out of a round hole eaten through the skin. Many of these-worm eaten peas will germinate, as the germ is seldom injured by the larva. Latreille and others recommend putting the seed peas in hot water a minute or two just before planting, by which means the weevils will be killed and the sprouting of the peas be quickened. Curtis states that an immersion of four minutes in boiling water will kill almost all the peas. The water should not be above 170 to 180° Fahr. Late sown peas escape their attacks, and if sown as late as the middle of June, are seldom infested with this weevil. If the peas are kept over the year, they are free from this pest, the beetle having deserted them. Mr. Curtis states that kiln-drying at a heat of 133° to 144° will kill the insects without altering the quality of the peas, but such seed will no longer vegetate. The New York weevil is a very large curculio of a gray color, marked with whitish lines and black dots. It destroys the buds and gnaws the young twigs of the pear, plum, cherry, maple, oak, etc. As they are not very numerous yet, and appear to be local, no remedy has been proposed. Hand-picking and shaking them off the trees in a similar manner to the plum weevil might answer, if they should increase so as to become very injurious. (See articles Curculio, Thrips, etc.)

WEIGHTS. (See Measures.)

WELSH CATTLE. Naturally we should look to Wales, in England, for types of the ancient race of English cattle, since its climate being comparatively mild, and its people not having been entirely conquered by either the Saxon or Roman invasions, we confidently expect to here find cattle preserving, in miniature, indeed, from the mountainous nature of the country, but yet clearly the old forms and characteristics of the original cattle of Great Britain. Consequently Welsh cattle do resemble the Devons, and Herefords, and also the Sussex cattle of 100 years ago, all these breeds being originally imbued with the prepotent blood of the old Devons. The Pembroke, the Glamorgans, and the Anglesey cattle are the principal breeds. Of these breeds Youatt says: Great Britain does not afford a more useful animal than the Pembroke cow or ox. It is black; the great majority are entirely so; a few have white faces, or a little white about the tail, or the udders; and the horns are white. The latter turn up in a way characteristic of the breed, and indeed the general form of the cattle undeniably betrays their early origin. They have a peculiarly lively look and good eye. The hair is rough, but short, and the hide is not thick. The bones, although not small, are far from large; and the Pembroke cattle are very fair milkers, with a propensity to fatten. The meat is generally beautifully marbled. They thrive in every situation. The Glamorgan cattle are thus described: The Glamorganshire farmers took great pride in their cattle, and evinced much judgment in their breeding and selection. There was one principle from which they never deviated—they admitted no mixture of foreign blood, and they produced the Glamorgan ox, so much admired for activity and strength, and aptitude to fatten; and the cow, if she did not vie with the best milkers, yielded a good remunerating profit for the dairyman. They were of a dark brown color, with white bellies, and a streak of white along the back from the shoulder to the tail. They had clean heads, tapering from the neck and shoulders; long white horns, turning upward; and a lively countenance. Their dewlaps were small, the hair short, and the coat silky. If there was any fault, it was that the rump, or setting on of the tail, was too high above the level of the back to accord with the modern notions of symmetry. Their aptitude to fatten rendered them exceedingly profitable when taken from the plow at six or seven years old, and they were brought to great perfection on the rich English pastures—frequently weighing more than twenty scores per quarter. The beef was beautifully veined and marbled, the inside of the animal was well lined with tallow, and the Glamorgans commanded the highest price both in the metropolitan and provincial market. During the French revolutionary war, the excessive price of corn attracted the attention of the Glamorganshire farmers to the increased cultivation of it, and a great proportion of the best pastures were turned over by the plow. The natural consequence of inattention and starvation was, that the breed greatly degenerated in its disposition to fatten, and, certainly, with many exceptions, but yet, in their general character, the Glamorganshire cattle became and are flat-sided, sharp in hip joints and shoulders, high in the rump, too long in the legs, with thick skins, and a delicate constitution. Therefore, it must be acknowledged at present, and perhaps it must long continue to be the fact, that the Glamorgans, generally, are far from being what they once were.

They continue, however, to maintain their character for stoutness and activity, and are still profitably employed in husbandry work. The beef is still good, marbled, and good tasted; and in proportion as the value of the ox to the grazier has decreased, the value of the cow has become enhanced for the dairy. He who is accustomed to cattle will understand the meaning of this; and the kind of incompatibility between an aptitude to fatten in a little time, and on spare keep, and the property of yielding a more than average quantity of milk. This is the breed which is established in the populous districts of Glamorgan. The Glamorgan cattle bear a close resemblance to the Herefords in figure, although inferior to them in size; they feed, when in confinement kindly—the flesh and fat are laid equally over them—the beef is beautifully marbled, and they yield a more than average quantity of milk. They are fattened to perfection at five years old, but not often at an earlier age: and will become sufficiently bulky on the good pastures of the vale without any artificial food. The Anglesey cattle are small and black, with moderate bone. deep chest, rather too heavy shoulders, enormous dewlap, round barrel, high and spreading haunches, the face flat, the horns long, and characteristic of the breed with which we will still venture to class them, almost invariably turning upward. The hair is apparently coarse, but the hide is mellow: they are hardy, easy to rear, and well-disposed to fatten when transplanted to better pasture than their native isle affords. The Anglesey cattle are principally destined for grazing. Great numbers of them are purchased in the midland counties, and prepared for metropolitan consumption; and not a few find their way directly to the vicinity of London, in order to be finished for the market. In point of size, they hold an intermediate rank between the English breeds of all kinds and the smaller varieties of Scotch cattle; and so they do in the facility with which they are brought into condition.

WELCH CLOVER. (See Rabbit-foot.)

WELDING. The union of two pieces of metal at a white heat by hammering; iron, steel and platinum are the only metals susceptible of welding. The surfaces are cleaned by borax in welding steel.

WHEAT. *Triticum vulgare.* Wheat has in all ages of the world been the chief reliance among nations for bread. Those countries exporting bread grains even to-day relying upon it as a great money crop. This is due to two reasons, it carries well, and its large and uniform price enables it to be sent longer distances than any other bread grain except rice, the latter only serving as food to the partially civilized nations of warm climates. In plants used as food by man, we find the following interesting and condensed history of wheat, which we reproduce: Wheat (*Triticum vulgare*), which is the most important and widely distributed of all breadstuffs, according to the Grecian fable, was originally native on the plains of Enna and in Sicily, but it is much more probable that, like barley, it was received from Central Asia, where Olivier seems to have found it growing wild on the banks of the Euphrates. In any event, it belongs to the longest cultivated cerealia. Even Theophrastes was acquainted with it; probably the grained summer variety, from which the winter wheat seems to have been subsequently developed. In a similar manner, Scripture points to its cultivation in Palestine. Even in China it was known 3,000 years before Christ as a cultivated plant. As Isis was supposed to have introduced wheat into Egypt, and Demeter into Greece, so the Emperor Chin-nong is said to have introduced it into China. The great variety of the ancient names used for indicating this plant points to the wide circle of distribution which it originally possessed. At the present day, wheat is cultivated in all parts of the earth, having been taken to America by the Spaniards, at the beginning of the sixteenth century. Besides the common wheat, several other species of wheat are to be considered as cultivated plants, although they have attained a much more restricted distribution. Among these may be mentioned the *Triticum turgidum,* which was cultivated even by the ancient Egyptians, and was known to the Romans in Pliny's time. As it has not even yet reached India, its native land is to be looked for rather to the south and west of the Mediterranean than in Central Asia. The many-eared or Egyptian wheat (*Triticum compositum,*) is only a variety. It is cultivated chiefly in southern Europe and in England. Two species of wheat, *Triticum durum,* and *Triticum Polonicum,* or Polish wheat, areonly cultivated to advantage in the warmer regions of Europe. The Spelt (*Triticum spelta*), at present cultivated only in Europe, here and there, was met with even by Alexander the Great as a cultivated plant in his campaign in Pontus. Its origin in Mesopotamia and Hamadan, in Persia, is doubtful; especially as its cultivation in these countries can not be carried back to any very remote antiquity, and it likewise seems to have been known in Egypt, even though at the present day it is not found there. The German name *Spalt* points to its early cultivation in Germany. We come finally to the little-cultivated, one-grained wheat, (*Triticum monococcum*), this is the *Kussemeth* of the Scriptures. From it the Syrians and Arabians made their bread. Its cultivation has not extended either to India, Egypt or Greece. Both the Crimea and the region of Eastern Caucasus have been indicated as the native country of the one-eared wheat. The *Emmercorn,* or German wheat, (*Triticum amyleum*), has had an equally ancient cultivation. It is cultivated more frequently in the southern than in the middle portions of Europe. Wheat occupies a broader belt than rye, and is cultivated as the principal crop in middle and southern France, England, (where it constitutes the chief object of culture among the cerealia), a part of Germany, Hungary, the lands of the southern Danube, the Crimea, and in the lands of the Caucasus, as well as Central Asia, wherever the soil is cultivated; along its northern border it is associated in culture with rye, in the southern with rice and maize (Indian corn). The latter is chiefly the case in the North American States, and in the region of the Mediterranean. Wheat is even cultivated in the southern hemishere, at the Cape, Buenos Ayres, and Chili, wherever the climatological conditions will allow. Coming to the United States we find that wheat was first sown in the United States at Cuttyhunk, Buzzard's bay, in 1602, by Gosworld, the first explorer of the coast. It was first sown in Virginia in 1611, in the Dutch colony of New

Netherlands, prior to 1626, since in that year samples were sent back to the mother country. The first record of wheat in the Plymouth colony, is that in 1629 wheat and other seed grains were sent for to the mother country. In all new countries capable of producing wheat it quickly becomes the staple crop, but quickly exhausting the soil under such indifferent cultivation as is usually given, it is soon replaced by other crops. Within the last thirty years, the Genesee valley in New York, East, and Virginia in the South, were the two greatest wheat raising sections of the United States. The report of the Commissioners of Agriculture in 1876 gives most interesting figures in relation to this hegira, the three tables of which are significant. The statement is as follows: Another point of inquiry has been the changes in kind and volume of production, caused by westward emigration, settlements of virgin tracts of territory, depreciation of rate of yield by irrational modes of culture, and the varying measure of foreign demand for food products. The movement of population westward across the continent has been one of the wonders of modern times. Not only is the volume of wheat of to-day more than threefold greater than in 1849, but the increase of that portion of it grown beyond the Mississippi is greater than the entire crop of that year. Five per cent. only was then produced west of the Mississippi; and in 1876, a year of comparative failure in the Northwest, it was forty per cent. Dividing the country into three sections, the first including the Atlantic coast States, with Pennsylvania, and the Virginias to the Ohio river, and the second and third sections separated by the Mississippi river, we find more than half of the wheat grown in the first in 1849, the percentages of each section changing rapidly, as follows:

Section.	1849.	1859.	1869.	1876.
Atlantic coast	51.4	30.7	20	19.6
Central belt	43.3	54.6	49	40.8
Trans-Mississippi belt	5.3	14.7	31	39.6

The first section has now a little more than one-third of its former proportion; even the second, which was swept with so heavy a wave of immigration in the first decennial period, exhibits a declining percentage, while the third has eight times its former prominence, even in a year of low production of spring wheat, and promises to make the proportion nine to one in 1877, or forty-five per cent. A few years more will find a preponderating weight of wheat production beyond the Father of Waters. Comparing relative quantities rather than proportions of the crop, we find that the Atlantic coast has held its own, and little more; the central belt produces three times as much; the trans-Mississippi belt, more than twenty times as much. The figures in the first table below will explain themselves. That the wheat crop, with a smaller volume and a more active foreign demand, should make so rapid extension is less strange than the nearly equal rate of acceleration of the immense volume of our great natural crop, maize. With less than an increase of 100 per cent. in population, this crop has more than doubled. The quantity produced has actually decreased in the East, it

Section.	1849.	1859.	1869.	1876.
Atlantic coast	51,057,020	53,294,137	57,476,371	56,480,500
Central belt	43,522,646	94,458,609	140,877,070	118,122,000
Trans-Mississippi belt	5,806,278	25,352,178	89,392,185	114,745,000
Total	100,485,944	173,104,924	287,745,626	289,356,500

has doubled in the Central States, and is seven times as large beyond the Mississippi. The proportions of the whole crop produced by the three sections are (nearly) as follows:

Section.	1849.	1859.	1869.	1875.
Atlantic coast	30	24	20	14
Central belt	58	55	53	51
Trans-Mississippi belt	12	21	27	35

The East has declined continuously and hopelessly; the center has held a determined struggle, yielding only inch by inch; the West has trod the track of destiny with accelerated step. In 1880 this Western preponderance had already been reached, the center of wheat production being a line running north and south, and touching the Mississippi river at St. Louis. In relation to varieties and to cross fertilization, selection and cultivation, in producing superior qualities, and also in the adaptation of certain soils in growing superior seed wheat, the following facts must suffice: From the well-defined species accepted by botanists, and which may be described in general terms, as the hard wheats, the soft wheats and the Polish wheats, all the innumerable varieties known to agriculturalists have descended. The hard wheats are the product of warm climates, such as Italy, Sicily and Barbary. The soft wheats are grown in the northern parts of Europe, as in England, Belgium, Denmark and Sweden. The Polish wheats grow in the country from which they derive their name, and are also hard wheats. The hard wheats contain much more gluten than the other varieties. This valuable ingredient is a tough, viscid substance, very nutritious, and which, as it abounds in nitrogen, readily promotes fermentation in the dough, and is essential to good light bread. The quantity of nitrogen varies with the soil and climate from five per cent. in some soft wheats to thirty per cent. in the hardest and most transparent. It is the higher proportion of gluten that exists in Italian wheats that fits them for use in the preparation of macaroni and the rich pastes that form so large a portion of the food of the people of that land. The softer wheats contain a larger proportion of starch. The latter are usually grown in England, and require to be well dried and hardened before they can be readily ground into flour. Many of these varieties of wheat have resulted from influences derived from the soil. Some soils are remarkable, far and wide, for producing good seed, and it is equally well known that this seed degenerates in other soils, so that the original is resorted to for fresh supplies of seed. This is so well known in England that the produce of a certain parish in Cambridgeshire is sold for seed at a price considerably above the average. It is not, however, the experience of all that the finest wheat makes the best seed, but in the choice of seed the nature of the soil upon which it is to be sown must be considered as well as that upon which it grew. It has been asserted that all the various noted seed wheats, when analyzed by the chemist, are found to contain the different elements of which they are composed in nearly the same proportion, especially the starch and gluten. For bread, that which contains the most gluten, is preferred; but to produce a perfect vegetation there should be no excess of this substance, and no deficiency, and the seed should have arrived at perfect maturity. Moreover, it has also been stated, and with great apparent probability of its truth, that if we wish to grow any peculiar sort of wheat, and find by our preparation of the soil or its original composition that we produce a wheat in which the gluten and starch are in different proportions from that of the original seed, we may conclude that this is owing to more or less nitrogenous matter in the soil—that is, more animal manure—or proportionally more vegetable humus; and by increasing the one or the other, we may bring our wheat to have all the properties of the original seed. By selecting seed from those ears which appeared superior to the others in a field of ripe wheat, sowing them in a garden or in a part of the field, the variety which may have been produced by some fortuitous impregnation, or by some peculiarity of the soil of the spot where it grew, may be perpetuated. By carefully adapting the seed to the soil, and by a careful and garden-like cultivation, and adding those manures which are found to be best adapted to favor its perfect vegetation, crops of wheat have been raised which at one time would have been thought miraculous, and in Great Britain, where only is its culture regarded as its importance demands, and the highest skill, the result of enlightened inquiry into the requirements of this invaluable grain, been persistently applied, the average product has been greatly increased on all soils. To original defect in the soil or inadequate fertilization, we may reasonably ascribe the deterioration observed to follow cultivation of varieties of wheat which at first appeared well adapted to the locality and the climate. The demand for new seed wheat to repair the loss arising from continued decline in the product from year to year, should induce cultivators to seek for a cause for this deterioration, either in the condition of the soil and its constituents, or in an unwise culture and indifference to the selection of the best product for continuing the crop. We have many recorded instances of the very valuable results of care in selecting the largest and heaviest grains for seed. In some instances the crop has been quadrupled in quantity and quality by the use of the choicest seed selected from that with which the rest of the field was sown. When importing seed wheat and any other seed of new or superior varieties of plants, attention should always be directed to the peculiarities of the soil and climate under which they originated, and those under which it is proposed to grow them. English varieties of spring wheat are sown in February or early in March, have the benefit of early spring growth, and of a milder and moister summer than a spring sown wheat can have in the northern United States. The failure that has attended attempts to introduce English varieties of wheat is no new thing, such having been the almost universal result for many years past. The distinction between winter and spring wheat is one which arises entirely from the season in which they have usually been sown, for they can readily be converted into each other by sowing earlier or later, and gradually accelerating or retarding their growths. If a winter variety is caused to germinate slightly, and then checked by exposure to a low temperature, or freezing, until it can be sown in spring, it may be converted into a spring wheat. The difference in color between red and white wheats is owing chiefly to the influence of the soil, while wheats gradually becoming darker and ultimately red in some stiff, wet soils, and red wheats losing their color and becoming first yellow and then white in rich, light and mellow soils. The grain changes color sooner than the chaff and straw, hence we have red wheats with white chaff, and white wheats with red chaff. The blue-stem, long cultivated in Virginia, was formerly a red, but at length became a beautiful white wheat. If it be true that each variety of grain is adapted to a specific climate in which it grows perfectly, and where it does not degenerate when supplied with proper and sufficient nourishment, may not the consideration of the origin of each variety we propose to sow be of more importance than has yet been accorded to it in the selection of minor varieties, the product of our country? The varieties of wheat that have originated, apparently by accident, (for there are no accidents in nature) or from peculiar culture, do not enjoy all the surroundings necessary for perfect continuous product. Causes yet unexplained are ever at work modifying the germ of the new growth, and the care of man is needed to preserve unimpaired, or to render perfect the already improved varieties. That cross-fecundation and hybridization are possible has been fully proved by the results of experiments made by Maund and Raynbird, whose Hybrid Ceréalia received the prize medals at the industrial exhibition in London as long ago as 1851; and that success has attended judicious efforts to improve upon the ordinary wheat by continued careful selection of seed, is evident from the product of the Giant wheat and Pedigree wheat, grown by F. F. Hallett, of Brighton, England. By selecting from year to year not only the best heads of wheat, but the best kernels of the finest ears, and using them for seed, this gentleman has produced a variety possessing great fecundity of grain, extraordinary strength of stem, and a uniformity in the size of the ear. Some of the heads of these new varieties measured seven inches in length, and were proportionately thick. In some instances one kernel has produced seventy-two heads, containing six thousand four hundred and eighty grains, and a maximum product was obtained of sixty and sixty-two, and in one instance seventy-two bushels per acre. The highest results on the farm of Mr. Hallett were six quarters or fifty-six bushels per acre, which appears to have been produced, not upon a chosen garden spot, but upon several acres. The large numbers named need not excite surprise or doubt of their probability, since Schuyler county, Ill., has produced wheat heads six and a half inches long, and Talbot county, Md., has exhibited a field of nearly thirty acres which in 1860 yielded very nearly fifty-five bushels of wheat, of sixty pounds each, to the acre, and nine of which produced sixty-four and a half bushels upon each acre. This last was a smooth-headed wheat brought from North Carolina a few years before. William Hotchkiss, of Niagara county, N. Y., exhibited at the industrial exhibition in London in 1851, the product of six acres in 1849-'50 which averaged sixty-three and a half bushels to the acre, weighing sixty-three pounds to the bushel. This extraordinary yield was, however exceeded in the summer of 1858 by Thomas Powell, of the same county, whose field of seven measured acres averaged within a small fraction of seventy bushels to the acre—namely, four hundred and eighty-nine bushels of wheat. Mr. Hallett describes the system by which he produced his Pedigree wheat as follows: The best plant is called the selection of the year (say 1861) in which it is thus obtained, and consists of numerous ears containing many hundreds, and even thousands, of grains, which are planted separately, those of each ear being kept quite distinct, as, although the best grain of any plant is nearly always found to lie in its best ear, it may be otherwise, and the successive parent ears must be preserved. At the following harvest (1862) the best plant forms the selection for 1863, and its produce is continued on the experimental ground, while that of the remaining plants furnishes the annual seed for the farm in the autumn of 1862, and the crops are in 1863 offered to the public. Thus the selection sold is that of 1861, or in any year that of two years before, the latest selection, that of the year immediately preceding, is not sold, being solely employed as the home seed. It is indeed true of late years, farmers have learned that not only must the land be in proper condition, and the season right, but that none but clean, well-ripened seed must be sown and that the soil must be carefully and honestly prepared. What is required for winter wheat is a winter in which it will not be heaved by freezing and thawing and succeeding weather to keep it growing, with dry and rather cool weather for harvesting. Spring wheat requires similar weather except as to the winter. The three seasons preceding 1880 were of this character. Hence the wonderful crops of wheat, whole Western States producing the best averages of England in her best years. The following table of the several States mentioned shows as follows. The proportionate area represented compared with the entire winter wheat area in each State. The proportion sown

STATES.	No of counties	Area represented. Percentage	Proportion sown	Proportion drilled	Increase of product by drilling.	Seed per acre. Bushels in broadcasting	Bushels in drilling
New York	21	63	50	50	13	1.80	1.60
New Jersey	10	22	45	55	6	1.95	1.80
Pennsylvania	33	62	30	70	12	1.74	1.49
Delaware	2	43	26	74	10	1.75	1.50
Maryland	8	66	24	76	7	1.70	1.43
Virginia	29	35	62	38	12	1.44	1.21
North Carolina	15	26	97	3		1.07	.83
South Carolina	4		99	1		1.00	.70
Georgia	16	14	99	1		1.00	.90
Alabama	8		99	1		1.00	
Mississippi	5		99	1		1.25	
Texas	9	21	98	2		1.15	.90
Arkansas	2		100			1.10	
Tennessee	27	37	96	4	10	1.20	1.10
West Virginia	17	57	58	42	12	1.53	1.33
Kentucky	23	22	92	8	10	1.36	1.11
Ohio	38	51	39	62	16	1.57	1.33
Michigan	22	52	49	51	9	1.64	1.40
Illinois	32	39	24	76	19	1.52	1.24
Indiana	41	44	49	51	15	1.48	1.21
Missouri	47	45	62	38	21	1.52	1.21
Kansas	23	36	55	45	16	1.49	1.23
Nebraska	2	4	51	49	17	1.56	1.25
California	9		98	2		1.33	
Oregon	7	21	81	19	5	1.50	1.21

and drilled respectively. The estimated relative increase of product by drilling over that obtained by sowing, collected for the year 1874. The proportion of spring wheat sown is about forty per cent. of the whole crop. It is grown mainly in Wisconsin, Minnesota, and Iowa, almost to the exclusion of fall-sown wheat in those States. Michigan, though as far north as either, produces almost exclusively winter wheat, owing to the modifying influences of the surrounding waters, and perhaps in some degree to the soil, much of which has good natural drainage. One-third of the crop of Illinois (in the northern counties) is spring wheat. A small portion of that of Kansas is sown in the spring, and nearly all of that of Nebraska. California is anomalous in wheat as in everything else. Wheat can be sown all through the summer to sprout when rains fall, or it may be put in all through the rainy season till spring. In point of fact, the planting season has actually a range of several months. The little grown in the New

England States is nearly all spring wheat. In the Middle and Southern States, and in the Western States not named above, fall sowing is almost the exclusive practice. A little is sown in the spring in New York and Pennsylvania. We have shown how the cultivation of wheat has steadily progressed westward, seeking the new and virgin soils. The time is coming however when this must cease. Then wheat will be grown in all the range of climate adapted to it, and form part of a regular rotation. When this is done, wheat may again be profitably grown wherever it has once succeeded, as it is now profitably grown, by that class of farmers who make it one of a series of crops, and who never exhausting their soil by running to one special crop for the present money it brings, from having cared to know that once the fertility of the soil is lost, it will cost more to again bring it back than it would to have kept it, as originally, fertile.

WHEAT BIRD. White-Throated Sparrow, *Zonotrichia albicollis*. A beautiful song sparrow of the Eastern States, arriving early in the season, but breeding in the extreme northern sections of the United States and Canada. It is innocent of harm and not destructive to crops as its name would suggest.

WHEAT GRASSES. Grasses of the same genus as wheat (*Triticum*), of which the couch grass (*T. repens*) is best known. They are not indigenous in the United States, and, although very nutritious, are not objects of special cultivation.

WHEAT PRODUCTION. (See Supplement.)

WHEEL-SHAPED COROLLA. A rotate corolla; it is monopetalous, with a spreading border and very short tube.

WHELP. The young of the dog.

WHEY. The refuse of milk, in making cheese, being separated from the curd, after coagulation. It is fed to calves of three weeks and upward by mixing a pint of buckwheat or rye flour to sixteen quarts of whey. It also has some value, if given to milch cows to drink, but is principally used to feed swine in connection with more solid food. It contains 4.54 parts of milk sugar, 0.35 butter, 0.47 caseine, 0.38 albumen, 0.42 lactic acid, 0.69 ash, and 93.12 water in 100 parts. (See Dairying.)

WHIPPING OUT GRAIN. Striking the ears against a stone or the edge of a board till the grain is separated from the straw.

WHIPPLE TREE. A swinging bar to which the traces of the horse are fastened.

WHIP-POOR-WILL. (See Night-hawk.)

WHIRLBONE. The knee pan. In the horse, the articulation of the thigh bone in the pelvis; the acetabulum.

WHIRLWIND. A revolving wind, blowing to a center. The tornado is a violent whirlwind.

WHISKY. A strong spirit distilled from a fermented mash of corn, barley, wheat or other grains.

WHISTLING. Wind broken, highblowing, roaring, and whistling are all the effect of chronic difficulty in the respiratory passages, or of some disease of the windpipe. In roaring there is generally a sharp cough. Medicines are really of but little use, except to alleviate the distress for a time. One drachm, each, of powdered opium, powdered nitre, and powdered camphor, made into a ball and given once or twice a day, before feeding, for several days, is probably as good as any, or the animal may be treated as recommended for heaves.

WHITE ARSENIC. Common arsenic, arsenious acid. It has been recommended for dusting grain after brining, but should never be used; for other substances, as blue vitriol, answer much better, and are not so dangerous.

WHITE CEDAR. (See Cedar.)

WHITE CLOVER. (See Clover.)

WHITE CROPS. Grain crops; the *Cerealia*. They are exhausting, from the quantity of seeds they form, and are foul crops, from allowing weeds to grow among them. White crops (an English term) require to be followed by clean crops, as Indian corn, etc.

WHITE LEAD. Carbonate of lead. It is the basis of all colors used in painting.

WHITE PRECIPITATE. A violent mercurial poison, used in ointments for destroying vermin.

WHITE ROOT. *Asclepias tuberosa*. Colic or pleurisy root; butter-fly weed. It is used in domestic practice as a cathartic, diaphoretic, and expectorant.

WHITE SCOUR. Diarrhœa.

WHITE SPOT. (See Eye Spot.)

WHITE THORN. The hawthorn.

WHITE TOP. *Agrostis alba*. A grass very similar to red top.

WHITE VITRIOL. Sulphate of zinc. A powerful emetic, and is used in lotions.

WHITE WASH. Ordinary lime wash is made by putting half a peck or a peck of lumps of quick-lime into a tight barrel, and pouring on hot water to slake it; when slaked add water to make it of the consistency of thin cream and it is ready for use. It is one of the best of materials for covering ordinary walls since it is beautifully white and conducive to health. For painting rough out-buildings, fences, etc., put half a bushel of quick-lime in a barrel and add boiling water until it is covered nearly six inches deep, cover the barrel to keep the steam in, and when the violent ebullition is over, add water enough to bring it to the consistency of cream; allowing four pounds of rice flour to each half bushel of lime; or, the rice flour may be mixed with the water for slaking, mixing the flour carefully in cold water before putting it in the hot water. Stir constantly in the hot water until thoroughly set, and then pour it all over the lime as directed. Another excellent wash, and one which will harden on wood work, is to slake the lime as before directed, then add water to bring it to the proper consistency, and add two pounds of sulphate of zinc and one pound of common salt. Add water to bring it to a fit state for spreading with the brush. For cream color, add three pounds, or as much as may be necessary, of yellow ochre. Four pounds umber, one pound Indian red, and one pound lampblack, or in these proportions, will give a fawn color. Four pounds of raw umber, and two pounds of lampblack, or in these proportions, will give a gray or stone color. An excellent wash for rough work is made in the following proportions: Three pecks of water lime, one peck silver sand, or any clean, sharp, fine sand, and half a peck of salt. This coat stands well on old or rough boards, etc.

WHITE WEED. The larger perennial May weed (*Chrysanthemum*), occurring in wheat fields and meadows.

WHITE WOOD. The tulip-tree.

WHITING. Prepared chalk, for cleaning brasses and silver.

WHITLOW. A painful inflammation near the bone, tending to suppuration.

WHITLOW GRASS. The genus *Draba;* cruciferous plants, some of which are ornamental.

WHORL. In botany, an arrangement of leaves or other organs around the stem, and apparently on the same level, as the leaves of madder.

WHORTLEBERRY. *Gaylussacia.* Also called Huckleberry. Both the huckleberry, the blueberry, the dewberry and the cranberry belong to the huckleberry—a subfamily, of the order *Ericaceæ*. The huckleberries differ from the blueberry, in having a spicy, rather sweet taste, the berry containing ten large seeds or rather small stones. It is also strictly deciduous. The blueberry, *vaccinium*, is ranked as an evergreen, and in the case of the cranberry, *V. oxycoccus*, and *macrocarpon*, they are strictly evergreen. The principal species of huckleberry are the black or common, *Gaylussacia resinosa*. The pale, blue tangle, *G. frondosa* and the dwarf *G. dumosa*. (See also Cranberry and Huckleberry.)

WILD INDIGO. *Baptisia tinctoria.* A perennial leguminous plant, with wedge-ovate leaves, and yellow terminal racemes, flowering in July, it grows three feet high, is common in the woods throughout the States, and affords a good amount of indigo dye.

WILDING. Young trees produced from seeds naturally distributed.

WILD MUSTARD. (See Mustard.)

WILD PEAR. The June berry.

WILD RICE. *Zizania aquatica.* (See Rice.)

WATER OATS. (See Rice.)

WILLOW. *Salix.* The willow family, *Salicaceæ*, is an important one to agriculture, especially western agriculture, since it contains the willows proper, and the poplar tribe, *populus*, in which are included the cottonwoods. The poplars have been noticed under cottonwood. The willows necessary to be noticed, here are: The White Willow, *Salix alba*, a most valuable tree for wind breaks, when quick growth, and a tolerable firewood are desired. It is upright in its growth, attaining an ultimate height of sixty to eighty feet, grows rapidly from cuttings, and as readily puts forth new wood when topped at any desired height. The wood is much sought for, its charcoal being used in the manufacture of powder. The Black Willow is the common willow of the west, a rugged tree of no particular value. Its wood is, however, used in the making of bowls and other wooden ware. The Yellow Willow, *S. vitellina*, is held to be simply a variety of the yellow willow, and is sometimes planted as a shade tree, but is not well adapted to the purpose. The Osier or Basket Willow, *S. viminalis*, is the well known shrub from which the rods are prepared for basket making. Its cultivation has been undertaken a number of times in the United States, but each time abandoned, from the fact that American labor could not compete with the cheap labor of women and children, in Europe, in peeling and preparing the shoots. The Bottle or Bedford Willow is also somewhat used for basket work.

WIND DROPSY. (See Blown).

WIND COLIC. (See Blown).

WIND FLOWER. *Anemone Virginiana.*

WIND GALLS. Small tumors near the fetlocks of horses, produced by strains and over-driving. They contain a serous fluid. The animal should have rest; astringent lotions may be used, and a bandage applied very tight. (See Spavin.)

WINDMILL. In mechanics, a mill which receives its motion from the wind. The building containing the machinery is usually circular.

WINDOW GARDENING. The culture of flowers, odorous plants, and those kept for the beauty of their foliage, in dwellings, is probably as old as the era of comfortable dwellings themselves. It is so old in fact that its beginning has never been chronicled. The love of flowers is as inherent in our natures as the love of life, and the desire to possess within the dwelling such objects as strike the eye, would naturally suggest the transplantation of curious or striking plants. Window gardening or the cultivation of plants in rooms, is almost exclusively confined to the middle and poorer classes, or at least to those classes whose wealth will not allow their cultivation in greenhouses and conservatories. It is a constant and striking proof of that innate love of the beautiful, found in the more sensitive natures as well of the savage as the most enlightened of mankind. It is a taste which the rich and the poor may alike enjoy; for the humblest window in an obscure alley of the crowded city may have its crock of plants or its single blooming flower, if no more, giving as unalloyed satisfaction as the most costly plants in the great conservatories of the most wealthy. One of the chief drawbacks to window gardening is that the range of plants for this culture is limited. No skill would enable the cultivator to keep certain classes of plants healthy in rooms. In crowded cities the list would be still less in number, since the confined air of such rooms are the very worst situation in which plants can be placed. Therefore, if healthy plants and an abundance of bloom are expected, variety must be sacrificed. Among the succulent species best adapted to a confined space and close atmosphere are many of the aloes, cactuses, etc. The orange and myrtle are well known among that class, having firm leaves, and a smooth, compact skin. Those plants having the leaves small and of a delicate texture, are illy adapted to house culture, and some tribes as the heaths, and probably the whole race of pinnate leaved, and papilionaceous flowered plants, of which lupins, clover, etc., are types, are entirely unfit for house cultivation. Pinnate-leaved plants have that class of foliage where a single petiole has several alternate leaves attached to each side of it. Water, heat, air and light are the four essentials to plant growth, a proper soil being supplied. The first three and the last all may command. The first three promote growth. Light renders the growth perfect, and over this we can not have perfect control, even in the most favored situations, indifferently so in houses in the country; in the city it is the most difficult factor to control in the cultivation of plants in houses. To reach favorable results light must come directly from the sun, and plants should be so placed, that there be as little refraction and decomposition, always present when it passes obliquely through glass or any other medium other than the air. Without good light it is impossible to grow healthy plants, and while it acts beneficially upon the upper surfaces of leaves, it seems to be injurious to the under surfaces, for however a plant may be placed, it will turn the upper surface of the leaves to the light. Plants in rooms turn not only their leaves but also their branches to the light, and this is in proportion to the light of the windows and the shadow of the room; therefore plants do nicely in a south window, and when light is also admitted to the room from an east and a west window. If this south exposure be a bay window that may be closed from the room, and where heat and moisture may be conserved, you have the best possible conditions, under the circumstances. Now-a-days portable stands are so cheap that almost any one may by their use grow at least some plants, and when the plants require washing or cleaning they are easily removed for the purpose. If saucers are used, they should be filled with coarse gravel upon which to set the pots. Thus any water they contain will be evaporated into the air and about the foliage and thus assist in keeping up a due and equable moisture in the apartment. Plants respire constantly by their leaves. In rooms these soon become choked with dust, and if not cleaned the plant becomes sickly and dies. When grown out of doors they are daily washed by dew, exercised by the wind, and thoroughly cleansed by every shower. Plants with large solid leaves may be sponged, while smaller and rough-leaved plants may be cleansed by inverting the pot on the hand and rinsing in a vessel of water. Loose dirt may be got rid of with a pair of bellows, and thus by giving the plants exercise, will essentially increase their vigor. Whenever possible plants should be taken out of doors, or some other suitable place, for washing, then it may be done with a garden syringe, or a fine rose watering pot held high above them, that they may get advantage of the force of the drops. House plants, especially roses and geraniums, are often subject to the attacks of lice, *Aphides*. They are easily removed by washing in rather weak tobacco water and often in clear water, or a cone of paper may be placed over the plant and a little tobacco smoke blown under. So also they may be destroyed by camphorated water. Mildew sometimes attacks plants. This fungi is the result of a bad condition of the plants. Sulphur or camphor are the proper remedies, and a due circulation of air the preventive. Scale insects—cocus—also attack the orange, camellia, and similar plants. They may be removed by a sponge and water. The idea entertained by some that plants in rooms are injurious to the health of those living in them is altogether unfounded. In fact theoretically the reverse should be the case. Plants exhale oxygen from their under surfaces, during the light. When large numbers of plants, especially those whose flowers are highly perfumed, or those with odorous leaves, are kept in close rooms, they may sometimes occasion faintness, but with the few that are usually kept the perfume will only be sufficient to give the delightful sensation we all so much admire. Plants in rooms, to the extent they are generally grown by persons of taste, are not only not injurious to the health, but will afford relaxation from ordinary routine duties, amusement to the mind, and pleasant exercise to those whose time is not fully occupied. The examination of the several parts, both botanically and physiologically, will afford a pleasant and instructive study that, once engaged in, will thereafter not be discontinued.

WINDROW. A line or row of grass, or other material exposed to dry. The untilled borders of the field.

WINE. In the article Gallizing we have treated of the manufacture of fruit wines, and of increasing the strength of wines by the addition of sugar. It is well known that the juice of any fruit containing acid, starch or sugar, may be converted into a kind of wine, by the addition of such constituents as they may lack. Hence any fruit juice, or the juice of the leaf-stalks of vegetables, as rhubarb, may be made into an innocent and pleasant juice. A well known authority says that starch readily passes into the saccharine fermentation, and sugar into the vinous; thus wheat, corn, rye, barley, etc., put in warm water, a certain portion of the starch within is changed into sugar, and if the fermentation is permitted to proceed till it passes on into the vinous or alcoholic, the sugar is changed into alcohol. The fluid now contains a portion of alcohol which is removed by distillation. As alcohol boils at a much less temperature than water, if the mixed fluid be gradually heated up to the alcoholic boiling point, the alcohol, being converted into vapor, will pass over into the receptacle, while the water will remain unaffected. In ripe apples, peaches, currants, blackberries, grapes, and similar fruits, there is a small per cent. of sugar with little or no starch. The juice is, therefore, so to say, already past the saccharine fermentation and ready for the vinous. Left to the action of the atmosphere, all these juices in a few days ferment, i. e., change whatever sugar there may be into alcohol, the amount of which will depend entirely upon the amount of sugar before fermentation. Such a juice is, in general terms, a cider; if its percentage of alcohol is increased by adding sugar before the fermentation, it is a wine. The process of checking the fermentation is similar in both, only that in the case of wine great caution is to be exercised not to cork too soon, as the energy of the fermentation, being much greater than that of cider, the safety of the corking may be exposed by too early closing. Mashing the fruit, but not so as to bruise the seeds, the juice on being pressed out is mixed with an equal amount of water, and from two to five pounds of sugar to a gallon of the mixture. Grapes usually require about three and a quarter pounds; currants four pounds; blackberry and raspberry, three and a half pounds; peach and cherry, the same as grape; orange wine, the juice of a dozen oranges and three pounds of sugar to a gallon of pure water; the sugar in all cases should be the best white, lump, or crystallized. After the fermentation has nearly ceased it must be stoutly corked, and four or five months later bottled tightly. Sealed well it keeps for years without change. From the invaluable medicinal qualities of grape, currant, and blackberry wines, the certainty of their purity, connected with the fact that nearly every wine of commerce is drugged and utterly unfit for the sick chamber, their manufacture for home use is daily becoming more extensive. No port, sherry, or madeira, as commonly found in our market, is at all comparable to these wines in medicinal excellence or grateful qualities. A practical writer on wine making, in a repor to the Department of Agriculture at Washington, some time since, wrote an exhaustive article on wine making, from which we collate such matter as will be of interest generally to those who have fruit which they wish to convert into wine. The writer says: To make a first class white wine, only white grapes are used; they are mashed in the apparatus, being fixed on the top of the fermenting vat, but not allowing the husks to fall into the vat, which, after being mashed, are put on the press, and when the whole mass is thus prepared, they are pressed out, and the juice, or must, put in the vat. As there are no husks in the vat, the false bottom is not required. The head, or cover, is now put on, and the temperature of the must ascertained by the thermometer. If it is lower than 50°, some must is taken out and heated, to warm up the whole mass till it comes up to 60°, which is the point it should be brought to when fermentation takes a proper course. This temperature must be maintained as evenly as possible, and therefore a proper room, as already described, with a stove or fireplace in it, will be the most serviceable. After the temperature of the must is regulated, the bung with the safety-valve and tube are fixed on, and a small vessel with water is placed under the other end of the tube, or cylinder, so that it will reach into the water about three inches. The whole work of mashing, pressing, regulating the temperature, and closing up the vat, must be performed with the greatest possible speed, as the juice begins to ferment as soon as it is extracted from the berries, and by coming in contact with the atmosphere, the most essential part of the wine, its chief strength, the alcohol, escapes. In proportion as the grape contains sugar, the fermentation of the must will proceed; hence the fermentation of the must from highly improved grapes of best qualities, containing much sugar, and a vintage favored with a hot, dry summer, will take twice as much time as poor and watery juice. By fermentation, the sugar of the grape-juice is converted into alcohol, which amalgamated with the other contents of the grape juice, forms the wine, at once fiery, aromatic, and pleasant in every respect. The dissolution of the greater part of the sugar, and the union with the acids, gluten, tannin, etc., will have been performed when the must begins to get a clear color, an aromatic vinous taste, and quiet; it is then time to draw it from the fermenting vat into the casks, in which it will slowly finish its fermenting process. Rich must will ferment in from five to eight days in the vat, while that of inferior quality gets through in two or three days. It is very important to have large casks in which to keep the wine, as thus its properties and character are much better preserved. When the casks have been filled, a similar tube is fixed, as on the fermenting vat, with one end in the bung-hole and the other in a small vessel of water. Schiller wine signifies a particular color of the wine, varying from one hue to another, and to be called neither white, yellow, nor red. Grapes of all colors are used in making this wine; they are mashed by putting the mill on the top of the vat, and the husks put in it, and fermented together with the must. When they are all mashed, or one vat is filled, the false or fermenting bottom is set in, to keep the husks under the must, and the head and other fixtures put on. The fermenting of schiller wine takes a longer time and is more stormy than white or claret wines; but this is stronger, more fiery, and aromatic, than either. The same temperature is required as for other kinds. Much care, however, must be taken to watch its culminating point, when the carbonic acid gas escapes furiously, the water begins to roar in the little tub, and the safety valve works like a hammer, that nothing may interfere with the action and function of those agents, on which depends, in this critical period, the safety of the whole contents of the vat. The agitation may be observed still better in the glass tube connected with the vat; but after a short time, only a few hours, the must will calm, the fermentation proceed more quietly, and, in two or three days, begin to get clear and vinous, which is the time for drawing the young wine into the casks, there to complete its fermentation. The husks are pressed and the juice obtained added to the rest. As soon as one cask is filled, the tube is fixed into the bung-hole, and a small vessel of water put under the other end, to keep the air from contact with the young wine. The ventilation of the cellar is so regulated as to get an even temperature of about 50°. The blue and Traminer-colored varieties are used for making red wine or claret; after the whole vintage, white, Traminer, and blue, or black, is made into claret. The color of the juice has to be examined, if it be not of the desired dark-red, some coloring matter must be used. There are several harmless substitutes, such as well-ripened elder berries, the berries of the hawthorn, etc. Whatever kind of berries may be used, they should, in all cases, be perfectly ripe; still better if they have been picked some time before they are wanted, and dried in the sun. The quantity of these must be ascertained by taking a sample of the must and adding berry juice till the desired color is obtained; but, as the red or claret wines become lighter by age, the color should at first be a few shades darker. Claret wine takes more time to finish its fermenting process than any other. It is perfected when the color becomes clear, and the taste changed from sweet to strong vinous. According to the state of the weather and the season, which influence the quality of the grape, the fermentation will proceed, but the ordinary period requisite to complete it is from eight to ten days. When finally fit to draw into the casks, the management is the same as with other varieties; the husks are put under the press, and the extracted juice into the casks and mixed with the juice first drawn. The sediment or lees, from either variety, is saved in a cask for further use. The husks, which still contain a considerable amount of wine-making properties, after the juice has been extracted from them by the press, are broken up fine, put into the fermenting vat, and water, in equal proportion to its bulk, is added—to each ten gallons of water one gallon of lees—to strengthen and facilitate its fermentation. A light but pleasant wine is obtained in this way, which is fit to drink the next summer, and will be found, in hot weather, a very agreeable cooling drink. All the seeds should be saved, carefully and thoroughly dried, and hung up in bags and in an airy, dry place. The young wine, after it has been brought into the cellar, will go through another second course of fermentation, and will be more or less agitated, for a certain time. The casks have to be filled occasionally, and kept full to the bung;

the dissolution of the sugar and of the different constituents of the wine will proceed slowly, and finally cease altogether; the undissolved matter settles on the bottom of the cask, and is called lees. When the wine gets to such a state, quiet and clean, it is time to draw it off into another cask. The casks, before using them, must be well cleaned and sulphured, which is done by dissolving sulphur in an iron pan over a fire, cutting strips of cotton cloth or linen two inches wide and nine long, and soaking them in the sulphur, then a piece of wire about a foot long is fastened to the bung, and the other end bent to a hook, on which is hung an ignited strip of the sulphured cotton, and introduced into the cask, the bung driven in, the cask rolled to and fro, and finally the sulphuric acid gas, which has not penetrated into the wood, let out by loosening the bung. A syphon, reaching about two-thirds to the bottom of the cask, is used for drawing. If the empty cask be placed near enough, so that the other end of the syphon reaches to its bung-hole, it is so much better, as there is less escape of the gaseous and flavoring ingredients of the wine. The rest of the wine which the syphon does not draw is drawn off by a faucet, about six inches above the bottom. When a cask is thus filled to the bung-hole, the bung is driven in tight. In order to preserve the fine, clear condition of the wine, all jerking and other rough treatment of the casks must be avoided. The lees from the emptied casks are collected into a cask by itself. White wines will have attained the proper condition for drawing in a couple of months, wine of inferior quality still sooner, and should be drawn immediately after showing a clear, bright color, as the sediment injures its taste and character. Schiller wine, according to its quality and intended use, may remain some time on the lees, especially if it is designed for preserving to an old age; but in most instances it will improve by drawing as soon as it is clear. Claret wine, however, should remain from five to six months in the first cask and lees. When fermentation is no longer perceptible, the cask is filled, the bung driven in, and it is left undisturbed till the drawing is finished. The exact period is a matter of fashion, according to the taste and habit predominating in the country where it is sold. By letting it stand on the lees for several months it obtains more of those peculiar principles, astringency, etc., preferred in good claret. No wine should be drawn, and no good wine-cooper will open a cask in cloudy or sultry weather, as the wine, coming in contact with such an atmosphere, gets turbid and excited; therefore cool and bright days must be chosen for that purpose. All articles used in the drawing, no matter how clean they may be kept, should be previously rinsed with wine. There are many instances when the wine loses its character, either by turning flat, or getting excited and turbid, when it will be necessary to attend at once to its restoration by applying proper remedies, and prevent it from total destruction. By acting according to the principles set down here, such cases can occur only by accident; but, to avoid the calamity, constant care is required. The causes may be different, but generally it will be found that neglect, merely, or perhaps ignorance of proper management, created the trouble. When wine becomes flat, it wants stimulating. This may be done by various means. The liquid from two pounds of raisins, cut fine, and soaked a few days in a gallon of good rectified alcohol, then pressed and strained, is mixed with a couple of gallons of the flat wine, heated to near boiling, and all put into the cask again. After it has been well stirred, the bung is replaced and left undisturbed for at least two months, when it may be drawn into another cask, previously well sulphured. Every thirty gallons will require a gallon of alcohol and two pounds of raisins. Another good remedy is, from each thirty gallons of flat wine, two gallons are taken out, two pounds of well-dried grape seed added, and brought over fire; while it is heating the seeds are stirred and rubbed with a beater, and after a while the liquid is strained and put hot into the cask again, which is bunged up immediately. Practical knowledge and experience are necessary to manage such wines; but the cause of the trouble may easily be prevented by adhering to the general principles of wine-making. If the cask produced the flatness, the wine must be drawn first into another, before anything is done with it. When the wine becomes excited, turbid, and ferments again, which may occur often in poor cellars, if the weather should change from cold to warm, or if the casks have been opened in close, sultry, and cloudy weather, the difficulty will be found most likely in the cellar. Wine can not be expected to keep and mature well in a poor cellar, which, perhaps, is also used for other purposes. Sulphur is a good remedy. An empty, clean cask is provided, two gallons of the infected wine put in, a strip of sulphured cotton ignited, the bung driven in, and the cask rolled. After a while, two gallons more of wine are put in, sulphured, and rolled again, according to the quantity to be cured; eight or ten gallons may be impregnated with sulphur, or even more; and finally restored to its stand, and well stirred, with the bung out. After the wine has been drawn once, there is still more or less undissolved matter in it, which will soon settle to the bottom of the cask and therefore render necessary another drawing. This must be done, generally, three or four times before the wine gets clear, well-fined, and fit for the market. The proper time for drawing will be at intervals of from three to five months; but experience and judgment alone can point out the exact period. If it is desired to sell the wine before it has attained its finish, it must be fined. This is done by taking out of the cask from four to five gallons, and adding to each thirty gallons the whites of ten eggs; these are beaten to foam with the wine, finally put into the cask, well stirred, and the cask bunged up. Or powdered gum arabic may be used, in the proportion of one ounce to fifty gallons of wine, well stirred with the whole contents. Both articles are perfectly harmless to the character of the wine, and entirely answer the purpose. In the course of from four to six days the wine will be in the desired condition to draw and bottle for market. It will keep best and improve more in the casks; but there are several instances when, after it has been drawn, and the casks filled, portions remain, for which no casks small enough can be provided; it is better to draw such portions at once into bottles. Simple as the bottling seems to be, yet there are many things to be observed, in order to keep the wine well and prevent it from becoming flat and turbid. The first and chief requirements are clean, sweet bottles, and new, fresh corks; it must be a rule, strictly adhered to, that as soon as a bottle is emptied it is to be rinsed out well with water and placed in the open air, on a shelf or frame erected for the purpose; before using, it is rinsed out once more, and then filled within two inches of the mouth. The cork, which should fit exactly, is dipped into wine, and driven well in. The bottles should always be placed in a horizontal position, so that the corks can not get dry and admit air, which is generally the reason why the wine gets flat. They keep best if put in dry sand, one above the other. As further protection, the corks may be waxed. The husks, lees, and seeds may be differently used; a pleasant wine can be made of them, in the way already described, but a real good marketable wine is obtained by adding sugar in proportion to the vinous principles, found out by proper instruments, by which all wines have to be brought up to a certain standard point, most favorable to their development. But, as a description of this modern art of wine making would require more room than has been allowed, it may only be mentioned that a vintage can be increased from 100 to 200 per cent. without the least detriment to its quality. If the husks are not wanted for this purpose, a good vinegar may be obtained from them. As soon as they come from the press they are broken up fine, and put into a vinegar vat, twice their bulk of rainwater added, with two gallons of lees and a quart of beer-yeast to each barrel. The vat is set in a warm room, but not in a fermenting room, cellar, or anywhere near wine, and allowed to stand till the vinegar is formed, which is then drawn into barrels, the husks being brought to the compost heap, or directly to the vineyard. The lees contain considerable undissolved sugar and other vinous substances, which, by distilling, make a highly flavored brandy. The quantity may be increased without affecting its good quality by adding to each barrel of lees half a barrel of well rectified alcohol; that from potatoes is the best. Let it stand a couple of weeks, turning the cask once or twice a day, and finally it will be fit for the still. The remainder in the still, too weak for brandy, makes a good vinegar. Lees are likewise a good stimulant for flat, insipid wine, and a portion should always be kept on hand to be thus applied. Grape seeds are very valuable for fining and strengthening the wine; they may be used either in the manner mentioned, or a few handfuls thrown into the cask just as they are. They must be well dried, and kept hung up in an airy place. In consequence of many failures in the ripening of the grape, and diseases spreading rapidly over the continent, more or less destroying the crops of whole districts, grape culturists and chemists began to look for remedies and substitutes for those principles in which the vintages are deficient. Much has been said against this method, and much suggested to neutralize predominating acids without resort to sugar and water, but all experiments have thus far failed, either the wine would get flat at once, or be unfit for use on account of its harshness. More than fifty years ago, Chaptal, Cadet de Vaux, and other eminent chemists, suggested that poor wines might be improved by adding sugar; later, Claudot-Dumont urged his countrymen to abstain from the bad practice of sweating and mixing their poor wines, and recommended sugar as the best agent to improve them. But neither of these chemists were able to point out in what proportion sugar should be used to obtain the desired result. This problem has finally been solved by Drs. Gall and Petiol, and approved by such men as Thénard, Döbeneiner, Von Babo, Bronner, and others. Drs. Gall and Petiol both discovered, after many analytical experiments and researches, that the surplus acids in the grape juice can be turned to good account, by bringing its other ingredients (sugar and water) to a proper proportion. Every kind of grape juice is nothing but clear water, in which are dissolved from six to thirty per cent. of sugar, two to four per cent. of free acids, and from three to five per cent. of other matter, or the essence of wine-making principles. Sugar converts itself into alcohol by fermenting, and two per cent. of sugar will produce, in the average, one per cent. of alcohol; the free acids, if they are in proportion to the other principles, give the wine its agreeable vinous character, its flavor, etc.; the last properties contain the principles necessary for fermenting, fining, and keeping. Dr. Gall has further proved the fact that these different acids in the grape do not require particular notice; it is sufficient to find out the whole sum, and then treat them alike. In order to ascertain what percentage of sugar and acids the must, or grape juice, contains, two different instruments are required, a must scale and an acidimeter; for the first purpose Oechsle's must scale is generally used, and Otto's acidimeter for the second; on both the following calculations are based, illustrative of the method, as given, of making wine. Experiments continued for eight years have proved that, in favorable seasons, grape-juice contains, in the average, in 1,000 pounds:

Material.	Pounds
Sugar	240
Free acids	6
Water	754
	1,000

These proportions may be set down as normal; therefore, to obtain good wine from a vintage of inferior quality, these proportions must be secured by adding sugar and water. It will be seen that the contents of the acids are the indicating point as to what quantities of sugar and water would be required to bring the wine to such a normal state; further, as has been the case generally, the less sugar the more acids. The per cent. of acid in the grape-juice is the basis on which a calculation must be founded. All practical grape-growers and wine-makers in Germany and France admit that a wine containing the proportion of sugar, acids, and water above described, is in every respect preferable to heavier or lighter wines. It has lately been called a normal wine, and will serve here as well as a standard. When a must contains, instead of twenty-four per cent., only fifteen per cent., or instead of two hundred and forty pounds, only one hundred and fifty pounds of sugar, but, instead of only six per cent. of pounds, nine per cent. of acids in one thousand pounds, the question arises, how much sugar and water will have to be added, to bring such a must to the proportion of a normal wine? To solve it, we calculate thus: if, in six pounds of acid, in a normal wine, two hundred and forty pounds of sugar appear, how much sugar is wanted for nine pounds of acids? Answer: three hundred and sixty pounds. And again: If, in six pounds of acids, in a normal wine, seven hundred and fifty-four pounds of water appear, how much water is required for nine pounds of acids? Answer: one thousand one hundred and thirty-one pounds. As, therefore, the must, which we intend to improve by neutralizing its acids, should contain 360 pounds of sugar, nine pounds of acids, and 1,131 pounds of water, but contains already 150 pounds of sugar, nine pounds of acids, and 841 pounds of water, there remains to be added 210 pounds of sugar, 0 pounds of acids, and 290 pounds of water. By ameliorating a quantity of 1,000 pounds must by 210 pounds sugar and 290 pounds water, we obtain 1,500 pounds of must, consisting of the same properties as the normal must, which makes a first class wine. The increase of the quantity is five hundred pounds, or two hundred and fifteen quarts, which, after deducting the outlay for sugar, two hundred and ten pounds, at twelve and a half cents per pound, amounts to twenty-six dollars and twenty-five cents, and, allowing fifty cents per quart, leaves a clear profit of eighty-one dollars and twenty-five cents. Another illustration, which probably comes near the qualities of northern wild native grapes may be thus calculated: Such grape-juice, or must, contains twelve per cent., or one hundred and twenty pounds of sugar, fifteen per cent., or pounds of acids. One thousand pounds of such must will consist, then, of one hundred and twenty pounds of sugar, fifteen pounds of acids, and eight hundred and sixty-five pounds of water. In order to neutralize these acids, and make them proportionate, corresponding with wine of a good character and normal state, it will require to fifteen pounds of acids, 600 pounds of sugar and 1,885 pounds of water; as the must contains fifteen pounds of acids, 120 pounds of sugar, and 865 pounds of water, have to be added 0 pounds of acids, 480 pounds of sugar, and 1,020 pounds of water. Such improved must will, therefore, consist of fifteen pounds of acids, 600 pounds of sugar, 1,885 pounds of water, or in all 2,500 pounds. Deducting one thousand pounds of must, which furnished the wine-making principles, acids, etc., gives a surplus of fifteen hundred pounds, or six hundred and forty-five quarts of must in a normal state. Value of six hundred and forty-five quarts, at fifty cents per quart, three hundred and twenty-two dollars and fifty cents. Cost of four hundred and eighty pounds of sugar, at twelve and a half cents per pound, sixty dollars. Net profit, two hundred and sixty two dollars and fifty cents. It will be seen that such wine is produced at the small expense of nine and a quarter cents per quart, omitting the one thousand pounds, or four hundred and thirty quarts, which furnished the wine-making principles. But a true estimate of the cost of such a wine from the wild native grapes when they have to be bought must be calculated thus:

3,000 pounds of grapes, at 3½ cents per pound. ... $105.00
480 pounds of sugar, at 12½ cents per pound..... 60.00

Total cost........................... $165.00

And as one hundred and sixty-five dollars make two thousand five hundred pounds of must, or one thousand seventy-five quarts, the actual expense is fifteen and one-third cents per quart; allowing interest on capital invested for apparatus, casks, shrinkage, and labor, the whole expense will not average twenty cents per quart. An immense field of profitable employment presents itself to industrious men. In a favorable season a man will gather five bushels of wild grapes in a day, from which he obtains at least eighty quarts of natural wine, while if ameliorated according to Drs. Gall and Petiol, he will get 120 quarts of good native wine. It is further proved that such wines made according to these principles mature at least in half the time required by natural wine, and keep better; consequently permitting a quicker return of invested capital, a better article for speculation, safe transport to distant markets, etc. Thus, too, a good wine can be made of an inferior vintage, grown in an unfavorable season, and the quantity of a rich vintage increased to 200 per cent., without the least detriment to its quality. It is very important that this method should be introduced into our country; it will not only encourage people to more activity in this lucrative branch of industry, but will furnish us with a wholesome and pleasant beverage; insuring as a pure, cheap article, a large consumption and a ready sale. Grapes properly cultivated in vineyards or gardens, and in favorable climates and localities, will generally contain sufficient sugar and no surplus of acids; so it may appear that there is no need to practice this method. But Dr. Gall and others found by analyzing the husks or pomace, after the juice had been extracted by means of powerful presses, that these not only still contained a considerable amount of juice, but also a great amount of extracts or wine-making principles, in many cases sufficient for three times the bulk of the juice previously obtained. This fact suggested the question: as there are so many of these valuable properties left, and only sugar and water exhausted, why can not these principles be substituted till the others are completely used up? It was found that it could be easily done. The secret of making wine from water was thus solved, and an all-important principle for wine-making established. By further experiments these speculations not only proved to be correct, but it was in most cases impossible to judge which was natural wine, or which the product of this new method; indeed, the preference is generally given to the latter. While natural wine is so very different, according to circumstances which prevailed in its growth, such Gallized wine is always in perfect harmony, because its contents are not the results of chance, but the close following of processes of nature. The practice of this method is quite simple; for instance, let the vintage be of an average good quality, the must containing twenty-four per cent. of sugar and six per cent. of acid, and the quantity 1,000 pounds. The grapes are mashed in the usual way, but not pressed; the juice, if it be white wine, drawn off into casks to ferment; if claret or red wine, it is fermented on the husks, as described in a former paragraph, and then drawn off into casks. Before this is done, however, 240 pounds of sugar are dissolved in 754 pounds of water, and as soon as the grape-juice is drawn off, this solution is put on the husks in the fermenting vat. It is absolutely necessary to have sugar-water prepared and ready for an infusion before the wine is drawn from the fermenting vat, and put immediately on the pomace as soon as the wine is off, to prevent their coming in contact with the air, getting dry, moldy, and spoiled. It is practicable to draw off this infusion once and put it on the husks again in order that their fatty substances may be better dissolved; but this operation has to be performed without delay, as fermentation commences immediately, and must not be interrupted. The water used for that purpose should be soft rain or cistern water. A large iron or copper kettle is put over a fire and heated, in which the sugar is thoroughly dissolved and then the whole brought to a temperature of 70° and poured over the husks in the vat. The mode of fermenting, temperature, and the entire operation, is the same as before described. To obtain a certain color, it may be necessary to let this second wine remain longer on the husks and in the vat. The proper period for drawing will be best found out by often examining samples till the desired result is obtained. When this is the case, the young wine is drawn off and filled into casks. Again, 240 pounds of sugar are dissolved in 754 pounds of water put on the husks and managed as before stated. Should this second wine, after it has fermented and been drawn off from the lees, contain less than five per cent. of acid, it will be necessary to add two ounces of tartaric acid to each 100 pounds, or twenty ounces to 1,000 pounds of wine; the tartar is pulverized and dissolved in two quarts of heated wine, which is then put into the casks and well stirred. After this third wine (second infusion) has fermented and been drawn off, the husks are taken out and put under the press, and the extracted juice added to the rest in the casks. This wine is treated like other wines, only left some time longer on the lees before drawing and fining. There is, from 1,000 pounds, of 430 quarts of must, an increase of 2,000 pounds, or 860 quarts of wine, which, after charging for 480 pounds of sugar, at twelve and a half cents per pound, will equal sixty dollars, or not quite seven cents per quart. The must-scale and acidimeter have to be used often while wine is in its fermenting process, and before it is drawn off from the vat, in order to examine and find out the capacity of the husks, whether they contain sufficient properties for another infusion, or only for a part. If the result of the examination of the young wine shows an undiminished amount of acids, the husks will bear another infusion of sugar-water to the same amount as before; or if there is found a deficiency of one and a half or two per cent., the quantity of sugar and water must be regulated accordingly. For instance, after the first infusion has fermented, the pomace shows a decrease of two per cent. of acids, or wine extracts, but there is still four per cent. remaining, which, if fermented with a proportionate quantity of sugar-water, will make as good a wine as any. Therefore, to determine of what proportion the second infusion should consist, we calculate thus: If six per cent. of acids require 240 pounds of sugar, how much is wanted for four per cent.? Answer: 160 pounds. Now, if six per cent. of acid required 754 pounds of water, how much is wanted for four per cent.? Answer: 502¾ pounds. There is consequently wanted for the second infusion 160 pounds of sugar and 502¾ pounds of water. It will sometimes be found that, after two infusions have been fermented, and 200 per cent. obtained, the pomace still contains several per cent. of wine extract; therefore, a third infusion of sugar-water may be applied, and a still larger quantity of wine obtained. The calculation in regard to the amount of sugar and water to be used is the same. In either case, should a stronger vinous taste be desired, tartaric acid is added by degrees till the object is attained. To facilitate these manipulations, it is necessary to construct tables, in which the proportion of weight and measure to each other are calculated. It will be found more convenient in practice to measure the must and water, instead of weighing, and as must will differ in its specific weight, according to its acids and saccharine properties, it is necessary to have a table, on which can be ascertained, according to the indication of the scales, the exact amount of each. On the table, for instance, which has been calculated and constructed to Oechsle's must-scale, when ninety-five per cent. is indicated, it will be found that the must contains 21.8 per cent. of sugar. The acids and extracts which the must contains increase its specific weight, and prevent the scale from sinking and showing the amount of sugar correctly, being deducted, and the exact amount of sugar found on it. For the acidimeter, a table is constructed, on which is found the calculation how the per cents. of acid compare with those of sugar, and how much water is required for certain per cents. of acids and sugar in weight and measure. These tables, as they are compiled in conformity with the scales, are generally supplied with the instruments, and with directions for use. As the sugar contains more or less water, even when it appears perfectly dry, it is necessary, after a certain quantity has been dissolved for such ameliorating purposes, to use the must-scale, find out how it compares with the intended purpose, and regulate the balance by either adding more sugar or water till the desired point on the scale is correct. It is a matter of course that only sugar of the best quality should be used; grape sugar is the best; but as this can not be had cheap and in large quantities, white loaf sugar must be used. Still there is no doubt that enough of the former will be manufactured as soon as a demand is manifested. Since the introduction of this method of wine-making into Germany, several grape-sugar factories have been established, and are all doing well, as the demand for this article increases from year to year. Grape sugar can be produced from forty to fifty per cent. cheaper than white loaf sugar; it is therefore, a great desideratum that this method should be adopted. It has been suggested to keep each part of the wine by itself: as the natural wine, the first, second, and third, that a fair chance of judgment may be had; but afterward, when the result has given satisfaction, and all doubts are removed, it will be found that no reason exists why they should not be mixed at once, as the care and management will be considerably facilitated, without interfering in the least with its quality. (See articles Cider and Gallizing for further information.)

WINE STONE. Crude tartar, argal or argol.

WINGS. *Alæ.* In botany, the side petals of pea-like flowers, the membranous expansions of the seeds of the ash, ailanthus, parsnip, and other seeds.

WINTER AND SUMMER PRUNING. The principal object to be kept in view in pruning is to calculate so we may keep the top in proper shape, and so equalize all that each portion of the tree may have a due proportion of light and air, so far as practicable; and, that the tree may form its head from a single stem regularly, and from a given height, keeping the branches regular, and of as equal size as possible, each having as due a proportion of sap as may be. In this the operator must have due regard to the variety, so that the natural habit of the tree may be preserved so far as possible. Therefore no rule can be laid down that will apply to all; for, some are pendulous, others upright, and others again are spreading. The operator must study the natural habit of each, and use his judgment accordingly. In the West, however, all orchard trees should have their trunks shaded so far as possible, and their tops should be kept as dense as possible, affording at the same time due amount of light in every part. Why? We know that all varieties of orchard fruit, whatever their natural locality, require free circulation of air, and a due proportion of sun-light; for, fruits grown in deep shade are never fine in color or flavor; and; this, in proportion to such exclusion. When the top is so dense as to exclude a proper circulation of air, and are deprived of proper light, the leaves are pale, watery, and consequently incapable of their proper functions as elaborators of sap, etc. But trees require a moist atmosphere, and hence, in the West, they may not be so severely pruned as on the seacoast, or near other large bodies of water. If, however, they be deprived of proper light and air, the weaker portions gradually sicken, and at length die and become harbors for insects, and the decay may gradually extend to other parts of the tree. Therefore all branches or shoots showing signs of disease or decay should be immediately removed. This accomplished, and the head kept sufficiently open so that the branches and foliage do not interfere, and yet kept sufficiently dense so the trunk and ground beneath may be well shaded, is about all that is required in ordinary orchard pruning in the West. In pruning, the natural habit of the tree must be preserved so far as possible. The three principal forms of growth are: First, conical shaped, second, round topped, and third, spreading. Types of these, with a strong upward tendency, are, Sweet June, and Paradise Winter Sweet; those with round heads, Fameuse, and Golden Russett, and those with spreading tops, Tallman Sweet, and Bellflower. To these may be added Primate, Rhode Island Greening, and Stannard, as crooked and irregular growers. It is evident that these will all require different systems of pruning. This should always be done with a view to preserve their natural inclination, so far as possible. The first two simply require to be kept in shape, and thinned only sufficiently to duly admit light and air. The two latter, to be shortened in only sufficiently to induce thicker growth, and induce, so far as may be, symmetry; always keeping the top thoroughly well clothed with leaves. No pruning is better than mutilation. And yet the usual rule is to send the hired man into the orchard some time in winter, with an axe and saw; and after, have him cart out the limbs on a hay rack to the brush heap. Is it any wonder, then, that the mutilated skeletons remaining, clothe themselves with water sprouts and refuse to bear fruit, or that they sicken, decay, and soon die? Is it any wonder that such pruning tends to intensify the idea that it is cheaper to buy fruit than to raise it? In conclusion, the following may be adopted as the ten commandments in fruit planting for the ordinary farmer, who does not profess to be a finished horticulturist: 1. Plant only such varieties as are generally known to be hardy. 2. Select only well formed, healthy trees. 3. Prepare for the orchard on a well drained spot, and bring the soil into good tilth. 4. Plant your trees carefully and pack the earth well around the roots. 5. Force them to remain upright by staking, or otherwise, until they get thoroughly established. 6. Induce twig growth on the stems, while young, to strengthen them, and cut back the young tops to induce a close, firm head. 7. Shade the stems until the top gets sufficient size to do so themselves. 8. Form the heads as low and as dense as possible, having due regard to convenience, and light and air; you have no business with a horse and plow next the trunks. 9. Keep the ground in good heart, and well stirred, up to the middle of July. 10. Keep the pruning knife and saw out of your orchard, except to reduce superabundant and struggling growth, and take this out whenever seen. Thus every farmer may grow sufficient fruit for home use, cheaper than he can buy it.

WINTER BERRY. *Prinos (Ilex) verticillata.* False alder, a shrub of four to eight feet, with permanent red berries, adapted to shrubberies.

WINTER CRESS. *Barbarea præcox.* An indigenous, perennial, cruciferous plant, growing near spring branches, similar to water-cress, but more pungent in flavor. *B. vulgaris,* also indigenous, is the water-radish, or rocket.

WINTER GREEN. The genus *Chimaphila;* pretty Alpine plants. They are perennial, with long roots, and grow in the shade of woods. The *C. umbellata*—pipsissewa—is used in domestic medicine as a tonic and as an astringent.

WIRE GRASS. (See Blue Grass.)

WIRE WORM. (See Elater.)

WISTARIA. The wistarias are so called hardy climbers, and are really so in the north, up to the latitude of Lake Erie, and even farther north in protected situations, where they may have the protection of a wall or the house. They require a light rich soil, and are among the most rapid and elegant of climbing plants, but are better if taken down late in the autumn and covered, as recommended for grape vines. There are two principal species, and a number of varieties. *Wistaria brachybotrys* is the Japan variety, with light blue and fragrant flowers. *W. Chinensis* is one of the most elegant and rapid growing of any, often reaching fifteen or twenty feet in a season. It has long, pendant clusters of pale blue flowers, in May or June, and again in autumn. The cut shows a shoot, leaves and bloom one quarter of the natural size. There is a white variety, *(alba,)* which is very fine. The double purple wistaria, introduced from Japan, has double flowers, and is deeper in color than the single Chinese wistaria which it otherwise resembles. Another desirable variety is the

Shrubby or cluster flowered wistaria, *W. frutescens*, less vigorous than the Chinese, the flowers pale blue and borne in short clusters; the variety *alba*, or white American wistaria has clear white flowers, and like its blue relative, they are borne in short bunches. This is a free bloomer. *W. magnifica*, has the flowers in dense-drooping racemes, of the size and general character of the Chinese, pale lilac in color, and is vigorous and a free bloomer.

WITHE. A flexible twig or bough that may be twisted and used as a cord.

WITHERITE. Mineral carbonate of baryta.

WITHERS. The high portion of an animal's back over the shoulders. Horses with high withers are said to have the fore hand well up; they go high above the ground and are quick and safe. In draft horses the breadth or weight of the fore hand is desirable. The word is sometimes applied to the womb of the cow. Casting the withers is inversion and protrusion of the womb. It should be returned by the hand and arm, and maintained in its place by a roll of linen introduced into the vagina in a wet state. The animal must be kept quiet and free from fever. (See Womb, Inversion of.)

WOLF'S BANE. Monk's hood.

WOLLASTONITE. A species of prismatic augite.

WOOD. The substance of the trunk of exogenous trees; it consists of an internal hard and colored portion, the heart-wood (*duramen*), and an external, softer, and more perishable part, the new wood, sap wood, or alburnum. It consists of woody fiber and ducts. Wood decays slowly, and yields water and carbonic acid when in contact with air.

WOODBINE. The honeysuckle.

WOODCHUCK. *Arctomys monax*. The ground hog, as the animal is familiarly called, is known all over the North, and is found West as far as the Rocky mountains. Its natural haunts are woodlands, the banks of streams, the edges of groves, and rocky bluffs. Though, as a coun try is cleared up, it often takes to the meadows or permanent pastures, where clover is found, of which it is fond. It likes green corn, peas, and various garden vegetables, and also eats insects and larvæ to some degree. Its burrows deface pastures, and although not so destructive as the rabbit, from its greater scarcity, it should be destroyed whenever found. Its fur is not valuable, but its tough skin, when tanned, makes the best of whip lashes and pouches.

WOODCOCK. *Grallatores*. The whole order of waders, comprising bitterns, cranes, herons, plovers, rails, sandpipers, snipes, and woodcock, are beneficial to the farmers, and should be preserved, since their food consists entirely of insects. The food of the woodcock (*Scolophax minor*) is earth worms and also such larvæ as it can draw out of the ground with its long bill. It is nocturnal and is seldom seen during the day, except it be roused from its covert. Their haunts during the day are woods and thickets, which they leave at night for the fields and moist places in search of food.

WOODPECKER. *Picus.* The red-headed woodpecker (*P. erythrocephalus*) is the most common of the family North. It may be regarded as a beneficial bird, since its habit of boring into trees is solely to take the borers and other insects which infest them. The Hairy Woodpecker (*P. villosus*) is a southern species, but is also a summer resident of the valley of the Mississippi up to the northern borders of the great lakes. Its food is insects and grain of various kinds. The Canada Woodpecker (*P. Canadensis*) somewhat resembles this species, but is found further north. The Golden Woodpecker, (*P. auratus*) known also as Yellow Hammer, High Holder, and Flicker. Their food is insects of various

CHINESE WISTARIA—ONE-QUARTER SIZE.

kinds and various fruits and berries. They can hardly be classed as beneficial to the horticulturist, but may be so to the mere farmer.

WOOD PEWEE. (See Pewee.)

WOOD SORREL. The genus *Oxalis*, the leaves of which are sour, and contain oxalate of potash. They grow in rich, shady places. Many species bear beautiful flowers.

WOOD WASPS. The saw flies.

WOOD WAXEN. *Genista tinctoria*. Dyer's broom, a perennial leguminous plant, with yellow flowers, growing one foot high, leaves lanceolate, smooth, stem round, upright, without spines. It is exotic, but grows readily in the Northern and Eastern States. The plant in flower yields a yellow dye, which is fixed by solution of tin or acetate of alumina. It may be readily raised from seed, in drills a foot apart, and the plants kept clean by the cultivator.

WOODY FIBER. Very slender, tapering, cellular tissue, containing lignin, and forming, when compacted together, the tough fiber of hemp, flax, and vegetables, as well as the bulk of wood.

WOOL. Ranking with cotton, as a clothing material, the wool industry of the world is, year by year assuming greater and greater proportions.

Large as is the area in the United States adapted to the keeping of sheep, the wool supply has always been unable to keep up with the yearly increasing demand of the manufacturers. Of late years, however, or since 1870, our imports of wool have not increased. For the first half of the decade, two-thirds of the manufactured product was home grown, the bulk of the imports being low grade carpet wool and unwashed merino, but constituting only about one-fourth of the value of the wool manufactured. Among the wool producing countries of the world, Australia has made the most marvelous growth in the production of this staple. In 1840, England imported thence only 10,000,000 pounds of wool. In 1874 England imported from that country 238,000,000 pounds of wool, and the flocks, including New Zealand, consisted of 55,496,907 sheep. The following table, compiled from late sources of information, carefully verified, places the sheep and the wool of the world as follows:

Countries.	Number of sheep.	Pounds of wool.
Europe:		
Great Britain	35,000,000	218,000,000
German Empire	29,000,000	125,000,000
Austria-Hungary	21,000,000	60,000,000
Russia	50,000,000	188,000,000
France	26,000,000	124,000,000
Spain	22,000,000	69,000,000
Portugal	2,750,000	11,000,000
Italy	11,000,000	38,000,000
Turkey	15,000,000	37,500,000
Greece	2,630,000	7,500,000
Switzerland	550,000	2,500,000
Denmark	1,900,000	8,000,000
Holland	900,000	4,500,000
Belgium	800,000	3,500,000
Sweden	1,700,000	6,000,000
Norway	1,750,000	6,250,000
Total	221,750,000	838,750,000
America:		
United States	36,000,000	185,000,000
Canada	2,000,000	8,000,000
South America and Mexico	58,000,000	174,000,000
Total	96,000,000	367,000,000
Asia	175,000,000	350,000,000
Africa:		
Northern	20,000,000	45,000,000
Cape of Good Hope	12,000,000	51,000,000
Total	32,000,000	96,000,000
Australia	60,000,000	235,000,000
Grand Total	584,750,000	1,926,750,000

The estimate of Great Britain is based upon four and three-quarter pounds of wool per fleece, with 52,000,000 pounds for wool of sheep butchered during the year. The number thus disposed of is usually reckoned at three-eighths of the standing numbers of the flocks. In the German Empire the average is placed at three and two-thirds pounds, with 6,000,000 fleeces of three pounds from slaughtered sheep. Hungarian fleeces are lighter, and in Austria-Hungary the extra fleeces are assumed to bring the average nearly to three pounds for each sheep. France produces heavier sheep and fleeces than the German States, more mutton sheep, with a larger proportion annually slaughtered, making 124,000,000 pounds for standing flocks of 26,000,000 sheep a reasonable estimate. The South American fleeces are variable, but the average is much lower than in South Africa or Australia, and the sheep of Asia can not be safely estimated to yield more than two pounds each. There are some sheep in the islands of the Pacific, rendering the total estimate of 2,000,000,000 pounds very probable, and the number of sheep of the world 600,000,000 in round numbers is at least approximately correct. In the United States the sheep are kept almost entirely for their wool. The mutton product is really a minor consideration, except in the vicinity of large cities. In some portions of the country the pelts are even yet considered the more valuable portion of the dead animal. In England, mutton is of fully as much importance as the wool; hence when an Englishman buys, he feels the animal and asks how much it will weigh. An American parts the wool and asks how much wool it will shear. Thus in the United States the efforts are in the direction of wool; in England in the production of mutton. The shearing and handling of wool may be summed up as follows: If the sheep have been washed, shearing should take place when the oily-feeling matter, termed yolk, has so far reappeared in the wool as to give it its natural brilliant appearance and silky feeling. The mode of shearing can not be described here in detail. The wool should be cut off evenly and smooth, reasonably close, but not leaving the skin naked and red, which renders the sheep very liable to receive injury from cold. Stubble shearing and trimming, leaving the wool long, so as to give the next fleece the appearance of extraordinary length, leaving it long in places, in order to affect the apparent shape of the animal, are both frauds. The fleece should be as little broken as possible in shearing. It should be gathered up carefully, placed on a smooth table, with the inside ends down, put into the exact shape in which it came from the sheep, and pressed close together. If there are dung-balls, they should be removed. Fold in each side one-quarter, next the neck and breech one-quarter, and the fleece will then be in an oblong square form, some twenty inches wide, and twenty-five or thirty inches long. Then fold it once more lengthwise and it is ready to be rolled up and tied, or placed in the press. The improved wool-press, worked by a lever, or a crank etc., does the work far more expeditiously, far better, and with much less labor than doing it up by hand. Three bands of moderate sized twine, flax or hemp once round are enough for the fleece. It is fraudulent to put the unwashed wool of sheep that have died of disease, or of those which have been killed, or unwashed tags, into washed fleeces. It is also fraudulent to sell burred wool so done up as to conceal the burs, without giving notice to the buyer. The burred wool should be put by itself, so that the buyer can open and examine it. Wool should be stored in a clean dry room, tight enough to keep out dust, vermin, and insects. If sacked and sent off to market, it is put up in bales nine feet long, formed of two breadths of burlaps thirty-five or forty inches wide.

WOLF TEETH. In so called moon-blindness, small, black, imperfect teeth, sometimes found between the nippers and grinders, and called wolf teeth, are credited with the cause of the disease. Both names are incorrect. So called moon blindness is periodical ophthalmia,

TOTAL ANNUAL PRODUCTION.

Share of Capital, Savings of the People, and Entire Annual Wages Fund.

"A"—Domestic consumption on farms and domestic product of families, which is not exchanged or does not come into the commercial product, $1,000,000,000.

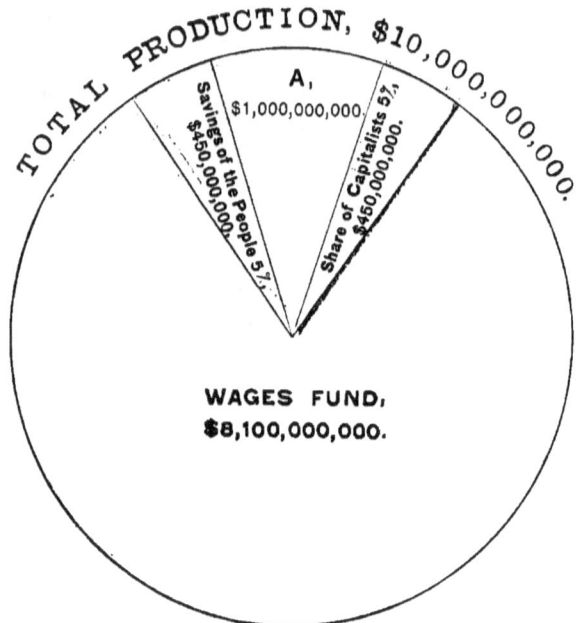

In the above Tabulation the "Wages Fund" is calculated from official statistics, and may be divided as follows:

FIRST.

Share of 1,100,000 persons assumed to be engaged in mental and administrative work.. $1,100,000,000
This class may be further subdivided: 200,000 teachers in lower grade schools, scientists, authors, artists, young lawyers, clergymen and others in similar employments, at an average of $550............ $ 110,000,000
900,000 merchants, tradesmen, officials, superintendents, etc., at an average of $1,100..... 990,000,000

Total, as above... $1,100,000,000

SECOND.

Share of 16,200,000 farmers, laborers, mechanics, artisans, operators, clerks, dressmakers and other wage-workers, at an average of $432 7,000,000,000

Grand Total, as shown in diagram............................ $8,100,000,000

which see. The teeth have nothing to do with the disease, except that when loose they should be extracted. So also the other teeth should be looked to, as a diseased condition of the teeth produces intensity of ophthalmia by sympathy of the several parts. (See Eyes, Inflammation of.)

WOMB, INVERSION OF. It is not unusual in protracted and difficult labor in farm animals, especially the mare and cow. Thus from excessive straining, the womb is inverted and protruded in the form of a large red or violet colored bag. If not discovered for some time, engorged and purple with thick blood. The treatment is to cleanse thoroughly with warm water. If it be much engorged, puncture lightly, just deep enough to draw blood, and with a sharp lancet, to relieve the engorged blood vessels. When the bleeding has proceeded far enough, stop the flow with cold water. Then while two helpers support the mass by means of a cloth held underneath it, the operator oils the bag, and placing his right hand, well oiled, against the horn or point of the bag furthest from the vagina, presses it gently, but steadily and firmly into its place, as far as may be possible. Then with the left hand the dependent parts are pressed inwards, the assistants helping by following the bag to keep it from again extruding, until it can be fixed by a pledget of oiled tow, supported by a bandage kept in place by attached to a surcingle and collar forward. If there is continued straining, give the cow half an ounce of chloroform and two ounces of laudanum in a quart of milk. In any case the bowels must be restrained from acting for twenty-four hours by means of laudanum. This accomplished and the pains having ceased, the tow may be removed, and finally the bandage; but the animal must have quiet for some time. (See article Parturition.)

WORMING. An operation performed on puppies, consisting in the removal of a vermiform ligament from under the tongue; it is ignorantly supposed to prevent madness, but, in fact, merely breaks them of their habit of gnawing.

WORMSEED. Goosefoot, Jerusalem oak. An oil is distilled from the seeds, and called worm-seed oil: it is exceedingly nauseous, and ts given to children in the dose of five to ten drops, and followed by cathartics. (See Goosefoot.)

WORMWOOD. The genus *Artemisia*, including southernwood, mugwort, etc. They are composite, bitter perennials, with a strong, rank odor, and have been much used as tonic bitters, and some species are vermifuges. Common wormwood is *A. absinthium*: the French flavor a cordial with it, but its habitual use is deleterious.

WIRT. A decoction of malt; an old name for an herb.

WOUNDS. The treatment of wounds, says the late Dr. Dadd, depends altogether upon their nature and cause. It is very difficult in the horse—although not so in man—to heal a wound by what is called first intention, which means union by medium of coagulable lymph without suppuration. The definition of wound, technically, is, a solution of continuity in the soft parts, produced by some mechanical agent. Wounds are divided into incised, contused, lacerated, punctured, and penetrating, of these our authority says: Incised wounds are those inflicted by
66

sharp instruments. On the human body they often heal without any subsequent inflammation, beyond what nature sets up in the restorative process; but the difficulty in the horse is, that we can not always keep the parts in contact, and therefore it is not so easy to unite them. In many cases, after having been at the trouble to adjust by sutures the edges of divided parts, and when all seems going on favorably, the animal gets his head round, and tears the wound open afresh, so that our labor is all in vain. This puts a damper on healing by first intention. There are several other difficulties in the way of healing by this method, well known to anatomists. We shall just merely refer to the principal one, because it may satisfy the reader that some wounds had better not be sutured, for they put the subject to a great deal of pain for no purpose. Horses, as well as some other animals, have, in lieu of hands, a peculiar muscular arrangement under the skin, by means of which they can shake off flies and other foreign bodies; and it is owing to the facility with which they can jerk or move the skin that we often fail in uniting flesh wounds. Other obstacles are to be met with, both in relation to the size of the wound and as regards its anatomical direction. If the wound is seen immediately after infliction, and there seems to be the least probability of healing by first intention, we place a twitch on the horse's nose, and examine the part. If there be found neither dirt nor foreign body of any kind, the blood had better not be washed off; for this is the best healing material in the world. The edges are then to be brought together by interrupted sutures, taking care not to include the hair between the edges of the wound, for that would effectually prevent union. Nothing more is needed but to secure the animal so that he can not get at it. If he is to be kept in the stable, without exercise, for any length of time, he had better be put on half diet. Pure air will not hurt him. Contused wounds are generally occasioned by hooks, or some blunt body connected with the harness or vehicle. They generally leave a gaping wound with bruised edges. We have only to remember that nature possesses the power of repairing injuries of this kind—of filling up the parts and covering them with new skin: all we have to do is, to attend to the general health of the animal, and keep the wound in a healthy condition. A usual application and a good one, is the compound tincture of myrrh. If the part assume an unhealthy aspect, a charcoal poultice will rectify that. If such can not be applied, owing to the situation of the wound, dress it with pyroligneous acid. Lacerated wounds are generally in the form of a rent rather than cut, inflicted by the calking of a shoe tearing off the integuments and subcellular tissue, leaving a sort of triangular flap. In these cures we generally employ sutures, and treat them the same as incised wounds. Punctured wounds are those inflicted by a pointed body, as a nail in the foot, point of a fork, or splinter of wood. These are the most dangerous kinds of wounds, for they are frequently the cause of fistula and lockedjaw. We make it an invariable rule, in the treatment of punctured wounds, to first examine by probe or otherwise, and remove any foreign body that may be present, and then poultice with flaxseed, into which we stir a small quantity of fir balsam. In puncture of the foot by nail, instead of plastering it with tar, and forcing a tent into the orifice, and then covering the sole with leather, as most backsmiths are wont to do, we have the shoe taken off, the foot washed clean, and a moderately warm poultice applied, and renewed daily, until the suppurative stage commences. That once established, we consider our patient safe; for many men, as well as animals, have lost their lives from the absorption of pus formed in the wound after the external breach had healed. When a bone is injured by the point of a nail, or fork, the cure is rather tedious; the primary means, however, are the same. The poultices may be followed by astringent injections as alum water, etc. In case of injury to the bone, we use pyroligneous acid; to be thrown into the wound by means of a small syringe. If extensive disease of the bone sets in, the services of a veterinary surgeon will be required. A very profuse or unhealthy discharge from a punctured wound must be met by constitutional remedies. Sulphur and sassafras, to the amount of half an ounce each, every other day, to the amount of three or four doses, will arrest the morbid phenomenon. The local remedy in all cases of this kind is diluted acetic or pyroligneous acid. Penetrating wounds are inflicted by the horns of cattle, stakes, shafts, etc., and have to be treated according to the nature of the case. A penetrating wound of the walls of the abdomen is generally followed by protusion of the intestines; this has to be returned; the wound is then closed by strong sutures, and the belly must be encircled with a long bandage. In such cases we generally keep the bowels soluble with scalded shorts, well seasoned with salt, and empty the rectum occasionally by enema. Of penetrating wounds of intestines, to illustrate the mode of procedure when they are wounded, the following case is introduced: The animal had a wound on the off side, about four inches in length, in the iliac region, through which a portion of the small intestine protruded. On exploring the breach, it was found to run in a slanting direction, and as it approached the peritoneum, was found quite small, scarcely admitting the little finger; here the bowel was both strangulated and lacerated, the intestinal opening being external to the stricture. Before proceeding to cast the horse, a twitch was placed on the nose, and the edges of the wounded intestine were neatly sewed together with a very fine suture needle. Our reason for doing this before casting was, lest in the animal's struggles the bowel might recede, and give us some trouble in getting hold of it again. There was not much danger of it, however; still we wanted to be on the safe side. The intestinal wound was not produced by the cow's horn, but took place some three hours afterwards, and two hours before we saw the case, in the following manner: the protruded bowel had then become distended with gas, and according to the owner's account, was about the size of his two fists. The animal, probably being in pain, got down and rolled on the injured side, and thus burst the gut. After sewing up the wounded intestine, it was cleansed with warm water, and attempts were made to return it within the abdomen, but to no purpose. The patient was then cast, and, by means of a huudle of straw on each side, propped him on his back; the bowel did not return so easily as we had expected, for it was found necessary to dilate the stricture by means of a button-pointed bistoury. The several layers of abdominal muscles were then sutured with as much nicety as the nature of the wound admitted; and lastly the integuments were brought together by interrupted suture. This case terminated unfavorably, for the animal died on the sixth day from peritonitis. It may be well to observe that the accident happened on a very cold day, in the depth of winter; and the bowel being so long exposed to the depressing influence of cold, probably led to the fatal result; for it is well known that operations of this kind often prove successful. It may be interesting to the reader to know that wounds of the intestines heal as readily as those of other parts, as the following cases will show: An incision one inch and a half in length was made in the bowels of a dog; the wound of the integuments was closed by suture; the animal was scarcely affected by the operation, took food as usual, and had natural evacuations. At the end of a fortnight, when perfectly recovered, he was killed for the purpose of examining the bowel, when the wound appeared to be completely healed. In the eighteenth volume of the Philosophical Transactions a similar experiment is related by Mr. W. Cooper: An opening was made in the abdomen of a dog; a large wound was made in the intestines, and the wound in the abdomen was stitched up, etc.; the dog recovered without any bad symptoms, and became perfectly well in a few days after. It should be observed that the bowel does not appear to have been stitched up when returned into the belly. The following experiment by Mr. Travers is still more remarkable: A ligature of thin packthread was firmly tied round the first intestine (duodenum) of a dog so as completely to obstruct it; the ends of the string were cut off, and the parts returned; the wound in the abdomen was closed, and the animal expressed no sign of suffering when the operation was concluded. On the following day he was frequently sick, and vomited some milk that was given him; his respiration was hurried. Third day his sickness continued, and he vomited some bilious fluid. Fifth day he passed a copious stool of the same appearance as the fluid discharged by vomiting; his sickness from this time ceased, and his breathing was natural; he took bread and milk, and drank abundantly of water. Seventh day he had three similar evacuations, and appeared well, eating animal food freely. On the fifteenth day, his cure being established, he was killed for the purpose of examination. The ligature which was fastened around the intestine divided the interior coats of the gut, in this respect resembling the operation of a ligature upon an artery; the peritoneal or outer coat alone maintained its integrity. The inflammation which the ligature induces on either side of it is terminated by the deposition of a coat of lymph, exterior to the ligature; this quickly becomes organized; and the ligature, thus enclosed, is liberated by the ulcerative process, falls of necessity into the canal, and passes off by stool. Penetrating wounds of the chest are not fatal, provided the lungs or heart are not perforated. All that can be done is to suture the wound, pass several turns of a roller round the chest, and adopt such constitutional means as the case seems to require.

WOUNDWORT. The genus *Stachys*, weeds.

WREN. All the wrens are beneficial to the farmer in the highest degree, and should be sedulously protected. The most of them will build in boxes put out for that purpose, and this should invariably be done. The common house wren, *Troglodytes ædon*, is a most familiar visitor, which, if allowed, will build in the piazza or window -casements of the house, especially if cosy breeding places are provided. They arrive in the North as soon as the trees begin to put forth their foliage, and remain while insect food lasts. Species less known at the North, are the long-billed, and the short-billed marsh wren, Bewick's Carolina, or mocking wren, said to be, in imitative powers, little short of the mocking bird, the ruby crowned and golden crested, and and wood and the winter wren.

WROUGHT. Materials which have been brought to a surface by hammering or other labor.

X

XANTHINE. A yellow principle in madder.

XANTHIUM. Cockle-bur, clot-bur. A class of vile weeds from their production of hooked spines, which become matted with the burs, in the manes and tails of horses, and fleeces of sheep, in the most annoying manner. The principal species are the common cockle-bur, *X. strumarium,* and its variety, *echinatum*, and the thorny clot-bur, *X. spinosum.*

XANTHOPHYL. The yellow coloring matter of autumnal foliage.

XYLITE. *Liguone*, an empyreumatic spirit existing in products of vinegar distilled from wood.

XYLOPHAGANS, XYLOPHAGA. A tribe of coleopterous insects, comprehending those of which the larvæ devour the wood of trees in which they are developed; also applied to a family of dipterous insects, the larvæ of which have similarly destructive habits.

XYLOPHILINS, XILOPHILI. A tribe of beetles, consisting of those which live on decayed wood.

XYLOTROGES, XYLOTROGI. A tribe of serricorn beetles, comprehending those which perforate timber. The Serricorn land beetles, include the Buprestidæ, and the Elateridæ.

Y

YAK. The Himalayan bison, resembling the buffalo, three and a half feet high, and with fine, long hair.

YAM. The yam—Iguame—*Dioscorea alata*, is cultivated in every tropical portion of the earth, and also some temperate climates, where the young plants are brought forward early in the season. The Indian archipelago and the southern portion of the Indian continent is said to be the native homes of this, the most widely cultivated of the Dioscorea family. It was carried thence to the eastern coast of Africa, next to the west coast and from there to America, under the name of yam, which, in the negro dialect of Guinea, means to eat. The other species of yam cultivated more or less, and all from the Indian archipelago and continent, are *Dioscorea pentaphylla, D. bulbifera, D. esculenta,* and *D. deltoides,* (or *Satara,*) the latter being known under both names. The Chinese yam, *Dioscorea batatas*, was widely disseminated in the United States some years ago, at high prices, and with the assurance that it would supersede the potato. It is entirely hardy, even well North, has some good qualities as an ornamental plant, and the roots have the remarkable quality of remaining sound for years in the ground. In fact it takes several years for them to attain full size. The labor of cultivating this running vine, and especially the labor of digging, precludes all profit, if indeed, it were equal as food to the common and sweet potato, which it is not, all of which the introducers ought to have known. They strike their long tubers into the ground, being thickest at the lower end, so that in gathering the earth must be moved to a depth of two feet, or even more

YARD, DISEASES OF. Diseases of the sex organs of both horses and mares are not uncommon, and for the reason that stallions are given undue and exhaustive connection together with artificial surroundings in care and exercise. The trouble generally is external and internal inflammation of the yard, and inflammation of the vagina. This last in the mare is rare and is due to violence in the service. In external inflammation of the yard, the parts should be washed clean by syringing with warm soapy water inside and out, followed by a wash of one drachm of carbolic acid to a quart of water. If there are granulations wash the yard in the following solution (a powerful caustic and painful but necessary: Two drachms chloride of zinc and one pint of water. Repeat this every day until the granulations are reduced, and the parts assume a healthy character. Internal inflammation attacks geldings as well as stallions. The symptoms are frequent desire to urinate, Ineffectual or with difficulty, extension of the yard, and a discharge of whitish or yellowish matter. As a first means relieve the bowels with four or five drachms of aloes. Foment the parts thoroughly with water as hot as can be borne, and give several times a day an· ounce of bicarbonate of soda in water. These means not succeeding ulcers may be suspected within the urethra. If so, the animal must be cast and the diseased parts touched with nitrate of silver, followed by injections of from one half to one drachm of sulphate of zinc to the pint of water. In any case, however, of disease of the genital organs, either in the horse or mare, the services of an experienced veterinary surgeon should be procured if possible. (See Vagina, Inflammation of.)

YARD-DUNG. Farm-Yard Manure. The ordinary manure of the farm.

YARD OF LAND. A quantity of land which, in some counties in England, signifies fifteen acres, in some twenty, and in others twenty-four, thirty and thirty-four acres.

YARROW. *Achillea.* The thousand-leaved Achillea. Yarrow, or milfoil, *A. Millefolium*, is a plant introduced from Europe, as a valuable pasture plant. It is an aromatic, bitter and astringent. It has proved quite inferior as a pasture plant, and has degenerated into a thoroughly naturalized weed, and should be eradicated wherever found.

YEARLINGS. A term applied to calves, colts, and other young stock, when they have completed their first year.

YEAST. The froth or scum which rises on beer during the act of fermentation. It contains a variety of components; among others, carbon, acetic and malic acids, alcohol, potassa, lime, a saccharine, mucilaginous extract, gluten, and water. Yeast is an article of the greatest importance in domestic economy, forming a necessary ingredient in the manufacture of bread, which would otherwise become heavy and unwholesome. When put in contact with saccharine matters, at a temperature of between 50° and 60°, it causes fermentation, and changes the sugar into alcohol and carbonic acid. Yeast may be dried and yet retain its properties, but a temperature of 212° destroys it. The substance called yeast or ferment, derives its name from the power it possesses of causing fermentation in sugar, or saccharine vegetable juices. It possesses,-says Liebig, all the characters of a compound of nitrogen in the state of putrefaction and eremacausis. Like wood in the state of eremacausis, yeast converts the oxygen of the surrounding air into carbònic acid, but it also evolves this gas from its own mass, like bodies in the state of putrefaction. When kept under water, it emits carbonic acid, accompanied by gases of an offensive smell, and is at last converted into a substance resembling old cheese. But when its putrefaction is completed, it has no longer the power of inducing fermentation in other bodies.

YELLOWBIRD. Yellow warbler, *Dendroica æstiva.* (See Warbler.)

YELLOW DYES. Persian berries, weld, quercitron bark, fustic, turmeric, dyer's broom, annotto, willow leaves, barberry roots, are the principal vegetable dyes. Chrome yellow, oxide of iron, sulphurets of antimony and arsenic, and nitric acid are obtained from the mineral kingdom. Solutions of alum and tin are used as mordants.

YELLOW-NECKED CATERPILLAR. Hand Maid Moth. *Datana ministra.* There are a number of caterpillars called "Tent worms." The true tent caterpillars build webs under which they feed. Others, as in the case of the Yellow-necked caterpillar, transform only under webs, within which they congregate, for the purpose, though they often spin webs as they progress in feeding. - These species are so nearly alike, in the moth state, as scarcely to be distinguished. Thus, the larvæ, found feeding on the hickory and black walnut, are black-necked, while those on the apple are yellow-necked. Those on the oak, elm, plum and other trees are orange pencilled. The preceding cut will show the form and peculiarities of these insects; *a*,

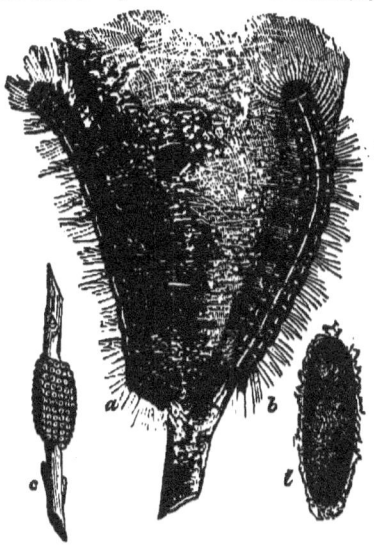

AMERICAN TENT CATERPILLAR.

larvæ, *b*, moth, *c*, egg mass, *d*, egg magnified. They should be assiduously sought for and killed where they gather together at night, during the molting season. For comparison, we append a discription of the true tent caterpillar, with illustration, above. The American tent caterpillar, *Clisiocampa Americana*, is most destructive. The report on the Rocky Mountain Locusts, 1877, says: At the same time that the canker-worms are breaking out of their egg-shells, the young tent-caterpillars are following suit. This occurs usually about the 1st of May, in the region of Boston, or a month or six weeks earlier in the latitude of St. Louis, just as the leaves are unfolding. At this time, if one will examine closely the conspicuous bunches of eggs on the twigs of the tree, he may be able to see the little caterpillars clustering about on the outside of the egg-mass. When hatched, they have large heads, and the body is provided with long, scattered hairs, they at once betake themselves to the opening buds, congregating at noon time, when the sun is hot among the axils of the branches, there forming a tent of silk for protection from the sun and rain. As they increase in size, they make extended journeys over different branches, laying pathways of silk wherever they go. The

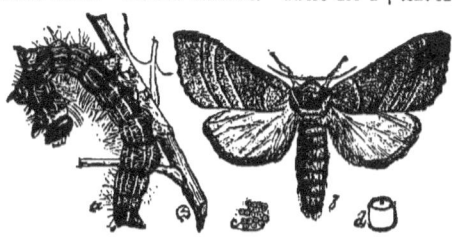

YELLOW-NECKED CATERPILLAR.

tent or nest increases in size until it becomes the conspicuous, but by no means ornamental, object so noticeable on the grounds of slovenly farmers early in June. The caterpillars become fully grown by the middle of June. Then they spin dense, tough, white cocoons under loose bark, or under boards and rails of fences, and the moth appears about the 1st of July. The American tent-caterpillar is about two inches in length, with long, rather dense hairs. Along the back runs a white stripe, accompanied by numerous fine, wrinkled black lines on a yellow ground, united below into a common black line. On the side of each segment of the body is a conspicuous blue spot. The moths hide by day about the garden, and when the lamps are lighted, in they dart and tumble about on the table under the light, in an insensate way, as if frightened out of their wits. So peculiar is their mode of entering a lighted room, that one can usually tell what moth is coming by its peculiar, noisy mode of entrance. The moth is reddish-brown, very thick-bodied, clothed in a thick coat of long hairs, and with short, broad, strong wings, as it flies swiftly. It is reddish-brown, with two oblique, dirty-white lines on the fore wings, which expand when outstretched, about an inch and a half. Early in June the female lays her eggs, in bunches of from 300 to 400. They are placed side by side, in a mass surrounding the twigs, and after they are thus stuck on so as to surround the branch like a collar, the entire mass is covered over with a gummy secretion, which hardens, and serves as a protection to the eggs. Remedies: In the early spring as well as late autumn the bunches of eggs should he picked off and burned. When the tents are formed in June the nest should be removed with a mop dipped in oil or kerosene, at noon-time, when the caterpillars are in the tent. By discharging a gun close to the nest it can be destroyed with a small charge of powder. The cut, page 1044, shows *a*, *b*, larvæ, *c*, mass of eggs on twig, *d*, cocoon.

YELLOW RATTLE. The weed *Rhinanthus crista-galli*, sometimes called rattle weed.

YELLOWS. For yellows in horses see Jaundice. In cattle the disease is much similar, and produced by congestion and inflammation of the liver. Over-feeding with rich and heating food, sudden changes in the weather, excessive milking, are the principal causes. The animal ceases to ruminate is dull, languid, hide-bound and has a staring, unhealthy coat of hair. The whites of the eyes and inside of the mouth, will be of a dirty yellow color. The bowels may be costive or there may be scouring, accompanied with a fœtid odor. In cows the secretion of milk also quickly fails. The first thing is change of diet, to plain, sweet, nutritious food. The grooming should be of the best and the comfort of the animal in every way cared for. Give the following as a laxative and tonic: one half ounce each of powdered sugar and of aloes, one ounce each of Castile soap, scraped fine, and of powdered Peruvian bark, mix in a pint of water and give one of the doses every three or four days as the animal may seem to need it. This is for the disease as brought about by ordinary causes. If this does not give relief and, if in addition to a yellow skin and jaundiced eye, there is loss of appetite, incessant thirst, hard and rapid pulse and heaving of the flanks; if the ears are alternately hot and cold, if the urine turns to a transparent, red, yellow or brown, give the following: two ounces laudanum, twenty drops of croton oil, and one pound of sulphate of magnesia, in a quart of linseed tea; hasten the action of the dose by mashes, or something of that kind, turn the animal out to grass, and repeat the dose if the bowels again become costive, and the evacuations are passed in hard dark balls.

YELLOW SEED. The weed *Thlaspi campestre*, false flax, mithridate mustard, a cruciferous annual with mustard-flavored pods, which abounds in flax fields, and is very troublesome. It can only be avoided by screening the flax seed carefully, and omitting the cultivation of flax for a season, introducing cleaning or hoed crops instead.

YELLOWS, IN THE PEACH. In the Middle States, especially upon sandy soils, peach trees have been subject for a long time to a disease known as Yellows, a remedy for which has not so far been found, except that of grubbing affected trees and burning. The applications that have produced most good have been iron filings, scales from the blacksmith's anvil, and hot wood ashes applied at the rate of a shovel full about each tree. Salt is also reported to have been beneficial. Trees grown from the seeds of affected fruit, will sometimes show the disease at one year old. Often it is not noticeable until the tree has borne one or two crops of fruit, when it is indicated by slender, erect branches starting up from the larger limbs, a general sickly appearance of the tree, and a dull color of the foliage. The fruit also becomes discolored, and so changes from the natural taste and appearance of the variety as not to be recognizable as the same. When first attacked, a single branch only is sometimes affected; but by the following season it spreads over the whole tree, which struggles feebly for life for a season or two, producing small, immature, and flavorless fruit. The yellows is a contagious disease, and is imparted to other trees by contact or propinquity, as well as by a knife used in pruning trees affected, from buds taken from infected trees, and from the soil in which such trees have grown. The cut will show the appearance of an infected branch. The disease has been known in the West for many years, but does not appear to make much headway except on the loess formation or other sandy soils. On the light sands of the Michigan lake shore region, long famous for its excellent peaches, it has of late years made such ravages that the legislature of the State has been obliged to pass the most stringent laws, involving the destruction even of whole orchards where found, and the appointment of commissioners to see that the law is carried into effect. In relation to this disease, the microscopist of the Department of Agriculture reports to the government experiments as follows: A series of experiments by the moist process with the bark of a peach-tree affected with the yellows, showed as follows: Into five glass receivers I placed respectively, a few drops of water, just sufficient to form a moist atmosphere in each. Into No. 1 I put a piece of bark affected with the yellows; into No. 2 a piece of bark from a healthy peach tree; into No. 3 a handful of peach leaves from the unhealthy tree; into No. 4 a similar quantity from the healthy tree; and into No. 5 portions of bark from the healthy and unhealthy trees mentioned.

All the specimens were secured from the outward atmosphere. The temperature of the room in which the specimens were kept was frequently at 90° Fahr. These conditions were highly favorable to the development of such fungi-germs as mature under excess of heat and moisture. Previous to arranging the specimens in the receivers they were examined minutely with a low power but no signs of fungi were visible. On the fifteenth day the unhealthy specimens in Nos. 1 and 5 exhibited on their external surface a spotted appearance. When

BRANCH AFFECTED WITH YELLOWS.

viewed by a power of seventy-five diameters they were seen to consist mostly of a translucent, yellowish-brown, spiral, thread-like fungus, genus *Næmaspora*. When a portion about .03 of an inch is placed under an object-glass of one inch, and secured in the usual manner by means of a disc, with dilute gum water, the spiral forms are seen to dissolve gradually, and ultimately to form a yellow stain. On viewing it with a power of one-eighth, it appears to be a mass of curved spores, resembling in form caraway seeds, but invisible to the naked eye. Each spore has a life-like motion confined to a center of its own. When they are treated to the action of nitric, muriatic, and nitro-muriatic acids, no immediate change is observable; and in those strong acids the life-like motion continues, which, I think, proves that the motions are not the result of any form of organic life, but simply what is known as Brownian motion, which is frequently seen when minute particles of inorganic matter are placed under a high power. When the spores are combined either with concentrated sulphuric acid or caustic potash they become completely destroyed, forming a homogeneous mass, and their organic structure is no longer visible. The figures in the cut, page 1047, represent a sectional view of the bark, showing fungus growth; 6, *Næmaspora*; 7, the same, when placed in water or acid, except sulphuric; 8, a very highly magnified form of the spores contained in 6. About the twentieth day mycelium was found in abundance growing from the spiral threads, resembling double-celled *Puccinia*, the spores varying in number from one to ten, and so small that a power of one-eighth was required to give good definition. Since contact with water dissolves this form of *Næmaspora* without destroying the life of the spores, it is evident that the action of rain or washes of pure water will only tend to diffuse the spores over the body of the tree and roots, while the applications of solutions of sulphuric acids and alkalies will destroy them. Hence a remedy may be found for peach-yellows in the application of alkalies and sulphates, and their compounds, to the bark and roots of the trees. Statements have frequently been made that the application of hot lye has been known to cure peach-yellows when applied to the bark and roots. My observations seem to confirm these common rumors. In receiver No. 5 the healthy bark was not contaminated, seemingly, with the *Næmaspora*, notwithstanding its immediate contact during several weeks with the unhealthy bark. As might be expected, the common molds, as *Penicillium* and *Mucors*, grew all over the surface of the specimens, healthy and unhealthy. The leaves in Nos. 3 and 4 were next examined. They had been subjected to the same treatment as the bark. The healthy leaves, although confined during four weeks in a moist atmosphere, at a temperature ranging from 80° to 90°, exhibited no signs of mildew. A split branch to which the leaves were attached exhibited a small portion of *Mucor* fruit, and *Mycelium* on the sap-wood and pith; but the unhealthy leaves were completely covered in two weeks with *Mycelium*, (mold,) and the fruit of the common blue, yellow, and black *Penicillium* and *Mucors*. I have repeated these experiments several times, always with the same results. It is evident that the healthy leaves possess an antiseptic substance, which prevents the growth of the common molds on them. A portion of healthy and unhealthy leaves from the trees above mentioned was analyzed in the laboratory to determine the respective amounts of moisture, organic matter, and ash in them, and gave the following results:

Healthy peach leaves.	Per cent.
Moisture	29.20
Organic matter	63.22
Ash	7.58
	100.00

Unhealthy leaves.	
Moisture	36.9
Organic matter	59.4
Ash	3.7
	100.00

The fact of the absence of ash or solid matter and of the increase of moisture in the unhealthy leaves, would of itself account for their greater tendency to mold. Since leaves do not absorb earthy matter from the atmosphere, it is evident that the cellular structure of the tree has in some way failed to perform its functions; for, had the ascending sap carried with it potash, lime, or other earthy matter, the leaves would have been stored with them, since the leaves have no power to evaporate them. The deficiency of earthy matters in the leaves may also account for the absence of ash in the fruit. If the theory is well founded that the leaves elaborate juice for the growth of the fruit, the leaves being deprived of proper nourishment, the fruit can not mature. It has been long observed that trees affected with the yellows fruit earlier and mature prematurely, and soon decay. The presence of a larger amount of sap in the unhealthy than in the healthy, indicates an earlier and greater flow than in that of the healthy tree. The presence of watery sap in the leaves, twigs, and buds would induce naturally an early growth of fruit and premature decay. From these and other observations the disease seems traceable to the body of the tree or roots. Applications of washes in this case to the leaves would probably prove useless, but if it should be applied to the bark and roots might possibly prove curative; and for that purpose, judging from microscopic observations, I would recommend the frequent application of hot lye as the best substance. J. M. Asher, National City, Cal., writes to the Department under date October 28, 1872, as follows: One of your writers suggests lye as a remedy for yellows of the peach trees. Our soil in California is more or less impregnated with alkali, and I never have seen a case of yellows in the State. Whether a specific for this disease will soon be found remains in doubt. In its attacks it seems to be epidemic, ravaging a district of country for years sometimes to such a degree as to destroy a majority of the orchards, those of negligent cultivators suffering first and most. It then declines, as it has done from time to time in the peach-raising districts of the Atlantic coast, again and again to reappear. So far, the best remedies are those we have named,' good fertilization and cultivation, setting no stocks but those perfectly sound, using no knife on healthy trees that has been used on affected ones, until thoroughly disinfected with carbolic acid, and promptly grubbing all trees at the first knowledge of their infection.

YELLOW THISTLE. (See Thistle.)
YELLOW THROAT. *Geothlypis tricas.* (See Warbler.)
YELLOW TOP. White top. *Agrostis alba.*
YELLOW WEED. The butter cup, Ranunculus. Cuckoo-bud of Shakespeare.
YEW. *Taxus.* The North American yew. *T. Canadensis*, is a low growing shrub, found from Canada to Virginia, spreading, but scarcely ever attaining a height of more than six feet, and found growing in rocky shady places. It is not worthy of general planting. In a collection a single specimen will suffice. The European yew,' *T. baccata*, has long been used in Great Britain for decorating cemeteries, and has there long been considered a funereal tree, as much so as the cypress is in the south of Europe.

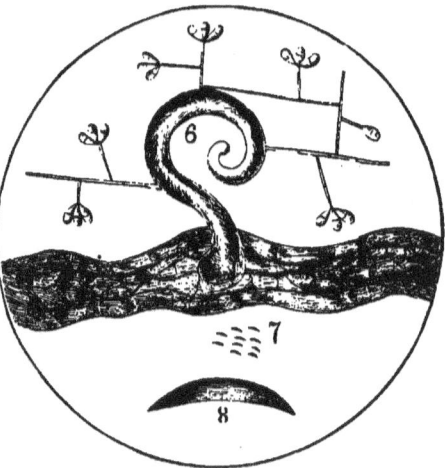

YELLOWS IN THE PEACH.

In the West, the yews, of which there are many elegant varieties, none can be called hardy. In the Atlantic States they stand better. Some of the new forms are quite striking, among them may be mentioned the Silver, the Golden, the Irish, and the variegated yew.' When the yew will stand it is well adapted to hedging, since it is compact, of slow growth and stands the shears well.

YOLK. The yellow of the egg. An animal soap, also called gum, secreted by the skin of sheep, and pervading the wool. The finest fleeces contain most yolk, especially that of the Merinos. It is readily softened by warm water, and may be washed out without trouble; but there remains an oil among the wool, which is only separated with trouble. The amount varies from twenty to fifty per cent. of the fleece, and is most in warm climates and fine fleeces.

YTTRIUM. The metallic base of yttria, a rare earth resembling alumina.

YUCCA. This class of plants are almost entirely of tropical origin and cultivated only in greenhouses and conservatories. _Yucca fila-mentosa_, called Adam's needle, is indigenous in Virginia and South, and hardy in the West up to and above the Wisconsin line, if planted in a dry situation, better if a bushel of sand be mixed in the soil in which it is planted. It is perennial, throwing up a flowered stalk sometimes six to eight feet high, and is worthy of a place on every lawn.

YULE. Christmas.

Z

ZAMIA. A genus of Cycadeous trees, the stems of which yield a kind of sago. The _Z. integrifolia_ and _Z. pumila_ grow in Florida, and furnish sago, or what is improperly called arrow-root.

ZANTE CURRANT. The small, stoneless raisins of commerce are made from the Corinth grape, long grown in the islands of the Mediterranean. It should be unnecessary to say that it is a true grape and not a currant. Its cultivation has been attempted in the South, but, we believe, abandoned, probably from the fact that the cost of cultivation, gathering, drying and packing did not give so good profits as the more staple crops. It is said not to be hardy outside of the Gulf States, and the South Atlantic states. In some portions of California, where irrigation is possible, it may perhaps be worthy of trial.

ZEA. The generic name of Indian corn, (_Z. Mays_).

ZEBRA. The zebra is of the size and general appearance of the mule, but with a skin striped with brown or black and white; it has not been domesticated.

ZEDOARY. _Curcuma Zedoaria._ An East Indian plant, of the same family as the ginger, but producing rhizomes not quite as pungent.

ZECKSTEIN. A magnesian limestone, lying below the red sandstone.

ZEIN. The azotized product of Indian corn, similar to albumen.

ZENITH. The vertical point in the sky of any place; the point immediately overhead.

ZEOLITE. A family of minerals which fuse and boil before the blow-pipe; they are silicates of alumina and lime, or soda with water. The soda zeolite is called Natrolite.

ZERO. Nothing; it is used to designate the 0° point of graduated scales, as the thermometer, areometer, and usually means a degree equal to a given test; thus the zero of the areometer is the specific gravity of pure water at 59° Fahr.; the zero of Fahrenheit's thermometer is the temperature of snow mixed with salt. The zero of the Centigrade and Reaumer scales is the freezing point. Degrees above zero are plus, (+), below it minus (—).

ZERUMBET. An East Indian rhizome, similar to ginger.

ZIMOME. That part of the gluten of wheat which is insoluble in alcohol.

ZINC. Spelter. A valuable metal for roofing and the construction of vessels, such as are made of tin plate, than which it is more durable and stronger. In chemistry it is of great use for the construction of galvanic circles and batteries, forming the positive surface or pole of single circles. It is rapidly acted on by the strong acids, and forms an oxide which combines with most acids. Of its salts, the sulphate, or white vitriol, is most employed; it is emetic and irritant, and used chiefly in lotions. Calamine is an impure native carbonate of zinc. Tutty is an impure artificial oxide.

ZINCOUS, ZINCOID, ZINCODE. Resembling zinc. This term is used to designate any metal or other body which, in a galvanic circle, occupies the place of the zinc. It is the same as positive metal or pole, positive electrode, anode, and the derivatives. _Zincolysis_ means the same as electrolysis; _zincolyte_, as electrolyte. These terms are indeed to be preferred over those previously in existence, because they refer to the zinc element, or its substitute, as the origin of its galvanic action.

ZINGIBER. The generic name of the ginger plant, (_Z. officinale_).

ZIRCONIUM. A rare metal, the base of zirconium.

ZIZANIA. Wild rice. (See Rice.)

ZIZIPHUS. The generic name of the shrubs yielding the jujube (_Z. jujuba_).

ZONE. A word much used by naturalists to denote a band or strip running around any object. In geography, a division of the earth's surface. There are five great zones. The tropic or torrid zone, occupying the central or equatorial regions of the earth to a distance of 23¼ degrees north and south, and therefore having a width of 47 degrees. The north temperate zone lies between 23½ N. lat. and 66½ N. lat., and occupies 43° of latitude. The south temperate zone lies in the same space on the south side of the globe. The north and south frigid zones occupy the space beyond 66½ degrees to the poles; they are also called the arctic and antarctic regions.

ZOOLOGY. The history and classification of animals. The objects of the animal kingdom are so extremely various that a classification of them is one of the severest labors. Numerous suggestions have been made as a basis for classification, but the advance of knowledge has shown them all to be wanting in comprehensiveness. When it is remembered that under the term animal is grouped thousands of species differing from the scarcely organized and imperceptible dots of jelly called monads, to the most complicated quadrupeds, the difficulty of classification will be apparent. (See Entomology, Mammalogy, Ornithology, etc.)

HOUSEHOLD DEPARTMENT.

ALLOYS

ALCOHOL, PER CENT. OF, in Liquors.
The table will explain itself. The first column shows the beverage, and the second the per cent. of alcohol:

Beverages.	Per cent.
Ale	6 to 8
Small beer	1¼
Lager beer	2
Brandy	50 to 55
Hard cider	6 to 10
Gin, true	50
London porter	4
Wine, Angelica	17 to 2)
" Catawba	12
" Claret	12 to 17
" Champagne	12
" Hock	12
" Malaga	17
" Madeira	24
" Muscat	19

ALLOYS, GOLD, SILVER, ETC.
Gold alloys. Standard gold for coin in Great Britain is: Pure gold, 22; pure copper, 2. This alloy is harder and more fusible but less ductile than pure gold. It is said to be 22 carats fine. Standard gold for coin in United States and France: Gold, 9; copper, 1. Jeweler's gold varies from 22 down to 9 parts gold, with sufficient silver, or copper and silver, to make up 24 parts. The number of parts of pure gold in 24 parts of an alloy denotes its fineness; thus gold 18 carats fine is an alloy containing 18 parts of pure gold and 6 parts silver or copper.

Silver alloys are as follows: Standard silver for coin and plate in Great Britain: Pure silver, 222; pure copper, 18. (Specific gravity, 10.2.) French standard silver for medals and plates: Silver, 95; copper, 5. American and French standard silver for coin: Silver, 90; copper, 10. French standard silver for jewelry work: Silver, 80; copper, 20. Silver solder: Silver, about 66 per cent., with zinc and copper.

Queen's Metal. Tin, 9; antimony, 1; lead, 1; bismuth, 1. Used for teapots, spoons, etc.

Brass is made of copper, 64 parts; zinc, 36 parts; proportions slightly varied to make the metal darker by increasing the copper even to 74 per cent.

Bronze is made of copper, 85 to 90 parts; tin, 10 to 15 parts; sometimes a little lead and zinc is added.

HOUSEHOLD DEPARTMENT

Bell metal is made of copper, 75 parts, and tin, 25 parts.
German silver is made of copper, 16 parts; zinc, 7 parts, and nickel; 8 parts.
Type metal is made of lead, 83 parts; metallic antimony, 7 parts.
Stereotyping metal is made of lead, 9 parts; metallic antimony and bismuth, each 2 parts.
Common solder is made of lead and tin equal parts.
Fine solder is made of lead, 1 part; tin, 2 parts.
Pewter is made of lead, 4 parts; tin, 1 part.

BEVERAGES.

Koumis. The following is a correct formula for making koumis: Best unskimmed milk, one quart; yeast, (brewer's or old baker's), 100 grains; cane sugar, 200 grains. Mix and keep it at 80° Fahr. until fermentation is brisk, stirring it frequently, then bottle and secure the corks with wire or stout cord. In twenty-four hours it may be used.

Ginger powder, effervescing. Powdered ginger, two drachms; bi-carbonate of soda, ten drachms; white sugar, four ounces; essence of lemon, ten drops. Make into twelve powders which fold into blue papers; each of which is to be accompanied by a white paper containing thirty grains of tartaric acid, and they are to be prepared for use the same as seidlitz powders.

Lemonade, effervescing. Bi-carbonate of potash, one-half drachm; sugar, two drachms; essence of lemon, ten drops; citric acid, crystal, two scruples; water to fill bottle. Nearly fill a strong mineral water bottle with water. Put in the potash, sugar and lemon, shake up well, add the citric acid and cork immediately and let it be placed in a cool place upside down until needed for use.

Citrate of Magnesia (effervescent). Take of powdered citric acid, four pounds; calcined magnesia, one and a half pounds; bi-carbonate of soda, three pounds; tartaric acid, three pounds; powdered white sugar, six pounds; oil of lemon, one and a half ounces; rectified spirits a sufficiency. Mix thoroughly the citric acid with the sugar, add the soda, magnesia and tartaric acid; pass the whole through a sieve to facilitate their mixture; moisten with the spirit, pass the whole through a coarser sieve, and place in a wooden tray to dry in a warm place. When dry add the oil of lemon, and bottle instantly.

Eff-rvescing powders, granulated. Mix well dried tartaric acid and bi-carbonate of soda in the proportion of five to six, with sufficient strong alcohol to reduce the mixture to a moist condition; pass it then through a somewhat coarser sieve, and thoroughly dry it. If desired it may be flavored with a little oil of lemon dissolved in alcohol. A mixture thus prepared effervesces. on the addition of water, to the last particle.

BUSINESS HABITS.

A strict attention to business matters is a principal integer to success in life. The following will be especially valuable to farmers as well as other classes: With a business man a sacred regard to the principles of justice forms the basis of every act. He is strict in keeping his engagements. Does nothing carelessly or in a hurry. Employs nobody to do what he can easily do himself. Keeps everything in its proper place. Leaves nothing undone that ought to be done, and which circumstances permit him to do. Is prompt and decisive with his customers, and does not overtrade his capital. He is clear and explicit in all his bargains. Prefers short credits to long ones, and cash to credit at all times, either in buying or selling, and small profits in credit cases, with little risk, to the chance of better gain, with more hazard. Leaves nothing of consequence to memory that he can and ought to commit to writing. Keeps copies of all his important letters which he sends away, and has every letter, invoice, etc., belonging to his business, clasped and put away. Is always at the head of his business, well knowing that if he leaves it, it will leave him. Holds as a maxim, that he whose credit is suspected is not one to be trusted. Is constantly examining his books and sees through all his affairs, as far as care and attention will enable him. He is economical in his expenditures, always living within his means. Keeps a memorandum in his pocket, in which he notes every particular relative to appointments and petty cash matters.

BUSHEL.

What makes a bushel by weight, often perplexes many. The following table will show the general standard: Wheat, sixty pounds; corn, shelled, fifty-six pounds; rye, fifty-six pounds; oats, thirty-two pounds; barley, forty-six pounds; buckwheat, fifty-six pounds; Irish potatoes, sixty pounds; sweet potatoes, sixty pounds; onions, fifty-seven pounds; beans, sixty pounds; bran, twenty-seven pounds; hemp seed, forty-four pounds; clover seed, sixty pounds; timothy seed, forty-five pounds; blue-grass seed, fourteen pounds; dried peaches, thirty-three pounds. Again, to find the measurement of a box the following table will show:

A box 24 by 16 inches square and 22 deep, contains 1 bbl.
" 24 by 16 " " " 11 " " ½ "
" 16 by 16.8 " " " 8 " " 1 "
" 12 by 11.2 " " " 8 " " ¼ "
" 8 by 8.4 " " " 8 " " ⅛ "
" 8 by 8 " " " 4.2 " " ½ "
" 7 by 4 " " " 4.8 " " ½ gal.
" 4 by 4 " " " 4.2 " " ¼ "

CALCIMINING AND PAINTING.

Calcimining. In calcimining, a great deal depends on the condition of the walls. If they are smoked, they should be thoroughly washed. If they are spongy, or very dry, and soak up too freely, they should be coated with a size made of glue and common soft soap. Take gilders' whiting or Paris white, or about equal parts of each, and soak it in water; put in a trifle of ultramarine blue to give it a blue tint. Dissolve good white glue in water in the proportion of one-fourth pound of glue to a common pail of calcimine. Mix the whiting and glue together and thin with cold water to about the consistency of paste. Strain the mixture through a sieve; lay it on the wall crosswise, viz: making the strokes with your brush to cross each other.

Oil for oiling floors. Mix four quarts raw linseed oil, two quarts spirits turpentine, one pint best coach japan.

To preserve paint brushes, when not in use. Cleanse them thoroughly after using and suspend them in water. Varnish brushes should always be kept in raw linseed oil when not in use.

Painting inside walls. First coat. The paint should be mixed quite thin with linseed oil. Second coat. A trifle thicker, with three parts oil and one part turpentine. Third coat. Thin glue size, made of about three ounces of good glue in one gallon of water. Fourth coat. Paint thinned with equal parts oil and turpentine. Fifth coat. Paint thinned with clear turpentine.

Fireproof paint for woodwork. Owing to the fact that waterglass is gradually dissolved out of the wood, while chloride of zinc is volatile at the temperature where wood ignites, the author, F. Siehurger, proposes the following: Two coats of a hot saturated solution of three parts alum and one part ferrous sulphate are first applied and allowed to dry. A third coat is a dilute solution of ferrous sulphate, into which white potter's clay is stirred until it has the consistency of good water colors. Another method is to apply hot glue water as long as it is absorbed into the pores of the wood. A thick coat of boiled glue is then applied, and, while fresh, is dusted over with a powder composed of one part sulphur, one part ochre of clap, and six parts ferrous sulphate.

COINS, VALUE OF, by U. S. Standard.

Country.	Gold.		Silver.	
Austria	Ducat........	$2 28	Rix Dollar	$1 02
Belgium........	Twenty-five Frc.	4 83		
Bolivia........	Doubloon	15 50		
Brazil			D'bl Milreis	1 04
Central America	Escudo	1 84		
"	Dollar........	98		
"	Four Reals.....	49		
Chili..........	Doubloon.....	15 50	Dollar......	96
Denmark	Ten Thaler....	7 90	Riga Daler.	54
France........	Twenty Francs.	3 84	Five Francs	96
German Empire	Mark.........	23	Five Marks.	96
"			Old Thaler.	71
Great Britain...	Pound Sterling.	4 86	Half Crown	56
"			Shilling	22
Italy..........	Twenty Lire...	3 84	Lire........	19
Japan..........	Yen..........	99	Fifty Sen..	42
Mexico........	Doubloon....	15 60	Dollar......	99
Netherlands ...	Ducat........	2 26	Guilder.....	40
"	Ten Guilders...	4 00	Florin......	38
Peru..........			Dollar......	92
Portugal.......	Crown........	5 80	Crown ,....	97
"	Milreis,.......	1 08		
Russia.........	Five Roubles...	3 97	Rouble.....	73
Spain	Ten Escudos...	5 00	Pistareen ..	17
"	Peseta	19	Peseta.....	19
Sweden	Five Pesetas...	94	Half Daler.	50
"	Crown........	26	Rix Daler..	27
Switzerland.....	Franc........	19	Franc	19

COOKING AND KITCHEN ART.
Cooking in General. Since the advent of cooking stoves, and especially since the later improvements in kitchen stoves and ranges, there is no reason why bad or indifferent cooking should be the rule. However simple the dishes, (and expensive dishes do not constitute good living), the exercise of care and judgment will enable them to be brought to the table, nicely cooked, palatable, and nourishing. In the United States there seems to be a strong objection to soups and stews. There is no reason why this should be so, for there are few dishes more easily prepared, more savory, or more nourishing. There is also a general lack of vegetable dishes. It has been said that the farmers' vegetables are cabbage and potatoes. It might have been said that they were potatoes and potatoes, since the odorous boiled cabbage is by no means a standing dish, nor should it be The increased attention given by farmers to the cultivation of gardens will enable them to have all the principal vegetables and fruits of the season in abundance, and thus allow them to live as well as the best, with some attention to the manner of preparing them. A good vegetable garden will yield nearly or quite half the living of the family. In the body of this Encyclopædia will be found, articles pertaining to the principal vegetables cultivated, under their respective names, with directions for cultivation. In this connection we propose to give plain directions for preparing them for the table, in connection with recipes for cooking and baking in the other departments of the culinary art. In these days of improved cooking utensils the cook is not obliged to depend upon iron pots, nor cheap tin ware, for making stews, sauces, etc., and the modern stove, whether hard or soft coal, coke or wood is used, leaves but little to be desired in baking, broiling or boiling. If the housewife have, in addition to the broiler, frying pan, baking pans, cutters for cake and vegetables, paste boards, rolling pin, skewers, sieves for flour, etc., meat saw and cleaver, various kitchen knives, colanders, basins, and the kitchen clock; if to these be added, a thermometer to mark up to 500°, a good set of scales and weights, a large and a small porcelain lined steam pan, she can do nice cooking and baking, at a pinch, whatever the company may be. It is, of course, better that she have other conveniences; as an egg bowl and whisk, wooden spoons, a fish kettle, steamers, tart moulds, brazing pan, stock (soup) pots, measures, funnels, moulds for jellies, creams, charlottes, and cake; dredgers, ladles, skimmers, a mortar and pestle, large forks, etc. Yet with those we have mentioned the farmer's wife, may easily get along until these can be had. In the making of soup, when it is part of the daily dinner, what is denominated stock, is used A strong soup, made of lean meat, the soup to be skimmed of all fat when cold. This may be made the basis of any soup. In the articles relating to cooking proper, we shall extract liberally from Buckmaster's Cookery, a late and common-sense English work on cooking. In addition, in the various branches of cooking, we shall give original recipes contributed by farmers, wives and daughters, and accumulated during years of editorial life. Any vegetable or meat prepared by simmering till the substance is sufficiently pulpy or soft to be passed through a horse-hair or tammy sieve is called purée. In the case of meat it is sometimes necessary to beat in a pestle and mortar after simmering. The sieve is placed bottom upwards over a dish or tin, and with a wooden spoon or purée-presser the substance is worked through, and what passes through is called purée. It is sometimes necessary to moisten with a little liquor, which facilitates the passing of the purée. The purée of any vegetable stirred into a clear beef stock makes a soup and gives it its characteristic name. Butter required for soups should be added at two different times, except in preparing a Julienne soup. The first butter goes to fry the vegetables and adds little or nothing to the flavor. But, just before serving, two or three small pieces of butter in the tureen are a very acceptable addition; the butter should only be melted, for if boiled it loses its flavor and freshness. The addition of cold butter to soups and sauces is sometimes called a liaison of butter. A less quantity of butter is required for sweating vegetables than for frying or browning them. Liaisons are methods for thickening soups. One liaison is prepared by mixing flour with water, or milk, or broth. Mix the flour smooth with one of the above liquids, strain through a pointed strainer into the soup, continually stirring with the hand. The proper way to mix a liaison is to add some of the soup to it, thoroughly mix, and then add all to the soup or take the yolk or yolks only of eggs, say the yolk of one egg for one pint of soup; separate the white or albumen from the yolk by pouring backwards and forwards, put the yolks into a basin, beat up with a little powdered loaf sugar, (if none has been used with the soup), a small piece of butter, add a quarter pint of cream or half a pint of milk for each yolk; when thoroughly mixed, add a little soup and stir; remove your soup from the fire, and then stir in the liaison with wooden spoon. But never allow your soups to go on the fire after adding the liaison. A faggot of herbs, is constantly referred to in cooking, and is a mixture of parsley, thyme, and bay-leaf, and sometimes marjoram, rosemary and a clove of garlic; these are tied into a bunch, and are used for seasoning; it is called bouquet garni. Wash the parsley, and arrange the other herbs so that they are enclosed within the parsley. The ends of the parsley should be folded over to more effectually enclose the herbs, and then tied round with a string. A small handful of parsley, weighing say one ounce, one-sixteenth in weight of thyme, the same weight of bay-leaves, the same weight of marjoram, and, if used, one clove only of garlic, constitute an ordinary bouquet garni, or faggot of herbs. For a small bouquet garni use half the quantity; for a large, double the quantity. Dried herbs should always be to hand, and are best prepared in the following way: Gather the herbs just before flowering, and dry them quickly in an oven or before a screen, and pick out all the stalks Gouffé recommends the following preparations: quarter ounce of thyme, one-eighth ounce of marjoram, quarter ounce of rosemary. These are to be pounded in a mortar, with half ounce of nutmeg, quarter ounce of whole pepper, half ounce of cloves, one-eighth ounce of cayenne pepper, and passed through a hair sieve, and kept in a dry place in a well-stoppered bottle. In these proportions a good seasoning is secured. The proportion for mixing

with salt is one ounce of the mixture with four ounces of dry salt. Before cooking, arrange all your things as nearly as possible in order; no time is lost with this preliminary arrangement, it saves a good many steps; and as soon as you have finished with an article put it out of your way; this will save overcrowding, or in the middle of your cooking you will have to leave off to make room for your work. Wash your hands, clean your nails, read over slowly and thoughtfully the recipe. If you can not understand it in all its details, perhaps it will be better to substitute one that you do understand. No two cooks work exactly to the same recipe, nor is it desirable with persons who think about what they are doing. Rain water is best for all cooking purposes, but it will be necessary sometimes to filter it. About half a pint of soup may be calculated for each person. Thick glutinous soups and sauces require constant stirring, and always use wooden spoons. A small teaspoonful of powdered loaf-sugar may be added to all vegetable soups, and green vegetables. Good oil may often be used instead of butter, or with butter, especially with beans and peas. In the use of butter, or dripping, remember a less quantity is required for sweating than frying or browning vegetables. In seasoning, be careful with vegetables, herbs and spices remarkable for strong flavors.

Custards. A pint of new milk, three ounces of loaf sugar, and the thin rind of half a lemon are to be boiled in a clean enameled saucepan for three minutes; take it off the fire for five minutes; beat up eight eggs, leaving out the whites of four of them, add the milk to the eggs, stirring quickly as it is poured in. Strain the custard into the saucepan, and stir with a wooden spoon over a gentle fire till it begins to thicken; then strain through a fine sieve into a basin. The custard should not be flavored too strongly, and never cease stirring. Watch for the small lumps on the side of the pan (this is the commencement of boiling), and remove immediately.

Orange Custard Pudding. Beat up, as for an omelette, four eggs, with four ounces of powdered loaf sugar, and one pint and a half of milk previously boiled and allowed to cool, then add the grated peel of one orange, beat all up together, strain into a shallow pie-dish, and put into a moderate oven to bake. The safer way is to put the dish containing the custard into a tin dish, with boiling water coming two thirds of the way up the dish containing the custard, then put it into a moderate oven for twenty minutes, and if at the end of this time it is not sufficiently firm let it remain until it is so. When cold, sprinkle over the pudding powdered loaf sugar. The materials should be well mixed, but not too much beaten; if the custard is baked without putting into another dish with water, then the dish containing the custard should be shallow.

Lemon Custard Pudding. Prepare in the same way, using lemon-peel instead of orange.

Bain-Marie Pudding. Take a quart of new milk, and add six ounces of pounded loaf sugar. Put the sweetened milk into a clean stewpan, and reduce to one pint. When reduced, put aside one gill for the sauce. When the milk is nearly cold, mix gradually the yolks of five eggs and the whites of three. Strain into a mould, and steam it for half an hour in a stewpan with boiling water, taking care the water does not enter the mould. Take it out and let it stand for a few minutes before turning out. Put the gill of milk into a stewpan, add the juice of any delicate fruit, let it come to the boil, stir in a little cream, and pour over the pudding. The careful preparation of the sauce is most important.

Marmalade Pudding. Take four ounces of suet chopped finely, four ounces of grated bread crumbs, four ounces of moist sugar, four ounces of marmalade, mix these ingredients well together with three eggs, allow the mixture to stand for an hour. Butter an earthenware mould, put in the mixture, and lay a buttered paper on the top, tie it over with a cloth, and boil for two hours. When turned out, sprinkle it over with powdered loaf sugar. Do not let the water come over the top of the mould.

Lemon Pudding. Take two fresh lemons and three ounces of moist sugar, grate the rind off the lemons into a basin with the sugar, squeeze all the juice out, and mix together. Line a shallow tin with short paste, about a quarter of an inch in thickness, then spread over it some of the mixture, then another layer of paste, then some more of the mixture, and a thin layer of paste to cover; bake in a quick oven and serve hot. Be very careful that the lemons are fresh, and have a clear, good rind.

Baked Rice Pudding. Wash in two or three waters four heaped tablespoonfuls of rice, and boil it in a pint and a half of new milk for half an hour, stir in two tablespoonfuls of pounded loaf sugar, and flavor with anything you like, let it get cold, then add two well beaten eggs, butter a pie dish, put in the pudding, grate a little nutmeg over the top, and bake in a moderate oven for half an hour. The pudding should be baked quickly.

Rice Soufflé. Boil in a quart of milk six tablespoonfuls of rice with two tablespoonfuls of orange flower water and six ounces of pounded loaf sugar. Take six fresh eggs and separate the yolks from the whites; stir in one yolk, then another, till they are all used, and three ounces of butter in parts of one ounce each; stir with a wooden spoon so as to thoroughly mix the ingredients, and continue stirring till the rice is tender and sufficiently thickened. Well whisk the whites of the eggs till they are very stiff; if these are insufficiently beaten the soufflé will never rise. Take the stewpan aside, and let the contents cool a little, then add the whites and mix them quickly with the rice. Have ready a warm tin or soufflé dish slightly buttered, pour in the soufflé mixture, sprinkle with pounded loaf sugar, and put it into a rather brisk oven for seven or ten minutes; a straw run through will indicate when it is sufficiently baked. Serve very hot with a napkin around the tin. A clean stewpan, the proper whisking of the eggs, and a good oven, are all necessary to success.

Apple and Rice Meringue. Peel six apples, core them, cut them in pieces, and place them in a stewpan with half a pint of water, four ounces of loaf sugar, a few cloves, and a little cinnamon, and let them boil gently until they become quite soft, remove the apples, and let the syrup boil away till it is reduced to three tablespoonfuls, then strain it over the apples. Boil half a pound of rice, drain off the water, and add one pint of milk, four ounces of pounded loaf sugar, and the thin rind of a lemon. When the rice has absorbed all the milk, let it get cold, then remove the lemon rind and work into the rice the yolks of three or four eggs. Put the whites aside in a basin to whip up. Then make a shallow wall of rice round the dish in which it is to be served, place the apples in the center, and cover the whole with the whites of the eggs beaten up with a tablespoonful of powdered lump sugar, into a stiff froth, neatly plaster over the whole surface; sprinkle powdered sugar over and bake about fifteen minutes till the surface is nicely browned. Gooseberries or other fruit may be substituted for apples. Use the best rice and spread the white of the eggs neatly over the surface.

Apple Charlotte. Peel fifteen tart apples, slice them, remove the cores, and put them for ten minutes into cold water, to which has been added the juice of half a lemon. Then put them into a clean stewpan over a moderate fire with half a pound of loaf sugar and a little cinnamon; cover the stewpan and occasionally shake it and stir the apples. When quite soft and pulpy pass them through a tammy. Cut the crumb of some stale bread into slices of about a quarter of an inch in thickness, cut out a center-piece to cover the bottom of a mould, then cut some heart-shaped, or other fancy forms, and dip each of them on one side in melted butter as they are wanted, beginning with the large piece, which place at the bottom of the mould, and arrange the heart-shaped pieces round it, overlapping one another, and with the points resting on the piece at the bottom. Cut the remainder of the slices of bread into strips one and a half inch wide, and of the height of the mould; dip them in butter, and stand them all round the mould, also overlapping one another like feather-edged boarding; fill the center with the cooked apples, and put the charlotte in the oven until the bread is well colored. Turn the charlotte out of the mould on to a dish, glaze it over with some boiled apricot jam and serve. Every part of the mould must be well covered with bread and butter or the charlotte will not turn out.

Charlotte Russe. Peel and core twelve large pippins and cook them as just described for apple charlotte. Melt a little sweet butter, and well cover the inside of the mould, using a brush. Line the mould with finger biscuits, and fill it up with the apples. Make a hole in the center; this is best done by standing a clean glass bottle in the mould, remove the bottle and fill up with red currant jelly or apricot jam. Cover with finger biscuits and put the mould into a good oven for five or seven minutes. Turn the charlotte on a dish and serve hot. Be very particular to well cover the mould with butter and biscuits, so that none of the fruit comes into contact with the mould.

Gooseberry Fool. Put the picked fruit with half a pint of water into a stewpan with pounded loaf sugar, and set it over a stove, or in boiling water, till the fruit will pulp, pass it through a hair sieve and mix the *purée* by degrees with cream, or with a plain custard. Green gooseberries are to be preferred.

Strawberry Cream. Soak two ounces of pure gelatine in cold water, just sufficient to cover it. Now take two punnets of strawberries, pick them, and put them in a basin with three quarters of a pound of pounded loaf-sugar. After five or ten minutes pass them through a fine sieve and add the juice of one lemon. Dissolve the gelatine in a small clean stewpan over the fire, and when cold mix it with the strawberries by straining through a pointed strainer into another stewpan containing the purée of strawberries. Surround the stewpan with ice and stir till the contents begin to freeze. Whip three half pints of cream, remove the stewpan from the ice, and lightly and gradually stir in the whipped cream. Take a cylinder mould (not tin) and fill it, place the filled mould in a basin with pounded ice round it, cover the top with the lid of a stewpan and cover the lid with ice, and in about two hours the cream will be set. Have ready a large basin of water, as hot as the hand can bear, dip the mould entirely in the water, take it out quickly, place a dish on the top of the mould, reverse it, and it is ready. If the cream does not leave the mould freely dip it again into hot water. Be careful not to break the jelly in turning out.

Strawberry Ice Pudding. Take two pints of strawberries, pick them, and put them in a basin with half a pound of pounded loaf-sugar, let them remain a few minutes, then pass them through a sieve, (purée.) Melt one ounce of isinglass in half a pint of water, and when cold strain it through a fine sieve into the purée, and thoroughly mix by constantly stirring. Take a plain mould, which may be decorated with blanched almonds, fill it with the purée, put it on ice, cover the top with a stewpan lid, and then with ice. Let it remain two hours and it is ready. Be careful in turning it out, and do not add the water until quite cold.

Clarified Sugar for Water Ices. The water for these ices is prepared by dissolving one pound and a half of sugar in one pint of water, then beat up and stir in half the white of one egg, let it come to the boil and continue boiling for ten minutes with frequent skimming; strain through a hair sieve, and when cold the water is ready for use. This is called clarified sugar. There is often a little difficulty in freezing, which generally arises from the water or cream being too sweet. It will then be necessary to add a little more water or milk. Too much sugar in solution prevents the liquid from freezing. Ices are a very agreeable luxury and easily made, and the quantities given in the following recipes are for one pint and a half of ice.

Cherry-Water Ice. Beat up in a mortar one pound of cherries with their stones, and make them into a purée, then add the juice of two lemons to one pint of clarified sugar and half a pint of water, mix thoroughly and freeze.

Lemon-Water Ice. Rub off the rind of two lemons on some lumps of sugar, add the juice of six lemons and one orange, a pint of clarified sugar, and a half a pint of water, strain through a hair sieve and freeze.

Strawberry and Raspberry-Water Ice. Place in a basin one pound of picked strawberries and half a pound of raspberries, make into a purée and mix with one pint of clarified sugar and half a pint of water, thoroughly mix and freeze.

Raspberry and Currant Ice Cream. Prepare a pound of strawberries and half a pound of red currants, pass them through a sieve, and mix with three-quarters of a pound of powdered loaf-sugar, and a pint of cream. Freeze.

Pine-Apple Cream. Remove the peel and seed from a pine-apple, take one pound and work it to a pulp in a marble mortar, pass the pulp through a large hair sieve, (purée), mix the purée with three-quarters of a pound of pounded loaf-sugar and one pint of cream. Thoroughly mix and freeze.

Ginger Ice Cream. Bruise in a mortar six ounces of the best preserved ginger, and pass it through a hair sieve, add the juice of a lemon, half a pound of powdered loaf-sugar, and a pint of cream. Thoroughly mix and freeze.

Lemon Ice Cream. Rub off the rind of two lemons on some lumps of loaf-sugar, squeeze the juice of the lemons into a basin with the pieces of sugar, and add half a pound of powdered loaf-sugar and one pint of cream. Thoroughly mix, pass through a horsehair sieve, and freeze. A glass of good brandy added will make Italian ice cream.

Strawberry Ice Cream. Take a pound of fresh strawberries, remove the stalks and cast aside the bad ones. Put them in a basin and sprinkle them with half a pound of powdered loaf-sugar, then add the juice of a lemon, make a purée by passing through a horsehair sieve, and add one pint of cream. Mix thoroughly and freeze.

Italian Cream. Simmer half an ounce of isinglass in a little milk with the thin outer rind of half a lemon. Whip up half a pint of cream with the juice of two lemons, half a gill of sherry, and a dessertspoonful of pounded loaf-sugar. When the isinglass is all dissolved, remove the lemon rind, and, while warm, stir the whole together in a basin. Put it into a mould, stirring to prevent any settlement. This cream may be flavored with any liqueur, with raspberry, strawberry, or any other fruits, instead of lemon, and colored, if necessary, with cochineal. The isinglass must be thoroughly dissolved in the milk before mixing.

Apple Fritters. Prepare a batter as for any fritters. Peel some tart apples, remove the core with a vegetable cutter, and cut the apples across into slices of about three-eighths of an inch. Roll in pounded loaf-sugar and dip the slices into frying batter and fry in hot fat till they are of a nice yellow color and crisp. Remove them on to a cloth and sprinkle with pounded loaf-sugar. Arrange them in a heap on a hot napkin and serve. The temperature of the fat should be slightly increased after adding the fritters, and they should be well covered with batter before frying.

Orange Salad. Take one or two good oranges, wipe them, and cut them with the peel into slices of not more than a quarter of an inch in thickness. Arrange them round a circular dish, and let each piece overtop its predecessor. Sprinkle over two ounces of pounded loaf-sugar and add a gill of brandy, or any liqueur; but if sweet liqueurs are used, only half the quantity of sugar need be employed.

Omelettes. In preparing omelettes remember that, the eggs are not too much beaten; that you have a clean pan; that the omelette is not too large—three or four eggs are enough; that it is quickly cooked; and, that it is eaten hot. In making a plain omelette, we must be careful that the frying pan is perfectly clean. Place in the frying-pan about one ounce of sweet butter. Break three eggs separately to see that they are fresh, beat them up with a little chopped parsley and a pinch of pepper and salt. The eggs should not be beaten too much, (about four seconds will be sufficient), or the white separates, and you produce a watery mixture, which destroys the flavor and appearance of the omelette. Now that the butter is melted and in a state of froth, pour into the frying-pan the omelette mixture, and stir till it begins to set or thicken; shake the pan occasionally, and when sufficiently firm, fold the omelette over neatly into an oval shape, strike the handle of the frying-pan so as to produce a gentle vibration, which keeps the omelette detached from the pan, and when the omelette is of a golden color turn it quickly into a dish. To be able to prepare a plain omelette is to be able to prepare every kind of omelette. The chief thing to be borne in mind in cooking an omelette, is that the mixture does not adhere to the frying-pan. A cheese omelette. If you require a cheese omelette, introduce into the omelette mixture about a dessertspoonful of grated dry cheese, with a little pepper and salt, and sometimes a few grains of cayenne pepper; sprinkle the omelette when it is turned out with a little grated cheese. Sweet omelette. Beat up a teaspoonful of pounded loaf-sugar with the eggs, and just before the omelette is ready, distribute evenly over it a little jam, and fold the omelette over it; turn it into a hot dish, and sprinkle it with pounded loaf-sugar. Bacon omelette. A few pieces of previously cooked bacon cut into small dice, added just before folding the omelette, and so on; for the principle is the same for all omelettes. Omelette soufflé. Take three eggs, separate the yolks from the whites, and turn the yolks into one basin and the whites into another. Add to the yolks a dessertspoonful of pounded loaf-sugar and a tablespoonful of cream stir these together with a wooden spoon. Whip the whites for four minutes into a stiffish froth, then add them to the yolks, and mix altogether same as for an omelette. Have ready in a state of froth about half an ounce of butter in a small clean frying-pan. Pour in the mixture and proceed in precisely the same way as for a sweet omelette. The only difference between a plain omelette and an omelette soufflé is that cream is used, and the whites are whipped, and added to the mixture for a soufflé. Keep the mixture free from the pan while cooking.

Paste, Pies, Puddings, etc. Farinaceous foods are characterized by their large amount of starch, but the proportion of carbon and nitrogen will give a better idea of the relative value of different starchy substances commonly used as food: One pound of household bread yields 1,994 grains of carbon and eighty-nine grains of nitrogen. One pound of oat-meal contains 2,800 grains of carbon and 140 grains of nitrogen. One pound of pearl barley contains 2,660 grains of carbon and ninety-one grains of nitrogen. One pound of maize contains 2,800 grains of carbon and 121 grains of nitrogen. One pound of rice contains 2,780 grains of carbon and seventy grains of nitrogen. One pound of potatoes contain 770 grains of carbon and twenty-four grains of nitrogen. One pound of sago and arrowroot contain 2,555 grains of carbon and thirteen grains of nitrogen. One pound of peas, or beans, contains 2,730 grains of carbon and 255 grains of nitrogen. When substances containing a large proportion of starch are used as food, milk is a valuable and almost a necessary addition. If we bear in mind the quantity of carbon, twelve and one-half ounces, and of nitrogen, 250 grains, required daily by a laboring man, we can form some idea of the relative value of cereals as food substances. The form in which they are chiefly used is as wheaten bread. In the conversion of wheat into bread we grind the grain and reject the lining membrane of the bran, which is rich in nitrogen and phosphates; but the presence of this inner lining of the bran and small portions of the bran itself give a brown color to the bread, and in our craze for white flour and white bread, a prejudice difficult to overcome, (especially among the poor), we waste a considerable portion of our food. The utility of finely bolting meal, by which all the bran and pollards are removed, is very doubtful, because you not only get rid of much nitrogen, but also of the salts which are especially valuable in the nourishment of the young.

Puff Paste. This paste can not be made with certainty in summer time without a refrigerator, because the butter is liable to become oily. Wash your hands using a nail brush, and place on a clean paste-board or marble slab one pound of fine sifted flour, make a hollow in the center of it, then add half a teaspoonful of salt and about half a pint of water. Mix the flour and water gradually, and when about half mixed sprinkle the paste with a little more water so as to collect all the flour. Work the paste lightly till it ceases to stick either to the board or the fingers. Take three-quarters of a pound of butter, work it in a clean cloth to remove the water. Have the paste about one inch in thickness, place the butter in the center of it and fold over the four sides of the paste so as to enclose the butter in a square. The paste will now be from two to three inches in thickness. Put it aside for five minute in a cold place or a refrigerator. Then roll the paste to a length of three feet, fold over from one end one-third of the length, and now fold over the other end. There are now three thicknesses of paste of equal lengths, and this folding into three is called one turn. Put the paste aside for ten minutes, then give it two turns, beginning at right angles to the first rolling, then in the same direction as the first rolling. Put it aside for another ten minutes, then give it two more turns, in all five or six turns. Gather the paste into a lump and finish by rolling to the required thickness, about a quarter of an inch.

Short Paste. Wash your hands and place on a clean paste-board or marble slab one pound of sifted flour, make a hole in the center and add two tablespoonfuls of pounded loaf-sugar, and half, or better three-quarters, of a pound of butter, previously freed from water. Mix gradually with half a pint of water. Work thoroughly but lightly with the hands. Roll it into a smooth lump, and, if you have time, it will be the better if put aside for one hour. Then roll it out two or three times, folding over each time, and the paste is ready. If fresh butter has been used, a small pinch of salt may be added.

Suet Crust. To every pound of flour allow five or six ounces of beef suet. Free the suet from the skin and mince it finely, then rub it well into the flour with a pinch of salt; work the whole to a smooth paste with a half pint of water, roll it out, and it is ready. This crust is quite rich enough for most purposes; but when a better one is desired, use from a half to three-quarters of a pound of suet to every pound of flour. For rich crusts pound the suet in a mortar, with a small quantity of sweet butter. It should then be laid on the paste in small pieces, the same as for puff crust, and will be found exceedingly good for hot tarts. Five ounces of suet to every pound of flour will make a good crust, and even a quarter of a pound will answer very well where the crust is wanted very plain.

Suet Pudding. Put a pound of sifted flour in a basin with half a pound of beef suet, finely chopped; add two eggs with a pinch of salt and a quarter of a pint of water; beat well together with a wooden spoon, making a rather thick batter; flour a pudding cloth and lay it in a small round-bottomed basin, pour in the mixture, tie the cloth tightly, and put the pudding to boil in boiling water; an hour and a quarter would be sufficient to cook it. When done, remove the cloth, turn the pudding over upon a dish, and serve very hot. The water must be kept boiling.

Pease Pudding. Soak a pint of peas for ten hours in rain or soft water—the bad ones float and can be removed. Drain them and tie them up loosely in a clean cloth, and put them into plenty of cold rain water; let them come to the boil and then simmer till the peas are tender; the time will vary with the kind of peas, but never less than two hours. Drain them over a colander and pass them through a clean wire sieve. Season the pulp with pepper and salt, bent up one or two eggs with an ounce of sweet butter and stir it into the pulp. Thoroughly mix with a wooden spoon. Have a clean cloth, and tightly tie up the pudding. Let it boil for another half hour. Turn it on to a dish and serve. This is usually served with fat pork, and is a very sensible and nutritious dish for working people. Be careful in the selection of the peas, and be sure that they are soft enough to pulp before turning them out.

Roly-Poly Pudding. Make a nice light suet crust and roll it out to the thickness of about half an inch. Spread jam, or currants and treacle, equally over it, leaving a small margin of paste without any treacle. Roll it up, fasten the ends securely, and tie it in a floured cloth; then put the pudding into boiling water and boil for two or three hours. Fresh suet and a light crust are necessary.

Apple Pudding. Take a basin, butter it, and line it with a suet crust; pare, core, and cut the apples into pieces, and fill the basin with them, with sugar according to taste; add one small teaspoonful of finely minced lemon-peel, one tablespoonful of lemon juice, and cover with crust; close the edges well together, flour the cloth, and tie it securely over the pudding, and put it into plenty of boiling water. Let it boil from one and a half to two and a half hours, according to the size, then turn it out of the basin and send to the table quickly. Apple pudding does not suffer by being boiled an extra hour, if care be taken to keep it well covered with the water all the time. The water must be kept constantly boiling, and if more is added, let it be boiling water.

Baked Batter Pudding. Take six ounces of fine flour, three eggs, and a pinch of salt; add by degrees as much milk as will, when well beaten, make it the consistency of thick cream; pour into a pudding dish, and bake three-quarters of an hour; or it may be boiled in a basin, or tied up in a cloth. It will require two hours' boiling. The milk should be added gradually.

Yorkshire Pudding. Use for every egg as much flour as a tablespoon will carry, and a small pinch of salt. Whisk the eggs well, strain and mix them gradually with the flour, then pour in by degrees as much new milk as will reduce the batter to the consistence of rather thin cream. The tin or pan which is to receive the pudding, must have been placed for some time previously, under a joint which has been put down to roast; one of beef is usually preferred. Beat the batter briskly and lightly the instant before it is poured into the pan, watch it carefully that it may not burn, and let the edges have an equal share of the fire. When the pudding is quite firm in every part and well colored on the surface, turn it round to brown on the under side. This is best accomplished by first dividing it into quarters. Be careful in mixing the batter, which should be rather more liquid than for a boiled pudding.

Pigeon Pie. Prepare three or four house pigeons, and take half a pound of tender beefsteak, cut into convenient pieces, lightly fry the steak first, and then the pigeons, in a clean stewpan with a little butter, season with chopped mushrooms, one eschalot, a little parsley, and pepper and salt. Place the steak at the bottom of the dish, upon this place the halves of the pigeons, rinse out the stewpan in which the things have been fried, with half a pint of stock or water, and strain into the dish; add the yolks only of five hard boiled eggs, cover with a puff paste, and bake for an hour and a quarter in a moderate oven. The pigeons must be young and the steak tender; and do not fry too long in the butter.

Giblet Pie. Clean and blanch the giblets (except the liver), and put them, with the wings, feet, head and neck, in boiling water; and remove the skin from the feet and beak. Put into a stewpan a piece of butter the size of a walnut, one onion cut in slices, a bay-leaf, a little salt, pepper and sugar; place them on the fire until the onion is brown; put in the giblets with the head cut in two, let them remain on the fire for about three minutes, stirring them round; then add nearly a quart of boiling water, and let them stew gently for two hours; remove from the fire and let them get cold. Take a pie dish and place a piece of steak on the bottom, then place over that the giblets with the liver, and steak again over them; add the liquor the giblets were stewed in, season and cover with good paste. The giblets must be fresh and well stewed.

Squab Pie. Trim part of the fat off some mutton cutlets, and season them with pepper and salt, place them in a pie dish, and cover with a layer of sliced apples sprinkled with sugar and chopped onions, previously blanched; if the pie is large, arrange another layer of cutlets, and again cover with onions and apples, then cover with a good suet crust and bake. When done, pour out all the gravy at the side, remove the fat, and add a spoonful of mushroom ketchup to the liquor; and return it to the pie. The fat must be well removed from the gravy.

Rumpsteak Pie. Take three pounds of tender rump steak, cut it into pieces half the size of your hand, trim off all the skin, the sinews, and every part which can not be eaten, and beat the steak with a chopper or a kreatone. Chop very finely half a dozen eschalots, and mix them with half an ounce of pepper and salt, strew some of the mixture at the bottom of the dish, then a layer of steak, then some more of the mixture, and so on till the dish is full; add half a gill of mushroom ketchup and the same quantity of rich stock; cover it with a good paste, and bake it two hours. Large oysters blanched, bearded, and laid alternately with the steak, is a great improvement, and the liquor in which they were blanched, when reduced, may be used instead of the ketchup or stock. The steak must be tender, or made so by beating.

Preparing Forcemeat. Remove the rind, gristle, bone, and brown parts from three-quarters of a pound of fat bacon, take three-quarters of a pound of veal with any trimmings, mince them very finely, and add a good dessertspoonful of spiced salt. Work all these well together in a mortar till it is of a rather stiff paste, and put it aside in a basin. Make a short paste and line the inside of a plain oval pie mould. Now arrange a layer of the forcemeat on the paste at the bottom of the mould; use about one-fourth. Then a layer of rashers of ham; then another layer of forcemeat; then the veal, cut into convenient pieces. Sprinkle over with spiced salt. Now another layer of forcemeat, then rashers of ham, then forcemeat. Cover the surface with three rashers of fat bacon and a bay-leaf; cover with paste, and bake for two hours in a moderate oven, covering the top with a piece of buttered paper. A fine plated skewer thrust in will enable you to judge when the meat is sufficiently baked. If the spice is at hand this pie is no more trouble, nor does it take more time, than an ordinary veal and ham pie, and is much better. The chief point to be borne in mind is not to have it too highly seasoned, and the meat should be free from gristle and skin.

Veal and Ham Pie. Take about two pounds of lean veal, from the breast or fillet, free it from fat, skin, bone, and gristle, and three-quarters of a pound of ham or bacon, in thin rashers free from rind and coarse parts. Cut these in convenient pieces. Prepare a short or puff paste and line the dish. Mince finely half-a-dozen button mushrooms, a sprig of parsley, and sweat these in a clean stewpan with an ounce of butter and a little flour; add a gill or half a pint of good stock, or in default water, and a dessertspoonful of ketchup. Bring these slowly to the boil and stand it aside. Prepare three hard boiled eggs and cut them into dice; if preferred use only the yolks. Now arrange the meat, a layer of veal, then ham, and so on, finishing with ham mingled with the egg, (some use a little grated lemon-peel, others add oysters, sweetbreads, mushrooms, etc.) The pie may be made rich and savory in a dozen ways, according to taste. Finish the pie and strain through the hole at the top all but a wineglassful of the gravy; cover the hole with an ornamental piece of paste and bake. When ready remove the ornament at the top, make the remainder of the gravy very hot and strain it in, cover the hole again and serve. In meat pies it is essential that the meat should be tender and free from skin and gristle.

Rissoles. Take the trimmings of puff paste; roll the paste out to the thickness of a penny piece; place small balls of meat, the same as those prepared for croquets, and put them at distances of two inches from each other; moisten the paste round these balls of meat with a brush dipped in water; fold the flap of the front part of the paste over the balls, just as you would fold a sheet of paper lengthwise; press all round them with the edge of the thumb; cut them out with a fluted round tin cutter, and place them on a dish sprinkled with flour: having cut out a sufficient number, fry them in hot fat, and serve up with fried parsley on a napkin. The difference between a croquet and a rissole is this,— the rissole is always fried in a paste, the croquet in egg and bread-crumb. Take care to have a good paste and the rissoles neatly made.

Open Jam Tarts. All fruit pies and tarts require a light, good crust. Take an open tart mould and line it with paste about a quarter of an inch in thickness. Make a few holes in the bottom; this is to prevent the paste puffing up in the center. Bake in a brisk oven ten or fifteen minutes. Let the paste cool, then add the preserve, but if the tart is to be served hot, warm the jam in a clean stewpan and add at once. The tart may be decorated with leaves, flowers, or stars, cut out of the paste and baked. It is not desirable to bake the jam in the tart; it spoils its flavor and appearance. A good oven is essential for all fruit pastry.

Apple Pie. Prepare the apples, by peeling and removing the cores, and cutting them into eight pieces, moisten the edge of the dish with a little butter and lay a slip of puff paste round it. Arrange a layer of apples at the bottom, then sugar, and flavor with cinnamon, cloves, lemon-peel, orange-peel, candied citron, or whatever flavoring you prefer; a little quince is a great improvement. Keep adding the apples till the dish is full and well heaped up in the center. Cover with puff paste and decorate the top. Cream is a good addition to apple pie. In baking pies and tarts a light crust is essential.

Plain Cake. Take half a quartern of common paste, four eggs, a quarter of a pound of sugar, a quarter of a pound of butter, or dripping, a quarter of a pound of currants, carefully washed and dried, and a little salt. Break the paste lightly in a basin, put in the sugar, the butter, and two eggs, thoroughly mix the whole together, then add the other two eggs, one at a time, work the mixture well, and, lastly, work in the currants. Fill a plain mould, previously buttered, with the mixture, and set it in a warm place to rise. As soon as it has risen put it into a moderate oven to bake to a brown color. The chief thing is to carefully mix the ingredients.

Seed Cake. Mix a half pound of pounded loaf-sugar with two pounds of flour in a large bowl or pan. Make a hole in the center, and pour into it a half pint of lukewarm milk and two spoonfuls of yeast. Draw a little of the surrounding flour into this, and throwing a cloth over the vessel, set it in a warm place for an hour or two. Then add half a pound of butter just liquefied, an ounce of caraway seeds, a little allspice, ginger, and very little nutmeg, and milk sufficient to make the whole of a proper stiffness. Mix it thoroughly; butter a plain mould, and pour in the mixture; let it stand half an hour at the mouth of the oven to rise, and then bake it. Be careful to prove your yeast before using it.

Ginger Cakes. Take one pound of flour, twelve ounces of fresh butter, twelve ounces of pounded loaf-sugar, two ounces of best ground ginger, add the yolks of eight eggs. Work the whole of these together on a paste board or slab, and after having gathered the paste up into a compact mass, separate it by cutting with a round patty cutter, and then place them on a slightly buttered baking sheet. Bake them to a light brown color in a moderate oven. The ingredients must be thoroughly well mixed.

*Roasting, Baking, Broiling, and Boiling.** Beef constitutes by far the larger portion of animal food consumed by man; and in selecting a piece of beef or mutton, see that the grain is not too coarse, that the meat is of a bright red color, soft to the touch, and that the fat is nicely intermixed with the lean. Mutton and beef will be more tender if the weather will admit of their being hung, knuckle downwards, some days before cooking; but two days in summer are often equal to a week in winter. The flavor and the quality of meat will depend on the breed, age, and food. The lean is the muscular part of the animal, and consists of fibrin, gelatine, and albumen. Experiments, which have been carefully made, show that a sirloin of beef, weighing twelve pounds, lost in roasting forty-four ounces, of which twenty-seven were water and seventeen fat or dripping. A flank of beef, weighing twelve pounds, made into pot-au-feu, or bouilli, lost twenty-five ounces. It is therefore quite clear that boiling, especially when the liquor is turned to an account, as it should be, is the most economic kind of cooking. When meat is boiled, much of the albumen remains in the water, and when flavored with vegetables and herbs, and thickened with meal, you have a highly nutritious soup, much used in every country except our own. Glue is an impure gelatine. The white of egg is nearly a pure albumen; this albumen surrounds the fibers of the meat; and the stringy threads of stewed meat afford an example of fibrin. The osmazome is that extract or essence which gives meat its peculiar odor and taste by long stewing. The osmazome is dissolved in the water, and this is the secret of all meat flavors in soup. Roasting appears to exalt the flavor of meat more than any other method of cooking. The best joints for roasting are the ribs and fillet, the rump and sirloin; for making soup, the neck, tail, and tops of ribs; and for stewing all the inferior pieces. To roast properly a good fire is most important: it should be evenly lighted, bright and radiant, and never allowed to get low. No reliable time can be given for roasting, because the nature and the qualities of meat vary. About two hours for seven pounds of beef, and one hour and three-quarters for a leg of mutton of the same weight, or roughly, about a quarter of an hour to the pound, will generally be found sufficient. To tell whether the meat is done, press the fleshy part with the thumb; if the meat yield to the pressure it is done. In the case of poultry or game, the flesh of the leg may be tried in the same manner. Cooks attach importance to the steams drawing to the fire. When the meat is nearly done, remove the buttered paper, if any has been used, and sprinkle over the meat a little salt, and put the ends of the joint to the fire; well baste the meat, and endeavor to obtain a clear brown color before the fire. If you wish the meat to be frothed, dredge very lightly a little well-dried flour over the surface, and give it time to crisp; do not baste after the flour. Practice is the only way to learn to roast properly. In the United States but little roasting is done before an open fire. Meats are baked. The general principles, however, are the same. Broiling is a very acceptable kind of cooking when well done, but anything broiled requires constant watching. It is an easy method of making a small portion of meat savory, and may be recommended to bachelors. It is not the cooking for families. Things broiled should be turned with steak tongs; a fork should on no account be used; and without a clear, bright fire broiling is impossible. The principle is the same as roasting; the albumen of the meat or fish is coagulated, which forms a crust, and so retains all the juices. Delicate appetites are often encouraged with a nice broiled fish. The bars of gridirons are often too large and obstruct much of the heat. The gridiron should be very clean, and if bright when purchased it should be kept so, and always be washed before putting away. Before putting anything on the gridiron let it get thoroughly hot; the reason for this is obvious; much of the heat of the fire is conducted away by the iron, and if a piece of meat be placed on at once the albumen coagulates but slowly, and allows the juices to drop into the fire instead of being preserved in the meat. When your gridiron is thoroughly clean and warm, rub the bars with a piece of suet, this prevents the meat sticking and coming to table with black stripes. If you like the flavor, just rub the gridiron with a clove of garlic, or eschalot. Perpendicular gridirons are objectionable, because there is always a current of cold air on one side of the thing broiled. For fish, the gridiron should be rubbed with chalk; as the things broiled are usually small they should be served on a very hot dish. When the fat smokes and blazes too much remove the gridiron for an instant, and just sprinkle the fire with a little salt. Arrange your gridiron, if possible, so that it may be from two to five inches above the fire and slightly inclined toward the cook. In relation to boiling, some cooks think, after a piece of meat has been placed in the saucepan, it requires no more attention, but boiling requires as much care as almost any kind of cooking. If you wish to retain all the flavors and juices of the meat plunge it into soft boiling water, and after three minutes stand it aside to simmer, at about 170° or 180°. Always remember that a boiling temperature coagulates the albumen on the surface. If you want to make stock or broth, on no account allow the water to boil; the scum must always be removed, and a little cold water facilitates its rising. Some cooks boil mutton and fowls in a floured cloth, to make them look whiter, but its utility is very doubtful.

Bouilli or Boiled Beef. Beef used for the pot-au-feu is called Bouilli, and has no doubt given much of its flavor to the broth; but it may be made into a very inviting dish. As soon as the beef broth has been prepared the meat should be taken out and placed on a dish, garnished with vegetables that can be eaten.

Bouilli with Sharp Sauce. Take about a pound and a half of cold beef and cut it across the grain into slices a quarter of an inch thick. Trim off the gristle and outside parts, put the meat into a small gratin dish, sprinkle with pepper and salt, and moisten with a gill of stock: let the meat bake for a quarter of an hour in a moderate oven. Serve either with piquante or tomato sauce poured over the meat. The preparation of the sauce is most important for this dish. In roasting we have given directions as though the meat were really to be roasted before an open fire. When stoves are used place it in the oven. The other directions will apply as well in this as in other cases.

Roast Sirloin of Beef. Take a piece of sirloin of beef, weighing seven or nine pounds, cut off the chine bone, flatten the flap part and tie it under the fillet, or cut it off. Trim up the joint, then tie a layer of suet over the fillet. Cover the meat with buttered paper, secure it with a piece of tape, and roast before an even fire. Put it close to the fire for ten minutes, then remove to a short distance. Ten minutes before the meat is ready, remove the paper and sprinkle with salt. A little water or stock without flavor should be put into the dripping-pan, but not butter nor dripping. Baste frequently, and if you have to add coals during the roasting, do so in such a way as not to deaden the fire.

Roast Ribs of Beef. Saw off the chine-bone, trim the joint, wrap it in buttered paper, and roast as sirloin.

Roast Neck of Veal. Roasted veal is rather tasteless; it is greatly improved by larding. Veal should be thoroughly cooked before a moderate fire. The neck, loin, and chump are best for roasting. Take a neck of veal and saw off the chine-bone, as for cutlets, and cut through the ribs about the middle, so as to roll the flaps underneath, and tie the meat with a piece of tape. It is better to wrap the veal in buttered paper; and about ten minutes before it is ready remove the paper, sprinkle with salt, and let it come to a golden color. Baste every ten minutes, skim off the fat, and strain the gravy over the meat. The French make a great many delicate dishes from the liver, tongues, ears, feet, brains, kidneys, and sweetbreads of calves.

Roast Loin of Veal. Take four or five pounds, including the kidney, remove the chine-bone, and trim off some of the fat, then roll the flap underneath, and tie it with a piece of tape, so as to enclose the kidney.

Roast Leg of Mutton. Mutton for roasting is all the better for having been kept a few days, if the weather be favorable, in a dry, airy place, free from flies. A short thick leg is the best; the lean rather of a dark red, and the fat firm and white. Saw off the shank bone two inches below the knuckle. A clove of garlic may be introduced near the knuckle for those who like the flavor. Place it before a sharp fire for fifteen minutes, to keep in the gravy, then remove it a short distance to finish roasting; put half a pint of broth in the dripping-pan, and five or ten minutes before taking from the fire, sprinkle with salt; place the mutton on a dish, and put a white paper frill around the knuckle-bone; skim off all the fat, and strain the gravy over the meat. You may serve with this joint white haricot beans, or macaroni under the meat or separately. Constant basting is necessary for all roast meat.

Roast Hind Quarter of Lamb. Saw off the knuckle-bone of a hind-quarter or leg of lamb, and roast before a sharp, even fire; when ready, place it on a dish, and garnish with watercresses. Horseradish or mint sauce may be served in a boat. Frequent basting and a clear uniform fire are necessary.

Roast Breast of Lamb. Select a nice breast or leg of lamb, and put it before a clear fire. Take some stale bread-crumbs, minced parsley, and a little salt and pepper; mix these thoroughly together. After about a quarter of an hour, when the fat begins to melt freely, sprinkle the mixture uniformly over the surface. When done, skim the fat from the gravy, and strain over the joint. Garnish with watercresses, and serve with hot mint sauce in a boat. A lemon is often sent up with roast lamb. A clear uniform fire and basting are essential for all roast meat.

Roast Duck. Stuff the duck with a stuffing prepared as follows:—Take two or three onions, say six ounces, cut them in slices with six or eight sage leaves, blanch both for five minutes; drain and chop them fine; put the whole in a stewpan with one ounce of butter, two pinches of salt, and two small pinches of pepper; simmer gently for ten minutes, stirring with a wooden spoon; add a handful of bread-crumbs, and stir for two minutes more; the stuffing is then ready for use; an apple mixed with the stuffing is thought by some to be an improvement. Truss the duck, and put it down to roast before a very hot fire. A young duck, a good fire, and occasional basting are necessary.

Roast Goose. A goose weighing six or eight pounds is to be preferred. Pick, draw, singe and wipe, and stuff it with stuffing as for roast duck. Sprinkle with a little salt, baste frequently, skim off all the fat, strain the gravy and serve separately or on the dish, as preferred. It is essential that the goose should be young, and roasted before a good fire, but not a fierce one. Try the pinion, and if the lower part of the beak breaks easily, the goose or duck is young.

Roast Fowl. Pick, draw, wipe, singe and truss a fowl. Unless stuffed, an onion inside and a piece of butter are thought to be an improvement. Tie a rasher of fat bacon over the breast and put the fowl before a bright, clear fire, then roast slowly, with occasional basting. When ready, strain the gravy and pour it under the fowl. Garnish with watercresses. A young fowl is essential, which may be known by the large size of its feet and knee joints, and the smallness of the spurs. Try the pinions and breast. Baste occasionally.

Roast Turkey. Prepare a turkey; one of about six or seven pounds is to be preferred. Put the turkey before a good fire and roast till of a golden color. Skim off the fat, strain the gravy, and garnish with watercresses. It is necessary to have a young turkey with white flesh. Avoid one with long hairs and flesh inclined to a violet tinge.

Boiled Leg of Mutton. Cut off the shank, wipe it, put it into a clean saucepan or stewpan with plenty of lukewarm water, and let it come slowly to the boil; skim when necessary. For a leg of eight pounds, let it simmer for two hours. The mutton should be well done, but not overdone, it should retain all the juices and look plump; when the meat is not very white it is sometimes blanched for ten minutes in hot water or wrapped in a floured cloth. A few minutes before it is ready add half a teaspoonful of salt. Wether mutton, four or five years old, is the best both for boiling or roasting; for boiling it is a whiter color if cooked fresh, but more tender if kept four or five days. Serve with boiled turnips, and caper sauce not poured over it, but served in a boat. Skimming and simmering are necessary, or the meat will be hard and tough.

A Fricasée of Fowl. To prepare a fricasée of chicken, which may be slightly varied from the following recipe, is one of the best examples of good English cooking. Draw, pick, wash and singe a chicken, cut off the head and legs at the first joint and the wings at the second. In singeing be careful not to break, burn or blacken the fowl. It is necessary to singe all fowls; it not only destroys the small down but tightens the skin. Put the chicken into a clean threequart stewpan with sufficient warm water to cover it; add one onion with a clove, a little salt and a bunch of parsley. Skim when necessary. Let it boil for ten minutes, remove it to sieve and let it drain for three minutes. With the liquor in which the chicken was boiled prepare a sauce by adding two ounces of butter and two tablespoonfuls of flour, and thoroughly stir. Prepare and blanch for five minutes a dozen mushrooms, in just sufficient water to cover them; add the juice of half a lemon. Strain into the sauce and put the mushrooms aside; be careful that they are not broken. Neatly cut up the fowl into ten pieces, keeping the skin on each piece, and finish cooking the pieces in the sauce, which will take from twenty to twenty-five minutes. Arrange them neatly on a dish, strain over them the sauce and garnish with the mushrooms. Four crayfish make a good garnish, or croutons of bread fried in butter. It is necessary to have a young fowl, and it must not remain in the sauce longer than is necessary for cooking.

Boiled Fowl. Neatly truss and prepare a fowl; be careful not to break the skin in picking, and wrap it in a sheet of white buttered paper, put it into a clean stewpan or saucepan with plenty of lukewarm water, and let it just boil, skim, and in fifteen minutes turn the fowl over for another fifteen minutes, and for a fowl of about three pounds this will be sufficient. Young fowls and all poultry will be the better for being kept two or three days before boiling. Serve with a white sauce, or bechamel sauce, or parsley and butter, according to taste. Choose a young fowl with white or pale-colored legs. Occasional skimming is necessary.

Calf's Liver and Bacon. The liver should be cut in slices, each about a quarter of an inch in thickness; cut also some streaky bacon into thin rashers of uniform thickness and fry them first, and drain on a plate, and add the fat to the frying pan; after having covered each piece of liver with flour, fry them in the fat from the bacon, and when nicely browned on both sides dish up the liver and bacon in a circular row, placing a piece of each alternately; strain off the fat from the pan in which the liver has been fried, add a little flour and a tablespoonful of ketchup, a little pepper and salt, and half a gill of stock or water; a few minced gherkins or mushrooms, pickled walnuts, or mixed pickles may be mixed with the sauce; stir all together over the fire until the sauce just boils, and pour it over the liver and bacon. Be careful to flour the pieces of liver uniformly; and the bacon should be young.

Beef or Rump Steak. A rump steak should be one and a half inch thick. Slightly flatten it with a chopper, which should be moistened on the side with water, to prevent its adhering to the meat. Trim it into an oval shape and oil the surfaces; this oiling is not to flavor the steak, but to prevent the outside hardening on the fire, and to quicken the cooking. Sprinkle with a little pepper and salt, and broil over a clear fire. Let the gridiron incline a little toward you. Have a clear, brisk fire and turn the steak with tongs; a fork should never be used for broiled meat or fish.

Veal Cutlets. Trim and flatten the cutlets taken from a neck of veal. Remove the chine-bone and all the skin and gristle. Sprinkle the cutlet with pepper and salt, oil it on both sides and put it on the gridiron over a clear fire, and dish up with brown gravy, or a sharp sauce, or with maitre-d'hotel butter under the cutlet, or with tomato sauce. A clear bright fire and the gridiron slightly inclined towards the cook are necessary.

Sweetbreads. Whatever the dish, sweetbreads are always first prepared as follows: Soak for three hours in cold water three sweetbreads, change the water occasionally if it becomes discolored, put them into boiling water for half an hour, or long enough to become firm, but not hard, press them into shape by placing them between two paste-boards or baking tins, with a four or five pound weight on the top, then lard them with bacon about one-eight of an inch in section. Bacon for larding should be cured without saltpetre, or it gives a pink tinge to all white meat. Put them in a clean stewpan with three gills of rich stock, and season with salt; when the stock thickens add another half-pint and baste frequently with the stock; arrange them on a dish, strain the gravy over them, and serve with sorrel, green peas, or tomato sauce. Throat sweetbreads are the best, and the gravy should be rich and free from fat. Do not allow the sweetbreads to harden in boiling or they will be difficult to lard.

Beans and Bacon. Put a pint of beans into cold water the over-night. Cut half a pound of bacon into half-inch dice, put the bacon and beans into a clean saucepan with just sufficient cold water to cover them; let the beans boil till they are tender, then stir in one or two tablespoonfuls of flour, a little pepper, and a bouquet garni, with a clove of garlic or an eschalot, Let the contents simmer slowly, and when the sauce is sufficiently thickened the beans and bacon are ready. The beans, if old, will require long soaking, or much longer boiling than is desirable for the bacon.

Fat Pork or Bacon and Beans. Soak a quart of beans in cold water for ten or twelve hours, then boil them with a little salt till they are tender. Take a common yellow dish, and put the beans at the bottom, and on a tripod place two pounds of fat bacon or pork and bake for an hour, or the meat may be roasted and the beans placed in the dripping-pan. The beans should be quite tender before baking.

Gravy for General Use. It is often necessary to prepare a gravy for general use. Take about two pounds of fillet of veal, remove any fat, cut it into three or four pieces and add any odd portions of uncooked meat. Put them all into a six-pint saucepan or stewpan with half a pint of soft water. Let it come slowly to the boil and continue reducing till it forms a glaze. Turn the pieces of meat over and add three pints of water, a teaspoonful of salt, a pinch of pepper, a bouquet garni, a small carrot split into four, and one onion, with two cloves. Let the contents come to the boil and simmer slowly for two hours with the lid removed. Skim as occasion requires and strain the liquor through a tammy sieve and put it aside for use. The pieces of meat can be served with a sharp sauce. The contents must not boil or the gravy will not be clear, and freedom from fat is most essential.

Stuffing. Melt in a clean stewpan one ounce of butter and season with pepper and salt. Blanch for seven minutes three-quarters of a pound of sliced onions and fifteen sage leaves, remove the stalks and mince them finely and then stir into the butter. Stir for ten minutes with a wooden spoon. Now add stale bread-crumbs, sufficient to bring the stuffing to its proper consistency, and the stuffing is ready for use. The mixture requires constant stirring. Or, take half a pound of stale bread-crumbs, four ounces of finely-chopped suet, two eggs, a dessertspoonful of minced parsley, a very small teaspoonful of minced eschalots, marjoram, and thyme, then season with pepper and salt and two grated nutmegs. Work these thoroughly well together with the hands and it is ready.

Salads. Salads are a very simple and harmless luxury, and they make an agreeable addition to our ordinary food, and if taken with plenty of oil, are very wholesome. In this country we are perfect savages in the making of salads. The dressing is often served up in a twisted bottle, and the wet vegetables are heaped up on a dish like food for cows, with the polite invitation to every one to help himself. A salad properly prepared should be one of the most attractive dishes on the table. There are many little things necessary to secure a good salad, and their variety is only limited by the ingenuity of the cook. The Spanish proverb is that four persons are necessary to make a good salad—"A spendthrift for oil, a miser for vinegar, a barrister for salt, and a madman to stir it up." Young ladies in the country, where they have an abundance and variety of vegetables, might render a national service if they would turn their attention to salads as well as croquet. If you wish to preserve the crispness and flavor of green vegetables for salads they should be gathered either early in the morning or late in the evening, and put in a cool, damp place. To soak green vegetables in water to keep them fresh, or to keep up the appearance of freshness, is a mistake. Lettuce, which is the chief thing in most green salads, should be eaten young, or the leaves are too strong for a delicate salad, and if possible, lettuce should never be washed or cut with a steel knife: the best way is to break the lettuce into the bowl, or to cut it with a silver knife. If you must wash the vegetables, do it quickly, and thoroughly dry them in a clean cloth before putting into the salad bowl. A salad should never be prepared till a few minutes before it is wanted. A variety of vegetables may be used according to taste, but the fewer the better; cress is often too thready to be used agreeably; the chief vegetables are lettuce, endive, radishes, onions, basil, mustard, watercress, cucumber, celery, mint, parsley, beetroot, dandelion, tarragon, chervil, sorrel and tomatoes. In Europe cold meat, fish, fowl and game are more often served as salads than green, uncooked vegetables. Our forefathers had the same notion of salads, which were frequently prepared by them from previously cooked meat and vegetables. Above all things be particular with the sauces and jellies, meat or fish, served as part of the salad.

Vegetable Salad. Boil separately equal weights, according to the quantity required, of the following vegetables:—French beans, carrots, green peas, turnips and asparagus points; dry these vegetables in a clean cloth, and when quite cold cut them into dice of one-quarter or three-eighths of an inch; the French beans should be cut into squares; now arrange them on a dish; begin by placing the French beans at the bottom and in the center, arrange round the French beans in about equal quantities in narrow rows the carrots then peas, then turnips, then asparagus points, and if the dish is large enough and the vegetables sufficient, proceed again in the same order; sprinkle the surface with a tablespoonful of Ravigote—*i. e.*, finely minced chervil, tarragon, burnet. chives and garden cress all previously blanched, strained, cooled and dried in a clean cloth. Serve with mayonnaise sauce in a boat. The success of this salad depends on the vegetables being young and tender.

Fish Salad. Take the remains of any cold boiled fish and cut them into small scallops about two inches, and dip them into mayonnaise sauce; wash, if necessary, two freshly gathered young Goss lettuce, a little endive and watercress, and drain over a colander and dry in a clean cloth, by shaking to remove all the water; break up the lettuce, watercress, and endive into pieces about three-quarters of an inch in length, mince a small sprig of chervil, two leaves of tarragon, and a few leaves of sorrel, peel and slice one cucumber and one beetroot, mix all together thoroughly, and begin by rubbing the dish with garlic; now arrange at the foundation a layer of the green vegetables, then a layer of cold fish, meat, chicken; lobster, shrimp, fowl or game; now a thin layer of mayonnaise sauce, then a layer of vegetable, and so on, finishing with mayonnaise sauce, and garnishing with nasturtium flowers; some of the beetroot and cucumber may be reserved to arrange alternately round the edge of the dish, or aspic jelly and hard boiled eggs, or olives may also be introduced: this makes a very pretty foundation. With all fish salads mayonnaise sauce should be served in a boat. The mayonnaise sauce must be good and the vegetables fresh, and taste should be shown in the arrangement of the materials.

Lettuce Salad. If necessary wash two lettuces, dry them thoroughly in a cloth, and break the leaves or cut them with a silver knife into convenient pieces; put the yolks of two hard-boiled eggs into a basin, (not boiled more than eight or nine minutes or the yolks will be dark colored), with a teaspoonful of dry mustard, pepper and salt to taste, and one tablespoonful of oil; work the mixture into a smooth paste and add gradually three tablespoonfuls of oil and two of vinegar; when mixed to the consistency of cream add two or three leaves of tarragon, and one small eschalot finely minced, and the whites of two eggs cut into half-inch dice, then add the lettuce and a small handful of garden cress, and when the sauce is thoroughly mixed with the vegetables the salad is ready. See that you have young tender lettuce, and be careful to mix the sauce thoroughly before adding the vegetables.

Tomato Salad. Take six tomatoes, but not too ripe to handle, cut them into slices and remove all the seeds, rub a dish with garlic and lay them in a mixture of oil and vinegar in the proportion of two of oil to one of vinegar; sprinkle pepper and salt over them according to taste, and a few leaves of fresh basil finely minced. Let them lie in the sauce for two hours, and the salad is ready. Be careful in the selection of the tomatoes and well free them from seed.

Potato Salad. Cold boiled potatoes make a very good salad. Take one pound, cut them into slices the thickness of a penny, arrange them neatly on a dish which has been rubbed with eschalot or garlic. Mince equal quantities of capers and parsley, two or three leaves of tarragon and thyme, altogether about a tablespoonful, add oil and vinegar in the proportion of two of oil to one of vinegar, and pepper and salt to taste; work all well together, and pour over the potatoes. For this salad the potatoes should be dry and well boiled.

Cauliflower Salad. Boil a cauliflower till tender, but not so as to break in pieces; when cold cut it up neatly into small sprigs. Beat up three tablespoonfuls of oil added gradually to one tablespoonful of tarragon vinegar, and half a tablespoonful of common vinegar, add pepper and salt to taste. Rub the dish very slightly with garlic; arrange the pieces of cauliflower on it, strew over them some capers, a little tarragon, chervil, and parsley, all finely minced, and the least bit of powdered dried thyme and marjoram. Pour the oil and vinegar over and serve. The cauliflower should be fresh and carefully boiled, and the salad not too much flavored. The garlic may be omitted, or an eschalot finely minced used instead.

Sauces. As beef stock is the foundation of all meat soups, so plain melted butter is the foundation of most of our sauces. All starchy compounds when exposed to heat and moisture begin to swell and then burst. If you were to see the starch of flour, or any kind of starch, under a microscope, the particles would appear something like the shape of a flattened egg. These particles are called granules, and they are made up of cells, which burst in cooking. Uncooked starch is anything but pleasant. Now the art of making melted butter consists in bursting the starch cells of flour in the presence of sufficient fat or butter, so that the starch is well cooked. Making melted butter is one of those simple things which every servant of all work is expected to know by instinct, but it is one of those things rarely ever properly done. It is often brought to the table more like starch, or billsticker's paste, than melted butter. It has always been our chief sauce, and has obtained for us the distinction of a nation with twenty religions and one sauce, a circumstance, probably, which led the late Earl of Dudley to speak of one of the Barons of the exchequer as a good man, sir, a most religious man, he had the best melted butter I ever tasted.

Plain Melted Butter. Suppose we wish to make a pint of melted butter:—Take three ounces of good butter; one ounce of flour; a pinch of pepper and salt; half a pint of warm water put one ounce of the three ounces of butter and the one ounce of flour into a quart stewpan, mix the butter and flour into a soft paste, add the pepper and salt and half a pint of warm water. Stir over the fire with a wooden spoon till the contents boil. If it should be too thick (which will depend on the flour, for some flour requires more water), add half a gill or so of warm water, before putting in the remainder of the butter. The sauce should then be thick enough to coat the spoon. Cut the remaining two ounces of butter into pieces to accelerate the melting, take the stewpan off the fire and stir till the butter is melted. It must not be placed on the fire again. The great point in preparing melted butter is this:—as soon as it has come to the boil to take it off the fire, and then add the cold butter, which gives it the flavor. The failure in properly making melted butter may arise from the flour being in excess, which destroys the flavor of the butter; or it may arise from mixing the whole quantity of butter with the flour at once. If too thin, mix a tablespoonful of flour with half an ounce of cold butter, take the sauce off the fire and allow it to cool for a few minutes, add the mixture of flour and butter and stir while off the fire. When melted, put the sauce over the fire again till just boiling, then add a small piece of butter before serving. The essential condition of success is that the flour and butter should be of the very best, or good, melted butter is impossible, no matter what recipe is followed. The butter, unless good and fresh, gives an unpleasant flavor to the sauce. Melted butter is sometimes preferred slightly acid, when a little lemon juice is stirred into the sauce before serving. All plain sauces should have a simple but decided character, and be served as hot as possible. They should, therefore, never be made until just before they are required for use. Sauces with liaisons or creams should be well stirred, and never allowed to boil after the liaison or cream is added. The same care must be exercised with lemon juice, pickles and other acid mixtures. For sauces use clean stewpans, those of enamel or porcelain are the best, and stir always with a wooden spoon.

Fennel, Parsley, and Tarragon Sauces. A little fennel blanched for a few minutes in boiling water and finely minced, then stirred into the butter, makes fennel sauce, and so with tarragon or parsley.

Mayonnaise Sauce. This sauce is used as a dressing for salad and cold meat or fowl, it is the foundation of all cold sauces, and must be well made. Separate thoroughly the yolk of one egg and put it into a basin with half a tablespoonful of tarragon vinegar, one tablespoonful of good vinegar, and just a little salt and pepper. Mix these with a wooden spoon, then take the oil bottle and place your thumb over the top and let the oil fall in at short intervals, drop by drop, and well mix. The great art is to thoroughly mix the oil before adding more. After adding about forty or fifty drops of oil you may now add it, in quantities of a teaspoonful, till you have used about four ounces altogether, which will make about half a pint of sauce. Taste it, and add more vinegar or pepper, and salt, if necessary. As a rule this sauce should be well seasoned. If desirable, slightly rub the basin in which the sauce is mixed with an eschalot or garlic. Some think a finely minced eschalot and parsley are agreeable additions to this sauce. Thoroughly stir in the oil till the sauce is of the consistency of cream.

Green Mayonnaise Sauce. Mince finely two or three tablespoonsful of chervil, garden cress, tarragon, burnet, and any other herbs you may fancy, mix these together then stir them into the sauce. This mixture is called *ravigote*, if tarragon vinegar has been used; in preparing the white mayonnaise sauce no tarragon should be used in the ravigote. When tarragon is scarce, tarragon vinegar may be used instead. The two or three tablespoonsful of ravigote are intended for the quantity of sauce indicated in the previous recipe. The herbs should be finely minced and used in equal quantities.

Piquant Sauce. Chop up a good half ounce of eschalots, a tablespoonful of parsley, and a tablespoonful of gherkins. Take a clean quart stewpan and put into it one ounce of butter, four tablespoonfuls of vinegar and the chopped eschalots, and stir over the fire with a wooden spoon; the vinegar is sufficiently reduced when the butter is clear. When the eschalots have absorbed all the vinegar add one ounce of flour and stir four or five minutes, then add a pint of broth or stock, (if unflavored with vegetables the better), season with pepper and salt according to the saltness of the broth, bring it to the boil and continue boiling gently for ten minutes and skim. Now add the parsley and gherkins. Boil up and skim again if necessary. Any additional seasoning may now be added and the sauce is ready. This reducing is necessary to produce the proper sharpness to the sauce and secure a right mixture of the flour and butter. A brisk boiling is necessary when anything has to be reduced.

Dutch Sauce. When well made this is the first and best of white sauces. Reduce two tablespoonfuls of vinegar to one tablespoonful in a clean stewpan, with a little salt and coarsely-ground white pepper (mignonette). Remove the stewpan from the fire, and add two tablespoonfuls of cold water and the yolks of two eggs. Put the stewpan on the fire and stir, but do not boil. Divide four ounces of sweet, fresh butter into six parts. Take the stewpan off the fire and stir in till melted one part only of the butter. Place the stewpan again on the fire for about a minute, constantly stirring. Remove it again from the fire and add another part of the butter and repeat in the same way till all the butter has been used. It will be necessary to add at intervals a tablespoonful of cold water, to prevent the sauce from thickening. Season with pepper and salt and serve hot. The yolks of the eggs are to be well freed from the white, and constant attention is necessary.

Hot Mint Sauce. Take a clean quart stewpan and reduce half a pint of vinegar with half an ounce of brown sugar. Add a pint of water, boil up, simmer for ten minutes, then add a tablespoonful of young mint finely minced. Well mix and serve. The large stalks should be removed from the mint before mincing.

Cold Mint Sauce. Take three ounces of brown sugar, three tablespoonfuls of young mint, previously picked and washed and then finely minced, and half a pint of vinegar, mix well in a basin, and when the sugar is melted put the sauce into a tureen and serve. Remove the large stalks from the mint.

Bechamel Sauce. If you have no rich white stock cut up some lean veal, free from fat, into two inch cubes, and put them into a three-quart stewpan. Add one moderate sized onion two and a half inches in diameter, one small carrot cut into pieces, and six ounces of butter. Fry the vegetables in the butter for ten minutes, without coloring, then stir in three ounces of flour and continue stirring five minutes longer. Add three pints of stock, one pint of cream, five ounces of sliced mushrooms, a small bouquet garni, half a teaspoonful of salt and a pinch of mignonette pepper (white pepper). Stir till it comes to the boil, skim occasionally to remove the fat, and simmer for two hours. Strain through a tammy sieve into an enameled or porcelain stewpan with a gill of cream. Simmer over the fire till it coats the spoon, strain again through a tammy sieve into a basin and stir till the sauce is cold. This sauce especially requires the cook's utmost attention.

Horseradish Sauce. Boil half a pint of rich cream or new milk, then add one ounce of finely-grated horseradish, a pinch of pounded loaf sugar, and a little salt. The horseradish should be young.

Onion Sauce. Peel the onions, blanch them, and roughly mince them, put an ounce of butter into a clean stewpan, then add a teaspoonful of flour, stir for two minutes, add the onions, and stir to prevent coloring, now add a little pounded loaf sugar, and pepper and salt to taste. When the onions are sufficiently soft, pass them through a sieve, return the pulp to the stewpan, and bring the sauce to its proper consistency with milk or cream, continually stirring. Serve hot. Do not let the sauce boil after adding the cream.

Tomato Sauce. This sauce is best made with fresh tomatoes. Take six or eight tomatoes and remove the stalks, then squeeze out the juice and seeds; take a three pint stewpan with a close-fitting lid, put in the tomatoes and add a gill of water, a little salt and pepper, and a small bouquet garni; boil for twenty minutes or half an hour, with frequent stirring. When soft, pass them through a wire sieve. Melt half an ounce of butter, and stir into it a teaspoonful of flour; stir for two or three minutes. Take it off the fire, and add in small portions the *purée* of tomatoes, constantly stirring; add a gill of stock, better if flavored with a rasher of ham or bacon, and boil for a quarter of an hour. Should the sauce be too thick, add a little more stock. If preserved tomatoes are used, begin with them as if a *purée*, and proceed as already described, and the sauce is ready. Almost constant stirring is required.

Bread Sauce. Take a clean stewpan and put in six ounces of stale bread-crumbs with one pint of new milk and one eschalot, boil for ten minutes and the sauce is ready. See that the bread-crumbs are good, and take care that the sauce does not boil over.

Oyster Sauce. Open a dozen oysters, and let them boil for two minutes in their own liquor, drain them over a colander, and strain the liquor. Mix to a smooth paste three-quarters of an ounce of butter with the same weight of flour, then add the liquor of the oysters, and make nearly a pint by adding milk; stir over the fire till it comes to the boil, take it off the fire and stir in half an ounce of butter till melted, remove the beards from the oysters, and return the oysters into the sauce to warm. The sauce must not boil after the oysters are added.

Mushroom Sauce. Wash and pick a pottle of mushrooms, remove the gritty part near the stalk, and put them into a basin of cold water for three or four minutes, then dry them on a cloth trim them, and, if you like, whiten them in a stewpan with a tablespoonful of lemon-juice and the same quantity of water, mince them, stalks and all, and put them into a clean quart saucepan with an ounce of butter; when the mushrooms are nearly done add half a pint of Bechamel sauce, and simmer for half an hour. Pass the whole through a strainer, and serve hot. Good Bechamel sauce and young mushrooms will be required.

Lemon and Liver Sauce. Wash and score the liver of a fowl or a rabbit, blanch it for a few minutes cut half a lemon into small slices, remove all the white and seeds, take a quarter of the lemon-rind and mince it and the liver finely, prepare half a pint of melted butter, add the minced liver and lemon, and season with a little salt. Let it come gradually to a good temperature without boiling, and then serve. Be sure the livers are fresh and healthy.

Liver and Parsley Sauce. Proceed as in the last recipe by blanching the parsley and liver, mincing them separately, and stirring the melted butter. The same as the preceding.

Roux. Melt three ounces of butter, and stir in one ounce of flour, until it becomes of a light brown color. Cover the stewpan and let it remain for half an hour on the stove, then add half a pint of boiling water, season with pepper and salt, and stir gently till well mixed. Continue the stirring five minutes after it comes to the boil. Stock, as I have before explained, is better than water. Roux is used for thickening sauces and gravies; when wanted white it must not remain on the fire long enough to brown. The difference between brown roux and white roux is simply in the browning of the butter. It can be kept for some days in a clean earthenware jar in a cool place. Great care must be given to the preparation of roux, for if the butter and flour are not good, or allowed to become too brown, the flavor of the sauce is strong and acrid.

Soups. In the article on Cooking some general directions are given for making soups and stews. In the making of soups the meat should be put into cold water and heated gradually, and throughout the cooking the water should only simmer, the object being to extract the juices of the meat. It may also be added that the broth should be thoroughly skimmed during the operation of bringing it to the scalding point.

Pea Soup. Take half a pound of good split peas, wash them in several waters, and let them soak all night in a pint of water. In the morning put two ounces of good butter or sweet dripping into a saucepan; when it is melted add the peas, well drained from the water, with a lump of sugar the size of a walnut; stir the peas frequently, and as they begin to thicken add from time to time a little water (half teacupful); when they have been on the fire about an hour add an onion, shredded very finely, half a teaspoonful of dried herbs, and half a teaspoonful of dried mint. Let all boil gently for two hours longer, add water as it thickens, and stir frequently to prevent burning, then rub through a coarse sieve, return the pulp to the saucepan with a quart of good stock; add salt and pepper to taste, let it boil five minutes and the soup is ready. This soup may be made with mutton broth, or the liquor in which beef has been boiled, if not too salt. Then the water may be omitted and the broth used instead. If the soup is required to be very thick, use one pound of peas instead of half a pound. This soup will require frequent stirring. Beans may be cooked in the same way.

Scotch Broth. Take a neck of mutton, and trim it as for cutlets, remove eight of the chops and put them aside on a dish. Put the remaining part of the neck into a three-quart saucepan with two quarts of cold water, with a little pepper and salt, and two onions, one with two cloves. When the water comes to the boil skim, add altogether half a pint of the following vegetables, made up of about equal quantities, carrots, turnips, leeks and onions, cut up into quarter inch dice. Simmer for three hours. Blanch two ounces of Scotch barley, and finish cooking it in water with a little butter and salt. Put the chops into another stewpan, with some of the broth or stock, and nicely cook them. Drain the barley and put it into the tureen with the chops. Remove the neck of mutton on to a dish, pour over it the broth, add a dessertspoonful of coarsely chopped parsley, previously blanched, and serve. Do not boil after adding the vegetables.

Mutton Broth. Take two pounds of scrag of mutton, and put it into a large basin, cover with cold water and a little salt to remove the blood, let it remain one hour. Then put it into a stewpan, with two quarts of water, with either one ounce of Scotch barley or rice or oatmeal according to taste, and one onion. Let it come to the boil slowly, skim, and add two or three turnips cut into quarters. Let the contents simmer for two hours. A little chopped parsley or petals of marigolds are sometimes added; season with salt, strain into the tureen and serve. For sick persons this broth should be prepared without any vegetable flavor, and should be carefully freed from fat. This broth should be prepared slowly, and not too strong with turnip.

Julienne Soup. Take carrots (three ounces), turnips (three ounces), onion (one ounce), leeks (one ounce), celery (half ounce)—shred in small strips about one and a quarter inch long, melt one ounce and a half of good butter in a stewpan, and add the shredded vegetables; fry to a nice brown color, add three pints and a half of stock, and leave it to boil at one corner of the fire. When the vegetables are cooked, skim, put in a few leaves of sorrel, and a sprig of chervil, chopped finely, add a little powdered loaf sugar, and serve in a soup tureen after having put in several crusts of bread cut up in small pieces. Wash and dry the vegetables before shredding.

Soup from Remnants of Joints. After all the meat available for a hash has been cut away from a leg of mutton, break the bones into pieces, the addition of a pound or two of fresh bones will be desirable, put them into a three-quart saucepan with two carrots and two turnips cut in quarters, and two whole onions and a *bouquet garni*. Nearly fill the saucepan with water, add three cloves, a full tablespoonful of whole pepper and allspice in equal parts, and salt to taste. Set the saucepan on the fire and let the contents simmer for four hours. Strain the broth, free it from fat, and use it as stock for any kind of thick soup. Pass through a hair sieve the carrots and one of the onions; melt an ounce of butter in a two-quart saucepan and stir in a tablespoonful of flour. When the two are well mixed add a little of the stock, then the carrot and onion pulp, and gradually the remainder of the stock, or so much as will produce a purée of the consistency of pea soup. Pour it boiling hot over small dice of toasted or fried bread. Take care that the soup is not too strongly flavored with the vegetables.

Chantilly Soup. Put into a two-quart stewpan one pint and a half of green peas, a small bunch of parsley, and a small bunch of mint with two finely shredded onions, (two and a half inches in diameter), and a small cucumber, peeled and cut into thin slices, add sufficient water to cover the vegetables, and boil with a teaspoonful of pounded loaf-sugar till they are soft enough to pass through a tammy sieve. Strain over a colander and make a purée of the vegetables. Stir the purée into three or four pints of stock, but do not boil after adding it or you will spoil the color of the soup. A proper mixture of the vegetables so as to agreeably blend the flavors, is requisite.

Soup Maigre. Melt slowly in a clean stewpan about one-half ounce of butter; when melted add two onions, a quarter of a head of celery, a small carrot and turnips, all coarsely shredded. Let these vegetables stew in the butter for fifteen or twenty minutes until they are nicely browned, and stir frequently with a wooden spoon to prevent burning. Add three pints of boiling water, and, if at the proper season, three-quarters of a pint of green peas and six white peppercorns. When the vegetables are quite tender let the soup stand for a few minutes to clear, then strain into another stewpan. Boil up and add an onion, half head of celery, a carrot and a turnip cut into fillets, or into wheels or into stars, with a vegetable cutter. When these vegetables are sufficiently cooked, the soup is ready. If necessary season with pepper and salt. Cleanliness, tender vegetables and good butter are essential. Stir occasionally to prevent burning.

Poor Man's Soup. Shred three ounces of onions and put them into a clean three-quart saucepan, with one ounce of butter or dripping or skimmings of saucepans, cook to a pale brown color, constantly stirring; now add one ounce of flour, and cook it for five minutes in the dripping, add three pints of boiling water and stir till it boils up, skim, add one pound of potatoes, shredded or cut into small slices, and boil till they are cooked, add pepper and salt and a dessertspoonful of chopped parsley, boil up, and pour into the tureen over half inch squares of bread. This soup can be made very nourishing by using oatmeal or pealmeal instead of flour. If too thick, add a little more water. A milk liaison is a valuable addition to this soup. See that the fat and onions do not burn, or get too dark a color.

Ox Tail Soup. Take two ox tails of average size, cut them up at the joints, obtain as nearly as possible pieces of the same bulk. Put them into cold water with a little salt, and let them remain two hours to remove the blood.

Drain them and dry them in a clean cloth; put them into a three-quart stewpan with two ounces of butter, and a few pieces of lean beef, and cook till nicely browned. add two quarts of stock, one onion with two cloves stuck in it, and a *bouquet garni*. Bring to the boil, and skim and simmer for three or four hours, till the tails are cooked. While the soup is simmering slice three young carrots, and cook them with fifteen, button onions in a little stock. Take the pieces of tail from the soup, remove the bones, and put the meat only into the tureen with the carrots and strain over the soup and serve. Careful cooking in the butter, and tender carrots are required.

Mulligatawny Soup. Take a small knuckle of veal, cut it up, break the bones, and put it into a stewpan with one half ounce of butter, a quarter of a pound of lean ham, a small carrot and turnip, two onions and four apples, all cut into quarters; add half a pint of water. Set the stewpan over a brisk fire, moving the meat frequently with a wooden spoon; let it remain until the bottom of the stewpan is covered with a brownish glaze, then add three tablespoonfuls of curry-powder, one of curry paste, and a quarter of a pound of flour; stir well in, and add four or five pints of water, a teaspoonful of salt, half a teaspoonful of sugar; when boiling place it at the corner of the fire, and let it simmer for two hours and a half, skimming off all the fat, then pass it through a tammy into a tureen. Trim some of the pieces of veal and put them back into the stewpan to boil up, and add them to the soup, and serve with plain boiled rice, on a separate dish. Ox-tails, or pieces of rabbit, or fowl, left from a previous dinner, may be served in it instead of veal, or the pieces of veal may be prepared separately, and the soup strained over them in the tureen. Have a good curry powder, and give constant attention until water is added.

Giblet Soup. Scald and pick very clean two sets of goose, or four of duck giblets, (the fresher the better), wash them well in two or three warm waters, cut off the beaks and split the heads, divide the gizzards and necks into mouthfuls. If the gizzards are not cut into pieces the rest of the meat will be done too much. Crack the bones of the legs, put them into a stewpan, cover them with cold water; when they boil take off the scum, then put in a bundle of herbs, such as lemon thyme, winter savory, or marjoram, about three sprigs of each, and double the quantity of parsley. Twenty berries of allspice, the same of black pepper; tie these up in a muslin bag and stew very gently till the gizzards are tender. This will take from an hour and a half to two hours and a half, according to the size and age of the giblets Take them up with a skimmer, put them into the tureen, and cover down close to keep warm till the soup is ready. Melt an ounce of butter in a clean stewpan, stir in a dessertspoonful of flour; then pour to it by degrees, a gill or half a pint of the giblet liquor, add the remainder by degrees; let it boil about ten minutes, stirring it all the while; skim it and strain through a fine sieve into a basin; wash out the stewpan, then return the soup into it, and season it with a glass of wine, a little mushroom catsup, and a little salt; let it have one boil up, and then put the giblets in to get hot, and the soup is ready. Young giblets and freedom from scum are essential.

Vegetable Soup. Shred three good sized onions, fry them to a nice brown color in an ounce and a half of sweet dripping or butter, then put them into a saucepan with three pints of water. Cut into small slices one large or two small turnips, and the same of carrots, add them to the onions with a pinch of dried herbs, pepper and salt. Boil gently three hours without the lid, then thicken with a spoonful of flour or oatmeal; boil ten minutes longer, and serve with pulled bread. Young turnips and sweet dripping are necessary, and the onions carefully fried.

Potato Soup. Take two pounds of potatoes, after they are peeled, and cut them into thin slices, or shred them; shred six ounces of onions. Take a three-quart saucepan and melt two ounces of butter or sweet beef dripping; put in the onions, let them cook five minutes in the butter, stir occasionally, then add the potatoes and three pints of water, or milk and water, or skim milk; when the potatoes and onions are thoroughly soft, strain through a horsehair sieve, return the liquor to the stewpan, and pass through the vegetables; stir the purée into the soup, season with pepper and salt. The addition of a milk or cream liaison is a great improvement. Do not blacken the onions; and frequently stir before making the purée.

Stewed Eels. Skin, and cut into pieces about two inches in length, two pounds of eels; wash in salt and water, and dry in a cloth. Take a three-pint stewpan, put into it one ounce and a half of butter, one onion shredded thinly; add a little flour, pepper and salt, an onion with two cloves, a bay-leaf or a bouquet garni, and a piece of lemon peel; add the pieces of eel and fry to a nice color, with constant stirring. Add a half pint or three gills of good stock. Stew gently till the eels are done. Take them out, arrange on a dish, strain over the sauce, and serve with toasted bread cut into triangles and arranged round the edge of the dish. The stew requires constant attention, and must only simmer.

Hotch-Potch. Grate rather coarsely two young carrots, and slice three carrots, three turnips, and three onions; shred one lettuce and a bunch of parsley, altogether any a quart. Take a pint of green peas when shelled, and the sprigs of a cauliflower. Put aside half the peas in a basin. Have ready, in a clean four-quart stewpan, three pints of mutton stock or broth. Put in all the vegetables except the peas put aside in the basin. Have ready cutlets as for Irish stew, and put them in the stewpan. Let the contents come slowly to a boil, then add two ounces of pearl barley or rice, previously blanched in a little water or stock, and simmer till the meat is ready. Skim and season with white pepper and a small teaspoonful of pounded loaf sugar. Boil the remaining peas separately, and add them just before serving. Hotch-potch should be thick. Young vegetables are very necessary in preparing a good hotch-potch.

Stewed Pigeons. Take three house pigeons, (they are the best), draw, pick, and singe them. Put the livers inside, and truss them with legs inside. If the pigeons are large you may divide them into halves. Take a quarter of a pound of streaky bacon, cut it into one and a half inch dice, and fry with an ounce of butter in a stewpan till of a light brown color. Put the pigeons in the stewpan and fry till they are of a light brown color. Then take out the bacon and pigeons and put them aside on a plate. Thicken the butter in the stewpan with flour; add a pint of stock with a few button mushrooms or ketchup. Season with pepper and salt, stir till it comes to the boil, and strain in a basin. Rinse out the stewpan with a little hot water, and put in the pigeons, breasts downwards, with the gravy and bacon and a bouquet garni; add ten button onions previously blanched and fried in a little butter to a nice brown color. Simmer about half an hour. Take out the pigeons, put them on a dish. Bring the sauce to a boil, skim, and strain the sauce over the pigeons, and garnish with the onions, bacon, and mushrooms. Instead of onions and mushrooms garnish with green peas or French beans. It will be necessary occasionally to move the pigeons in the stewpan, or they are liable to burn.

Stewed Fowls. Prepare and cut up at the joints a fowl or chicken. Take a six-pint stewpan, melt two ounces of butter, and fry in it for five minutes one ounce of sliced carrot, and one sliced onion, stirring with a wooden spoon. Put in the pieces of fowl, with a little pepper and salt; add two tablespoonfuls of flour, stirring so as to thoroughly mix with the butter. When mixed, add at intervals about a pint of good stock, and four ounces of picked tomatoes with the skins and seeds removed, and broken in pieces. Stir, and let it come slowly to the boil, then simmer. Now add six button mushrooms cut into slices and a tablespoonful of chopped parsley. Let it come to the boil, simmer for ten minutes, then skim, haste and serve. Fresh tomatoes and mushrooms are essential.

Stewed Rabbits. Cut up a young rabbit into small joints, and put them aside. Take a quarter of a pound of streaky bacon, and cut it into small slices. Melt in a clean stewpan one ounce and a half of butter, or sweet dripping; add the bacon, and when lightly fried add the pieces of rabbit, and fry to a nice brown, constantly stirring the whole with a wooden spoon. Now add a tablespoonful of flour, work it well, and add at short intervals a little water or stock, stirring all the time till the pieces are just covered, season with pepper and salt, and a small piece of lemon peel. Skim, then simmer slowly, and add a dozen button onions and six mushrooms, both previously blanched. When the rabbit is done, take it out, and arrange it on a dish. Boil the sauce, which should just coat the wooden spoon, skim, and pour it over the rabbit. The rabbit must be young, and see that it does not burn or boil. The flavoring should be delicate, and the sauce free from fat.

Stewed Breast of Veal. Cut off the neck, and remove the bone from a breast of veal, and stew them for stock. Stuff the thin part of the breast with some savory forcemeat. Secure the stuffing nicely by sewing or with skewers. Simmer for nearly two hours the veal in the stock made with the neck and bones. Take a pint of the stock for sauce, and thicken it with a little flour and a dozen oysters previously stewed, the beards removed, and cut up six button mushrooms, minced, and a dozen white peppercorns in a muslin bag. Strain the sauce hot over the veal, and garnish with slices of lemon and forcemeat balls. Cream, wine, truffles, ketchup, anchovy, are all occasionally put into this dish. The stock should be made some time and allowed to cool before putting in the veal.

Stewed Steak. Take two pounds of beefsteak, or better rumpsteak, an inch and a quarter or inch and a half in thickness, and not too fat. Beat it with the flat side of a chopper, or what is better a kreatone, which is an instrument invented by an English medical man to make steaks tender, and which may be used for such purposes with advantage. Cut the steak into convenient pieces, and fry them in two ounces of butter to a nice brown on each side. Cut into thin slices two onions and two young carrots, and cut into quarter-inch dice two young turnips, or cut them into shapes with a vegetable cutter, and fry these vegetables in the same butter. Put the meat and vegetables into a clean stewpan, with half a pint or three gills of water or stock, simmer slowly till the meat is tender. When half done, turn the meat on the other side. Skim, season with a little salt and pepper, add a little ketchup or six button mushrooms, or flavor the gravy with anything you prefer. Take out the meat, thicken the gravy with a little flour, let it come to the boil, skim, pour over the steak, and serve. Garnish with green peas or French beans. The steak must stew very slowly, be free from fat, and by all means be not too highly seasoned.

Minced Veal. Cut up with a sharp knife, into small slices, the remains of any cold veal; trim off all the fat, gristle and brown parts which have seen the fire. If you have no stock, prepare a little in the following manner: Take a clean stewpan, break up the bones, add the trimmings of the veal and any odd pieces in the larder, (a slice of ham is acceptable), cover with water, and season with pepper and salt, a bouquet garni, a blade of mace, and fifteen peppercorns, a slice or two of lemon peel (and a small sliced carrot and onion if the flavors are liked). Let these simmer for two or three hours. Strain into a basin, let the stock cool, and remove all the fat. Melt in a stewpan an ounce of butter, stir in a tablespoonful of flour, add the stock, boil, skim if necessary, and stand it aside to cool a little; then stir in the veal; let it gently simmer, just sufficient to warm the meat through. A spoonful of cream is an acceptable addition to the mince. Serve with toasted or fried sippets of bread. The careful preparation of the sauce is important, and the meat should be cut into pieces of uniform size.

Haricot Mutton. Haricot properly means French beans; it now means meat cut into chops, and stewed with vegetables. Divide three pounds of the best end of neck of mutton into chops; trim and shape them and remove the fat. Cut two onions into slices, cut three moderate-sized turnips and three carrots into fancy shapes with a vegetable cutter. Take a clean fryingpan and fry the cutlets lightly in butter over a brisk fire, but do not cook them. Fry the vegetables in the same butter for three or four minutes, but do not brown them or change their color. Put the cutlets into a stewpan, lay the vegetables on them, and cover with stock, and let the contents come slowly to the boil. Skim off all the fat, then put aside to simmer until the chops are tender; season with pepper and salt, and finish with a teaspoonful of mushroom or walnut ketchup, and mixed pickles finely minced. Dish the chops in a soup dish, pour over the gravy and vegetables, and serve. Freedom from fat and delicate flavoring are necessary.

Stewed Onions. Take half a dozen large onions, peel them, and cut off the tops and bottoms, but not so as to fall into pieces. Blanch them in two quarts of boiling water for twenty minutes, drain on a colander and take out the center of each onion and fill it with fine meat flavored with chopped parsley, eschalot, and button mushrooms, butter the onions, put them into a stewpan with white stock, and let them simmer over a slow fire, turn them over, and, when tender and covered with a glaze, they are ready. Be careful in the selection of the onions, and let them stew gently.

Stewed Lentils and Bacon. Soak for three hours in cold water half a pint of beans, put them into a saucepan with plenty of cold water, and let them boil for half an hour, then strain them over a colander. Return the beans to the saucepan, and cover with barley water, which is the water in which pearl barley has been boiled; add an onion with three cloves, and a *bouquet garni*. Scrape and trim a pound of bacon or salt pork, which will be all the better if previously blanched for a few minutes. Put it in the saucepan with the lentils, and simmer till the beans are thoroughly cooked; season with pepper and salt, and a little chopped parsley. Turn on a dish, and place the bacon on them, and serve. The bacon or pork should not be old or coarse; and add just sufficient water to cover.

Tripe and Onions. Tripe is usually purchased ready boiled, it should be thick, white and fresh; but it still requires cooking. Cut it into pieces about three inches by two inches, trim off the fat, wash it well in cold water, and dry it on a clean cloth. It may be whitened like veal, chicken or turbot, by rubbing over with lemon-juice. First blanch the tripe for five or ten minutes in water, then take some new milk, put it into a stewpan, and add the tripe. Simmer very gently for two or three hours, stir frequently with a wooden spoon to prevent the tripe sticking or burning at the bottom of the saucepan. Boil six or eight onions, and when done, chop them up, add to the tripe, and season with pepper and salt, and a small teaspoonful of pounded loaf-sugar. Two dessertspoonfuls of flour may be stirred into the milk to thicken it, a quarter of an hour before serving. Tripe may be boiled in plain water, and served with onion sauce and mustard, or it may be boiled in veal stock with fresh beef bones, or baked in milk and served with onion sauce, or, after it is boiled, it may be dipped in batter, and fried for five minutes in butter with finely minced eschalots to a golden-brown color. It is necessary that the tripe should be fresh and slowly simmered, with frequent attention.

Stewed Kidneys. Skin half a dozen kidneys, and remove all the fat. Cut them across into slices the thickness of a penny. Mince a small eschalot, two mushrooms, and a little thyme finely, and use double the quantity of minced parsley. Sprinkle the sliced kidneys with the mixture and a little salt and pepper, with just the smallest sprinkle of cayenne. Melt two ounces of butter in a clean stewpan, and fry the kidneys to a brown color, first on one side then the other. Thicken with a little flour, and finish with a gill or half a pint of hot stock or gravy, and a squeeze of lemon. Let it come to the boil, skim if necessary, and serve with sippets of fried bread. The kidneys are not to be opened but cut into slices across, and be careful not to fry them too much before adding the flour and stock.

Stewed Cheese. Cut into thin slices half a pound of good Gloucester or Cheddar cheese. Take a clean quart stewpan and put in the cheese with a little old ale or chablis, and stir over the fire till it is melted, beat up the yolks only of two eggs and a small teaspoonful of dry mustard and a very little cayenne; stir for two minutes over the fire, and serve very hot with toasted or fried sippets of bread. The top may be browned with a hot iron or salamander, or in front of a brisk fire. Sometimes the cheese is spread over toast and served. Do not let it burn, and if the cheese is not very rich add a little butter or salad oil; serve hot, and be careful with the cayenne.

Beef a la Mode. This is a very popular dish, and, if nicely prepared, is one which never fails to give satisfaction. Take five pounds of thick flank of beef, and two slices of fat bacon half an inch in thickness. Remove the rind and cut the bacon into strips of half an inch; this will give you pieces half an inch in section; sprinkle the strips of bacon with pepper; lard the beef in the direction of its grain, and tie it up. Place it in a stewpan, with three pints of stock, the rind of bacon, and two calf's feet, all previously blanched, and the feet boned. Proceed exactly as for the pot au feu, add a teaspoonful of salt, let it come gradually to the boil, and skim; then add four small carrots, one onion with three cloves stuck in it, a bouquet garni with a clove of garlic, and a little pepper. Close the stewpan tightly, and simmer slowly for four hours. When the beef is done take it out, with the calf's feet and carrots, and put aside to keep hot. Remove all the fat and strain the liquor through a pointed strainer into another stewpan, reduce it over a brisk fire for half an hour. Remove the string, place the beef on a dish, and garnish with carrots and calf's feet. Pour over the reduced liquor, and serve. If required cold, put it into a basin, or earthenware mould, with the calf's feet, vegetables, and liquor, which will gelatinize into a solid mass. When cold it can be turned on to a dish. The gravy should be thick and gelatinous, and cooking very slowly is necessary.

Vegetables. All vegetables intended for boiling should be well washed, but not soaked, in water; a little vinegar in the water will be more effectual in removing insects than salt. Green vegetables should have plenty of room, and be plunged into boiling water with a small teaspoonful of pounded loaf sugar. The saucepan should be uncovered and the contents occasionally skimmed, and the vegetables should not remain in the water an instant after they are cooked. We do not attach sufficient importance to vegetables; they may be prepared in different ways, and eaten as separate dishes. In many countries they form quite a distinct part of the dinner. It is sometimes said that plain boiled vegetables are the best; but this would also apply to plain boiled meat and fish. Carefully cooked vegetables are more wholesome and digestible. Very few vegetables can be eaten with safety without cooking, and if some of the following recipes are rather more expensive they may often economically replace meat, which is the most costly thing on a table.

Potatoes, Plain Boiled. To boil potatoes properly they should all be of the same sort, and as nearly as possible of the same size. Wash off the dirt, and scrub them very clean with a hard brush, but neither scoop nor apply a knife to them in any way, even to clear the eyes. Rinse them well and arrange them compactly in a saucepan so that they may not lie loose in the water, and that a small quantity may be sufficient to cover them. Pour the water in cold and when it boils throw in one large teaspoonful of salt to each quart of water, and simmer the potatoes till they are nearly done, but for the last two or three minutes let them boil rapidly. When they are tender quite through, which may be known by probing them with a fork, pour all the water from them immediately, lift the lid of the saucepan to allow the steam to escape, and place them by the side of the fire till the moisture has entirely evaporated, then peel and send them to table as quickly as possible, either in a hot napkin or in a dish in which the cover is so placed that the steam may pass off. There should be no delay in serving after they have been once taken from the fire. Irish families always prefer them served in their skins. Some kinds will be sufficiently boiled in twenty minutes, others in not less than half an hour. Pour away the water as soon as the potatoes are cooked, and dry them.

Mashed Potatoes. Boil or steam the potatoes half an hour, turn them into a basin, and with a wooden spoon bruise them into flour, to three pounds of potatoes add a teaspoonful of salt, three ounces of fresh butter, and a gill of cream or hot milk. Stand the basin in a saucepan of boiling water and beat the potatoes for five minutes. Serve on a very hot dish, either in a rough cone shape or smoothed over with a knife. The potatoes should be well mixed with the butter and cream.

Potatoes with Milk. Have ready some boiled potatoes, and when nearly cold, cut them into slices and cover them with a clean cloth. Take a stewpan and melt three ounces of butter with two ounces of flour, stir with a wooden spoon, and add gradually a gill of warm milk; season with pepper and salt and a little grated nutmeg. When the sauce comes to the boil put in the sliced potatoes, and let them gently boil for about fifteen minutes, then stand the stewpan aside. Mix the yolks of two eggs with a gill of cream and pour into the stewpan, stirring until it becomes thick. Turn it on to a hot dish and serve. Take care to prepare the sauce carefully.

Potatoes and Spinach. Boil a pound of potatoes and mash them. Have ready the same quantity of boiled spinach, chop it up, and thoroughly mix with the potatoes; add salt, pepper, a little grated nutmeg, and three ounces of sweet butter. Work the whole together, put it into a pie-dish and bake. When the top is of a nice brown color, it is ready. The ingredients should be well mixed before baking.

Potatoes and Bacon. Take half a pound of bacon, scrape it and cut it into half-inch dice. Put the pieces into a stewpan with three ounces of sweet dripping or butter; let the bacon brown lightly. Then add a tablespoonful of flour, and when thoroughly mixed add a pint of hot water, or, better, stock, and a bouquet garni, with a clove of garlic. Cover the stewpan and let the contents come to the boil. Wash and peel about a pound of good potatoes, (the kidney variety is the best), slice them in pieces about a quarter of an inch in thickness. Cover the stewpan and let the potatoes boil till they are cooked. Take out the seasoning and serve. Good potatoes and careful preparation of the sauce is essential.

Potato Soufflé. Boil six large potatoes and mash them with three ounces of sweet butter, a little pepper and salt, and four ounces of grated cheese, (half Parmesan and half Gruyere is the best mixture), add the yolks of four eggs and the whites, previously whisked to a rather stiff paste. Mix these thoroughly and put into a pie-dish and bake. When the top is nicely browned in the oven it is ready. The ingredients should be thoroughly mixed before baking and the whites well whisked before mixing.

Fried Potato Chips. Peel six large potatoes, and cut them in slices each an eighth of an inch in thickness; wash and dry them in a cloth. Melt your frying fat over a brisk fire, and when the temperature rises to 385° throw the potatoes in; stir with the skimmer occasionally to secure an even cooking; eight or ten minutes' frying will be sufficient. Drain them on a wire sieve, sprinkle with salt, and serve. When potatoes are required very crisp, let them fry three or four minutes longer. Do not put in too many potato chips or the fat will fall too low for frying. A slight increase of temperature while the potatoes are frying is desirable.

Fried Potatoes and Onions. The remains of cold potatoes may be used thus: Put two ounces of butter and one of oil in a frying pan, in which fry three sliced onions; put on the potatoes, cut in thin slices each about the thickness of half a crown, and toss them now and then until they have a nice yellow color; add a spoonful of chopped parsley, salt, pepper, and the juice of a lemon. Shake the pan well that they may mix thoroughly together, dish, and serve very hot. An excellent dish to serve with a chop, a steak, or a joint. A clean fryingpan and good oil are essential.

Potato Croquets. Cold mashed potatoes may be used up as croquets. Stir an egg or two into your potatoes, add a little spice, pepper and salt to taste, and some minced parsley; mix well, and roll the mixture into balls, or in the shape of corks; cover with egg and bread-crumbs, and fry to a nice golden color in hot fat, and garnish with fried parsley. Careful frying of the croquets to a nice color is essential.

Cauliflowers. Wash the cauliflower thoroughly clean, and remove the coarse outer leaves, split the stalk into four by cutting it across, but not deep enough to separate the flower. Plunge the flower downward into plenty of boiling water with a teaspoonful of sugar and salt; keep the saucepan lid off, and skim; when it is cooked, (which will be in about ten or fifteen minutes), remove the cauliflower carefully with a slice, and drain on a sieve. Plenty of boiling water and plenty of room are essential.

Spinach. Pick and wash perfectly clean two or three pounds of spinach; put it into a saucepan with a very little water, and let it boil till quite done. Turn the spinach on to a colander to drain, squeeze the water out between two plates, and pass the spinach through a sieve. Put two ounces of butter into another saucepan, fry the butter a light brown, add a small teaspoonful of flour, mix well, and then put in the spinach with pepper and salt to taste, and a little milk. The spinach should only remain in the second saucepan long enough to thoroughly mix with the butter and seasoning.

Cabbage. Wash and trim off the outer leaves of a cabbage, divide it, or split the stalk into four, throw the cabbage stalk upward into boiling water, with a teaspoonful of pounded loaf sugar or salt. When cooked well, drain it on a colander and serve, if preferred, with a white sauce. The cabbage should be young and have plenty of room in the saucepan.

Asparagus. Scrape the sticks of the asparagus, wash them, and cut them into equal lengths. Divide the sticks into bundles of ten or twelve, tie them together, and put them into plenty of salted boiling water and a tablespoonful of vinegar. Take care not to over-cook—about fifteen or twenty minutes will be sufficient — or the heads, which are the most delicate part, will break off in the saucepan. When sufficiently cooked, remove them carefully and serve on buttered toast. Care is necessary to prevent the heads breaking off.

Carrots. Scrape clean and wipe, but not wash, fifteen or twenty small young carrots. Put them in a stewpan with three ounces of butter, cover the stewpan, and from time to time give it a shake. After fifteen minutes add a little pepper and salt, and some finely minced parsley or chives, or eschalots. Put on the lid, occasionally shake till the carrots are tender. Old carrots should be previously well blanched, and cut into slices and finished cooking in the sauce. If the carrots are not young they should be nearly cooked before adding to the sauce.

Carrots with Ham or Bacon. Melt in a stewpan three ounces of butter, and mix with it one ounce of flour; stir for five minutes. Now add a gill of boiling stock or water, stirring with a wooden spoon. Add half a pound of ham or bacon, cut into half-inch dice, with a little pepper, (and, perhaps, a little salt, but this will depend on the saltness of the ham or bacon), a bouquet garni, with a clove of garlic, or a large onion instead of the garlic. Cut into slices, about the thickness of a penny, six large carrots and put them in the stewpan. Let the contents boil till the carrots are tender. Remove the onion and bouquet garni and serve. Constant attention is necessary after adding the sliced carrots.

Colcannon. Boil potatoes and greens or spinach separately; mash the potatoes; squeeze the greens dry; chop them quite fine, and mix altogether in a basin, with a little butter, pepper, and salt; put the whole into a mould, previously well buttered with a brush. Let it stand in a hot oven for ten minutes and then turn out. Let the vegetables be firm and the mould properly buttered, or the colcannon breaks on turning out.

Green Peas. Tie into a small bunch a small head of lettuce and one or two onions, and throw them with the peas into plenty of boiling water, with some salt, and a little pounded loaf-sugar. When cooked strain off all the water and remove the bunch. Mix with about an ounce of butter a small quantity of finely minced mint, previously blanched, put this in a dish and turn the peas over it. The peas should be young, quickly boiled, and not shelled before wanted.

String Beans, Plain. Take fresh beans, remove the strings and stalks, and, if they are old, split them. Turn them into a saucepan with plenty of boiling water and a teaspoonful of sugar and salt to each quart, boil them till they are tender, which can be ascertained by trying them. When this vegetable is too old, no cooking will ever make it good. In boiling green vegetables the color can only be retained by quick boiling in plenty of water in an uncovered saucepan.

Diet for the Sick Room. In no branch of domestic economy is it more desirable or important to know how to prepare tempting dishes than in that pertaining to such light, nourishing foods as are commonly allotted to the sick. To this end rules, for the proper preparation of articles of diet for the sick, are given below. The capricious appetites, often the attendant of sickness, will tax the ingenuity and resources alike of nurses and cooks; hence the necessity for plain, simple modes of serving dainty dishes for the sick room.

Arrow Root Custard. Dry Bermuda arrow root, two drachms or two teaspoonfuls; sugar, one drachm or one teaspoonful. Mix by rubbing or careful stirring with a little cold milk until all lumps are broken, and it forms a perfect mixture a little thicker than heavy cream. Boil half a pint of milk or water, and as soon as it comes to a boil pour it over the paste, stirring until it thickens. If any flavor is desired add it just before pouring on the boiling milk.

Oat Meal Gruel. Oat meal, of medium fineness, four drachms or a tablespoonful; salt to season to the taste. Mix with enough milk to form a paste and stir well, then add half a pint of milk and heat to a boil, maintaining this temperature five or six minutes while constantly stirring. Remove from the fire and add an even teaspoonful of sugar and a piece of butter as large as a cherry. Mix thoroughly.

Restorative Jelly. Russian isinglass, one ounce; gum arabic, two drachms; sugar, two ounces; cassia buds, broken, ten ounces; lemon juice, one drachm; pure port wine, half a pint. Mix altogether and let them stand in a glass or porcelain vessel about two hours, then place the dish in a vessel of warm water, heat gently and stir until the isinglass and gum are dissolved, and finally bring the water to a boil a few minutes; then remove and strain the jelly into shallow moulds. A small slice of this jelly placed in the mouth of an unconscious or helpless invalid will gradually dissolve and pass into the stomach without effort of the patient.

Beef Tea, quickly made. Put any desired quantity of thoroughly lean beef, cut across the grain and into small pieces, in a dry saucepan and allow it to rest over a slow fire for a few minutes, stirring to keep it from sticking to the pan; when of a whitish color pour on its own weight (pint for pound) of cold water and bring it to the boil, let it gently simmer ten minutes and strain under ordinary pressure into a shallow dish; if any fat appears on the surface remove it with white filter or blotting paper. This makes a strong and excellent beef tea.

Toast Water. Take one slice stale bread, half inch thick and four by four inches in length and breadth, thoroughly toasted without scorching, put while hot into half pint boiling water, cover tightly and allow to cool, and then strain. This is quite refreshing to invalids unable to use stronger food.

Panada. Take two slices stale bread one-half inch thick, toast well without scorching, cut into small squares, put into a bowl, sprinkle a little salt over them and pour on a pint of boiling water, and grate in a little nutmeg.

Sago Jelly. Sago, four tablespoonfuls; juice or rind of one lemon; sugar, to suit the taste, perhaps two ounces; water, one quart. Mix and let them stand an hour, then boil, stirring frequently, until all is dissolved, and add one ounce of port wine. Mix, and allow to cool.

Castillon's Powder. Powdered tragacanth, powdered sago, powdered salep, and sugar, each one ounce; prepared carbonate lime, two drachms. Mix thoroughly and make into powders containing one drachm; for use, put one powder in four tablespoonfuls of cold milk, put into a pan and stir well, and add slowly one pint of boiling milk, and boil for fifteen minutes and add sugar to the taste.

Fluid Extract of Coffee. A good article may be prepared on a small scale as follows: Light brown coffee, roasted, five ounces; dark brown, five ounces; alcohol, three ounces; cold water, twelve ounces; hot water, sufficient. Grind the two kinds of coffee together, and macerate them for two days in a closed percolator with the alcohol and the cold water. Then add enough hot water to obtain fifteen ounces of percolate. Set this aside, and continue the percolation till ten ounces more have passed through. Evaporate this down to five ounces, filter, and add to the reserved liquor. Dose, two or three teaspoonsful to a cup of hot water.

Dried Meat for Medicinal Purposes is prepared by cutting fresh meat finely, spreading upon muslin, drying rapidly in a current of air, and rubbing into a brown powder, which is almost inodorous, and has a slightly saline taste. It is readily taken by patients, spread upon bread or a teaspoonful of it mixed with a cupful of broth or soup, or by children if baked into biscuits.

Ice Cream and Beef Juice. The following is an excellent dietary article: Cream, 120 grams; sugar, thirty grams; extract of vanilla, 8 grams; beef juice, eight grams. Any confectioner can make it, or it may readily be prepared at home with a freezer.

DIGESTION OF VARIOUS FOODS.

	Average Time.
Apples, sweet	1 hours, 30 minutes
" sour	2 " 00 "
Beans, pod, boiled	2 " 30 "
Beef, fresh, rare, roasted	3 " 00 "
" " dried	3 " 30 "
" " fried	4 " 00 "
Beets, boiled	4 " 45 "
Bread, wheat, fresh	3 " 30 "
" corn	3 " 15 "
Butter (melted)	3 " 30 "
Cabbage, with vinegar, raw	2 " 00 "
" boiled	4 " 30 "
Cheese (old, strong)	3 " 30 "
Codfish	2 " 00 "
Custard (baked)	2 " 45 "
Ducks (domestic), roasted	4 " 00 "
" (wild)	4 " 30 "
Eggs, fresh, hard boiled	3 " 30 "
" soft "	3 " 00 "
" fried	3 " 30 "
Goose, roast	2 " 00 "
Lamb, fresh, boiled	2 " 30 "
Liver, beef, boiled	2 " 00 "
Milk, boiled	2 " 00 "
" raw	2 " 15 "
Parsnips, boiled	2 " 30 "
Mutton, roast	3 " 15 "
" broiled	3 " 00 "
" boiled	3 " 00 "
Oysters, raw	2 " 55 "
" roast	3 " 15 "
" stewed	3 " 30 "
Pork (fat and lean), roast	5 hours, 15 minutes
" " " boiled	3 " 15 "
" " " raw	3 " 00 "
Potatoes, boiled	3 " 30 "
" baked	2 " 30 "
Rice, boiled	1 " 00 "
Sago, "	1 " 45 "
Salmon (salted), boiled	4 " 00 "
Soup (beef, vegetable)	4 " 00 "
" (chicken), boiled	3 " 00 "
" (oyster), "	3 " 30 "
Tapioca, boiled	2 " 00 "
Tripe (soused), boiled	1 " 00 "
Trout, fresh, boiled or fried	1 " 30 "
Turkey (domestic), roast	2 " 00 "
" (wild)	2 " 18 "
Turnips (boiled)	3 " 30 "
Veal, fresh, boiled	4 " 00 "
" " fried	4 " 30 "
Venison steak, broiled	1 " 35 "

DISINFECTANTS.

In addition to what may be found, in the body of this work, upon disinfection in connection with the diseases of animals, the following will be found valuable: The value of chloride of lime and sulphuric acid, which form the most effectual disinfecting material, is here expressed by 100, while the remaining numbers show the value of the other materials as compared with this standard:

Chloride of Lime with Sulphuric Acid	100-0
Chloride of Lime with Sulphate of Iron	99-0
Carbolic Acid—disinfecting Powder	85-6
Slaked Lime	84-6
Alum	80-4
Sulphate of Iron	76-7
Chloralum	74-0
Sulphate Magnesia	57-1
Permanganate of Potash with Sulphuric Acid	51-3

Dry Earth. Makes an excellent disinfectant of privy vaults, cesspools and sinks.

To Disinfect Clothing. Subject it to dry heat, as great as it will bear without injury to the texture.

Condie's Disinfectant. Crude permanganate of potash half ounce; water half pint. Put a few teaspoonfuls in the room to be disinfected and renew as often as the solution loses its color. For purifying foul water a teaspoonful to the barrel is sufficient to sweeten, and if added until a faint tinge of color shows in the water, all injurious organic matter will be destroyed. If the water is for drinking put in a little coffee or tea, a teaspoonful, and the tinge will disappear leaving the water pure and wholesome.

For Privy Vaults or Cess Pools—having a rotten egg smell, sulphuretted hydrogen, use copperas in coarse powder. One or two pounds to an ordinary vault will be ample, as a general rule, to remove all unpleasant odor. Where the odor of carbolic acid or chloride of lime is not objectionable, they will prove valuable disinfectants, especially for drains, etc.

To Ascertain Whether the Air of a Sick Room is Pure or Not. Dampen a piece of white linen or muslin in a solution of nitrate of lead. If impure the cloth will darken, otherwise remain white.

FOOD, in Relation to Hunger and Thirst.

Food consists of substances taken into the stomach for the purpose of digestion, or of conversion into blood. Food is rendered necessary by the waste of the system. Food is the primary source of nervous and muscular power. Food which supplies calorific power is termed heat-forming, respiratory, carbonaceous, or fuel food, and consists of starchy, saccharine, of oleaginous bodies which contain a preponderance of carbon, or of carbon and hydrogen. Food which supplies dynamical (mechanical and mental power) is termed histogenetic,(tissue-forming), nitrogenous, azotized, proteinous, or albuminous; and consists of substances which are comparatively rich in nitrogen, as milk, eggs, flesh, cheese, peas, beans, and other bodies containing fibrin, albumen, caseine, or gluten. A small portion of the respiratory food also probably contributes to the formation of the tissues; and likewise a portion of histogenetic or albuminous food to the development of the animal heat. The student and the hard-laboring professional man require even more tissue-forming food than the ordinary physical laborer. A due supply of animal food is necessary to the development of a high civilization; that is, to the development of races who are capable of sustained muscular and mental labor. Alcohol, either strong or dilute, can not possess any histogenetic power from its deficiency of nitrogen; and, as far as the results of modern experiments can show, is neither oxidized nor burnt in the system, and therefore is probably neither a heat-former nor a flesh-former. It is consequently deficient in true food power, or, in other words, can neither nourish the body nor develop heat. A due mixture of heat-forming and flesh-forming food is most beneficial, economizing both food and digestive (vital or nervous) power. An excess of animal food is much more injurious than a corresponding excess of vegetable food. Cooking renders food more savory, wholesome, and digestible, and destroys the parasitic animals which might otherwise excite serious if not fatal disease; it saves food, and enables the same amount of digestive (vital) power to do more effective work, and diminishes the quantity which would otherwise pass away undigested. Any system of instruction in cooking which does not include some knowledge of the chemistry and physiology of food must be defective. What is food? how is it converted into blood? how does the blood circulate? and how is the body nourished and kept in health? are questions of the greatest importance in their relation to public health and morality, and should be generally taught in our schools. The following may be taken as correct as to the qualities of human food mentioned, and their characteristics when introduced into the stomach. Beef. When it is the flesh of a bullock of middle age, it affords good and strong nourishment, and is peculiarly well adapted to those who labor, or take much exercise. It will often sit easy upon stomachs that can digest no other kind of food; and its fat is almost as easily digested as that of veal. Veal is a proper food for persons recovering from indisposition, and may even be given to febrile patients in a very weak state, but it affords less nourishment than the flesh of the same animal in a state of maturity. The fat of it is lighter than that of any other animal, and shows the least disposition to putrescency. Veal is a very suitable food in costive habits; but, of all meat it is the least calculated for removing acidity from the stomach. Mutton, from the age of four to six years, and fed on dry pasture, is an excellent meat. It is of a middle kind between the firmness of beef and the tenderness of veal. The lean part of mutton, however, is the most nourishing and conducive to health, the fat being hard of digestion. The head of the sheep, especially when divested of the skin, is very tender; and the feet, on account of the jelly they contain, are highly nutritive. Lamb is not so nourishing as mutton; but it is light, and extremely suitable to delicate stomachs. House lamb, though much esteemed by many, possesses the bad qualities common to the flesh of all animals reared in an unnatural manner. Pork affords rich and substantial nourishment; and its juices are wholesome when properly fed, and when the animal enjoys pure air and exercise. But the flesh of hogs reared in towns is both hard of digestion and unwholesome. Pork is particularly improper for those who are liable to any foulness of the skin. It is almost proverbial, that a dram is good for promoting its digestion; but this is an erroneous notion, for though a dram may give a momentary stimulus to the coats of the stomach, it tends to harden the flesh, and of course to make it more indigestible. Smoked hams are a strong meat, and rather fit for a relish than a diet. It is the quality of all salted meat that the fibers become rigid; and therefore more difficult of digestion; and when to this is added smoking, the heat of the chimney occasions the salt to concentrate, and the fat between the muscles sometimes to become rancid. Bacon is also of an indigestible quality, and is apt to turn rancid on weak stomachs; but for those in health it is an excellent food, especially when used with fowl or veal, and even eaten with peas, cabbages, or cauliflowers. Goat's flesh is hard and indigestible, but that of kids is tender as well as delicious, and affords good nourishment. Venison, or the flesh of deer, and that of hares, is of a nourishing quality, but it is liable to the inconvenience, that, though much disposed to putrescency of itself, it must be kept for a little time before it becomes tender. The blood of animals is used as an aliment by the common people, but they could not long subsist upon it unless mixed with oatmeal, etc., for it is not very soluble, alone, by the digestive powers of the human stomach, and therefore can not prove nourishing. Milk is of very different consistence in different animals; but that of cows being the kind used in diet, is at present the object of our attention. Milk, where it agrees with the stomach, affords excellent nourishment for those who are weak and can not digest other aliments. It does not readily become putrid, but it is apt to become sour on the stomach, and thence to produce flatulence, heart-burn, or gripes, and in some constitutions a looseness. The best milk is from a cow at three or four years of age, about two months after producing a calf. It is lighter, but more watery than the milk of sheep and goats; while, on the other hand, it is more thick and heavy than the milk of asses and mares, which are next in consistence to human milk. On account of the acid which is generated after digestion, milk coagulates in all stomachs; but the caseous or cheesy part is again dissolved by the digestive juices, and rendered fit for the purposes of nutrition. It is improper to eat acid substances with milk, as these would tend to prevent the due digestion of it. Cream is very nourishing, but, on account of its fatness, is difficult to be digested in weak stomachs. Violent exercise, after eating it, will, in a little while, convert it into butter. Butter. Some writers inveigh against the use of butter as universally pernicious; but they might with equal reason condemn all vegetable oils, which form a considerable part of diet in the southern climates, and seem to have been beneficially intended by nature for that purpose. Butter, like every other oily substance, has doubtless a relaxing quality, and if retained long in the stomach is liable to become rancid; but, if eaten in moderation, it will not produce those effects. It is, however, improper in bilious constitutions. The worst consequence produced by butter, when eaten with bread, is that it obstructs the discharge of the saliva in the act of mastication or chewing, by which means the food is not so easily digested. To obviate this effect, it would be a commendable practice at breakfast, first to eat some dry bread, and chew it well, till the salivary glands were exhausted, and afterwards to eat it with butter. By these means such a quantity of saliva might be carried into the stomach as would be sufficient for the purpose of digestion. Cheese is likewise reprobated by many as extremely unwholesome. It is doubtless not easy of digestion; and when eaten in a great quantity, may overload the stomach; but if eaten sparingly, its tenacity may be dissolved by the digestive juices, and it may yield a wholesome, though not very nourishing, chyle. Toasted cheese is agreeable to most palates, but it is rendered more indigestible by that process. The flesh of birds differs in quality according to the food on which they live. Such as feed upon grain and berries, afford, in general, good nourishment; if we except geese and ducks, which are hard of digestion, especially the former. A young hen or chicken is a tender, delicate food, and extremely well adapted where the digestive powers are weak. But of all tame fowls, the capon is the most nutritious. Turkeys, as well as guinea or India fowls, afford a substantial nutriment, but are not so easy of digestion as the common domestic fowls. In all birds those parts are the most firm, which are most exercised; in the small birds, therefore, the wings, and in the larger kinds, the legs, are commonly the most difficult of digestion. The flesh of wild birds, in general, though more easily digested, is less nourishing than that of quadrupeds, as being more dry on account of their almost constant exercise. Those birds are not wholesome which subsist upon worms, insects and fishes. The eggs of birds are a simple and wholesome aliment. Those of the turkey are superior in all the qualifications of food. The white of eggs is dissolved in a warm temperature, but by much heat it is rendered tough and hard. The yolk contains much oil, and is highly nourishing, but has a strong tendency to putrefaction; on which account, eggs are improper for people of weak stomachs, especially when they are not quite fresh. Eggs boiled hard or fried are difficult of digestion, and are rendered still more indigestible by the addition of butter. All eggs require a sufficient quantity of salt, to promote their solution in the stomach. Fish, though some of them be light and easy of digestion, afford less nourishment than vegetables, or the flesh of quadrupeds, and are, of all the animal tribes, the most disposed to putrefaction. Salt water fish are, in general, the best; but when salted, though less disposed to putrescency, they become more difficult of digestion. Whitings and flounders are the most easily digested. Acid sauces, and pickles, by resisting putrefaction, are a proper addition to fish, both as they retard putrescency, and correct the relaxing tendency of butter, so generally used with this kind of aliment. Oysters and cockles are eaten both raw and dressed; but in the former state they are preferable, because heat dissipates considerably their nutritious parts as well as the salt water, which promotes their digestion in the stomach; if not eaten very sparingly, they generally prove laxative. Muscles and periwinkles are far inferior to oysters, both in point of digestion and nutriment. Sea muscles are by some supposed to be of a poisonous nature; but though this opinion is not much countenanced by experience, the safest way is to eat them with vinegar, or some other vegetable acid. Bread. At the head of the vegetable class stands bread, that article of diet which, from general use, has received the name of the staff of life. Wheat is the grain chiefly used for the purpose in this country, and is among the most nutritive of all the farinaceous kinds, as it contains a great deal of starch. Bread is very properly eaten with animal food, to correct the disposition to putrescency; but is most expedient with such articles of diet as contain much nourishment in a small bulk, because it then serves to give the stomach a proper degree of expansion. But as it produces a slimy chyle, and disposes to costiveness, it ought not to be eaten in a large quantity. To render bread easy of digestion, it ought to be well fermented and baked, and it never should be used till it has stood twenty-four hours after being taken out of the oven, otherwise it is apt to occasion various complaints in those who have weak stomachs; such as flatulence, heartburn, watchfulness, and the like. The custom of eating butter with bread, hot from the oven, is compatible only with very strong digestive powers. Pastry, especially when hot, has all the disadvantages of hot bread and butter, and even buttered toast, though the bread be stale, is scarcely inferior in its effects on a weak stomach. Dry toast, with butter, is by far the wholesomest breakfast. Brown wheaten bread, in which there is a good deal of rye, though not so nourishing as that made of fine flour, is both palatable and wholesome, but apt to become sour on weak stomachs. Oats, barley, and rice. —Oats, when deprived of the husk, and particularly barley, when properly prepared, are each of them softening, and afford wholesome and cooling nourishment. Rice likewise contains a nutritious mucilage, and is less used in Great Britain than it deserves, both on account of its wholesomeness and economical utility. The notion of its being hurtful to the sight is a vulgar error. In some constitutions it tends to induce costiveness; but this seems to be owing chiefly to flatulence, and may be corrected by the addition of some spice, such as caraways, aniseed, and the like. Potatoes are an agreeable and wholesome food, and yield nearly as much nourishment as any of the roots used in diet. The farinaceous or mealy kind is in general the most easy of digestion, and they are much improved by being toasted or baked. They ought almost always to be eaten with meat, and never without salt. The salt should be boiled with them. Green peas and beans, boiled in their fresh state, are both agreeable to the taste and wholesome, being neither so flatulent, nor so difficult of digestion, as in their ripe state; in which they resemble the other leguminous vegetables. French beans possess much the same qualities; but yield a more watery juice, and have a greater disposition to produce flatulence. They ought to be eaten with some spice. Salads, being eaten raw, require good digestive powers, especially those of the cooling kind; and the addition of oil and vinegar, though qualified with mustard, hardly renders the free use of them consistent with a weak stomach. Spinach affords a soft lubricating aliment, but contains little nourishment. In weak stomachs it is apt to produce acidity, and frequently a looseness. To obviate these effects, it ought always to be well beaten, and but little butter mixed with it. Asparagus is a nourishing article in diet, and promotes the secretion of urine; but in common with the vegetable class, disposes a little to flatulence. Artichokes resemble asparagus in their qualities, but seem to be more nutritive, and less diuretic. Cabbages are some of the most conspicuous plants in the garden. They do not afford much nourishment, but are an agreeable addition to animal food, and not quite so flatulent as the common greens. They are likewise diuretic, and somewhat laxative. Cabbage has a stronger tendency to putrefaction than most other vegetable substances; and, during its putrefying state, sends forth an offensive smell, much resembling that of putrefying animal bodies. So far, however, from promoting a putrid disposition in the human body, it is on the contrary, a wholesome aliment in the true putrid scurvy. Turnips are a nutritious article of vegetable food, but not very easy of digestion, and are flatulent. This effect is in a good measure obviated, by pressing the water out of them before they are eaten. Carrots contain a considerable quantity of nutritious juice, but are among the most flatulent of vegetable productions. Parsnips are more nourishing and less flatulent than carrots, which they also exceed in the sweetness of their mucilage. By boiling them in two different waters, they are rendered less flatulent, but their other qualities are thereby diminished in proportion. Parsley is of a stimulating and aromatic nature, well calculated to make agreeable sauces. It is also a gentle diuretic, but preferable in all its qualities when boiled. Celery affords a root both wholesome and fragrant, but is difficult of digestion in its raw state. It gives an agreeable taste to soups, as well as renders them diuretic. Onions, garlic, and shallots are all of a stimulating nature, by which they assist digestion, dissolve slimy humors, and expel flatulency. They are, however, most suitable to persons of a cold and phlegmatic constitution. Radishes of all kinds, particularly the horse radish, agree with the three preceding articles in powerfully dissolving slimy humors. They excite the discharge of air lodged in the intestines. Apples are a wholesome vegetable aliment, and in many cases medicinal, particularly in diseases of the breast and complaints arising from phlegm. But, in general, they agree best with the stomach when eaten either roasted or boiled. The more aromatic kinds of apples are the fittest for eating raw. Pears resemble much in their effects the sweet kinds of apples, but have more of a laxative quality, and a greater tendency to flatulence. Cherries are in general a wholesome fruit, when they agree with the stomach, and they are beneficial in many diseases, especially those of the putrid kind. Plums are nourishing, and have, besides, an attenuating as well as a laxative, quality, but are apt to produce flatulence. If eaten fresh, and before they are ripe, especially in large quantities, they occasion colics, and other complaints of the bowels. Peaches are not of a very nourishing quality, but they abound in juice, and are serviceable in bilious complaints. Apricots are more pulpy than peaches, but are apt to ferment, and produce acidities in weak stomachs. Where they do not disagree they are cooling, and tend likewise to correct a disposition to putrescency. Gooseberries and currants, when ripe, are similar in their qualities to cherries, and when used in a green state, they are agreeably cooling. Strawberries are an agreeable, cooling aliment, and are accounted good in cases of gravel. Cucumbers are cooling, and agreeable to the palate in hot weather; but to prevent them from proving hurtful to the stomach, the juice ought to be squeezed out after they are sliced, and vinegar, pepper, and salt, afterward added. Tea, by some, is condemned in terms the most vehement and unqualified, while others have either asserted its innocence, or gone so far as to ascribe to it salubrious, and even extraordinary virtues. The truth seems to lie between these two extremes; there is, however, an essential difference in the effects of green tea and of black, or of bohea; the former of which is much more apt to affect the nerves of the stomach than the latter, more especially when drank without cream, and likewise without bread and butter. That, taken in a large quantity, or at a later hour than usual, tea often produces watchfulness, is a point that can not be denied; but if used in moderation, and accompanied with the additions just now mentioned, it does not sensibly discover any hurtful effects, but greatly relieves an oppression of the stomach, and abates a pain of the head. It ought always to be made of a moderate degree of strength: for if too weak it certainly relaxes the stomach. As it has an astringent taste, which seems not very consistent with a relaxing power, there is ground for ascribing this effect not so much to the herb itself as to the hot water, which not being impregnated with a sufficient quantity of tea, to correct its own emollient tendency, produces a relaxation, unjustly imputed to some noxious quality of the plant. But tea, like every other commodity, is liable to damage, and when this happens, it may produce effects not necessarily connected with its original qualities. It is allowed that coffee promotes digestion, and exhilarates the animal spirits; besides which, various other qualities are ascribed to it, such as dispelling flatulency, removing dizziness of the head, attenuating viscid humors, increasing the circulation of the blood, and consequently perspiration; but if drank too strong, it affects the nerves, occasions watchfulness, and tremor of the hands; though in some phlegmatic constitutions it is apt to produce sleep. Indeed, it is to persons of that habit that coffee is well accommodated; for to people of a thin and dry habit of body it seems to be injurious. Turkey coffee is greatly preferable in flavor to that of the West Indies. Drank, only in the quantity of one dish, after dinner, to promote digestion, it answers best without either sugar or milk; but if taken at other times, it should have both; or in place of the latter, rather cream, which not only improves the beverage, but tends to mitigate the effect of coffee upon the nerves. Chocolate is a nutritive and wholesome composition, if taken in a small quantity, and not repeated too often; but is generally hurtful to the stomach of those with whom a vegetable diet disagrees. By the addition of vanilla and other ingredients, it is made too heating, and so much affects particular constitutions as to excite nervous symptoms, especially complaints of the head.

FREEZING MIXTURES WITHOUT ICE.

Use water not warmer than 50° Fahrenheit:

Mixtures.	Down to	Change
Nitrate Ammonia, Water, } each one part..	50°	4°	46°
Muriate Ammonia Nitrate of Potash, } each five parts..	50	10	40
Water, sixteen parts....			
Muriate Ammonia, Nitrate of Potash, } each five parts..			
Sulphate of Soda, eight parts	50	4	46
Water, sixteen parts			
Sulphate of Soda, three parts	50	−3	53
Dilute Nitric Acid, two parts			
Nitrate of Ammonia, Carbonate Soda, } each one part	50	−7	57
Water,			
Phosphate Soda, nine parts	50	−12	62
Dilute Nitric Acid, four parts			
Sulphate of soda, five parts.	50	3	47
Dilute Sulphuric Acid, four parts			
Sulphate of Soda, six parts			
Muriate Ammonia, four parts	50	−10	60
Nitrate of Potash, two parts			
Dilute Nitric Acid, four parts			
Sulphate of Soda, six parts			
Nitrate of Ammonia, five parts	50	−14	64
Dilute Nitric Acid, four parts.			

FREEZING, FUSING & BOILING POINTS.

The following table will explain itself, and will be valuable to many readers:

Substances.	Reaumer.	Centigrade.	Fahr h't.
Bromine freezes at	−16°	−20°	−4°
Oil Anise "	8	10	50
" Olive "	8	10	50
" Rose "	12	15	63
Quicksilver "	−31.5	−39.4	−39
Water "	−1	0	32
Bismuth metal fuses at	200	264	507
Cadmium "	248.8	315	592
Copper "	874.6	1093	2000
Gold "	961	1200	2200
Iodine "	92	115	239
Iron "	1280	1538	2800
Lead "	255.5	325	617
Potassium "	46	58	136
Phosphorus "	44		111
Silver "	816.8	1021	1870
" Nitrate "	159	198	389
Sodium "	72	90	194
Steel "	1452	1856	3300
Sulphur "	72	90	194
Tin "	173	230	446
Zinc "	328	410	770
Alcohol boils at	63	78	173
Bromine "	50	63	145
Ether "	28	55	95
" Nitrous boils at	11	14	57
Iodine "	140	175	347
Olive Oil "	252	315	600
Quicksilver "	280	350	662
Water "	80	100	212

HAIR.

A Safe Depilatory. Take a strong solution of sulphuret of barium, and add enough finely powdered starch to make a paste. Apply to the roots of the hair and allow it to remain on a few minutes, then scrape off with the back edge of a knife-blade, and rub with sweet oil.

Quick Depilatory for Removing Hair. Best slaked lime, 6 ounces; orpiment, fine powder, 1 ounce. Mix with a covered sieve and preserve in a dry place in closely stoppered bottles. In using mix the powder with enough water to form a paste, and apply to the hair to be removed. In about five minutes, or as soon as it is caustic action is felt on the skin, remove, as in shaving, with an ivory or bone paper knife, wash with cold water freely, and apply cold cream.

Tricopherous for the Hair. Castor oil, alcohol, each, 1 pint; tinct. cantharides, one ounce; oil bergamot, ¼ ounce; alkanet coloring, to color as wished. Mix and let it stand forty-eight hours, with occasional shaking, and then filter.

Liquid Shampoo. Take bay rum, 2½ pints, water, ¼ pint, glycerine, 1 ounce, tinct. cantharides, 2 drachms, carbonate of ammonia, 2 drachms, borax, ¼ ounce; or take of New England rum, 1½ pints, bay rum, 1 pint, water, ¼ pint, glycerine, 1 ounce, tinct. cantharides, 2 drachms, ammon. carbonate, 2 drachms, borax, ¼ ounce; the salts to be dissolved in water and the other ingredients to be added gradually.

Moustache Grower. Simple cerate, 1 ounce, oil bergamot, 10 minims, saturated tinct. of cantharides, 15 minims. Rub them together thoroughly, or melt the cerate and stir in the tincture while hot, and the oil as soon as it is nearly cold, then run into moulds or rolls. To be applied as a pomade, rubbing in at the roots of the hair. Care must be used not to inflame the skin by too frequent application.

Cleaning Hair Brushes. Put a teaspoonful or dessertspoonful of aqua ammonia into a basin half full of water, comb the loose hairs out of the brush, then agitate the water briskly with the brush, and rinse it well with clear water.

Burns and Scalds. Glycerite of lime is recommended as soothing the pain and lessening the inflammation of burns. It is made as follows: Freshly slaked lime, 1 part, glycerine, 50 parts, hydrochloric ether, 1 part. Rub the lime with a small portion of the glycerine into a smooth cream, then add the remaining glycerine and ether and thoroughly mix. Another recipe is, lime water and pure olive or linseed oil, equal parts, shake thoroughly to form a uniform and rather thin or liquid salve. Apply freely to burns or scalds, and bind the wounds in rags saturated with it. Lime water is made by pouring a gallon of water on a pound of unslaked lime, and after standing twelve hours decant or filter, and preserve for use when needed. An excellent and available remedy for burns at hand in almost every house, is the bi-carbonate or ordinary baking soda. Make a thin paste with water and apply promptly; it will quickly remove the pain and check inflammation.

MEDICINES, Active, Maximum Doses.

Every person should know the largest doses, which it is safe to give of active medicines. The following table shows the largest doses admissible, in grammes, and also the equivalent in grains for solids, and in minims for liquids. The doses are expressed in fractions, thus: 1-18, 1-64, meaning one thirteenth, one sixty-fourth. In non-professional hands it is the safest plan to strictly observe the rule of never giving the maximum dose of any medicine. Unless in case of some idiosyncrasy, it is rare that a medium, safe dose will not serve the end desired, and, should it become necessary to increase the dose to obtain the full remedial effects, the point of toleration may thus be cautiously reached without detriment to the patient. The table is as follows:

Medicines.	Grammes.	Grains.
Arsenious Acid	.005	1-13
Acid, Carbolic	.05	¾
" Hydrocyanic	.06	1
Aconitia	.004	1-16
Aconite Root	.15	2¼
Arsenic, Iodide	.025	⅜
Atropia	.001	1-64
Atropia Sulph	.001	1-64
Barium, Chlor	.12	1⅞
Belladonna, Herb	.2	3
" Root	.1	1½
Codia	.05	¾
Conia	.001	1-64
Digitalis	.3	4½
Ext. Aconite Leaves	.1	1½
" " Root	.025	⅜
" Belladonna	.1	1¾
" Cannabis Indica	.1	1½
" Conium	.18	2¾
" Digitalis	2	3
" Nux Vomica, Alc	.05	¾
" Opium	.1	1½
" Stramon. Seed	.05	¾
Fowler's Solution	.4	6 min.
Lead, Sugar of	.06	9 10
Mercury, Corrosive Chlor	.03	9-20
" Red Iodide	.03	9-20
Morphia and its Salts	.03	9-20
Nitrate Silver	.03	9-20
Oil, Croton	.06	9-10
Opium	.15	2¼
Phosphorus	.015	2-9
Potassa, Arsenite	.005	1-13
" Cyanide	.03	9-20
Santonine	.1	1½
Soda, Arsenite	.005	1-13
Strychnia and Salts	.01	1-6
Tartar Emetic	.2	3
Veratria	.005	1-13
Veratrum Virido	.3	4½
Zinc, Chloride	.015	2-9
" Valerianate	.06	9-10

PASTE.

The following paste, it is said, will adhere to any substance to which it is applied: Sugar of lead, 1½ ounces; alum, 1½ ounces; gum arabic, 2½ ounces; wheat flour, 1 pound; water, sufficient. Dissolve the gum arabic in two quarts of warm water; when cold, mix in the wheat flour, and add the sugar of lead and alum dissolved in water. Place the whole on a a fire, stirring constantly, and take it off when it shows signs of ebullition. Let it cool, and the paste is made. If the paste is too thick, add to it some gum water to bring it to the proper consistence.

PERFUMES.

Cologne. Deodorized proof spirit or dil. alcohol, 4 pints; oil lemon, 2 drachms; oil rose, 2 minims; oil citronella, 4 minims; oil bergamot, 2 drachms. Rub the oil thoroughly with one ounce of carbonate magnesia, then add alcohol gradually, rubbing the paste until it is very thin, pour in two pints of alcohol, stir well, and pour into a filter; after most of the liquid has passed, put the remainder of the alcohol into the filter and let it pass through. Another recipe for an excellent cologne, is as follows: Strong cologne spirits, 1 gallon; oil lemon, 2 drachms; oil bergamot, 1 ounce; oil lavender flowers, 4 drachms; oil of rose, ½ drachm; oil jasmin, 1 ounce; tinc. musk, 1 drachm. Dissolve the oils and musk, allow the mixture to stand forty-eight hours, and then filter and keep two weeks, well stoppered, before using.

Inexhaustible Smelling Salts. Sal tartar, 3 drachms; mur. ammonia, granulated, 6 drachms; oil neroli, 5 minims; oil lavender flowers, 5 minims; oil rose, 3 minims; spirits ammonia, 15 minims. Put into the pungent a small piece of sponge filling about one-fourth the space, and pour on it a due proportion of the oils; then put in the mixed salts until the bottle is three-fourths full, and pour on the spirits of ammonia in proper proportion and close the bottle.

Volatile Salts for Pungents. Liquor ammon., fort, 1 pint; oil lavender flowers, 1 drachm; oil rosemary, fine, 1 drachm; oil bergamot, ½ drachm; oil peppermint, 10 minims. Mix thoroughly and fill pungents or keep in well stoppered bottle. Another formula is, sesqui-carbonate of ammonia, small pieces, 10 ounces; concentrated liq. ammonia, 5 ounces. Put the sesqui-carb. in a wide mouth jar with air-tight stopper, perfume the liquor ammonia to suit and pour over the carbonate, close tightly the lid and place in a cool place; stir with a stiff spatula every other day for a week, and then keep it closed for two weeks, or until it becomes hard, when it is ready for use.

Aromatic Spirit of Vinegar. Acetic acid, No. 8, pure, 8 ounces; camphor, ½ ounce. Dissolve, and add oil lemon, oil lavender flowers, each 2 drachms; oil cassia, oil cloves, ½ drachm each. Thoroughly mix and keep in well stoppered bottle.

Rose Vinegar. Best red rose leaves, freshly dried, ½ pound; dilute acetic acid, 1 gallon. Macerate for two weeks with frequent stirring and filter, or macerate twenty-four hours and pour off the vinegar; rub up the leaves with well washed fine sand and pack in percolator and displace with the vinegar taken from the leaves; to this add oil rose, ten drops. Shake well and filter.

Lavender Vinegar. Lavender flowers, freshly dried, ½ pound; dilute acetic acid, 6 pints. Treat as for rose vinegar, and add to the liquid, before filtering, 2 drachms oil lavender flowers.

Orange Flower Vinegar. Fresh orange leaves, 1 pound; dilute acetic acid, 6 pints. Macerate or displace as above, and add oil neroli, 10 minims, and filter.

PLANTS, ETC., USED IN MEDICINE.

The following complete list gives the botanical names in alphabetical order, and the common names and synonyms of plants, etc., used in medicine. It will be valuable for reference:

Achillea Millefolium—Yarrow, Milfoil, Thousand Leaf.
Aconitum Napellus—Aconite, Monkshood, Wolfsbane.
Actæa Alba—White Cohosh, White Beads, Necklace Weed, White Baneberry.
Actæa Rubra—Red Cohosh, Baneberry.
Adiantum Pedatum—Maiden Hair, Rock Fern.
Æsculus Glabra—Ohio Buckeye, Horse Chestnut.
Æsculus Hipocastanum—English Horse Chestnut.
Agathotes Chirayita—Chiretta, Cherayita, Bitter Stick.
Agrimonia Eupatoria—Common Agrimony, Stick Wort.
Ajuga Chamæpithys—Yellow Bugle, Ground Pine.
Ajuga Reptans—Common Bugle.
Aletris Farinosa—Star Grass, Star Root, Blazing Star, Mealy Starwort, True Unicorn Root, Bitter Grass, Aloe Root, Colic Root, Ague Root, Crowcorn, Ague Grass.
Alisma Plantago—Water Plantain.
Alnus Rubra—Red Alder, Tag Alder, Swamp Alder, Smooth Alder.

HOUSEHOLD DEPARTMENT 1076 PLANTS, ETC., USED IN MEDICINE

Alotonia—Dita Bark.
Althaea Officinalis—Marsh Mallows, Bismalva, Hibiscus, Ibiscus, Mortification Root.
Amaranthus Hypochondriacus—Prince's Feather, Red Cockscomb, Pilewort, Amaranth.
Amaranthus Melancholicus—Love-lies-bleeding.
Ambrosia Artemisaefolia—Rag Weed, Roman Wormwood, Hog Weed.
Ampelopsis—Virginia Creeper.
Anacyclus Pyrethrum—Pellitory Root, Pellitory of Spain, Pyrethrum Root.
Anagallis Arvensis—Scarlet Pimpernel, Poor-man's Weather-glass.
Anchusa Tinctoria—Alkanet, Bugloss, Dyers' Alkanet.
Andira—Cabbage Tree Bark.
Anemone Pulsatilla—Pulsatilla.
Anethum Graveolens—Dill Seed, Garden Dill, Dilly.
Angelica Atropurpurea—Purple Angelica, High Angelica.
Angelica Archangelica—Wild Archangel.
Angelica Sylvestris—Wild Angelica.
Anthemis Cotula—May Weed, Dog Fennel, Wild Chamomile, Stinking Chamomile, Dill Weed, Field Weed, Mathen, Flake.
Anthemis Nobilis—Roman Chamomile, Low Chamomile, English Chamomile.
Apium Petroselinum—Parsley Leaves, Seed and Root.
Apocynum Androsaemifolium—Bitter Root, Dogsbane, Bitter Dogsbane, Wandering Milk Weed, Ipecac Milk, Honey Bloom, Catch-fly.
Apocynum Cannabinum—Indian Hemp, Black Hemp.
Aralia Hispida—Dwarf Elder, Wild Elder, Bristly Aralia, Bristle Stem, Sarsaparilla.
Aralia Racemosa—Spikenard, Petty-morel, Life of Man, Spignet.
Aralia Spinosa—Angelica Tree, Toothache Bush, Hercules' Club, Prickly Elder.
Aralia Nudicaulis—Wild Sarsaparilla, Shotbush, Sea Ash.
Arnica Montana—Leopard-bane, Mountain Tobacco.
Artemisia Abrotanum—Southern Wood, Old Man, Boy's Love, Lad's Love.
Artemisia Absinthium—Wormwood.
Artemisia Vulgaris—Mugwort, Wild Wormwood.
Arum Triphyllum—Wild Turnip, Indian Turnip, Pepper Turnip, Bog Onion, Marsh Turnip, Dragon's Root, Dragon's Turnip, Jack in the Pulpit, Canada Turnip.
Arum Maculatum—Wake Robin, Cuckoo's Pint.
Asarum Canadense—Wild Ginger, Indian Ginger, Canada Ginger, Wild Turnip, Kidney-leaved Asarabacca, Canada Snake Root, Heart Root, Coltsfoot, Coltsfoot Snake Root, False Coltsfoot, Vermont Snake Root, Heart Snake Root.
Asclepias Incarnata—Rose-colored Silk Weed, Swamp Milk Weed Root, White Indian Hemp, Flesh-colored Asclepias.
Asclepias Syriaca—Milk Weed, Silk Weed Root, Wild Cotton.
Asclepias Tuberosa—Pleurisy Root, Butterfly Weed, Flux Root, White Flux Root, White Root, Canada Root, Orange Swallow Root, Swallowwort, Windwort, Tuber Root.
Asplenium Angustifolium—Swamp Spleenwort.
Asplenium Filix Faemina—Female Fern, Backache-brake.
Aster Puniceus—Red-Stalked Aster, Cold Water Root, Cocash Root, Meadow Scabish.
Atropa Belladonna—Belladonna, Deadly Nightshade, Dwale.
Azedarach—Pride of China, Bead Tree, Pride of India.
Baptisia Tinctoria—Wild Indigo Weed, Indigo Broom, Yellow Broom, Horse-fly Weed Rattlebush.
Berberis Vulgaris—Barberry, Pipperidge.
Betula Lenta—Birch Bark, Sweet Birch, Cherry Birch, Spice Birch.
Borago Officinalis—Borage, Burrage.
Brayera—Kooso.
Bursa Pastoris—Shepherd's Purse.
Calamus Aromaticus—Flag Root, Sweet Flag, Sweet Rush.
Calendula Officinalis—Marigold.
Callitriche—Water Starwort.
Canella Alba—Wild Cinnamon.
Cannabis Indica—Foreign Indian Hemp, Cannabis Ganja.
Capsicum Annuum—Cayenne Pepper, Red Pepper, Bird Pepper, Cockspur Pepper, Guinea Pods.
Carduus Benedicta—Spotted Cardus, Blessed Thistle, Spotted Thistle, Cursed Thistle, Holy Thistle, Star Thistle, Lovely Thistle, Thistle Root, Cardus Plant.
Carthamus Tinctorius—Safflower, Dyers' Saffron, American Saffron.
Cassia Marilandica—American Senna, Wild Senna, Maryland Cassia, Locust Plant.
Castanea—Chestnut Leaves.
Caulophyllum Thalictroides (see *Leontice Thalictroides*)—Blue Cohosh, Leontice, Pappoose Root, Squaw Root, Blueberry Root.
Ceanothus Americana—Jersey Tea, Bohea, Red Root, Wild Snow Ball.
Celastrus Scandens—Bittersweet Bark, Climbing Bittersweet, False Bittersweet, Shrubby Bittersweet, Fevertwig, Wax Work, Staff Wine, Staff Tree.
Centaurea Americana—Great American Century, Wild Succory, Rose Pink.
Chamaelirium Luteum—Devil's Bit, False Unicorn.
Chelidonium Majus—Celandine, Tetterwort.
Chelone Glabra—Balmony, Snake Head, Bitterbarb, Turtle Bloom, Salt Rheum Weed, Fishmouth, Turtle Head, Shell Flower.
Chenopodium Anthelminticum—Wormseed, Jerusalem Oak, Worm Gooseroot, Jesuit's Tea.
Chimaphila Umbellata—Pipsissewa, Prince's Pine, Ground Leaf, Ground Holly, American Wintergreen, King's Cure, Rheumatism-weed.
Cicuta Maculata—American Water Hemlock, Spotted Cowbane, Beaver Poison, Musquash Root.
Cicuta Virosa—Water Hemlock, Cowbane, Poison Hemlock.
Cimicifuga Racemosa (see *Macrotys Racemosa*)—Black Snake Root, Black Cohosh, Deer Weed, Rattle Root, Bugbane.
Cinchona Pallida—Peruvian Bark, Crown Bark, Jesuit's Bark.
Cistus Canadensis—Rock Rose, Holly Rose.
Clematis Virginica—Virgin's Bower, Traveler's Joy.
Cochlearia Officinalis—Scurvy Grass.
Collinsonia Canadensis—Horse Weed, Horse Balm, Ox Balm, Rich Weed, Heal-all, Knob's Grass, Knob Root, Knot Root, Stone Root, Woundwort.
Comptonia Asplenifolia—Sweet Fern, Sweet Bush, Fern Gale, Sweet Ferry, Meadow Fern.
Convolvulus Panduratus—Bind Weed, Man Root, Wild Scammony, Wild Jalap, Hog Potato, Mechameck, Wild Rhubarb, Kusauda, Wild Potato.
Coptis Trifolia—Gold Thread, Mouth Root, Canker Root.
Corallorhiza Odontorhiza—Coral Root, Crawley, Dragoo's Claw, Coral Teeth.
Corallorhiza Hyemale (see *Aplectrum Hyemale*)—Adam and Eve, Putty Root, Chicken's Toes.
Cornus Circinata—Round-leaved Dogwood or Cornel, Cornea, Green Osier.
Cornus Florida—Dogwood, Boxwood, Dog Tree, Box Tree, Budwood.
Cornus Cericea—Swamp Dogwood, Rose Willow, Red Osier, Red Willow, Red Rod, Silky Cornel.
Corydalis Formosa—Turkey Corn, Turkey Pea, Stagger Weed, Squirrel Corn.
Cucumis Colocynthis—Colocynth, Bitter Apple, Bitter Cucumber.
Cunila Mariana—American Dittany, Mountain Dittany, Mint-leaved Cunila, Wild Basil, Stone Mint.
Cynoglossum Officinalis—Hound's Tongue.
Cypripedium Pubescens—Lady's Slipper, Nerve Root, Nervine, Moccasin Root, Umbil Root, Noah's Ark, Indian Shoe, Bleeding Heart, American Valerian, Pine Tulip.
Datura Stramonium—Jimson Weed, Devil's Apple, Stink Weed, Thorn Apple.
Delphinium Staphisagria—Stavesacre, Larkspur.
Digitalis Purpurea—Foxglove, Fairy's Glove.
Dioscorea Villosa—Wild Yam, China Root.
Doratenia Contrayerva—Counter Poison, Antidote.
Dracocephalum Canariense—Dragon's Head.
Dracontium Faetidum—Skunk Cabbage, Skunk Weed, Collard, Polecat Weed, Bear's-leaf, Bear's-foot.
Drosera—Sundew.
Dulcamara—Bittersweet, Woody Nightshade, Scarlet Berry, Violet Bloom.
Epigaea Repens—Trailing Arbutus, Gravel Plant, Ground Laurel, Winter Pink, Mountain Pink.
Epilobium Angustifolium—Wickup, Willow Herb.
Epiphegus Americanus—Cancer Root, Beech Drop, Broom Rape.
Erigeron Canadense—Canada Fleabane, Butter Horse Weed, Blood Staunch, Butter Weed, Mare's Tail, Pride Weed.
Erigeron Philadelphicum, Erigeron Purpurum—Philadelphia Fleabane, Cocash, Sweet Scabious, Skavish.
Eriodictyon—Mountain Balm, Consumptive's Weed, Bear's Weed.
Eryngium Aquaticum—Water Eryngo, Rattlesnake's Master, Corn Snake Root.
Erythronium Americanum—Erythronium, Yellow Adder's Tongue, Yellow Snake Leaf, Dogtooth Violet, Rattlesnake Violet.
Euonymus Atropurpureus—Wahoo, Burning Bush, Spindle Tree, Strawberry Tree, Indian Arrow Wood.
Eupatorium Aromaticum—Pool Root.
Eupatorium Perfoliatum—Boneset, Thoroughwort, Crosswort, Indian Sage, Feverwort, Ague Weed, Sweating Plant.
Eupatorium Purpureum—Queen of the Meadow, Gravel Root, Trumpet Weed, Purple Boneset, Joe Pye.
Eupatorium Urticifolium—White Snake Root.

Euphorbia Corallata—Large Flowering Spurge, Wild Ipecac, Wild Hippo.
Euphorbia Ipecacuanha—Ipecacuanha Spurge, Carolina Ipecac.
Euphrasia Officinalis—Eyebright.
Filix Mas—Male Fern, Golden Fern.
Fraseri Walteri—American Columbo, Pyramid Flower, Yellow Gentian, Meadow Pride, Indian Lettuce, Wild Columbo.
Fucus Vesiculosus—Sea Wrack, Bladder Wrack, Kelp Ware, Blacktang.
Fumaria Officinalis—Fumitory.
Galanga Major and Minor—Catarrh Root, East India Root, Galangal, Kassamac.
Galium Aparine—Cleavers Root, Goose Grass, Milkaweet, Clabber Grass, Poor Robin, Catch Weed, Bed Straw, Savoyan.
Gaultheria Procumbens—Wintergreen, Partridge Berry, Spicy Wintergreen, Deer Berry, Grouse Berry, Checker Berry, Tea Berry, Box Berry, Spice Berry, Mountain Tea, Red Berry, Ground Berry.
Gelsemium Sempervirens—Yellow Jessamine, Wild Jessamine, Carolina Jessamine, Bignonia, Woodbine.
Gentiana Catesbæi—Blue Gentian, Southern Gentian.
Gentiana Lutea—Great Yellow Gentian.
Gentiana Quinqueflora—Bitter Plantain, Five-flowered Gentian.
Gentiana Saponaria—Sampson Snake Root.
Geranium Maculatum—Cranesbill, Stork's Bill, Crowfoot, Dovefoot.
Geum Rivale—Avens Root, Water Avens, Purple Avens, Throat Root.
Geum Virginianum—White Avens, Evan Root, Chocolate Root, Cure-all.
Gillenia Trifoliata—Indian Physic, Bowman's Root, Beaumont's Root, American Ipecac, Dropwort, Indian Hippo.
Glechoma Hederacea—Ground Ivy, Gill Run, Gill go over the Ground, Catloot, Alehoof.
Glycyrrhiza Glabra—Licorice, Sweetwood, Spanish Root.
Gnaphalium—Life Everlasting, Cud-Weed, Field Balsam, Live Forever, Sweet Balsam, White Balsam, Indian Posey, Mouse Ear, Dysentery Root.
Goodyera Pubescens—Rattlesnake Root, Adder Violet, Netleaf Plantain.
Gossypium Herbaceum—Cotton Root.
Guaiac Wood—Lignum Vitæ.
Hamamelis Virginica—Witch Hazel, Striped Alder, Winter Bloom, Snapping Hazelnut, Spotted Alder.
Hedeoma Pulegioides—Pennyroyal, Squaw Mint, Tick Weed, Stinking Balm.
Helenium—Sneeze Weed, Sneezewort.
Helianthemum Canadense—Frostwort, Frost Weed, Scrofula, Weed.
Helonias Dioica—Starwort, False Unicorn, Unicorn's Horn, Drooping Starwort.
Helleborus Fœtidus—Bear's Foot, Setterwort.
Helleborus Niger—Black Hellebore, Christmas Rose.
Hepatica Americana—Liverwort, Liver Leaf.
Heracleum Lanatum—Masterwort, Cow Parsnip.
Heuchera Americana—Alum Root, Cliff Weed, Ground Maple, Split Rock.
Hieracium—Hawk Weed, Rattlesnake Weed.
Hydrangea Arborescens—Hydrangea, Wild Hydrangea, Seven-Barks.
Hydrastis Canadensis—Golden Seal, Yellow Root, Yellow Puccoon, Orange Root, Ground Raspberry, Eye Balm.
Hyoscyamus Niger—Black Henbane, Fœtid Nightshade, Poison Tobacco.
Hypericum Perforatum—St. Johnswort, Johnswort.
Impatiens Balsamina, Impatiens fulva and Pallida—Wild Celandine, Balsam Weed, Jewel Weed, Touch-me-not.
Imperatoria—Masterwort.
Inula Helenium—Elecampane, Scabwort.
Iris Versicolor—Blue Flag, Flag Lily, Fleur-de-lis, Liver Lily, Poison Flag, Snake Lily, Water Flag.
Kalmia Angustifolia—Sheep Laurel, Narrow-leaved Laurel, Sheep Poison.
Kalmia Glauca—Swamp Laurel.
Kalmia Latifolia—Laurel, Mountain Laurel, Lambkill, Spoonwood, Calico Bush, Calfkill.
Krameria Triandra—Rhatany.
Lactuca Elongata—Wild Lettuce, Snake Bite.
Lappa Minor—Burdock Leaves, Clot Burr.
Laurus Benzoin—Fever Wood, Spice Bush, Spice Wood, Wild Allspice, Allspice Bush.
Ledum—Marsh Tea, Wild Rosemary.
Leontice Thalictroides—Blueberry.
Leonurus Cardiaca—Motherwort, Cardiaca, Wolfstrap.
Leptandra Virginica—Culvers Root, Culvers Physic, Black Root, Brinton Root, Tall Veronica.
Levisticum—Lovage, Lavose, Smellage.
Liatris Spicata—Button Snake Root, Gayfeather, Backache Root.

Linaria—Toad Flax, Snap Dragon.
Liriodendron Tulipifera—Tulip Tree Bark, Whitewood, White Poplar, Yellow Poplar, Len-nik-hi, Cucumber Tree.
Lobelia Cardinalis—Red Cardinal Flower, Red Cardinal Plant, Red Lobelia, Indian Pink.
Lobelia Inflata—Lobelia, Indian Tobacco, Wild Tobacco, Asthma Root, Emetic Herb, Emetic Weed, Puke Root.
Lycopodium Clavatum—Club Moss, Vegetable Sulphur.
Lycopus Europæus—Green Archangel, Water Hoarhound, Water Bugle, Bugle, Gipseywort.
Lycopus Virginicus—American Archangel, Red Archangel, Gipsey Weed, Virginia Hoarhound, Paul's Betony, Sweet Bugle, Bugle Weed, Bitter Bugle.
Lythrum Salicaria—Loose Strife, Spiked Strife, Purple Willow Herb.
Magnolia Glauca—Sweet Magnolia, Beaver Tree, Sweet Bay, White Bay, Swamp Sassafras.
Malva Rotundifolia—Low Mallows, Cheese Plant.
Malva Sylvestris—High Mallows.
Marrubium Vulgare—Prassium, White Hoarhound.
Mecenium Virginica—Indian Cucumber, Cucumber Root.
Melilotus Officinalis—Kings's Clover, Sweet Clover, Yellow Melilot.
Melissa Officinalis—Lemon Balm, Dropsy Plant, Sweet Balm.
Menispermum Canadense—Texas Sarsaparilla, Yellow Parilla, Canada Wormwood, Canadian Moonseed, Vine Maple.
Mentha Piperita—Peppermint.
Mentha Viridis—Spearmint, Julep Grass, Garden Mint, Flavoring Herb.
Menyanthes Trifoliata—Buck Bean, Bog Bean, Marsh Trefoil, Water Shamrock, Bitter-worm.
Mimulus Moschatus—Musk Plant, Monkey Flower.
Mitchella Repens—Squaw Vine, Winter Clover, Partridgeberry, Hive Vine.
Momordica Balsamina—Balsam Apple, Balsamine.
Monarda Didyma—Mountain Balm, Oswego Tea, Red Balm, Square Stalk.
Monarda Punctata—Horse Mint.
Monotropa Uniflora—Fit Root, Fit Plant, Pie Plant, Pine Sap, Corpse Plant, Ice Plant, Indian Pipe, Ova-ova.
Mucuna—Cowhage.
Myrica Cerifera—Bayberry, Candleberry, Waxberry, Wax Myrtle.
Myrica Gale—Sweet Gale, Sweet Willow, Dutch Myrtle, Bog Myrtle.
Nabula Albus—Lion's foot, White Lettuce.
Nasturtium Amphibium—Water Radish, Water Cress, Amphibious Cress.
Nasturtium Palustre—Marsh Water Cress.
Nepeta Cataria—Catnip, Catmint, Catwort.
Nuphar Advena—Yellow Pond Lily, Toad Lily, Frog Lily, Cow Lily, Water Lily, Water Nymph, Cow Cabbage, White Lily, White Pond Lily, Sweet Water Lily, Water Cabbage, Spatter Dock, Beaver Root.
Nux Vomica—Dog Button.
Nymphæa Odorata—(See *Nuphar Advena*.)
Ocymum Basilicum—Sweet Basil, Royal Ocimum, Basilicum.
Œnothera Biennis—Evening Primrose, Tree Primrose.
Origanum Majorana—Sweet Marjoram, Amaracus.
Origanum Vulgare—Mountain Mint, Wild Marjoram.
Orobanche Virginiana, Orobanche Uniflora—Cancer Root, Beech Drop, Broom Rape, Squaw Root.
Osmorrhiza Brevistylis—Sweet Cicily, Short-styled Cicily, Hairy Sweet Cicily.
Oxalis Acetosella—Wood Sorrel, Acetosella, Cuckoo's Bread.
Panax Quinquefolia—Ginseng, Ninsin, Garantogen, Sang.
Papaver Somniferum—Poppy, Opium Poppy.
Pareira Brava—Ice Vine, Violet Leaf.
Parthenium Integrifolium—Prairie Dock, Nephritic Plant, Cutting Almond.
Pedicularis Canadensis—Wood Betony, Betony Weed, Lousewort.
Petroselinum Sativum—Parsley Root, Rock Parsley.
Phytolacca Decandra—Poke, Garget, Cocum, Pigeon Berry, American Nightshade, Jalap, Cancer Root, Pecatacalleloe, Scoke Root.
Pinckneya Pubens—Pinckneya, Carolina Cinchona, Georgia Bark, Fever Tree, Florida Bark.
Pinus Canadensis—Hemlock Spruce.
Pinus Balsamea—Balsam Fir.
Piper Angustifolium—Matico, Narrow-leafed Piper.
Plantago Major—Plantain, Way Bread, Rib Grass.
Podophyllum Peltatum—May Apple, Mandrake, Wild Lemon, Indian Apple, Raccoon Berry, Duck's Foot, Ipecacuanha.
Polemonium Reptans—Abscess Root, Blue Bell, Sweat Root, Greek Valerian.
Polygala Rubella—Bitter Polygala, Ground Flower.
Polygala Senega—Seneka Snake Root, Seneka, Senega, Mountain Flax, Milkwort.
Polygonum Hydropiper—Smart Weed, Arsmart.

Polygonum Punctatum—Water Pepper, Dead Arsmart, Knot Weed, Biting Persicaria, Biting Knot Weed.
Polypodium Vulgare—Common Polypody, Brake Root, Rock Polypody.
Polytrichum Juniperinum—Hair-cap Moss, Robin's Rye, Bear's Bed, Ground Moss.
Populus Balsamifera—Balsam Poplar, Tacamahac, Balm of Gilead.
Populus Tremuloides—Trembling Poplar, Aspen, American Aspen, Quaking Aspen, Quiver Leaf.
Potentilla Canadensis—Cinque Foil, Five Finger.
Prenanthes—Rattlesnake Root, Lion's-foot, Cancer Weed, White Lettuce.
Prinos Verticillatus—Black Alder, False Alder, Striped Alder, Winter-berry, Fever Bush.
Prunella Pennsylvanica—Self Heal.
Prunus Virginiana—Wild Cherry Bark, Black Cherry.
Ptelea Trifoliata—Water Ash, Shrubby Trefoil, Hop Tree, Ague Bark, Wing Seed.
Pteris Atropurpurea—Rock Brake, Winter Fern, Indian Dream.
Pulmonaria Officinalis—Lungwort, Cowslips of Jerusalem, Gum Plant, Sage of Jerusalem, Spotted Comfrey, Spotted Lungwort, Maple Lungwort.
Pyrethrum Parthenium—Feverfew, Featherfew, Chrysanthemum.
Pyrola Rotundifolia—Wild Lettuce, Round-leafed Pyrola.
Pyrola Umbellata—Round-leafed Consumption Weed, Shin Leaf.
Quassia Bitter Wood, Bitter Ash, Bitter Weed, Simaruba, Mountain Zarnum.
Ranunculus Acris—Buttercup, Meadow Crowfoot, Yellow Weed, Meadow Bloom, Blister Weed.
Ranunculus Bulbosus—Bulbous Crowfoot.
Rhamnus Catharticus—Buck Thorn, Purging Berries.
Rhus Glabra—Smooth Sumach, Upland Sumach.
Rhus Toxicodendron—Poison Oak, Poison Ivy, Poison Ash, Poison Vine.
Rubus Occidentalis—Blackberry, Thimbleberry, Black Raspberry.
Rudbeckia Laciniata Thimble Weed, Cone-disk, Sun Flower, Tall Cone Flower.
Rumex Anaticus—Water Dock, Zanthoriza.
Rumex Crispus—Yellow Dock, Curled Dock, Narrow Dock, Sour Dock, Garden Patience.
Sabbatia Angularis—Red Century, Sabbatia, Bitter Bloom, Bitter Clover, Rose Pink, Wild Succory.
Salvia Lyrata—Wild Sage, Meadow Sage, Lyre-leaved Sage, Caucer Weed.
Salvia Sclarey—Clary, Clammy Sage.
Sambucus Canadensis—Elder Blooms, Common Elder, Sweet Elder.
Sanguinaria Canadensis—Blood Root, Red Root, Puccoon, Indian Paint.
Sanicula Marilandica—Black Sanicle.
Saponaria Officinalis Soapwort, Bouncing Bet, Old Maid's Pink, London Pride.
Sarracenia Purpurea, Sarracenia Officinalis—Side-saddle Plant, Fly-trap, Water Cup, Pitcher Plant, Eve's Cup, Huntsman's Cup, Small Pox Plant.
Scoparius Cytisus - Broom.
Scrophularia Nodosa—Figwort, Scrofula Plant, Carpenter's Square, Heal-all.
Scutellaria Lateriflora—Scullcap, Hooded Willow Herb, Hoodwort, Mad Weed, Mad Dog Scullcap, Blue Scullcap, Blue Pimpernel.
Sedum—Stone Crop, Mossy Stone Crop.
Senecio Aureus—Life Root, Golden Ragwort, Uncum, Golden Senecio.
Senecio Hieracifolius—Fire Weed.
Senecio Obovatus—Squaw Weed.
Senecio Vulgaris Common Groundsel.
Serpentaria—Virginia Snake Root, White Snake Root, Snargel, Birthwort, White Sanicle.
Silene Virginica—Wild Pink, Virginia Catch-fly.
Sisymbrium Officinale—Hedge Mustard.
Sium Nodiflorum—Water Parsnip.
Smilax Herbacea—Carrion Flower.
Smilax Peduncularis—Jacob's Ladder.
Solidago Odora—Golden Rod, Sweet-scented Golden Rod.
Sorbus—Mountain Ash.
Spigelia Marilandica—Carolina Pink Root, Wormgrass, Indian Pink Root, Unsteetle, Star Bloom.
Spiræa Tomentosa—Hardhack, Steeplebush, Whitecap, Meadow Sweet, White Leaf.
Statice Caroliniana—Marsh Rosemary, Seathrift, Meadow Root, Ink Root, Sea Lavender.
Stillingia Sylvatica—Queen's Root, Queen's Delight, Cock-up-hat, Yaw Root, Silver Leaf.
Stramonium—Thorn Apple, Jimson Weed.
Sumbul—Musk Root.
Symphytum Officinale—Comfrey, Healing Herb.
Taraxicum—Dandelion.
Taxus—Yew.
Tephrosia Virginiana—Goat's Rue, Hoary Pea, Devil's Shoestring, Catgut.
Thuja Occidentalis—Arbor Vitæ.
Toxicodendron—Poison Oak, Poison Ivy, Poison Ash, Poison Vine.
Trifolium Pratense—Red Clover.
Trifolium Repens—White Clover.
Trillium Pendulum Beth Root, Birth Root, Cough Root, Ground Lily, Indian Balm, Jewsharp, Lamb's Quarter, Parlawort, True Love.
Triosteum Perfoliatum—Fever Root, Feverwort, Wild Ipecac, Bastard Ipecac, Dr. Tinker's Weed, False Ipecac, Cinque, Horse Ginseng, White Gentian, Wild Coffee, Sweet Bitter.
Triticum Repens—Couch Grass, Quich Grass, Quitch Grass, Dog Grass, Knot Grass, Witch Grass, Quickens.
Tropaolum Majus—Nastartium, Indian Cress.
Tussilago Farfara—Coltsfoot, Bull's Foot, Flower Velure.
Ulmus Fulva—Slippery Elm, Indian Elm, Sweet Elm.
Urtica Dioica—Nettle Root, Stinging Nettle.
Uva Ursi—Bearberry, Wild Cranberry, Bear's Whortleberry, Mountain Box, Mountain and Upland Cranberry.
Veratrum Viride—American Hellebore, Itch Weed, Indian Poke.
Verbascum Thapsus—Mullein, Yellow Moth, Blattaria.
Verbena Hastata—Blue Vervain, Purvain, Simpler's Joy.
Veronica Officinalis—Speedwell, Fluellin, Virginia Speedwell.
Viburnum Opulus—Cramp Bark, High Cranberry, Snowball, Cranberry Tree, Nanny Bush Bark, Guelder's Rose, Sheep's Berry.
Viburnum Prunifolium—Black Haw, Sloe.
Viscum—Mistletoe.
Xanthium Strumarium—Cockle Bur.
Xanthoria Apifolia—Yellow Root, Shrub Yellow Root.
Xanthoxylum Fraxineum—Yellow Wood, Prickly Ash, Suterberry, Toothache Tree, Parsley.

POISONING.

In the case of animals, the subject has been treated of in the body of this work. In cases of poisoning of any member of the family, send for a physician at once. But the following general treatment will be indicated, when the poison is not known: Vomit the patient freely with warm water and mustard, ipecac or salt water, then give white of eggs freely, or of lard, olive, or other bland oil, except in phosphorus poisoning. If an acid has been taken give freely of calcined magnesia, chalk, or other alkali. If the poison has been an alkali, give oil freely, and after the vomiting neutralize with acid drinks, followed by more oil and second vomiting, if acids will not make poisonous compounds with the alkali. If the source of the poisoning is known, the following special treatment will be indicated.

For Arsenical Poisoning. Vomit with ipecac. Solution of alum and salt water. Give white of egg freely, and follow with weakened solution of perchloride of iron or dialised iron. If the patient is very weak use hot applications, and very cautiously of alcoholic stimulants.

For Aconite, Belladonna, and Digitalis. Vomiting, stimulants, strong coffee, opium, and hot applications. Opium only under the care of a physician or experienced person.

Chloral Hydrate or Chloroform. Vomiting, stimulants, strong coffee, hot baths, and dropping the head lower than the rest of the body, to cause a flow of blood to the brain.

Lead Poisoning. Epsom salts in large doses, with ipecac until vomiting and purging sets in. Use white of egg if poison is a lead salt taken into the stomach, and give plenty of fresh milk. Strychnia is often found valuable when there is paralysis. Fresh milk used regularly in diet is said to prevent lead colic, with those who work in paint or lead.

Lye Poisoning. Give freely of oil, or warm lard and white of egg, and if possible cause vomiting after giving the oil.

Opium or Morphia. Vomiting and white of egg. If the poison has been just taken give a solution of tannin to prevent ready absorption of the poison. If already diffused in the system, use tinct. belladonna in full doses until the pulse quickens, and the pupils of the eye begin to dilate, observing great caution after these signs appear. Strong coffee is beneficial, also electric currents, and frequent application of cold water so as to shock the system. Keep the patient in motion constantly if practicable.

Silver, Nitrate. Use moderately strong solution of common salt, and after the vomiting give freely of fresh milk.

Strychnia and its Salts. Vomiting, and if the poison has been recently taken use solution of tannin, and very freely of white of egg. If convulsions appear use chloroform, chloral hydrate, or opium.

Antidotes for Strychnia. Prof. Bellini, after a long series of experiments on poisoning by strychnia and its salts, arrives at the following conclusions: That the best antidotes are tannic acid, chlorine, and the tinctures of iodine and bromine. Chlorine attacks the strychnia even after it is diffused through the system. He believes the arrest in the symptoms by tannin to be due, not to chemical action, but to its astringent effects on the mucous membrane of the stomach, whereby the absorption of the poison is rendered difficult.

Chloroform. Death from chloroform need never occur, according to the doctrine of Syme, Lister and Hughes, if this simple rule be observed: "Never mind the pulse, never mind the heart, leave the pupil to itself. Keep your eye on the breathing, and if it becomes embarrassed to a grave extent, take an artery forceps and pull the tongue well out." Syme never lost a case from chloroform, although he gave it 5,000 times. This simple rule enabled him (so he thought) to make this excellent record. Another remedy is to lay the patient so that his head will hang lower than the rest of the body, and cause a flow of blood to the brain.—To avoid mistakes with poisons when not intending to use them: Keep all active poisons as arsenic, corrosive sublimate, Hall's and Fowler's solutions, etc, in bottles painted with rings of black, or a large black square under the label, in the center of which a death's head label might be pasted. This not only prevents using such medicines by mistake in place of comparatively harmless remedies, but also calls attention to their dangerous character when using properly and incites closer notice of quantities prescribed. For eruptions of poison oak or poison ivy, the following prescription is most valuable. Get the prescription filled by a druggist:

Acid Carbolic..........................Half drachm.
Ol. Sassafras..........................｜｜｜
Ol. Juniperi..........................Each one drachm.
Ung. Zinci Oxide (Benz.).........One ounce.

Apply from two to four times daily, and before going to bed wash the inflamed part thoroughly with warm water and soap.

POULTICES.

Bread Poultice. Dry bread crumbs, a sufficient quantity, boiling water to make a stiff mush of the crumbs, stirring well to remove all hard lumps, then stir in a half teaspoonful of glycerine to the teacupful of poultice, and it is ready for use.

Slippery Elm Poultice. Powdered elm, hot water or milk, enough of each to make a good paste, and then add glycerine half teaspoonful to a cupful of poultice.

When either of these two poultices are to be applied to very painful surfaces, a little laudanum can be added to advantage.

Mild Mustard Poultice. Good ground mustard, ground flax seed, each one ounce, water to make a thick paste and spread on muslin.

Strong Mustard Poultice. Best ground mustard, vinegar enough to make a paste, spread on muslin. This poultice will often blister nicely.

Linseed Poultice. Powdered flaxseed four ounces, hot water half pint. Add the seed gradually, stirring well till a soft paste is formed.

SINGING AND CAGE BIRDS.

The birds now kept in cages either for the beauty of their plumage or their song, now embrace a great variety, running all the way through the finches, linnets, sparrows, thrushes, up to the parrots, and the more magnificent plumaged araras and cockatoos. The musical canary is however, the universal pet, found in almost every household, and is generally admired for its sprightly action, delicate coloring, and its pleasing and varied song. Their original home is in the Canary Islands, but over 300 years of domestication has so changed their color and instincts that the domesticated bird would no longer be recognized, except by the naturalist, either in his songs or plumage. In confinement more birds are ruined by too much coddling, and mistaken kindness than by all other causes put together. They are semi-tropical birds and can not stand extremes of heat and cold, drafts, or a confined atmosphere. All the feathered tribes require plenty of air and light, and when at liberty take a large amount of exercise. This in confinement must be liberally supplied as to the first two; and the third their natural instincts will tempt them to so far as their cages will allow. Canary birds are classified, as German Harz, which resemble the wild birds more than others, and as Dutch Belgian, or Parisian, which have longer legs, a more arched back, and a somewhat ruffled breast. The first class are bright yellow, straw color, or nearly white, yellowish white, green or gray, cream colored filberts, and spotted or mottled. These latter may be smooth-headed single-colored birds, the head alone shaded, or they may be green, gray, brown, or black-headed with brilliant plumage as to their body; this with the depth of color on the head constituting value. There is another strain of birds called swallows; their value consists in the regularity of their markings. The most prized are the capped, filbert-colored birds, but swallows are not necessarily capped, since if the wings only are marked they are called wing swallows. The Belgian (Holland) canary is pure yellow in color. They are divided into Parisian, large birds, with ruffled shoulders and breast; the Holland smaller, and the ruffles less developed; and the Brussels, a slender, deep colored bird with a flat head. The German canaries, however, are generally considered to be the best singers. The shape of the cage is immaterial, but the larger the better. They must always be hung above the reach of cats; they should always have the morning sun, and in summer the cages should be hung out of doors, in the shade as much as possible. If painted cages are used, the paint should be kept well covered with varnish. The utensils should be of china or glass, the perches of soft wood of a size large enough so the claws of the bird may grasp half way round. And the utmost cleanliness should be used. Give them a water bath every day. The principal food should be clean, sweet canary seed, with a little rape added. A cuttle-fish bone should always be kept in the cage, and also a little clean, sharp, fine gravel should be allowed once a week. Chick weed and lettuce should also be given them, and occasionally, during the moulting season, the yolk of a hard-boiled egg rubbed up in Indian meal. Sweet apple is also good, and occasionally a piece of stale bread, but no cake of any kind. Until the bird is six months old, it should have the yolk of hard-boiled eggs as a part of the diet. If the birds are lean, give a little flax seed every other day, and occasionally to all birds, a little poppy seed, and coarse oatmeal grits. In relation to breeding and raising young birds, a writer describes the manner of breeding in the Harz mountains, Germany, as follows: According to the size of the space at your disposal, place from three to six males in your room, and three times as many females. Place a large number of jumping-bars at different heights and distances. Arrange, also, two nests for each hen. In the center of the breeding room a little table must be placed, for feeding and drinking purposes. Water vessels must be so arranged that the birds can not bathe in them. On the floor place building material, such as short-cut hemp, Manila, animal hair, feathers, etc.; the birds will take care of the rest. Supply fresh food and drink each day; the birds must be disturbed as little as possible. The principal food for them while breeding is German rape-seed mixed with a little canary seed. After the have been hatched give them, twice or three times daily, eggs boiled hard, grated, equally mixed with soaked or grated crackers; instead of crackers, stale bread, moistened with water, may be served. One egg will be sufficient for fifteen or twenty birds each day. Lettuce should also be supplied in abundance; also, cuttle-fish, egg-shells, and gravel. Soaked rape-seed can not be sufficiently recommended; with it the old birds feed the young, and the young soon learn to feed themselves. To save time the egg may be cut in halves, and thus served. The egg-shells are eaten with great relish by the old birds, on account of the limy substance contained in them. If the egg be not grated, but served as before described, it will be well to add soaked (wheat) bread. Food and drinking vessels of china are preferable to all others. Greens, such as lettuce, chickweed, etc., can be supplied daily during hot weather; but on cold, damp days green food should be administered with great care, as it tends to induce diarrhœa, which, in many cases, proves fatal to the little songsters. During the first few days there will generally be well-contested fights among the males; unfortunately, this can not be avoided. After the birds have been mated, and each cock has obtained his hens, there will be peace and harmony in the breeding-room. The hens will then select their nests and labor diligently in their construction, the cock affording all the assistance in his power. The bird-raiser must now pay strict attention to his breeding-room or cage. It will be expedient to number the nests; observe carefully when the first, as well as the last, egg has been laid, in order to ascertain when the twelve days have passed, and when the young birds must come from the shell. Examine the nests daily, and remove the dead young. Watch closely lest there be among the flock a growler, who can do considerable mischief, destroying nests and eggs, as well as killing the young birds. Such ill-mannered growlers must be immediately removed. After the first brood have left their nests, and are no longer dependent for food on the parent birds, they must be separated from them and placed in a large cage, that the next brood may not be disturbed by them. They must then be well cared for, so that they may not catch cold. They must be carefully kept from every draft. As soon as the young cock can be distinguished by his singing, he must be separated from the others, and placed in a cage by himself near good singers, who will serve as his instructors. A breeding-room must have an abundance of light, and should have the morning sun. One or more evergreen trees, planted in boxes and placed in the bird-room will give it a pleasant appearance, and afford great pleasure to the birds. If no live trees can be had a few fir-trees, cut in the month of February, will answer instead, and remain green for some time. Nest-boxes of tin or wire are most desirable, as those of wood or pasteboard are suited for the generation of insects. After the young birds have left the nest, it is desirable to remove it and cleanse it thoroughly, in order that all the vermin may be destroyed. It will be well to keep constantly on hand some insect powder, and to strew, from time to time, a little in the nests. The genuine Parisian insect powder, although it completely destroys lice, is harmless to birds. Lice are dangerous enemies to the young brood. Want of cleanliness is the cause of the increase of insects, which annoy the breeding-hen, especially at night. Through this the little sufferer is compelled to scratch with her feet, in order to remove her enemy. Again, particles of excrement are thus collected on the claws, which becoming hard, increases the pressure on the delicate egg-shell and ultimately ruptures it. Under these circumstances, the nest may be purified by dipping it in boiling water, or by strewing in it Parisian insect powder. Should the bird have soiled claws it must be caught and have its claws purified by immersion in lukewarm water. The building material having been placed in the cage, becomes saturated with excrements and rendered unfit for use. Building material must, therefore, never be supplied in large quantities, but from time to time, as may be necessary. It may also be placed outside the cage, and accessible to the birds only through the wires. Nests placed inside the cages have not generally the necessary protection. The young bird of the preceding brood, and even the cock in the breeding cage, will often busy themselves about the nest, thereby causing the breeding-hen to leave the nest, while they inspect the eggs and in many cases break them. Sometimes they will peck at the materials of the nest, and, in so doing, break the eggs. A nest which is open at the top is not useful; nay, it is even unfit for use, because the excrements of birds whose nests are above will fall into them; soiled eggs will not be hatched out; the excrements will, moreover, harden, and with their sharp, pointed edges will often injure the coming brood. It will, therefore, be advisable to give the nest a covering of strong paper, or pasteboard, leaving only one part open in front; such protected nests are preferred by the birds. In such cases the birds do not rob each other of the building material, and the breeding birds are not disturbed by the approach of others. In cages the same general rule should be used. The nests too should be placed in corners opposite so the hen may take her choice, and covered so they may be retired. The material may be of short cotton wool as to the bottom with a little fine down for the surface. Sometimes the male bird is cruel. Unless very quiet he should be removed once the hen bird begins to sit; but if the male conducts himself properly and feeds his mate let him remain. While sitting the hen must be supplied with extra food about the tenth day or at least before the twelfth day. The food of the young birds should be hard-boiled yolk of egg rubbed up with stale bread crumbs. After the young birds leave the nest on or about the twenty-first day the old birds will continue to feed them, but it is better that there be a separation in the cage when the young birds are of this age, since the old birds often begin to lay for a second brood before the young birds are able to take care of themselves. Hence the advantage of a double cage for breeding purposes. During the whole time the old birds are feeding the young in addition to hard boiled yolk of eggs and bread crumbs, there should be soaked rape seed, canary seed, greens, and the usual food of the birds, and this should be continued for the young birds. When the young males begin to sing they should be separated from the females and hung where they may hear a first-class singer, and also the notes of out-door birds, if possible. Since thus they may learn to adapt their song to that of other birds. To learn a bird to whistle a tune: Select a strong, loud-voiced bird and place in a room where it can hear no other sound. Procure a good toned bird organ and play the tune selected for an hour at a time two or three times a day. It may take three months or more for the bird to catch the notes fully, and thereafter they will sing nothing else. The foregoing instructions will apply to all the sparrow and finch tribes or hard billed birds. In relation to the diseases of birds and their treatment, Our Pets or the Book of Birds says: It is much easier to prevent disease, by taking proper care of birds, than to cure them. It would, however, be ridiculous to state that birds, whose treatment is in every respect proper, never get sick. Even at liberty the bird is subject to diseases of various kinds. Whosoever watches his birds carefully will soon observe that the sick bird is exactly opposite to the same when well. The healthy bird is fond of exercise; and views his surroundings with bright eyes, while the sick bird will remain sitting on one spot, his plumage puffed and ruffled, his eyelids drawn down, and his head for the most part hidden behind his wing. The sick bird does not refuse to eat, but attacks his food with a greediness which immediately arouses the suspicions of the fancier. According to the nature of the disease other symptoms will soon appear. The sick bird opens his bill as widely as the healthy bird, during oppress-

ively warm days, but the eyes of the healthy bird are wide open while so doing, whereas the sick bird will keep them closed. The breathing of the bird is accompanied by strange unnatural sounds, while the motion of the feathers on the bosom is irregular. The throat looks pale; he is feverish and cold, as shown by his shaking his body, which motion he repeats oftener and oftener. Fits generally follow, and the bird drops from his perch and lies a corpse in the bottom of the cage. Many diseases show symptoms of this kind, and even the doctor's power is of no avail; but a few hours elapse from the beginning of the disease till death. *Consumption.* Many birds perish from irregular and improper nourishment. Such, as a matter of course, will induce extremely poor blood (*Anæmia*), leanness, weakness, and pains in the bowels; a disease which is very commonly called (*Darre*) consumption. The bird may have this disease and appear lively. He eats the food given him; it may be, however, that he does not eat with his usual appetite; he takes but little, flies away, and again returns to his food. He stops singing. In a few days diarrhœa and consumption ensue, when he ruffles his feathers and dies. The consumption is more chronic if it derives its origin from the bowels. Birds frequently labor under this disease as the result of improper food and of colds. The symptoms are various. Sometimes they will continue to eat, though affected with costiveness or diarrhœa. The excrements will tell when birds are sick. Should costiveness or diarrhœa continue for any length of time, inflammation of the intestines will ensue, and defecation will become painful, as is manifested by the bird shaking his rump and tail. These alone will produce a fatal result. If, however, the food be changed during the early stages of the disease, the bird may be saved. In insect-eaters, meal-worms in many cases are very effectual, and should be given with a few drops of castor oil. Besides healthy food in this, as in all other diseases, the first and most necessary remedy is a good supply of fresh air, plenty of room for the cage, on which as much sunlight as possible, without burning rays, may fall. Plenty of gravel should be placed in the bottom of the cage; drafts should be avoided. Stacklen says in his report on singing birds: "In many cases diarrhœa and costiveness will be cured if, for example, you feed birds of prey with raw meat without removing the hair or feathers; fruit, or grain-eaters with nightingale food and greens; soft-eaters with meal-worms, drowned in olive or sweet oil, spiders, and ground hemp-seeds as much as they desire, and distilled water for drink. Their bathing-cup should, from time to time, be removed. As a rule, such diet will have a better effect than all quack prescriptions, such as liniments, (butter, oil, or lard), syringing, and other humbugs, such as we see recommended in many books. Many bird-fanciers believe that the consumption (*Darre*) results from induration of the excretory glands, from which birds take the oil necessary to grease their wings, or that it is merely a disease of this organ. They believe it advantageous to squeeze them open with the thumb nail, or to prick them with a pin. Dr. Richter has designated this method as nonsensical. For such mal-treatment there is not the slightest excuse. Should a bird thus treated become well, the wound will heal, the same disease will recur, and the bird doomed to die only a little later. The only thing that can be done without injury is to oil this gland carefully with a feather. When we have a surplus of fat, it will be well to simplify the food, and to sprinkle the bird with lukewarm water about noon-time. This will compel the bird to clean itself, and thus, by regreasing his plumage, remove the surplus fat.

Fatness. This disease results from irregular food, and is the opposite of the *Darre.* It attacks grain-eaters most frequently; soft-eaters are rarely affected by it. Want of sufficient exercise is also a potent cause of it. Birds sometimes, when supplied with mixed food, consume only the most nutritious, and thus induce a surplus of fat. Some canary birds, when fed on German rape and canary seed, will eat only the latter, and never touch the former. If nothing be done to mend this habit, and compel the bird to eat rape seed and greens, he will soon become too fat and too lazy to sing. In the case of too much fat, grain-eaters should be supplied with plenty of greens; soft-eaters with berries, sweet turnips, or their juice, and well salted water to drink. The birds should, moreover, be excited to exercise more freely. Whoever lets a bird in this condition fly around a room for a few weeks generally cures him. When the disease is too far advanced, it will be useless to withhold his food, as the organs no longer perform their proper functions. In such cases they are sure to die, and the less we disturb them the better.

Apoplexy. Food which is too rich and nutritive, often produces this disease, many times resulting fatally to birds in a state of captivity as well as free. It often occurs that while they sing, eat or sleep, they suddenly drop and expire in a few minutes. Grain eaters are more subject to this disease than others, as their generally lazy mode of living makes them more fitting subjects of fat disease. These birds are sometimes saved by cutting the nail of the back toe until it bleeds, and then immerse them several times in cold water. A shower or plunge bath is, under these circumstances, advantageous; but it is of the utmost importance to protect the wet bird from draft, and afford him an opportunity of drying his feathers.

Epileptic Fits. Improper food may be considered as the cause of this disease, although brain disease and worms may also induce it. This terrible disease, very common among seed eating birds, and observed among other birds also, is incurable. The remedies which have been applied, may, for a time, alleviate the pain of the sufferer, but are wholly inadequate to eradicate the disease. The best thing to be done is to remove them at once, as no pleasure can be derived from a bird suffering from this disease.

Catarrh, Cold, (Pips). The care of captive birds is as important as their food. A great many diseases are brought on by colds induced by drafts, change of temperature, or unseasonable baths. The first of the diseases incurred from the above mentioned causes is pips, which is most frequently found among seed eating birds. The sick bird opens his bill because his nostrils are clotted with phlegm. He sneezes, coughs from time to time, with a view to clear his breathing organs; he gasps, ruffles the feathers on his head, and sinks exhausted on the floor of his cage. After the disease has continued for some time, the skin of the tongue and throat hardens, inflammation sets in, and all the symptoms of a severe catarrh fever may be observed. This disease kills many birds, yet a cure may be effected if they are taken in time. The first and best method is to place the bird in a sunny room with an even temperature; rinse his bill with lukewarm and moderately salt water; grease his nostrils with sweet oil; remove his bathing vessels, and supply him with the proper food. The experiment often resorted to by bird fanciers, of placing a greased feather in his nostrils, and of permitting it to remain there for several days, is not only useless, but detrimental, as it induces inflammation of the nasal organs—an effect worse than the original disease. It is equally dangerous, though sometimes recommended, to remove the diseased skin with a knife or needle. Many who know nothing of birds act as surgeons in these cases. No one understands what possible good it can do. I can only warn you against such maltreatment. It will not be dangerous to mix some well known cough medicines with sugar and their drink. These remedies are at least harmless. The proper treatment is: let the air be warm, moist, and of an even temperature. Should catarrh suddenly supervene, a vapor bath may be given in the following manner: wrap the bird in a damp woolen cloth, and place it in close proximity to the stove. During the operation the air must be kept damp by keeping a waterpot on the stove.

Diarrhœa and Costiveness. The same treatment may be observed as in the above diseases. Should they result from colds, a warm and damp air will be better than medicines, though the last should not be neglected in connection with the sweating process. As soon as one of our favorites looks sick, his nurse should examine his excrements. From these any one skilled in birds can tell what ails the sufferer. Again, the excretory organs should be examined. In the case of a liquid excrement, the feathers will be fastened together so that excretion becomes impossible. This alone will endanger the life of the bird. The male can resist an obstruction of this kind from twenty-four to thirty hours; the female from forty to fifty hours. Both may be saved at the last moment. The bird must be taken in the hand, the adhering feathers carefully cut away with scissors, and the parts anointed with sweet oil. Internal remedies may also be supplied. For canary birds a little fat pork suspended in the cage, carrot juice, a little of the tincture of rhubarb added to the water, say six to eight drops, rotsum bi-carbonicum salt, and a little rochelle salts should be given. In cases of diarrhœa, give them in their drink about two drops of laudanum. The food must be changed, as previously directed.

Gout. This disease, to which only cage-birds are subject, has been proved to arise from colds. Some say that the gout is contagious between man and the bird. This, however, is nonsense. Suitable food, exercise in a large cage or room having plenty of the sun's rays, a good clear air, and plenty of water for bathing, are the chief and only remedies.

Reeling Disease. Among the diseases resulting from wrongly-constructed and ill-furnished cages this is the most prevalent. By this disease the regular giddiness is not meant, as the latter is caused by worms, disease of the brain, and is incurable, while the former is induced by habit. The symptoms of the disease are as follows: The bird keeps his head bent backwards, is almost constantly turning his body, as if he were endeavoring to perform a somersault; he rocks to and fro and appears as if wholly incapable of supporting his body on his legs. Ultimately this disease becomes annoying; the bird at times falls as if in fits from his perch, and remains for some minutes senseless on the floor of his cage. This disease is generally observed in birds kept in small round cages, especially when the upper perch is fixed too high in the cage. Birds afflicted with this disease can not be cured with medicines. The only remedy is their timely removal to a larger cage.

Foot Disease—(Foot Gout). Foot disease generally results from unclean cages. This disease may be prevented by carefully cleaning the floor of the cage and the perches, as well as the birds which do not bathe themselves; washing their feet, and afterwards rubbing them with glycerine, which keeps their skin soft and tender. Every bird's feet should be bathed in lukewarm water from time to time, although this may at first glance appear a useless luxury. Leave their feet at least one minute in the bath, so that all matter adhering to them may be softened; remove the dirt, and dry well with a soft cloth before the sand again touches it. In this manner the birds will enjoy the full benefit of the bath. Old and hard corns may be removed at this time. When birds have sore feet they should be well washed and then touched with caustic, nitrous acid silver. Keep the bird in the hand until the caustic is dry, then put him back in his cage. If possible, place him on a perch, on which he will remain for some time owing to the pain caused by the caustic. Many valuable birds are saved in this way.

Moulting. Moulting, strictly considered, is not a disease, but a regular and necessary change. Should, however, the bird not properly treated during the moulting season, skin and feather diseases are easily contracted. Most birds moult from July to September, many foreign birds moult twice in the year, in spring and autumn. Nothing definite can be stated with regard to the beginning and duration of the moulting season, they being irregular even for the same bird. A bird may moult one year in July, while in the following year he may not moult before August or September. An observant bird-fancier will be able to mark the moulting season of his birds, not only from the loss, but also from the growth, of their feathers. The moulting bird is not actually sick, but the change of his plumage makes him feel ill and irritable, and will disturb his regular mode of life to such a degree that he will always be sullen, nor will he sing. He always sits on the same spot, ruffles his feathers and pecks at them, with the idea of helping the growth of the young, sprouting feathers, to remove those that are no longer useful, and to grease those that have attained a sufficient size. These actions are so remarkable that the inexperienced will easily take them for the symptoms of disease. Moulting does undoubtedly require peculiar treatment, but no nonsensical quackery should be resorted to. Those who keep their birds properly need do nothing but increase the quantity and quality of their food, while those who have paid but little attention to them, and would now during the moulting season place them in a more sunny locality, or expose them to the drafts, or give them richer food, would act injudiciously. Do not, during the moulting season, change the food of your birds. Increase your attention, supply fresh food frequently, give the seed-eaters, beside their usual food, such seeds as poppy, hemp, also some eggs. To soft-eaters supply as many different sorts of insects as possible; plenty of meal-worms; give them a frequent change of bathing-water, and an abundance of clean, dry gravel in the cage; protect them from intrusion, from drafts, and from too much sunshine. It is an evil custom to carry a moulting bird to and fro, or to otherwise disturb or frighten him. When birds moult too heavily, we should suspend a cloth around their cage to protect them from draft. This I can recommend as an excellent plan. A light colored cloth must be used, as one of another color would render the cage too dark. Should these rules be observed, moulting will pass off quietly and quickly. It sometimes happens that birds in moulting lose their feathers altogether. This arises from their having caught cold, or from being kept in an overheated apartment.

Scrofulous. Such eruptions on the root of the bill and around the eyes, closing up the nostrils and injuring the eyelids, and sometimes causing blindness, are the result of uncleanliness and entire want of proper bathing arrangements. The only and best remedy for this is to wash the diseased parts several times each day with a solution of caustic; one to two grains to one ounce of water.

Bird Lice. If the bird seems to suffer from vermin, it is best to give the cage a thorough cleaning. Restlessness and moving around the cage after sunset are a sure sign that these parasites, which keep quiet during the day, are at work, and are depriving our little favorites of sleep. In a clean cage vermin seldom harbor; should they, however, be found there, it will be well to remove the cage at once. Should this not suffice they must be got rid of by other means. In winter time they can be exterminated by hanging the cage (without the bird) out of doors during a few cold nights. At other times I would advise to give the cage a thorough cleansing, washing the same with hot water; to examine the extremities of the perches carefully, and rub them with oil, as this will kill the lice. Brass cages should be sent to the factory to have them renewed and revarnished. After the cage has been well cleaned, and the bird placed in some other cage, strew its bottom with genuine Parisian insect powder. The best time for doing this is the evening. Then cover the cage well with a clean cloth. The lice will leave the bird and take refuge on the cloth. This must be removed in the morning and washed in boiling water. The process must be continued for eight days.

Worms in the Wind-pipe. The wind-pipe worm (*Syngamus Trachealis*, or *Sclerostomum Syngamus*) is one of the most terrible animals that annoy our favorite. The signs of his existence are a restless shaking of the head, opening of the bill, gasping and coughing; in short, all the symptoms of a severe catarrh. In the early stages of disease it sometimes happens that the worm is coughed out; but later, when it has settled and increased in numbers, this is impossible. These parasites increase with wonderful rapidity. Whether the disease is contagious has not been fully ascertained; it will be well, however, to keep the birds thus affected separate from the others. Unfortunately, we are acquainted with no means by which these parasites may be destroyed to a certainty. Cronon recommends to feed these birds with meal-worms soaked in olive-oil, or to directly put this oil on the wind-pipe with a quill. He says that by this means some birds have been cured.

Melancholy. The wonderful intelligence of birds affords a sufficient proof that they can suffer from depression of spirits, and even die of melancholy. The numerous instances of these facts on record leave no further doubt on the subject. Birds which have lost their mate, or have been robbed of their young, have grieved unto death; others, taken from their playmate, have fallen into a fit of dejection; others pined from missing their usual attendants. Their removal causes sadness. While so suffering, it is advantageous to dress the cage with green branches. Fresh air, sunlight, variety of food, a more roomy place for exercise, are advisable.

Mocking Birds—Are the very finest of singing birds, when we take into consideration the great variety and wonderful modulation of their notes. They will easily catch the song of any singing bird and repeat it with fidelity. Thus if the famous nightingale be placed within hearing, the mocking bird will repeat the notes with the utmost fidelity, and as a night singing bird they excel the nightingale itself. The food of the mocking bird is insects of various kinds, especially grasshoppers, fruits, ripe berries. Berries especially should be liberally supplied all during the season, and the carefully dried fruit may be softened in water and fed sparingly in winter. During the season when grasshoppers are about half grown, they may be caught in large numbers in a bag net, dried in the oven, and fed during winter, first being softened with water. A good mocking bird food, is to take sound, mealy potatoes, boiled, two-thirds, and yolk of hard-boiled eggs, one-third; mash the potatoes and then thoroughly mix with the egg. This is an excellent general food, and birds if fed also liberally on berries and insects, thrive wonderfully. Mocking birds should be supplied daily with pure water for bathing; must not be exposed to drafts of cold air, but should be kept where the air is pure and fresh. The cage should be at least thirty inches long by twenty inches wide, and if much larger it is better, since if allowed the bird will be in continual motion while singing.

STAINS.

Silver Stains, to remove. Put half a pound of glauber salts, a quarter of a pound of the chloride of lime, and eight ounces of water, into a wide-mouthed bottle, and when required for use pour some of the thick sediment into a saucer, and rub it well over the hands with pumice stone or a nail brush, and it will clean the fingers quite equal to cyanide, but without any danger. This will do to use over again until exhausted, and should be kept corked up. The disagreeable smell may be entirely avoided by the liberal use of lemon juice, which not only entirely removes the smell, but whitens the hands.

Stains, Iodine. By adding a few drops of liquid carbolic acid to the iodine tincture, the latter will not stain. According to Dr. Bogs, carbolic acid also renders the efficacy of tincture of iodine more certain.

STOPPERS, to Loosen.

Hold the hand around the neck of the bottle ten or fifteen seconds, until its warmth expands the glass of the bottle, when the stopper will move easily. If it does not, try a higher heat by means of a rag dipped in hot water and wrapped around the neck of the bottle for a minute or so. Another way is to hold the neck of the bottle, cautiously turning it so as not to expose any part too much, or to too sudden a heat, near or over a gas jet or heat from a lamp. Or rub a little salad oil, with a feather, round the stopper close to the mouth of the decanter, then place it a short distance from the fire, that the heat may cause the oil to run between the stopper and decanter. When warm, strike the stopper gently with any light wooden instrument, first on one side, then on the other; if not movable, repeat the process till you can draw the stopper out.

TEETH.

Toothache Cure. Compound tinct. benzoin is said to be one of the most certain and speedy cures for toothache; pour a few drops on cotton, and press at once into the diseased cavity, when the pain will almost instantly cease.

Toothache Tincture. Mix tannin, 1 scruple; mastic, 3 grains; ether, 2 drachms. Apply on cotton wool, to the tooth previously dried.

Austrian Tooth Powder. Powdered soap, 100 parts; chalk, 40 parts; carmine, 1 part; oil peppermint, 2½ parts; alcohol, 15 parts. Mix and dry.

Charcoal Tooth Paste. Chlorate of potash, ¼ drachm; mint water, 1 ounce. Dissolve and add powdered charcoal, 2 ounces; honey, 1 ounce.

Excellent Mouth Wash. Powdered White Castile Soap, 2 drachms; alcohol, 3 ounces; honey, 1 ounce; essence or extract jasmine, 2 drachms. Dissolve the soap in alcohol and add honey and extract.

WASHING FLUID.

Alcohol, 1 pint; spirits turpentine, 1 pint; aqua ammonia, 4f. 2 ounces. Mix: Put three or four tablespoonsful to one pint of soft soap or one pound of hard soap. The clothes should be in soak over night, if possible, before using this mixture, but if soaked an hour or two it will aid much.

Washing Fluid for Fine Linen, Laces, Etc. Borax, 4 ounces; water, 5 gallons. For crinoline or any stiff fabric increase the quantity of borax to six ounces.

WATER, Tests of.

Water Containing Iron. Dissolve a crystal of prussiate of potash in it. If it turns blue there is iron in it.

Water Containing Copper. A few drops of liquid ammonia will turn it blue if copper be present.

Water, Hard or Soft, Tests for. Dissolve a small quantity of soap in alcohol, and let fall a few drops of it into a glass of the water. If the water becomes milky it is hard, but if little or no milkiness appears the water may be said to be soft.

Water, Test for Lead. Add to the water a little sulphuret of ammonia or potash. If lead be present it will be known by the color of the water, which will have a dark brown or blackish tinge.

Gilt Articles, Test for. To ascertain whether an article is gilt or made of a gold-colored alloy, Weber uses a solution of bichloride of copper, which gives a brown spot on an alloy, but produces no effect on a surface of gold.

WEIGHTS AND MEASURES.

The following tables of weights and measures will be found valuable for reference in the household:

Apothecaries Weight, U. S.

20 grains	1 scruple.
3 scruples	1 drachm.
8 drachms	1 ounce.
12 ounces	1 pound.

Troy Weight, as used in the Pharmacopœia.

480 grains	1 ounce.
12 ounces	1 pound.

Apothecaries, or Wine Measure, U. S.

60 minims	1 fluid drachm.
8 fluid drachms	1 fluid ounce.
16 fluid ounces	1 pint.
8 pints	1 gallon.

Imperial Measure.

60 minims	1 fluid drachm.
8 fluid drachms	1 fluid ounce.
20 fluid ounces	1 pint.
8 pints	1 gallon.

Avoirdupois Weight.

Used in weighing drugs, etc., in the wholesale and retail trade, excepting prescriptions, formulæ, etc.

16 drachms	1 ounce = 437½ grains.
16 ounces	1 pound = 7,000 "

Relative Value of Apothecaries and Imperial Measure.

Apothecaries.	Imperial.
1 gallon equals...6 pints, 13 ounces, 2 drachms, 23 minims.	
1 pint " 16 " 5 " 16 "
1 fluid ounce equals 1 " 0 " 20 "
1 fluid drachm " 1 " 2½ "

Metric Weights.

10 Milligrams	1 Centigram.
10 Centigrams	1 Decigram.
10 Decigrams	1 Gram.
10 Grams	1 Dekagram.
10 Dekagrams	1 Hektogram.
10 Hektograms	1 Kilogram.

Metric Measures.

One Milliliter or Cubic Centimeter.

10 Milliliters	1 Centiliter.
10 Centiliters	1 Deciliter.
10 Deciliters	1 Liter.
10 Liters	1 Dekaliter.
10 Dekaliters	1 Hektoliter.
10 Hektoliters	1 Kiloliter.

Metric Lengths.

10 Millimeters	1 Centimeter.
10 Centimeters	1 Decimeter.
10 Decimeters	1 Meter.
10 Meters	1 Dekameter.
10 Dekameters	1 Hektometer.
10 Hektometers	1 Kilometer.

Metric Weights and Measures Equivalents.

1 Gram	1 Cubic Centimeter.
1 Gram, 15 grs	15 Minims.
4 Grams, 1 drachm	1 fluid drachm.
1 Milligram	1.65 gr. or Minim.
1 Centigram	2-18 gr. or Minim.
1 Decigram	1½ grs. or Minims.
1 Gram	15.4 grs. or Minims.
1 Dekagram	154 grs. or Minims.
1 Hektogram	1543 grs. or Minims.
1 Kilogram	2 1-5 lbs. Avoirdupois.
1 Cubic Centimeter	15 Minims.
1 Cubic Centimeters	1 f. drachm.
16 Cubic Centimeters	half an ounce.
32 Cubic Centimeters	one ounce.

Metric Length Equivalents.

1 Millimeter	.039 inch.
1 Centimeter	.39 inch.
1 Decimeter	3.9 inches.
1 Meter	39.37 inches.
1 Dekameter	32¾ feet.
1 Hectometer	328¼ feet.
1 Kilometer	1089 yards.

Domestic and Drop Measures Approximated.

A teaspoonful, one fluid drachm	4 grams.
A dessertspoonful, two fluid drachms	3 grams.
A tablespoonful, half fluid ounce	16 grams.
A wineglassful, two fluid ounces	64 grams.
A tumblerful, half pint	256 grams.

Weights of Oils to Gallon of Measure.

Sperm Oil	6¾ lbs. Avoirdupois.
Paraffine	6¾ lbs. Avoirdupois.
Olive Oil	7 lbs. Avoirdupois.
Cod Liver Oil	7¼ lbs. Avoirdupois.
Whale W. B.	7¼ lbs. Avoirdupois.
Lard Oil	7½ lbs. Avoirdupois.
Castor Oil	7½ lbs. Avoirdupois.
Linseed Oil	7½ lbs. Avoirdupois.

SUPPLEMENT.

CEREALS

BARLEY. This crop is one of restricted area and use. It is not sufficiently abundant or cheap to take the place of corn or other cattle grains, and is not used except in a very limited way in competition with other breadstuffs. California, however, is a local exception to this statement, producing more than a fourth of the crop and using it extensively in feeding. New York, the Northwest and the Pacific coast region produce nearly all of this grain. The crop of 1886 was a full average, or over twenty-two bushels per acre, and the product nearly 60,000,000 bushels. The following statement shows the course of production and values since 1880:

Calendar Years.	Total Production.	Total Area of Crop.	Total Value of Crop.
	Bushels.	Acres.	Dollars.
1880	45,165,346	1,843,329	30,090,742
1881	41,161,330	1,967,510	33,862,513
1882	48,953,926	2,272,103	30,768,015
1883	50,136,097	2,379,009	29,420,423
1884	61,208,000	2,608,816	29,779,170
1885	58,360,000	2,729,359	32,867,696
Total	304,979,699	13,800,126	186,788,559
Annual average	50,829,950	2,300,021	31,131,427
Annual average for preceding ten years	33,704,652	1,529,357	24,885,505

BUCKWHEAT. Buckwheat is the smallest in value of our cereal crops. The reason can only be that farmers consider it an undesirable crop; in some respects it is so—the scattered seed is apt to come up the next season and hence

Calendar Years.	Total Production	Total Area of Crop.	Total Value of Crop.
	Bushels.	Acres.	Dollars.
1880	14,617,535	822,802	8,683,488
1881	9,486,200	828,615	9,305,705
1882	11,019,353	847,112	8,036,862
1883	7,668,954	857,349	6,303,080
1884	11,116,000	879,403	6,549,020
1885	12,626,000	914,394	7,057,363
Total	66,534,042	5,149,675	44,537,418
Annual Average	11,089,007	858,313	7,472,903
Annual average for preceding ten years	9,747,272	551,104	6,972,974

the slack farmer considers it as a weed. The sagacious man sows some buckwheat, yearly, in all that region where the seed will ripen during the cool nights of Autumn. The East, the West and Northwest are generally adapted to the crop; but as we go west, beyond the Mississippi, the crop is less and less valuable. In 1886 the crop was light, scarcely 10,000,000 bushels. The crop of 1887 will probably be found lighter still from the great drought of that year. The foregoing table gives the record for the series of years named.

CEREAL PRODUCTS, EXTENSION AND AREA OF. The reading of statistics to the thinking man sometimes reveals marvelous changes. The increase in productive capacity of the United States is shown from the fact, as stated in the Report of the Commissioner of Agriculture, that, while the number of people in 1880 were more than double those of 1850, the production of cereals not only kept pace with population, but furnished fifty-three bushels for each inhabitant in place of thirty-eight of the earlier date. With an increase of seven millions of people in the first half of the present decade, the aggregate of cereals exceeded 3,000,000,000 bushels in 1885, still keeping up the extraordinary rate of supply attained in 1880, and showing in wheat a product five times as large as in 1850, a corn crop nearly four times as large. The year 1886 was one of medium productiveness, with less corn and more wheat than in 1885, or nearly 1,700,000,000 bushels of corn, and something more than 450,000,000 bushels of wheat. The recent extension of area and product has been remarkable, as shown by a comparison of the averages of the decade between 1870 and 1880, and those of the six years of the present decade, as follows:

Cereal.	1870–1879.		1880–1885.	
	Acres.	Bushels.	Acres.	Bushels.
Corn	43,741,381	1,184,486,954	67,225,872	1,685,357,755
Wheat	25,187,414	312,152,728	37,147,276	446,163,098
Oats	11,075,822	314,441,178	19,320,530	517,526,065
Rye	1,305,061	18,460,935	2,094,438	25,610,067
Barley	1,529,357	33,704,652	2,300,021	50,829,950
Buckwheat	551,104	9,747,272	858,313	11,089,007
All cereals	83,391,089	1,872,993,769	128,947,550	2,686,875,942

SUPPLEMENT.

CEREALS

BARLEY. This crop is one of restricted area and use. It is not sufficiently abundant or cheap to take the place of corn or other cattle grains, and is not used except in a very limited way in competition with other breadstuffs. California, however, is a local exception to this statement, producing more than a fourth of the crop and using it extensively in feeding. New York, the Northwest and the Pacific coast region produce nearly all of this grain. The crop of 1886 was a full average, or over twenty-two bushels per acre, and the product nearly 60,000,000 bushels. The following statement shows the course of production and values since 1880:

Calendar Years.	Total Production.	Total Area of Crop.	Total Value of Crop.
	Bushels.	Acres.	Dollars.
1880	45,165,346	1,843,329	30,000,742
1881	41,161,330	1,967,510	33,802,513
1882	48,953,946	2,272,103	30,768,015
1883	50,136,097	2,379,009	29,420,423
1884	61.203,000	2,608,816	29,779,170
1885	58,360,000	2,729,359	32,867.696
Total	304,979,699	13,800,126	186,788,559
Annual average	50,829,950	2,300,021	31,131,427
Annual average for preceding ten years	33,704,652	1,529,357	24,885,505

BUCKWHEAT. Buckwheat is the smallest in value of our cereal crops. The reason can only be that farmers consider it an undesirable crop; in some respects it is so—the scattered seed is apt to come up the next season and hence

Calendar Years.	Total Production	Total Area of Crop.	Total Value of Crop.
	Bushels.	Acres.	Dollars.
1880	14,517,535	822,809	8,682,468
1881	9,486,200	828,615	8,905,705
1882	11,010,353	847,112	8,036,862
1883	7,668,954	857,349	6,303,980
1884	11,116,000	879,403	6,549,020
1885	12,626,000	914,394	7,057,363
Total	66,534,042	5,149,875	44,837,418
Annual Average	11,089,007	858,313	7,472,903
Annual average for preceding ten years	9,747,272	551,104	6,972,974

the slack farmer considers it as a weed. The sagacious man sows some buckwheat, yearly, in all that region where the seed will ripen during the cool nights of Autumn. The East, the West and Northwest are generally adapted to the crop; but as we go west, beyond the Mississippi, the crop is less and less valuable. In 1886 the crop was light, scarcely 10,000,000 bushels. The crop of 1887 will probably be found lighter still from the great drought of that year. The foregoing table gives the record for the series of years named.

CEREAL PRODUCTS, EXTENSION AND AREA OF. The reading of statistics to the thinking man sometimes reveals marvelous changes. The increase in productive capacity of the United States is shown from the fact, as stated in the Report of the Commissioner of Agriculture, that, while the number of people in 1880 were more than double those of 1850, the production of cereals not only kept pace with population, but furnished fifty-three bushels for each inhabitant in place of thirty-eight at the earlier date. With an increase of seven millions of people in the first half of the present decade, the aggregate of cereals exceeded 3,000,000,000 bushels in 1885, still keeping up the extraordinary rate of supply attained in 1880, and showing in wheat a product five times as large as in 1850, a corn crop nearly four times as large. The year 1886 was one of medium productiveness, with less corn and more wheat than in 1885, or nearly 1,700,000,000 bushels of corn, and something more than 450,000,000 bushels of wheat. The recent extension of area and product has been remarkable, as shown by a comparison of the averages of the decade between 1870 and 1880, and those of the six years of the present decade, as follows:

Cereal.	1870–1879.		1880–1885.	
	Acres.	Bushels.	Acres.	Bushels.
Corn	43,741,331	1,184,486,954	67,225,872	1,835,357,755
Wheat	25,187,414	312,152,723	37,147,276	446,163,098
Oats	11,076,823	314,441,178	19,320,630	517,826,065
Rye	1,305,061	18,460,985	2,094,438	25,610,087
Barley	1,529,357	33,704,652	2,300,021	50,829,950
Buckwheat	551,104	9,747,272	858,313	11,089,007
All cereals	83,391,089	1,872,993,769	128,947,550	2,886,875,943

The increase of production, in this brief period, is over 43 per cent., while the enlargement of area is still greater, amounting to 54 per cent. This advance was attained in a series of years with a comparatively low rate of yield, including the unfavorable seasons of 1881 and 1883.

According to *The Cotton World* there was about double the land devoted to corn, wheat and oats in the Southern States in 1887 that was planted in cotton, and the value of the cereal production of these States was in excess of that of the cotton crop. In round figures there were 85,000,000 acres planted in corn last year, against 18,500,000 in cotton. The corn crop of the South in 1887 was worth over $200,000,000, and if that portion of it which was converted into meal be taken into consideration, it would doubtless be found that the corn-crib now furnishes more wealth than the cotton-gin even in the extreme Southern States.

The wheat production of India, which has been a bugbear to many in this country and Europe, is not likely to produce any extraordinary increase. For the past four years the crop has averaged 262,937,511 bushels, but the crop of 1884–5 was 80,000,000 bushels, and that of 1885–6 was 20,000,000 bushels more than the crop of 1886–7. The area under wheat remains year after year pretty uniformly about 27,000,000 acres.

CEREAL GRAINS, EXTENSION OF CANADA. The crops of Ontario and Manitoba constitute the great bulk of the cereal wealth of the Canadian provinces of Great Britain. The following table shows acres, bushels and yield per acre for Ontario for a series of years, and also the crops for 1887, as given by the Bureau of Statistics, the same being total averages:

the four years 1883–'86, and the average yield per acre for each of the two periods. The average yields per acre given for the periods 1883–'86, in wheat, oats and barley are from the returns made by thrashers, in the other crops during the two periods the yields are made up from the returns of the regular crop correspondents of the Manitoba department of agriculture.

CORN. The subject of Indian corn is extensively treated on pages 613 to 617. The area planted in 1887 was increased more than 2,000,000 acres over that of the previous year, or nearly 78,000,000 acres. The disastrous season of drought reduced this acreage to 72,393,720 acres. It also reduced the yield to twenty bushels per acre. Yet the actual value per acre was greater than since 1884. Thus we see that it is not always the greatest yield that gives the most money to the farmer. The following table will show the status of the crop and development from 1880 to 1887:

Years.	Total Production.	Total Area of Crop.	Total Value of Crop.
	Bushels.	Acres.	Dollars.
1880	1,717,434,543	62,317,842	679,714,499
1881	1,194,916,000	64,262,025	759,482,170
1882	1,617,025,100	65,659,546	783,867,175
1883	1,551,066,895	68,301,889	658,051,485
1884	1,795,528,000	69,683,780	640,735,360
1885	1,936,176,000	73,130,150	635,674,630
1886	1,665,441,000	75,694,208	510,311,000
1887	1,456,161,000	72,392,720	546,106,770
Total	12,933,748,538	551,442,160	5,413,943,299
Annual average	1,616,718,567	68,930,270	676,742,911
Annual average for preceding ten years	1,184,486,954	43,741,331	504,571,043

Crops.	1887.			1882–'87.		
	Total Area.	Total Yield.	Yield per Acre.	Area.	Average Yield.	Average Yield per Acre.
	Acres.	Bushels.	Bushels.	Acres.	Bushels.	Bushels.
Rye	68,362	894,867	13.1	115,206	1,700,115	14.8
Corn (in ear)	162,893	8,404,792	51.5	173,307	11,261,501	64.8
Buckwheat	64,143	1,025,353	16.0	62,516	1,396,456	22.3
Beans	20,275	275,975	13.6	22,133	451,313	20.4
Potatoes	140,283	10,878,000	75.1	155,075	18,360,115	117.6
Mangel-wurzels	17,924	5,695,761	317.8	17,313	7,460,475	430.9
Carrots	9,110	2,105,686	231.1	9,936	3,539,728	355.3
Turnips	105,322	30,513,486	289.7	98,001	36,059,549	388.4
		Tons.	Tons.		Tons.	Tons.
Hay and Clover	2,250,643	3,063,610	1.36	2,202,352	3,098,547	1.41

The table below gives statistics for Manitoba, of the estimated area and yield of the leading crops for the reported average area and yield for

The home consumption of this eight-year period was about 27.5 bushels per capita, an increase over that of the ten years previous of 2.5

Crops.	1887.			1883–'86.		
	Total Area.	Total Yield.	Yield per Acre.	Area.	Average Yield.	Average Yield per Acre.
	Acres.	Bushels.	Bushels.	Acres.	Bushels.	Bushels.
Wheat	432,134	12,351,724	27.7	316,903	6,141,580	19.3
Oats	155,176	7,255,237	46.2	155,851	5,083,859	32.6
Barley	66,110	1,925,231	36.3	52,707	1,278,144	24.2
Peas	872	16,680	20.5	2,969	51,101	17.2
Flax	8,539	163,572	15.3	11,534	197,554	13.6
Potatoes	10,791	2,510,086	233.0	11,508	2,250,982	194.0
		Tons.	Tons.		Tons.	Tons.
Hay		265,896	1.67		282,204	1.77

bushels, or a ten per cent. increase. The constantly increasing area planted keeps the price from increasing; nevertheless, the man who converts his corn into meat, milk, butter and cheese, is the wise man, for only in very bad years can money be made in selling corn. So far as export goes, the amount is so insignificant in comparison to the total yield—about one per cent.—that it will at once be seen that the legitimate use for the crop is for feeding purposes. The table below shows the total acres, bushels and values of Indian corn for 1887 by States, as well as the grand totals:

States and Territories.	Acres.	Bushels.	Value.
Maine	32,165	1,132,000	$769,760
New Hampshire	38,678	1,323,000	912,870
Vermont	62,001	2,204,000	1,498,720
Massachusetts	59,997	2,124,000	1,486,800
Rhode Island	12,046	414,000	290,800
Connecticut	58,140	1,977,000	1,324,590
New York	706,406	23,410,000	13,343,700
New Jersey	346,866	10,406,000	5,723,300
Pennsylvania	1,394,561	44,905,000	22,452,500
Delaware	216,595	4,332,000	1,862,760
Maryland	719,073	19,415,000	8,736,750
Virginia	2,153,126	37,680,000	17,709,600
North Carolina	2,673,910	85,830,000	21,139,700
South Carolina	1,501,322	15,013,000	9,308,060
Georgia	2,915,140	32,067,000	20,202,210
Florida	454,306	4,816,000	3,419,300
Alabama	2,464,827	33,522,000	18,101,880
Mississippi	1,866,319	32,633,000	17,295,490
Louisiana	1,001,226	18,022,000	9,191,290
Texas	4,499,405	76,490,000	39,009,900
Arkansas	2,068,349	41,367,000	20,683,500
Tennessee	3,497,848	75,204,000	37,602,000
West Virginia	658,755	12,516,000	6,758,640
Kentucky	3,160,668	57,840,000	30,685,200
Ohio	2,805,961	71,400,000	35,422,560
Michigan	841,816	18,930,000	9,086,400
Indiana	3,569,094	71,400,000	32,130,000
Illinois	7,347,915	141,080,000	57,842,800
Wisconsin	1,018,776	25,775,000	10,825,500
Minnesota	812,750	19,081,000	6,689,970
Iowa	7,196,148	183,502,000	64,225,700
Missouri	8,406,785	140,949,000	52,151,130
Kansas	6,242,979	76,547,000	28,322,390
Nebraska	3,865,158	93,150,000	27,945,000
California	156,752	4,708,000	2,868,830
Oregon	6,673	182,000	116,480
Nevada	863	24,000	14,880
Colorado	31,207	938,000	590,940
Arizona	3,111	59,000	38,350
Dakota	636,120	20,992,000	7,347,200
Idaho	1,989	56,000	33,600
Montana	906	25,000	15,000
New Mexico	51,056	970,000	698,400
Utah	13,197	285,000	213,750
Washington	3,375	74,000	49,580
Total	72,352,720	1,456,161,000	$646,106,770

The United States Statistician, Mr. Dodge, says in relation to the crops, that, "with a steady increase of area, amounting to about 20 per cent. since 1879, the product of this year is the smallest of the series, excepting only that of 1881. It is less by 9.9 per cent. than the average for the period. This average product of eight years is 16.6 per cent. larger than that of the ten years preceding." (See also pages 613–617.)

COTTON. This has always been considered an exhausting crop to the land. There is no reason why this should be when only the lint is used. The real reason for impoverishment, from cropping, is undoubtedly the land lying bare to washing rains in winter, and without the proper rotation of crops. The cotton crop of 1887 can not be more than approximately given since the real totals are not known for a year after the crop is gathered. It may be stated at 6,806,150 bales on 18,614,067 acres. The table below will give the figures for 1880 to 1885, namely:

Years.	Acres.	Bales.	Per Acre.
1880	15,475,300	6,605,750	.427
1881	16,249,065	5,456,048	.336
1882	16,276,691	6,949,756	.427
1883	16,777,993	5,713,200	.841
1884	17,439,612	5,706,165	.327
1885	18,300,865	6,575,691	.359
Total	100,519,526	37,006,610	.368

(See also page 243.)

The next table gives the total by States for 1887:

States.	Acres.	Bales.	Pounds per Acre.
Virginia	40,331	12,907	147
North Carolina	1,066,301	394,531	170
South Carolina	1,622,185	583,947	169
Georgia	2,941,486	867,738	141
Florida	262,616	68,280	81
Alabama	2,809,599	800,355	143
Mississippi	2,548,074	973,593	181
Louisiana	1,066,854	461,948	210
Texas	3,900,327	1,318,786	170
Arkansas	1,388,058	527,600	187
Tennessee	855,709	205,298	153
Missouri	78,234	25,035	155
Total	18,641,067	6,306,150	164

DAIRYING. Modern dairying has fully kept pace with other modern improvements in farm processes. In the making of butter, to-day, if cleanliness is exercised all the way from the milking-stool to the packing of the butter, and thence forward, the butter does not go above 60° Fahrenheit in the place of storage. Thus, if kept from contact of air, the butter will keep sweet, if it has been eliminated of everything but the fat and the salt necessary to bring it to the popular taste, whether the number of cows be five, fifty or more. This has been made possible by the use of tanks submerged in cold water for the raising of cream. These are what are known as the Cooley process, the cabinet creamery, and others of like nature, which take up but little space, and being encased, may be kept anywhere where it is fairly cool and not subject to a foul atmosphere. A step has also been taken in advance of the old way of churning. The temperature of the cream, the ripening having been proper, is now considered of importance. It should go into the churn at about 58° in summer and at 60° in winter. When the butter forms granules in the churn, of the size of small shot, the churning is discontinued and the buttermilk having been drawn off, very cold water is added to cool down the mass. This is slightly agitated, and drawn off when a little saturated brine is added. The butter is then taken from the churn, and the water carefully pressed out, wiping the butter worker from time to time, and also drying the moisture from the butter with a pure linen cloth free from lint. The butter is then salted at the rate of one-half an ounce (or somewhat more), to the pound of butter according to the taste of the consumers in the particular market in which it is sold. The science of getting the most money from butter, now, is not in packing down for winter use, but to send it to market, kept perfectly cool, and, also, kept in cold storage until sold. Thus, whatever good flavor was originally in the butter will be measurably preserved; and, it should be remembered, if the flavor is bad it will get no better. In the body of the work among other interesting matter will be found a table showing the pounds of butter and cheese, and the value of the product at intervals from 1790 to 1859, and thence forward yearly up to 1878. The table below, for which we are indebted to Mr. R. Lespinasse, Secretary of the Illinois Dairymen's Association, will show at a glance, the aggregate value of dairy products for each succeeding ten years from 1850 to 1870; for 1877, and thence forward to 1887. The table is as follows:

VALUE OF DAIRY PRODUCTS.

1850	$163,565,700 00	1881	$407,163,127 60
1860	254,546,309 00	1882	540,000,000 00
1870	280,363,600 00	1883	527,083,976 93
1877	327,800,000 00	1884	575,000,000 00
1878	350,000,000 00	1885	541,563,800 00
1879	427,800,000 00	1886	560,000,000 00
1880	440,622,600 00	1887	564,985,900 00

This table is curious in some respects. It shows the gradual increase of the dairy interests up to 1881, and between that and 1882, a great jump in value; in 1883, a decided decrease; in 1884, another large increase in value, for 1884 and 1885; following in 1886 by a decrease; the value for 1887 being less than in 1884. It is true, without doubt, that our dairy interests have now settled down to that basis where the name and reputation of the maker of butter and cheese must be the test of value at home and abroad. The time has passed when adulterated and inferior goods can be sneaked on the sharp sense of expert buyers, either for home use or export. The export of dairy products forms an essential integer in agricultural values. They are no less interesting as showing fluctuations. The table given below will show the whole matter in a nut shell, from 1881 to 1887, inclusive, and was kindly furnished by Col. R. M. Littler, Secretary Chicago Produce Exchange. The table is as follows:

EXPORTS OF BUTTER AND CHEESE FROM THE UNITED STATES.
—YEARS ENDING JUNE 30.

Years.	BUTTER.		CHEESE.	
	Pounds.	Value.	Pounds.	Value.
1881	31,560,000	$6,255,000	147,995,000	$14,380,000
1882	14,794,000	2,864,000	127,989,000	14,058,000
1883	12,358,000	2,290,000	92,200,000	11,134,000
1884	20,621,000	3,749,000	112,840,000	11,663,000
1885	21,583,000	3,643,000	111,092,000	10,444,000
1886	18,953,000	2,958,000	91,877,000	7,882,000
1887	12,76,0000	2,050,000	88,835,000	6,358,000

ENSILAGE AND SILOS. Since the introduction of ensilage into the United States, its importance and value, especially to the dairyman, was early and carefully examined. Year by year its value came more and more to be acknowledged until now there are few who have tried it but testify to its economy and value. The writer, as long ago as 1869, eight years before other attempts had been made in the United States to preserve green fodder in pits, succeeded perfectly in so preserving beet tops. In November of that year a pit was dug eight feet square and deep, in stiff clay upon a knoll where there was no danger of seepage of water. Into this the beet tops were thrown and tramped thoroughly and constantly while being filled. The pit was filled and the material piled up about three feet above the surface. Two feet of earth was then thrown over all and the whole again carefully tramped. When settled, in a few days, additional earth was cast on, well beaten down, and the pit was then left until the middle of February. Upon being opened, the ensilage was found blackened somewhat next the upper sides of the pit, and on the top it was blackened for about four inches in depth. This of course hermetically sealed the remainder, and it came out" in perfect condition—what the German workmen on the farm called "wine sour." The stock to which it was fed ate it greedily. This crude effort, therefore, demonstrated the fact that fodder could thus be measurably well saved. Previous to this time, however, M. Goffert had experimented in France. In 1873 he obtained real success. In 1876 Mr. Francis Morris, of Maryland, bricked up three silos inside his stone barn, each ten feet deep, four feet wide, and twenty-four feet long. It was filled by tramping during the filling. If the silo had been a single pit, it would have been better. Nevertheless, the inference is, it was fairly successful, since the record shows that although some animals refused it at first, yet when once tasted all farm animals consumed it. These two experiments, therefore, may be considered as the first successful attempts in the United States to cure fodder in its green state. The experiment of Mr. Periam, of Illinois, in 1869, is undoubtedly the first fairly successful attempt, either in Europe or America. Since this time, the saving of ensilage in pits, has been constantly improved on, both in the cost of the silo and the labor of preparing and putting in the crop. Within the last three years, the extension of silos, especially in the East and West, has been wonderful; and in the South this means of saving forage for winter is also receiving attention, especially in Maryland, Virginia, Tennessee and Kentucky. In the East many expensive structures have been erected and costly appliances used. In the West, so far, wooden silos with double walls have given the best satisfaction. It has come now also to be generally conceded that Indian corn is the cheapest fodder, and when cut into one-inch lengths, at the time when the small ears produced by thick planting are in the stage where glazing of the kernel has taken place, the most satisfactory results are reached. Many practical men have also found that partially wilted corn is better than that containing the full amount of sap, and also that filling from time to time to allow settling, allowing the heat of the silo to rise to 130° to 140° Fahrenheit, destroys bacterial germs that, in the presence of air, may cause putrefactive degeneration, one of the most dangerous forms that can attack ensilage. This, however, is only the case where the cruder forms of silos are erected. In England, fair success has been attained in stacking green fodder compactly in the open air, and weighting the whole heavily. The mild, moist climate there seems to prevent undue access of air to the stack. In the United States this means cannot be used, since our strong autumn winds and dry atmosphere will act against success. Ensilage is a French word, the meaning being to preserve watery foods by compressing in air-tight pits to prevent access to air, and hence undue fermentation. The French word, silo, is the place for holding these substances. The canning or putting any substance in sealed jars, for preserving green fruits or vegetables, is simply a most perfect manner of saving such foods Hence the soldered can or sealed jar may be called a miniature silo, and the product ensilage. It is not necessary to enter further into an argument to prove the value of ensilage. It has proved itself to be most valuable. In the East, silos of stone or brick seem yet to be the rule. In the West, wooden silos meet with most favor. However built, we advocate that it should communicate directly with the feeding stable, and if the lay of the land is right, the preference would be that it may be eight feet below and four to six feet above ground. Above this may be a permanent roof, and a room for storage of many things when the silo is not being filled. In this case the upper portion may be banked against with the excavated earth. On the side next the stable should be double doors, as security against frost, for ease in emptying the silo, and inside all should be planks, fitting into an inset or groove, removable at pleasure, as the ensilage is taken out. It is also preferable, we think, that the bottom be water tight, with a drainage pipe, ⌒ formed, with the outer end open to the air. The sides should be of stone or brick, laid in water cement, and strong enough to resist the pressure of the ensilage, smoothly plastered within. The superstructure may be of timber and lumber. The ensilage will weigh about fifty pounds per cubic foot. Thus the dimensions of the silo will be easily calculated for the desired number of cattle to be fed. The simplest silos of wood have been estimated as low as fifty cents per ton, and the more elaborate as high as five dollars per ton of material contained. Any material that stock will eat in summer makes good ensilage for winter—clover, alfalfa, millet, Hungarian grass, sorghum, etc.—but when the large leafy Southern corn will mature to come into roasting ears before frost, this will be found the cheapest material. Any material, however, is better when so nearly ripe as to contain its normal quantity of sap; corn, for instance, at that time when the grain is fairly glazed. Opinions vary as to the relative value per acre as between ensilage and the dry product. Mr. Hiram Smith, of Wisconsin, than whom there are few more practical men, after using ensilage for dairy cows, believes in it, and believes in corn for this purpose. He puts it in the silo just when the corn begins to glaze. The proper length for cutting the writer believes to be in one-inch lengths, using buts and all of the corn. The corn ensilage is estimated all the way up to 30 or 40 per cent. above the value of corn cut up and dried. The relative value of other material is estimated lower and lower until we come to clover, which shows a relatively small per cent. of value ensilaged, over the crops cut and cured dry in the best possible manner. But then it must be remembered, that perfectly cured clover is the most digestible of fodder crops, and curing without loss is most difficult. Siloing is undoubtedly the cheapest as it is the best means of securing all coarse fodders, like Indian corn and the larger growths of the sorghum tribe. In relation to the value of ensilage East, the following is reported as coming from Hon. George B. Loring, ex-Commissioner of Agriculture of the United States, and whose home is in Massachusetts: "I know of six silos in my immediate vicinity at Salem. I think they all give perfect satisfaction. They have been in use from four to seven years. They are esteemed more and more highly as time goes on, and none so far as I know have been abandoned. The users of ensilage have made no other change of feeding than is involved in a new system. The cultivation of corn for ensilage has undoubtedly improved since the system of silos was first adopted. It is found that immature corn fodder and frost-bitten stalks do not make good ensilage. The corn grown in this section is the white Virginia corn which grows to great height and size. It is the best plant known to me for ensilage purposes, and, according to my judgment and experience, far excels green rye or clover, or any other crop. Of the economy of the silo for those who are engaged in feeding cattle during the winter months, for any purpose whatever, there can be no doubt. The adoption of the silos constitutes an era in the agriculture of this country. Ensilage should be fed morning and evening with a supply of grain, the intermediate feed at noon being hay. It is a good substitute for roots, of which I have fed large quantities; and while it preserves the health of the animals it increases in milch cows the flow of milk. I suppose ten acres of well-grown corn ensilage will feed forty cows in the way I have suggested through the winter months—if it is well cultivated and of a good variety. A silo well managed makes all the difference to the farmer between consuming his entire hay-crop and having hay to sell. A silo built of wood is better than a silo built of stone and cement; and if it is placed in the bays of the barn, and built from the cellar bottom to the plates it can be constructed with great economy." This brings us to the question of silos of wood. The studding should be of 2 x 6, or 2 x 8 stuff, according to the size of the silo. It should be boarded outside and in with matched plank, and then, preferably, lined inside with tarred building paper. For taking out the ensilage there should be movable plank, as heretofore stated. To facilitate filling, the owner must be guided by circumstances. A horse power will furnish means of cutting the fodder, though steam would be preferable, and the straw carrier of a thrashing machine will be found a practical means of elevating the cut material. Professor W. A. Henry, Director of the Experiment Station, University of Wisconsin, at Madison, is well known for his conservative ideas and careful conclusions. Considering the extreme care and, of course, cost in preserving the corn fodder, the conclusions arrived at are distinctly in favor of ensilage; for it is well known that as generally saved in the field, corn fodder has but little value as food, compared with that of the fresh, green stalks and leaves. In fact the leaf surface of dried stalks is the principal valuable portions of the fodder. In the fourth annual report of the Wisconsin Agricultural Experiment Station, Professor Henry makes public the following: "The ensilage and fodder corn of the two trials here reported were made by taking an equal number of rows of fodder corn for each lot and shocking one part and cutting and putting the other into a small silo made for the purpose. The varieties were dent corn, sweet corn and southern ensilage corn in equal amounts by weight. The pit in which the ensilage was kept was a small one, made for the purpose of boards and building paper. Most of the ensilage made by slow filling was of excellent quality, having that sweet smell characteristic of good ensilage, but here and there through the mass was a patch of mould. This was carefully separated and only good ensilage fed. It seems much more difficult to keep ensilage in small quantities than in large bulk. The fodder corn was stored in the barn after it was cured, and was run through the fodder cutter and made fine for feeding. We had then, it will be noted, ensilage and dry fodder corn from the same field in the same proportions and each cut up fine for feeding trial. Four fresh cows were selected, placed two and two, and one lot fed ensilage and the other corn fodder for twenty-two days. At the close of this trial the feeds were reversed and the trial repeated for twenty-two days. The first seven days of each trial were thrown out as preliminary feeding, and only the data of the last fifteen days of each trial here reported. It was deemed advisable not to feed the cows a heavy grain ration, as by so doing we might conceal the real value of coarse food; accordingly each cow received daily only two pounds of corn meal and four pounds of bran, fed dry in two feeds. As much fodder and ensilage was fed as the cows would eat up without waste, but no more. The milk and butter from each lot was saved separately, and is given in the accompanying tables. The trial began November 20, 1886." The tables give the data of the two trials in a condensed form:

pounds of milk from fodder were required for one pound of butter. The fodder and ensilage were sampled for analysis, but only the amounts of water were determined. The analysis shows:

Water in ensilage as fed.................. 79.28 per cent.
Solids in ensilage as fed .... 20.82 per cent.
Water in fodder as fed.................... 44.15 per cent.
Solids in fodder as fed .... 55.85 per cent.

From this it will be found that there was fed 932.87 pounds of dry matter in the corn fodder and 942.86 pounds of dry matter in the ensilage. Ignoring the grain fed, we have as the value of the dry matter the following:

16.11 lbs. dry matter in corn fodder=1 lb. butter.
15.69 lbs. dry matter in ensilage=1 lb. butter.

It will be noted that practically equal results were obtained with fodder corn and ensilage in this case. The results, it is true, are slightly in favor of ensilage, but the difference falls within what is styled in the laboratory, "the limits of error." The fall of 1886 was with us, says Professor Henry, on the whole the most favorable for curing fodder we had seen since coming into the State seven years ago. The fodder, when dried, was taken to the barn and reshocked on an upper floor. As it had not suffered in the least from storms before being taken to the barn, it may be said to have been in perfect condition. While this is just as it should have been for experimental work, it is quite different in practice. Had we compared ensilage with fodder corn brought from the field in winter with many of the leaves blackened by rains and the stalks full of frozen moisture, we would not have been able to show such excellent results for fodder as we have done in this case. Coming now to the

RESULT OF FEEDING ENSILAGE.

	Feed Consumed.			Product.	
	Ensilage.	Bran.	Corn Meal.	Milk.	Butter.
	Lbs.	Lbs.	Lbs.	Lbs. Oz.	Lbs. Oz.
Lot I. Emma and Rose, 15 days	2,294½	120	60	696 11	26 5
Lot II. Sylvia and Palmer, 15 days	2,256	120	60	585 11	33 12
Total, 4 cows, 15 days each....	4,550½	240	120	1,282 6	60 1

RESULT OF FEEDING CORN FODDER.

	Feed Consumed.			Product.	
	Corn Fodder.	Bran.	Corn Meal.	Milk.	Butter.
	Lbs.	Lbs.	Lbs.	Lbs. Oz.	Lbs. Oz.
Lot II. Sylvia and Palmer......	955	120	60	625 10	31 10
Lot I. Emma and Rose........	735	120	60	619 1	26 4
Total, 4 cows, 15 days each....	1,690	240	120	1,244 11	57 14

Simplifying results, we have:

1,690 lbs. corn fodder plus 360 lbs. bran and corn meal equal 1,234 lbs., 11 oz. milk, equal 57 lbs., 14 oz. butter.
1,550 lbs. ensilage plus 380 lbs. bran and corn meal equal 1,282 lbs., 6 oz. milk, equal 60 lbs., 1 oz. butter.
Excess in favor of ensilage, 37 lbs., 11 oz. milk, 2 lbs. 3 oz. butter.

This shows there was obtained about 3 per cent. more milk and butter by feeding ensilage than from feeding the same material in the shape of corn fodder, cut fine with the feed cutter; 21.8 pounds of milk from ensilage, and 21.7

proper filling of the silo, it used to be the plan to fill quickly, tramping as hard as possible. The plan now generally adopted in the West, is to fill so slowly that the temperature of the material reaches 130° to 140°, and to so fill that the temperature is kept at this point until the silo is full. Thus bacterial germs are killed, the air is pressed out, and heat and vapor take the place of air. The silo then being filled and properly weighted, after covering with boards, tarred paper and leaves or sawdust to exclude air, the silo may be considered safe until wanted for use. There are various patented devices for accomplishing the exclusion of air and governing temperature. The matter here given will, we think, practically cover essentials, economically considered. We have already spoken of stacked green crops, as practiced in England. It is not there considered the best way of making ensilage, nevertheless the results show conclusively the value of this system there, and of course the profit would be far greater where the ensilage could be more perfectly saved. Leaving out the carefully tabulated elaboration of the whole matter, and this includes milk fed to young calves, for the animal was fed during the whole life of the individual, including the fattening as conducted by the Ensilage Press Company of England, the conclusions are as stated, the money value being English coin — as follows: "The silage used consisted chiefly of what is commonly called the sweet, green sort, made by cutting the crop young, and keeping the temperature of the stack between 130° and 140° Fahr. The temperature can be regulated by means of pressure. The experiment began when the calf was from four to five months old; and during the time he was having milk, three other calves were reared with him, and the quantity of new milk allowed for in the estimate is probably rather in excess of the quantity actually given. The amount of silage allowed for as consumed is in every case the amount weighed for a week together at the end of each period. For instance, the twenty-eight pounds given as being the amount consumed during the first three months is what it was found he was eating at the time he was six months old. The amount of cake may be taken as what was actually consumed by the steer. The amount allowed for labor and bedding is an estimate, but considering that the silage was given whole and merely shaken up when taken from the stack, 6d per week would be sufficient to cover this expense. The same with the bedding if moss litter is used. How much should be charged to the steer, and how much allowed for manure, is an open question. If the moss litter is capable of absorbing moisture to the extent of nine times its own weight, which is claimed for it, then one-third to the steer and two-thirds to the manure would be about the right proportion; but in this, as well as in the case of the milk and silage, the steer is debited with the maximum amount, viz.: one-half the cost of the moss litter. In arriving at the consuming value of the silage per ton, the calculation is based on the value of a green crop being 10s per ton to sell off, or 7s 6d per ton its consuming price. To this must be added 20 per cent. for loss by fermentation and waste. When the temperature of the stack is kept below 140°, 10 or 12 per cent. is probably sufficient to allow for loss under this head; and if a stack is well built and properly weighted, the loss by waste should not exceed 5 per cent. This experiment goes a long way towards, if it does not conclusively prove, that silage, when properly made, is a very healthy food, and may be used in the same manner and as freely as grass or clover in their natural green condition. The steer was never out of health, nor was ever known to refuse his food; and on being slaughtered, all the internal organs were found to be in a most healthy state. Certainly this experiment proves that the best quality of beef can be produced by means of silage, without hay or turnips. The analysis of the milk was much in favor of ensilage, and shows that silage produces exactly the same quality of milk as grass does in the summer time. And also show such a great reduction in the cost of keeping during the winter months, that the conclusions drawn were that the ensilage system must very shortly revolutionize dairy farming in the country."

FEEDING FOR FAT AND LEAN. — The remarkable results obtained by Prof. W. A. Henry, Director of the Experiment Station, Wisconsin University, during the past year, have attracted the attention, not only of scientists, in America and Europe, but of practical feeders as well. The subjects were pigs, but the facts and conclusions are no less important in relation to all farm stock. The subject matter and the illustrations are kindly furnished by Professor Henry, the reading matter being a condensation from his elaborate report in the volume prepared for the University of Wisconsin. In relation to the experiments it is stated: "Out of a litter of eight pigs, six were selected, which were even in size and form, for the trial, when they were 100 days old. Up to the beginning of the trial, the pigs were all fed alike, from the same trough, a mixture consisting of shorts, corn meal, skimmilk and buttermilk. The pigs were cross-bred Jersey Reds and Poland Chinas. At the beginning of the trial the six were divided into two lots of three each, and to Lot A was fed a ration consisting of one part of dried blood, six parts of shorts and fourteen parts of sweet skimmilk by weight. To Lot B was fed all the fine ground corn meal they could properly consume. Water was freely provided for each lot, and each had the run of a small yard back of the feeding-pen in which exercise could he taken; all went on with remarkable uniformity from first to last, with no accident of any kind to either lot during the whole period of 136 days. The following shows in a condensed form the amount of food consumed by the two lots during the trial of 136 days:

LOT A, FED FOR LEAN.

Amount of sweet skimmilk consumed .... 3302 lbs.
Amount of shorts consumed................ 1415 1-7 lbs.
Amount of dried blood consumed........ . 235 6-7 lbs.

LOT B, FED FOR FAT.

Amount of corn meal consumed .... 1690 lbs.

The digestible matter in the food fed to the two lots was as follows:

	Protein.	Carbhydrates.
Total digestible matter fed to Lot A.	428 lbs.	833 lbs.
Total digestible matter fed to Lot B.	153 lbs.	1193 lbs.

It will be seen that each lot received about the same number of pounds of actual food, but that the proportions of the protein to the carbhydrates varied greatly. Protein goes to make muscle, though it may be used for heat and fat in the body. The carbhydrates (starch, sugar, etc.) cannot make muscle in the body of an animal, though they may save it from waste and decay, but are used for maintaining the bodily heat and for making fat. Our corn-fed hogs then were fed a very fattening food, while the other lot were given a large amount of muscle— (or lean meat)—making material. Here we have our feeds so widely different in character that the effect should be very evident in the carcasses of the hogs, if the character of the food affects the composition of the body. The hogs were slaughtered Nov. 8, 1886, a skilled butcher assisting, every operation being conducted with great care and precision. After taking the live weight of each animal, it was killed by slow bleeding and the blood caught and weighed. The viscera were taken out and each organ weighed and the dressed hogs hung up to cool and stiffen. Upon being taken to the block each dressed hog was lain on his back, and first the head was severed, next the body was cut square across between the fifth and sixth ribs, and again at the loin or small of the back. A painter was employed to sketch the appearance and disposition of the fat and lean meat as exposed by the cuts. Fearing the painter was not exact enough, a photographer was employed for the same purpose, and we were thus enabled to preserve for future reference and study that which would have otherwise soon been lost.

The engravings which are herewith presented show the proportion and disposition of the fat and lean in some of the cuts. We present six illustrations, three of each lot. The second two

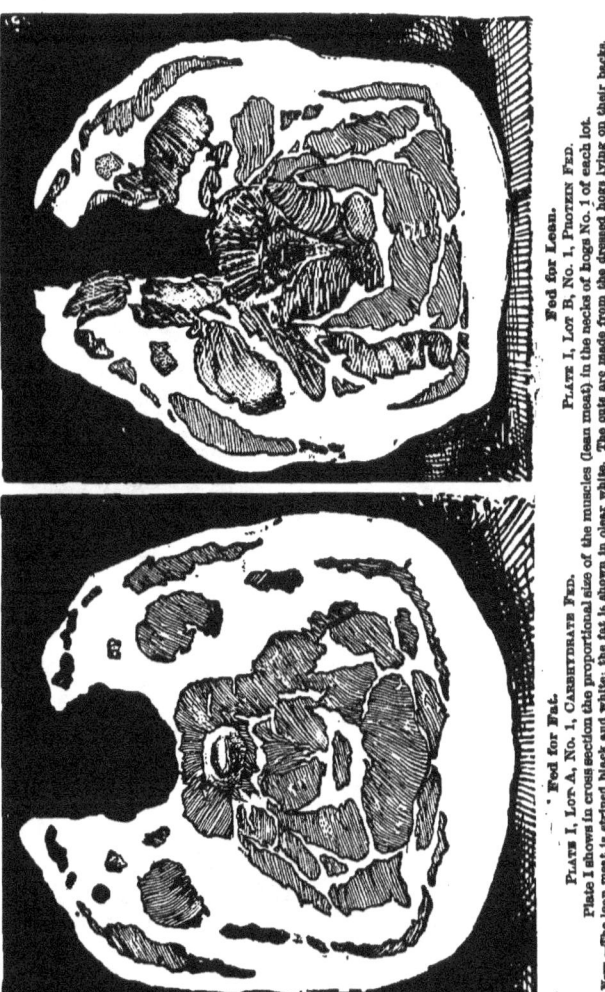

PLATE I, LOT A, No. 1, CARBHYDRATE FED.   Fed for Fat.
PLATE I, LOT B, No. 1, PROTEIN FED.   Fed for Lean.

Plate I shows in cross section the proportional size of the muscles (lean meat) in the necks of hogs No. 1 of each lot. The cuts are made from the dressed hogs lying on their backs.

Note.—The lean meat is striped black and white; the fat is shown in clear white.

show in the same way the cuts made between the fifth and sixth ribs of the hogs, numbered "two" in each lot, while the last two engravings show the loin cut of the hogs numbered "three" of each lot. In each of the engravings the dark shaded parts represent lean meat or muscle, be seen in each case the muscles (red or lean meat) of the protein-fed hogs are larger than the same muscles of those fed the ration rich in carbhydrates. Even the muscles of the neck are stronger, as shown in the first two cuts. On the back over the heart, the muscles of Lot A

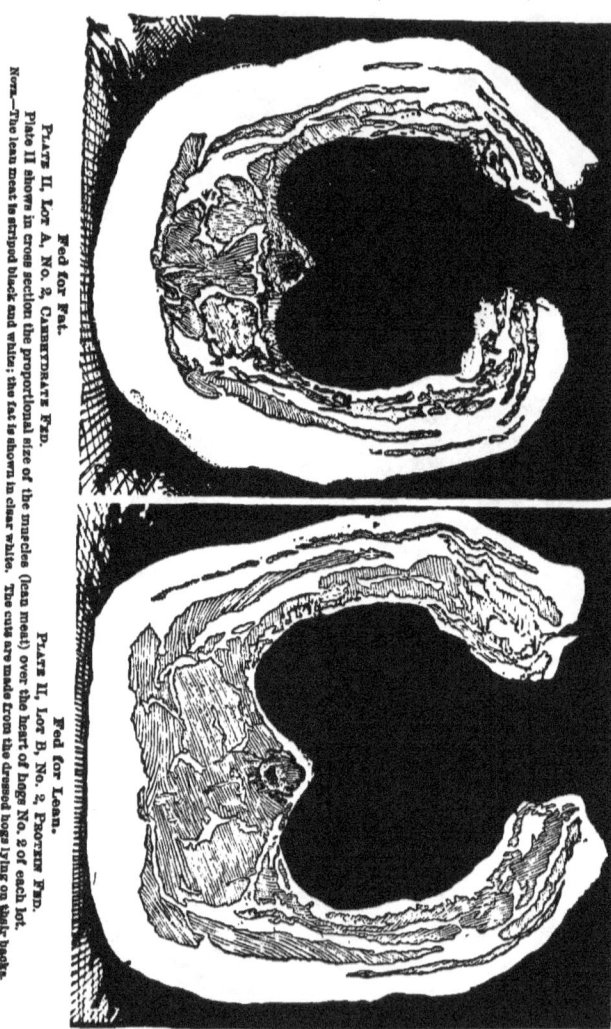

PLATE II, LOT A, NO. 2, CARBOHYDRATE FED.
Fed for Fat.

PLATE II, LOT B, NO. 2, PROTEIN FED.
Fed for Lean.

NOTE.—The lean meat is striped black and white; the fat is shown in clear white. The cuts are made from the dressed hogs lying on their backs. Plate II shown in cross section the proportional size of the muscles (lean meat) over the heart of hogs No. 2 of each lot.

while the fat is shown by the white parts. As in cutting across the body at the three places named we cut square across most of the muscles, the reader can see the relative size of each muscle, in cross section in two hogs of each lot. The reader is asked to give these illustrations more than a passing glance—to study each. It will show far less fat between them than of Lot B. The most remarkable difference, though, is in the small of the back, where it will be noted that Lot A has about twice as much muscle as Lot B. The viscera of each lot was carefully dissected out and weighed and some most remarkable differences between the two lots were found.

The hair was saved and weighed. Each hog was carefully skinned and skins weighed. The large muscle of the back, also the tenderloin muscles were dissected and weighed. The bones were freed from tendons and flesh by boiling, and the thigh bones were broken on a testing

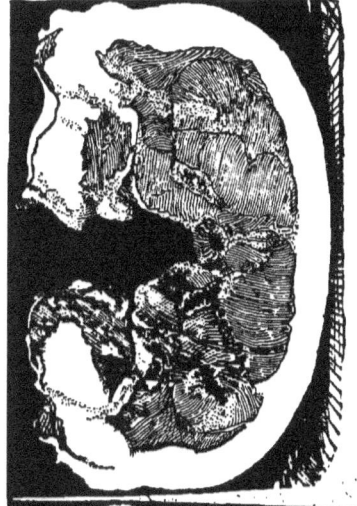

PLATE III, LOT B. NO. 3, PROTEIN FED.
Plate III, Lot B, No. 3 of each lot cut rough from the dressed hogs lying on their backs

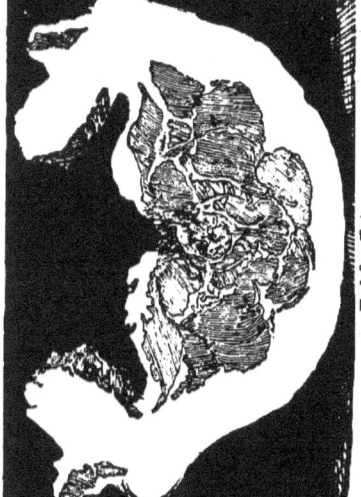

PLATE III, LOT A, NO. 3, CARBHYDRATE FED.
Plate III shows in cross section the proportional size of muscles (lean meat) of the hogs
Note.—The lean meat is striped black and white; the fat is shown in clear white. The cuts are made from the dressed hogs lying on their backs

machine, to determine the strength of each. Each bone was laid on two iron edges about a quarter of an inch thick set four inches apart; a similar iron edge was brought down from above just midway between the two edges below. This plate was crowded down by a lever until the bone broke. In this way we broke five thigh bones of Lot A, and the same of Lot B. We found that the aggregate pressure required to break five thigh bones with the protein-fed hogs was 4550 lbs., or an average of over 909 lbs. per each bone; against 2855 lbs., or 571 lbs. per each bone with the corn-fed hogs. Here was a weakening of the bones of over 300 lbs. each in 136 days. The following table gives the most important facts in the case, the weights being of three hogs in each lot.

	Lot A. Fed for Lean.	Lot B. Fed for Fat.
Total live weight	669¼ lbs.	561¼ lbs.
Total dressed weight	541½ lbs.	451 lbs.
Total external fat	150 lbs.	156 lbs.
Total lean meat	244 lbs.	178½ lbs.
Total weight of kidneys	27 oz.	19 oz.
Total weight of spleens	16 oz.	12 oz.
Total weight of livers	146½ oz.	109¼ oz.
Total weight of blood	296 oz.	186 oz.
Breaking strain 5 thigh bones	4550 lbs.	2855 lbs.

But figures placed in this way are largely lost to the general reader, so we take the liberty of placing them in a different form:

1. The live weight of Lot A (fed for lean) is 19 per cent. greater than Lot B, fed for fat.
2. The dressed weight of Lot A is 21 per cent. greater than Lot B.

These differences should be borne in mind in considering what follows.

3. The kidneys of Lot A weighed 42 per cent. more than those of Lot B.
4. The spleens of Lot A weighed 33 per cent. more than those of Lot B.
5. The livers of lot A weighed 32 per cent. more than those of Lot B.
6. The blood (caught on killing) of Lot A weighed 59 per cent. more than that of Lot B.
7. The hair on Lot A weighed 36 per cent. more than that of Lot B.
8. The skin of Lot A weighed 36 per cent. more than that of Lot B.
9. The large muscles of the back (Ilio spinalis) of Lot A weighed 64 per cent. more than those of Lot B.
10. The two tenderloin muscles (Psoas magnus) of Lot A weighed 38 per cent. more than those of Lot B.
11. Thirty-eight per cent. of all the meat that could be cut from the carcasses of Lot A was fat, while the fat of Lot B was 46 per cent. of all that could be separated.
12. The bones of Lot A were 23 per cent. heavier than those of Lot B.
13. The thigh bones of Lot A were 62 per cent. stronger with the testing machine than those of Lot B.

Before making any deduction we wish to make plain, possible, that which seems a most important consideration, and one that must be clearly understood before we can use these experiments as we should. All through this discussion, we have carried the impression that we could put lean meat or fat on the hog at will; but can we? Is it not true that in every animal there is a certain limitation to muscular development beyond which it cannot go? The blacksmith or the baseball player develops a large amount of muscle, but the limit is not very high, after all, with them, and probably a man weighing 175 lbs. cannot add, either by what he eats or the exercise he takes, over a very few pounds of real meat or muscle to his body; indeed when men "go into training" they reduce their weight as a rule instead of increasing it, getting rid of fat and water in the body. On the other hand, when men have a tendency to laying on fat, the limit they may reach may double their normal weight. We may say, then, that the possible muscular development of an animal has a narrow limit comparatively, while the possible fatty development has a much wider range. We should hold, then, it would seem, that our hogs which show the best muscular development are only normally developed, or at least have not departed far from the normal, and that whatever we find in them is a condition to be held as a standard, while our hogs which have grown fat and show a variation from the lean hogs, are abnormal. Having assumed the above as correct we can make a much clearer statement of the deductions which may be drawn from the experiments. We may claim that the experiments show that when we feed to our hogs a ration rich in carbhydrates but lacking in protein, like corn meal, we will find:

(1.) That there is an extensive development of fat not only on the outside of the muscles and beneath the skin, but also among the muscles.
(2.) That the muscles of the body fail to develop to their normal size, especially some of the most important ones, as those along the back.
(3.) That an abnormally small amount of hair and a thin skin result.
(4.) That while the brain, heart and lungs do not seem to change in weight, the spleen, liver and kidneys are unusually small.
(5.) The amount of blood in the body is greatly reduced from the normal.
(6.) The strength of the bones may be reduced one-half.

It would seem that we may conclude that a system of feeding which robs the hog of half his blood and half the natural strength of his bones, and produces other violent changes, is a most unnatural one, and must, if persisted in, end in giving us a race of animals which will be unsatisfactory to all concerned. From the parents thus weakened must come descendants that will fall easy victims to disease and disaster. Knowing the facts as here set forth, can we any longer wonder that our hogs are weak in constitution and easily break down when attacked by disease? Nor is this all; the meat from such animals can hardly be of flavor and composition satisfactory to the consumer. If even a part of what has been set forth is correct, is it not high time we turned our energies toward better methods? To do this calls for higher thought, better care, but I fully believe no extra outlay of money; rather, I believe, we can feed hogs more profitably by rational methods than by the unscientific and shiftless ways now only too common. First of all, we must see to it that breeding sows are fed a proper ration in which protein compounds form a liberal share. The young pigs must likewise have a goodly allowance of protein, while the mature hogs, when fattening, can be fed a large proportion of carbhydrates, especially if we wish to make a large proportion of lard. The food articles at our command which are rich in protein are skimmilk, buttermilk, shorts, bran, peas, green clover and the like. No farmer can afford to manage his farm with a minimum of these muscle-making foods; they should be supplied abundantly and at a reasonable cost if we will only study to do so. Shall we raise less corn, then? Not at all. The corn crop is the best of all we raise, and let the word be "more," rather than "less." We need it all, but we must not forget that protein is somewhat lacking in the corn. We may compare our corn to the brick which go into a building, and the protein foods to the mortar which cements the brick together. He who would lay up brick without mortar builds foolishly, and his house will tumble. Should he find out his mistake, such a man should not from that date neglect the brick and turn his whole attention to the mortar. Plenty of good strong mortar and an abundance of brick are what he needs. We do not want less corn, but we want more clover, more shorts, more bran, more peas, more skimmilk and such foods to bring the highest results. Without attempting to give any exact rules for guidance, the following statements may not be out of place: During gestation, breeding sows should have only a small allowance of corn, the feed being mainly that which will go to give her young good sound bodies. Such feed would be shorts (middlings or shipstuff), bran, skimmilk, buttermilk and clover. When suckling her young, of course milk is one of the best articles at our command. When weaned, the pigs may get, say two parts of milk by weight, one part of shorts and one part of corn meal. A run on good clover would go far to make a good frame. When nearing maturity the ration can be changed more and more to the carbonaceous, and for the last two months, when fattening, the feed can be largely corn, if one desires fat pork, but if lean, juicy meat be desired, the muscle-making foods must be continued.

[NOTE BY THE EDITOR. Where protein is mentioned, food rich in muscle constituents are understood, as skimmilk, shorts, dried blood, beans, peas, etc. When carbhydrates are spoken of, foods rich in fat producing elements, as Indian corn and other starchy and oily foods are to be understood.]

FLAX. This product has shown some curious changes in the areas of production. Flax is raised almost entirely in the United States for its seed, the lint being used only in the coarsest fabrics. The reason for this is, labor in the United States cannot compete with the cheap labor of Europe, where nearly all the manipulation must be done by hand. When machinery can be brought into competition we can compete. Machinery can reduce the fiber for paper stock, bagging, etc., and hence flax fiber is confined in the United States to such uses. When machinery may be devised for pulling thickly sown flax, and cheaply reducing the fiber for manufacturing into fine linen, we can easily produce the world's supply. The table below shows the relative productions of the States principally interested in the production of the seed, for the years 1879 and 1887:

States.	1879.	1887.
Ohio	593,217	118,643
Indiana	1,419,172	113,534
Illinois	1,812,436	94,247
Wisconsin	547,104	65,652
Minnesota	98,689	1,246,442
Iowa	1,511,131	1,888,914
Missouri	379,535	360,558
Kansas	513,616	1,068,321
Nebraska	77,805	665,283
Dakota	26,757	3,237,597
All other	191,487	142,258
Total	7,170,951	9,001,399

It will be seen that in 1879 the four States east of the Mississippi River produced 63 per cent. of the total of the States named, while in the present year the same region grows but little more than 4 per cent. of the whole, the six trans-Mississippi States producing considerably more than nine-tenths of all. Even in this region the industry is now beginning to decline, and the causes are the same as have caused its virtual abandonment farther east. Many returns from Iowa and Wisconsin agree that under existing conditions it is not a profitable crop, being very hard on any but fresh soil, and the seed alone not paying for its growth. The great markets of the United States for flaxseed are Chicago, St. Louis and Milwaukee, the bulk of the seed goes directly or indirectly to these cities. From the returns of the various State Boards of Agriculture are collected the following as the latest information on the subject of flaxseed. These are probably much under the true status—perhaps to the amount of 10 per cent.—but the approximation is close enough.

States.	Acres, 1886.	Bushels of Seed, 1886.	Acres, 1887
Indiana	18,268	153,128	14,000
Illinois	13,231	117,593	10,184
Wisconsin			
Minnesota	204,147	1,508,771	170,225
Iowa	291,580	2,332,480	271,161
Kansas	87,904	879,040	132,560
Dakota	549,189	3,544,328	366,126

GRASSES. In grasses there is very little new that has not been treated of in the body of this work; nevertheless, since the South and Southwest are largely interested in the extension of grasses, indigenous or introduced, many of which were heretofore considered simply as pests in the cotton fields, but now are found of prime value either for pasture or as forage crops for cutting green, we give a review of species. In Texas, particularly, some most valuable grasses have been found, and the best of which is Texas blue grass (*Poa arachnifera*). Another valuable grass, better known in Texas than elsewhere in the United States, is Rescue Grass (*Bromus unioloides*). In the Far West a plant of the geranium family (*Erodium cicutarium*) has lately grown into great repute under various names, as alfilaria, pin clover, pin grass, filree. Alfalfa (*Medicago sativa*) is coming more and more into use in all that region South and West where red clover has not succeeded. Dr. George Vasey, United States Botanist, has given careful attention to the subject of native and introduced grasses for the South and West, and in 1887 made public his investigations relating to some of the grasses considered valuable West and South, but not generally known. We, therefore, give short descriptions of species deemed most valuable, not found in the body of this encyclopædia. One of these that may be named, is the Hairy flowered Paspalum. A Texas correspondent, Charles N. Ely, of southeastern Texas, writes Dr. Vasey as follows: "*Paspalum dilatatum* was brought to this country about twelve years ago and planted by S. B. Wallis. It is a promising grass for hay and pasture, growing best on moist lands, but doing well on upland. It is easily subdued by cultivation and is not inclined to encroach on cultivated lands. It is best propagated by roots or sets, the seed not being reliable. It is rather slow in starting, but when well rooted it spreads and overcomes all other grasses. Tramping and grazing is more of an advantage to it than otherwise. I think that this grass will succeed in a great variety of soils and climates, but those planting it must have patience with it at first." Mr. Wallis says : "This I consider the most valuable of all the grasses with which I am acquainted; it is perennial and grows here all the year round, furnishing excellent green feed for stock at all seasons, except that the green blades freeze in our very coldest weather, perhaps two or three times in the winter. It increases rapidly from seeds, and also reproduces itself from suckers, which sprout from the nodes of the culm after the first seed has ripened. I have seen these suckers remain green for six or eight weeks after the old stalks were as dead and dry as hay, and then when the old stalk had fallen to the ground take root and form new plants. It grows well on all kinds of dry land. Plants two or three years old form stools twelve to eighteen inches across. The grass has very strong roots, and grows in the longest drought almost as fast as when it rains." Another species, *P. platycaule*, sometimes called Louisiana Grass, is well regarded in the Gulf States, and said to make fine pasture grass, giving a sod equal to Bermuda grass. Tramping does not hurt it, it is drought resisting, but is not cut for hay, and if wished to be destroyed, one plowing kills it. Teosinte (*Euchlæna luxurians*) is a semi-tropical forage plant. The plant resembles Indian corn, but is more slender, suckers far more, the seeds being produced in small tufts or husks. It ripens its seeds only in Florida and other favored portions of the Gulf States. Upon rich land it makes immense growth. It endures heat, drought and rains as well as sorghum, and better than corn, and cures well into hay. Dr. Charles Mohr, Mobile, Ala., says of this plant: "This tropical grass does not ripen its seeds in this latitude, it scarcely unfolds its blossoms before the advent of the first frost. It is very tender, being easily affected by frost or drought. During a cold spring it is difficult to secure a good stand, and it is only after warm weather has fairly set in that it begins to make a rapid growth, affording three cuttings and over of rich fodder on well-manured ground in a season of genial showers. It is too succulent to be easily cured for hay. On that account, and from the difficulty in securing a good stand, and from the necessity of procuring each season a supply of seed from abroad, this grass has not found the favor with the cultivators of this section with which it is held in the subtropical zone." The general expression by those who have cultivated it in the Gulf States is that it is valuable. The seed is now sold by the best class of seedsmen. Millo Maize (*Sorghum vulgare*) variety. This plant produces profusely and ripens its seeds in the Gulf States. The bulk of the testimony is that cattle do not relish the plant, and that it is inferior to many other forage plants. American Canary Grass, (*Phalaris intermedia*)— Reed Canary Grass, Gilbert's Relief Grass, California Timothy, etc. This grass, a biennial, indigenous through the Gulf States and across into California and Oregon, has seeds resembling flaxseed, and its habit of growth is that of wheat. It is natural to wet ground and seems to have acquired a good reputation in California. It may be valuable in the South as a winter grass.

Velvet Grass, (*Holcus lanatus*), known as Meadow Soft Grass in the catalogues, and in some parts of the South as Velvet Mesquit, was introduced from Europe. It does best on rich, moist lands, but also grows fairly on dry sandy land. It is worthy of trial in the West. It will not stand on lands liable to overflow by water. Mr. H. W. L. Lewis, Secretary of the Louisiana State Grange, writes Dr. Vasey in relation to this grass as follows: "It is hardy and cultivated in small lots, doing best on rich, sandy loam, yielding two to three tons per acre. I have experimented more than any one else in my section with forage plants, especially winter grains and grasses. Have used rye and barley for winter feed, but have given them up in favor of the *Holcus lanatus;* have had this in cultivation for thirty years. It is a perennial, but owing to its shallow roots it dies out during our long, dry summer and fall from 50 to 75 per cent. One lot kept the third year had less than 10 per cent. of the grass alive. Hence I have for twenty years or more used it as an annual, sowing it with turnips, collards, or by itself. A good way is to sow the seed broadcast and cover lightly in a late crop of turnips after the last cultivation. After the turnip crop is removed the first warm days in January or February will start the grass into rapid growth. It is cut frequently through the spring for green feed, and after oats are ready to cut, is allowed to mature seed." Tall Oat Grass, (*Arrhenatherum avenaceum*). This is known as Tall Meadow Oat Grass, Ray Grass and by other local names, is perennial, vigorous in growth, and is widely distributed North and South. It is hardy, withstands drought well, but likes moist sandy loam, where it yields heavy crops. Prof. D. L. Phares, of Mississippi, says: "It is well adapted to a great variety of soils. On sandy and gravelly soils it succeeds admirably, growing two to three feet high. On rich dry upland it grows five to seven feet high. It has an abundance of perennial long fibrous roots, penetrating deeply in the soil, enabling it to resist drought and cold and yield a large amount of foliage winter and summer. These advantages render it one of the very best grasses for the South, both for grazing, being evergreen, and for hay, admitting of being cut twice a year. It is probably the best winter grass that can be obtained. It will make twice as much hay as Timothy. To make good hay it must be cut as soon as it blooms, and after cut must not be wet by dew or rain, which damages it greatly in quality and appearance. For green soiling it may be cut four or five times in favorable seasons. In from six to ten days after blooming the seeds begin to ripen and fall, the upper ones first. It is therefore somewhat troublesome to save the seed; as soon as those at the top of the panicle ripen sufficiently to begin to drop, they should be cut and dried, when they will mature and thrash out readily. It may be sowed in March or April, and be mowed the same season; but if sown in September or October, the yield the next season will be heavier. Not less than two bushels (fourteen pounds) per acre should be sown. The annual yield of this grass in the Southern belt is probably twice as great as in Pennsylvania and the Northern States." Texas Blue Grass, (*Poa arachnifera*), was first found in the head-waters of the Trinity River, in Northern Texas, in 1852. It is yet but little known, but where tried is highly spoken of, especially South. It stands drought well, and holds to the ground as well as Kentucky Blue Grass, yet it is as easily subdued by cultivation. It does not come to full perfection until the third or fourth year. We have seen no statement where it was not well liked, east or west of the Mississippi River, but seems to do best West, well up into Kansas. South it is one of the best of winter pasture grasses. Cactus, (*Opuntia Englemanni*). This Southern cactus has within the last few years attracted attention in the Southwest, and especially in Texas, for its value as a forage plant. It grows often to the height of ten to twelve feet, and is greedily eaten by all classes of farm stock when the spines are clipped. A Texas correspondent says of it: "The pears should be cut and hauled to the feed-lots while the sap is in the roots, or before the warm days come, for if it is fed when the sap is in the tops it is liable to cause laxness and weaken the animals. We prepare it for feeding by holding it for a moment over a blaze. I believe that in the southern part of the State they have a burner with which they burn off the prickles, without cutting the plants from the ground, and then let the cattle eat them as they please, but we prefer to cut and feed as above stated. One good man can prepare the Cactus and feed about 100 head of cattle in this way. A poor or half-starved animal should be fed only a small quantity at first, which may be gradually increased until the animal is allowed to eat all it wants. When fed in this manner to range cattle, we have never known any injurious results. But if it is fed to steers, and they are worked immediately afterwards, even if the feed is small, and not accustomed to it, they are liable to swell up. We have had them do so when we thought there was danger of its proving fatal. They can be given a feed at night, however, and then worked the following morning without danger of any injurious results."

HAY. The hay crop is one of the most important of the country. The annual average for the last six years, as reported, is 33,838,247 tons, carrying a money value of $387,771,207. In the South this crop is receiving more and more attention yearly, and especially is attention being paid to the grasses natural for the climate, and to forage crops natural there; among these latter may be mentioned Japan clover and Lucerne, generally called by its Spanish name Alfalfa. (See "Clover," also in Supplement "Japan Clover.") The following table will show production and averages of hay for the series of years reported up to date:

Calendar Years.	Total Production	Total Area of Crop.	Total Value of Crop.
	Tons.	Acres.	Dollars.
1880	31,925,233	25,863,955	371,811,084
1881	35,135,064	30,888,700	415,131,365
1882	38,138,049	34,339,585	369,958,158
1883	46,864,009	35,515,948	383,834,451
1884	48,470,460	38,571,593	396,139,309
1885	44,731,550	39,849,701	389,752,873
Total	245,264,365	209,029,482	2,326,627,241
Annual average	40,877,394	34,838,217	387,771,207
Annual average for preceding ten years	28,526,750	23,142,841	323,935,991

Japan Clover (*Lespedeza striata*). Of this legume a partial description is given on pages 231 and 234, and also illustrated. Since that article was written, the plant has gained more and more reputation in the South. Dr. Vasey, writing of it in 1887, says it now furnishes thousands of acres of excellent grazing in every one of the Gulf States, and is still spreading northward in Kentucky and Virginia, and westward in Texas, Indian Territory, and Arkansas. It is an annual, and furnishes pasture only during summer and until killed by frost in the fall. The small purplish blossoms are produced singly in the axils between the leaf and stem, and the seeds ripen, a few at a time, from about the first of August until the close of the season. It reproduces itself from seed on the same ground year after year, and on this account has been erroneously called a perennial. It will grow on poor soils, either sand or clay, but prefers the latter. It is better adapted to poor soils than Bermuda Grass, both from giving a more certain and perhaps larger yield, and from being more useful in restoring their fertility. On poor upland soils it is seldom cut for hay, growing only from six inches to one foot in height, and being inclined to spread out flat upon the surface. On rich bottom lands it grows thicker, taller, and more upright, and is largely cut for hay. It has been sown artificially only to a limited extent as yet, but seed is now offered in the market, and its cultivation is likely to be considerably extended, especially on lands too dry or poor for Alfalfa and where the true clovers do not succeed. Japan clover is remarkable for holding its own against other plants. It will run out broom sedge and other inferior plants, and even Bermuda in some localities. It does not withstand drought as well as either Bermuda or Johnson grass, but soon recovers after a rain. The young plants are easily killed by drought or frost, and for this reason a good catch is more certain on an unbroken sod than on well-prepared land. Still there is believed to be less difficulty in obtaining a catch with this than with some other forage plants. A good method of seeding is to sow in March, at the rate of one-half bushel per acre, on small grain sown the previous autumn or winter. For hay it should be cut early, before it becomes woody.

It is cured in the same manner as clover, and the hay is apparently relished by all kinds of stock. There is some complaint that stock do not at first eat it readily while growing, and that horses and mules are liable to be salivated if allowed to eat it freely while very luxuriant. In both these respects, however, it probably differs little from the ordinary clovers. No cases have been reported of bloat or hoven being caused by it. (See page 231.)

LANDED ESTATES AND FARMS. In the body of this work is an exhaustive article after the title as above. The statistical tables were brought down to the latest date at the time of the writing. At the close of 1887 there were about 5,000,000 owners of farms in the United States. Since 1880 there have been added about 1,000,000 farms to the country. There is no later data than that of the census of 1880, nor will there be until that of 1890. To give an idea of the land development and increase of farms, the following table will show those States in comparison with 1870, when the most marked change has occurred. An interesting point is the diminution in the size of farms. This means, as one of the important integers, better cultivation and increased crops per acre. The table is as follows:

States.	Number of Farms.		Land in Farms.		Average size of Farms.		Per cent. Unimproved.	
	1880.	1860.	1880.	1860.	1880.	1860.	1880.	1860.
			Acres.	Acres.	Acres.	Acres.		
New York	241,058	196,990	23,780,754	20,974,958	99	106	25.5	31.5
Pennsylvania	213,542	156,357	19,791,211	17,012,140	93	109	32.2	38.5
Ohio	247,189	179,889	24,529,226	20,472,141	99	114	26.3	38.3
Michigan	154,008	62,422	13,807,240	7,030,834	90	113	39.9	50.5
Kentucky	166,453	90,814	21,495,240	19,163,261	129	211	50.1	60.1
Indiana	194,013	131,826	20,420,983	16,388,292	105	124	31.8	49.7
Illinois	255,741	143,310	31,673,645	20,911,989	124	146	17.5	32.6
Missouri	215,575	92,792	27,879,276	19,984,810	129	215	39.9	66.7
Kansas	138,561	10,400	21,417,468	1,778,400	155	171	49.9	77.2
Nebraska	63,387	2,789	9,944,826	631,214	157	226	44.6	81.3
North Carolina	157,609	75,203	22,363,558	23,762,969	142	316	71.0	72.6
South Carolina	93,864	33,171	13,457,613	16,195,919	143	488	69.3	71.8
Florida	23,438	6,568	3,297,324	2,920,228	141	444	71.3	77.6
Alabama	135,864	55,128	18,855,334	19,104,545	139	346	66.2	66.6
Mississippi	101,772	42,840	15,855,462	15,839,684	156	370	67.1	68.0
Louisiana	48,292	17,328	8,273,506	9,298,576	171	536	66.9	70.9
Texas	174,184	42,891	36,292,219	25,344,028	208	591	65.1	69.5
Arkansas	94,433	39,004	12,061,547	9,573,706	128	245	70.2	79.3

The statistician who formulated the above, in relation to the whole matter says: The points of greatest significance in this table are the small proportion of unimproved land in the Ohio Valley, less than three-tenths of the area, and the great reduction in size of farms in the cotton States and increase of their number. The latter fact is due largely to the renting of old estates on shares or otherwise to several tenants who report separately, making the number of farms far more than the number of proprietors. There is no immediate prospect of a change of this system, though the individual tenants hold by a very uncertain tenure. The tendency will, doubtless, still be strong towards subdivision of lands, both by sale and rent. There are, however, significant figures lately made public, showing that in proportion to the increase of non-agricultural population is the increase in farm land values, and in the value of the productions. The table given below is striking in this direction. It gives us a result of the value of land, $5.18 per

LANDED ESTATES AND FARMS

acre for States averaging 77 per cent. in agriculture, $13.53 where 58 per cent. are in agriculture, $30.65 for 42 per cent., and $38.65 for 18 per cent. employed in agriculture. The four classes are in groups of States; and the table explains itself, the actual area and value being shown in these four classes of States·

farm lands are also suburban property, with prices beyond the mere agricultural value. The lands next in value are those of New Jersey, so near to four millions of urban population just across its borders as to make practically a lower proportion in agriculture than Massachusetts or Rhode Island.

VALUE BY CLASSES.

Classes.	Number of States and Territories.	Acres.	Value.	Value per Acre.	Workers in Agriculture.
					Per Cent.
First class	15	77,250,742	$2,985,641,197	$38 65	18
Second class	13	112,321,257	3,430,915,767	30 55	42
Third class	13	237,873,040	3,212,108,970	13 53	58
Fourth class	6	108,636,706	562,430,642	5 16	77

The first class has 82 per cent. of all labor in industries producing nothing from the soil, and dependent on 18 per cent. employed in food production, or else upon products of other States. These are the more advanced manufacturing States, and mining States and Territories, as follows:

Class third (on page 1102) includes all States having one-half and not exceeding seven-tenths employed in agriculture, the newer States of the West, and the older and more diversified of the districts of the South. The values in class fourth represent highest per cent. in workers, but lowest cash price of farm values. In this,

VALUES IN CLASS FIRST.

States and Territories.	Farms.			Workers in Agriculture.
	Acres.	Value.	Value per Acre.	
				Per Cent.
District of Columbia	18,146	$ 3,632,403	$200 18	2
Massachusetts	3,350,079	146,197,415	43 52	9
Rhode Island	514,813	25,682,079	50 27	9
Colorado	1,165,378	25,109,223	21 55	13
Nevada	530,802	5,408,325	10 19	13
Arizona	135,573	1,127,946	8 32	15
New Jersey	2,929,773	190,895,833	65 16	15
Wyoming	124,433	835,895	6 72	16
Connecticut	2,453,541	121,063,910	49 34	18
Montana	405,683	3,234,504	7 97	20
New York	23,780,754	1,056,176,741	44 41	20
Pennsylvania	19,791,341	975,689,410	49 30	21
California	16,503,742	262,051,282	15 79	21
Idaho	327,706	2,832,890	8 64	25
Maryland	5,110,831	165,503,341	32 33	28
Total	77,250,742	$2,985,641,197	$38 65	31

In the District of Columbia the farm lands are so near to a city of nearly 200,000 people that its

Alabama shows the lowest cash price per acre, and Arkansas the largest price.

VALUES IN CLASS SECOND.

[This list includes the smaller manufacturing States and those of the West where less than half the labor is in agriculture.]

States and Territories.	Farms.			Workers in Agriculture.
	Acres.	Value.	Value per Acre.	
				Per Cent.
New Hampshire	3,721,173	$ 75,834,389	$20 38	31
Delaware	1,090,245	36,789,072	33 74	33
New Mexico	631,131	5 514,399	8 74	35
Maine	6,552,578	102,357,615	15 62	35
Utah	655,524	14,015,178	21 38	36
Ohio	24,529,226	1,127,497,353	45 97	40
Oregon	4,214,712	56,908,575	13 50	40
Washington	1,409,421	13,844,222	9 82	42
Michigan	13,807,240	499,103,181	36 15	42
Illinois	31,673,645	1,000,594,580	31 87	44
Wisconsin	15,353,118	357,709,507	23 30	47
Vermont	4,882,586	109,346,010	22 40	47
Dakota	3,800,656		5 89	49
Total	112,321,257	$3,430,915,765	$30 55	42

VALUES IN CLASS THIRD.

States.	Farms.			Workers in Agriculture.
	Acres.	Value.	Value per Acre.	
				Per Cent.
Virginia	19,835,785	$ 216,028,107	$10.89	51
Missouri	27,879,276	375,633,307	13.47	51
Minnesota	13,403,019	193,724,260	14.45	52
Indiana	20,420,983	635,236,111	31.11	52
Louisiana	8,273,506	59,982,117	7.13	57
Iowa	24,752,700	567,430,227	22.92	57
Nebraska	9,944,826	105,932,541	10.65	59
West Virginia	10,193,779	133,147,175	13.06	61
Kentucky	21,495,240	299,298,631	13.92	62
Florida	3,297,324	20,291,835	6.15	64
Kansas	21,417,468	235,178,936	10.98	64
Tennessee	20,666,915	206,749,837	10.00	66
Texas	36,292,219	170,468,866	4.70	69
Total	237,873,040	$3,218,108,970	$13.52	58

VALUES IN CLASS FOURTH.

States.	Farms.			Workers in Agriculture.
	Acres.	Value.	Value per Acre.	
				Per Cent.
Georgia	26,043,282	$111,910,540	$4.30	72
North Carolina	22,363,558	135,793,602	6.07	75
South Carolina	13,457,613	68,677,482	5.10	75
Alabama	18,855,334	78,954,648	4.19	77
Mississippi	15,855,462	92,844,915	5.86	82
Arkansas	12,061,547	74,249,655	6.16	83
Total	108,636,796	$562,430,842	$5.18	77

LANDED ESTATES AND FARMS OF ONTARIO. The values of farm property for 1885 and 1886, and the average for the five years' period 1882-'86 are as follows:

	1886.	1885.	1882-'86.
Farm Lands	$648,009,828	$626,422,024	$637,409,217
Buildings	183,749,212	182,477,905	167,071,058
Implements	50,530,936	48,569,725	45,496,743
Live Stock	107,208,935	100,690,086	98,325,787
Total	$989,497,911	$958,159,740	$948,302,805

LIVE STOCK OF CANADA. The report of the Ontario Bureau of Industries, 1887, gives the following details as to the number of farm animals in the province in 1886 and 1887, respectively:

Animals.	1886.	1887.
Cattle:		
Working Oxen	14,414	13,763
Milch Cows	746,807	748,321
Store Cattle over two years old	418,079	392,580
Young and other Cattle	838,783	793,600
Total Cattle	2,018,173	1,948,264
Horses:		
Working Horses	800,682	296,504
Breeding Mares	107,000	111,907
Unbroken Horses	151,967	166,950
Total Horses	559,649	575,361

Animals.	1886.	1887.
Sheep:		
Coarse wooled, over one year old	790,652	672,935
Coarse wooled, under one year old	476,970	413,775
Fine wooled, over one year old	206,371	183,478
Fine wooled, under one year old	136,956	124,973
Total Sheep	1,510,949	1,395,161
Pigs over one year old	207,487	206,944
Pigs under one year old	652,638	625,873
Total Pigs	860,125	832,817
Poultry:		
Turkeys	522,714	409,596
Geese	493,756	426,055
Other Fowls	5,952,445	5,600,708
Total Poultry	6,968,915	6,436,361

The figures for Manitoba given for 1886 are from the British Statistical Abstract of the Colonial and Other Possessions of the United Kingdom. Those for 1887 are from the Manitoba Crop Bulletin, July 1, 1887:

NUMBERS OF LIVE STOCK IN 1886 AND 1887.

	1886.	1887.
Cattle	144,685	101,681
Horses	37,485	29,915
Sheep	16,053	12,540
Pigs	101,490	85,713

The number of young dropped in the season of 1887 as compared with that of 1886 is stated in the Crop Bulletin as follows: Calves, 109 per cent.; colts, 119 per cent.; lambs, 106 per cent., and pigs, 85 per cent. Of the cattle in 1887, 95 per cent. were grades and only 5 per cent. pure breeds. Of the sheep and hogs, the number marketable as compared with 1886, was 108 per cent. in the case of sheep and 80 per cent. in the case of hogs.

LIVE STOCK OF THE UNITED STATES.

The latest statistics in relation to farm animals in the United States is up to March, 1888. From the report the following will give the gist of the salient matter for reference. Relating to increase and decrease we find: Cattle were highest in 1869, $25.12 in 1870, declining until 1879 shows increase and decrease from 1887 to 1888. As given, it shows the average value of horses and cattle, the minus and plus marks showing the increase and decrese in per cent. of values as given.

Stock.	1887.	1888.	Increase or Decrease.
Horses	72.15	71.82	—.33
Mules	78.91	79.78	+.87
Milch Cows	26.08	24.65	—1.43
Oxen and other Cattle	19.79	17.79	—2.00
Sheep	2.01	2.05	+.04
Swine	4.48	4.98	+.50

Taking the reports from 1879 to 1888, we find the record of ten years' prices to be as follows:

Years.	Horses.	Mules.	Milch Cows.	Other Cattle.	Sheep.	Swine.
1879	$52.41	$56.06	$21.73	$15.39	$2.07	$3.18
1880	54.75	61.26	23.27	16.10	2.21	4.28
1881	58.44	69.79	23.95	17.33	2.39	4.70
1882	58.52	71.35	25.80	19.89	2.37	5.98
1883	70.59	79.49	30.21	21.50	2.53	6.75
1884	74.64	84.22	31.37	23.52	2.59	5.57
1885	73.70	82.38	29.70	23.25	2.14	5.02
1886	71.27	79.60	27.40	21.17	1.91	4.25
1887	72.15	78.91	26.08	19.79	2.01	4.48
1888	71.82	79.78	24.65	17.79	2.05	4.96

to $15.39, then rising annually to 1884, the average being $23.52, and declining constantly since, standing now at $17.79. This is higher than at the lowest depression, and at the gold value about the same as at the commencement of the monetary panic of 1873. From 1879 to 1884 the annual estimates of prices of milch cows and other cattle advanced yearly, and the decline has since been uninterrupted, without exception, for either class of stock. The fall in milch cows has been from $26.08 to $24.65, over 5 per cent.; and in oxen and in other cattle from $19.79 to $17.79, a decline of 10 per cent. in the last year. In sheep, as in other stock, the annual advance was quite steady after 1879, and amounted to 22 per cent. in four years. From 1883 to 1886 the decline was over 25 per cent., or from $2.53 to $1.91. The next year's average was $2.01, and the present average $2.05, or nearly as much as in the depression of 1879, when prices were the lowest in twenty years. There has been an advance in the average for swine of all ages from $4.48 to $4.98, or 11 per cent. The annual advance was continuous from 1879 to 1883, then declining to 1886 and slightly advancing again since. The following table

The comparison of aggregate values with those of 1887 shows an increased valuation of over $8,000,000, cattle and sheep only showing decrease, while horses, mules, and swine have an increased valuation. From this we may fairly conclude that milch cows, oxen and other cattle, and sheep are decreasing in price, while other stock is increasing.

Stock.	1887.	1888.	Increase or Decrease.
Horses	$ 901,685,755	$ 946,096,154	+$14,410,399
Mules	167,057,538	174,853,563	+ 7,796,025
Milch Cows	378,789,589	366,252,173	— 12,537,416
Oxen and other Cattle	663,137,926	611,750,520	— 51,387,406
Sheep	89,872,830	89,279,926	— 592,913
Swine	200,043,291	220,811,082	+ 20,767,791
Total	$2,400,586,938	$2,409,043,418	+$ 8,456,480

It will be seen that the stock interests of the United States are in a fairly prosperous condition. Cattle will probably advance in prices. The farm stock interest represents $2,400,000,000, and, including horses and other animals in cities, not far from $3,000,000,000. It is one of the very first in agricultural importance, and demands the most intelligent endeavor of farmers to obtain the largest possible annual income from the investment at the lowest possible cost. How to do this will be found in the several pages of the original work. As enabling the reader to form a comparison of the animals of the United States, in connection with the various matters in the body of this work, the following table will be instructive and interesting. We give on the following pages three tables concerning the farm animals, including dairy cattle.

SUPPLEMENT   1104   LIVE STOCK OF THE UNITED STATES

TABLE SHOWING THE ESTIMATED NUMBER OF ANIMALS ON FARMS, TOTAL VALUE OF EACH KIND, AND AVERAGE PRICE, JANUARY, 1888.

States and Territories.	Horses.			Mules.		
	Number.	Average Price.	Value.	Number.	Average Price.	Value.
Maine	94,657	$91.07	$8,838,353			
New Hampshire	49,878	86.18	4,296,944			
Vermont	84,841	84.22	7,145,111			
Massachusetts	65,194	107.61	7,015,576			
Rhode Island	10,055	105.13	1,057,126			
Connecticut	49,361	100.77	4,976,036			
New York	674,018	96.96	65,365,391	5,210	$106.02	$552,366
New Jersey	94,397	105.46	9,955,374	9,501	118.99	1,130,482
Pennsylvania	594,972	93.71	55,757,103	24,143	109.35	2,640,083
Delaware	23,000	94.75	2,179,250	4,102	116.23	476,787
Maryland	130,316	86.00	11,207,590	13,625	108.35	1,476,294
Virginia	243,319	70.89	17,249,636	35,726	87.36	3,121,130
North Carolina	149,708	74.59	11,167,289	89,945	84.13	7,567,086
South Carolina	65,966	90.05	5,940,100	75,451	95.51	7,206,052
Georgia	110,060	83.62	9,203,490	149,654	96.27	14,407,417
Florida	32,743	80.87	2,647,961	12,496	96.02	1,199,295
Alabama	130,853	82.54	10,800,925	137,695	87.01	11,980,835
Mississippi	134,065	71.95	9,645,784	159,548	87.08	13,988,374
Louisiana	119,810	57.15	6,847,597	84,478	88.46	7,472,811
Texas	1,225,803	31.09	38,115,135	193,488	51.85	10,032,254
Arkansas	179,955	59.34	10,678,480	132,457	74.02	9,063,669
Tennessee	300,264	68.92	20,693,284	194,771	73.09	14,236,061
West Virginia	138,281	66.62	9,212,076	6,475	73.70	477,223
Kentucky	390,733	72.30	28,250,002	162,285	71.97	11,680,018
Ohio	723,156	87.30	63,132,979	24,724	89.42	2,210,795
Michigan	458,918	91.80	42,126,410	6,095	103.62	636,572
Indiana	641,716	81.09	52,039,440	54,382	84.32	4,585,456
Illinois	1,069,639	77.25	82,649,687	115,661	83.73	9,684,515
Wisconsin	412,687	78.61	32,441,507	7,930	90.34	716,424
Minnesota	379,489	82.86	31,445,299	10,969	94.30	1,034,415
Iowa	1,008,022	73.81	74,032,082	45,649	86.23	3,936,640
Missouri	783,104	57.59	45,040,996	225,553	66.59	15,019,534
Kansas	634,893	67.34	42,754,975	86,104	83.32	7,173,954
Nebraska	413,980	75.82	31,311,968	41,165	90.40	3,721,963
California	307,004	71.00	21,797,255	38,824	85.08	3,301,399
Oregon	177,842	49.90	8,874,804	3,155	68.38	215,789
Nevada	45,547	51.43	2,342,496	2,154	75.49	162,602
Colorado	127,483	58.34	7,437,666	8,247	92.12	759,897
Arizona	10,267	49.00	503,063	1,882	72.00	135,504
Dakota	247,459	76.21	18,858,150	12,323	97.89	1,206,340
Idaho	102,375	50.00	5,118,750	1,705	65.00	110,825
Montana	187,344	50.96	9,547,985	5,537	63.53	351,746
New Mexico	40,533	34.46	1,396,768	10,803	61.33	662,504
Utah	120,692	40.65	4,906,026	3,686	54.71	201,668
Washington	96,122	61.96	5,955,637	1,243	80.07	99,529
Wyoming	99,000	43.80	4,336,279	2,936	77.64	227,964
Total	13,172,936	71.82	$946,096,154	2,191,727	$79.78	$174,853,563

ESTIMATED NUMBER OF ANIMALS ON FARMS, TOTAL VALUE OF EACH KIND, ETC.—Continued.

States and Territories.	Milch Cows.			Oxen and other Cattle.		
	Number.	Average Price.	Value.	Number.	Average Price.	Value.
Maine	167,507	$29.00	$4,857,703	185,160	$27.51	$5,093,108
New Hampshire	99,021	30.50	3,020,141	141,670	29.94	4,241,119
Vermont	225,552	28.70	6,473,342	180,362	28.06	5,059,093
Massachusetts	180,319	34.17	6,161,500	105,022	28.47	2,990,105
Rhode Island	22,868	35.75	818,067	19,226	32.27	424,463
Connecticut	127,153	30.71	4,286,328	109,926	31.34	3,434,104
New York	1,540,053a	30.50	46,971,617	851,126	31.92	27,184,608
New Jersey	175,114	35.92	6,397,855	68,541	32.35	2,217,487
Pennsylvania	929,371	28.60	26,580,011	867,059	26.09	22,620,105
Delaware	28,683	30.00	860,490	27,137	28.00	759,825
Maryland	135,021	28.25	3,814,343	138,182	24.18	3,340,798
Virginia	257,793	21.50	5,542,550	423,761	17.37	7,360,725
North Carolina	243,758	16.00	3,900,128	419,383	10.99	4,607,133
South Carolina	140,195	19.00	2,777,705	212,521	12.48	2,651,835
Georgia	337,603	17.00	5,739,251	598,636	11.01	6,588,980
Florida	52,822	16.32	862,055	576,912	8.56	4,941,076
Alabama	296,787	15.40	4,570,520	445,139	9.41	4,187,82
Mississippi	285,904	15.55	4,445,807	428,909	9.48	4,064,009
Louisiana	162,649	18.30	2,851,179	270,816	11.33	3,069,187
Texas	772,718	14.20	10,972,567	6,336,004	9.95	63,077,904
Arkansas	304,404	14.68	4,453,431	469,057	9.81	4,603,415
Tennessee	329,572	19.75	6,706,547	461,239	12.61	5,815,073
West Virginia	171,273	24.07	4,122,541	290,802	18.50	5,196,913

LIVE STOCK OF THE UNITED STATES 1105   SUPPLEMENT

ESTIMATED NUMBER OF ANIMALS ON FARMS, TOTAL VALUE OF EACH KIND, ETC.—Continued.

States and Territories.	Milch Cows.			Oxen and other Cattle.		
	Number.	Average Price.	Value.	Number.	Average Price.	Value.
Kentucky	313,953	24.30	7,629,058	520,018	21.24	11,237,076
Ohio	783.481	29.20	22,877,645	967,540	25.60	24,766,690
Michigan	437.303	29.00	12,681,787	511,406	25.16	12,863,948
Indiana	556 961	27.75	15,455,068	894,344	22.44	22,008,941
Illinois	937,478	26.50	24 843 114	1,485,754	22.23	33,029,792
Wisconsin	548,222	23.83	13,064,130	640,732	20 97	13,488,103
Minnesota	433,966	23.75	10,306,693	468,886	20.36	9,974,676
Iowa	1,255,432	23.30	29,251,506	2,095,259	20.35	42,633,705
Missouri	737,250	20.25	14,929,495	1,429,453	18.24	26,077,367
Kansas	640,081	22.41	14,344,215	1,583,915	20.37	32,271,946
Nebraska	357,202	25.50	9,108,651	1,079,940	21.08	22,763,690
California	250,773	33.00	8,275,509	609,207	20.50	14,194,447
Oregon	78,097	29.60	2,338,311	598 216	20.35	12,172,122
Nevada	18,037	35.00	631,295	323.400	18.00	5,819,848
Colorado	63,023	37.21	2,345,086	1,049 353	19.93	20,918,327
Arizona	16,298	37.20	606,266	420.000	18.00	7,560,000
Dakota	223,418	21.67	4,841,468	767,809	21.73	16,687,171
Idaho	26,458	26.67	705.635	424,316	18.75	7,955,925
Montana	31,132	28.40	884.149	934,500	19.21	17,948,007
New Mexico	19,394	23.75	460,608	1,257,507	15.04	18.911,121
Utah	49,878	25.25	1,259,420	435,000	16.76	7,292,733
Washington	65,523	33.30	2,181,016	300,070	23.48	7,060,177
Wyoming	6,994	35.00	244,790	1,230,192	19.11	23,504,668
Indian Territory				620.937	14.50	9,003.587
Total	14,856,414	$24.65	$366,252,173	34,278,363	$17.79	$611,750,520

ESTIMATED NUMBER OF ANIMALS ON FARMS, TOTAL VALUE OF EACH KIND, ETC.—Continued.

States and Territories.	Sheep.			Hogs.		
	Number.	Average Price.	Value.	Number.	Average Price.	Value.
Maine	547,725	$3.01	$1,645,914	73,188	$9.13	$667,917
New Hampshire	205,023	2.98	610,968	54,309	10.93	594,311
Vermont	393,301	2.85	1,120 279	76,353	9.02	688,385
Massachusetts	62,037	3.30	206,702	65,314	10.30	672,602
Rhode Island	20,852	3.81	79,496	13,261	9.50	125,978
Connecticut	49,199	3.81	187,317	61,776	9.00	561,543
New York	1,504,067	3.40	5,413 582	686,390	8.45	5,803,084
New Jersey	105,378	3.70	389,100	191,818	9.19	1,762,326
Pennsylvania	984,801	2.80	2,756,119	1,027,477	8.03	8,254,748
Delaware	22,294	3.27	72,790	42,054	6.80	200,018
Maryland	160,254	3.35	537,171	281,397	6.24	1,756,021
Virginia	444,741	2.42	1,078,053	811.362	4.34	3,521,313
North Carolina	427,500	1.36	581,054	1,266,438	3.53	4,464,194
South Carolina	107,384	1.72	184,400	550,166	3.92	2,159,072
Georgia	442,274	1.50	664,826	1,534,189	3.17	4,859,083
Florida	92,888	1.96	182,061	307,051	2.05	628,840
Alabama	310,622	1.46	456.135	1,376,148	3.39	4,661,014
Mississippi	247,830	1.57	380,332	1,226 680	3.10	3,801.754
Louisiana	113,965	1.64	186,891	573,821	3.06	1 709,663
Texas	4,528,739	1.52	6,964,774	2,276,082	2.82	6,436,126
Arkansas	220,107	1.41	310,127	1,536,360	2.56	3,938,202
Tennessee	516,504	1.61	832,440	1,853 070	3.06	6,774,825
West Virginia	474,938	2.26	1,073,834	432,778	4.20	1,819.744
Kentucky	797,908	2.43	1,936,741	1,718,178	4.27	7,320,727
Ohio	4,106,622	2.61	10,714,177	2,668,381	5.72	15,261.021
Michigan	2,113,004	2.72	5,743,090	1,082,500	6.30	5,780.700
Indiana	1,003,068	2.55	2,553,611	2,371,085	5.94	11,082,349
Illinois	814,177	2.49	2,023,804	3 102,945	6.47	20,088,408
Wisconsin	911,662	2.15	1,902,261	1,123,860	6.02	6,766,798
Minnesota	268,725	2.38	674,698	549,793	5.92	3,254,775
Iowa	408,478	2.41	985,249	4,148,811	6.74	27,969,624
Missouri	1,097,090	1.74	1,804,973	3,798,799	3.96	15,043 246
Kansas	830,139	1.76	1,457,558	2,377,561	5.66	13,457,469
Nebraska	422,112	2.02	852,450	2,384,525	5.72	13,341,813
California	5,452 728	1.88	10,291,779	1,047,642	4.62	4,836.000
Oregon	2,930,123	1.70	4,987,060	220,728	3.01	664,819
Nevada	660,006	1.91	1,259,600	21 087	5.30	111,846
Colorado	1,137,686	1.98	2,257,109	23,419	6.54	153,109
Arizona	658,561	1.75	1,152 484	16,441	5.75	94,536
Dakota	269,019	2.60	700,520	533,970	5.94	3,173,918
Idaho	312,408	2.05	640,436	42,150	6.00	252,900
Montana	1,265,000	2.10	2,658.208	22,289	6.77	150,898
New Mexico	3 623,168	1.09	3,953,298	19,941	5.64	112,466
Utah	1,335,000	1.94	1,068,970	40,118	7.15	286,818
Washington	549,885	1.94	1,068,970	91 054	5.01	455,997
Wyoming	523,340	2.08	1,089,855	2,613	6.64	17,358
Indian Territory				841,500	2.50	2,103,750
Total	43,544,755	$2.05	$89,278,920	44,346,525	$4.98	$220,811,082

70

LIVE STOCK OF THE WORLD

LIVE STOCK OF THE WORLD. A large class of citizens, including merchants and business men, are interested in knowing the numbers of the several classes of live animals on farms in the world. The following table will show this as existing up to the latest date made known, 1887. This table will be of especial value for reference, since, except in the United States, there is comparatively little change in numbers. The table is as follows:

Countries, etc.	Years.	Cattle.	Horses.	Mules and Asses.	Sheep and Lambs.	Swine.	Goats.
NORTH AMERICA.							
United States	1888	49,234,777	13,172,936	2,191,727	43,544,755	44,346,525	
Canada:							
Ontario and Quebec	1881	2,732,500	864,150		2,249,011	1,030,121	
Nova Scotia	1881	325,003	57,167		377,801	47,256	
New Brunswick	1881	212,500	52,975		221,163	53,087	
Manitoba	1881	60,261	16,739		6,078	17,358	
Prince Edward Island	1881	90,722	31,335		166,496	40,181	
British Columbia	1881	80,451	26,122		27,788	16,841	
Northwest Territory, etc	1881	12,872	10,870		346	2,775	
Total – Canada	1881	3,514,980	1,059,358		3,048,678	1,207,619	
Ontario	1887	1,948,264	575,361		1,396,161	832,817	
Manitoba	1887	101,681	29,915		12,540	35,713	
Northwest Territory, etc	1886	86,536	24,125		19,398	22,542	
Newfoundland	1869					6,417	
Newfoundland	1884	19,884	5,436		40,326		
Jamaica	1885	130,532	62,945		13,390		
Nicaragua	1884	400,000					
Guadeloupe	1880	9,615	5,988	7,519	13,590	14,116	14,709
Guatemala	1885	494,180	117,860	45,501	460,426		
Total – North America		53,803,927	14,424,443	2,244,857	47,121,265	45,574,677	14,709
SOUTH AMERICA.							
Argentine Republic	1885	18,000,000	5,000,000		80,000,000		
Argentine Republic	1883			600,000			3,000,000
Falkland Islands	1885	7,934	3,009		516,975		
Paraguay	1884	600,000					
Uruguay	1884	5,952,340	480,686	5,742	15,921,069	100,000	5,656
Venezuela	1883	2,926,733	291,603	906,467	3,490,563	976,500	
Total – South America		27,487,016	5,776,298	1,512,209	99,928,607	1,076,500	3,005,656
EUROPE.							
Austria-Hungary:							
Austria	1880	8,584,077	1,463,282	49,618	3,841,340	2,721,541	1,006,675
Hungary	1880	5,311,378	2,078,528	33,746	9,838,133	4,160,127	333,233
Total – Austria-Hungary		13,895,455	3,541,810	83,354	13,679,473	6,881,668	1,339,908
Hungary	1884	4,879,038	1,748,859	22,993	10,594,831	4,803,639	270,192
Belgium	1880	1,382,815	271,974	10,120	365,400	646,375	248,755
Denmark	1881	1,470,078	347,561	882	1,548,613	527,417	9,331
France	1886	13,275,021	2,938,489	624,873	22,688,230	5,774,924	1,420,112
Germany	1883	15,786,764	3,522,545	9,795	19,189,715	9,206,195	2,639,994
Great Britain and Ireland:							
Great Britain	1887	6,441,268	1,428,383		25,958,768	2,298,323	
Ireland	1887	4,157,409	495,330		3,378,417	1,408,485	
Isle of Man, etc	1887	41,283	9,212		64,565	13,149	
Total – United Kingdom	1887	10,639,960	1,936,925		29,401,750	3,720,957	
Greece	1875					179,602	
Greece	1877	279,445	97,176	142,835	2,921,917		1,836,668
Italy	1881	4,783,232		968,114	8,596,108	1,163,916	2,016,307
Italy	1882		660,123				
Netherlands	1888	1,510,100	270,100		774,100	442,000	158,900
Portugal	1870	624,658			2,977,454	971,085	836,863
Roumania	1860		600,000			2,810,000	
Roumania	1884	2,376,066			4,654,776		
Russia in Europe	1883	23,528,031	17,880,798		46,724,736	9,361,680	1,067,137
Servia	1882	826,580	129,500		3,620,750	1,067,940	725,700
Spain	1878	2,353,247		1,832,635	16,939,288	2,348,802	3,813,000
Sweden and Norway:							
Sweden	1885	2,366,286	460,830		1,442,396	515,556	96,891
Norway	1875	1,016,617	151,903		1,686,306	101,020	322,861
Switzerland	1886	1,210,849	98,212	2,792	337,905	304,330	414,584
Eastern Roumelia	1883	370,862	43,001	33,415	1,558,839	107,442	425,569
Malta	1881	7,485	6,659		13,497		
Total – Europe		97,803,521	32,969,700	3,706,165	179,421,258	45,721,009	17,472,575

Countries, etc.	Years.	Cattle.	Horses.	Mules and Asses.	Sheep and Lambs.	Swine.	Goats.
ASIA.							
Russia:							
Caucasia		1,816,200	300,000		4,544,300		1,227,00
Transcaucasia		1,900,000	770,000		5,067,500		
British India:							
Madras	1884-85	9,105,697	36,951	137,002	8,495,856		
Bombay	1884-85	7,483,561	137,533	65,191	3,231,844		
Oudh	1884-85	5,144,723	101,035	52,464	1,491,565		
Punjab	1884-85	6,707,903	124,664	351,890	4,906,883		
Central Provinces	1877-88	5,200,000	94,000	22,000	641,000	132,000	
Lower Burmah	1884-85	1,566,402	8,364	4	31,893		
Mysore	1877-88	2,300,000	18,900	37,000	1,590,000	32,000	
Coorg	1884-85	97,866	550		325	5,555	
Berar	1884-85	1,850,758	89,543	23,355	400,594		
Ceylon	1885	951,805	3,983			46,684	
Cyprus	1881	30,119	38,611			212,904	
Japan	1884	1,093,471	1,564,993				
Total — Asia		45,197,805	3,238,747	699,321	30,660,628	164,000	1,227,000
AFRICA.							
Egypt	1879	228,326	8,741	87,882	320,047		
Algeria	1880		350,000			300,000	
Algeria	1884	1,126,886			6,810,579		3,999,367
Cape of Good Hope	1875	1,329,445	241,342		11,279,743	132,373	3,065,202
Natal	1880	629,735	50,012		569,556	22,927	282,506
Mauritius	1884	15,000	12,000		30,000	30,000	
Orange Free State	1881	464,575	131,504		5,056,301		673,424
Total — Africa		3,793,957	793,680	87,882	24,066,226	485,300	8,021,299
AUSTRALASIA.							
Australia:							
New South Wales	1886	1,367,844	361,063		39,169,304	209,576	
Victoria	1886	1,303,265	306,553		10,700,403	240,057	
South Australia	1884	389,726	168,420		6,695,400	168,807	
Western Australia	1886	88,254	38,360		1,809,071	24,655	
Queensland	1886	4,071,563	278,094		9,690,445	61,861	
Total — Australia		7,220,652	1,155,690		68,065,629	700,856	
Tasmania	1886	148,665	29,684		1,608,946	73,118	
New Zealand	1886	853,358	187,382		16,564,595	277,901	
Fiji Islands	1885	5,953	590		6,850	1,578	8,733
Total — Australasia		8,228,628	1,323,346		86,245,520	1,053,453	8,733
OCEANIA.							
Tahiti and Morea	1883	3,000	1,000	15	3,000	20,000	1,300

RECAPITULATION.

Countries, etc.	Cattle.	Horses.	Mules and Asses.	Sheep and Lambs.	Swine.	Goats.
North America	53,803,927	14,424,443	2,244,647	47,121,265	45,574,677	14,709
South America	27,487,016	5,775,298	1,512,200	90,928,607	1,076,500	3,005,656
Europe	97,803,521	32,369,700	3,708,165	179,421,253	45,721,000	17,472,575
Asia	45,197,805	3,238,747	699,321	30,666,628	164,000	1,227,000
Africa	3,793,957	793,689	87,582	24,066,226	785,300	8,021,299
Australasia	8,228,628	1,373,346		86,245,520	1,053,453	8,733
Oceania	3,000	1,000	15	3,000	20,000	1,300
Grand Total	236,317,854	58,576,223	8,242,439	467,452,499	94,094,939	29,751,272

LUCERNE, ALFALFA (MEDICAGO SATIVA). The remarkable success of late years attending the cultivating of Lucerne, now generally known by its Spanish name, Alfalfa, makes it necessary that it be again written up in this supplement. In the South and in the region west of the Missouri River, and in California, it is the most valuable single legume known, fully taking the place of red clover in territory not natural to this plant. But, where red clover is natural to the soil, Alfalfa will be found inferior to it. The testimony of Dr. Vasey is, that in the Southern States east of the Mississippi it is especially desirable that its merits should be better known. The climate of that section is nearly as favorable to its growth as Southern California, but much of its soil less suitable, hence reports from different localities vary somewhat as to its value. Alfalfa is less hardy than red clover and is adapted to a milder climate; still, it has stood the winters safely as far north as Vermont, New York, and Michigan, though farther west, where less protected by snow, it winter-kills more or less even as far south as Texas. The young plants are very susceptible to frost, and the mature plants, if not killed by the cold winters of the Northern States, are so weakened that they endure there for a much shorter period than in milder climates. A cold of 25° is said to kill the tops, but in the Southern States the plant quickly recovers from the effect of frost and grows most

OATS. (See also page 679). The steady annual increase in the area of oats sown is suggestive. It is proportionally more than that of wheat and corn, while the price has declined less. The figures given show that the decline in value per acre in a comparison of the periods 1880 to 1887, is 13.2 per cent. for oats, 14.9 per cent. for corn, and 22.6 per cent. for wheat. The whole matter is shown in the table below.

Years.	Total Production.	Total Area of Crop.	Total Value of Crop.	Average Value per Bushel.	Average Yield per Acre.	Average Value per Acre.
	Bushels.	Acres.	Dollars.	Cents.	Bushels.	
1880	417,885,380	16,187,977	150,243,565	36.0	25.8	$ 9.28
1881	416,481,000	16,831,600	193,198,970	40.4	24.7	11.48
1882	488,250,610	18,494,691	182,978,022	37.5	26.4	9.64
1883	571,302,400	20,324,962	187,040.264	33.0	28.1	9.27
1884	583,628,000	21,300,917	161,528,470	28.0	27.4	7.56
1885	629,409,000	22,783,680	179,631,860	28.5	27.6	7.66
1886	624,134,000	23,658,474	186,137,930	29.8	26.4	7.87
1887	659,618,000	25,920,906	200,699,790	30.4	25.4	7.74
Total	4,390,706,390	165,503,157	1,441,458,871			
Annual average	548,838,549	20,687,895	180,182,350	32.8	26.5	8.71
Annual average for preceding ten years.	314,441,175	11,076,822	111,075,228	35.3	28.4	10.08

of the winter. In the Northern States, even where it endures the winter, the yield is so much less than at the South, that it has little or no advantage over the common red clover. Farther south, however, even where both may be grown, Alfalfa is often preferred, not only for its larger yield, but also for its perennial character. Alfalfa is especially adapted to dry climates, and withstands drought much better than the ordinary clovers. Although Alfalfa improves the fertility of the soil, it must have a rich soil to start with, and it therefore is of little value as a renovator of worn-out lands. It prefers sandy soils, if fertile. The failure on sandy soils in the East and South has been mainly due to the lack of fertility to give the young plants a good start and enable them to become deeply rooted before the advent of drought. On this account it usually thrives best on rich bottom lands. Lands that are tenacious and hold water are not adapted to its culture unless well drained. Most of the lands in the West upon which it is grown successfully have a permeable subsoil. When the soil permits, its roots penetrate to a great depth. Cases have frequently been observed of their reaching a depth of twelve or fifteen feet, and depths of more than twenty feet have been reported. Hence, after the plant is established, the character of the subsoil is of more importance than that of the surface. In relation to cultivation, sow at any time that the ground is in suitable condition, and when there will be time for the plants to become well established before they are subjected either to drought or extreme cold. In the Northern States the month of May will be about the right time. Farther south, in the latitude of Northern Mississippi, September is probably the best month, and in the extreme South, or the warm valleys of California, any time will answer from fall until spring. The soil should be thoroughly prepared, and the seed sown at the rate of fifteen to twenty pounds to the acre. If sown broadcast, about the latter quantity will be required; if in drills, the former amount will be sufficient. (See also page 608.)

As an index to the relative standing of the various States in the production of oats, the following table will give the required information:

States and Territories.	Acres.	Bushels.	Value.
Maine	93,205	2,684,000	$ 1,127,280
New Hampshire	39,749	965,000	414,950
Vermont	107,723	2,736,000	1,094,400
Massachusetts	24,752	703,000	302,290
Rhode Island	6,353	165,000	70,950
Connecticut	39,417	1,088,000	456,960
New York	1,413,068	32,206,000	12,226,280
New Jersey	138,830	3,221,000	1,159,560
Pennsylvania	1,330,234	33,921,000	11,872,350
Delaware	21,623	458,000	151,140
Maryland	117,798	2,438,000	804,540
Virginia	652,665	11,095,000	3,883,250
North Carolina	654,110	8,504,000	3,741,760
South Carolina	397,196	4,607,000	2,718,130
Georgia	612,561	7,044,000	4,086,520
Florida	52,496	761,000	456.600
Alabama	422,101	4,649,000	2,692,940
Mississippi	358,551	4,410,000	2,513,700
Louisiana	36,861	498,000	263,940
Texas	580,614	12,198,000	4,511,410
Arkansas	369,125	4,710,000	1,884,000
Tennessee	645,086	9,325,000	3,505,500
West Virginia	147,207	2,531,000	885,850
Kentucky	491,400	8,847,000	3,307,980
Ohio	1,003,278	30,098,000	9,631,360
Michigan	765,000	22,644,000	7,946,080
Indiana	1,054,923	27,943,000	8,103,470
Illinois	3,090,385	108,866,000	29,393,820
Wisconsin	1,440,299	34,855,000	9,759,400
Minnesota	1,354,532	40,636,000	10,565,360
Iowa	2,438,746	74,382,000	17,851,680
Missouri	1,258,119	39,793,000	10,346,180
Kansas	1,505,291	40,041,000	11,611,890
Nebraska	922,309	25,365,000	5,326,650
California	81,955	2,196,000	1,273,680
Oregon	203,183	5,547,000	2,218,800
Nevada	7,858	196,000	98,000
Colorado	50,617	1,509,000	708,050
Arizona			
Dakota	1,180,800	37,266,000	9,316,500
Idaho	36,509	1,095,000	492,750
Montana	60,180	1,566,000	839,700
New Mexico	15,389	362,000	108,860
Utah	29,058	786,000	337,980
Washington	91,045	3,309,000	1,482,360
Wyoming	2,921	88,000	39.600
Total	25,920,906	659,018,000	200,099,790

The increase in the area of oats is undoubtedly due to two principal reasons: first, farmers and feeders are coming more and more to understand its value as a feeding material, in comparison with corn, where the money value is nearly equal, pound for pound. Oats contain all the elements of life in fairly proper proportions; corn does not. Hence larger and larger yearly quantities of this grain are used for feeding to animals, and its use as food for man, under improved processes of preparation, is also steadily increasing.

POISONING INSECTS, RECIPES FOR. The Bureau of Entomology, Department of Agriculture, Washington, sends out the following, for use as insecticides on or about plants, etc.: London purple.—To twenty pounds flour from one-quarter to one-half pound is added and well mixed. This is applied with a sifter or blower. With forty gallons of water one-quarter to one-half pound is mixed for spraying. Paris green.—With twenty pounds of flour from three-quarters to one pound is mixed and applied by sifting or by a blower. The same amount of the insecticide to forty gallons of water is used as a spray. Bisulphite of Carbon.—For use in the ground a quantity is poured or injected among the roots that are being infected. Against insects damaging stored grain of museum material a small quantity is used in an air-tight vessel. Carbolic acid.—A solution of one part in 100 of water is used against parasites on domestic animals and their barns and sheds; also on the surface of plants and among the roots in the ground. Helebore.—The powder is sifted on alone or mixed one part to twenty of flour. With one gallon of water one-quarter pound is mixed for spraying. Kerosene-Milk Emulsion.—To one part milk add two parts kerosene, and churn by force pump or other agitator. The butter-like emulsion is diluted ad libitum with water. An easier method is to simply mix one part kerosene with eight of milk. Soap Emulsion.—In one gallon hot water one-half pound whale-oil soap is dissolved. This, instead of milk, is mixed to an emulsion with kerosene in the same manner and proportion as above. Pyrethrum, Persian Insect Powder.—Is blown or sifted on dry; also applied in water, one gallon to a tablespoonful of the powder, well stirred and then sprayed. Tobacco Decoction.—This is made as strong as possible as a wash or spray to kill insect pests on animals and plants. Prof. A. J. Cook, of the Michigan Agricultural College, as to the use of gas lime as an insecticide for leaf-eating pests, says it may be scattered on as a powder, or it may be mixed with water and sprinkled on the plants. He has reason to believe that if a little of it is incorporated with the soil in beds where radishes and cabbages are growing, that the destructive maggot will not appear. It was tried on plants already attacked, and all the maggots actually touched by the powder were speedily killed. Like the kerosene emulsion, to give perfect satisfaction it must be applied as early as the fleas come to deposit their eggs. It is also stated to be very possible that by scattering this gas lime on squash vines in June, we may stay the ravages of that dreaded pest, the squash borer. We would, however, remind the reader that gas lime will kill plants if too strong, hence experiment is necessary in reducing or diluting it. (See also Entomology.)

POTATOES. The potato crop of 1887 was the smallest for years, while the acreage, 2,300,000 acres, is larger than that of any previous year. The total crop is recorded at 134,000,000 bushels, or a little above fifty-six bushels per acre, as compared with seventy-three bushels per acre, or a total crop of 163,000,000 bushels. The crop of 1879, was 169,458,539 bushels. In fact, so small a crop has not been harvested since 1881, and the quality is very generally bad. The table below will give the status of the crop from 1880 to 1886. The crop for 1887 will be subject to some modifications, yet, and probably will be placed still lower than stated above. The table is as follows:

Year.	Acres.	Per Acre.	Product.
		Bushels.	Bushels.
1880	1,842,510	91.0	167,659,570
1881	2,041,670	53.5	109,145,494
1882	2,171,636	78.7	170,912,508
1883	2,289,275	91.0	208,164,425
1884	2,220,980	85.8	190,642,000
1885	2,265,823	77.2	175,029,000
1886	2,237,000	73.0	163,000,000

The only State showing above an average is Dakota, while California and the Territories show a medium production. A curious feature in our potato crop is, we do not produce potatoes enough for home consumption. Of potatoes imported, those from Germany are best. Holland sends some good potatoes. Those from Scotland are fair in quality and those from Ireland are most uncertain; some will be of first-rate quality, others most inferior. This is said to be from the fact that they are bought in small lots from farms, and hence the quality does not run as even as those from Scotland. To show at a glance the relative yearly export and import of potatoes for the years 1877 to 1887, inclusive, the table below will give information. The fiscal period ends June 1st, each year:

Exports, bu.	Imports, bu.	Exports, bu.	Imports, bu.
1877....520,650	3,935,535	1883....439,443	2,803,962
1878... 744,409	524,584	1884....554,618	425,408
1879... 635,842	2,024,149	1885....340,860	638,693
1880... 606,080	721,808	1886... 404,948	1,937,418
1881... 638,840	2,170,372	1887....437,029	1,439,487
1882....408,286	8,789,800		

For the eleven months ending Nov. 30, 1887, the exports were 389,015 bushels and the imports 1,943,745 bushels. These figures, however, include part of the exports and imports for the period ending June 30, 1887. One more statement in relation to European cost, carriage and duty will be interesting. It is as follows:

Cents per brl.
Cost of product.................................... 50
Carriage... 65
Duty... 45
$1.60

Thus the price in New York would be $1.15 per barrel, and delivered in Chicago $1.60 per barrel. The price of potatoes in Europe for export is stated to average about fifteen to twenty-five cents per bushel, some grades running higher and some lower. The ocean rate from Liverpool or from France is from twenty-five to thirty-five cents per barrel of 180 pounds to New York; the rate from New York to Chicago, about fifty-five cents per barrel. These figures are given as a curiosity, showing that in 1887-88, there was a profit in the export of potatoes, including duty and transportation 1,000 miles inland from the seaport.

POULTRY—MANAGEMENT, CROSSES, ETC. In relation to show birds, crosses, eligible breeds for the farm, an English authority says, of the various breeds, the Dorkings were of great antiquity, having been bred from fowls brought over to England by the Romans. They required dry, sandy soil, were indifferent layers, good table birds, and excellent birds in almost every respect in which they could be considered. The Brahmas were very hardy, good layers in winter, and were large, growing to twelve or thirteen pounds weight. The Black Spanish were showy birds, but second or third rate in respect of production of eggs, and not to be recommended as table birds. The Minorcas were non-sitters, but produced large eggs, and gave a good return for their food. Their flesh was not first class, but they bred very true. The Leghorns were handsome birds that came originally from Italy. They were prolific layers, non-sitters, matured early, were hardy, but not good table birds, being rather suited for egg production. The Cochins, for which such extravagant prices were paid when they were first brought out in 1843, were large birds, easily reared, hardy, and tolerably good on the table if killed within eight months; large eaters, good sitters and mothers. Of the Dutch poultry, the Hamburgs were sprightly and elegant in shape, non-sitters, but grand layers as to numbers of eggs; flesh good, but size small, ranging from four to five pounds weight; game fowls were unequalled for courage, and were among fowls what race horses were among equines; they were good layers, splendid sitters and mothers, easily reared, magnificent for table, and well adapted for crossing. The Langshan, from the north of China, was a good and prolific winter layer, a good mother, and excellent sitter, and very valuable for crossing. The Black Orpington, really a cross-breed, were good table birds, good winter layers and bred very true. The Plymouth Rocks are a cross between the Black Javas (now so scarce in England) and the American Dominiques, and are becoming the most popular variety for general and especially for farm purposes. It is a vigorous, hardy fowl, active, and a good forager, and stands the extremes of heat and cold well. The hens are fine, excellent layers, producing richly-flavored eggs of average size; good sitters, tractable mothers, and the birds can be killed for table when twelve or fourteen weeks old. The Wyandottes stand about second to the Plymouth Rocks, and will be sure to maintain that position. The Malays, a pugnacious breed, are moderate layers, but good on the table. In the French varieties, the La Flèche make good layers, but are rather difficult to rear. The Houdans are hardy and good on table, but their crests constitute rather a drawback. The Crèvecœurs are also good birds. The Polish are more of a fancy breed, as are also the Bantams, of which there were so many varieties. In crossing, pure-bred stock should be used, and light varieties should be crossed with other light varieties to preserve uniformity of color. The following are stated to make good crosses: Brahmas and Dorkings, Plymouth Rocks and Dorkings, Plymouth Rocks and Hamburgs, Hamburgs and Dorkings (a small sized bird), white Cochins and white Dorkings (a splendid table bird), white Cochins and light Brahmas, Langshans and Plymouth Rocks (good winter layers), Game and Dorking, and Leghorns with Plymouth Rocks. For farm poultry there was nothing to come up to the Minorca crossed with the Plymouth Rock. Turkeys do best when reared on sandy soil, and they must have plenty of liberty. The Austrian white turkeys are the best layers in England. The best varieties of ducks were found to be the Aylesbury, Rouen, Pekin and Muscovy breeds. The ordinary geese are very hardy, but not big enough. The Chinese geese, either brown or white, are good varieties. The Guinea fowl is intermediate between pheasant and turkey; its eggs and flesh are delicious. In order to give a general idea of some of the most valuable breeds of turkeys and barn-yard fowls, it may be stated that the Bronze turkey stands at the head of the list for size, hardiness and good laying qualities. The color is a rich lustrous bronze. The White Holland comes next in size. It is pure white throughout. The Narragansett turkey is next to the Bronze in good qualities. It has a dark metallic plumage. The other varieties of turkeys are not so popular as the first mentioned, they are the Black, Buff and Slate. The Black turkey is pure black in plumage and has very dark legs. The Buff turkey is a buff color throughout, with flesh-colored legs. The Slate turkey has a bluish coat of feathers, with blue or light-colored legs. Of French fowls there are three principal breeds: Houdan, La Flèche and Crèvecœur. The Houdan is the most popular and has a coat of black and white with a large crest. In plumage the La Flèche is black. It has a prong-shaped comb, two spikes projecting. Like the La Flèche, the Crèvecœur is black with a small crest. Of Minorcas there are two varieties, the White and the Black. The White Minorcas have a white plumage throughout, with white beak, earlobes and legs. The Black Minorcas have a greenish black plumage and legs, with yellowish beak and white earlobes. Both varieties are hardy and are good layers. There are four varieties of Polands: The White Crested White, White Crested Black, Silver Spangled and Golden Spangled. The White Crested White Polands are beautiful fowls. They are solid white with a crest. The White Crested Black Poland is an ornamental variety. They have a black plumage, with a large white crest. The Golden Polands is red and black, with a small crest, and the Silver Poland is black and white. The Black Java is of a lustrous black color. They have small single combs, clean black legs, are good table fowls and weigh heavy, are good layers and breed true to feather. Coming now to a correct and definite general description of every point, it would take a large amount of space to describe them in detail. Nevertheless, every poultry raiser wishes definite information in relation to the breeds of barn yard fowls. To this end a careful tabulation of the observations of E. Lemain Cresne, France, a gentleman who united patience with scientific accuracy, and whose ser-

POULTRY.—Table Showing the Most Minute Characteristics of Every Known Breed.

No.	Races.	Soil.—Climate.	Development.	Incubation.	Color of Chick at its Birth.	Weight of Chick, one day old.	Daily Increase of the Weight of Chick during 20 days.	Annual Laying.	Weight of Eggs.	Quantity of Food Daily.	Flesh.	Average Weight of Flesh at 6 months.	Average Weight of Bone.	No.
						oz.	oz.	Eggs	oz.	oz		lbs. oz.	oz. d.	
1	Crevecœur	Grass, mild climate, fears the fog.	Rapid; fattens easily.	Does not sit.	Black, crest black and white, yellow neck and breast.	1 9-16	5-16	122	2 3-4	7	Exquisite, white, delicate.	4 10	7 15	1
2	Houdan	Calcareous, thrives in all climates	Very rapid	Nil.	Black and white.	1 3-8	11-32	125	2 3-16	5 13-16	Delicate.	3 15	7 0¾	2
3	La Bresse (black)	Grass, hardy in all climates.	Rapid; fattens easily.	Good sitter; does not steal nest	Black, yellow breast.	1 7-16	1-4	160	2 13-16	6 13-16	Exquisite, and fine taste.	3 8	5 4½	3
4	La Bresse (grey)	In any climate.	Rapid; fattens easily	Nil.	Grey, brown, black.	1 5-16	1-4	160	1 7-8	6 1-4	Very good.	3 7	5 1½	4
5	Barbezieux	Dry, mild climate.	Slow.	Good.	Black, yellow breast.	1 10-16	5-16	1[illegible]0	2 7-16	6 10-16	Delicate.	4 11	8 7½	5
6	La Fleche	Dry, mild climate.	Slow; fattens easily.	Nil.	Black, white breast.	1 1-2	7-32	110	2 7-16	6 13-16	Very delicate.	3 6	6 5½	6
7	Le Mans	Dry, in all climates.	Rapid.	Rarely	Black, grey breast.	1 10-16	5-16	111	2 1-4	6 14-16	Delicate	4 5	7 12	7
8	Gournay	Grass, in all climates.	Pretty rapid.	Rarely.	Black and white.	1 3-16	3-16	140	2 7-16	4 11-16	Good.	2 10	4 9	8
9	Courtes Pattes	Hardy breed, dry soil, all climates	Middling.	Good, but late.	Black, yellowish white breast.	1 1-4	3-16	150	2 2-16	6 10-16	Good.	3 10	5 7½	9
10	Andalusian	Dry, warm climate.	Middling.	Nil.	Grey, slaty light-grey breast.	1 5-16	1-4	165	2 7-16	6 12-16	Delicate.	3 1	5 13	10
11	Brahma	Hardy race, dry soil, all climates.	Slow.	Excellent; good mother.	Yellowish white.	1 5-8	7-32	120	2 1-4	9 1-2	Pretty good.	4 11	10 15	11
12	Campine (silver-spangled)	Hardy race, requires great space, all climates.	Middling.	Nil.	Black, greyish white.	1 1-16	3-16	225	1 11-16	5 1-2	Good.	2 3	4 3¾	12
13	Cochin (cinnamon	Hardy in all climates	Very slow.	Excellent; good mother, but heavy.	Yellow.	1 13-16	3-16	115	2 1-16	10 1-2	Stringy.	4 9	14 4½	13
14	Game	Hardy in all climates.	Rapid.	Capital; good mother.	Brown and black.	1 6-16	7-32	100	2 7-16	6 1-4	Excellent.	3 10	4 6½	14
15	Cosaque	Very hardy race in all climates	Rapid.	Nil.	Black, yellowish breast.	1 3-16	1-4	120	2 3-16	4 1 4	Delicate.	2 15	4 16	15
16	Dominique	Hardy in all climates.	Middling.	Very good; and excellent mother.	Light grey; dark grey.	1 1-4	7-32	110	2 7-32	4 3-4	Good.	3 11	5 6¾	16
17	Dorking	Grass, mild climate.	Very rapid.	Very good; and very good mother	Dark yellow, brown and white.	1 7-16	11-32	130	1 15-16	6 13-16	Very delicate and juicy.	6 4	7 6½	17
18	Spanish	Sandy soil, warm climate, delicate	Slow; long time feathering	Rare.	Black, yellow breast.	1 5-16	7-32	160	2 3-4	5 13-16	Delicate.	3 1	9 8¼	18
19	Hamburg (silver-spangled)	Any soil, all climates.	Middling.	Very rare.	Head white, the remainder of the body black and white.	1 2-16	7-32	239	1 11-16	5 1-4	Delicate.	2 3½	4 6½	19
20	Dutch (black)	Grass, delicate breed.	Middling	Nil.	Black back, white breast.	1 1-16	2-16	93	2	6 1-2	Pretty good	2 3	4 9	20
21	Langshan	Very hardy race in any climate.	Rapid.	Good; most excellent mother.	Black, breast and neck yellowish white	1 10-16	5-16	11[illegible]	2 3-16	7	Excellent	6 4	10 10½	21
22	Leghorn (golden-spangled)	Very hardy race in all climates.	Rapid	Very rarely.	Brown, black, light Havana.	1 1-4	1-4	190	2 7-32	6	Indifferent.	3 15	7 0¾	22
23	Polands (silver-spangled)	Delicate race, fears the damp.	Not very rapid.	Rare.	Light grey, dark grey.	1 3-16	3-16	100	2 1-16	4	Delicate.	2 13	4 13	23
24	Scotch Grey	Grass, delicate race.	Middling.	Nil.	Light grey, dark grey.	1 1-4	7-32	110	2 7-32	6 13.16	Good	3 4½	4 15	24
25	Bantam (silver-spangled)	Very delicate breed, dry soil	Middling.	Pretty good.	Grey, light grey and white.	9-16	.....	80	1 1-8	2 7-8	.....	.....	.....	25
26	Game Bantam	Delicate breed, dry soil.	Middling.	Good; must not be disturbed.	Black, brown, light Havana.	7-16	.....	93	1 1-32	2 3-4	.....	.....	.....	26
27	Nagasaki	Sandy soil.	Middling	Indifferent.	Light grey, yellowish white.	1-3	.....	95	1 3-32	3 1-8	Good	.....	.....	27
28	Silkies	Very hardy race in all climates.	Rapid.	Excellent; very good mother	Silky down, straw yellow, very light.	3-4	.....	96	1 1-4	3 9-16	Very bad, horrible.	.....	.....	28

vices have been recognized by the French Government, will be most valuable. It shows at a glance all that it is possible to convey in many pages of print. There is nothing left to chance, and the whole matter is complete, except in the column "incubation." Where the word "nil" occurs, no full observation was made. On general principles, it may be stated that the breeder or farmer who does not leave to chance the future of his poultry yard can, by consulting this table, make his choice of the poultry most probably suitable to the soil he cultivates, and which is likely to prove the most profitable, whether for egg producing or for the table. Our authority says, should any be undecided about the choice of a breed, let him look first to the nature of the land, whether it is dry, damp, calcareous, sandy, or grass land; then he may consult the table, (page 1111,) and make his choice accordingly. Certain breeds of fowls cannot live in damp, foggy atmosphere; others, on the contrary, can live in all climates, and the fact is stated that fowls native of torrid zones are often more hardy than birds native of temperate zones. The table will be useful in various ways. It shows even in the chick as soon as hatched to which breed it belongs; it also gives the daily increase in weight during the period of the first twenty days. It shows the produce of eggs in each race; it gives the weight of the different eggs, also the average weight of flesh at six months old, as also the weight of bone, and on this account the table ought to be carefully studied. Suppose you wish to know which breed produces the most flesh. The table gives the Langshan as the heaviest; but with five pounds four ounces of flesh, there are ten ounces, ten and a-half drachms of bone. The Dorking, five pounds three and a-half ounces of flesh, has only seven ounces, six and a-half drachms of bone. (See table on preceding page.)

PROTECTION AGAINST FLOODS. The yearly destruction caused by river floods, the protection of levees and natural river banks and artificial embankments against erosion from various causes, demand the best attention of those who may be subject to inundation, or to the abrasion of natural and artificial banks through the action of water. Every person having banks of rivers to protect, or levees to be held intact, road overseers and railway companies who have property to be protected against encroachment, are especially interested in this matter. Encroachments by whatever cause must be promptly met by counteracting means. It is an important subject for discussion before every horticultural body, and by all whose interests lie in protecting lines of transportation. The higher civilization of to-day must meet results brought about by the cutting away of forest growths in the past. The mischief already accomplished can never be fully met. On the contrary, it will go on increasing from year to year so long as the remaining hills and forests are denuded by their owners. There are yet enormous areas to be cut away. In a Government like ours it does not seem practicable that legislation should undertake the regeneration of our forests. Individuals must be shown that their interests lie in this preservation or regeneration. Every declivity, rocky ridge, hillside and mountain liable to wash will pay better in trees and grass than in any other crop. It is easy of demonstration. The price of timber and lumber is yearly increasing. It will continue so to be. A wild forest contains twenty trees of little commercial value, to one of general utility. The planted grove or forest contains just such species as are planted and required and just where they are wanted. The remedy is in planting valuable trees when others are cut away, to leave enough underbrush on hillsides for nurses to planted trees, and to cause the water to percolate through the soil rather than to allow it to run over the surface; or else to plant new forests and cultivate them to increase their size as rapidly as possible. Along all such natural obstructions to the passage of water, osier willows, strong-rooted grasses, and trees having fibrous, interlacing roots, should be planted. These will gradually catch the debris. The collections will thus be more or less held, so the water in passing by must percolate more or less slowly. Thus it will be taken up into the soil below. The aggregate temporary water surface thus secured will be enormous in checking sudden floods. Artificial reservoirs to hold surplus water to be given off gradually in summer will also be of great value. These, however, must, as a rule, be undertaken by the General Government for this reason: Their effects reach far beyond the boundary of individual States. Nevertheless, the profits would be ample in isolated cases, to individuals, in assisting the water power in time of drought. Levees should especially be protected by the planting of osier and other fibrous-rooted willows, and strong-rooted grasses, in addition to the more artificial means of protection. This will be found the cheapest means of preventing erosion of the banks, and especially valuable on the silt levees of the lower Mississippi, using varieties found most natural to the climate and situation. The South is especially rich in grasses tenacious to the soil, and these means should in no respect be neglected. In a majority of cases they will check the tearing out by water breaks, and give time to apply means that otherwise would be futile. If to the various means which would naturally suggest themselves to the competent engineer having charge of works in the several localities, in addition to those suggested, could be added a system for closing all ditches to enable them to hold in check their utmost capacity, such as the temporary closing of sloughs, gulches and ravines, as might be found practicable, it would solve, measurably at least, the recurrence of terribly destructive floods, except at comparatively rare intervals. The suggestions, as given, are the natural remedies to be employed, as embodying those least destructive to private interests. Only in the closing temporarily of ditches, sloughs and gulches could damage ensue, and here only through a false view of the case. The flooding of lands along these water courses for a short time in the spring, being chiefly grass lands, would be a benefit in nine cases out of ten. Grass lands may be flooded for forty-eight hours at a time at any season during their earlier growth, and often with benefit. When vegetation is dormant this flooding may be extended to a week or ten days. The same rule will hold good where there are no crops, and except winter wheat, rye, barley and oats, no crop would be injured by flooding with back water in the spring. Railway and other raised embankments may also be perfectly protected from washing by planting them us to their sides with osier and other dwarf willows and tenacious grasses. Where they are subject also to the wash of water at times this means will be found invaluable The objection to these growths, that "they obstruct the repair of tracks," is invalid, since the planting need not extend high enough to thus interfere. The real difficulty has been that the work has been entrusted to laborers whose ignorance has led them to suppose the planting would reduce their days of service. The other objection, that they must yearly be cut, to prevent obstruction to the sight, is scarcely worth noticing. The same scythe employed in cutting other brush and grass will here suffice, unless the labor be unduly neglected. The yearly decrease in our timber and lumber supplies has long since called for substitutes in building. Brick, stone and iron have, in a great measure so far, and better and more economically supplied the want in outside work, and especially in cities. The increasing scarcity of finishing lumber, and that for ties and other railroad work, vehicles, furniture and various manufactures, has caused forest growths to be carefully examined from Maine to Georgia, and from the Alleghanies to Indiana—the last great remaining timber belt east of the Sierra Nevadas. Prices have doubled and trebled in respect to many species of timber within the last ten years. The time has now come when the man who plants timber, in suitable situations, will as surely reap profit as in any other direction in agriculture. Abundant crops of wheat, corn and other cereals may glut the markets of the world; a glut of merchantable lumber can never come. It is wanted every day and everywhere. Before the crop can be matured of trees planted now, still further advance in price will be reached, and thus the cultivator will receive compound interest on his investment. (See also Moisture, Rain and Vapor.)

PRUNING AND CARE OF ORCHARDS.

It is a somewhat general opinion that the agriculture of 100 years ago was crude and of the simplest kind. It was especially supposed that horticulture was given but little attention. It is true the implements of cultivation were crude and inefficient, as compared with our day, and the cultivation laborious. Practically, however, the cultivation was most excellent, the soil, climate and condition seem carefully to have been studied. In respect to pruning, the system of well furnished heads for fruit trees was then advocated as is now the case by the better informed in the United States, and especially in the West. Knight, upon the subject of pruning, is coincided with by Dickson, a voluminous and competent English authority of the early part of the century, and is quoted as advocating the protection of trees by allowing the foliage to grow dense and thick. The cutting away of branches is especially condemned, as is the opening out of centers of trees. There seems to have been tree butchers then as now. Upon this subject Knight says: "The ignorant pruner gets into the middle of the tree, and lays about him right and left, till he leaves only small tufts of branches on the extremity of the large boughs. The branches now receiving the whole nourishment of the tree of course increases rapidly, and soon become, when loaded with fruit or snow, too heavy for the long naked boughs—which are, of necessity, full of dead knots from the former labors of the pruner—to support. Many hundreds of trees perish annually from this cause. It is believed the present system of pruning ought to be precisely reversed, and that the pruner should confine himself almost entirely to the extremity of the branches and leave the internal parts of the tree nearly as he finds it. Large branches should rarely or never be amputated." He also instances the protection afforded to trees by their thick foliage. From the above it is seen that light pruning was considered the best in England more than 100 years ago. If correct in the humid climate of England with its low temperature, how much more important in the West with its dry, hot, summer climate. We now advocate as little pruning as may be compatible with habit and due symmetry of form of the trees. Abrasion of the branches should be prevented. The habit of the variety should, in every case, be taken into account in pruning. Some trees bear the fruit at or near the extremity of the branches, others do so within the shelter of the foliage. The olden writers on horticulture gave special attention to the varieties of the apple fit for cider. The apple was then regarded as of special value if it made good, sound cider. The uses for which the apple is now used are changed, in this country, to what it was 100 years ago. The superior old cider fruits have almost disappeared from our lists, and apples superior for cooking and for dessert have taken their place. Soils would seem to have been carefully considered in the olden time. There were various opinions then as to the best soils, and the quality of soils adapted to the varieties of the apple just as there are now. A century before Knight wrote, the best apples were thought to be raised on light sandy loams, especially so for cider of fine body and quality. In Knight's time a soil of entirely different nature was chosen, strong red clays, but Mr. Knight is careful to explain that much of the soil, then called clay, is really an argillaceous marl, some of it containing so large a proportion of calcareous earth that it effervesced strongly, under the action of an acid. This was considered a most superior soil for producing sound cider, free from austerity. Upon soils so underlaid were found the best orchards of that day. Nevertheless, it was held that the best cider apples were produced on a "shallow loam on a limestone basis." The best orchards to-day are upon precisely such soils. A limestone soil, if well drained, is a good fruit soil anywhere, and no soils are better adapted to fruits than our marly clays and the loess formations of the West. A Herefordshire, English, report of the early part of the century, gives some interesting information as to soils adapted to varieties, varieties adapted to a special purpose, and also upon a question which has long excited controversy—in this country—the effect of graft on stock, and the influence of soils upon grafted varieties. Upon this subject the report says:

"There can be no doubt but the apple tree is capable of succeeding in soils of very different qualities, provided they be perfectly free from stagnant (excessive) moisture; that from many trials in retentive soils, where the bottom is wet, they begin to grow mossy, and decline in the course of a very few years. Experiment, it says, had shown that early fruits obtain their greatest perfection in a sandy soil, and the late ones answer best when they are planted in a strong loamy or clayey one. The more celebrated of the cider fruits there known for light, sandy soils, were the Styre, Hagloe Crab and the Golden Pippin. It was stated as beyond controversy that cuttings from the same tree grafted on similar stocks, but planted in different soils, produced different liquors. And, it was also admitted that liquors of the strongest body, and which kept best, were produced from trees grown on clayey soils."

The following was compiled some years ago by the editor and is introduced here as valuable to pomologists now: "Of the varieties of reputable cider fruits given in Dickson's Agriculture, those that have come down to us as retaining their original names in Downing and Warder's works are: Styre, Hagloe Crab, Red Streak, Golden Pippin, Russet, Wine Apple, Margil Green (Aromatic ?), Cornish, Cats-head, and Brandy Apple. Of these, the Styre, an early sort, is noted for the strength and excellence of its cider. The yellowest, or forest Styre, from which we infer there were others of that name, is described by Mr. Crocker as being small, red on one side, and a fine yellow on the other; of a mild, pleasant acid, making an excellent cider." In relation to productiveness of sorts, Crocker says of the Normandy, of which there are three varieties, "the yellow, white and green; all of a bitter sweet taste, make rich cider and of a high color, and the trees are abundant bearers; thirty trees of this variety in the fifth year from grafting produced five hogsheads of cider of 100 gallons each. Allowing ten bushels of apples to the barrel of thirty-two gallons, this would give an average of nearly six bushels per tree, at five years from grafting." This would seem to show that we have not gained much in early maturity of sorts during this century. It shows, also, that our forefathers did not take much stock in the assertions of leading cultivators of a later day, that the grafter could not expect to gather the fruit of the trees he might plant. (See also Horticulture, Orcharding, etc.)

ROTATION FOR THE SOIL. The value of rotation is no longer denied by any. It has long been accepted as one of the most important in conserving the fertility of the soil, but a rotation to be valuable must include not only the smaller cereal grains, but as large a variety of cultivated crops as possible. In connection with the foregoing, meadows and pastures are the most important in assisting to restore fertility, and in connection with the great fallow crop of the United States, Indian corn. The fertility of originally fertile land may by these means be kept up fully and indefinitely. All the small cereal grains are exhausting, and none more so than oats, of valuable constituents. A soil that will produce fifty bushels of oats per acre should produce twenty bushels of wheat. The oat crop will exhaust nearly as much potash, nearly half as much of the phosphates, and nearly 50 per cent. more nitrogen than the crop of wheat named, in the grain. The value of straw as manure is about equal in each, but wheat is always sold to be carried away from the farm, while oats may or should be fed at home. Thus a large amount of the valuable fertilizing materials are returned to the soil as manure if carefully saved. The reason why Indian corn is so little exhausting to the soil is that it is nearly all fed on the farm, and the stalks, being fed off in the fields, these and the manure dropped are again plowed under. Another reason why Indian corn is not excessively exhausting to the soil is that it contains more largely of carbon and less of phosphate and nitrogen, but more potash. Neither the elements of carbon—starch, sugar, oil, etc.—nor potash are deficient in fertile soils, neither do they wear out so easily as the phosphates and albuminoids, or, as the latter may be properly classed, nitrogen. Indian corn, also, must receive clean and careful cultivation, in order to produce a good crop. Hence it is the cheapest and best fallow or cleaning crop known to American agriculture. Flax is generally classed as an exhausting crop. It is not especially so, however, certainly not more so than wheat and oats, if reaped and the straw is returned to the soil. It, however, unless especially cleaned, brings into the soil all manner of foul weeds, difficult to eradicate. The difficulty with a rotation that includes only the small cereal grains, and flax is, these grains are constantly exhausting the soil of one class of constituents, and largely of the more difficult to replace, phosphorous and nitrogen. The great value of pasture, then, is that nearly all the manure made is returned directly to the soil, and the manure made from the hay of meadows may easily be returned. The true value of straw on the farm is as an absorbent of the liquid manure, more valuable by far than that of the solids. Plenty of pasture and plenty of Indian corn, therefore, are the most valuable in the long run in the rotation of crops. These conserve, while the selling of the cereal grain carries away fertility that can never be replaced for the price of that carried away, unless the land is cultivated to other crops to such an extent as to allow the soil naturally to recuperate. In the West, or on any virgin soils, not less than three-quarters of the land should be in pasture, meadow and fallow crops one year with another, to hold the full fertility of the soil. In order to fully accomplish this, all the manure should be saved and again be carted on to the soil. In this connection, Prof. J. W. Sanborn, reporting experiments in crop rotation, gives the following which are valuable upon the philosophy of rotation: Rotations are valuable because plants vary in the area of the soil in which the roots grow, and from which they derive the sustenance of the plant, thus more completely utilizing the soil within their reach. There is a remarkable variation in the power of plants to appropriate the various elements of plant growth, due, at least in part, to the character of the acids secreted by their roots. Thus one plant, like clover, has a high power of gathering nitrogen, and another, like wheat, a very low power. Plants vary in their weight of roots; as an illustration, clover carries several times the weight of roots that wheat does; it will be seen that, inasmuch as clover roots are very much richer in nitrogen than wheat, and carry enough nitrogen to grow a crop of wheat, that wheat will most advantageously follow clover. Thus, likewise, other plants follow each other advantageously. Rotation of crops baffles, in a large measure, the root enemies, both insect and fungus, that prey upon them. Each plant having its own peculiar enemies, changing of plants removes them to fields unoccupied by such enemies. This is true of the above-ground growth of plants to an important degree. Plants vary in the amounts of varying elements of nutrition actually taken up in growth; thus, while wheat takes only one and one-fourth pounds of potash for every pound of phosphoric acid, potatoes take three and one-fourth pounds of potash for each pound of phosphoric acid. Continuous growth of potatoes would exhaust the potash of the soil or of supplied manure long before the phosphoric acid would give out. The leaves of plants vary in their power of gaining food and of vaporizing water, and are roughly divided into broad and narrow leaved. Leaves vary in their season of active growth. Those plants maturing in midsummer and early fall generally gather nitrogen (corn and turnips are good examples), following in their growth the decomposing influence of the sun, more easily and fully than other crops do. Rotation conserves soil fertility and yet aids in soil decomposition by alternation of grass, or clover crops and hoed crops. Under a continuation of plow and tillage crops, leaching, volatilization and washing of fertility is rapid and may be or is more than carried away by crops, especially so of nitrogen. Rotation of crops distributes labor over the year, and therefore economizes labor and gives regular help and aids in the solution of the labor problem of the farm. (See also Rotation of Crops, Soil, etc.)

RYE. The rye crop of the United States is insignificant in comparison with the other cereals. The Statistician of the Department of Agriculture, in his latest report, says of this crop and those following, that it is used to a limited extent for bread in combination with maize in New England and by the people coming from continental Europe, and in a still smaller proportion for distillation. The crop of 1886 was about an average, 26,000,000 bushels, in round numbers, yielding a little less than twelve bushels per acre. The following statement shows the previous production and value.

driven by a small engine. On this shafting and five feet apart are cast-iron wheels two feet in diameter, each wheel having one side of its flange slightly beveled. Six feet six inches above the shearing floor, and attached to each post by back screws, and five feet apart, is a cast-iron bracket with an extension of three feet of right angle iron. On each bracket is a small leather wheel four inches in diameter, with a bevel of one and one-half inches, corresponding to the bevel of the iron wheel above. This wheel, which rotates on a spindle, is formed by compressing several layers of leather between brass plates. On the end of the spindle is a steel hook, and outside the bearing is screwed a brass coupling, which is attached to a flexible tube six feet six inches long. Inside this tube is a piece of round gut half an inch in diameter, with a hook at one end and an eye at the other; the eye is placed in the hook at the end of the spindle carrying the small leather friction wheel, and the hook is placed in the eye at the end of the universal joint forming part of the shearing machine. The connection is made complete by a thin brass coupling slipping over a light brass ferule on the end of the flexible tube and screwed to the end of the universal joint. By pulling a small cord hanging from the bracket, a spring liberates the catch and instantly the bevel leather wheel is pushed into position and contact with the bevel of the iron wheel revolving on the shaft, and thus it communicates a rotary motion to the core inside the flexible tube, and so to the small rods working their crank inside the casing of the machine. This crank moves from side to side of the cylinder, and thus causes the fork with cutter attached at the end to reciprocate over the comb, and as the comb is pushed into the wool, so does the small cutter cut. An eight horse-power engine will drive one hundred shears, one man attending each, and their construction is not so complex but that a shearer of ordinary intelligence can learn to work them in a few hours. The time required for the shearing of one sheep is from three and a half to five

Calendar Years.	Total Production.	Total Area of Crop.	Total Value of Crop.	Average Value per Bushel.	Average Yield per Acre.	Average Value of Yield per Acre.
	Bushels.	Acres.	Dollars.	Cents	Bushels.	Dollars.
1880	24,540,829	1,767,619	18,564,560	75 6	13.9	1,050
1881	20,704,050	1,789,100	19,327,415	93 3	11 6	1,080
1882	29,960,037	2,227,889	18,480,194	61.5	13.4	828
1883	28,058,583	2,314,754	16,300,503	58.0	12 1	704
1884	28,640,000	2,343,040	14,857,040	52.0	12.2	634
1885	21,756,000	2,129,301	12,504,820	57.9	10.2	592
Total	153,660,399	12,572,626	100,083,532			
Annual Average	25,610,067	2,095,438	16,680,589	65.1	12.2	706
Annual Average for preceding ten years	18,460,985	1,305,061	12,945,136	70.1	14.1	992

SHEARING SHEEP BY MACHINERY. There have been many attempts to perfect machines for shearing sheep. They have been all either partial or total failures. Lately, however, a machine has been invented in Australia, and after two years' trial it has been pronounced a success. The *Mark Lane Express*, one of the foremost agricultural journals of Great Britain, speaking of this machine, says it consists of a length of shafting facing the shearing floor,

minutes. In this connection we see no reason why such a machine may not be practically applied on the great sheep ranches of the United States. We also think there is room for improvement in the system of washing and shearing followed in many parts of this country. The smaller flocks are generally shorn by gangs of shearers, who start fair enough, but who get out of their regular engagements as the work goes on, simply because A has washed his sheep earlier than he expected, whilst B has not washed his so soon as he expected, and D has not washed his at all. The weather after washing makes a great difference to the date of shearing, and thus it often falls out that A's sheep are shorn too late, and B's too early; in either case it would have been better had the sheep not been washed at all. In fact we are decidedly of opinion that it would be economy to give up the practice of sheep-washing entirely. It would be supposed that the finer wools of Australia would pay for washing, because of freightage on, say, one-third extra weight, but of late years this idea has been dispelled. It pays to wash the finer fleeces on the sheep's back with warm water in an elaborate bath, but for the rest it appears that, whereas, in 1869, the proportion of wool exported in the grease from Australia amounted to only 30 per cent. of the whole, in 1886 it amounted to 70 per cent. of the whole. In the United States and in the La Plata districts the increase of the wool marketed in the grease of late years has been very marked. In the former country the wool crop for 1886 was returned as 261,469,650 pounds, of which 52,874,-524 pounds were washed wool, and 208,595,126 pounds greasy wool. The principle of selling greasy wool must, therefore, be right, and we think the practice will commend itself to our flock-masters. If middlemen object, let steps be taken to sell direct to the manufacturers. Meanwhile, shearing by mechanical means is worthy of more extended trial than it has yet had in this country, for the idea is not a novel one. The principle is one which only needs perfection in detail, to which the Australian invention would seem to have more nearly approached than anything by which it has been preceded.

SISAL AND MANILLA FIBER. Among the new fiber plants lately growing in importance in the United States, Sisal and Manilla may be mentioned. The history and uses and statistics thereof, as stated by Mr. A. M. Earle, of Akron, Ohio, are worthy of record, as we find it stated, in 1877, in the *Farm, Field and Stockman*, and of which we give an account of its uses in agriculture, especially for binder twine. Agave Sisalana, or Sisal hemp, is the agave or aloe plant, a genus of the cactus family. It derives its name "Sisal" from the port of Sisal, where it was formerly exported from. It is a native of Yucatan, a State of the Mexican Confederation. There are several varieties of the agave plant, all deriving their name from the country which produces them, as Agave Americana, Agave Mexicana, Agave Yucatana. The agave has only been grown successfully, as a fiber plant, n the State of Yucatan, the worn-out soil of which is peculiarly adapted to it. The plant is best propagated by cuttings, the young plants being allowed to grow at will until three years old, after which they are transplanted into regular rows in fields. They require but little cultivation and are of rather slow growth, taking about eight years to mature into plants to bear the cutting, after which time, if moderate care be exercised, they will last for many years. In arid soils and upon the uplands the leaves cluster around the stalk, which reaches but a few inches, often not more than a foot or so, above the ground, with the broad leaves six or eight inches wide, coarse and very thick. On the lowlands the leaves are much narrower, much longer and produce better and finer fiber, from three to six inches long. If they are allowed to remain on the stalk they continue to grow and increase in length during the entire life of the plant. Hemp that is grown upon the lowlands is much the best. The hemp, until 1862, was cleaned by a very primitive method, as pounding the leaves between stones, and whipping them to cleanse them of the outer coat. It is now cleansed by passing it over a toothed wheel of large diameter and driven by steam. The long, pulpy leaf is thrust in toward the wheel; the teeth seize it, and in a second a mass of fiber is left hanging to the butt of the leaf, still held in the hands of the operator. A similar process converts the whole into a bunch of fiber, which it does without loss of very much good material. The increasing attention paid to the agave as a fiber plant has opened a field

AGAVE SISILANA

YASHQUI.)

and caused a demand for new machines, and devices to be used in its preparation for the market. After the hemp is cleaned it is tied into small hanks and these hanks are then pressed into bales weighing from 350 to 500 pounds, bound with ropes, the special mark of the shipper or grower is placed on them, and the bales are then shipped to New York, Boston and other seaboard points. Over six-sevenths of all Sisal hemp exported from Yucatan goes to the various parts of the United States, New York leading the past year with over 209,095 bales. The following figures are believed to be accurate: In 1860 there were imported and used in the United States, 1,393 bales of Sisal hemp, weighing 445,-760 pounds; in 1870, 19,893 bales, weighing 6,962,550 pounds; in 1880, 80,252 bales, weighing 25,910,094 pounds; from January 1st, 1860, to January 1st, 1884, 859,945,750 pounds; from January 1st, 1884, to January 1st, 1887, 435,586 bales, weighing 139,387,520 pounds. Total amount, from date of first shipment of Sisal hemp to this country (in any quantity), January

1st, 1860, to January 1st, 1887, 599,333,270 pounds, exceeding that of Manilla the past year by 37,863,290 pounds. During the past six years as much Sisal hemp was used as had been imported in the twenty years previous. Manilla hemp (fiber), of the Musa genus, endogenous plants indigenous to Asia, and including the banana and plantain. It very much resembles the banana and derives its name from the port of Manilla, where it is now mostly and formerly was exported from. It is a native of Suzon, the largest of the Phillipine Islands, a group lying in the tropics, north of Australia, and east and south of Asia. It grows readily from seeds and also from shoots or suckers. When cut down it easily sprouts from the same root, and can be grown in any tropical country, often reaching the height of twenty or twenty-five feet, having a tuft of leaves only at the top. After the hemp is dried and cleaned it is tied in hanks and put in bales weighing 270 pounds, covered with grass matting, bound tightly with rattan, and shipped to England, France and the United States, the voyage taking about four months. The following figures are believed to be correct: In 1843 there was imported and used in the

MUSA ROSACEA

(BANANA OR PLANTAIN TREE.)

United States 27,820 bales, weighing 7,511,400 pounds; in 1860, 143,618 bales, weighing 38,-766,860 pounds; in 1870, 133,338 bales, weighing 36,001,260 pounds; in 1880, 44,570,367 pounds. From January 1st, 1843, to January 1st, 1884, the amount aggregated 1,346,589,745 pounds, together with the amount 100,403,870 pounds, imported in the years 1885 and 1886, gives a total number of pounds imported and used in the United States from January 1st, 1843, to January 1st, 1887, as 1,446,998,615 pounds. Entire total amount of Sisal and Manilla hemp received into the United States, for the past forty-three years, 1,946,331,885 pounds. The above figures do not include Canada or the quantity of Sisal hemp exported to England. There is at this time capacity enough in the United States (to say nothing of Canada and its provinces) to manufacture three or four times more cordage and binder twine of the above material, than there is demand for. The consequence is the market is overstocked, competition strong and prices low, which increases the tendency of some manufacturers to make an inferior article. The above figures will show the immense amount of Manilla and Sisal hemp which has been used in this country since 1843, to what extent the material is required, and how much we are dependent upon these two productions of tropical countries. The annual product of cordage manufactured in the United States is estimated at 120,000,000 pounds. Of this quantity, 7 per cent. is exported to foreign countries, and of the remainder, one-half, or about 27,000 tons, consists of binder twine, and the amount now used for that purpose alone is equal in quantity to the whole amount of cordage annually manufactured in this country previous to the year 1887. (See also Fiber.)

SORGHUM SUGAR. More than fifteen years ago the writer stated the opinion that the time was not far off when sugar from sorghum, in paying quantities, would be a fixed fact, and also, the probability was, the Western States would compete successfully with European countries manufacturing beet sugar, as an article for use at home and for export. This was founded upon the fact, first, that the saccharine elements were amply present in sorghum to fully as great a degree as in the beet; and, second, only time and improved methods were necessary to discover the proper method of eliminating and manufacturing it at a profit. The experiments of the last few years, and particularly the work of the last two years, have practically demonstrated this. There is plenty of sucrose (true sugar), as well as glucose (grape sugar), in the plant. During the autumn and winter of 1877–78, this was demonstrated both in Kansas and in New Jersey. In Louisiana, the process was successfully established in the treatment of the juice of the true sugar cane of the tropics. When we reflect that it required a generation of our race to fully establish the successful cultivation and working of the beet for sugar in Europe, and further, that now the beet furnishes more than two-thirds of the entire sugar product of the world, the sorghum growers of the United States may well be congratulated on the measure of success, so far. The sugar is in the cane, and the last year has demonstrated that it can be successfully and profitably manufactured. Ten or fifteen years more may, in all probability, work as great results in sorghum sugar for the United States as has beet sugar for Europe. At this time it seems the Western and Northwestern States, west of the Mississippi, are destined to become one of the great regions of the world in the production of sugar. The record of experiments as carried out by the Department of Agriculture of the United States, under the direction of Commissioner Colman, who for many years previously had given his best endeavors in the direction of sorghum and sorghum sugar, is interesting. Commissioner of Agriculture, Le Duc, extended a strong helping hand to the sorghum-sugar industry while in office. His successor in office, Commissioner Loring, while being skeptical as to results, had the work continued during his term of office. The present commissioner, Norman J. Colman, has extended all the aid at his command, and, assisted by liberal appropriations from Congress, he has every reason to feel gratified at the great success attained the present year. The history of experimental sugarmaking in Kansas—which may be called the central region in the West for the cultivation of sorghum cane—is as follows: From 1878 to 1882, much attention was given to the study of sorghum juices from canes cultivated in the Department of Agriculture, at Washington, under the direction of Dr. Peter Collier, Chief Chemist of the Department. The records of the Department show that, stimulated by the analytical results published by Dr. Collier, interested parties erected large sugar factories and provided them with costly appliances. Hon. John Bennyworth erected one of these at Larned, in Kansas. S. A. Liebold & Co. subsequently erected one at Great Bend. Both of these factories made some sugar, both lost money, and both quit the business. Sterling and Hutchinson followed with factories which made considerable amounts of merchantable sugar at no profit. The factory at Sterling was erected by R. M. Sandys & Co., of New Orleans, who sought, by combining Mr. Sandys' thorough knowledge of sugar with the best practical skill of the South, to establish the sorghum-sugar industry on a proper basis. For two seasons this combination worked faithfully, and while the syrup produced paid the expenses of the factory, not a crystal of sugar was made. The factory then, in 1883, changed hands, and passed under the superintendency of Prof. M. A. Scovell, then of Champaign, Ill., who, with Professor Weber, had worked out, in the laboratories of the Illinois Industrial University, a practical method for obtaining sugar from sorghum in quantities which, at prices then prevalent, would pay a profit on the business. But prices declined, and after making sugar for two years in succession, the Sterling factory succumbed. The Hutchinson factory at first made no sugar, but subsequently passed under the management of Prof. M. Swenson, who had successfully managed sugar in the laboratory of the University of Wisconsin. Large amounts of sugar were made at a loss, and the Hutchinson factory closed its doors. In 1884, Hon. W. L. Parkinson fitted up a complete sugar factory at Ottawa, Kansas, and for two years made sugar at a loss. Mr. Parkinson was assisted during the first year by Dr. Wilcox, and during the second year by Professor Swenson. In 1886 and 1886, Congress made further appropriations. It had been previously shown that by the process of diffusion and carbonization, crystallized sugar could be produced, and that 95 per cent. of the sugar in the cane could be marketed, either as syrup or dry sugar. In 1887, sugar in paying quantities was produced by a company of which Hon. W. L. Parkinson was manager,

at Fort Scott, Kansas. The success has been due, first, to the almost complete extraction of the sugars from the cane by the diffusion process; second, the prompt and proper treatment of the juice in defecating and evaporating; third, the efficient manner in which the sugar was boiled to grain in the strike-pan. The total product and status at the end of the season of 1887, is given below from notes in the report of M. Parkinson, as follows:

Sugar, 235,896 pounds, at 5¾ cents	$18,559.98
Sugar, State bounty, at 2 cents	4,716.52
	17,276.50
Syrups, 51,000 gallons (estimated), at 20 cents.	10,200.00
Seed (estimated)	7,000.00
Value of total product	34,476.50

TOTAL COST.

Cane, 3,840 tons, at $2	7,680.00
Seed, 967 tons, at $2	1,934.00
	9,614.00
Labor bill from August 15 to October 15, including labor for Department experiments	5,737.16
Coal, including all experiments	1,395.77
Salaries, etc.	3,500.00
Insurance, sundries, etc.	1,500.00
Total	21,746.93
Total value	34,476.50
Total cost	21,246.93
Net	$13,229.57

It will be interesting to follow the production of saccharine matter, and its inversion in the cane. The chemist produces glucose, or grape sugar, from either starch or sugar by treatment with acid, but all attempts have failed to produce cane sugar from either starch or grape sugar. The farmer, then, or perhaps more accurately the power which impels the plant to select and combine in proper form and proportions the three elements, carbon, hydrogen and oxygen, is the real sugar-maker. All after processes are merely devices for separating the sugar from the other substances with which it grows. The process of the formation of sugar in the cane is not fully determined; but analyses made of canes at different stages of growth show that the sap of growing cane contains a soluble substance having a composition and giving reactions similar to starch. As maturity approaches, grape sugar is also found in the juice. A further advance towards maturity discloses cane sugar with other substances, and at full maturity perfect canes contain much cane sugar and little grape sugar and starchy matter. In sweet fruits the change from grape sugar to cane sugar does not take place, or takes place but sparingly. The grape sugar is very sweet, however. Cane sugar, called also sucrose or crystallizable sugar, when in dilute solution is changed very readily into grape sugar or glucose, a substance which is much more difficult than cane sugar to crystallize. This change, called inversion, takes place in overripe canes; it sets in very soon after cutting in any cane during warm weather; it occurs in cane which has been injured by blowing down or by insects or by frost, and it probably occurs in cane which takes a second growth after nearly or quite reaching maturity. Since sugar is produced only by nature's processes of growth and is easily lost through inversion, it is evident that the farmer's part in the process of sugar-making is first and most important of all. It is a subject which invites most careful, scientific, and practical attention, and will be further considered under the subject "Improving the cane." It is apparent from what has already been said, that to insure a successful outcome from the operations of the factory, the cane must be so planted, cultivated, and matured as to make the sugar in its juice; that it must be delivered to the factory very soon after cutting; and that it must be taken care of before the season of heavy frosts. As to what is diffusion and how it operates in the cells, the record of experiments shows as follows: The condition in which the sugar and other soluble substances exist in the cane is that of solution in water. This sweetish liquid is contained, like the juices of plants generally, in cells. The walls of these cells are porous. It has long been known that if a solution of sugar in water be placed in a porous or membranous sack and the sack placed in water, an action called osmose takes place, whereby the water from the outside and the sugar solution from the inside of the sack each pass through until the liquids on the two sides of the membrane are equally sweet. Other substances soluble in water behave similarly, but sugar and other readily crystallizable substances pass through much more readily than uncrystallizable or difficultly crystallizable bodies. To apply this property to the extraction of sugar, the cane is first cut into fine chips, and put into the diffusion cells, where water is applied and the sugar is displaced. For the purpose of illustration, let us assume that, when a cell has been filled with chips, just as much water is passed into the cell as there was juice in the chips. The process of osmose or diffusion sets in, and in a few minutes there is as much sugar in the liquid outside of the cane cells as in the juice in these cane cells; in other words, the water and the juice have divided the sugar, each taking half. Again, assume that as much liquid can be drawn from one as there was water added. It is plain that if the osmotic action is complete the liquid drawn off will be half as sweet as cane juice. It has now reached fresh chips in two, and again equalization takes place. Half of the sugar from one was brought into two, so that it now contains 1½ portions of sugar, dissolved in two portions of liquid, or the liquid has risen to ¾ of the strength of cane juice. This liquid having ¾ strength passes to three, and we have in three 1¾ portions of liquid, or after the action has taken place the liquid in three is ⅞ strength. One portion of this liquid passes to four, and we have 1⅞ portions of sugar in two portions of liquid, or the liquid becomes 1⅝ strength. One portion of this liquid passes to five, and we have in five 1 15/16 portions of sugar in two portions of liquid, or the liquid is 31/32 strength. It is now called juice, and is drawn off and subjected to the processes of the subsequent operations of the factory. From this time forward, a cell is drawn for every one filled. The following table will illustrate the working of the saccharine matters of the stalks cut up in fine chips in the cell. The process will be readily understood from the diagram, in which the columns represent the cells of the battery, the numbers at the left the number of diffusions; w, water; l, liquid in the cells, or passing through them, and j, juice to be drawn. Throughout the operation the temperature is kept as near the boiling point as can be done conveniently without danger of filling some of the battery cells with steam. Diffusion takes place more rapidly at high than at low temperature, and the danger of fermentation, with the consequent loss of sugar, is avoided. To round out the subject, we quote from the report of the Commissioner, in which it is stated that the grape-sugar content of sorghum is very large. When freed from such of the "not sugar" products as have an unpleasant taste, this constitutes an elegant syrup constituent. It is composed chiefly of two sugars, called, respectively, dextrose and levulose. The last is sweeter than cane sugar. This grape sugar is that to which most sweet fruits owe their sweetness. The large amount of it—over fifty-three pounds to the ton of cane—is likely to be recognized in the near future as one of the most valuable contents of sorghum cane. At present we are able to separate only a portion of the cane sugar from the other constituents of the juice. It is believed to be impossible by methods at present used to separate more than the difference between the cane sugar and the grape sugar. Thus the sorghum of 1883 could have yielded not more than 162.7−73.44=89.26 pounds per ton, while that of 1884 should, by the same computation, have yielded 264.9−22.32=242.58 pounds per ton. The available sugar in the sorghum crop of 1887, by the same method, was 171.8−60=111.8 pounds, and the average available sugar in the sorghum for the five years was 193.1−53.55=139.55 pounds. This is supposing that the juice is all obtained from the cane, and that there is no waste in the subsequent processes. At Fort Scott, however, only a little more than 92 per cent. of the sugar was obtained from the cane, so that the above figures should be multiplied by .92, making the mean available sugar with this extraction 128.38 pounds, and the available sugar of 1887, 102.8 pounds per ton of cleaned cane. The actual yield obtained at Fort Scott was 234,607 pounds of first sugar, from 2,501 cells. If, now, the cell be taken as a ton, the yield of first sugar was 234,607+2,501= 93.8 pounds. Enough of the molasses was reboiled for a second crop of crystals, and the sugar separated to ascertain that fifteen to twenty pounds, per ton of cane represented, could be obtained. Calling it fifteen, we have for the entire yield 93.8+15=108.8 pounds per ton of cleaned cane. This is a larger yield than is obtainable according to the heretofore accepted theory. There is some uncertainty about the weight of a cell, which may account for the discrepancy between the theoretical and the actual results. It is possible, however, that the theory may need reconstruction. In any case, the yield actually obtained is most gratifying. I have made no mention in the above of the exceptionally large yields of some special strikes made during the season. One strike gave 109 pounds of merchantable sugar for each cellful (ton) of chips. The seconds from this would doubtless have brought the yield up to 130 pounds. But the general reader and the prospective manufacturer are more interested in average than in special results. It seems safe to assume that a mean of 100 pounds of sugar and twelve gallons of molasses can be made from each ton of cleaned sorghum cane of average richness. The price paid for cane delivered at the sugar factory has heretofore been $2 per ton. It needs only to be stated that long hauls by wagon would cost too much to leave any profit to the farmer at this price. It is doubtful whether the farmer who lives more than three miles from the factory, can afford to raise cane unless he can transport it most of the way by rail. Again, the factory will easily obtain all it can work from farmers whose distance does not exceed two miles, and will prefer to patronize these on account of the greater regularity with which they can deliver their crops, as well as the greater facility with which the supervision of the factory may be extended. Farmers living on a line of railroad may be able to ship their cane on such favorable terms as to avail themselves of the market at the factory. In Cuba and in some parts of Louisiana, light railroads are constructed where the distance is too great for hauling on ordinary roads. On these a team hauls about thirteen tons at a load. The system of central and auxiliary factories seems, however, to offer the best solution for the problem of distance.

THRESHING SHOCKED CORN. The idea of threshing shocked corn, and at the same time tearing and shredding the stalks by means of a common threshing machine, has lately attracted considerable attention. We have lately seen the statement, however, that it is difficult to get the stalks dry enough to prevent the fodder heating when thrown into bulk. This point is well taken. It is often difficult to cure the shocks so dry that when the shredded stalks are stacked serious heating will not ensue. But if this be the only difficulty, it is easily obviated in the winter by a dry system of slight ventilation, rails, etc., being used. There is, however, another strong objection to the threshing of corn; the grains are much broken, thus seriously impairing the commercial value, but of course not impairing it for use on the farm. The idea is reported by Mr. Henry Collins, in the *New York Tribune*, to have occurred to Mr. J. T. Cobb, of the *Grange Visitor*, who says the only preparation necessary is to remove a section of the concave, put a board in its place and lower the other section a little: just how much can best be determined by actual trial. If you have barn room, stick the end of the straw carrier into the barn somewhere. If into the big doors, fix up a little platform to catch the fodder if there be space for it in the upper part of the barn, and much less space is required for twenty acres of corn than one would suppose. To get the shocks to the thresher, Mr. Cobb gives suggestions, and says if the cornstalks are dry when threshed, the fodder will keep all right and be worth twice as much as when fed in the ordinary way. Cattle will eat it better when torn into shreds than when cut into pieces. It should not be pressed down in the mow, but left loose as it falls from the straw carrier. The directions for hauling are as follows: Prepare a strip of wood nine inches long, one and one-fourth inches wide and one-third inch thick. Bore a one-fourth inch hole near one end and saw a one-fourth inch notch at a holding angle near the other end. Cut one-fourth inch rope into pieces five or six feet long, tie a knot in one end; run the rope through this block binder, tie a knot in the other end and two more knots eight inches apart. With a half bushel of these binding ties, three wagons with good hay racks and plenty of help you are ready, with all other necessary preparations made, to harvest your corn crop in a day. With these ties drawn tightly around the shocks, if not too large, two men with strong forks will pitch the shocks to a loader, who will find it very convenient to have an assistant to drive and help unload. The binders are not removed until the shocks are on the table of the machine. There is still another matter that must be taken into consideration. If the fodder is damp the corn will be so. Indeed, corn seldom dries out in the shock during the winter sufficiently so the shelled corn will keep sound in the bin, but the corn can be thrown on a platform and shoveled over occasionally until dry enough to bin. So far as the West is concerned, where the bulk of the crop is husked on the stalk in the field as it grew, this mode will not be applicable, but for corn, shocked to be fed stalks and grain, the plan is worthy of trial. (See Threshing.)

TOBACCO. Until 1880, the estimates of the tobacco crop, one of great importance to the country, was neither complete nor satisfactory. Since that time, great care has been exercised in gathering correct figures. The crops of 1869 and 1870 were small, and prices high; and that of 1874 was very small, made so by a very unfavorable season; and the export price advanced from 9.6 cents to 11.3 cents in the export year 1874–75. Three large crops followed that of 1874, in succession, 522, 585, and 580 millions of pounds, which reduced the export price, at first gradually, from 11.3 in 1874–75 to 7.6 cents in 1879–80, when the reduction was checked by a succession of medium crops scarcely equal to the demand for consumption and exportation. Since, the crop of 1882 exceeded the distribution and left a surplus, as have the last three in succession. The price swung upward as the result of several moderate crops, and did not reach its turning point till 1885–86, when it pointed at the average of 9.6 cents, but fell to 8.7 during 1887. Thus the law of supply and demand, the potent factor in the trade with Europe, has regulated prices of exports firmly, so that in the two decades for 1868 to 1887, inclusive, the range of yearly averages has only been from 7.6 to 11.4 cents, while the annual product has ranged from 315,000,000 to 580,000,000 pounds. The table below gives the figures approximately up to 1880, and thence forward the figures may be taken to be quite correct. They are as follows:

Years.	Quantity.	Total Value.	Value per Pound.
	Pounds.	Dollars.	Cents.
1866	190,896,248	29,456,145	15.4
1867	184,803,065	19,620,159	10.6
1868	206,020,504	22,898,623	11.1
1869	181,527,630	20,552,943	11.3
1870	185,748,881	21,100,420	11.4
1871	215,667,604	19,908,797	9.2
1872	234,936,892	24,136,166	10.3
1873	213,995,176	22,589,135	10.6
1874	318,097,604	30,399,181	9.6
1875	223,901,913	25,241,549	11.3
1876	216,310,265	22,737,383	10.4
1877	282,366,426	29,825,521	10.2
1878	285,973,198	24,303,165	8.7
1879	322,279,540	25,157,364	7.8
1880	215,910,187	16,379,107	7.6
1881	227,026,605	18,737,043	8.3
1882	223,665,980	19,067,721	8.5
1883	235,626,360	19,438,066	6.2
1884	192,130,820	17,405,234	9.1
1885	219,221,207	21,799,251	9.9
1886	281,737,190	20,926,544	9.6
1887	293,666,995	25,537,983	8.7

The distribution is world wide, including nearly all countries with which the United States has any trade. Yet nearly all goes to Europe, nine-tenths to seven countries, Germany, Great Britain, France, Italy, Netherlands, Spain and Belgium, in the order named. The proportion taken by the several countries has somewhat changed since 1880, Germany taking much less, Great Britain and the Netherlands less, and France, Italy and Spain more.

UNDERDRAINING AND MOISTURE. In addition to what has been stated in the body of the work, we give place to some new matter just made public by a practical drainage expert of Ohio, who, speaking of earlier days, says: Many have probably passed through this country in an early day, who will remember it as a low, swampy land, unfit for anything but muskrats and fish to live in, full of ague, or "the shakes," as it was called. In consequence, this part of the country was given a wide berth until within the last fifteen years, when the farmers began to wake up to the fact that they had the best land that lies out of doors. The writer then relates his experience as follows: We first tried mole ditching, but this would not last but a year or so. Then our outlets were not good. Then we got the county interested, and our main ditches were dug by the county, each man being taxed, or he could dig his part to the value to which he was benefited. Our township ditches were constructed on the same plan. These big ditches cost a great deal of money; most of them require cleaning out every year. Into these other ditches were dug to drain off the fields, but it was found they took up valuable ground, and would not draw the water from any distance. We found tile would draw the water a rod on each side for each foot in depth; this an open ditch will not do. In other words, in a good tile drain there is always a suction. An open ditch does not pay. It is a big expense to dig it, and then it is a constant source of expense, requiring cleaning. Stock gets in, especially sheep, while the first crop over the ditch would pay for the tile. The tile drain will last a life time. We have tile drains here that have six rows of six-inch tile in them, carrying enough water to run a saw mill. Does it pay? Yes. Before the tile was put in, the land was worth nothing; now it will sell for $75 to $100 per acre, and will produce seventy-five to 100 bushels of corn per acre. Does tile draining lessen the soil moisture during droughts? No, emphatically no! It increases it, rather. If there is no moisture above the tile, it comes up from below; not water, but moisture such as the roots of corn or other plants need. This moisture goes up through the stalks of the plant, and into the air through the leaves. If you are the happy possessor of a farm, underdrain it, no matter whether it is wet or not. Our heavy, clayey soils need underdraining worse than the black ground. Talk about your fertilizers! Five hundred dollars invested in good underdraining will produce more corn and wheat than one thousand dollars in fertilizers. Hark! I hear some big Eastern farmer say, "I don't believe it; how do you make that out?" Fertilizing has got to be done one year after year; but it is a good thing, and it beats nothing. But did you ever stop to think that Mother Earth has lying within her all the properties for plant life? The elements not in the earth are in the air. All you have to do is to get them together. The plant life of which the air is composed must circulate in the ground to a greater or less extent; and that of the earth must combine with that of the air. Mix the two greater producers of plant life above and below ground. Then plant your seeds, tend them well, and you will be repaid a hundred fold. Underdraining is of vast importance. By a thorough system the ground which heretofore has run together, been muddy, sticky, and so close that water would never get through it, and would only get away by evaporation, if rendered porous, the air circulates through the tile and up into the soil, carrying moisture to the roots of the plants. In a wet time, when there is a surplus of water, it is carried off within two or three hours, so there can be no damage to the growing crops. If your ground is underdrained it will never bake and crack, but it will break up like an ash heap. Another great advantage is that it takes only about half the labor to put out a crop and take care of it. The ground can be plowed while your neighbors are waiting for theirs to dry off. You need no roller, as there are no clods. The cost of digging the drains can be done for about seven cents per foot, or twenty-one cents per yard, for a ditch three feet deep. It is necessary to have good outlets where there is much water to carry off. Sometimes it is well to put in two or three rows of tile in one drain. Each foot in depth will draw the water from a rod on each side. After a heavy rain is the best time to lay off drains. In a great many soils an outlet can be dispensed with. An outlet is better if it can be had; if it cannot, lay off the drain, dig about two and a half or three feet deep. In throwing out the dirt you can tell ground that is porous, such as gravel or sandy soil. Such a place will be the outlet. Now lay about a three-inch tile, costing about seven cents per rod, cover them, and you have a good drain. A great many ponds and low places are merely basins; when once broken through the water all seeps away. Where tile cannot be had, a drain can be dug with a shoulder in it, or, as some would call it, a step. Boards can be cut and laid in the drain, one end on the step, the other on the bottom of the drain, on the opposite side. There is another way. Lay down two logs in the bottom of the drain and another on top of the two. This makes a cheap drain, and will last for years. Do not stop at draining the black, swampy land, but drain your heavy, clayey soil as well. Within a few years you will have a valuable farm. A breaking plow, with three horses, is a good thing to take off the top soil with. It can be made to cut a furrow eight inches deep. To fill in a drain after the tile are laid, take a spade and cave the dirt in around the tile, so there will be no danger of disturbing them. Then hitch two horses to a scraper; have them hitched out long so they will not get in the drain. It will take two men, one to drive and the other to hold the scraper. Get the scraper back of the dirt, then drive up until the scraper comes to the brink of the drain so the dirt will fall in; then back the horses, pull the scraper over, and go again. Two men, with a team, will lay the tile and fill in two hundred rods of a drain a day. The dirt must be all on one side of the drain to be filled in to an advantage with above plan. To fill in a drain where it is too wide for a scraper and a team, take a plank ten or twelve feet long. To this bolt the wheels of a sulky corn-plow on each end. One-third the distance of the plank bore a hole for a clevis. To this a plow. Hitch two horses on the short end of the plank and one on the long end. With this arrangement the horses are away from all danger. You can fill in, with three hands, two hundred and fifty rods in a day. In digging the drains, a common hand will throw out six rods three feet deep in a day, while a good hand will do nine to ten rods. So a man can estimate the cost any way he chooses. On underdraining he will clear on his investment one hundred to a thousand per cent., provided he does the work in a good, systematic way. In relation to soil moisture, of soils drained and undrained, Prof. T. F. Hunt, assistant in Agirculture University of Illinois, has continually made elaborate experiments, this very dry season, to test soil moisture in land tile-drained and undrained. We have already stated that the guesswork theory of visionaries that drainage caused drought was entirely unfounded. So far as increased soil moisture in drained as against undrained soil is concerned, the experience of practical men is in favor of the drained land during droughts. It is also a fixed fact that the soil moisture in cultivated land under the same condition is superior to that in undrained soil. It is not necessary to give the long details by which Prof. Hunt arrived at his conclusions. The summary is as follows: Eighty samples of soil, forty from the first foot in depth, and forty from second, taken in Champaign, Marion and Hancock Counties, between August 1 and 19, 1887, gave an average of 13.2 per cent. of water. This in two feet of soil is equal to four inches of rainfall or 110,000 gallons of water per acre. This is about equal to the average monthly rainfall in this region, and is over four times the rainfall in Champaign County during the two months previous to making the tests as reported by the observer for the Illinois State Weather Service. Forty-four samples taken in Champaign County gave an average of 13.5 per cent. of water. This is a little more than one-fourth the amount contained by a thoroughly saturated soil. Twenty-two samples of first foot contained on an average 12.0 per cent., and a like number of second foot 15.0 per cent. of water. The lowest per cent. of water found in first foot of soil was 8.5. It was found in two instances—in an oat stubble and a clover stubble. The clover was green and growing, while blue grass and timothy on adjacent soil containing an average of 9.7 per cent. of water, was parched. The highest per cent. in first foot, 16.0, was found in a broom-corn field in two instances, in one instance tiled and one untiled. Twelve per cent. was the lowest found in second foot, being in an oat stubble, and 18.4 the highest, being in a corn field. Comparing the average of forty samples taken on tiled and untiled land, which are in some measure comparable, there was found to be in two feet of tiled soil 14.1 per cent. of water, and 13.2 in untiled land. In first foot, 13.6 in tiled and 11.8 in untiled; in second foot, 14.5 in tiled and 15.0 in untiled. Comparing the average of samples, Nos. 9 to 16, which for reasons before given are the only samples strictly comparable as to the tiled and untiled land, there was found in two feet of soil 15.3 per cent. of water in tiled, and 14.0 in untiled land; in first foot, 14.4 in tiled and 13.3 in untiled; in second foot, 16.2 in tiled and 14.8 in untiled. As to conclusions: on the whole, it may be said, that no striking difference was found in the amount of water in tiled and untiled land. The difference in all probability amounts practically to nothing, but such as it is, it is in favor of tiled land. There need be no fear, therefore, that the laying of tile, which has been pushed forward with such enterprise and good judgment by the Illinois farmer, in the last ten years, will ever prove anything but a benefit, and he may keep on laying it at the rate of 12,000 miles annually with the perfect assurance that he will get abundant returns for the capital invested. On the other hand, the increased yield of crops claimed to be produced on tiled land during drought must be explained on other grounds than the increased percentage of moisture. Fifty-six samples of soil taken in fields growing cultivated and uncultivated crops, show somewhat more moisture in soil growing cultivated than in that growing uncultivated crops. In two feet deep there was an average of 13.6 per cent.; in first foot 12.0 vs. 10.3, and in second foot 15.0 vs. 12.8 per cent. respectively. In an artificial test of cultivated and uncultivated fallow land, the uncultivated was found to lose nearly twice as much moisture as the cultivated land. The excess of water lost in uncultivated land in one week was equal to a rainfall of one-fourth of an inch. (See also Draining.)

VENTILATION IN STABLES. The absence of proper ventilation in stock barns and stables is one of the most serious evils known in the care of stock. These buildings have either no means of ventilation except the doors and windows, causing thorough drafts and suddenly reducing the temperature, or else the building is left so open that there are currents of air passing in all directions. As to correct ventilation either in country or city it seems to be the last thing thought of. Correct ventilation consists in such means of gently moving the air, that while the temperature of the stable shall be fairly equable, there shall be little or no animal odor or that of decaying excrement. It may best be conserved by a simple system that while admitting fresh air, and carrying off the foul air, by equally simple means of deodorization, the proper effect is secured. First, the stable must be made so tight that air can not pour in through cracks and ill-fitting windows and doors. If we place a louvre on the roof of the barn—an extension of the roof upwards, protected by slat blinds, communicating with a hollow shaft two to three feet square connecting between the stable and roof, the air will rise through this carrying off the foul gases. If in addition to this we provide narrow slits in the wall, with a board arranged so the incoming air shall be deflected downward, and furnished with a trap that may be closed as required, we can get plenty of pure air, and in the proper quantities as wanted. This is one of the most simple means, and also effective. Now, if we make the shaft large enough inside, so hay and other fodder may be passed down it by means of tightly fitting doors, at proper distances through the mow, we may have two economies at once, the shaft and chute leading to the feeding floor. Of course, if the building is only of one story, no air shafts will be needed; the air may escape directly from the louvre, or even from slits properly guarded under the eaves. In relation to deodorization: This may be by means of dry, finely pulverized clay or loam in the stalls. This will absorb the liquids, the essence of the manure, and only the saturated portions are removed to the manure pile. It will pay far more than the cost, and with plenty of bedding, another important economy, you conserve the comfort of the animals as well. If you have not the prepared earth, use ground gypsum freely. It will act both mechanically and chemically, is in itself a valuable fertilizer, and cheap. The other plan is to sprinkle the stalls with a solution of copperas (sulphate of iron). It is safe to say that the liquid manure treated as we have described would give double the value, than where treated in the ordinary manner. (See Ventilation, page 1005.)

WHEAT. The increased production of wheat, through the opening of vast farm areas over the productive West, has been most wonderful. Between 1875 and 1880, a series of crop failures in Western Europe stimulated demand never existing before, and which may not again be brought about in this generation, unless in the case of a general European war. For we have seen that the world's production during the last few years has kept up without diminution. India and Australia are beginning to export large quantities, and the unplowed fields of the southern portions of the South American continent are yet undeveloped, but increase of wheat production has been in excess of con-

Years.	Total Production.	Total Area of Crop.	Total Value of Crop.	Average Value per Bushel.	Average Yield per Acre.	Average Value per Acre.
	Bushels.	Acres.	Dollars.	Cents.	Bushels.	Dollars.
1880	498,549,868	37,986,717	474,201,850	95.1	13.1	12.48
1881	383,280,090	37,709,020	456,880,427	119.8	10.2	12.12
1882	504,185,470	37,067,194	444,602,125	88.2	13.6	11.99
1883	421,086,160	36,455,593	383,649,272	91.0	11.6	10.52
1884	512,765,000	39,475,885	330,862,260	64.5	13.0	8.38
1885	357,112,000	34,189,246	275,520,390	77.1	10.4	8.05
1886	457,218,000	36,806,184	314,226,020	68.7	12.4	8.54
1887	456,329,000	37,641,783	310,612,960	68.1	12.1	8.25
Total	3,590,525,588	297,331,622	2,990,355,304			
Annual average	448,815,699	37,166,453	373,794,413	83.3	12.1	10.06
Annual average for preceding ten years	312,152,726	25,187,414	337,407,258	104.9	12.4	13.00

States and Territories.	Acres.	Bushels.	Value.
Maine	39,460	481,000	$ 505,050
New Hampshire	10,485	110,000	114,400
Vermont	21,351	320,000	307,200
Massachusetts	1,080	16,000	16,000
Rhode Island			
Connecticut	2,171	37,000	38,600
New York	666,883	10,137,000	8,312,340
New Jersey	143,068	1,459,000	1,269,330
Pennsylvania	1,421,151	13,785,000	11,165,850
Delaware	94,790	920,000	760,360
Maryland	562,836	5,797,000	4,811,510
Virginia	635,638	4,832,000	3,018,920
North Carolina	717,442	9,094,000	4,482,720
South Carolina	192,637	1,233,000	1,220,670
Georgia	382,094	2,522,000	2,398,900
Florida			
Alabama	207,115	1,305,000	1,278,900
Mississippi	41,770	315,000	207,350
Louisiana			
Texas	544,977	5,450,000	4,360,000
Arkansas	231,357	2,290,000	1,877,800
Tennessee	1,199,400	9,595,000	7,388,150
West Virginia	302,177	2,840,000	2,158,400
Kentucky	1,069,493	11,113,000	8,112,490
Ohio	2,740,087	35,845,000	26,921,250
Michigan	1,629,467	21,672,000	16,037,280
Indiana	2,502,063	37,528,000	27,236,160
Illinois	2,425,092	36,861,000	25,802,700
Wisconsin	1,368,208	13,063,000	8,360,320
Minnesota	3,129,208	30,299,000	21,416,410
Iowa	2,683,076	26,837,000	16,370,570
Missouri	1,712,028	27,744,000	17,301,360
Kansas	762,394	7,607,000	4,642,270
Nebraska	1,842,127	16,585,000	8,700,050
California	2,766,235	30,429,000	23,517,460
Oregon	920,026	16,100,000	10,948,000
Nevada	5,570	111,000	88,800
Colorado	119,709	2,514,000	1,885,500
Arizona	22,450	303,000	248,460
Dakota	3,664,737	52,400,000	27,251,120
Idaho	64,015	1,120,000	862,400
Montana	97,756	1,760,000	1,337,600
New Mexico	81,372	1,221,000	1,098,900
Utah	108,738	1,971,000	1,478,310
Washington	463,610	8,345,000	5,591,150
Total	37,641,783	456,329,000	310,612,960

sumption. The average of the ten-year period (1870-79) was 312,152,728 bushels; of the recent period of eight years, 448,815,699 bushels, an increase of 44 per cent., while the increase of population has been only about 25 per cent. At prices that have ruled for the last four years, the crop has paid little or no profit to the farmer, and the average value of an acre of wheat has

large portion of their supply from the West. Those States consume five bushels, and the West quite as much, while some of the Southern States require but three or four bushels.

To round out the whole, the table on the preceding page will show the production of wheat by States, including acreage and value of crop. We may naturally expect, without doubt,

Fig. 1.—CATTLE, HOG AND SHEEP FENCE.

been less than an acre of Indian corn, as a comparison of the tables of these crops will show. The table on the preceding page gives the totals and other matter interesting for comparison.

Statistician Dodge says, the estimates of production average 448,000,000 bushels, in round numbers, for seven years since 1880, not including 1887. The exportation averages nearly 121,000,000 bushels, and with estimates of seed and

to find our wheat production steadily diminishing, per capita. The best wheat lands are already taken up. The raising of wheat after wheat steadily depletes the soil. Our population is steadily increasing; and we may therefore conclude, that, unless a general European war should cause a demand, and largely increasing production, our export of wheat will be a steadily decreasing quantity, since in the opening

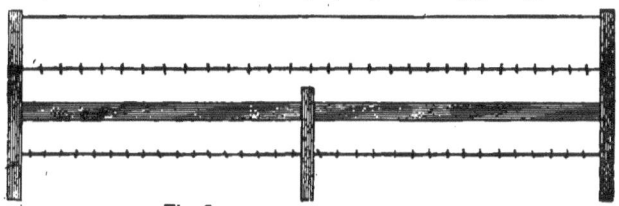

Fig. 2.—CATTLE AND HORSE FENCE.

bread, the entire distribution averages 447,000,000 bushels. These figures may not be absolute proof of the accuracy of the estimates, because the consumption itself is estimated. As the range of annual variation is more than 150,000,000 bushels, and that of exportation as large proportionally, the estimates made in advance of consumption are entirely independent of the

of new farms, the pioneer ceases to raise wheat as a principal money crop, as soon as his means allow him to acquire live stock and undertake diversified farming.

WIRE FENCING. A correspondent of the *Farm, Field and Stockman* furnishes that paper some very practically illustrated matter on wire fencing, and the means of bracing gates and the

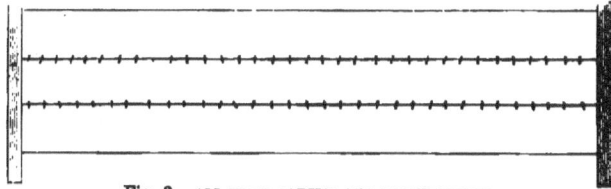

Fig. 3.—ALL-WIRE CATTLE AND HORSE FENCE.

ultimate facts of distribution, and are made entirely from the crop records of the year. The per capita rate of consumption is almost a bushel less than that of Great Britain, and it corresponds with all data to local distribution that has been found available, especially in New England and the Middle States, which obtain a

fences at each side. That journal has kindly loaned the cuts and hence we present the matter entire, as stated. In introducing the subject the editor of the journal states, that the constantly increasing use of wire fence, or of fencing that combines wire and lumber, shows its adaptability to general economic uses by the masses. It will

WIRE FENCING — SUPPLEMENT

turn any stock, and where lumber and wire are used together there is little liability of danger from the wounding of stock. A reference to Fig. 1 will show an excellent plan of building a fence for cattle, hogs and sheep, as it will perfectly turn all three of these animals. The posts are set so as to use sixteen-feet fence boards, a stake being used for the center post, of which there are usually plenty on the farm. When a post of ordinary length rots off at the surface, it is sufficiently long for such work. The bottom wire is a hog wire, three inches from the ground; it will prevent little pigs from going under. The first is a four-inch space, second five inches, third twelve inches, fourth fourteen inches, making the fence fifty inches high. Fig. 2 shows a good cattle and horse fence. The single

The posts should be sixteen feet apart properly, but in case posts are scarce they can be placed twenty to thirty feet apart by using one or more ties, as shown in the cut. This makes a very substantial and cheap fence. The bottom wire is twenty-two inches from the ground; first space fourteen inches, second fourteen, making the fence fifty inches high. It should be remembered, however, that only absolute necessity, from lack of timber, renders an all-wire fence desirable, for the reason that stock cannot see it plainly, and hence may be injured by running against it. Any pale or narrow board on top of the upper wire, if whitewashed, will prevent this. Coming now to wire gates and bracing, it is correctly stated that gates require to be much wider now than formerly. Mowers, self-raking

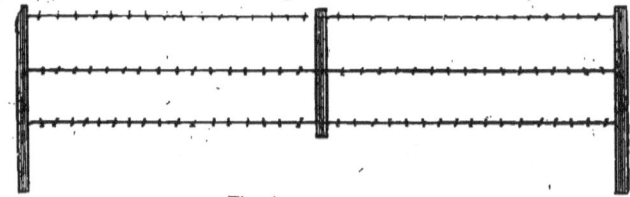

Fig. 4.—CATTLE FENCE.

board will prevent horses from running into it, and the upper wire being a plain galvanized number nine wire, it makes it doubly secure, for if the horse should jump it would not be cut or lacerated. The two barb wires, the barbs not over three or four inches apart, are sufficiently close to the board to prevent stock from breaking it. A stake can be used for the center the same as with Fig. 1. The bottom wire is twelve inches from the ground; first space ten inches, second ten, third fourteen, making this fence fifty-two inches high. Fig. 3 gives a view of the best all-wire cattle and horse fence that can be built. The two barb wires are sufficient

reapers and binders require plenty of room. Much wider and heavier loads of hay are now carried than formerly. Hence in the case of reapers, etc., a gate of good width saves much handling and loading. Since the use of wire has come into use, gates are made light and cheaply. At the same time they are firm and strong. There is so much less strain on the hinges that a very wide gate combination of wire and lumber is easy to swing, and in the case of slide gates much easier to slide, since it is necessary that a slide gate be fourteen feet to admit a six and a-half foot binder to pass through. To enable any person handy with tools to make

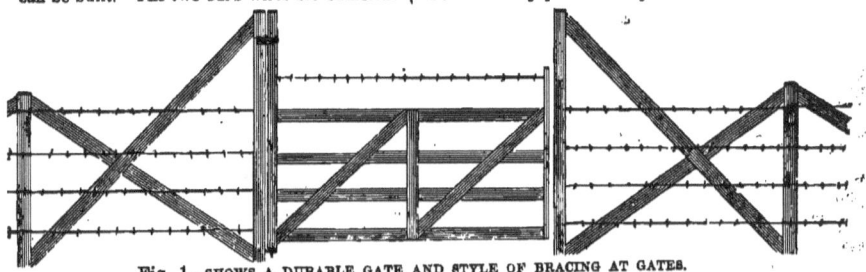

Fig. 1—SHOWS A DURABLE GATE AND STYLE OF BRACING AT GATES.

to prevent stock from going through, while the top and bottom wires, of number nine, plain galvanized wire, will prevent horses from being cut, either by pawing over the bottom wire, which is frequently the case, or by jumping upon the upper one. The bottom wire is fourteen inches from the ground; first space twelve inches, second twelve, third fourteen, making this fence fifty-two inches high. The posts are sixteen feet apart. Fig. 4 illustrates the most common barb wire fence in use. It can be changed to various styles to suit the builder.

and put up their own gates, various designs are illustrated. Fig. 1 shows plan of a cheap and durable farm gate. The hinge post is 4x4, the head a piece of 2x4. The balance is made of six-inch fence boards, with a wire at the top. The mode of hanging is cheap, and far more durable than the ordinary hinges. The lower hinge is an eye bolt, the eye of which is three inches in diameter, and made of inch-iron. Bore a hole in center of gate post and drive into the eye. Then round the 4x4 piece until it will slip in the eye. The upper hinge is a piece of band iron, or a piece of wagon tire as the best and most durable. Cut a ïtch in the front side of the 4x4 for it to turn in. Then bend in shape to fit the notch, and draw back on gate post as far as necessary, and pass a bolt through the holes made in the iron, and bolt fast to the post. This mode of hanging is far better than hinges, for the reason that the post will not split. The gate of Fig. 2 is built the same as in Fig. 1, except that it is half wire, which makes it lighter and cheaper. In place of the wooden braces as in Fig. 1, it has a wire brace running from the bottom of the gate in front, to top of 4x4, which has a small eye-bolt that the wire is fastened into, so that it can be drawn up with a wrench, to take the sag out of the gate when necessary. The

Fig. 2.—CHEAP RAISING GATE.

Fig. 3.—CHEAP AND DURABLE SLIDE GATE.

wire is stapled every place where it crosses in contact with the wood. Fig. 3 shows a light and durable slide gate. It is made entirely of fence boards and wire. In Fig. 1 is also shown a good plan of bracing wire fences next to gates. The posts are eight feet apart, one board from the bottom of gate post to top of first post is all that is necessary, but it requires two boards from bottom of first post to top of gate post (one

Fig. 4.—CENTER BRACING.

on each side to keep the gate post from twisting) as the wires will pull it around if strained tight. Then nail one board from top of first post to bottom of second. Then by bracing every fifteen or twenty rods, as shown in Fig. 4, and the corners as shown in Fig. 5, you have a wire fence that will remain as tight as when first built. The old-fashioned way of bracing which is used altogether too much, using a rail or post for a brace at the corners, with a stake driven in the ground to hold it, is a very poor plan, for when the stake gives out the wires pull the post over and that lets it all loose. It stands to reason that a poorly stretched wire fence is almost as bad as no fence at all.

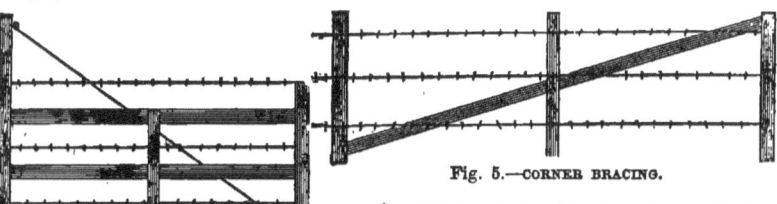

Fig. 5.—CORNER BRACING.

WOOD PULP. The invention of forming paper pulp from wood has revolutionized the paper trade in the United States, especially in printing paper. It now constitutes a vast industry. The poplars—quaking ash is the best—and others, soft without being gummy, are especially useful. In Europe, the industry is a large one, and as in this country, increasing yearly. In Europe much soft pine is used. There are three methods of reducing the wood in pulp. In two the initial processes are the same. Cut transversely by machinery into small pieces, after having been barked—or it would be more correct to say thin slices—the wood is boiled in water under high pressure. In one process, known as the "soda process," it is afterwards treated likewise under great heat, with caustic soda, which leaves it a pure cellulose mass. This mass is subsequently washed and passed through an ordinary "breaker," then over a machine with an endless sieve or felt, from which it issues as a roll, or what is known in commerce as wood-pulp. In the other process, known as the "acid process," the wood is treated with sulphuric acid instead of caustic soda. In color, the "wood-pulp" is light gray, and when dry it is of great tenacity. By the soda process, two to four and one-half tons of wood are required for one ton of pulp. Considerable controversy exists as to the merits of the two processes, but the respective pulps sell at about the same price, and, except by very experienced paper-makers, it is said, could not be distinguished. The other process is known as the "mechanical process," the wood being simply ground—practically in water—into minute fibers and partially dried in the usual manner. The logs are brought in a "lade" up to the saws and cut into pieces varying from a foot to two feet in length. These pieces are in turn barked and split by machinery, and passed on to have the knots bored out and the pith removed. Upright grinding-stones are kept revolving in water or, at all events, are kept drenched with water, and against these stones the wood is held by a hydraulic piston, which can be adjusted so as to produce long or short fiber. Open pipes carry the water with the fiber in suspension—the mass resembling a cloudy stream—onto the knotters or sieves, which check the passage of unground chips, while the strained material is carried onto an ordinary paper-making machine with an endless web or fine sieve, whence it issues in the shape of large sheets, with 50 per cent. of the water squeezed out of them.